THE INTERNATIONAL BIBLIOGRAPHY OF ANTHROPOLOGY

This bibliography, with its sister publications, Economics, Political Science, and Sociology (known together as the *International Bibliography of the Social Sciences* (*IBSS*)) is an essential tool for librarians, academics and researchers wishing to keep up to date with the published literature in the social sciences.

The *IBSS* lists journal articles and monographs from all over the world and in over 70 languages, all with English title translations where needed.

From 1991, users already familiar with the bibliography will notice major improvements in contents and currency. There is greater coverage of monographs as well as journals, with continued emphasis on international publications, especially those from the developing world and Eastern Europe. Indexing techniques have been refined: the *IBSS* now offers more specific subject and geographical indexes together with an author index. A subject index in French continues to be provided.

Prepared until 1989 at the Fondation nationale des sciences politiques in Paris, the *IBSS* is now compiled and edited by the British Library of Political and Economic Science at the London School of Economics. The International Committee for Social Science Information and Documentation and UNESCO continue to support the publication. The new *International Bibliography* not only maintains its traditional extensive coverage of periodical literature, but considerably extends its coverage of monographic material by incorporating most of that which would previously have been included in the *London Bibliography of the Social Sciences*, publication of which has now been discontinued.

Also available from Routledge

Copies of the *International Bibliography of the Social Sciences* for previous years.

Thematic Lists of Descriptors. Four subject volumes published in 1989, following the classification and index terms of the relevant volume of the *IBSS*.

Copies of the *London Bibliography of the Social Sciences* for previous years are available from Schmidt Periodicals, Dettendorf, D-8201 Bad Feilnbach 2, Germany.

INTERNATIONAL BIBLIOGRAPHY OF THE SOCIAL SCIENCES

BIBLIOGRAPHIE INTERNATIONALE DES SCIENCES SOCIALES

published annually in four parts since 1961: UNESCO, Paris
paraissant chaque année en quatre parties jusqu'en 1961: UNESCO, Paris

International bibliography of sociology / Bibliographie internationale de sociologie [red cover / couverture rouge] Vol.1:1951 (publ. 1952)

International bibliography of political science / Bibliographie internationale de science politique [grey cover / couverture grise] Vol.1:1952 (publ. 1954)

International bibliography of economics / Bibliographie internationale de sciences économiques [yellow cover / couverture jaune] Vol.1:1952 (publ. 1955)

International bibliography of social and cultural anthropology / Bibliographie internationale d'anthropologie sociale et culturelle [green cover / couverture verte] Vol.1:1955 (publ. 1958)

Prepared by

THE BRITISH LIBRARY OF POLITICAL AND ECONOMIC SCIENCE

with the support of the International Committee for Social Science Information
and Documentation with the assistance of UNESCO

Editor
Jean Sykes
Librarian, British Library of Political and Economic Science

Editorial Manager
Csanád Z. Siklós

Assistant Editorial Manager
Liam Earney

Database Design
Robert H. Browne

Editorial Assistants
Michelle Brattle Juliette Chivers
Kath Farrell Jocelyn Guttery
Rebecca Ursell Anna Vaughan

INTERNATIONAL BIBLIOGRAPHY OF THE SOCIAL SCIENCES

2001

INTERNATIONAL BIBLIOGRAPHY OF ANTHROPOLOGY

VOLUME XLVII

BIBLIOGRAPHIE INTERNATIONALE DES SCIENCES SOCIALES

BIBLIOGRAPHIE INTERNATIONALE D'ANTHROPOLOGIE

Prepared with the support of the International Committee for Social Science Information and Documentation with the assistance of UNESCO

Établie avec le concours du Comité international pour l'information et la documentation en sciences sociales avec l'assistance de l'UNESCO

LONDON AND NEW YORK

First published in 2002 by
Routledge
(on behalf of The British Library of Political and Economic Science)

11 New Fetter Lane
London EC4P 4EE
&
29 West 35th Street
New York NY 10001

Routledge is an imprint of the Taylor & Francis Group

© 2002 British Library of Political and Economic Science

Printed in Great Britain by
Biddles Ltd, Guildford and King's Lynn

British Library Cataloguing in Publication Data

A CIP catalogue record for this book is available from the British Library.
ISBN 0-415-28400-7
ISSN 0085-2074

Editorial Correspondence should be sent to:

International Bibliography of the Social Sciences
British Library of Political and Economic Science
London School of Economics
10 Portugal Street
London WC2A 2HD
United Kingdom

Telephone: (U.K.) 020-7955-7455
Fax: (U.K.) 020-7955-6923
email: ibss@lse.ac.uk
http://www.lse.ac.uk/ibss/

CONTENTS

International Committee for Social Science
    Information and Documentation   vi

Preface   vii

Selection criteria   ix

List of periodicals consulted   xi

List of abbreviations used   lxvii

Classification scheme   lxxxix

Bibliography for 2001   1

Author index   243

Placename index   305

Subject index   315

Index des matières   395

INTERNATIONAL COMMITTEE FOR SOCIAL SCIENCE INFORMATION AND DOCUMENTATION

LE COMITÉ INTERNATIONAL POUR L'INFORMATION ET LA DOCUMENTATION EN SCIENCES SOCIALES

Krishna G. Tyagi, National Social Science Documentation Centre, New Delhi (President)

Arnaud Marks, SWIDOC/KNAW, Amsterdam (Secretary General)

ACKNOWLEDGEMENTS

The Editor would like to thank the members of the International Committee, and all those who have contributed to the production of these volumes, particularly: Kaarlo Mäkelä of Eduskunnan Kirjasto, the Library of Parliament at Helsinki; Dr Csaba Nagy of the Library of the Hungarian Parliament, Budapest; Ekkehart Seusing of the Zentralbibliothek der Wirtschaftswissenschaften, Bibliothek des Instituts für Weltwirtschaft, Kiel; and, Yusuke Iijima and the Database Committee of the Japan Sociological Society.

PREFACE

The **International Bibliography of the Social Sciences** is an annual four volume publication covering Economics, Political Science, Sociology and Anthropology. It is compiled by the British Library of Political and Economic Science under the auspices of the International Committee for Social Science Information and Documentation. Until recently UNESCO gave financial support for the preparation of the IBSS volumes, but in consultation with the ICSSD it was decided that UNESCO's support should be transferred to the distribution of the IBSS volumes. This has greatly benefitted a number of information and documentation centres in developing countries.

Some 100,000 articles (from over 2,500 journals) and 20,000 books are scanned each year in the process of compiling the **International Bibliography**. Coverage is international with publications in over 70 languages from more than 60 countries. All titles are given in their original language and in English translation.

The selection policy (criteria appear on page ix) is designed to provide a tool for retrospective search rather than current awareness. Each volume represents the most significant new material published in that discipline in a given year.

With the increase in interdisciplinary material published in the social sciences, some items will be listed in more than one of the four volumes. It is nonetheless advisable to check other disciplines in the series to avoid missing relevant items which may for some reason be cited in only one volume.

Production of the **International Bibliography** is computerized. The database from which it is extracted is available on CD-ROM, providing access to a broader range of material than is cited in these volumes, and updated quarterly. There is also an online service available in the United Kingdom.

PRÉFACE

La **Bibliographie internationale des sciences sociales** est un ouvrage annuel en 4 volumes couvrant la science économique, la science politique, la sociologie et l'anthropologie. Elle est préparée par la British Library of Political and Economic Science sous les auspices du Comité international pour l'information et la documentation en sciences sociales. Jusqu'ici l'assistance financière de l'UNESCO était consacrée à la préparation des volumes de la Bibliographie internationale des sciences sociales. Cependant, et en consultation avec le CIDSS, il a été décidé de transférer cette assistance financière à la distribution de la BISS, ce dont bénéficient un certain nombre de centres d'information et de documentation dans les pays en voie de développement.

Chaque année, quelques 100,000 articles (provenant de 2,500 périodiques) et 20,000 livres sont analysés et indexés en vue de la préparation de la **Bibliographie internationale**. Il s'agit d'une bibliographie véritablement internationale puisqu'elle comprend des publications en plus de 70 langues, provenant de plus de 60 pays. Tous les titres sont présentés dans la langue originale avec une traduction en anglais.

Dans le choix des références, on a davantage cherché à fournir un instrument de recherche retrospective plutôt qu'un service d'information courante. Chaque volume présente les publications les plus significatives parues dans cette discipline au cours d'une année donnée.

Du fait du nombre croissant de publications de nature interdisciplinaire dans les sciences sociales, certains éléments peuvent apparaître dans plus d'un des 4 volumes. Il est cependant conseillé de se reporter aux autres volumes disciplinaires de la série, au cas où des références importantes ne figuraient que dans un seul volume.

La préparation de la **Bibliographie internationale** est informatisée. La base de données dont elle est issue est disponible sur CD-ROM. Elle donne accès à une plus large sélection de publications que celles citées dans ces volumes, et sera mise à jour 4 fois par an. En Grande Bretagne il existe aussi un service en ligne.

SELECTION CRITERIA

1. Subject.

Documents relevant to anthropology.

2. Nature and form.

Publications of known authorship and lasting significance to anthropology, whether in serial or monographic form, typically works with a theoretical component intending to communicate new knowledge, new ideas or making use of new materials.

Previously published materials in all formats are omitted, including most translations. Also excluded are textbooks, materials from newspapers or news magazines, popular or purely informative papers, presentations of predominantly primary data and legislative or judicial texts and items of parochial relevance only.

LIST OF PERIODICALS CONSULTED

LISTE DES PERIODIQUES CONSULTÉS

Abacus: Journal of accounting, finance and business studies. (0001-3072). Oxford.
Aboriginal history. (0314-8769). Canberra.
Academy of Management review. (0363-7425). Ada OH.
Acadiensis: Journal of the history of the Atlantic Region. (0044-5851). Fredericton.
Accounting and business research. (0001-4788). London.
Accounting review. (0001-4826). Sarasota FL.
Accounting, auditing and accountability journal. (0951-3574). Bradford.
Accounting, business and financial history. (0958-5206). London.
Accounting, organizations and society. (0361-3682). Oxford.
Acta asiatica. (0567-7254). Tokyo.
Acta baltica. (0567-7289). Taunus.
Acta ethnographica. (1216-9803). Budapest.
Acta juridica hungarica. (1216-2574). Budapest.
Acta oeconomica. (0001-6373). Budapest.
Acta orientalia. (0001-6438). Copenhagen.
Acta politica. (0001-6810). Meppel.
Acta sociologica [Mexico]. (0186-6028). Mexico City.
Acta sociologica [Norway]. (0001-6993). Oslo.
Acta Universitatis Łódziensis: Folia oeconomica. (0208-6018). Łódz.
Acta Universitatis Łódziensis: Folia sociologica. (0208-600X). Łódz.
Actualité économique. (0001-771X). Montreal.
ACU bulletin. (0044-9563). London.
Addiction. (0965-2140). Abingdon.
Administration. (0001-8325). Dublin.
Administration [Kumamoto]. Kumamoto.
Administration and society. (0095-3997). Thousand Oaks CA.
Administration for development. (0311-4511). Boroko.
Administrative science quarterly. (0001-8392). Ithaca NY.
Affari sociali internazionali. Milan.
Africa [Rome]. Rome.
Africa development = Afrique & développement. (0850-3907). Dakar.
Africa insight. (0256-2804). Pretoria.
Africa perspective. Witwatersrand.
Africa quarterly. (0001-9828). New Delhi.
Africa today. (0001-9887). Denver CO.
Africa: Journal of the International African Institute. (0001-9720). Edinburgh.
African affairs. (0001-9909). Oxford.
African anthropology = Anthropologie africaine. (1024-0969). Yaounde.
African arts. (0001-9933). Los Angeles CA.
African development review = Revue africaine de développement. Abidjan.
African economic history. (0145-2258). Madison WI.

African journal of international and comparative law = Revue africaine de droit international et comparé. (0954-8890). London.
African notes. (0002-0087). Ibadan.
African review. (0856-0056). Dar es Salaam.
African sociological review = Revue Africaine de sociologie. (1027-4332). Grahamstown.
African studies. (0002-0184). Witwatersrand.
African studies review. (0002-0206). New Brunswick, NJ.
African urban quarterly. (0747-6108). Nairobi.
Africana. (0871-2336). Porto.
Africana Marburgensia. (0174-5603). Berlin.
Africana research bulletin. Freetown.
Afrika Spectrum. (0002-0397). Hamburg.
Afrika Zamani: An annual journal of African history. (0850-3079). Dakar.
Afrique 2000. (1017-0952). Brussels.
Afrique contemporaine. (0002-0478). Paris.
Afrique et l'Asie modernes. (0399-0370). Paris.
Ageing and society. (0144-686X). Cambridge.
Agenda. (1013-0950). Dalbridge.
Agrekon. (0303-1853). Pretoria.
Agricultura y sociedad. (0211-8394). Madrid.
Agricultural history. (0002-1482). Berkeley CA.
Al-Abhath. Beirut.
Al-Qantara. (0211-3589). Madrid.
Aletheia. (1413-0394). Canoas.
Allgemeines statistisches Archiv. (0002-6018). Heidelberg.
Alternatives. (0304-3754). Boulder CO.
Amazonia peruana. (0252-886X). Lima.
América indígena. (0002-7081). Mexico City.
American anthropologist. (0002-7294). Arlington VA.
American behavioral scientist. (0002-7642). Thousand Oaks CA.
American economic review. (0002-8282). Nashville TN.
American education studies review. Osaka.
American ethnologist. (0094-0496). Arlington VA.
American historical review. (0002-8762). Washington DC.
American journal of agricultural economics. (0002-9092). Ames IA.
American journal of comparative law. (0002-919X). Berkeley CA.
American journal of economics and sociology. (0002-9246). New York NY.
American journal of international law. (0002-9300). Washington DC.
American journal of Islamic social sciences. (0742-6763). Herndon VA.
American journal of orthopsychiatry. (0002-9432). New York NY.
American journal of physical anthropology. (0002-9483). New York NY.
American journal of political science. (0092-5853). Madison WI.
American journal of primatology. (0275-2565). New York NY.
American journal of sociology. (0002-9602). Chicago IL.
American philosophical quarterly. (0003-0481). Bowling Green OH.
American political science review. (0003-0554). Washington DC.
American politics research. (1532-673X). Thousand Oaks CA.
American psychologist. (0003-066X). Washington DC.
American sociological review. (0003-1224). Washington DC.
American sociologist. (0003-1232). New Brunswick NJ.
Amerindia. (0221-8852). Paris.

Análise social. (0003-2573). Lisbon.

Analysis. (0003-2638). Oxford.

Anarchist studies. (0967-3393). Cambridge.

Anatolian studies. (0066-1546). London.

Ancient Nepal. Kathmandu.

ANEMOS. Hasekô Sôgôkenkyusho.

Annales æquatoria. (0254-4296). Lovenjoel.

Annales d'économie et de statistique. (0769-489X). Paris.

Annales d'études internationales = Annals of international studies. (0066-2135). Brussels.

Annales de géographie. (0003-4010). Paris.

Annales de l'économie publique sociale et coopérative = Annals of public and cooperative economics. (1370-4788). Brussels.

Annales internationales de criminologie = International annals of criminology = Anales internacionales de criminología. (0003-4452). Paris.

Annales universitatis Mariae Curie-Skłodowska: Sectio H. Oeconomia. (0459-9586). Lublin.

Annales: Histoire, sciences sociales. Paris.

Annali della fondazione Luigi Einaudi. Turin.

Annali di ca'foscari. Venice.

Annals of family studies. Tokyo.

Annals of human biology. (0301-4460). London.

Annals of regional science. (0570-1864). Heidelberg.

Annals of the American Academy of Political and Social Science. (0002-7162). Thousand Oaks CA.

Annals of the Association of American Geographers. (0004-5608). Washington DC.

Annals of the Institite of Statistical Mathematics. Tokyo.

Année sociologique. (0066-2399). Paris.

Annuaire des pays de l'Ocean indien. (0247-400X). Paris.

Annuaire français de droit international. (0066-3085). Paris.

Annual bulletin. Kobe.

Annual bulletin of the Faculty of Humanities Matsuyama Shinonome College. Matsuyama.

Annual journal of the Japanese Association of Labor Sociology. Tokyo.

Annual of economic jurisprudence. Tokyo.

Annual of Institute Kanazawa Economical College. Kanazawa City.

Annual of the Department of Antiquities of Jordan. Amman.

Annual of the Institute of Economic Research Chuo University. Tokyo.

Annual of the Society of Economic Sociology. Kobe.

Annual report of Shizuoka Kenritsu Daigaku. Hamamatsu.

Annual report of studies in humanities and social sciences. Nara City.

Annual report of University of Shizuoka, Hamamatsu College. Shizuoka.

Annual reports of the Faculty of Arts and Letters Tohoku University. Tohoku.

Annual research report of Education Department of Rikkyo University. Tokyo.

Annual review of anthropology. (0084-6570). Palo Alto CA.

Annual review of energy and the environment. (0362-1626). Palo Alto CA.

Annual review of public health. (0163-7525). Palo Alto CA.

Annual review of Shukutoku University. Shukutoku.

Annual review of sociology. (0360-0572). Palo Alto CA.

Annual review of sociology [Japan]. Tokyo.

Annuals of Japan Association for Urban Sociology. Japan.

Annuals of sociology. Tokyo.

Anthropological forum. (0066-4677). Nedlands WA.

Anthropological linguistics. (0003-5483). Bloomington IN.

Anthropological papers of the American Museum of Natural History. (0065-9452). New York NY.

Anthropological quarterly. (0003-5491). Washington DC.
Anthropological science. (0918-7960). Tokyo.
Anthropological theory. (1463-4996). London.
Anthropologie [Paris]. (0003-5521). Paris.
Anthropologie visuelle. Paris.
Anthropology and aesthetics. (0277-1322). Santa Monica CA.
Anthropology and humanism. (0193-5615). Arlington VA.
Anthropology today. (0268-540X). London.
Anthropos [Athens]. (1105-2155). Athens.
Anthropos [St. Augustin]. (0257-9774). Sankt Augustin.
Anti-slavery international. London.
Antipode. (0066-4812). Oxford.
Antiquités africaines. (0066-4871). Paris.
Antiquity. (0003-598X). Cambridge.
Antropologia portuguesa. (0870-0990). Coimbra.
Antropologica. (0003-6110). Caracas.
Antropologiska studier. (0003-6129). Stockholm.
Anuario de estudios centroamericanos. (0377-7316). San José.
Anuario de eusko folklore. (0210-7732). San Sebastián.
Anuarul arhivei de folclor. (0255-4895). Bucharest.
Anuarul Institutului de Etnografie şi Folclor „Constantin Brăiloiu". (1220-5230). Bucharest.
Applied economics. (0003-6846). London.
Applied economics letters. (1350-4851). London.
Applied financial economics. (0960-3107). London.
Appropriate technology. (0305-0920). London.
Apuntes. (0252-1865). Lima.
Arab affairs. (0950-0731). London.
Arab studies journal. (1083-4753). Washington DC.
Arab studies quarterly. (0271-3519). Belmont MA.
Arabica. (0570-5398). Leiden.
Archaeologia polona. (0066-5924). Warsaw.
Archaeology in Oceania. (0003-8121). Sydney.
Archeologia. (0066-605X). Warsaw.
Archeologia polski. (0003-8180). Warsaw.
Archipel. (0044-8613). Paris.
Archiv des öffentlichen Rechts. (0003-8911). Tübingen.
Archiv des Völkerrechts. (0003-892X). Tübingen.
Archiv für Kommunalwissenschaften. (0003-9209). Stuttgart.
Archiv für Rechts- und Sozialphilosophie = Archives de philosophie du droit et de philosophie sociale =
    Archives for philosophy of law and social philosophy = Archivo de filosofía jurídica y social.
    (0001-2343). Stuttgart.
Archiv für Sozialgeschichte. (0066-6505). Bonn.
Archív orientální. (0044-8699). Prague.
Archives européennes de sociologie = European journal of sociology = Europäisches Archiv für
    Soziologie. (0003-9756). Cambridge.
Archives of economic history. Athens.
Archives of suicide research. (1381-1118). Dordrecht.
Area. (0004-0894). London.
Arena magazine. (1039-1010). Victoria.
Argumentation. (0920-427X). Dordrecht.
Armed forces and society. (0095-327X). New Brunswick NJ.

Arquivo. Maputo.
ART AsiaPacific. (1039-3625). Sydney.
Artha vijñāna. (0971-586X). Pune.
Artibus asiae. (0004-3648). Ascona.
ASEAN economic bulletin. (0217-4472). Singapore.
Asia journal of theology. (0218-0812). Bangalore.
Asia major. (0004-4482). Princeton NJ.
Asia Pacific business review. (1360-2381). London.
Asia Pacific journal of anthropology. (1444-2213). Canberra.
Asia Pacific journal of environmental law. (1385-2140). London.
Asia Pacific journal on environment and development. (1023-7895). Dhaka.
Asia Pacific review. (1343-9006). Tokyo.
Asian and Pacific migration journal. (0117-1968). Quezon City.
Asian culture (Asian-Pacific culture) quarterly. (0378-8911). Taipei.
Asian Development Bank Occasional Papers. Manila.
Asian economic journal. Hong Kong.
Asian economic review. (0004-4555). Hyderabad.
Asian economies. (0304-260X). Seoul.
Asian folklore studies. (0385-2342). Nagoya.
Asian journal of communication. (0129-2986). Singapore.
Asian journal of political science. Singapore.
Asian journal of public administration. (0259-8272). Hong Kong.
Asian music. (0044-9202). Ithaca NY.
Asian Pacific communication. (0957-6851). Clevedon.
Asian perspective [S. Korea]. (0258-9184). Seoul.
Asian perspectives [Hawaii]. (0066-8435). Honolulu HI.
Asian profile. (0304-8675). Hong Kong.
Asian research trends. (0917-1479). Tokyo.
Asian studies review. (0314-7533). Sydney.
Asian survey. (0004-4687). Berkeley CA.
Asian thought and society. (0361-3968). New York NY.
Asian-Pacific economic literature. (0818-9935). Oxford.
Atlal. The journal of Saudi Arabian archaeology. Riyadh.
Aus der Südosteuropa-Forschung. Munich.
Aussenpolitik. (0587-3835). Bielefeld.
Aussenwirtschaft. (0004-8216). Zurich.
Australian Aboriginal studies. (0729-4352). Canberra.
Australian and New Zealand journal of sociology. Bundoora.
Australian and New Zealand journal of statistics. (1369-1473). Oxford.
Australian cultural history. (0728-8433). Kensington NSW.
Australian economic history review. (0004-8992). Oxford.
Australian economic papers. (0004-900X). Adelaide.
Australian economic review. (0004-9018). Oxford.
Australian feminist studies. (0816-4649). Basingstoke.
Australian geographer. (0004-9182). Gladesville NSW.
Australian geographical studies. (0004-9190). Campbell.
Australian historical studies. (1031-461X). Carlton.
Australian journal of agricultural economics. (0004-9395). East Melbourne.
Australian journal of anthropology. (1035-8811). Sydney.
Australian journal of Chinese affairs. (0156-7365). Canberra.
Australian journal of early childhood. (0312-5033). Watson ACT.

Australian journal of international affairs. (1035-7718). Canberra.
Australian journal of linguistics. (0726-8602). Cambridge.
Australian journal of political science. (1036-1146). Oxford.
Australian journal of politics and history. (0004-9522). Queensland.
Australian journal of public administration. (0313-6647). Sydney.
Australian journal of social issues. (0157-6321). Sydney.
Australian quarterly. (0005-0091). Balmain.
Australian studies. (0954-0954). Stirling.
Australian year book of international law. (0084-7658). Canberra.
Australian-Canadian studies. (0810-1906). Nathan QLD.
Austrian history yearbook. (0667-2378). Minneapolis MN.
AWR Bulletin. (0014-2492). Vienna.
Azania. (0067-270X). Nairobi.
Aziia i Afrika segodnia. Moscow.
Baessler-Archiv. (0005-3856). Berlin.
Baishin. Osaka.
Balkanologie. (1279-7952). Paris.
Banca Nazionale del Lavoro quarterly review. (0005-4607). Rome.
Bancaria. (0005-4623). Rome.
Bangladesh development studies. (0304-095X). Dhaka.
Bangladesh journal of political economy. Dhaka.
Bangladesh journal of public administration. Dhaka.
Bank of England quarterly bulletin. (0005-5166). London.
BC studies. (0005-2949). Vancouver.
Behavioral and brain sciences. (0140-525X). New York NY.
Beiträge zur Japanologie. (0522-6759). Vienna.
Belizean studies. (0250-6831). Belize City.
Benefits: a journal of social security research policy and practice. (0962-7898). Nottingham.
Berkeley journal of sociology. (0067-5830). Berkeley CA.
Berkeley technology law journal. (0885 2715). Berkeley CA.
Berliner indologische Studien. Reinbek.
Berliner Journal für Soziologie. (0863-1808). Berlin.
Bevolking en gezin. (0772-764X). Brussels.
Biblical archaeologist. (0006-0895). Baltimore MD.
Biblioteka etnografii polskiej. (0067-7655). Warsaw.
BIISS journal. (1010-9356). Dhaka.
Bijdragen tot de taal-, land- en volkenkunde. (0006-2294). Leiden.
Bilig. (1301-0549). Ankara.
Bioethics. (0269-9702). Oxford.
Biography. (0162-4962). Honolulu HI.
Biométrie humaine et anthropologie. (1279-7863). Paris.
Body and society. (1357-034X). London.
Boekmancahier: kwartaalschrift voor kunst, onderzoek en beleid. (0925-0239). Amsterdam.
BOFIT discussion papers. (1456-4564). Helsinki.
Boletim do Museu Paraense Emílio Goeldi: Série antropologia. (0522-7291). Belém.
Boletín de antropología americana. (0252-841X). Mexico City.
Boletín de la Asociación Española de Orientalistas. (0571-3692). Madrid.
Boletín. Centro de estudios monetarios latinoamericanos. (0186-7229). Mexico City.
Borneo research bulletin. (0006-7806). Williamsburg VA.
Borneo review. Sabah.
Botswana notes and records. (0525-5059). Gaborone.

Boundary and security bulletin. (0967-411X). Durham.
British accounting review. (0890-8389). London.
British elections and parties review. (1368-9886). Ilford.
British journal for the history of science. (0007-0874). Cambridge.
British journal of Canadian studies. (0269-9222). London.
British journal of clinical psychology. (0144-6657). Leicester.
British journal of criminology. (0007-0955). London.
British journal of developmental psychology. (0261-510X). Leicester.
British journal of educational studies. (0007-1005). Oxford.
British journal of ethnomusicology. (0968-1221). London.
British journal of industrial relations. (0007-1080). Oxford.
British journal of management. (1045-3172). Chichester.
British journal of Middle Eastern studies. (1353-0194). Durham.
British journal of political science. (0007-1234). Cambridge.
British journal of psychology. (0007-1269). Leicester.
British journal of social psychology. (0144-6665). Leicester.
British journal of social work. (0045-3102). Oxford.
British journal of sociology. (0007-1315). London.
British review of New Zealand studies. (0951-6204). Edinburgh.
British year book of international law. (0068-2691). Oxford.
Brookings papers on economic activity. (0007-2303). Washington DC.
Brookings review. (0745-1253). Washington DC.
Bulletin. Yokohama.
Bulletin d'études indiennes. (0761-3156). Paris.
Bulletin de l'École française d'Extrême-Orient. (0336-1519). Paris.
Bulletin de la Société d'archéologie copte. Cairo.
Bulletin de la Société des études océaniennes. Papeete.
Bulletin des études africaines de l'INALCO. (0249-728X). Paris.
Bulletin du Centre genevois d'Anthropologie. Louvain.
Bulletin for international fiscal documentation. (0007-4624). Amsterdam.
Bulletin of Aichi University of Education. Aichi.
Bulletin of Chukyo Gakuin University. Gifu.
Bulletin of comparative labour relations. The Hague.
Bulletin of Eastern Caribbean affairs. (0254-7406). Cave Hill.
Bulletin of economic research. (0307-3378). Oxford.
Bulletin of education. Tokyo.
Bulletin of Faculty of Education, Okayama University. Okayama.
Bulletin of graduate studies. Tokyo.
Bulletin of Hirosaki Gakuin College. Hirosaki.
Bulletin of Hokkaido Tokai University. Sapporo.
Bulletin of Holy Cross College. Mie.
Bulletin of Indonesian economic studies. (0007-4918). Canberra.
Bulletin of International Research Center for Japanese Studies. Kyoto.
Bulletin of Ishinomaki Senshu University. Ishinomaki.
Bulletin of Joetsu University education. Japan.
Bulletin of Kanto Gakuin University. Yokohama.
Bulletin of Latin American research. (0261-3050). Oxford.
Bulletin of liberal arts and sciences of the National Defense Medical College. Tokyo.
Bulletin of Musashino Women's College. Tokyo.
Bulletin of Shiga Junior College of Cultural Studies. Shiga.
Bulletin of Shukugawa Gakuin Junior College. Nishinomiya.

Bulletin of sociology. Tokyo.
Bulletin of Tanzanian affairs. (0952-2948). London.
Bulletin of the Akita Prefectural College of Agriculture. Akita City.
Bulletin of the American Schools of Oriental Research. (0003-097X). Baltimore MD.
Bulletin of the Bihar Tribal Welfare Research Institute. Ranchi.
Bulletin of the Department of Management and Information Science Jôbu University. Gunma.
Bulletin of the doctoral research course in human culture. Tokyo.
Bulletin of The Faculty of Education. Tokyo.
Bulletin of the Faculty of Education [Sapporo]. Sapporo.
Bulletin of the Faculty of Education [Wakayama]. Wakayama.
Bulletin of the Faculty of Education Hokkaido University. Hokkaido.
Bulletin of the Faculty of Education, Chiba University. Chiba.
Bulletin of the Faculty of General Education of Utsunomiya University. Tochigi.
Bulletin of the Faculty of Humanities and Social Science. Tsu.
Bulletin of the Faculty of Humanities of Aichi Gakuin University. Aichi.
Bulletin of the Faculty of Literature Aichi Prefectural University. Aichi.
Bulletin of the Faculty of Sociology. Kyoto.
Bulletin of the Faculty of Sociology [Ôtsu]. Ôtsu.
Bulletin of the Graduate Division of Literature. Tokyo.
Bulletin of the Indian Institute of History of Medicine. (0304-9558). New Delhi.
Bulletin of the Institute of Ethnology, Academia Sinica. (0001-3935). Taipei.
Bulletin of the Institute of Oriental Philosophy. Tokyo.
Bulletin of the Institute of Socio-Information and Communication Studies. Tokyo.
Bulletin of the International Committee on Urgent Anthropological and Ethnological Research. (0538-5865). Vienna.
Bulletin of the Japan Society for the Study of Adult Education. Tokyo.
Bulletin of the Museum of Far Eastern Antiquities. (0081-5691). Stockholm.
Bulletin of the Nanzan Institute for Religion and Culture. (0386-720X). Nagoya.
Bulletin of the Polytechnic University. Tokyo.
Bulletin of the Research Institute Chuo-Gakuin University. Tokyo.
Bulletin of the School of Education. Nagoya.
Bulletin of the School of Oriental and African Studies. (0041-977X). London.
Bulletin of Tibetology. (0007-5159). Gangtok.
Bulletin of Tohoku Fukushi University. Sendai.
Bulletin, Yokohama City University. Yokohama.
Bulletin. Bank of Finland. (0784-6509). Helsinki.
Bulletin. Kagawa University. Takamatsu.
Bulletin. Oita University, Faculty of Education. Oita City.
Bulletin. Tokyo University, Graduate School. Tokyo.
Bulletin. University of the Ryukyus, College of Law and Letters. Okinawa.
Bulletin: Bank of Botswana. Gaborone.
Bungaku-kenkyuka Kiyo (Journal of the Waseda Graduate School). Waseda.
Bungakubu ronshu (Journal of the Aichi Prefectural University). Aichi.
Business economist. (0306-5049). Watford.
Business ethics quarterly. (1052-150X). Charlottesville VA.
Business ethics: a European review. (0962-8770). Oxford.
Business history. (0007-6791). Ilford.
Business history review. (0007-6805). Boston MA.
Cahiers africains d'administration publique = African administrative studies. (0007-9588). Tangiers.
Cahiers d'études africaines. (0008-0055). Paris.
Cahiers d'études arabes. (0985-1909). Paris.

Cahiers d'études sur la Méditerranée orientale et le monde turco-iranien. (0764-9878). Paris.
Cahiers d'outre-mer. (0373-5843). Bordeaux.
Cahiers de l'Asie du Sud-Est. (0399-1652). Paris.
Cahiers de l'homme. (0068-5046). Paris.
Cahiers de l'ISSP. Neuchâtel.
Cahiers de linguistique. Asie orientale. (0153-3320). Paris.
Cahiers des Amériques latines. (0008-0020). Paris.
Cahiers du monde russe. (1252-6576). Paris.
Cahiers économiques et monétaires. (0396-4701). Paris.
Cahiers internationaux de sociologie. (0008-0276). Paris.
Cahiers ivoiriens de recherche linguistique. (0252-9386). Abidjan.
Cakalele: Maluku research journal. (1053-2285). Honolulu HI.
California management review. (0008-1256). Berkeley CA.
Cambridge anthropology. Cambridge.
Cambridge journal of economics. (0309-166X). London.
Cambridge law journal. (0008-1973). Cambridge.
Cambridge review of international affairs. (0955-7571). Cambridge.
Canadian Association of African Studies newsletter = Association canadienne des études africaines
    bulletin. (0228-8397). Ottawa.
Canadian ethnic studies = Études ethniques au Canada. (0008-3496). Montréal.
Canadian geographer. (0008-3658). Montreal.
Canadian historical review. (0008-3755). Toronto.
Canadian journal of African studies = Revue canadienne des études africaines. (0008-3968). Ottawa.
Canadian journal of agricultural economics = Revue canadienne d'économie rurale. (0008-3976).
    Ottawa.
Canadian journal of economics = Revue canadienne d'économique. (0008-4085). Downsview.
Canadian journal of human sexuality. (1188-4517). Ontario.
Canadian journal of philosophy. (0045-5091). Calgary.
Canadian journal of political and social theory. (0380-9420). Montreal.
Canadian journal of political science = Revue canadienne de science politique. (0008-4239). Ottawa.
Canadian journal of sociology = Cahiers canadiens de sociologie. (0318-6431). Edmonton.
Canadian journal of statistics = Revue canadienne de statistiques. (0319-5724). Ottawa.
Canadian public administration = Administration publique du Canada. (0008-4840). Toronto.
Canadian review of sociology and anthropology = Revue canadienne de sociologie et d'anthropologie.
    (0008-4948). Montréal.
Canadian review of studies in nationalism = Revue canadienne des études sur le nationalisme. (0317-
    7904). Charlottetown.
Canadian yearbook of international law = Annuaire canadien de droit international. (0069-0058).
    Vancouver.
Canberra anthropology. (0314-9099). Canberra.
Capital and class. (0309-8168). London.
Capitalism, nature, socialism. (1045-5752). New York NY.
Caravelle. (1147-6753). Toulouse.
Caribbean quarterly. (0008-6495). Kingston.
Caribbean studies = Estudios del Caribe = Études des Caraïbes. (0008-6533). Puerto Rico.
Caribe contemporáneo. (0185-2426). Mexico City.
Cato journal. (0273-3072). Washington DC.
Central Asia and the Caucasus: journal of social and political studies. Luleå.
Central Asian survey. (0263-4937). Abingdon.
Central Asiatic journal. (0008-9192). Wiesbaden.
Central European history. (0008-9389). Boston.

Central European Political Science Review. (1586-4197). Budapest.
Centro: Journal of the center of Puerto Rican studies. New York.
CEPAL review. (0251-2920). Santiago.
Challenge. (0577-5132). Armonk NY.
Child abuse and neglect. (0145-2134). Denver CO.
Child care in practice. (1357-5279). Belfast.
Child development. (0009-3920). Chicago IL.
Child welfare. (0009-4021). Washington DC.
Children and society. (0951-0605). London.
China city planning review. (1002-8447). Beijing.
China information. (0920-203X). Leiden.
China journal. Canberra.
China law reporter. Chicago IL.
China quarterly. (0009-4439). London.
China report. (0009-4455). New Delhi.
China review international. (1069-5834). Honolulu HI.
Chinese culture. (0009-4544). Taiwan.
Chinese economy. (0009-4552). Armonk NY.
Chinese sociology and anthropology. (0009-4625). Armonk NY.
Ching feng. (0009-4668). Hong Kong.
Choices. New York.
Chukyo daigkau shakaigaku kiyo. Aichi.
Ciclos. (0327-4063). Buenos Aires.
CIRIEC-España: Revista de economía pública, social y cooperativa. (0213-8093). Valencia.
Cities. (0264-2751). London.
City. (1360-4813). London.
Civilisations. (0009-8140). Brussels.
Civilization study. Japan.
Cognition. (0010-0277). Amsterdam.
Cognitive linguistics. (0936-5907). Berlin.
Cognitive science. (0364-0213). Norwood NJ.
Cold war history. (1468-2745). Ilford.
Collection. Purusartha. (0339-1744). Paris.
Collegium antropologicum. (0350-6134). Zagreb.
Columbia journal of transnational law. (0010-1931). New York NY.
Columbia journal of world business. (0022-5428). New York NY.
Columbia law review. (0010-1958). New York NY.
Commonwealth and comparative politics. (1466-2043). Ilford.
Communicateur. Paris.
Communication & society. Nagareyama.
Communication research. (0093-6502). Thousand Oaks CA.
Communication review. (1071-4421). New York NY.
Communication theory. (1050-3293). Cary NC.
Communist and post-communist studies. (0967-067X). Exeter.
Community development in Japan. Japan.
Community development journal. (0010-3802). Oxford.
Community welfare study. Osaka.
Comparative and international law journal of Southern Africa. (0010-4051). Pretoria.
Comparative political studies. (0010-4140). Thousand Oaks CA.
Comparative politics. (0010-4159). New York NY.
Comparative social research. (0195-6310). Greenwich CT.

Comparative studies in society and history. (0010-4175). New York NY.
Comparative studies of South Asia, Africa and the Middle East. (1089-201X). Durham NC.
Complutum. (1131-6993). Madrid.
Comprehensive urban studies. (0386-3506). Tokyo.
Computational and mathematical organization theory. (1381-298X). Dordrecht.
Computational economics. (0927-7099). Dordrecht.
Comunicación y sociedad. (0214-0039). Navarre.
Comunidades y culturas peruanas. Lima.
Comunità internazionale. (0010-5066). Padua.
Conflict resolution quarterly. (1536-5581). San Francisco CA.
Constitutional political economy. (1043-4062). Dordrecht.
Contemporary accounting research. (0823-9150). Toronto.
Contemporary British history. (1361-9462). Ilford.
Contemporary economic policy. (1074-3529). Oxford.
Contemporary economic problems. (0732-4308). Washington DC.
Contemporary Pacific. (1043-898X). Honolulu HI.
Contemporary policy issues. (0735-0007). Huntington Beach CA.
Contemporary security policy. (1352-3260). Ilford.
Contemporary sociological studies. Hokkaido.
Contemporary sociology - a journal of reviews. (0094-3061). Washington DC.
Contemporary South Asia. (0958-4935). Abingdon.
Contemporary Southeast Asia: A journal of international and strategic affairs. (0129-797X). Singapore.
Contention: Debates in society, culture, and science. (1056-1072). Bloomington IN.
Continuity and change. (0268-4160). Cambridge.
Contributions to Indian sociology. (0069-9667). New Delhi.
Contributions to Nepalese studies. Kirtipur.
Contributions to political economy. (0277-5921). London.
Cooperation and conflict. (0010-8367). London.
Coyuntura económica. (0120-3576). Bogota.
Coyuntura social. (0121-2532). Bogotá.
Crime and delinquency. (0011-1287). Thousand Oaks CA.
Crime and delinquency. Tokyo.
Crime and justice. (0192-3234). Chicago IL.
Crime, law and social change. (0925-4994). Dordrecht.
Criminal justice: the international journal of policy and practice. (1466-8025). London.
Criminology. (0011-1384). Columbus OH.
Critica marxista. (0011-152X). Rome.
Critica sociologica. (0011-1546). Rome.
Critical Asian studies. (1467-2715). London.
Critical perspectives on accounting. (1045-2354). London.
Critical review. (0891-3811). Chicago IL.
Critical social policy. (0261-0183). London.
Critical sociology. (0896-9205). Eugene OR.
Critique of anthropology. (0308-275X). London.
Croatian economic survey. (1330-4860). Zagreb.
Cross-cultural research. (1069-3971). Thousand Oaks CA.
Crossings. Queensland.
Crossroads. (0741-2037). DeKalb IL.
Cuadernos americanos. (0185-156X). Mexico City.
Cuadernos de administracion. (0120-3592). Bogota.
Cuadernos de nuestra América. Havana.

Cuadernos de sección antropologia-etnografia. (0213-0297). San Sebastián.
Cuadernos del sur. (1405-1966). Oaxaca.
Cuestiones políticas. (0798-1406). Maracaibo.
Cultural anthropology. (0886-7356). Arlington VA.
Cultural critique. (0882-4371). Minneapolis.
Cultural dynamics. (0921-3740). London.
Cultural geographies. (1474-4740). London.
Cultural studies. (0950-2386). London.
Cultural values. (1362-5179). Oxford.
Culture & psychology. (1354-067X). London.
Culture, health and sexuality. (1369-1058). London.
Culture, medicine and psychiatry. (0165-005X). Dordrecht.
Curator. (0011-3069). New York NY.
Current anthropology. (0011-3204). Washington DC.
Current English studies. Tokyo.
Current history. (0011-3530). Philadelphia PA.
Current issues in language and society. (1352-0520). Clevedon.
Current politics and economics of Europe. (1057-2309). Huntington NY.
Current research on peace and violence. (0356-7893). Tampere.
Current sociology. (0011-3921). London.
Current world leaders. (0192-6802). Santa Barbara CA.
Cyprus review. (1015-2881). Nicosia.
Czech sociological review. (1210-3861). Prague.
Dædalus. (0011-5266). Cambridge MA.
Daigaku jiho. Japan.
Daigaku ronshu. Hiroshima.
De Economist. (0013-063X). Dordrecht.
Debates de coyuntura económica. (0120-8969). Bogota.
Defence and peace economics. (1024-2694). Reading.
Delhi law review. Delhi.
Democracy & nature. (1085-5661). Basingstoke.
Democratization. (1351-0347). Ilford.
Demográfia. (0011-8249). Budapest.
Demografie. (0011-8265). Prague.
Demography. (0070-3370). Washington DC.
Derechos humanos. (0327-1846). Buenos Aires.
Desarrollo económico. (0046-001X). Buenos Aires.
Desarrollo y sociedad. (0120-3584). Bogota.
Deutschland Archiv: Zeitschrift für das vereinigte Deutschland. (0012-1428). Cologne.
Developing economies. (0012-1533). Tokyo.
Developing world bioethics. (1471-8731). Oxford.
Development. (1011-6370). Rome.
Development & socio-economic progress. Cairo.
Development and change. (0012-155X). London.
Development anthropologist. (1087-9900). Binghamton NY.
Development bulletin. (1035-1132). Canberra.
Development dialogue. (0345-2328). Uppsala.
Development in practice. (0961-4524). Oxford.
Development policy review. (0950-6764). Oxford.
Development Southern Africa. (0376-835X). Halfway House.
Developmental psychology. (0012-1649). Washington.

Developments: the international development magazine. (1461-474X). Glasgow.

Diachronica. (0176-4225). Amsterdam.

Dialectical anthropology. (0304-4092). Dordrecht.

Dialogue. St. Augustine.

Diaspora. (1044-2057). Toronto.

Die Welt des Orients. Göttingen.

Diplomacy and statecraft. (0959-2296). Ilford.

Diplomatic history. (0145-2096). Wilmington, DE.

Dirasat: Administrative Sciences. (1026-373X). Amman.

Dirasat: Educational Sciences. (1026-3713). Amman.

Dirasat: Human and Social Sciences. (1026-3721). Amman.

Dirasat: the humanities. (0255-8033). Amman.

Disability and society. (0968-7599). Abingdon.

Disasters: Journal of disaster studies, policy and management. (0361-3666). Oxford.

Discourse & society. (0957-9265). London.

Discourse studies. (1461-4456). London.

Discussion papers. Nagoya.

Documents. (0151-0827). Paris.

Dohodaigaku ronso. Nagoya.

Dokumente. (0012-5172). Bonn.

Dor ledor. Tel Aviv.

Douwa mondai kenkyu. Osaka.

Dreptul. Bucharest.

Druzhba narodov. Moscow.

Early China. (0362-5028). Berkeley CA.

East Asian review. Seoul.

East European Jewish affairs. (1350-1674). London.

East European meetings in ethnomusicology. (1221-9711). Bucharest.

East European politics and societies. (0888-3254). Berkeley CA.

East European quarterly. (0012-8449). Boulder CO.

Eastern Africa social science research review. Addis Ababa.

Eastern anthropologist. (0012-8686). Lucknow.

Eastern Buddhist. (0012-8708). Kyoto.

Ecological economics. (0921-8009). Amsterdam.

Ecology of food and nutrition. (0367-0244). New York NY.

Econometric reviews. (0747-4938). New York NY.

Econometric theory. (0266-4666). New York NY.

Econometrica. (0012-9682). Evanston IL.

Economia & lavoro. (0012-978X). Rome.

Economia [Lisbon]. (0870-3531). Lisbon.

Economia [Quito]. (0012-9704). Quito.

Economia chilena. (0717-3830). Santiago.

Economia e banca. (0393-9243). Trento.

Economia internazionale. (0012-981X). Genoa.

Economía y administración. (0716-0100). Concepción.

Economia y desarrollo. (0252-8584). Havana.

Economic affairs [Calcutta]. (0424-2513). Calcutta.

Economic and business review for Central and South-Eastern Europe. (1580-0466). Ljubljana.

Economic and industrial democracy. (0143-831X). London.

Economic and social review. (0012-9984). Dublin.

Economic bulletin. Norges bank. (0029-1676). Oslo.

Economic development and cultural change. (0013-0079). Chicago IL.
Economic development quarterly. (0891-2424). Thousand Oaks CA.
Economic eye. (0389-0503). Tokyo.
Economic geography. (0013-0095). Worcester MA.
Economic history review. (0013-0117). Oxford.
Economic inquiry. (0095-2583). Oxford.
Economic issues. (1363-7029). Stoke-on-Trent.
Economic journal. (0013-0133). Oxford.
Economic modelling. (0264-9993). Guildford.
Economic notes. (0391-5026). Siena.
Economic papers [Australia]. (0812-0439). East Hawthorn.
Economic papers. Bank of Korea. (1226-7589). Seoul.
Economic policy. (0266-4658). Oxford.
Economic record. (0013-0249). Sydney.
Economic roundup. Canberra.
Economic systems. (0939-3625). Heidelberg.
Economic systems research. (0953-5314). Abingdon.
Economic theory. (0938-2259). Heidelberg.
Económica [Argentina]. (0013-0419). La Plata.
Economica [London]. (0013-0427). London.
Economics and philosophy. (0266-2671). New York NY.
Economics and politics. (0954-1985). Oxford.
Economics letters. (0165-1765). Amsterdam.
Economics of planning. (0013-0451). Dordrecht.
Economics of transition. (0967-0750). Oxford.
Économie appliquée. (0013-0494). Paris.
Économie et statistique. (0336-1454). Paris.
Économie internationale. (1240-8093). Paris.
Économies et sociétés. (0013-0567). Paris.
Economisch en sociaal tijdschrift. (0013-0575). Antwerp.
Economy and society. (0308-5147). London.
Economy and society [Japan]. Tokyo.
Edinburgh anthropology. (0953-2919). Edinburgh.
Education action. London.
Education and urban society. (0013-1245). Thousand Oaks CA.
Education economics. (0964-5292). London.
Educational gerontology. (0360-1277). London.
Educational research. (0013-1881). London.
Ekistics. (0013-2942). Athens.
Ekonomia. (1025-5508). Nicosia.
Ekonomisk debatt. (0345-2646). Stockholm.
Ekonomist. (0869-4672). Moscow.
Ekonomista. (0013-3205). Warsaw.
Ekonomski pregled. (0424-7558). Zagreb.
Electoral studies. (0261-3794). Kidlington.
Electronic markets: The international journal of electronic commerce & business media. (1019-6781). London.
Elementa: Journal of Slavic studies and comparative cultural semiotics. (1064-6663). London.
Emergences: journal for the study of media and composite cultures. (1045-7224). Basingstoke.
Empirica. (0340-8744). Dordrecht.
Empirical economics. (0377-7332). Heidelberg.

Employee relations. (0142-5455). Bradford.
Energy economics. (0140-9883). Oxford.
Energy policy. (0301-4215). Guildford.
English in Africa. (0376-8902). Grahamstown.
English in Africa. Grahamstown.
English world-wide. (0172-8865). Amsterdam.
Ensayos sobre política económica. (0120-4483). Bogota.
Enterprise & society: the international journal of business history. (1467-2227). Oxford.
Entrepreneurship & regional development. (0898-5626). London.
Entrepreneurship, innovation, and change. (1059-0137). New York NY.
Entrepreneurship: Theory and practice. (1042-2587). Waco TX.
Entreprises et histoire. (1161-2770). Paris.
Environment. (0013-9157). Washington DC.
Environment and behavior. (0013-9165). Thousand Oaks CA.
Environment and planning A. (0308-518X). London.
Environment and planning B: Planning and design. (0265-8135). London.
Environment and planning C: Government and policy. (0263-774X). London.
Environment and planning D: Society and space. (0263-7758). London.
Environment and urbanization. (0956-2478). London.
Environmental & resource economics. (0924-6460). Dordrecht.
Environmental impact assessment review. (0195-9255). New York NY.
Environmental information science. Tokyo.
Environmental law. (0046-2276). Portland OR.
Environmental politics. (0964-4016). Ilford.
Environmental values. (0963-2719). Cambridge.
ESP. Tokyo.
Espace géographique. (0046-2497). Paris.
Espace populations sociétés. (0755-7809). Villeneuve d'Ascq.
Esprit. (0014-0759). Paris.
Estrategia económica y financiera. (0121-4802). Bogota.
Estudios de Asia y Africa. (0185-0164). Mexico City.
Estudios de economía. (0304-2758). Santiago.
Estudios demográficos y urbanos. (0186-7210). Mexico City.
Estudios económicos. Mexico City.
Estudios internacionales. (0716-0240). Santiago.
Estudios latinoamericanos. (0187-1811). Mexico City.
Estudios políticos. (0185-1616). Mexico City.
Estudos de antropologia cultural e social. (0870-4457). Lisbon.
Ethical theory and moral practice. (1386-2820). Dordrecht.
Ethics. (0014-1704). Chicago IL.
Ethics and international affairs. (0892-6794). New York.
Ethnic and racial studies. (0141-9870). London.
Ethnic studies report. (1010-5832). Kandy.
Ethnicities. (1468-7968). London.
Ethnographisch archäologische Zeitschrift. (0012-7477). Berlin.
Ethnography. (1466-1381). London.
Ethnologia Balkanica: Journal for Southeast European Anthropology. Sofia.
Ethnologia Polona. (0137-4079). Warsaw.
Ethnologica helvetica. Bern.
Ethnologie française. (0046-2616). Paris.
Ethnologies. (1481-5974). Quebec.

Ethnology. (0014-1828). Pittsburgh PA.
Ethnomusicology. (0014-1836). Bloomington IN.
Ethnos. (0014-1844). Stockholm.
Etnografia polska. (0071-1861). Warsaw.
Etnograficheskoe obozrenie. Moscow.
Etnologiska studier. (0374 7530). Gothenburg.
Etnoloska tribina. (0351-1944). Zagreb.
Études balkaniques. Sofia.
Études et documents. (0182-788X). Paris.
Études et documents berbères. (0295-5245). Paris.
Études inter-ethniques. (0761-7291). Lille.
Études internationales. (0014-2123). Quebec.
Études maliennes. Bamako.
Études mésoaméricaines. (0378-5726). Mexico City.
Études mongoles et sibériennes. (0766-507S). Nanterre.
Études rurales. (0014-2182). Paris.
Études sociales. Paris.
Eurasian studies. (1300-1604). Ankara.
Eurasian studies yearbook. (0042-0786). Bloomington IN.
Eure: Revista latinoamericana de estudios urbanos regionales. (0250-7161). Santiago.
Eurobalkans. Aegina.
Euromoney. (0014-2433). London.
Europa ethnica. Vienna.
Europe-Asia studies. (0966-8136). Abingdon.
European accounting review. (0963-8180). London.
European business organization law review. (1566-7529). The Hague.
European economic review. (0014-2921). Amsterdam.
European financial management. (1354-7798). Oxford.
European foreign affairs review. (1384-6299). The Hague.
European history quarterly. (0265-6914). London.
European journal of archaeology. (1461-9571). London.
European journal of communication. (0267-3231). London.
European journal of crime, criminal law and criminal justice. (0928-9569). Deventer.
European journal of cultural studies. (1367-5494). London.
European journal of development research. (0957-8811). Ilford.
European journal of finance. (1351-847X). London.
European journal of housing policy. (1461-6718). London.
European journal of industrial relations. (0959-6801). London.
European journal of international relations. (1354-0661). London.
European journal of law and economics. (0929-1261). Dordrecht.
European journal of philosophy. (0966-8373). Oxford.
European journal of political research. (0304-4130). Oxford.
European journal of population = Revue européenne de démographie. (0168-6577). Amsterdam.
European journal of social psychology. (0046-2772). Chichester.
European journal of social theory. (1368-4310). London.
European journal of social work. (1369-1457). Oxford.
European journal of the history of economic thought. (0967-2567). London.
European journal of women's studies. (1350-5068). London.
European journal on criminal policy and research. (0928-1371). Dordrecht.
European law journal. (1351-5993). Oxford.
European legacy: towards new paradigms. (1084-8770). Basingstoke.

European review of agricultural economics. (0165-1587). Oxford.
European review of history = Revue européenne d'histoire. (1350-7486). Abingdon.
European review of Latin American and Caribbean studies = Revista europea de estudios latinoamericanos y del Caribe. (0924-0608). Amsterdam.
European security. (0966-2839). Ilford.
European societies. (1461-6696). London.
European sociological review. (0266-7215). Oxford.
European Union politics. (1465-1165). London.
European urban and regional studies. (0969-7764). London.
Evaluation. (1356-3890). London.
Evaluation review. (0193-841X). Thousand Oaks CA.
Evolution and human behavior. (1090-5138). New York NY.
Evolutionary anthropology. (1060-1538). New York NY.
Explorations in economic history. (0014-4983). Duluth MN.
Extrême-orient, extrême-occident: Cahiers de recherches comparatives. (0754-5010). Paris.
Fabula. (0014-6242). Berlin.
Faculty bulletin humanity and science. Kobe.
Family and community history. (1463-1180). Leeds.
Family studies. Kobe.
Far Eastern affairs. (0206-149X). Moscow.
Fasciculi archaeologiae historicae. (0860-0007). Warsaw.
Fashion theory. (1362-704X). Oxford.
Federal Reserve Bank of New York economic policy review. New York NY.
Federal Reserve bulletin. (0014-9209). Washington DC.
Federalist. (0393-1358). Pavia.
Feminism & psychology. (0959-3535). London.
Feminist economics. (1354-5701). London.
Feminist legal studies. (0966-3622). Liverpool.
Feminist media studies. (1468-0777). London.
Feminist review. (0141-7789). London.
Feminist studies. (0046-3663). College Park MD.
Feminist theory. (1464-7001). London.
Field methods. (1525-822X). Thousand Oaks CA.
Finance & development. (0015-1947). Washington DC.
Finance India. (0970-3772). Delhi.
Financial analysts journal. (0015-198X). Charlottesville VA.
Financial history review. (0968-5650). Cambridge.
Financial management. (0046-3892). Tampa FL.
Financial markets, institutions and instruments. (0963-8008). Malden MA.
Finansy. (0869-446X). Moscow.
Finanzarchiv. (0015-2218). Tübingen.
Finnish economic papers. (0784-5197). Helsinki.
Finnish review of East European studies. Helsinki.
Finsk tidskrift. (0015-248X). Turku.
First language. (0142-7237). Chalfont St Giles.
Fiscal studies. (0143-5671). London.
Flux: Cahiers scientifiques internationaux réseaux et territoires. (1154-2721). Marne la Vallée.
Folia linguistica. (0165-4004). Berlin.
Folia linguistica historica. Berlin.
Folia primatologica. (0015-5713). Basle.
Folk. (0085-0756). Copenhagen.

Folk life: journal of ethnological studies. Leeds.
Folklore. (0015-587X). London.
Folklore [Calcutta]. (0015-5896). Calcutta.
Food and foodways. (0740-9710). New York NY.
Food policy. (0306-9192). Oxford.
For new sociology. Tokyo.
Foreign affairs. (0015-7120). New York NY.
Foreign policy. (0015-7228). Washington DC.
Foreign trade review. New Delhi.
Forensic linguistics. (1350-1771). Birmingham.
Forschungsjournal neue soziale Bewegungen. (0933-9361). Wiesbaden.
Forum. Tokyo.
Forum for development studies. (0803-9410). Oslo.
French cultural studies. (0957-1558). Chalfont St Giles.
French politics, culture, and society. (0882-1267). Oxford.
French studies. (0016-1128). Belfast.
Games and economic behavior. (0899-8256). Orlando FL.
Garcia de Orta: série de antropobiologia. (0870-0168). Lisbon.
Gendai no Esupuri. Japan.
Gendai shakairion kenkyu. Tokyo.
Gendaishakaigaku kenkyu. Sapporo.
Gender and development. (1355-2074). Oxford.
Gender and history. (0953-5233). Oxford.
Gender and Japanese history. Tokyo.
Gender and society. (0891-2432). Thousand Oaks CA.
Gender, place and culture: A journal of feminist geography. (0966-369X). Abingdon.
Gender, technology and development. (0971-8524). New Delhi.
Gender, work and organization. (0968-6673). Manchester.
Genders. Boulder Co.
Genèses. (1155-3219). France.
Geneva papers on risk and insurance theory. (0926-4957). Dordrecht.
Genus. (0016-6987). Rome.
Geoforum. (0016-7185). Oxford.
Geografiska annaler: Series B — Human geography. (0435-3684). Uppsala.
Geographia polonica. (0016-7282). Warsaw.
Geographical analysis. (0016-7363). Columbus OH.
Geographical journal. (0016-7398). London.
Geographical review. (0016-7428). New York NY.
Geographical review of India. (0375-6386). Calcutta.
Geographical review of Japan. (0016-7444). Tokyo.
Geographische Rundschau. (0016-7460). Braunschweig.
Geography. Sheffield.
Geojournal. (0343-2521). Dordrecht.
Geopolitics. (1465-0045). Ilford.
Geopolitique. (0752-1693). Paris.
George Washington international law review. (0748-4305). Washington DC.
Georgica. (0232-4490). Konstanz.
German history: the journal of the German history society. (0266-3554). London.
German politics. (0964-4008). London.
German studies review. (0149-7952). Northfield MN.
Gerontologist. Washington DC.

Geschichte und Gesellschaft. (0340-613X). Göttingen.
Gewerkschaftliche Monatshefte. (0016-9447). Wiesbaden.
Giornale degli economisti e annali di economia. (0017-0097). Milan.
Glasnik Slovenskega etnološkega društva = Bulletin of the Slovene ethnological society. Ljubljana.
Global dialogue. (1450-0590). Nicosia.
Global economic review. Seoul.
Global environmental change. (0959-3780). New York.
Global eye. Coulsdon.
Global governance. (1075-2846). Boulder CO.
Global networks: a journal of transnational affairs. (1470-2266). Oxford.
Global social policy: an interdisciplinary journal of public policy and social development. (1468-0181).
    London.
Global society. (1360-0826). Abingdon.
Global thinking. London.
Gospodarka narodowa. (0867-0005). Warsaw.
Gosudarstvo i pravo. (0132-0769). Moscow.
Gothenburg studies in social anthropology. (0348-4076). Gothenburg.
Governance. (0952-1895). Oxford.
Government and opposition. (0017-257X). London.
Grassroots development. (0733-6608). Rosslyn VA.
Greek economic review. Athens.
Greener management international. (0966-9671). Sheffield.
Group analysis: The journal of group analytic psychotherapy. (0533-3164). London.
Group decision and negotiation. (0926-2644). Dordrecht.
Group processes and intergroup relations. (1368-4302). London.
Groupwork. (0951-824X). London.
Growth and change. (0017-4815). Oxford.
Gyosei shakai ronshu. Fukushima.
Habitat international. (0197-3975). Oxford.
Hacienda pública española. (0210-1173). Madrid.
Hallinnon tutkimus. Tampere.
Hamburger Jahrbuch für Wirtschafts- und Gesellschaftspolitik. Tübingen.
Hannan ronshu. Osaka.
Harsunan Nijeriya. Kano.
Harvard journal of Asiatic studies. (0073-0548). Cambridge MA.
Harvard law review. (0017-811X). Cambridge MA.
Health and human rights. (1079-0969). Cambridge MA.
Health and social work. (0360-7283). Washington DC.
Health care for women international. (0739-9332). London.
Health policy. (0168-8510). Shannon.
Health policy and planning. (0268-1080). Oxford.
Health sciences. Tokyo.
Health transition review. (1036-4005). Canberra.
Health, risk & society. (1369-8575). Oxford.
Hebrew annual review. Columbus OH.
Hebrew studies. (0146-4094). Madison WI.
Hemispheres. (0239-8818). Warsaw.
Heritage of Zimbabwe. (0556-9605). Harare.
Hespëris Tamuda. Rabat.
Hessische Blätter für Volks- und Kulturforschung. (1075-3479). Marburg.
Hevrah u-revahah = Society and welfare. Jerusalem.

Higher education. (0018-1560). Dordrecht.
Hikone ronso. Shiga.
Himal. (1012-9804). Lalitpur.
Himalayan research bulletin. (0891-4834). New York NY.
Hiroshima Hogaku. Hiroshima.
Hispanic American historical review. (0018-2168). Durham NC.
Historical archaeology. (0440-9213). Tucson AZ.
Historical journal. (0018-246X). Cambridge.
Historical social research = Historische Sozialforschung. (0172-6404). Cologne.
History. (0018-2648). London.
History and anthropology. (0275-7206). London.
History and technology. (0734-1512). London.
History and theory. (0018-2656). Middletown CT.
History in Africa. (0361-5413). New Jersey.
History of political economy. (0018-2702). Durham NC.
History of political thought. (0143-781X). Thorverton.
History of psychiatry. (0957-154X). Chalfont St Giles.
History of religions. (0018-2710). Chicago IL.
History of the family. (1081-602X). Greenwich CT.
History of the human sciences. (0952-6951). London.
Hitotsubashi journal of commerce and management. (0018-2796). Tokyo.
Hitotsubashi journal of economics. (0018-280X). Tokyo.
Hitotsubashi journal of law and politics. (0073-2796). Tokyo.
Hitotsubashi journal of social studies. (0073-280X). Tokyo.
Hitotsubashi ronsô. Tokyo.
Hogaku (Bulletin of Kokugakuin University). Kokugakuin.
Hogaku (Journal. Surugadai University). Surugadai.
Hogaku kenkyu. Tokyo.
Hogaku kenyū. Tokyo.
Hogaku ronshu. Yamanashi.
Hogaku seijigaku ronkyu. Tokyo.
Hokuriku hogaku. Kanazawa.
Homines. (0252-8908). Hato Rey.
Homme. (0439-4216). Paris.
Homme et la société. (0018-4306). Paris.
Hong Kong anthropologist. Hong Kong.
Hong Kong economic papers. (0018-4578). Hong Kong.
Hong Kong journal of the social sciences. (1021-3619). Hong Kong.
Hong Kong law journal. (0378-0600). Hong Kong.
Horizontes antropológicos. (0104-7183). Porto Alegre.
Hosei Kenkyu. Fukuoka.
Hosogaku kenkyu. Tokyo.
Housing policy debate. (1051-1482). Washington DC.
Housing, theory and society. (1403-6096). Stockholm.
Howard journal of criminal justice. (0265-5527). Oxford.
Hudai keizai ronshû. Toyama.
Human communication studies. Tokyo.
Human development. (0018-716X). Basel.
Human ecology: the CHEC journal. (0268-4918). London.
Human ethology bulletin. (0739-2036). Orono ME.
Human nature. (1045-6767). Hawthorne NY.

Human organization. (0018-7259). Temple Terrace FL.
Human relations. (0018-7267). London.
Human resource development international. (1367-8868). London.
Human rights quarterly. (0275-0392). Baltimore MD.
Human studies. (0163-8548). Dordrecht.
Humor. (0933-1719). Berlin.
Hyogo University of Teacher Education journal. Hyogo.
Identities: global studies in culture and power. (1070-289X). Newark NJ.
IDS bulletin. (0265-5012). Brighton.
Ifo-Studien. (0018-9731). Berlin.
IFRA: Les cahiers. Nairobi.
Immigrants and minorities. (0261-9288). Ilford.
Impact assessment and project appraisal. (1461-5517). Guildford.
Ind-Africana. Delhi.
India quarterly. (0019-4220). New Delhi.
Indian economic and social history review. (0019-4646). New Delhi.
Indian economic journal. (0019-4662). Bombay.
Indian economic review. (0019-4671). Delhi.
Indian geographical journal. (0019-4824). Madras.
Indian journal of agricultural economics. (0019-5014). Bombay.
Indian journal of economics. (0019-5170). Allahabad.
Indian journal of gender studies. (0971-5215). New Delhi.
Indian journal of industrial relations. (0019-5286). New Delhi.
Indian journal of labour economics. (0971-7927). Patna.
Indian journal of political science. (0019-5510). Madras.
Indian journal of public administration. (0019-5561). New Delhi.
Indian journal of regional science. (0046-9017). Calcutta.
Indian journal of social work. (0019-5634). Bombay.
Indian labour journal. (0019-5723). Shimla.
Indian psychological abstracts and reviews. (0971-524X). New Delhi.
Indian social science review. (0972-0731). New Delhi.
Indiana journal of global legal studies. (1080-0727). Bloomington IN.
Indigenous affairs. (1024-3283). Copenhagen.
Indigenous world. (1024-0217). Copenhagen.
Indo Asia. (0019-719X). Sachsenheim-Hohenhaslach.
Indo-Iranian journal. (0019-7246). Dordrecht.
Indonesia. Ithaca NY.
Indonesia and the Malay world. (1363-9811). Oxford.
Indonesian quarterly. (0304-2170). Jakarta.
Industria. Bologna.
Industrial and corporate change. (0960-6491). Oxford.
Industrial and labor relations review. (0019-7939). Ithaca NY.
Industrial and social relations. (0258-7181). Bellville.
Industrial archaeology review. (0309-0728). Leicester.
Industrial relations. (0019-8676). eng.
Industrial relations journal. (0019-8692). Oxford.
Industrielle Beziehungen. (0943-2779). Mering.
Industry and innovation. (1366-2716). Abingdon.
Industry of free China. (0019-946X). Taipei.
Información comercial española. (0019-977X). Madrid.
Information & society. Tokyo.

Information economics and policy. (0167-6245). Amsterdam.
Information, communication & society. (1369-118X). London.
Informationen zur Raumentwicklung. (0303-2493). Bonn.
Informations sociales. (0046-9459). Paris.
Inner Asia. (1464-8172). Cambridge.
Innovation: the European journal of social sciences. (1351-1610). Oxford.
Inquiry. (0020-174X). Oslo.
Instructional science. (0020-4277). Dordrecht.
Insurance mathematics & economics. (0167-6687). Amsterdam.
Intelligence and national security. (0268-4527). Ilford.
Inter-Asia cultural studies. (1464-9373). London.
Interchange. (0826-4805). Dordrecht.
Intercultural communication studies. (1057-7769). San Antonio TX.
Intereconomics. (0020-5346). Hamburg.
Interfaces. (0092-2102). Providence RI.
Internasjonal politikk. (0020-577X). Oslo.
International affairs [London]. (0020-5850). London.
International affairs [Moscow]. (0130-9641). Minneapolis, MN.
International and comparative law quarterly. (0020-5893). London.
International business and management forum. Japan.
International development planning review. (1474-6743). Liverpool.
International development policies: review of the activities of international organizations. (0964-699X).
    London.
International economic journal. (1016-8737). Seoul.
International economic review. (0020-6598). Philadelphia PA.
International feminist journal of politics. (1461-6742). London.
International history review. (0707-5332). Burnaby, British Columbia.
International interactions. (0305-0629). Philadelphia.
International journal. (0020-7020). Toronto.
International journal for philosophy of religion. (0020-7047). Dordrecht.
International journal for the semiotics of law = Revue internationale de sémiotique juridique. (0952-
    8059). Liverpool.
International journal of accounting. (0020-7063). Heidelberg.
International journal of African historical studies. (0361-7882). Boston MA.
International journal of American linguistics. (0020-7071). Chicago IL.
International journal of children's rights. (0927-5568). The Hague.
International journal of comparative and applied criminal justice. Wichita KS.
International journal of comparative labour law and industrial relations. (0952-617X). The Hague.
International journal of comparative sociology. (0020-7152). Leiden.
International journal of cross cultural management. (1470-5958). London.
International journal of cultural studies. (1367-8779). London.
International journal of Dravidian linguistics. Trivandrum.
International journal of drug policy. (0955-3959). Amsterdam.
International journal of entrepreneurship and innovation. (1465-7503). London.
International journal of game theory. (0020-7276). Heidelberg.
International journal of health services. (0020-7314). Amityville NY.
International journal of human resource management. (0958-5192). London.
International journal of industrial organization. (0167-7187). Amsterdam.
International journal of Japanese sociology. (0918-7545). Tokyo.
International journal of Kurdish studies. (0885-386X). New York NY.
International journal of law, policy, and the family. (1360-9939). Oxford.

International journal of Middle East studies. (0020-7438). New York NY.
International journal of offender therapy and comparative criminology. (0306-624X). New York NY.
International journal of organizational analysis. (1055-3185). Bowling Green KY.
International journal of pharmacy practice. (0961-7671). London.
International journal of philosophical studies. (0967-2559). London.
International journal of politics, culture and society. (0891-4486). New York NY.
International journal of primatology. (0164-0291). New York NY.
International journal of psychoanalysis. (0020-7578). London.
International journal of public opinion research. (0954-2892). Oxford.
International journal of Punjab studies. (0971-5223). New Delhi.
International journal of social economics. (0306-8293). Bradford.
International journal of social psychiatry. (0020-7640). London.
International journal of social research methodology: theory & practice. (1364-5579). London.
International journal of sustainable development. (0960-1406). Geneva.
International journal of the economics of business. (1357-1516). Abingdon.
International journal of the history of sport. (0952-3367). Ilford.
International journal of the sociology of language. (0165-2516). Berlin.
International journal of the sociology of law. (0194-6595). London.
International journal of transport economics. (0391-8440). Rome.
International journal of urban and regional research. (0309-1317). Sevenoaks.
International journal on minority and group rights. (1385-4879). Dordrecht.
International labour review. (0020-7780). Geneva.
International migration = Migrations internationales = Migraciones internacionales. (0020-7985).
    Geneva.
International migration review. (0197-9183). New York NY.
International minds. (0957-1299). London.
International negotiation: a journal of theory and practice. (1382-340X). The Hague.
International organization. (0020-8183). Cambridge MA.
International peacekeeping. (1353-3312). Ilford.
International perspectives. (0381-4874). Ottawa.
International political science review = Revue internationale de science politique. (0192-5121). London.
International politics. (1384-5748). The Hague.
International regional science review. (0160-0176). Thousand Oaks CA.
International relations. London.
International relations. (0047-1178). London.
International relations [Japan]. Japan.
International review of administrative sciences. (0020 8523). London.
International review of applied economics. (0269-2171). Abingdon.
International review of education. (0020-8566). The Hague.
International review of law and economics. (0144-8188). New York NY.
International review of retail, distribution and consumer research. (0959-3969). London.
International review of social history. (0020-8590). Cambridge.
International review of the Red Cross. (1560-7755). Geneva.
International security. (0162-2889). Cambridge MA.
International small business journal. (0266-2426). Macclesfield.
International social science journal. (0020-8701). Oxford.
International social work. (0020-8728). London.
International sociology. (0268-5809). London.
International spectator. (0393-2729). Rome.
International studies. (0020-8817). New Delhi.
International studies in the philosophy of science. (0269-8595). Abingdon.

International studies quarterly. (0020-8833). Malden MA.

International studies review. (1521-9488). Malden MA.

International tax and public finance. (0927-5940). Dordrecht.

Internationale Politik. (0014 2476). Bonn.

Internationale Politik und Gesellschaft. (0945-2419). Bonn.

Internationales Asienforum. (0020-9449). Cologne.

Internet archaeology. (1363-5387). York.

Investigaciones economicas. (0210-1521). Madrid.

Iran nameh. Bethesda MD.

Iranian journal of international affairs. (1016-6130). Tehran.

Iranica antiqua. (0021-0870). Louvain.

Iraq. (0021-0889). London.

Irian. (0304-2189). Jayapura.

Irish banking review. (0021-1060). Dublin.

Irish journal of sociology. (0791-6035). Maynooth.

Irish political studies. (0790-7184). Limerick.

Irish review. (0790-7850). Cork.

Isis. (0021-1753). Chicago IL.

ISLA: Journal of Micronesian studies. Mangiloa.

Islam et sociétés au sud du Sahara. (0984-7685). Paris.

Islamic law and society. Leiden.

Israel affairs. (1353-7121). Ilford.

Israel exploration journal. (0021-2059). Jerusalem.

Israel law review. (0021-2237). Jerusalem.

Israel oriental studies. (0334-4401). Tel Aviv.

Israel yearbook on human rights. (0333-5925). Dordrecht.

Issue. (0047-1607). Emory GA.

Issues & studies. (1013-2511). Taipei.

Italia contemporanea. (0392-3568). Milan.

IWK: Internationale wissenschaftliche Korrespondenz zur Geschichte der deutschen Arbeiterbewegung. (0046-8428). Berlin.

Iyu Machi. Okinawa.

Iztapalapa. (0185-4259). Mexico City.

Jahrbuch des öffentlichen Rechts der Gegenwart. (0075-2517). Tübingen.

Jahrbuch Extremismus & Demokratie. Bonn.

Jahrbuch für Antisemitismusforschung. (0941-8563). Frankfurt.

Jahrbuch für christliche Sozialwissenschaften. (0075-2584). Münster.

Jahrbuch für Ethnomedizin und Bewußtseinsforschung = Yearbook for ethnomedicine and the study of consciousness. (0942-1408). Berlin.

Jahrbuch für Geschichte Lateinamerikas. (1438-4752). Cologne.

Jahrbuch für musikalische Volks- und Völkerkunde. Eisenach.

Jahrbuch für Soziologiegeschichte. Leverkusen.

Jahrbuch für Wirtschaftsgeschichte. (0075-2800). Berlin.

Jahrbuch für Wirtschaftswissenschaften: Review of Economics. (0948-5139). Göttingen.

Jahrbücher für Geschichte Osteuropas. (0021-4019). Stuttgart.

Jahrbücher für Nationalökonomie und Statistik. (0021-4027). Stuttgart.

Jain journal. (0021-4043). Calcutta.

Jamaica journal. (0021-4124). Kingston.

Japan and the world economy. (0922-1425). Amsterdam.

Japan Christian review. (0918-516X). Tokyo.

Japan digest. (0960-1473). Folkestone.

Japan echo. (0388-0435). Tokyo.
Japan election studies. Tokyo.
Japan journal of sport sociology. Tsukuba.
Japan labor bulletin. Tokyo.
Japan marketing journal. Tokyo.
Japan quarterly. (0021-4590). Tokyo.
Japan review of international affairs. (0913-8773). Tokyo.
Japanese annual of international law. (0448-8806). Tokyo.
Japanese economic review. (1352-4739). Tokyo.
Japanese journal of administrative behavior. Nagoya.
Japanese journal of educational research. Tokyo.
Japanese journal of family sociology. Tokyo.
Japanese journal of gerontology. Tokyo.
Japanese journal of nursing science. Tokyo.
Japanese journal of religious studies. (0304-1042). Nagoya.
Japanese journal of sociological criminology. Tokyo.
Japanese journal of women's studies. Tokyo.
Japanese journalism review. Tokyo.
Japanese religions. (0448-8954). Kyoto City.
Japanese scientific review. Tokyo.
Japanese sociological review. Tokyo.
Javnost = Public. (1318-3222). Ljubljana.
Jewish journal of sociology. (0021-6534). London.
Jewish quarterly review. (0021-6682). Philadelphia PA.
Jewish social studies. (0021-6704). New York NY.
Jimbun ronsō. Osaka.
Jinbun gakuho. Tokyo.
Jinbun-ronkyu. Nishinomiya.
Jinbun: Journal of Kyoto University. Kyoto.
Jinbungakubu kiyo. Toyama.
Jinko mondai kenkyu. Tokyo.
Jinko to Kaihatsu. Tokyo.
Jogtudományi közlöny. (0021-7166). Budapest.
Joho to shakai (Journal of Edogawa University). Nagareyama.
Jomin bunka. Tokyo.
Josei kukan. Tokyo.
Journal de la Société de Statistique de Paris. (0037 911X). Paris.
Journal de la Société des américanistes. (0037-9174). Paris.
Journal de la Société des Océanistes. (0300-953X). Paris.
Journal des Africanistes. (0399-0346). Paris.
Journal du droit international. (0021-8170). Paris.
Journal for East European management studies. (0949-6181). Mering.
Journal for the scientific study of religion. (0021-8294). Provo UT.
Journal for the theory of social behaviour. (0021-8308). Oxford.
Journal für Entwicklungspolitik. (0258-2384). Frankfurt.
Journal Japan Women's University Faculty of Integrated Arts and Social Sciences. Kawasaki.
Journal of accounting and economics. (0165-4101). Amsterdam.
Journal of accounting and public policy. (0278-4254). New York NY.
Journal of African economies. (0963-8024). Oxford.
Journal of African history. (0021-8537). Cambridge.
Journal of African languages and linguistics. (0167-6164). Berlin.

Journal of African law. (0221-8553). London.
Journal of African Marxists. (0263-2268). London.
Journal of African religion and philosophy. Kampala.
Journal of agricultural economics. (0021-857X). Reading.
Journal of agricultural economics research. Washington DC.
Journal of American studies. (0021-8758). Cambridge.
Journal of American-East Asian relations. (1058-3947). Chicago IL.
Journal of anthropological archaeology. (0278-4165). San Diego CA.
Journal of anthropological research. (0091-7710). Albuquerque NM.
Journal of applied behavioral science. (0021-8863). Thousand Oaks.
Journal of applied econometrics. (0883-7252). Chichester.
Journal of applied economics. (1514-0326). Buenos Aires.
Journal of applied psychoanalytic studies. (1521-1401). New York.
Journal of applied psychology. (0021-9010). Washington DC.
Journal of applied social psychology. (0021-9029). Silver Spring MD.
Journal of architectural and planning research. (0738-0895). Chicago IL.
Journal of Asian and African affairs. (1044-2979). Washington DC.
Journal of Asian and African studies [Leiden]. (0021-9096). Leiden.
Journal of Asian business. (1068-0055). Ann Arbor MI.
Journal of Asian history. (0021-910X). Wiesbaden.
Journal of Asian studies. (0021-9118). Ann Arbor MI.
Journal of Australian political economy. (0156-5826). Sydney.
Journal of Australian studies. Bundoora.
Journal of Baltic studies. (0162-9778). Portland OR.
Journal of banking and finance. (0378-4266). Amsterdam.
Journal of BARD. Comilla.
Journal of behavioral education. (1053-0819). New York NY.
Journal of biosocial science. (0021-9320). Cambridge.
Journal of black psychology. (0095-7984). Thousand Oaks CA.
Journal of black studies. (0021-9347). Thousand Oaks CA.
Journal of British studies. (0021-9371). Chicago IL.
Journal of business. (0021-9398). Chicago IL.
Journal of business & economic statistics. (0735-0015). Alexandria VA.
Journal of business and society. (1012-2591). Nicosia.
Journal of business ethics. (0167-4544). Dordrecht.
Journal of business finance and accounting. (0306-686X). Oxford.
Journal of Canadian studies = Revue d'études canadiennes. (0021-9495). Peterborough.
Journal of Caribbean studies. (0190-2008). Lexington KY.
Journal of child and family studies. (1062-1024). New York NY.
Journal of Chinese law. (1041-7567). Lincoln NE.
Journal of Chinese philosophy. Honolulu HI.
Journal of church and state. (0021-969X). Waco TX.
Journal of classical sociology. (1468-795X). London.
Journal of common market studies. (0021-9886). Oxford.
Journal of communication. (0021-9916). New York NY.
Journal of communist studies and transition politics. (1352-3279). Ilford.
Journal of community and applied social psychology. (1052-9284). Chichester.
Journal of comparative economics. (0147-5967). Duluth MN.
Journal of comparative family studies. (0047-2328). Calgary.
Journal of comparative policy analysis: research and practice. (1387-6988). Dordrecht.
Journal of conflict resolution. (0022-0027). Thousand Oaks CA.

Journal of conflict studies. (1198-8614). New Brunswick.
Journal of constitutional and parliamentary studies. New Delhi.
Journal of consumer affairs. (0022-0078). Madison WI.
Journal of consumer culture. (1469-5405). London.
Journal of consumer policy. (0342-5843). Dordrecht.
Journal of contemporary African studies. (0258-9001). Abingdon.
Journal of contemporary Asia. (0047-2336). Manila.
Journal of contemporary ethnography. (0891-2416). Thousand Oaks CA.
Journal of contemporary history. (0022-0094). London.
Journal of contingencies and crisis management. (0966-0879). Oxford.
Journal of cooperative studies. (0961-5784). Buxton.
Journal of corporate citizenship. (1470-5001). Sheffield.
Journal of cost management. (0899-5141). Boston MA.
Journal of criminal law. (0022-0183). London.
Journal of criminal law and criminology. (0091-4169). Chicago IL.
Journal of cross-cultural gerontology. (0169-3816). Dordrecht.
Journal of cultural studies. (1595-0956). Lagos.
Journal of democracy. (1045-5736). Baltimore MD.
Journal of developing areas. (0022-037X). Macomb IL.
Journal of developing societies. (0169-796X). Leiden.
Journal of development assistance. (1341-3953). Tokyo.
Journal of development economics. (0304-3878). Amsterdam.
Journal of development planning. (0085-2392). New York NY.
Journal of development studies. (0022-0388). Ilford.
Journal of East Asian affairs. (1010-1608). Seoul.
Journal of Eastern African research & development. (0251-0405). Nairobi.
Journal of econometrics. (0304-4076). Amsterdam.
Journal of economic and social measurement. (0747-9662). Amsterdam.
Journal of economic behavior and organization. (0167-2681). Amsterdam.
Journal of economic cooperation among Islamic countries. (0252-953X). Ankara.
Journal of economic dynamics and control. (0165-1889). Amsterdam.
Journal of economic growth. (1381-4338). Dordrecht.
Journal of economic history. (0022-0507). New York NY.
Journal of economic issues. (0021-3624). Lewisburg PA.
Journal of economic literature. (0022-0515). Nashville TN.
Journal of economic methodology. (1350-178X). London.
Journal of economic perspectives. (0895-3309). Nashville TN.
Journal of economic psychology. (0167-4870). Amsterdam.
Journal of economic studies. (0144-3585). Bradford.
Journal of economic surveys. (0950-0804). Oxford.
Journal of economic theory. (0022-0531). Bruges.
Journal of economics & management strategy. (1058-6407). Cambridge MA.
Journal of economics [Austria] = Zeitschrift für Nationalökonomie. (0931-8658). Vienna.
Journal of educational sociology. Tokyo.
Journal of environment and development. (1070-4965). Thousand Oaks CA.
Journal of environmental economics and management. (0095-0696). Duluth MN.
Journal of environmental law. (0952-8873). Oxford.
Journal of environmental management. (0301-4797). London.
Journal of environmental planning and management. (0964-0568). Abingdon.
Journal of environmental sociology. Tokyo.
Journal of ethnic and migration studies. (1369-183X). Abingdon.

Journal of European economic history. (0391-5115). Rome.
Journal of European integration history = Revue d'histoire de l'intégration européenne = Zeitschrift für Geschichte der europäischen Integration. (0947-9511). Baden-Baden.
Journal of European public policy. (1350-1763). London.
Journal of European social policy. (0958-9287). London.
Journal of evolutionary economics. (0936-9937). Berlin.
Journal of experimental child psychology. (0022-0965). Duluth MN.
Journal of experimental social psychology. (0022-1031). Duluth MN.
Journal of Family Education Center. Yokohama.
Journal of family history. (0363-1990). Thousand Oaks, CA.
Journal of family therapy. (0163-4445). Oxford.
Journal of family violence. (0885-7482). New York NY.
Journal of finance. (0022-1082). New York NY.
Journal of financial and quantitative analysis. (0022-1090). Seattle WA.
Journal of financial economics. (0304-405X). Amsterdam.
Journal of financial intermediation. (1042-9573). Orlando FL.
Journal of financial services research. (0920-8550). Dordrecht.
Journal of forecasting. (0277-6693). Chichester.
Journal of forensic economics. (0898-5510). Kansas City KS.
Journal of forensic psychiatry. (0958-5184). London.
Journal of forest economics. Tokyo.
Journal of futures markets. (0270-7314). New York NY.
Journal of gender studies. (0958-9236). Abingdon.
Journal of health economics. (0167-6296). Amsterdam.
Journal of health politics, policy and law. (0361-6878). Durham NC.
Journal of Himeji Gakuin Women's Junior College. Himeji.
Journal of historical sociology. (0952-1909). Oxford.
Journal of home economics of Japan. Tokyo.
Journal of homosexuality. (0091-8369). Binghampton NY.
Journal of housing and the built environment. (1566-4910). Dordrecht.
Journal of housing economics. (1051-1377). Orlando FL.
Journal of housing research. (1052-7001). Washington DC.
Journal of human development. (1464-9888). Basingstoke.
Journal of human evolution. (0047-2484). London.
Journal of human resources. (0022-166X). Madison WI.
Journal of human sciences [Osaka]. Osaka.
Journal of human sciences [Tokyo]. Tokyo.
Journal of humanities and natural sciences. (0495-8012). Tokyo.
Journal of Hyogo Educational University. Yashiro.
Journal of Imperial and Commonwealth history. (0308-6534). Ilford.
Journal of Indian philosophy. (0022-1791). Dordrecht.
Journal of Indo-European studies. (0092-2323). Washington DC.
Journal of industrial economics. (0022-1821). Oxford.
Journal of industrial history. (1463-6174). Lancaster.
Journal of industrial relations. (0022-1856). Sydney.
Journal of industry and management. Osaka.
Journal of inquiry and research. Osaka.
Journal of institutional and theoretical economics = Zeitschrift für die gesamte Staatswissenschaft. (0932-4569). Tübingen.
Journal of interdisciplinary economics. (0260-1079). Bicester.
Journal of interdisciplinary history. (0022-1953). Cambridge MA.

Journal of interdisciplinary studies: An international journal of interdisciplinary and interfaith dialogue. (0890-0132). Santa Monica CA.
Journal of international accounting auditing and taxation. (1061-9518). Greenwich CT.
Journal of international affairs. (0022-197X). New York NY.
Journal of international business studies. (0047-2506). New Orleans LA.
Journal of international development. (0954-1748). Chichester.
Journal of international economic law. (1369-3034). Oxford.
Journal of international economics. (0022-1996). Amsterdam.
Journal of international financial management and accounting. (0954-1314). Oxford.
Journal of international financial markets, institutions & money. (1042-4431). Binghampton NY.
Journal of international money and finance. (0261-5606). Guildford.
Journal of international politics and economics. Tokyo.
Journal of international relations. Tokyo.
Journal of international relations and development. (1408-6980). Ljubljana.
Journal of international studies. Tokyo.
Journal of international trade and economic development. (0963-8199). London.
Journal of Israeli history: studies in Zionism and statehood. (1353-1042). Ilford.
Journal of Japanese studies. (0095-6848). Seattle WA.
Journal of Jewish studies. (0022-2097). Oxford.
Journal of Kibi International University. Okayama.
Journal of Kobe Yamate College. Japan.
Journal of Korean studies. Los Angeles CA.
Journal of Kyoto Medical Association. Kyoto.
Journal of labor economics. (0734-306X). Chicago IL.
Journal of labor research. (0195-3613). Fairfax VA.
Journal of Laboratory Institute. Tokyo.
Journal of language and social psychology. (0261-927X). Clevedon.
Journal of Latin American studies. (0022-216X). Cambridge.
Journal of law. Tokyo.
Journal of law and economics. (0022-2186). Chicago IL.
Journal of law and political studies. Tokyo.
Journal of law and society. (0263-323X). Oxford.
Journal of law, economics, & organization. (8756-6222). Cary NC.
Journal of legal pluralism and unofficial law. (0732-9113). Birmingham.
Journal of legal studies. (0047-2530). Chicago IL.
Journal of legislative studies. (1357-2334). London.
Journal of leisure research. (0022-2216). Alexandria VA.
Journal of libertarian studies. (0363-2873). Burlingame CA.
Journal of linguistics. (0022-2267). Cambridge.
Journal of Literary Society of Yamaguchi University. Yamaguchi.
Journal of macroeconomics. (0164-0704). Baton Rouge LA.
Journal of management and governance. (1385-3457). Dordrecht.
Journal of management studies. (0022-2380). Oxford.
Journal of market history. Kumamoto.
Journal of marriage and the family. (0022-2445). Minneapolis MN.
Journal of mass communication studies. Tokyo.
Journal of material culture. (1359-1835). London.
Journal of mathematical economics. (0304-4068). Amsterdam.
Journal of mathematical sociology. (0022-250X). New York NY.
Journal of Mauritian studies. Moka.
Journal of medicine and philosophy. (0360-5310). SZ Lisse.

Journal of Mediterranean studies. (1016-3476). Msida.
Journal of modern African studies. (0022-278X). Cambridge.
Journal of modern history. (0022-2801). Chicago IL.
Journal of modern Italian studies. (1354-571X). London.
Journal of modern Korean studies. Fredericksburg VA.
Journal of monetary economics. (0304-3932). Amsterdam.
Journal of money, credit and banking. (0022-2879). Columbus OH.
Journal of multilingual and multicultural development. (0143-4632). Clevedon.
Journal of multinational financial management. (1042-444X). Oxford, U.K.
Journal of Natal and Zulu history. Durban.
Journal of Near Eastern studies. (0022-2968). Chicago IL.
Journal of Nigerian languages and literatures. (0943-1640). Munich.
Journal of North African studies. (1362-9387). Ilford.
Journal of Northeast Asian studies. (0738-7997). Washington DC.
Journal of northwest semitic languages. (0259-0131). Stellenbosch.
Journal of occupational and organizational psychology. (0963-1798). Leicester.
Journal of occupational rehabilitation. (1053-0487). New York NY.
Journal of Okazaki College of Foreign Studies. Okinawa.
Journal of Osaka Sangyo University social sciences. Osaka.
Journal of Pacific Asia. Tokyo.
Journal of Pacific history. (0022-3344). Canberra.
Journal of Pacific studies. (1011-3029). Suva.
Journal of Palestine studies. (0377-919X). Berkeley CA.
Journal of peace research. (0022-3433). London.
Journal of peasant studies. (0306-6150). Ilford.
Journal of personality. (0022-3506). Malden MA.
Journal of personality and social psychology. (0022-3514). Washington DC.
Journal of philosophy. (0022-362X). New York NY.
Journal of pidgin and creole languages. (0920-9034). Amsterdam.
Journal of planning literature. (0885-4122). Thousand Oaks CA.
Journal of policy analysis and management. (0276-8739). New York NY.
Journal of policy history. (0898-0306). University Park PA.
Journal of policy modeling. (0161-8938). New York NY.
Journal of political economy. (0022-3808). Chicago IL.
Journal of political ideologies. (1356-9317). Abingdon.
Journal of political philosophy. (0963-8016). Oxford.
Journal of politics. (0022-3816). Malden MA.
Journal of popular culture. (0022-3840). Bowling Green OH.
Journal of population economics. (0933-1433). Heidelberg.
Journal of population research. Canberra.
Journal of post Keynesian economics. (0160-3477). Armonk NY.
Journal of pragmatics. (0378-2166). Amsterdam.
Journal of psychology. (0022-3980). Washington DC.
Journal of public administration research and theory. (1053-1858). New Brunswick NJ.
Journal of public economics. (0047-2727). Amsterdam.
Journal of public policy. (0143-814X). Cambridge.
Journal of quantitative anthropology. (0922-2995). Dordrecht.
Journal of real estate finance and economics. (0895-5638). Dordrecht.
Journal of real estate literature. (0927-7544). Grand Forks ND.
Journal of real estate portfolio management. (1083-5547). Grand Forks ND.
Journal of real estate research. (0896-5803). Grand Forks ND.

Journal of refugee studies. (0951-6328). Oxford.
Journal of regional policy. Naples.
Journal of regional science. (0022-4146). Malden MA.
Journal of regulatory economics. (0922-680X). Dordrecht.
Journal of religion in Africa. (0022-4200). Leiden.
Journal of research in crime and delinquency. (0022-4278). Thousand Oaks CA.
Journal of risk and uncertainty. (0895-5646). Dordrecht.
Journal of risk research. (1366-9877). London.
Journal of ritual studies. (0890-1112). Pittsburgh PA.
Journal of rural development and administration. (0047-2751). Peshawar.
Journal of rural problem. Tokyo.
Journal of rural studies. (0743-0167). Oxford.
Journal of rural studies [Japan]. Tokyo.
Journal of semantics. (0167-5133). Oxford.
Journal of Slavic military studies. (1351-8046). Ilford.
Journal of social and clinical psychology. (0736-7236). New York NY.
Journal of social and evolutionary systems. (1061-7361). Stamford CT.
Journal of social and personal relationships. (0265-4075). London.
Journal of social archaeology. (1469-6053). London.
Journal of social development in Africa. (1012-1080). Harare.
Journal of social distress and the homeless. (1053-0789). New York NY.
Journal of social history. (0022-4529). Pittsburgh PA.
Journal of social issues. (0022-4537). New York NY.
Journal of social policy. (0047-2794). Cambridge.
Journal of social problems. Tokyo.
Journal of social psychology. (0022-4545). Washington DC.
Journal of social studies. Dhaka.
Journal of social studies. Japan.
Journal of social work. (1468-0173). London.
Journal of social work practice. (0265-0533). Abingdon.
Journal of social, political and economic studies. (0193-5941). Washington DC.
Journal of sociology: The journal of Australian Sociological Association. (0004-8690). London.
Journal of Southeast Asian studies. (0022-4634). Cambridge.
Journal of Southeast European and Black Sea studies. (1468-3857). London.
Journal of Southern African studies. (0305-7070). Abingdon.
Journal of Southern Europe and the Balkans. (1461-3190). Oxford.
Journal of strategic studies. (0140-2390). Ilford.
Journal of structural learning and intelligent systems. (1027-1015). Newark NJ.
Journal of studies in contemporary social theory. Tokyo.
Journal of Sugiyama Jogakuen University. Japan.
Journal of the American Oriental Society. (0003-0279). Ann Arbor MI.
Journal of the American Statistical Association. (0162-1459). Alexandria VA.
Journal of the Anthropological Society of Oxford. (0044-8370). Oxford.
Journal of the Asia Pacific economy. (1354-7860). London.
Journal of the Asiatic Society. (0368-3303). Calcutta.
Journal of the Asiatic Society of Bangladesh. Dhaka.
Journal of the Assam Research Society. Guwahati.
Journal of the Australian Population Association. (0814-5725). Canberra.
Journal of the British archaeological association. (0068-1288). Leeds.
Journal of the Center for Women's Studies. Tokyo.
Journal of the College of Business Administration and Information Science. Japan.

Journal of the Culture Research Institute. Tokyo.
Journal of the economic and social history of the orient. (0022-4995). Leiden.
Journal of the history of economic thought. (1042-7716). London.
Journal of the history of ideas. (0022-5037). Baltimore MD.
Journal of the history of philosophy. (0022-5053). St. Louis MO.
Journal of the history of sexuality. (1043-4070). Chicago IL.
Journal of the history of the behavioral sciences. (0022-5061). New York NY.
Journal of the Institute of International Sociology. Japan.
Journal of the International Phonetic Association. Los Angeles CA.
Journal of the Japanese and international economies. (0889-1583). Duluth MN.
Journal of the Madras University: Section A — Humanities. Madras.
Journal of the Maharaja Sayajirao University of Baroda. (social science number). Baroda.
Journal of the Malaysian branch of the Royal Asiatic Society. (0126-7353). Kuala Lumpur.
Journal of the Mysore University: Section A-Arts. Mysore.
Journal of the Oriental Institute. (0030-5324). Baroda.
Journal of the Pakistan Historical Society. Karachi.
Journal of the Polynesian Society. (0032-4000). Auckland.
Journal of the Research Society of Buddhism and Cultural Heritage. Japan.
Journal of the Research Society of Pakistan. Lahore.
Journal of the Royal Asiatic Society (Sri Lanka branch). Colombo.
Journal of the Royal Australian Historical Society. (0035-8762). Sydney.
Journal of the Royal Statistical Society: Series A (statistics in society). (0964-1998). London.
Journal of the Royal Statistical Society: Series B (statistical methodology). (1369-7412). London.
Journal of the Royal Statistical Society: Series C (applied statistics). (0035-9254). Oxford.
Journal of the Royal Statistical Society: Series D (the statistician). (0039-0526). London.
Journal of the Rural Life Society of Japan. Tsukuba.
Journal of the Siam Society. (0857-7099). Bangkok.
Journal of the study of human rights. Tokyo.
Journal of the Third World spectrum. (1072-5040). Washington DC.
Journal of the Walter Roth Museum of Anthropology. (0256-4653). Georgetown DC.
Journal of theoretical politics. London.
Journal of Third World studies. (8755-3449). Americus GA.
Journal of time series analysis. (0143-9782). Oxford.
Journal of Tokyo Keizai University. (0493-4091). Tokyo.
Journal of transport economics and policy. (0022-5258). Bath.
Journal of urban economics. (0094-1190). Duluth MN.
Journal of urban history. (0096-1442). Thousand Oaks CA.
Journal of West African languages. (0022-5401). Dallas TX.
Journal of women's education. Tokyo.
Journal of women's history. (1042-7961). Bloomington IN.
Journal of world business. (1090-9516). Stamford CT.
Journal of world history. (1045-6007). Honolulu HI.
Journal of world trade. (1011-6702). London.
Journal of Yasuda Women's University. Hiroshima.
Journal. Institute of Muslim Minority Affairs. (0266-6952). London.
Journal. Konan University, Faculty of Letters. Kobe.
Journal. Okayama University, School of General Education. Okayama.
Journal. Yamaguchi University, Literary Society. Yamaguchi.
Kabar seberang. (0314-5786). Townsville.
Kagoshima keizai daigaku shakaigakubu ronshu. Kagoshima.
Kagoshima law review. Kagoshima.

Kaiho shakaigaku kenkyu. Tokyo.
Kailash: A journal of Himalayan studies. Kathmandu.
Kajian Malaysia. (0127-4082). Penang.
Kanagawa University review. Kanagawa.
Kano studies. Kano.
Kansai University review of law and politics. Osaka.
Kanto toshigakkai ronshû. Tokyo.
Kasarinlan. Quezon City.
Kazoku shakaigaku kenkyu. Tokyo.
Keiei Johogakubu Kiyo (Bulletin of Jobu University). Gumma.
Keieisenryaku kiso koza. Tokyo.
Keio business review. (0453-4557). Tokyo.
Keio communication review. Tokyo.
Keio economic studies. (0022-9709). Tokyo.
Keizai orai. Japan.
Keizai ronshu: Journal of Toyama University. Toyama.
Keizaigaku ronshû. Kagoshima.
Keizaigaku zasshi (Journal of Osaka Municipal University). Osaka.
Keizaigaku-ronshu of Kagoshima University. Kagoshima.
Kenkyu kiyo (Bulletin of Hyogo Kyoiku University). Nishiwaki.
Kenkyu kiyo (Journal of Aomori University). Aomori.
Kenkyu kiyo (Journal of Kibi Kokusai University). Takahashi.
Kenkyu kiyo (Journal. Tamagwa Fukushi University). Sendai.
Kenkyu-kiyo. Tokyo.
Kenkyu-kiyo (Bulletin of Osaka Kyoiku University). Osaka.
Kenkyunenpo (Bulletin of Rissho University). Tokyo.
Kenmin Katsudo kenkyu. Saitama.
Kesu Kenkyu. Tokyo.
Kigyo-kenkyusho Nenpo. Nagoya.
Kikan fukushi rodo. Tokyo.
Kikan Tomorrow. Amagasaki.
Kindai. Kobe.
Kindai Fudo. Osaka.
Kinki daigaku kyouyou gakuba kenkyū kiyou. Osaka.
Kisebbségkutatás: szemle a hazai és külföldi irodalomból. (1215-2684). Budapest.
Kiyo (Bulletin of Tyukyo University). Nagoya.
Kiyo (Journal of Seitoku College). Tokyo.
Kiyo shakaigakka. Tokyo.
Knowledge, technology & policy. (0897-1986). New Jersey.
Kobe economic and business review. (0075-6407). Kobe.
Kobe International University review. Kobe.
Kobe journal of higher education. Kobe.
Kokugakuin daigaku nihonbunka kenkyushoho. Tokyo.
Kokugakuin hougaku. Tokyo.
Kokumin Seikatsu Kenkyu. Tokyo.
Kölner Zeitschrift für Soziologie und Sozialpsychologie. (0340-0425). Wiesbaden.
Komodo Science. Tokyo.
Konjunkturpolitik. (0023-3498). Berlin.
Korea and world affairs. Seoul.
Korea economic report. Seoul.
Korea focus. (1225-8113). Seoul.

Korea journal. (0023-3900). Seoul.
Korea observer. (0023-3919). Seoul.
Korean culture. (0270-1618). Los Angeles CA.
Korean financial review. Seoul.
Korean social science journal. Seoul.
Korean studies. (0145-840X). Honolulu HI.
Közgazdasági szemle. (0023-4346). Budapest.
Kredit und Kapital. (0023-4591). Berlin.
Kroeber anthropological society papers. (0023-4869). Berkeley CA.
Kumamoto journal of culture and humanities. Kumamoto.
Kunapipi: Journal of post-colonial writing. (0106-5734). Wollongong.
Kunnallistieteellinen aikakauskirja. Finland.
Kwansai Gakuin University annual studies. Hyogo.
Kwansei Gakuin daigaku shakaigakubu kiyo. Hyogo.
Kwansei Gakuin law review. (0452-9480). Nishinomiya.
Kwartalnik historii kultury materialnej. (0023-5881). Warsaw.
Kyklos. (0023-5962). Basle.
Kyoiku-shakaigaku kenkyu. Tokyo.
Kyoikugakubu kenkyu hokoku (Bulletin of Yamanashi University). Kohu.
Kyoto journal of sociology. Kyoto.
Kyoto University economic review. (0023-6055). Kyoto.
Kyoto University research studies in education. Kyoto.
Kyoyobu kiyo (Bulletin of Rissho University). Tokyo.
Labour [Canada] = Travail. (0700-3862). St. John's.
Labour [Italy]. (1121-7081). Oxford.
Labour, capital and society = Travail, capital et société. (0706-1706). Montreal.
Lakimies. Helsinki.
Lalit kalā. New Delhi.
Land economics. (0023-7639). Madison WI.
Land reform, land settlement and cooperatives. (0251-1894). Rome.
Language. (0097-8507). Baltimore MD.
Language & communication. (0271-5309). New York NY.
Language in society. (0047-4045). New York NY.
Language problems and language planning. (0272-2690). Amsterdam.
Latin American business review. (1097-8526). Binghampton NY.
Latin American Indian literatures journal. (0888-5613). McKeesport PA.
Latin American perspectives. (0094-582X). Thousand Oaks CA.
Latin American politics and society. (1531-426X). Coral Gables FL.
Latin American research review. (0023-8791). Albuquerque NM.
Law and contemporary problems. (0023-9186). Durham NC.
Law and critique. (0957-8536). Liverpool.
Law and philosophy. (0167-5249). Dordrecht.
Law and policy. (0265-8240). Oxford.
Law and society review. (0023-9216). Amherst MA.
Ledelse og Erhvervsøkonomi. (0902-3704). Copenhagen.
Legislative studies. (0816-9152). Canberra.
Legislative studies quarterly. (0362-9805). Iowa City IA.
Leiden journal of international law. (0922-1565). The Hague.
Leisure sciences. (0149 0400). London.
Levante. (0024-1504). Rome.
Leviatán. (0210-6337). Madrid.

Liberian studies journal. (0024-1989). Bloomington IL.
Libyan studies. (0263-7189). London.
Linguistic inquiry. (0024-3892). Cambridge MA.
Linguistic review. (0167-6318). Hawthorne NY.
Linguistics. (0024-3949). Berlin.
Linguistics and philosophy. (0165-0157). Dordrecht.
Linguistics of the Tibeto-Burman area. (0731-3500). Berkeley CA.
Linguistique africaine. (0994-7744). Paris.
Literatura ludowa. (0024-4708). Wroclaw.
Littérature orale arabo-berbère. (0336-5654). Paris.
Local economy. (0269-0942). London.
Local economy quarterly. Luton.
Local environment. (1354-9839). Abingdon.
Local government review in Japan. (0288-7622). Tokyo.
Local government studies. (0300-3930). Ilford.
Lokayan bulletin. (0970-5406). New Delhi.
Lotus. Shiga.
Low intensity conflict and law enforcement. (0966-2847). Ilford.
Lud. (0076-1435). Wroclaw.
Maandschrift economie. (0013-0486). Tilburg.
Macedonian review. Skopje.
Magyar jog. (0025-0147). Budapest.
Magyar közigazgatás. (0865-736X). Budapest.
Magyar tudomány. (0025-0325). Budapest.
Malaysian journal of tropical geography. (0127-1474). Kuala Lumpur.
Man in India. (0025-1569). Ranchi.
Management accounting research. (1044-5005). London.
Management science. (0025-1909). Providence RI.
Managerial and decision economics. (0143-6570). Chichester.
Manchester School. (1463-6786). Oxford.
Mandenkan. (0752-5443). Paris.
Mankind quarterly. (0025-2344). Washington DC.
Manusia dan Masyarakat. (0126-8678). Kuala Lumpur.
Marga. Colombo.
Marine policy. (0308-597X). Guildford.
Marketing letters. (0923-0645). Dordrecht.
Marx-Engels Jahrbuch. (0232-6132). Berlin.
Marxistische Blätter. (0542-7770). Essen.
Masculinities. (1072-8538). New York NY.
Mathematical finance. (0960-1627). Oxford.
Mathematical social sciences. (0165-4896). Amsterdam.
Media culture and society. (0163-4437). London.
Mediation quarterly. (0739-4098). San Francisco CA.
Medical anthropology. (0145-9740). London.
Medical anthropology quarterly. (0745-5194). Arlington VA.
Medicine, conflict and survival. (1362-3699). Ilford.
Medina, mimshal vihasim benleumiyim. (0334-2514). Jerusalem.
Mediterranean politics. (1362-9395). Ilford.
Mediterranean quarterly: A journal of global issues. (1047-4552). Durham NC.
Medizin Mensch Gesellschaft. (0340-8183). Stuttgart.
Megamot. (0025-8679). Jerusalem.

Meiji daigaku kyouyou ronshuu. Tokyo.
Meiji gakuin ronso. Tokyo.
Melanesian law journal. Papua New Guinea.
Melbourne journal of politics. (0085-3224). Melbourne.
Memoirs of Osaka Kyoiku University. Osaka.
Memoirs of Taisho University. Tokyo.
Memoirs. Bukkyo University, Postgraduate Research Institute. Kyoto.
Men and masculinities. (1097-184X). Thousand Oaks CA.
Mens en maatschappij. (0025-9454). Houten.
Mesoamérica. (0252-9963). Guatemala.
Mesopotamia. (0076-6615). Florence.
Metapolítica. (1405-4558). Mexico City.
Method and theory in the study of religion. (0943-3058). New York NY.
Metroeconomica. (0026-1386). Bologna.
Mezinárodní vztahy. (0323-1844). Prague.
Middle East business and economic review. Australia.
Middle East journal. (0026-3141). Bloomington IN.
Middle East policy. (1061-1924). Washington DC.
Middle East quarterly. (1073-9467). Lawrence KS.
Middle East report. (0899-2851). Washington DC.
Middle East Studies Association bulletin. (0026-3184). Tucson AZ.
Middle Eastern studies. (0026-3206). Ilford.
Migracijske teme. (0352-5600). Zagreb.
Milbank quarterly. (0887-378X). New York NY.
Millennium. (0305-8298). London.
Mind. (0026-4423). Oxford.
Mind and language. (0268-1064). Oxford.
Minerva. (0026-4695). Dordrecht.
Mir Rossii: Universe of Russia, Sotsiologiia, Etnologiia. Moscow.
Mirovaia ekonomika i mezhdunarodnye otnosheniia. (0131-2227). Moscow.
Mitologicas. (0326-5676). Buenos Aires.
Mitteilungen der Deutschen Orient-Gesellschaft zu Berlin. (0342-118X). Berlin.
Mobilization. (1086-671X). San Diego CA.
Moct-Most: Economic policy in transitional economies. (1120-7388). Dordrecht.
Modern Asian studies. (0026-749X). Cambridge.
Modern China. (0097-7004). Thousand Oaks CA.
Modern law review. (0026-7961). Oxford.
Monatsberichte der Deutschen Bundesbank. (0012-0006). Frankfurt am Main.
Monatsberichte. Österreichisches Institut für Wirtschaftsforschung. (0029-9898). Vienna.
Monde arabe maghreb machrek. (1241-5294). Paris.
Monde copte. (0399-905X). Limoges.
Mondes en développement. (0302-3052). Paris.
Monetaria. (0185-1136). Mexico City.
Monetary and economic studies. (0288-8432). Tokyo.
Money affairs. (0187-7615). Mexico City.
Mongolia survey. (1081-5082). Bloomington IN.
Mongolian studies. (0190-3667). Bloomington IN.
Monthly report of the Deutsche Bundesbank. (0418-8292). Frankfurt am Main.
Monthly review: State Bank of India, Economic Research Department. (0039-0003). Bombay.
Monumenta Nipponica. (0027-0741). Tokyo.
Monumenta serica. (0254-9948). St. Augustin.

Morocco: The journal of the society for Moroccan studies. London.
MOST Journal of multicultural studies. (1564-4901). Paris.
Most: Economic journal on Eastern Europe and the former Soviet Union. Bologna.
Mouvement social. (0027-2671). Paris.
Multilingua. (0167-8507). Berlin.
Municipal problems. Tokyo.
Nagoya daigaku shakaigaku ronshu. Nagoya.
Nampo-bunka. Tenri.
Nanzan shûkyô bunka kenkyûjo kenkyûjohô. Nagoya.
Nara Women's University sociological studies. Nara.
Narodna tvorchist' ta etnografiia. Kiev.
National Institute economic review. (0027-9501). London.
National interest. (0884-9382). Washington DC.
National tax journal. (0028-0283). Columbus OH.
Nationalism and ethnic politics. (1353-7113). Ilford.
Nationalities papers. (0090-5992). Omaha NE.
Nations and nationalism. (1354-5078). Cambridge.
Natural resources forum. (0165-0203). Guildford.
Natural resources journal. (0028-0739). Albuquerque NM.
Nature and resources. (0028-0844). Carnforth.
Negotiation journal. (0748-4526). New York NY.
NEHA-bulletin. (0920-9875). Amsterdam.
NEHA-jaarboek voor economische, bedrijfs- en techniekgeschiedenis. (1380-5517). Amsterdam.
Nenpo shakaigaku ronshu. Tokyo.
Netherlands international law review. (0165-070X). Dordrecht.
Netherlands journal of social sciences = Sociologia Neerlandica. (0038-0172). Assen.
Netherlands quarterly of human rights. (0169-3441). Dordrecht.
Netherlands yearbook of international law. (0167-6768). Dordrecht.
Neue Gesellschaft / Frankfurter Hefte. (0177-6738). Bonn.
Neue politische literatur. (0028-3320). Frankfurt am Main.
New economy. (1070-3535). London.
New England economic review. Boston MA.
New European. (0953-1432). Bradford.
New formations. (0950-2378). London.
New genetics and society. (1463-6778). Basingstoke.
New left review. (0028-6060). London.
New media & society. (1461-4448). London.
New perspectives on Turkey. (0896-6346). Great Barrington MA.
New political economy. (1356-3467). Abingdon.
New politics. (0028-6494). Brooklyn NY.
New quest. (0258-0381). Pune.
New technology, work and employment. (0268-1072). Oxford.
New York University journal of international law and politics. (0028-7873). New York NY.
New Zealand economic papers. (0077-9954). Wellington.
New Zealand international review. (0110-0262). Wellington.
New Zealand journal of history. (0028-8322). Auckland.
New Zealand sociology. (0112-921X). Palmerston.
NIAS. (0904-597X). Copenhagen.
Nieuwe West-Indische gids = New West Indian guide. (0028-9930). Dordrecht.
Nigerian field. (0029-0076). Ibadan.
Nigerian forum. (0189-0816). Lagos.

Nigerian journal of economic and social studies. (0029-0092). Ibadan.
Nigerian journal of international affairs. (0331-3646). Lagos.
Nigerian journal of policy and strategy. Kuru.
Nigerian journal of political science. (0031-8524). Zaria.
Nigerian journal of public administration and local government. Nsukka.
Nihon Keizaiseisaku Gakkai Nenpo. Tokyo.
Nihon rôdô shakai gakkai nenpô. Tokyo.
Nilo-Ethiopian studies. (1340-329X). Kyoto.
Nilo-Ethiopian studies newsletter. (0919-8210). Kyoto.
Nineteenth-century contexts. (0890-5495). London.
Ningen kagaku kenkyu (Journal of Waseda University). Tokyo.
Nogyo mondai kenkyu. Tokyo.
Nogyo sogo kenkyu. Tokyo.
Nonprofit management and leadership. (1048-6682). San Francisco CA.
NORA: Nordic journal of women's studies. (0803-8740). Oslo.
Nord nytt. (0008-1345). Copenhagen.
Nordic journal of African studies. (1235-4481). Helsinki.
Nordic journal of linguistics. (0332-5865). Oslo.
Norsk økonomisk tidsskrift. (0039-0720). Oslo.
North Korea quarterly. (0340-104X). Hamburg.
Noson seikatsu kenkyu. Tsukuba.
Notas mesoamericanas. Puebla.
Noticario de historia agraria. (1132-1261). Zaragoza.
Nougyo shijo kenkyu. Sapporo.
Nova economia: revista do Departamento de Ciências Econômicas da UFMG. (0103-6351). Belo Horizonte.
Nueva sociedad. (0251-3552). Caracas.
Numen. (0029-5973). Leiden.
Nuova antologia. Florence.
Obshchestvennye nauki i sovremennost'. (0869-0499). Moscow.
Ocean development and international law. (0090-8320). London.
Oceania. (0029-8077). Sydney.
Oceanic linguistics. (0029-8115). Honolulu HI.
OECD economic studies. (0255-0822). Paris.
Omni-management. Japan.
OPEC review. (0277-0180). Oxford.
Open economies review. (0923-7992). Dordrecht.
Opinião pública. (0104-6276). São Paulo.
Oral history. (0143-0955). Colchester.
Orbis. (0030-4387). Philadelphia PA.
Ordo. (0048-2129). Stuttgart.
Organization and environment. (1086-0266). Thousand Oaks CA.
Organization science. (1047-7039). Linthicum MD.
Organization studies. (0170-8406). Berlin.
Organization: the interdisciplinary journal of organization, theory and society. (1350-5084). London.
Organizational behavior and human decision processes. (0749-5978). Duluth MN.
Oriens Extremus. (0030-5197). Wiesbaden.
Orient. (0030-5227). Leverkusen.
Orientalia. (0030-5367). Rome.
Orissa historical research journal. (0474-7267). Orissa.
Orita. (0030-5596). Ibadan.

Osaka daigaku ningenkagakubu kiyō. Osaka.
Osaka economic papers. (0473-4548). Osaka.
Osaka shogyo daigaku ronshu. Osaka.
Osaka studies in sociology of education. Osaka.
Österreichische Zeitschrift für Politikwissenschaft. (1615-5548). Vienna.
Osteuropa. (0030-6428). Stuttgart.
Osteuropa Wirtschaft. (0030-6460). Stuttgart.
Otemon economic studies. (0475-0756). Osaka.
Overseas social security news. Tokyo.
Oxford agrarian studies. (0264-5491). Abingdon.
Oxford bulletin of economics and statistics. (0305-9049). Oxford.
Oxford development studies. (1360-0818). Abingdon.
Oxford economic papers. (0030-7653). Oxford.
Oxford international review. (0966 0054). Oxford.
Oxford journal of archaeology. (0262-5253). Oxford.
Oxford review of economic policy. (0266-903X). Oxford.
Oyo-shakaigaku kenkyu (Journal of Rikkyo University). Tokyo.
Pacific affairs. (0030-851X). Vancouver.
Pacific economic bulletin. (0817-8038). Canberra.
Pacific historical review. (0030-8684). Berkeley CA.
Pacific perspective. (0379-626X). Suva.
Pacific review. (0951-2748). London.
Pacific Rim law and policy journal. (1066-8632). Seattle WA.
Pacific studies. (0275-3596). Laie HI.
Pacific viewpoint. (0030-8978). Wellington.
Paideuma. (0078-7809). Stuttgart.
Pakistan development review. (0030-9729). Islamabad.
Pakistan economic and social review. (1011-002X). Lahore.
Pakistan horizon. (0030-980X). Karachi.
Pakistan journal of applied economics. (0254-9204). Karachi.
Pakistan journal of history and culture. (1012-7682). Islamabad.
Palaeoslavica: International journal for the study of Slavic medieval literature, history, language and
    ethnology. (1070-5465). Cambridge MA.
Palestine-Israel journal of politics, economics and culture. (0793-1395). Jerusalem.
Państwo i prawo. (0031-0980). Warsaw.
Papeles de economía española. (0210-9107). Madrid.
Papers in regional science. (0486-2902). Urbana IL.
Papers: revista de sociologia. (0210-2862). Barcelona.
Parliamentary affairs. (0031-2290). Oxford.
Party politics. (1354-0688). London.
Past and present. (0031-2746). Oxford.
Patterns of prejudice. (0031-322X). London.
Peace and conflict. (1078-1919). Mahwah NJ.
Peasant studies. Salt Lake City UT.
Penant. (0336-1551). Le Vésinet.
Péninsule. Paris.
Pensamiento iberoamericano. (0212-0208). Madrid.
Pensée. (0031-4773). Paris.
Pensiero politico. (0031-4846). Florence.
Pénzügyi szemle. (0031-496X). Budapest.
People and place. (1039-4788). Victoria.

Perfiles Latinoamericanos. (0188-7653). Mexico City.
Peripherie. (0173-184X). Berlin.
Perspectiva económica. (0100-039X). São Leopoldo.
Perspectives on science. (1063-6145). Chicago IL.
Perspectives on social problems. Greenwich CT.
Pesquisa e planejamento econômico. (0100-0551). Rio de Janeiro.
Petersburg journal of cultural studies. (0136-0159). St. Petersburg.
Peuples méditerranéens = Mediterranean peoples. (0399-1253). Paris.
Philippine economic journal. Quezon City.
Philippine journal of public administration. (0031-7675). Quezon City.
Philippine quarterly of culture and society. (0115-0243). Cebu City.
Philippine studies. (0031-7837). Quezon City.
Philosophical quarterly. (0031-8094). Oxford.
Philosophie politique. Paris.
Philosophy. Tokyo.
Philosophy & public affairs. (0048-3915). Princeton NJ.
Philosophy & social criticism. (0191-4537). London.
Philosophy east and west. (0031-8221). Honolulu HI.
Philosophy of science. (0031-8248). Chicago IL.
Philosophy of the social sciences. (0048-3931). Thousand Oaks CA.
Planeación y desarrollo. (0034 8686). Colombia.
Planning practice and research. (0269-7459). London.
Planning theory & practice. (1464-9357). London.
Police studies. (0141-2949). Bradford.
Policing and society. (1043-9463). London.
Policy and politics. (0305-5736). Bristol.
Policy sciences. (0032-2687). Dordrecht.
Policy studies. (0144-2872). London.
Polis [Bologna]. Bologna.
Polis [Moscow]. (0321-2017). Moscow.
Polis [York]. (0412-257X). Thorverton.
Polish quarterly of international affairs. (1230-4999). Warsaw.
Política internacional. (0873-6650). Lisbon.
Politica: tiddskrift for politisk videnskab. (0105-0710). Aarhus.
Political communication. (1058-4609). London.
Political economy journal of India. (0971-2097). Chandigarh.
Political geography. (0962-6298). Oxford.
Political power and social theory. Greenwich CT.
Political psychology. (0162-895X). Malden MA.
Political quarterly. (0032-3179). Oxford.
Political research quarterly. (1065-9129). Salt Lake City UT.
Political science. (0032-3187). Wellington.
Political science and politics. (1049-0965). Washington DC.
Political science quarterly. (0032-3195). New York NY.
Political studies. (0032-3217). Oxford.
Political theory. (0090-5917). Thousand Oaks CA.
Politička misao. (0032-3241). Zagreb.
Politico. (0032-325X). Milan.
Politics. (0263-3957). London.
Politics and society. (0032-3292). Thousand Oaks, CA.

Politics and the individual: International journal of political socialization and political psychology. (0939-6071). Hamburg.

Politics and the life sciences. (0730-9384). Guildford, Surrey.

Politics, groups and the individual: International journal of political psychology and political socialization. (1430-0230). Norderstedt.

Politics, philosophy & economics. (1470-594X). London.

Politiikka. Tampere.

Politikon. (0258-9346). Stellenbosch.

Politique africaine. (0244-7827). Paris.

Politique et sociétés. (1203-9438). Montreal.

Politique étrangère. (0032-342X). Paris.

Politique internationale. (0221-2781). Paris.

Politiques et management public. (0758-1726). Paris.

Politische Vierteljahresschrift. (0032-3470). Wiesbaden.

Politisches Denken Jahrbuch. (0942-2307). Stuttgart.

Politix. (0295-2319). Paris.

Population. (0032-4663). Paris.

Population and development review. (0098-7921). New York NY.

Population and environment. (0199-0039). New York NY.

Population research and policy review. (0167-5923). Dordrecht.

Population review. (0032-471X). La Jolla CA.

Population studies [London]. (0032-4728). London.

Population studies [New York]. (0082-805X). New York NY.

Post-communist economies. (1463-1377). Abingdon.

Post-Soviet affairs. (1060-586X). Silver Spring MD.

Postgraduate Research Institute Bukkyo University. Kyoto.

Pouvoirs. (0152-0768). Paris.

Praca i zabezpieczenie społeczne. (0032-6186). Warsaw.

Practice. (0950-3153). Birmingham.

Présence africaine. (0032-7638). Paris.

Presidential studies quarterly. (0360-4918). New York NY.

Primates. (0032-8332). Aichi.

Problèmes d'Amérique latine. (0765-1333). Paris.

Problèmes politiques et sociaux. (0015-9743). Paris.

Probus. (0921-4771). Berlin.

Proceedings for Annual Conference of Japan Institute of Tourism Research. Tokyo.

Proceedings. American Statistical Association. Alexandria VA.

Professional geographer. (0033-0124). Oxford.

Progress in human geography. (0309-1325). Sevenoaks.

Progress in planning. (0305-9006). Oxford.

Projet. (0033-0884). Paris.

Prokla: Zeitschrift für kritische Sozialwissenschaft. (0342-8176). Berlin.

Prometheus. (0810-9028). Basingstoke.

Przegląd archeologiczny. (0079-7138). Warsaw.

Przegląd orientalistyczny. (0033-2283). Warsaw.

Przegląd polonijny. (0137-303X). Wroclaw.

Przegląd socjologiczny. (0033-2356). Lódz.

Przegląd statystyczny. (0033-2372). Warsaw.

Psychoanalytic review. (0033-2836). New York NY.

Psychoanalytic studies. (1460-8952). Oxford.

Psychological bulletin. (0033-2909). Washington DC.

Psychological review. (0033-295X). Washington DC.
Psychological science in the public interest: a journal of the American Psychological Society. (1529-1006). Oxford.
Psychological science: a journal of the American Psychological Association. (0956-7976). Oxford.
Psychology and developing societies. (0971-3336). New Delhi.
Psychology of women quarterly. (0361-6843). New York NY.
Psychology, evolution & gender. (1461-6661). London.
Public administration. (0033-3298). Oxford.
Public administration and development. (0271-2075). Chichester.
Public administration and policy. (1022-0275). Hong Kong.
Public administration review. (0033-3352). Washington DC.
Public affairs quarterly. (0887-0373). Bowling Green OH.
Public choice. (0048-5829). Dordrecht.
Public culture. (0899-2363). Durham NC.
Public enterprise. (0351-3564). Ljubljana.
Public finance = Finances publiques. (0033-3476). Frankfurt am Main.
Public finance review. (1091-1421). Thousand Oaks CA.
Public interest. (0033-3557). Washington DC.
Public law. (0033-3565). London.
Public management review. (1471-9037). London.
Public money and management. (0954-0962). Oxford.
Public opinion quarterly. (0033-362X). Chicago IL.
Publius: the journal of federalism. (0048-5950). Easton PA.
Publizistik. (0033-4006). Konstanz.
Punishment & society. (1462-4745). London.
Quaderni dell'osservatorio elettorale. Florence.
Quaderni della rivista di economia agraria. Bologna.
Quaderni di sociologia. (0033-4952). Turin.
Quaderni di studi arabi. Venice.
Quaderni storici. (0301-6307). Bologna.
Qualitative inquiry. (1077-8004). Thousand Oaks CA.
Qualitative research. (1468-7941). London.
Quarterly bulletin. Central Bank of Ireland. (0069-1542). Dublin.
Quarterly economic bulletin. (0952-0724). Liverpool.
Quarterly economic commentary. (0306-7866). Glasgow.
Quarterly economic review. Bank of Korea. Seoul.
Quarterly ethnology. Osaka.
Quarterly journal of economics. (0033-5533). Cambridge MA.
Quarterly of social research. Tokyo.
Quarterly of social security research. Tokyo.
Quarterly review of economics and finance. (0033-5797). Champaign IL.
Quarterly review. Federal Reserve Bank of New York. (0147-6580). New York NY.
Quest. (1011-226X). Lusaka.
Race and class. (0306-3968). London.
Radical history review. (0163-6545). New York NY.
Rand journal of economics. (0741-6261). Santa Monica CA.
Rassegna economica. Naples.
Rassegna italiana di sociologia. (0486-0349). Bologna.
Rassegna parlamentare. Rome.
Rationality and society. (1043-4631). London.
Recherches contemporaines. (1251-2419). Paris.

Recherches économiques de Louvain. (0770-4518). Louvanin-la-Neuve.
Recherches sociographiques. (0034-1282). Quebec.
Recherches sociologiques. (0771-677X). Leuven.
Refuge. (0229-5113). Toronto.
Regards sur l'actualité. (0337-7091). Paris.
Region and community studies bulletin. Kobe.
Regional and federal studies. (1359-7566). Ilford.
Regional science and urban economics. (0166-0462). Amsterdam.
Regional studies. (0034-3404). Abingdon.
Rekishi to shakai. Tokyo.
Relaciones internacionales. (0185-0814). Mexico City.
Relations internationales. (0335-2013). Paris.
Religion. (0048-721X). London.
Religion, state and society. (0963-7494). Abingdon.
Report of the Institute of Social Sciences. Tokyo.
Report of the Sociology & Social Work Institute. Tokyo.
Reports of the Research Institute for Japanese Culture. Sendai.
Reproductive health matters. (0968-8080). London.
Res publica [Brussels]. (0486-4700). Brussels.
Res publica [Liverpool]. (1356-4765). Liverpool.
Resarun. Itanagar.
Research bulletin. Kyushu.
Research bulletin of Kagoshima Women's College. Kagoshima.
Research bulletin of sociology. Tokyo.
Research bulletin. Meisei University. Tokyo.
Research bulletin. Tokyo University, Graduate School of Sociology. Tokyo.
Research Bulletin: Bank of Botswana. Gabarone.
Research evaluation. (0958-2029). Guildford.
Research in African literatures. (0034-5210). Bloomington IN.
Research in economic anthropology. (0190-1281). Greenwich CT.
Research in education. (0034-5237). Manchester.
Research in law and economics. Greenwich CT.
Research in Melanesia. (0254-0665). Port Moresby.
Research in political economy. (0161-7230). Greenwich CT.
Research in population economics. (0163-7878). Greenwich CT.
Research in social movements, conflicts and change. (0163-786X). Greenwich CT.
Research in social psychology. Tokyo.
Research in social stratification and mobility. (0276-5624). Greenwich CT.
Research in the sociology of work. (0277-2833). Greenwich CT.
Research papers in education — policy and practice. (0267-1522). London.
Research report. National Institute for Educational Research. Tokyo.
Reserve Bank of India bulletin. (0034-5512). Bombay.
Resources policy. (0301-4207). Oxford.
Rethinking Marxism. (0893-5696). New York NY.
Review. Suva.
Review of African political economy. (0305-6244). Abingdon.
Review of Association of Region and Community Studies. Tokyo.
Review of Austrian economics. (0889-3047). Dordrecht.
Review of black political economy. (0034-6446). New Brunswick NJ.
Review of Central and East European law. (0925-9880). Dordrecht.
Review of contemporary ideas. Tokyo.

Review of economic conditions in Italy. (0034-6799). Rome.
Review of economic studies. (0034-6527). Oxford.
Review of economics and statistics. (0034-6535). Cambridge.
Review of economies in transition. (1235-7405). Helsinki.
Review of financial studies. (0893-9454). Cary NC.
Review of income and wealth. (0034-6586). New York NY.
Review of Indonesian and Malaysian affairs. (0034-6594). Sydney.
Review of industrial organization. (0889-938X). Dordrecht.
Review of international economics. (0965-7576). Oxford.
Review of international political economy. (0969-2290). London.
Review of international studies. (0260-2105). Cambridge.
Review of Islamic economics. (0962-2055). Leicester.
Review of Middle East studies. Buckhurst Hill.
Review of modern thought. Tokyo.
Review of Osaka University of Commerce. Osaka.
Review of policy issues. (1355-6223). Sheffield.
Review of political economy. (0953-8259). Abingdon.
Review of politics. (0034-6705). Notre Dame IN.
Review of population and social policy. (0918-788X). Tokyo.
Review of quantitative finance and accounting. (0924-865X). Dordrecht.
Review of radical political economics. (0486-6134). Stamford CT.
Review of rural and urban planning in Southern and Eastern Africa. Harare.
Review of social economy. (0034-6764). London.
Review of the Osaka University of Commerce. Osaka.
Review of urban and regional development studies. (0917-0553). Tokyo.
Review. Federal Reserve Bank of St. Louis. (0014-9187). St. Louis MO.
Review. Fernand Braudel Center. (0147-9032). Binghamton NY.
Reviews in anthropology. (0093-8157). Newark NJ.
Revista Andina. (0259-9600). Cusco.
Revista brasileira de ciência política. (0103-3352). Brasilia.
Revista brasileira de ciências sociais. (0102-6909). São Paulo.
Revista brasileira de economia. (0034-7140). Rio de Janeiro.
Revista brasileira de estudos de população. (0102-3098). Brazil.
Revista brasileira de estudos políticos. (0034-7191). Belo Horizonte.
Revista de administración pública. (0034-7639). Madrid.
Revista de ciência política. (0034-8023). Rio de Janeiro.
Revista de ciências sociais. (0041-8862). Ceará.
Revista de ciencias sociales. (0034-7817). Puerto Rico.
Revista de economía institucional. (0124-5996). Bogota.
Revista de economía y estadística. (0034-8066). Córdoba.
Revista de estudios políticos. (0048-7694). Madrid.
Revista de etnografie şi folclor. (0034-8198). Bucharest.
Revista de fomento social. (0015-6043). Madrid.
Revista de historia económica. (0212-6109). Madrid.
Revista de humanidades: Tecnológico de Monterrey. (1405-4167). Monetrrey.
Revista de planeación y desarrollo. (0034-8686). Bogota.
Revista de sociologia e política. (0104-4478). Curitiba.
Revista econômica do nordeste. (0100-4956). Fortaleza.
Revista internacional de estudos africanos. (0871-2344). Lisbon.
Revista latinoamericana de estudios avanzados. (1316-0486). Caracas.
Revista mexicana de ciencias politicas y sociales. (0185-1918). Mexico City.

Revista mexicana de sociología. (0035-0087). Mexico City.

Revista mexicana del Caribe. (1405-2962). Chetumal, Quintana Roo.

Revista paraguaya de sociología. Asunción.

Revista Universidad EAFIT. (0120-033X). Medellín.

Revue belge de droit international = Belgian review of international law = Belgisch tijdschrift voor internationaal recht. (0035-0788). Brussels.

Revue canadienne d'études de développement = Canadian journal of development studies. (0225-5189). Ottawa.

Revue d'assyriologie et d'archéologie orientale. Paris.

Revue d'économie politique. (0373-2630). Paris.

Revue d'économie régionale et urbaine. (0180-7307). Paris.

Revue d'études comparatives Est-Ouest. (0338-0599). Paris.

Revue d'études palestiniennes. (0252-8290). Paris.

Revue d'histoire moderne et contemporaine. (0048-8003). Paris.

Revue de Corée. Seoul.

Revue de l'économie meridionale. (0987-3813). Montpellier.

Revue de l'histoire des religions. (0035-1423). Paris.

Revue de l'Institut de sociologie. (0770-1055). Brussels.

Revue de l'OFCE: Observations et diagnostics économiques. (1265-9576). Paris.

Revue de science criminelle et de droit pénal comparé. (0035-1733). Paris.

Revue de statistique appliquée. (0035 175X). Paris.

Revue des mondes musulmans et de la Méditerranée. (0997-1327). Aix-en-Provence.

Revue diplomatique. Tokyo.

Revue du droit public: et de la science politique en France et à l'étranger. (0035-2578). Paris.

Revue du travail. (0035-2705). Brussels.

Revue économique. (0035-2764). Paris.

Revue économique et sociale. (0035-2772). Lausanne-Dorigny.

Revue européenne des sciences sociales: Cahiers Vilfredo Pareto. (0048-8046). Geneva.

Revue française d'administration publique. (0152-7401). Paris.

Revue française d'histoire d'outre-mer. (0300-9513). Paris.

Revue française d'histoire des idées politiques. (1266-7862). Paris.

Revue française de science politique. (0035-2950). Paris.

Revue française de sociologie. (0035-2969). Gap.

Revue générale de droit international public. (0035-3094). Paris.

Revue hellénique de droit international. (0035-3256). Athens.

Revue internationale de droit comparé. (0035-3337). Paris.

Revue internationale de droit pcnal − International review of penal law. (0223-5404). Ramonville St. Agne.

Revue juridique, politique et économique du Maroc. (0251-4761). Rabat.

Revue politique et parlementaire. (0035-385X). Paris.

Revue roumaine des sciences économiques − Romanian economic review. (1220-5397). Bucharest.

Revue Tiers Monde. (0040-7356). Paris.

Revue trimestrielle de droit européen. (0035-4317). Paris.

Revue tunisienne des sciences sociales. (0035-4333). Tunis.

Rig. (0035-5267). Stockholm.

Rinrigaku Nenpo. Tokyo.

Riron to hoho = Sociological theory and methods. (0913-1442). Sapporo.

Risk, decision and policy. (1357-5309). Cambridge.

Risparmio. (0035-5615). Milan.

Ritsumeikan kokusaikankei kenkyu. Kyoto.

Ritsumeikan review of industrial society. Kyoto.

Ritsumeikan sangyoshakai ronsyu. Kyoto.
Rivista di diritto finanziario e scienza delle finanze. (0035-6131). Milan.
Rivista di economia agraria. (0035-6190). Bologna.
Rivista di politica economica. (0391-6170). Rome.
Rivista di storia economica. (0393-3415). Turin.
Rivista di studi politici internazionali. (0035-6611). Florence.
Rivista internazionale di scienze economiche e commerciali. (0035-6751). Padua.
Rivista internazionale di scienze sociali. (0035-676X). Milan.
Rivista italiana di scienza politica. (0048-8402). Bologna.
Rivista storica italiana. (0035-7073). Naples.
Rivista trimestrale di diritto pubblico. (0557-1464). Milan.
Rock art research. (0813-0426). Melbourne.
Roma. Chandigarh.
Romani studies. (1528-0748). Cheverly MD.
Ronshu (Bulletin of Tohoku Gakuin University). Sendai.
Ronshu (Bulletin of Tokyo Women's University). Tokyo.
Ronshu (Journal of Komatsu College). Komatsu.
Ronshu (Journal of Matsuyama University). Matsuyama.
Ronso. Mizunami.
Ronso. Japan.
Ronso Shinrigaku Kiyo (Journal of Meiji Gakuin University). Tokyo.
Rosei jiho. Tokyo.
Round table. (0035-8533). Abingdon.
Royal Bank of Scotland review. (0267-1190). Edinburgh.
Rural africana. (0085-5839). East Lansing MI.
Rural development in Nigeria. Ibadan.
Rural history: Economy, society, culture. (0956-7933). Cambridge.
Rural sociology. (0036-0112). College Station TX.
Russian politics and law. (1061-1940). Armonk NY.
Russian review. (0036-0341). Malden MA.
RWI-Mitteilungen. (0933-0089). Berlin.
Ryudai law review. Okinawa.
Ryukoku Kiyo. Kyoto.
Saeculum. (0080-5319). Freiburg.
SAIS review. (0036-0775). Washington DC.
Sangeet natak. New Delhi.
Santé mentale au Québec. (0383-6320). Montreal.
Sapientia. Amagasaki.
Sarawak gazette. (0036-4762). Kuching.
Sarawak Museum journal. (0375-3050). Kuching.
Sari. (0127-2721). Selangor.
Sarjana. Kuala Lumpur.
Savanna. (0331-0523). Zaria.
Savings and development. (0393-4551). Milan.
Scandinavian economic history review. (0358-5522). Lund.
Scandinavian journal of development alternatives and area studies. (0280-2791). Stockholm.
Scandinavian journal of economics. (0347-0520). Oxford.
Scandinavian journal of history. (0346-8755). Oslo.
Scandinavian journal of social welfare. (0907-2055). Copenhagen.
Scandinavian journal of the Old Testament. (0901-8328). Aarhus.
Scandinavian political studies. (0080-6757). Oxford.

School field. (0353-6807). Ljubljana.
Schweizerische Zeitschrift für Soziologie = Revue suisse de sociologie. (0379-3664). Zurich.
Schweizerische Zeitschrift für Volkswirtschaft und Statistik = Revue suisse d'économie et de statistique. (0303-9692). Basel.
Science and education. (0926-7220). Dordrecht.
Science and public policy. (0302-3427). Guildford.
Science and society. (0036-8237). New York NY.
Science as culture. (0950-5431). London.
Science, technology & development. (0950-0707). Ilford.
Science, technology and society. (0971-7218). Thousand Oaks CA.
Scottish geographical journal. (0036-9225). Glasgow.
Scottish journal of political economy. (0036-9292). Oxford.
Scripta ethnologica. (0325-6669). Buenos Aires.
Searchlight South Africa. (0954-3384). London.
Security dialogue. (0967-0106). London.
Security studies. (0963-6412). Ilford.
Seguridad estratégica regional. Buenos Aires.
Seijo communication review. Tokyo.
Seijo University economic papers. Tokyo.
Seikatsubunkakenkyû. Nagoya.
Selected reports in ethnomusicology. Los Angeles CA.
Semiotica. (0037-1998). Berlin.
Senri ethnological studies. Osaka.
Senriyama bungaku-ronshu. Osaka.
Senshu sociology. Kanagawa.
Sexualities: studies in culture and society. (1363-4607). London.
Shakai bunseki. Tokyo.
Shakai-kagaku Tokyu. Tokyo.
Shakai-undo. Tokyo.
Shakaibunka kenkyu. Hiroshima.
Shakaigaku hyoron. Tokyo.
Shakaigaku kenkyuka kiyo (Bulletin of Keio-Gijuku Graduate School). Tokyo.
Shakaigaku nenpō. Sendai.
Shakaigaku ronko. Tokyo.
Shakaigaku ronshu (Bulletin of Momoyama University). Osaka.
Shakaigaku ronshu [Nagoya]. Nagoya.
Shakaigaku ronso. Tokyo.
Shakaigaku-nenshi. Tokyo.
Shakaigaku-senko kiyo. Tokyo.
Shakaigaku-zasshi. Kobe.
Shakaigakubu kiyo (Bulletin of Ryukoku University). Otsu.
Shakaigakubu kiyo (Journal of Kansai University). Osaka.
Shakaigakubu ronso. Ibaraki.
Shakaijinruigaku nenpo. Tokyo.
Shakaishinrigaku kenkyu. Tokyo.
Shaman. (1216-7827). Szeged.
Shimbun kenkyu. Tokyo.
Shinbungaku hyoron. Japan.
Shisei. Tokyo.
Shiseikenkyu. Osaka.
Shizen, ningen, shakai. Yokohama.

Shnaton. Tel-Aviv.
SIER Bulletin. Kwaluseni.
Signs. (0097-9740). Chicago IL.
Sikh review. (0037-5123). Calcutta.
Simmei shakaigaku kenkyu. Kawasaki.
Simulation and gaming. (0037-5500). Thousand Oaks CA.
Singapore economic review. (0217-5908). Singapore.
Singapore journal of tropical geography. (0129-7619). Singapore.
Sino-American relations. Taiwan.
Siso no Kagaku. Tokyo.
Slavic review. (0037-6779). Stanford CA.
Slavonic and East European review. (0037-6795). London.
Slovo. (0954-6839). London.
Small business economics. (0921-898X). Dordrecht.
Small enterprise development. (0957-1329). London.
Small wars and insurgencies. (0959-2318). Ilford.
Smithsonian contributions to anthropology. (0081-0223). Washington DC.
Social & cultural geography. (1464-9365). London.
Social action [New Delhi]. (0037-7627). New Delhi.
Social analysis [Adelaide]. (0155-977X). Adelaide.
Social analysis [Fukuoka]. Fukuoka.
Social and economic studies. (0037-7651). Kingston.
Social and legal studies. (0964-6639). London.
Social anthropology. (0964-0282). Cambridge.
Social biology. (0037-766X). New York NY.
Social choice and welfare. (0176-1714). Heidelberg.
Social cognition. (0278-016X). New York NY.
Social compass. (0037-7686). London.
Social dynamics. (0253-3952). Rondebosch.
Social forces. (0037-7732). Chapel Hill NC.
Social history. (0307-1022). London.
Social identities: Journal for the study of race, nation and culture. (1350-4630). Abingdon.
Social indicators research. (0303-8300). Dordrecht.
Social information. Sapporo.
Social justice. (0094-7571). San Francisco CA.
Social networks. (0378-8733). Amsterdam.
Social philosophy & policy. (0265-0525). Cambridge.
Social policy. (0037-7783). New York NY.
Social policy and administration. (0144-5596). Oxford.
Social politics: international studies in gender, state and society. (1072-4745). Cary NC.
Social problems. (0037-7791). Berkeley CA.
Social psychology quarterly. (0190-2725). Washington DC.
Social science & medicine. (0277-9536). Exeter.
Social science history. (0145-5532). Durham NC.
Social science information. (0539-0184). London.
Social science Japan. (1340-7155). Tokyo.
Social science Japan journal. (1369-1465). Oxford.
Social science Japan review. Tokyo.
Social science quarterly. (0038-4941). Austin TX.
Social science research. (0049-089X). Orlando FL.
Social science review of Kagoshima University. Kagoshima.

Social sciences [Kyoto]. Kyoto.
Social sciences in China. (0252-9203). Beijing.
Social sciences review. Tokyo.
Social sciences review. Tokyo.
Social scientist. (0970-0293). New Delhi.
Social security: Journal of welfare and social security studies. (0334-231X). Jerusalem.
Social semiotics. (1035-0330). Queensland.
Social service review. (0037-7961). Chicago IL.
Social studies of science. (0306-3127). London.
Social work and social sciences review. (0953-5225). London.
Social work education. (0261-5479). London.
Socialism and democracy. New York NY.
Socialismo y participación. Lima.
Socialist alternatives. Quebec.
Socialist history. (0969-4331). London.
Sociedad. (0327-7712). Buenos Aires.
Sociétés contemporaines. (1150-1944). Paris.
Society. (0147-2011). New Brunswick NJ.
Society & Animals. (1063-1119). Cambridge.
Society of Malaŵi journal. (0037-993X). Blantyre.
Socio-economic planning sciences. (0038-0121). Exeter.
Sociolinguistics. (0257-7135). Dordrecht.
Sociologia [Bratislava] = Sociology [Bratislava]. (0049-1225). Bratislava.
Sociologia [Rome]. (0038-0156). Rome.
Sociologia internationalis. (0038-0164). Berlin.
Sociologia ruralis. (0038-0199). Oxford.
Sociologia urbana e rurale. (0392-4939). Bologna.
Sociologica. Tokyo.
Sociological bulletin. (0038-0229). New Delhi.
Sociological forum. (0884-8971). New York NY.
Sociological methodology. (0081-1750). Oxford.
Sociological methods and research. (0049-1241). Thousand Oaks CA.
Sociological perspectives. (0731-1214). Las Vegas NV.
Sociological practice: a journal of clinical and applied psychology. (1522-3442). New York.
Sociological quarterly. (0038-0253). Greenwich CT.
Sociological research online. (1360-7804). Guildford.
Sociological review. (0038-0261). London.
Sociological review [Kobe]. Kobe.
Sociological review of Ryukoku University. Kyoto.
Sociological theory. (0735-2751). Malden MA.
Sociologický časopis. (0038-0288). Prague.
Sociologie du travail. (0038-0296). Paris.
Sociologische gids. (0038-0334). Meppel.
Sociologos. Tokyo.
Sociologus. (0038-0377). Berlin.
Sociology [U.K.]. (0038-0385). Cambridge.
Sociology of health and illness. (0141-9889). Oxford.
Sociology of health care. Hampton Hill.
Sociology of law. Tokyo.
Sociology of religion. (0038-0210). Holiday FL.
Sociology today. Tokyo.

Sôgô toshi kenkyû. Tokyo.
Sogokagakubu-kiyo. Hiroshima.
SOJOURN: Journal of social issues in Southeast Asia. (0217-9520). Singapore.
Sophia. Tokyo.
Sophia University studies in sociology. Tokyo.
Soshiolojika. Tokyo.
Soshioroji. Kyoto.
Sotsial'no-gumanitarnye Znaniia. (0869-8120). Moscow.
Sotsiologicheski problemi. (0324-1572). Sofia.
Sotsiologicheskie issledovaniia (sotsis). (0132-1625). Moscow.
South African archaeological bulletin. (0038-1969). Vlaeberg.
South African Archaeological Society: Goodwin series. (0304-3460). Vlaeberg.
South African geographical journal = Suid-Afrikaanse geografiese tydskrif. (0373-6245). Wits.
South African historical journal = Suid-Afrikaanse historiese joernaal. (0258-2473). Pretoria.
South African journal of African languages = Suid-Afrikaanse tydskrif vir Afrikatale. (0257-2117).
    Pretoria.
South African journal of economic history. Pretoria.
South African journal of economics = Suid-Afrikaanse tydskrif vir ekonomie. (0038-2280). Pretoria.
South African journal of ethnology = Suid-Afrikaanse tydskrif vir etnologie. (0258-0144). Pretoria.
South African journal of international affairs. (1022-0461). Johannesburg.
South African journal of sociology = Suid-Afrikaanse tydskrif vir sosiologie. Pretoria.
South African labour bulletin. Johannesburg.
South African law journal. (0258-2503). Kenwyn.
South Asia. (0085-6401). Armidale.
South Asia research. (0262-7280). New Delhi.
South Asian anthropologist. (0257-7348). Ranchi.
South Asian studies. (0266-6030). London.
South Asian survey. (0971-5231). New Delhi.
South East Asia research. (0967-828X). London.
South East Asian review. Gaya.
South East Europe Review for Labour and Social Affairs. Baden-Baden.
South European society & politics. (1360-8746). Ilford.
Southeast Asia: history and culture. Tokyo.
Southeast Asian affairs. (0377-5437). Singapore.
Southeast Asian research materials group newsletter. (0311-290X). Canberra.
Southeast Asian studies. Kyoto.
Southern Africa record. (0377-5445). Braamfontein.
Southern economic journal. (0038-4038). Stillwater OK.
Soziale Welt. (0038-6073). Baden Baden.
Soziologie. (0340-918X). Stuttgart.
Space & polity. (1356-2576). Abingdon.
Spanish economic review. (1435-5469). Heidelberg.
Spoudai. (1105-8919). Piraeus.
Sprawozdania archeologiczne. (0081-3834). Warsaw.
Sri Lanka journal of social sciences. (0258-9710). Colombo.
Sri Lanka journal of the humanities. Peradeniya.
St. Andrew's University sociological review. Osaka.
Staat und Recht. (0038-8858). Berlin.
Staff papers. International Monetary Fund. (0020-8027). Washington DC.
State politics & policy quarterly. (1532-4400). Illinois.
Statistica. (0039-0380). Bologna.

Statistical papers = Statistische Hefte. (0932-5026). Heidelberg.
Statistics in transition. (1234-7655). Warsaw.
Statsvetenskaplig tidskrift. (0039-0747). Lund.
Statute law review. (0144-3593). Oxford.
Storia contemporanea. (0039-1875). Bologna.
Storia politica società. Turin.
Strategic management journal. (0143-2095). Chichester.
Studi bresciani. (1121-6557). Brescia.
Studia africana. (1130-5703). Barcelona.
Studia demograficzne. (0039-3134). Warsaw.
Studia diplomatica. (0770-2965). Brussels.
Studia ethnica. (1427-0110). Warsaw.
Studia fennica. (0085-6835). Helsinki.
Studia fennica: Folkloristica. (1235-1946). Helsinki.
Studia iranica. (0772-7852). Lésigny.
Studia orientalia. (0039-3282). Helsinki.
Studia prawno-ekonomiczne. (0081-6841). Łódź.
Studia rosenthaliana. (0039-3347). Amsterdam.
Studia socjologiczne. (0039-3371). Warsaw.
Studies and essays — behavioral sciences and philosophy. (1342-4262). Kanazawa.
Studies in American political development. (0898-588X). New York NY.
Studies in comparative culture. Tokyo.
Studies in comparative history of circum-Japan Sea areas. Niigata.
Studies in comparative international development. (0039-3606). New Brunswick NJ.
Studies in conflict and terrorism. (1057-610X). London.
Studies in East European thought. (0925-9392). Dordrecht.
Studies in family planning. (0039-3665). New York NY.
Studies in history. (0257-6430). New Delhi.
Studies in history and philosophy of modern physics. (1355-2198). Oxford.
Studies in history and philosophy of science. (0039-3681). Oxford.
Studies in human sciences. Tokyo.
Studies in language and culture. Hiroshima.
Studies in law, politics, and society. London.
Studies in philosophy and education. (0039-3746). Dordrecht.
Studies in political economy. (0707-8552). Ottawa.
Studies in social science. Fukuoka.
Studies in social sciences. Hiroshima.
Studies in sociology, psychology and education. Tokyo.
Studies in the humanities. Matsumoto.
Studies in the humanities and sciences. Hiroshima.
Studies in the linguistic sciences. (0049-2388). Urbana IL.
Studies in Third World societies. (1056-9189). Williamsburg VA.
Studies in Western Australian history. Nedlands WA.
Studies in Western history. Osaka.
Studies of broadcasting. Tokyo.
Studies of The Japan Institute of Labour. Tokyo.
Studies on the history of sociology. Tokyo.
Studies. Kwansei Gakuin university, Sociology Department. Hyogo.
Studii şi comunicări etnologie. (1221-6518). Bucharest.
Study for the history of social services. Japan.
Study of sociology. Sendai.

Südosteuropa Aktuell. Munich.
Südosteuropa Mitteilungen. (0340-174X). Munich.
Südosteuropa-Jahrbuch. Munich.
Südosteuropa-Schriften. (1430-8770). Munich.
Südosteuropa-Studie. Munich.
SUGIA: Sprache und Geschichte in Afrika. (0170-5946). Cologne.
Suomalais-Ugrilaisen Seuran Aikakauskirja. (0355-0214). Helsinki.
Suomalais-Ugrilaisen Seuran kansatieteellisiä julkaisuja. (0359-7679). Helsinki.
Surugadai University studies. Japan.
Survey of Jewish affairs. (0741-6571). Oxford.
Survival. (0039-6338). Oxford.
Svobodnaia mysl'. (0869-4435). Moscow.
Swedish economic policy review. (1400-1829). Stockholm.
Swiss political science review. (1424-7755). Zurich.
Symbolon. (0082-0660). Frankfurt am Main.
Systems research and behavioral science. (1092-7026). Chichester.
Szociológia. (0133-3461). Budapest.
Tama Gakkai. Tokyo.
Tamkang journal of area studies. Taipei.
Tanzanian economic trends. (0856-3373). Dar es Salaam.
Tareas. (0494-7061). Panama City.
Társadalmi szemle. (0039-971X). Budapest.
Társadalomkutatás. (0580-4795). Budapest.
Te reo. (0494-8440). Auckland.
Technology analysis & strategic management. (0953-7325). London.
Technology and culture. (0040-165X). Baltimore MD.
Technology and development. (0914-918X). Tokyo.
Teikyo journal of sociology. Tokyo.
Tel Aviv: Journal of the Institute of Archaeology of Tel Aviv University. (0334-4355). Tel Aviv.
Telecommunications policy. (0308-5961). Amsterdam.
Television & new media. (1527-4764). Thousand Oaks CA.
Telos. (0090-6514). New York NY.
Tempo social. (0103-2070). São Paulo.
Temps modernes. (0040-3075). Paris.
Teoria politica. (0394-1248). Milan.
Terra. Helsinki.
Terrain. (0760-5668). Paris.
Terrorism and political violence. (0954-6553). Ilford.
Text. (0165-4888). Berlin.
The journal of energy literature. (1359-3714). Oxford.
Theory and decision. (0040-5833). Dordrecht.
Theory and psychology. (0959-3543). London.
Theory and society. (0304-2421). Dordrecht.
Theory culture and society. (0263-2764). London.
Thesis eleven. (0725-5136). London.
Third World quarterly. (0143-6597). Abingdon.
Tibet journal. (0970-5368). Dharamshala.
Tidsskriftet antropologi. (0906-3021). Copenhagen.
Tijdschrift voor economie en management. (0772-7664). Louvain.
Tijdschrift voor economische en sociale geografie = Journal of economic and social geography. (0040-747X). Oxford.

Time & society. (0961-463X). London.
Tochi-seido shigaku. Tokyo.
Tohoku daigaku bungakuba nenpo. Sendai.
Tohoku daigaku kyoyobu kiyo. Miyagi.
Tokai law review. Tokyo.
Tokiwa journal of human science. Mita.
Toledo journal of Great Lakes' law, science & policy. (1097-9328). Toledo.
Toshi mondai. Tokyo.
Toshi-mondai kenkyu. Osaka.
Totalitarian movements and political religions. (1469-0764). Ilford.
Toukei. Tokyo.
Tourism geographies. (1461-6688). London.
Town planning review. (0041-0020). Liverpool.
Toyama daigaku keizai ronshu. Toyama City.
Transactions of the Asiatic Society of Japan. Tokyo.
Transactions of the Institute of British Geographers: New series. London.
Transactions of the Institute of Humanities. Yokohama.
Transactions of the Philological Society. (0079-1636). Oxford.
Transafrican journal of history. (0251-0391). Nairobi.
Transfer: European review of labour and research. (1024-2589). Antwerp.
Transformation. (0258-7696). Durban.
Transit: Europäische Revue. (0938-2062). Frankfurt am Main.
Transition. (1012-8263). Georgetown.
Transitions. (1211-0205). Prague.
Translator: Studies in intercultural communication. (1355-6509). Manchester.
Transnational organized crime. (1357-7387). Ilford.
Transportation. (0049-4488). Dordrecht.
Transportation research. (0191-2615). Tarrytown NY.
Transportation science. (0041-1655). Linthicum MD.
Tri-view. Tokyo.
Tribus. (0082-6413). Stuttgart.
Trimestre económico. (0041-3011). Mexico City.
Tsukuba annals of sociology. Tsukuba.
Tsukuba journal of sociology. Tsukuba.
Turkish review of Middle East studies. Istanbul.
Turkish studies. (1468-3849). Ilford.
Turkish yearbook of international relations – Milletlerarasi münasebetler Türk yilli&gi. (0544-1943)
    Ankara.
Twentieth century British history. (0955-2359). Oxford.
Tyuo tyosa ho. Tokyo.
Ufahamu. (0041-5715). Los Angeles CA.
Ukrainian economic review. (1080-725X). Philadelphia PA.
Ulkopolitiikka. (0501-0659). Helsinki.
Unisa Latin American report. (0256-6060). Pretoria.
Universitas. (0049-5530). Legon.
University of Western Australia Anthropological Research Museum occasional papers. (0810-8536).
    Perth.
University studies. Ibaruki-Ken.
Uomo. Rome.
Uomo & cultura. Palermo.
Urban advance. Nagoya.

Urban affairs annual reviews. (0083-4688). Thousand Oaks CA.

Urban affairs review. (1078-0874). Thousand Oaks CA.

Urban anthropology. (0894-6019). Brockport NY.

Urban forum. (1015-3802). Johannesburg.

Urban geography. (0272-3638). Silver Spring MD.

Urban studies. (0042-0980). Abingdon.

US-Japan women's journal. (0898-8900). Palo Alto CA.

Utilitas. (0953-8208). Edinburgh.

Utilities policy. (0957-1787). Oxford.

Valóság. (0324-7228). Budapest.

Venture capital. (1369-1066). London.

Verfassung und Recht in Übersee = Law and politics in Africa, Asia and Latin America. (0506-7286). Baden-Baden.

Vestnik Moskovskogo universiteta. Seriia 12 Politicheskie nauki. (0201-7385). Moscow.

Vestnik Moskovskogo universiteta. Seriia 5 Geografiia. Moscow.

Vestnik Moskovskogo universiteta. Seriia 6 Ekonomika. (0130-0105). Moscow.

Vestnik Moskovskogo universiteta. Seriia 9 Filologiia. (0130-0075). Moscow.

Vestnik Sankt-Peterburgskogo universiteta. Seriia 5 Ekonomika. (0233-755X). St. Petersburg.

Vestnik Sankt-Peterburgskogo universiteta. Seriia 6 Filosofiia, politologiia, sotsiolgiia, psikhologiia, pravo. St. Petersburg.

Vestnik Sankt-Peterburgskogo universiteta. Seriia 6 Filosofiia, politologiia, sotsiologiia, psikhologiia, pravo, mezhdunarodnye otnosheniia. (0132-4624). Saint Petersburg.

Vestsi natsyianalnai akademii navuk Belarusi: Seryia gumanitarnykh navuk. (0321-1649). Minsk.

Vierteljahrschrift für Sozial- und Wirtschaftsgeschichte. (0340-8728). Stuttgart.

Vierteljahrshefte für Zeitgeschichte. (0042-5702). Munich.

Vierteljahrshefte zur Wirtschaftsforschung. (0340-1707). Berlin.

Vietnam social sciences. (1013-4328). Hanoi.

Vietnamese studies. (0085-7823). Hanoi.

Visual anthropology. (0894-9468). New York NY.

Visual anthropology review. (1058-7187). Arlington VA.

Volkskundig bulletin. (0166-0667). Amsterdam.

Volonta. (0392-5013). Milan.

Voluntas. (0957-8765). New York NY.

Voprosy ekonomiki. (0042-8736). Moscow.

Wage & social security. Tokyo.

WAMP: West African Museums Programme bulletin. London.

War studies journal. (1363-1225). London.

Waseda bulletin of comparative law. (0285-9211). Tokyo.

Waseda economic papers. (0511-1943). Tokyo.

Waseda koto gakuin kennkyu nenshi. Tokyo.

Waseda shogaku. Tokyo.

Washington quarterly. (0163-660X). Cambridge MΛ.

Welsh history review = Cylchgrawn hanes Cymru. (0083-792X). Cardiff.

Welt des Islams. (0043-2539). Leiden.

Welt Trends: internationale Politik und vergleichende Studien. (0944-8101). Potsdam.

Weltwirtschaft. (0043-2652). Tübingen.

Weltwirtschaftliches Archiv. (0043-2636). Tübingen.

Werkdocumenten over etnische kunst = Working papers in ethnic art. Ghent.

West African journal of archaeology. (0331-3158). Ibadan.

West European politics. (0140-2382). Ilford.

Wirtschaftsdienst. (0043-6275). Hamburg.

Wirtschaftspolitische Blätter. (0043-6291). Vienna.
Wirtschaftswissenschaft. (0043-633X). Berlin.
Women's studies. (0049-7878). Philadelphia.
Women's studies international forum. (0277-5395). Oxford.
Work and occupations. (0730-8884). Thousand Oaks CA.
Work, employment and society. (0950-0170). Cambridge.
Working papers in linguistics. Columbus OH.
World archaeology. (0043-8243). London.
World Bank economic review. (0258-6770). Washington DC.
World Bank research observer. (0257-3032). Washington DC.
World development. (0305-750X). Oxford.
World economy. (0378-5920). Oxford.
World futures. (0260-4027). London.
World in Slavic society. Kobundo.
World of music. (0043-8774). Bamberg.
World politics. (0043-8871). Baltimore MD.
World review. Indooroophilly QLD.
World today. (0043-9134). London.
WSI Mitteilungen. (0342-300X). Frankfurt am Main.
Wuqûf. (0930-9306). Hamburg.
Yagl-Ambu. (0254-0681). Papua New Guinea.
Yale journal on regulation. (0741-9457). New Haven CT.
Yale law journal. (0044-0094). New Haven CT.
Yamaguchi daigaku kyoikugakuba ronsoh. Yamaguchi.
Yapi kredi economic review. (1019-1232). Istanbul.
Yearbook of co-operative enterprise. (0952-5556). Oxford.
Yearbook of Finnish foreign policy. (0355-0079). Helsinki.
Yhtyneet kuvalehdet oy. (0355-0303). Helsinki.
York papers in linguistics. (0307-3238). York.
Yoron. Tokyo.
Youth problems study. Osaka.
Yugoslav law = Droit yougoslave. (0350-2252). Belgrade.
Zagreb journal of economics. (1331-4599). Zagreb.
Zaïre-Afrique. (0049-8513). Kinshasa.
Zambezia. (0379-0622). Harare.
Zambia journal of history. Lusaka.
Zeitschrift fur ausländisches öffentliches Recht und Völkerrecht. (0044-2348). Stuttgart.
Zeitschrift für Balkanologie. (0044-2356). Wiesbaden.
Zeitschrift für Ethnologie. (0044-2666). Berlin.
Zeitschrift für öffentliches recht. (0948-4396). Vienna.
Zeitschrift für Parlamentsfragen. (0340-1758). Wiesbaden.
Zeitschrift für Politik. (0044-3360). Cologne.
Zeitschrift für Recht und Wirtschaft: Betriebs-Berater. Heidelberg.
Zeitschrift für Sexualforschung. (0932-8114). Stuttgart.
Zeitschrift für Soziologie. (0340-1804). Stuttgart.
Zeitschrift für Unternehmensgeschichte. (0342-2852). Stuttgart.
Zeitschrift für vergleichende Rechtswissenschaft [Heidelberg]. (0044-3638). Heidelberg.
Zeitschrift für Verkehrswissenschaft. (0044-3670). Düsseldorf.
Zeitschrift für Wirtschafts- und Sozialwissenschaften. (0342-1783). Berlin.
Zeitschrift für Wirtschaftspolitik. (0721-3808). Stuttgart.
Zimbabwe journal of economics. Harare.

LIST OF ABBREVIATIONS USED

LISTE DES ABRÉVIATIONS UTILISÉES

A. Dept. Antiq. Jordan Annual of the Department of Antiquities of Jordan. Directorate General of Antiquities: P.O. Box 88, Amman, Jordan.

Acadiensis Acadiensis: Journal of the history of the Atlantic Region. (0044-5851). University of New Brunswick: Fredericton, New Brunswick, E3B 5A3, Canada.

Acta Orient. Acta orientalia. (0001-6438). Munksgaard: Copenhagen, Denmark.

Acta Sociol. [Mexico] Acta sociologica [Mexico]. (0186-6028). Universidad Nacional Autónoma de México, Facultad de Ciencias Políticas y Sociales: Ciudad Universitaria, Coyoacán, 04510 México D.F., Mexico.

Af. Spec. Afrika Spectrum. (0002-0397). Institut für Afrika-Kunde: Neuer Jungfernstieg 21, D-20354 Hamburg, Germany.

Afr. Affairs African affairs. (0001-9909). Oxford University Press: Great Clarendon Street, Oxford OX2 6DP, U.K., in association with Royal African Society: 18 Northumberland Avenue, London WC2N 5BJ, U.K.

Afr. Arts African arts. (0001-9933). University of California, James S. Coleman African Studies Center: Los Angeles, CA 90024-1310, U.S.A.

Afr. Devel. Africa development = Afrique & développement. (0850-3907). Council for the Development of Social Science Research in Africa / Conseil pour le développement de la recherche en sciences sociales en Afrique: B.P. 3304, Dakar, Senegal.

Afr. Econ. Hist. African economic history. (0145-2258). University of Wisconsin, African Studies Program: 205 Ingraham Hall, 1155 Observatory Drive, Madison, WI 53706, U.S.A.

Afr. Q. Africa quarterly. (0001-9828). Indian Council for Cultural Relations: Azad Bhavan, Indraprastha Estate, New Delhi 110 002, India.

Afr. Stud. African studies. (0002-0184). Witwatersrand University Press: P.O. Wits, Johannesburg, 2050, South Africa.

Afr. Stud. R. African studies review. (0002-0206). African Studies Association: Rutgers, State University of New Jersey, Douglass Campus, 132 George Street, New Brunswick, NJ 08901-1400, U.S.A.

Africa Africa: Journal of the International African Institute. (0001-9720). International African Institute: School of Oriental and African Studies, Thornhaugh Street, Russell Square, London, WC1 0XG.

Africana Africana. (0871-2336). Centro de estudos Africanos e Orientais: Universidade Portucalense, Rua Dr. António Bernardino de Almeida, 541-619, 4200 Porto, Portugal.

Age. Soc. Ageing and society. (0144-686X). Cambridge University Press: The Edinburgh Building, Shaftesbury Road, Cambridge CB2 2RU, U.K., in association with Centre for Policy on Ageing / British Society of Gerontology.

Agr. Hist. Agricultural history. (0002-1482). University of California Press Journals: 2120 Berkeley Way, Berkeley, CA 94720-5812, U.S.A., in association with Agricultural History Society: ERS, 1301 New York Avenue N.W., Washington DC 20205, U.S.A.

Al-Qantara Al-Qantara. (0211-3589). Consejo Superior de Investigaciones Científicas, Instituto de Filología: Duque de Medinaceli 6, 28014 Madrid, Spain.

Alternatives Alternatives. (0304-3754). Lynne Rienner Publishers: 1800 30th Street, Boulder, CO 80301, U.S.A.

Am. Anthrop. American anthropologist. (0002-7294). American Anthropological Association: 4350 North Fairfax Drive, Suite 640, Arlington, VA 22203-1620, U.S.A.

Am. Behav. Sc. American behavioral scientist. (0002-7642). Sage Publications: 2455 Teller Road, Newbury Park, Thousand Oaks, CA 91320, U.S.A.

Am. Econ. Rev. American economic review. (0002-8282). American Economic Association: 2014 Broadway, Suite 305, Nashville, TN 37203, U.S.A.

Am. Ethn. American ethnologist. (0094-0496). American Anthropological Association: 4350 North Fairfax Drive, Suite 640, Arlington VA 22203-1620, U.S.A.

Am. Hist. Rev. American historical review. (0002-8762). American Historical Association: 400 A Street S.E., Washington DC 20003, U.S.A.

Am. J. Agr. Ec. American journal of agricultural economics. (0002-9092). American Agricultural Economics Association: 415 South Duff Avenue, Suite C, Ames, IA 50011-6600, U.S.A.

Am. J. Prim. American journal of primatology. (0275-2565). John Wiley & Sons: 605 Third Avenue, New York, NY 10158-0012, U.S.A., in association with American Society of Primatologists.

Am. Psychol. American psychologist. (0003-066X). American Psychological Association: 750 First Street, NE Washington, DC 20002-4242.

Amerindia Amerindia. (0221-8852). Association d'Ethnolinguistique Amérindienne: B.P. 431, 75233 Paris Cedex 05, France.

An. Est. Cent.Am. Anuario de estudios centroamericanos. (0377-7316). Universidad de Costa Rica, Instituto de Investigaciones Sociales: Apartado 75, 2060 Ciudad Universitaria, Rodrigo Facio, 2050 San Pedro de Montes de Oca, San José, Costa Rica.

An. Eusko. Folk. Anuario de eusko folklore. (0210-7732). Editorial Eusko-Ikaskuntza.

Anál. Soc. Análise social. (0003-2573). Instituto de Ciências Sociais da Universidade de Lisboa: Avenida das Forças Armadas, Edificio I.S.C.T.E., Ala Sul, 1º andar, 1600 Lisbon, Portugal, in association with Junta Nacional de Investigação Científica e Tecnológia / Instituto Nacional de Investigação Científica.

Anatol. St. Anatolian studies. (0066-1546). British Institute of Archaeology at Ankara: 10 Carlton House Terrace, London, SW1Y 5AH, U.K.

Ann. Annales: Histoire, sciences sociales. Éditions de l'École des hautes études en sciences sociales: 54 boulevard Raspail, 75006 Paris, France.

Ann. Æqua. Annales æquatoria. (0254-4296). Aequatoria: Stationsstraat 48, B-3360 Lovenjoel, Belgium.

Ann. Géogr. Annales de géographie. (0003-4010). Armand Colin: 21, rue du Montparnasse - F - 75283 PARIS CEDEX 06, France.

Ann. R. Anthr. Annual review of anthropology. (0084-6570). Annual Reviews: 4139 El Camino Way, P.O. Box 10139, Palo Alto, CA 94303-0139, U.S.A.

Ann. Sociol. Année sociologique. (0066-2399). Presses Universitaires de France: 108 boulevard Saint-Germain, 75006 Paris, France, in association with Bibliothèque de Philosophie Contemporaine.

Annales Annales: Économies, sociétés, civilisations. (0395-2649). Armand Colin: 21, rue du Montparnasse - F - 75283 PARIS CEDEX 06, France, in association with C.N.R.S. / École des hautes études en sciences sociales: 54, boulevard Raspail 75006 - PARIS.

Anth. Sci. Anthropological science. (0918-7960). Anthropological Society of Nippon: Business Centre for Academic Studies Japan, Honkomagome 5-16-9, Bunkyo-ku, Tokyo 113, Japan.

Anth. Th. Anthropological theory. (1463-4996). Sage Publications: 6 Bonhill Street, London EC2A 4PU, U.K.

Anthr. Quart. Anthropological quarterly. (0003-5491). Catholic University of America Press: 620 Michigan Avenue, N.E., Administration Building Room 303, Washington DC 20064, U.S.A., in association with Catholic University of America, Department of Anthropology: Washington, DC 20064, U.S.A.

Anthr. Today Anthropology today. (0268-540X). Royal Anthropological Institute of Great Britain and Ireland: 50 Fitzroy Street, London W1P 5HS, U.K.

Anthro. forum Anthropological forum. (0066-4677). University of Western Australia, Department of Anthropology: Nedlands, WA 6009, Australia.

Anthrop. Ling. Anthropological linguistics. (0003-5483). Anthropological Linguistics: Indiana University, Student Building 130, 701 E. Kirkwood Avenue, Bloomington, IN 47405-7100, USA.

Anthropologie [Paris] Anthropologie [Paris]. (0003-5521). Masson: 120 boulevard Saint-Germain, 75280 Paris Cedex 06, France.

Anthropos [St. Augustin] Anthropos [St. Augustin]. (0257-9774). Anthropos Institut: Arnold-Janssen-Str. 20, D-53754 Sankt Augustin, Germany.

Antiquity Antiquity. (0003-598X). Antiquity Publications: c/o 85 Hills Road, Cambridge CB2 1PG, U.K.

Arabica Arabica. (0570-5398). Brill Academic Publishers: P.O. Box 9000, 2300 PA Leiden, The Netherlands.

Arch. Orient. Archív orientální. (0044-8699). Academia Publishing House: Legerova 61, 120 00 Prague 2 Czech Republic, in association with Czechoslovak Academy of Sciences, Oriental Institute.

Archaeol. Ocean. Archaeology in Oceania. (0003-8121). Oceania Publications: 116 Darlington Road, University of Sydney, NSW 2006, Australia.

Archaeol. Polona Archaeologia polona. (0066-5924). Instytut Archeologii i etnologii: Polskiej Akademii Nauk, Al. Solidarnosci 105, 00-140 Warszawa, Poland, in association with Polska Akademia Nauk, Instytut Historii Kultury Materialnej: Al. Swierczewskiego 105, 00-140 Warsaw, Poland.

Archeol. Pol. Archeologia polski. (0003-8180). Instytut Archeologii i etnologii: Polskiej Akademii Nauk, Al. Solidarnosci 105, 00-140 Warszawa, Poland, in association with Polska Akademia Nauk, Instytut Historii Kultury Materialnej: Al. Swierczewskiego 105, 00-140 Warsaw, Poland.

Archeologia Archeologia. (0066-605X). Institute of Archaeology and Ethnnology: Polish Academy of Sciences, Aleja Solidarnosci 105, 00-140 Warszawa, Warsaw, Poland.

Archipel Archipel. (0044-8613). Editions de l'École des hautes études en sciences sociales: 54 boulevard Raspail, 75006 Paris, France, in association with Association Archipel.

Area Area. (0004-0894). Royal Geographical Society (with IBG): 1 Kensington Gore, London SW7 2AR, U.K.

Asia Pacific J. Anthr. Asia Pacific journal of anthropology. (1444-2213). Department of Anthropology: Research School of Pacific and Asian Studies, The Australian National University, Canberra ACT 0200, Australia.

Asian Cult. (Asian-Pac. Cult.) Q. Asian culture (Asian-Pacific culture) quarterly. (0378-8911). Asian-Pacific Cultural Center: Asian-Pacific Parliamentarians' Union, 6F, 66 Aikuo East Road, Taipei, Taiwan 10726.

Asian Folk. S. Asian folklore studies. (0385-2342). Nanzan University, Anthropological Institute: 18 Yamazato-chō, Shōwa-ku, 466-8673 Nagoya, Japan.

Asian Mus. Asian music. (0044-9202). Society for Asian Music: Department of Asian Music, Lincoln Hall, Cornell University, Ithaca, NY 14853, U.S.A.

Asian Persp. [Hawaii] Asian perspectives [Hawaii]. (0066-8435). University of Hawaii Press: 2840 Kolowalu Street, Honolulu, HI 96822-1888, U.S.A.

Asian Prof. Asian profile. (0304-8675). Asian Research Service: Rm. 704, Federal Building, 369 Lockhart Road, Hong Kong.

Aus. Fem. St. Australian feminist studies. (0816-4649). Carfax Publishing, Taylor & Francis Ltd: Rankine Road, Basingstoke, Hants, RG24 8PR, UK.

Aus. J. Anth. Australian journal of anthropology. (1035-8811). Australian Anthropological Society: University of Sydney, Department of Anthropology, Sydney, NSW 2006, Australia.
Aust. Geogr. Australian geographer. (0004-9182). Carfax Publishing: P.O. Box 25, Abingdon, Oxfordshire OX14 3UE, U.K.
Aust. Geogr. Stud. Australian geographical studies. (0004-9190). Blackwell Publishers: 108 Cowley Road, Oxford OX4 1JF, U.K., in association with Australian Defence Force Academy, Campbell, ACT 2600, Australia.
Aust. J. Ling. Australian journal of linguistics. (0726-8602). Carfax Publishing, Taylor and Francis Ltd: P.O. Box 25, Abingdon, Oxfordshire OX14 3UE, U.K., in association with Australian Linguistic Society: Department of Linguistics, La Trobe University, Bundoora 3083, Victoria, Australia.
B. Am. Sch. Orient. R. Bulletin of the American Schools of Oriental Research. (0003-097X). Johns Hopkins University Press: 2715 North Charles Street, Baltimore, MD 21218-4363, U.S.A., in association with American Schools of Oriental Research: 711 West 40th Street, Suite 354, Baltimore, MD 21211, U.S.A.
B. Éc. Fr. Ex.-Or. Bulletin de l'École française d'Extrême-Orient. (0336-1519). École française d'Extrême-Orient: 22 avenue du Président Wilson, 75116 Paris, France.
B. Ét. Afr. INALCO Bulletin des études africaines de l'INALCO. (0249-728X). Institut national des langues et civilisations orientales: 2 rue de Lille, 75007 Paris, France.
B. Ind. Inst. Hist. Med. Bulletin of the Indian Institute of History of Medicine. (0304-9558). Indian Institute of History of Medicine: Osmania Medical College Buildings, Putlibowli, Hyderabad 500 195, India, in association with Central Council for Research in Ayurveda and Siddha.
B. Inst. Ethn. Ac. Sin. Bulletin of the Institute of Ethnology, Academia Sinica. (0001-3935). Institute of Ethnology Academia Sinica: Nankang, Taipei, Taiwan.
B. Int. Com. Urg. Anthrop. Ethnol. R. Bulletin of the International Committee on Urgent Anthropological and Ethnological Research. (0538-5865). International Committee on Urgent Anthropological and Ethnological Research: c/o Institut für Völkerkunde, Universitätsstraße 7, A-1010 Vienna I, Austria, in association with UNESCO.
B. Lat. Am. Res. Bulletin of Latin American research. (0261-3050). Elsevier Science: PO Box 211, 1000 AE Amsterdam, The Netherlands, in association with Society for Latin American Studies.
B. Sch. Orient. Afr. Stud. Bulletin of the School of Oriental and African Studies. (0041-977X). Oxford University Press: Great Clarendon Street, Oxford OX2 6DP, U.K., in association with School of Oriental and African Studies: Thornhaugh Street, Russell Square, London WC1H 0XG, U.K.
Baes-A. Baessler-Archiv. (0005-3856). Museum für Völkerkunde Berlin: Arnimallee 27, 14195 Berlin, Germany.
Bang. Dev. Stud. Bangladesh development studies. (0304-095X). Bangladesh Unnayan Gobeshona Protishthan = Bangladesh Institute of Development Studies: G.P.O. Box No.3854, E-17 Agargaon, Sher-e-Bangla Nagar, Dhaka, Bangladesh.
BC Stud. BC studies. (0005-2949). University of British Columbia: Vancouver BC, V6T 1Z2, Canada.
Bijdragen Bijdragen tot de taal-, land- en volkenkunde. (0006-2294). Koninklijk Instituut voor Taal-, Land -en Volkenkunde: P.O. Box 9515, 2300 RA Leiden, The Netherlands.
Bilig Bilig. (1301-0549). Foundation of Ahmet Yesevi University: Bilig Editörlügü, Ahmet Yesevi Üniversitesi, Mütevelli Heyet Baskanligi, Tashkent Caddesi, 10.sok. No:30, 06430 Bahçelievler, Anakara, Turkey.
Bio. Hum. Anthrop. Biométrie humaine et anthropologie. (1279-7863). Société de biometrie humaine: 28 rue de Charenton, 75571 Paris Cedex 12, France, in association with Centre national de la recherche scientifique.
Biography Biography. (0162-4962). University of Hawaii Press: 2840 Kolowalu Street, Honolulu, HI 96822-1888, U.S.A., in association with Center for Biographical Research: Varsity College, University of Hawaii, Honolulu, HI. 96822, U.S.A.

Cult. Health. Sex. Culture, health and sexuality. (1369-1058). Taylor & Francis Ltd: 1 Gunpowder Square, London, EC4A 3DF, UK., in association with International Association for Study of Sexuality, Culture and Society.

Cult. Medic. Psych. Culture, medicine and psychiatry. (0165-005X). Kluwer Academic Publishers: P.O. Box 322, 3300 AH Dordrecht, The Netherlands.

Cult. St. Cultural studies. (0950-2386). Routledge, Taylor and Francis Ltd: 11 New Fetter Lane, London EC4P 4EE, U.K.

Cult. Val. Cultural values. (1362-5179). Blackwell Publishers Ltd: 108 Cowley Road, Oxford, OX4 1JF, U.K., in association with Institute for Cultural Research, Lancaster University.

Curr. Anthr. Current anthropology. (0011-3204). University of Chicago Press: 5720 S. Woodlawn Avenue, Chicago, IL 60637, U.S.A., in association with Wenner-Gren Foundation for Anthropological Research.

Czech Soc. Rev. Czech sociological review. (1210-3861). Institute of Sociology of the Czech Academy of Sciences: Jilská 1, 110 00 Praha 1, Czech Republic.

Dædalus Dædalus. (0011-5266). American Academy of Arts and Sciences: 136 Irving Street, Cambridge, MA 02138, U.S.A.

Demography Demography. (0070-3370). Population Association of America: 1722 N. Street N.W., Washington DC 20036, U.S.A.

Dev. Anthrop. Development anthropologist. (1087-9900). Institute for Development Anthropology: 99 Collier Street, Suite 302, P.O. Box 2207, Binghamton, NY 13902-2207, U.S.A.

Dev. Bul. Development bulletin. (1035-1132). Development Studies Network Ltd: Research School of Social Sciences, Australian National University, Canberra ACT 0200, Australia.

Dev. Dialog. Development dialogue. (0345-2328). Dag Hammarskjöld Foundation: Övre Slottsgatan 2, SE-753 10 Uppsala, Sweden.

Develop. Eco. Developing economies. (0012-1533). Institute of Developing Economies: 42 Ichigaya-Hommura-chō, Shinjuku-ku, Tokyo 162, Japan.

Develop. Pract. Development in practice. (0961-4524). Carfax Publishing: P.O. Box 25, Abingdon, Oxfordshire OX14 3UE, U.K., in association with Oxfam: 274 Banbury Road, Oxford OX2 7DZ, U.K.

Development Development. (1011-6370). Sage Publications Ltd: 6 Bonhill Street, London EC2A 4PU, U.K., in association with Society for International Development: 207 via Panisperna, 00184, Rome, Italy Città del Lavoro, Rome 00144, Italy.

Diachronica Diachronica. (0176-4225). John Benjamins Publishing: P.O. Box 75577, Amsteldijk 44, 1070 Amsterdam, The Netherlands.

Dialect. Anthrop. Dialectical anthropology. (0304-4092). Kluwer Academic Publishers: P.O. Box 17, 3300 AA Dordrecht, The Netherlands.

Diaspora Diaspora. (1044-2057). University of Toronto Press: 5201 Dufferin St., Toronto, ON M3H 5T8 Canada, in association with Zoryan Institute of Canada.

Dirasat Ad. Sc. Dirasat: Administrative Sciences. (1026-373X). Deanship of Academic Research: University of Jordan, Amman, Jordan.

Dirasat Hum. Soc. Sc. Dirasat: Human and Social Sciences. (1026-3721). Deanship of Academic Research: University of Jordan, Amman, Jordan.

Disasters Disasters: Journal of disaster studies, policy and management. (0361-3666). Blackwell Publishers: 108 Cowley Road, Oxford OX4 1JF, U.K.

Ecol. Eco. Ecological economics. (0921-8009). Elsevier Science: PO Box 211, 1000 AE Amsterdam, The Netherlands, in association with International Society for Ecological Economics.

Econ. Aff. [Calcutta] Economic affairs [Calcutta]. (0424-2513). Himansu Roy: BC144, Sector 1, Salt Lake City, Calcutta 700064, India.

Econ. Desar. Economia y desarrollo. (0252-8584). Universidad de la Habana, Facultad de Economia: Calle O No.262 e/ 25 y 27, Vedado, Havana 4, Cuba.

Econ. Dev. Cult. Change Economic development and cultural change. (0013-0079). University of Chicago Press: 5720 S. Woodlawn Avenue, Chicago, IL 60637, U.S.A.

Ecumene Ecumene: a journal of cultural geographies. (0967-4608). Arnold Publishers: Journals Department, 338 Euston Road, London, NW1 3BH, U.K.

Ekistics Ekistics. (0013-2942). Athens Technological Organization, Athens Center of Ekistics: 24 Strat. Syndesmou St., 10673 Athens, Greece.

Eng. Afr. English in Africa. (0376-8902). Rhodes University, Institute for the Study of English in Africa: Grahamstown 6140, South Africa.

Eng. Wor.-wide English world-wide. (0172-8865). John Benjamins Publishing: P.O. Box 75577, Amsteldijk 44, 1070 Amsterdam, The Netherlands.

Environ. Urban. Environment and urbanization. (0956-2478). International Institute for Environment and Development: 3 Endsleigh Street, London WC1H 0DD, U.K.

Espace Géogr. Espace géographique. (0046-2497). Éditions BELIN: 8 rue Férou, 75278 Paris cedex 06, France.

Espace Pop. Soc. Espace populations sociétés. (0755-7809). Université des Sciences et Techniques de Lille-Flandres-Artois: 59655 Villeneuve d'Ascq Cedex, France.

Esprit Esprit. (0014-0759). Esprit: 212 rue Saint-Martin, 75003 Paris, France.

Eth. Balk. Ethnologia Balkanica: Journal for Southeast European Anthropology. Prof. Marin Drinov Academic Publishing House: Sofia, Bulgaria.

Ethn. Fr. Ethnologie française. (0046-2616). PUF: 6, avenue Reille, 75685 Paris Cedex 14, France.

Ethn. Racial Ethnic and racial studies. (0141-9870). Routledge, Taylor and Francis Ltd: 11 New Fetter Lane, London EC4P 4EE, U.K.

Ethnog. Ethnography. (1466-1381). Sage Publications: 6 Bonhill Street, London EC2A 4PU, U.K.

Ethnol. Pol. Ethnologia Polona. (0137-4079). Instytut Archeologii i etnologii: Polskiej Akademii Nauk, Al. Solidarnosci 105, 00-140 Warszawa, Poland, in association with Polskiej Akademii Nauk, Zakład Etnografii Instytutu Historii Kultury Materialnej = Polish Academy of Sciences, Institute for the History of Material Culture: ul. Zwierzyniecka 20, 60-814 Poznań, Poland.

Ethnologies Ethnologies. (1481-5974). Folklore Studies Association of Canada / L'Association canadienne d'ethnologie et de folklore: CÉLAT, Université Laval, Québec, Canada G1K 7P4.

Ethnology Ethnology. (0014-1828). University of Pittsburgh: Department of Anthropology, Pittsburgh, PA 15260, U.S.A.

Ethnomusicology Ethnomusicology. (0014-1836). Indiana University, Society for Ethnomusicology: Morrison Hall 005, Indiana University, Bloomington, IN 47405, U.S.A.

Ethnos Ethnos. (0014-1844). Routledge, Taylor and Francis Ltd: 11 New Fetter Lane, London EC4P 4EE, U.K.

Ethos Ethos. (0091-2131). American Anthropological Association: 4350 North Fairfax Drive, Suite 640, Arlington, VA 22203-1620, U.S.A.

Etn. Polska Etnografia polska. (0071-1861). Instytut Archeologii i etnologii: Polskiej Akademii Nauk, Al. Solidarnosci 105, 00-140 Warszawa, Poland.

Etnograf. Oboz. Etnograficheskoe obozrenie. (0869-5415). Nauka: Profsoiuznaia ul. 90, 117864 Moscow, Russia.

Etnoloska Etnoloska tribina. (0351-1944). Croatian Ethnological Society: Faculty of Philosophy, Zagreb, Ivana Lučića 3, Croatia.

Eur. J. Soc. Archives européennes de sociologie = European journal of sociology = Europäisches Archiv für Soziologie. (0003-9756). Cambridge University Press: The Edinburgh Building, Shaftesbury Road, Cambridge CB2 2RU, U.K.

Eur. J. Wom. Stud. European journal of women's studies. (1350-5068). Sage Publications: 6 Bonhill Street, London EC2A 4PU, U.K., in association with European Women's Studies Association: Heidelberglaan 2, 3584 CS Utrecht, Netherlands.

Eur. Stud. Y. Eurasian studies yearbook. (0042-0786). Eurolingua: P.O. Box 101, Bloomington, Indiana 47402-0101, USA.

Euro. J. Arch. European journal of archaeology. (1461-9571). Sage Publications Ltd: 6 Bonhill Street, London EC2A 4PU, U.K., in association with European Association of Archaeologists.

Euro. J. Dev. Res. European journal of development research. (0957-8811). Frank Cass: Newbury House, 890-900 Eastern Avenue, Newbury Park, Ilford, Essex IG2 7HH, U.K.

Euro. Journ. Cult. Stud. European journal of cultural studies. (1367-5494). Sage Publications Ltd: 6 Bonhill Street, London, EC2A 4PU, U.K.

Evol. Hum. Behav. Evolution and human behavior. (1090-5138). Elsevier Science: PO Box 211, 1000 AE Amsterdam, The Netherlands.

Evolut. Anthrop. Evolutionary anthropology. (1060-1538). John Wiley & Sons: 605 Third Avenue, New York, NY 10158-0012, U.S.A.

Fabula Fabula. (0014-6242). Walter de Gruyter: Genthiner Strasse 13, D-10785 Berlin, Germany.

Fas. Arch. Hist. Fasciculi archaeologiae historicae. (0860-0007). Instytut Archeologii i etnologii: Polskiej Akademii Nauk, Al. Solidarnosci 105, 00-140 Warszawa, Poland.

Fash. Theory Fashion theory. (1362-704X). Berg Publishers: 150 Cowley Road, Oxford OX4 1JJ, U.K.

Fem. Med. St. Feminist media studies. (1468-0777). Routledge, Taylor and Francis Ltd: 11 New Fetter Lane, London EC4P 4EE, U.K.

Fem. Stud. Feminist studies. (0046-3663). Feminist Studies: University of Maryland, Women's Studies Program, College Park, MD 20742, U.S.A.

Fie. Meth. Field methods. (1525-822X). Sage Publications: 2455 Teller Road, Thousand Oaks, CA, 91320 U.S.A.

Folia Ling. Folia linguistica. (0165-4004). Mouton de Gruyter: Postfach 303421, 10728 Berlin, Germany, in association with Societas Linguistica Europaea: Olshausenstraße 40-60, DW 2300 Kiel, Germany.

Folia Ling. Hist. Folia linguistica historica. Mouton de Gruyter: Postfach 303421, 10728 Berlin, Germany, in association with Societas Linguistica Europaea.

Folia Prim. Folia primatologica. (0015-5713). Karger: Allschwilerstraße 10, CH 4009, Basle, Switzerland.

Folklore Folklore. (0015-587X). Routledge, Taylor and Francis Ltd: 11 New Fetter Lane, London EC4P 4EE, U.K., in association with Folklore society.

Food Food. Food and foodways. (0740-9710). Harwood Academic Publishers, Taylor and Francis Ltd: 11 New Fetter Lane, London, EC4P 4EE, UK.

Fr. Cult. Stud. French cultural studies. (0957-1558). Alpha Academic: Halfpenny Furze, Mill Lane, Chalfont St. Giles, Buckinghamshire HP8 4NR, U.K.

Fr. Stud. French studies. (0016-1128). Society for French Studies.

Fre. Pol. Cult. Soc. French politics, culture, and society. (0882-1267). Berghahn Books: 3, Newtec Place, Magdalen Road, Oxford OX4 1RE, U.K.

Gen. Dev. Gender and development. (1355-2074). Oxfam Publishing: 274 Banbury Road, Oxford OX2 7DZ, U.K.

Gen. Tech. Dev. Gender, technology and development. (0971-8524). Sage Publications India: 32 M-Block Market, Greater Kailash I, New Delhi 110 048, India, in association with Asian Institute of Technology, Thailand.

Genèses Genèses. (1155-3219). Éditions Belin: 8 rue Férou, 75278 Paris Cedex 06.

Genus Genus. (0016-6987). Comitato Italiano per lo Studio dei Problemi della Popolazione: Via Nomentana 41, 00161 Rome, Italy.

Geoforum Geoforum. (0016-7185). Elsevier Science: PO Box 211, 1001 AE Amsterdam, The Netherlands.

Geogr. J. Geographical journal. (0016-7398). Royal Geographical Society (with IBG): 1 Kensington Gore, London SW7 2AR, U.K.

Geogr. Rev. Geographical review. (0016-7428). American Geographical Society: 120 Wall Street, Suite 100; New York; NY 10005; U.S.A.

Geogr. Rev. Jpn. Geographical review of Japan. (0016-7444). Association of Japanese Geographers: Japan Academic Societies Center, 2-4-16 Yayoi, Bunkyo-ku, Tokyo 113-0032 , Japan.

Geogr. Rund. Geographische Rundschau. (0016-7460). Westermann Schulbuchverlag: Georg-Westermann-Allee 66, 3300 Braunschweig, Germany.

Geojournal Geojournal. (0343-2521). Kluwer Academic Publishers: P.O. Box 17, 3300 AA Dordrecht, The Netherlands.

German St. R. German studies review. (0149-7952). German Studies Association: History Department, Carleton College, Northfield, MN 55057-4025, U.S.A.

Glo. Environ. Chan. Global environmental change. (0959-3780). Pergamon: Elsevier Science, PO Box 945, New York, NY 10010, U.S.A.

Heb. St. Hebrew studies. (0146-4094). National Association of Professors of Hebrew: Department of Hebrew and Semitic Studies, 1346 Van Hise Hall, 1220 Linden Drive, University of Wisconsin, Madison WI 53706-1558, U.S.A.

Herit. Zimb. Heritage of Zimbabwe. (0556-9605). History Society of Zimbabwe: P.O. Box 8268, Causeway, Harare, Zimbabwe.

Hisp. Am. Hist. Rev. Hispanic American historical review. (0018-2168). Duke University Press: Box 90660, Durham, NC 27708-0660, U.S.A., in association with American Historical Association, Conference on Latin American History.

Hist. Afr. History in Africa. (0361-5413). African Studies Association: Rutgers, State University of New Jersey, Douglass Campus, 132 George Street, New Brunswick, NJ 08901-1400, U.S.A.

Hist. Anthrop. History and anthropology. (0275-7206). Harwood Academic Publishers, Taylor and Francis Ltd: 11 New Fetter Lane, London, EC4P 4EE, UK.

Hist. Archaeol. Historical archaeology. (0440-9213). Society for Historical Archaeology: P.O. Box 30446, Tucson, AZ 85751-0446, U.S.A.

Hist. Fam. History of the family. (1081-602X). JAI Press: 100 Prospect Street, P.O. Box 811, Stamford, CT 06904-0811, U.S.A.

History History. (0018-2648). Blackwell publishers Ltd: 108 cowley Road, Oxford, OX4 1JF, UK, in association with Historical Association.

Hom. Soc. Homme et la société. (0018-4306). Editions l'Harmattan: 5-7 rue de l'École-Polytechnique, 75005 Paris, France, in association with Centre National des Lettres / Centre National de la Recherche Scientifique.

Homme Homme. (0439-4216). Éditions de l'École des hautes études en sciences sociales: 54 boulevard Raspail, 75006 Paris, France, in association with Laboratoire d'anthropologie sociale: Collège de France, 52 rue du Cardinal-Lemoine, 75005 Paris, France.

Hum. Dev. Human development. (0018-716X). S. Karger AG: PO Box, CH-4009, Basel, Switzerland.

Hum. Nature Human nature. (1045-6767). Aldine de Gruyter: 200 Saw Mill River Road, Hawthorne, NY 10532, U.S.A.

Hum. Rights Q. Human rights quarterly. (0275-0392). Johns Hopkins University Press: 2715 North Charles Street, Baltimore, MD 21218-4363, U.S.A.

Human ecology Human ecology: the CHEC journal. (0268-4918). Commonwealth Human Ecology Council: Church House, Newton Road, Bayswater, London W2 5LS, UK.

Human. Org. Human organization. (0018-7259). Society for Applied Anthropology: 5205 E.Flowler Avenue, Suite 310, Temple Terrace, FL 33617, U.S.A.

Humor Humor. (0933-1719). Mouton de Gruyter: Postfach 303421, 10728 Berlin, Germany.

Identities Identities: global studies in culture and power. (1070-289X). Harwood Academic Publishers, Taylor and Francis Ltd: 11 New Fetter Lane, London, EC4P 4EE, UK.

IDS Bull. IDS bulletin. (0265-5012). Institute of Development Studies: University of Sussex, Brighton BN1 9RE, U.K.

IFRA IFRA: Les cahiers. Institut Français de Recherche en Afrique: Nairobi, Kenya.

Imm. Minor. Immigrants and minorities. (0261-9288). Frank Cass: Newbury House, 890-900 Eastern Avenue, Newbury Park, Ilford, Essex IG2 7HH, U.K.

Ind. Geograph. J. Indian geographical journal. (0019-4824). Indian Geographical Society: c/o The editor, Indian Geographical Journal, Department of Geography, University of Madras, Madras 600 005, India.

Ind. J. Eco. Indian journal of economics. (0019-5170). University of Allahabad, Department of Economics: Post Box No. 2005, Allahabad 211.002, India.

Ind. J. Gend. Stud. Indian journal of gender studies. (0971-5215). Sage Publications India: 32 M-Block Market, Greater Kailash I, New Delhi 110 048, India, in association with Centre for Women's Development Studies: New Delhi, India.

Ind. Soc. Sci. R. Indian social science review. (0972-0731). Sage Publications India: 32 M-Block Market, Greater Kailash I, New Delhi 110 048, India, in association with Indian Council of Social Science Research.

India Q. India quarterly. (0019-4220). Indian Council of World Affairs: Sapru House, Barakhamba Road, New Delhi 110001, India.

Indian Ec. Soc. His. R. Indian economic and social history review. (0019-4646). Sage Publications India: 32 M-Block Market, Greater Kailash I, New Delhi 110 048, India, in association with Indian Economic and Social History Association.

Indian J. Publ. Admin. Indian journal of public administration. (0019-5561). Indian Institute of Public Administration: Indraprastha Estate, Ring Road East, New Delhi 110002, India.

Indian J. Soc. W. Indian journal of social work. (0019-5634). Tata Institute of Social Sciences: PB No. 8313 Deonar, Bombay 400 088, India.

Indig. Aff. Indigenous affairs. (1024-3283). International Work Group for Indigenous Affairs: Classensgade 11E, DK-2100, Copenhagen, Denmark.

Indo-Iran. J. Indo-Iranian journal. (0019-7246). Kluwer Academic Publishers: P.O. Box 322, 3300 AH Dordrecht, The Netherlands.

Int. J. Afr. H. S. International journal of African historical studies. (0361-7882). Boston University, African Studies Center: 270 Bay State Road, Boston, MA 02215, U.S.A.

Int. J. Drav. Ling. International journal of Dravidian linguistics. Dravidian Linguistics Association: Kerala Paanini Building, Trivandrum 86, Kerala, India.

Int. J. Hist. Sport International journal of the history of sport. (0952-3367). Frank Cass: Newbury House, 890-900 Eastern Avenue, Newbury Park, Ilford, Essex IG2 7HH, U.K.

Int. J. M. E. Stud. International journal of Middle East studies. (0020-7438). Cambridge University Press: 40 West 20th Street, New York, NY 10011-4211, U.S.A., in association with Middle East Studies Association of North America: University of Arizona, 1232 North Cherry, Tuscon, AZ 85721, U.S.A.

Int. J. Pol. C. S. International journal of politics, culture and society. (0891-4486). Human Sciences Press: 233 Spring Street, New York, NY 10013-1578, U.S.A.

Int. J. Primat. International journal of primatology. (0164-0291). Plenum Publishing: 233 Spring Street, New York, NY 10013-1578, U.S.A.

Int. J. S. Lang. International journal of the sociology of language. (0165-2516). Mouton de Gruyter: Postfach 303421, 10728 Berlin, Germany.

Int. J. Soc. Psyc. International journal of social psychiatry. (0020-7640). Avenue Publishing: 55 Woodstock Avenue, London NW11 9RG, U.K.

Int. Peace. International peacekeeping. (1353-3312). Frank Cass: Newbury House, 890-900 Eastern Avenue, Newbury Park, Ilford, Essex IG2 7HH, U.K.

Int. R. Educat. International review of education. (0020-8566). Kluwer Academic Publishers: P.O. Box 322, 3300 AH Dordrecht, The Netherlands.

Int. Secur. International security. (0162-2889). MIT Press: 55 Hayward Street, Cambridge, MA 02142, U.S.A., in association with Harvard University Center for Science and International Affairs: 79 John F. Kennedy Street, Cambridge, MA 02138, U.S.A.

Int. Soc. Work International social work. (0020-8728). Sage Publications Ltd: 6 Bonhill Street, London, EC2A 4PU, U.K., in association with International Association of Schools of Social Work.

Iran. Ant. Iranica antiqua. (0021-0870). Peeters Press: Bondgenolenlaan 153, Louvain, Belgium.

Is. Orient. Stud. Israel oriental studies. (0334-4401). Brill Academic Publishers: P.O. Box 9000, 2300 PA Leiden, The Netherlands, in association with Tel-Aviv University.

Isis Isis. (0021-1753). University of Chicago Press: 5720 S. Woodlawn Avenue, Chicago, IL 60637, U.S.A., in association with History of Science Society.

Islam. Law Soc. Islamic law and society. (0928-9380). Brill Academic Publishers: P.O. Box 9000, 2300 PA Leiden, The Netherlands.

Israel Explor. J. Israel exploration journal. (0021-2059). Israel Exploration Society: 5 Avida Street, P.O. Box 7041, Jerusalem 91070, Israel.

J. Afr. Hist. Journal of African history. (0021-8537). Cambridge University Press: The Edinburgh Building, Shaftesbury Road, Cambridge CB2 2RU, U.K.

J. Am. Stud. Journal of American studies. (0021-8758). Cambridge University Press: The Edinburgh Building, Shaftesbury Road, Cambridge CB2 2RU, U.K.

J. Anthr. Res. Journal of anthropological research. (0091-7710). Journal of anthropological research, University of New Mexico, Department of Anthropology: Albuquerque, NM 87131-1086, U.S.A.

J. Anthrop. Arch. Journal of anthropological archaeology. (0278-4165). Academic Press: 1250 Sixth Avenue, San Diego, CA 92101, U.S.A.

J. Anthrop. Soc. Oxford Journal of the Anthropological Society of Oxford. (0044-8370). Anthropology Society of Oxford: Institute of Social and Cultural Anthropology, 51 Banbury Road, Oxford OX2 6PE, U.K.

J. Arch. Plan. Res. Journal of architectural and planning research. (0738-0895). Locke Science Publishing: P.O. Box 146413, Chicago, IL 60614, U.S.A.

J. As. Afr. S. Journal of Asian and African studies [Leiden]. (0021-9096). E.J. Brill: P.O. Box 9000, 2300 PA Leiden, The Netherlands.

J. Asian Hist. Journal of Asian history. (0021-910X). Otto Harrassowitz: Taunusstrasse 14, D-65183 Wiesbaden, Germany.

J. Asian St. Journal of Asian studies. (0021-9118). University of Michigan: 1 Lane Hall, Ann Arbor, MI 48109, U.S.A., in association with Association for Asian Studies.

J. Balt. St. Journal of Baltic studies. (0162-9778). Association for the Advancement of Baltic Studies: 3465 East Burnside Street, Portland OR, 97214-2050, U.S.A.

J. Biosoc. Sc. Journal of biosocial science. (0021-9320). Biosocial Society: Department of Biological Anthropology, Downing Street, Cambridge CB2 3DZ, U.K.

J. Br. Stud. Journal of British studies. (0021-9371). University of Chicago Press: 5720 S. Woodlawn Avenue, Chicago, IL 60637, U.S.A.

J. Ch. Philos. Journal of Chinese philosophy. Dialogue Publishing: P.O. Box 11071, Honolulu, HI 96826, U.S.A.

J. Comp. Fam. Stud. Journal of comparative family studies. (0047-2328). Journal of comparative family studies: Department of Sociology, University of Calgary, Calgary, Alberta, T2N 1N4 Canada.

J. Cons. Cult. Journal of consumer culture. (1469-5405). Sage Publications: 6 Bonhill Street, London EC2A 4PU, U.K.

J. Contemp. Ethnog. Journal of contemporary ethnography. (0891-2416). Sage Publications: 2455 Teller Road, Newbury Park, Thousand Oaks, CA 91320, U.S.A.

J. Cr-Cult. Gerontol. Journal of cross-cultural gerontology. (0169-3816). Kluwer Academic Publishers: P.O. Box 17, 3300 AA Dordrecht, The Netherlands.

J. Cult. St. Journal of cultural studies. (1595-0956). African Cultural Initiatives: 346 Herbert Macaulay Street, Yaba, Lagos, Nigeria.

J. Dev. Stud. Journal of development studies. (0022-0388). Frank Cass: Newbury House, 890-900 Eastern Avenue, Newbury Park, Ilford, Essex IG2 7HH, U.K.

J. Ec. Soc. Hist. O. Journal of the economic and social history of the orient. (0022-4995). Brill Academic Publishers: P.O. Box 9000, 2300 PA Leiden, The Netherlands.

J. Econ. Soc. Geogr. Tijdschrift voor economische en sociale geografie = Journal of economic and social geography. (0040-747X). Blackwell Publishers: 108 Cowley Road, Oxford OX4 1JF, U.K., in association with Royal Dutch Geographical Society = Koninklijk Nederlands Aardrijkskundig Genootschap: Weteringschans 12, 1017 SG Amsterdam, The Netherlands.

J. Ethnobio. Journal of ethnobiology. (0278-0771). Society of Ethnobiology: c/o Virginia Popper, UCLA, Los Angeles, CA 90095, USA.

J. Fam. Hist. Journal of family history. (0363-1990). Sage Publications Inc.: 2455 Teller Road, Newbury Park, Thousand Oaks, CA 91320, U.S.A., in association with National Council on Family Relations.

J. Folk. Res. Journal of folklore research. (0737-7037). Indiana University Folklore Institute: 504 North Fess, Bloomington, IN 47405, U.S.A., in association with Folklore Institute.

J. Gender St. Journal of gender studies. (0958-9236). Carfax Publishing: P.O. Box 25, Abingdon, Oxfordshire OX14 3UE, U.K., in association with Hull Centre for Gender Studies, University of Hull: HU6 7RX, U.K.

J. Hist. Sexual. Journal of the history of sexuality. (1043-4070). University of Chicago Press: 5720 S. Woodlawn Avenue, Chicago, IL 60637, U.S.A.

J. Hum. Dev. Journal of human development. (1464-9888). Carfax Publishing, Taylor & Francis Ltd: Rankine Road, Basingstoke, Hants, RG24 8PR, UK, in association with United Nations Development Programme.

J. Hum. Nat. Sci. Journal of humanities and natural sciences. (0495-8012). Tokyo Keizai University: 1-7 Minami-cho, Kokubunji-shi, Tokyo 185-8502, Japan.

J. Ind. Phil. Journal of Indian philosophy. (0022-1791). Kluwer Academic Publishers: P.O. Box 17, 3300 AA Dordrecht, The Netherlands.

J. Indo-Eur. S. Journal of Indo-European studies. (0092-2323). Institute for the Study of Man: 1133 13th Street N.W., Suite C-2, Washington DC 20005-4297, U.S.A.

J. Int. Dev. Journal of international development. (0954-1748). John Wiley & Sons: Baffins Lane, Chichester, West Sussex PO19 1UD, U.K., in association with Institute for Development Policy and Management: University of Manchester, Precinct Centre, Oxford Road, Manchester M13 9QS, U.K.

J. Inter. Phon. Ass. Journal of the International Phonetic Association. International Phonetic Association: Phonetics Laboratory, Department of Linguistics, UCLA, Los Angeles, CA 90024-1543, U.S.A.

J. Interd. Ec. Journal of interdisciplinary economics. (0260-1079). A.B. Academic Publishers: P.O. Box 42, Bicester, Oxon OX26 6NW, U.K.

J. Jew. Stud. Journal of Jewish studies. (0022-2097). Oxford Centre for Postgraduate Hebrew Studies: 45 St. Giles, Oxford OX1 2LP, U.K.

J. Jpn. Stud. Journal of Japanese studies. (0095-6848). Society for Japanese Studies: University of Washington, Box 353650, Seattle, WA 98195-3650, U.S.A.

J. Lang. Soc. Psychol. Journal of language and social psychology. (0261-927X). Multilingual Matters: Frankfurt Lodge, Clevedon Hall, Victoria Road, Clevedon, BS21 7HH, U.K.

J. Mat. Cult. Journal of material culture. (1359-1835). Sage Publications: 6 Bonhill Street, London EC2A 4PU, U.K.

J. Multiling. Journal of multilingual and multicultural development. (0143-4632). Multilingual Matters: Frankfurt Lodge, Clevedon Hall, Victoria Road, Clevedon, BS21 7HH, U.K.

J. N. African Stud. Journal of North African studies. (1362-9387). Frank Cass: Newbury House, 890-900 Eastern Avenue, Newbury Park, Ilford, Essex IG2 7HH, U.K.

J. Near East. Journal of Near Eastern studies. (0022-2968). University of Chicago Press: 5720 S. Woodlawn Avenue, Chicago, IL 60637, U.S.A., in association with University of Chicago.

J. N.W. Sem. Lang. Journal of northwest semitic languages. (0259-0131). University of Stellenbosch, Department of Ancient Studies: Stellenbosch 7600, South Africa.

J. Orient. Inst. Journal of the Oriental Institute. (0030-5324). Maharaja Sayairao University of Baroda, Oriental Institute: Baroda 390 002, Gujarat, India.

J. Pak. Hist. Soc. Journal of the Pakistan Historical Society. Pakistan Historical Society: Bait al-Hikmah, Hamdard University, Muhammad Bin Qasim Avenue, Karachi 74700, Pakistan.

J. Peasant Stud. Journal of peasant studies. (0306-6150). Frank Cass: Newbury House, 890-900 Eastern Avenue, Newbury Park, Ilford, Essex IG2 7HH, U.K.

J. Pid. Creo. Lang. Journal of pidgin and creole languages. (0920-9034). John Benjamins Publishing: P.O. Box 75577, Amsteldijk 44, 1070 Amsterdam, The Netherlands.

J. Pop. Cult. Journal of popular culture. (0022-3840). Popular Press: Bowling Green State University, Bowling Green, OH 43402, U.S.A., in association with Modern Language Association of America, Popular Literature Section / Midwest Modern Language Association, Folklore Section.

J. Pop. Ec. Journal of population economics. (0933-1433). Springer-Verlag: Tiergartenstrasse 17, D-69121 Heidelberg, Germany.

J. Relig. Afr. Journal of religion in Africa. (0022-4200). Brill Academic Publishers: P.O. Box 9000, 2300 PA Leiden, The Netherlands.

J. Res. Soc. Pakist. Journal of the Research Society of Pakistan. University of the Punjab, Punjab University Library: Old Campus, Lahore, Pakistan.

J. Rit. Stud. Journal of ritual studies. (0890-1112). Deixis Publishing: Ste 264, 414 Craig Street, Pittsburgh, PA 15213-3709, USA.

J. Roy. Aust. H. Soc. Journal of the Royal Australian Historical Society. (0035-8762). Royal Australian Historical Society: History House, 133 Macquarie Street, Sydney NSW 2000, Australia.

J. Royal Anth. Inst. Journal of the Royal Anthropological Institute. (0025 1496). Royal Anthropological Institute of Great Britain and Ireland: 50 Fitzroy Street, London W1P 5HS, U.K.

J. S. Afr. Stud. Journal of Southern African studies. (0305-7070). Carfax Publishing: P.O. Box 25, Abingdon, Oxfordshire OX14 3UE, U.K.

J. Siam Soc. Journal of the Siam Society. (0857-7099). Siam Society: 131 Soi Asoke, Sukhumvit 21, Bangkok 10110, Thailand.

J. Soc. Amér. Journal de la Société des américanistes. (0037-9174). Musée de l'Homme, Société des Américanistes: 17 place du Trocadéro, 75116 Paris, France.

J. Soc. Arch. Journal of social archaeology. (1469-6053). Sage Publications: 6 Bonhill Street, London EC2A 4PU, U.K.

J. Soc. Clin. Psychol. Journal of social and clinical psychology. (0736-7236). Guilford Publications: 72 Spring Street, New York, NY 10012, U.S.A.

J. Soc. Hist Journal of social history. (0022-4529). Carnegie Mellon University: 242C Baker Hall, Pittsburgh, PA 15213-3890, U.S.A.

J. Wom. Hist. Journal of women's history. (1042-7961). Indiana University Press: 601 N. Morton, Bloomington, IN 47404-3797, U.S.A.

Jahrb. Ges. Lat.am. Jahrbuch für Geschichte Lateinamerikas. (1438-4752). Böhlau-Verlag GmbH & Cie, Ursulaplatz 1, D-50668 Cologne, Germany.

Jain J. Jain journal. (0021-4043).

Jap. J. Relig. St. Japanese journal of religious studies. (0304-1042). Nanzan Institute for Religion and Culture: 18 Yamazato-chō, Shōwa-ku, Nagoya 466, Japan.

Jew. Q. Rev. Jewish quarterly review. (0021-6682). Annenberg Research Institute: 420 Walnut Street, Philadelphia, PA 19106, U.S.A.

Jew. Soc. Stud. Jewish social studies. (0021-6704). Indiana University Press: 601 North Morton Street, Bloomington, IN 47404-6797, U.S.A., in association with Conference on Jewish Social Studies.

Journ. Mod. Italian Studs. Journal of modern Italian studies. (1354-571X). Routledge, Taylor and Francis Ltd: 11 New Fetter Lane, London EC4P 4EE, U.K.

Jpn. Relig. Japanese religions. (0448-8954). NCC Center for the Study of Japanese Religions: Karasuma-Shimotachiun, Kamikyo-ku, Kyoto-shi 602, Japan.

Kor. Stud. Korean studies. (0145-840X). University of Hawaii Press: 2840 Kolowalu Street, Honolulu, HI 96822-1888, U.S.A.

Korea J. Korea journal. (0023-3900). Korean National Commission for Unesco: C.P.O. Box 64, Seoul, 100-022 Korea.

Kroeber Anthr. Soc. Pap. Kroeber anthropological society papers. (0023-4869). Kroeber Anthropological Society: Department of Anthropology, University of California, Berkeley, CA 94720, U.S.A.

Kunapipi Kunapipi: Journal of post-colonial writing. (0106-5734). University of Wollongong: English Studies Program, University of Wollongong, Wollongong, NSW 2522, Australia, in association with European Association of Commonwealth Languages and Literatures.

Kwart. Hist. Kult. Mater. Kwartalnik historii kultury materialnej. (0023-5881). Instytut Archaeologii i Etnologii: 00-140 Warszawa, Al. Solidarności 105, Poland, in association with Polskiej Akademii Nauk, Dawniej Instytut Historii Kultury Materialnej PAN.

Lang. Prob. Lang. Plan. Language problems and language planning. (0272-2690). John Benjamins Publishing: P.O. Box 75577, Amsteldijk 44, 1070 Amsterdam, The Netherlands.

Lang. Soc. Language in society. (0047-4045). Cambridge University Press: 40 West 20th Street, New York, NY 10011-4211, U.S.A.

Language Language. (0097-8507). Linguistic Society of America: 428 East Preston Street, Baltimore, MD 21202, U.S.A.

Lat. Am. Res. R. Latin American research review. (0023-8791). Latin American Studies Association: Latin American Institute, 801 Yale NE, University of New Mexico, Albuquerque, NM 87131-1016, U.S.A.

Lib. Stud. Libyan studies. (0263-7189). Society for Libyan Studies: c/o Institute of Archaeology, 31-34 Gordon Square, London WC1H 0PY, U.K.

Ling. Tib.Bur. Area Linguistics of the Tibeto-Burman area. (0731-3500). Sino-Tibetan Etymological Dictionary and Thesaurus Project: c/o Institute for International Studies, 215 Moses Hall, University of California, Berkeley, CA 94720, U.S.A.

Linguist. Afr. Linguistique africaine. (0994-7744). Groupe d'Études et de Recherches en Linguistiques Africaine: Université Paris 7, U.F.R. Linguistique, T.C. 9ét., 2 place Jussieu, 75251 Paris Cedex 05, France.

Linguist. In. Linguistic inquiry. (0024-3892). MIT Press: 55 Hayward Street, Cambridge, MA 02142, U.S.A.

Linguist. R. Linguistic review. (0167-6318). Walter de Gruyter: 200 Saw Mill River Road, Hawthorne, NY 10532, U.S.A.

Mag. Tud. Magyar tudomány. (0025-0325). Akadémiai Kiadó: P.O. Box 245, H-1519 Budapest, Hungary, in association with Magyar Tudományos Akadémia: Roosevelt-tér 9, 1051 Budapest, Hungary.

Man India Man in India. (0025-1569). Sudarshan Press: Church Road, Ranchi 834 001 Bihar, India.

Mankind Q. Mankind quarterly. (0025-2344). Council for Social and Economic Studies: Suite C-2, 1133 13th Street N.W., Washington DC 20005-4297, U.S.A.

Med. Anthrop. Medical anthropology. (0145-9740). Harwood Academic Publishers, Taylor and Francis Ltd: 11 New Fetter Lane, London, EC4P 4EE, UK.

Mesopotamia Mesopotamia. (0076-6615). Casa Editrice le Lettere: Costa San Giorgio 28, 1-50125 Florence, Italy, in association with Università di Torino, Centro Ricerche Archeologiche e Scavi di Torino per il Medio Oriente e l'Asia: Dipartimento di Scienze Archeologiche, Via S. Ottavio 20, 10122 Turin, Italy.

Metapolítica Metapolítica. (1405-4558). Centro de Estudios de Política Comparada: Playa Eréndira 19, Barrio Santiago Sur, México D.F. 08800, Mexico.

Mir Rossii Mir Rossii. Vysshaia Shkola Ekonomiki: Rossiia 101987, Moskva, ul. Miasnitskaia 20, kom. 217, Russia, in association with Institut ekonomicheskikh problem perekhodnogo perioda.

Mod. Asian S. Modern Asian studies. (0026-749X). Cambridge University Press: The Edinburgh Building, Shaftesbury Road, Cambridge CB2 2RU, U.K.

Mod. Chi. Modern China. (0097-7004). Sage Publications: 2455 Teller Road, Newbury Park, Thousand Oaks, CA 91320, U.S.A.

Mon. St. Mongolian studies. (0190-3667). Mongolia Society: Goodbody Hall 321-322, Indiana University Campus, Bloomington, IN 47405-2401, U.S.A.

Monu. Nippon. Monumenta Nipponica. (0027-0741). Sophia University: 7-1 Kioi-chō, Chiyoda-ku, Tokyo 102, Japan.

Morocco Morocco: The journal of the society for Moroccan studies. Society for Moroccan Studies: SOAS, Thornhaugh Street, London WC1H 0XG, U.K.

Multilingua Multilingua. (0167-8507). Mouton de Gruyter: Postfach 303421, 10728 Berlin, Germany.

Nar. Umjetn. Narodna umjetnost. (0547-2504). Institut za etnologiju i folkloristiku: Ulica kralja Zvonimira 17, HR-10000 Zagreb, PP 287, Croatia.

Nat. Nat. Nations and nationalism. (1354-5078). Cambridge University Press: The Edinburgh Building, Shaftesbury Road, Cambridge CB2 2RU, U.K., in association with Association for the Study of Ethnicity and Nationalism.

New Gen. & Soc. New genetics and society. (1463-6778). Carfax Publishing, Taylor & Francis Ltd: Rankine Road, Basingstoke, Hants, RG24 8PR, UK.

Niger. F. Nigerian field. (0029-0076). Nigerian Field Society.

Nilo-Ethiop. St. Nilo-Ethiopian studies. (1340-329X). Japan Association for Nilo-Ethiopian Studies: Shimotachiuri Ogawa-Higashi, Kamikyou-ku, Kyoto 602, Japan.

Nineteen.-C. Ctxt. Nineteenth-century contexts. (0890-5495). Routledge, Taylor and Francis Ltd: 11 New Fetter Lane, London, EC4P 4EE, United Kingdom.

Nord. J. Afr. St. Nordic journal of African studies. (1235-4481). Helsinki University Press: Helsinki, Finland, in association with Nordic Association of African Studies: Uppsala, Sweden.

Nordic J. Linguist. Nordic journal of linguistics. (0332-5865). Scandinavian University Press: P.O. Box 2959, Tøyen, N-0608 Oslo 6, Norway, in association with Nordic Association of Linguists.

Numen Numen. (0029-5973). Brill Academic Publishers: P.O. Box 9000, 2300 PA Leiden, The Netherlands, in association with International Association for the History of Religions.

N.Z. J. Hist. New Zealand journal of history. (0028-8322). University of Auckland, History Department: Private Bag 92019 Auckland, New Zealand.

Oceania Oceania. (0029-8077). Oceania Publications: University of Sydney, 116 Darlington Road, NSW 2006, Australia.

Oceanic Ling. Oceanic linguistics. (0029-8115). University of Hawaii Press: 2840 Kolowalu Street, Honolulu, HI 96822-1888, U.S.A.

Oral Hist. Oral history. (0143-0955). Oral History Society: Colchester, U.K.

Orientalia Orientalia. (0030-5367). Pontificio Istituto Biblioc, Facoltà degli studi dell'Antico Oriente: Via della Pilotta 25, I-00187 Rome, Italy.

Oris. Hist. R. J. Orissa historical research journal. (0474-7267). Orissa State Museum.

Ox. J. Archaeol. Oxford journal of archaeology. (0262-5253). Blackwell Publishers: 108 Cowley Road, Oxford OX4 1JF, U.K.

Pac. Stud. Pacific studies. (0275-3596). Institute for Polynesian Studies: Brigham Young University-Hawaii, 55-220 Kulanui Street, Box 1979, Laie, HI 96762, U.S.A.

Paideuma Paideuma. (0078-7809). Franz Steiner Verlag: Birkenwaldstraße 44, Postfach 10 15 26, D-7000 Stuttgart 1, Germany, in association with Frobenius Institut: Liebigstrasse 41, 6000 Frankfurt am Main, Germany.

Pak. Dev. R. Pakistan development review. (0030-9729). Pakistan Institute of Development Economics: P.O. Box 1091, Islamabad, Pakistan.

Pak. Ec. Soc. R. Pakistan economic and social review. (1011-002X). University of the Punjab, Department of Economics: Quaid-i-Azam Campus, Lahore 54590, Pakistan.

Patt. Prej. Patterns of prejudice. (0031-322X). Sage Publications: 6 Bonhill Street, London EC2A 4PU, U.K., in association with Institute of Jewish Affairs: 11 Hertford Street, London W1Y 7DX, U.K.

Péninsule Péninsule. Association Péninsule: 30 rue Boissière, 75116 Paris, France.

Pensée Pensée. (0031-4773). Institut de recherches marxistes: 64, boulevard Auguste-Blanqui, 75013 Paris, France.

Phil. Q. Cult. Soc. Philippine quarterly of culture and society. (0115-0243). University of San Carlos: Publications Office, Cebu City 6000, Philippines.

Phil. Stud. Philippine studies. (0031-7837). Ateneo de Manila University Press: P.O. Box 154, Manila 1099, Philippines.

Philos. E.W. Philosophy east and west. (0031-8221). University of Hawaii Press: 2840 Kolowalu Street, Honolulu, HI 96822-1888, U.S.A.

Philos. S. Sc. Philosophy of the social sciences. (0048-3931). Sage Publications: 2455 Teller Road, Newbury Park, Thousand Oaks, CA 91320, U.S.A.

Pol. Afr. Politique africaine. (0244-7827). Éditions Karthala: 22-24 boulevard Arago, 75013 Paris, France, in association with Association des chercheurs de politique africaine.

Pol. Geogr. Political geography. (0962-6298). Elsevier Science: PO Box 211, 1000 AE Amsterdam, The Netherlands.

Pop. Res. Pol. R. Population research and policy review. (0167-5923). Kluwer Academic Publishers: P.O. Box 17, 3300 AA Dordrecht, The Netherlands.

Population Population. (0032-4663). Éditions de l'Institut national d'études démographiques: 133 boulevard Davout, 75980 Paris Cedex 20, France.

Prés. Afr. Présence africaine. (0032-7638). Société africaine de culture: 25 bis, rue des Écoles, 75005 Paris, France.

Primates Primates. (0032-8332). Japan Monkey Centre: Kanrin Inuyama, Aichi 484-0081, Japan.

Prof. Geogr. Professional geographer. (0033-0124). Blackwell Publishers: 108 Cowley Road, Oxford OX4 1JF, United Kingdom, in association with Association of American Geographers.

Przeg. Archeolog. Przegląd archeologiczny. (0079-7138). Instytut Archeologii i etnologii: Polskiej Akademii Nauk, Al. Solidarnosci 105, 00-140 Warszawa, Poland, in association with Instytut Historii Kultury Materialnej PAN: Świerczewskiego 105, 00-140 Warszawa, Poland.

Psych. St. Psychoanalytic studies. (1460-8952). Carfax Publishing, Taylor & Francis Ltd: P.O. Box 25, Abingdon, Oxfordshire OX14 3UE, U.K.

Psychol. B. Psychological bulletin. (0033-2909). American Psychological Association: 750 First Street N.E., Washington DC 20002-4242, U.S.A.

Publ. Adm. D. Public administration and development. (0271-2075). John Wiley & Sons: Baffins Lane, Chichester, West Sussex PO19 1UD, U.K., in association with Royal Institute of Public Administration: Regent's College, Inner Circle, Regent's Park, London NW1 4NS, U.K.

Publ. Aff. Q. Public affairs quarterly. (0887-0373). Philosophy Documentation Center: Bowling Green State University, Bowling Green, OH 43403-0189, U.S.A.

Publ. Cult. Public culture. (0899-2363). Duke University Press: Box 90660, Durham, NC 27708-0660, S.A.

Qual. Res. Qualitative research. (1468-7941). Sage Publications: 6 Bonhill Street, London EC2A 4PU, U.K.

R. African Lit. Research in African literatures. (0034-5210). Indiana University Press: 601 N. Morton, Bloomington, IN 47404-3797, U.S.A.

R. Et. Palest. Revue d'études palestiniennes. (0252-8290). Editions de Minuit: 7 rue Bernard-Palissy, 75006 Paris, France, in association with Institut des études palestiniennes / Fondation Diana Tamari Sabbagh.

R. Ind. Malay. Aff. Review of Indonesian and Malaysian affairs. (0034-6594). RIMA, University of Sydney, Department of Southeast Asian Studies: Sydney, NSW 2006, Australia.

R. Inst. Sociol. Revue de l'Institut de sociologie. (0770-1055). Institut de Sociologie: 44 avenue Jeanne, (CP 124) B-1050 Brussels, Belgium.

R. T. Monde Revue Tiers Monde. (0040-7356). Presses Universitaires de France: 108 boulevard Saint-Germain, 75006 Paris, France, in association with Université de Paris, Institut d'étude du développement économique et social: 58 boulevard Arago, 75013 Paris, France.

Rass. It. Soc. Rassegna italiana di sociologia. (0486-0349). Società editrice il Mulino: Strada Maggiore 37, 40125 Bologna, Italy.

Recher. Sociolog. Recherches sociologiques. (0771-677X). Université Catholique de Louvain: Place Montesquieu 1/1, B-1348 Louvain-la-Neuve, Belgium.

Regio Regio. (0865 557X).

Relig. State Soc. Religion, state and society. (0963-7494). Carfax Publishing: P.O. Box 25, Abingdon, Oxfordshire OX14 3UE, U.K., in association with Keston College: 33a Canal Street, Oxford OX2 6BQ, U.K.

Religion Religion. (0048-721X). Academic Press: 24-28 Oval Road, London NW1 7DX, U.K.

Reprod. Health Mat. Reproductive health matters. (0968-8080). Blackwell Science Ltd: Osney Mead, Oxford OX2 0EL, U.K.

Rev. Cien. Soc. Revista de ciencias sociales. (0034-7817). Universidad de Puerto Rico, Facultad de Ciencias Sociales, Centro de Investigaciones Sociales: Rio Piedras, Puerto Rico 00931.

Rev. de Human. Revista de humanidades: Tecnológico de Monterrey. (1405-4167). División de Humanidades y Ciencias Sociales: Instituto Tecnológico y de Estudios Superiores de Monterrey, Campus Monterrey, Ave. Eugenio Garza Sada 2501 sur, Col. Tecnológico, C.P. 54849, Monterrey, N.L. Mexico.

Rev. Fr. Hist. O.mer. Revue française d'histoire d'outre-mer. (0300-9513). Société française d'histoire d'outre-mer, in association with Centre Nationale de la Recherche Scientifique.

Rev. Fr. Soc. Revue française de sociologie. (0035-2969). Éditions Ophrys: B.P. 87, 05003 Gap Cx, France, in association with Institut de recherche sur les sociétés contemporaines: 59-61 rue Pouchet, 75017 Paris, France.

Rig Rig. (0035-5267). Föreningen för svensk kulturhistoria: Nordiska museet, 11521 Stockholm, Sweden.

Rom. Stud. Romani studies. (1528-0748). Gypsy Lore Society: 5607 Greenleaf Road, Cheverly, MD 20785, U.S.A.

Rural Stud. Études rurales. (0014-2182). Éditions de l'École des hautes études en sciences sociales: 54 boulevard Raspail, 75006 Paris, France, in association with Laboratoire d'anthropologie sociale: Collège de France, 52 rue du Cardinal Lemoine, 75005 Paris, France.

S. Afr. Geogr. J. South African geographical journal = Suid-Afrikaanse geografiese tydskrif. (0373-6245). South African Geographical Society = Suid-Afrikaanse Geografiese Vereniging: Department ofEnvironmental and Geographical Science, University of Cape Town, Private Bag, Rondebosch 7700, South Africa.

S. Afr. Hist. J. South African historical journal = Suid-Afrikaanse historiese joernaal. (0258-2473). South African Historical Society: Department of History, University of South Africa, P.O. Box 392, Pretoria 0001, South Africa.

S. Afr. J. Afr. Lang. South African journal of African languages = Suid-Afrikaanse tydskrif vir Afrikatale. (0257-2117). Foundation for Education, Science and Technology, Bureau for Scientific Publications: P.O. Box 1758, Pretoria 0001, South Africa, in association with African Languages Association of Southern Africa / Afrikatale-Vereniging van Suider-Afrika: Department of African Languages, University of South Africa, P.O. Box 392, Pretoria 0001, South Africa.

S. Afr. J. Ethnol. South African journal of ethnology = Suid-Afrikaanse tydskrif vir etnologie. (0379-8860). Foundation for Education, Science and Technology, Bureau for Scientific Publications: P.O. Box 1758, Pretoria 0001, South Africa, in association with Association of Afrikaans Ethnologists / Vereniging van Afrikaanse Volkekundiges.

S. Afr. J. Ethnol. South African journal of ethnology = Suid-Afrikaanse tydskrif vir etnologie. (0258-0144). Forum Press: PO Box 93895, Boordfontein, 0201 South Africa South Africa, in association with South African Society of Cultural Anthropologists.

S. Asia R. South Asia research. (0262-7280). Sage Publications India: 32 M-Block Market, Greater Kailash I, New Delhi 110 048, India, in association with School of Oriental and African Studies, Thornhaugh Street, Russell Square, London WC1H 0XG, U.K.

S. Asian Surv. South Asian survey. (0971-5231). Sage Publications India: 32 M-Block Market, Greater Kailash I, New Delhi 110 048, India, in association with Indian Council for South Asian Cooperation.

Saeculum Saeculum. (0080-5319). Verlag Karl Alber: Hermann-Herder-Straße 4, 7800 Freiburg im Breisgau, Germany.

San. Nat. Sangeet natak. Sangeet Natak Akademi: Rabindra Bhavan, Feroze Shah Road, New Delhi 110-001, India.

Scan. J. Old. Test. Scandinavian journal of the Old Testament. (0901-8328). Taylor & Francis Ltd: 11 New Fetter Lane, London EC4P 4EE, UK, in association with University of Aarhus, Department of Old Testament Studies.

Scand. J. Hist. Scandinavian journal of history. (0346-8755). Taylor & Francis Ltd: PO Box 2562 Solli, N-0202 Oslo, Norway.

Sci. Cult. Science as culture. (0950-5431). Carfax Publishing, Taylor and Francis Ltd: 11 New Fetter Lane, London, EC4P 4EE, U.K., in association with Free Association Books: 26 Freegrove Road, London N7 9RQ,.

Scot. Geog. J. Scottish geographical journal. (0036-9225). Royal Scottish Geographical Society: Graham Hills Building, 40 George Street, Glasgow, G1 1QE, UK.

S.E. Asia Res. South East Asia research. (0967-828X). IP Publishing Ltd: 4-5 Coleridge Gardens, London NW6 3QH, UK, in association with School of Oriental and African Studies.

Semiotica Semiotica. (0037-1998). Walter de Gruyter: Genthiner Strasse 13, D-10785 Berlin, Germany, in association with International Association for Semiotic Studies.

Senri Ethn. Stud. Senri ethnological studies. National Museum of Ethnology: Senri Expo Park, Suita, Osaka, 565 Japan.

Signs Signs. (0097-9740). University of Chicago Press: 5720 S. Woodlawn Avenue, Chicago, IL 60637, U.S.A.

Sikh Rev. Sikh review. (0037-5123). Sikh Cultural Centre: 116 Karnani Mansion, 25A Park Street, Calcutta 700 016, India.

Sing. J. Trop. Geogr. Singapore journal of tropical geography. (0129-7619). Blackwell Publishers: 108 Cowley Road, Oxford OX4 1JF, U.K., in association with National University of Singapore: Department of Geography, Kent Ridge, Republic of Singapore 0511.

Slav. E. Eur. Rev. Slavonic and East European review. (0037-6795). School of Slavonic and East European Studies: Malet Street, London WC1E 7HU, U.K.

Slavic R. Slavic review. (0037-6779). American Association for the Advancement of Slavic Studies: 128 Encina Commons, Stanford University, Stanford, CA 94305, U.S.A.

Slov. Národop. Slovensky národopis. (0037-7023). Slovak Academic Press: P.O. Box 57, Nám. Svobody 6, 81005 Bratislava, Slovakia, in association with Slovenska Akademia Vied, Narodopisny Ustav.

Soc. Anal. [Adelaide] Social analysis [Adelaide]. (0155-977X). University of Adelaide, Department of Anthropology: G.P.O. Box 498, Adelaide 5A 5001, Australia.

Soc. Anthrop. Social anthropology. (0964-0282). Cambridge University Press: The Edinburgh Building, Shaftesbury Road, Cambridge CB2 2RU, U.K.

Soc. Biol. Social biology. (0037-766X). Society for the Study of Social Biology: c/o Population Council, One Dag Hammarskjold Place, New York, NY 10017, U.S.A.

Soc. Compass Social compass. (0037-7686). Sage Publications: 6 Bonhill Street, London EC2A 4PU, U.K., in association with International Federation of Institutes for Social and Socio-Religious Research (FERES) / Centre de Recherches Socio-Religieuses: Université Catholique de Louvain, Belgium.

Soc. Cult. Geog. Social & cultural geography. (1464-9365). Routledge, Taylor and Francis Ltd: 11 New Fetter Lane, London EC4P 4EE, U.K.

Soc. Ét. Océan. Bulletin de la Société des études océaniennes. Société des études océaniennes: B.P. 110 Papeete, French Polynesia.

Soc. Ident. Social identities: Journal for the study of race, nation and culture. (1350-4630). Carfax Publishing: P.O. Box 25, Abingdon, Oxfordshire OX14 3UE, U.K.

Soc. Leg. Stud. Social and legal studies. (0964-6639). Sage Publications: 6 Bonhill Street, London EC2A 4PU, U.K.

Soc. Sci. China Social sciences in China. (0252-9203). China Social Sciences Publishing House: Jia 158 Gulouxidajie, Beijing 100720, China, in association with Chinese Academy of Social Science.

Soc. Sci. Info. Social science information. (0539-0184). Sage Publications: 6 Bonhill Street, London EC2A 4PU, U.K., in association with Maison des sciences de l'homme / École des hautes études en science sociales.

Soc. Sci. Med. Social science & medicine. (0277-9536). Elsevier Science: PO Box 211, 1000 AE Amsterdam, The Netherlands.

Soc. Sem. Social semiotics. (1035-0330). Carfax Publishing: P.O. Box 25, Abingdon, Oxfordshire OX14 3UE, U.K.

Soc. Stud. Sci. Social studies of science. (0306-3127). Sage Publications: 6 Bonhill Street, London EC2A 4PU, U.K.

Sociol. For. Sociological forum. (0884-8971). Plenum Publishing: 233 Spring Street, New York, NY 10013-1578, U.S.A.

Sociol. Q. Sociological quarterly. (0038-0253). JAI Press: 100 Prospect Street, P.O. Box 811, Stamford, CT 06904-0811, U.S.A.

Sociol. Trav. Sociologie du travail. (0038-0296). Editions Elsevier: 23 rue Linois, 75724 Paris cedex 15, France.

Sociologia [Rome] Sociologia [Rome]. (0038-0156). Istituto Luigi Sturzo: Via delle Coppelle 35, 00186 Rome, Italy.

SOJOURN SOJOURN: Journal of social issues in Southeast Asia. (0217-9520). Institute of Southeast Asian Studies: 30 Heng Mui Keng Terrace, Pasir Panjang, Singapore 119614, Singapore.

Soz. Welt. Soziale Welt. (0038-6073). Nomos Verlagsgesellschaft: Waldseestraße 3-5, 76530 Baden-Baden, Germany, in association with Arbeitsgemeinschaft sozialwissenschaftlicher Institute: Universität Bamberg, Feldkirchenstraße 21, 8600 Bamberg, Germany.

Spraw. Arch. Sprawozdania archeologiczne. (0081-3834). Instytut Archeologii i Etnologii: Polskiej Akademii Nauk, Al. Solidarnosci 105, 00-140 Warszawa, Poland Poland.

Sri Lanka J. Soc. Sci. Sri Lanka journal of social sciences. (0258-9710). Natural Resources, Energy & Science Authority of Sri Lanka: 47/5 Maitland Place, Colombo 7, Sri Lanka.

St. Ess. Beh. Sc. Phil. Studies and essays — behavioral sciences and philosophy. (1342-4262). The Faculty of Letters, Kanazawa University, Kanazawa, 920-1192 Japan.

St. Ros. Studia rosenthaliana. (0039-3347). Stichting Bibliotheca Rosenthaliana: P.O. Box 19185, 1000 GD Amsterdam, The Netherlands.

Statistica Statistica. (0039-0380). Cooperitiva Libraria Universitaria Editrice.

Stud. Afr. Studia africana. (1130-5703). Centre d'Estudis Africans: Barcelona, Spain.

Stud. Hist. Studies in history. (0257-6430). Sage Publications India: 32 M-Block Market, Greater Kailash I, New Delhi 110 048, India.

Stud. Iran. Studia iranica. (0772-7852). Association pour l'avancement des études iraniennes: c/o Institut d'Études iraniennes, 13 rue de Santeuil, 75005 Paris.

Stud. Orient. Studia orientalia. (0039-3282). Finnish Oriental Society: Snellmaninkatu 9-11, SF-00170 Helsinki, Finland.

Suomal.-Ugril. Seur. Aikak. Suomalais-Ugrilaisen Seuran Aikakauskirja. (0355-0214). Suomalais-Ugrilaisen Seura: Mariankatu 7, B.P. 320, 00171, Helsinki, Finland.

Tel Aviv Tel Aviv: Journal of the Institute of Archaeology of Tel Aviv University. (0334-4355). Tel Aviv University, Institute of Archaeology: The Emery and Claire Yass Publications in Archaeology, P.O. Box 39040, Tel Aviv 69978, Israel.

Temps Mod. Temps modernes. (0040-3075). Gallimard: 4 rue Férou, Paris 6, France.

Terrain Terrain. (0760-5668). Ministère de la Culture et de la Communication, Mission du Patrimoine ethnologique: 65 rue de Richelieu, 75002 Paris, France.

Text Text. (0165-4888). Mouton de Gruyter: Postfach 303421, 10728 Berlin, Germany.

Theory Cult. Soc. Theory culture and society. (0263-2764). Sage Publications: 6 Bonhill Street, London EC2A 4PU, U.K.

Thes. Elev. Thesis eleven. (0725-5136). Sage Publications: 6 Bonhill Street, London EC2A 4PU, U.K.

Third World Plan. R. Third World planning review. (0142-7849). Liverpool University Press: 4 Cambridge Street, Liverpool L69 7ZU, U.K.

Tibet J. Tibet journal. (0970-5368). Library of Tibetan Works and Archives: Gangchen Kyishong, Dharamshala 176 215, India.

Tids. Antrop. Tidsskriftet antropologi. (0906-3021). Stofskifte: Frederiksholms Kanal 4, 1220 Copenhagen, Denmark.

Tour. Geog. Tourism geographies. (1461-6688). Routledge, Taylor and Francis Ltd: 11 New Fetter Lane, London EC4P 4EE, U.K.

Trans. Philolog. Soc. Transactions of the Philological Society. (0079-1636). Blackwell Publishers: 108 Cowley Road, Oxford OX4 1JF, U.K.

Tribus Tribus. (0082-6413). Linden-Museum Stuttgart: Staatliches Museum für Völkerkunde, Hegelplatz 1, D-70174 Stuttgart, Germany.

Unisa Lat.Am. Rep. Unisa Latin American report. (0256-6060). University of South Africa: P.O. Box 392, 0003 Pretoria, South Africa, in association with Unisa Centre for Latin American Studies.

Urban Anthro. Urban anthropology. (0894-6019). The Institute: 56 Centennial Avenue, Brockport, NY 14420, U.S.A.

V. Aka. Belarusi Vestsi natsyianalnai akademii navuk Belarusi: Seryia gumanitarnykh navuk. (0321-1649). Belaruskaia navuka: Natayianalnai akademii navuk Belarusi, Kuprevicha 18, 220141 Minsk, Belarus.

Vest. Lenin. Univ. 6 Vestnik Sankt-Peterburgskogo universiteta. Seriia 6 Filosofiia, politologiia, sotsiologiia, psikhologiia, pravo, mezhdunarodnye otnosheniia. (0132-4624). Universiteta Nab. 7/9, 199034 Sankt Peterbur, Russia.

Vest. Mosk. Univ. Ser. 9 Filol. Vestnik Moskovskogo universiteta. Seriia 9 Filologiia. (0130-0075). Izdatel'stvo Moskovskogo Universiteta: ul. B. Nikitskaia, 5-7, 103009 Moscow, Russia.

Vis. Anthrop. Visual anthropology. (0894-9468). Harwood Academic Publishers, Taylor and Francis Ltd: 11 New Fetter Lane, London, EC4P 4EE, UK.

Wom. St. Inter. For. Women's studies international forum. (0277-5395). Elsevier Science: PO Box 211, 1000 AE Amsterdam, The Netherlands.

Wom. Stud. Women's studies. (0049-7878). Gordon and Breach Publishing, Taylor & Francis Group: 325 Chestnut Street, Suite 800, Philadelphia, PA 19106, U.S.A.

Wor. Futur. World futures. (0260-4027). Harwood Academic Publishers, Taylor and Francis Ltd: 11 New Fetter Lane, London, EC4P 4EE, UK.

World Bank Res. Obser. World Bank research observer. (0257-3032). International Bank for Reconstruction and Development: 1818 H Street N.W., Washington DC 20433, U.S.A.

World Dev. World development. (0305-750X). Elsevier Science: PO Box 211, 1000 AE Amsterdam, The Netherlands.

Z. Balkan. Zeitschrift für Balkanologie. (0044-2356). Otto Harrassowitz: Wiesbaden, Germany, in association with Friedrich-Schiller-Universität Jena, Institut für Slawistik: Grietgasse 6, 07743 Jena.

Z. Ethn. Zeitschrift für Ethnologie. (0044-2666). Dietrich Reimer Verlag: Unter den Eichen 57, 1000 Berlin 45, Germany, in association with Deutsche Gesellschaft für Völkerkunde / Berliner Gesellschaft für Anthropologie, Ethnologie und Urgeschichte.

Z. Soziol. Zeitschrift für Soziologie. (0340-1804). Lucius & Lucius Verlagsgesellschaft mbH: Gerokstraße 51, D-70184, Stuttgart, Germany.

CLASSIFICATION SCHEME
PLAN DE CLASSIFICATION

A.   **General studies / Études générales.**

A.1.   History of anthropology / Histoire de l'anthropologie.

A.2.   Teaching and research / Enseignement et recherche.

A.3.   Reference works / Ouvrages de référence.

A.4.   Anthropologists — life and works / Anthropologues — vie et œuvre.

B.   **Materials and methods of anthropology / Sources et méthodes de l'anthropologie.**

B.1.   Anthropology, its scope and its relations to other sciences / L'anthropologie, son domaine et ses rapports avec les autres sciences.

B.2.   Anthropological theory / Théorie anthropologique.

B.3.   Methods and techniques / Méthodes et techniques.
Collections / Collections; Ethnography / Ethnographie; Media / Médias

B.4.   Historical and archaeological material / Matériaux historiques et archéologiques.

B.4.1.   Historical material / Matériaux historiques.
Ancient history / Histoire ancienne; Anthropology and history / Anthropologie et histoire; Colonial history / Histoire coloniale; Prehistory / Préhistoire

B.4.2.   Archaeology / Archéologie.
Archaeological theory / Théorie archéologique; Arts and architecture of prehistory and antiquity / Arts et architecture de la préhistoire et de l'Antiquité; Excavation reports / Rapports sur fouilles; Funerary archaeology / Archéologie funéraire; Inscriptions / Inscriptions; Material culture / Culture matérielle

B.5.   Physical anthropology / Anthropologie physique.
Craniology / Crâniologie; Dentition / Dentition; Genetics / Génétique; Human evolution / Évolution humaine; Human growth and development / Croissance et développement de l'homme; Primatology / Primatologie

B.6.   Language and communication / Langage et communication.
> Media and communication / Médias et communication; Multilingualism and linguistic contact / Plurilinguisme et contact linguistique; Names and naming / Noms et appellations; Afro-Asiatic languages / Langues afro-asiatiques; Altaic languages / Langues altaïques; Austronesian languages / Langues austronésiennes; Dravidian languages / Langues dravidiennes; Indo-European languages / Langues indo-européennes; Languages of the Americas / Langues des Amériques; Niger-Congo languages / Langues du bassin Niger-Congo; Nilo-Saharan languages / Langues nilo-sahariennes; Pidgin and Creole languages / Langues créoles et pidgins; Sino-Tibetan languages / Langues sino-tibétaines; Uralic languages / Langues ouraliennes

C.   Ecology, Technology, Economy. / Écologie, Technologie, Économie.

C.1.   Ecology / Écologie.
> Demography / Démographie; Migration / Migration; Rural anthropology / Anthropologie rurale; Urban anthropology / Anthropologie urbaine

C.2.   Technology / Technologie.
> Crafts / Artisanat

C.3.   Economy / Économie.
> Agriculture / Agriculture; Consumption / Consommation; Exchange, commerce and property / Échanges, affaires et propriété; Land tenure / Régimes fonciers; Production systems / Systèmes de production; Work / Travail

D.   Ethnographic studies of peoples and communities / Études ethnographiques des peuples et des communautés.

E.   Socio-political structure and relations / Structure et relations socio-politiques.

E.1.   Political structure and power / Structure et pouvoir politique.
> Political leadership / Leadership politique

E.2.   Social structure / Structure sociale.

E.2.1.   Social organization and social groups / Organisation sociale et groupements sociaux.
> Classes and castes / Classes et castes

E.2.2.   Family and kinship systems / Systèmes familiaux et de parenté.

E.2.3.   Life cycle / Cycle de vie.
> Birth and childhood / Naissance et enfance; Adolescence / Adolescence; Marriage / Mariage; Ageing / Vieillissement; Death / Mort

E.2.4. The body, gender and sexuality / Le corps, genre et sexualité.
   Gender / Genre; Sexuality / Sexualité; The body / Le corps

E.3. Legal systems and moral codes / Systèmes juridiques et codifications morales.
   Crime / Crime; Traditional and modern law / Loi traditionnelle et moderne; Violence / Violence

E.4. Interethnic and intraethnic relations / Rapports interethniques et intraethniques.
   Africa / Afrique; Americas / Amériques; Asia / Asie; Europe / Europe; Oceania / Océanie

F. Religion, magic and sorcery / Religion, magie, sorcellerie.

F.1. Cosmology and myth / Cosmologie et mythe.

F.2. Major religions / Religions principales.
   Buddhism / Bouddhisme; Christianity / Christianisme; Hinduism / Hindouisme; Islam / Islam; Jainism / Jaïnisme; Judaism / Judaïsme; Sikhism / Sikhisme

F.3. Local religions and rituals / Religions locales et rites.

F.4. Magic and sorcery / Magie et sorcellerie.

F.5. Religious change / Processus de changement religieux.

G. Knowledge, folk traditions, arts and science / Connaissance, traditions populaires, arts et science.

G.1. Categories of thought and meaning / Catégories de la pensée et de la signification.
   Invention of tradition / Invention de la tradition

G.2. Symbolism / Symbolisme.

G.3. Anthropology of science and medicine / Anthropologie de la science et de la médecine.
   Medical anthropology / Anthropologie de la médecine; Anthropology of science / Anthropologie de la science

G.4. Creative expression / Expressions créatrices.
   Architecture / Architecture; Dance and theatre / Danse et théâtre; Music and songs / Musique et chanson; Oral tradition / Tradition orale; Poetry / Poésie; Visual arts / Arts visuels; Written materials / Matériaux écrits

G.5. Games, leisure and tourism / Jeux, loisirs et tourisme.

G.6. Food and festivals / Nourriture et fêtes.
   Food and drink / Alimentation

H.   Culture, personality, identity / Culture, personnalité, identité.
Ethnicity / Ethnicité; Identity / Identité; National identity / Identité nationale; Psychology / Psychologie

H.1.   Educational systems / Systèmes d'enseignement.

H.2.   Biographical material / Matériaux biographiques.

I.   Social change / Changements sociaux.
Globalization and localization / Mondialisation et localisation

J.   Applied anthropology / Anthropologie appliquée.

J.1.   Borders and rights / Frontières et droits.
Indigenous rights / Droits indigènes

J.2.   Social development and welfare / Développement et bien-être social.
Agricultural development / Développement agricole; Development policy, aid and management / Politique, aide et gestion du développement; Education / Éducation; Environment and development / Environnement et développement; Food supply and nutrition / Approvisionnement alimentaires et nutrition; Gender and development / Genre et développement; Health / Santé; Rural development / Développement rural; Urban development / Développement urbain

BIBLIOGRAPHY FOR 2001

BIBLIOGRAPHIE POUR 2001

A: **GENERAL STUDIES**
ÉTUDES GÉNÉRALES

A.1: **History of anthropology**
Histoire de l'anthropologie

1 Aboriginal overkill overstated errors in Charles Kay's hypothesis. Michael J. Yochim. **Hum. Nature** 12:2 2001 pp.141-167.
2 Afterword: the usual suspects. Adam Kuper. **Patt. Prej.** 35:2 4:2001 pp.81-86.
3 The anthropology of reform and the reform of anthropology: anthropological narratives of recovery and progress in China. Stevan Harrell. **Ann. R. Anthr.** 30 2001 pp.139-161.
4 Bugs in the system: insects, agricultural science, and professional aspirations in Britain, 1890-1920. J.F.M. Clark. **Agr. Hist.** 75:1 Winter:2001 pp.83-116.
5 Comparative religion, taxonomies and 19th century philosophies of science: Chantepie de la Saussaye and Tiele. Thomas Ryba. **Numen** XLVIII:3 2001 pp.309-338.
6 De l'histoire des études orientales à Paris: Anton et Liza Zigmund-Cerbu. *[In French]*; [The history of oriental studies in Paris: Anton and Liza Zigmund-Cerbu]. Arion Roşu. **Bull. Ét. Indien.** 17-18 1999-2000 pp.21-32.
7 The funding of social anthropological research: a preliminary note to a fragment of history written by E.M. Chilver in 1955. Shirley Ardener. **J. Anthrop. Soc. Oxford** XXIX:3 1998 pp.243-250.
8 Fünfzig Jahre Ethnologie. *[In German]*; [Fifty years of ethnology]. Hans Fischer. **Paideuma** 47 2001 pp.7-24.
9 Germaine Dieterlen and Meyer Fortes. Susan Drucker-Brown. **Cam. Anthrop.** 22:2 2000-2001 pp.50-59.
10 The Gypsy question and the Gypsy expert in Sweden. Norma Montesino. **Rom. Stud.** 11:1 6:2001 pp.1-24.
11 A history of anthropology. Thomas Hylland Eriksen; Finn Sivert Nielsen. London, Sterling VA: Pluto Press, 2001. viii, 207p. *ISBN: 074531385X, 0745313906. Includes bibliographical references (p. 179-191) and index. (Series: Anthropology, culture and society).*
12 «Korennoi perelom» v otechestvennoi etnografii (diskussiia o predmete etnologicheskoi nauki: konets 1920-kh - nachalo 1930-kh godov). *[In Russian]*; ('A radical turn' in our domestic ethnography (discussion on the object of ethnological science: late 1920's — early 1930's).) *[Summary]*. T.D. Solovei. **Etnograf. Oboz.** 3 5-6:2001 pp.101-122.
13 Object lessons and ethnographic displays: museum exhibitions and the making of American anthropology. David Jenkins. **Comp. Stud. S.** 36:2 4:1994 pp.242-292.
14 Orientalism and Gypsylorism. Ken Lee. **Soc. Anal. [Adelaide]** 44(2) 11:2000 pp.129-156.
15 Poleska ekspedycja etnosocjologiczna Józefa Obrębskiego w latach 1934-1937. Organizacja. Metody badań. Problematyka. Uczestnicy. *[In Polish]*; (Ethno-sociological expedition of Józef Obrębski to Polesie in the years 1934-1937: organization, research

methods, problems, participants.) *[Summary]*. Anna Engelking. **Etn. Polska** XLV:1-2 2001 pp.23-46.

16　Rivers lecture: the disappearance of useful sciences. Simon Schaffer. **Cam. Anthrop.** 22:1 2000-2001 pp.1-23.

17　Slovenska etnologija med ljudsko in alternativno medicino. *[In Slovene]*; (Slovene ethnology between popular and alternative medicine.) *[Summary]*. Nena Židov. **Bull. Slov. Ethno. Soc.** 41:1-2 2001 pp.134-137.

18　A social history of anthropology in the United States. Thomas Carl Patterson. Oxford: Berg Publishers, 2001. x, 212p. *ISBN: 1859734944, 1859734898. Includes bibliographical references (p. 165-205) and index.*

A.2:　**Teaching and research**
Enseignement et recherche

19　12th annual meeting of *La Société Francophone de Primatologie*, Besançon, September 2000. B.L. Deputte. **Folia Prim.** 72:3 2001 pp.115-127.

20　13th international ethnological food research conference. Rastislava Stoličná. **Slov. Národop.** 48:2 2000 pp.236-239.

21　14th meeting of the Italian Primatological Society, Pisa-Calci, October 2000. A. Gregorace; E. Palagi; S.M Borgognini-Tarli. **Folia Prim.** 72:3 2001 pp.128-152.

22　50 years of Vedic research — retrospect and prospects. S.K. Lal. **J. Orient. Inst.** XLVII:1-2(47) 9-12:1997 pp.119-128.

23　7th congress of the German Primate Society, Zurich, September-October 2001. A.E. Müller; W. Scheffrahn. **Folia Prim.** 72:3 2001 pp.153-194.

24　Anthropology and public culture: the Yanomami, science and ethics. Steve Nugent. **Anthr. Today** 17:3 6:2001 pp.10-14.

25　The archives and library of the Berlin Mission Society. Ulrich van der Heyden. **Hist. Afr.** 23 1996 pp.411-428.

26　C.A. Schmitz — Ein Betriebsunfall am Frobenius-Institut? *[In German]*; [C.A. Schmitz - a mishap at the *Frobenius-Institut*?] Justin Stagl. **Paideuma** 47 2001 pp.25-42.

27　Central Eurasian Studies Society conference. U. Schamiloglu. **Eur. Stud. Y.** 73 2001 pp.177-178.

28　A debate about our canon. Paul Atkinson; Amanda Coffey; Sara Delamont. **Qual. Res.** 1:1 4:2001 pp.5-21.

29　A decade of Filipino-Dutch academic cooperation: the Cagayan Valley Programme on Environment and Development. Andres B. Masipiqueña; Gerard A. Persoon; Denyse J. Snelder. **Bijdragen** 157:3 2001 pp.691-712.

30　L'entreprise internationale de l'*Onomasticon Arabicum* en avril 2000. *[In French]*; [The international *Onomasticon Arabicum* project in April 2000]. J. Sublet. **Arabica** XLVIII:3 7:2001 pp.383-391.

31　Esquisse ethnographique d'un projet: le Musée du Quai Branly. *[In French]*; [Ethnographic outline of a project: the Quai Branly Museum]. Nélia Dias. **Fre. Pol. Cult. Soc.** 19:2 Summer:2001 pp.81-101.

32　Etnologija in študijski krožki. *[In Slovene]*; (Ethnology and academic circles.) *[Summary]*. Tatjana Dolžan Eržen. **Bull. Slov. Ethno. Soc.** 41:1-2 2001 pp.100-105.

33　Field science ethnography: methods for systematic observation on an Arctic expedition. William J. Clancey. **Fie. Meth.** 13:3 8:2001 pp.223-243.

34　From social to cognitive archaeology. Colin Renfrew; Lynn Meskell [Interviewer]. **J. Soc. Arch.** 1:1 6:2001 pp.13-34.

35　Gehan Wijeyewardene (1932-2000). Ananda Rajah. **Asia Pacific J. Anthr.** 2:1 4:2001 pp.89-108.

36　Guide to African archives in Belgium. Hugues Legros; Curtis A. Keim. **Hist. Afr.** 23 1996 pp.401-410.

37 In memoriam Professor Koentjaraningrat (15 June 1923 - 23 March 1999). James J. Fox. **Bijdragen** 157:2 2001 pp.239-246.

38 Introduction: new directions in bereavement research and theory. George A. Bonanno. **Am. Behav. Sc.** 44:5 1:2001 pp.718-725.

39 Kruglyi stol «Moskovskaia baltistika na poroge XXI veka». *[In Russian]*; (Round table: 'Moscow Baltic Sea area studies on the brink of the 21ˢᵗ century'.) S.I. Ryzhakova. **Etnograf. Oboz.** 1 1-2:2001 pp.157-159.

40 Looking to the past: the role of oral history research in recording the visual history of Britain's deaf community. Martin Atherton; Dave Russell; Graham Turner. **Oral Hist.** 29:2 Autumn:2001 pp.35-47.

41 Nativizing Chinese anthropology: take two. Gregory Eliyu Guldin; Zhou Daming; Huang Shuping; Zhang Dunfu; Fan Ke; Gao Chong; Zou Jing; Naran Bilik; Wang Jianmin; Ma Guoqing. **Chin. Soc. Anth.** 33:4 Summer:2001 pp.3-98. *Collection of 8 articles.*

42 The ninth international Finno-Ugric congress in Tartu/Estland. A.A. Kim. **Eur. Stud. Y.** 73 2001 pp.155-160.

43 The organization of social and economic research in the British colonial territories. E.M. Chilver. **J. Anthrop. Soc. Oxford** XXIX:3 1998 pp.251-272.

44 Prevention of sexually transmitted infections in different populations: a review of behaviourally effective and cost-effective interventions. Alexander McKay. **Canad. J. Human Sex.** 9:2 2000 pp.95-120.

45 Prikladnye issledovaniia v zapadnoi sotsial'noi/kul'turnoi antropologii. *[In Russian]*; (Applied research in Western social/cultural anthropology.) *[Summary]*. A.A. Nikishenkov. **Etnograf. Oboz.** 5 9-10:2000 pp.18-30.

46 Proceedings of the XVIII congress of the International Primatological Society, Adelaide, January 2001. Dorothy M. Fragaszy; J.A.R.A.M. van Hooff; Katherine A. Leighty. **Int. J. Primat.** 22:6 12:2001 pp.1057-1086.

47 Recherches ethnographiques en Europe et en Amérique du Nord. *[In French]*; [Ethnographic research in Europe and North America]. Ana Vásquez-Bronfman [Ed.]; Isabel Martinez [Ed.]; Angela Xavier de Brito [Tr.]. Paris: Anthropos, Diffusion, Economica, 1999. xii, 294p. *ISBN: 2717837809. Text in English and French. Includes bibliographical references.*

48 Rossiiskoe etnograficheskoe sibirevedenie v XX v. *[In Russian]*; (Russian ethnographic Siberian studies of the 20ᵗʰ century.) *[Summary]*. N.A. Tomilov. **Etnograf. Oboz.** 3 5-6:2001 pp.92-100.

49 Rückkehr zur Feldforschung? *[In German]*; [Return to field work?] Irene Albers. **Anthropos [St. Augustin]** 95:2 2000 pp.568-570.

50 Select contents of Oriental journals. P.H. Joshi. **J. Orient. Inst.** XLVII:1-2(47) 9-12:1997 pp.129-136.

51 Select contents of Oriental journals. P.H. Joshi. **J. Orient. Inst.** XLVII:3-4(47) 3-6:1998 pp.303-308.

52 Sexuality, culture, and power in HIV/AIDS research. Richard Parker. **Ann. R. Anthr.** 30 2001 pp.163-179.

53 Social science research and the Africanist: the need for intellectual and attitudinal reconfiguration; *[Summary in French]*. Wisdom J. Tettey; Korbla P. Puplampu. **Afr. Stud. R.** 43:3 12:2000 pp.81-102.

54 Taïwan et le Viêt-Nam, un survol d'ouvrages en langue chinoise de l'Institut d'Ethnologie de l'*Academia Sinica*. *[In French]*; [Taiwan and Vietnam: a synopsis of work in the Chinese language by the Institute of Ethnology at the *Academia Sinica*]. Josiane Cauquelin. **Péninsule** 40 2000 pp.155-158.

55 Teaching visual anthropology. Notes from the field. Anna Grimshaw. **Ethnos** 66:2 2001 pp.237-258.

56 Temporal'naia antropologiia: novoe napravlenie issledovanii ili sostavnaia chast' istoricheskoi psikhologii. *[In Russian]*; (Temporal anthropology: a new branch of investigations, or a component of historical psychology.) V.K. Karnaukh. **Vest. Lenin. Univ. 6** 4(30) 12:2000 pp.24-30.

57 Uralic linguistic studies at the University of Tartu 1995-2000. A. Künnap. **Eur. Stud. Y.** 73 2001 pp.162-171.
58 Der „Verdienst-Komplex": Rückblick auf einen Forschungsschwerpunkt der deutschen Ethnologie. *[In German]*; (The 'meritorious complex': a review of a research focus in German anthropology.) Ulrich Braukämper. **Z. Ethn.** 126:2 2001 pp.209-236.
59 'We make the law and the law makes us': some ideas on a law in development research agenda. Peter P. Houtzager. **IDS Bull.** 32:1 1:2001 pp.8-18.
60 Why teach Heisenberg to archaeologists? A.M. Pollard. **Antiquity** 69:263 6:1995 pp.242-247.

A.3: **Reference works**
Ouvrages de référence

61 Bhīsma's sources. Alf Hiltebeitel. **Stud. Orient.** 94 2001 pp.261-278.
62 A brief on Ayurvedic manuscripts preserved at Utkal University, Bhubaneswar. M.M. Padhi; B. Das; N. Srikanth; N.N. Pathak; K.K. Chopra. **B. Ind. Inst. Hist. Med.** XXIX:2 7:1999 pp.159-164.
63 Cambridge practice tests for IELTS 1. Vanessa Jakeman; Clare McDowell. Cambridge: Cambridge University Press, 1996. iv, 154p. *ISBN: 0521497671, 0521497663. Cassette.*
64 Collins Cobuild English dictionary. Glasgow: HarperCollins, 1995. 1951p.
65 Collins Diccionario Inglés. *[In Spanish]*; Collins Spanish dictionary. London: Collins, 2000. 2141p. *ISBN: 0004707583, 0004701518.*
66 Colloquial Portuguese of Brazil: the complete course for beginners. Esmenia Simões Osborne; João Sampaio; Barbara McIntyre. London: Routledge, 1997. vi, 302p. *ISBN: 0415161371. Includes indexes. (Series: The colloquial).*
67 Diccionario de la lengua española. *[In Spanish]*; [Dictionary of the Spanish language]. Real Academia Española. Madrid: Real Academia Española, 1992. *ISBN: 842399418X, 8423994163, 8423994171. 2 Volumes.*
68 English-Portuguese, Portuguese-English dictionary. John Whitlam; Vitoria Davies; Mike Harland. London: Collins, 2001. 367p. *ISBN: 0004724194.*
69 Erklärungen und Übungen. Grundstufen-Grammatik für Deutsch als Fremdsprache. *[In German]*; [Explanations and exercises - grammatical rules for German as a foreign language]. Monika Reimann. Ismaning: Max Hueber Verlag, 1996. 237p. *ISBN: 3190015759.*
70 Exploring spoken English. Ronald Carter; Michael McCarthy. Cambridge: Cambridge University Press, 1997. 160p. *ISBN: 0521568609, 0521567777, 0521560497. Cassette. Includes bibliographical references.*
71 Gramática activa 1. *[In Portuguese]*; [Active grammar]. Olga Mata Coimbra; Isabel Coimbra Leite. Lisbon: Lidel, 2000. 129p. *ISBN: 9727571425. Volume 1.*
72 Handbook of ethnography. Paul Atkinson [Ed.]; et al. London: Sage Publications, 2001. 640p. *ISBN: 076195824X.*
73 Historical dictionary of pre-colonial Africa. Robert O. Collins. Lanham MD: Scarecrow Press, 2001. 688p. *ISBN: 0810839784. Includes index. (Series:* Historical dictionaries of ancient civilizations and historical eras).
74 Marktchance Wirtschaftsdeutsch: Mittelstufe. *[In German]*; [Business German: middle level]. Jurgen Bolten. Klett, 1999. 159p. *ISBN: 3126751407.*
75 Le nouveau petit Robert: dictionnaire alphabétique et analogique de la langue française. *[In French]*; [The new *Petit Robert*: an alphabetical and analogical dictionary of the French language]. Paul Robert; Josette Rey-Debove [Ed.]; Alain Rey [Ed.]. Paris: Dictionnaires Le Robert, 1996. xxxv, 2551p. *ISBN: 2850365068.*
76 Of mice and manuscripts: a memoir of the National Archives of Zimbabwe. Anthony King. **Hist. Afr.** 25 1998 pp.405-412.
77 An overview of the African National Congress archives at the University of Fort Hare. T.J. Stapleton; M. Maamoe. **Hist. Afr.** 25 1998 pp.413-422.

78 Predstavitev zbirnega registra kulturne dediščine in etnološke dediščine v njem. *[In Slovene]*; [Introduction to the central register of cultural and ethnological heritage]. Ksenija Kovačec Naglič. **Bull. Slov. Ethno. Soc.** 41:3-4 2001 pp.12-16.

79 Recent bibliography in classical Chinese philosophy. Helmolt Vittinghoff [Ed.]. **J. Ch. Philos.** 28:1-2 3-6:2001 pp.1-188.

80 The regional archive at Addi Qäyyeh, Eritrea. Irma Taddia. **Hist. Afr.** 25 1998 pp.423-426.

81 Retrieving hidden traces of the intercultural past: an introduction to archival resources in Cameroon, with special reference to the Central Archives of the Presbyterian Church in Cameroon. Guy Thomas. **Hist. Afr.** 25 1998 pp.427-440.

82 Salvaging manuscripts from 1947 Lahore: the making of an Indology library. Mahesh Sharma; P.V. Rao. **Bull. Ét. Indien.** 17-18 1999-2000 pp.491-500.

83 Schlüssel. Grundstufen-Grammatik für Deutsch als Fremdsprache. *[In German]*; [Grammatical rules for German as a foreign language]. Monika Reimann. Ismaning: Max Hueber Verlag, 1996. 48p. *ISBN: 3190115753.*

84 *Sueños*: world Spanish, activity book. Aurora Longo; Almudena Sánchez. London: BBC Books, 1995. 78p. *ISBN: 0563399295. British Broadcasting Corporation.*

A.4: Anthropologists — life and works
Anthropologues — vie et œuvre

85 'A rich and promising site': Winifred Lamb (1894-1963), Kusura and Anatolian archaeology. David W.J. Gill; Winifred Lamb. **Anatol. St.** 50 2000 pp.1-10.

86 Une anthropologie religieuse en Lorraine: hommage à Serge Bonnet. *[In French]*; [Religious anthropology in Lorraine: a tribute to Serge Bonnet]. Serge Bonnet [Dedicatee]; Serge Bonnet; Richard Lioger [Ed.]. Metz: Éditions Serpenoise, 2000. 292p. *ISBN: 2876924358. Papers presented at Une anthropologie religieuse en Lorraine?, Metz, September 1998. Includes bibliographical references.*

87 Bedřich Hrozný and the Bible. Stanislav Segert. **Arch. Orient.** 67:4 11:1999 pp.629-648.

88 Bernardo Kohnen (1876.-1939.) *[In Croatian]*; (Bernardo Kohnen (1876-1939).) Koraljka Kuzman. **Etnoloska** 23:30 2000 pp.93-104.

89 Bernth Lindfors and the archive of African literature. Kenneth W. Harrow. **R. African Lit.** 32:4 Winter:2001 pp.147-154.

90 Beyond the visible and the material: the Amerindianization of society in the work of Peter Rivière. Neil L. Whitehead [Ed.]; Laura M. Rival [Ed.]. New York, Oxford: Oxford University Press, 2001. xiii, 301p. *ISBN: 0199244766. Includes bibliographical references and index.*

91 Bronislaw Malinowski: collected works. Bronislaw Malinowski. London: Routledge, 2001. 3000p. *ISBN: 0415216710. 9 volumes.*

92 Bronisław Piłsudski. Zesłaniec, etnograf, polityk. *[In Polish]*; (Bronisław Piłsudski: exile, ethnographer, politician.) *[Summary]*. Antoni Kuczyński. Wrocław: Atla 2, 2000. 188p *ISBN: 8388555014.*

93 C.A. Schmitz — Ein Betriebsunfall am Frobenius-Institut? *[In German]*; [C.A. Schmitz - a mishap at the *Frobenius-Institut*?] Justin Stagl. **Paideuma** 47 2001 pp.25-42.

94 De l'histoire des études orientales à Paris: Anton et Liza Zigmund-Cerbu. *[In French]*; [The history of oriental studies in Paris: Anton and Liza Zigmund-Cerbu]. Arion Roşu. **Bull. Ét. Indien.** 17-18 1999-2000 pp.21-32.

95 Deromanticizing subalterns or recolonializing anthropology? Denial of indigenous agency and reproduction of northern hegemony in the work of David Stoll. John Gledhill. **Identities** 8:1 3:2001 pp.135-161.

96 Donald Moodie: South Africa's pioneer oral historian. V.C. Malherbe. **Hist. Afr.** 25 1998 pp.171-198.

97 The Elmina *dagregister* of William Butler, 1721. Jan J. Clement. **Hist. Afr.** 24 1997 pp.409-412.

98   Envisioning power: ideologies of dominance and crisis. Stanley R. Barrett; Sean Stokholm; Jeanette Burke. **Am. Anthrop.** 103:2 6:2001 pp.468-480.
99   Ernst Wilhelm Middendorf: medical doctor — Andean scholar. Henning Bischof. **Baes-A.** XLVII:2 6:2001 pp.397-445.
100   Der Ethnologe als Utopist. Zu Lahontan's *Bon Sauvage-Utopie*. *[In German]*; [The ethnologist as utopianist. Lahontan's *Bon Sauvage-Utopie*]. Richard Saage. **Paideuma** 47 2001 pp.43-60.
101   Etnografsko-fotografski doprinos Radivoja Simonovića hrvatskoj etnologiji. *[In Croatian]*; (Radivoj Simonović's ethnographic and photographic contributions to Croatian ethnology.) Aleksandra Muraj. **Etnoloska** 23:30 2000 pp.49-64.
102   Floyd Glenn Lounsbury (1914-1998). Harold C. Conklin. **Am. Anthrop.** 102:4 12:2000 pp.860-864.
103   Gabriel Martínez. *[In French]*; [Gabriel Martínez]. Antoinette Molinié. **J. Soc. Amér.** 86 2000 pp.225-228.
104   Gehan Wijeyewardene (1932-2000). Ananda Rajah. **Asia Pacific J. Anthr.** 2:1 4:2001 pp.89-108.
105   Gender, power and ritual in cross-cultural perspective — essays in honour of Michael Allen. Mary Patterson; Robert Tonkinson; Michael Allen [Dedicatee]; Les Hiatt; Jeremy Beckett; Chris Eipper; Kenneth Maddock; Geoffrey Samuel; Vivienne Kondos. **Anthro. forum** 11:1 5:2001 pp.7-108. *Collection of 7 articles.*
106   Georges Baudot — Alfredo J. Bablot. *[In Spanish]*; [Georges Baudot and Alfredo J. Bablot]. Clementina Díaz de Ovando. **Caravelle** 76-77 12:2001 pp.455-459.
107   Georges Perec's experiments in social description. Howard Becker. **Ethnog.** 2:1 3:2001 pp.63-76.
108   Germaine Dieterlen and Meyer Fortes. Susan Drucker-Brown. **Cam. Anthrop.** 22:2 2000-2001 pp.50-59.
109   La «*Grammaire et vocabulaire du lingala ou langue du Haut-Congo*» d'Egide De Boeck de 1904: commentaires historiques, présentation et texte. *[In French]*; [The *Grammar and Vocabulary of Lingala or the Language of Haut-Congo* by Egide De Boeck in 1904: historical commentary, presentation and text] *[Summary]*. M. Meeuwis. **Ann. Æqua.** 22 2001 pp.327-421.
110   Hommage a Paul Broca (1824-1880) Sainte-Foy-la-Grande (Gironde), 2 et 3 février 2001. *[In French]*; [A tribute to Paul Broca (1824-1880), Sainte-Foy-la-Grande (Gironde), 2-3 February 2001]. P. Monod-Broca; Cl. Massé; J.Cl. Drouin; F. Boller; P. Marcie; T. Hamanaka; E.A. Cabanis; M.T. Iba-Zizen; R. Saban; C.L. Hamonet. **Bio. Hum. Anthrop.** 19:3-4 7-12:2001 pp.127-188. *Collection of 8 articles.*
111   In memoriam: Ali M.A. Salih (1943-1997). I. Melhim. **A. Dept. Antiq. Jordan** XLII 1998 pp.5-6.
112   In memoriam: James A. Sauer (1945-1999). Ghazi Bisheh. **A. Dept. Antiq. Jordan** XLIV 2000 pp.9-10.
113   In memoriam Michel Dieu. *[In French]*; [In memory of Michel Dieu]. D. Barreteau. **B. Ét. Afr. INALCO** 19-20 1993 p.237.
114   In memoriam Professor Koentjaraningrat (15 June 1923 - 23 March 1999). James J. Fox. **Bijdragen** 157:2 2001 pp.239-246.
115   An interview with Adam Kuper. Robert Gibb [Interviewer]; Adam Kuper; David Mills [Interviewer]. **Soc. Anthrop.** 9:2 6:2001 pp.207-216.
116   Interview with Apollon Davidson. Apollon Davidson; Irina Filatova [Interviewer]. **S. Afr. Hist. J.** 42 2000 pp.307-340.
117   Karl Heinrich Menges. H. Anetshofer. **Cent. Asia. J.** 45:1 2001 pp.3-6.
118   Kenneth Howard Peacock 1922-2000. Anna K. Guigné. **Ethnologies** 22:2 2000 pp.289-294.
119   Kenneth Lee Pike (1912-2000). Thomas N. Headland. **Am. Anthrop.** 103:2 6:2001 pp.505-509.
120   Laura Maud Thompson (1905-2000). Nancy J. Parezo; Rebecca A. Stephenson. **Am. Anthrop.** 103:2 6:2001 pp.510-514.

121   Lectures de De Martino en France aujourd'hui. *[In French]*; [De Martino's lectures in France today] *[Summary]*; *[Summary in German]*. Christine Bergé. **Ethn. Fr.** XXXI:3 7-9:2001 pp.537-548.

122   Lettres au Marabout: messages touaregs au Père de Foucauld. *[In French]*; [Letters to Marabout: Tuareg messages to Père de Foucauld]. Lionel Galand [Ed.]; Mohamed Aghali Zakara; Paulette Galand-Pernet; Ariane Aron; Lamara Bougchiche; Jeannine Drouin; Dominique Casajus. Paris: Belin, 1999. 256p. *ISBN: 2701121027. Includes bibliographical references (p. 249-254) and index.*

123   Lev Pavlovich Lashuk. *[In Russian]*; (Lev Pavlovich Lashuk.) V.V. Karlov. **Etnograf. Oboz.** 3 5-6:2001 pp.3-6.

124   Linguistique historique et histoire de la langue: 80 ans après *La Formation de la langue marathe* de Jules Bloch. *[In French]*; [Historical linguistics and history of language: 80 years after Jules Bloch's *The Formation of the Marathi Language*]. Jean Pacquement. **B. Éc. Fr. Ex.-Or.** 87:2 2000 pp.741-764.

125   Making the James Stuart Archive. John Wright. **Hist. Afr.** 23 1996 pp.333-350.

126   Max Gluckman and the critique of segregation in South African anthropology, 1921-1940. Paul Cocks. **J. S. Afr. Stud.** 27:4 12:2001 pp.739-756.

127   Miyata Noboru: the folklorist and his scholarship. Watching the tide, knowing the time. Takanori Shintani. **Asian Folk. S.** LIX:2 2000 pp.285-322.

128   M.O. Kosven - kavkazoved. *[In Russian]*; (M.O. Kosven — explorer of the Caucasus.) *[Summary]*. B.A. Kaloev. **Etnograf. Oboz.** 3 5-6:2000 pp.122-134.

129   Naphtali Kinberg, 1948-1997. Yishai Peled. **Is. Orient. Stud.** XIX 1999 pp.263-266.

130   The native collector: Louis Shotridge and the contests of possession. Elizabeth P. Seaton. **Ethnog.** 2:1 3:2001 pp.35-62.

131   Netzwerkanalyse, oder: die Fraktionen der deutschen Ethnologie. Zu Thomas Schweizers „Muster sozialer Ordnung". *[In German]*; [Network analysis, or: fractions of German ethnology. On Thomas Schweizer's *Muster sozialer Ordnung*]. Thomas Hauschild. **Anthropos [St. Augustin]** 95:2 2000 pp.564-567.

132   La obra cartográfica de don Carlos de Sigüenza y Góngora. *[In Spanish]*; [The cartographic work of Carlos de Sigüenza y Góngora]. Elías Trabulse. **Caravelle** 76-77 12:2001 pp.265-275.

133   Out of words: the æsthesodic cine-eye of Robert Gardner: an exegesis and interview. Robert Gardner; Ilisa Barbash [Interviewer]. **Vis. Anthrop.** 14:4 2001 pp.369-414.

134   The passion of Franz Boas. Herbert S. Lewis. **Am. Anthrop.** 103:2 6:2001 pp.447-467.

135   Perspectives on Tierney's *Darkness in El Dorado*. Fernando Coronil; Alan G. Fix; Peter Pels; Charles L. Briggs; Raymond Hames; Susan Lindee; Alcida Rita Ramos. **Curr. Anthr.** 42:2 4:2001 pp.265-276.

136   Poleska ekspedycja etnosocjologiczna Józefa Obrębskiego w latach 1934-1937. Organizacja. Metody badań. Problematyka. Uczestnicy. *[In Polish]*; (Ethno-sociological expedition of Józef Obrębski to Polesie in the years 1934-1937: organization, research methods, problems, participants.) *[Summary]*. Anna Engelking. **Etn. Polska** XLV:1-2 2001 pp.23-46.

137   Preemstvennost' i preobrazovanie v istoricheskom razvitii etnosa. *[In Russian]*; (Continuity and change in the historical development of ethnos. List of major works of L.P. Lashuk.) *[Summary]*. L.P. Lashuk. **Etnograf. Oboz.** 3 5-6:2001 pp.20-31.

138   The relevance of Ernest Gellner's thought today. Jiří Musil; Chris Hann; Sukumar Periwal; Martin Ottenheimer; Jiří Šubrt; Zdeněk Suda; Peter Salner; Zdeněk Uherek. **Czech Soc. Rev.** IX:2 Fall:2001 pp.153-257. *Collection of 8 articles.*

139   Robert Austerlitz in Hungarian context. P. Hajdú. **Eur. Stud. Y.** 73 2001 pp.153-154.

140   Rozhovor s Konradom Köstlinom. *[In Slovak]*; (Interview with Konrad Köstlin.) Gabriela Kiliánová [Interviewer]; Konrad Köstlin. **Slov. Národop.** 47:1 1999 pp.51-64.

141   Rudolf Schenda (1930-2000). *[In German]*; (Rudolf Schenda (1930-2000).) Hermann Bausinger. **Fabula** 42:1-2 2001 pp.134-138.

142   Saints and spirits and their significance in Moroccan cultural beliefs and practices: an analysis of Westermarck's work. Mohamed Chtatou. **Morocco** 1 1996 pp.62-84.

143 Scholarship and Margaret Murray. Jacqueline Simpson. **Ethnologies** 22:2 2000 pp.281-288.

144 Sherwood Larned Washburn (1911-2000). Russell H. Tuttle. **Am. Anthrop.** 102:4 12:2000 pp.865-869.

145 S.M. Abramzon - issledovatel' tsentral'noaziatskikh kirgizov. *[In Russian]*; (S.M. Abramzon — a student of Central Asian Kirghizes.) *[Summary]*. A.M. Reshetov. **Etnograf. Oboz.** 1 1-2:2001 pp.142-148.

146 Sud'by teorii etnosa. Pamiati Iu.V. Bromleia. *[In Russian]*; (Fortunes and misfortunes of the theory of ethnos. In memory of Iu.V. Bromley.) *[Summary]*. S.E. Rybakov; Iu.V. Bromley [Dedicatee]. **Etnograf. Oboz.** 1 1-2:2001 pp.3-22.

147 Vatra kao domovina smrti u Nodilovoj religiji groba. *[In Croatian]*; (Fire as the homeland of death in Nodilo's *Religija Groba* [*The Grave Religion*].) *[Summary]*. Suzana Marjanić. **Nar. Umjetn.** 37:2 2000 pp.87-108.

148 Vivre parmi les «anthros». *[In French]*; [To live among the 'anthros']. Clifford Geertz. **Esprit** 276 7:2001 pp.20-33.

149 Wilhelm Heinrich Riehl and the scientific-literary formation of *Volkskunde*. Mary Beth Stein. **German St. R.** XXIV:3 10:2001 pp.487-512.

150 The work and archives of Chokan Valikhanov as a source of information about the trade and prices in east Turkestan and adjacent regions of Central Asia. M. Fedorov. **Cent. Asia. J.** 45:2 2001 pp.230-242.

151 Worldmaking, metaphors and montage in the representation of cultures: cross-cultural filmmaking and the poetics of Robert Gardner's *Forest of Bliss*. Roderick Coover. **Vis. Anthrop.** 14:4 2001 pp.415-438.

B.1:   Anthropology, its scope and its relations to other sciences
             L'anthropologie, son domaine et ses rapports avec les autres sciences

152   Academic folklore research in Canada: trends and prospects (part 1). Gerald L. Pocius.
        Ethnologies 22:2 2000 pp.255-280.
153   Academic folklore research in Canada: trends and prospects (part 2); *[Summary in
        French]*. Gerald L. Pocius. **Ethnologies** 23:1 2001 pp.289-318.
154   Academic nomadism: the relationship between social anthropology and history of religion.
        Berit Thorbjørnsrud. **Numen** XLVIII:2 2001 pp.204-223.
155   American historical archaeology. Laura Nader; Charles E. Orser, Jr.; Bonnie G. McEwan;
        Adrian Praetzellis; Mary Praetzellis; Paul A. Shackel; Elizabeth M. Scott; Amy L. Young;
        Michael Tuma; Cliff Jenkins. **Am. Anthrop.** 103:3 9:2001 pp.621-704. *Collection of 6
        articles.*
156   Anthropological knowledge and scientific fact. John Edward Terrell. **Am. Anthrop.** 102:4
        12:2000 pp.808-817.
157   Anthropologie sans frontières. *[In French]*; [Anthropology without borders]. Albert
        Doutreloux. **Recher. Sociolog.** XXXII:1 2001 pp.7-14.
158   Anthropology and consultancy. Andrew Strathern [Ed.]; Pamela J. Stewart [Ed.]; Marta
        Rohatynskyj; Richard Scaglion; Paige West; John Wagner; Lorenzo Brutti; Martha
        MacIntyre. **Soc. Anal. [Adelaide]** 45(2) 10:2001 pp.3-142. *Collection of 7 articles.*
159   Anthropology in Disneyworld: Rapport, Gardner and the 'discipline' of anthropology.
        Declan Quigley. **Aus. J. Anth.** 12:2 8:2001 pp.182-189.
160   Anthropology in France. Susan Carol Rogers. **Ann. R. Anthr.** 30 2001 pp.481-504.
161   Antropologia codzienności. *[In Polish]*; (Anthropology of everyday life.) *[Summary]*.
        Roch Sulima. Krakow: Wydawnictwo Uniwersytetu Jagiellońskiego, 2000. 194p. *ISBN:
        8323313393.*
162   Antropológia, história, archeológia. *[In Slovak]*; (Anthropology, history and archaeology.)
        Martin Kanovský. **Slov. Národop.** 48:2 2000 pp.206-210.
163   Antropološki vidik slovstvene folklore. *[In Slovene]*; (An anthropological view of literary
        folklore.) *[Summary]*. Marija Stanonik. **Bull. Slov. Ethno. Soc.** 41:1-2 2001 pp.121-133.
164   Archaeology, anthropology and subsistence; *[Summary in French]*. Mark Pluciennik. **J.
        Royal Anth. Inst.** 7:4 12:2001 pp.741-758.
165   Bugs in the system: insects, agricultural science, and professional aspirations in Britain,
        1890-1920. J.F.M. Clark. **Agr. Hist.** 75:1 Winter:2001 pp.83-116.
166   Bulgarie: voix d'hier, paroles d'aujourd'hui. *[In French]*, [Bulgaria: a voice from the past
        and present]. Stefana Stoykova; Stoyanka Boyadzhieva; Anna Ilieva; Anna Shtarbanova;
        Dimitrina Kaufman; Nikolai Kaufman; Ivanichka Georgieva; Elka Bakalova; Mila
        Santova; Iveta Todorova-Pirgova; Doroteya Dobreva; Petar Petrov; Haralan Aleksandrov;
        Ivaylo Ditchev; Frédéric Saumade. **Ethn. Fr.** XXXI:2 4-6:2001 pp.199-336. *Collection of
        13 articles.*
167   Comparison: some suggestions for improving the inevitable. Benson Saler. **Numen**
        XLVIII:3 2001 pp.267-275.
168   (Constructing belief: the actuality of the sociology of religion.); *[Text in Japanese]*. Eiichi
        Otani; Toshinori Kawamata; Hiroo Kikuchi. Tanashi: Harvest-sha, 2000. 185p.
169   Un dilemme: micro ou macro-anthropologie? *[In French]*; [A dilemma: micro- or macro-
        anthropology?] Charles-Henry Pradelles de Latour. **Homme** 158-159 4-9:2001 pp.377-
        382.
170   The emergence of social cognitive neuroscience. Kevin N. Ochsner; Matthew D.
        Lieberman. **Am. Psychol.** 56:9 9:2001 pp.717-734.

171   Estéticas e políticas do folclore. *[In Portuguese]*; (The aesthetics and politics of folklore.) *[Summary]*; *[Summary in French]*. João Vasconcelos. **Anál. Soc.** XXXVI:158-159 Spring-Summer:2001 pp.399-434.

172   Ethnographie et économétrie: pour une coopération empirique. *[In French]*; (Ethnography and econometrics: in favour of empirical cooperation.) *[Summary]*. Agnès Gramain; Florence Weber. **Genèses** 44 9:2001 pp.127-144.

173   Etnonatsional'naia refleksiia i predmet etnologii (k probleme samosoznaniia nauki). *[In Russian]*; (Ethnonational reflexion versus the object of ethnology (on the notions and terminology of science).) *[Summary]*. V.V. Karlov. **Etnograf. Oboz.** 4 7-8:2000 pp.3-21.

174   Fashion research and its discontents. Efrat Tseëlon. **Fash. Theory** 5:4 12:2001 pp.435-452.

175   French anthropology and material culture. Laurence Faure-Rouesnel. **J. Mat. Cult.** 6:2 7:2001 pp.237-247.

176   Freud in the field. Beatrice B. Whiting. **Ethos** 29:3 9:2001 pp.247-258.

177   Global 'disjuncture' and the 'sites' of anthropology. Peter Metcalf. **Cult. Anthro.** 16:2 5:2001 pp.165-182.

178   The globalization of archaeology and heritage: a discussion with Arjun Appadurai. Arjun Appadurai; Ashish Chadha [Discussant]; Ian Hodder [Discussant]; Trinity Jackman [Discussant]; Chris Witmore [Discussant]. **J. Soc. Arch.** 1:1 6:2001 pp.35-49.

179   Globalizatsiia etnologii na poroge novogo tysiacheletiia. *[In Russian]*; (Globalization of ethnology on the eve of the new millennium.) *[Summary]*. N.A. Dubova. **Etnograf. Oboz.** 1 1-2:2000 pp.19-38.

180   Hinsides postmodernismen — hen imod en kritisk engageret antropologi. *[In Danish]*; [Beyond postmodernism - towards a critically engaged anthropology]. Christian Groes-Green. **Tids. Antrop.** 42 2000 pp.105-108.

181   In memoriam: Nelly Naumann. Maria-Verena Blümmel; Klaus Antoni. **Asian Folk. S.** LX:1 2001 pp.135-148.

182   In pursuit of anthropology. Mariza G.S. Peirano. **Ind. Soc. Sci. R.** 1:1 1-6:1999 pp.153-179.

183   International AIDS research in anthropology: taking a critical perspective on the crisis. Brooke G. Schoepf. **Ann. R. Anthr.** 30 2001 pp.335-362.

184   Introduction: an overview of Philippine studies. Gerard A. Persoon. **Bijdragen** 157:3 2001 pp.451-470.

185   Jaina studies in Japan. Atsushi Uno. **Jain J.** XXXV:4 4:2001 pp.173-178.

186   Ken Wilber's spectrum model: identifying alternative soteriological perspectives. Leon Schlamm. **Religion** 31:1 1:2001 pp.19-39.

187   Means and meanings: methodological issues in Africanist interdisciplinary research. Ato Quayson. **Hist. Afr.** 25 1998 pp.307-318.

188   Med tradicijo in inovacijo ali položaj folkloristike v sodobni znanosti. *[In Slovene]*; (The state of folklore studies in modern science.) *[Summary]*. Marjetka Golež Kaučič. **Bull. Slov. Ethno. Soc.** 41:1-2 2001 pp.116-120.

189   Moving from indigenization toward globalization. Xu Jieshun; Fei Xiaotong; Weng Naiqun; Zhou Daming; Naran Bilik; Rong Guanqiong. **Chin. Soc. Anth.** 33:1 Fall:2000 pp.6-72. *Collection of 6 articles.*

190   Nativizing Chinese anthropology: take two. Gregory Eliyu Guldin; Zhou Daming; Huang Shuping; Zhang Dunfu; Fan Ke; Gao Chong; Zou Jing; Naran Bilik; Wang Jianmin; Ma Guoqing. **Chin. Soc. Anth.** 33:4 Summer:2001 pp.3-98. *Collection of 8 articles.*

191   Opyt polevykh issledovanii islama na Severo-Zapadnom Kavkaze. *[In Russian]*; (Experience of Islamic field studies in the north-west Caucasus.) A.A. Iaarlykapov. **Etnograf. Oboz.** 3 5-6:2001 pp.132-135.

192   Organic purity and the role of anthropology in Cambodia and Rwanda. Scott Straus. **Patt. Prej.** 35:2 4:2001 pp.47-62.

193   A perspective on anthropology. Walter Goldschmidt. **Am. Anthrop.** 102:4 12:2000 pp.789-807.

194   Povratnik s terena: konceptualni ideal i izvedbene mogućnosti dijaloga u etnografskom tekstu. *[In Croatian]*; (Returnee from the field: the conceptual ideal and the operative

possibilities of dialogue in an ethnographic paper.) *[Summary]*. Ines Prica. **Nar. Umjetn.** 37:2 2000 pp.47-66.

195 Probleme und Grenzen der Anwendung psychoanalytischer Begriffe in der Religionswissenschaft. *[In German]*; [Problems with and limits to the use of psychoanalytical concepts in religious studies]. Hartmut Zinser. **Paideuma** 46 2000 pp.189-206.

196 Reflexivity and critique in discourse analysis. Mary Bucholtz. **Crit. Anthr.** 21:2 6:2001 pp.165-184.

197 Refolucija Slovenske etnologije in kulturne antropologije. *[In Slovene]*; [The revolution in Slovene ethnology and cultural anthropology] *[Summary]*. Borut Brumen. **Bull. Slov. Ethno. Soc.** 41:1-2 2001 pp.8-16.

198 A remembrance of kinship studies past: a call for their rebirth. Susan Bedford. **Hist. Anthrop.** 12:4 2001 pp.315-341.

199 Rire d'ethnologues. *[In French]*; [Laughing at ethnologists]. Wiktor Stoczkowski. **Homme** 160 10-12:2001 pp.91-114.

200 Rossiiskoe etnograficheskoe sibirevedenie v XX v. *[In Russian]*; (Russian ethnographic Siberian studies of the 20th century.) *[Summary]*. N.A. Tomilov. **Etnograf. Oboz.** 3 5-6:2001 pp.92-100.

201 Secret spaces, forbidden places: rethinking culture. Fran Lloyd [Ed.]; Catherine O'Brien [Ed.]. New York: Berghahn Books, 2000. xxii, 298p. *ISBN: 1571817891, 1571817883. Includes bibliographical references (p. [227]-283) and index. (Series: Polygons - v. 4).*

202 Seminar «Perspektivy etnograficheskogo izucheniia islama v Srednei Azii i sopredel'nikh regionakh». *[In Russian]*; (Seminar on 'The prospects of ethnographic studies in the Islam of Central Asia and adjoining areas'.) S.N. Abashin; V.I. Bushkov. **Etnograf. Oboz.** 3 5-6:2001 pp.123-124.

203 Settings, interactions and things: a plea for multi-integrative ethnography. Florence Weber. **Ethnog.** 2:4 12:2001 pp.475-500.

204 Slovenska etnologija in Marksizem: v vrtincu stoterih možnosti. *[In Slovene]*; [Slovene ethnology and Marxism: the development of Slovene ethnological thought and contemporary attitudes in the field] *[Summary]*. Rajko Muršič. **Bull. Slov. Ethno. Soc.** 41:1-2 2001 pp.19-26.

205 Small places, large issues: an introduction to social and cultural anthropology. Thomas Hylland Eriksen. London: Pluto Press, 2001. 336p. *ISBN: 0745317723, 0745317731.* (*Series:* Anthropology, culture and society).

206 Studies of traditional Chinese poetry in the U.S., 1962-1996 (part II). William H. Nienhauser, Jr. **Chin. Cult.** XL:2 6:1999 pp.45-72.

207 Temporal'naia antropologiia: novoe napravlenie issledovanii ili sostavnaia chast' istoricheskoi psikhologii. *[In Russian]*; (Temporal anthropology: a new branch of investigations, or a component of historical psychology.) V.K. Karnaukh. **Vest. Lenin. Univ. 6** 4(30) 12:2000 pp.24-30.

208 Theology comes home: the role of theology in the academic study of religion and the role of theology of Judaism in the academic study of Judaism. Jacob Neusner. **Religion** 31:1 1:2001 pp.1-18.

209 Universals, general terms and the comparative study of religion. Jeppe Sinding Jensen. **Numen** XLVIII:3 2001 pp.238-266.

210 Universals revisited: human behaviors and cultural variations. William Paden. **Numen** XLVIII:3 2001 pp.276-289.

211 VII Mezhdunarodnyi seminar «Integratsiia arkheologicheskikh i etnograficheskikh issledovanii». *[In Russian]*; (The 7th international seminar: 'Integration of Archaeological and Ethnographic Studies'.) M.L. Bereznhova; S.N. Korusenko; N.A. Tomilov. **Etnograf. Oboz.** 1 1-2:2001 pp.149-153.

212 Virtual society? Get real! Abstraction and decontextualisation: an anthropological comment or: e for ethnography. Marilyn Strathern. **Cam. Anthrop.** 22:1 2000-2001 pp.52-66.

213 When: a conversation about culture. Robert Borofsky; Fredrik Barth; Richard A. Shweder; Lars Rodseth; Nomi Maya Stolzenberg. **Am. Anthrop.** 103:2 6:2001 pp.432-446.

B.2: **Anthropological theory**
Théorie anthropologique

214 Acquis, problèmes et perspectives dans l'étude des sources ethnohistoriques de l'ancien Mexique. *[In French]*; [Acquisitions, problems and perspectives in the study of ethnohistorical sources from ancient Mexico]. Jacqueline de Durand-Forest; Michael W. Swanton; Monique Cohen; Henry B. Nicholson; Marc Thouvenot; Susan Spitler; Eloise Quiñones Keber; Patrick Lesbre; Maarten Jansen; Martine Simonin; José Rubén Romero Galván; Elke Ruhnau; Berthold Riese; Ethelia Ruiz Medrano; Perla Valle; Stephanie Wood. **J. Soc. Amér.** 84:2 1998 pp.9-276. *Collection of 14 articles.*

215 Anthropological perspectives on alcohol and drugs at the turn of the new millennium. Mac Marshall; Genevieve M. Ames; Linda A. Bennett; Geoffrey Hunt; Judith C. Barker; Robin Room; Merrill Singer; Lee Strunin; Paul Spicer; David N. Suggs; Christine Eber. **Soc. Sci. Med.** 53:2 7:2001 pp.153-262. *Collection of 8 articles.*

216 Anthropology and modernity. Joel S. Kahn. **Curr. Anthr.** 42:5 12:2001 pp.651-680.

217 Anthropology in Disneyworld: Rapport, Gardner and the 'discipline' of anthropology. Declan Quigley. **Aus. J. Anth.** 12:2 8:2001 pp.182-189.

218 An anthropology of Marxism. Cedric J. Robinson. Aldershot: Ashgate, 2001. xxii, 169p. *ISBN: 1840147008. Includes bibliographical references and index. (Series:* Race and representation).

219 Anthropology! Distinguished lecture — 2000. Laura Nader. **Am. Anthrop.** 103:3 9:2001 pp.609-620.

220 The assessment of the analytic group treatment efficiency according to Yalom's classification; *[Summary in Croatian]*. M. Vlastelica; I. Urlić; S. Pavlović. **Coll. Antrop.** 25:1 6:2001 pp.227-238.

221 L'attitude prospective en anthropologie le point de vue d'une anthropologie clinique d'inspiration psychanalytique. *[In French]*; (The prospective attitude in anthropology as seen from the angle of a psychoanalytically-oriented clinical anthropology.) Robert Steichen. **Recher. Sociolog.** XXXII:1 2001 pp.55-75.

222 Being lost at sea: ontology, epistemology and a whale hunt. Anita Lundberg. **Ethnog.** 2:4 12:2001 pp.533-558.

223 Categories and classifications: Maussian reflections on the social. N.J. Allen. New York, Oxford: Berghahn Books, 2000. 165p. *ISBN: 1571818243, 1571818081. Includes bibliographical references and index. (Series:* Methodology and history in anthropology - 8).

224 Causal thinking and its anthropological misrepresentation. Pascal Boyer. **Philos. S. Sc.** 22:2 6:1992 pp.187-213.

225 Clearing a path: theorizing the past in Native American studies. Nancy Shoemaker [Ed.]. London: Routledge, 2001. 215p. *ISBN: 0415926750, 0415926742.*

226 Comparative religion, taxonomies and 19th century philosophies of science: Chantepie de la Saussaye and Tiele. Thomas Ryba. **Numen** XLVIII:3 2001 pp.309-338.

227 Comparativism and sociobiological theory. Luther H. Martin. **Numen** XLVIII:3 2001 pp.290-308.

228 Conceptualizing/re-conceptualizing Africa. Maghan Keita; Lamont DeHaven King; Jesse Benjamin; Jeremy Prestholdt; Thomas Ricks; Robert Launay; Richard J. Payne; Cassandra R. Veney. **J. As. Afr. S.** XXXVI:4 2001 pp.331-450. *Collection of 7 articles.*

229 Le conte et la théorie. *[In French]*; [The theory of storytelling]. Harold Neemann. **Fabula** 42:3-4 2001 pp.297-303.

230 Context is/as critique. Jan Blommaert. **Crit. Anthr.** 21:1 3:2001 pp.13-32.

231 Contextualizing and decontextualizing African historical photographs. Carolyn Keyes Adenaike. **Hist. Afr.** 23 1996 pp.429-438.

232 De l'épaississement empirique à l'interpellation interprétative en passant par l'ampliation analogique: une méthode pour l'anthropologie prospective. *[In French]*; [From the empirical depths to questions of interpretation via analogical expansion: long-term anthropological methods]. Mike Singleton. **Recher. Sociolog.** XXXII:1 2001 pp.15-40.

233 Den magiske illusion? En kognitiv tilgang til magiske ritualer. *[In Danish]*; (The magic illusion: a cognitive approach to magic rituals.) *[Summary]*. Jesper Sørensen. **Tids. Antrop.** 41 2000 pp.65-82.

234 Deromanticizing subalterns or recolonializing anthropology? Denial of indigenous agency and reproduction of northern hegemony in the work of David Stoll. John Gledhill. **Identities** 8:1 3:2001 pp.135-161.

235 Discourse and critique: part two. Monica Heller; James Collins; Mary Bucholtz; Sari Wastell. **Crit. Anthr.** 21:2 6:2001 pp.117-210. *Collection of 4 articles.*

236 Ethnographic critique and techno-scientific narratives: the old mole, ethical plateaux, and the governance of emergent biosocial polities. Michael M.J. Fischer. **Cult. Medic. Psych.** 25:4 12:2001 pp.355-393.

237 Ethnographic encounters. Positioning within and outside the insider frame; *[Summary in French]*. Narmala Halstead. **Soc. Anthrop.** 9:3 10:2001 pp.307-324.

238 Ethnohistoire ou anthropologie prospective? Quelques balises pour sortir d'un tunnel épistémologique. *[In French]*; (Ethnohistory or prospective anthropology? A few markers on the way out of the epistemological tunnel.) Alain Reyniers; Olivier Servais. **Recher. Sociolog.** XXXII:1 2001 pp.41-54.

239 Etnografia dei confini: dilemma clinico e polisemia. *[In Italian]*; (Bounded places and ethnography: facing clinical dilemma and polyphony.); *[Summary]*. Gianmarco Navarini. **Rass. It. Soc.** XLII:2 4-6:2001 pp.283-308.

240 Etnografia dei mondi contemporanei. Limiti e potenzialità del metodo etnografico nell'analisi della complessità. *[In Italian]*; [Ethnographies for the contemporary world. Limitations and potential of ethnography in the study of complexity]; *[Summary]*. Enzo Colombo. **Rass. It. Soc.** XLII:2 4-6:2001 pp.205-230.

241 Etnografia e riflessività. Le pratiche riflessive costrette nei binari del discorso scientifico. *[In Italian]*; [Ethnography and reflexivity]; *[Summary]*. Mario Cardano. **Rass. It. Soc.** XLII:2 4-6:2001 pp.173-204.

242 L'etnografo allo specchio: racconti dal campo e forme di riflessività. *[In Italian]*; (The ethnographer at the mirror: tales from the field and forms of reflexivity.); *[Summary]*. Marco Marzano. **Rass. It. Soc.** XLII:2 4-6:2001 pp.257-282.

243 Etnonatsional'naia refleksiia i predmet etnologii (k probleme samosoznaniia nauki). *[In Russian]*; (Ethnonational reflexion versus the object of ethnology (on the notions and terminology of science).) *[Summary]*. V.V. Karlov. **Etnograf. Oboz.** 4 7-8:2000 pp.3-21.

244 The fate of 'culture': Geertz and beyond. Sherry B. Ortner [Ed.]. Berkeley CA, London: University of California Press, 1999. vii, 169p. *ISBN: 0520216016, 0520216008. Includes bibliographical references and index.* (*Series:* Representations books - 8).

245 Feminist theory, embodiment, and the docile agent: some reflections on the Egyptian Islamic revival. Saba Mahmood. **Cult. Anthro.** 16:2 5:2001 pp.202-236.

246 Hanihara's conundrum revisited: theoretical estimates of the immigration into Japan during the 1,000 year period from 300 B.C. to A.D. 700. Kenichi Aoki; Shripad Tuljapurkar. **Anth. Sci.** 108:4 10:2000 pp.305-320.

247 Inequality. Charles Tilly; Keith Hart; Caroline Humphrey; Katherine Verdery. **Anth. Th.** 1:3 9:2001 pp.299-392. *Collection of 5 articles.*

248 Language and agency. Laura M. Ahearn. **Ann. R. Anthr.** 30 2001 pp.109-137.

249 Lecture notes toward a theory of applied anthropology. Walter Goldschmidt. **Human. Org.** 60:4 Winter:2001 pp.423-429.

250 Linguistics and post-modernism. F. Manjali. **Int. J. Drav. Ling.** XXX:1 1:2001 pp.59-68.

251 Local histories and global theories in Colombian Pacific coast archaeology. David M. Stemper; Héctor Salgado López. **Antiquity** 69:263 6:1995 pp.248-269.

252 A look at the acts of identity theory through a social network analysis of Portuguese-based Creoles in West Africa. Steve Graham. **J. Pid. Creo. Lang.** 16:1 2001 pp.1-51.

253   The materiality of diaspora. Pnina Werbner; Karen Leonard; Bennetta Jules-Rosette; Sally Howell; Henry Goldschmidt; Khachig Tölölyan; André Levy. **Diaspora** 9:1 Spring:2000 pp.5-158. *Collection of 7 articles.*

254   Native Pacific cultural studies on the edge. Margaret Jolly; Geoffrey M. White; Ty Kāwika Tengan; Jonathan Kamakawiwo'ole Osorio; Teresia K. Teaiwa; Vicente M. Diaz; J. Kēhaulani Kauanui; James Clifford; David Welchman Gegeo; Karin von Strokirch; David A. Chappell; John Moffat Fugui; Anita Jowitt; Sandra Tarte. **Cont. Pac.** 13:2 Fall:2001 pp.315-563. *Collection of 9 articles.*

255   Negations and ambiguities in the cultures of organization. Allen W. Batteau. **Am. Anthrop.** 102:4 12:2000 pp.726-740.

256   „Nowa antropologia" wobec dawniejszch koncepcji religii i magii. *[In Polish]*; ('New anthropology' in relation to former concepts of religion and magic.) Adam Szafrański. Krakow: Nomos, 2000. 126p. *ISBN: 8385527990.*

257   Obraz osobliwy - hermeneutyczna lektura źródeł etnograficznych. Wielkie opowieści. *[In Polish]*; [A peculiar image - hermeneutic readings of ethnographic sources: large narratives]. Joanna Tokarska-Bakir. Krakow: Universitas, 2000. 412p. *ISBN: 8370527736.*

258   On archaeological praxis, gender bias and indigenous peoples in South America. Gustavo Politis. **J. Soc. Arch.** 1:1 6:2001 pp.90-107.

259   On going native: Thomas Kuhn and anthropological method. John Tresch. **Philos. S. Sc.** 31:3 9:2001 pp.302-322.

260   On the concept of axial space: orientalism and the originary. Bryan S. Turner. **J. Soc. Arch.** 1:1 6:2001 pp.62-74.

261   Penser la connaissance de sens commun dans la modernité avancée. *[In French]*; [Common sense knowledge theory in advanced societies] *[Summary]*. Geneviève Daudelin. **Can. R. Soc. A.** 38:3 8:2001 pp.293-308.

262   Penser le temps culturel du droit. Le destin anthropologique du concept de coutume. *[In French]*; (Thinking the cultural time of law: the anthropological destiny of the concept of custom.) *[Summary]*. Louis Assier-Andrieu. **Homme** 160 10-12:2001 pp.67-90.

263   Philosophical aspects of the 'AAA Statement on 'Race". Naomi Zack; Lee D. Baker [Comments by]. **Anth. Th.** 1:4 12:2001 pp.445-472.

264   Postbook: working the ruins of feminist ethnography. Patti Lather. **Signs** 27:1 Autumn:2001 pp.199-227.

265   Pour une socio-anthropologie urbaine... prospective. *[In French]*; (Towards a prospective urban socioanthropology.) Bernard Francq; Xavier Leloup; Margarita Becerra; F. Bodeux; E. Goovaerts; J. Pierart. **Recher. Sociolog.** XXXII:1 2001 pp.77-85.

266   Predicaments of criticism. Jef Verschueren. **Crit. Anthr.** 21:1 3:2001 pp.59-82.

267   Preemstvennost' i preobrazovanie v istoricheskom razvitii etnosa. *[In Russian]*; (Continuity and change in the historical development of ethnos. List of major works of L.P. Lashuk.) *[Summary]*. L.P. Lashuk. **Etnograf. Oboz.** 3 5-6:2001 pp.20-31.

268   Presuming scale, making diversity: on the mischiefs of measurement and the global: local metonym in theories of law and culture. Sari Wastell. **Crit. Anthr.** 21:2 6:2001 pp.185-210.

269   The question of cultural difference: anthropological perspectives in South Africa; *[Summary in Afrikaans]*. John Sharp. **S. Afr. J. Ethnol.** 24:3 2001 pp.67-74.

270   Right and Left as political categories. An exercise in 'not-so-primitive' classification. H.F. Bienfait; W.E.A. van Beek. **Anthropos [St. Augustin]** 96:1 2001 pp.169-178.

271   Ritual communication and linguistic ideology: a reading and partial reformulation of Rappaport's theory of ritual. Joel Robbins. **Curr. Anthr.** 42:5 12:2001 pp.591-614.

272   Schefflers Lösung. Brauchbarkeitsanalyse eines Deszendenzbegriffs. *[In German]*; [Scheffler's solution: analysis of the usefulness of a concept of evolution]. Hartmut Lang. **Anthropos [St. Augustin]** 95:2 2000 pp.558-563.

273   Science and/or art: aerial photographs in archaeological discourse. Włodzimierz Rączkowski. **Archaeol. Polona** 39 2001 pp.127-146.

274   Science, theory and archaeology in Britain: a minimalist view of the debate. Peter Rowley-Conwy. **Archaeol. Polona** 39 2001 pp.17-36.

275   Secularism: personal values and professional evaluations. Charles Stewart; João De Pina-Cabral; Lale Yalçin-Heckmann; David N. Gellner; Bruce Kapferer. **Soc. Anthrop.** 9:3 10:2001 pp.325-344. *Collection of 5 articles.*

276   Social aspects of abstraction; *[Summary in French]*. James G. Carrier. **Soc. Anthrop.** 9:3 10:2001 pp.243-256.

277   La spiona, il parassita, l'ortodosso. Tre racconti di osservazione partecipante. *[In Italian]*; (The spy, the parasite and the orthodox.); *[Summary]*. Luca Bobbio; Giovanna Resta; Lorenzo Venturini. **Rass. It. Soc.** XLII:2 4-6:2001 pp.309-322.

278   Thinking temporally or modernizing anthropology. Donald L. Donham; John L. Comaroff [Comments by]; Jean Comaroff [Comments by]. **Am. Anthrop.** 103:1 3:2001 pp.134-160.

279   Using phylogenetically based comparative methods in anthropology: more questions than answers. Monique Borgerhoff Mulder. **Evolut. Anthrop.** 10:3 2001 pp.99-111.

280   Woman, sexual difference and the dance of undecidability in Nietzsche's *Thus Spoke Zarathustra*. Iva Popovicova. **Dialect. Anthrop.** 25:3-4 2000 pp.281-295.

B.3:   **Methods and techniques**
        Méthodes et techniques

281   Anthropologische Implikationen der Hermeneutik und die Frage nach dem 'radikal Fremden' im Kontext der Ethnologie. *[In German]*; [Anthropological implications of hermeneutics and the question of the 'radical foreigner' in the context of ethnology]. Heike Kämpf. **Paideuma** 46 2000 pp.149-160.

282   A case in case study methodology. Christine Benedichte Meyer. **Fie. Meth.** 13:4 11:2001 pp.329-352.

283   Chislennost' kochevogo sotsiuma: istochniki i sposoby podcheta. *[In Russian]*; (Nomad populations: sources and methods of their counting.) *[Summary]*. V.V. Trepavlov. **Etnograf. Oboz.** 4 7-8:2000 pp.95-101.

284   Classifying the material food, textiles and status in North Vanuatu. Lissant Bolton. **J. Mat. Cult.** 6:3 11:2001 pp.251-268.

285   Community-based survey on female genital excision in Faranah district, Guinea; *[Summary in Spanish]*; *[Summary in French]*. Daman Keita; David Blankhart. **Reprod. Health Mat.** 9:18 11:2001 pp.135-142.

286   Comparing two methods for estimating network size. Christopher McCarty; Peter D. Killworth; H. Russell Bernard; Eugene C. Johnsen; Gene A. Shelley. **Human. Org.** 60:1 Spring:2001 pp.28-39.

287   The consensus group technique in social research. Dennis List. **Fie. Meth.** 13:3 8:2001 pp.277-290.

288   Le Crédit rural de Guinée vu par les acteurs: l'étude socio-anthropologique comme outil institutionnel. *[In French]*; [Rural credit in Guinea as seen by the actors: the social anthropological study as institutional tool]. Kefing Condé; Stéphane Bouju; Dominique Gentil. Paris: GRET, 2001. 95p. *ISBN: 2868441157. Crédit rural de Guinée. Institut de recherches et d'applications des méthodes et développement rural.*

289   Description of structure of the folktale: using a bioinformatics multiple alignment program. Jun'ichi Oda. **Senri Ethn. Stud.** 55 2001 pp.153-174.

290   Discomfort, discord and discontinuity as data: using focus groups to research sensitive topics. Kaye Wellings; Patrick Branigan; Kirsti Mitchell. **Cult. Health. Sex.** 2:3 7-9:2000 pp.255-267.

291   Doing fieldwork. Wilbur Zelinsky; John B. Wright; Cathy Whitlock; Bret Wallach; Gregory Veeck; Yi-Fu Tuan; Karen E. Till; Richard Symanski; Stan Stevens; Paul F. Starrs; Carlin F. Starrs; Genoa I. Starrs; Lynn Huntsinger; Ralph H. Saunders; Yamuna Sangarasivam; Christopher L. Salter; Paul Routledge; Karl B. Raitz; Lydia Mihelic Pulsipher; Marie D. Price; Eric P. Perramond; Hester Parr; Kathleen C. Parker; Bernard Q. Nietschmann; Heidi J. Nast; Garth Andrew Myers; Linda McDowell; Kent Mathewson; Julie Matheson; Ben Marsh; W. George Lovell; Thomas D. Jones; Jennifer Hyndman;

André Humbert; Joseph J. Hobbs; Melinda Herrold; Steve Herbert; Maureen Hays-Mitchell; John Fraser Hart; Cole Harris; Susan W. Hardwick; Holly M. Hapke; Devan Ayyankeril; Josefina Gómez Mendoza; Peter Goin; Daniel W. Gade; Larry R. Ford; Thomas Eley; Cheryl Northon; James S. Duncan; Nancy G. Duncan; Christine Drennon; Lorraine Dowler; William E. Doolittle; Jerome E. Dobson; Vincent J. Del Casino, Jr.; Diana K. Davis; Lowell Ben Bennion; Jerry Rohde; Daniel D. Arreola; Nigel J.R. Allan; Stuart C. Aitken. **Geogr. Rev.** 91:1-2 1-4:2001 pp.1-508. *Collection of 57 articles.*

292   Du danger et du terrain en Algérie. *[In French]*; (Danger and fieldwork in Algeria.) *[Summary]*; *[Summary in German]*. Abderrahmane Moussaoui. **Ethn. Fr.** XXXI:1 1-3:2001 pp.51-59.

293   The ethnographer's eye: ways of seeing in anthropology. Anna Grimshaw. Cambridge, New York: Cambridge University Press, 2001. xiii, 222p. *ISBN: 0521774756, 0521773105. Includes bibliographical references (p. 174-212) and index.*

294   Ethnographic mapmaking: part 2 — practical concerns and triangulation. Oswald Werner; Lawrence A. Kuznar. **Fie. Meth.** 13:3 8:2001 pp.291-296.

295   Evaluating five models of human colonization. John H. Moore. **Am. Anthrop.** 103:2 6:2001 pp.395-408.

296   Évaluation anthropométrique d'un échantillon d'étudiants de la province de cunéo. *[In French]*; (Anthropometric evaluation of a student's sample of Cuneo province.) *[Summary]*. S. Galaverna; A. Barello; E. Fubini. **Bio. Hum. Anthrop.** 19:3-4 7-12:2001 pp.235-246.

297   (Experiences of fieldwork.); *[Text in Japanese]*. Hiroaki Yoshii; Atsushi Sakurai. Tokyo: Serika Shobo, 2000. 249p.

298   Grand hypotheses: palaeodemographic modelling in Western Australia's south-west. C.E. Dortch; M.V. Smith. **Archaeol. Ocean.** 36:1 4:2001 pp.34-46.

299   In and out of culture: fieldwork in war-torn Uganda. Sverker Finnström. **Crit. Anthr.** 21:3 9:2001 pp.247-258.

300   In defense of the comparative method. Robert A. Segal. **Numen** XLVIII:3 2001 pp.339-373.

301   Interaction with the environment: anthropological cybernetic model; *[Summary in Croatian]*. J. Bončina; V. Ivković; V. Jovanović. **Coll. Antrop.** 25:2 12:2001 pp.413-424.

302   List task and a cognitive salience index. Urmas Sutrop. **Fie. Meth.** 13:3 8:2001 pp.263-276.

303   Metodologické východiská k etnologickému výskumu Radošinskej doliny. *[In Slovak]*; (Methodological starting-points to ethnological research of Radošina Valley.) *[Summary]*. Jaroslav Čukan. **Slov. Národop.** 48:2 2000 pp.185-194.

304   My best informant's dress: the erotic equation in fieldwork. Esther Newton. **Cult. Anthro.** 8:1 2:1993 pp.3-23.

305   Participatory developmental research: a working model. F.J. Coughlan; K.J. Collins. **Int. Soc. Work** 44:4 10:2001 pp.505-518.

306   Participatory rural appraisal as qualitative research: distinguishing methodological issues from participatory claims. John R. Campbell. **Human. Org.** 60:4 Winter:2001 pp.380-389.

307   Perceptions of relative wealth in a Tibetan community: a note on research methodology. Geoff Childs. **Tibet J.** XXVI:2 Summer:2001 pp.26-38.

308   Perepis' 2002 g.: igry po Vitgenshteinu. *[In Russian]*; (Russian Federation census of 2002: Wittgensteinian language games.) *[Summary]*. S.V. Sokolovskii. **Etnograf. Oboz.** 4 7-8:2000 pp.91-94. *This is a comment on Population censuses: who is to be counted and how? by S.V. Cheshko which appeared in Etnograficheskoe obozrenie 4 7-8:2000 pp. 82-90.*

309   Perepis' naseleniia: kogo schitat' i kak schitat'? *[In Russian]*; (Population censuses: who is to be counted and how?) *[Summary]*. S.V. Cheshko. **Etnograf. Oboz.** 4 7-8:2000 pp.82-90.

310   Propriétés statistiques des indices en anthropologie. *[In French]*; (Statistical properties of the index in anthropology.) *[Summary]*. J.C. Pineau; Y. Deloison; G. Ignazi; E.A. Cabanis. **Bio. Hum. Anthrop.** 19:3-4 7-12:2001 pp.265-274.

311   Rückkehr zur Feldforschung? *[In German]*; [Return to field work?] Irene Albers. **Anthropos [St. Augustin]** 95:2 2000 pp.568-570.

312   'Twixt the cup and the lip:' field notes on the way to print. David Henige. **Hist. Afr.** 25 1998 pp.119-132.

313   Using electronic scanning forms for data entry. Susan C. Weller; Roberta D. Baer. **Fie. Meth.** 13:2 5:2001 pp.198-203.

Collections
Collections

314   African art at the Nelson-Atkins museum of art. Joyce M. Youmans. **Afr. Arts** XXXIII:4 Winter:2000 pp.40-61.

315   African art in the Ethnologisches Museum in Berlin. Paola Ivanov. **Afr. Arts** XXXIII:3 Autumn:2000 pp.18-39.

316   Architekturdekor aus dem Panjab: Die Sammlung des Linden-Museums Stuttgart, III: Baukeramik/Fliesen. *[In German]*; [Architectural decoration from the Punjab: the Linden Museum Stuttgart's collection, III: ceramics and tiles]. Margareta Pavaloi. **Tribus** 50 12:2001 pp.107-134.

317   Archival research in Antananarivo, Madagascar: the national archives. Jeffrey C. Kaufmann. **Hist. Afr.** 24 1997 pp.413-430.

318   The archives of the Consolata Mission and the formation of the Italian Empire, 1913-1943. Alberto Sbacchi. **Hist. Afr.** 25 1998 pp.319-340.

319   Arguing with the KGB archives. Archival and narrative memory in post-Soviet Latvia. Vieda Skultans. **Ethnos** 66:3 2001 pp.320-343.

320   Arkhetip 'arkhiva': razmyshleniia o novom tipe uchrezhdeniia i ego aktual'nykh problemaka. *[In Russian]*; [The archetype of 'archives': reflections on a new type of institution and its current problems]. E. Schmidt. **Suomal.-Ugril. Seur. Aikak.** 89 2001 pp.267-280.

321   Ayyubid and Mamluk coins preserved in the Oriental Institute of the University of Chicago. Warren C. Schultz. **J. Near East.** 60:4 10:2001 pp.269-274.

322   Bronzekessel aus der Sammlung des Linden-Museums Stuttgart. *[In German]*; [A bronze pot in the Linden Museum collection in Stuttgart]. Jangar Ilyasov; Margareta Pavaloi. **Tribus** 50 12:2001 pp.91-100.

323   Cabo Verde - do século XV ao fim do segundo milénio: permanências e rupturas numa sociedade em transformação. *[In Portuguese]*; [Cape Verde - from the 15th century to the end of the second millennium: permanence and change in a society in transformation]. Ilídio Do Amaral; Maria Emília Madeira Santos; Iva Cabral; Maria Manuel Ferraz Torrão; Maria João Soares; Zelinda Cohen; Raquel Monteiro; Maria Teresa De Oliveira Ramos; Carla Teixeira E. Cruz; Gonçalves Guimarães; Cecília Matias; Margarida Tavares Da Conceição; Anouk Faria Da Costa; José Maria Lobo de Carvalho; Teresa De Deus Ferreira; Adriano Vasco Rodrigues; José Silva Évora; Paulo Frederico Ferreira Gonçalves; Cláudia Correia; Abel Dos Santos Cruz; Isabel L. Morgado De S.E. Silva; Octávio Do Nascimento; António Germano Lima; Salvador Magalhães Mota; Fernanda Paula Sousa Maia; João Lopes Filho. **Africana** 6 2001 pp.13-324. *Collection of 19 articles.*

324   A catalogue as a research tool: the Arabic MSS from the Yahuda collection at the JNUL. Camilla Adang. **Is. Orient. Stud.** XIX 1999 pp.495-499.

325   The catalogues of the Pitt-Rivers Museum, Farnham, Dorset. Michael Thompson; Colin Renfrew. **Antiquity** 73:280 6:1999 pp.377-393.

326   Collectes et collections ethnologiques: une histoire d'hommes et d'institutions. *[In French]*; [Collectors of ethnography and ethnographic collections: a history of men and institutions]. J. Rivallain; F. Coulon; X. Cadet; E. Patole-Edoumba; E. Desramaut; C. Mériot; F. Angleviel; B. Dupaigne; M. Lobligeois; M. Gessain; A.A. Dembélé; G. Rassinier; M. Balard; E. Maestri; E. Rieth; C.H. Perrot; J. Tubiana; P. Mongne; P. Riviale;

Laurent Dartigues; Christopher Goscha; Sylvie Ducas; Bertrand Jalla; Tramor Quemeneur. **Rev. Fr. Hist. O.mer.** 2(332-333) 2001 pp.5-427. *Collection of 23 articles.*

327   The collecting passion in America. Paula Rubel; Abraham Rosman. **Z. Ethn.** 126:2 2001 pp.313-330.

328   Les collections d'insulinde du musée de l'homme inventaire sommaire d'un trésor méconnu (1ère partie). *[In French]*; [Collections from ethnographic museums]. Christian Pelras. **Archipel** 62 2001 pp.163-208.

329   Colonialism and knowledge in Algeria: the archives of the Arab Bureau. Abdelmajid Hannoum. **Hist. Anthrop.** 12:4 2001 pp.343-379.

330   The comparative study of collection and representation. Tadao Umesao. **Senri Ethn. Stud.** 54 2001 pp.1-14.

331   The composition of the Siebold collection in the National Museum of Ethnology in Leiden. Ken Vos. **Senri Ethn. Stud.** 54 2001 pp.39-50.

332   Cuneiform texts in the Archaeological Museum of Strasbourg. János Everling. **Arch. Orient.** 68:4 11:2000 pp.587-600.

333   Descent from privilege: a researcher's memoir of the national archives of Zimbabwe, 1984-1993. Leslie Bessant. **Hist. Afr.** 24 1997 pp.401-408.

334   Drohbriefe der Karo-Batak. *[In German]*; [Threatening letters of the Karo Batak]. Uli Kozok. **Tribus** 50 12:2001 pp.101-106.

335   Dust to dust: a user's guide to local archives in Mali. Gregory Mann. **Hist. Afr.** 26 1999 pp.453-456.

336   Fon brass genre figures in Náprstek's Museum in Prague. Jana Jiroušková; Lucie Loosová. **Arch. Orient.** 68:1 2:2000 pp.1-10.

337   From 'collection royale' to 'collection publique': the formation of the Louvre. Yoshiaki Nishino. **Senri Ethn. Stud.** 54 2001 pp.51-66.

338   From weapon to work of art: 'sword hunts' in modern Japan. Naoyuki Kinoshita. **Senri Ethn. Stud.** 54 2001 pp.119-136.

339   Guide to African archives in Belgium. Hugues Legros; Curtis A. Keim. **Hist. Afr.** 23 1996 pp.401-410.

340   Guide to the Asian Collections at the International Institute of Social History. Emile Schwidder [Ed.]; Eef Vermeij [Ed.]. Amsterdam: Stichting beheer IISG, 2001. 184p. *ISBN: 9068612131. Includes index.*

341   Human skeletal remains in the University of San Carlos Museum. Aloysius Ma.L. Cañete; Wenda R. Trevathan. **Phil. Q. Cult. Soc.** 28:4 12:2000 pp.512-527.

342   Illicit antiquities and international litigation — the Turkish experience. Janet Blake. **Antiquity** 72:278 12:1998 pp.824-830.

343   An inscribed ossuary from a private collection. Tal Ilan. **Israel Explor. J.** 51:1 2001 pp.92-95.

344   Inscripciones árabes inéditas en el museo provincial de Almería. *[In Spanish]*; [Unedited Arabic inscriptions in the Almeria museum]. Jorge Lirola Delgado. **Al-Qantara** XXI:1 2000 pp.97-142.

345   Istoriia Muzeia narodov SSSR v Moskve. *[In Russian]*; (History of the Moscow Museum of Peoples of the USSR.) *[Summary]*. A.B. Ippolitova. **Etnograf. Oboz.** 2 3-4:2001 pp.144-160.

346   Izbiranje, zbiranje in interpretiranje. *[In Slovene]*; [Selecting, collecting and interpreting: criteria and strategies for collecting material culture and its ethnological interpretation] *[Summary]*. Irena Keršič; Bojana Rogelj Škafar; Polona Sketelj; Janja Žagar. **Bull. Slov. Ethno. Soc.** 41:1-2 2001 pp.88-92.

347   Japan at the exhibition, 1867-1877: from representation to practice. Angus Lockyer. **Senri Ethn. Stud.** 54 2001 pp.67-76.

348   Kolonialwaren und Trophäen. Die Abgabe von Dubletten an das Berliner Museum für Völkerkunde im Kontext des Kolonialrevisionismus. *[In German]*; [Colonial wares and trophies. The delivery of duplicates to the Berlin Museum of Ethnology in the context of colonial revisionism]. Markus Schindlbeck. **Paideuma** 47 2001 pp.83-102.

349   Loom weights of Ugento. Krzysztof Nawotka. **Archeologia** LI 2000 pp.61-66.

350 A 'lost' seal from Harappa in the Nicholson Museum (Sydney). D.T. Potts. **Stud. Orient.** 94 2001 pp.405-416.

351 Museum collections as sources for African history. Colleen E. Kriger. **Hist. Afr.** 23 1996 pp.129-154.

352 Museums: using keyworkers to deliver lifelong learning. David Gray; Alan Chadwick. **Int. R. Educat.** 47:5 9:2001 pp.427-441.

353 The native collector: Louis Shotridge and the contests of possession. Elizabeth P. Seaton. **Ethnog.** 2:1 3:2001 pp.35-62.

354 A note on the São Tomé archives. Stanley B. Alpern. **Hist. Afr.** 24 1997 pp.399-400.

355 Of mice and manuscripts: a memoir of the National Archives of Zimbabwe. Anthony King. **Hist. Afr.** 25 1998 pp.405-412.

356 On the coins found at al-Fustāt. Mutsuo Kawatoko. **Senri Ethn. Stud.** 55 2001 pp.55-72.

357 Oral history at the extremes of human experience: Holocaust testimony in a museum setting. Tony Kushner. **Oral Hist.** 29:2 Autumn:2001 pp.83-94.

358 Orissa State Museum copper plate grant of Silabhanja, regnal year 11. Snigdha Tripathy. **Oris. Hist. R. J.** XLV:1-4 2000 pp.14-28.

359 An overview of the African National Congress archives at the University of Fort Hare. T.J. Stapleton; M. Maamoe. **Hist. Afr.** 25 1998 pp.413-422.

360 The Paruai malagan in the Linden-Museum Stuttgart. Gerry Barton; Sabine Weik. **Tribus** 50 12:2001 pp.45-66.

361 Plant collecting and the history of Japan in eighteenth-century London. Timon Screech. **Senri Ethn. Stud.** 54 2001 pp.29-38.

362 Plant hunters and Japan: plants, collection, and exhibition. Yozaburo Shirahata. **Senri Ethn. Stud.** 54 2001 pp.15-28.

363 Plated Iron Age coins: official issues or contemporary forgeries? G.L. Cottam. **Ox. J. Archaeol.** 20:4 11:2001 pp.377-390.

364 Postmodernism and the symbols of history: the relationship between collection, display, and materials in the Hiroshima Peace Memorial Museum and the Museum of Kamigata Performing Arts. Lisa Yoneyama. **Senri Ethn. Stud.** 54 2001 pp.137-148.

365 Problemy istochnikovedeniia i atributsii etnograficheskoi kollektsii N.N. Miklukho-Maklaia iz MAE (na primere 'barabana' i 'podstavki' s o-va Mangareva). *[In Russian]*; [Sourcing and attributing problems of the Nikolai Milukho-Maklai ethnographic collections at the Museum of Anthropology and Ethnography (the examples of a 'drum' and a 'bier to support a corpse' from Mangareva Island) *[Summary]*. L.A. Ivanova. **Etnograf. Oboz.** 5 9-10:2000 pp.88-105.

366 La province sassanide d'Abhar. Nouvelles données dans les collections des Musées Royaux d'Art et d'Histoire de Bruxelles. *[In French]*; [The Sassanian province of Abhar. New features of the collections of the Royal Museums of Art and History in Brussels] *[Summary]*. R. Gyselen. **Stud. Iran.** 30:1 2001 pp.31-44.

367 Raw histories: photographs, anthropology and museums. Elizabeth Edwards. Oxford: Berg Publishers, 2001. xiii, 270p. *ISBN: 1859734979, 1859734928. Includes index.*

368 Reflections on 'African voices' at the Smithsonian's national museum of natural history. Mary Jo Arnoldi; Christine Mullen Kreamer; Michael Atwood Mason. **Afr. Arts** XXXIV:2 Summer:2001 pp.16-35.

369 The regional archive at Addi Qäyyeh, Eritrea. Irma Taddia. **Hist. Afr.** 25 1998 pp.423-426.

370 Salvaging manuscripts from 1947 Lahore: the making of an Indology library. Mahesh Sharma; P.V. Rao. **Bull. Ét. Indien.** 17-18 1999-2000 pp.491-500.

371 Samling. *[In Danish]*; [Collecting] *[Summary]*. Kirsten Marie Raahauge; Kirsten Ramløv; Mikael Bøgh Rasmussen; Inger Sjørslev; Nana Vaaben; Mark Vacher; Hanne Veber; Espen Wæhle; Hans Harrestrup Andersen; Bryan Cleal; Torkil Funder; Rolf Gilberg; Jørn Duus Hansen; Kirsten Winther Jørgensen; Lene Otto; Jens Paaske; Vibeke Petersen; Lars Holmberg; Tidsskriftet antropologi [Interviewer]. **Tids. Antrop.** 43-44 2001 pp.5-217. *Collection of 18 articles.*

372 Der schriftliche Archivbestand des Fachreferates Afrika im Ethnologischen Museum Berlin: Das Projekt seiner Erfassung und Erschliessung. *[In German]*; [The written

archival holdings of the Africa department of the Ethnological Museum, Berlin] *[Summary]*. Christine Stelzig; Johannes Röhm. **Baes-A.** XLVIII:1 12:2001 pp.107-270.

373 The social life of local museums. Berardino Palumbo. **Journ. Mod. Italian Studs.** 6:1 Spring:2001 pp.19-37.

374 The tea ceremony and collection: the prehistory of private art museums. Isao Kumakura. **Senri Ethn. Stud.** 54 2001 pp.105-118.

375 *The Century Speaks*: a public history partnership. Rob Perks. **Oral Hist.** 29:2 Autumn:2001 pp.95-105.

376 Tiumenskii oblastnoi kraevedcheskii muzei i ego etnograficheskie raboty. *[In Russian]*; (The Tyumen regional museum of local lore, history and literature and its ethnographic works.) *[Summary]*. N.A. Tomilov. **Etnograf. Oboz.** 1 1-2:2000 pp.129-139.

377 Tōhaku and Minpaku within the history of modern Japanese civilization: museum collections in modern Japan. Kenji Yoshida. **Senri Ethn. Stud.** 54 2001 pp.77-104.

378 Die »Unbekleidete Frau« von Nasca: Eine Figurenplastik des Ethnologischen Museums, Berlin. *[In German]*; [The naked woman of Nazca: a ceramic figurine at the Ethnological Museum, Berlin] *[Summary]*. Christiane Clados. **Baes-A.** XLVIII:1 12:2001 pp.25-42.

379 Unprovenanced material culture and Freud's collection of antiquities. Peter Ucko. **J. Mat. Cult.** 6:3 11:2001 pp.269-322.

380 Vehicles of meaning: ethnographic artefacts in a corporate environment; *[Summary in Afrikaans]*. Barbara Freemantle; Eulalie van Heerden. **S. Afr. J. Ethnol.** 24:4 2001 pp.138-146.

381 The white father archives at Mwanza, Tanzania. Kathleen Smythe. **Hist. Afr.** 24 1997 pp.431-432.

382 The work and archives of Chokan Valikhanov as a source of information about the trade and prices in east Turkestan and adjacent regions of Central Asia. M. Fedorov. **Cent. Asia. J.** 45:2 2001 pp.230-242.

Ethnography
Ethnographie

383 At the margins of death: ritual space and the politics of location in an Indo-Himalayan border village. Ravina Aggarwal. **Am. Ethn.** 28:3 8:2001 pp.549-573.

384 Being lost at sea: ontology, epistemology and a whale hunt. Anita Lundberg. **Ethnog.** 2:4 12:2001 pp.533-558.

385 Beyond the visible and the material: the Amerindianization of society in the work of Peter Rivière. Neil L. Whitehead [Ed.]; Laura M. Rival [Ed.]. New York, Oxford: Oxford University Press, 2001. xiii, 301p. *ISBN: 0199244766. Includes bibliographical references and index.*

386 Bronislaw Malinowski: collected works. Bronislaw Malinowski. London: Routledge, 2001. 3000p. *ISBN: 0415216710. 9 volumes.*

387 Chronological separation, geographical segregation, or ethnic demarcation? Ethnography and the Iron Age low chrononology. Shlomo Bunimovitz; Avraham Faust. **B. Am. Sch. Orient. R.** 322 5:2001 pp.1-10.

388 Conceptual modeling as a toolbox for grounded theorists. Danielle Soulliere; David W. Britt; David R. Maines. **Sociol. Q.** 42:2 Spring:2001 pp.253-270.

389 Doing visual ethnography: images, media and representation in research. Sarah Pink. London: Sage Publications, 2001. vii, 196p. *ISBN: 0761960546, 0761960538. Includes bibliographical references and index.*

390 Entre sédiments, strates et failles: le «terrain», une métaphore minée? *[In French]*; (Between sediments, layers, and fault-lines: is the 'field' a mined metaphor?) *[Summary]*; *[Summary in German]*. Jean-Yves Durand. **Ethn. Fr.** XXXI:1 1-3:2001 pp.127-141.

391 Ethnographic appropriations: German exploration and fieldwork in West-Central Africa. Beatrix Heintze. **Hist. Afr.** 26 1999 pp.69-128.

392   Ethnographic encounters. Positioning within and outside the insider frame; *[Summary in French]*. Narmala Halstead. **Soc. Anthrop.** 9:3 10:2001 pp.307-324.

393   Ethnographic mapmaking: part 1 — principles. Lawrence A. Kuznar; Oswald Werner. **Fie. Meth.** 13:2 5:2001 pp.204-213.

394   Ethnography. John D. Brewer. Buckingham, Philadelphia PA: Open University Press, 2000. viii, 211p. *ISBN: 0335202691, 0335202683. Includes bibliographical references and index. (Series:* Understanding social research).

395   Ethnography under the gun: fieldwork in zones of conflict, war, and peace. John T. Crist; Cynthia Keppley Mahmood; Avram Bornstein; Patrick G. Coy; David R. Segal; Kevin Avruch. **J. Contemp. Ethnog.** 30:5 10:2001 pp.516-648. *Collection of 6 articles.*

396   Etnografia dei confini: dilemma clinico e polisemia. *[In Italian]*; (Bounded places and ethnography: facing clinical dilemma and polyphony.); *[Summary]*. Gianmarco Navarini. **Rass. It. Soc.** XLII:2 4-6:2001 pp.283-308.

397   Etnografia dei mondi contemporanei. Limiti e potenzialità del metodo etnografico nell'analisi della complessità. *[In Italian]*; [Ethnographies for the contemporary world. Limitations and potential of ethnography in the study of complexity]; *[Summary]*. Enzo Colombo. **Rass. It. Soc.** XLII:2 4-6:2001 pp.205-230.

398   L'etnografo allo specchio: racconti dal campo e forme di riflessività. *[In Italian]*; (The ethnographer at the mirror: tales from the field and forms of reflexivity.); *[Summary]*. Marco Marzano. **Rass. It. Soc.** XLII:2 4-6:2001 pp.257-282.

399   Exploring new worlds in American Romani studies: social and cultural attitudes among the American Mačvaia. Rena C. Gropper; Carol Miller. **Rom. Stud.** 11:2 12:2001 pp.81-110.

400   Faire de l'ethnologie en Croatie dans les années quatre-vingt-dix. *[In French]*; (Doing ethnological work in Croatia in the 1990s.) *[Summary]*; *[Summary in German]*. Jasna Čapo Žmegač. **Ethn. Fr.** XXXI:1 1-3:2001 pp.41-50.

401   Fermeture et transfert de trois hôpitaux parisiens. L'ethnologue accompagnateur social. *[In French]*; (Closing down and moving three Parisian hospitals: the ethnologist as a social worker.) *[Summary]*; *[Summary in German]*. Anne Monjaret. **Ethn. Fr.** XXXI:1 1-3:2001 pp.103-115.

402   A flood, Friday mosques and the formation of local identity: Hausa politics and the impact of ethnographic fieldwork in a village divided, Maradi (Niger). Sean E. Pratt. **Cam. Anthrop.** 22:2 2000-2001 pp.20-36.

403   From how to why: on luminous description and causal inference in ethnography (part 1). Jack Katz. **Ethnog.** 2:4 12:2001 pp.443-474.

404   From 'reading over the shoulders of natives' to 'reading alongside natives' literally: toward a collaborative and reciprocal ethnography. Luke Eric Lassiter. **J. Anthr. Res.** 57:2 Summer:2001 pp.137-149.

405   Georges Perec's experiments in social description. Howard Becker. **Ethnog.** 2:1 3:2001 pp.63-76.

406   Handbook of ethnography. Paul Atkinson [Ed.]; et al. London: Sage Publications, 2001. 640p. *ISBN: 076195824X.*

407   Learning how to find out: theories of knowledge and learning in field research. Cati Coe. **Fie. Meth.** 13:4 11:2001 pp.392-411.

408   Lectures de De Martino en France aujourd'hui. *[In French]*; [De Martino's lectures in France today] *[Summary]*; *[Summary in German]*. Christine Bergé. **Ethn. Fr.** XXXI:3 7-9:2001 pp.537-548.

409   *Man of Aran* revisited: an anthropological critique. John C. Messenger, Jr. **Vis. Anthrop.** 14:4 2001 pp.343-368.

410   O metodologii issledovaniia etnicheskikh fenomenov. *[In Russian]*; (On the methodology of studying ethnic phenomena.) *[Summary]*. S.E. Rybakov. **Etnograf. Oboz.** 5 9-10:2000 pp.3-17.

411   Un mode de prospection ethnographique: le reportage. *[In French]*; [Reporting — an ethnographic research tool]. Gérard Derèze. **Recher. Sociolog.** XXXII:1 2001 pp.87-100.

412   O nekim znanstvenopovijesnim uzrocima dualizma hrvatske etnologije. *[In Croatian]*; (On some scholarly-historical grounds for the dualism in Croatian ethnology.) Ines Prica. **Etnoloska** 23:30 2000 pp.79-92.

413   Ocherednye zadachi etnograficheskogo izucheniia islama v Turkestane. *[In Russian]*; (Immediate ethnographic tasks to study Islam in Turkestan.) L.A. Chvyr'. **Etnograf. Oboz.** 3 5-6:2001 pp.124-127.

414   On going native: Thomas Kuhn and anthropological method. John Tresch. **Philos. S. Sc.** 31:3 9:2001 pp.302-322.

415   Performing comparisons: ethnography, globetrotting, and the spaces of social knowledge. Michael Herzfeld. **J. Anthr. Res.** 57:3 Fall:2001 pp.259-276.

416   Perspectives on Tierney's *Darkness in El Dorado*. Fernando Coronil; Alan G. Fix; Peter Pels; Charles L. Briggs; Raymond Hames; Susan Lindee; Alcida Rita Ramos. **Curr. Anthr.** 42:2 4:2001 pp.265-276.

417   La photo volée. Les pièges de l'ethnographie en cité de banlieue. *[In French]*; (The stolen snapshot. The traps for ethnography in the suburbs.) *[Summary]*; *[Summary in German]*. David Lepoutre. **Ethn. Fr.** XXXI:1 1-3:2001 pp.89-102.

418   The political uses of ethnography: a workshop report. Carola Lentz. **Paideuma** 47 2001 pp.147-160.

419   Postbook: working the ruins of feminist ethnography. Patti Lather. **Signs** 27:1 Autumn:2001 pp.199-227.

420   Povratnik s terena: konceptualni ideal i izvedbene mogućnosti dijaloga u etnografskom tekstu. *[In Croatian]*; (Returnee from the field: the conceptual ideal and the operative possibilities of dialogue in an ethnographic paper.) *[Summary]*. Ines Prica. **Nar. Umjetn.** 37:2 2000 pp.47-66.

421   Recherches ethnographiques en Europe et en Amérique du Nord. *[In French]*; [Ethnographic research in Europe and North America]. Ana Vásquez-Bronfman [Ed.]; Isabel Martinez [Ed.]; Angela Xavier de Brito [Tr.]. Paris: Anthropos, Diffusion, Economica, 1999. xii, 294p. *ISBN: 2717837809. Text in English and French. Includes bibliographical references.*

422   Researching from afar: distance, ethnography, and testing the edge. D. Angus Vail. **J. Contemp. Ethnog.** 30:6 12:2001 pp.704-725.

423   Settings, interactions and things: a plea for multi-integrative ethnography. Florence Weber. **Ethnog.** 2:4 12:2001 pp.475-500.

424   Teilnehmende Beobachtung als dichte Teilnahme. *[In German]*; [Participant observation as full participation] *[Summary]*. Gerd Spittler. **Z. Ethn.** 126:1 2001 pp.1-26.

425   «Terrain désigné», observation sous contrôle: quelques enjeux d'une ethnographie des Tsiganes. *[In French]*; ('Assigned area', observation under surveillance: some stakes in the ethnography of Gypsies.) *[Summary]*; *[Summary in German]*. Marc Bordigoni. **Ethn. Fr.** XXXI:1 1-3:2001 pp.117-126.

426   Terrains minés. *[In French]*; [Minefields]. Dionigi Albera. **Ethn. Fr.** XXXI:1 1-3:2001 pp.5-14.

427   Trenutek slovenskega etnografskega filma. *[In Slovene]*; (Ethnological film.) *[Summary]*. Naško Križnar. **Bull. Slov. Ethno. Soc.** 41:1-2 2001 pp.72-77.

428   Truth and intentionality: an ethnographic critique. Alessandro Duranti. **Cult. Anthro.** 8:2 5:1993 pp.214-245.

429   Using emergy analysis in ethnographic field research. Jorge M. Rocha. **Fie. Meth.** 13:3 8:2001 pp.244-262.

430   VII Mezhdunarodnyi seminar «Integratsiia arkheologicheskikh i etnograficheskikh issledovanii». *[In Russian]*; (The 7th international seminar: 'Integration of Archaeological and Ethnographic Studies'.) M.L. Berezhnova; S.N. Korusenko; N.A. Tomilov. **Etnograf. Oboz.** 1 1-2:2001 pp.149-153.

431   Virtual society? Get real! Abstraction and decontextualisation: an anthropological comment or: e for ethnography. Marilyn Strathern. **Cam. Anthrop.** 22:1 2000-2001 pp.52-66.

432   When the camera won't focus: tensions in media ethnography. Vicki Mayer. **Fem. Med. St.** 1:3 11:2001 pp.307-322.

433   'Writing culture' under the gaze of my country. Meira Weiss. **Ethnog.** 2:1 3:2001 pp.77-92.

Media
Médias

434   Consuming history and memory through mass media products. Alejandro Baer. **Euro. Journ. Cult. Stud.** 4:4 11:2001 pp.491-502.

435   Demonstrating Pertex: a new method for improving text interpretation. Helge Helmersson; Jan Mattsson. **Fie. Meth.** 13:2 5:2001 pp.115-136.

436   Handheld computers as tools for writing and managing field data. Paul D. Greene. **Fie. Meth.** 13:2 5:2001 pp.181-197.

437   La obra cartográfica de don Carlos de Sigüenza y Góngora. *[In Spanish]*; [The cartographic work of Carlos de Sigüenza y Góngora]. Elías Trabulse. **Caravelle** 76-77 12:2001 pp.265-275.

438   Od dokumentarne k etnološki fotografiji. *[In Slovene]*; [From documentary to ethnological photography] *[Summary]*. Mihaela Hudelja. **Bull. Slov. Ethno. Soc.** 41:1-2 2001 pp.81-85.

439   Out of words: the æsthesodic cine-eye of Robert Gardner: an exegesis and interview. Robert Gardner; Ilisa Barbash [Interviewer]. **Vis. Anthrop.** 14:4 2001 pp.369-414.

440   Renewing ethnographic film: is digital video changing the genre? David MacDougall. **Anthr. Today** 17:3 6:2001 pp.15-21.

441   Schlummernde Schätze — Unbekannte Bestände historischer Photographien aus der nichtwestlichen Welt und Prinzipien ihrer Erschliessung. *[In German]*; [Sleeping beauties: unknown holdings of historical photographs from Asia, Africa and Latin America] *[Summary]*. Paul Jenkins. **Baes-A.** XLVIII:1 12:2001 pp.1-23.

442   Teaching visual anthropology. Notes from the field. Anna Grimshaw. **Ethnos** 66:2 2001 pp.237-258.

443   What we learned from a photographic component in a study of Latino children's health. Lauren Clark; Lorena Zimmer. **Fie. Meth.** 13:4 11:2001 pp.303-328.

444   Worldmaking, metaphors and montage in the representation of cultures: cross-cultural filmmaking and the poetics of Robert Gardner's *Forest of Bliss*. Roderick Coover. **Vis. Anthrop.** 14:4 2001 pp.415-438.

B.4:   **Historical and archaeological material**
    Matériaux historiques et archéologiques

B.4.1:   **Historical material**
    Matériaux historiques

Ancient history
Histoire ancienne

445   Absolute age range of the late Cypriot IIC Period on Cyprus. Sturt W. Manning; Bernhard Weninger; Alison K. South; Barbara Kling; Peter Ian Kuniholm; James D. Muhly; Sophocles Hadjisavvas; David A. Sewell; Gerald Cadogan. **Antiquity** 75:288 6:2001 pp.328-340.

446   The advent of Sultān Jalāl al-Dīn Khwārizmshāh in the trans-Indus territories (present Pakistan). N.A. Baloch. **J. Pak. Hist. Soc.** XLVIII:4 10-12:2000 pp.5-14.

447   Antagonistic neighbours: Ashkelon, Judaea, and the Jews. Gideon Fuks. **J. Jew. Stud.** LI:1 Spring:2000 pp.42-62.

448   Archaic Greeks in the Orient: textual and archaeological evidence. Wolf-Dietrich Niemeier. **B. Am. Sch. Orient. R.** 322 5:2001 pp.11-32.

449   Aspects of 'colonization'. John Boardman. **B. Am. Sch. Orient. R.** 322 5:2001 pp.33-42.

450   Der Assur-Katalog der Serie *Enūma Anu Enlil* (EAE). *[In German]*; [The Assur catalogue for the *Enūma Anu Enlil* series]. J.C. Fincke. **Orientalia** 70:1 2001 pp.19-39.

451   (The attitude of early Latin Christian thinkers toward classical culture (200-580).) *[Summary]*; *[Text in Arabic]*. Mona Hammad. **Dirasat Hum. Soc. Sc.** 28:2 8:2001 pp.527-543.

452   Between fasting and feasting: the literary and archaeobotanical evidence for monastic diet in Late Antique Egypt. Mary Harlow; Wendy Smith. **Antiquity** 75:290 12:2001 pp.758-768.

453   Broken fingers: classic Maya scribe capture and polity consolidation. Kevin J. Johnston. **Antiquity** 75:288 6:2001 pp.373-381.

454   Camels in antiquity: Roman period finds from Slovenia. László Bartosiewicz; Janez Dirjec. **Antiquity** 75:288 6:2001 pp.279-285.

455   Ceramic Age seafaring and interaction potential in the Antilles: a computer simulation. Richard T. Callaghan. **Curr. Anthr.** 42:2 4:2001 pp.308-313.

456   Complexity in archaic states. Robert McC. Adams. **J. Anthrop. Arch.** 20:3 9:2001 pp.345-360.

457   The concept of national unity in the Vedic Age. L.M. Joshi. **J. Orient. Inst.** XLVII:3-4(47) 3-6:1998 pp.297-302.

458   Crossing the Euphrates in antiquity: Zeugma seen from space. Anthony Comfort; Catherine Abadie-Reynal; Rifat Ergeç. **Anatol. St.** 50 2000 pp.99-126.

459   Curing cut or ritual mutilation? Some remarks on the practice of female and male circumcision in Graeco-Roman Egypt. Mary Knight. **Isis** 92:2 6:2001 pp.317-350.

460   Datation par RPE et U-Th des sites pléistocènes d'Atapuerca, Trinchera Dolina et Trinchera Galería. Bilan géochronologique. *[In French]*; (U-series and ESR dating of Atapuerca Pleistocene sites: Sima de los Huesos, Gran Dolina and Trinchera Galería.) *[Summary]*. C. Falguères; J.J. Bahain; Y. Yokoyama; J.L. Bischoff; J.L. Arsuaga; J.M. Bermúdez de Castro; E. Carbonell; J.M. Dolo. **Anthropologie [Paris]** 105:1 1-3:2001 pp.71-82.

461   La dea Ops nel *pantheon* romano-africano. *[In Italian]*; [The goddess Ops in the Roman-African 'pantheon']. Silvia Bullo. **Cah. Tunis.** XLIX:178 1997 pp.29-60.

462   Dromedaries in antiquity: Iberia and beyond. Jose A. Riquelme; Corina Liesua von Lettow-Vorbeck; Arturo Morales Muñiz. **Antiquity** 69:263 6:1995 pp.368-375.

463   Economy and exchange in the east Mediterranean during late antiquity. Michael Decker [Ed.]; Sean A. Kingsley [Ed.]. Oxford: Oxbow, 2001. vi, 178p. *ISBN: 1842170449. Includes bibliographical references.*

464   Elementary, my dear Lycians: a pronouncement on physics from Diogenes of Oinoanda. Martin Ferguson Smith. **Anatol. St.** 50 2000 pp.133-138.

465   The elite in the Lower Danube provinces of the Roman Empire in the time of Principate. Marek Żyromski. Mosina: ALPIM Book Company, 1995. 124p. *ISBN: 8385186050. Includes bibliographical references (p. 121-124).*

466   L'espace urbain du grand Pètra, les routes et les stations caravanières. *[In French]*; [Urban space in Greater Petra - roads and caravan stops]. F. Zayadine. **A. Dept. Antiq. Jordan** XXXVI 1992 pp.217-240.

467   Ethnicity and culture in late antiquity. Geoffrey Greatrex [Ed.]; Stephen Mitchell [Ed.]. London: Duckworth, 2001. 350p. *ISBN: 0715630431.*

468   Exarchon: an unsuspected Jewish liturgical title from ancient Rome. Margaret H. Williams. **J. Jew. Stud.** LI:1 Spring:2000 pp.77-87.

469   The excavation and restoration of the Hippodrome at Jerash: a synopsis. A. Ostrasz. **A. Dept. Antiq. Jordan** XXXV 1991 pp.237-250.

470   (The failure of the Hawwārite state formation under Abū Yazīd.) *[Summary]*; *[Text in Japanese]*. Fukuzo Amabe. **J. Hum. Nat. Sci.** 110 9:2000 pp.3-24.

471 The first century historians of Roman Britain. E.W. Black. **Ox. J. Archaeol.** 20:4 11:2001 pp.415-428.

472 The first discovered leaves of *Sefer Hefes*. Neil Danzig. **Jew. Q. Rev.** 82 1991-1992 pp.51-262.

473 'For the vineyard of the Lord of hosts was the house of Israel': Cyprian of Carthage and the Jews. Charles A. Bobertz. **Jew. Q. Rev.** 82 1991-1992 pp.1-240.

474 Géographie et politique dans le Viêt-Nam ancien. *[In French]*; (Geography and politics in ancient Vietnam.) *[Summary]*. Philippe Papin. **B. Éc. Fr. Ex.-Or.** 87:2 2000 pp.609-628.

475 A glimpse at Moche Phase III occupation at the Huacas of Moche site, northern Peru. Claude Chapdelaine; Victor Pimentel; Hélène Bernier. **Antiquity** 75:288 6:2001 pp.361-372.

476 Gnostic myth in Jewish garb: Niriyah (Norea), Noah's bride. Reimund Leicht. **J. Jew. Stud.** LI:1 Spring:2000 pp.133-140.

477 Hammurabi oder Hammurapi? *[In German]*; [Hammurabi or Hammurapi?] Michael P. Streck. **Arch. Orient.** 67:4 11:1999 pp.655-670.

478 Hethitische Kleinigkeiten. *[In German]*; [Hittite details]. Johann Tischler. **Arch. Orient.** 67:4 11:1999 pp.683-694.

479 Hethitisch-hurritische und armasische (georgische) „Triaden". *[In German]*; [Hittite-Hurrian and Georgic 'triads']. Gregor Giorgadze. **Arch. Orient.** 67:4 11:1999 pp.547-566.

480 History of the Western Kshatrapas of Gujarat. Atusha Bharucha Irani. **J. Orient. Inst.** XLVII:3-4(47) 3-6:1998 pp.289-296.

481 Hsia Wu-chu: physician to the first Ch'in emperor. Lanny B. Fields. **J. Asian Hist.** 28 1994 pp.97-108.

482 Die *igisûm*-Abgabe in den altbabylonischen Quellen. *[In German]*; [The *igisûm* tax in ancient Mesopotamia]. Lukáš Pecha. **Arch. Orient.** 69:1 2:2001 pp.1-20.

483 Les implantations Omeyyades dans la Balqa: l'apport d'Umm-el-Walid. *[In French]*; [Umayyad settlements in Balqa: the role of Umm-el-Walid]. M.A. Haldimann. **A. Dept. Antiq. Jordan** XXXVI 1992 pp.307-324.

484 The Islamic conquest of southern Jordan. Z.T. Fiema. **A. Dept. Antiq. Jordan** XXXVI 1992 pp.325-332.

485 (Judges' salaries in Abbasid state (132-334 A.H.)); *[Text in Arabic]*. Hussein Kassasbeh. **Dirasat Hum. Soc. Sc.** 28:1 2:2001 pp.131-157.

486 Julia Crispina, daughter of Berenicianus, a Herodian princess in the Babatha archive: a case study in historical identification. Tal Ilan. **Jew. Q. Rev.** 82 1991-1992 pp.361-382.

487 Kul'tura altaitsev - naslednitsa drevnei tsivilizatsii kochevnikov Tsentral'noi Azii. *[In Russian]*; (Culture of the Altaians — heir of the ancient civilization of the nomads of Central Asia.) *[Summary]*. L.P. Potapov. **Etnograf. Oboz.** 5 9-10:2000 pp.31-41.

488 Linseed oil and oil mills in central Turkey. Flax/linum and eruca, important oil plants of Anatolia. Füsun Ertug. **Anatol. St.** 50 2000 pp.171-185.

489 Der Mann aus Babylonien — Steuerhinterzieher, Flüchtling, Immigrant oder Agent? Zu einem aramäischen Dekret aus neuassyrischer Zeit. *[In German]*; [The Babylonians - tax evaders, refugees, immigrants or agents? An Aramaic decree of a new Assyrian period]. I. Kottsieper. **Orientalia** 69:4 2000 pp.368-392.

490 Membership in private associations in Ptolemaic Tebtunis; *[Summary in French]*. Brian Muhs. **J. Ec. Soc. Hist. O.** 44:1 2:2001 pp.1-21.

491 Money and its uses in the ancient Greek world. Andrew Meadows [Ed.]; Kirsty Shipton [Ed.]. Oxford: Oxford University Press, 2001. xx, 167p. *ISBN: 0199240124. Papers presented at two conferences held in Oxford, 1995 and 1997. Includes bibliographical references and index.*

492 Nabataean and Roman presence between Petra and Wādī 'Arabah survey expedition 1997/98: Umm Ratam. Manfred Lindner; Ulrich Hübner; Johannes Hübl. **A. Dept. Antiq. Jordan** XLIV 2000 pp.535-568.

493 A neo-Babylonian colony in Transpotamia (?) Muhammad A. Dandamayev. **Arch. Orient.** 67:4 11:1999 pp.541-546.

494 No slow dusk: Maya urban development and decline at La Milpa, Belize. Norman Hammond; Gair Tourtellot; Sara Donaghey; Amanda Clarke. **Antiquity** 72:278 12:1998 pp.831-837.

495 Non-royal women in Old Kingdom Egypt. Vivienne Gae Callender. **Arch. Orient.** 68:2 5:2000 pp.219-236.

496 Notes préliminaires a l'étude de la voie romaine Gerasa/Philadelphia. *[In French]*; [Preliminary notes on the study of the Roman road between Gerasa and Philadelphia]. Anne-Michèle Rasson-Seigne; Jacques Seigne. **A. Dept. Antiq. Jordan** XXXIX 1995 pp.193-210.

497 On the Dravidian axis 27N-27S (Mohenjo Daro — Easter Island). Benon Zb. Szalek. **J. Orient. Inst.** XLVII:1-2(47) 9-12:1997 pp.1-28.

498 The order of battle in the Roman army: evidence from marching camps. Alan Richardson. **Ox. J. Archaeol.** 20:2 5:2001 pp.171-185.

499 Pacbitun (Belize) and ancient Maya use of slate. Paul F. Healy; Jaime J. Awe; Gyles Iannone; Cassandra Bill. **Antiquity** 69:263 6:1995 pp.337-348.

500 The *Passio Sanctorum Quattuor Coronatorum*: a petrological approach. D.P.S. Peacock. **Antiquity** 69:263 6:1995 pp.362-368.

501 (The people and emperor of the late Meiji period.); *[Text in Japanese]*. Makihara Norio. **J. Hum. Nat. Sci.** 111 3:2001 pp.69-84.

502 The perils of love: magic and countermagic in Coptic Egypt. David Frankfurter. **J. Hist. Sexual.** 10:3-4 7-10:2001 pp.480-500.

503 Petra, the periplus and ancient Indo-Arabian maritime trade. V.D. Gogte. **A. Dept. Antiq. Jordan** XLIII 1999 pp.299-304.

504 Politics with style: identity formation in pre-Hispanic southeastern Mesoamerica. Edward M. Schortman; Patricia A. Urban; Marne Ausec. **Am. Anthrop.** 103:2 6:2001 pp.312-330.

505 'Priam's treasure': clearly a composite. David A. Traill. **Anatol. St.** 50 2000 pp.17-36.

506 The processing of gold and silver tax in the Achaemenid Empire: Herodotus 3.96.2 and the archeological realities; *[Summary in French]*. A. Zournatzi. **Stud. Iran.** 29:2 2000 pp.241-272.

507 Rameses II and the tobacco beetle. P.C. Buckland; E. Panagiotakopulu. **Antiquity** 75:289 9:2001 pp.549-556.

508 Reading Mesopotamian law cases, PBS 5 100: a question of filiation; *[Summary in French]*. Martha T. Roth. **J. Ec. Soc. Hist. O.** 44:3 8:2001 pp.243-292.

509 Redating the schism between the Judaeans and the Samaritans. Alan D. Crown. **Jew. Q. Rev.** 82 1991-1992 pp.17-50.

510 The rhetoric of justice: strategies of reconciliation and revenge in the restoration of Athenian democracy in 403 BC; *[Summary in French]*; *[Summary in German]*. David Cohen. **Eur. J. Soc.** XLII:2 2001 pp.335-356.

511 Un roi Nabatéen à Délos? *[In French]*; [A Nabatean king in Delos?] S. Schmid. **A. Dept. Antiq. Jordan** XLIII 1999 pp.279-298.

512 Roman interaction in North-Western Iberia. Martin Millett. **Ox. J. Archaeol.** 20:2 5:2001 pp.157-170.

513 The Roman street of the Petra project, 1997: a preliminary report. Z.T. Fiema. **A. Dept. Antiq. Jordan** XLII 1998 pp.395-424.

514 Sexuality in late antiquity. Daniel Boyarin [Ed.]; Elizabeth A. Castelli [Ed.]; Dina Stein; Charlotte Elisheva Fonrobert; Jill Gorman; Virginia Burrus; David Frankfurter; David Brakke. **J. Hist. Sexual.** 10:3-4 7-10:2001 pp.357-535. *Collection of 7 articles.*

515 The silent women of Yehud: notes on Ezra 9-10. H. Zlotnick-Sivan. **J. Jew. Stud.** LI:1 Spring:2000 pp.3-18.

516 Social justice and creative jurisprudence in late Bronze Age Syria; *[Summary in French]*. Raymond Westbrook. **J. Ec. Soc. Hist. O.** 44:1 2:2001 pp.22-43.

517 Staat und Wirtschaft im Alten Ägypten. *[In German]*; [State and economy in ancient Egypt]. M. Römer. **Orientalia** 69:4 2000 pp.407-429.

518 A statue of Dionysos from the sanctuary of Apollo at Cyrene: a recent join. Neil Adams. **Lib. Stud.** 32 2001 pp.87-92.

519   Suetonius' *Claudius* 25.4, acts 18, and Paulus Orosius' *Historiarum Adversum Paganos Libri VII* : dating the Claudian expulsion(s) of Roman Jews. Dixon Slingerland. **Jew. Q. Rev.** 83 1992-1993 pp.127-144.

520   Thalatta, Thalatta: Xenophon's view of the Black Sea. Tim Mitford. **Anatol. St.** 50 2000 pp.127-132.

521   Der thebanische 'Gottesstaat'. *[In German]*; [The Theban 'god state']. K. Jansen-Winkeln. **Orientalia** 70:2 2001 pp.153-182.

522   Turks and Uighurs during the rebellion of An Lu-shan Shih Ch'ao-yi (755-762). A. Kamalov. **Cent. Asia. J.** 45:2 2001 pp.243-265.

523   An ultra-low chronology of Iron Age Palestine. Graham Hagens. **Antiquity** 73:280 6:1999 pp.431-439.

524   The *Via Nova Traiana* in northern Jordan: a cultural resource under threat. David Kennedy. **A. Dept. Antiq. Jordan** XXXIX 1995 pp.221-228.

525   Water resources of the Chunchucmil Maya. Sheryl Luzzadder-Beach. **Geogr. Rev.** 90:4 10:2000 pp.493-510.

526   Were ancient seals secure? Roger G. Johnston; Debbie D. Martinez; Anthony R.E. Garcia. **Antiquity** 75:288 6:2001 pp.299-305.

527   Were customs dues levied at the time of the prophet Muhammad? Michael Lecker. **Al-Qantara** XXII:1 2001 pp.19-44.

528   Women and slaves in Greco-Roman culture: differential equations. Sandra R. Joshel [Ed.]; Sheila Murnaghan [Ed.]. London: Routledge, 2001. 287p. *ISBN: 0415261597, 0415162297. Includes bibliographical references.*

Anthropology and history
Anthropologie et histoire

529   Amalfi et la Tunisie au Moyen Âge. *[In French]*; [Amalfi and Tunisia in the Middle Ages]. Emanuele Riverso. **Cah. Tunis.** XLIX:178 1997 pp.11-28.

530   American historical archaeology. Laura Nader; Charles E. Orser, Jr.; Bonnie G. McEwan; Adrian Praetzellis; Mary Praetzellis; Paul A. Shackel; Elizabeth M. Scott; Amy L. Young; Michael Tuma; Cliff Jenkins. **Am. Anthrop.** 103:3 9:2001 pp.621-704. *Collection of 6 articles.*

531   American nations: encounters in Indian country, 1850 to the present. Frederick E. Hoxie; Peter C. Mancall; James H. Merrell. New York, London: Routledge, 2001. 519p. *ISBN: 0415927501, 0415927498.*

532   The anthropology and historiography of Central-South Nigeria before and since Igbo-Ukwu. A.E. Afigbo. **Hist. Afr.** 23 1996 pp.1-16.

533   Archéologie du massif du Barajas. Premières données sur l'évolution des sociétés préhispaniques du sud-ouest du Guanajuato, Mexique. *[In French]*; [Archaeology of the massif of Barajas. First data about the evolution of pre-Hispanic societies of south-west Guanajuato, Mexico]. Grégory Pereira; Gérald Migeon; Dominique Michelet. **J. Soc. Amér.** 87 2001 pp.265-281.

534   The arms and armour of the municipal war wagon escort in 1521. Jan Szymczak. **Fas. Arch. Hist.** XV 1999-2000 pp.27-34.

535   Aryan destruction of Indus Valley civilization - myth or reality. M. Qasim Jan. **J. Pak. Hist. Soc.** XLIX:2 4-6:2001 pp.31-36.

536   Barbed-wire bonnat? The case of the clueless text. David Henige. **Hist. Afr.** 23 1996 pp.439-452.

537   The Benin kinglist/s: some questions of chronology. Stefan Eisenhofer. **Hist. Afr.** 24 1997 pp.139-156.

538   Bioarchaeology of the African diaspora in the Americas: its origins and scope. Michael L. Blakey. **Ann. R. Anthr.** 30 2001 pp.387-422.

539   Clearing a path: theorizing the past in Native American studies. Nancy Shoemaker [Ed.]. London: Routledge, 2001. 215p. *ISBN: 0415926750, 0415926742.*

540   Colonizing language? Missionaries and Gikuyu dictionaries, 1904 and 1914. Derek Peterson. **Hist. Afr.** 24 1997 pp.257-272.
541   A concise history of India. Barbara Daly Metcalf; Thomas R. Metcalf. Cambridge: Cambridge University Press, 2001. xxiii, 321p. *ISBN: 0521639743, 0521630274. Includes bibliographical references and index. (Series:* Cambridge concise histories).
542   Consideraciones epistemológicas sobre la historiografia del México pre-hispánico. *[In Spanish]*; [Epistemological reflections on pre-Hispanic Mexican historiography]. Patrick Johansson. **Caravelle** 76-77 12:2001 pp.27-35.
543   Culture history of the Toalean of South Sulawesi, Indonesia. David Bulbeck; Monique Pasqua; Adrian Di Lello. **Asian Persp. [Hawaii]** 39:1-2 Spring-Fall:2000 pp.71-108.
544   De la mémoire communicative à la mémoire culturelle. Le passé dans les témoignages d'Arezzo et de Sienne (1177-1180). *[In French]*; (From communicative memory to cultural memory. The past in the testimonies of Arezzo and Siena (1177-1180).) *[Summary]*. Guy P. Marchal. **Annales** 56:3 5-6:2001 pp.563-590.
545   De l'espace iconique à l'écriture. *[In French]*; (From iconic space to writing.) *[Summary]*. A.M. Christin. **Anthropologie [Paris]** 105:4 10-12:2001 pp.627-636.
546   Debilidades y grandeza humana de Bernardo Reyes: historia y leyenda. *[In Spanish]*; [The weakness and human greatness of Bernardo Reyes: history and legend]. Rogelio Arenas Monreal. **Caravelle** 76-77 12:2001 pp.461-474.
547   Descent from privilege: a researcher's memoir of the national archives of Zimbabwe, 1984-1993. Leslie Bessant. **Hist. Afr.** 24 1997 pp.401-408.
548   'Desperate men': the 1914 rebellion and the politics of poverty. Sandra Swart. **S. Afr. Hist. J.** 42 2000 pp.161-175.
549   The doom of early African history? Jan Vansina. **Hist. Afr.** 24 1997 pp.337-344.
550   Early Swahili history reconsidered. Thomas Spear. **Int. J. Afr. H. S.** 33:2 2000 pp.257-290.
551   L'économie indochinoise dans la guerre (1945-1954). *[In French]*; [The economy of Indochina during the war (1945-1954)] *[Summary]*. Hugues Tertrais. **Rev. Fr. Hist. O.mer.** 1(330-331) 6:2001 pp.113-128.
552   Editing nineteenth-century intelligence reports on the Sokoto caliphate and Borno; the delights of the collaborative approach. A.S. Kanya-Forstner; Paul E. Lovejoy. **Hist. Afr.** 24 1997 pp.195-204.
553   'Elephants for want of towns:' the interethnic and international history of Bulama Island, 1456-1870. P.E.H. Hair. **Hist. Afr.** 24 1997 pp.177-194.
554   Ethnicity and the slave trade: *lucumi* and *nago* as ethnonyms in West Africa. Robin Law. **Hist. Afr.** 24 1997 pp.205-220.
555   Ethnohistory of the Bedul Bedouin of Petra. Kenneth W. Russell. **A. Dept. Antiq. Jordan** XXXVII 1993 pp.15-36.
556   Evolutions in the Lapita cultural complex: a view from the Southern Lapita Province. Christophe Sand. **Archaeol. Ocean.** 36:2 7:2001 pp.65-76.
557   The expansion of the nuclear family unit in Great Britain between 1910 and 1920. Magali Gente. **Hist. Fam.** 6:1 2001 pp.125-142.
558   Firearms and political power: the military decline of the Turkana of Kenya 1900-2000. Nene Mburu. **Nord. J. Afr. St.** 10:2 2001 pp.148-162.
559   The first migration wave of Indo-Iranians to the South. E.E. Kuzmina. **J. Indo-Eur. S.** 29:1-2 Spring-Summer:2001 pp.1-40.
560   For which types of speech would a Jew have studied Greek rhetoric in seventeenth-century Amsterdam? Shlomo Berger. **St. Ros.** 34:2 2000 pp.153-167.
561   Frühneuzeitliche Argumentationsmuster der Entbarbarisierung Europas. *[In German]*; [Early modern examples of argumentation in the barbarization of Europe]. Hans Grünberger. **Paideuma** 46 2000 pp.161-188.
562   The gay oral history project in Zimbabwe: Black empowerment, human rights, and the research process. Marc Epprecht. **Hist. Afr.** 26 1999 pp.25-42.
563   The Gdańsk *Landsknechts* in the second half of the 16th century and their arms and armour. Marek Plewczyński. **Fas. Arch. Hist.** XV 1999-2000 pp.21-26.

564   Gender roles in history: women as hunters. K.S. Singh. **Gen. Tech. Dev.** 5:1 1-4:2001 pp.113-124.

565   Greying in the cloister: the Ursuline life course in eighteenth-century France. Sherri Klassen. **J. Wom. Hist.** 12:4 Winter:2001 pp.87-112.

566   La grippe espagnole à Tahiti en 1918 — extrait des cahiers de Berthe Rougier 12 nov. 1918-1er janv. 1919. *[In French]*; [Spanish flu in Tahiti in 1918 - an extract from Berthe Rougier's journals from 12 November 1918 to 1 January 1919]. Paul-Emmanuel Boulagnon. **Soc. Ét. Océan.** 288 3:2001 pp.16-43.

567   La guerre de 1940-45 vécue à Coquilhatville. *[In French]*; [The 1940-45 war as experienced in Coquilhatville] *[Summary]*. H. Vinck. **Ann. Æqua.** 22 2001 pp.21-102.

568   Halakhah, Kabbalah, and heresy: a controversy in early eighteenth-century Amsterdam. Matt Goldish. **Jew. Q. Rev.** 84 1993-1994 pp.153-176.

569   Herodotus on the Garamantes: a problem of protohistory. Daniel E. McCall. **Hist. Afr.** 26 1999 pp.197-218.

570   Heury's *Ya-Heywat tarik* and Mahtama-Sellase's *che balaw*: two perceptions of a biographical dictionary. Bahru Zewde. **Hist. Afr.** 23 1996 pp.387-400.

571   Histoire des Alaouites (1268-1971). *[In French]*; [A history of the 'Alawites (1268-1971)]. Jacques Benoist-Méchin; Alain Decaux [Foreword]. Paris: Perrin, 1994. 285p. *ISBN: 226201597X.*

572   Historicization of the culture concept. Emiko Ohnuki-Tierney. **Hist. Anthrop.** 12:3 2001 pp.213-254.

573   History and historiography in precolonial Nigerian societies: the case of the Ekiti. C.O.O. Agboola. **Hist. Afr.** 26 1999 pp.1-10.

574   The history of the Baga in early written sources. P.E.H. Hair. **Hist. Afr.** 24 1997 pp.381-392.

575   History, oral transmission and structure in Ibn Khaldun's chronology of Mali rulers. Ralph A. Austen; Jan Jansen. **Hist. Afr.** 23 1996 pp.17-28.

576   Hitler and the occult: the magical thinking of Adolf Hitler. Raymond L. Sickinger. **J. Pop. Cult.** 34:2 Fall:2000 pp.107-126.

577   How the 1965 Indo-Pak war was won. Patwant Singh. **Sikh Rev.** 49:9(573) 9:2001 pp.44-46.

578   Identificación de «al-Qurtubī», autor de al-I'lām bimā fī dīn al-nasārà min al-fasād wa-l-awhām. *[In Spanish]*; [The attribution of *al-I'lām bimā fī dīn al-nasārà min al-fasād wa-l-awhām* to al-Qurtubī]. Samir Kaddouri. **Al-Qantara** XXI:1 2000 pp.215-220.

579   The identity of one of the Ismaili *dā'īs* sent by the Fatimids to Ibn Hafsūn. Paul E. Walker. **Al-Qantara** XXI:2 2000 pp.387-388.

580   If I had known that 35 years ago: contextualizing the copper mines of Central Africa. Bruce Fetter. **Hist. Afr.** 26 1999 pp.449-452.

581   Ikonograficzne źródło do historii artylerii w drugiej połowie XV wieku. *[In Polish]*; (An iconographic source to the history of artillery in the second half of the 15th century.) Beata Możejko. **Kwart. Hist. Kult. Mater.** XLVIII:3-4 2000 pp.171-176.

582   L'image des peul dans l'oeuvre du General Faidherbe. *[In French]*; [The image of the Fulani in the works of General Faidherbe]. Anna Pondopoulo. **Hist. Afr.** 23 1996 pp.279-300.

583   Images of an African ruler: *Kabaka* Mutesa of Buganda, ca. 1857-1884**Hist. Afr.** 26 1999 pp.269-298.

584   In the raw: some reflections on transcribing and editing Lieutenant Hugh Clapperton's writings on the Borno mission of 1822-1825. Jamie Bruce Lockhart. **Hist. Afr.** 26 1999 pp.157-196.

585   India and Japan — migration in pre-historic times — cultural and spiritual interaction through the ages and its role in India's struggle for freedom. P.N. Chopra. **India Q.** LVII:1 1-3:2001 pp.89-98.

586   Inscripciones árabes inéditas en el museo provincial de Almería. *[In Spanish]*; [Unedited Arabic inscriptions in the Almeria museum]. Jorge Lirola Delgado. **Al-Qantara** XXI:1 2000 pp.97-142.

587   Intellectual aspects of strong kingship in the late nineteenth century. Attachak Sattayanurak. **J. Siam Soc.** 88:1-2 2000 pp.72-95.

588   Is human history predestined in Wang Fuzhi's cosmology? Jeeloo Liu. **J. Ch. Philos.** 28:3 9:2001 pp.321-338.

589   Is there a baby in this bathwater? Disquieting thoughts on the value of content in history. G.R. Allen. **S. Afr. Hist. J.** 42 2000 pp.290-306.

590   IV Vserossiiskaia konferentsiia «Russkii vopros: istoriia i sovremennost'». *[In Russian]*; (The fourth all-Russia conference: 'The Russian question: history and the present'.) M.A. Zhigunova; T.N. Zolotova. **Etnograf. Oboz.** 1 1-2:2001 pp.154-156.

591   Jewish and Christian astrology in late antiquity — a new approach. Kocku von Stuckrad. **Numen** XLVII:1 2000 pp.1-40.

592   The Jewish officials of Willemsoord and Veenhuizen, 1818-1890. Iet Erdtsieck. **St. Ros.** 35:1 2001 pp.23-47.

593   Jews, semites and their cultures in Fergus Millar's *Roman Near East*. Tessa Rajak. **J. Jew. Stud.** LI:1 Spring:2000 pp.63-68.

594   The journals of Captain Cook. James Cook; J.C. Beaglehole [Ed.]; Philip Edwards [Ed.]. London: Penguin, 1999. xiv, 646p. *ISBN: 0140436472.* (*Series:* Penguin classics).

595   Korean history studies in Japan: the 2000 *Shigaku zasshi* historiography review. Hamanaka Noboru; Kuwano Eiji; Nagashima Hiroki; James Lewis [Tr.]; Kenneth R. Robinson [Tr.]. **Kor. Stud.** 25:1 2001 pp.111-127.

596   (The land of Ash-Sham in Ibn Jubair's journey.) *[Summary]*; *[Text in Arabic]*. Shafeeq Al-Raqab. **Dirasat Hum. Soc. Sc.** 28:2 8:2001 pp.341-360.

597   Language, culture, history and the fieldworker: what I did on my Christmas holidays on Malakula (Vanuatu). Terry Crowley. **Anthro. forum** 11:2 11:2001 pp.195-215.

598   Lapita on the periphery. New data on old problems in the Kingdom of Tonga. David V. Burley; William R. Dickinson; Andrew Barton; Richard Shutler, Jr. **Archaeol. Ocean.** 36:2 7:2001 pp.89-104.

599   Lawlessness on the frontier: the Anglo-Scottish borderlands in the fourteenth to sixteenth century. John Gray. **Hist. Anthrop.** 12:4 2001 pp.381-408.

600   Lettres au Marabout: messages touaregs au Père de Foucauld. *[In French]*; [Letters to Marabout: Tuareg messages to Père de Foucauld]. Lionel Galand [Ed.]; Mohamed Aghali Zakara; Paulette Galand-Pernet; Ariane Aron; Lamara Bougchiche; Jeannine Drouin; Dominique Casajus. Paris: Belin, 1999. 256p. *ISBN: 2701121027. Includes bibliographical references (p. 249-254) and index.*

601   Majimaji and the millennium: Abrahamic sources and the creation of a Tanzanian resistance tradition. Thaddeus Sunseri. **Hist. Afr.** 26 1999 pp.365-378.

602   Making the James Stuart Archive. John Wright. **Hist. Afr.** 23 1996 pp.333-350.

603   Mamki w Rzymie i w Państwie kościelnym w XVII i XVIII wieku. *[In Polish]*; (Wet-nurses in Rome and the papal state in the 17th and 18th centuries.) Marian Surdacki. **Kwart. Hist. Kult. Mater.** XLIX:4 2001 pp.327-344.

604   Meaninglessness, meaningfulness, and super-meaningfulness in scripture: an analysis of the controversy surrounding Dan 2:12 in the Middle Ages. Richard C. Steiner. **Jew. Q. Rev.** 82 1991-1992 pp.431-570.

605   Medical anthropology, subaltern traces, and the making and meaning of Western medicine in South Africa: 1895-1899. Premesh Lalu. **Hist. Afr.** 25 1998 pp.133-160.

606   The Mediterranean family. Nimrod Hurvitz; Edward Fram; David S. Powers; Yossef Rapoport; Dror Ze'Evi; Bettina Dennerlein; Miriam Frenkel; Howard Tzvi Adelman. **Contin. Change** 16:2 8:2001 pp.169-319. *Collection of 7 articles.*

607   The missing Golden Horde chronicles and historiography in the Mongol Empire. Charles J. Halperin. **Mon. St.** XXIII 2000 pp.1-16.

608   Missionary researchers and researching missions: a South African view of cultural colonisation at the millennium. Stephen Gray. **Eng. Afr.** 26:2 10:1999 pp.55-68.

609   Le monument des martyrs de l'indépendance à Mbandaka. *[In French]*; [The monument to the martyrs of independence in Mbandaka] *[Summary]*. Lewono Lufungula. **Ann. Æqua.** 22 2001 pp.103-124.

610 Museum collections as sources for African history. Colleen E. Kriger. **Hist. Afr.** 23 1996 pp.129-154.

611 North Africa, Islam and the Mediterranean world: from the Almoravids to the Algerian War. Julia Clancy-Smith; Amira K. Bennison; James A. Miller; Ronald A. Messier; Mohamed El Mansour; Dalenda Larguèche; Abdelhamid Larguèche; Edmund Burke, III; Jonathan G. Katz; James D. Le Sueur. **J. N. African Stud.** 6:1 Spring:2001 pp.1-186. *Collection of 10 articles.*

612 Not quite Venus from the waves: the Almoravid conquest of Ghana in the modern historiography of western Africa. Pekka Masonen; Humphrey J. Fisher. **Hist. Afr.** 23 1996 pp.197-232.

613 Not telling — secrecy, lies and history. Arnold Temu; Luise White; Tim Nuttall; John Wright; Uma Dhupelia-Mesthrie; Cynthia Kros; Marijke du Toit; Paul Maylam. **S. Afr. Hist. J.** 42 2000 pp.2-135. *Collection of 7 articles.*

614 Not telling: African history at the end of the millennium. Arnold Temu. **S. Afr. Hist. J.** 42 2000 pp.2-10.

615 *Nota biographica*: Maklouf Levi and Evariste Lévi-Provençal. David J. Wasserstein. **Al-Qantara** XXI:1 2000 pp.211-214.

616 On being a historian of Tuvalu: further thoughts on methodology and mindset. Doug Munro. **Hist. Afr.** 26 1999 pp.219-238.

617 On the coins found at al-Fustāt. Mutsuo Kawatoko. **Senri Ethn. Stud.** 55 2001 pp.55-72.

618 Organic purity and the role of anthropology in Cambodia and Rwanda. Scott Straus. **Patt. Prej.** 35:2 4:2001 pp.47-62.

619 The origins and early history of the kingdom of Kongo, c. 1350-1550. John Thornton. **Int. J. Afr. H. S.** 34:1 2001 pp.89-120.

620 El palacio de los Leones de la Alhambra: ¿madrasa, *zāwiya* y tumba de Muhammad V? Estudio para un debate. *[In Spanish]*; [The Palace of the Lions in the Alhambra: a tomb for Muhammad V?] Juan Carlos Ruiz Souza. **Al-Qantara** XXII:1 2001 pp.77-120.

621 The past altered by the present: a Melanesian village after twenty years. Simon Harrison. **Anthr. Today** 17:5 10:2001 pp.3-9.

622 The *Pate Chronicles* revisited: nineteenth-century history and historiography. Randall L. Pouwels. **Hist. Afr.** 23 1996 pp.301-318.

623 The pattern of Lapita settlement in Fiji. Geoffrey Clark; Atholl Anderson. **Archaeol. Ocean.** 36:2 7:2001 pp.77-88.

624 Peasants in the medieval Bohemian army. Wojciech Iwańczak. **Fas. Arch. Hist.** XV 1999-2000 pp.15-20.

625 La perception du Mande et de l'identite Mandingue dans les textes européens, 1453-1508. *[In French]*; [Perceptions of Mande and Mande identity in early modern European texts, 1453-1508]. José da Silva Horta. **Hist. Afr.** 23 1996 pp.75-86.

626 Persian religious and cultural influence in Siam/Thailand and maritime Southeast Asia in historical perspective: a plea for a concerted interdisciplinary approach. Muhammad Ismail Marcinkowski. **J. Siam Soc.** 88:1-2 2000 pp.186-194.

627 A personal journey into custom, identity, power and politics: researching and writing the life and times of Buganda's Queen Mother Irene Drusilla Namaganda (1896-1957). Nakanyike B. Musisi. **Hist. Afr.** 23 1996 pp.369-386.

628 The poetics of race in 1890s Ireland: an ethnography of the Aran Islands. Scott Ashley. **Patt. Prej.** 35:2 4:2001 pp.5-18.

629 Polities and political discourse: was Mande already a segmentary society in the Middle Ages? Jan Jansen. **Hist. Afr.** 23 1996 pp.121-128.

630 La Polynésie, Tahiti et la «conjoncture romanesque rationnelle». *[In French]*; [Polynesia, Tahiti and the 'rational romantic circumstances']. Gérard Messeiller. **Soc. Ét. Océan.** 288 3:2001 pp.132-149.

631 Poniatie uzla etnogonicheskogo protsessa v sovremennom osveshchenii. *[In Russian]*; (An ethnogenetic nexus in its modern interpretation.) *[Summary]*. L.P. Lashuk. **Etnograf. Oboz.** 3 5-6:2001 pp.7-19.

632   Prevalence of powerful chief ministers in southern Sung China, 1127-1279 A.D. Gong Wei Ai. **Chin. Cult.** XL:2 6:1999 pp.103-114.

633   Princes as highway men. A consideration of the phenomenon of armed banditry in precolonial Borgu. Olayemi Akinwumi. **Cah. Ét. Afr.** XLI(2):162 2001 pp.333-350.

634   The quadripartite division of the intellect in medieval Jewish thought. Dov Schwartz. **Jew. Q. Rev.** 84 1993-1994 pp.227-237.

635   *Quilombos* on São Tomé, or in search of original sources. Jan Vansina. **Hist. Afr.** 23 1996 pp.453-460.

636   Reading *South Pacific*: colonialism and anthropology in an Australian journal. George D. Westermark. **Hist. Anthrop.** 12:2 2001 pp.159-178.

637   Reassessing Robert Drury's journal as a historical source for southern Madagascar. Mike Parker Pearson. **Hist. Afr.** 23 1996 pp.233-256.

638   Die reflexive Anthropologie des Zivilisationsprozesses. *[In German]*; (The reflexive anthropology of the process of civilization.) *[Summary]*. Gesa Lindemann. **Soz. Welt.** 52:2 2001 pp.181-198.

639   The reign of *Kabaka* Nakibinge of Buganda: myth or watershed? Richard Reid. **Hist. Afr.** 24 1997 pp.287-298.

640   Religious oratory and the improvement of congregants: Dutch-Jewish preaching in the first half of the nineteenth century. Bart Wallet. **St. Ros.** 34:2 2000 pp.168-193.

641   The representation of status in Mande: did the Mali Empire still exist in the nineteenth century? Jan Jansen. **Hist. Afr.** 23 1996 pp.87-110.

642   Ru thog district before the Chinese occupation (1900-1958): a preliminary study of its cultural history. Korpon Lobsang Khenrap. **Tibet J.** XXV:4 Winter:2000 pp.33-77.

643   The salt-gold alchemy in the eighteenth and nineteenth century Mande world: if men are its salt, women are its gold. B. Marie Perinbam. **Hist. Afr.** 23 1996 pp.257-278.

644   The scandal of Rev. James Read and the taming of the London Missionary Society by 1820. Julia Wells. **S. Afr. Hist. J.** 42 2000 pp.136-160.

645   Scottish life and society. A compendium of Scottish ethnology: institutions of Scotland education. European Ethnological Research Centre; Heather Holmes [Ed.]. East Linton: Tuckwell Press, 2000. xviii, 558p. *ISBN: 1862321868. Volume 11. Includes bibliographical references and index. European Ethnological Research Centre.*

646   Seasonality of marriages and ecological contexts in rural communities of central-southern Italy (Abruzzo), 1500-1871; *[Summary in Croatian]*. A. Coppa; L. Di Donato; F. Vecchi; M.E. Danubio. **Coll. Antrop.** 25:2 12:2001 pp.403-412.

647   Sequels of colonialism: Edward Bunting's ancient Irish music. Leith Davis. **Nineteen.-C. Ctxt.** 23:1 2001 pp.29-58.

648   Shanguo is not a Shan kingdom: to correct a mistake related to the early history of Tai-speaking peoples in China and Mainland Southeast Asia. He Ping. **J. Siam Soc.** 88:1-2 2000 pp.178-185.

649   A short note on a few uncertain links in the Han lineage. Bing Siong Han; Claudine Salmon [Comments by]. **Archipel** 62 2001 pp.43-64.

650   Siting translation: history, post-structuralism, and the colonial context. Tejaswini Niranjana. Berkeley CA, Oxford: University of California Press, 1992. xii, 203p. *ISBN: 0520074505, 0520074513.*

651   Situating social history: Orissa (1800-1997). Biswamoy Pati. London: Sangam Books, 2001. xiv, 182p. *ISBN: 0863118585. Includes bibliographical references and index. (Series: New perspectives in South Asian History - 2).*

652   Sobre la supernova del 1006. *[In Spanish]*; [The 1006 supernova]. Mónica Rius. **Al-Qantara** XXI:1 2000 pp.225-226.

653   Sobre los cometas en el *Rawd al-qirtās*. *[In Spanish]*; [Comets in *Rawd al-qirtās*]. J.M. Vaquero; M.C. Gallego; J.M. Cobos. **Al-Qantara** XXI:1 2000 pp.221-224.

654   Social suffering and the politics of pain: observations on the concentration camps in the Anglo-Boer War 1899-1902. Jenny De Reuck. **Eng. Afr.** 26:2 10:1999 pp.69-88.

655   Sources v. text: an 'integrated edition of sources'. Jan Vansina. **Hist. Afr.** 23 1996 pp.461-466.

656   Studying ritual in the past. Christine A. Hastorf. **Kroeber Anthr. Soc. Pap.** 85 2001 pp.1-15.

657   Tamactún-Acalán: interpretación de una hegemonía política maya de los siglos XIV-XVI. *[In Spanish]*; [Tamatún-Acalán: interpretation of a Mayan political hegemony from the 14th 16th centuries]. Andrés Ciudad Ruiz; Alfonso Lacadena García-Gallo. **J. Soc. Amér.** 87 2001 pp.9-38.

658   Tangier, Russia and the Soviet Union (1777-1956). Andrei M. Ledovski. **Morocco** 1 1996 pp.3-51.

659   A text that contains the truth on the origin of the Tibetans — an interpretation of the legendary genesis of the Tibetans from a macaque and a rock demon. Shi Shuo. **Soc. Sci. China** XXII:3 Autumn:2001 pp.162-172.

660   The theatricality of history making and the paradoxes of acting. Greg Dening. **Cult. Anthro.** 8:1 2:1993 pp.73-95.

661   Tibet: another world. A look at the French press's vision of Tibet in 1950. Claude Arpi. **Tibet J.** XXVI:1 Spring:2001 pp.73-99.

662   Timeline history and the Anzac myth: settler narratives of local history in a north Australian town. Elizabeth Furniss. **Oceania** 71:4 6:2001 pp.279-297.

663   Toward historicizing gender in Polynesia: on Vilsoni Hereniko's *Woven Gods* and regional patterns. Jeannette Marie Mageo. **Pac. Stud.** 22:1 3:1999 pp.93-122.

664   The transformation of America: Georgian sensibility, capitalist conspiracy, or consumer revolution? Dennis J. Pogue. **Hist. Archaeol.** 35:2 2001 pp.41-57.

665   Two lives of Mpamizo: understanding dissonance in oral history. Justin Willis. **Hist. Afr.** 23 1996 pp.319-332.

666   Two models of medieval Jewish marriage: a preliminary study. Michael S. Berger. **J. Jew. Stud.** LII:1 Spring:2001 pp.59-84.

667   Varstvo in obnova kulturne dediščine v Naravnem parku Lonjsko polje. *[In Slovene]*; (Protection and renovation of cultural heritage in the Lonjsko Polje Nature Reserve.) *[Summary]*. Ksenija Petrić. **Bull. Slov. Ethno. Soc.** 41:3-4 2001 pp.75-78.

668   A view from a village: popular political culture in sixteenth-century England. Judy Ann Ford. **J. Pop. Cult.** 34:2 Fall:2000 pp.1-20.

669   Were the Scots Irish? Ewan Campbell. **Antiquity** 75:288 6:2001 pp.285-292.

670   'What do you mean there were no tribes in Africa?' Thoughts on boundaries — and related matters — in precolonial Africa. Donald R. Wright. **Hist. Afr.** 26 1999 pp.409-426.

671   Whispers and shouts: some recent writings on medieval south India. Sanjay Subrahmanyam. **Indian Ec. Soc. His. R.** XXXVIII:4 10-12:2001 pp.453-466.

672   The white father archives at Mwanza, Tanzania. Kathleen Smythe. **Hist. Afr.** 24 1997 pp.431-432.

673   'Why is that White man pointing that thing at me?' Representing the Maasai. Tim Youngs. **Hist. Afr.** 26 1999 pp.427-448.

674   'Wondering with an unending wonder': remarks on Ham Mukasa's journey to England in 1902. Heike Behrend. **Hist. Afr.** 25 1998 pp.55-68.

675   Writing biographies of Boorana: social histories at the time of Kenya's independence. Mario I. Aguilar. **Hist. Afr.** 23 1996 pp.351-368.

676   Young women in France and England, 1050-1300. Fiona Harris Stoertz. **J. Wom. Hist.** 12:4 Winter:2001 pp.22-46.

677   Z.K. Sentongo and the Indian question in East Africa. Michael Twaddle. **Hist. Afr.** 24 1997 pp.309-336.

Colonial history
Histoire coloniale

678   The 1598-1599 siege of Pegu and the expansion of Arakanese imperial power into Lower Burma. Michael W. Charney. **J. Asian Hist.** 28 1994 pp.39-58.

679   The 1805 Forékariah conference: a case of political intrigue, economic advantage, network building. Bruce L. Mouser. **Hist. Afr.** 25 1998 pp.219-262.

680   Abolitionism and issues of race and gender. John R. McKivigan [Ed.]. New York: Garland Publishing, 1999. 405p. *ISBN: 0815331088. Includes bibliographical references. (Series:* The American abolitionist movement - 4).

681   Abolitionnistes de l'esclavage et réformateurs des colonies, 1820-1851: analyse et documents. *[In French]*; [Slavery abolitionists and reformers of the colonies, 1820-1851: analysis and documents]. Nelly Schmidt. Paris: Karthala, 2000. 1196p. *ISBN: 2845861028. Includes bibliographical references (p. [1071]-1145) and index.*

682   Aboriginal Khoikhoi servants and their masters in colonial Swellendam, South Africa, 1745-1795. Russel Viljoen. **Agr. Hist.** 75:1 Winter:2001 pp.28-51.

683   (Abu Al-Kasim Al-Hifnawi and his book: acquainting the successors with their predecessors.) *[Summary]*; *[Text in Arabic]*. M. Zarman. **Dirasat Hum. Soc. Sc.** 28:Supp. 12:2001 pp.605-623.

684   Administrators' knowledge and state control in colonial Zimbabwe: the invention of the rural-urban divide in Buhera district, 1912-80. Jens A. Andersson. **Espace Pop. Soc.** 43:1 2002 pp.119-143.

685   Africa's 'last wilderness': reordering space for political and economic control in colonial Tanzania; *[Summary in French]*. Roderick P. Neumann. **Africa** 71:4 2001 pp.641-665.

686   Agency and action in colonial Africa: essays for John E. Flint. Christopher P. Youé [Ed.]; Timothy Joseph Stapleton [Ed.]; John E. Flint [Dedicatee]. Basingstoke, New York: Palgrave, 2001. x, 219p. *ISBN: 0333778855. Includes bibliographical references and index.*

687   Agricultural improvement and technological innovation in a slave society: the case of early national northern Virginia. A. Glenn Crothers. **Agr. Hist.** 75:2 Spring:2000 pp.135-167.

688   Alliance and warfare in an Eastern Indonesian principality Kédang in the last half of the nineteenth century. R.H. Barnes. **Bijdragen** 157:2 2001 pp.271-312.

689   The Anglo-Indianness of Geoffrey Firmin: deracination in *Under the Volcano*. Paul Matthew St. Pierre. **Kunapipi** XXIII:2 2001 pp.167-177.

690   Angola's eastern hinterlands in the 1750s: a text edition and translation of Manoel Correia Leitão's *Voyage* (1755-1756). Evá Sebestyén; Jan Vansina. **Hist. Afr.** 26 1999 pp.299-364.

691   Apprendre à dire l'espace. L'invention du triangle polynésien dans les récits de circumnavigation (1817-1845). *[In French]*; (Learning to read space. The invention of the Polynesian triangle in accounts of circumnavigation (1817-1845).) *[Summary]*. Hélène Blais. **Genèses** 45 12:2001 pp.91-113.

692   Arsénio Pompílio Pompeu de Carpo: um percurso negreiro no século XIX. *[In Portuguese]*; (Arsénio Pompílio Pompeu de Carpo: the path of a slave-trader in the 19th century.) *[Summary]*; *[Summary in French]*. João Pedro Marques. **Anál. Soc.** XXXVI:160 Autumn:2001 pp.609-638.

693   Associative socialism and slave emancipation in French Guiana, 1839-1848; *[Summary in French]*. Lawrence C. Jennings. **Rev. Fr. Hist. O.mer.** 1(330-331) 6:2001 pp.167-188.

694   At home in the empire. Susan Pedersen; Mary A. Procida; Mrinalini Sinha; M. Page Baldwin; Wendy Webster. **J. Br. Stud.** 40:4 10:2001 pp.447-584. *Collection of 5 articles.*

695   The Atlantic slave trade was not a 'Black-on-Black Holocaust'; *[Summary in French]*. Lansiné Kaba. **Afr. Stud. R.** 44:1 4:2001 pp.1-20.

696   Attitudes to Africans in English primary sources on Guinea up to 1650. P.E.H. Hair. **Hist. Afr.** 26 1999 pp.43-68.

697   Automobilismus und Kolonialherrschaft. Zur Bedeutung des Autoverkehrs für die Herrschaftsstrukturen in der westafrikanischen Kolonie Dahomey. *[In German]*; [Motor vehicle use and colonial society. The impact of motor traffic on social structure in the West African colony of Dahomey]. Erdmute Alber. **Paideuma** 46 2000 pp.279-300.

698   Les bagnes des Indochinois en Guyane (1931-1963). *[In French]*; [Indochinese penal colonies in Guiana (1931-1966)] *[Summary]*. Danielle Donet-Vincent. **Rev. Fr. Hist. O.mer.** 1(330-331) 6:2001 pp.209-222.

699 Big chief Elizabeth: how England's adventurers gambled and won the New World. Giles Milton. London: Hodder & Stoughton, 2000. xiii, 416p. *ISBN: 0340748818. Includes bibliographical references and index.*

700 Bishop Alfred Tucker and the establishment of a British protectorate in Uganda 1890-94. Tudor Griffiths. **J. Relig. Afr.** XXXI:1 2001 pp.92-114.

701 Un breve apunte de Antonio Tello, cronista de Xalisco. *[In Spanish]*; [A brief note on Antonio Tello, chronicler of Jalisco]. José Murià. **Caravelle** 76-77 12:2001 pp.243-254.

702 British culture and the end of empire. Stuart Ward [Ed.]. Manchester, New York: Manchester University Press, 2001. 241p. *ISBN: 0719060486, 0719060478. Includes bibliographical references and index.* (*Series:* Studies in imperialism).

703 The British Empire. Jane Samson [Ed.]. Oxford, New York: Oxford University Press, 2001. xii, 330p. *ISBN: 0192892932. Includes bibliographical references and index.* (*Series:* Oxford readers).

704 The British occupation of Tangier 1662-1684. Peter Collier. **Morocco** 1 1996 pp.52-61.

705 The British occupation of Tangier, 1674-80. Peter Collier. **Morocco** 2 1997 pp.77-87.

706 Bushmen of Australia in Rhodesia: 1900. Roger Howman. **Herit. Zimb.** 10 1991 pp.64-86.

707 Cabo Verde - do século XV ao fim do segundo milénio: permanências e rupturas numa sociedade em transformação. *[In Portuguese]*; [Cape Verde - from the 15th century to the end of the second millennium: permanence and change in a society in transformation]. Ilídio Do Amaral; Maria Emília Madeira Santos; Iva Cabral; Maria Manuel Ferraz Torrão; Maria João Soares; Zelinda Cohen; Raquel Monteiro; Maria Teresa De Oliveira Ramos; Carla Teixeira E. Cruz; Gonçalves Guimarães; Cecília Matias; Margarida Tavares Da Conceição; Anouk Faria Da Costa; José Maria Lobo de Carvalho; Teresa De Deus Ferreira; Adriano Vasco Rodrigues; José Silva Évora; Paulo Frederico Ferreira Gonçalves; Cláudia Correia; Abel Dos Santos Cruz; Isabel L. Morgado De S.E. Silva; Octávio Do Nascimento; António Germano Lima; Salvador Magalhães Mota; Fernanda Paula Sousa Maia; João Lopes Filho. **Africana** 6 2001 pp.13-324. *Collection of 19 articles.*

708 A case of mistaken identity? Suikerlords and ladies, tempo doeloe and the Dutch colonial communities in nineteenth century Java. G. Roger Knight. **Soc. Ident.** 7:3 9:2001 pp.379-391.

709 'Cash for his turnups': agricultural production for local markets in colonial Pennsylvania, 1725-1783. Michael V. Kennedy. **Agr. Hist.** 74:3 Summer:2000 pp.587-608.

710 Cecil John Rhodes. Richard Wood. **Herit. Zimb.** 10 1991 pp.123-130.

711 Chief Makoni and the Shona rebellion. Tim Tanser. **Herit. Zimb.** 10 1991 pp.105-111.

712 Le choc des cultures: plusieurs histoires coloniales et des conflits toujours en suspens. *[In French]*; [Culture shocks: numerous colonial histories and unresolved conflicts]. Mohamed Mohamed-Abdi. **Stud. Afr.** 12 3:2001 pp.7-20.

713 La *Cité des Césars* de James Burgh: de l'utopie à la réalité. *[In French]*; [James Burgh's *An Account of the Cessares* from Utopia to reality]. Jean-Pierre Sanchez. **Caravelle** 76-77 12:2001 pp.363-373.

714 Collecting colonialism: material culture and colonial change. Christopher Gosden; Chantal Knowles. Oxford: Berg Publishers, 2001. xxi, 234p. *ISBN: 1859734081, 1859734030. Includes bibliographical references and index.*

715 The colonial history of the Norman conquest? Francis James West. **History** 84:274 4:1999 pp.219-236.

716 Colonialism as a continuing project: the Portuguese experience. Bela Feldman-Bianco. **Identities** 8:4 12:2001 pp.477-482.

717 Community, gender and violence. Partha Chatterjee [Ed.]; Pradeep Jeganathan [Ed.]. London: Hurst, 2000. viii, 347p. *ISBN: 1850655812, 1850655804. Papers presented at the Fifth Subaltern Studies Conference, Colombo, June 1995. Includes bibliographical references and index.* (*Series:* Subaltern studies - 11).

718 La compétitivité des productions indochinoises et les plans de mise en valeur. *[In French]*; [Competitiveness of Indochinese products and development plans] *[Summary]*. Jean-Dominique Giacometti. **Rev. Fr. Hist. O.mer.** 1(330-331) 6:2001 pp.71-90.

719   Conflicting views of 'coloured' people in the South African liquor bill debate of 1928. Jeremy Creighton Martens. **Can. J. Afr. St.** 35:2 2001 pp.313-365.

720   Conquering categories: the problem of pre-history in nineteenth century Puerto Rico and Cuba. Christopher Schmidt-Nowara. **Centro** XIII:1 Spring:2001 pp.4-21.

721   O Consulado de Paulo Dias de Novais. Angola no último quartel do século XVI e primeiro do século XVII. *[In Portuguese]*; [The consulate of Paulo Dias de Novais. Angola at the end of the 16th and beginning of the 17th century]. Ilídio do Amaral. Lisbon: Instituto de Investigação Científica Tropical, 2000. 280p. *ISBN: 972672886X. Ministério da Ciência e da Tecnologia.*

722   Creating the moral body: missionaries and the technology of power in early Papua New Guinea. Wayne Fife. **Ethnology** XL:3 Summer:2001 pp.251-269.

723   La crise de la banane à la Martinique en 1998: un révélateur de la crise d'un système social et économique? *[In French]*; [The 1998 banana crisis in Martinique: indicator of crisis in the social and economic system?] *[Summary]*. Soléane Duplan. **Rev. Fr. Hist. O.mer.** 1(330-331) 6:2001 pp.143-158.

724   Dahomey's royal road. Stanley B. Alpern. **Hist. Afr.** 26 1999 pp.11-24.

725   La découverte des Américains. *[In French]*; [The American discovery]. Tzvetan Todorov. **Caravelle** 76-77 12:2001 pp.309-316.

726   Le destin des exploitations rizicoles françaises dans le delta du Mekong. *[In French]*; [The fate of the exploitation of French ricefields in the Mekong delta] *[Summary]*. Pierre Brocheux. **Rev. Fr. Hist. O.mer.** 1(330-331) 6:2001 pp.103-112.

727   Destined to fail: forced settlement at the *Office du Niger*, 1926-45. Jean Filipovich. **J. Afr. Hist.** 42:2 2001 pp.239-260.

728   The discovery and conquest of Peru: chronicles of the New World encounter. Pedro de Cieza de León; Alexandra Parma Cook [Ed.]; Noble David Cook [Ed.]. Durham NC, London: Duke University Press, 1998. xviii, 501p. *ISBN: 0822321467, 0822321270. Translated from the Spanish Descubrimiento y conquista del Perú. Includes bibliographical references (p. [479]-487) and index. (Series: Latin America in translation/en traducción/em tradução).*

729   Doctors for the empire: the Medical School of Goa and its narratives. Cristiana Bastos. **Identities** 8:4 12:2001 pp.517-548.

730   Du taureau au dindon. La domestication du métissage dans le nouveau monde mexicain. *[In French]*; (From bulls to turkeys: domesticating '*métissage*' in the Mexican new world.) Frédéric Saumade. **Rural Stud.** :157-158 1-6:2001 pp.107-140.

731   A Dutch embassy to Asante in 1857: the journal of David Mill Graves. Larry W. Yarak. **Hist. Afr.** 24 1997 pp.363-380.

732   Un échec relatif: la mission des engagés indiens aux Antilles et à la Réunion (seconde moitié du XIXème siècle). *[In French]*; [A relative failure: the mission to committed Indians of the Antilles and Réunion (second half of the 19th century)] *[Summary]*. Philippe Delisle. **Rev. Fr. Hist. O.mer.** 1(330-331) 6:2001 pp.189-204.

733   La 'embaxada por los indios' del cacique zapoteca Patricio Antonio López. *[In Spanish]*; [Zapotec chief Patricio Antonio Lopez's 'Indian embassy']. Beatriz Mariscal Hay. **Caravelle** 76-77 12:2001 pp.277-287.

734   English merchants and Brazilian banks during the second reign: the *Sociedade Bancária Mauá*, MacGregor & Co. (1854-1866). Carlos Gabriel Guimarães. **Rev. Fr. Hist. O.mer.** 1(330-331) 6:2001 pp.39-52.

735   Epilogue of empire: East Timor and the Portuguese postcolonial catharsis. Miguel Vale de Almeida. **Identities** 8:4 12:2001 pp.583-605.

736   Un esempio di inculturazione della fede in Oceania: l'attività evangelizzatrice del primo missionario cattolico nella Nuova Guinea Britannica del 1885. *[In Italian]*; [An example of religious socialization in Oceania: the evangelism of the first catholic missionaries in British Papua New Guinea (1885)]. P. Lucio De Stefano. **Sociologia [Rome]** XXXV:1 2001 pp.151-168.

737   España en América: estudios sobre la historia de las ideas en Hispanoamérica. *[In Spanish]*; [Spain in America: studies on the history of ideas in Spanish America]. Enrique

Zuleta Alvarez. Buenos Aires: Editorial Confluencia, 2000. 390p. *ISBN: 9879362128.*
Includes bibliographical references and index.

738   The essence of commodification: caffeine dependencies in the early modern world. Ross W. Jamieson. **J. Soc. Hist** 35:2 Winter:2001 pp.269-294.

739   Ethnic intercession: leadership at Kalaupapa leprosy colony, 1871-1887. Pennie Moblo. **Pac. Stud.** 22:2 6:1999 pp.27-70.

740   Der Ethnologe als Utopist. Zu Lahontan's *Bon Sauvage-Utopie*. *[In German]*; [The ethnologist as utopianist. Lahontan's *Bon Sauvage-Utopie*]. Richard Saage. **Paideuma** 47 2001 pp.43-60.

741   Farghana's contacts with India in the 18th and 19th centuries (according to the Khokand chronicles). T.K. Beisembiev. **J. Asian Hist.** 28 1994 pp.124-135.

742   A female conquistador: contradictions of colonial discourse in the countess of Merlin's *Viaje a La Habana*. Luz Mercedes Hincape. **Kunapipi** XXIII:2 2001 pp.31-47.

743   Flooded with foreign coins: Spanish and American administrators dealing with currency problems in the Philippines, 1890-1905. Willem G. Wolters. **Bijdragen** 157:3 2001 pp.511-538.

744   Foodways on two colonial whaling stations: archaeological and historical evidence for diet in nineteenth-century Tasmania. Susan Lawrence. **J. Roy. Aust. H. Soc.** 87:2 12:2001 pp.209-229.

745   Fray Alonso de Molina, lexicógrafo e indigenista. *[In Spanish]*; [Fray Alonso de Molina, lexicographer and supporter of the Indian cause]. Ascensión Hernández de León-Portilla. **Caravelle** 76-77 12:2001 pp.235-241.

746   Frederick Courteney Selous (1851-1917). C. John Ford. **Herit. Zimb.** 10 1991 pp.131-148.

747   French administrators in Maharaja Ranjit Singh's court. Jean Marie Lafont. **Sikh Rev.** 49:11(575) 11:2001 pp.44-45.

748   From law to custom: the shifting legal status of Muslim *originaires* in Kayes and Medine, 1903-13. Rebecca Shereikis. **J. Afr. Hist.** 42:2 2001 pp.261-284.

749   From pack animals to railways: transport and the expansion of peanut production and trade in Senegal, 1840-1940; *[Summary in French]*. Bernard Moitt. **Rev. Fr. Hist. O.mer.** 1(330-331) 6:2001 pp.241-268.

750   From the counting house to the field and loom: ecologies, cultures, and economies in the missions of Sonora (Mexico) and Chiquitaná (Bolivia). Cynthia Radding. **Hisp. Am. Hist. Rev.** 81:1 2:2001 pp.45-87.

751   Galvão among the cannibals: the emotional constitution of colonial power. João de Pina-Cabral. **Identities** 8:4 12:2001 pp.483-515.

752   Georges Baudot — Alfredo J. Bablot. *[In Spanish]*; [Georges Baudot and Alfredo J. Bablot]. Clementina Díaz de Ovando. **Caravelle** 76-77 12:2001 pp.455-459.

753   Le grand patronat colonial français face à la décolonisation, 1945-1962: problématiques, sources, conclusions. *[In French]*; [The great French colonial employers faced with decolonization, 1945-1962: problems, sources, conclusions]. Catherine Hodeir. **Rev. Fr. Hist. O.mer.** 1(330-331) 6:2001 pp.129-142.

754   Henrique Paiva Couceiro — um colonialista e um conservador. *[In Portuguese]*; (Henrique Paiva Couceiro — colonialist and conservative.) *[Summary]*; *[Summary in French]*. Vasco Pulido Valente. **Anál. Soc.** XXXVI:160 Autumn:2001 pp.767-802.

755   Historia de las mujeres en la Argentina: colonia y siglo XIX, siglo XX. *[In Spanish]*; [The history of women in Argentina: colonies and the 19th century/20th century]. Fernanda Gil Lozano [Ed.]; María Gabriela Ini [Ed.]; Valeria Silvina Pita [Ed.]; Mercedes Sacchi [Ed.]. Buenos Aires: Taurus, 2000. *ISBN: 9505116454, 9505116462, 9505116497. Volumes 1 and 2. Includes bibliographical references.*

756   History of a voyage to the land of Brazil, otherwise called America: containing the navigation and the remarkable things seen on the sea by the author; the behavior of Villeganon in that country; the customs and strange ways of life of the American savages; together with the description of various animals, trees, plants, and other singular things completely unknown over here. Jean de Léry; Janet Whatley [Tr.]; Janet Whatley [Intro.].

Berkeley CA: University of California Press, 1990. lxii, 276p. *ISBN: 0520068491. Translation of: Histoire d'un voyage fait en la terre du Brésil. (Series:* Latin American literature and culture - 6).

757   Holding the line: the rural enclosure movement in the Cape colony, c.1865-1910. Lance van Sittert. **Espace Pop. Soc.** 43:1 2002 pp.95-118.

758   El humanismo español y la crónica oficial de Indias de Pedro de Valencia. *[In Spanish]*; [Spanish humanism and the offical chronicles of Pedro de Valencia]. Jesús Paniagua Pérez. **Caravelle** 76-77 12:2001 pp.223-234.

759   Images de Timor en France (1812-1824). *[In French]*; [French images of Timor (1812-1825)]. Pierre Labrousse. **Archipel** 62 2001 pp.71-90.

760   Imperial bodies: the physical experience of the Raj, c.1800-1947. E.M. Collingham. Oxford: Polity, 2001. 256p. *ISBN: 0745623700, 0745623697.*

761   The Indian mutiny of 1857: why Britain succeeded and the rebels failed. Sanjay Radav. **J. Asian Hist.** 28 1994 pp.136-153.

762   Indian pundits and the Russian exploration of Tibet: an unknown story of the Great Game era. A. Andreyev. **Cent. Asia. J.** 45:2 2001 pp.163-180.

763   Indígenas y neohispanos en las áreas fronterizas de Costa Rica (1800-1860). *[In Spanish]*; [Indians and the Spanish colonists on Costa Rica's borderlands (1800-1860)] *[Summary]*. Juan Carlos Solórzano Fonseca. **An. Est. Cent.Am.** 25:2 1999 pp.73-102.

764   Indo-britanniques et indo-portugais: la présence marchande dans le Sud du Mozambique au moment de l'implantation du système colonial portugais (de la fin du XIXème siècle aux années 1930). *[In French]*; [The British and Portuguese Indies: merchant presence in Southern Mozambique at the time of the establishment of the Portuguese colonial system (from the end of the 19th century to the 1930's] *[Summary]*. Joana Pereira Leite. **Rev. Fr. Hist. O.mer.** 1(330-331) 6:2001 pp.13-38.

765   L'Indochine, les droits humains entre colonisateurs et colonisés, la Ligue des Droits de l'Homme (1898-1954). *[In French]*; [Indochina, human rights between colonizers and colonized, the French League for Human Rights (1898-1954)] *[Summary]*. Daniel Hémery. **Rev. Fr. Hist. O.mer.** 1(330-331) 6:2001 pp.223-240.

766   Inka bodies and the body of Christ: Corpus Christi in colonial Cusco, Peru. Carolyn Dean. Durham NC: Duke University Press, 1999. *ISBN: 0822323672, 082232332X. Includes bibliographical references and index.*

767   An innocent woman, unjustly accused? Charwe, medium of the Nehanda Mhondoro spirit, and the 1896-97 Central Shona rising in Zimbabwe. D.N. Beach. **Hist. Afr.** 25 1998 pp.27-54.

768   Las Islas Malvinas: descubrimiento, primeros mapas y ocupación: siglo XVI. *[In Spanish]*; [The Falkland Islands: discovery, first maps and occupation in the 16th century]. Vicente Guillermo Arnaud. Buenos Aires: Academia Nacional de Geografía, 2000. 255p. *ISBN: 9509953865. Includes bibliographical references (p. 247-255).*

769   Japan's first cyborg? Miss Nippon, eugenics and wartime technologies of beauty, body and blood. Jennifer Robertson. **Bod. Soc.** 7:1 3:2001 pp.1-34.

770   Late colonial development in British West Africa: the Gonja development project in the northern territories of the Gold Coast, 1948-57; *[Summary in French]*. Jeff D. Grischow. **Can. J. Afr. St.** 35:2 2001 pp.282-312.

771   Law and colonial cultures: legal regimes in world history, 1400-1900. Lauren A. Benton. New York: Cambridge University Press, 2001. 285p. *ISBN: 052100926X, 0521804140. Includes bibliographical references and index. (Series:* Studies in comparative world history).

772   Livrets scolaires coloniaux: méthodes d'analyse — approche herméneutique. *[In French]*; [Colonial records: analytical methodology and hermeneutics]. Honoré Vinck. **Hist. Afr.** 26 1999 pp.379-408.

773   Lost lion of empire: the life of Cape-to-Cairo Grogan. Edward Paice. London: HarperCollins, 2001. 470p. *ISBN: 0002570033.*

774 Luís de Molina e a escravização dos negros. *[In Portuguese]*; (Luís de Molina and black slavery.) *[Summary]*. António Manuel Hespanha. **Anál. Soc.** XXXV:157 Winter:2001 pp.937-960.

775 Madness and colonization: psychiatry in the British and French empires, 1800-1962. Richard Keller. **J. Soc. Hist** 35:2 Winter:2001 pp.295-326.

776 'Many divorces and many spinsters': marriage as an invented tradition in southern Malawi, 1946-1999. Amy Kaler. **J. Fam. Hist.** 26:4 10:2001 pp.529-556.

777 The many faces of cosmo-polis: border thinking and critical cosmopolitanism. Walter D. Mignolo. **Publ. Cult.** 12:3 Fall:2000 pp.721-748.

778 The many-headed hydra: sailors, slaves, commoners, and the hidden history of the revolutionary Atlantic. Peter Linebaugh; Marcus Buford Rediker. Boston MA: Beacon Press, 2000. 433p. *ISBN: 0807050067. Includes bibliographical references (p. 355-411) and index.*

779 Marco Polo and the discovery of the world. John Larner. New Haven CT, London: Yale University Press, 2001. xiii, 250p. *ISBN: 0300089007, 0300079710. Includes bibliographical references and index.* (*Series: Nota bene*).

780 Moçambique e as múltiplas formas da violência colonial. *[In Portuguese]*; [Mozambique and the many forms of colonial violence]. João Paulo Borges Coelho. **Stud. Afr.** 12 3:2001 pp.21-36.

781 The Moravian, Berlin, and Leipzig mission archives in Eastern Germany. Thaddeus Sunseri. **Hist. Afr.** 26 1999 pp.457-462.

782 Mosques, mawlanas and muharram: Indian Islam in colonial Natal, 1860-1910. Goolam H. Vahed. **J. Relig. Afr.** XXXI:3 2001 pp.305-335.

783 La muy temprana aportación etnográfica de Paulmier de Gonneville en 1504. *[In Spanish]*; [The early ethnographic contributions of Paulmier de Gonneville, 1504]. Miguel León-Portilla. **Caravelle** 76-77 12:2001 pp.177-181.

784 Nationalité et citoyenneté en Afrique occidentale français: originaires et citoyens dans le Sénégal colonial. *[In French]*; [Nationality and citizenship in French West Africa: indigenous peoples and citizens in colonial Senegal] *[Summary]*. Catherine Coquery-Vidrovitch. **J. Afr. Hist.** 42:2 2001 pp.285-306.

785 Negotiating India in the nineteenth-century media. Douglas M. Peers [Ed.]; David Finkelstein [Ed.]. Basingstoke: Macmillan, 2000. 288p. *ISBN: 0333711467. Includes index.*

786 New England encounters: Indians and Euroamericans ca. 1600-1850. Alden T. Vaughan. Boston MA: Northeastern University Press, 1999. xiv, 427p. *ISBN: 155553404X. Includes bibliographical references and index.*

787 The odyssey of Japanese colonists in the Dominican Republic. Oscar H. Horst; Katsuhiro Asagiri. **Geogr. Rev.** 90:3 7:2000 pp.335-358.

788 Of cargoes, colonies and kings: diplomatic and administrative service from Africa to the Pacific. Andrew Stuart. London: Radcliffe, 2001. 225p *ISBN: 1860647138.*

789 Old World irrigation technology in a New World context: *qanats* in Spanish colonial western Mexico. Christopher S. Beekman; Phil C. Weigand; John J. Pint. **Antiquity** 73:280 6:1999 pp.440-446.

790 On the origins of the Amazons of Dahomey. Stanley B. Alpern. **Hist. Afr.** 25 1998 pp.9-26.

791 The optimistic years: the Ayrshire mine, 1892-1909 and beyond. Robert Burrett. **Herit. Zimb.** 10 1991 pp.17-30.

792 Our fourth judge — Sir Fraser Russell. Michael J. Kimberley. **Herit. Zimb.** 10 1991 pp.31-50.

793 Philippine-Dutch social relations, 1600-2000. Otto van den Muijzenberg. **Bijdragen** 157:3 2001 pp.471-510.

794 The Pioneer Column and the occupation of Mashonaland. Tim Tanser. **Herit. Zimb.** 10 1991 pp.112-122.

795 Pioneer farmers and family dynasties in Marirangwe purchase area, colonial Zimbabwe, 1931-1947; *[Summary in French]*. Allison K. Shutt. **Afr. Stud. R.** 43:3 12:2000 pp.59-80.

796   La platica breve de la *Doctrina Christiana* (1584). *[In French]*; (The *platica breve* forming part of the *Doctrina Christiana* (1584).) *[Summary]*. Gerald Taylor. **Amerindia** 25 2000 pp.173-188.

797   The politics of land settlement in Namibia, 1890-1960. Christo Botha. **S. Afr. Hist. J.** 42 2000 pp.232-276.

798   'Portuguese' architecture and Luso-African identity in Senegambia and Guinea, 1730-1890. Peter Mark. **Hist. Afr.** 23 1996 pp.179-196.

799   Postcolonial perspectives on the cultures of Latin America and Lusophone Africa. Robin Fiddian [Ed.]. Liverpool: Liverpool University Press, 2000. x, 218p. *ISBN: 085323566X, 0853235767. Includes bibliographical references and index.*

800   Radama's smile: domestic challenges to royal ideology in early nineteenth-century Imerina. Gerald M. Berg. **Hist. Afr.** 25 1998 pp.69-92.

801   Reappropriating colonial documents in Kolhapur (Maharashtra): variations on a nationalist theme. Véronique Bénéï. **Mod. Asian S.** 33:4 10:1999 pp.913-950.

802   Reflexiones acerca del plano de Tenochtitlan publicado en Nuremberg en 1524. *[In Spanish]*; [A study of the map of Tenochtitlan published in Nuremberg in 1524]. Eduardo Matos Moctezuma. **Caravelle** 76-77 12:2001 pp.183-195.

803   Réserves indigènes et périmètres de colonisation à Madagascar (1895-1960). *[In French]*; [Indigenous reserves and the perimeters of colonisation in Madagascar (1895-1960) *[Summary]*. Francis Koerner. **Rev. Fr. Hist. O.mer.** 1(330-331) 6:2001 pp.91-102.

804   Rethinking ancestors and colonial power in Madagascar; *[Summary in French]*. Jennifer Cole; Karen Middleton. **Africa** 71:1 2001 pp.1-37.

805   The rhetoric of empire: colonial discourse in journalism, travel writing, and imperial administration. David Spurr. Durham NC, London: Duke University Press, 1993. 212p. *ISBN: 0822313170, 0822313030. (Series:* Post-contemporary interventions).

806   O Rio Cuanza (Angola), da Barra a Cambambe: reconstituição de aspectos geográficos e acontecimentos históricos dos séculos XVI e XVII. *[In Portuguese]*; [The Kwanza River in Angola, from the coast to Cambambe: piecing together geographical features and historical events from the 16th and 17th centuries] *[Summary]*. Ilídio do Amaral. Lisbon: Instituto de Investigação Científica Tropical, 2000. 110p. *ISBN: 9726728851. Ministério da Ciência e da Tecnologia.*

807   Slavery. Robert L. Paquette [Ed.]; Stanley L. Engerman [Ed.]; Seymour Drescher [Ed.]. New York: Oxford University Press, 2001. *ISBN: 0192893025. Includes bibliographical references and index. (Series:* Oxford readers).

808   Social and cultural conditions of religious conversion in colonial southwest Tanzania, 1891-1939. Wolfgang Gabbert. **Ethnology** XL:4 Fall:2001 pp.291-308.

809   Steel to stone: a chronicle of colonialism in the southern highlands of Papua New Guinea. Jeffrey Clark; Chris Ballard [Ed.]; Michael Nihill [Ed.]. New York: Oxford University Press, 2001. 187p. *ISBN: 0198233779. Includes bibliographical references. (Series:* Oxford studies in social and cultural anthropology).

810   Subjecting the natives: aborigines, property and possession under early colonial rule. Bruce Buchan. **Soc. Anal. [Adelaide]** 45(2) 10:2001 pp.143-162.

811   Südsee-Babys erinnern an Kolonialgebiete im Pazifik. *[In German]*; [South Sea babies: a reminder of the Pacific regions's colonial past]. Susanne Fenske. **Tribus** 50 12:2001 pp.87-90.

812   A sugar factory and its swimming pool: incorporation and differentiation in Dutch colonial society in Java. G. Roger Knight. **Ethn. Racial** 24:3 5:2001 pp.451-471.

813   'The abandoned mother': ageing, old age and missionaries in early and mid-nineteenth century south-east Africa. Andreas Sagner. **J. Afr. Hist.** 42:2 2001 pp.173-198.

814   Tropical Versailles: empire, monarchy, and the Portuguese Royal Court in Rio de Janeiro, 1808-1821. Kirsten Schultz. New York, London: Routledge, 2001. 325p. *ISBN: 0415929881, 0415929873.*

815   Um homem para todas as causas — perfil político do duque de Ávila e Bolama. *[In Portuguese]*; (A man for all causes — a political profile of the Duke of Ávila and

Bolama.) *[Summary]*; *[Summary in French]*. José Miguel Sardica. **Anál. Soc.** XXXVI:160 Autumn:2001 pp.639-684.

816 Venezuela. República negra en los informes a España. *[In Spanish]*; [Venezuela: the *Black Republic* of Spanish reports] *[Summary]*. Consuelo Cal. **Jahrb. Ges. Lat.am.** 38 2001 pp.207-232.

817 The view across the river: Harriette Colenso and the Zulu struggle against imperialism. Jeff Guy. Oxford: James Currey, 2001. 498p. *ISBN: 086486373X, 0813921333, 0852557914.*

818 *Virtù* and *fortuna* in Radama's nascent bureaucracy, 1816-1828. Gerald M. Berg. **Hist. Afr.** 23 1996 pp.29-74.

Prehistory
Préhistoire

819 Accelerator radiocarbon dating of the initial Upper Palaeolithic in southeast Siberia. Ted Goebel; Mikhail Aksenov. **Antiquity** 69:263 6:1995 pp.349-357.

820 Adriatic sailors and stone knappers: Palagruža in the 3rd millennium BC. Timothy Kaiser; Stašo Forenbaher. **Antiquity** 73:280 6:1999 pp.313-324.

821 Aspects of the prehistory of Freetown and creoledom. P.E.H. Hair. **Hist. Afr.** 25 1998 pp.111-118.

822 Atapuerca, le conte de deux sites. *[In French]*; (Atapuerca, a tale of two sites.) *[Summary]*. Y. Fernández-Jalvo; P. Andrews. **Anthropologie [Paris]** 105:2 4-6:2001 pp.223-236.

823 Le Bâtiment G de Rumeilah (oasis d'Al Ain). Remarques sur les salles à poteaux de l'âge du Fer en Péninsule d'Oman. *[In French]*; [Building G, Rumeilah (Al Ain oasis). The Oman peninsular during the Iron Age]. R. Boucharlat; P. Lombard. **Iran. Ant.** XXXVI 2001 pp.213-238.

824 Les carnivores (Mammalia) des sites du pléistocène ancien et moyen d'Atapuerca (Espagne). *[In French]*; (The carnivores (Mammalia) from the Lower and Middle Pleistocene sites of Atapuerca (Spain).) *[Summary]*. N. Garcia; J.L. Arsuaga. **Anthropologie [Paris]** 105:1 1-3:2001 pp.83-94.

825 Chalcolithic dwelling remains, cup marks and olive (*Olea europaea*) stones at Nevallat. Edwin C.M. van den Brink; Nili Liphschitz; Dorit Lazar; Georges Bonani. **Israel Explor. J.** 51:1 2001 pp.36-43.

826 The chronology of the Iron Age 'moats' of northeast Thailand. R.J. McGrath; W.E. Boyd. **Antiquity** 75:288 6:2001 pp.349-360.

827 Circular earthwork Krek 52/62: recent research on the prehistory of Cambodia. Gerd Albrecht; Miriam Noël Haidle; Chhor Sivleng; Heang Leang Hong; Heng Sophady; Heng Than; Mao Someaphyvath; Sirik Kada; Som Sophal; Thuy Chanthourn; Vin Laychour. **Asian Persp. [Hawaii]** 39:1-2 Spring-Fall:2000 pp.20-46.

828 Cosmovision and metaphor: monsters and shamans in Gallo-British cult-expression; *[Summary in French]*; *[Summary in German]*. Miranda Aldhouse Green. **Euro. J. Arch.** 4:2 8:2001 pp.203-232.

829 Dolna Grashtitsa-90: frakiiskie ochagi-zhertvenniki. *[In Russian]*; (*Dolna grashtitza-90*: Thracian sacrificial altar hearths.) *[Summary]*. S.M. Krykin. **Etnograf. Oboz.** 1 1-2:2000 pp.81-87.

830 Early agriculturalist population diasporas? Farming, languages, and genes. Peter Bellwood. **Ann. R. Anthr.** 30 2001 pp.181-208.

831 The Eastern al-Hasa late Pleistocene project: preliminary report on the 1998 season. N.R. Coinman; D.I. Olszewski; K. Abdo; T.G. Clausen; J.B. Cooper; J.R. Fox; M. al-Nahar; E. Richey; L.S. Saele. **A. Dept. Antiq. Jordan** XLIII 1999 pp.9-26.

832 Éléments pour une préhistoire de la géométrie. *[In French]*; [Towards a prehistory of geometry] *[Summary]*. O. Keller. **Anthropologie [Paris]** 105:3 7-9:2001 pp.327-350.

833 Environmental crisis in prehistory: hunter-gatherers and mass extinction. Martin Spence. **Cap. Nat. Social.** 12(3):47 9:2001 pp.105-118.

834   An Epipalaeolithic sequence from Wādī Hisbān in the east Jordan Valley. P.C. Edwards; M.J. Head; P.G. Macumber. **A. Dept. Antiq. Jordan** XLIII 1999 pp.27-48.

835   Expressions of inequality: settlement patterns, economy and social organization in the southwest Iberian Bronze Age (c.1700-1100 BC). Leonardo García Sanjuán. **Antiquity** 73:280 6:1999 pp.337-351.

836   La fin du paléolithique moyen et le début du paléolithique supérieur en Grèce: la séquence de la grotte 1 de Klissoura. *[In French]*; [The end of the Middle Palaeolithic and the beginning of the Upper Palaeolithic in Greece: the sequence of cave 1 at Klissoura] *[Summary]*. M. Koumouzelis; J. Kozlowski; C. Escutenaire; V. Sitlivy; K. Sobczyk; H. Valladas; N. Tisnerat-Laborde; P. Wojtal; B. Ginter. **Anthropologie [Paris]** 105:4 10-12:2001 pp.469-504.

837   'Fish-tail' projectile points and megamammals: new evidence from Paso Otero 5 (Argentina). Gustavo A. Martínez. **Antiquity** 75:289 9:2001 pp.523-528.

838   From the Bronze Age to the Iron Age in Thailand: applying the heterarchical approach. Dougald J.W. O'Reilly. **Asian Persp. [Hawaii]** 39:1-2 Spring-Fall:2000 pp.1-19.

839   Géologie de la Sierra de Atapuerca et stratigraphie des remplissages karstiques de galería et Dolina (Burgos, Espagne). *[In French]*; (Geology of Sierra de Atapuerca and stratigraphy of karst fillings from Galería and Dolina (Burgos, Spain).) *[Summary]*. A. Pérez-Gonzàlez; J. María Parés; E. Carbonell; T. Aleixandre; A.I. Ortega; A. Benito; M.A. Martín Merino. **Anthropologie [Paris]** 105:1 1-3:2001 pp.27-44.

840   GIS-backed analysis and modeling for the early Bronze Age settlement site in Bruszczewo (Poland). Benjamin Ducke. **Archaeol. Polona** 39 2001 pp.165-172.

841   Le gisement de Galería (Sierra de Atapuerca, Burgos, Espagne): un modèle archéozoologique de gestion du territoire durant le Pléistocène. *[In French]*; (The site of Galería (Sierra de Atapuerca, Burgos, Spain): an archaeozoological pattern for territory gestion during Pleistocene.) *[Summary]*. R.H. Pàmies; C.D. Fernàndez-Lomana; J. Rosell Ardèvol; I. Cáceres Cuello de Oro; V. Moreno Lara; Núria Ibañez Lòpez; P. Saladié Ballesté. **Anthropologie [Paris]** 105:2 4-6:2001 pp.237-258.

842   Le gisement pléistocène de la «sima del elefante» (Sierra de Atapuerca, Espagne). *[In French]*; (Sima del Elefante: a new Pleistocene site at the Sierra of Atapuerca (Spain).) *[Summary]*. A. Rosas; A. Pérez-González; E. Carbonell; J. van der Made; A. Sánchez; C. Laplana; G. Cuenca-Bescós; J.M. Parés; R. Huguet. **Anthropologie [Paris]** 105:2 4-6:2001 pp.301-312.

843   Die Herkunft der zu Kyrene ansässigen Perioiken. *[In German]*; [The origins of the Perioikoi settlers of Kyrene] *[Summary]*. F.X. Ryan. **Lib. Stud.** 32 2001 pp.79-86.

844   Hermeneutics and natural science in prehistoric archaeology. Johannes Müller. **Archaeol. Polona** 39 2001 pp.147-152.

845   High-tech in the Middle Palaeolithic: Neandertal-manufactured pitch identified. Johann Koller; Ursula Baumer; Dietrich Mania. **Euro. J. Arch.** 4:3 12:2001 pp.385-397.

846   Historique des découvertes préhistoriques de la Sierra de Atapuerca (Burgos, Espagne), et perspectives du futur. *[In French]*; (The history of the Sierra de Atapuerca (Burgos, Spain) prehistoric findings, and the future of the research.) *[Summary]*. X.P. Rodríguez; E. Carbonell; A.I. Ortega. **Anthropologie [Paris]** 105:1 1-3:2001 pp.3-12.

847   Holocene climatic changes in an archaeological landscape: the case study of Wadi Tanezzuft and its drainage basin (SW Fezzan, Libyan Sahara). Mauro Cremaschi. **Lib. Stud.** 32 2001 pp.3-28.

848   Household units in the analysis of prehistoric social complexity, Cook Islands. Julie M.E. Taomia. **Asian Persp. [Hawaii]** 39:1-2 Spring-Fall:2000 pp.139-164.

849   The initial Upper Paleolithic in Northeast Asia. P. Jeffrey Brantingham; Andrei I. Krivoshapkin; Li Jinzeng; Ya. Tserendagva. **Curr. Anthr.** 42:5 12:2001 pp.735-746.

850   Interprétation fonctionnelle d'un site gravettien à burins de Noailles. *[In French]*; (Functional interpretation of a Gravettian settlement of Noailles Burins Facies.) *[Summary]*. B. Aranguren; A. Reverdin. **Anthropologie [Paris]** 105:4 10-12:2001 pp.533-546.

851   An interview with Richard S. MacNeish. Helke Ferrie; Richard S. MacNeish. **Curr. Anthr.** 42:5 12:2001 pp.715-734.

852   Island identities: ritual, travel and the creation of difference in Neolithic Malta; *[Summary in French]*; *[Summary in German]*. John Robb. **Euro. J. Arch.** 4:2 8:2001 pp.175-202.

853   Kultura badeńska w regionie wielicko-bocheńskim — stan i problematyka badań. *[In Polish]*; (The Baden culture in the Wieliczka-Bochnia region — state of research and key issues.) *[Summary]*. Albert Zastawny. **Spraw. Arch.** 52 2000 pp.9-47.

854   Kultura ceramiki wstęgowej rytej w zachodniej części Małopolski — materiały do badań nad geografią osadnictwa. *[In Polish]*; (The linear band pottery culture in western Lesser Poland — settlement geography sources.) *[Summary]*. Agnieszka Czekaj-Zastawny. **Spraw. Arch.** 52 2000 pp.49-95.

855   Kultura przeworska we wschodniej części Niecki Nidziańskiej. *[In Polish]*; (The Przeworsk culture in the eastern part of the Nida Basin.) *[Summary]*. Krzysztof Garbacz. **Spraw. Arch.** 52 2000 pp.329-356.

856   The last Pleniglacial and the human settlement of Central Europe: new information from the Rhineland site of Wiesbaden-Igstadt. Martin Street; Thomas Terberger. **Antiquity** 73:280 6:1999 pp.259-272.

857   The late Quaternary of the western Amazon: climate, vegetation and humans. J. Stephen Athens; Jerome V. Ward. **Antiquity** 73:280 6:1999 pp.287-302.

858   Later Neolithic woodland regeneration in the Long Barrow ditch fills of the Avebury area: the molluscan evidence. Paul Davies; Colleen Wolski. **Ox. J. Archaeol.** 20:4 11:2001 pp.311-318.

859   Later prehistory in south-east Scotland: a critical review. D.W. Harding. **Ox. J. Archaeol.** 20:4 11:2001 pp.355-376.

860   Life on the edge: prehistoric settlement and economy on Utrok Atoll, northwest Marshall Islands. Marshall I. Weisler. **Archaeol. Ocean.** 36:3 10:2001 pp.109-133.

861   Long-distance transport of bulk goods in the pre-Hispanic American Southwest. Nancy J. Malville. **J. Anthrop. Arch.** 20:2 6:2001 pp.230-243.

862   Masterov Kliuch and the early Upper Palaeolithic of the Transbaikal, Siberia. Ted Goebel; Michael R. Waters; Mikhail N. Meshcherin. **Asian Persp. [Hawaii]** 39:1-2 Spring-Fall:2000 pp.47-70.

863   Megalithic engineering techniques: experiments using axe-based technology. Clifford J. Osenton. **Antiquity** 75:288 6:2001 pp.293-298.

864   Méthodes, objectifs et flexibilité d'un système de production Levallois dans le nord de l'Italie. *[In French]*; [Methods, objectives and flexibility in north Italian Levallois production] *[Summary]*. M. Peresani. **Anthropologie [Paris]** 105:3 7-9:2001 pp.351-368.

865   Microburins and microliths of the Levantine Epipalaeolithic. Daniel Kaufman. **Antiquity** 69:263 6:1995 pp.375-381.

866   Modeling prehistoric populations: the case of Neolithic Brittany. Chris Scarre. **J. Anthrop. Arch.** 20.3 9.2001 pp.285 313.

867   Neolithic diet at the Brochtorff circle, Malta; *[Summary in German]*. M.P. Richards; R.E.M. Hedges; I. Walton; S. Stoddart; C. Malone. **Euro. J. Arch.** 4:2 8:2001 pp.253-262.

868   New AMS radiocarbon dates for the North Ferriby boats — a contribution to dating prehistoric seafaring in northwestern Europe. Edward V. Wright; Robert E.M. Hedges; Alex Bayliss; Robert Van de Noort. **Antiquity** 75:290 12:2001 pp.726-734.

869   A new megalithic dolmen from the Balearic island of Mallorca: its radiocarbon dating and artefacts. W. Waldren. **Ox. J. Archaeol.** 20:3 8:2001 pp.241-262.

870   Nouvelles perspectives sur le peuplement humain de l'Asie extrême-orientale depuis le pléistocène supérieur récent. *[In French]*; (New perspectives on human settlement in far eastern Asia from the late Upper Pleistocene period.) *[Summary]*. F. Demeter. **Bio. Hum. Anthrop.** 19:3-4 7-12:2001 pp.247-256.

871   Obiekt gospodarczy kultury badeńskiej odkryty z pełnym wyposażeniem w Szarbi Zwierzynieckiej, gm. Skalbmierz. *[In Polish]*; (The Baden culture utility feature with complete outfit from Szarbia Zwierzyniecka, Skalbmierz commune.) *[Summary]*. Barbara Baczyńska. **Spraw. Arch.** 52 2000 pp.113-130.

872   Les ongulés d'Atapuerca. Stratigraphie et biogéographie. *[In French]*; (The ungulates from Atapuerca: stratigraphy and biogeography.) *[Summary]*. J. van der Made. **Anthropologie [Paris]** 105:1 1-3:2001 pp.95-114.

873   Paviland Cave: contextualizing the 'Red Lady'. Stephen Aldhouse-Green; Paul Pettitt. **Antiquity** 72:278 12:1998 pp.756-772.

874   Personhood and social relations in the British Neolithic with a study from the Isle of Man. Chris Fowler. **J. Mat. Cult.** 6:2 7:2001 pp.137-164.

875   Perspectives méthodologiques de l'analyse fonctionnelle des ensembles lithiques du pléistocène inférieur et moyen d'Atapuerca (Burgos, Espagne). *[In French]*; (Methodological perspectives of usewear analysis applied to lithic assemblages from Atapuerca's (Burgos, Spain) Lower and Middle Pleistocene.) *[Summary]*. B. Márquez; A. Ollé; R. Sala; J.M. Vergès. **Anthropologie [Paris]** 105:2 4-6:2001 pp.281-300.

876   Prehistoric context of Mayurbhanj district of Orissa (India). Sudipta DasGupta. **Anthropos [St. Augustin]** 95:2 2000 pp.485-500.

877   Prehistoric human migration in the *Linearbandkeramik* of Central Europe. T. Douglas Price; R. Alexander Bentley; Jens Lüning; Detlef Gronenborn; Joachim Wahl. **Antiquity** 75:289 9:2001 pp.593-603.

878   La région de Téhéran à l'aube de l'âge du Fer: reflections et commentaires sur les nécropoles du IIe millénaire av. J.-C. *[In French]*; [The Tehran region at the dawn of the Iron Age: reflections and commentaries on cemeteries in 2000 BC]. A. Mousavi. **Iran. Ant.** XXXVI 2001 pp.151-212.

879   Risk and invention in human technological evolution. Ben Fitzhugh. **J. Anthrop. Arch.** 20:2 6:2001 pp.125-167.

880   Ritual control and transformation in middle-range societies: an example from the American Southwest. Gregson Schachner. **J. Anthrop. Arch.** 20:2 6:2001 pp.168-194.

881   O roli krzemienia u niektórych społeczności epok metali. *[In Polish]*; [About the role of flint in some societies of metal periods] *[Summary]*; *[Summary in French]*. Tadeusz Malinowski. **Przeg. Archeolog.** 48 2000 pp.127-140.

882   The seasonal cycle of grassland use in the Caspian sea steppe during the Bronze Age: a new approach to an old problem. Natalia I. Shishlina. **Euro. J. Arch.** 4:3 12:2001 pp.346-366.

883   The second phase of Neolithization in East-Central Europe. Marek Nowak. **Antiquity** 75:289 9:2001 pp.582-592.

884   La séquence des rongeurs (Mammalia) des sites du pléistocène inférieur et moyen d'Atapuerca (Burgos, Espagne). *[In French]*; (The rodent sequence (Mammalia) of the Lower to Middle Pleistocene sites of Atapuerca (Burgos, Spain).) *[Summary]*. G. Cuenca Bescos; J. Ignacio Canudo; C. Laplana. **Anthropologie [Paris]** 105:1 1-3:2001 pp.115-130.

885   Settlement patterns in the Ayalon Valley in the Bronze and Iron ages. Alon Shavit. **Tel Aviv** 27:2 2000 pp.189-230.

886   Social and monumental space in Neolithic Thessaly, Greece. Stratos Nanoglou. **Euro. J. Arch.** 4:3 12:2001 pp.303-322.

887   The stone tool technology of Ishi and the Yana of north central California: inferences for hunter-gatherer cultural identity in historic California. M. Steven Shackley. **Am. Anthrop.** 102:4 12:2000 pp.693-712.

888   Stonehenge: is the medium the message? John C. Barrett; Kathryn J. Fewster. **Antiquity** 72:278 12:1998 pp.847-852.

889   Structure de la communauté de mammifères pléistocènes de Gran Dolina (Sierra de Atapuerca, Burgos, Espagne). *[In French]*; (Pleistocene mammalian community structure of Gran Dolina (Sierra de Atapuerca, Burgos, Spain).) *[Summary]*. J. Rodríguez. **Anthropologie [Paris]** 105:1 1-3:2001 pp.131-157.

890   Structure morphotechnique de l'industrie lithique du pléistocène inférieur et moyen d'Atapuerca (Burgos, Espagne). *[In French]*; (Morphotechnical structure of the lithic industry of Atapuerca's Lower and Middle Pleistocene sites (Burgos, Spain).) *[Summary]*.

E. Carbonell; M. Mosquera; A. Ollé; X.P. Rodríguez; M. Sahnouni; R. Sala; J.M. Vergès. **Anthropologie [Paris]** 105:2 4-6:2001 pp.259-280.

891   Tabaqat al-Būma: 1990 excavations at a Kebaran and late Neolithic site in Wādī Ziqlāb. E.B. Banning; R.R. Dods; J. Field; I. Kujit; J. McCorriston; J. Siggers; H. Taani; J. Triggs. **A. Dept. Antiq. Jordan** XXXVI 1992 pp.43-70.

892   Tågerup — fifteen hundred years of Mesolithic occupation in western Scania, Sweden: a preliminary view; *[Summary in French]*; *[Summary in German]*. Per Karsten; Bo Knarrström. **Euro. J. Arch.** 4:2 8:2001 pp.165-174.

893   Towards an environmental history of the Amazon: from prehistory to the nineteenth century. David Cleary. **Lat. Am. Res. R.** 36:2 2001 pp.65-96.

894   La transition vers le paléolithique supérieur dans la grotte du Castillo (Cantabrie, Espagne): la couche 18. *[In French]*; (The transition to the Upper Palaeolithic in the Castillo cave (Cantabria, Spain): level 18.) *[Summary]*. V. Cabrera; J.M. Maillo; M. Lloret; F. Bernaldo de Quiros. **Anthropologie [Paris]** 105:4 10-12:2001 pp.505-532.

895   Tribes, trade, and towns: a new framework for the late Iron Age in southern Jordan and the Negev. Piotr Bienkowski; Eveline van der Steen. **B. Am. Sch. Orient. R.** 323 8:2001 pp.21-47.

896   Unusual food plants from Oakbank Crannog, Loch Tay, Scottish Highlands: cloudberry, opium poppy and spelt wheat. Jennifer J. Miller; James H. Dickson; T. Nicholas Dixon. **Antiquity** 72:278 12:1998 pp.805-811.

B.4.2:   **Archaeology**
            Archéologie

897   4Q348, 4Q343 and 4Q345: three economic documents from Qumran cave 4? Hanan Eshel. **J. Jew. Stud.** LII:1 Spring:2001 pp.132-135.

898   Analyse morphométrique comparée des dents humaines de Gran Dolina (TD6) et de Sima de los Huesos d'Atapuerca. *[In French]*; (Comparative morphometric analysis of the human dental samples of Gran Dolina (TD6) and Sima de los Huesos caves sites at Atapuerca.) *[Summary]*. J.M. Bermúdez de Castro; S. Sarmiento. **Anthropologie [Paris]** 105:2 4-6:2001 pp.203-222.

899   Analyse phylogénétique des hominidés de la Sierra de Atapuerca (Sima de los Huesos et Gran Dolina TD-6): l'évidence crânienne. *[In French]*; [Phylogenetic analysis of hominids from Sierra de Atapuerca (Sima de los Huesos and Gran Dolina TD6): the cranial evidence] *[Summary]*. J.L. Arsuaga; I. Martínez; A. Gracia. **Anthropologie [Paris]** 105:2 4-6:2001 pp.161-178.

900   Archaeobotanical evidence for pearl millet (*Pennisetum glaucum*) in sub-Saharan West Africa. A.C. D'Andrea; M. Klee; J. Casey. **Antiquity** 75:288 6:2001 pp.341-348.

901   Archaeo-geology in Petra, Jordan. Friedrich Pflüger. **A. Dept. Antiq. Jordan** XXXIX 1995 pp.281-296.

902   Archaeological remarks on the 4th and 5th dynasty chronology. Miroslav Verner. **Arch. Orient.** 69:3 8:2001 pp.363-418.

903   The archaeological study of empires and imperialism in pre-Hispanic central Mexico. Michael E. Smith; Lisa Montiel. **J. Anthrop. Arch.** 20:3 9:2001 pp.245-284.

904   Archaeology of Bamanghaty-Mayurbhanj, Orissa. Basanta K. Mohanta. **Oris. Hist. R. J.** XLV:1-4 2000 pp.87-99.

905   The archaeology of hermits: a reply. Yizhar Hirschfeld. **Tel Aviv** 27:2 2000 pp.286-291.

906   The archaeology of Myanma Pyay (Burma). Miriam T. Stark; Michael A. Aung-Thwin; Elizabeth Moore; Pauk Pauk; Bob Hudson; Nyein Lwin; Win Maung Tanpawady; Peter Grave; Mike Barbetti; John N. Miksic; Pamela Gutman; Ian G. Glover; C.F.W. Higham. **Asian Persp. [Hawaii]** 40:1 Spring:2001 pp.1-138. *Collection of 9 articles.*

907   The archaeology of the southern Fazzan and prospects for future research. David N. Edwards. **Lib. Stud.** 32 2001 pp.49-66.

908   Archaeology, science-based archaeology and the Mediterranean Bronze Age metals trade: a contribution to the debate. Noel Gale. **Euro. J. Arch.** 4:1 4:2001 pp.113-132.

909   Becoming New York: the Five Points neighborhood. Rebecca Yamin; Stephen A. Brighton; C. Milne; Pamela Crabtree; Michael C. Bonasera; Leslie Raymer; Cheryl J. LaRoche; Gary S. McGowan; Heather J. Griggs; Reginald H. Pitts; Paul E. Reckner; Robert Fitts; Diana diZerega Wall. **Hist. Archaeol.** 35:3 2001 pp.1-135. *Collection of 11 articles.*

910   Bioarchaeological research in northwestern Argentina: analyses by classification and regression trees. B. Wiese; M.G. Colaneri; E. Bru de Labanda; R. Raya. **Statistica** LXI:1 1-3:2001 pp.135-142.

911   Ceremonial households and domestic temples: 'fuzzy' definitions in the Andean formative. Emily Dean; David Kojan. **Kroeber Anthr. Soc. Pap.** 85 2001 pp.109-135.

912   Chemical composition and lead isotopy of copper and bronze from Nuragic Sardinia. Friedrich Begemann; Sigrid Schmitt-Strecker; Ernst Pernicka; Fulvia Lo Schiavo. **Euro. J. Arch.** 4:1 4:2001 pp.43-86.

913   A comparison of the environmental changes of the post-European period with those of the preceding 2000 years at Lake Keilambete, south-western Victoria. S.D. Mooney; J.R. Dodson. **Aust. Geogr.** 32:2 7:2001 pp.163-180.

914   Comparisons and the case for interaction among Neanderthals and early modern humans in the Levant. Daniel Kaufman. **Ox. J. Archaeol.** 20:3 8:2001 pp.219-240.

915   Cremna in Pisidia: a re-appraisal of the siege works. G. Davies. **Anatol. St.** 50 2000 pp.151-158.

916   Cross-cultural links in ancient Iberia: socio-economic anatomy of hospitality. Eduardo Sánchez-Moreno. **Ox. J. Archaeol.** 20:4 11:2001 pp.391-414.

917   The end of town-life in Scythia Minor. Alexandru Madgearu. **Ox. J. Archaeol.** 20:2 5:2001 pp.207-217.

918   Evidence of flax cultivation from the temple-granary complex Et-Tell (Bethsaida/Julias). Patrick Scott Geyer. **Israel Explor. J.** 51:2 2001 pp.231-234.

919   Far Western, Western, and Eastern Lapita: a re-evaluation. Glenn R. Summerhayes. **Asian Persp. [Hawaii]** 39:1-2 Spring-Fall:2000 pp.109-138.

920   The faunal remains from Molokwane, capital of the Bakwena ba Modimosana, Northwest Province, South Africa. Julius C.C. Pretorius; Ina Plug. **S. Afr. J. Ethnol.** 24:1 2001 pp.25-39.

921   Formation of the Phrygian state: the early Iron Age at Gordion. Mary M. Voigt; Robert C. Henrickson. **Anatol. St.** 50 2000 pp.37-54.

922   The Galatian settlement in Asia minor. Gareth Darbyshire; Stephen Mitchell; Levent Vardar. **Anatol. St.** 50 2000 pp.75-98.

923   Gharandal survey 1997: air photo interpretation and ground verification. D. Kennedy; J. Kennedy [Contrib.]. **A. Dept. Antiq. Jordan** XLII 1998 pp.573-586.

924   Hazor XII-XI with an addendum on Ben-Tor's dating of Hazor X-VII. Israel Finkelstein. **Tel Aviv** 27:2 2000 pp.231-247.

925   The Indo-Iranian problem in the light of the latest excavations in Margiana. V. Sarianidi. **Stud. Orient.** 94 2001 pp.417-442.

926   Investigations at Jabal Quiesa, Jordan (1993): a reconsideration of chronology and occupational history. Ian Kuijt; Meredith S. Chesson. **A. Dept. Antiq. Jordan** XXXVIII 1994 pp.33-40.

927   An Iron Age (Edomite) occupation of Jabal al-Khubtha (Petra) and other discoveries on the 'mountain of treachery and deceit'. M. Lindner; E.A. Knauf; J. Hübl; J.P. Zeitler. **A. Dept. Antiq. Jordan** XLI 1997 pp.177-188.

928   The Iron Age I at Tel Hazor in light of the renewed excavations. Doron Ben-Ami. **Israel Explor. J.** 51:2 2001 pp.148-170.

929   The jaguars of Altar Q, Copan, Honduras: faunal analysis, archaeology, and ecology; *[Summary in Spanish]*; *[Summary in French]*. D.A. Ballinger; J. Stomper. **J. Ethnobio.** 20:2 Winter:2000 pp.223-238.

930 Jeszcze raz w sprawie „zaleceń" pióra Zbigniewa Kobylińskiego. *[In Polish]*; (One more time on the 'recommendations' of Zbigniew Kobyliński.) *[Summary]*. Eugeniusz Tomczak. **Spraw. Arch.** 52 2000 pp.435-442.

931 The Lapita site at Votua, northern Lau islands, Fiji. Geoffrey Clark; Atholl Anderson; Sepeti Matararaba. **Archaeol. Ocean.** 36:3 10:2001 pp.134-145.

932 A limestone landscape from the air: le Causse Méjean, Languedoc, France. Peter Fowler. **Antiquity** 73:280 6:1999 pp.411-419.

933 The Median Empire reconsidered: a view from Kerkenes Dag. Geoffrey D. Summers. **Anatol. St.** 50 2000 pp.55-74.

934 A Moabite sanctuary at Khirbat al-Mudayna. P.M. Michèle Daviau; Margreet Steiner. **B. Am. Sch. Orient. R.** 320 11:2000 pp.1-21.

935 A new dating sequence for Çatalhöyük. Craig Cessford. **Antiquity** 75:290 12:2001 pp.717-725.

936 New Late Iron Age spatial identities in the Bankeveld. J.C.C. Pistorius. **S. Afr. J. Ethnol.** 23:4 2000 pp.150-163.

937 Phū Phra Bāt: a remarkable archaeological site in northeastern Thailand. Nandana Chutiwongs. **J. Siam Soc.** 88:1-2 2000 pp.42-52.

938 The potential for heavy metal soil analysis on low status archaeological sites at Shapwick, Somerset. M.A. Aston; M.H. Martin; A.W. Jackson. **Antiquity** 72:278 12:1998 pp.838-847.

939 A preliminary report on the Bedouin ethnoarchaeological survey project in southern Jordan. Benjamin Adam Saidel. **A. Dept. Antiq. Jordan** XLIV 2000 pp.569-580.

940 A preliminary report on the Dhībān plateau survey project, 1999: the Versacare expedition. Chang-Ho C. Ji; Jong Keun Lee. **A. Dept. Antiq. Jordan** XLIV 2000 pp.493-506.

941 Recent research at Abu Hamid. Geneviève Dollfus; Zeidan Kafafi. **A. Dept. Antiq. Jordan** XXXVII 1993 pp.241-262.

942 Recherches archéologiques dans le Haut Xingu, Mato Grosso, Brésil. *[In French]*; (Archaeological research in the Upper Xingu, Mato Grosso, Brazil.) *[Summary]*; *[Summary in Portuguese]*. Pierre Becquelin. **J. Soc. Amér.** 86 2000 pp.9-48.

943 Relative Chronologie der mittelalterlichen Siedlung in Bielovce/Slowakei. *[In German]*; [Relative chronology for the medieval settlement in southwestern Slovakia] *[Summary]*. Gabriel Fusek. **Przeg. Archeolog.** 48 2000 pp.115-126.

944 Results of archaeological reconnaissance in West Aqaba: evidence of the pre-Islamic settlement. J.L. Meloy. **A. Dept. Antiq. Jordan** XXXV 1991 pp.397-411.

945 Results of the Southeast 'Arabah archaeological reconnaissance. Andrew M. Smith, II; Tina M. Niemi. **A. Dept. Antiq. Jordan** XXXVIII 1994 pp.469-484.

946 El Sabinito, Soto La Marina, Tamaulipas. Un sitio arqueológico norestense con cultura sedentaria. *[In Spanish]*; [Sabinito, Soto La Marina, Tamaulipas. A northeast Mexican archaeological site of sedentary culture] *[Summary]*. Araceli Rivera Estrada. **Rev. de Human.** 11 Autumn:2001 pp.187-200.

947 Scientific and interpretive components in social zooarchaeology: the case of early farming communities in Kujavia. Arkadiusz Marciniak. **Archaeol. Polona** 39 2001 pp.87-110.

948 Sea-level change and the archaeology of early Venice. A.J. Ammerman; C.E. McClennen; M. De Min; R. Housley. **Antiquity** 73:280 6:1999 pp.303-312.

949 A small-scale reconnaissance in Qā' al-Jinz. Michael P. Neeley. **A. Dept. Antiq. Jordan** XLIV 2000 pp.99-108.

950 Stayt: a 13th century Iron Age site, Soutpansberg district, Northern Province, South Africa. H.P. Prinsloo; F.P. Coetzee. **S. Afr. J. Ethnol.** 24:3 2001 pp.81-87.

951 Studnia z Bochenia a problem chronologii starszych faz wczesnego średniowiecza na Mazowszu zachodnim. *[In Polish]*; [The well in Bocheń and the problem of the chronology of older phases of the early Middle Ages in western Mazovia]; *[Summary in German]*. Felix Biermann; Marek Dulinicz. **Archeol. Pol.** XLVI:1-2 2001 pp.85-118.

952 Summary results of the archaeological project at Khirbat an-Nawāfla/Wādī Mūsā. Khairieh 'Amr; Ahmed al-Momani; Naif al-Nawafleh; Sami al-Nawafleh. **A. Dept. Antiq. Jordan** XLIV 2000 pp.231-256.

953 The survey of al-Wu'ayra: a contribution to the knowledge of the crusader castles in Jordan. M. Bini; S. Bertocci. **A. Dept. Antiq. Jordan** XLI 1997 pp.403-414.

954 Survey of Sabra (Jordan) 1990, preliminary report. M. Lindner. **A. Dept. Antiq. Jordan** XXXVI 1992 pp.193-216.

955 The Tafīla-Busayra archaeological survey: phase 1 (1999). B. MacDonald; A. Bradshaw; L. Herr; M. Neeley; S. Quaintance. **A. Dept. Antiq. Jordan** XLIV 2000 pp.507-522.

956 The Tawaāhīn as-Sukkar and Khirbat ash-Shaykh 'Isa project phase I: the surveys. R.E. Jones; G. Tompsett; K.D. Politis; E. Photos-Jones. **A. Dept. Antiq. Jordan** XLIV 2000 pp.523-534.

957 Uncertain supplies: water availability and regional archaeological structure in the Palmer River catchment, central Australia. Peter Thorley. **Archaeol. Ocean.** 36:1 4:2001 pp.1-14.

958 The unique Nabataean high place of Rās Slaysil northwest of Petra and its topographical context. Manfred Lindner; Elisabeth Gunsam. **A. Dept. Antiq. Jordan** XXXIX 1995 pp.267-280.

959 Uwagi o kulturze mikockiej na górnym Śląsku. Przyczynek do genezy kultury mikockiej w Europie środkowej. *[In Polish]*; (Remarks on the Micoquian culture in Upper Silesia. A contribution on the genesis of the Micoquian culture in Central Europe.) *[Summary]*. Maria Fajer; Edelgarda M. Foltyn; Eugeniusz Foltyn; Janusz K. Kozłowski. **Archeol. Pol.** XLVI:1-2 2001 pp.31-66.

960 The water catchment system of Nakhl, Jordan. G.L. Mattingly; J.H. Pace; R.A. Stephenson; E.P. Wagnon. **A. Dept. Antiq. Jordan** XLII 1998 pp.331-340.

961 West Africa during the Atlantic slave trade: archaeological perspectives. Christopher R. DeCorse [Ed.]. London, New York: Leicester University Press, 2001. 194p. *ISBN: 0718502477. Includes bibliographical references and index. (Series:* New approaches to anthropological archaeology).

962 The world cultural heritage site of Sukur. Raymond Hickey. **Niger. F.** 66:1 4:2001 pp.19-28.

963 Wykrywacz metali w rękach archeologa — zagrożenie czy niezbędne narzędzie? *[In Polish]*; (Metal detector in an archeologist's hands — useful tool or a danger?) *[Summary]*. Zenon Woźniak. **Spraw. Arch.** 52 2000 pp.455-466.

964 Yasileh: a new site in northern Jordan. Z. al-Muheisen. **A. Dept. Antiq. Jordan** XXXV 1991 pp.341-346.

965 Zagadnienie obronności osiedli typu biskupińskiego. O potrzebie alternatywnej interpretacji. *[In Polish]*; [The issue of the Biskupin's type settlement defences. On the necessity of an alternative interpretation] *[Summary]*; *[Summary in German]*. Andrzej Mierzwiński. **Przeg. Archeolog.** 48 2000 pp.141-152.

966 Zwierzęcy materiał kostny z obiektu kultury badeńskiej z Szarbii Zwierzynieckiej, gm. Skalbmierz. *[In Polish]*; (Animal bones from the Baden culture feature in Szarbia Zwierzyniecka, Skalbmierz commune.) *[Summary]*. Danuta Makowicz-Poliszot. **Spraw. Arch.** 52 2000 pp.131-138.

Archaeological theory
Théorie archéologique

967 'A rich and promising site': Winifred Lamb (1894-1963), Kusura and Anatolian archaeology. David W.J. Gill; Winifred Lamb. **Anatol. St.** 50 2000 pp.1-10.

968 African archaeology today. Paul Lane; Colin Breen; Wes Forsythe; Tom McErlean; Rosemary McConkey; Athman Lali Omar; Rory Quinn; Brian Williams; Cornelia Kleinitz; Rudolph Kuper; Bertram B.B. Mapunda; Mats Eriksson; Christophe Mbida Mindzie; Raymond Asombang; Michèle Delneuf; Siyakha Mguni; Thomas Plummer; Joseph Ferraro; Peter Ditchfield; Laura Bishop; Richard Potts; Andrew Reid; Derek Watson; James Woodhouse; Mauro Cremaschi; Savino di Lernia; Zoë Crossland; Rogier Bedaux; Kevin MacDonald; Alain Person; Jean Polet; Kléna Sanogo; Annette Schmidt; Samuel

Sidibé; Peter R. Schmidt; Matthew C. Curtis; Antonieta Jerardino; Scott MacEachern; M. Rowlands. **Antiquity** 75:290 12:2001 pp.793-876. *Collection of 16 articles.*

969 American historical archaeology. Laura Nader; Charles E. Orser, Jr.; Bonnie G. McEwan; Adrian Praetzellis; Mary Praetzellis; Paul A. Shackel; Elizabeth M. Scott; Amy L. Young; Michael Tuma; Cliff Jenkins. **Am. Anthrop.** 103:3 9:2001 pp.621-704. *Collection of 6 articles.*

970 Archaeologists as forensic investigators: defining the role. Douglas D. Scott; Melissa Connor; G. Clark Davenport; Robert C. Sonderman; William D. Haglund; Thomas A.J. Crist; Douglas W. Owsley; Eric Stover; Molly Ryan. **Hist. Archaeol.** 35:1 2001 pp.1-104. *Collection of 10 articles.*

971 Archaeology and archaeological science: past, present and future. Arkadiusz Marciniak; Włodzimierz Rączkowski. **Archaeol. Polona** 39 2001 pp.5-16.

972 Archaeology, archaeologists and 'Europe'. Mark Pluciennik. **Antiquity** 72:278 12:1998 pp.816-824.

973 The archaeology of a 'destroyed' site: surface survey and historical documents at the civilian conservation corps camp, Bandelier National Monument, New Mexico. Monica L. Smith. **Hist. Archaeol.** 35:2 2001 pp.31-40.

974 Archaeozoology or zooarchaeology? A problem from the last century. Laszlo Bartosiewicz. **Archaeol. Polona** 39 2001 pp.75-86.

975 Bedřich Hrozný and the Bible. Stanislav Segert. **Arch. Orient.** 67:4 11:1999 pp.629-648.

976 Bedřich Hrozný und die *Ahhiiaua*-Frage. *[In German]*; [Bedřich Hrozný and the *Ahhiiaua* question]. Susanne Heinhold-Krahmer. **Arch. Orient.** 67:4 11:1999 pp.567-584.

977 A bioarchaeological perspective on the history of violence. Phillip L. Walker. **Ann. R. Anthr.** 30 2001 pp.573-596.

978 A Black feminist-inspired archaeology? Maria Franklin. **J. Soc. Arch.** 1:1 6:2001 pp.108-125.

979 A conversation with Edward B. Jelks. Robert L. Schuyler [Interviewer]; Edward B. Jelks. **Hist. Archaeol.** 35:4 2001 pp.8-37.

980 Cross-cultural comparative approaches in archaeology. Peter N. Peregrine. **Ann. R. Anthr.** 30 2001 pp.1-40.

981 Defining and integrating sequences in site analysis: the evidence from hillforts and other sites. D.V. Clarke. **Ox. J. Archaeol.** 20:3 8:2001 pp.293-306.

982 Delaware archaeology and the revolutionary eighteenth century. John Bedell. **Hist. Archaeol.** 35:4 2001 pp.83-104.

983 Development of large-scale digital orthophotographs from balloon-borne aerial photos of archaeological ruins in Angkor, Cambodia. B. Babu Madhavan; Sachio Kubo; Watanabe Nobuya. **Ind. Geograph. J.** 73:1 6:1998 pp.23-34.

984 Empires: perspectives from archaeology and history. Susan E. Alcock [Ed.]. New York: Cambridge University Press, 2001. 523p. *ISBN: 0521770203. Includes bibliographical references.*

985 A feminist critique of recent archaeological theories and explanations of the rise of state-level societies. Carol Jane Key; J. Jefferson MacKinnon. **Dialect. Anthrop.** 25:2 2000 pp.109-121.

986 From Croatia to Cape Town: the future of the World Archaeological Congress. Julian Thomas [Comments by]; Willy Kitchen. **Antiquity** 72:278 12:1998 pp.747-753.

987 From social to cognitive archaeology. Colin Renfrew; Lynn Meskell [Interviewer]. **J. Soc. Arch.** 1:1 6:2001 pp.13-34.

988 Historical archaeology adrift? Charles E. Cleland; Douglas V. Armstrong [Comments by]; Lu Ann de Cunzo [Comments by]; Gregory A. Waselkov [Comments by]; Donald L. Hardesty [Comments by]; Roberta S. Greenwood [Comments by]. **Hist. Archaeol.** 35:2 2001 pp.1-30.

989 In memoriam: Michael Meinecke (1941-1995). Thomas Weber. **A. Dept. Antiq. Jordan** XXXIX 1995 pp.11-12.

990 In memoriam: Musa M. al-Zayyat (1945-1998). S. Balqar; A. Naghawai. **A. Dept. Antiq. Jordan** XLII 1998 pp.7-8.

991   *Lebenswelt* and doxa. Adam T. Smith; Diana DiPaolo Loren; Stephen Silliman; Bettina Arnold; Laurie A. Wilkie; Ulrike Sommer; Sherry B. Ortner. **J. Soc. Arch.** 1:2 10:2001 pp.155-278. *Collection of 7 articles.*

992   Making history in Banda: anthropological visions of Africa's past. Ann Brower Stahl. Cambridge: Cambridge University Press, 2001. xix, 268p. *ISBN: 0521801826. Includes bibliographical references and index. (Series:* New studies in archaeology).

993   Multilevel selection and political evolution in the valley of Oaxaca, 500-100 B.C. Charles S. Spencer; Elsa M. Redmond. **J. Anthrop. Arch.** 20:2 6:2001 pp.195-229.

994   People as an agent of environmental change. Rebecca A. Nicholson [Ed.]; T.P. O'Connor [Ed.]. Oxford: Oxbow, 2000. vii, 133p. *ISBN: 1842170023. Selected papers from the annual conference of the Association for Environmental Archaeology, 1995. Includes bibliographical references. (Series:* Symposia of the Association for Environmental Archaeology - 16).

995   The *pfahlbauproblem* and the history of lake-dwelling research in the Alps. Francesco Menotti. **Ox. J. Archaeol.** 20:4 11:2001 pp.319-328.

996   Problems, functions and conditions of archaeological knowledge. Felipe Criado Boado. **J. Soc. Arch.** 1:1 6:2001 pp.126-146.

997   O przydatności metody planigraficznej we wstępnej fazie badań stanowisk archeologicznych. *[In Polish]*; (Concerning the use of the planigraphic method in the initial phase of the research of archaeological sites.) *[Summary]*. Maciej Karczewski. **Archeol. Pol.** XLVI:1-2 2001 pp.7-30.

998   Rola i znaczenie pojęcia doświadczenia w archeologii. *[In Polish]*; (The importance and meaning of category of experience in archaeology.) *[Summary]*. Danuta Minta-Tworzowska. **Przeg. Archeolog.** 48 2000 pp.5-18.

999   Science and/or art: aerial photographs in archaeological discourse. Włodzimierz Rączkowski. **Archaeol. Polona** 39 2001 pp.127-146.

1000   Society and nature — forests, trees and lures. Lars Larsson. **Archaeol. Polona** 39 2001 pp.37-54.

1001   Stosowanie wykrywacza metali podczas badań archeologicznych. *[In Polish]*; (The use of metal detectors during archaeological investigations.) *[Summary]*. Paul Barford. **Spraw. Arch.** 52 2000 pp.443-454.

1002   Theorising the practice or practicing the theory: archaeology and GIS. Gary Lock. **Archaeol. Polona** 39 2001 pp.153-164.

1003   Three-dimensional imaging in archaeology: its history and future. Paul T. Nicholson. **Antiquity** 75:288 6:2001 pp.402-409.

1004   Von der Schwierigkeit ein Fach zu bestimmen: Überlegungen zur kognitiven Identität der Ur- und Frühgeschichtsforschung. *[In German]*; [Determining a subject from difficulties: reflections on the cognitive identity of pre- and ancient history]. Ulrich Veit. **Saeculum** 52:1 2001 pp.73-90.

Arts and architecture of prehistory and antiquity
Arts et architecture de la préhistoire et de l'Antiquité

1005   Adjetivos iconográficos en el arte mexica. *[In Spanish]*; [Iconographic adjectives in Aztec art]. José Alcina Franch. **Caravelle** 76-77 12:2001 pp.47-58.

1006   Alcuni aspetti della glittica sacro-magica sasanide: il "cavaliere nimbato". *[In Italian]*; [Aspects of sacred and magic Sasanian glyptics: the 'haloed horseman'] *[Summary]*. M.R. Magistro. **Stud. Iran.** 29:2 2000 pp.167-194.

1007   Analyse de la peinture de quelques sites postglaciaires du Sud Est de la France. *[In French]*; (Paint analysis of some post-glacial sites in south-eastern France.) *[Summary]*. Ph. Hameau; V. Cruz; E. Laval; M. Menu; C. Vignaud. **Anthropologie [Paris]** 105:4 10-12:2001 pp.611-626.

1008   Analysis of sandstone weathering of the Roman theater in Petra, Jordan. T.R. Paradise. **A. Dept. Antiq. Jordan** XLIII 1999 pp.353-368.

1009   The archaeology of military politics: the case of Castle Clinton. William A. Griswold. **Hist. Archaeol.** 35:4 2001 pp.105-118.

1010   Architectural investigation on the building techniques of the Nabataeans with reference to tomb 825. M. Shaer; Z. Aslan. **A. Dept. Antiq. Jordan** XLI 1997 pp.219-230.

1011   Architecture and sound: an acoustic analysis of megalithic monuments in prehistoric Britain. Aaron Watson; David Keating. **Antiquity** 73:280 6:1999 pp.325-336.

1012   Arquitectura y rebelión: construcción de iglesias durante la revuelta de 'Umar b. Hafsūn. *[In Spanish]*; [Architecture and rebellion: church construction during the Hafsūnid revolt]. Fernando Arce Sainz. **Al-Qantara** XXII:1 2001 pp.121-146.

1013   L'art schématique linéaire dans le sud-est de la France. *[In French]*; (Schematic linear art in the southeast of France.) *[Summary]*. P. Hameau. **Anthropologie [Paris]** 105:4 10-12:2001 pp.565-610.

1014   The Artemis statue excavated at Abila of the Decapolis in 1994. W. Harold Mare. **A. Dept. Antiq. Jordan** XLI 1997 pp.277-282.

1015   Un aspecto constructivo de las bóvedas en al-Andalus. *[In Spanish]*; [The construction of Islamic vaults in Andalucia]. Antonio Almagro. **Al-Qantara** XXII:1 2001 pp.147-170.

1016   Bench decorations of Structure XX, Chicanná Campeche. Karl Herbert Mayer. **Baes-A.** XLVII:2 6:2001 pp.323-344.

1017   A bronze ingot-bearer from Cyprus. Vassos Karageorghis; George Papasavvas. **Ox. J. Archaeol.** 20:4 11:2001 pp.339-354.

1018   The buildings under the 'cathedral' of Gerasa: the second interim report on the Jarash cathedral project. Beat Brenk; Carola Jäggi; Hans-Rudolf Meier. **A. Dept. Antiq. Jordan** XXXIX 1995 pp.211-220.

1019   Bulguksa Temple and Seokbulsa Temple. Kang Woobang. **Korea J.** 41:2 Summer:2001 pp.320-343.

1020   The bull and its two masters: moon and storm deities in relation to the bull in ancient Near Eastern art. Tallay Ornan. **Israel Explor. J.** 51:1 2001 pp.1-26.

1021   A Byzantine building with a cruciform plan in the citadel of Amman. Antonio Almagro. **A. Dept. Antiq. Jordan** XXXVIII 1994 pp.417-428.

1022   The Byzantine church at Darat al-Funun. Pierre M. Bikai; May Shaer; Brian Fitzgerald. **A. Dept. Antiq. Jordan** XXXVIII 1994 pp.401-416.

1023   Cave art without the caves. Paul G. Bahn. **Antiquity** 69:263 6:1995 pp.231-237.

1024   El *chacmool* mexica. *[In Spanish]*; [The Mexica *chacmool*]. Alfredo López Austin; Leonardo López Lujan. **Caravelle** 76-77 12:2001 pp.59-84.

1025   The changing face of Nubian religion: the lion temples at Musawwarat Es Sufra and Naqa and the three-headed and four-armed Apedemak. Christiaan Nel. **J. N.W. Sem. Lang.** 27:1 2001 pp.101-120.

1026   La chapelle de la Theotokos dans le Wādī 'Ayn al-Kanīsah au mont Nébo en Jordanie. *[In French]*; [The Theotokos Chapel in Wādī 'Ayn al-Kanīsah on Mount Nebo in Jordan]. Michele Piccirillo. **A. Dept. Antiq. Jordan** XXXIX 1995 pp.409-420.

1027   The cisterns of the al-Karak plateau. James H. Pace. **A. Dept. Antiq. Jordan** XL 1996 pp.369-374.

1028   The citadel of Amman: the conservation and restoration of the Ayyubid tower. A.A. Ostrasz. **A. Dept. Antiq. Jordan** XLI 1997 pp.395-402.

1029   The Cleaven Dyke: a Neolithic cursus monument/bank barrow in Tayside region, Scotland. Gordon J. Barclay; Gordon S. Maxwell; Ian A. Simpson; Donald A. Davidson. **Antiquity** 69:263 6:1995 pp.317-326.

1030   Comprehensive characterization and rating of the weathering state of rock carved monuments in Petra-Jordan — weathering forms, damage categories and damage index. K. Heinrichs; B. Fitzner. **A. Dept. Antiq. Jordan** XLIII 1999 pp.321-352.

1031   Considerazioni sul teatro di Marcello nei resti monumentali e nella tradizione grafica rinascimentale. *[In Italian]*; [Thoughts on the Theatre of Marcellus in the monumental ruins and the Renaissance tradition of graphic arts] *[Summary]*. Alessandra Tomasello; Jerzy Żelazowski. **Archeologia** LI 2000 pp.7-36.

1032   El Cristo de la Luz de Toledo. Dos supuestas mezquitas en una. *[In Spanish]*; [The Mosque of the Christ of Light in Toledo: two mosques or one?] Basilio Pavón Maldonado. **Al-Qantara** XXI:1 2000 pp.155-184.

1033   Croire aux arts premiers. *[In French]*; [Believing in the early arts]. Gaetano Ciarcia. **Homme** 158-159 4-9:2001 pp.339-352.

1034   Designs on painted Ayyubid/Mamluk pottery from Rujm el-Kursi, 1990 season. L. Khadija. **A. Dept. Antiq. Jordan** XXXVI 1992 pp.345-419.

1035   Documents of cultural heritage in Baghdad: traditional houses in al-Kraimat quarter. R. Parapetti; Rajiha Mrawuih Ibrahim. **Mesopotamia** XXXIV-XXXV 1999-2000 pp.202-228.

1036   Doorway orientation, settlement planning and cosmology in ancient Israel during Iron Age II. Avraham Faust. **Ox. J. Archaeol.** 20:2 5:2001 pp.129-155.

1037   An Edomite fortress and a late Islamic village near Petra (Jordan): Khirbat al-Mu'allaq. M. Lindner; E.A. Knauf; J.P. Zeitler. **A. Dept. Antiq. Jordan** XL 1996 pp.111-136.

1038   Les églises géminées d'Umm er-Rasas. Fouilles de la mission archéologique Suisse (foundation Max van Berchem). *[In French]*; [Gemelled churches in Umm er-Rasas. Excavations by the Swiss Archaeological Mission (Max van Berchem Foundation)]. J. Bujard; M. Piccirillo; M. Poiatti-Haldimann. **A. Dept. Antiq. Jordan** XXXVI 1992 pp.291-306.

1039   An Egyptian statuette in Petra. Alicia I. Meza. **A. Dept. Antiq. Jordan** XXXVII 1993 pp.427-432.

1040   The Egyptian statuette in Petra and the Isis cult connection. Alicia I. Meza. **A. Dept. Antiq. Jordan** XL 1996 pp.167-176.

1041   Emerging trends in rock art research: hunter-gatherer culture, land and landscape. Mairi Ross. **Antiquity** 75:289 9:2001 pp.543-548.

1042   An engraved bone fragment from c.70,000-year-old Middle Stone Age levels at Blombos cave, South Africa: implications for the origin of symbolism and language. Francesco d'Errico; Christopher Henshilwood; Peter Nilssen. **Antiquity** 75:288 6:2001 pp.309-318.

1043   Evaluation of weathering damages on monuments carved from rocks in Petra-Jordan: research project 1996-1999. B. Fitzner; K. Heinrichs. **A. Dept. Antiq. Jordan** XLII 1998 pp.341-360.

1044   Évocation allusive des maximes des Sept Sages. A propos de la «Colère d'Achille» sur la mosaïque de Mérida. *[In French]*; [An allusive evocation of the maxim of the Seven Sages: on the 'Anger of Achilles' on the Mérida mosaic] *[Summary]*. Marek T. Olszewski. **Archeologia** LI 2000 pp.37-46.

1045   The façade of the vaulted rooms along the so-called cardo in Umm Qays (ancient Gadara), area III: architectural design and reconstruction. R.L.J.J. Guinée; N.F. Mulder; K.J.H. Vriezen. **A. Dept. Antiq. Jordan** XL 1996 pp.207-216.

1046   The fountain court of Jarash Cathedral reconsidered: the first report of a new Swiss research project. Beat Brenk; Carola Jäggi; Hans-Rudolf Meier. **A. Dept. Antiq. Jordan** XXXVIII 1994 pp.351-358.

1047   The four seasons in zodiac mosaics: the Tallaras baths in Astypalaea, Greece. Ruth Jacoby. **Israel Explor. J.** 51:2 2001 pp.225-230.

1048   Ganga Cuttack, 1112-1435 A.D. Pramod Kumar Mohanty. **Oris. Hist. R. J.** XLV:1-4 2000 pp.35-44.

1049   The great Temenos at Naukratis once again. Květa Smoláriková. **Arch. Orient.** 68:4 11:2000 pp.571-578.

1050   The Hasmonean period 'synagogue' at Jericho and the 'council chamber' building at Qumran. Yehudah Rapuano. **Israel Explor. J.** 51:1 2001 pp.48-56.

1051   A head of the goddess Tyche from Petra, Jordan. J.J. Basile. **A. Dept. Antiq. Jordan** XLI 1997 pp.255-266.

1052   Hearth structures in the religious pattern of early Bronze Age northeast Anatolia. Turan Takaoglu. **Anatol. St.** 50 2000 pp.11-16.

1053   Hillforts, monumentality and place: a chronological and topographic review of first millennium BC hillforts of south-east England. Sue Hamilton; John Manley. **Euro. J. Arch.** 4:1 4:2001 pp.7-42.

1054   Historical residential houses in as-Salt. Remarks on their shape and function. A. Mollenhauer. **A. Dept. Antiq. Jordan** XLI 1997 pp.415-432.

1055   The iconography of pre-Islamic women in Iran. A. Daems. **Iran. Ant.** XXXVI 2001 pp.1-150.

1056   The Indus-like symbols on megalithic pottery: new evidence. Iravatham Mahadevan. **Stud. Orient.** 94 2001 pp.379-386.

1057   The Iron Age fortifications of Tel Beth Shemesh: a 1990-2000 perspective. Shlomo Bunimovitz; Zvi Lederman. **Israel Explor. J.** 51:2 2001 pp.121-147.

1058   Jabal al-Qseir: a fortified Iron II (Edomite) mountain stronghold in southern Jordan, its pottery and its historical context. Manfred Lindner; Ernst A. Knauf; John P. Zeitler; Hannes Hübl. **A. Dept. Antiq. Jordan** XL 1996 pp.137-166.

1059   Jerash: notes sur l'étude et la restauration de la porte sud. *[In French]*; [Jerash: notes on the study and restoration of the South Gate]. J. Seigne; C. Wagner. **A. Dept. Antiq. Jordan** XXXVI 1992 pp.241-260.

1060   Keftiu in context: Theban tomb-paintings as a historical source. D. Panagiotopoulos. **Ox. J. Archaeol.** 20:3 8:2001 pp.263-283.

1061   Late Islamic villages in the greater Petra region and medieval 'Hormuz'. M. Lindner. **A. Dept. Antiq. Jordan** XLIII 1999 pp.479-500.

1062   Lithotypes of rock-carved monuments in Petra-Jordan — classification and petrographical properties. Kurt Heinrichs; Bernd Fitzner. **A. Dept. Antiq. Jordan** XLIV 2000 pp.283-312.

1063   Megalithic architecture and funerary practices in the late prehistory of Wadi Tanezzuft (Libyan Sahara). Savino di Lernia; Giovanni B. Bertolani; Francesca Merighi; Francesca R. Ricci Giorgio Manzi; Mauro Cremaschi. **Lib. Stud.** 32 2001 pp.29-48.

1064   Methodology for the conservation of the façades in Petra. Zaki Aslan; May Shaer. **A. Dept. Antiq. Jordan** XL 1996 pp.467-472.

1065   The monastery of Saint Aaron. Glen Peterman; Robert Schick. **A. Dept. Antiq. Jordan** XL 1996 pp.473-480.

1066   Monuments, power and personhood in the British Neolithic. Joanna Brück. **J. Royal Anth. Inst.** 7:4 12:2001 pp.649-668.

1067   Das mysteriöse Doppelmasken-Motiv an Megalithen von Long Pulung in Ost-Kalimantan/Indonesien. *[In German]*; [The mysterious double mask motif on megaliths in Long Pulung, East Kalimantan, Indonesia] *[Summary]*. Herwig Zahorka. **Tribus** 50 12:2001 pp.151-172.

1068   Nabataean faces from Petra. P.C. Hammond; T. Mellott-Khan. **A. Dept. Antiq. Jordan** XLII 1998 pp.319-330.

1069   A new building on the main street in Gerasa North of the sanctuary of Artemis: a preliminary report of an architectural study. R. Parapetti. **A. Dept. Antiq. Jordan** XLII 1998 pp.361-368.

1070   New data for the chronology of the early Christian cathedral of Gerasa: the third interim report on the Jarash cathedral project. C. Jäggi; H.R. Meier; B. Brenk; I. Kehrberg [Contrib.]. **A. Dept. Antiq. Jordan** XLI 1997 pp.311-320.

1071   New light on the equestrian figures from ancient Benin. O.I. Pogoson. **Niger. F.** 66:1 4:2001 pp.5-18.

1072   Une nouvelle peinture murale sogdienne dans le temple de Džartepa II. *[In French]*; [A new Sogdian mural painting in the temple of Džartepa II] *[Summary]*. A. Berdimuradov; M. Samibaev; F. Grenet; B. Marshak. **Stud. Iran.** 30:1 2001 pp.45-66.

1073   A Paradeisos in Petra: new light on the 'lower market'. L.A. Bedal. **A. Dept. Antiq. Jordan** XLIII 1999 pp.227-240.

1074   La peinture d'un tombeau à as-Salt. *[In French]*; [Tomb painting at as-Salt]. C. Vibert-Guigue. **A. Dept. Antiq. Jordan** XLII 1998 pp.369-374.

1075   The Petra church project, 1992-93: a preliminary report. Robert Schick; Zbigniew T. Fiema; Khairieh 'Amr. **A. Dept. Antiq. Jordan** XXXVII 1993 pp.55-66.

1076   Les ponts en pierre du Cambodge ancien aménagement ou contrôle du territoire? *[In French]*; (The stone bridges of ancient Cambodia: national development or military control?) *[Summary]*. Bruno Bruguier. **B. Éc. Fr. Ex.-Or.** 87:2 2000 pp.529-552.

1077   Portrety mumiowe — nowe dyskusje, nowe problemy. *[In Polish]*; [Mummy portraits - new discussions, new problems] *[Summary]*. Maria Nowicka. **Archeologia** LI 2000 pp.119-130.

1078   Preliminary report of the notes on the head of the goddess Tyche from Petra, Jordan. J.J. Basile. **A. Dept. Antiq. Jordan** XLIII 1999 pp.223-226.

1079   Preliminary report on the excavations and architectural survey in Gadara (Umm Qeis) in Jordan, area I (1992). Ute Wagner-Lux; Karel J.H. Vriezen; Ferdinand van der Bosch; Nicole Mulder; Robert Guinée. **A. Dept. Antiq. Jordan** XXXVII 1993 pp.385-396.

1080   Preliminary report on the excavations of the lower church at el-Quweisma 1989. R. Schick; E. Suleiman. **A. Dept. Antiq. Jordan** XXXV 1991 pp.325-340.

1081   Le Ramayana au palais de Phnom-Penh. 1 — les peintures du Vat Prah Keo. *[In French]*; [The Ramayana in the palace of Phnom-Penh. The paintings of Vat Prah Keo]. Jacques Nepote; Marie Gamonet. **Péninsule** 40 2000 pp.5-104.

1082   Rapport d'activités à Qusayr 'Amra. *[In French]*; [A report on the work at Qusayr 'Amra]. G. Bisheh; T. Morin; C. Vibert-Guigue. **A. Dept. Antiq. Jordan** XLI 1997 pp.375-394.

1083   Remarks on some Zoroastrian architectural features; *[Summary in French]*. P. Jamzadeh. **Stud. Iran.** 30:1 2001 pp.17-30.

1084   Representations of the north Syrian landscape in neo-Assyrian art. Allison Karmel Thomason. **B. Am. Sch. Orient. R.** 323 8:2001 pp.63-96.

1085   The Ridge Church at Petra. Patricia M. Bikai. **A. Dept. Antiq. Jordan** XL 1996 pp.481-486.

1086   La sculpture susienne à l'époque de l'Empire parthe. *[In French]*; [Susian sculpture during the Parthian Empire]. P. Amiet. **Iran. Ant.** XXXVI 2001 pp.239-292.

1087   The Sela' sculpture: a neo-Babylonian rock relief in southern Jordan. S. Dalley; A. Goguel. **A. Dept. Antiq. Jordan** XLI 1997 pp.169-176.

1088   O semantike kamennykh labirintov Severa. *[In Russian]*; (On the hidden meaning of the stone labyrinths in the Russian north.) *[Summary]*. V.A. Burov. **Etnograf. Oboz.** 1 1-2:2001 pp.53-65.

1089   Site d'un arc à Tokra et l'aménagement urbain de la ville. *[In French]*; [The site of an arch at Tocra and the development of the town] *[Summary]*. Fuaad Bentaher. **Lib. Stud.** 32 2001 pp.95-106.

1090   The South Theatre at Jarash, 1994 campaign. Frank Sear. **A. Dept. Antiq. Jordan** XL 1996 pp.217-230.

1091   Une structure d'accueil des visiteurs à l'entrée de Qusayr 'Amra. *[In French]*; [A visitor reception at the entrance of Qusayr 'Amra]. Thierry Morin; Claude Vibert-Guigue. **A. Dept. Antiq. Jordan** XLIV 2000 pp.581-591.

1092   Temple, kiln and church — fourth interim report on the Jarash Cathedral project (autumn 1997). C. Jäggi; H.R. Meier; B. Brenk; I. Kehrberg [Contrib.]. **A. Dept. Antiq. Jordan** XLII 1998 pp.425-432.

1093   A terracotta statuette of Artemis with a deer at the Israel Museum. Sonia Klinger. **Israel Explor. J.** 51:2 2001 pp.208-224.

1094   Traditional arts of Jordan. Carol Palmer; Kenneth W. Russell. **A. Dept. Antiq. Jordan** XXXVII 1993 pp.37-54.

1095   Tranceinduzierte Felsbilder in der Ile-de-France? *[In German]*; [Trance-inducing rock paintings in the Ile-de-France?] Joest Leopold. **Anthropos [St. Augustin]** 95:2 2000 pp.501-518.

1096   Trois bas-reliefs parthes dans les monts Bakhtiaris. *[In French]*; [Three Parthian bas-reliefs from the Bakhtiari mountains]. J. Mehr Kian. **Iran. Ant.** XXXVI 2001 pp.293-298.

1097   Two engraved Tridacna shells from Tel Miqne-Ekron. Baruch Brandl. **B. Am. Sch. Orient. R.** 323 8:2001 pp.49-62.

1098   Two Hellenistic heads from Petra. Eve French. **A. Dept. Antiq. Jordan** XXXVIII 1994 pp.267-270.

1099   The Umayyad mosque of the Citadel of Amman. Antonio Almagro; Pedro Jiménez. **A. Dept. Antiq. Jordan** XLIV 2000 pp.459-476.

1100   Umm al-Walīd et Khān Az-Zabīb, cinq qusūr omeyyades et leurs mosquées revisités. *[In French]*; [Umm al-Walīd and Khān Az-Zabīb, the Ummmayeds and their mosques]. J. Bujard; W. Trillen [Contrib.]. **A. Dept. Antiq. Jordan** XLI 1997 pp.351-374.

1101   Una ciudadela estilo Recuay en el valle de Chacas (Perú): el sitio Pinchay-Riway. Una nota preliminar. *[In Spanish]*; [A Recuay style fortress in the Chacas Valley (Peru): the Pinchay-Riway area. A preliminary note]. Laura Laurencich-Minelli; Alberto Minelli; Carolina Orsini. **J. Soc. Amér.** 87 2001 pp.325-338.

1102   Das Wandbild aus dem Palast K von Dur-Scharrukin als Machtproklamation. *[In German]*; [The mural on Palace K at Dur-Sargon as a proclamation of power]. Burchard Brentjes. **Arch. Orient.** 67:4 11:1999 pp.535-540.

1103   Was the second Jerusalem temple a primarily Persian project? James Trotter. **Scan. J. Old. Test.** 15:2 2001 pp.276-294.

1104   Who were the builders of the Tibetan forts? Siegbert Hummel; G. Vogliotti [Tr.]. **Tibet J.** XXV:3 Autumn:2000 pp.3-7.

1105   Why digital enhancement of rock paintings works: rescaling and saturating colours. Bruno David; John Brayer; Ian J. McNiven; Alan Watchman. **Antiquity** 75:290 12:2001 pp.781-792.

1106   Wine production in the hills of southern Ammon and the founding of Tall al-'Umayrī in the sixth century BC. Larry G. Herr. **A. Dept. Antiq. Jordan** XXXIX 1995 pp.121-126.

Excavation reports
Rapports sur fouilles

1107   The 1988 season of excavation at Abila of the Decapolis. W.H. Mare. **A. Dept. Antiq. Jordan** XXXV 1991 pp.203-222.

1108   The 1990 excavations at Abu Snesleh: preliminary report. G. Lehmann; R. Lamprichs; S. Kerner; R. Bernbeck. **A. Dept. Antiq. Jordan** XXXV 1991 pp.41-66.

1109   The 1990 Wadi el-Yabis survey project and soundings at Khirbet um el-Hedamus. G. Palumbo. **A. Dept. Antiq. Jordan** XXXVI 1992 pp.25-42.

1110   The 1992 season of excavation at Abila of the Decapolis. W. Harold Mare. **A. Dept. Antiq. Jordan** XXXVIII 1994 pp.359-378.

1111   The 1992 season of excavations and 1993 season of restorations at Deir 'Ain 'Abata. Konstantinos D. Politis. **A. Dept. Antiq. Jordan** XXXVII 1993 pp.503-520.

1112   The 1992 season of excavations in Wādī Ziqlāb, Jordan. E.B. Banning; D. Rahimi; J. Siggers; H. Taani. **A. Dept. Antiq. Jordan** XL 1996 pp.29-50.

1113   1993 archaeological excavations and survey of the Southern Temple at Petra, Jordan. Martha Sharp Joukowsky. **A. Dept. Antiq. Jordan** XXXVIII 1994 pp.293-332.

1114   The 1993 season at 'Ain Ghazal: preliminary report. Gary O. Rollefson; Zeidan Kafafi. **A. Dept. Antiq. Jordan** XXXVIII 1994 pp.11-32.

1115   The 1994 and 1995 seasons of excavation at Abila of the Decapolis. W. Harold Mare. **A. Dept. Antiq. Jordan** XL 1996 pp.259-270.

1116   1994 archaeological excavations and survey of the Southern Temple at Petra, Jordan. Martha Sharp Joukowsky; Erika Schluntz. **A. Dept. Antiq. Jordan** XXXIX 1995 pp.241-266.

1117   The 1994 excavations at 'Ayn Ghazāl: preliminary report. Zeidan Kafafi; Gary O. Rollefson. **A. Dept. Antiq. Jordan** XXXIX 1995 pp.13-30.

1118   1995 archaeological excavation of the Southern Temple at Petra, Jordan. Martha Sharp Joukowsky. **A. Dept. Antiq. Jordan** XL 1996 pp.177-206.

1119   The 1995 season at 'Ayn Ghazāl: preliminary report. Gary O. Rollefson; Zeidan Kafafi. **A. Dept. Antiq. Jordan** XL 1996 pp.11-28.

1120   The 1995-1996 excavation of Dayr al-Qaṭṭār al-Byzantī: a preliminary report. R. Holmgren; A. Kaliff; J. Svensson [Contrib.]. **A. Dept. Antiq. Jordan** XLI 1997 pp.321-340.

1121   The 1996 Brown University archaeological excavations at the 'great' Southern Temple at Petra. Martha Sharp Joukowsky. **A. Dept. Antiq. Jordan** XLI 1997 pp.195-218.

1122   The 1996 excavation season at Khirbat as-Samrā'. The Byzantine cemetery site B. A.J. Nabulsi; J.B. Humbert; A.A. Abbadi. **A. Dept. Antiq. Jordan** XLII 1998 pp.615-620.

1123   The 1996 season at 'Ayn Ghazāl: preliminary report. G.O. Rollefson; Z. Kafafi. **A. Dept. Antiq. Jordan** XLI 1997 pp.27-48.

1124   The 1996 season of excavation at Abila of the Decapolis. W. Harold Mare. **A. Dept. Antiq. Jordan** XLI 1997 pp.303-310.

1125   The 1998 excavations at 'Ayn Ghazāl: a preliminary report. Gary O. Rollefson; Zeidan Kafafi. **A. Dept. Antiq. Jordan** XLIV 2000 pp.91-98.

1126   The 1998 Finnish Jabal Hārūn project: a preliminary report. J. Frösén; Z.T. Fiema; M. Lavento; K. Koistinen; R. Holmgren. **A. Dept. Antiq. Jordan** XLIII 1999 pp.369-410.

1127   The 1998 season of archaeological survey in the regions of 'Irāq al-'Amir and Wādī al-Kafrayn: a preliminary report. Chang-Ho C. Ji; J.K. Lee. **A. Dept. Antiq. Jordan** XLIII 1999 pp.521-543.

1128   The 1998 season of excavation at Abila of the Decapolis. W. Harold Mare. **A. Dept. Antiq. Jordan** XLIII 1999 pp.451-458.

1129   The 1999 Finnish Jabal Hārūn project: a preliminary report. Jaakko Frösén; Zbigniew T. Fiema; Mika Lavento; Katri Koistinen; Richard Holmgren; Yvonne Gerber. **A. Dept. Antiq. Jordan** XLIV 2000 pp.395-424.

1130   The age of the Bellows Dune site O18, O'ahu, Hawai'i, and the antiquity of Hawaiian colonization. H. David Tuggle; Matthew Spriggs. **Asian Persp. [Hawaii]** 39:1-2 Spring-Fall:2000 pp.165-188.

1131   Al-Karak resources project 1995: a preliminary report on the pilot season. Gerald L. Mattingly. **A. Dept. Antiq. Jordan** XL 1996 pp.349-368.

1132   Al-Karak resources project 1997: excavations at Khirbat al-Mudaybī'. G.L. Mattingly; J.I. Lawlor; J.D. Wineland; J.H. Pace; A.M. Bogaard; M.P. Charles. **A. Dept. Antiq. Jordan** XLIII 1999 pp.127-144.

1133   Al-Marājim, implantation rurale du IIIème millenaire en Jordanie du nord. *[In French]*; [Al-Marājim, a three thousand year old rural site in northern Jordan]. Ch. Nicolle; T. Steimer; J.B. Humbert. **A. Dept. Antiq. Jordan** XLIII 1999 pp.91-98.

1134   American expedition to Petra: the 1990-1993 seasons. Philip C. Hammond; David J. Johnson. **A. Dept. Antiq. Jordan** XXXVIII 1994 pp.333-344.

1135   Amman ring road archaeological project phase I (survey). M. Waheeb. **A. Dept. Antiq. Jordan** XLII 1998 pp.621-626.

1136   (Archaeological and epigraphical survey results in Samrat Abu at-Trefiyat in the southeastern Badiyah-Al Jafr region.) *[Summary]*; *[Text in Arabic]*. Jum'ah M. Kareem; Sultan A. al-Ma'ani. **Dirasat Hum. Soc. Sc.** 28:2 8:2001 pp.414-440.

1137   Archaeological and palaeontological research in central Flores, east Indonesia: results of fieldwork 1997-98. M.J. Morwood; F. Aziz; Nasruddin; D.R. Hobbs; Paul O'Sullivan; Asaf Raza. **Antiquity** 73:280 6:1999 pp.273-286.

1138   Archaeological excavation at Rās an-Naqab -'Aqaba road alignment: preliminary report (1995). Mohammad Waheeb. **A. Dept. Antiq. Jordan** XL 1996 pp.339-348.

1139   Archaeological excavations at the late Neolithic site of ash-Shalaf: a preliminary report on the 1998 season. H.D. Bienert; D. Vieweger; K. Bastert [Contrib.]; L. Herling [Contrib.]; J. Meadows [Contrib.]. **A. Dept. Antiq. Jordan** XLIII 1999 pp.49-68.

1140   Archaeological excavations at the late Neolithic site of ash-Shalaf in northern Jordan: a preliminary report on the 1999 season. Hans-Dieter Bienert; Dieter Vieweger; Katrin Bastert [Contrib.]; Lothar Herling [Contrib.]. **A. Dept. Antiq. Jordan** XLIV 2000 pp.109-118.

1141   Archaeological expedition to Khirbat Iskandar and its vicinity, 1994. Suzanne Richard; Jesse C. Long, Jr. **A. Dept. Antiq. Jordan** XXXIX 1995 pp.81-92.

1142   Archaeological explorations in the vicinity of Khirbat ath-Thamāyil — 1992. Bruce Routledge. **A. Dept. Antiq. Jordan** XXXIX 1995 pp.127-148.

1143   Archaeological investigation of Omis cave: a Yapese stone money quarry in Palau. Scott M. Fitzpatrick. **Archaeol. Ocean.** 36:3 10:2001 pp.153-162.

1144   Archaeological rescue survey of the Ras an-Naqab-Aqaba highway alignment, 1992. Ghazi Bisheh; Suleiman Farajat; Gaetano Palumbo; Mohammad Waheeb. **A. Dept. Antiq. Jordan** XXXVII 1993 pp.119-134.

1145   Archaeological rescue survey of the Tafileh-Ghor Feifeh road alignment, sections I and II. Mohammad Waheeb. **A. Dept. Antiq. Jordan** XXXVII 1993 pp.135-146.

1146   Archaeological research on medieval Petra: a preliminary report. Guido Vannini; Andrea Vanni Desideri. **A. Dept. Antiq. Jordan** XXXIX 1995 pp.509-540.

1147   Archaeological survey and excavation at Wādī al-Yutum and Tall Al-Magass area — 'Aqaba (ASEYM): a preliminary report on the first season 1998. L. Khalil [Contrib.]; R. Eichmann; H. Brückner [Contrib.]; J. Görsdorf [Contrib.]; A. Hauptmann [Contrib.]; L. Herling [Contrib.]; H. Kallweit [Contrib.]; S. Kerner [Contrib.]; R. Miqdadi [Contrib.]; R. Neef [Contrib.]. **A. Dept. Antiq. Jordan** XLIII 1999 pp.501-520.

1148   Archaeological survey and settlement patterns in the region of 'Irāq al-'Amīr, 1996: a preliminary report. Chang-Ho C. Ji. **A. Dept. Antiq. Jordan** XLII 1998 pp.587-610.

1149   Archaeological survey of greater Amman, phase 1: final report. A.S. Abu Dayyah; J.A. Greene; I. Haj Hassan; E. Suleiman. **A. Dept. Antiq. Jordan** XXXV 1991 pp.361-396.

1150   Archaeological survey of the Dhībān plateau, 1996: a preliminary report. Chang-Ho C. Ji; T. 'Attiyat. **A. Dept. Antiq. Jordan** XLI 1997 pp.115-128.

1151   Archaeological survey of the east coast of the Dead Sea phase I: Suwayma, az-Zāra and Umm Sidra. Khairieh 'Amr; Khalil Hamdan; Svend Helms; Luay Mohamadieh. **A. Dept. Antiq. Jordan** XL 1996 pp.429-450.

1152   Archaeological survey of the Wādī al-'Ājib, al-Mafraq. Alison Betts; Samantha Eames; Maria Schroder; Abed al-Qader al Husan. **A. Dept. Antiq. Jordan** XXXIX 1995 pp.149-168.

1153   Ar-Rasfa, a stratified Middle Paleolithic open-air site in northwest Jordan: a preliminary report on the 1997 excavations. J.J. Shea. **A. Dept. Antiq. Jordan** XLII 1998 pp.41-52.

1154   Ayla-'Aqaba in the light of recent excavations. Fawzi Zayadine. **A. Dept. Antiq. Jordan** XXXVIII 1994 pp.485-506.

1155   Ba'ja - the archaeology of a landscape - 9000 years of human occupation: a preliminary report on the 1999 field season. Hans-Dieter Bienert; Roland Lamprichs; Dieter Vieweger; Katrin Bastert [Contrib.]; Janet Haberkorn [Contrib.]; Nasser Hindawi [Contrib.]; Zeidoun al-Muheisen [Contrib.]; Bernd Müller-Neuhof [Contrib.]; Isabelle Ruben [Contrib.]. **A. Dept. Antiq. Jordan** XLIV 2000 pp.119-148.

1156   The Brown University 1998 excavations at the Petra Great Temple. Martha Sharp Joukowsky. **A. Dept. Antiq. Jordan** XLIII 1999 pp.195-222.

1157   Brown University 1999 excavations at the Petra Great Temple. Martha Sharp Joukowsky. **A. Dept. Antiq. Jordan** XLIV 2000 pp.313-334.

1158   The Chalcolithic and early Bronze cemeteries near 'Irāq al-Amīr and the preliminary report on salvage excavations. Chang-Ho C. Ji. **A. Dept. Antiq. Jordan** XLI 1997 pp.49-68.

1159   The credibility of the Tel Jezreel excavations: a rejoinder to Amnon Ben-Tor. David Ussishkin. **Tel Aviv** 27:2 2000 pp.248-256.

1160   The Dāna-Faynān-Al-Ghuwayr early prehistory project, spring 2000 season. Bill Finlayson; Anne Pirie; Steve J. Mithen. **A. Dept. Antiq. Jordan** XLIV 2000 pp.19-36.

1161   Découvertes récentes sur le sanctuaire de Zeus à Jerash (rapport préliminaire à la campagne de fouille de 1992). *[In French]*; [Recent discoveries at the Sanctury of Zeus at Jerash]. Jacques Seigne. **A. Dept. Antiq. Jordan** XXXVII 1993 pp.341-358.

1162   Deep sounding on the lower terrace of the Amman Citadel: final report. J.A. Greene; K. 'Amr. **A. Dept. Antiq. Jordan** XXXVI 1992 pp.113-144.

1163   The electrical resistivity survey at the EB IV — MB II cemetery near Tell el-'Umeiri. Mohammad Waheeb. **A. Dept. Antiq. Jordan** XXXVIII 1994 pp.75-80.

1164   The eleventh and twelfth seasons of excavations at Pella (Tabaqat Fahl), 1989-1990. Alan G. Walmsley; Phillip G. Macumber; Phillip C. Edwards; Stephen J. Bourke; Pamela M. Watson. **A. Dept. Antiq. Jordan** XXXVII 1993 pp.165-240.

1165   Etude du temple antique de Qasr ar-Rabba dans le Moab rapport sommaire d'une première campagne de relevés (1996). *[In French]*; [The temple at Qasr ar-Rabba: a summary report of the first season (1996)]. J. Calzini Gysens; L. Marino. **A. Dept. Antiq. Jordan** XLI 1997 pp.189-194.

1166   Excavation of building F of the Umayyad Palace of Amman: preliminary report. Antonio Almagro; Pedro Jiménez; Julio Navarro. **A. Dept. Antiq. Jordan** XLIV 2000 pp.433-458.

1167   The excavation of the Hūwāra church: Irbid 1996. W. Karasneh; A. al-Zibda. **A. Dept. Antiq. Jordan** XLII 1998 pp.19-24.

1168   The excavation of the Khirbat ad-Duwayr church/Jinīn as-Safā. I. Melhim. **A. Dept. Antiq. Jordan** XLII 1998 pp.25-38.

1169   Excavations and restorations at Dayr 'Ayn 'Abātā 1995. K.D. Politis. **A. Dept. Antiq. Jordan** XLI 1997 pp.341-350.

1170   Excavations and restorations of Dayr 'Ayn 'Abāta 1994. Konstantinos D. Politis. **A. Dept. Antiq. Jordan** XXXIX 1995 pp.477-492.

1171   Excavations at Deir 'Ain 'Abata 1991. K.D. Politis. **A. Dept. Antiq. Jordan** XXXVI 1992 pp.281-290.

1172   Excavations at Tall Dayr 'Allā; seasons 1987 and 1994. M.M. Ibrahim; G. van der Kooij. **A. Dept. Antiq. Jordan** XLI 1997 pp.95-114.

1173   Excavations at Tell Jawa, Jordan (1993): preliminary report. P.M. Michèle Daviau. **A. Dept. Antiq. Jordan** XXXVIII 1994 pp.173-194.

1174   The fifth season of excavations at Tall Jāwā (1994) a preliminary report. P.M. Michèle Daviau. **A. Dept. Antiq. Jordan** XL 1996 pp.83-100.

1175   The Finnish Jabal Hārūn project report on the 1997 season. J. Frösén; Z.T. Fiema; H. Haggrén; K. Koistinen; M. Lavento; G.L. Peterman. **A. Dept. Antiq. Jordan** XLII 1998 pp.483-502.

1176   A first season of renewed excavation by the University of Sydney at Tulaylāt al-Ghassūl. Stephen J. Bourke; Peta L. Seaton; Rachael T. Sparks; Jaimie L. Lovell; Lachlan D. Mairs. **A. Dept. Antiq. Jordan** XXXIX 1995 pp.31-64.

1177   Fouilles et travaux en Égypte et au Soudan, 1998-1999 (tab. XII-XXXIII). *[In French]*; [Archaeological excavations in Egypt and Sudan, 1998-1999]. J. Leclant; A. Minault-Gout. **Orientalia** 69:5 2000 pp.209-329.

1178   Four seasons of excavations at Khirbat al-Mudayna on Wādī ath-Thamad, 1996-1999. Robert Chadwick; P.M. Michèle Daviau; Margreet Steiner. **A. Dept. Antiq. Jordan** XLIV 2000 pp.257-270.

1179   The fourth gate at Ayla: a report on the 1992 excavations at Aqaba. Donald Whitcomb. **A. Dept. Antiq. Jordan** XXXVII 1993 p.533.

1180   Gadara — Umm Qeis: preliminary report on the 1991 and 1992 seasons. Susanne Kerner; Adolf Hoffmann. **A. Dept. Antiq. Jordan** XXXVII 1993 pp.359-384.

1181   Gadara 1998. The excavation of the five-aisled Basilica at Umm Qays: a preliminary report. T. Weber; U. Hübner [Contrib.]. **A. Dept. Antiq. Jordan** XLII 1998 pp.443-456.

1182   Gadara of the Decapolis: preliminary report on the 1990 season at Umm Qeis. T. Weber. **A. Dept. Antiq. Jordan** XXXV 1991 pp.223-236.

1183   Geoarchaeological research of Holocene occupations in Wādī al-Hasa: a preliminary report on the 1999 season. J. Brett Hill. **A. Dept. Antiq. Jordan** XLIV 2000 pp.11-18.

1184   Geoelectric and archaeological work at Sāl, Jordan: a preliminary report on the 1999 season at the Chalcolithic and early Bronze Age site. Zeidan Kafafi; Dieter Vieweger; Muhammad Jaradat [Contrib.]; Patrick Leiverkus [Contrib.]; Erich Lippmann [Contrib.]. **A. Dept. Antiq. Jordan** XLIV 2000 pp.173-192.

1185   Geophysical and palynological investigations of the Tell El Dabaa archaeological site, Nile Delta, Egypt. Salah Y. el Beialy; Kevin J. Edwards; Ahmed S. el Mahmoudi. **Antiquity** 75:290 12:2001 pp.735-744.

1186   Gharandal in Jibāl: first season report. A. Walmsley; M.C. Ricklefs [Contrib.]; N. Ricklefs [Contrib.]. **A. Dept. Antiq. Jordan** XLII 1998 pp.433-442.
1187   The Humeima excavation project: preliminary report of the 1991-1992 seasons. John P. Oleson; Khairieh 'Amr; Robert Schick; Rebecca M. Foote; John Somogyi-Csizmazia. **A. Dept. Antiq. Jordan** XXXVII 1993 pp.461-502.
1188   The international Wādī Farasa Project (IWFP) exploration season 1999. Stephan G. Schmid. **A. Dept. Antiq. Jordan** XLIV 2000 pp.335-354.
1189   Khirbet Salameh 1992. Pierre M. Bikai. **A. Dept. Antiq. Jordan** XXXVII 1993 pp.521-532.
1190   A large area archaeological excavation at Cuddie Springs. Judith Field; Richard Fullagar; Garry Lord. **Antiquity** 75:290 12:2001 pp.696-702.
1191   Mādabā Plains project 1994: excavations at Tall al-'Umayrī, tall Jalūl and vicinity. Larry G. Herr; Lawrence T. Geraty; Øystein S. Labianca; Randall W. Younker; Douglas R. Clark. **A. Dept. Antiq. Jordan** XL 1996 pp.63-82.
1192   Mādabā plains project 1996: excavations at Tall al'Umayrī, Tall Jalūl and vicinity. L.G. Herr; L.T. Geraty; Ø.S. Labianca; R.W. Younker; D.R. Clark. **A. Dept. Antiq. Jordan** XLI 1997 pp.145-168.
1193   Mādabā Plains project 1997: excavations and restoration work at Tall Hisbān and vicinity. Ø.S. Labianca; P.J. Ray, Jr. **A. Dept. Antiq. Jordan** XLIII 1999 pp.115-126.
1194   Mādabā Plains project: excavations at Tall al-'Umayrī, 1998. L.G. Herr; D.R. Clark; L.T. Geraty; Ø.S. Labianca. **A. Dept. Antiq. Jordan** XLIII 1999 pp.99-114.
1195   Mādabā Plains project: the 1989 excavations at Tell el-'Umeiri and vicinity. L.G. Herr; L.T. Geraty; Ø.S. LaBianca; W. Younker. **A. Dept. Antiq. Jordan** XXXV 1991 pp.155-180.
1196   Mādabā Plains project: the 1992 excavations at Tell el-'Umeiri, Tell Jalul, and vicinity. Larry G. Herr; Lawrence T. Geraty; Oystein S. LaBianca; Randall W. Younker. **A. Dept. Antiq. Jordan** XXXVIII 1994 pp.147-172.
1197   Mapping and preliminary survey in Wādī Faynān, south Jordan. I. Ruben; R.H. Barnes; R. Kana'an. **A. Dept. Antiq. Jordan** XLI 1997 pp.433-454.
1198   Notes and news on the excavations at Ghawr an-Numayra. Mohammad Waheeb. **A. Dept. Antiq. Jordan** XL 1996 pp.451-456.
1199   Novae — western sector (*principia*), 1998-1999. Preliminary report on the excavations of the Warsaw University Archaeological Expedition. Tadeusz Sarnowski. **Archeologia** LI 2000 pp.79-88.
1200   Novae — western sector (section IV), 1997-1999. Preliminary report on the excavations of the Center for Archaeological Research — Novae, Warsaw University. Piotr Dyczek. **Archeologia** LI 2000 pp.89-104.
1201   Pella/Tall al-Husn excavations 1993, the University of Sydney — 15th season. Pamela Watson; John Tidmarsh. **A. Dept. Antiq. Jordan** XL 1996 pp.293-314.
1202   The Petra National Trust site projects archaeological survey of the Wādī Mūsā water supply and wastewater project area K. 'Amr; A. Al-Momani; S. Farajat; H. Falahat. **A. Dept. Antiq. Jordan** XLII 1998 pp.503-548.
1203   The Petra National Trust site projects: excavation and clearance at Petra and Beida. F. Zayadine; S. Farajat. **A. Dept. Antiq. Jordan** XXXV 1991 pp.275-312.
1204   The Petra National Trust site projects: preliminary report on the 1991 season at Zurrabah. K. 'Amr. **A. Dept. Antiq. Jordan** XXXV 1991 pp.313-324.
1205   Polish excavations at tell el-'Umeiri in 1994, 1996 and 1998, by the Madaba Plains Project. Mariusz Górniak; Elżbieta Dubis; Maryla Kapica. **Archeologia** LI 2000 pp.105-118.
1206   A preliminary note on the Wādī Mūsā salvage excavation 1996. K. 'Amr; S. al-Nawafleh; H. Qrarhi. **A. Dept. Antiq. Jordan** XLI 1997 pp.469-474.
1207   Preliminary report of excavations at Khirbat al-Mudayna on Wādī ath-Thamad (1996-1999) the Nabataean buildings. P.M. Michèle Daviau; Noor Mulder-Hymans; Laura Foley; Christopher J. Simpson [Contrib.]. **A. Dept. Antiq. Jordan** XLIV 2000 pp.271-282.
1208   Preliminary report of the 1990 excavation at Tell Nimrin. J.W. Flanagan; D.W. McCreery; K.N. Yassine. **A. Dept. Antiq. Jordan** XXXVI 1992 pp.89-112.

1209   Preliminary report of the al-Humayma excavation project, 1995, 1996, 1998. J.P. Oleson; K. 'Amr; R. Foote; J. Logan; M.B. Reeves; R. Schick. **A. Dept. Antiq. Jordan** XLIII 1999 pp.411-450.

1210   Preliminary report of the excavations at Tell Jawa in the Madaba Plains (1991). P.M.M. Daviau. **A. Dept. Antiq. Jordan** XXXVI 1992 pp.145-162.

1211   Preliminary report of the Humayma excavation project, 1993. John P. Oleson; Khairieh 'Amr; Rebecca M. Foote; Robert Schick. **A. Dept. Antiq. Jordan** XXXIX 1995 pp.317-354.

1212   Preliminary report of the Swiss-Liechtenstein excavations at ez-Zantur in Petra 1992: the fourth campaign. Bernhard Kolb; Rolf A. Stucky. **A. Dept. Antiq. Jordan** XXXVII 1993 pp.417-426.

1213   Preliminary report of the third season of excavations at Tell Jawa, Jordan (1992). P.M. Michèle Daviau. **A. Dept. Antiq. Jordan** XXXVII 1993 pp.325-340.

1214   Preliminary report on a reconnaissance survey in the region of Wādī Bāyir. Jacqueline Calzini Gysens; Fawwaz al-Khraysheh. **A. Dept. Antiq. Jordan** XXXIX 1995 pp.355-364.

1215   Preliminary report on Brigham Young University's first season of excavation and survey at Wādī al-Matāha, Petra, Jordan. D.J. Johnson; J. Janetski; M. Chazan; S. Witcher; R. Meadow. **A. Dept. Antiq. Jordan** XLIII 1999 pp.249-260.

1216   Preliminary report on the excavation at al-Bālū' and a first sounding at al-Misna in 1997. U. Worschech; F. Ninow. **A. Dept. Antiq. Jordan** XLIII 1999 pp.169-174.

1217   Preliminary report on the excavations and architectural survey at Umm Qays (ancient Gadara), areas I and III (1997). Ute Wagner-Lux; Karel J.H. Vriezen; Nicole F. Mulder; Robert L.J.J. Guinée. **A. Dept. Antiq. Jordan** XLIV 2000 pp.425-432.

1218   Preliminary report on the fifth (1990) season of excavations at Tell es-Sa'idiyeh. J.N. Tubb. **A. Dept. Antiq. Jordan** XXXV 1991 pp.181-194.

1219   Preliminary report on the first (1991) season of excavations at Tell esh-Shuna North. D. Baird; G. Philip. **A. Dept. Antiq. Jordan** XXXVI 1992 pp.71-88.

1220   A preliminary report on the human remains from a rock-cut chamber tomb near 'Irāq al-'Amīr. Cindy M. Loh; Chang-Ho C. Ji. **A. Dept. Antiq. Jordan** XLIV 2000 pp.201-210.

1221   A preliminary report on the results of the salvage excavation at Dayr Ghubār/Amman. I. az- Zabin; H. al-Taher. **A. Dept. Antiq. Jordan** XLII 1998 pp.9-14.

1222   Preliminary report on the survey of the Dhībān plateau, 1997. Chang-Ho C. Ji; J.K. Lee. **A. Dept. Antiq. Jordan** XLII 1998 pp.549-572.

1223   Preliminary report on the third campaign at the ancient site of el-Balu' in 1991. Udo F.Ch. Worschech; Friedbert Ninow. **A. Dept. Antiq. Jordan** XXXVIII 1994 pp.195-204.

1224   Preliminary report on the third campaign at the ancient site of el-Balu' in (1991). U.F.Ch. Worschech; F. Ninow. **A. Dept. Antiq. Jordan** XXXVI 1992 pp.167-174.

1225   Preliminary report on the university of Sydney's fourteenth season of excavations at Pella (Tabaqat Fahl) in 1992. S.J. Bourke; R.T. Sparks; K.N. Sowada; L.D. Mairs. **A. Dept. Antiq. Jordan** XXXVIII 1994 pp.81-126.

1226   Problems, functions and conditions of archaeological knowledge. Felipe Criado Boado. **J. Soc. Arch.** 1:1 6:2001 pp.126-146.

1227   Qā' Abū Tulayha West: an interim report of the 1998 season. Sumio Fujii. **A. Dept. Antiq. Jordan** XLIII 1999 pp.69-90.

1228   Qā' Abū Tulayha West: an interim report of the 1999 season. Sumio Fujii. **A. Dept. Antiq. Jordan** XLIV 2000 pp.149-172.

1229   Recent excavations at the 'Ammān Nymphaeum: preliminary report. Mohammad Waheeb; Zuhair Zu'bi. **A. Dept. Antiq. Jordan** XXXIX 1995 pp.229-240.

1230   Report on the excavations at Basta 1988. H.J. Nissen; M. Muheisen; H.G. Gebel. **A. Dept. Antiq. Jordan** XXXV 1991 pp.13-40.

1231   Report on the excavations at Wādī al-Kufrayn Southern Ghors (Al-Aghwār). M. Waheeb. **A. Dept. Antiq. Jordan** XLI 1997 pp.463-468.

1232   The resumption of the archaeological investigation at Qal'at el-Mishnaqa, 1992
        excavation: a preliminary report. Susanna Bianchi; Fabio Faggella. **A. Dept. Antiq.
        Jordan** XXXVII 1993 pp.407-416.

1233   The Roman 'Aqaba project: the 1994 campaign. S. Thomas Parker. **A. Dept. Antiq.
        Jordan** XL 1996 pp.231-258.

1234   The Roman 'Aqaba project: the 1996 campaign. S. Thomas Parker. **A. Dept. Antiq.
        Jordan** XLII 1998 pp.375-394.

1235   The Roman 'Aqaba project: the 1997 and 1998 campaigns. S. Thomas Parker. **A. Dept.
        Antiq. Jordan** XLIV 2000 pp.373-394.

1236   Roman vineyards in Britain: stratigraphic and palynological data from Wollaston in the
        Nene Valley, England. A.G. Brown; I. Meadows; S.D. Turner; D.J. Mattingley. **Antiquity**
        75:290 12:2001 pp.745-757.

1237   Sa'ad: notes on the 1996 excavations. J.C. Rose; M. el-Najjar; N. Tourshan; S. Sari. **A.
        Dept. Antiq. Jordan** XLI 1997 p.475.

1238   A salvage excavation at a 6th 7th century C.E. site on Palmach Street, Beersheba. Alexander
        Fantalkin. **Tel Aviv** 27:2 2000 pp.257-272.

1239   Salvage excavations at 'Tell Faysal', Jarash. Gaetano Palumbo; Khairieh 'Amr; Ali Musa;
        Michelle Rasson-Seigne. **A. Dept. Antiq. Jordan** XXXVII 1993 pp.89-118.

1240   A salvage operation at Bāb adh-Dhrā'. David W. McCreery. **A. Dept. Antiq. Jordan** XL
        1996 pp.51-62.

1241   Second and third season of excavations at Tell Abu Sarbut, Jordan Valley (preliminary
        report). H. de Haas; H.E. LaGro; M. Steiner. **A. Dept. Antiq. Jordan** XXXVI 1992
        pp.333-344.

1242   A second and third season of renewed excavation by the University of Sydney at Tulaylāt-
        Ghassūl (1995-1997). Stephen Bourke; Jaimie Lovell; Rachael Sparks; Peta Seaton;
        Lachlan Mairs; John Meadows. **A. Dept. Antiq. Jordan** XLIV 2000 pp.37-90.

1243   The second season of excavation at al-Magass-'Aqaba, 1990. Lutfi A. Khalil. **A. Dept.
        Antiq. Jordan** XXXIX 1995 pp.65-80.

1244   A short note on the excavations of Yājūz 1994-1995. Emsaytif Suleiman. **A. Dept. Antiq.
        Jordan** XL 1996 pp.457-462.

1245   A site in history: archaeology at Dolní Věstonice/Unterwisternitz. Silvia Tomášková.
        Antiquity 69:263 6:1995 pp.301-316.

1246   A street and the beach at Ayla: the fall season of excavations at 'Aqaba, 1992. Donald
        Whitcomb. **A. Dept. Antiq. Jordan** XXXIX 1995 pp.499-508.

1247   Survey and excavation: a comparison of survey and excavation results from sites of the
        Wādī al-Hasa and the Southern al-Aghwār and North-East 'Arabah archaeological surveys.
        Burton MacDonald. **A. Dept. Antiq. Jordan** XL 1996 pp.323-338.

1248   Survey and excavation in Wadi al-Hasa: a preliminary report of the 1993 field season. G.A.
        Clark; D.I. Olszewski; J. Schuldenrein; N. Rida; J.D. Eighmey. **A. Dept. Antiq. Jordan**
        XXXVIII 1994 pp.41-56.

1249   Survey of prehistoric sites, Wadi Araba, southern Jordan. Donald O. Henry; Heather A.
        Bauer; Kristopher W. Kerry; Joseph E. Beaver; J. Joel White. **B. Am. Sch. Orient. R.** 323
        8:2001 pp.1-19.

1250   Swiss — Liechtenstein excavations at ez-Zantur in Petra 1989: the second campaign. R.A.
        Stucky; et al. **A. Dept. Antiq. Jordan** XXXV 1991 pp.251-274.

1251   Swiss-Liechtenstein excavations at az-Zantūr in Petra 1994: the sixth campaign. Rolf A.
        Stucky; Bernhard Kolb; Stephan G. Schmid; Yvonne Gerber; Ulrich Bellwald; Christiane
        Jacquat. **A. Dept. Antiq. Jordan** XXXIX 1995 pp.297-316.

1252   Swiss-Liechtenstein excavations at az-Zantūr in Petra 1996: the seventh season. B. Kolb;
        D. Keller [Contrib.]; R. Fellmann Brogli [Contrib.]. **A. Dept. Antiq. Jordan** XLI 1997
        pp.231-254.

1253   Swiss-Liechtenstein excavations at az-Zantūr/Petra: the tenth season. Bernhard Kolb;
        Daniel Keller. **A. Dept. Antiq. Jordan** XLIV 2000 pp.355-372.

1254   Swiss-Liechtenstein excavations at ez-Zantur in Petra 1991, the third campaign. R.A.
        Stucky; et al. **A. Dept. Antiq. Jordan** XXXVI 1992 pp.175-192.

1255   Swiss-Liechtenstein excavations at ez-Zantur in Petra 1993: the fifth campaign. Rolf A. Stucky; Yvonne Gerber; Bernhard Kolb; Stephan G. Schmid. **A. Dept. Antiq. Jordan** XXXVIII 1994 pp.271-292.

1256   Swiss-Liechtenstein excavations on az-Zantūr in Petra, 1998. B. Kolb; L. Gorgerat; M. Grawehr. **A. Dept. Antiq. Jordan** XLIII 1999 pp.261-278.

1257   Tall Abū al-Kharaz: the Swedish Jordan expedition 1994, fifth season, preliminary excavation report. Peter M. Fischer. **A. Dept. Antiq. Jordan** XL 1996 pp.101-110.

1258   Tall Abū al-Kharaz: the Swedish Jordan expedition 1995-1996. Sixth and seventh season preliminary excavation report. Peter M. Fischer; H. Ingemarsdotter [Contrib.]. **A. Dept. Antiq. Jordan** XLI 1997 pp.129-144.

1259   Tall Abū al-Kharaz. The Swedish Jordan expedition 1993: fourth season preliminary excavation report. Peter M. Fischer; Alan G. Walmsley [Contrib.]. **A. Dept. Antiq. Jordan** XXXIX 1995 pp.93-120.

1260   Tall Nimrīn: preliminary report on the 1995 excavation and geological survey. James W. Flanagan; David W. McCreery; Khair N. Yassine. **A. Dept. Antiq. Jordan** XL 1996 pp.271-292.

1261   Tell Abu al-Kharaz: the Swedish Jordan expedition 1989, first season preliminary report from trial soundings. Peter M. Fischer. **A. Dept. Antiq. Jordan** XXXV 1991 pp.67-104.

1262   Tell Abu al-Kharaz: the Swedish Jordan expedition 1991, second season preliminary excavation report. Peter M. Fischer. **A. Dept. Antiq. Jordan** XXXVII 1993 pp.279-306.

1263   Tell Abu al-Kharaz. The Swedish Jordan expedition 1992: third season preliminary excavation report. Peter M. Fischer. **A. Dept. Antiq. Jordan** XXXVIII 1994 pp.127-146.

1264   Tell Nimrin: preliminary report on the 1993 season. James W. Flanagan; David W. McCreery; Khair N. Yassine. **A. Dept. Antiq. Jordan** XXXVIII 1994 pp.205-244.

1265   Town and village: site transformations in south Jordan (the Gharandal archaeological project, second season report). A. Walmsley; P. Karsgaard; T. Grey; M. Choat [Contrib.]; K. Barrett [Contrib.]. **A. Dept. Antiq. Jordan** XLIII 1999 pp.459-478.

1266   Umm al-Jimāl area R 1994 field season. Ahmad Momani; Michael Horstmanshof. **A. Dept. Antiq. Jordan** XXXIX 1995 pp.469-476.

1267   The Umm al-Jimāl project, 1993 and 1994 field seasons. Bert de Vries. **A. Dept. Antiq. Jordan** XXXIX 1995 pp.421-436.

1268   The Umm el-Jimal project, 1981-1992. Bert de Vries. **A. Dept. Antiq. Jordan** XXXVII 1993 pp.433-460.

1269   Umm Qays-Gadara: a preliminary report 1993-1995. S. Kerner. **A. Dept. Antiq. Jordan** XLI 1997 pp.283-302.

1270   University of Jordan excavations at Khirbat Yājūz. L. Khalil. **A. Dept. Antiq. Jordan** XLII 1998 pp.457-472.

1271   University of Jordan excavations at Khirbet Salameh, 1993. Pierre M. Bikai. **A. Dept. Antiq. Jordan** XXXVIII 1994 pp.395-400.

1272   Urban life in the highlands of central Jordan: a preliminary report of the 1996 tall Mādabā excavations. Timothy P. Harrison; Brian Hesse; Stephen H. Savage; Douglas W. Schnurrenberger. **A. Dept. Antiq. Jordan** XLIV 2000 pp.211-230.

1273   Wadi al-Hasa Paleolithic project-1992: preliminary report. G.A. Clark; M.P. Neeley; B. MacDonald; J. Schuldenrein; K. 'Amr. **A. Dept. Antiq. Jordan** XXXVI 1992 pp.13-24.

1274   Wādī al-Kharrār archaeological project (Al-Maghtas). M. Waheeb. **A. Dept. Antiq. Jordan** XLII 1998 pp.635-638.

1275   Wadi al-Qattar salvage excavation 1989. Khairieh 'Amr; Mohammad Najjar; Susanne Kerner; Kevin Rielly; David W. McCreery. **A. Dept. Antiq. Jordan** XXXVII 1993 pp.263-278.

1276   The Wādī az-Zarqā'/ Wādī ad-Dulayl archaeological project, report on the 1996 fieldwork season. Z. Kafafi; G. Palumbo; A.H. al-Shiyab; F. Parenti; E. Santucci; M. Hatamleh; M. Shunnaq; M. Wilson. **A. Dept. Antiq. Jordan** XLI 1997 pp.9-26.

1277   The Wādī az-Zarqā'/Wādī ad-Dulayl excavations and survey project: report on the October-November 1993 fieldwork season. Gaetano Palumbo; Massimiliano Munzi; Sarah

Collins; Fouad Hourani; Alessandra Peruzzetto; Martin D. Wilson. **A. Dept. Antiq. Jordan** XL 1996 pp.375-428.

1278   The Wadi el-Yabis survey and excavations project: report on the 1992 season. Gaetano Palumbo; Jonathan Mabry; Mohammad Abu Abileh; Elena Avellino; Michèle Biewers; Cecilia Conati; Ruba Kana'an; Stefano Mammini. **A. Dept. Antiq. Jordan** XXXVII 1993 pp.307-324.

Funerary archaeology
Archéologie funéraire

1279   The 1994 Umm al-Jimāl cemetery excavations: areas and Z. Janet Brashler. **A. Dept. Antiq. Jordan** XXXIX 1995 pp.457-468.

1280   Anthropological and cultural features of a skeletal sample of horsemen from the medieval necropolis of Vicenne-Campochiaro (Molise, Italy); *[Summary in Croatian]*. M.G. Belcastro; F. Facchini. **Coll. Antrop.** 25:2 12:2001 pp.387-402.

1281   Archaeological skeletal part profiles and differential transport: an ethnoarchaeological example from Hadza bone assemblages. Karen D. Lupo. **J. Anthrop. Arch.** 20:3 9:2001 pp.361-378.

1282   Archaeology and the Anglo-Boer War (1899-1902): a report on the discovery of the Black refugee camp and cemetery at Brandfort, Free State; *[Summary in Afrikaans]*. J. Dreyer. **S. Afr. J. Ethnol.** 24:4 2001 pp.131-137.

1283   The archaeology of osteoporosis; *[Summary in French]*; *[Summary in German]*. Gordon Turner-Walker; Unni Syversen; Simon Mays. **Euro. J. Arch.** 4:2 8:2001 pp.263-272.

1284   Assyrian king-lists, the royal tombs of Ur, and Indus origins. Julian Reade. **J. Near East.** 60:1 1:2001 pp.1-30.

1285   Bronze Age Myanmar (Burma): a report on the people from the cemetery of Nyaunggan, Upper Myanmar. Nancy Tayles; Kate Domett; U. Pauk Pauk. **Antiquity** 75:288 6:2001 pp.273-278.

1286   The burial ground of ar-Raha al-Mu'arrajah. Udo Worschech. **A. Dept. Antiq. Jordan** XLIV 2000 pp.193-200.

1287   The Byzantine cemetery at Khirbat as-Samrā': preliminary human osteological analysis. Abdalla J. Nabulsi. **A. Dept. Antiq. Jordan** XL 1996 pp.315-322.

1288   Cmentarzysko wczesnoprzeworskie ze Stradowa, pow. Kazimierza Wielka. *[In Polish]*; (The early Przeworsk culture cemetery in Stradów, Kazimierza Wielka district.) *[Summary]*. Leszek Gajewski; Zenon Woźniak. **Spraw. Arch.** 52 2000 pp.231-328.

1289   Correlates of contact: epidemic disease in archaeological context. Dale L. Hutchinson; Jeffrey M. Mitchem. **Hist. Archaeol.** 35:2 2001 pp.58-72.

1290   Dating the first New Zealanders: the chronology of Wairau Bar. Thomas Higham; Atholl Anderson; Chris Jacomb. **Antiquity** 73:280 6:1999 pp.420-427.

1291   Dating women and becoming farmers: new palaeodietary and AMS dating evidence from the Breton Mesolithic cemeteries of Téviec and Hoëdic. Rick J. Schulting; Michael P. Richards. **J. Anthrop. Arch.** 20:3 9:2001 pp.314-344.

1292   An early Bronze Age IV cemetery at al-Bassah, near 'Iraq Al-Amir. Mohammed Waheeb; Gaetano Palumbo. **A. Dept. Antiq. Jordan** XXXVIII 1994 pp.57-62.

1293   Excavations in the Byzantine cemetery at Khirbat as-Samrā' site B — 1995. A.J. Nabulsi; J.B. Humbert. **A. Dept. Antiq. Jordan** XL 1996 pp.491-493.

1294   Expiración, luto y defunción. Evidencias sobre prácticas mortuorias de los antiguos norestenses. *[In Spanish]*; [Expiration, mourning and death. Evidence of mortuary customs of the ancient northeasterners]. Moisés Valadez Moreno. **Rev. de Human.** 10 Spring:2001 pp.121-134.

1295   Fouille de sauvetage dans la nécropole nord-ouest de Jérash. *[In French]*; [Rescue excavation of the necropolis north west of Jerash]. M. Smadeh; A.M. Rasson; J. Seigne. **A. Dept. Antiq. Jordan** XXXVI 1992 pp.261-280.

1296 Fragmentary endings: a discussion of 3rd millennium BC burial practices in the Oman Peninsula. Soren Blau. **Antiquity** 75:289 9:2001 pp.557-570.

1297 Further investigation of the human skeletal remains from the hippodrome at Jarash. K.B. Hendrix. **A. Dept. Antiq. Jordan** XLII 1998 p.639.

1298 Grave markers: Middle and early Upper Paleolithic burials and the use of chronotypology in contemporary Paleolithic research. Julien Riel-Salvatore; Geoffrey A. Clark; Current Anthropology [Comments by]. **Curr. Anthr.** 42:4 8-10:2001 pp.449-480.

1299 Grób niszowy ze Złotej, pow. Pińczów na tle znalezisk kultury ceramiki sznurowej z nad dolnej Nidy. *[In Polish]*; (The niche grave from Złota, Pinczów district settlement of the corded ware culture in the lower basin of the Nida River.) *[Summary]*. Andrzej Kempisty; Piotr Włodarczak. **Spraw. Arch.** 52 2000 pp.151-170.

1300 Groby kultury ceramiki wstęgowej rytej z Aleksandrowic, stan. 2, gm. Zabierzów, woj. małopolskie. *[In Polish]*; (Graves of the linear band pottery culture from Aleksandrowice, site 2, Zabierzów commune, Małopolskie voivodship.) *[Summary]*. Agnieszka Czekaj-Zastawny. **Spraw. Arch.** 52 2000 pp.97-112.

1301 The late Ottoman cemetery in field L, Tall Hisban. Bethany J. Walker. **B. Am. Sch. Orient. R.** 322 5:2001 pp.47-78.

1302 A late Roman soldier's grave by the Dead Sea. S. Thomas Parker. **A. Dept. Antiq. Jordan** XXXVIII 1994 pp.385-394.

1303 Life and death in the 'Neolithic': dwelling-scapes in southern Britain. Martin P. King. **Euro. J. Arch.** 4:3 12:2001 pp.323-345.

1304 Mesolithic mortuary ritual at Franchthi Cave, Greece. Tracey Cullen. **Antiquity** 69:263 6:1995 pp.270-289.

1305 A middle Bronze Age tomb near Tall al-'Umayrī. M. Waheeb. **A. Dept. Antiq. Jordan** XLI 1997 pp.75-80.

1306 Możliwości interpretacji znalezisk z łużycko-kloszowej osady we Władysławowie, stan. 2, woj. mazowieckie. *[In Polish]*; (The interpretation possibilities of the finds from the Lusatian and Cloche-graves cultures settlement at Władysławów, site 2, Mazowieckie Voivodeship.) *[Summary]*. Violetta Lis. **Archeol. Pol.** XLVI:1-2 2001 pp.67-84.

1307 A new middle Bronze Age tomb from the citadel of Amman. M. Najjar. **A. Dept. Antiq. Jordan** XXXV 1991 pp.105-134.

1308 A note on ossuary burial and the resurrection of the dead in first-century Jerusalem. Steven Fine. **J. Jew. Stud.** LI:1 Spring:2000 pp.69-76.

1309 Osada kultury łużyckiej na stanowisku Iwanowice-Babia Góra II. *[In Polish]*; (The settlement of the Lusatian culture on site Babia Góra II in Iwanowice.) *[Summary]*. Wojciech Suder. **Spraw. Arch.** 52 2000 pp.171-220.

1310 The Pella hinterland tomb project: a short report on the 1996 season. F. Baker. **A. Dept. Antiq. Jordan** XLI 1997 pp.69-74.

1311 Preliminary report on a mausoleum at the turn of the BC/AD century at Jarash. Jacques Seigne; Thierry Morin. **A. Dept. Antiq. Jordan** XXXIX 1995 pp.175-192.

1312 A preliminary report on the human remains from a rock-cut chamber tomb near 'Irāq al-'Amīr. Cindy M. Loh; Chang-Ho C. Ji. **A. Dept. Antiq. Jordan** XLIV 2000 pp.201-210.

1313 Rescue excavations in the Nabataean cemetery at Khirbat Qazone 1996-1997. K.D. Politis. **A. Dept. Antiq. Jordan** XLII 1998 pp.611-614.

1314 Salvage excavations at a Bronze Age cemetery near Tell el-'Umeiri. Mohammad Waheeb; Gaetano Palumbo. **A. Dept. Antiq. Jordan** XXXVII 1993 pp.147-164.

1315 Salvage excavations at the bronze age cemetery of Khirbet Umm Zaytuna, Wadi Kufrenjeh. Mohammad Waheeb; Gaetano Palumbo; Mohammad Abu Abileh. **A. Dept. Antiq. Jordan** XXXVIII 1994 pp.63-74.

1316 Les stèles funéraires musulmanes dites *batu Aceh* de l'état de Johor (Malaisie). *[In French]*; (Muslim graves with *batu Aceh* tombstones from Johor (Malaysia).) *[Summary]*. Daniel Perret. **B. Éc. Fr. Ex.-Or.** 87:2 2000 pp.579-608.

1317 Die *Tabella defixionis* KAI 89 und die Magie des Fluches. *[In German]*; [The *Tabella defixionis* KAI 89 and the magic of curses]. H.P. Müller. **Orientalia** 69:4 2000 pp.393-406.

1318   Three tombs near the hippodrome at Jarash: a preliminary report. Ruba Abu-Dalu. **A. Dept. Antiq. Jordan** XXXIX 1995 pp.169-174.

1319   (The tombstone of the Marwanite Prince Mohammed bn Khaled bn 'Abd el-Malik bn al-Harth bn Al-Hakam from the southern part of Jordan: epigraphical and analytical study.) *[Summary]*; *[Text in Arabic]*. Juma'h M. Kareem. **Dirasat Hum. Soc. Sc.** 28:1 2:2001 pp.158-186.

1320   L'udová kozmovízia v bielych karpatoch. *[In Slovak]*; (The folk cosmovision in the White Carpathian mountains.) *[Summary]*. Milan Kováč. **Slov. Národop.** 47:2-3 1999 pp.173-181.

1321   Umm al-Jimāl 1993: a cist burial. Melissa Cheyney. **A. Dept. Antiq. Jordan** XXXIX 1995 pp.447-456.

1322   The use of cattail (*Typha latifolia L.*) down as a sacred substance by the interior and Coast Salish of British Columbia. Joanna Ostapkowicz; et al. **J. Ethnobio.** 21:2 Winter:2001 pp.77-90.

1323   Vatra kao domovina smrti u Nodilovoj religiji groba. *[In Croatian]*; (Fire as the homeland of death in Nodilo's *Religija Groba* [*The Grave Religion*].) *[Summary]*. Suzana Marjanić. **Nar. Umjetn.** 37:2 2000 pp.87-108.

1324   Vozmozhnosti rekonstruktsii pogrebalnoi pishchi v keramicheskikh sosudakh iz kurganov bronzovogo i rannezheleznogo vekov. *[In Russian]*; (New means for the reconstruction of funeral foods found in the ceramic vessels from the Bronze and early Iron Age kurgans.) *[Summary]*. V.A. Demkin; T.S. Demkina. **Etnograf. Oboz.** 4 7-8:2000 pp.73-81.

1325   Wczesnośredniowieczne cmentarzysko szkieletowe w Trześni, pow. Tarnobrzeg, woj. podkarpackie. *[In Polish]*; (Early medieval inhumation cemetery in Trześń, Tarnobrzeg district, Podkarpackie voivodship.) *[Summary]*. Marek Florek; Halina Gajewska; Leszek Gajewski. **Spraw. Arch.** 52 2000 pp.373-388.

1326   Wczesnośredniowieczny grób wojownika odkryty w Krakowie. *[In Polish]*; (Early medieval warrior grave discovered in Cracow.) *[Summary]*. Marian Myszka; Radosław Myszka. **Spraw. Arch.** 52 2000 pp.357-372.

1327   Where are the children? Age-dependent burial practices in Peqi'in. Yossi Nagar; Vered Eshed. **Israel Explor. J.** 51:1 2001 pp.27-35.

1328   Where is Herod's tomb at Herodium? Jodi Magness. **B. Am. Sch. Orient. R.** 322 5:2001 pp.43-46.

Inscriptions
Inscriptions

1329   An Achaemenid royal inscription: the text of paragraph 13 of the Aramaic version of the Bisitun inscription. Jan Tavernier. **J. Near East.** 60:3 7:2001 pp.161-176.

1330   Assyrian deportations to the province of Samerina in the light of two cuneiform tablets from Tel Hadid. Nadav Na'aman; Ran Zadok. **Tel Aviv** 27:2 2000 pp.159-188.

1331   Der babylonische König Nabonid und der RBSRS in einigen neu publizierten frühnordarabischen Inschriften aus Taymā'. *[In German]*; [The Babylonian king Nabonid and the *RBSRS* in some newly published early north Arabic inscriptions from Taymā']. Hani Hayajneh. **Acta Orient.** 62 2001 pp.22-64.

1332   Cuneiform texts in the Archaeological Museum of Strasbourg. János Everling. **Arch. Orient.** 68:4 11:2000 pp.587-600.

1333   De Almanzor a Felipe II: la inscripción del Puente de Alcántara de Toledo (387/997-998) y su curiosa historia. *[In Spanish]*; [From Muhammad b. Ab 'Amir alMansur to Felipe II: the strange story of the inscription of the Alcántara Bridge in Toledo]. María José Rodríguez; Juan Antonio Souto. **Al-Qantara** XXI:1 2000 pp.185-210.

1334   Des traces de la déesse Spenta Ārmaiti à Persépolis. Et proposition pour une nouvelle lecture d'un logogramme élamite. *[In French]*; [Traces of the goddess Spenta Ārmaiti in Persepolis: proposing a new interpretation of an Elamite logogram] *[Summary]*. Sh. Razmjou. **Stud. Iran.** 30:1 2001 pp.7-16.

1335   Edfu and the eastern desert: Žába's rock inscriptions, no. A22 reconsidered. Andrés Diego Espinel. **Arch. Orient.** 68:4 11:2000 pp.579-586.

1336   Estelas funerarias de época califal aparecidas en Orihuela (Alicante). *[In Spanish]*; [Funerary inscriptions from the age of the Caliphate in Alicante]. Mª Antonia Martínez Núñez. **Al-Qantara** XXII:1 2001 pp.45-76.

1337   A fragment of a monumental inscription from the City of David. Frank Moore Cross. **Israel Explor. J.** 51:1 2001 pp.44-47.

1338   Hebrew graffiti from the first temple period. Joseph Naveh. **Israel Explor. J.** 51:2 2001 pp.194-207.

1339   Inscripciones árabes inéditas en el museo provincial de Almería. *[In Spanish]*; [Unedited Arabic inscriptions in the Almeria museum]. Jorge Lirola Delgado. **Al-Qantara** XXI:1 2000 pp.97-142.

1340   L'inscription de type dédanite de Abū ad-Dibā'/Wādī Ramm: une nouvelle lecture. *[In French]*; [Dedanite inscriptions in Abū ad-Dibā'/Wādī Ramm: a new interpretation]. Saba Farès-Drappeau. **A. Dept. Antiq. Jordan** XXXIX 1995 pp.493-498.

1341   The inscription of Sargon II at Tang-i Var and the chronology of Dynasty 25. D. Kahn. **Orientalia** 70:1 2001 pp.1-18.

1342   Les inscriptions de l'Arabie antique et les études arabes. *[In French]*; [Inscriptions of ancient Arabia and Arab studies]. Chr.J. Robin. **Arabica** XLVIII:4 10:2001 pp.509-577.

1343   Israel in Merenptah's inscription and reliefs. Anson F. Rainey. **Israel Explor. J.** 51:1 2001 pp.57-75.

1344   (Kufic inscription dated to the Umayyad period from the southeastern part of Wadi al-Gharra (al-Jafr).) *[Summary]*; *[Text in Arabic]*. Juma'ah Mahmoud Kareem. **Dirasat Hum. Soc. Sc.** 28:2 8:2001 pp.391-413.

1345   Die Maya-Hieroglyphe Z 33.707 *ch'ach'* „abschlagen". *[In German]*; [The Maya hieroglyph Z 33.707 *ch'ach'*]. Berthold Riese. **Paideuma** 46 2000 pp.267-278.

1346   A new Nabataean inscription from Qasr al-Hallabat. Giancarlo Lacerenza. **A. Dept. Antiq. Jordan** XXXVIII 1994 pp.345-350.

1347   (New Thamudic inscriptions from ar-Rajif.) *[Summary]*; *[Text in Arabic]*. Sultan A. al-Ma'ani. **Dirasat Hum. Soc. Sc.** 28:1 2:2001 pp.195-205.

1348   Notes and inscriptions on the cult of Apollo at Oinoanda. N.P. Milner. **Anatol. St.** 50 2000 pp.139-150.

1349   An Old Nubian lectionary fragment. G.M. Browne. **Orientalia** 70:1 2001 pp.113-116.

1350   The Parvatipati Temple marble inscription: Parvatipatipur, Sonepur. P.M. Nayak. **Oris. Hist. R. J.** XLV:1-4 2000 pp.29-34.

1351   Petra church project, Petra Papyri. Pierre M. Bikai. **A. Dept. Antiq. Jordan** XL 1996 pp.487-490.

1352   A possible reconstruction of the name of Haza'el's father in the Tel Dan inscription. William M. Schniedewind; Bruce Zuckerman. **Israel Explor. J.** 51:1 2001 pp.88-91.

1353   The road to Jezreel. Primary history and the *Tel Dan* inscription. Jan-Wim Wesselius. **Scan. J. Old. Test.** 15:1 2001 pp.83-103.

1354   Two inscriptions from Petra. S. Tracy. **A. Dept. Antiq. Jordan** XLIII 1999 pp.305-310.

1355   Two new inscriptions from Umm Qeis. Taha Batayneh; Wajih Karasneh; Thomas Weber. **A. Dept. Antiq. Jordan** XXXVIII 1994 pp.379-384.

1356   Two north-Arabian inscriptions from Jordan. F. Zayadine. **A. Dept. Antiq. Jordan** XLIII 1999 pp.311-320.

1357   Two wall mosaic inscriptions from the Umayyad market place in Bet Shean/Baysān. Elias Khamis. **B. Sch. Orient. Afr. Stud.** 64:2 2001 pp.159-176.

1358   Vie, mort et résurrection des inscriptions latines. Remarques sur la représentativité de la documentation épigraphique. *[In French]*; [Life, death and resurrection in Latin inscriptions: comments on the representativity of epigraphic documentation] *[Summary]*. Jerzy Kolendo. **Archeologia** LI 2000 pp.67-78.

Material culture
Culture matérielle

1359 Across forests and savannas: later Stone Age assemblages from Ituri and Semliki, Democratic Republic of Congo. Julio Mercader; Alison S. Brooks. **J. Anthr. Res.** 57:2 Summer:2001 pp.197-218.

1360 Archaeological textiles: a review of current research. Irene Good. **Ann. R. Anthr.** 30 2001 pp.209-226.

1361 Archaeology and nationalism. Margarita Díaz-Andreu; Anthony D. Smith; Timothy Champion; Athena S. Leoussi; Neil Asher Silberman; John Hutchinson; D.A. Brading. **Nat. Nat.** 7:4 10:2001 pp.429-531. *Collection of 7 articles.*

1362 L'axe Rhin-Rhône au paléolithique supérieur récent: l'exemple des mollusques utilisés comme objets de parure. *[In French]*; (The Rhine-Rhone axis in the late Upper Palaeolithic: the example of molluscs used as ornament objects.) *[Summary]*. E. Alvarez Fernandez. **Anthropologie [Paris]** 105:4 10-12:2001 pp.547-564.

1363 Beyond characterisation. Polished stone exchange in the western Mediterranean 5500-2000 BC. R.J. Harrison; T. Orozco Köhler. **Ox. J. Archaeol.** 20:2 5:2001 pp.107-127.

1364 Bone objects from Polish excavations at Kom el-Dikka, Alexandria (1988-1990). Part I. Jolanta Jabłonowska-Taracha. **Archeologia** LI 2000 pp.51-60.

1365 Byzantine and early Islamic oil lamp fragments from house 119 at Umm al-Jimāl. Eric C. Lapp. **A. Dept. Antiq. Jordan** XXXIX 1995 pp.437-446.

1366 A cache of hippopotamus ivory at Gao, Mali; and a hypothesis of its use. Timothy Insoll. **Antiquity** 69:263 6:1995 pp.327-336.

1367 Camels in antiquity: Roman period finds from Slovenia. László Bartosiewicz; Janez Dirjec. **Antiquity** 75:288 6:2001 pp.279-285.

1368 Caves, ursids, and artifacts: a natural-trap hypothesis. Steve Wolverton. **J. Ethnobio.** 21:2 Winter:2001 pp.55-76.

1369 Cerámica monocroma esgrafiada/incisa de la Gran Nicoya (siglos I-XVI d.C.) *[In Spanish]*; [Engraved/incised monochrome ceramics of the Great Nicoya]. Gilles Desrayaud. **J. Soc. Amér.** 87 2001 pp.39-88.

1370 La céramique comme document sur la guerre chez les anciens Mayas. *[In French]*; [Ceramics as a document of war among the ancient Maya]. Jean Michel Hoppan. **Amerindia** 24 1999 pp.91-118.

1371 The cisterns of the al-Karak plateau. James H. Pace. **A. Dept. Antiq. Jordan** XL 1996 pp.369-374.

1372 Classic Maya state, urbanism, and exchange: chipped stone evidence of the Copán Valley and its hinterland. Kazuo Aoyama. **Am. Anthrop.** 103:2 6:2001 pp.346-360.

1373 The classification and chronology of the Islamic glass bracelets from al-Tūr, Sinai. Yoko Shindo. **Senri Ethn. Stud.** 55 2001 pp.73-100.

1374 Communities of practice in the early pottery traditions of the American Southeast. Kenneth E. Sassaman; Wictoria Rudolphi. **J. Anthr. Res.** 57:4 Winter:2001 pp.407-426.

1375 La construcción de canoas monoxilas en la cuenca del Plata. *[In Spanish]*; [The construction of *monoxila* canoes in the La Plata River valley]. Verónica Aldazabal; María Agueda Castro. **J. Soc. Amér.** 86 2000 pp.185-228.

1376 Contribution de la thermoluminescence à la chronologie de la culture du Gaudo: datation de céramiques du site de La Trinita, Piano di Sorrento, Italie. *[In French]*; (The contribution of thermoluminescence to the chronology of Gaudo culture: dating pottery from the site of La Trinita, Piano di Sorrente, Italy.) *[Summary]*. E. Vartanian; P. Guibert; F. Bechtel; M. Schvoerer; C. Albore-Livadie. **Anthropologie [Paris]** 105:3 7-9:2001 pp.421-436.

1377 The corpus of west Semitic stamp seals: review article. Alan Millard. **Israel Explor. J.** 51:1 2001 pp.76-87.

1378 Dating Shuidonggou and the Upper Palaeolithic blade industry in north China. David B. Madsen; Li Jingzen; P. Jeffrey Brantingham; Gao Xing; Robert G. Elston; Robert L. Bettinger. **Antiquity** 75:290 12:2001 pp.706-716.

1379   Dépôts fossilifères du karst de Atapuerca, premiers 20 ans. *[In French]*; (Fossiliferous karst of Atapuerca: the first 20 years of research.) *[Summary]*. E. Aguirre. **Anthropologie [Paris]** 105:1 1-3:2001 pp.13-26.

1380   The discovery of two additional pottery kilns at az-Zurrāba/Wādī Mūsā. K. 'Amr; A. al-Momani. **A. Dept. Antiq. Jordan** XLIII 1999 pp.175-194.

1381   Do problematyki świętych gajów pogańskich — z komparatystyki archeologii słowiańskiej. *[In Polish]*; (Concerning the issue of pagan sacred groves — from comparative studies of Slav archaeology.) *[Summary]*. Witold Hensel. **Archeol. Pol.** XLVI:1-2 2001 pp.119-124.

1382   The Donghulin Woman from western Beijing: ^{14}C age and an associated compound shell necklace. Shou-Gang Hao; Xue-Ping Ma; Si-Xun Yuan; John Southon. **Antiquity** 75:289 9:2001 pp.517-522.

1383   The earliest evidence for metal bridle bits. M.A. Littauer; J.H. Crouwel. **Ox. J. Archaeol.** 20:4 11:2001 pp.329-338.

1384   Encoding information: unique Natufian objects from Hayonim Cave, western Galilee, Israel. O. Bar-Yosef; A. Belfer-Cohen. **Antiquity** 73:280 6:1999 pp.402-410.

1385   El estilo cerámico Santamariano de Los Andes Del Sur (siglos XI a XVI). *[In Spanish]*; [The Santa Maria pottery style of the southern Andes (11th to 16th centuries)] *[Summary]*. Javier Nastri. **Baes-A.** XLVII:2 6:2001 pp.361-396.

1386   Evidentiranje, inventariziranje in revizija etnološke dediščine oz. Etnološka stavbna dediščina v občini Idrija. *[In Slovene]*; (Keeping records of fixed cultural heritage in the case of revising ethnological heritage in the municipality of Idrija.) *[Summary]*. Andrejka Ščukovt. **Bull. Slov. Ethno. Soc.** 41:1-2 2001 pp.109-115.

1387   The ewer of Ibn Jaldak (623/1226) at the Metropolitan Museum of Art: the inquiry into the origin of the Mawsilī school of metalwork revisited. Howayda Al Harithy. **B. Sch. Orient. Afr. Stud.** 64:3 2001 pp.355-368.

1388   The excavation of two seventh century pottery kilns at Aqaba. Ansam Melkawi; Khairieh 'Amr; Donald S. Whitcomb. **A. Dept. Antiq. Jordan** XXXVIII 1994 pp.447-468.

1389   Excavations of kilns near the old city of Sisatchanalai, Thailand: prompt redevelopment of pottery production. Karen Randolph. **J. Siam Soc.** 88:1-2 2000 pp.34-41.

1390   Fair prehistory: archaeological exhibits at French *Expositions Universelles*. Nils Müller-Scheeßel. **Antiquity** 75:288 6:2001 pp.391-401.

1391   Figurka zoomorficzna z cmentarzyska kultury łużyckiej w Opatowie, stanowisko 1, pow. Kłobuck, woj. śląskie. *[In Polish]*; (A zoomorphic figurine from the cemetery of the Lusatian culture in Opatów, site 1, Kłobuck district Śląskie voivodship.) *[Summary]*. Anita Szczepanek; Magdalena Wieczorek-Szmal; Paweł Jarosz. **Spraw. Arch.** 52 2000 pp.221-230.

1392   French beads in France and northeastern North America during the sixteenth century. Laurier Turgeon. **Hist. Archaeol.** 35:4 2001 pp.58-82.

1393   Grinding implements and material found at Tall Dayr 'Alla, Jordan: their place and role in archaeological research. L.P. Petit. **A. Dept. Antiq. Jordan** XLIII 1999 pp.145-168.

1394   The head of the MUBARRŪ-men on Hittite seals. Itamar Singer. **Arch. Orient.** 67:4 11:1999 pp.649-654.

1395   The history and culture of boats and boat-building in the western Visayas. Henry F. Funtecha. **Phil. Q. Cult. Soc.** 28:2 6:2000 pp.111-132.

1396   Identification of 'jet' artefacts by reflected light microscopy; *[Summary in French]*; *[Summary in German]*. L. Allason-Jones; J.M. Jones. **Euro. J. Arch.** 4:2 8:2001 pp.233-252.

1397   Innovation, production and specialization in early prehistoric copper metallurgy. B.S. Ottaway. **Euro. J. Arch.** 4:1 4:2001 pp.87-112.

1398   The Iron Age bread ovens from Tell Deir 'Alla. E.J. van der Steen. **A. Dept. Antiq. Jordan** XXXV 1991 pp.135-154.

1399   An Iron Age II cemetery and wine presses at an-Nabi Danyal. David Amit; Irit Yezerski. **Israel Explor. J.** 51:2 2001 pp.171-193.

1400   Jarash bowls and other related local wares from the Spanish excavations at the Macellum of Gerasa (Jarash). Alexandra Uscatescu. **A. Dept. Antiq. Jordan** XXXIX 1995 pp.365-408.

1401   Kaloli copper-plates of Rāstrakūta Dhārāvarsa Dhruvarāja (I) of the Lāta branch of Gujarat, Śaka Sam. 744 (A.D. 822). Bharati Shelat. **J. Orient. Inst.** XLVII:1-2(47) 9-12:1997 pp.29-42.

1402   Knobbed spearbutts of the British and Irish Iron Age: new examples and new thoughts. Andrew Heald. **Antiquity** 75:290 12:2001 pp.689-696.

1403   Kopalnia krzemienia grimes graves w świetle nowych badań. *[In Polish]*; (The Grimes Graves flint mine site in the light of new research.) *[Summary]*. Jacek Lech; Ian Longworth. **Przeg. Archeolog.** 48 2000 pp.19-74. *Article in English and Polish.*

1404   Lapita in the Far West: recent developments. Glenn R. Summerhayes. **Archaeol. Ocean.** 36:2 7:2001 pp.53-64.

1405   Learning to make pottery in the prehispanic American Southwest. Patricia L. Crown. **J. Anthr. Res.** 57:4 Winter:2001 pp.451-470.

1406   A Levallois point embedded in the vertebra of a wild ass (*Equus africanus*): hafting, projectiles and Mousterian hunting weapons. Eric Boëda; J.M. Geneste; C. Griggo; N. Mercier; S. Muhesen; J.L. Reyss; A. Taha; H. Valladas. **Antiquity** 73:280 6:1999 pp.394-402.

1407   Linking artifact assemblages to household cycles: an example from the Gibbs site. Mark D. Groover. **Hist. Archaeol.** 35:4 2001 pp.38-57.

1408   Lithic assemblages from the Chang Tang region, northern Tibet. P. Jeffrey Brantingham; John W. Olsen; George B. Schaller. **Antiquity** 75:288 6:2001 pp.319-327.

1409   Lithic technology and discard at Marki, Cyprus: consumer behaviour and site formation in the prehistoric Bronze Age. Jennifer M. Webb. **Antiquity** 72:278 12:1998 pp.796-804.

1410   A 'lost' seal from Harappa in the Nicholson Museum (Sydney). D.T. Potts. **Stud. Orient.** 94 2001 pp.405-416.

1411   Marmaric wares: New Kingdom and later examples. Linda Hulin. **Lib. Stud.** 32 2001 pp.67-78.

1412   Materiały archeologiczne z wieży „B" zamku w Szydłowie. *[In Polish]*; (Archaeological materials from tower 'B' of the castle in Szydłów.); *[Summary in French]*. Leszek Kajzer. **Kwart. Hist. Kult. Mater.** XLVIII:3-4 2000 pp.153-162.

1413   Le mésolithique du bassin Pannonien et la formation du Rubané. *[In French]*; (The Mesolithic of the Pannonian basin and the formation of the LBK.) *[Summary]*. M. Otte; P. Noiret. **Anthropologie [Paris]** 105:3 7-9:2001 pp.409-420.

1414   Metallographic investigation of two miner's tools from Wadi Khalid/Feinan. A. Hauptmann; R. Maddin; G. Weisgerber. **A. Dept. Antiq. Jordan** XXXV 1991 pp.195-202.

1415   Motor skills and the learning process: the conservation of cordage final twist direction in communities of practice. C. Jill Minar. **J. Anthr. Res.** 57:4 Winter:2001 pp.381-406.

1416   A Nabataean graffito. a sherd from the Swiss-Liechtenstein excavation at az-Zantūr, Petra (1994). Yvonne Gerber; Hanna Jenni. **A. Dept. Antiq. Jordan** XL 1996 pp.463-466.

1417   Nabataean pottery from the 'cistern': some finds from the Brown University excavations at the Petra Great Temple. L.D. Bestock. **A. Dept. Antiq. Jordan** XLIII 1999 pp.241-248.

1418   A new milestation from the Roman road Gerasa/Philadelphia. J. Seigne; S. Agusta-Boularot; A.M. Rasson-Seigne. **A. Dept. Antiq. Jordan** XLI 1997 pp.267-276.

1419   Notes on Roman milestones from Khirbat Badrān: preliminary report. J. Seigne; S. Agusta-Boularot; A.M. Rasson-Seigne. **A. Dept. Antiq. Jordan** XLI 1997 pp.455-458.

1420   Notes on the history of the art of mother-of-pearl in Thailand with particular reference to the doors on the *ubōsot* of Wat Phra Chetuphon. Klaus Wenk. **J. Siam Soc.** 88:1-2 2000 pp.1-14.

1421   An olive press at Gal'ad/as-Salt. S. Hadidi; I. Melhim. **A. Dept. Antiq. Jordan** XLII 1998 pp.15-18.

1422   Paradna głowica buławy ze starego miasta we Wrocławiu. *[In Polish]*; (The ceremonial head of a baton from Wrocław old town.); *[Summary in German]*. Krzysztof Kamiński. **Kwart. Hist. Kult. Mater.** XLVIII:3-4 2000 pp.163-170.

1423   Parthian belts and belt plaques. V. Sarkhosh Curtis. **Iran. Ant.** XXXVI 2001 pp.299-328.

1424   Podkrakowska ceramika „biała" w świetle nowszych badań. *[In Polish]*; (Cracow 'white' pottery in the light of recent studies.) *[Summary]*. Ewa Kubica-Kabacińska. **Spraw. Arch.** 52 2000 pp.405-418.

1425   Pots and potters in the central Jordan Valley. Eveline J. van der Steen. **A. Dept. Antiq. Jordan** XLI 1997 pp.81-94.

1426   Pots, Slavs and 'imagined communities': Slavic archaeologies and the history of the early Slavs. Florin Curta. **Euro. J. Arch.** 4:3 12:2001 pp.367-384.

1427   Prehistoric children working and playing: a southwestern case study in learning ceramics. Kathryn A. Kamp. **J. Anthr. Res.** 57:4 Winter:2001 pp.427-450.

1428   Producción de plata en México 1804-1826, según Henry George Ward. *[In Spanish]*; [Silver production in Mexico 1804-1826, according to Henry George Ward]. Óscar Alatriste Guzmán. **Cuad. Am.** XV:3(87) 5-6:2001 pp.133-147.

1429   Provenience of eighteenth-century British porcelain sherds from sites 3B and 4E, fortress of Louisbourg, Nova Scotia: constraints from mineralogy, bulk paste, and glaze compositions. J. Victor Owen. **Hist. Archaeol.** 35:2 2001 pp.106-121.

1430   Ritual, change, and the pre-pottery Neolithic figurines of the central-southern Levant. Kathy Twiss. **Kroeber Anthr. Soc. Pap.** 85 2001 pp.16-48.

1431   A sixth-seventh century ceramic assemblage from Madaba, Jordan. Timothy P. Harrison. **A. Dept. Antiq. Jordan** XXXVIII 1994 pp.429-446.

1432   Social archaeology and the theatres of memory. Martin Hall. **J. Soc. Arch.** 1:1 6:2001 pp.50-61.

1433   A Sogdian incense-burner of the late VII-early VIII c. AD from Koshoi Korgon hillfort. M. Fedorov. **Iran. Ant.** XXXVI 2001 pp.361-381.

1434   Some Byzantine bronze objects from Beycesultan. G.R.H. Wright. **Anatol. St.** 50 2000 pp.159-170.

1435   A stamp seal of the Persian period from Khirbet Salameh (Amman). Pierre Bikai; Jürg Eggler. **J. N.W. Sem. Lang.** 27:1 2001 pp.63-70.

1436   Survey and rescue collections in the Ghawr as-Sāfī. K.D. Politis. **A. Dept. Antiq. Jordan** XLII 1998 pp.627-634.

1437   Tarabh plates of Chalukya Bhima II (Vikrama) Samvat 1263. Jai Prakash. **Oris. Hist. R. J.** XLV:1-4 2000 pp.107-116.

1438   Tell Nimrin: the Byzantine gold hoard from the 1993 season. James W. Flanagan; David W. McCreery; Khair N. Yassine. **A. Dept. Antiq. Jordan** XXXVIII 1994 pp.245-266.

1439   Temper for the sake of coherence: analyses of bone- and chaff-tempered ceramics from Iron Age Scandinavia. Ole Stilborg. **Euro. J. Arch.** 4:3 12:2001 pp.398-406.

1440   A tentative synchronisation of the local late Chalcolithic ceramic horizons of northern Syro-Mesopotamia. E. Rova. **Mesopotamia** XXXIV-XXXV 1999-2000 pp.175-201.

1441   'The oldest British industry': continuity and obsolescence in a flintknapper's sample set. John C. Whittaker. **Antiquity** 75:288 6:2001 pp.382-390.

1442   Two stamped jar impressions of the Persian province of Ammon from Tell el-'Umeiri. L.G. Herr. **A. Dept. Antiq. Jordan** XXXVI 1992 pp.163-166.

1443   W kwestii genezy i rozprzestrzenienia umb z kolcem z młodszego okresu przedrzymskiego. *[In Polish]*; [The question of the origin and distribution of the early pre-Roman shield boss with spike] *[Summary]*; *[Summary in German]*. Piotr Łuczkiewicz. **Przeg. Archeolog.** 48 2000 pp.83-114.

1444   Wczesnośredniowieczny piec do wytopu srebra i ołowiu w Dąbrowie Górniczej — Łosniu, st. 2. *[In Polish]*; (Early medieval kiln for melting silver and lead in Dąbrowa Górnicza — Łosień, site 2.) *[Summary]*. Jerzy Roś; Dariusz Rozmus. **Spraw. Arch.** 52 2000 pp.389-404.

1445   Wyniki badań mineralogicznych ceramiki „białej" ze stanowisk w Krakowie-Nowej Hucie. *[In Polish]*; (Results of mineralogical research of 'white' pottery from archaeological sites in Kraków-Nowa Huta.) *[Summary]*. Maciej Pawlikowski. **Spraw. Arch.** 52 2000 pp.419-434.

1446 Zdobiony toporek ślężański z Buska-Zdroju, woj. świętokrzyskie. *[In Polish]*; (Decorated shaft-holed axe of the *śłęża* type from Busko-Zdrój Świętokrzyskie province.) *[Summary]*. Czesław Hadamik. **Spraw. Arch.** 52 2000 pp.143-150.

1447 Znaki na butelkach szklanych z XVIII-XIX wieku ze Starego Fordonu nad wisłą. *[In Polish]*; (Marks on bottles from Stary Fordon on the Vistula from the 18th-19th century.); *[Summary in German]*. Jacek Woźny. **Kwart. Hist. Kult. Mater.** XLIX:3 2001 pp.245-252.

B.5: Physical anthropology
Anthropologie physique

1448 The alienation of body tissue and the biopolitics of immortalized cell lines. Margaret Lock. **Bod. Soc.** 7:2-3 6-9:2001 pp.63-92.

1449 Do you see what I see? Facial attractiveness and weight preoccupation in college women. Caroline Davis; Barbara Shuster; Michelle Dionne; Gordon Claridge. **J. Soc. Clin. Psychol.** 20:2 Summer:2001 pp.147-160.

1450 Fat distribution patterns in young amenorrheic females. Sylvia Kirchengast; Johannes Huber. **Hum. Nature** 12:2 2001 pp.123-140.

1451 Genomics: technics and writing the 'posthuman'. Mark Zuss. **Dialect. Anthrop.** 25:3-4 2000 pp.255-279.

1452 Mate choice trade-offs and women's preference for physically attractive men. David Waynforth. **Hum. Nature** 12:3 2001 pp.207-220.

1453 Non-random mating among Oraons of Purulia. Subha Sankar Das. **Man India** 80:3-4 7-12:2000 pp.351-358.

1454 Observing dermatoglyphic differentiation among Oraons: a study of finger prints. Udai Pratap Singh. **Man India** 80:3-4 7-12:2000 pp.259-272.

1455 A study on Palmar interdigital ridge counts among the Lodha of West Bengal. Basanta Kumar Mandal; K.K.N. Sharma. **Man India** 80:3-4 7-12:2000 pp.359-366.

1456 Tallest in the world: Native Americans of the Great Plains in the nineteenth century. Richard H. Steckel; Joseph M. Prince. **Am. Econ. Rev.** 91:1 3:2001 pp.287-294.

1457 Variability in the timing of stepping movement. Mari Ogiue-Ikeda; Tasuku Kimura. **Anth. Sci.** 109:2 4:2001 pp.167-182.

Craniology
Craniologie

1458 Analyse phylogénétique des hominidés de la Sierra de Atapuerca (Sima de los Huesos et Gran Dolina TD-6): l'évidence crânienne. *[In French]*; [Phylogenetic analysis of hominids from Sierra de Atapuerca (Sima de los Huesos and Gran Dolina TD6): the cranial evidence] *[Summary]*. J.L. Arsuaga; I. Martínez; A. Gracia. **Anthropologie [Paris]** 105:2 4-6:2001 pp.161-178.

1459 Bony bridging of the mylohyoid groove of the human mandible. Kentaro Jidoi; Takashi Nara; Yukio Dodo. **Anth. Sci.** 108:4 10:2000 pp.345-370.

1460 Etude en céphalométrie 3d de l'effet d'un traitement par hormone de croissance chez l'enfant. *[In French]*; (Analysis of craniofacial modifications by three dimensional cephalometry of children on GH treatment) *[Summary]*. F. Vaysse; C. Madrid; M. Tauber; J. Treil; R. Benitah. **Bio. Hum. Anthrop.** 19:3-4 7-12:2001 pp.197-204.

1461 Metric and non-metric characters of the Jomon skulls from the Ebishima shell-mound in northeastern Honshu, Japan. Yuji Mizoguchi; Yukio Dodo. **Anth. Sci.** 109:1 1:2001 pp.23-56.

1462 Metric data of the Ryukyuan crania. Yukio Dodo; Naomi Doi; Osamu Kondo. **Anth. Sci.** 109:2 4:2001 pp.183-190.

1463 The mismeasure of man. Stephen Jay Gould. London: Penguin, 1997. 444p. *ISBN: 0140258248. Includes bibliographical references (p. [425]-432) and index.*

1464   A morphometric analysis of Jomon skeletons from the Funadomari site on Rebun Island, Hokkaido, Japan. Hirofumi Matsumura; Tomoko Anezaki; Hajime Ishida. **Anth. Sci.** 109:1 1:2001 pp.1-21.

1465   Note sur l'ontogenèse crânienne et les hétérochronies chez *Gorilla gorilla* et *Pan troglodytes*. *[In French]*; (Cranial ontogeny and heterochronies in *Gorilla gorilla* and *Pan troglodytes*.) *[Summary]*. J.J. Millet; B. Viguier; F. Courant; F. Magniez-Jannin; D. Marchand; J. Chaline. **Anthropologie [Paris]** 105:3 7-9:2001 pp.317-326.

1466   Sexually dimorphic ontogenetic trajectories of frontal sinus cross sections; *[Summary in Croatian]*. H. Prossinger. **Coll. Antrop.** 25:1 6:2001 pp.1-12.

Dentition
Dentition

1467   Analyse morphométrique comparée des dents humaines de Gran Dolina (TD6) et de Sima de los Huesos d'Atapuerca. *[In French]*; (Comparative morphometric analysis of the human dental samples of Gran Dolina (TD6) and Sima de los Huesos caves sites at Atapuerca.) *[Summary]*. J.M. Bermúdez de Castro; S. Sarmiento. **Anthropologie [Paris]** 105:2 4-6:2001 pp.203-222.

1468   Croissance dentaire chez l'homme de néandertal — élaboration d'une nouvelle méthode d'estimation de leur âge dentaire. *[In French]*; (Neanderthals' dental growth — elaboration of a new method to estimate their dental age.) *[Summary]*. J. Granat; J.L. Heim. **Bio. Hum. Anthrop.** 19:3-4 7-12:2001 pp.205-216.

1469   Croissance osseuse chez les enfants néandertaliens. *[In French]*; (Skeletal growth of Neanderthal children.) *[Summary]*. J.L. Heim; J. Granat. **Bio. Hum. Anthrop.** 19:3-4 7-12:2001 pp.217-224.

1470   Croissance saltatoire de l'enfant: conséquences sur la chronologie du traitement orthodontique. *[In French]*; (Saltatory growth in children: consequences [of] the timing of orthodontic treatment.) J.P. Loreille. **Bio. Hum. Anthrop.** 19:1-2 1-6:2001 pp.37-46.

1471   Dental size and morphology of precontact Marshall Islanders (Micronesia) compared with other Pacific Islanders. Daris R. Swindler; Marshall I. Weisler. **Anth. Sci.** 108:3 7:2000 pp.261-282.

1472   Developmental aspects of sexual dimorphism in hominoid canines. Gary T. Schwartz; Don J. Reid; Christopher Dean. **Int. J. Primat.** 22:5 10:2001 pp.837-860.

1473   Distribution of tubercle-shaped incisors in South Pacific populations. Eisaku Kanazawa; Yuji Shirono; Mitsuko Nakayama; Hiroyuki Yamada; Hajime Hanamura; Shintaro Kondo. **Anth. Sci.** 109:3 7:2001 pp.225-238.

1474   Evaluation of denture stomatitis in Croatian adult population; *[Summary in Croatian]*. R. Ćelić; D. Knezović Zlatarić; I. Baučić. **Coll. Antrop.** 25:1 6:2001 pp.317-326.

1475   Factors predisposing to early childhood caries (ECC) in children of pre-school age in the city of Zagreb, Croatia; *[Summary in Croatian]*. O. Lulić-Dukić; H. Jurić; W. Dukić; D. Glavina. **Coll. Antrop.** 25:1 6:2001 pp.297-302.

1476   Hypohidrotic ectodermal dysplasia: dental features and carriers' detection; *[Summary in Croatian]*. D. Glavina; M. Majstorović; O. Lulić-Dukić; H. Jurić. **Coll. Antrop.** 25:1 6:2001 pp.303-310.

1477   Maturation et usure dentaire: estimation de l'âge. *[In French]*; (Maturation and dental wear: towards an age estimate.) *[Summary]*. E. Peyre; J. Granat. **Bio. Hum. Anthrop.** 19:3-4 7-12:2001 pp.189-196.

1478   Metrical studies of the crown components of the Japanese mandibular molars. Shintaro Kondo; Hiroyuki Yamada; Eisaku Kanazawa. **Anth. Sci.** 109:3 7:2001 pp.213-223.

1479   Morphometric analysis of hominoid lower molars from Yuanmou of Yunnan Province, China. W. Liu; L.J. Hlusko; L. Zheng. **Primates** 42:2 4:2001 pp.123-134.

1480   Morphometric evolutionary trends in the dental complex of *Pongo*. David W. Cameron. **Primates** 42:3 7:2001 pp.253-266.

1481   Primate molar crown formation times and life history evolution revisited. Gabriele A. Macho. **Am. J. Prim.** 55:4 12:2001 pp.189-202.

1482   Short and broad dental arch in Papua New Guinea highlanders. Yuriko Igarashi; Masanobu Matsuno; Atsushi Majima; Yoshimitsu Kawasaki; Kenji Kobayashi; Kazutaka Kasai; Hirofumi Aboshi; Eisaku Kanazawa. **Anth. Sci.** 109:3 7:2001 pp.239-251.

1483   Tubercle-shaped incisor of the Cook Islanders. Hiroyuki Yamada; Hajime Hanamura; Shintaro Kondo. **Anth. Sci.** 108:4 10:2000 pp.321-330.

1484   Was extensive tooth wear normal in our ancestors? A preliminary examination in the genus *homo*. Yousuke Kaifu. **Anth. Sci.** 108:4 10:2000 pp.371-386.

1485   What can developmental defects of enamel reveal about physiological stress in nonhuman primates? Debbie Guatelli-Steinberg. **Evolut. Anthrop.** 10:4 2001 pp.138-149.

Genetics
Génétique

1486   ABO blood group incompatibility and fertility among the Bhatras of Bastar. Manjula Guha; Jaya Mukherjee; Moyna Chakravarty. **Man India** 80:3-4 7-12:2000 pp.313-320.

1487   Are we hardwired? The role of genes in human behavior. William R. Clark; Michael Grunstein. Oxford, New York: Oxford University Press, 2000. ix, 322p. *ISBN: 0195138260. Includes bibliographical references (p. [295]-312) and index.*

1488   Behavior genetic modeling of human fertility: findings from a contemporary Danish twin study. Joseph Lee Rodgers; Hans-Peter Kohler; Kirsten Ohm Kyvik; Kaare Christensen. **Demography** 38:1 2:2001 pp.29-42.

1489   Demonic affliction or contagious disease? Changing perceptions of smallpox in the late Edo period. Hartmut O. Rotermund. **Jap. J. Relig. St.** 28:3-4 Fall:2001 pp.373-398.

1490   Distribution and variation of LH blood types among the Yerukala and Sugali tribes of Andhra Pradesh. V. Rami Reddy; C. Alivelu; G.P. Naidu. **Man India** 80:3-4 7-12:2000 pp.309-312.

1491   Effects of antigenic incompatibility on reproductive performances of four ethnic groups of Orissa. U. Deka; B. Mohanty; P.K. Das. **Man India** 80:3-4 7-12:2000 pp.231-250.

1492   Ethnic differences in pain perception: a biological basis. Aldric Hama. **Mankind Q.** XLII:2 Winter:2001 pp.201-218.

1493   Facial attractiveness signals different aspects of 'quality' in women and men. Deborah K. Hume; Robert Montgomerie. **Evol. Hum. Behav.** 22:2 3:2001 pp.93-112.

1494   Facial symmetry and judgements of apparent health: support for a 'good genes' explanation of the attractiveness-symmetry relationship. B.C. Jones; A.C. Little; I.S. Penton-Voak; B.P. Tiddeman; D.M. Burt; D.I. Perrett. **Evol. Hum. Behav.** 22:6 11:2001 pp.417-430.

1495   Indigenous and independent origin of the B*-mutation in ancient India: is it a myth or reality? R.S. Balgir. **Mankind Q.** XLII:2 Winter:2001 pp.99-116.

1496   The influence of genomic imprinting on brain development and behavior. Lisa M. Goos; Irwin Silverman. **Evol. Hum. Behav.** 22:6 11:2001 pp.385-408.

1497   JC virus genotypes in northwestern China: implications for its population history. Zheng Guo; Shu Ping Zheng; Chie Sugimoto; Yue Ling Wang; Huai-Ying Zheng; Tomokazu Takasaka; Tadaichi Kitamura; Jing Guo; Yoshiaki Yogo. **Anth. Sci.** 109:3 7:2001 pp.203-212.

1498   The kin in the gene: the medicalization of family and kinship in American society. Kaja Finkler; Janet Dolgin [Comments by]; Sarah Franklin [Comments by]; Hugh Gusterson [Comments by]; Norman M. Hadler [Comments by]; James P. Evans [Comments by]; Marit Melhuus [Comments by]; Dorothy Nelkin [Comments by]; Martin Richards [Comments by]; Lisbeth Sachs [Comments by]. **Curr. Anthr.** 42:2 4:2001 pp.235-264.

1499   Living with our genes: why they matter more than you think. Dean H. Hamer; Peter Copeland. London: Pan, 2000 |e r. 355p. *ISBN: 0330376039. Includes bibliographical references (p. 321-344).*

1500   Maternal or fetal origin of rhesus monkey (*Macaca mulatta*) amniotic fluid leukocytes can be identified by polymerase chain reaction using the zinc finger Y gene. A.E. Macias; S.W. Wong; D.W. Sadowsky; C.M. Luetjens; M.K. Axthelm; M.G. Gravett; G.J. Haluska; M.J. Novy. **Am. J. Prim.** 55:3 11:2001 pp.159-170.

1501   Meiosis and chromosome painting of sex chromosome systems in Ceboidea. M.D. Mudry; I.M. Rahn; A.J. Solari. **Am. J. Prim.** 54:2 6:2001 pp.65-78.

1502   Patterns of variation in a caste-cluster of Dhangars of Maharashtra, India; *[Summary in Croatian]*. B.M. Reddy; D.A. Demarchi; K.C. Malhotra. **Coll. Antrop.** 25:2 12:2001 pp.425-442.

1503   Polymorphism of the C1R subcomponent of the first complement component in Indonesians, Bangladeshis, Tibetans, South Africa Blacks, South Africa Whites and Samoans. Akira Kido; Rie Susukida; Masakazu Oya; Noboru Fujitani; Hiroshi Kimura; Masaaki Hara. **Anth. Sci.** 108:3 7:2000 pp.283-288.

1504   Polymorphisms of HLA-A and -B genes in the Kyrgyz population. Olga Tarasenko; Jun Ohashi; Mikhail Kitaev; Avtandil Alisherov; Bakhtygul Tyurebaeva; Toktogazy Kutukeev; Katsushi Tokunaga. **Anth. Sci.** 108:4 10:2000 pp.293-304.

1505   Professional constructions of family and kinship in medical genetics. Paul Atkinson; Evelyn Parsons; Katie Featherstone. **New Gen. & Soc.** 20:1 4:2001 pp.5-24.

1506   PTC taste sensitivity and red green colour blindness among Paidies. M. Ramesh; V. Govindaiah; I. Subba Rao. **Man India** 80:3-4 7-12:2000 pp.367-370.

1507   The science of desire: the search for the gay gene and the biology of behavior. Dean H. Hamer; Peter Copeland. New York: Simon & Schuster, 1994. 272p. *ISBN: 0671887246. Includes bibliographical references (p. 250-258) and index.*

1508   Sexual dimorphism: asymmetry and diversity of 38 dermatoglyphic traits in five endogamous populations of West Bengal, India; *[Summary in Croatian]*. B. Karmakar; K. Yakovenko; E. Kobyliansky. **Coll. Antrop.** 25:1 6:2001 pp.167-188.

1509   Subspecific genetic differences in the saddle-back tamarin (*Saguinus fuscicollis*) postcranial skeleton. Luci Ann P. Kohn; Laura Bishoff Langton; James M. Cheverud. **Am. J. Prim.** 54:1 5:2001 pp.41-56.

1510   Testing the reliability of noninvasive genetic sampling by comparing analyses of blood and fecal samples in barbary macaques (*Macaca sylvanus*). M. Lathuillière; N. Ménard; A. Gautier-Hion; B. Crouau-Roy. **Am. J. Prim.** 55:3 11:2001 pp.151-158.

1511   Toward developing a genome-wide microsatellite marker set for linkage analysis in the rhesus macaque (*Macaca mulatta*): identification of 76 polymorphic markers. Ruth M. Hadfield; Jan G. Pullen; Kay F. Davies; Sarah E. Wolfensohn; Joseph W. Kemnitz; Daniel E. Weeks; Simon T. Bennett; Stephen H. Kennedy. **Am. J. Prim.** 54:4 8:2001 pp.223-232.

1512   Tribal health status on socio-cultural and genetic determinants - a study among Kamars, an identified primitive tribal group of Raipur district in Madhya Pradesh, India. Nitin Malik. **B. Int. Com. Urg. Anthrop. Ethnol. R.** 40 1999-2000 pp.141-148.

1513   Understanding individual differences: critical human service component. Ralph Scott. **Mankind Q.** XLII:2 Winter:2001 pp.133-150.

Human evolution
Évolution humaine

1514   Adaptations to altitude: a current assessment. Cynthia M. Beall. **Ann. R. Anthr.** 30 2001 pp.423-456.

1515   Age and origin of the human species. Ronald Alan Fonda. **Mankind Q.** XLII:2 Winter:2001 pp.189-200.

1516   Blind in a cloud of data: problems with the chronology of Neanderthal extinction and anatomically modern human expansion. P.B. Pettitt; A.W.G. Pike; J.P. Bocquet-Appel [Comments by]; P.Y. Demars [Comments by]. **Antiquity** 75:288 6:2001 pp.415-420.

1517   Bringing in Darwin: evolutionary theory, realism, and international politics. Bradley A. Thayer. **Int. Secur.** 25:2 Fall:2000 pp.124-151.

1518   Comparisons and the case for interaction among Neanderthals and early modern humans in the Levant. Daniel Kaufman. **Ox. J. Archaeol.** 20:3 8:2001 pp.219-240.

1519   Creation: from nothing until now. Willem B. Drees. London: Routledge, 2001. 115p. *ISBN: 0415256534, 0415256526.*

1520   The debated mind: evolutionary psychology versus ethnography. Harvey Whitehouse [Ed.]. Oxford: Berg Publishers, 2001. ix, 229p. *ISBN: 1859734324, 1859734278. Includes bibliographical references and index.*

1521   Dmanisi and dispersal. Leo Gabunia; Susan C. Antón; David Lordkipanidze; Abesalom Vekua; Antje Justus; Carl C. Swisher, III. **Evolut. Anthrop.** 10:5 2001 pp.158-170.

1522   DNA analysis and the evolutionary history of the Basque population: a review. Neskutes Izagirre; Santos Alonso; Concepción de la Rúa. **J. Anthr. Res.** 57:3 Fall:2001 pp.325-344.

1523   Evolution de la morphologie claviculaire au sein du genre *homo*. Conséquences architecturales et fonctionnelles sur la ceinture scapulaire. *[In French]*; (Evolution of the clavicular morphology within the genus *homo*. Architectural and functional consequences on the shoulder girdle.); *[Summary in]*. J.L. Voisin. **Anthropologie [Paris]** 105:4 10-12:2001 pp.449-468.

1524   The evolutionary history of humans in Australasia from an environmental perspective. Paul Storm. **Anth. Sci.** 108:3 7:2000 pp.225-260.

1525   Habitats for humanity: effects of visual affordance on the evolution of hominid antipredator communication. Nicholas Nicastro. **Evolut. Anthrop.** 10:5 2001 pp.153-157.

1526   Handaxe-Hurling hominids: an unlikely story. John C. Whittaker; Grant McCall. **Curr. Anthr.** 42:4 8-10:2001 pp.566-572.

1527   Human skeletal remains in the University of San Carlos Museum. Aloysius Ma.L. Cañete; Wenda R. Trevathan. **Phil. Q. Cult. Soc.** 28:4 12:2000 pp.512-527.

1528   Metric variation and species recognition in the fossil record. J. Michael Plavcan; Dana A. Cope. **Evolut. Anthrop.** 10:6 2001 pp.204-222.

1529   Mind the gap: hierarchies, health and human evolution. Richard G. Wilkinson. London: Weidenfeld & Nicolson, 2000. 70p. *ISBN: 0297646486.* (*Series:* Darwinism today).

1530   Novaia interpretatsiia roli «Geidel'bergskogo cheloveka» v evoliutsii roda *Homo*. *[In Russian]*; (New interpretation of Heidelberg Man's significance in the evolution of the genus *homo*.) *[Summary]*. A.A. Zubov. **Etnograf. Oboz.** 1 1-2:2001 pp.91-111.

1531   Of monsters and fossils: the making of racial difference in Malvina Hoffman's Hall of the Races of Mankind. Jeff Rosen. **Hist. Anthrop.** 12:2 2001 pp.101-158.

1532   Peking Man and the politics of paleoanthropological nationalism in China. Barry Sautman. **J. Asian St.** 60:1 2:2001 pp.95-124.

1533   Présentation paléo-environnementale du remplissage de la Baume Moula-Guercy à Soyons (Ardèche): implications paléoclimatiques et chronologiques. *[In French]*; (Baume Moula-Guercy, Soyons (Ardèche): palaeoclimatic and chronological implications [of a French site].) *[Summary]*. A. Defleur; É. Crégut-Bonnoure; E. Desclaux; M. Thinon. **Anthropologie [Paris]** 105·3 7-9:2001 pp.369-408.

1534   Restes post-crâniens du niveau TD6 du site en grotte du pléistocène inférieur de Gran Dolina, Sierra de Atapuerca, Espagne. *[In French]*; (Human postcranial bones from the Gran Dolina site, Sierra de Atapuerca, Burgos, Spain.) *[Summary]*. J.M. Carretero; C. Lorenzo; J.L. Arsuaga. **Anthropologie [Paris]** 105:2 4-6:2001 pp.179-202.

1535   Les sédiments d'*homo* antecessor de Gran Dolina (Sierra de Atapuerca, Burgos, Espagne). Interprétation micromorphologique des processus de formation et enregistrement paléoenvironnemental des sédiments. *[In French]*; (*Homo* antecessor sediments of Gran Dolina (Sierra de Atapuerca, Burgos, Spain). Micromorphological interpretation of the formation process and palaeoenvironmental record of the sediments.) *[Summary]*. J. Vallverdú; M.A. Courty; E. Carbonell; A. Canals; F. Burjachs. **Anthropologie [Paris]** 105:1 1-3:2001 pp.45-70.

1536   Southern Africa and modern human origins. Richard G. Klein. **J. Anthr. Res.** 57:1 Spring:2001 pp.1-16.

1537   Theoretical evolutionary ecology. Michael George Bulmer. Sunderland MA: Sinauer Associates, 1994. xi, 352p. *ISBN: 0878930795, 0878930787.*

1538   We hold these truths to be self-evident. Kenneth Weiss. **Evolut. Anthrop.** 10:6 2001 pp.199-203.

1539   Who dares, wins: heroism versus altruism in women's mate choice. Susan Kelly; R.I.M. Dunbar. **Hum. Nature** 12:2 2001 pp.89-106.

Human growth and development
Croissance et développement de l'homme

1540   Allaitement maternel, niveau socio-économique et état nutritionnel des nourrissons Marocains. *[In French]*; [Breast-feeding, socioeconomic level and nutritional status of Moroccan infants]. N. Belkeziz; H. Amor; A. Baali; F. Rovillé-Sausse. **Bio. Hum. Anthrop.** 19:1-2 1-6:2001 pp.97-102.

1541   Anthropometric parameters for the assessment of nutritional status in (0-6) years children in Varanasi. Lipi Das; Indira Bishnoi; B.K. Das. **Man India** 80:3-4 7-12:2000 pp.345-350.

1542   Application of nonpregnant and pregnant women's anthropometric data in medicine. H. Kaarma; J. Kasmel; J. Peterson; G. Veldre. **Mankind Q.** XLII:2 Winter:2001 pp.169-188.

1543   Assessing the biological status of human populations. Napoleon Wolański; Anna Siniarska. **Curr. Anthr.** 42:2 4:2001 pp.301-307.

1544   Association between maternal age at menarche and newborn size. Sylvia Kirchengast. **Soc. Biol.** 47:1-2 Spring-Summer:2000 pp.114-126.

1545   Auxologie et maturation squelettique. *[In French]*; (Auxology and skeletal maturation.) M. Sempé; C. Pavia; M. Bouchard. **Bio. Hum. Anthrop.** 19:1-2 1-6:2001 pp.1-8.

1546   Beyond lifetime averages: tracing life histories through isotopic analysis of different calcified tissues from archaeological human skeletons. Judith Sealy; Richard Armstrong; Carmel Schrire. **Antiquity** 69:263 6:1995 pp.290-300.

1547   Brain evolution and cognition. Gerhard Roth [Ed.]; Mario F. Wullimann [Ed.]. New York: Wiley, 2000. *ISBN: 0471331708. Includes index.*

1548   Breastfeeding behavior and infant survival with emphasis on reverse causation bias: some evidence from Nigeria. Clement Ahiadeke. **Soc. Biol.** 47:1-2 Spring-Summer:2000 pp.94-113.

1549   The compact formulation of anthropodynamical measures in physiological anthropology; *[Summary in Croatian]*. O. Muftić; L. Ibrahimagić; D. Milčić. **Coll. Antrop.** 25:1 6:2001 pp.269-278.

1550   Considérations sur la stature des populations sub-actuelles de Patagonie et extrême sud d'Amérique. *[In French]*; [Considerations on the stature of past populations of Patagonia and the extreme south of America] *[Summary]*. P. Soto-Heim. **Bio. Hum. Anthrop.** 19:3-4 7-12:2001 pp.257-264.

1551   Croissance et alimentation d'enfants (0 à 18 mois) d'origine Maghrébine dans trois pays européens (France, Belgique et Espagne). *[In French]*; [Comparative study of the diet and growth of children born to Magrebi parents in France, Belgium and Spain]. F. Rovillé-Sausse; M. Vercauteren; C. Prado-Martinez. **Bio. Hum. Anthrop.** 19:1-2 1-6:2001 pp.47-54.

1552   Croissance et état nutritionnel des enfants Marocains d'âge préscolaire. *[In French]*; (Growth and nutritional status of pre-school age Moroccan children.) H. Amor; A. Baali; F. Rovillé-Sausse; E. Crognier; G. Boëtsch. **Bio. Hum. Anthrop.** 19:1-2 1-6:2001 pp.63-70.

1553   Croissance pubertaire: à partir du modèle pubertés précoces. *[In French]*; [Pubertal growth: [a] study using the model of early puberty]. R. Brauner. **Bio. Hum. Anthrop.** 19:1-2 1-6:2001 pp.83-88.

1554   Deti Kalmykii: trudy i igry. *[In Russian]*; (Children of Kalmykia: works and games.) *[Summary]*. O.Iu. Artemova; M.L. Butovskaia. **Etnograf. Oboz.** 3 5-6:2000 pp.30-45.

1555   The development of blood and lymph vessels of human parathyroid glands in embryonal, fetal and postnatal period; *[Summary in Croatian]*. R. Pezerović-Panijan; Đ. Grbeša; Lj. Banek; D. Ježek; Dž. Pezerović; J. Čavčić; R. Čanić. **Coll. Antrop.** 25:1 6:2001 pp.333-340.

1556   Dietary variety, energy regulation, and obesity. Hollie A. Raynor; Leonard H. Epstein. **Psychol. B.** 127:3 5:2001 pp.325-341.

1557   Différences de croissance et de composition corporelle au cours de la puberté entre adolescentes Sénégalaises ayant été ou non malnutries lors de leur petite enfance. *[In French]*; [Pubertal growth and body composition in Senegal: a study of adolescent girls with malnourished and non-malnourished infancies]. E. Bénéfice; D. Garnier; K.B. Simondon; R.M. Malina. **Bio. Hum. Anthrop.** 19:1-2 1-6:2001 pp.55-62.

1558   The effect of age on time until ovulation in female menstrual cycles. A longitudinal data analysis based on mixed models; *[Summary in Italian]*; *[Summary in French]*. F.C. Billari; A. Rosina. **Genus** LVII:2 4-6:2001 pp.71-88.

1559   Effect of specially programmed physical and health education on motor fitness of seven-year-old school children; *[Summary in Croatian]*. J. Babin; R. Katić; D. Ropac; D. Bonacin. **Coll. Antrop.** 25:1 6:2001 pp.153-166.

1560   Effects of maternal body morphology, morning sickness, gestational diabetes and hypertension on fluctuating asymmetry in young women. Devendra Singh; Valerie C. Rosen. **Evol. Hum. Behav.** 22:6 11:2001 pp.373-384.

1561   Emotional symptoms of neurological disorders in children. Ralph Scott. **Mankind Q.** XLI:4 Summer:2001 pp.399-414.

1562   Environment sensitive human development index: issues and alternatives. B. Ramanathan. **Ind. Soc. Sci. R.** 1:1 1-6:1999 pp.193-201.

1563   Estimation of sex from the talus in prehistoric native Americans; *[Summary in Croatian]*. Ch. Barrett; W. Cavallari; P.W. Sciulli. **Coll. Antrop.** 25:1 6:2001 pp.13-20.

1564   Évaluation de la maturation squelettique au niveau du coude en orthopédie. *[In French]*; [The elbow as a determiner of skeletal maturity]. T. Craviari; M. Sempé; F. Chotel; M. Bouchard; J. Berard. **Bio. Hum. Anthrop.** 19:1-2 1-6:2001 pp.13-28.

1565   Évolution de la croissance de l'enfant Tunisien au cours des 3 dernières décennies: facteurs déterminants. *[In French]*; [Changes in growth patterns of Tunisian children over the last three decades: determinant factors]. F. Khaldi; A. Ben Mansour. **Bio. Hum. Anthrop.** 19:1-2 1-6:2001 pp.115-120.

1566   L'évolution du poids à la naissance en fonction des conditions socio-économiques différentes. *[In French]*; [Changing birth-weights in correlation with differing social and economic conditions: Romania 1966-1996]. C. Glavce; L. Dragomirescu; C. Valentin; L. Apâvâloae. **Bio. Hum. Anthrop.** 19:1-2 1-6:2001 pp.89-96.

1567   Evolution of human growth. Steven R. Leigh. **Evolut. Anthrop.** 10:6 2001 pp.223-236.

1568   Gender differentials in malnutrition — a case study of preschool children. K. Visweswara Rao; D. Krishna; N. Balakrishna. **Man India** 80:3-4 7-12:2000 pp.289-294.

1569   Growth and development of male children and youth in Tuzla's region after the war in Bosnia and Herzegovina; *[Summary in Croatian]*. J. Hadžihalilović; R. Hadžiselimović. **Coll. Antrop.** 25:1 6:2001 pp.41-58.

1570   Hepatocyte growth factor levels in Croatian healthy and alcoholic liver cirrhosis patients. N. Antoljak; E. Topić; M. Duvnjak; N. Vrkić; I. Žuntar. **Coll. Antrop.** 25:1 6:2001 pp.341-348.

1571   The human development index and sustainability — a constructive proposal. E. Neumayer. **Ecol. Eco.** 39:1 10:2001 pp.101-114.

1572   Hypertension artérielle chez les enfants en Silésie (Pologne). *[In French]*; [Arterial hypertension in Polish children]. W. Rokicki; A. Skierska; T. Bilewicz-Wyrozumska. **Bio. Hum. Anthrop.** 19:1-2 1-6:2001 pp.77-82.

1573   Inaugural lecture: desperately seeking security. G. Wood. **J. Int. Dev.** 13:5 7:2001 pp.523-534.

1574   Influence of father's weight and height on weight of male and female newborns; *[Summary in Croatian]*. F. Mikulandra; I. Tadin; J. Grgurić; Z. Zakanj; M. Periša. **Coll. Antrop.** 25:1 6:2001 pp.59-64.

1575   Lung lavage neutrophils, neutrophil elastase and albumin in the prognosis of pulmonary sarcoidosis; *[Summary in Croatian]*. T. Peroš-Golubičić; A. Ivičević; A. Bekić; M. Alilović; J. Tekavec-Trkanjec; S. Smojver-Ježek. **Coll. Antrop.** 25:1 6:2001 pp.349-356.

1576   The need for specific stature standards for children in an urban area in Sardinia; *[Summary in French]*. E. Sanna; L. Palmas; N. Tedesco; G. Floris. **Bio. Hum. Anthrop.** 19:3-4 7-12:2001 pp.225-234.

1577   Parental investment and child health in a Yanomamö village suffering short-term food stress. Edward H. Hagen; Raymond B. Hames; Nathan M. Craig; Matthew T. Lauer; Michael E. Price. **J. Biosoc. Sc.** 33:4 10:2001 pp.503-528.

1578   Physical development of rural adolescents: a cross sectional study in Andhra Pradesh. K. Mayuri; K. Madhavilatha. **Man India** 80:3-4 7-12:2000 pp.337-344.

1579   Physical growth among the affluent and non-affluent Meitei boys of Manipur. L. Dibamani Singh; T. Shyamacharan Singh. **Man India** 80:3-4 7-12:2000 pp.295-308.

1580   Prevention of sexually transmitted infections in different populations: a review of behaviourally effective and cost-effective interventions. Alexander McKay. **Canad. J. Human Sex.** 9:2 2000 pp.95-120.

1581   Un problème pour la biométrie: la variation de la composition corporelle pendant le cycle menstruel après la puberté. *[In French]*; (A problem in biometry: variation of body composition during the menstrual cycle.) C. Prado-Martinez; E. Delgado. **Bio. Hum. Anthrop.** 19:1-2 1-6:2001 pp.71-76.

1582   Race and the inheritance of low birth weight. Dalton Conley; Neil G. Bennett. **Soc. Biol.** 47:1-2 Spring-Summer:2000 pp.77-93.

1583   Race/ethnic differentials in heavy weight and cesarean births. R. Frank; W.P. Frisbie; S.G. Pullum. **Pop. Res. Pol. R.** 19:5 10:2000 pp.459-476.

1584   Recent anthropological perspectives on human weaning. Daniel W. Sellen; Thomas W. McDade; Hillary N. Fouts; Barry S. Hewlett; Michael E. Lamb; Daniel W. Sellen; Diana B. Smay. **Hum. Nature** 12:1 2001 pp.1-87. *Collection of 4 articles.*

1585   The relationship between left ventricular filling shortly after an uncomplicated myocardial infarction and subsequent exercise capacity; *[Summary in Croatian]*. R. Urek; M. Čubrilo-Turek; M. Crnčević-Urek. **Coll. Antrop.** 25:1 6:2001 pp.279-288.

1586   Reproductive health and culture among the Mapuche and Tehuelche of South America. Maria Christina Chiriguini; Maria Elina Vitello. **Mankind Q.** XLII:2 Winter:2001 pp.117-132.

1587   Ressemblance familiale de traits anthropométriques. I. Évaluation d'une influence liée à l'activité professionnelle de la mère. *[In French]*; [Shared familial anthropometric traits, part I: an evaluation of the influences linked to the occupation of the mother]. I. Salces; E. Rebato; Ch. Susanne; L. San Martin; J. Rosique; A. Vinagre. **Bio. Hum. Anthrop.** 19:1-2 1-6:2001 pp.103-110.

1588   Sexual dimorphism in body composition, weight status and growth in prepubertal school children from rural areas of eastern Austria; *[Summary in Croatian]*. S. Kirchengast; V. Steiner. **Coll. Antrop.** 25:1 6:2001 pp.21-30.

1589   Some anthropometric characteristics, reactions on physical stress, and blood pressure in males aged 18 in Primorsko-Goranska County, Croatia; *[Summary in Croatian]*. I. Kontošić; E. Mesaroš-Kanjski; J. Božin-Juračić; M. Vukelić; H. Grubišić-Greblo; A. Jonjić. **Coll. Antrop.** 25:1 6:2001 pp.31-40.

1590   Temporal changes in maxillary alveolar profile angle and inclination of incisor in Japan. Miho Ohsako. **Anth. Sci.** 108:4 10:2000 p.387.

1591   Transcranial doppler in smoking relapse prevention strategy. N. Blažić-Čop; V. Šerić; V. Bašić; N. Thaller; V. Demarin. **Coll. Antrop.** 25:1 6:2001 pp.289-296.

1592   Variabilité du rythme de développement et de la période pubertaire chez des sujets belges. *[In French]*; [Variations in the tempo of development and puberty among Belgians]. M. Vercauteren. **Bio. Hum. Anthrop.** 19:1-2 1-6:2001 pp.29-36.

1593   Women in transition — menopause and body composition in different populations; *[Summary in Croatian]*. J. Aréchiga; C. Prado; M. Cantó; M. Carmenate. **Coll. Antrop.** 25:2 12:2001 pp.443-448.

Primatology
Primatologie

1594   12th annual meeting of *La Société Francophone de Primatologie*, Besançon, September
        2000. B.L. Deputte. **Folia Prim.** 72:3 2001 pp.115-127.

1595   14th meeting of the Italian Primatological Society, Pisa-Calci, October 2000. A. Gregorace;
        E. Palagi; S.M Borgognini-Tarli. **Folia Prim.** 72:3 2001 pp.128-152.

1596   7th congress of the German Primate Society, Zurich, September-October 2001. A.E.
        Müller; W. Scheffrahn. **Folia Prim.** 72:3 2001 pp.153-194.

1597   Abundance, diversity, and patterns of distribution of primates on the Tapiche River in
        Amazonian Peru. Cynthia L. Bennett; Suzi Leonard; Scott Carter. **Am. J. Prim.** 54:2
        6:2001 pp.119-126.

1598   Abundance, use of space, and activity patterns of white-faced sakis (*Pithecia pithecia*) in
        French Guiana. Jean-Christophe Vié; Cécile Richard-Hansen; Christine Fournier-
        Chambrillon. **Am. J. Prim.** 55:4 12:2001 pp.203-222.

1599   Activity and ranging patterns of guerezas in the Kakamega Forest: intergroup variation and
        implications for intragroup feeding competition. Peter J. Fashing. **Int. J. Primat.** 22:4
        8:2001 pp.549-578.

1600   Activity budget and positional behavior of the Mysore slender loris (*Loris tardigradus
        lydekkerianus*): implications for slow climbing locomotion. K.A.I. Nekaris. **Folia Prim.**
        72:4 2001 pp.228-241.

1601   The adaptive significance of geophagy for Japanese macaques (*Macaca fuscata*) at
        Arashiyama, Japan. J.V. Wakibara; M.A. Huffman; M. Wink; S. Reich; S. Aufreiter; R.G.V.
        Hancock; R. Sodhi; W.C. Mahaney; S. Russel. **Int. J. Primat.** 22:3 6:2001 pp.495-520.

1602   Adult male-infant interactions in wild muriquis (*Brachyteles arachnoides hypoxanthus*).
        Vanessa Da Oliveira Guimarães; Karen B. Strier. **Primates** 42:4 10:2001 pp.395-400.

1603   Analysis of infant handling and the effects of female rank among Tana River adult female
        yellow baboons (*Papio cynocephalus cynocephalus*) using permutation/randomization
        tests. Vicki K. Bentley-Condit; Thomas Moore; E.O. Smith. **Am. J. Prim.** 55:2 10:2001
        pp.117-130.

1604   Are bonobos (*Pan paniscus*) really more bipedal than chimpanzees (*Pan troglodytes*)?
        Elaine N. Videan; W.C. McGrew. **Am. J. Prim.** 54:4 8:2001 pp.233-239.

1605   An attempted within-group infanticide in wild chimpanzees. Tetsuya Sakamaki; Noriko
        Itoh; Toshisada Nishida. **Primates** 42:4 10:2001 pp.359-366.

1606   Behavioral and hormonal analysis of social relationships between oldest females in a wild
        monogamous group of common marmosets (*Callithrix jacchus*). Ana Cláudia S.R.
        Albuquerque; Maria B.C. Sousa; Herbert M. Santos; T.E. Ziegler. **Int. J. Primat.** 22:4
        8:2001 pp.631-646.

1607   Behavioral responses of an infant gorilla to maternal separation in a captive social group of
        lowland gorillas (*Gorilla gorilla gorilla*). Masayuki Nakamichi; April Silldorff; Peggy
        Sexton. **Primates** 42:3 7:2001 pp.245-252.

1608   Behavioural diversity among the wild chimpanzee populations of Bossou and
        neighbouring areas, Guinea and Côte d'Ivoire, West Africa. A preliminary report. T.
        Humle; T. Matsuzawa. **Folia Prim.** 72:2 2001 pp.57-68.

1609   Benefits of polyspecific associations for the Goeldi's monkey (*Callimico goeldii*). Lelia M.
        Porter. **Am. J. Prim.** 54:3 7:2001 pp.143-158.

1610   A biomechanical study of the long bones in Platyrrhines. L. Llorens; A. Casinos; C. Berge;
        M. Majoral; F.K. Jouffroy. **Folia Prim.** 72:4 2001 pp.201-216.

1611   Can concurrent speed and directness of travel indicate purposeful encounter in the yellow
        baboons (*Papio hamadryas cynocephalus*) of Ruaha National Park, Tanzania? Sharon T.
        Pochron. **Int. J. Primat.** 22:5 10:2001 pp.173-786.

1612   Can rhesus monkeys spontaneously subtract? Gregory M. Sulkowski; Marc D. Hauser.
        Cognition 79:3 5:2001 pp.239-262.

1613   Changes in urinary steroid conjugates and gonadotropin excretion in the menstrual cycle and pregnancy in the Yunnan snub-nosed monkey (*Rhinopithecus bieti*). Yimei He; Yijin Pei; Rujin Zou; Weizhi Ji. **Am. J. Prim.** 55:4 12:2001 pp.223-232.

1614   Changes in yearling rhesus monkeys' relationships with their mothers after sibling birth. B.J. Devinney; C.M. Berman; K.L.R. Rasmussen. **Am. J. Prim.** 54:4 8:2001 pp.193-210.

1615   Characterization and screening of microsatellite loci in a wild lemur population (*Propithecus verreauxi verreauxi*). Richard R. Lawler; Alison F. Richard; Margaret A. Riley. **Am. J. Prim.** 55:4 12:2001 pp.253-259.

1616   Cloning, sequencing, and functional characterization of the vitamin D receptor in vitamin D-resistant New World primates. Rene F. Chun; Hong Chen; Lorrie Boldrick; Connie Sweet; John S. Adams. **Am. J. Prim.** 54:2 6:2001 pp.107-118.

1617   Colony specificity in a social call of mouse lemurs (*Microcebus ssp.*) Elke Zimmermann; Thomas G. Hafen. **Am. J. Prim.** 54:3 7:2001 pp.129-141.

1618   Comparative methods for studying primate adaptation and allometry. Charles L. Nunn; Robert A. Barton. **Evolut. Anthrop.** 10:3 2001 pp.81-98.

1619   Comparison of reproductive characteristics and changes in body weight between captive populations of rufous and gray mouse lemurs. Dorothea Wrogemann; Ute Radespiel; Elke Zimmermann. **Int. J. Primat.** 22:1 2:2001 pp.91-108.

1620   Confidence intervals for morphology-based cladistic trees: a Platyrrhine phylogeny test case. Robert S. Corruccini. **Int. J. Primat.** 22:6 12:2001 pp.1007-1020.

1621   Contest versus scramble competition for mates: the composition and spatial structure of a population of gray mouse lemurs (*Microcebus murinus*) in north-west Madagascar. Ute Radespiel; Petra Ehresmann; Elke Zimmermann. **Primates** 42:3 7:2001 pp.207-220.

1622   Contrast of estrus in accordance with social contexts between two troops of wild Japanese macaques on Yakushima. Naobi Okayasu. **Anth. Sci.** 109:2 4:2001 pp.121-140.

1623   Correlates of intergroup transfer in male grey-cheeked mangabeys. William Olupot; Peter M. Waser. **Int. J. Primat.** 22:2 4:2001 pp.169-188.

1624   Daily torpor in free-ranging gray mouse lemurs (*Microcebus murinus*) in Madagascar. Jutta Schmid. **Int. J. Primat.** 22:6 12:2001 pp.1021-1032.

1625   Demography and pedigree structure of an SPF colony of rhesus monkeys (*Macaca mulatta*). Lisa Ludvico; Susan Slifer; Kristina Massey; Kathryn Mosman; Carlos Mohamed; William Stone; Michale Keeling; Bruce Bernacky; Bennett Dyke. **Am. J. Prim.** 53:4 4:2001 pp.155-166.

1626   Detection of antibodies to selected human pathogens among wild and pet macaques (*Macaca tonkeana*) in Sulawesi, Indonesia. Lisa Jones-Engel; Gregory A. Engel; Michael A. Schillaci; Rosany Babo; Jeffery Froehlich. **Am. J. Prim.** 54:3 7:2001 pp.171-178.

1627   Dietary differences among sympatric Callitrichinae in northern Bolivia: *Callimico goeldii, Saguinus fuscicollis* and *S. labiatus*. Leila M. Porter. **Int. J. Primat.** 22:6 12:2001 pp.961-992.

1628   Differential energy budget and monopolization potential of harem holders and bachelors in hanuman langurs (*Semnopithecus entellus*): preliminary results. Oliver Schülke. **Am. J. Prim.** 55:1 9:2001 pp.57-63.

1629   Dissociation of cortisol and behavioral indicators of stress in an orangutan (*Pongo pygmaeus*) during a computerized task. Christopher M. Elder; Charles R. Menzel. **Primates** 42:4 10:2001 pp.345-358.

1630   Distribution and habitat associations of baboons (*Papio hamadryas*) in central Eritrea. D. Zinner; F. Peláez; F. Torkler. **Int. J. Primat.** 22:3 6:2001 pp.397-414.

1631   Dominance style in female guerezas (*Colobus guereza* Rüppell 1835). Thalia Grunau; Jutta Kuester. **Primates** 42:4 10:2001 pp.301-308.

1632   Dynamics of estrous synchrony in captive gray mouse lemurs (*Microcebus murinus*). Ute Radespiel; Elke Zimmermann. **Int. J. Primat.** 22:1 2:2001 pp.71-90.

1633   Effect of aging on circadian activity in gray mouse lemurs. Alain Schilling; Jean-Pierre Richard; Jacques Servière. **Int. J. Primat.** 22:1 2:2001 pp.25-42.

1634   Effect of ambient temperature on the body temperature rhythm of male gray mouse lemurs (*Microcrocebus murinus*). F. Aujard; F. Vasseur. **Int. J. Primat.** 22:1 2:2001 pp.43-56.

1635 Effect of male emigration on the vigilance behavior of coresident males in white-faced capuchins (*Cebus capucinus*). Katharine M. Jack. **Int. J. Primat.** 22:5 10:2001 pp.715-732.

1636 Effects of cognitive challenge on self-directed behaviors by chimpanzees (*Pan troglodytes*). David A. Leavens; Filippo Aureli; William D. Hopkins; Charles W. Hyatt. **Am. J. Prim.** 55:1 9:2001 pp.1-14.

1637 Episodic memory in primates. Bennett L. Schwartz; Siân Evans. **Am. J. Prim.** 55:2 10:2001 pp.71-86.

1638 Extended application of a marked nest census method to examine seasonal changes in habitat use by chimpanzees. Takeshi Furuichi; Chie Hashimoto; Yasuko Tashiro. **Int. J. Primat.** 22:6 12:2001 pp.913-928.

1639 Factors affecting feeding decisions in a group of black lemurs confronted with novel food. Delphine Gosset; Jean-Jacques Roeder. **Primates** 42:3 7:2001 pp.175-182.

1640 Fecal analysis of ovarian cycles in female black-handed spider monkeys (*Ateles geoffroyi*). C.J. Campbell; S.E. Shideler; H.E. Todd; B.L. Lasley. **Am. J. Prim.** 54:2 6:2001 pp.79-90.

1641 Feeding, diet, and jaw form in West African *Colobus* and *Procolobus*. David J. Daegling; W. Scott McGraw. **Int. J. Primat.** 22:6 12:2001 pp.1033-1056.

1642 Feeding ecology of guerezas in the Kakamega forest, Kenya: the importance of Moraceae fruit in their diet. Peter J. Fashing. **Int. J. Primat.** 22:4 8:2001 pp.579-610.

1643 Female dominance in captive gray mouse lemurs (*Microcebus murinus*). Ute Radespiel; Elke Zimmermann. **Am. J. Prim.** 54:4 8:2001 pp.181-192.

1644 Food habits of Formosan rock macaques (*Macaca cyclopis*) in Jentse, northeastern Taiwan, assessed by fecal analysis and behavioral observation. Hsiu-Hui Su; Ling-Ling Lee. **Int. J. Primat.** 22:3 6:2001 pp.359-378.

1645 Food resource characteristics in two nocturnal lemurs with different social behavior: *Avahi occidentalis* and *Lepilemur edwardsi*. Urs Thalmann. **Int. J. Primat.** 22:2 4:2001 pp.287-324.

1646 Food sharing in pied bare-faced tamarins (*Saguinus bicolor bicolor*): development and individual differences. Eluned C. Price; Anna T.C. Feistner. **Int. J. Primat.** 22:2 4:2001 pp.231-242.

1647 Food transfer among adult lion tamarins: mutualism, reciprocity or one-sided relationship? Lisa G. Rapaport. **Int. J. Primat.** 22:4 8:2001 pp.611-630.

1648 Fruit availability and habitat use by chimpanzees in the Kalinzu Forest, Uganda: examination of fallback foods. Takeshi Furuichi; Chie Hashimoto; Yasuko Tashiro. **Int. J. Primat.** 22:6 12:2001 pp.929-946.

1649 Genetic characterization of long-tailed macaques (*Macaca fascicularis*) on Tabuan Island, Indonesia. Dyah Perwitasari-Farajallah; Yoshi Kawamoto; Randall C. Kyes; R.P. Agus Lelana; Dondin Sajuthi. **Primates** 42:2 4:2001 pp.141-152.

1650 Genetic comparison of wild populations of *Lepilemur septentrionalis* and *Lepilemur dorsalis* using RAPD markers. Berthine Ravaoarimanana; Jean-Luc Fausser; Yves Rumpler. **Primates** 42:3 7:2001 pp.221-231.

1651 Geophagy by the bonnet macaques (*Macaca radiata*) of southern India: a preliminary analysis. J. Voros; W.C. Mahaney; M.W. Milner; R. Krishnamani; S. Aufreiter; R.G.V. Hancock. **Primates** 42:4 10:2001 pp.327-344.

1652 The Great Ape Project and disability rights: ominous undercurrents of eugenics in action. Nora Ellen Groce; Jonathan Marks. **Am. Anthrop.** 102:4 12:2000 pp.818-822.

1653 Greeting behavior during party encounters in captive chimpanzees. Kyoko Okamoto; Naoki Agetsuma; Shozo Kojima. **Primates** 42:2 4:2001 pp.161-166.

1654 Group composition and adult sex-ratio of hamadryas baboons (*Papio hamadryas hamadryas*) in central Eritrea. D. Zinner; F. Peláez; F. Torkler. **Int. J. Primat.** 22:3 6:2001 pp.415-430.

1655 Group fission in moor macaques (*Macaca maurus*). Kyoko Okamoto; Shuichi Matsumura. **Int. J. Primat.** 22:3 6:2001 pp.481-494.

1656   Habitat use and structural preferences of captive western lowland gorillas (*Gorilla gorilla gorilla*): effects of environmental and social variables. T.S. Stoinski; M.P. Hoff; T.L. Maple. **Int. J. Primat.** 22:3 6:2001 pp.431-448.

1657   Health evaluation of translocated free-ranging primates in French Guiana. Benoît de Thoisy; Ingrun Vogel; Jean-Marc Reynes; Jean-François Pouliquen; Bernard Carme; Mirdad Kazanji; Jean-Christophe Vié. **Am. J. Prim.** 54:1 5:2001 pp.1-16.

1658   Hormonal correlates of maternal style in captive macaques (*Macaca fuscata* and *M. mulatta*). Massimo Bardi; Keiko Shimizu; Shiho Fujita; Silvana Borgognini-Tarli; Michael A. Huffman. **Int. J. Primat.** 22:4 8:2001 pp.647-662.

1659   Immigration and hybridization patterns of yellow and anubis baboons in and around Amboseli, Kenya. Susan C. Alberts; Jeanne Altmann. **Am. J. Prim.** 53:4 4:2001 pp.139-154.

1660   Influence of fluctuation in the operational sex ratio to mating of troop and non-troop male Japanese macaques for four years on Kinkazan Island, Japan. Hiroyuki Takahashi. **Primates** 42:3 7:2001 pp.183-191.

1661   Integration of new males into four social groups of tufted capuchins (*Cebus apella*). Matthew A. Cooper; Irwin S. Bernstein; Dorothy M. Fragaszy; Frans B.M. de Waal. **Int. J. Primat.** 22:4 8:2001 pp.663-683.

1662   Is there adaptive value to reproductive termination in Japanese macaques? A test of maternal investment hypotheses. Linda Marie Fedigan; Mary S. McDonald Pavelka. **Int. J. Primat.** 22:2 4:2001 pp.109-126.

1663   Limb injuries resulting from snares and traps in chimpanzees (*Pan troglodytes schweinfurthii*) of the Budongo Forest, Uganda. John C. Waller; Vernon Reynolds. **Primates** 42:2 4:2001 pp.135-140.

1664   Manipulating the affiliative interactions of group-housed rhesus macaques using positive reinforcement training techniques. Steven J. Schapiro; Jaine E. Perlman; Brock A. Boudreau. **Am. J. Prim.** 55:3 11:2001 pp.137-150.

1665   Measurement of urinary and fecal steroid metabolites during the ovarian cycle in captive and wild Japanese macaques, *Macaca fuscata*. Shiho Fujita; Fusako Mitsunaga; Hideki Sugiura; Keiko Shimizu. **Am. J. Prim.** 53:4 4:2001 pp.167-176.

1666   Molecular phylogenetic relationships among Sichuan snub-nosed monkeys (*Rhinopithecus roxellanae*) inferred from mitochondrial cytochrome-b gene sequences. Ming Li; Bing Liang; Zoujian Feng; Hidetoshi B. Tamate. **Primates** 42:2 4:2001 pp.153-160.

1667   Monitoring the reproductive status of female gorillas (*Gorilla gorilla gorilla*) by measuring the steroid hormones in fecal samples. Sachiko Miyamoto; Yang Chen; Hidetoshi Kurotori; Tadashi Sankai; Takashi Yoshida; Takeo Machida. **Primates** 42:4 10:2001 pp.291-300.

1668   Monitoring the reproductive status of Japanese monkeys (*Macaca fuscata*) by measurement of the steroid hormones in fecal samples. Takashi Yoshida; Mie Matsumuro; Sachiko Miyamoto; Yasuyuki Muroyama; Yasuko Tashiro; Yuji Takenoshita; Tadashi Sankai. **Primates** 42:4 10:2001 pp.367-374.

1669   Neotropical primates in a regenerating Costa Rican dry forest: a comparison of howler and capuchin population patterns. Linda Marie Fedigan; Katharine Jack. **Int. J. Primat.** 22:5 10:2001 pp.689-714.

1670   Novel hyperprolactinemia and hyperprolactinemic anovulation model using the cynomolgus monkey (*Macaca fascicularis*). Makoto Moro; Ryuzo Torii; Hajime Ishii; Yoshikuni Tanioka; Yoichi Inada; Masami Kojima; Hirotada Tsujii. **Primates** 42:4 10:2001 pp.375-390.

1671   Nutritional aspects of western lowland gorilla (*Gorilla gorilla gorilla*) diet during seasons of fruit scarcity at Bai Hokou, Central African Republic. M.J. Remis; E.S. Dierenfeld; C.B. Mowry; R.W. Carroll. **Int. J. Primat.** 22:5 10:2001 pp.807-836.

1672   Observation of a wild Japanese macaque mother pacifying her distressed infant with an acorn. Miki Matsubara; Miho Funakoshi. **Primates** 42:2 4:2001 pp.171-173.

1673   On the nomenclature of *Pan paniscus*. Jo A. Myers Thompson. **Primates** 42:2 4:2001 pp.101-112.

1674   Orangutan home range size and its determinants in a Sumatran swamp forest. Ian Singleton; Carel P. van Schaik. **Int. J. Primat.** 22:6 12:2001 pp.877-912.

1675   Parental failure in captive cotton-top tamarins (*Saguinus oedipus*). Massimo Bardi; Andrew J. Petto; David E. Lee-Parritz. **Am. J. Prim.** 54:3 7:2001 pp.159-169.

1676   Park or ride? Evolution of infant carrying in primates. Caroline Ross. **Int. J. Primat.** 22:5 10:2001 pp.749-772.

1677   Party size and diet of syntopic atelids (*Ateles chamek* and *Lagothrix cana*) in southwestern Brazilian Amazonia. S. Iwanaga; S.F. Ferrari. **Folia Prim.** 72:4 2001 pp.217-227.

1678   Patterns of positional behavior in mixed-species troops of *Callimico goeldii*, *Saguinus labiatus*, and *Saguinus fuscicollis* in northwestern Brazil. P.A. Garber; S.R. Leigh. **Am. J. Prim.** 54:1 5:2001 pp.17-32.

1679   Phylogeny of lion tamarins (*Leontopithecus* spp) based on interphotoreceptor retinol binding protein intron sequences. Nicholas I. Mundy; Joanne Kelly. **Am. J. Prim.** 54:1 5:2001 pp.33-40.

1680   Positional behavior and social organization of the Philippine tarsier (*Tarsius syrichta*). Marian Dagosto; Daniel L. Gebo; Cynthia Dolino. **Primates** 42:3 7:2001 pp.233-243.

1681   Postconflict behavior of spectacled leaf monkeys (*Trachypithecus obscurus*) II. Contact with third parties. Kate Arnold; Robert A. Barton. **Int. J. Primat.** 22:2 4:2001 pp.267-286.

1682   Postconflict behavior of spectacled leaf monkeys (*Trachypithecus obscurus*) I. Reconciliation. Kate Arnold; Robert A. Barton. **Int. J. Primat.** 22:2 4:2001 pp.243-266.

1683   Practising infanticide, observing narrative: controversial texts in a field science. Amanda Rees. **Soc. Stud. Sci.** 31:4 8:2001 pp.507-532.

1684   Primate innovation: sex, age and social rank differences. Simon M. Reader; Kevin N. Laland. **Int. J. Primat.** 22:5 10:2001 pp.787-806.

1685   Primate nepotism: what is the explanatory value of kin selection? Bernard Chapais. **Int. J. Primat.** 22:2 4:2001 pp.203-230.

1686   Primate population decline in response to habitat loss: Borajan Reserve Forest of Assam, India. Arun Srivastava; Jayanta Das; Jihosuo Biswas; Pranab Buzarbarua; Prabal Sarkar; Irwin S. Bernstein; Surendra Mal Mohnot. **Primates** 42:4 10:2001 pp.401-406.

1687   Primate population densities and sizes in Atlantic Forest remnants of northern Espírito Santo, Brazil. Adriano G. Chiarello; Fabiano R. de Melo. **Int. J. Primat.** 22:3 6:2001 pp.379-396.

1688   Probable genetic origin for a large number of cataracts among captive-bred vervet monkeys (*Chlorocebus aethiops*). Charon de Villiers; Jürgen V. Seier; Muhammada A. Dhansay. **Am. J. Prim.** 55:1 9:2001 pp.43-48.

1689   Proceedings of the XVIII congress of the International Primatological Society, Adelaide, January 2001. Dorothy M. Fragaszy; J.A.R.A.M. van Hooff; Katherine A. Leighty. **Int. J. Primat.** 22:6 12:2001 pp.1057-1086.

1690   Ranging behavior of two species of guenons (*Cercopithecus lhoesti* and *C. mitis doggetti*) in the Nyungwe Forest Reserve, Rwanda. Beth A. Kaplin. **Int. J. Primat.** 22:4 8:2001 pp.521-548.

1691   Ranging pattern and use of space in a group of red howler monkeys (*Alouatta seniculus*) in a southeastern Colombian rainforest. Erwin Palacios; Adriana Rodriguez. **Am. J. Prim.** 55:4 12:2001 pp.233-252.

1692   Rank and grooming reciprocity among females in a mixed-sex group of captive hamadryas baboons. Iris Leinfelder; Han de Vries; Rebekka Deleu; Mark Nelissen. **Am. J. Prim.** 55:1 9:2001 pp.25-42.

1693   Recognition and categorization of biologically significant objects by rhesus monkeys (*Macaca mulatta*): the domain of food. Lucia R. Santos; Marc D. Hauser; Elizabeth S. Spelke. **Cognition** 82:2 12:2001 pp.127-155.

1694   Red-tailed guenons (*Cercopithecus ascanius*) and *Strychnos mitis*: evidence for plant benefits beyond seed dispersal. Joanna E. Lambert. **Int. J. Primat.** 22:2 4:2001 pp.189-202.

1695   Regulation by photoperiod of seasonal changes in body mass and reproductive function in gray mouse lemurs (*Microcebus murinus*): differential responses by sex. M. Perret; F. Aujard. **Int. J. Primat.** 22:1 2:2001 pp.5-24.

1696   Relevance of studbook data to the successful captive management of grey mouse lemurs. Angela R. Glatston. **Int. J. Primat.** 22:1 2:2001 pp.57-70.

1697   Reproductive behavioral changes during the ovarian cycle of lesser bushbabies (*Galago moholi*) in captivity. David L. Lipschitz; Jacqueline S. Galpin; Denny Meyer. **Am. J. Prim.** 55:2 10:2001 pp.101-116.

1698   Reproductive socioecology of tufted capuchins (*Cebus apella nigritus*) in northeastern Argentina. Mario S. Di Bitetti; Charles H. Janson. **Int. J. Primat.** 22:2 4:2001 pp.127-142.

1699   Seasonal ultrastructural modifications of the seminiferous epithelium in two *Eulemur* species: *E. fulvus* and *E. macaco*. B. Brun; R. Djlelati; Y. Rumpler; C. Koehl; M. Fabre. **Primates** 42:4 10:2001 pp.281-290.

1700   Seasonal variation in the feeding ecology of the grey-cheeked mangabey (*Lophocebus albigena*) in Cameroon. John R. Poulsen; Connie J. Clark; Thomas B. Smith. **Am. J. Prim.** 54:2 6:2001 pp.91-106.

1701   Self-induced increase of gut motility and the control of parasitic infections in wild chimpanzees. M.A. Huffman; J.M. Caton. **Int. J. Primat.** 22:3 6:2001 pp.329-346.

1702   Semifree-ranging tufted capuchins (*Cebus apella*) spontaneously use tools to crack open nuts. Eduardo B. Ottoni; Massimo Mannu. **Int. J. Primat.** 22:3 6:2001 pp.347-358.

1703   The sensory ecology of primate food perception. Nathaniel J. Dominy; Peter W. Lucas; Daniel Osorio; Nayuta Yamashita. **Evolut. Anthrop.** 10:5 2001 pp.171-186.

1704   'Separating the wheat from the chaff': a novel food processing technique in captive gorillas (*Gorilla g. gorilla*). Simone Pika; Michael Tomasello. **Primates** 42:2 4:2001 pp.167-170.

1705   Shifts in social structure of black howler (*Alouatta pigra*) groups associated with natural and experimental variation in population density. Linde E.T. Ostro; Scott C. Silver; Fred W. Koontz; Robert H. Horwich; Robin Brockett. **Int. J. Primat.** 22:5 10:2001 pp.733-748.

1706   Social organization, reproduction and rearing strategies of *Callimico goeldii*: new clues from the wild. L.M. Porter. **Folia Prim.** 72:2 2001 pp.69-79.

1707   Socioecology of hanuman langurs: the story of their success. Andreas Koenig; Carola Borries. **Evolut. Anthrop.** 10:4 2001 pp.122-137.

1708   Sources of variability in numbers of live births in wild golden lion tamarins (*Leontopithecus rosalia*). Karen Bales; Michelle O'Herron; Andrew J. Baker; James M. Dietz. **Am. J. Prim.** 54:4 8:2001 pp.211-222.

1709   Sources of variation in the nesting behavior of chimpanzees (*Pan troglodytes schweinfurthii*) in the Budongo Forest, Uganda. A.R. Brownlow; A.J. Plumptre; V. Reynolds; R. Ward. **Am. J. Prim.** 55:1 9:2001 pp.49-56.

1710   Spatial facilitation in a probing task in wedge-capped capuchins (*Cebus olivaceus*). Michel Dubois; Jean-François Gerard; Elineuza Sampaio; Olavo de Faria Galvão; Colette Guilhem. **Int. J. Primat.** 22:6 12:2001 pp.993-1006.

1711   Spontaneous tool use in captive, free-ranging golden lion tamarins (*Leontopithecus rosalia rosalia*). Tara S. Stoinski; Benjamin B. Beck. **Primates** 42:4 10:2001 pp.319-326.

1712   Status and distribution of golden langurs (*Trachypithecus geei*) in Assam, India. A. Srivastava; J. Biswas; J. Das; P. Bujarbarua. **Am. J. Prim.** 55:1 9:2001 pp.15-23.

1713   Strategies used by bonnet macaques (*Macaca radiata*) to reduce predation risk while sleeping. Uma Ramakrishnan; Richard G. Coss. **Primates** 42:3 7:2001 pp.193-206.

1714   The subspecies concept in primatology: the case of mountain gorillas. Craig B. Stanford. **Primates** 42:4 10:2001 pp.309-318.

1715   Substrate and tool use by brown capuchins in Suriname: ecological contexts and cognitive bases. Sue Boinski; Robert P. Quatrone; Hilary Swartz. **Am. Anthrop.** 102:4 12:2000 pp.741-761.

1716   Territory characteristics among three neighboring chimpanzee communities in the Taï National Park, Côte d'Ivoire. Ilka Herbinger; Christophe Boesch; Hartmut Rothe. **Int. J. Primat.** 22:2 4:2001 pp.143-168.

1717   Time allocation patterns of lowland woolly monkeys (*Lagothrix lagotricha poeppigii*) in a neotropical terra firma forest. Anthony Di Fiore; Peter S. Rodman. **Int. J. Primat.** 22:3 6:2001 pp.449-480.

1718   Timing of births in sympatric brown howler monkeys (*Alouatta fusca clamitans*) and northern muriquis (*Brachyteles arachnoides hypoxanthus*). Karen B. Strier; Sergio L. Mendes; Rogerio R. Santos. **Am. J. Prim.** 55:2 10:2001 pp.87-100.

1719   The use of hair morphology in the classification of galagos (primates, subfamily Galagoninae). Matthew J. Anderson. **Primates** 42:2 4:2001 pp.113-122.

1720   What factors affect the size of chimpanzee parties in the Kalinzu Forest, Uganda? Examination of fruit abundance and number of estrous females. Chie Hashimoto; Takeshi Furuichi; Yasuko Tashiro. **Int. J. Primat.** 22:6 12:2001 pp.947-960.

1721   Why taxonomic stability is a bad idea, or why are there so few species of primates (or are there?) Colin Groves. **Evolut. Anthrop.** 10:6 2001 pp.192-198.

B.6:   **Language and communication**
Langage et communication

1722   *Albounout* 'frankincense' and *Alsounalph* 'ox-tongue': Phoenician-Punic botanical terms with prothetic vowels from an Egyptian papyrus and a Byzantine codex. R.C. Steiner. **Orientalia** 70:1 2001 pp.97-103.

1723   Anna Wierzbicka and the trivialization of Australian culture. W.S. Ramson. **Aust. J. Ling.** 21:2 10:2001 pp.181-194.

1724   Another look at the typology of serial verb constructions: the grammaticalization of temporal relations in Bislama (Vanuatu). Miriam Meyerhoff. **Oceanic Ling.** 40:2 12:2001 pp.247-268.

1725   Article accretion and article creation in Southern Oceanic. John Lynch. **Oceanic Ling.** 40:2 12:2001 pp.224-246.

1726   Aspects of plurality in ‡Hoan. Chris Collins. **Language** 77:3 9:2001 pp.456-476.

1727   Atlas of the world's languages in danger of disappearing. S.A. Wurm [Ed.]. Paris: UNESCO Publishing, 2001. 90p. *ISBN: 9231037986.*

1728   Australian culture and Australian English: a response to William Ramson. Anna Wierzbicka. **Aust. J. Ling.** 21:2 10:2001 pp.195-214. *This is a comment on Anna Wierzbicka and the trivialization of Australian culture by W.S. Ramson which appeared in Australian Journal of Linguistics 21:2 October 2001, pp. 181-194.*

1729   Basic Nostratic: a second look. Harvey E. Mayer. **Eur. Stud. Y.** 73 2001 pp.25-34.

1730   Brain-language coevolution in lexical change. Mieko Ogura. **Folia Ling. Hist.** XX:1-2 1999 pp.3-24.

1731   Burushaski --*skir* 'father-in-law' and --*skus* 'mother-in-law'. Bertil Tikkanen. **Stud. Orient.** 94 2001 pp.479-482.

1732   Chukchi women's language: a historical-comparative perspective. Michael Dunn. **Anthrop. Ling.** 42:3 Fall:2000 pp.305-328.

1733   Constructing identity through ceremonial language in rural Fiji. Karen J. Brison. **Ethnology** XL:4 Fall:2001 pp.309-328.

1734   Convergence in language change: morpho-syntactic patterns in Mingrelian (and Laz). George Hewitt. **Trans. Philolog. Soc.** 99:1 2001 pp.99-145.

1735   Critique in interaction. Ben Rampton. **Crit. Anthr.** 21:1 3:2001 pp.83-107.

1736   Discourse and critique: part one introduction. Jan Blommaert; James Collins; Monica Heller; Ben Rampton; Stef Slembrouck; Jef Verschueren. **Crit. Anthr.** 21:1 3:2001 pp.5-12.

1737   The elusive concept of 'map': semantic insights into the cartographic heritage of Japan. S.R. Potter. **Geogr. Rev. Jpn.** 74:1 2001 pp.1-14.

1738   Etymology and magic: Yāska's *Nirukta*, Plato's *Cratylus*, and the riddle of semantic etymologies. Johannes Bronkhorst. **Numen** XLVIII:2 2001 pp.147-203.

1739 Exploratory notes on the origin of language. Yoav Yigael. **Wor. Futur.** 57:1 2001 pp.21-48.

1740 Gendernaia lingvistika i istoricheskie nauki. *[In Russian]*; (Gender linguistics and historical sciences.) *[Summary]*. N.L. Pushkareva. **Etnograf. Oboz.** 2 3-4:2001 pp.31-40.

1741 Genetic affiliations of the Yeniseian languages. B. Comrie. **Eur. Stud. Y.** 73 2001 pp.161-171.

1742 Headlessness and extraposition: another look at syntax. Robert Holmstedt. **J. N.W. Sem. Lang.** 27:1 2001 pp.1-16.

1743 How not to explain the great divide. Diederick Raven. **Soc. Sci. Info.** 40:3 9:2001 pp.373-410.

1744 The indigenous linguistic response to missionary authority in the Pacific. Terry Crowley. **Aust. J. Ling.** 21:2 10:2001 pp.239-260.

1745 Istoki sovremennoi kul'turno-iazykovoi situatsii v Kazakhstane. *[In Russian]*; (Origins of the present day culture and language situation in Kazakhstan.) *[Summary]*. I.S. Savin. **Etnograf. Oboz.** 5 9-10:2000 pp.117-128.

1746 The Jungar Tuvas: language and national identity in the PRC. Talant Mawkanuli. **C. Asian Sur.** 20:4 12:2001 pp.497-518.

1747 The /ka-/ and /kra-/ prefixes in Thai. Leela Bilmes. **Ling. Tib.Bur. Area** 21:2 Fall:1998 pp.73-96.

1748 Language and societal attitudes: a study of Malawi's 'new language'. Francis Moto. **Nord. J. Afr. St.** 10:3 2001 pp.320-343.

1749 Langues déliées. *[In French]*; [The gift of the gab]. Cécile Canut; Robert Nicolaï; Katja Ploog; Didier de Robillard; Éloi Ficquet; Benjamin Nicholas Lawrance; Marie-Louise Moreau; Salamatou Sow; Marie-Ève Humery-Dieng; César Cumbe; Afonso Muchanga; Cécile Van Den Avenne; Saïd Bennis; Pascal Singy; Fabrice Rouiller; Martine Dreyfus; Caroline Juillard; Abou Napon; Michelle Auzanneau; Dominique Caubet; Senamin Amédégnato; Amadou Bissiri; Alain Joseph Sissao; Gisèle Prignitz. **Cah. Ét. Afr.** XLI(3-4):163-164 2001 pp.399-832. *Collection of 21 articles.*

1750 Linguistics and post-modernism. F. Manjali. **Int. J. Drav. Ling.** XXX:1 1:2001 pp.59-68.

1751 The mental representation of inflected words: an experimental study of adjectives and verbs in German. Harald Clahsen; Sonja Eisenbeiss; Meike Hadler; Ingrid Sonnenstuhl. **Language** 77:3 9:2001 pp.510-543.

1752 Neuter designations of humans and norms of social interaction in the Balkans. Olga M. Mladenova. **Anthrop. Ling.** 43:1 Spring:2001 pp.18-53.

1753 On social deixis. H.Paul Manning. **Anthrop. Ling.** 43:1 Spring:2001 pp.54-105.

1754 On the conversational performance of narrative jokes: toward an account of timing. Neal R. Norrick. **Humor** 14:3 2001 pp.255-274.

1755 On the translation of God. Suzuki Norihisa. **Jpn. Relig.** 26:2 7:2001 pp.131-148.

1756 The ordering distribution of main and adverbial clauses: a typological study. Holger Diessel. **Language** 77:3 9:2001 pp.433-455.

1757 The origins of empty categories in Singapore English. Bao Zhiming. **J. Pid. Creo. Lang.** 16:2 2001 pp.275-320.

1758 Patrimonio oral: la experiencia de Marraquech. *[In Spanish]*; [Oral heritage: the experience of Marrakesh]. Juan Goytisolo. **Rev. de Human.** 11 Autumn:2001 pp.69-76.

1759 Plus de breton? Conflit linguistique en Bretagne rurale. *[In French]*; [Not more Breton? Linguistic conflict in rural Brittany]. Eva Vetter. Ar Releg-Kerhuon: An Here, 1999. 254p. *ISBN: 2868431933. Translated from the German Nicht mehr Bretonisch? Includes bibliographical references (p. [227]-245).*

1760 Poniatie uzla etnogonicheskogo protsessa v sovremennom osveshchenii. *[In Russian]*; (An ethnogenetic nexus in its modern interpretation.) *[Summary]*. L.P. Lashuk. **Etnograf. Oboz.** 3 5-6:2001 pp.7-19.

1761 'Rats fell from the ceiling and pestered me:' phrase books as sources for colonial Mozambican history. Kathleen Sheldon. **Hist. Afr.** 25 1998 pp.341-360.

1762 'Remember Shushan?' counter-nostalgia in gendered discourse. Esther Schely-Newman. **Text** 21:3 2001 pp.411-436.

1763   Resemiotization. Rick Iedema. **Semiotica** 137:1-4 2001 pp.23-40.
1764   Some acoustic effects of speaking style on utterances for automatic speaker verification. Jana Dankovičová; Francis Nolan. **J. Inter. Phon. Ass.** 29:2 12:1999 pp.115-128.
1765   Split intransitivity and Saweru. Mark Donohue. **Oceanic Ling.** 40:2 12:2001 pp.291-306.
1766   Towards a definition of Egyptian complimenting. Ahmad Aly Mursy; John Wilson. **Multilingua** 20:2 2001 pp.133-154.
1767   Towards a model of story puns. Kim Binsted; Graeme Ritchie. **Humor** 14:3 2001 pp.275-292.
1768   Traditional economy and folk beliefs as reflected in the vocabulary of the Ket language. Elizaveta Kotorova. **Eur. Stud. Y.** 73 2001 pp.35-42.
1769   (The use of English-Japanese dictionaries and computational lexicography (XI).) *[Summary]*; *[Text in Japanese]*. Yoshiaki Otani. **J. Hum. Nat. Sci.** 110 9:2000 pp.25-58.
1770   (The use of English-Japanese dictionaries and computational lexicography (XII).) *[Summary]*; *[Text in Japanese]*. Yoshiaki Otani. **J. Hum. Nat. Sci.** 111 3:2001 pp.15-30.
1771   The verbal art of Nenets' shamanism. Péter Simoncsics. **Eur. Stud. Y.** 73 2001 pp.43-126.

Media and communication
Médias et communication

1772   The anthropology of indirect communication. Joy Hendry [Ed.]; C.W. Watson [Ed.]. London: Routledge, 2001. 308p. *ISBN: 0415247454, 0415247446.*
1773   Computer-mediated communication in Australian anthropology and sociology. Helen Morton; John Goldlust; Kevin C. Thompson; Alberto G. Gomes; John Marshall. **Soc. Anal. [Adelaide]** 45(1) 4:2001 pp.3-102. *Collection of 6 articles.*
1774   Consuming Ireland: Lucky Charms cereal, Irish Spring soap and 1-800-SHAMROCK. Diane Negra. **Cult. St.** 15:1 1:2001 pp.76-97.
1775   De la différence, de la hiérarchie et du jeu des sexes. Ethnographie des gestes et du langage dans un quartier de Naples. *[In French]*; [On difference, hierarchy and the game of the sexes: an ethnography of gestures and language in an area of Naples]. Patrick Ténoudji. **Temps Mod.** 56:615-616 9-11:2001 pp.240-256.
1776   Discourse patterns in the language of election campaign. A.R. Fatihi. **Int. J. Drav. Ling.** XXX:1 1:2001 pp.111-118.
1777   Displaced persons: symbols of South Asian femininity and the returned gaze in U.S. media culture. Meenakshi Gigi Durham. **Commun. Theory** 11:2 5:2001 pp.201-217.
1778   Electronic corpora as a basis for the compilation of African-language dictionaries, part 1: the macrostructure. Gilles-Maurice de Schryver; D.J. Prinsloo. **S. Afr. J. Afr. Lang.** 20:4 2000 pp.291-309.
1779   Electronic corpora as a basis for the compilation of African-language dictionaries, part 2: the microstructure. Gilles-Maurice de Schryver; D.J. Prinsloo. **S. Afr. J. Afr. Lang.** 20:4 2000 pp.310-330.
1780   Explanation, interpretation and critique in the analysis of discourse. Stef Slembrouck. **Crit. Anthr.** 21:1 3:2001 pp.33-58.
1781   Genetic optimism: framing genes and mental illness in the news. Peter Conrad. **Cult. Medic. Psych.** 25:2 6:2001 pp.225-247.
1782   Ghosts in the cyber world. An analysis of folklore sites on the Internet; *[Summary in French]*; *[Summary in German]*. Larisa Fialkova; Maria N. Yelenevskaya. **Fabula** 42:1-2 2001 pp.64-89.
1783   Go kgobana ga bana ba batswana: setso se se nyelelang. *[In Setswana]*; (Mockery by Setswana children: a disappearing cultural practice.) *[Summary]*. L.J. Zerwick. **S. Afr. J. Afr. Lang.** 20:4 2000 pp.331-341.
1784   *Kipu*: ne pis'mo, no… *[In Russian]*; (*Quipu*: it is not a script, but…) *[Summary]*. N.V. Rakuts. **Etnograf. Oboz.** 2 3-4:2001 pp.52-67.
1785   Late-stage standardization and language ideology in the Colombian press. Mercedes Niño-Murcia. **Int. J. S. Lang.** 149 2001 pp.119-144.

1786   (Management of a small-scale community broadcasting FM station in Japan; case study: FM West Tokyo.) *[Summary]*; *[Text in Japanese]*. Harumichi Yamada. **J. Hum. Nat. Sci.** 110 9:2000 pp.59-84.

1787   Oralidad y escritura: une encrucijada para las lenguas indígenas. *[In Spanish]*; [Orality and writing: a crossroads for indigenous languages]. Rebeca Barriga Villanueva. **Caravelle** 76-77 12:2001 pp.611-621.

1788   Proverbs in Zimbabwean advertisements. Liveson Tatira. **J. Folk. Res.** 38:3 9-12:2001 pp.229-242.

Multilingualism and linguistic contact
Plurilinguisme et contact linguistique

1789   Atlantic, Pacific, and world-wide features in English-lexicon contact languages. Philip Baker; Magnus Huber. **Eng. Wor.-wide** 22:2 2001 pp.157-208.

1790   Bilingualism in development: language, literacy, and cognition. Ellen Bialystok. Cambridge, New York: Cambridge University Press, 2001. xii, 288p. *ISBN: 0521632315, 0521635071. Includes bibliographical references (p. [249]-279) and index.*

1791   Caribbean Creoles as a convergence conduit: English 'boss' and 'overseer', Ndjuká *basía*, Sranan *basja*, Jamaican *busha*, and Dutch *baas(-je)*. Mark R.V. Southern. **Folia Ling. Hist.** XXI:1-2 2000 pp.189-246.

1792   Colonial linguistics. Joseph Errington. **Ann. R. Anthr.** 30 2001 pp.19-39.

1793   Comparing bilinguals' quoted performances of self and others in tellings of the same experience in two languages. Michèle Koven. **Lang. Soc.** 30:4 12:2001 pp.513-558.

1794   Contact features in colonial Peruvian Spanish. Anna María Escobar. **Int. J. S. Lang.** 149 2001 pp.79-94.

1795   Contacto de dialectos y lenguas en el nuevo mundo: la vernacularización del español en América. *[In Spanish]*; [Dialect - and language contact in the New World: the vernacularization of Spanish in America] *[Summary]*. Claudia Parodi. **Int. J. S. Lang.** 149 2001 pp.33-54.

1796   Cooperative and intrusive interruptions in inter- and intracultural dyadic discourse. Han Z. Li. **J. Lang. Soc. Psychol.** 20:3 9:2001 pp.259-284.

1797   English in South Africa: expansion and nativization in concert. Jan Bernsten. **Lang. Prob. Lang. Plan.** 25:3 Fall:2001 pp.219-235.

1798   'Fish in the river': experiences of bicultural bilingual speakers. Bettina Heinz. **Multilingua** 20:1 2001 pp.85-108.

1799   Floyd Glenn Lounsbury (1914-1998). Harold C. Conklin. **Am. Anthrop.** 102:4 12:2000 pp.860-864.

1800   From one (Chinese) into many (European languages). Zdenka Heřmanová. **Arch. Orient.** 69:1 2:2001 pp.67-72.

1801   The great vowel shift and Anglo-French loanwords: a rejoinder to Diensberg 1998. Antonio Bertacca. **Folia Ling. Hist.** XXI:1-2 2000 pp.125-148.

1802   In memoriam Michel Dieu. *[In French]*; [In memory of Michel Dieu]. D. Barreteau. **B. Ét. Afr. INALCO** 19-20 1993 p.237.

1803   L2 lexis in L1: reluctance to translate out of concern for referential meaning. David C.S. Li. **Multilingua** 20:1 2001 pp.1-26.

1804   Linguistic contacts between Arabic and other languages. K. Versteegh. **Arabica** XLVIII:4 10:2001 pp.470-508.

1805   Linguistique historique et histoire de la langue: 80 ans après *La Formation de la langue marathe* de Jules Bloch. *[In French]*; [Historical linguistics and history of language: 80 years after Jules Bloch's *The Formation of the Marathi Language*]. Jean Pacquement. **B. Éc. Fr. Ex.-Or.** 87:2 2000 pp.741-764.

1806   Modern Rapanui adaptation of Spanish elements. Miki Makihara. **Oceanic Ling.** 40:2 12:2001 pp.191-223.

1807   On the mechanisms of morphological change. Guy Deutcher. **Folia Ling. Hist.** XXII:1-2 2001 pp.41-48.

1808   A profile of the Fiji English lexis. Jan Tent. **Eng. Wor.-wide** 22:2 2001 pp.209-245.

1809   Questions in cross-linguistic medical encounters: the role of the hospital interpreter. Brad Davidson. **Anthr. Quart.** 74:4 10:2001 pp.170-178.

1810   Reflexiones sobre la integración de los americanismos en el español peninsular. *[In Spanish]*; [Reflections on the integration of Americanisms into peninsular Spanish]. Nicolás Balutet. **Rev. de Human.** 8 Spring:2000 pp.175-180.

1811   The relation between syntax, semantics and pragmatics. Armado González Salinas. **Rev. de Human.** 11 Autumn:2001 pp.13-20.

1812   Supletivismo según la persona del perceptor en en el verbo 'dar' de algunas lenguas otomangues. *[In Spanish]*; [Recipient person suppletion for the verb *dar* in three Otomanguean languages]. Thomas Smith Stark. **Caravelle** 76-77 12:2001 pp.95-103.

1813   Die westfränkische Lautverschiebung nach dem Zeugnis der französischen Etymologie. *[In German]*; [The West Frankish sound shift on the evidence of French etymology]. Klaus-Peter Lange. **Folia Ling. Hist.** XXII:1-2 2001 pp.149-177.

1814   Where did it all start? Dialect contact, the 'founder principle' and the so called <-own> split in New Zealand English. David Britain. **Trans. Philolog. Soc.** 99:1 2001 pp.1-28.

1815   World Englishes. Rakesh M. Bhatt. **Ann. R. Anthr.** 30 2001 pp.527-550.

1816   Yiddish and Hebrew in Canada: the current situation; *[Summary in French]*. Leo Davids. **Can. Ethn. Stud.** XXXII:2 2000 pp.95-104.

Names and naming
Noms et appellations

1817   Annelie och Zoran, Rasmus och Matilda. *[In Swedish]*; (Annelie and Zoran, Rasmus and Matilda.) *[Summary]*. Charlotte Hagström. **Rig** 2 2001 pp.65-81.

1818   Bêtes et plantes. *[In French]*; [Animals and plants]. Denis Lemordant; Catherine Chadefaud; Jean-Luc Ville; Gérard Dumestre; Alain Rouaud; Michel Perret; Marguerite Razarihelisoa. **B. Ét. Afr. INALCO** 19-20 1993 pp.1-196. *Collection of 7 articles.*

1819   The birds named *kurkī* and *ghirnīq* in classical Arabic and their philological description and zoological identification — a case study in the processing of ancient scientific knowledge in classical Arabic literature. Philippe Provençal. **Acta Orient.** 61 2000 pp.7-22.

1820   Comment trouver le «meilleur nom géographique»? Les voyageurs français et la question de la dénomination des îles océaniennes au XIXe siècle. *[In French]*; (Finding the 'best' geographical name. French travellers and the naming of Oceanian islands in the 19th century.) *[Summary]*. Hélène Blais. **Espace Géogr.** 30:4 2001 pp.348-357.

1821   The cultural meaning of names among Basotho of South Africa: a historical and linguistic analysis. Mthobeli Guma. **Nord. J. Afr. St.** 10:3 2001 pp.265-279.

1822   Culture and biology: surnames in evaluating genetic relationships among the ethnic minorities of southern Italy and Sicily; *[Summary in Croatian]*. A. Vienna; G. Biondi. **Coll. Antrop.** 25:1 6:2001 pp.189-194.

1823   Exploring kinship in anthropology and history: surnames and social transformation in the Bolivian Andes. Harry Sanabria. **Lat. Am. Res. R.** 36:2 2001 pp.137-156.

1824   Indeterminacy and history in Britton Goode's *Western Apache Placenames*: ambiguous identity on the San Carlos Apache reservation. David Samuels. **Am. Ethn.** 28:2 5:2001 pp.277-302.

1825   K interpretatsii nekotorykh zagadochnykh etnonimov arkticheskogo poberezh'ia Chukotki. *[In Russian]*; (On the interpretation of some mysterious names of the Arctic coast peoples of Chukotka.) *[Summary]*. A.A. Burykin. **Etnograf. Oboz.** 4 7-8:2000 pp.45-58.

1826   Mumbaization: a linguistic by-product of globalization? J.V. McOrec. **Eur. Stud. Y.** 73 2001 pp.178-180.

1827   Names for Tobago. Arie Boomert. **J. Soc. Amér.** 87 2001 pp.339-349.

1828   Naming the past in a 'scattered' land: memory and the powers of women's naming practices in southern Mozambique. Heidi Gengenbach. **Int. J. Afr. H. S.** 33:3 2000 pp.523-542.
1829   Nicknaming patterns and traditions among Cape Breton coal miners. William Davey; Richard MacKinnon. **Acadiensis** XXX:2 Spring:2001 pp.71-83.
1830   Persistence and change in names on the North African landscape: Berber tribes in Ibn Khaldun's genealogies and as they appear today. David M. Hart. **J. N. African Stud.** 5:1 Spring:2000 pp.121-146.
1831   The personal names in Jeremiah as a source for the history of the period. David A. Glatt-Gilad. **Heb. St.** XLI 2000 pp.31-46.
1832   Reduplication in Sotho plant names and the cognitive salience of life forms; *[Summary in Afrikaans]*. L.J. Louwrens. **S. Afr. J. Ethnol.** 24:4 2001 pp.147-161.
1833   Rossiiskie onimy v kontekste otkrytiia V'etnamom zapadnogo mira (po sochineniiam v'etnamskikh avtorov XVIII - nachala XIX v.) *[In Russian]*; (Russian names in the context of the discovery of the Western world by Vietnam (as based on the works of Vietnamese authors of the 18ᵗʰ — early 19ᵗʰ centuries).) *[Summary]*. N.I. Nikulin. **Etnograf. Oboz.** 5 9-10:2000 pp.57-69.
1834   The social use of personal names among the Kyrgyz. Erlend H. Hvoslef. **C. Asian Sur.** 20:1 3:2001 pp.85-96.
1835   'The names spread in all directions': hereditary titles in Tsimshian social and political life. Christopher Roth. **BC Stud.** 130 Summer:2001 pp.69-109.
1836   Türk ad bilimine malzemeler: *Kitābu'l-İdrāk li Lisāni'l-Etrāk'te Kişi Adları*. *[In Turkish]*; (Materials for Turkish onomastics: personal names in *Kitābu'l-İdrāk li Lisāni'l-Etrāk*.) Melek Özyetgin. **Bilig** 19 Autumn:2001 pp.21-32.
1837   Who is *súnuḷqaʔ*? A Salish quest. Jan P. van Eijk. **Anthrop. Ling.** 43:2 Summer:2001 pp.177-197.

Afro-Asiatic languages
Langues afro-asiatiques

1838   1 Chron 22:12: the Chronicler in *Actu Scribendi*. Piet B. Dirksen. **J. N.W. Sem. Lang.** 26:2 2000 pp.135-142.
1839   The 1ˢᵗ sg. suffix -ay in Western Neo-Aramaic: a historical perspective. St. Fassberg. **Orientalia** 70:1 2001 pp.104-112.
1840   Acquisition of Israeli Hebrew and Palestinian Arabic: a review of current research. Ruth A. Berman; Dorit D. Ravid. **Heb. St.** XLI 2000 pp.83-98.
1841   Arabic in Madagascar. Kees Versteegh. **B. Sch. Orient. Afr. Stud.** 64:2 2001 pp.177-187.
1842   Arabic sociolinguistics. J. Owens. **Arabica** XLVIII:4 10:2001 pp.419-469.
1843   Biblical Hebrew nominal clause: definitions of subject and predicate. Tamar Zewi; Christo van der Merwe. **J. N.W. Sem. Lang.** 27:1 2001 pp.81-100.
1844   The colometry of Hebrew verse and the Masoretic accents: evaluation of a recent approach (part II). Raymond de Hoop. **J. N.W. Sem. Lang.** 26:2 2000 pp.65-100.
1845   Ethiopian-Semitic. The situation in Gurage land. Jack Fellman. **Anthropos [St. Augustin]** 96:1 2001 p.206.
1846   (Free) direct discourse in Biblical Hebrew. Galia Hatav. **Heb. St.** XLI 2000 pp.7-30.
1847   Is Nigerian Arabic an Arabic language?; *[Summary in French]*; *[Summary in German]*. Jonathan Owens. **Diachronica** XIII:2 1996 pp.283-318.
1848   Is there a tripartite nominal sentence in Biblical Hebrew? Tamar Zewi. **J. N.W. Sem. Lang.** 26:2 2000 pp.51-64.
1849   Is there an 'Ethiopian language area'? Mauro Tosco. **Anthrop. Ling.** 42:3 Fall:2000 pp.329-365.
1850   Lexical matters in LXX Proverbs. Johann Cook. **J. N.W. Sem. Lang.** 26:2 2000 pp.163-173.
1851   Loanwords from Arabic and the merger of d/d. Kees Versteegh. **Is. Orient. Stud.** XIX 1999 pp.273-286.

1852   A missing link between law and grammar, the *Intisār* of Ibn Wallād. M.G. Carter. **Arabica** XLVII:1 1:2001 pp.51-65.

1853   Naphtali Kinberg, 1948-1997. Yishai Peled. **Is. Orient. Stud.** XIX 1999 pp.263-266.

1854   The 'negative preterite' in Kabyle Berber. S. Bendjaballah. **Folia Ling.** XXXIV:3-4 2000 pp.185-223.

1855   The obscure combination in Isaiah 30:27: another description for anger? Paul A. Kruger. **J. N.W. Sem. Lang.** 26:2 2000 pp.155-162.

1856   Le parler des Arabes de Cyrénaïque vu par un voyageur Marocain du XIIIe siècle. *[In French]*; [Language of the Arabs of Cyrenaica according to a 13th century traveller]. P. Larcher. **Arabica** XLVIII:3 7:2001 pp.368-382.

1857   *Peshat* and *Derash* in medieval Hebrew lexicons. Aharon Maman. **Is. Orient. Stud.** XIX 1999 pp.343-358.

1858   The phonetics and phonology of Tashlhiyt Berber syllabic consonants. John Coleman. **Trans. Philolog. Soc.** 99:1 2001 pp.29-64.

1859   Physiological and philological notes to Psalm 137. Gary A. Rendsburg; Susan L. Rendsburg. **Jew. Q. Rev.** 83 1992-1993 pp.385-400.

1860   Predicate formation: the case of participial relatives. Ilan Hazout. **Linguist. R.** 18:2 2001 pp.97-124.

1861   Probeschnitt an Textschichten: Ein neuer Beitrag zur Textgeschichte der koptischen Bibelübersetzungen. *[In German]*; [A new contribution to text history of Coptic Bible translations]. T.S. Richter. **Orientalia** 70:1 2001 pp.117-127.

1862   Puntualización sobre el manuscrito J-XXXIII y otros manuscritos aljamiados. *[In Spanish]*; [Punctuation in Spanish texts written with Arabic characters]. Soha Abboud-Haggar. **Al-Qantara** XXI:1 2000 pp.237-258.

1863   Le rasoir d'Occam et la tradition grammaticale arabe. *[In French]*; [Occam's razor and the Arabic grammatical tradition]. G. Bohas. **Arabica** XLVII:1 1:2001 pp.1-19.

1864   Sarcasm, irony, wordplay, and humor in the Hebrew Bible: a response to Hershey Friedman. John Morreall. **Humor** 14:3 2001 pp.293-302.

1865   Sobre la estructura convencional del título en los libros árabes. *[In Spanish]*; [The construction of Arabic book titles]. Alfonso Carmona. **Al-Qantara** XXI:1 2000 pp.85-96.

1866   Stress placement as a morphological and semantic marker in Israeli Hebrew. Shmuel Bolozky. **Heb. St.** XLI 2000 pp.53-82.

1867   Sur le statut linguistique du *tanwīn*. Contribution à l'étude du système déterminatif de l'arabe. *[In French]*; [On the *tanwīn* code: a study of modifiers in Arabic]. D.E. Kouloughli. **Arabica** XLVII:1 1:2001 pp.20-50.

1868   Translating it-cleft constructions into Arabic: a discoursal perspective; *[Summary in Arabic]*. Nawaf Obiedat. **Dirasat Hum. Soc. Sc.** 28:1 2:2001 pp.283-301.

1869   (The trilateral theory of Arabic roots.) *[Summary]*; *[Text in Arabic]*. M. Jaffal. **Dirasat Hum. Soc. Sc.** 28:Supp. 12:2001 pp.847-868.

1870   Vowel reduction in modern Hebrew: traces of the past and current variation. Dorit Ravid; Yitzhak Shlesinger. **Folia Ling.** XXXV:3-4 2001 pp.371-398.

1871   *Yā-btā l-lādī fī l-samāwāt…* Notas sobre antiguas versiones árabes del «Padre Nuestro». *[In Spanish]*; [Comments on ancient Arabic versions of The Lord's Prayer] *[Summary]*. Juan Pedro Monferrer Sala. **Al-Qantara** XXI:2 2000 pp.277-306.

Altaic languages
Langues altaïques

1872   Causatives as honorifics. Heiko Narrog. **Folia Ling. Hist.** XX:1-2 1999 pp.47-62.

1873   Karaçay-Malkar Türkçesinin kelime hazinesi ve ses değişmeleri bakımından eski Türkçe ile mukayesesi. *[In Turkish]*; (The comparison of Karachay-Balkar Turkish with Old Turkish according to vocabulary and phonetics.) Ufuk Tavkul. **Bilig** 19 Autumn:2001 pp.123-146.

1874   Kazak Türkçesinde anlam kaymasına ugrayan arapça kelimeler. *[In Turkish]*; (The Arabic words in Kazak Turkish whose meanings have changed.); *[Summary in Russian]*. Emrullah İşler. **Bilig** 18 Summer:2001 pp.87-100.

1875   Logical structures of Japanese texts. Keizo Nanri. **Text** 21:3 2001 pp.373-409.

1876   Tribal meditative consciousness and change of ethnonyms in the Tuva Republic area. N.V. Abayev. **Eur. Stud. Y.** 73 2001 pp.172-173.

Austronesian languages
Langues austronésiennes

1877   Austronesian roots and Sino-Tibetan: some lexical correspondences. Lee C. Hogan. **Ling. Tib.Bur. Area** 21:2 Fall:1998 pp.111-222.

1878   Bruce Biggs, 1921-2000: a tribute. Andrew Pawley. **Oceanic Ling.** 40:1 6:2001 pp.1-19.

1879   The history of Proto-Oceanic *ma. Bethwyn Evans; Malcolm Ross. **Oceanic Ling.** 40:2 12:2001 pp.269-290.

1880   Language and space in Tonga: 'the front of the house is where the chief sits!'. Giovanni Bennardo. **Anthrop. Ling.** 42:4 Winter:2000 pp.499-544.

1881   Mangarevan doublets: preliminary evidence for Proto-Southeastern Polynesian. Steven Roger Fischer. **Oceanic Ling.** 40:1 6:2001 pp.112-124.

1882   The marking of sex distinctions in Polynesian kinship terminologies. Per Hage; Jeff Marck. **Oceanic Ling.** 40:1 6:2001 pp.156-166.

1883   Negation in Saisiyat: another perspective. Elizabeth Zeitoun. **Oceanic Ling.** 40:1 6:2001 pp.125-134.

1884   The numeral confix *i- -(e)n. David Mead. **Oceanic Ling.** 40:1 6:2001 pp.167-176.

1885   A quantitative study of voice in Malagasy. Edward L. Keenan; Cécile Manorohanta. **Oceanic Ling.** 40:1 6:2001 pp.67-84.

1886   A reevaluation of Proto-Polynesian *h. Lawrence Kenji Rutter. **Oceanic Ling.** 40:1 6:2001 pp.20-32.

1887   Rotuman and Fijian case-marking strategies and their historical development. Ritsuko Kikusawa. **Oceanic Ling.** 40:1 6:2001 pp.85-111.

1888   Some shared developments in pronouns in languages of southern Oceania. John Lynch; Françoise Ozanne-Rivierre. **Oceanic Ling.** 40:1 6:2001 pp.33-66.

1889   Thao triplication. Robert Blust. **Oceanic Ling.** 40:2 12:2001 pp.324-335.

1890   Tongan accent. Albert J. Schütz. **Oceanic Ling.** 40:2 12:2001 pp.307-323.

Dravidian languages
Langues dravidiennes

1891   The articulation of Malayalam coronal stops and nasals. Sarah N. Dart; Paroo Nihalani. **J. Inter. Phon. Ass.** 29:2 12:1999 pp.129-142.

1892   Aspects of sociology of grammar of early middle-Tamil period. S.V. Shanmugam. **Int. J. Drav. Ling.** XXX:1 1:2001 pp.15-22.

1893   Bengali Bible translation. Alison Mukherjee. **Arch. Orient.** 68:3 8:2000 pp.407-418.

1894   Caldwell and Gundert. S. Guptan Nair. **Int. J. Drav. Ling.** XXX:1 1:2001 pp.1-6.

1895   Cognitive organisation of Tamil simple sentences by monolinguals and bilinguals. P. Chandramathi; P. Prakash. **Int. J. Drav. Ling.** XXX:2 6:2001 pp.165-188.

1896   A contrastive analysis of gender in Hindi and Malayalam. V. Geethakumary. **Int. J. Drav. Ling.** XXX:1 1:2001 pp.105-110.

1897   Dravidian tribal language studies since Caldwell. B.R. Reddy. **Int. J. Drav. Ling.** XXX:2 6:2001 pp.107-140.

1898   Dravidians and Dravidian languages spoken in India. S. Manoharan. **Int. J. Drav. Ling.** XXX:1 1:2001 pp.69-104.

1899   Echo formations in Asamiya: its morphophonemic patterning. S. Dattamajumdar. **Int. J. Drav. Ling.** XXX:1 1:2001 pp.37-44.

1900   The evolution of Dravidian kinship systems in Oceania: linguistic evidence; *[Summary in French]*. Per Hage. **J. Royal Anth. Inst.** 7:3 9:2001 pp.487-508.

1901   The genesis of Oriya dative case. U.P. Dalai. **Int. J. Drav. Ling.** XXX:2 6:2001 pp.189-208.

1902   Making of Panini. K. Meenakshi. **Int. J. Drav. Ling.** XXX:1 1:2001 pp.45-58.

1903   Proto-Dravidian agricultural terms. C.A. Winters. **Int. J. Drav. Ling.** XXX:1 1:2001 pp.23-28.

1904   A sociolinguistic study of Raji/Rawati language. K. Rastogi. **Int. J. Drav. Ling.** XXX:2 6:2001 pp.209-216.

1905   Substrate languages in Old-Indo Aryan. M. Witzel. **Int. J. Drav. Ling.** XXX:2 6:2001 pp.1-94.

1906   Survey of Bengali dialects - an overview. S.S. Bhattacharya. **Int. J. Drav. Ling.** XXX:2 6:2001 pp.141-152.

1907   Syllable in Sanskrit. H.S. Ananthanarayana. **Int. J. Drav. Ling.** XXX:1 1:2001 pp.29-36.

1908   System reduction and system re-analysis in Dravidian. R. Kothandaraman. **Int. J. Drav. Ling.** XXX:1 1:2001 pp.7-14.

1909   Systemic treatment of sound changes: a comparative study of Telugu and Russian. J.P. Rao. **Int. J. Drav. Ling.** XXX:2 6:2001 pp.95-106.

1910   Verb reduplication in Asamiya. S.D. Majumdar. **Int. J. Drav. Ling.** XXX:2 6:2001 pp.217-226.

Indo-European languages
Langues indo-européennes

1911   *æ* and *eo* development in the *Cotton Nero A.x* : a new dialect feature. Judith Mara Kish. **Folia Ling. Hist.** XXI:1-2 2000 pp.99-117.

1912   *Al-* and *Albho-*. Philip Thornhill. **Mankind Q.** XLI:4 Summer:2001 pp.355-398.

1913   Der albanische Alphabetkongreß 1908. Reflexionen aus standard-sprachgeschichtlicher Sicht. *[In German]*; [The Albanian alphabet congress of 1908. Reflections from the point of view of standard language history]. Gerd-Dieter Nehring. **Z. Balkan.** 36:1 2000 pp.57-75.

1914   Die Anfänge der Balkanlinguistik in Deutschland im 18. und 19. Jahrhundert. Ivan Duridanov zum 80. Geburtstag. *[In German]*; [The beginnings of Balkan linguistics in Germany in the 18th and 19th centuries. Ivan Duridanov on his 80th birthday]. Helmut W. Schaller. **Z. Balkan.** 36:1 2000 pp.76-91.

1915   Between koineization and standardization: New World Spanish revisited. Margarita Hidalgo; Claudia Parodi; Anna María Escobar; Germán de Granda; Mercedes Niño-Murcia; Roland Breton. **Int. J. S. Lang.** 149 2001 pp.9-144. *Collection of 6 articles.*

1916   Les Bretons et la langue bretonne: ce qu'ils en disent. *[In Breton]*; [The Bretons and the Breton language: in their own words]. Anna Quéré. Brest: Brud Nevez, 2000. 104p. *ISBN: 286775195X. Includes bibliographical references (p. 99-102).*

1917   Der bulgarische Rhodopendialekt im Lichte der Balkanologie. *[In German]*; [The Bulgarian Rhodope dialect in the light of Balkanology]. Andrej N. Sobolev. **Z. Balkan.** 36:1 2000 pp.92-108.

1918   The case of the 'impersonal' construction in Old English. Hanna Pishwa. **Folia Ling. Hist.** XX:1-2 1999 pp.129-152.

1919   Une cause nationale: l'orthographe française. *[In French]*; [A national cause: French orthography]. Bernard Traimond. Paris: Presses universitaires de France, 2001. 287p. *ISBN: 2130514146. Includes bibliographical references (p. [251]-269) and index.*

1920   Comparative-historical Indo-European linguistics: old and new. Philip Baldi. **Diachronica** XIII:2 1996 pp.347-364.

1921   Constraining explicit and implicit content by means of a Norwegian scalar particle. Thorstein Fretheim. **Nordic J. Linguist.** 23:2 2000 pp.115-162.

1922   Cyprus Greek. Amalia Arvaniti. **J. Inter. Phon. Ass.** 29:2 12:1999 pp.173-178.

1923   The dialect of Maastricht. Carlos Gussenhoven; Flor Aarts. **J. Inter. Phon. Ass.** 29:2 12:1999 pp.155-166.

1924   A dialect with seven names. Petra Cech; Mozes Heinschink. **Rom. Stud.** 11:2 12:2001 pp.137-184.

1925   Discurso por la lengua española. *[In Spanish]*; [A treatise for the Spanish language]. Jaime Labastida. **Caravelle** 76-77 12:2001 pp.603-610.

1926   (An etymological approach to building up vocabulary.); *[Text in Japanese]*: Osaki Masaru. **J. Hum. Nat. Sci.** 111 3:2001 pp.55-68.

1927   The etymology of modern English 'girl' revisited. Bernhard Diensberg. **Folia Ling. Hist.** XXI:1-2 2000 pp.119-124.

1928   The function and typology of absolute and conjunct flexion in early Celtic: some hints from ancient Egyptian. Graham R. Isaac. **Trans. Philolog. Soc.** 99:1 2001 pp.147-170.

1929   Germanic dative personal pronouns in *-s. Kenneth Shields. **Folia Ling. Hist.** XX:1-2 1999 pp.25-36.

1930   Indo-European *sem/sm-in the pronouns: 'singulative' plurals. Onofrio Carruba. **J. Indo-Eur. S.** 28:3-4 Fall-Winter:2000 pp.341-358.

1931   Indo-Iranian *vayu* and Gogolean *viy*: an old hypothesis revisited. Yaroslav Vassilkov. **Stud. Orient.** 94 2001 pp.483-496.

1932   Italian lexical influence on modern Albanian. (A Balkan comparative survey). Kristina Jorgaqi. **Z. Balkan.** 36:2 2000 pp.143-157.

1933   Iterativity and contemporary aspect selection in Upper Sorbian. G.H. Toops. **Slav. E. Eur. Rev.** 79:3 7:2001 pp.401-414.

1934   Linguistic evidence for a prehistoric Eurasian empire of '3 races and 1 language'. Benon Zb. Szalek. **J. Orient. Inst.** XLVII:3-4(47) 3-6:1998 pp.173-188.

1935   Lithuanian and Indo-European parallels. William R. Schmalstieg. **J. Indo-Eur. S.** 28:3-4 Fall-Winter:2000 pp.385-398.

1936   The maturation of grammatical principles: evidence from Russian unaccusatives. Maria Babyonyshev; Jennifer Ganger; David Pesetsky; Kenneth Wexler. **Linguist. In.** 32:1 Winter:2001 pp.1-44.

1937   A medieval phonetic Balkanism. Irena Sawicka. **Folia Ling. Hist.** XXI:1-2 2000 pp.155-158.

1938   Natürlicher morphologischer Wandel: Die Entwicklung des Imperfekt Aktiv im Albanischen. *[In German]*; [Natural morphological change: the development of the imperfect active in Albanian]. Norbert Boretzky. **Z. Balkan.** 36:1 2000 pp.1-28.

1939   A note on the sanskrit verb *pā-*. Minoru Hara. **Stud. Orient.** 94 2001 pp.225-242.

1940   On MV/VM order in Old English. Masayuki Ohkado. **Folia Ling. Hist.** XX:1-2 1999 pp.79-106.

1941   On the Baltic theonyms: Baltic-Italic correspondences in divine-names. Václav Blažek. **J. Indo-Eur. S.** 29:3-4 Fall-Winter:2001 pp.351-366.

1942   On the etymology of Lat. *urbs*. C. Michiel Driessen. **J. Indo-Eur. S.** 29:1-2 Spring-Summer:2001 pp.41-68.

1943   On the origin of the PIE *o-* stems. Paul Brosman. **Folia Ling. Hist.** XIX:1-2 1998 pp.65-78.

1944   On the plausability of Old English dialectology: the ninth-century Kentish charter material. Kathryn Lowe. **Folia Ling. Hist.** XXII:1-2 2001 pp.67-102.

1945   On translating the *Kamasutra*: a *gurudakshina* for Daniel H. H. Ingalls. Wendy Doniger. **J. Ind. Phil.** 29:1-2 4:2001 pp.81-94.

1946   One century of study in New World Spanish. Margarita Hidalgo. **Int. J. S. Lang.** 149 2001 pp.9-32.

1947   Perceptual factors and word order change in English. Mieko Ogura. **Folia Ling. Hist.** XXII:1-2 2001 pp.233-253.

1948   Periphrastic 'do' in Early Modern English. Bjørg Bækken. **Folia Ling. Hist.** XX:1-2 1999 pp.107-128.

1949   Position of subject pronouns and finite verbs in old English. Masayuki Ohkado. **Folia Ling. Hist.** XXII:1-2 2001 pp.255-276.

1950   Pour décrire un commentaire traditionnel sur une œuvre littéraire sanskrite. *[In French]*; [A traditional commentary on a Sanskrit literary work]. François Grimal. **B. Éc. Fr. Ex.-Or.** 87:2 2000 pp.765-786.

1951   Pragmatic factors in language change: XVS and XSV clauses in Old and Middle English. Kristin Bech. **Folia Ling. Hist.** XIX:1-2 1998 pp.79-102.

1952   Procesos de estandarización revertida en la configuración histórica del español americano: el caso del espacio surandino. *[In Spanish]*; [Processes of *reverse standardization* in the historical configuration of American Spanish: the case of the south Andes area] *[Summary]*. Germán de Granda. **Int. J. S. Lang.** 149 2001 pp.95-118.

1953   Punctuation practice in a late medieval English medical remedy book. Francisco Alonso Almeida. **Folia Ling. Hist.** XXII:1-2 2001 pp.207-232.

1954   Reanalysing 'whose': the actuation and spread of the invariable 'who' relative in Early Modern English. Patricia Poussa. **Folia Ling. Hist.** XXI:1-2 2000 pp.159-188.

1955   Sociolinguistic stratification in New Spain. Margarita Hidalgo. **Int. J. S. Lang.** 149 2001 pp.55-78.

1956   Some more possible relationships between Indo-European and Dravidian. Stephan Hillyer Levitt. **J. Indo-Eur. S.** 28:3-4 Fall-Winter:2000 pp.407-439.

1957   A spectrographic analysis of vowel fronting in Bradford English. Dominic Watt; Jennifer Tillotson. **Eng. Wor.-wide** 22:2 2001 pp.269-302.

1958   Speech perception, sound change, and the Slavic palatalizations. Geoff Schwartz. **Folia Ling. Hist.** XXII:1-2 2001 pp.277-300.

1959   Standard modern Greek. Amalia Arvaniti. **J. Inter. Phon. Ass.** 29:2 12:1999 pp.167-172.

1960   Syntactic and semantic devices in the *astādhyāyī* of Pānini. S.D. Joshi. **J. Ind. Phil.** 29:1-2 4:2001 pp.155-167.

1961   The syntax of mood particles in the history of English. Elly van Gelderen. **Folia Ling. Hist.** XXII:1-2 2001 pp.301-330.

1962   Transitivity alternation and neutral-verbs in Korean. Jaehoon Yeon. **B. Sch. Orient. Afr. Stud.** 64:3 2001 pp.381-391.

1963   Virtual and actual existentials in English, Swedish and Icelandic. Piotr Twardzisz. **Nordic J. Linguist.** 23:2 2000 pp.163-190.

1964   Why Old Frisian is really Middle Frisian. Germen J. de Haan. **Folia Ling. Hist.** XXII:1-2 2001 pp.179-206.

1965   Le yiddish: la langue et la crypte. *[In French]*; [Yiddish: language and the crypt]. Rachel Ertel. **Temps Mod.** 56:615-616 9-11:2001 pp.75-89.

1966   Zum altpersischen *h y /hyal*. *[In German]*; [On the Old Persian *h y /hyal*]. Jan Tavernier. **Arch. Orient.** 67:4 11:1999 pp.695-702.

Languages of the Americas
Langues des Amériques

1967   Amuzgo and Zapotec: two more cases of laryngeally complex languages. Esther Herrera Z. **Anthrop. Ling.** 42:4 Winter:2000 pp.545-563.

1968   Aspects of the phonetics of Tlingit. Ian Maddieson; Caroline L. Smith; Nicola Bessell. **Anthrop. Ling.** 43:2 Summer:2001 pp.135-176.

1969   Bilingual education and language use among the Shipibo of the Peruvian Amazon. Kathleen Tacelosky. **J. Multiling.** 22:1 2001 pp.39-56.

1970   Las coplas indígenas de México. *[In Spanish]*; [Indigenous Mexican verse]. Victoria Bricker; Munro Edmonson. **Caravelle** 76-77 12:2001 pp.13-26.

1971   Culture-specific notions of causation in Matses grammar. David W. Fleck. **J. Soc. Amér.** 87 2001 pp.177-196.

1972   De la lecture des personnages dans l'écriture pictographique nahuatl. *[In French]*; (How to read the figures representing human beings in Nahuatl pictographic writing.) *[Summary]*. Marc Thouvenot. **Amerindia** 25 2000 pp.137-172.

1973   De quelques notions spatiales dans le dialecte nahuatl de la région de Huauchinango (Puebla, Mexique). *[In French]*; (Some spatial concepts in the Nahuatl dialect of the Huauchinango region (Puebla, Mexico).) Marie Noëlle Chamoux. **Amerindia** 25 2000 pp.107-136.

1974   El desarrollo actual de la literatura quechua. *[In Spanish]*; [Current developments in Quechua literature]. César Itier. **Amerindia** 24 1999 pp.31-46.

1975   La enseñanza de la lengua aborigen en el Perú. *[In Spanish]*; [Teaching indigenous language in Peru]. Felipe Huayhua Pari. **Amerindia** 24 1999 pp.47-52.

1976   Guaraní voiceless stops in oral versus nasal contexts: an acoustical study. Rachel Walker. **J. Inter. Phon. Ass.** 29:1 6:1999 pp.63-94.

1977   Une interaction entre localisation et aspect. *[In French]*; (An interaction between localization and aspect.) *[Summary]*; *[Summary in Spanish]*. Eliane Camargo. **Amerindia** 25 2000 pp.1-24.

1978   Kichwa kwintukuna patsaatsinan. *[In Quechua]*; [How stories are constructed in the Quechua language]. S. Hernán Aguilar. **Amerindia** 25 2000 pp.189-206.

1979   La lengua maya. *[In Spanish]*; [The Mayan language]. Munro Edmonson. **Caravelle** 76-77 12:2001 pp.85-94.

1980   -n, localisateur général dans la langue arawak des Guyanes. *[In French]*; (—n, a polyfunctional marker in the Arawak language of the Guianas.) *[Summary]*; *[Summary in Spanish]*. Marie France Patte. **Amerindia** 25 2000 pp.25-48.

1981   On the fricativization of /r/ and the French-Cree connection. Marc Picard. **Folia Ling. Hist.** XXII:1-2 2001 pp.137-147.

1982   Le participatif, une solution moyenne en arawak. *[In French]*; [The participative - an intermediate solution in Arawak]. Marie France Patte. **Amerindia** 24 1999 pp.53-72.

1983   Planificación del corpus del quechua en el Perú. *[In Spanish]*; [Planning the body of Quechua literature in Peru]. Serafin M. Coronel-Molina. **Amerindia** 24 1999 pp.1-30.

1984   Synopsis of a Boruca terminal speaker; *[Summary in French]*; *[Summary in Spanish]*. J. Diego Quesada. **Amerindia** 25 2000 pp.65-86.

1985   Transferencias náhuatl-español en el Balsas (Guerrero, México). *[In Spanish]*; [Language contact between Náhuatl and Spanish in the Balsas River area of Mexico]. J.A. Flores Farfan. **Amerindia** 25 2000 pp.87-106.

1986   Les verbes empruntés au français par le garifuna: des verbes d'état? *[In French]*; (French verbal loan-words in Garifuna: stative verbs?) *[Summary]*; *[Summary in Spanish]*. Sybille de Pury. **Amerindia** 25 2000 pp.49-64.

Niger-Congo languages
Langues du bassin Niger-Congo

1987   Areal grammaticalization: the case of the Bantu-Nilotic borderland. T.A. Kuteva. **Folia Ling.** XXXIV:3-4 2000 pp.267-283.

1988   Bantu expansions: re-envisioning a central problem of early African history. Christopher Ehret. **Int. J. Afr. H. S.** 34:1 2001 pp.5-41.

1989   Classes nominales et radicaux verbaux en isiamba (Tulungu, Kindu). *[In French]*; [Nominal and radical verbal classes in Isiamba (Tulungu, Kindu)] *[Summary]*. John Jacobs; Barthélémy Omeonga. **Ann. Æqua.** 22 2001 pp.205-220.

1990   Comments on Ehret, *Bantu expansions*. Christopher Ehret; Roland Oliver [Comments by]; Thomas Spear [Comments by]; Kairn Klieman [Comments by]; Jan Vansina [Comments by]; Scott MacEachern [Comments by]; David Schoenbrun [Comments by]; James Denbow [Comments by]; Yvonne Bastin [Comments by]; H.M. Batibo [Comments by]; Bernd Heine [Comments by]; Michael Mann [Comments by]; Derek Nurse [Comments by]. **Int. J. Afr. H. S.** 34:1 2001 pp.43-87.

1991   Consonant meanings in Emai ideophones. Francis O. Egbokhará. **Linguist. Afr.** 22 2000 pp.29-56.

1992   Eléments pour la dialectologie mongo. III. Lexique. *[In French]*; [Elements of Mongo dialectology part III, vocabulary] *[Summary]*. G. Hulstaert. **Ann. Æqua.** 22 2001 pp.221-258.

1993   Esquisse du parler lohangó. *[In French]*; [An outline of the Lohangó dialect] *[Summary]*. Mputu Alphée Bakamba. **Ann. Æqua.** 22 2001 pp.185-204.

1994   État de la recherche en linguistique descriptive sur les langues du Congo, dix ans après Kadima Kamuleta. *[In French]*; [Research in descriptive linguistics on the languages of the Congo, ten years after Kadima Kamuleta] *[Summary]*. Mangulu Motingea. **Ann. Æqua.** 22 2001 pp.125-136.

1995   La «*Grammaire et vocabulaire du lingala ou langue du Haut-Congo*» d'Egide De Boeck de 1904: commentaires historiques, présentation et texte. *[In French]*; [The *Grammar and Vocabulary of Lingala or the Language of Haut-Congo* by Egide De Boeck in 1904: historical commentary, presentation and text] *[Summary]*. M. Meeuwis. **Ann. Æqua.** 22 2001 pp.327-421.

1996   Guthrie et la zone C. Traduction et commentaire du point de vue Atetela. *[In French]*; [Guthrie and zone C. Translation and commentary from the Atetela point of view] *[Summary]*. H. Labaere. **Ann. Æqua.** 22 2001 pp.163-184.

1997   Kikuyu vowel harmony. Long Peng. **S. Afr. J. Afr. Lang.** 20:4 2000 pp.370-384.

1998   Negation marking in Ikwere. Sylvester Osu. **Linguist. Afr.** 22 2000 pp.57-108.

1999   Notes sur le parler Séngele de Mbéle. *[In French]*; [Notes on the Séngele dialect of Mbéle] *[Summary]*. Mangulu Motingea. **Ann. Æqua.** 22 2001 pp.259-326.

2000   An Old Nubian lectionary fragment. G.M. Browne. **Orientalia** 70:1 2001 pp.113-116.

2001   The phonetic status of the labial flap. Kenneth S. Olson; John Hajek. **J. Inter. Phon. Ass.** 29:2 12:1999 pp.101-114.

2002   La pluralité verbale dans une dizaine de langues des monts du Mandara. *[In French]*; [Verbal plurality in a dozen languages from the Mandara mountains]. Véronique de Colombel. **Linguist. Afr.** 22 2000 pp.5-28.

2003   Representing the Bantu expansions: what's at stake? David Schoenbrun. **Int. J. Afr. H. S.** 34:1 2001 pp.1-4.

2004   La standardisation de la langue dogon. *[In French]*; [Standardization of the Dogon language]. Gérard Galtier. **B. Ét. Afr. INALCO** 19-20 1993 pp.197-220.

2005   Varieties of Nigerian English: Igbo English in Nigerian literature. Herbert Igboanusi. **Multilingua** 20:4 2001 pp.361-378.

2006   When does 'become' BECOME 'be'? Lionel Posthumus. **S. Afr. J. Afr. Lang.** 20:4 2000 pp.342-352.

Nilo-Saharan languages
Langues nilo-sahariennes

2007   Areal grammaticalization: the case of the Bantu-Nilotic borderland. T.A. Kuteva. **Folia Ling.** XXXIV:3-4 2000 pp.267-283.

2008   Double articulations in some Mangbutu-Efe languages. Didier Demolin; Alain Soquet. **J. Inter. Phon. Ass.** 29:2 12:1999 pp.143-154.

2009   État de la recherche en linguistique descriptive sur les langues du Congo, dix ans après Kadima Kamuleta. *[In French]*; [Research in descriptive linguistics on the languages of the Congo, ten years after Kadima Kamuleta] *[Summary]*. Mangulu Motingea. **Ann. Æqua.** 22 2001 pp.125-136.

2010   Kunama. John Abraha Ashkaba; Richard Hayward. **J. Inter. Phon. Ass.** 29:2 12:1999 pp.179-186.

Pidgin and Creole languages
Langues créoles et pidgins

2011 Arguments against a British dialect source for UM in Bajan English Creole. Jeffrey P. Williams. **J. Pid. Creo. Lang.** 16:2 2001 pp.355-364.

2012 Implications of abstract grammatical structure: two targets in Creole formation. Carol Myers-Scotton. **J. Pid. Creo. Lang.** 16:2 2001 pp.217-274.

2013 A look at the acts of identity theory through a social network analysis of Portuguese-based Creoles in West Africa. Steve Graham. **J. Pid. Creo. Lang.** 16:1 2001 pp.1-51.

2014 Multifunctionality and the concept of lexical entry. Claire Lefebvre; Mikael Parkvall [Comments by]. **J. Pid. Creo. Lang.** 16:1 2001 pp.107-151.

2015 The nature of derivational morphology in Creoles and non-Creoles. Ingo Plag. **J. Pid. Creo. Lang.** 16:1 2001 pp.153-160.

2016 On the semantic opacity of Creole languages. Claire Lefebvre. **J. Pid. Creo. Lang.** 16:2 2001 pp.321-354.

2017 The past and present in marking futurity in Sango. William J. Samarin. **J. Pid. Creo. Lang.** 16:1 2001 pp.53-106.

2018 *'Yu mas kamap wan nesen* . The mainstream churches, Tok Pisin and national identity in Papua New Guinea. Philip Cass. **Paideuma** 46 2000 pp.253-266.

Sino-Tibetan languages
Langues sino-tibétaines

2019 À propos de l'écriture chinoise. *[In French]*; [On Chinese writing]. Viviane Alleton. **Arch. Orient.** 69:3 8:2001 pp.437-446.

2020 The affinal kin register in Dhimal. John T. King. **Ling. Tib.Bur. Area** 24:1 Spring:2001 pp.163-182.

2021 Austronesian roots and Sino-Tibetan: some lexical correspondences. Lee C. Hogan. **Ling. Tib.Bur. Area** 21:2 Fall:1998 pp.111-222.

2022 Counting the family: family group classifiers in Yi (Tibeto-Burman) languages. David Bradley. **Anthrop. Ling.** 43:1 Spring:2001 pp.1-17.

2023 Discussion on the history of Tibetan grammar. Sangye Tandar Naga; Riika Virtanen [Tr.]. **Tibet J.** XXV:3 Autumn:2000 pp.39-47.

2024 An empathy-based approach to the description of the verb system of the Dege dialect of Tibetan. Katrin Häsler. **Ling. Tib.Bur. Area** 24:1 Spring:2001 pp.1-34.

2025 Final auxiliary verbs in literary Tibetan and in the dialects. Nicolas Tournadre. **Ling. Tib.Bur. Area** 24:1 Spring:2001 pp.49-112.

2026 Four-member tonal oppositions in standard Chinese. Gyula Décsy. **Eur. Stud. Y.** 73 2001 pp.5-134.

2027 Glottal stop and glottalization in Lai (connected speech). Rungpat Roengpitya. **Ling. Tib.Bur. Area** 20:2 Fall:1997 pp.21-56.

2028 *Ho ne* (she) is Hmongic: one final argument. Martha Ratliff. **Ling. Tib.Bur. Area** 21:2 Fall:1998 pp.97-110.

2029 The impersonal construction in Manipuri (Meithei). Chungkham Yashawanta Singh. **Ling. Tib.Bur. Area** 21:2 Fall:1998 pp.5-12.

2030 Lai psycho-collocation. Kenneth Van Bik. **Ling. Tib.Bur. Area** 21:1 Spring:1998 pp.201-234.

2031 Lai verb lists. Jason D. Patent. **Ling. Tib.Bur. Area** 20:2 Fall:1997 pp.57-162.

2032 Limbu *nous autres* and first person morphology. Boyd Michailovsky. **Ling. Tib.Bur. Area** 24:1 Spring:2001 pp.145-156.

2033 The middle voice in Lai. Tomoko Yamashita Smith. **Ling. Tib.Bur. Area** 21:1 Spring:1998 pp.1-52.

2034 The morphosyntax of transitivization in Lai (Haka Chin). David A. Peterson. **Ling. Tib.Bur. Area** 21:1 Spring:1998 pp.87-154.

2035   Notes on Brian Hodgson's Limbu paradigms (1857). Boyd Michailovsky. **Ling. Tib.Bur. Area** 24:1 Spring:2001 pp.157-162.

2036   The origin of the suffix -men in Chinese. Robert Iljic. **B. Sch. Orient. Afr. Stud.** 64:1 2001 pp.74-97.

2037   Person and evidence in Himalayan languages. Balthasar Bickel; John Peterson; Bettina Zeisler; Roland Bielmeier; Marianne Volkart; Brigitte Huber; Felix Haller. **Ling. Tib.Bur. Area** 23:2 Fall:2000 pp.1-192. *Collection of 7 articles.*

2038   Person-marking in TB languages, northeastern India. François Jacquesson. **Ling. Tib.Bur. Area** 24:1 Spring:2001 pp.113-144.

2039   Phom phonology and word list. Robbins Burling; L. Amon Phom. **Ling. Tib.Bur. Area** 21:2 Fall:1998 pp.13-42.

2040   The role of the speaker in the verbal system of the Tibetan dialect of Tabo/Spiti. Veronika Hein. **Ling. Tib.Bur. Area** 24:1 Spring:2001 pp.35-48.

2041   The sound system of Lai. Nurit Melnik. **Ling. Tib.Bur. Area** 20:2 Fall:1997 pp.9-20.

2042   Structure of verbs in Karbi. A. Konwar. **Int. J. Drav. Ling.** XXX:2 6:2001 pp.153-164.

2043   Tense and aspect in Lai Chin. Darya Kavitskaya. **Ling. Tib.Bur. Area** 20:2 Fall:1997 pp.173-214.

2044   Tiddim Chin tones in historical perspective. Weera Ostapirat. **Ling. Tib.Bur. Area** 21:1 Spring:1998 pp.235-248.

2045   *Tsuu kaa tii hla?* Deixis, demonstratives and discourse particles in Lai Chin. Jonathan Barnes. **Ling. Tib.Bur. Area** 21:1 Spring:1998 pp.53-86.

2046   Verbal alternations in Lai. Nurit Melnik. **Ling. Tib.Bur. Area** 20:2 Fall:1997 pp.163-172.

2047   Views of outsiders as reflected in Chinese words of foreign origin. Dan Myers. **Chin. Cult.** XL:2 6:1999 pp.115-132.

2048   Wancho phonology and word list. Robbins Burling; Mankai Wangsu. **Ling. Tib.Bur. Area** 21:2 Fall:1998 pp.43-72.

2049   A willy-nilly look at Lai ideophones. Jason D. Patent. **Ling. Tib.Bur. Area** 21:1 Spring:1998 pp.155-200.

Uralic languages
Langues ouraliennes

2050   Havaintoja komin konverbeistä. *[In Finnish]*; [Observations on Komi adverbs]. Jussi Ylikoski. **Suomal.-Ugril. Seur. Aikak.** 89 2001 pp.199-226.

2051   Die Herkunft des estnischen Vokals õ. *[In German]*; [The origin of the Estonian vowel õ]. Jan Henrik Holst. **Suomal.-Ugril. Seur. Aikak.** 89 2001 pp.57-98.

2052   K probleme poiskov ural'skoi prarodiny. *[In Russian]*; [Problems in the searches for a Uralic primogenitor]. M.F. Kosarev; S.V. Kuz'minych. **Suomal.-Ugril. Seur. Aikak.** 89 2001 pp.99-126.

2053   Komin kielteinen eksistentiaali *abu. [In Finnish]*; [The use of the existential form *abu* in the Komi language]. Arja Hamari. **Suomal.-Ugril. Seur. Aikak.** 89 2001 pp.33-56.

2054   Konechnoe slovo *da* v komi iazyke s areal'no-tipologicheskoi tochki zreniia. *[In Russian]*; [The final word *da* in the Komi language from regional typological viewpoints]. Marja Leinonen; Valentina Ludykova. **Suomal.-Ugril. Seur. Aikak.** 89 2001 pp.127-165.

2055   Mansin murresanakirjatyön leksikografisia ongelmia. *[In Finnish]*; [Lexicographical problems of Mansi dialect dictionaries]. Vuokko Eiras. **Suomal.-Ugril. Seur. Aikak.** 89 2001 pp.7-20.

2056   Pohjoisudmurtin murteiden ja komin kielen areaalisia leksikaalisia yhtäläisyyksiä. *[In Finnish]*; [North Udmurt dialects and Komi language lexical similarities]. S.A. Maksimov. **Suomal.-Ugril. Seur. Aikak.** 89 2001 pp.167-184.

2057   Proekt sozdaniia tsentral'nogo iazykovogo fonda khantyiskogo i mansiiskogo iazykov dlia dialektologicheskikh slovarei. *[In Russian]*; [Project for the creation of a central language fund of Khanty and Mansi languages for dialect words]. E. Prilozhenies Schmidt; E.A. Nemysova; Z.S. Riabchikova. **Suomal.-Ugril. Seur. Aikak.** 89 2001 pp.280-288.

2058   The treatment of initial *l- in Proto-Samoyed. Peter A. Michalove. **Suomal.-Ugril. Seur. Aikak.** 89 2001 pp.185-189.

2059   Zum frühen iranischen und indoiranischen lexikalischen Einfluss auf das Finnisch-Ugrische. *[In German]*; [On Early Iranian and Indo-Iranian lexical influences on Finno-Ugric]. Jorma Koivulehto. **Stud. Orient.** 94 2001 pp.359-378.

C:	ECOLOGY, TECHNOLOGY, ECONOMY.
	ÉCOLOGIE, TECHNOLOGIE, ÉCONOMIE.

C.1: Ecology
Écologie

2060   Analysis of explorers' records of aboriginal landscape burning in the Kimberley region of Western Australia. Tom Vigilante. **Aust. Geogr. Stud.** 39:2 7:2001 pp.135-155.

2061   Annual flooding of parts of Osogbo. Bisi Durotoye. **Niger. F.** 66:1 4:2001 pp.35-45.

2062   The battlefield of water rights: rule making amidst conflicting normative frameworks in the Ecuadorian highlands. Rutgerd Boelens; Bernita Doornbos. **Human. Org.** 60:4 Winter:2001 pp.343-355.

2063   Bêtes et plantes. *[In French]*; [Animals and plants]. Denis Lemordant; Catherine Chadefaud; Jean-Luc Ville; Gérard Dumestre; Alain Rouaud; Michel Perret; Marguerite Razarihelisoa. **B. Ét. Afr. INALCO** 19-20 1993 pp.1-196. *Collection of 7 articles.*

2064   Birds of the bush: Wodaabe distinctions of society and nature. Kristín Loftsdóttir. **Nord. J. Afr. St.** 10:3 2001 pp.280-298.

2065   Climatic perspectives on Sahelian desiccation: 1973-1998. Mike Hulme. **Glo. Environ. Chan.** 11:1 4:2001 pp.19-29.

2066   Contributions to the ethnobotany of the Cup'it Eskimo, Nunivak Island, Alaska. Dennis Griffin. **J. Ethnobio.** 21:2 Winter:2001 pp.91-132.

2067   Decentralization, natural resource management and community-based conservation institutions in South Africa. Robert K. Hitchcock. **Indig. Aff.** 4 2001 pp.38-49.

2068   Dingo discourse: constructions of nature and contradictions of capital in an Australian eco-tourist location. Adrian Peace. **Anthro. forum** 11:2 11:2001 pp.175-194.

2069   Earth and nature-based spirituality (part 1): from deep ecology to radical environmentalism. Bron Taylor. **Religion** 31:2 4:2001 pp.175-193.

2070   L'eau. *[In French]*; (Water.) Camille Talkeu Tounouga; Mervyn Claxton; Laurent Laoukissam Feckoua; Paul N'Gouah-Beaud; Cornelius Kogbe; Jean Tape Bidi; Ndiawar Kane; Mamadou Abdoul Wane; Marie-Aïda Diop-Wane; Fatou Diome; Willy Alante Lima; Lucie-Mami Noor Nkaké. **Prés. Afr.** 161-162 2000 pp.29-213. *Collection of 13 articles.*

2071   L'eau dans la vie et la pensée de l'Inde: philologie et réalités. *[In French]*; [Water in the life and thought of India: philology and reality]. Arion Roşu. **Bull. Ét. Indien.** 17-18 1999-2000 pp.33-112.

2072   The ecological Indian: myth and history. Shepard Krech, III. New York: W.W. Norton & Company, 2000. 318p. *ISBN: 0393321002. Includes bibliographical references (p. 231-308) and index.*

2073   Ecology and power in the periphery of Maasina. the case of the Hayre in the nineteenth century. Mirjam de Bruijn; Han Van Dijk. **J. Afr. Hist.** 42:2 2001 pp.217-238.

2074   Ekologiia i etika otnoshenii s okruzhaiushchei sredoi y korennykh narodov Avstralii. *[In Russian]*; (Indigenous ecologies and environmental ethics.) *[Summary]*. D.B. Rose. **Etnograf. Oboz.** 2 3-4:2001 pp.41-51.

2075   Elizabeth's walk - Tshakuesh's *Meshkanu*. Jane McGillivray. **Indig. Aff.** :4 2001 pp.34-37.

2076   'Environmental conflict' and the social life of environmental security discourse. Christopher T. Timura. **Anthr. Quart.** 74:3 7:2001 pp.104-113.

2077   Ethnic diversity and its environmental determinants: effects of climate, pathogens, and habitat diversity. Elizabeth Cashdan. **Am. Anthrop.** 103:4 12:2001 pp.968-991.

2078   The evolving meanings of region in Canada. Gerald Friesen. **Can. Hist. R.** 82:3 9:2001 pp.529-545.

2079   Factors accounting for the rapid siltation of Hazelmere Dam, KwaZulu-Natal. F. Russow; G. Garland. **S. Afr. Geogr. J.** 82:3 2000 pp.182-188.

2080   Folkbiology. Douglas L. Medin [Ed.]; Scott Atran [Ed.]. Cambridge MA, London: MIT Press, 1999. ix, 504p. *ISBN: 026263192X, 0262133490. Includes bibliographical references and index.*

2081   Forest management in Mosuo matrilineal society, Yunnan, China. He Zhonghua. **Gen. Tech. Dev.** 5:1 1-4:2001 pp.33-62.

2082   From the counting house to the field and loom: ecologies, cultures, and economies in the missions of Sonora (Mexico) and Chiquitaná (Bolivia). Cynthia Radding. **Hisp. Am. Hist. Rev.** 81:1 2:2001 pp.45-87.

2083   Fuelwood and fodder extraction and deforestation: mainstream views in India discussed on the basis of data from the semi-arid region of Rajasthan. U.S. Nagothu. **Geoforum** 32:3 8:2001 pp.319-332.

2084   The function of *guachiplin*, *Dyphysa robiniodes*, in the Lenca landscape; *[Summary in Spanish]*; *[Summary in French]*. S. Brady. **J. Ethnobio.** 21:1 Summer:2001 pp.39-56.

2085   Habiter la nature? Le camping. *[In French]*; [Camping - living in nature?] Olivier Sirost; Bernard Kalaora; André Rauch; Arnaud Baubérot; Catherine Bertho Lavenir; Aude Tissandier; Jean Griffet; Martin de La Soudière; Gilles Raveneau; Sergio Dalla Bernardina. **Ethn. Fr.** XXXI:4 10-12:2001 pp.581-694. *Collection of 11 articles.*

2086   Histoire de l'Ouzboï, cours fossile de l'Amou Darya: synthèse et éléments nouveaux. *[In French]*; [History of the Uzboy and fossil course of the Amu Darya River - summary and new features] *[Summary]*. R. Létolle. **Stud. Iran.** 29:2 2000 pp.195-240.

2087   The historical ecology of southeastern longleaf pine and its southernmost expression; *[Summary in Spanish]*; *[Summary in French]*. K.J. Walker. **J. Ethnobio.** 20:2 Winter:2000 pp.269-302.

2088   Honduran folk entomology. Jeffery W. Bentley; Gonzalo Rodríguez. **Curr. Anthr.** 42:2 4:2001 pp.285-300.

2089   Industrious women: resource use and gender norms among the Kalanguya of the Philippines. Bernadette P. Resurrección. **Gen. Tech. Dev.** 5:2 5-8:2001 pp.245-265.

2090   Internal constraints on community-based forest management in a post-logging, upland community: the case of Ilagan, Isabela. Yoshiki Seki. **Phil. Q. Cult. Soc.** 28:4 12:2000 pp.399-437.

2091   Local perceptions about forests and water in two tropical catchments. J. Wilk. **Geojournal** 50:4 2000 pp.339-348.

2092   The Mediterranean: theories and histories. Franco Cassano; Peter Murphy; Elizabeth Jane Bellamy; Sandhya Shetty; Grant Parker; Timothy J. Reiss; Artemis Leontis. **Thes. Elev.** 67 11:2001 pp.1-117. *Collection of 6 articles.*

2093   The moral economy of water: equity and antiquity in the Andean Commons. Paul Trawick. **Am. Anthrop.** 103:2 6:2001 pp.361-379.

2094   Narratives of Embu rural women: gender roles and indigenous knowledges. Njoki Wane. **Gen. Tech. Dev.** 5:3 9-12:2001 pp.383-408.

2095   Perceiving the forest: early India. Romila Thapar. **Stud. Hist.** 17:1 1-6:2001 pp.1-16.

2096   Perceptions of nature and responses to environmental degradation in New Caledonia. Leah Sophie Horowitz. **Ethnology** XL:3 Summer:2001 pp.237-250.

2097   Pro-environment attitudes, values and behavior of Tibetan students. R.S. Pirta; Kavita Goswami. **Tibet J.** XXVI:2 Summer:2001 pp.60-67.

2098   Rain forest habitat classification among the Matsigenka of the Peruvian Amazon; *[Summary in Spanish]*; *[Summary in French]*. G. Shepard; et al. **J. Ethnobio.** 21:1 Summer:2001 pp.1-38.

2099   Religion and ecology: can the climate change? Mary Evelyn Tucker; John A. Grim; George Rupp; Michael B. McElroy; Donald A. Brown; J. Baird Callicott; Hava Tirosh-Samuelson; Sallie McFague; S. Nomanul Haq; Vasudha Narayanan; Christopher Key Chapple; Donald K. Swearer; Tu Weiming; James Miller; Jack D. Forbes; Bill McKibben. **Dædalus** 130:4 Fall:2001 pp.1-307. *Collection of 15 articles.*

2100   The resurgence of tradition in a post-communist society: the role of the Mongolian *ger* as a vehicle for the maintenance of ideology and practice in the diachronic process of Mongolian society. Ch. Sauer. **Cent. Asia. J.** 45:1 2001 pp.63-127.

2101 A river runs through us. Brett Williams. **Am. Anthrop.** 103:2 6:2001 pp.409-431.

2102 The Sahara's indigenous peoples, the Tuareg, fear environmental catastrophe. Jeremy Keenan. **Indig. Aff.** :4 2001 pp.50-57.

2103 Siedlungsgeschichten bei den Kassena: orale Traditionen und Lokalität. *[In German]*; [Settlement narratives among the Kasena: oral traditions and locality] *[Summary]*. Hans Peter Hahn. **Z. Ethn.** 125:2 2000 pp.241-263.

2104 Siedlungsgeschichten: Die Konstruktion von Lokalität und Gemeinschaft. Eine Einleitung. *[In German]*; [Settlement narratives: the construction of locality and community - an introduction] *[Summary]*. Carola Lentz. **Z. Ethn.** 125:2 2000 pp.177-188.

2105 Societies and nature in the Sahel: ecological diversity and social dynamics. Claude Raynaut. **Glo. Environ. Chan.** 11:1 4:2001 pp.9-18.

2106 Soil erosion in the West African Sahel: a review and an application of a 'local political ecology' approach in south west Niger. Andrew Warren; Simon Batterbury; Henny Osbahr. **Glo. Environ. Chan.** 11:1 4:2001 pp.79-95.

2107 Source to discard: patterns of lithic raw material procurement and use in Sturt National Park, northwestern New South Wales. Trudy Doelman; John Webb; Marian Domanski. **Archaeol. Ocean.** 36:1 4:2001 pp.15-33.

2108 Spectacular quetzals, ecotourism, and environmental futures in Monte Verde, Costa Rica. Luis A. Vivanco. **Ethnology** XL:2 Spring:2001 pp.79-92.

2109 Taxonomic identity of 'hallucinogenic' harvester ant (*Pogonomyrmex californicus*) confirmed. Kevin P. Groark. **J. Ethnobio.** 21:2 Winter:2001 pp.133-144.

2110 Towards an environmental history of the Amazon: from prehistory to the nineteenth century. David Cleary. **Lat. Am. Res. R.** 36:2 2001 pp.65-96.

2111 The use and abuse of nature. Madhav Gadgil; Ramachandra Guha. New Delhi: Oxford University Press, 2000. xv, 213p. *ISBN: 0195649273. Includes bibliographical references (p. [247]-266, p. 96-203) and indexes.*

2112 Water resources of the Chunchucmil Maya. Sheryl Luzzadder-Beach. **Geogr. Rev.** 90:4 10:2000 pp.493-510.

2113 Water under the sea, or water under the bridge? Foreign direct investment, public consultation, and the Bohol-Cebu water supply issue. Karen T. Fisher; Peter B. Urich. **Phil. Q. Cult. Soc.** 28:4 12:2000 pp.438-463.

2114 Wind, traffic and dust: the recycling of wastes. R. Thomas Rosin. **Contr. I. Soc.** 34:3 9-12:2000 pp.361-408.

2115 Women and forest: a study of the Warlis of western India. Indra Munshi. **Gen. Tech. Dev.** 5:2 5-8:2001 pp.177-198.

2116 Worldviews and decision making: natural resource management of the Laka of Mapela in an anthropological perspective; *[Summary in Afrikaans]*. Britta Eckert; F.C. de Beer; L.P. Vorster. **S. Afr. J. Ethnol.** 24:3 2001 pp.88-98.

2117 The yellow mangrove: its ethnobotany, history of maritime collection, and needed rehabilitation in the central and southern Philippines. J.H. Primavera; Lilian de la Peña. **Phil. Q. Cult. Soc.** 28:4 12:2000 pp.464-475.

Demography
Démographie

2118 ABO blood group incompatibility and fertility among the Bhatras of Bastar. Manjula Guha; Jaya Mukherjee; Moyna Chakravarty. **Man India** 80:3-4 7-12:2000 pp.313-320.

2119 The accuracy of mortality reporting in displaced persons' camps during the post-emergency phase. Paul B. Spiegel; Mani Sheik; Bradley A. Woodruff; Gilbert Burnham. **Disasters** 25:2 6:2001 pp.172-180.

2120 Administrators' knowledge and state control in colonial Zimbabwe: the invention of the rural-urban divide in Buhera district, 1912-80. Jens A. Andersson. **Espace Pop. Soc.** 43:1 2002 pp.119-143.

2121 Age at first birth and fertility level of women in Kerala: a cohort analysis. M.N. Sivakumar. **Man India** 80:3-4 7-12:2000 pp.273-288.

2122 The age pattern of fecundability: an analysis of French Canadian and Hutterite birth histories. Ulla Larsen; Sharon Yan. **Soc. Biol.** 47:1-2 Spring-Summer:2000 pp.34-50.

2123 Chislennost' kochevogo sotsiuma: istochniki i sposoby podcheta. *[In Russian]*; (Nomad populations: sources and methods of their counting.) *[Summary]*. V.V. Trepavlov. **Etnograf. Oboz.** 4 7-8:2000 pp.95-101.

2124 Comparing two methods for estimating network size. Christopher McCarty; Peter D. Killworth; H. Russell Bernard; Eugene C. Johnsen; Gene A. Shelley. **Human. Org.** 60:1 Spring:2001 pp.28-39.

2125 The Crimean Tatars in Uzbekistan: speaking with the dead and living homeland. Greta Lynn Uehling. **C. Asian Sur.** 20:3 9:2001 pp.391-404.

2126 Demise of the *sepaade* tradition: cultural and biological explanations. Eric Abella Roth. **Am. Anthrop.** 103:4 12:2001 pp.1014-1023.

2127 Demographic dimensions of an intervillage land dispute in Nubri, Nepal. Geoff Childs. **Am. Anthrop.** 103:4 12:2001 pp.1096-1113.

2128 Development and death: reinterpreting malaria, economics and ecology in British India. Ira Klein. **Indian Ec. Soc. His. R.** XXXVIII:2 4-6:2001 pp.147-179.

2129 The effects of breastfeeding and birth spacing on infant and early childhood mortality in Ethiopia. David P. Lindstrom; Betemariam Berhanu. **Soc. Biol.** 47:1-2 Spring-Summer:2000 pp.1-17.

2130 Evaluating five models of human colonization. John H. Moore. **Am. Anthrop.** 103:2 6:2001 pp.395-408.

2131 Fecundity of daughters born after short, intermediate, or long birth intervals: an analysis of family reconstitutions from the Netherlands, late 19th-early 20th century. Luc J. Smits; Piet H. Jongbloet; Gerhard A. Zielhuis. **Soc. Biol.** 47:1-2 Spring-Summer:2000 pp.18-33.

2132 Genealogical structuring of a population; *[Summary in Croatian]*. M. Kujundžić Tiljak; J. Kern; D. Ivanković; H. Tiljak; S. Vuletić. **Coll. Antrop.** 25:1 6:2001 pp.127-140.

2133 Geographical distribution of elderly people in Croatia; *[Summary in Croatian]*. I. Heim; S. Vuletić; M. Hromadko; H. Maver. **Coll. Antrop.** 25:1 6:2001 pp.65-76.

2134 Grand hypotheses: palaeodemographic modelling in Western Australia's south-west. C.E. Dortch; M.V. Smith. **Archaeol. Ocean.** 36:1 4:2001 pp.34-46.

2135 Hanihara's conundrum revisited: theoretical estimates of the immigration into Japan during the 1,000 year period from 300 B.C. to A.D. 700. Kenichi Aoki; Shripad Tuljapurkar. **Anth. Sci.** 108:4 10:2000 pp.305-320.

2136 Ideas, economics and 'the sociology of supply': explanations for fertility decline in Bangladesh. Naila Kabeer. **J. Dev. Stud.** 38:1 10:2001 pp.29-70.

2137 Impact of urinary schistosomiasis on rural land use: empirical evidence from Nigeria. J.C. Umeh; O. Amali; E.U. Umeh. **Soc. Sci. Med.** 52:2 1:2001 pp.293-304.

2138 Implications of health care provision on acute lower respiratory infection mortality in Bangladeshi children. M. Ali; M. Emch; F. Tofail; A.H. Baqui. **Soc. Sci. Med.** 52:2 1:2001 pp.267-278.

2139 (Influence of females' age at first marriage on human fertility in Jordan.) *[Summary]*; *[Text in Arabic]*. A. Al-Kareem Al-Fayez. **Dirasat Hum. Soc. Sc.** 28:1 2:2001 pp.206-224.

2140 The main determinants of infant mortality in Nepal. Juhee V. Suwal. **Soc. Sci. Med.** 53:12 12:2001 pp.1667-1682.

2141 Marital fertility in Lebanon: a study based on the population and housing survey. May A. Beydoun. **Soc. Sci. Med.** 53:6 9:2001 pp.759-772.

2142 Mortality responses to rice price fluctuations and household factors in a farming village in central Tokugawa, Japan. Noriko O. Tsuya; Kiyoshi Hamano. **Hist. Fam.** 6:1 2001 pp.1-31.

2143 On the role of families and kinship networks in pre-industrial agricultural societies: an analysis of the 1698 Slavonian census. H.P. Kohler; E.A. Hammel. **J. Pop. Ec.** 14:1 2001 pp.21-50.

2144 Paleodemography and taphonomy. Janusz Piontek. **Archaeol. Polona** 39 2001 pp.55-74.

2145   Perepis' 2002 g.: igry po Vitgenshteinu. *[In Russian]*; (Russian Federation census of 2002: Wittgensteinian language games.) *[Summary]*. S.V. Sokolovskii. **Etnograf. Oboz.** 4 7-8:2000 pp.91-94. *This is a comment on Population censuses: who is to be counted and how? by S.V. Cheshko which appeared in Etnograficheskoe obozrenie 4 7-8:2000 pp. 82-90.*

2146   Perepis' naseleniia: kogo schitat' i kak schitat'? *[In Russian]*; (Population censuses: who is to be counted and how?) *[Summary]*. S.V. Cheshko. **Etnograf. Oboz.** 4 7-8:2000 pp.82-90.

2147   La population de la Moselle au XIXe siècle. *[In French]*; [The population of Moselle in the 19th century]. Pierre Brasme. Metz: Editions Serpenoise, 2000. 196p. *ISBN: 287692448X. Includes bibliographical references (p. 183-192).*

2148   Rapid assessment of population size by area sampling in disaster situations. Vincent Brown; Guy Jacquier; Denis Coulombier; Serge Balandine; François Belanger; Dominique Legros. **Disasters** 25:2 6:2001 pp.164-171.

2149   Risk factors and child mortality among the Miao in Yunnan, southwest China. Peter Foggin; Nagib Armijo-Hussein; Céline Marigaux; Hui Zhu; Zeyuan Liu. **Soc. Sci. Med.** 53:12 12:2001 pp.1683-1696.

2150   The role of cultural and economic determinants in mortality decline in the Netherlands, 1875/1879-1920/1924: a regional analysis. J.H. Wolleswinkel-van den Bosch; F.W.A. van Poppel; C.W.N. Looman; J.P. Mackenbach. **Soc. Sci. Med.** 53:11 12:2001 pp.1439-1454.

2151   Rooted in the soil: farm family persistence in Burton Parish, Sunbury County, New Brunswick, 1851-1901. Timothy D. Lewis. **Acadiensis** XXXI:1 Autumn:2001 pp.35-54.

2152   Social policy and mortality decline in East Asia and Latin America. J.W. McGuire. **World Dev.** 29:10 10:2001 pp.1673-1697.

2153   Some aspects of social factors affecting fertility behaviour of Gond women. P.L. Pandey; D.C. Jain; G.D. Pandey; R. Choubey; R.S. Tiwary. **Man India** 80:3-4 7-12:2000 pp.251-258.

2154   Tbilisi — mała ojczyzna gruzińskiej Polonii. *[In Polish]*; (Tbilisi — the 'little homeland' of the Polish colony in Georgia.) *[Summary]*. Justyna Doboszyńska. **Etn. Polska** XLV:1-2 2001 pp.155-182.

2155   'Ten million families': statistic or metaphor? James A. Foley. **Kor. Stud.** 25:1 2001 pp.96-110.

2156   Where have all the young men gone? Evidences and explanations of changing age-sex ratios in Kampala; *[Summary in French]*. Sandra Wallman; Valdo Pons. **Africa** 71:1 2001 pp.113-127.

Migration
Migration

2157   The anthropology of Afro-Latin America and the Caribbean: diasporic dimensions. Kevin A. Yelvington. **Ann. R. Anthr.** 30 2001 pp.227-260.

2158   Creating options: forming a Marshallese community in Orange County, California. Jim Hess; Karen L. Nero; Michael L. Burton. **Cont. Pac.** 13:1 Spring:2001 pp.89-123.

2159   Déplacements forcés et urbanisation dans une petite ville de province: l'exemple de Garissa. *[In French]*; [Forced displacement and urbanization in a small provincial town: the example of Garissa]. Marc Antoine Pérouse de Montclos. **IFRA** 15 1-2:1999 pp.4-16.

2160   Effects of migration, ethnicity, and religiosity on cohabitation. Ruth Katz. **J. Comp. Fam. Stud.** XXXII:4 Autumn:2001 pp.587-600.

2161   The Filipino diaspora. E. San Juan, Jr. **Phil. Stud.** 49:2 2001 pp.255-264.

2162   The first migration wave of Indo-Iranians to the South. E.E. Kuzmina. **J. Indo-Eur. S.** 29:1-2 Spring-Summer:2001 pp.1-40.

2163   From sea and garden to school and town: changing gender and household patterns among Pollap Atoll migrants. Juliana Flinn. **Pac. Stud.** 17:3 9:1994 pp.117-132.

2164 Gender impact of resettlement: the case of Babagon Dam in Sabah, Malaysia. Carol Yong Ooi Lin. **Gen. Tech. Dev.** 5:2 5-8:2001 pp.223-244.

2165 Going home: giving voice to memory strategies of young Mayan refugees who returned to Guatemala as a community. Cécile Rousseau; Maria Morales; Patricia Foxen. **Cult. Medic. Psych.** 25:2 6:2001 pp.135-168.

2166 The impact of labor migration on African families in South Africa: yesterday and today. Ria Smit. **J. Comp. Fam. Stud.** XXXII:4 Autumn:2001 pp.533-548.

2167 Indo-Guyanese migration: from plantation to metropolis. Lomarsh Roopnarine. **Imm. Minor.** 20:2 7:2001 pp.1-25.

2168 It never happened: Kinguri's exodus and its consequences. Jan Vansina. **Hist. Afr.** 25 1998 pp.387-404.

2169 Kinship ties of Mexican migrant women on the United States/Mexico border. Elena Bastida. **J. Comp. Fam. Stud.** XXXII:4 Autumn:2001 pp.549-570.

2170 Landscapes on-the-move. Barbara Bender. **J. Soc. Arch.** 1:1 6:2001 pp.75-89.

2171 Living in migration in Austria. Rudolf Richter; Johannes Pflegerl. **J. Comp. Fam. Stud.** XXXII:4 Autumn:2001 pp.517-532.

2172 Locations for South Asian diasporas. Sandhya Shukla. **Ann. R. Anthr.** 30 2001 pp.551-572.

2173 Migration and mortality in Africa and the Atlantic world, 1700-1900. Philip D. Curtin. Aldershot, Burlington VT: Ashgate, 2001. *ISBN: 0860788334. Includes bibliographical references and index. (Series:* Variorum collected studies series - CS701).

2174 Migration and old age: Japanese women growing older in British society. Misa Izuhara; Hiroshi Shibata. **J. Comp. Fam. Stud.** XXXII:4 Autumn:2001 pp.571-586.

2175 The migration theory of Marija Gimbutas. V. Dergachev. **J. Indo-Eur. S.** 28:3-4 Fall-Winter:2000 pp.257-340.

2176 Narrations of authority and mobility. Ninna Nyberg Sørensen; Finn Stepputat. **Identities** 8:3 9:2001 pp.313-342.

2177 Prehistoric human migration in the *Linearbandkeramik* of Central Europe. T. Douglas Price; R. Alexander Bentley; Jens Lüning; Detlef Gronenborn; Joachim Wahl. **Antiquity** 75:289 9:2001 pp.593-603.

2178 Refugees from Tibet: structural causes of successful settlements. Dawa Norbu. **Tibet J.** XXVI:2 Summer:2001 pp.3-25.

2179 Reinterpreting the rural-urban connection: migration practices and socio-cultural dispositions of Buhera workers in Harare; *[Summary in French].* Jens A. Andersson. **Africa** 71:1 2001 pp.82-112.

2180 La relocalisation des populations déplacés: l'exemple de Nyahururu. *[In French]*; [Relocation of displaced populations: the Nyahururu example]. Arnaud Tranchant. **IFRA** 15 1-2:1999 pp.33-70.

2181 Rural-urban migration of the Iban of Sarawak and changes in long-house communities. R. Soda. **Geogr. Rev. Jpn.** 74:1 2001 pp.92-112.

2182 The Senegalese murid trade diaspora and the making of a vernacular cosmopolitanism. Mamadou Diouf. **Publ. Cult.** 12:3 Fall:2000 pp.679-702.

2183 The temporary migration of males and the power of females in a stem-family society: the case of nineteenth-century Auvergne. Rose Duroux. **Hist. Fam.** 6:1 2001 pp.33-49.

2184 Topoi in oralen Traditionen über Siedlungsgründungen in Borno (Nigeria). *[In German]*; [Topoi in oral settlement narratives in Borno state, Nigeria] *[Summary]*. Editha Platte; Holger Kirscht. **Z. Ethn.** 125:2 2000 pp.215-240.

2185 Transnational migration in rural Oaxaca, Mexico: dependency, development, and the household. Jeffrey H. Cohen. **Am. Anthrop.** 103:4 12:2001 pp.954-967.

2186 UK decisions on Sikh asylum claims. Simon Malcolm. **Sikh Rev.** 49:6(570) 6:2001 pp.37-61.

Rural anthropology
Anthropologie rurale

2187   La borde de moyenne montagne en haute-Soule et en Labourd. *[In French]*; [The *borda* in Soule and the Laburdi mountains] *[Summary]*; *[Summary in Spanish]*; *[Summary in Basque]*. Michel Duvert. **An. Eusko. Folk.** 42 2000 pp.125-136.

2188   Conflits villageois dans la Chine du XXe siècle. *[In French]*; (Village conflicts in 20th century China.) Lucien Bianco. **Rural Stud.** :157-158 1-6:2001 pp.45-64.

2189   Consumer preferences and the uptake of animal healthcare by the poor: a case study from Kenya. C. Heffernan. **J. Int. Dev.** 13:7 10:2001 pp.847-861.

2190   Ecology, alterity and resistance in Sardinia; *[Summary in French]*. Tracey Heatherington. **Soc. Anthrop.** 9:3 10:2001 pp.289-306.

2191   In search of *nyo*: Lyela farmers' perceptions of the forest in Burkina Faso; *[Summary in French]*. Sten Hagberg. **Africa** 71:3 2001 pp.481-501.

2192   Jest taka wieś. Typowa czy inna. *[In Polish]*; (There is such a village: typical or not.) Anna Szyfer. Wagrowiec, 2000. 124p. *ISBN: 8391294838.*

2193   Kultura wobec kręgów tożsamości. Materiały konferencji przedkongresowej, Poznań 19-21 października 2000. *[In Polish]*; [Culture on the basis of identity]. Teresa Kostyrko [Ed.]; Tafeusz Zgółka [Ed.]. Poznan, Wroclaw: Kongres Kultury Polskiej, 2000. 238p. *ISBN: 8385689397. Conference proceedings.*

2194   Life on the Amazon: the anthropology of a Brazilian peasant village. Mark Harris. Oxford: Oxford University Press, 2000. xii,236p. *ISBN: 0197262392.* (*Series:* British Academy postdoctoral fellowship monographs).

2195   Lokalität und Siedlungsgeschichte im Cross River-Gebiet. *[In German]*; [Locality and settlement history in the Cross River region] *[Summary]*. Ute Röschenthaler. **Z. Ethn.** 125:2 2000 pp.189-214.

2196   Markets, class and social change: trading networks and poverty in rural South Asia. Ben Crow; et al; K.A.S. Murshid [Contrib.]. New York: Palgrave, 2001. 265p. *ISBN: 0333946006. Includes bibliographical references and index.*

2197   Movimientos socio-rurales en las actuales Huastecas hidalguense y veracruzana (México), en la primera mitad del siglo XIX. *[In Spanish]*; [Socio-rural movements in the Huasteca region, during the first half of the 19th century] *[Summary]*. Antonio Escobar Ohmstede. **Jahrb. Ges. Lat.am.** 38 2001 pp.157-181.

2198   Nymphs, shepherds, and vampires: the agrarian myth on film. Tom Brass. **Dialect. Anthrop.** 25:3-4 2000 pp.205-238.

2199   The other Western Highlands; *[Summary in French]*; *[Summary in German]*; *[Summary in Spanish]*. Anton Ploeg. **Soc. Anthrop.** 9:1 2:2001 pp.25-43.

2200   A peasant's view of peasant life and its categories: a study of the proverbs of north India. Hetukar Jha. **Ind. Soc. Sci. R.** 3:1 1-6:2001 pp.101-114.

2201   Pursuing the fruits of knowledge: cognitive cthnobotany in Missouri's little Dixie. Justin M. Nolan. **J. Ethnobio.** 21:2 Winter:2001 pp.29-54.

2202   The Shan-Dany museum: community, economics, and cultural traditions in a rural Mexican village. Jeffrey H. Cohen. **Human. Org.** 60:3 Fall:2001 pp.272-280.

2203   Stanje mlinov in žag v krajinskem parku Kolpa. *[In Slovene]*; (Water mills and sawmills of the Kolpa nature reserve.) *[Summary]*. Dušan Štepec. **Bull. Slov. Ethno. Soc.** 41:3-4 2001 pp.98-103.

2204   (The study of formation process of the rural production group.); *[Text in Japanese]*. Junji Hirata. Kyoto: Kourosha, 2000. 540p.

2205   La terre et le paysan. *[In French]*; [Land and peasant]. Emmanuel Le Roy Ladurie [Foreword]; Marc Léopold Benjamin Bloch; Etienne Bloch [Comp.]. Paris: Armand Colin, 1999. xxviii, 571p. *ISBN: 2200219784. Includes bibliographical references.*

2206   'The changing face of clay': continuity and change in the transition from village to urban life in the Near East. David Wengrow. **Antiquity** 72:278 12:1998 pp.783-795.

2207   Transnational livelihood and landscapes. homas Perreault; Anthony Bebbington; Simon Batterbury; Dianne Rocheleau; Laurie Ross; Julio Morrobel; Luis Malaret; Ricardo Hernandez; Tara Kominiak. **Ecumene** 8:4 10:2001 pp.369-492. *Collection of 5 articles.*

Urban anthropology
Anthropologie urbaine

2208   Becoming New York: the Five Points neighborhood. Rebecca Yamin; Stephen A. Brighton; C. Milne; Pamela Crabtree; Michael C. Bonasera; Leslie Raymer; Cheryl J. LaRoche; Gary S. McGowan; Heather J. Griggs; Reginald H. Pitts; Paul E. Reckner; Robert Fitts; Diana diZerega Wall. **Hist. Archaeol.** 35:3 2001 pp.1-135. *Collection of 11 articles.*

2209   The bishopric of Fes. K. Sinclair-Loutit. **Morocco** 1 1996 pp.116-128.

2210   Civil society in action — transforming opportunities for the urban poor. Diana Mitlin; Somsook Boonyabancha; Arjun Appadurai; Sheela Patel; Sundar Burra; Celine D'Cruz; Beth Chitekwe; Ted Baumann; Joel Bolnick; Pedro Moctezuma; David Satterthwaite; Michael Edwards; Alexander J. Loftus; David A. McDonald; Malick Gaye; Loly Diouf; Nicola Keller; Ronald G.J. Boon; Nancy Alexaki; Herrera Becerra; Guillaume Iyenda; Asian Coalition for Housing Rights; Vincentian Missionaries Social Development Foundation Incorporated (VMSDFI). **Environ. Urban.** 13:2 10:2001 pp.3-241. *Collection of 18 articles.*

2211   La commémoration du 5 mai à Mexico au XIXᵉ siècle. *[In French]*; [The commemoration of May 5 in 19th century Mexico]. Verónica Zárate Toscano. **Cah. Amer. Lat.** 35 2000 pp.161-183.

2212   Creolized Utopias: squatter colonies and the post-colonial city in Malaysia. Yeoh Seng Guan. **SOJOURN** 16:1 4:2001 pp.102-124.

2213   Environment, living spaces, and health: compound-organisation practices in a Bamako squatter settlement, Mali. Paule Simard; Maria De Koninck. **Gen. Dev.** 9:2 7:2001 pp.28-39.

2214   Fragment d'une enquête dans un bidonville de Casablanca. *[In French]*; (Fragments of a research project in a Casablanca slum.) *[Summary]*; *[Summary in German]*. Abdelmajid Arrif. **Ethn. Fr.** XXXI:1 1-3:2001 pp.29-39.

2215   From rural migrant to urban citizen: a brief social history of the development of an urban poor suburb in Mexico. Cheleen Mahar. **Urban Anthro.** 29:4 Winter:2000 pp.359-402.

2216   Globalization and urban social movements: the case of Metro Manila, the Philippines. Ton van Naerssen. **Bijdragen** 157:3 2001 pp.677-690.

2217   Gorod Poshekhon'e: segodniashnii den' rossiiskoi provintsii. *[In Russian]*; (Poshekhonye city: the present day of the provinces of Russia.) *[Summary]*. O.R. Budina. **Etnograf. Oboz.** 3 5-6:2001 pp.42-60.

2218   'Like Nixon coming to China': finding common ground in a multi-ethnic coalition for environmental justice. Melissa Checker. **Anthr. Quart.** 74:3 7:2001 pp.135-146.

2219   Newcastle: the development of a model apartheid town and beyond. A.E. Todes. **S. Afr. Geogr. J.** 83:1 2001 pp.69-77.

2220   The oldest profession. A latent urban subculture. Ghaus Ansari. **B. Int. Com. Urg. Anthrop. Ethnol. R.** 40 1999-2000 pp.133-140.

2221   Rethinking urban poverty: a look inside the Indonesian household. Victoria A. Beard. **Third World Plan. R.** 22:4 11:2000 pp.361-378.

2222   Urban Brazil. E. Fernandes; M.M. Valença; A. Cristina Fernandes; R. Negreiros; M. Lopes de Souza; R. Antunes; A. Rodríguez-Pose; J. Tomaney; J. Klink; R. Rolnik; F.A.M. de Souza; J.J. Lima; C. Acioly, Jr.; E. Riley; J. Fiori; R. Ramirez; L.L. Martins; M.A. Abreu; S. Abakerli. **Geoforum** 32:4 11:2001 pp.415-565. *Collection of 11 articles.*

2223   Urchins, loafers and the cult of the cowboy: urbanization and delinquency in Dar es Salaam, 1919-61. Andrew Burton. **J. Afr. Hist.** 42:2 2001 pp.199-216.

2224   'We come to the garden'... again: Garden city, Kansas, 1990-2000. Donald D. Stull; Michael J. Broadway. **Urban Anthro.** 30:4 Winter:2001 pp.269-300.

C: ÉCOLOGIE, TECHNOLOGIE, ÉCONOMIE.

C.2: Technology
Technologie

2225   Ceramic Age seafaring and interaction potential in the Antilles: a computer simulation. Richard T. Callaghan. **Curr. Anthr.** 42:2 4:2001 pp.308-313.

2226   Cost, benefit and value in the organization of early European copper production. Stephen Shennan. **Antiquity** 73:280 6:1999 pp.352-363.

2227   Minaret building and apprenticeship in Yemen. Trevor H.J. Marchand. Richmond: Curzon Press, 2001. 304p. *ISBN: 0700715118.*

2228   Notes préliminaires a l'étude de la voie romaine Gerasa/Philadelphia. *[In French]*; [Preliminary notes on the study of the Roman road between Gerasa and Philadelphia]. Anne-Michèle Rasson-Seigne; Jacques Seigne. **A. Dept. Antiq. Jordan** XXXIX 1995 pp.193-210.

2229   La révolution informationnelle et le travail humain. *[In French]*; (The information revolution and human labour.) *[Summary]*. Claude Gindin. **Pensée** 326 4-6:2001 pp.9-20.

2230   Russkie lyzhi: istoriia razvitiia. *[In Russian]*; (Russian skis: history of development.) *[Summary]*. M.I. Vasil'ev. **Etnograf. Oboz.** 2 3-4:2001 pp.91-102.

2231   Stockholms stads sidenmanufactorie. *[In Swedish]*; (Stockholm city silk manufacture 1688-1693.) *[Summary]*. Jonas Berg; Elisabet Stavenow-Hidemark. **Rig** 2 2001 pp.82-91.

2232   La technique et son autre. Philosophie de Fernand Dumont. *[In French]*; [Technology and the other: Fernand Dumont's philosophy]. Serge Cantin. **Esprit** 276 7:2001 pp.84-103.

Crafts
Artisanat

2233   An approach to the study of contemporary earthenware technology in mainland Southeast Asia. Louise Cort; Leedom Lefferts. **J. Siam Soc.** 88:1-2 2000 pp.204-211.

2234   Artistic kites in the Asian tradition. Derek Lee. **Asian Cult. (Asian-Pac. Cult.) Q.** XXVIII:4 Winter:2000 pp.47-50.

2235   Jomon pottery production at Honmura-cho and Isarago sites: insights from geochemistry. Junko Habu; Mark E. Hall. **Anth. Sci.** 109:2 4:2001 pp.141-166.

2236   Learning and craft production: an introduction. C. Jill Minar; Patricia L. Crown. **J. Anthr. Res.** 57:4 Winter:2001 pp.369-380.

2237   Learning how to make the right pots: apprenticeship strategies and material culture, a case study in handmade pottery from Cameroon. Hélène Wallaert-Pêtre. **J. Anthr. Res.** 57:4 Winter:2001 pp.471-493.

2238   Michael Cardew and the Abuja potters. Liz Moloney. **Niger. F.** 66:2 10:2001 pp.113-124.

2239   Nadlak — remeselnícke centrum hrnčiarstva. *[In Slovak]*; (Nadlak — handicraft pottery centre.) Mária Štefanková. **Slov. Národop.** 48:2 2000 pp.217-234.

2240   Pacbitun (Belize) and ancient Maya use of slate. Paul F. Healy; Jaime J. Awe; Gyles Iannone; Cassandra Bill. **Antiquity** 69:263 6:1995 pp.337-348.

2241   The patent and the Malanggan. Marilyn Strathern. **Theory Cult. Soc.** 18:4 8:2001 pp.1-26.

2242   Petrol-box furniture. P.G. Locke. **Herit. Zimb.** 10 1991 pp.6-16.

2243   Prialki zoo-ornitomorfnogo tipa v kontekste etnicheskoi istorii Russkogo Severa. *[In Russian]*; (Zoo- and ornithological type distaffs in the context of ethnic history of the Russian North.) *[Summary]*. I.M. Denisova. **Etnograf. Oboz.** 2 3-4:2001 pp.68-90.

2244   Rural handicraft production in Mpumalanga, South Africa: organization, problems and support needs. Christian M. Rogerson; Perseverence M. Sithole. **S. Afr. Geogr. J.** 83:2 2001 pp.149-158.

2245   Shifting visions: along the routes of Sumba cloth. Jill Forshee. **Asia Pacific J. Anthr.** 1:2 10:2000 pp.1-25.

2246   Sign writers in Ibadan. Segun Oke. **Niger. F.** 66:2 10:2001 pp.105-109.

2247   Sitar-making today: problems and prospects of the craft. Suvarnalata Rao. **San. Nat.** 135-136 2000 pp.47-62.

2248   The sling and the inflated skin boat in Tibet. Siegbert Hummel; G. Vogliotti [Tr.]. **Tibet J.** XXV:3 Autumn:2000 pp.14-18.

2249   Stanaulenne asnounykh form gancharnai keramiki na Belarusi. *[In Belorussian]*; (Origination of main pottery forms in Belarus.) *[Summary]*; *[Summary in Russian]*. V.U. Ugrynovich-Kaminskaia. **V. Aka. Belarusi** 1 2000 pp.92-98.

2250   Thai ceramics, Lan Na and Sawanakalok: an interview with John Shaw. Ray Hearn. **J. Siam Soc.** 88:1-2 2000 pp.212-217.

2251   'Thread in her hands — cash in her pockets': women and domestic textile production in 19th century New Brunswick. Judith Rygiel. **Acadiensis** XXX:2 Spring:2001 pp.56-70.

2252   The use of *aso-oke* in Yoruba marriage ceremonies. A.A. Amubode; S.A. Adetoro. **Niger. F.** 66:1 4:2001 pp.29-34.

2253   Woodblock dyeing and printing technology in China, c. 700 A.D.: the innovations of Ms. Liu and other evidence. T.H. Barrett. **B. Sch. Orient. Afr. Stud.** 64:2 2001 pp.240-247.

C.3:   **Economy**
              Économie

Agriculture
Agriculture

2254   Agricultural improvement and technological innovation in a slave society: the case of early national northern Virginia. A. Glenn Crothers. **Agr. Hist.** 75:2 Spring:2000 pp.135-167.

2255   Agriculture et «développement durable» en Asie du Sud-Est. *[In French]*; (Agriculture and 'sustainable development' in South-East Asia.) *[Summary]*. Marc Dufumier. **R. T. Monde** XLI:162 4-6:2000 pp.257-276.

2256   The annual round of agricultural tasks in Dongyang county: synoptic illusion or symbolic capital? Eugene Cooper. **Asian Folk. S.** LIX:2 2000 pp.239-264.

2257   Au carrefour de l'économique et du culturel. La filière castanéicole corse comme marqueur de l'identité. *[In French]*; (At the crossroads between economics and culture: the Corsican chestnut business as a marker of identity.) Philippe Pesteil. **Rural Stud.** 157-158 1-6:2001 pp.211-228.

2258   L'avenir des cultures pérennes en Indonésie. Cacao et clou de girofle après la tempête monétaire. *[In French]*; (The future of perennial agriculture in Indonesia: cocoa and cloves after the financial crisis.) *[Summary]*. François Ruf. **R. T. Monde** XLI:162 4-6:2000 pp.431-452.

2259   Beyond the dust bowl: Lawrence Svobida, 1908-1984. Peter Hoehnle. **Agr. Hist.** 75:3 Summer:2001 pp.271-278.

2260   Catos Hut: Zum Ideal der „Kühle" in Weltbild und Anbau der Bauern der kolumbianischen Karibikküste. *[In German]*; [Cato's hand: the 'coolness' ideal in the world view and cultivation practices among farmers on Colombia's Caribbean coast]. Josef Drexler. **Tribus** 50 12:2001 pp.67-86.

2261   Cereals at Ebla. Alfonso Archi. **Arch. Orient.** 67:4 11:1999 pp.503-518.

2262   La chinampa, "cosa jamás vista en este mundo". *[In Spanish]*; [*Chinampa* - 'a thing never seen in this world' *[Summary]*. Erwin Stephan Otto Parrodi. **Acta Sociol. [Mexico]** 31 1-4:2001 pp.65-94.

2263   Conditions of agricultural production in North Korea, 1946-1950. Mitsuhiko Kimura. **Korea J.** 40:4 Winter:2000 pp.266-298.

2264   The contested role of heterogeneity in collective action: some evidence from community forestry in Nepal. G. Varughese; E. Ostrom. **World Dev.** 29:5 5:2001 pp.747-765.

2265   The Correll family and technological change in Australian agriculture. Lionel Frost. **Agr. Hist.** 75:2 Spring:2000 pp.217-243.

2266   The cultural life of early domestic plant use. Christine Hastorf. **Antiquity** 72:278 12:1998 pp.773-782.

2267   A currant affair: E.D. Smith and agricultural change in nineteenth-century Saltfleet township, Ontario. Sean W. Gouglas. **Agr. Hist.** 75:4 Fall:2001 pp.438-497.

2268   De la crise financière à la crise alimentaire: l'Indonésie en 1997-1999. *[In French]*; (From financial crisis to food crisis: Indonesia from 1997 to 1999.) *[Summary]*. Françoise Gérard. **R. T. Monde** XLI:162 4-6:2000 pp.411-430.

2269   Des paysans reconnus en Guinée et en France: les producteurs de pommes de terre des Timbis s'organisent. Problèmes, blocages et soutiens. *[In French]*; [North-South relations featuring peasants recognised in France and Guinea: how the potato producers of Timbi organize themselves] *[Summary]*. Marie-Christine Allart. **R. T. Monde** XLI:163 7-9:2000 pp.693-704.

2270   Destined to fail: forced settlement at the *Office du Niger*, 1926-45. Jean Filipovich. **J. Afr. Hist.** 42:2 2001 pp.239-260.

2271   Diversité des utilisations agricoles associées aux retenues d'eau du nord de la Côte-d'Ivoire. *[In French]*; (Diversity of agricultural uses associated with water barriers in northern Côte-d'Ivoire.) *[Summary]*. Tanguy Le Guen; Luis Tito De Moraïs. **Cah. Outre-mer** 54:215 7-9:2001 pp.283-304.

2272   Documenting the effects of veld burning on soil and vegetation characteristics in Giant's Castle Game Reserve, Kwazulu-Natal Drakensberg. H.J. Bijker; P.D. Sumner; K.J. Meiklejohn; G.J. Bredenkamp. **S. Afr. Geogr. J.** 83:1 2001 pp.28-33.

2273   Le dynamisme agricole malaysien. *[In French]*; (The dynamism of Malaysian agriculture.) *[Summary]*. Rodolphe de Koninck. **R. T. Monde** XLI:162 4-6:2000 pp.389-410.

2274   L'eau de la montagne et le pouvoir étatique au Maroc: entre le passé et le présent. *[In French]*; (The water from the mountains and state power in Morocco: between past and present.) M.D. El Jihad. **Ann. Géogr.** 110:622 11-12:2001 pp.665-672.

2275   Échanges croisés entre nouveau monde et ancien monde. Maïs, pomme de terre, tomate et cacao. *[In French]*; (Exchanges between the new and old worlds: maize, potatoes, tomatoes and cocoa.) *[Summary]*. Nikita Harwich. **Rural Stud.** 155-156 7-12:2001 pp.239-260.

2276   The Great Plains: agriculture and the environment in the late twentieth century. R. Douglas Hurt. **Agr. Hist.** 75:4 Fall:2001 pp.395-405.

2277   A health production function for quasi-autarkic agricultural households in Rwanda. Christophe Muller. **Euro. J. Dev. Res.** 13:1 6:2001 pp.87-105.

2278   The insoluable conflicts of agricultural collectivization in Vietnam. Chad Raymond. **Crossroads** 15:2 2001 pp.41-70.

2279   Les interactions agriculture-industrie en Thaïlande. Dynamiques agraires et mobilités de la main-d'œuvre. *[In French]*; (Interactions of agriculture and industry: Agricultural dynamics and labour mobility in Thailand.) *[Summary]*. Doryane Kermel-Torrès; Philippe Schar. **R. T. Monde** XLI:162 4-6:2000 pp.323-342.

2280   Introduction: mutations de l'agriculture en Asie du Sud-Est. *[In French]*; (Introduction: agricultural transformation in South-East Asia.) *[Summary]*. Marc Dufumier. **R. T. Monde** XLI:162 4-6:2000 pp.249-256.

2281   José do Canto, um *gentleman farmer* açoriano. *[In Portuguese]*; (José do Canto — an Azorean gentleman farmer.) *[Summary]*; *[Summary in French]*. Carlos Guilherme Riley. **Anál. Soc.** XXXVI:160 Autumn:2001 pp.685-710.

2282   Kings and commerce on an agrarian frontier: Kālketu's story in Mukunda's *Candīmangal*. David L. Curley. **Indian Ec. Soc. His. R.** XXXVIII:3 7-9:2001 pp.299-324.

2283   Lazy gardening. Margaret Brook. **Niger. F.** 66:1 4:2001 pp.51-68.

2284   A livelihood from the forest: gendered visions of social, economic and environmental change in Southern Cameroon. K. Brown; S. Lapuyade. **J. Int. Dev.** 13:8 11:2001 pp.1131-1149.

2285   The meaning of kinship in sharecropping contracts. Elisabeth Sadoulet; Alain de Janvry; Seiichi Fukui. **Am. J. Agr. Ec.** 79:2 5:1997 pp.394-406.

2286   Mind and labor on the farm in black-earth Russia, 1861-1914. David Kerans. Budapest, New York: Central European University Press, 2001. xiii, 491p. *ISBN: 9639116947. Includes bibliographical references (p. [449]-482) and index.*

2287   Monitoring land use change in the Badia transition zone in Jordan using aerial photography and satellite imagery. J.T. al-Bakri; J.C. Taylor; T.R. Brewer. **Geogr. J.** 167:3 9:2001 pp.248-276.

2288   More effective natural resource management through democratically elected, decentralised government structures in Uganda. Thomas Raussen; Geoffrey Ebong; Jimmy Musiime. **Develop. Pract.** 11:4 8:2001 pp.460-470.

2289   Les nouvelles politiques de l'eau enjeux urbains, ruraux, régionaux. *[In French]*; (Water: new management policies and the urban, rural and regional stakes.) Guy Meublat; Claude Ménard; Sylvy Jaglin; Fatiha Chikhr Saïdi; Gérard Grellet; Emmanuel Bon; Paul Mathieu; Ahmed Benali; Olivia Aubriot; Philippe Le Lourd; Rosa Maria Formiga Johnsson; Sébastien Treyer. **R. T. Monde** XLII:166 4-6:2001 pp.249-474. *Collection of 11 articles.*

2290   Oasis or mirage: the farming of black pearl in the Northern Cook Islands. Cluny MacPherson. **Pac. Stud.** 23:3-4 9-12:2000 pp.33-55.

2291   Obnove i lokalna značenja običaja: kumpanije na otoku Korčuli. *[In Croatian]*; (Revival and local meanings of customs: *kumpanije* on the island of Korčula.) *[Summary]*. Zorica Vitez. **Nar. Umjetn.** 37:2 2000 pp.27-46.

2292   On-farm testing and dissemination of agroforestry among slash-and-burn farmers in Nagaland, India. Merle D. Faminow; K.K. Klein; Project Operations Unit. **Develop. Pract.** 11:4 8:2001 pp.471-486.

2293   Optimization of shallow tubewell owners' income in a selected area of Tangail district, Bangladesh. Md. Saidur Rahman; M.A.S. Mandal; S.M.M. Murshed. **Econ. Aff. [Calcutta]** 45:4 10-12:2000 pp.210-222.

2294   Organizing the farm bureau: family, community, and professionals, 1914-1928. Nancy K. Berlage. **Agr. Hist.** 75:4 Fall:2001 pp.406-437.

2295   The origin of the irrigation technique in Tibet. Siegbert Hummel; G. Vogliotti [Tr.]. **Tibet J.** XXV:3 Autumn:2000 pp.8-13.

2296   Le pavot à opium et l'homme. Origines géographiques et premières diffusions d'un cultivar. *[In French]*; (The opium poppy and mankind: geographic origins and early diffusion of a cultivar.) *[Summary]*. P.A. Chouvy. **Ann. Géogr.** 110:618 3-4:2001 pp.182-194.

2297   Perception and management of cassava (*Manihot esculenta* Crantz) diversity among Makushi Amerindians of Guyana; *[Summary in Spanish]*; *[Summary in French]*. M. Elias; et al. **J. Ethnobio.** 20:2 Winter:2000 pp.239-268.

2298   Pink stripes and obedient servants: an agriculturalist in Tanganyika. John Ainley. Driffield: J.M. Ainley, 2001. 249p. *ISBN: 0954094409. Includes bibliographical references and index.*

2299   Pioneer farmers and family dynasties in Marirangwe purchase area, colonial Zimbabwe, 1931-1947; *[Summary in French]*. Allison K. Shutt. **Afr. Stud. R.** 43:3 12:2000 pp.59-80.

2300   Promoting the 'practical': science and agricultural modernization in Puerto Rico and Colombia, 1920-1940. Stuart McCook. **Agr. Hist.** 75:1 Winter:2001 pp.52-82.

2301   Proto-Dravidian agricultural terms. C.A. Winters. **Int. J. Drav. Ling.** XXX:1 1:2001 pp.23-28.

2302   Proto-Uto-Aztecan: a community of cultivators in central Mexico? Jane H. Hill. **Am. Anthrop.** 103:4 12:2001 pp.913-934.

2303   Resource limitations in Sahelian agriculture. Henk Breman; J.J. Rob Groot; Herman van Keulen. **Glo. Environ. Chan.** 11:1 4:2001 pp.59-68.

2304   Rice domestication. Gary W. Crawford; Chen Shen; Charles Higham; Tracey L.D. Lu; Pei Anping; Zhao Zhijun; Zhang Juzhong; Wang Xiangkun; Tracey L.D. Lu. **Antiquity** 72:278 12:1998 pp.858-907. *Collection of 6 articles.*

2305   La riziculture thaïlandaise face à la crise. *[In French]*; [Thailand rice production facing a crisis] *[Summary]*. Pascale Phélinas. **R. T. Monde** XLI:162 4-6:2000 pp.301-322.

2306   Rooted in the soil: farm family persistence in Burton Parish, Sunbury County, New Brunswick, 1851-1901. Timothy D. Lewis. **Acadiensis** XXXI:1 Autumn:2001 pp.35-54.

2307   Scaling up adoption and impact of agroforestry technologies: experiences from western Kenya. Qureish Noordin; Amadou Niang; Bashir Jama; Mary Nyasimi. **Develop. Pract.** 11:4 8:2001 pp.509-523.

2308   Scaling up the benefits of agroforestry research: lessons learned and research challenges. Steven Franzel; Peter Cooper; Glenn L. Denning. **Develop. Pract.** 11:4 8:2001 pp.524-534.

2309   Scaling up the use of fodder shrubs in central Kenya. Charles Wambugu; Steven Franzel; Paul Tuwei; George Karanja. **Develop. Pract.** 11:4 8:2001 pp.487-494.

2310   Sheepwatching. Sarah Franklin. **Anthr. Today** 17:3 6:2001 pp.3-9.

2311   Sir Albert Howard and the forestry roots of the organic farming movement. Gregory Barton. **Agr. Hist.** 75:2 Spring:2000 pp.168-187.

2312   Small-scale farmers expand the benefits of improved maize germplasm: a case study from Chiapas, Mexico. M.R. Bellon; J. Risopoulos. **World Dev.** 29:5 5:2001 pp.799-811.

2313   Soils and land use on lithologically diverse ophiolitic alluvia on the coastal plain of Palawan, Philippines. I.C. Baillie; N.B. Inciong; P.M. Evangelista. **Sing. J. Trop. Geogr.** 22:1 3:2001 pp.1-14.

2314   Le système agraire du delta du Chao Phraya: transformations et impact de la crise de 1997. *[In French]*; (The agrarian system of the Chao-Phraya delta: transformations and impact of the 1997 crisis.) *[Summary]*. François Molle; Thippawal Srijantr. **R. T. Monde** XLI:162 4-6:2000 pp.343-364.

2315   Transition and enterprise restructuring: the development of individual farming in Romania. M. Rizov; D. Gavrilescu; H. Gow; E. Mathijs; J.F.M. Swinnen. **World Dev.** 29:7 7:2001 pp.1257-1274.

2316   Urban agriculture in Mwanza, Tanzania; *[Summary in French]*. Karen Coen Flynn. **Africa** 71:4 2001 pp.666-691.

2317   L'utilisation publicitaire des paysages de terrasses. *[In French]*; (Using terraced landscapes in advertisements.) Françoise Alcaraz. **Rural Stud.** :157-158 1-6:2001 pp.195-210.

2318   Vietnam: la crise économique et l'intégration régionale sonnent-elles la fin de l'économie socialiste de marché? *[In French]*; (Are economic crises and regional integration signalling the end of the 'socialist market economy' in Vietnam?) *[Summary]*. Pascal Bergeret. **R. T. Monde** XLI:162 4-6:2000 pp.453-472.

2319   Weed vegetation and land use of upland maize fields in north-west Vietnam. A. Wezel. **Geojournal** 50:4 2000 pp.349-358.

2320   Yoruba rural women and alley farming. Elizabeth A. Ogunlana. **Gen. Tech. Dev.** 5:3 9-12:2001 pp.409-424.

2321   Zemledenlie u balkartsev. *[In Russian]*; (Land cultivation among the Balkars.) *[Summary]*. B.Kh. Kuchmezov. **Etnograf. Oboz.** 1 1-2:2001 pp.66-78.

Consumption
Consommation

2322   Consuming life. Zygmunt Bauman. **J. Cons. Cult.** 1:1 6:2001 pp.9-29.

2323   The consuming or the consumed? Virtual Hmong in China. Nicholas Tapp. **Asia Pacific J. Anthr.** 1:2 10:2000 pp.73-101.

2324   The consumption of mass. Nick Lee [Ed.]; Rolland Munro [Ed.]. Oxford: Blackwell Publishers, 2001. *ISBN: 0631228195.* (*Series:* Sociological Review Monographs).

2325   Economics and icons: identifying the issues in emergent cultural production. Elizabeth Morrell. **Asia Pacific J. Anthr.** 1:2 10:2000 pp.26-48.

2326   From counterculture to consumer culture: Vespa and the Italian youth market, 1958-78. Adam Arvidsson. **J. Cons. Cult.** 1:1 6:2001 pp.47-71.

2327   How Blacks use consumption to shape their collective identity: evidence from marketing specialists. Michèle Lamont; Virág Molnár. **J. Cons. Cult.** 1:1 6:2001 pp.31-45.

Exchange, commerce and property
Échanges, affaires et propriété

2328   Airborne *kula*: the appropriation of birds by Danish ornithologists. John Liep. **Anthr. Today** 17:5 10:2001 pp.10-15.
2329   Die Akan-Goldgewichte Westafrikas. Neue Aspekte Zum Gewichtssystem Und Zur Funktion Geometrischer Und Figürlicher Formen. *[In German]*; [The gold weights of Aka, West Africa. New aspects of the weights system and the function of geometric and figurative forms] *[Summary]*. Hartmut Mollat. **Baes-A.** XLVII:2 6:2001 pp.259-276.
2330   The Andrew Jackson administration and the Orient, 1829-1837. Jonathan Goldstein. **Asian Cult. (Asian-Pac. Cult.) Q.** XXVIII:2 Summer:2000 pp.55-79.
2331   The anthropology of economy: community, market and culture. Stephen Gudeman. Oxford: Blackwell Publishers, 2001. 189p. *ISBN: 0631225668. Includes bibliographical references and index.*
2332   The anthropology of economy: community, market, and culture. Stephen Gudeman. Malden MA, Oxford: Blackwell Publishers, 2001. viii, 189p. *ISBN: 0631225676, 0631225668. Includes bibliographical references (p. [165]-182) and index.*
2333   The British occupation of Tangier 1662-1684. Peter Collier. **Morocco** 1 1996 pp.52-61.
2334   Carnival and contestation in the Aztec marketplace. Scott R. Hutson. **Dialect. Anthrop.** 25:2 2000 pp.123-149.
2335   'Cash for his turnups': agricultural production for local markets in colonial Pennsylvania, 1725-1783. Michael V. Kennedy. **Agr. Hist.** 74:3 Summer:2000 pp.587-608.
2336   Circuits réels d'un objet virtuel. Monnaie, doubles et dette dans les Andes au XVI⁽ᵉ⁾ siècle. *[In French]*; (A virtual object's real circuit: money, doubles and debts in the 16th century Andes.) *[Summary]*. Carmen Bernand. **Rural Stud.** 155-156 7-12:2001 pp.261-276.
2337   Coca cola and *kolo*: land, ancestors and development. Jerry Jacka. **Anthr. Today** 17:4 8:2001 pp.3-8.
2338   Commodity flow and national market access: a case study from interior Alaska. William Hampton Adams; Peter M. Bowers; Robin Mills. **Hist. Archaeol.** 35:2 2001 pp.73-107.
2339   Development of commerce and commercial policy during the reign of King Chongjo. Donghwan Ko. **Korea J.** 40:4 Winter:2000 pp.202-226.
2340   The dynamics of wealth and poverty in the transegalitarian societies of Southeast Asia. Brian Hayden. **Antiquity** 75:289 9:2001 pp.571-581.
2341   Échange marchand, échange non marchand. *[In French]*; [Commercial and non-commercial exchange]; *[Summary in French]*. Alain Testart. **Rev. Fr. Soc.** 42:4 10-12:2001 pp.719-748.
2342   Économie: pour un retour à la valeur-travail. *[In French]*; (Economics: for a return to labour value.) *[Summary]*. Maurice Decaillot. **Pensée** 325 1-3:2001 pp.113-128.
2343   Economy and exchange in the east Mediterranean during late antiquity. Michael Decker [Ed.]; Sean A. Kingsley [Ed.]. Oxford: Oxbow, 2001. vi, 178p. *ISBN: 1842170449. Includes bibliographical references.*
2344   Ekonomsko-antropološki pristup u izučavanju creskoga ribarstva. *[In Croatian]*; (An economic-anthropological approach to the study of fishing trade on the island of Cres.) *[Summary]*. Goran Pavel Šantek. **Nar. Umjetn.** 37:2 2000 pp.133-150.
2345   The enchanting spirit of Thai capitalism: the cult of Luang Phor Khoon and the post-modernization of Thai Buddhism. Peter A. Jackson. **S.E. Asia Res.** 7:1 3:1999 pp.5-60.
2346   Enchères et émotions. *[In French]*; (Auctions and emotions.) *[Summary]*; *[Summary in German]*. Rolande Bonnain-Dulon. **Ethn. Fr.** XXXI:3 7-9:2001 pp.511-526.
2347   Enterpreneurs at home: secluded Muslim women and hidden economic activities in northern Nigeria. Zakaria Yakubu. **Nord. J. Afr. St.** 10:1 2001 pp.107-123.
2348   Flooded with foreign coins: Spanish and American administrators dealing with currency problems in the Philippines, 1890-1905. Willem G. Wolters. **Bijdragen** 157:3 2001 pp.511-538.

2349   From regional relations to ethnic groups? On the transformation of value relations to property claims in the Kula ring of Papua New Guinea. Frederick H. Damon. **Asia Pacific J. Anthr.** 1:2 10:2000 pp.49-72.

2350   Gender differences in land inheritance, schooling and lifetime income: evidence from the rural Philippines. Jonna P. Estudillo; Agnes R. Quisumbing; Keijiro Otsuka. **J. Dev. Stud.** 37:4 4:2001 pp.23-48.

2351   Gift, marriage and the denial of reciprocity. J.C. Heesterman. **Stud. Orient.** 94 2001 pp.243-260.

2352   Hadza meat sharing. K. Hawkes; J.F. O'Connell; N.G. Blurton Jones. **Evol. Hum. Behav.** 22:2 3:2001 pp.113-142.

2353   High art down home: an economic ethnography of a local art market. Stuart Plattner. Chicago IL, London: University of Chicago Press, 1996. xiii, 250p. *ISBN: 0226670848, 0226670821. Includes bibliographical references (p. 241-245) and index.*

2354   Die *igisûm*-Abgabe in den altbabylonischen Quellen. *[In German]*; [The *igisûm* tax in ancient Mesopotamia]. Lukáš Pecha. **Arch. Orient.** 69:1 2:2001 pp.1-20.

2355   Imperial policy and the decline of the Bengal salt industry under colonial rule: an episode in the 'de-industrialisation' process. Indrajit Ray. **Indian Ec. Soc. His. R.** XXXVIII:2 4-6:2001 pp.181-206.

2356   Indian merchant networks outside India in the nineteenth and twentieth centuries: a preliminary survey. Claude Markovits. **Mod. Asian S.** 33:4 10:1999 pp.883-911.

2357   India's trade with Tibet: early British attempts. Bir Good Gill. **Tibet J.** XXV:4 Winter:2000 pp.78-82.

2358   Initial social complexity in Southwestern Asia: the Mesopotamian advantage. Guillermo Algaze; B. Brentjes [Comments by]; Petr Charvát [Comments by]; Claudio Cioffi-Revilla [Comments by]; Rene Dittman [Comments by]; Jonathan Friedman [Comments by]; Kajsa Ekholm Friedman [Comments by]; A. Bernard Knapp [Comments by]; C.C. Lamberg-Karlovsky [Comments by]; Joy McCorriston [Comments by]; Hans Nisson [Comments by]; John Oates [Comments by]; Charles Stanish [Comments by]; T.J. Wilkinson [Comments by]. **Curr. Anthr.** 42:2 4:2001 pp.199-234.

2359   Integration of a tribal economy through market relations. Amiya Kanti Gupta; Dikshit Sinha; Srabani Chakraborty. **Ind. Soc. Sci. R.** 1:2 7-12:1999 pp.291-310.

2360   The Isle of Portland: an Iron Age port-of-trade. John Taylor. **Ox. J. Archaeol.** 20:2 5:2001 pp.187-205.

2361   (Judges' salaries in Abbasid state (132-334 A.H.)); *[Text in Arabic]*. Hussein Kassasbeh. **Dirasat Hum. Soc. Sc.** 28:1 2:2001 pp.131-157.

2362   The maritime trade on the northern Moroccan coast in the early nineteenth century. C.R. Pennell. **Morocco** 1 1996 pp.85-96.

2363   Marketing and commoditization. Kalman Applbaum. **Soc. Anal. [Adelaide]** 44(2) 11:2000 pp.106-128.

2364   Modeli ekonomicheskogo povedeniia i ikh verbalizatsiia v russkom narodnom fol'klore. *[In Russian]*; (Economic behaviour models and their verbalisation in Russian folklore.) *[Summary]*. V. Verkhovin. **Mir Rossii** X:1 2001 pp.106-124.

2365   Money and its uses in the ancient Greek world. Andrew Meadows [Ed.]; Kirsty Shipton [Ed.]. Oxford: Oxford University Press, 2001. xx, 167p. *ISBN: 0199240124. Papers presented at two conferences held in Oxford, 1995 and 1997. Includes bibliographical references and index.*

2366   Les monnaies de Muqanna'. *[In French]*; [Muqanna'ah money]. B. Kochnev. **Stud. Iran.** 30:1 2001 pp.143-152.

2367   Motivations, negotiations, and animal individuality: livestock exchange of the Turkana in northwestern Kenya. Itaru Ohta. **Nilo-Ethiop. St.** 7 2001 pp.45-61.

2368   Motor or millstone? The managing agency system in Bombay and Ahmedabad, 1850-1930. Gusbert Oonk. **Indian Ec. Soc. His. R.** XXXVIII:4 10-12:2001 pp.419-452.

2369   Negations and ambiguities in the cultures of organization. Allen W. Batteau. **Am. Anthrop.** 102:4 12:2000 pp.726-740.

2370   On the generification of culture: from blow fish to Melanesian; *[Summary in French]*. Frederick Errington; Deborah Gewertz. **J. Royal Anth. Inst.** 7:3 9:2001 pp.509-526.

2371   Peasant society and the perception of a moral economy: redistribution and risk aversion in traditional peasant culture. Peter Henningsen. **Scand. J. Hist.** 26:4 2001 pp.271-296.

2372   Petra, the periplus and ancient Indo-Arabian maritime trade. V.D. Gogte. **A. Dept. Antiq. Jordan** XLIII 1999 pp.299-304.

2373   Property effects. Social networks and compensation claims in Melanesia; *[Summary in French]*; *[Summary in German]*; *[Summary in Spanish]*. Stuart Kirsch. **Soc. Anthrop.** 9:2 6:2001 pp.147-164.

2374   Property, substance, and effect: anthropological essays on persons and things. Marilyn Strathern. London: Athlone Press, 1999. xii,336p. *ISBN: 0485121492, 0485115344. Includes bibliographical references (p. [307]-331) and index.*

2375   Prophets and profits: gendered and generational visions of wealth and value in Senegalese Murid households. Beth Anne Buggenhagen. **J. Relig. Afr.** XXXI:4 2001 pp.373-401.

2376   Reconsidering institutional change: property rights in northern Spain. David Guillet. **Am. Anthrop.** 102:4 12:2000 pp.713-725.

2377   Relational properties: understanding ownership in the Namib desert and beyond. Thomas Widlok. **Z. Ethn.** 126:2 2001 pp.237-268.

2378   A review of ancient and medieval coins found in Zimbabwe. P.G. Locke. **Herit. Zimb.** 10 1991 pp.51-60.

2379   Reziprozität und die Einführung des Fernsehens. *[In German]*; [Reciprocity and the introduction of television]. Hans W. Giessen. **Anthropos [St. Augustin]** 95:2 2000 pp.409-418.

2380   The Sahel in West Africa: countries in transition to a full market economy. Jean Marie Cour. **Glo. Environ. Chan.** 11:1 4:2001 pp.31-48.

2381   Semen as gift, semen as goods: reproductive workers and the market in altruism. Diane M. Tober. **Bod. Soc.** 7:2-3 6-9:2001 pp.137-160.

2382   Sharing, hoarding, and theft: exchange and resistance in forager-farmer relations. Jana Fortier. **Ethnology** XL:3 Summer:2001 pp.193-212.

2383   Slavery, Atlantic trade and the British economy, 1660-1800. Kenneth Morgan. Cambridge: Cambridge University Press, 2001. 134p. *ISBN: 0521588146, 052158213X.*

2384   Stone money in Yap. Peter E. Patacsil. **Asian Cult. (Asian-Pac. Cult.) Q.** XXVIII:4 Winter:2000 pp.61-64.

2385   Sur l'Amérique latine, miroir de la mondialisation. *[In French]*; (On Latin America, mirror of the world-wide economy.) *[Summary]*. J.P. Deler. **Cah. Outre-mer** 53:212 10-12:2000 pp.305-316.

2386   The Swahili: the social landscape of a mercantile society. Mark Horton; John Middleton. Malden MA: Blackwell Publishers, 2001. 282p. *ISBN: 063118919X. Includes bibliographical references and index.* (*Series:* The peoples of Africa).

2387   Symbolic technologies: machines and the Marxian notion of fetishism. Alf Hornborg. **Anth. Th.** 1:4 12:2001 pp.473-496.

2388   *Tempora et mores*: family values and the possessions of a post-apartheid countryside. Hylton White. **J. Relig. Afr.** XXXI:4 2001 pp.457-479.

2389   Tibetan monastic token currency. Wolfgang Bertsch. **Tibet J.** XXVI:2 Summer:2001 pp.39-55.

2390   Trade and trade-offs: using resources, making choices, and taking risks. M. Estellie Smith. Prospect Heights IL: Waveland Press, 2000. x, 250p. *ISBN: 1577660927. Includes bibliographical references (p. 219-234) and index.*

2391   Tuzemtsy Aliaski, russkie promyshlenniki i Rossiisko-Amerikanskaia kompaniia: sistema ekonomicheskikh otnoshenii. *[In Russian]*; (Aboriginals of Alaska, Russian traders and Russian-American companies: the system of economic relations.) *[Summary]*. A.V. Grinev. **Etnograf. Oboz.** 3 5-6:2000 pp.74-88.

2392   The value of coins in a Sakalava polity: money, death, and historicity in Mahajanga, Madagascar. Michael Lambek. **Comp. Stud. S.** 43:4 10:2001 pp.735-762.

2393   Voyaging and basalt exchange in the Phoenix and Line archipelagoes: the viewpoint from three mystery islands. Anne Di Piazza; Erik Pearthree. **Archaeol. Ocean.** 36:3 10:2001 pp.146-152.

2394   Vozvedenie zhilogo doma i organizatsiia uslad'by u narodov Iugo-Vostochnoi Evropy. *[In Russian]*; (Dwelling house construction and farmstead organization among the peoples of Southeast Europe.) *[Summary].* Iu.V. Ivanova. **Etnograf. Oboz.** 1 1-2:2001 pp.79-90.

2395   Were customs dues levied at the time of the prophet Muhammad? Michael Lecker. **Al-Qantara** XXII:1 2001 pp.19-44.

Land tenure
Régimes fonciers

2396   Access to land, rural poverty, and public action. Alain de Janvry [Ed.]; et al. New York: Oxford University Press, 2001. 451p. *ISBN: 0199242178. Includes bibliographical references and index. World Institute for Development Economics.* (*Series:* WIDER studies in development economics).

2397   Agrarian change in the peasant economy of a paddy producing village in the southern dry zone of Sri Lanka: the Gambaraya system in transition. Kumudu Kusum Kumara. **Sri Lanka J. Soc. Sci.** 22:1-2 6-12:1999 pp.77-114.

2398   The Bushmen of Southern Africa: slaughter of the innocent. Sandy Gall. London: Chatto & Windus, 2001. xxxix, 264p. *ISBN: 0701169060. Includes index.*

2399   Capitalist development, peasant differentiation and the state: survey findings from West Bengal. Sudipta Bhattacharyya. **J. Peasant Stud.** 28:4 7:2001 pp.95-126.

2400   Cocoa booms, the legalisation of land relations and politics in Cote d'Ivoire and Ghana: explaining farmers' responses. Richard C. Crook. **IDS Bull.** 32:1 1:2001 pp.35-45.

2401   Communal land rights in Zimbabwe as state sanction and social control: a narrative. Beacon Mbiba. **Africa** 71:3 2001 pp.426-448.

2402   Community and conservation land ownership in highland Scotland: a common focus in a changing context. Hamish Chenevix-Trench; Lorna J. Philip. **Scot. Geog. J.** 117:2 2001 pp.139-156.

2403   Dingo makes us human: life and land in an Australian aboriginal culture. Deborah Bird Rose. Cambridge, New York: Cambridge University Press, 2000. 249p. *ISBN: 0521794846. Includes bibliographical references and index.*

2404   Environmental governance in an uncertain world. Lyla Mehta; Melissa Leach; Ian Scoones; Ruth S. Meinzen-Dick; Rajendra Pradhan; Nathalie A. Steins; Frances Cleaver; Richard Chase Smith; Danny Pinedo; Percy M. Summers; Angelica Almeyda; Christian Lund; Ben Cousins; T. Ngaido; F. Shomo; G. Arab; Le Thi Van Hue; Dianne Rocheleau; Tania Murray Li. **IDS Bull.** 32:4 10:2001 pp.1-94. *Collection of 11 articles.*

2405   Hacendados brujos y hacendadas vírgenes en los Andes. *[In Spanish]*; [Sorcerers and virgins as landowners in the Andes]. Carlos M. Tur Donatti. **Cuad. Am.** XV:3(87) 5-6:2001 pp.148-157.

2406   Holding the line: the rural enclosure movement in the Cape colony, c.1865-1910. Lance van Sittert. **Espace Pop. Soc.** 43:1 2002 pp.95-118.

2407   Land administration reforms and social differentiation: a case study of Ghana's Lands Commission. Kasim Kasanga. **IDS Bull.** 32:1 1:2001 pp.57-64.

2408   Land and freedom: law, property rights and the British diaspora. A.R. Buck [Ed.]; John McLaren [Ed.]; Nancy E. Wright [Ed.]. Aldershot: Ashgate, 2001. xvii, 201p. *ISBN: 0754622096. Includes bibliographical references and index.*

2409   Land conflict of the Cotabato Manobo people. Douglas M. Fraiser. **Phil. Stud.** 49:2 2001 pp.215-235.

2410   Land inheritance and schooling in matrilineal societies: evidence from Sumatra. A.R. Quisumbing; K. Otsuka. **World Dev.** 29:12 12:2001 pp.2093-2110.

2411 Land, labour and the family in southern Ghana: a critique of land policy under neo-liberalisation. Kojo Amanor. Uppsala: Nordiska Afrikainstitutet, 2001. 127p. *ISBN: 9171064680.*

2412 Land reform implications of the distribution of badlands in the Mfolozi catchment, KwaZulu-Natal. H.K. Watson. **S. Afr. Geogr. J.** 82:3 2000 pp.143-148.

2413 Land tenure and natural resource management: a comparative study of agrarian communities in Asia and Africa. Keijiro Otsuka [Ed.]; Frank Place [Ed.]. Baltimore MD: Johns Hopkins University Press, 2001. 389p. *ISBN: 0801867479, 0801867460. Includes bibliographical references and index. International Food Policy Research Institute.*

2414 Life is not ours: land and human rights in the Chittagong Hill Tracts, Bangladesh. Chittagong Hill Tracts Commission. Amsterdam: Organising Committee, Chittagong Hill Tracts Campaign, 1991. 127p. *International Work Group for Indigenous Affairs.*

2415 Negotiating rights: access to land in the cotton zone, Burkina Faso. Lacinan Paré. Stevenage: International Institute for Environment and Development, 2001. 28p. *ISBN: 1899825835. (Series:* Land tenure and resource access in West Africa).

2416 Population growth and customary land law: the case of Cordillera villages in the Philippines. Lorelei Crisologo-Mendoza; Dirk Van de Gaer. **Econ. Dev. Cult. Change** 49:3 4:2001 pp.631-658.

2417 Prégnance du droit coutumier. *[In French]*; [The significance of customary law]. Geneviève Bédoucha; Gianni Albergoni; Anie Montigny; Andre Gingrich; Pierre Bonte; Négib Bouderbala; Gerhard Lichtenthäler; Stefan Kohler; Alain Mahé. **Rural Stud.** 155-156 7-12:2001 pp.11-214. *Collection of 10 articles.*

2418 Producing possession: labour, law and land on a Brazilian agricultural frontier, 1920-1945. C. Brannstrom. **Pol. Geogr.** 20:7 9:2001 pp.859-884.

2419 Resettlement revisited: land reform results in resource-poor regions in Zimbabwe. A. Harts-Broekhuis; H. Huisman. **Geoforum** 32:3 8:2001 pp.285-298.

2420 Searching for livelihood security: land and mobility in Burkina Faso. Mark Breusers. **J. Dev. Stud.** 37:4 4:2001 pp.49-80.

2421 Selling the ancestors' land: a Hong Kong lineage adapts. Selina Ching Chan. **Mod. Chi.** 27:2 4:2001 pp.262-284.

2422 State lands and rural development in mandatory Palestine, 1920-1948. Warwick P.N. Tyler. Brighton: Sussex Academic Press, 2001. 260p. *ISBN: 1902210751.*

2423 La terre et le paysan. *[In French]*; [Land and peasant]. Emmanuel Le Roy Ladurie [Foreword]; Marc Léopold Benjamin Bloch; Etienne Bloch [Comp.]. Paris: Armand Colin, 1999. xxviii, 571p. *ISBN: 2200219784. Includes bibliographical references.*

2424 Tierra y relaciones de dependencia económica en Cuba. *[In Spanish]*; (Land and economic dependency relations in the Cuban economy.) Julio A. Díaz Vázquez. **Econ. Desar.** 126:1 1:2000 pp.95-117.

2425 Tribal land rights in central Morocco: a call for comparative research. Wolfgang Kraus. **Morocco** 2 1997 pp.16-32.

2426 'Wedded to the marshes': salt marshes and socio-economic differentiation in early Prince Edward Island. Matthew Hatvany. **Acadiensis** XXX:2 Spring:2001 pp.40-55.

2427 Women's land rights in the transition to individualized ownership: implications for tree-resource management in western Ghana. Agnes R. Quisumbing; Ellen Payongayong; J.B. Aidoo; Keijiro Otsuka. **Econ. Dev. Cult. Change** 50:1 10:2001 pp.157-181.

Production systems
Systèmes de production

2428 Anthropology of shellfish-gathering. Philippe Lacombe. **Dialect. Anthrop.** 25:2 2000 pp.161-187.

2429 Coastal resource use by camel pastoralists: a case study of gathering and fishing activities among the Beja in eastern Sudan. Hiroshi Nawata. **Nilo-Ethiop. St.** 7 2001 pp.23-43.

2430   Colonist farm income, off-farm work, cattle, and differentiation in Ecuador's northern Amazon. Laura L. Murphy. **Human. Org.** 60:1 Spring:2001 pp.67-79.

2431   The contexts of female hunting in Central Africa. Andrew J. Noss; Barry S. Hewlett. **Am. Anthrop.** 103:4 12:2001 pp.1024-1040.

2432   Coping strategies in an ethnic minority group: the Aeta of Mount Pinatubo. Stefan Seitz. **Disasters** 22:1 3:1998 pp.76-90.

2433   Deferred harvests: the transition from hunting to animal husbandry. Michael S. Alvard; Lawrence Kuznar. **Am. Anthrop.** 103:2 6:2001 pp.295-311.

2434   Diversity in income-generating activities for sedentarized pastoral women in northern Kenya. Immaculate Nduma; Patti Kristjanson; John McPeak. **Human. Org.** 60:4 Winter:2001 pp.319-325.

2435   Ecological mutualism in Navajo corrals: implications for Navajo environmental perceptions and human/plant coevolution. Lawrence A. Kuznar. **J. Anthr. Res.** 57:1 Spring:2001 pp.17-39.

2436   From beach seining to *sapyaw* fishing: innovation, competition, and conflict avoidance in a municipal fishery in central Philippines. Aloysius Ma.L. Cañete. **Phil. Q. Cult. Soc.** 28:2 6:2000 pp.158-223.

2437   La ganadería y el pastoreo actualmente y a principios de siglo en Valderejo (Álava). *[In Spanish]*; [Cattle raising and grazing now and at the beginning of the century in Valderejo (Álava)] *[Summary]*; *[Summary in French]*; *[Summary in Basque]*. Javier Ortiz Vadillo. **An. Eusko. Folk.** 42 2000 pp.71-98.

2438   Ganadería y pastoreo en Aoiz (Navarra). *[In Spanish]*; [Cattle raising and grazing in Aoiz (Navarre)] *[Summary]*; *[Summary in French]*; *[Summary in Basque]*. Maria Pilar Sáez De Albéniz; Teresa Leache. **An. Eusko. Folk.** 42 2000 pp.99-124.

2439   Gefährliches Gold und bitteres Geld. Zum Umgang mit einer außergewöhnlichen Ressource in Burkina Faso. *[In German]*; (Dangerous gold and bitter money. On the treatment of an extraordinary resource.) *[Summary]*; *[Summary in French]*; *[Summary in German]*. Katja Werthmann. **Af. Spec.** 36:3 3:2001 pp.363-381.

2440   A people in travail III: veteran *Muro-Ami* families in cooperatives. Harold Olofson; Farah de Jose; Bernie Cañizares. **Phil. Q. Cult. Soc.** 28:4 12:2000 pp.498-511.

2441   Perceptions of drudgery in agricultural and animal husbandry operations: a gender analysis from Haryana state, India. S. Thakur; S.K. Varma; P.A. Goldey. **J. Int. Dev.** 13:8 11:2001 pp.1165-1178.

2442   Pig men and women, big men and women: gender and production in the New Guinea Highlands. Paul Sillitoe. **Ethnology** XL:3 Summer:2001 pp.171-192.

2443   A question of breeding: zootechny and colonial attitudes toward the tropical environment in late nineteenth-century Philippines. Greg Bankoff. **J. Asian St.** 60:2 5:2001 pp.413-438.

2444   A reconstruction of Middle Preclassic Maya subsistence economy at Cahal Pech, Belize. Terry G. Powis; Norbert Stanchly; Christine D. White; Paul F. Healy; Jaime J. Awe; Fred Longstaffe. **Antiquity** 73:280 6·1999 pp.364-376.

2445   Régi magyar háziállatfajtáink. A genetikai sokféleség megőrzése. *[In Hungarian]*; (The ancient domestic animal breeds in Hungary: preservation of genetic diversity.) *[Summary]*. Imre Bodó. **Mag. Tud.** 46:5 2001 pp.535-555.

2446   Sahel pastoralists: opportunism, struggle, conflict and negotiation. A case study from eastern Niger. Brigitte Thébaud; Simon Batterbury. **Glo. Environ. Chan.** 11:1 4:2001 pp.69-78.

2447   The Samburu livestock trader in north-central Kenya. Shinya Konaka. **Nilo-Ethiop. St.** 7 2001 pp.63-79.

2448   Les savanes de la République Dominicaine et leur exploitation par le système «*hatos*». *[In French]*; [The savannahs of the Dominican Republic and their exploitation by the '*hatos*' system]; *[Summary in Spanish]*. R. Camara. **Cah. Outre-mer** 53:212 10-12:2000 pp.343-366.

2449   The social economy of sharing: resource allocation and modern hunter-gatherers. George Wenzel [Ed.]; Grete Hovelsrud-Broda [Ed.]; Nobuhiro Kishigami [Ed.]. Osaka: National

Museum of Ethnology, 2000. i, 219p. *Includes bibliographical references.* (*Series:* Senri ethnological studies - 53).

2450   What's in a pig? 'State', 'market' and process in private pig production and consumption in Romania. Sabina Stan. **Dialect. Anthrop.** 25:2 2000 pp.151-160.

2451   Wherever the waves carry us: historical development of a Visayan fisherfolk's livelihood strategies. Koki Seki. **Phil. Q. Cult. Soc.** 28:2 6:2000 pp.133-157.

2452   Women in small-scale aquaculture in north-west Bangladesh. Benoy Kumar Barman. **Gen. Tech. Dev.** 5:2 5-8:2001 pp.267-287.

Work
Travail

2453   Anthropologie ouvrière et enquêtes d'usine. *[In French]*; [Anthropology of work and factory research]. Sylvain Lazarus; Samia Moucharik; Anne Duhin; Athena Kassapi; Marianne Hérard; Delphine Corteel; Judith Hayem; Laure Pitti; Martin Kuhlmann; Michael Schumann; Pierre-Noël Giraud; Myriam Hidouci; Laurence Kundid. **Ethn. Fr.** XXXI:3 7-9:2001 pp.389-502. *Collection of 11 articles.*

2454   Attention dangers! Enquête sur le travail dans le nucléaire. *[In French]*; (Danger! An inquiry into working conditions in the nuclear industry.) *[Summary]*; *[Summary in German]*. Pierre Fournier. **Ethn. Fr.** XXXI:1 1-3:2001 pp.69-80.

2455   Balancing budgets on women's backs: a case study of Pakistan urban working women. Khadija Ali. **Pak. Ec. Soc. R.** XXXVIII:1 Summer:2000 pp.87-127.

2456   Border enforcement in daily life: Palestinian day laborers and entrepreneurs crossing the green line. Avram S. Bornstein. **Human. Org.** 60:3 Fall:2001 pp.298-307.

2457   Brèves remarques sur le travail comme vecteur de la citoyenneté. *[In French]*; [Some brief remarks on work as a carrier of citizenship] *[Summary]*. Jacques Hamel. **Can. R. Soc. A.** 38:1 2:2001 pp.1-18.

2458   Chômage, malchance et traitement social. *[In French]*; (The dole, tough luck, and social treatment.) *[Summary]*; *[Summary in German]*. Sophie Divay. **Ethn. Fr.** XXXI:1 1-3:2001 pp.153-160.

2459   Dependência da empregada: o espaço da exclusão. *[In Portuguese]*; [The dependent maid: the space of exclusion]. Leda Teles. **Bol. Mus. Par. Emílio Goeldi** 14:2 12:1998 pp.117-267.

2460   Free and unfree labor in Qing China: emigration and escape among the bannermen of northeast China, 1789-1909. Cameron Campbell; James Lee. **Hist. Fam.** 6:4 2001 pp.455-476.

2461   House work, and outside work. Muppala Ranganayakamma. Hyderabad: Sweet Home Publications, 1999. 95p. *Translated from the Telugu I.n.tipanī, bai.tipanī.*

2462   How everyday life became virtual: mundane work at the juncture of production and consumption. Nicola Green. **J. Cons. Cult.** 1:1 6:2001 pp.73-92.

2463   The limits of policy: rural children and work in the United States and New Zealand, 1870-1920. Pamela Riney-Kehrberg. **Hist. Fam.** 6:1 2001 pp.51-68.

2464   'Local girls' and 'lab boys': gender, skill and medical laboratories in Nova Scotia in the 1920s and 1930s. Peter L. Twohig. **Acadiensis** XXXI:1 Autumn:2001 pp.55-75.

2465   Un oficio a través de los siglos: bibliotecario. *[In Spanish]*; [Librarianship: a centuries old profession] *[Summary]*. José Luis Ramírez. **Rev. de Human.** 11 Autumn:2001 pp.221-234.

2466   The other breadwinners: mobilization of secondary wage earners in early twentieth-century Black families. Andrea G. Hunter. **Hist. Fam.** 6:1 2001 pp.69-94.

2467   A people in travail I: labor relations history of veteran *Muro-Ami* fisherfolk in the central Philippines. Harold Olofson; Bernie Cañizares; Farah de Jose. **Phil. Q. Cult. Soc.** 28:2 6:2000 pp.224-267.

2468   Performance motivation among employees of a wholesale company. Stephné Herselman. **S. Afr. J. Ethnol.** 24:1 2001 pp.1-10.

2469   Stakeholder participation, gender, and codes of conduct in South Africa. Stephanie Barrientos; Sharon McClenaghan; Liz Orton. **Develop. Pract.** 11:5 11:2001 pp.575-586.

2470   Towards gender balance: but will women physicians have an impact on medicine? E. Riska. **Soc. Sci. Med.** 52:2 1:2001 pp.179-188.

2471   Le travail et l'économique, pour un regard anthropologique. *[In French]*; (Labor and the economy: for an anthropological view.) *[Summary]*. Alexandra Bidet. **Sociol. Trav.** 43:2 4-6:2001 pp.215-234.

D: ETHNOGRAPHIC STUDIES OF PEOPLES AND COMMUNITIES
ÉTUDES ETHNOGRAPHIQUES DES PEUPLES ET DES COMMUNAUTÉS

2472   An Amazonian myth and its history. Peter Gow. Oxford: Oxford University Press, 2001. xiii, 338p. *ISBN: 0199241961, 0199241953. Includes bibliographical references and index.* (*Series:* Oxford studies in social and cultural anthropology).

2473   Bedouin society in the Sinai Peninsula. Masaki Horiuchi. **Senri Ethn. Stud.** 55 2001 pp.13-40.

2474   Dualism and hierarchy: processes of binary combination in Keo society. Gregory Forth. Oxford: Oxford University Press, 2001. xix, 341p. *ISBN: 0198234244. Includes bibliographical references and index.*

2475   Histoire des populations mahi. À propos de la controverse sur l'ethnonyme et le toponyme «Mahi». *[In French];* (A history of the Mahi populations: on the controversy about the 'Mahi' ethnonym and toponym.) *[Summary].* Sylvain C. Anignikin. **Cah. Ét. Afr.** XLI(2):162 2001 pp.243-266.

2476   Italiani: racconto etnografico. *[In Italian];* [An ethnography of Italians]. Gian Luigi Bravo. Rome: Meltemi, 2001. 287p. *ISBN: 8883530616. Includes bibliographical references.*

2477   Materialy po sovremennoi kul'ture i sotsial'no-ekonomicheskomu polozheniiu severnoi gruppy uil'ta. *[In Russian];* (Materials on the modern culture and socioeconomic status of the northern group of the Uilta.) *[Summary].* D.A. Funk; A.P. Zenko; L. Sillanpää. **Etnograf. Oboz.** 3 5-6:2000 pp.14-29.

2478   Mediterranean islands: a concept; *[Summary in Croatian].* A. Lopašić. **Coll. Antrop.** 25:1 6:2001 pp.363-370.

2479   The Ottoman peoples and the end of empire. Justin McCarthy. London: Arnold Publishing Ltd., 2001. 234p. *ISBN: 0340706570, 0340706562.* (*Series:* Historical endings).

2480   Russian culture. Margaret Mead; Geoffrey Gorer; John Rickman. New York, Oxford: Berghahn Books, 2001. xx, 324p. *ISBN: 1571812342, 157181230X. Includes bibliographical references and index. Volume 3. Institute for Intercultural Studies.* (*Series:* Margaret Mead, researching Western contemporary cultures).

2481   Tradition and society in Turkmenistan: gender, oral culture and song. Carole Blackwell. Richmond: Curzon Press, 2000. 288p. *ISBN: 0700713549.*

2482   Z problematyki przemian kultury polskiej w XX wieku. *[In Polish];* (On changes of Polish culture in the 20th century.) Dorota Skotarczak [Ed.]. Poznan: Instytut historii UAM, 2000. 295p. *ISBN: 8386650133.*

E.1: **Political structure and power**
Structure et pouvoir politique

2483   1984 assault on Amritsar — Sardar Khushwant Singh's protest in parliament. Sikh Review
[Ed.]. **Sikh Rev.** 49:6(570) 6:2001 pp.34-36.

2484   Administrative tradition and civil jurisdiction of the Cordoban *sāhib al-ahkām* (I).
Christian Müller. **Al-Qantara** XXI:1 2000 pp.57-84.

2485   The Akali and Dravidian movements: perspectives on federalism in India. N.
Muthumohan. **Sikh Rev.** 49:7(571) 7:2001 pp.52-55.

2486   An anthropology of the European Union: building, imagining and experiencing the new
Europe. Irène Bellier [Ed.]; Thomas M. Wilson [Ed.]. Oxford: Berg Publishers, 2000. x,
205p. *ISBN: 1859733298, 1859733247. Includes bibliographical references and index.*

2487   Being of 'one heart': power and politics among the Iraqw of Tanzania; *[Summary in
French].* Katherine A. Snyder. **Africa** 71:1 2001 pp.128-148.

2488   Brothers, chiefdoms, and empires: on Jan Jansen's *The Representation of Status in Mande.*
Stephen Bühnen. **Hist. Afr.** 23 1996 pp.111-120.

2489   The burden of history: obstacles to power sharing in Sri Lanka. Michael Roberts. **Contr. I.
Soc.** 35:1 1-4:2001 pp.65-96.

2490   Características negroafricanas del poder en Haití: una aproximación. *[In Spanish]*; [Black
African characteristics of power in Haiti: an approach]. Joan Gimeno Prats. **Stud. Afr.** 12
3:2001 pp.119-130.

2491   The Chadian Tubu: contemporary nomads who conquered a state; *[Summary in French].*
Robert Buijtenhuijs. **Africa** 71:1 2001 pp.149-170.

2492   Chinese-Philippine diplomatic relations 1946-1975. Shi-ching Hsiao. **Chin. Cult.** XL:2
6:1999 pp.73-102.

2493   La chute de la Dynastie des Sisse: considerations sur la dislocation de l'Empire du Ghana à
partir de l'histoire de Gao. *[In French]*; [The collapse of the Sisse dynasty: the collapse of
the Ghanian Empire and the history of Gao]. Dierk Lange. **Hist. Afr.** 23 1996 pp.155-178.

2494   The Circassian *qubba-s* of Abbas Avenue, Khartoum: governors and soldiers in 19th
century Sudan. Andrew McGregor. **Nord. J. Afr. St.** 10:1 2001 pp.28-40.

2495   Co-existence with Pakistan. Patwant Singh. **Sikh Rev.** 49:8(572) 8:2001 pp.61-66.

2496   Commentary and contestation: on violence and the truth of narration. Nina Glick Schiller;
Holger Henke; Peggy Antrobus; Nan Peacocke; Don Robotham. **Identities** 8:3 9:2001
pp.411-466. *Collection of 4 articles.*

2497   La désignation territoriale des quatre *spāhbed* de l'Empire sassanide d'après les sources
primaires sigillographiques. *[In French]*; [Territorial designation of the Sassanian Empire's
four *spāhbed* according to primary sigillographic sources]. R. Gyselen. **Stud. Iran.** 30:1
2001 pp.137-142.

2498   Deszendenz, politische Macht und das Verhältnis der Geschlechter auf Yap, Westkarolinen.
[In German]; [Descent, political power and gender relations in Yap, western Caroline
Islands]. Corinna Erckenbrecht. **Anthropos [St. Augustin]** 96:1 2001 pp.119-140.

2499   The dramaturgy of power and politics in post-colonial Kenya: a comparative re-reading of
'forms' in texts by Ngugi wa Thiongo and Francis Imbuga. G. Odera Outa. **Nord. J. Afr. St.**
10:3 2001 pp.344-365.

2500   Eddie, Brian, Jack and let's phone Rusty: is this the history of the communist party of
South Africa (1921-1950)? Mia Roth. **S. Afr. Hist. J.** 42 2000 pp.191-209.

2501   The emergence of the the the Taifa kingdom of Toledo. David J. Wasserstein. **Al-Qantara**
XXI:1 2000 pp.17-56.

2502   Enfants, jeunes et politiques. *[In French]*; [Children, youth and politics]. Filip De Boeck;
Alcinda Honwana; Tshikala K. Biaya; Ahmadou Kourouma; Jean Comaroff; John

Comaroff; Michel Cahen; Jean-Pierre Chrétien; Jean-Pierre Olivier de Sardan; Abdoua Elhadji Dagobi; Pierre-Joseph Laurent. **Pol. Afr.** 80 12:2000 pp.5-110. *Collection of 5 articles.*

2503   Envisioning power: ideologies of dominance and crisis. Stanley R. Barrett; Sean Stokholm; Jeanette Burke. **Am. Anthrop.** 103:2 6:2001 pp.468-480.

2504   Ethnic militancy and national stability in Nigeria: a case study of the Oodua People's Congress. R.T. Akinyele. **Afr. Affairs** 100:401 10:2001 pp.623-640.

2505   An ethnographic theory of democracy. Politics from the viewpoint of Ilhéus's Black movement (Bahia, Brazil). Marcio Goldman. **Ethnos** 66:2 2001 pp.157-180.

2506   Une évolution lente et des perspectives contrastées. *[In French]*; [Contrasting perspectives of a slow evolution]. Farid Benbouzid. **Cah. Orient** 63 2001 pp.39-52.

2507   *Faly aux vazaha*: Eugène Bastard, taboo, and Mahafale autarky in southwest Madagascar, 1899. Jeffrey C. Kaufmann. **Hist. Afr.** 26 1999 pp.129-156.

2508   Firearms and political power: the military decline of the Turkana of Kenya 1900-2000. Nene Mburu. **Nord. J. Afr. St.** 10:2 2001 pp.148-162.

2509   Herrschaftsgeschichte und Konstruktion des Raums. *[In German]*; [Political order and the construction of space] *[Summary]*. Andreas Dafinger. **Z. Ethn.** 125:2 2000 pp.265-280.

2510   Historical account or discourse on identity? A reexamination of Fulbe hegemony and autochthonous submission in Banyo. Quentin Gausset. **Hist. Afr.** 25 1998 pp.93-110.

2511   Indian constitution in a federal perspective. Jasbir Singh Ahluwalia. **Sikh Rev.** 49:8(572) 8:2001 pp.57-60.

2512   Der Jäger, die Ziegen und der Erdschrein. Politik mit oralen Traditionen zur Siedlungsgeschichte in Nordghana. *[In German]*; [The hunter, the goats and the shrine: politics and oral narratives of settlement histories in northern Ghana] *[Summary]*. Carola Lentz. **Z. Ethn.** 125:2 2000 pp.281-304.

2513   Kinship and corruption in contemporary Nigeria. Daniel Jordan Smith. **Ethnos** 66:3 2001 pp.344-364.

2514   La *Lega Nord*: entre volonté de subversion et désir de légitimité. *[In French]*; (The *Lega Nord*: between the will to subvert and the desire for legitimacy.) *[Summary]*; [Summary in German]. Lynda Dematteo. **Ethn. Fr.** XXXI:1 1-3:2001 pp.143-152.

2515   Legacy of Longowal: an appraisal. Prithipal Singh Kapur. **Sikh Rev.** 49:7(571) 7:2001 pp.56-57.

2516   Living in the era of liquid modernity. Zygmunt Bauman. **Cam. Anthrop.** 22:2 2000-2001 pp.1-19.

2517   Maîtres de la pluie et chefs de terre. Ordres territoriaux et acteurs politiques dans la région Nord-Samo (Burkina Faso). *[In French]*; [Masters of the rain and lords of the land. Territorial order and political actors in the north Samo region, Burkina Faso]. Andrea Reikat. **Anthropos [St. Augustin]** 95:2 2000 pp.371-384.

2518   Making democracy count: opinion polls and market surveys in the Chilean political transition. Julia Paley. **Cult. Anthro.** 16:2 5:2001 pp.135-164.

2519   Le manuel administratif d'Ujīr Simha Thāpā: esquisse d'un code népalais du début du XIXe siècle. *[In French]*; [The administrative textbook of Ujīr Simha Thāpā: an outline of a Nepalese code at the start of the 19th century]. Jean Fezas. **Bull. Ét. Indien.** 17-18 1999-2000 pp.181-294.

2520   Militancy in Punjab: a viewpoint. Dipankar Gupta. **Sikh Rev.** 49:7(571) 7:2001 pp.40-41.

2521   Military examinations in late Chosôn: elite substratification and non-elite accommodation. Eugene Y. Park. **Kor. Stud.** 25:1 2001 pp.1-50.

2522   The nation in heterogeneous time. Partha Chatterjee. **Indian Ec. Soc. His. R.** XXXVIII:4 10-12:2001 pp.399-418.

2523   Nation-building in South Africa — exploring the ethnic landscape; *[Summary in Afrikaans]*. F.C. de Beer. **S. Afr. J. Ethnol.** 24:4 2001 pp.105-112.

2524   Nunavut: the still small voice of indigenous governance. P. Jull. **Indig. Aff.** 3 2001 pp.42-51.

2525   Of condoms, biculturalism, and political correctness. The Maori renaissance and cultural politics in New Zealand. Erich Kolig. **Paideuma** 46 2000 pp.231-252.

2526   On the Qusiqul army and the Tamaci army. Qu Dafeng. **Cent. Asia. J.** 45:2 2001 pp.266-272.
2527   The origin of state societies in South America. Charles Stanish. **Ann. R. Anthr.** 30 2001 pp.41-180.
2528   Perpetuating Mughal imperial authority in the region of Orissa. Sashikanta Dash. **Oris. Hist. R. J.** XLV:1-4 2000 pp.1-5.
2529   Politics and language planning in Sierra Leone. David J. Francis; Mohamed C. Kamanda. **Afr. Stud.** 60:2 12:2001 pp.225-244.
2530   Politics with style: identity formation in pre-Hispanic southeastern Mesoamerica. Edward M. Schortman; Patricia A. Urban; Marne Ausec. **Am. Anthrop.** 103:2 6:2001 pp.312-330.
2531   Polities and political discourse: was Mande already a segmentary society in the Middle Ages? Jan Jansen. **Hist. Afr.** 23 1996 pp.121-128.
2532   Pouvoirs sorciers. *[In French]*; [Witchcraft and power]. Florence Bernault; Joseph Tonda; Peter Geschiere; Michael G. Schatzberg; Stephen Ellis; Luise White; Jane I. Guyer; Murray Last; Catherine Boudet. **Pol. Afr.** 79 10:2000 pp.5-164. *Collection of 9 articles.*
2533   Power in America: nationhood and ethnicity. Eileen Boris; Robert Garson; Rocío G. Davis; Priscilla Roberts; Bridget Kevane; Victor J. Viser. **J. Am. Stud.** 35:1 4:2001 pp.1-109. *Collection of 6 articles.*
2534   The prophet of two revolutions. Victor V. Sumsky. **Phil. Stud.** 49:2 2001 pp.236-254.
2535   Reproducing culture and society: women and the politics of gender, age, and social rank in Walāta; *[Summary in French]*. Timothy Cleaveland. **Can. J. Afr. St.** 34:2 2000 pp.189-217.
2536   The rhetoric of justice: strategies of reconciliation and revenge in the restoration of Athenian democracy in 403 BC; *[Summary in French]*; *[Summary in German]*. David Cohen. **Eur. J. Soc.** XLII:2 2001 pp.335-356.
2537   Right and Left as political categories. An exercise in 'not-so-primitive' classification. H.F. Bienfait; W.E.A. van Beek. **Anthropos [St. Augustin]** 96:1 2001 pp.169-178.
2538   Samoopredelenie narodov: analiz ideino-politicheskikh podkhodov. *[In Russian]*; (Self-determination of peoples: an analysis of ideological and political approaches.) I.M. Sampiev; S.V. Sokolovskii [Comments by]. **Etnograf. Oboz.** 3 5-6:2001 pp.61-76.
2539   Secularism: personal values and professional evaluations. Charles Stewart; João De Pina-Cabral; Lale Yalçin-Heckmann; David N. Gellner; Bruce Kapferer. **Soc. Anthrop.** 9:3 10:2001 pp.325-344. *Collection of 5 articles.*
2540   Self-government in Greenland. J. Dahl. **Indig. Aff.** 3 2001 pp.36-41.
2541   The share of the Muslim Cutchi Khatri community in the Pakistan movement. Khatri Ismat Ali Patel. **J. Pak. Hist. Soc.** XLVIII:4 10-12:2000 pp.81-84.
2542   A Sikh regiment in the British army? Kim Sengupta. **Sikh Rev.** 49:9(573) 9:2001 p.43.
2543   The Sikhs in Indian polity. Rajinder Singh Vidyarthi. **Sikh Rev.** 49:9(573) 9:2001 pp.31-33.
2544   Social justice as religious responsibility in Near Eastern religions: historic ideal and ideological illusion. Philip J. Nel. **J. N.W. Sem. Lang.** 26:2 2000 pp.143-154.
2545   The star in the East: South African socialist expectations and responses to the outbreak of the Russian Revolution. W.P. Visser. **S. Afr. Hist. J.** 44 2001 pp.40-71.
2546   *Strīrājya*: Indian accounts of kingdoms of women. William L. Smith. **Stud. Orient.** 94 2001 pp.465-478.
2547   Tamactún-Acalán: interpretación de una hegemonía política maya de los siglos XIV-XVI. *[In Spanish]*; [Tamatún-Acalán: interpretation of a Mayan political hegemony from the 14th 16th centuries]. Andrés Ciudad Ruiz; Alfonso Lacadena García-Gallo. **J. Soc. Amér.** 87 2001 pp.9-38.
2548   'They made the freedom for themselves': popular interpretations of post-communist discourse in the Czech Republic. Revan Schendler. **Oral Hist.** 29:2 Autumn:2001 pp.73-82.
2549   Thinking the unthinkable: meditations on the events of 11.09.2001. Glenn Bowman. **Anthr. Today** 17:6 12:2001 pp.16-23.

2550 Tobia, Sanballat und die Persische Provinz Juda. *[In German]*; [Tobia, Sanballat and the Persian province of Judah] *[Summary]*. Siegfried Mittmann. **J. N.W. Sem. Lang.** 26:2 2000 pp.1-50.

2551 A tomb for Columbus in Santo Domingo. Political cosmology, population and racial frontiers; *[Summary in French]*; *[Summary in German]*; *[Summary in Spanish]*. Christian Krohn-Hansen. **Soc. Anthrop.** 9:2 6:2001 pp.165-192.

2552 Tribalisme et pouvoirs. *[In French]*; [Tribalism and powers]. Hosham Dawod. **Pensée** 325 1-3:2001 pp.5-8.

2553 «Tribu» et «état» au Maroc du XXe siècle: quelques réflexions. *[In French]*; [Some reflections on 'tribe' and 'state' in 20th century Morocco] *[Summary]*. Kenneth Brown. **Pensée** 325 1-3:2001 pp.35-42.

2554 Tribus et pouvoirs dans le monde arabe et ses périphéries. *[In French]*; [Tribes and powers in and around the Arab world] *[Summary]*. Pierre Bonte. **Pensée** 325 1-3:2001 pp.43-66.

2555 The use and abuse of power: multiple perspectives in the causes of corruption. John A. Bargh [Ed.]; Annette Y. Lee-Chai [Ed.]. Hove: Psychology Press, 2001. xiv, 312p. *ISBN: 1841690228.*

2556 A view from a village: popular political culture in sixteenth-century England. Judy Ann Ford. **J. Pop. Cult.** 34:2 Fall:2000 pp.1-20.

2557 Villagers into national revolutionaries? Shifting 'communities' in a period of revolutionary mobilization in the Philippines. Rosanne Rutten. **Bijdragen** 157:3 2001 pp.629-660.

2558 Violence et clientélisme comme moyens de gouvernement: le cas de Madagascar 1975-2000. *[In French]*; [Violence and clientelism as a means of government: the case of Madagascar, 1975-2000]. Manassé Esoavelomandroso. **Stud. Afr.** 12 3:2001 pp.95-104.

2559 Westminster democracy: a comparison of small island states varieties in the Pacific and the Caribbean. Dag Anckar. **Pac. Stud.** 23:3-4 9-12:2000 pp.57-76.

Political leadership
Leadership politique

2560 'Beer used to belong to older men': drink and authority among the Nyakusa of Tanzania; *[Summary in French]*. Justin Willis. **Africa** 71:3 2001 pp.373-390.

2561 Biros, books and big-men: literacy and the transformation of leadership in Simbu, Papua New Guinea. Eamonn McKeown. **Oceania** 72:2 12:2001 pp.105-116.

2562 Broken fingers: classic Maya scribe capture and polity consolidation. Kevin J. Johnston. **Antiquity** 75:288 6:2001 pp.373-381.

2563 Captain Cook and the roots of precedence in Tonga: 'leading' and 'following' as naturalised concepts. Arne Aleksej Perminow. **Hist. Anthrop.** 12:3 2001 pp.289-314.

2564 Chiefs for the nation: containing ethnonationalism and bridging the ethnic divide in Fiji. Robert Norton. **Pac. Stud.** 22:1 3:1999 pp.21-50.

2565 L'État en Afrique face à la chefferie: le cas du Togo. *[In French]*; [The African state and chiefdom: the case of Togo]. Emile Adriaan Benvenuto van Rouveroy van Nieuwaal. Paris: Karthala, 2000. 332p. *ISBN: 2845860315. Includes bibliographical references (p. [297]-316) and indexes.*

2566 The 'ethnic origin' of Iran's Safawid dynasty (907-1145/1501-1722): reflections on selected prevailing views and requirements for further research. Muhammad Ismail Marcinkowski. **J. Pak. Hist. Soc.** XLIX:2 4-6:2001 pp.5-20.

2567 (The failure of the Hawwārite state formation under Abū Yazīd.) *[Summary]*; *[Text in Japanese]*. Fukuzo Amabe. **J. Hum. Nat. Sci.** 110 9:2000 pp.3-24.

2568 Formes et fonctions du pouvoir politique. A propos des concepts de tribu, ethnie et état. *[In French]*; (Forms and functions of political power: on the concepts of tribe, ethnic group and state.) *[Summary]*. Maurice Godelier. **Pensée** 325 1-3:2001 pp.9-20.

2569 The genre of women leaders in local bodies: experience from Tamil Nadu. G. Palanithurai. **Indian J. Publ. Admin.** XLVII:1 1-3:2001 pp.38-50.

2570   Human rights in the Gambela national state, Ethiopia. N.A. Ochalla. **Indig. Aff.** 2 2001 pp.48-53.

2571   Inside, outside, and inside out masks, rulers, and gender among the Dii and their neighbors. Jean-Claude Muller. **Afr. Arts** XXXIV:1 Spring:1999 pp.58-71.

2572   Intellectual aspects of strong kingship in the late nineteenth century. Attachak Sattayanurak. **J. Siam Soc.** 88:1-2 2000 pp.72-95.

2573   The Jewish officials of Willemsoord and Veenhuizen, 1818-1890. Iet Erdtsieck. **St. Ros.** 35:1 2001 pp.23-47.

2574   King Chongjo: Confucianism, enlightenment, and absolute rule. Tae-Jin Yi. **Korea J.** 40:4 Winter:2000 pp.168-201.

2575   Kings and commerce on an agrarian frontier: Kālketu's story in Mukunda's *Candīmangal*. David L. Curley. **Indian Ec. Soc. His. R.** XXXVIII:3 7-9:2001 pp.299-324.

2576   The Kwajalein atoll and the new arms race. The US anti-ballistic weapons system and consequences for the Marshall Islands of the Pacific. PCRC. **Indig. Aff.** 2 2001 pp.38-43.

2577   Militarization and the Chittagong hill tracts. Chandra Roy. **Indig. Aff.** 2 2001 pp.14-19.

2578   Militarization in the Cordillera region, the Philippines. J. Carling; B. Solang. **Indig. Aff.** 2 2001 pp.20-25.

2579   Le pouvoir et l'interdit: royauté et religion en Afrique noire: essais d'ethnologie comparative. *[In French]*; [Power and the forbidden: royalty and religion in Black Africa - essays on comparative ethnology]. Alfred Adler. Paris: Albin Michel, 2000. 334p. *ISBN: 2226116648. Includes bibliographical references (p. [315]-324) and index.*

2580   Prevalence of powerful chief ministers in southern Sung China, 1127-1279 A.D. Gong Wei Ai. **Chin. Cult.** XL:2 6:1999 pp.103-114.

2581   Social problems and the active use of petitions during the reign of King Chongjo. Sang-kwon Han. **Korea J.** 40:4 Winter:2000 pp.227-246.

2582   Stories of the voiceless. A. Longchari. **Indig. Aff.** 2 2001 pp.8-13.

2583   Violence and social life in Colombia. Myriam Jimeno. **Crit. Anthr.** 21:3 9:2001 pp.221-246.

2584   The Yorùbá royal bards: their work and relevance in the society. Akintunde Akinyemi. **Nord. J. Afr. St.** 10:1 2001 pp.98-106.

E.2:   **Social structure**
          Structure sociale

E.2.1:   **Social organization and social groups**
          Organisation sociale et groupements sociaux

2585   The assessment of the analytic group treatment efficiency according to Yalom's classification; *[Summary in Croatian]*. M. Vlastelica; I. Urlić; S. Pavlović. **Coll. Antrop.** 25:1 6:2001 pp.227-238.

2586   La contestation chez les Toubou du Sahara central. *[In French]*; [Protest among the Tubu in the central Sahara]. Catherine Baroin. **Rural Stud.** :157-158 1-6:2001 pp.159-172.

2587   Co-opting justice: transformation of a multiracial environmental coalition in southern Alabama. Mark Moberg. **Human. Org.** 60:2 Summer:2001 pp.166-177.

2588   Cultural transmission and the diffusion of innovations: adoption dynamics indicate that biased cultural transmission is the predominate force in behavioral change. Joseph Henrich. **Am. Anthrop.** 103:4 12:2001 pp.992-1013.

2589   The evolution of prestige: freely conferred deference as a mechanism for enhancing the benefits of cultural transmission. Joseph Henrich; Francisco J. Gil-White. **Evol. Hum. Behav.** 22:3 5:2001 pp.165-196.

2590   Expressions of inequality: settlement patterns, economy and social organization in the southwest Iberian Bronze Age (c.1700-1100 BC). Leonardo García Sanjuán. **Antiquity** 73:280 6:1999 pp.337-351.

2591   A feminist critique of recent archaeological theories and explanations of the rise of state-level societies. Carol Jane Key; J. Jefferson MacKinnon. **Dialect. Anthrop.** 25:2 2000 pp.109-121.

2592   A forgotten people: the Ati community of Aklan. Karabi Baruah. **Phil. Q. Cult. Soc.** 28:3 9:2000 pp.301-316.

2593   From regional relations to ethnic groups? On the transformation of value relations to property claims in the Kula ring of Papua New Guinea. Frederick H. Damon. **Asia Pacific J. Anthr.** 1:2 10:2000 pp.49-72.

2594   House and hierarchy: politics and domestic space in northern Ghana; *[Summary in French]*. Susan Drucker-Brown. **J. Royal Anth. Inst.** 7:4 12:2001 pp.669-686.

2595   L'immoralité fondatrice. Bien commun et expression de l'intérêt individuel chez les Winye (Burkina Faso). *[In French]*; (Immorality at the foundations: common and individual interests among the Winye (Burkina Faso).) *[Summary]*. Jean-Pierre Jacob. **Cah. Ét. Afr.** XLI(2):162 2001 pp.315-332.

2596   Inequality. Charles Tilly; Keith Hart; Caroline Humphrey; Katherine Verdery. **Anth. Th.** 1:3 9:2001 pp.299-392. *Collection of 5 articles.*

2597   The Inka conical clan. David Jenkins. **J. Anthr. Res.** 57:2 Summer:2001 pp.167-195.

2598   Introduced writing and Christianity: differential access to religious knowledge among the Asabano. Roger Ivar Lohmann. **Ethnology** XL:2 Spring:2001 pp.93-111.

2599   Kartki z dziejów prawosławnej parafii św. Aleksandry w Stanisławowie koło Modlina. *[In Polish]*; (Some pages from the history of the St. Alexandra Russian Orthodox parish in Stanisławów near Modlin.) *[Summary]*. Andrzej Woźniak. **Etn. Polska** XLV:1-2 2001 pp.183-194.

2600   Keepers of the land: ideology and identities in the Scottish rural elite. Robert Stewart; Frank Bechhofer; David McCrone; Richard Kiely. **Identities** 8:3 9:2001 pp.381-410.

2601   Kultura w społeczności lokalnej - Podmiotowość odzyskana. *[In Polish]*; (Culture in local society: subjectivity regained.) *[Summary]*. Izabella Bukraba-Rylska. Warsaw: Instytut Rozwoju Wsi i Rolnictwa PAN, 2000. 252p. *ISBN: 8385369473.*

2602   La *maison* de Lévi-Strauss y la casa grande Wixarika. *[In Spanish]*; (Lévi-Strauss' *maison* and the Wixarika 'Great Houses'.) *[Summary]*; *[Summary in French]*. Johannes Neurath. **J. Soc. Amér.** 86 2000 pp.113-128.

2603   Multiple hierarchies and the duplex nature of groups; *[Summary in French]*. Frans J. Schryer. **J. Royal Anth. Inst.** 7:4 12:2001 pp.705-722.

2604   Personhood and social relations in the British Neolithic with a study from the Isle of Man. Chris Fowler. **J. Mat. Cult.** 6:2 7:2001 pp.137-164.

2605   Prophets and profits: gendered and generational visions of wealth and value in Senegalese Murid households. Beth Anne Buggenhagen. **J. Relig. Afr.** XXXI:4 2001 pp.373-401.

2606   Psychodynamics and regression of social groups; *[Summary in Croatian]*. Ž. Vukšić-Mihaljević; N. Mandić. **Coll. Antrop.** 25:1 6:2001 pp.213-226.

2607   Reciprocal work bees and the meaning of neighbourhood. Catharine Anne Wilson. **Can. Hist. R.** 82:3 9:2001 pp.431-464.

2608   The representation of status in Mande: did the Mali Empire still exist in the nineteenth century? Jan Jansen. **Hist. Afr.** 23 1996 pp.87-110.

2609   The social mobility of the Haratine and the re-working of Bourdieu's *Habitus* on the Saharan frontier, Morocco. Hsain Ilahiane. **Am. Anthrop.** 103:2 6:2001 pp.380-394.

2610   Socio-political characteristics of pastoral nomadism: flexibility among the Bodi (*mela-me'en*) in southwest Ethiopia. Katsuyoshi Fukui. **Nilo-Ethiop. St.** 7 2001 pp.1-21.

2611   The ties that bind: social networks of men and women in a Kipsigis community of Kenya. Sara Harkness; Charles M. Super. **Ethos** 29:3 9:2001 pp.357-370.

2612   *Trifunctionalia redivivia*: a note on some Greek possibilities. Dean Miller. **J. Indo-Eur. S.** 29:1-2 Spring-Summer:2001 pp.173-184.

2613   La vie à pas contés: génération, âge et société dans les hautes terres du Kénya (Meru Tigania-Igembe). *[In French]*; [A life not told: generation, age and society in the Kenyan highlands (Meru Tigania-Igembe)]. Anne-Marie Peatrik. Nanterre: Société D'ethnologie,

1999. 571p. *ISBN: 2901161596. Includes bibliographical references (p. 525-543) and index.*

Classes and castes
Classes et castes

2614 Anti-reservation protests and the Uttarakhand pro-autonomy movement: caste and regional identities in the Indian Himalayas. Joanne Moller. **S. Asia R.** 20:2 Spring:2000 pp.147-170.

2615 Beware of charitable souls: contagion, roguish ghosts and the poison(s) of Hindu alms; *[Summary in French]*. Jeffrey G. Snodgrass. **J. Royal Anth. Inst.** 7:4 12:2001 pp.687-704.

2616 Captives, kin, and slaves in Xiao Liangshan. Ann Maxwell Hill. **J. Asian St.** 60:4 11:2001 pp.1033-1050.

2617 Caste and clientage in an eighteenth-century Quebec convent. Jan Noel. **Can. Hist. R.** 82:3 9:2001 pp.465-490.

2618 Explorations of class and consciousness in the U.S. E. Paul Durrenberger. **J. Anthr. Res.** 57:1 Spring:2001 pp.41-60.

2619 The fall of the Bardados planter class: an interpretation of the 1980s crisis in the Barbados sugar industry. Robert Goddard. **Agr. Hist.** 75:3 Summer:2001 pp.329-351.

2620 Income status of Scheduled Castes in rural Uttar Pradesh. Gurupada Chakrabarty. **Ind. J. Eco.** LXXXI:322 1:2001 pp.361-378.

2621 Indian men, Afro-Creole women: 'casting' doubt on interracial sexual relationships in the late nineteenth-century Caribbean. Audra A. Diptee. **Imm. Minor.** 19:3 11:2000 pp.1-24.

2622 Nanny/mammy: comparing Lady Gregory and Jessie Fauset. Anthony Hale. **Cult. St.** 15:1 1:2001 pp.161-172.

2623 The rise and fall of *Varna-Vyavastha*. S.S. Gupta. **Indian J. Soc. W.** 62:2 4:2001 pp.169-179.

2624 Rūparām's *Dharma mangal*: an epic of the low castes? France Bhattacharya. **Arch. Orient.** 68:3 8:2000 pp.359-386.

2625 Samurai status, class and bureaucracy: a historiographical essay. Douglas R. Howland. **J. Asian St.** 60:2 5:2001 pp.353-380.

2626 Toward a balanced approach to the study of equality. Philip Carl Salzman. **Curr. Anthr.** 42:2 4:2001 pp.281-284.

2627 Untouchables in India's civil/uncivil democracy. A review article. Owen Lynch. **Ethnos** 66:2 2001 pp.259-268.

E.2.2: **Family and kinship systems**
Systèmes familiaux et de parenté

2628 Affinités électives et parenté arabe. *[In French]*; (Elective affinities and Arab kinship.) Édouard Conte. **Rural Stud.** :157-158 1-6:2001 pp.65-94.

2629 'An epidemic of runaway wives': discourses by Dani men on sex and marriage in highlands Irian Jaya, Indonesia. Leslie Butt. **Crossroads** 15:1 2001 pp.55-88.

2630 Changing contours of kinship: the impacts of social and economic development on kinship organization in the South Pacific. Cluny MacPherson. **Pac. Stud.** 22:2 6:1999 pp.71-96.

2631 Changing patterns of commitment to island homelands: a case study of Western Samoa. Cluny MacPherson. **Pac. Stud.** 17:3 9:1994 pp.83-116.

2632 Charged artifacts and the detonation of liminality. Teddy-bear diplomacy in the newborn incubator machine. Kyra Marie Landzelius. **J. Mat. Cult.** 6:3 11:2001 pp.323-344.

2633 The circulation of children through households in Yap and Kosrae. Michael L. Burton; Karen L. Nero; James A. Egan. **Ethos** 29:3 9:2001 pp.329-356.

2634 Correlations between frequencies of kin. Thomas Pullum; Douglas Wolf. **Demography** 28:3 8:1991 pp.391-410.

2635   Cultural narratives, violence, and mother-son loyalty: an exploration into Gusii personification of evil. Justus M. Ogembo. **Ethos** 29:1 3:2001 pp.3-29.

2636   The dynamics of household structure in the event of the father's death: Québec City in the 18th century. Jacques Légaré; Jean-François Naud. **Hist. Fam.** 6:4 2001 pp.519-530.

2637   Economics and fertility: changing family structure among Chamorros on the island of Guam. Ann M. Pobutsky. **Hist. Fam.** 6:1 2001 pp.95-123.

2638   The evolution of Dravidian kinship systems in Oceania: linguistic evidence; *[Summary in French]*. Per Hage. **J. Royal Anth. Inst.** 7:3 9:2001 pp.487-508.

2639   The expansion of the nuclear family unit in Great Britain between 1910 and 1920. Magali Gente. **Hist. Fam.** 6:1 2001 pp.125-142.

2640   Factors affecting unmet need for contraception. M. Kabir; Ubaidur Rob. **Asian Prof.** 29:2 4:2001 pp.147-158.

2641   The faded bond: calligraphesis and kinship in Abdelwahab Meddeb's *Talismano*. Dina Al-Kassim. **Publ. Cult.** 13:1 Winter:2001 pp.113-138.

2642   Family archives and the social use of space in old Babylonian houses at Ur. P. Brusasco. **Mesopotamia** XXXIV-XXXV 1999-2000 pp.1-174.

2643   (The family argument examined through the tomb.); *[Text in Japanese]*. Haruyo Inoue. Tokyo: Heibon-sha, 2000. 222p.

2644   Family enterprises and family life. Tamara K. Hareven; Andrejs Plakans; Ulrich Pfister; Antoinette Fauve-Chamoux; Josef Ehmer; Juanjo Romero-Marin; Tom Ericsson; Michael Blim; Rae Lesser Blumberg. **Hist. Fam.** 6:2 2001 pp.143-299. *Collection of 8 articles.*

2645   Gender and age differences in inheritance patterns. Why men leave more to their spouses and women more to their children: an experimental analysis. Bernd Bossong. **Hum. Nature** 12:2 2001 pp.107-122.

2646   Genealogical structuring of a population; *[Summary in Croatian]*. M. Kujundžić Tiljak; J. Kern; D. Ivanković; H. Tiljak; S. Vuletić. **Coll. Antrop.** 25:1 6:2001 pp.127-140.

2647   A Greek island cosmos: kinship and community on Meganisi. Roger Just. Oxford: James Currey, 2000. xi, 276p. *ISBN: 0852552688, 085255267X. (Series: World anthropology).*

2648   Growing up alone. Barbara Prynn. **Oral Hist.** 29:2 Autumn:2001 pp.62-72.

2649   Hawaiki: ancestral Polynesia - an essay in historical anthropology. Patrick Vinton Kirch; Roger Curtis Green. New York: Cambridge University Press, 2001. 375p. *ISBN: 052178879X, 0521783097. Includes bibliographical references.*

2650   Home alone: the effects of out-migration on Niuean elders' living arrangements and social supports. Judith C. Barker. **Pac. Stud.** 17:3 9:1994 pp.41-82.

2651   Hunting and nuclear families: some lessons from the Hadza about men's work. K. Hawkes; J.F. O'Connell; N.G. Blurton Jones. **Curr. Anthr.** 42:5 12:2001 pp.681-710.

2652   Hybrid identities: the Pomak community of Breznitza (southwest Bulgaria) in search of genealogy; *[Summary in German]*; *[Summary in French]*. Elka Agoston-Nikolova. **Fabula** 42:1-2 2001 pp.110-116.

2653   Imjjat: genesis of a Rifian lineage, genesis of a Rifian vendetta. David M. Hart. **Morocco** 2 1997 pp.33-54.

2654   The impact of grandparental proximity on maternal childcare in China. F. Chen; S.E. Short; B. Entwisle. **Pop. Res. Pol. R.** 19:6 12:2000 pp.571-590.

2655   Intergenerational relationships in rural areas. G. Clare Wenger; Thomas Scharf; Vanessa Burholt; Dena Shenk; Sally Keeling; Anitha Kumari Bhat; Raj Dhruvarajan; I.N. Keasberry. **Age. Soc.** 21:5 9:2001 pp.537-665. *Collection of 6 articles.*

2656   Kavkazskaia zhenshchina: mirovozzrencheskie predposylki obshchestvennogo statusa. *[In Russian]*; (Caucasian women: ideological prerequisites of social status.) *[Summary]*. Iu.Iu. Karpov. **Etnograf. Oboz.** 4 7-8:2000 pp.22-31.

2657   The kin in the gene: the medicalization of family and kinship in American society. Kaja Finkler; Janet Dolgin [Comments by]; Sarah Franklin [Comments by]; Hugh Gusterson [Comments by]; Norman M. Hadler [Comments by]; James P. Evans [Comments by]; Marit Melhuus [Comments by]; Dorothy Nelkin [Comments by]; Martin Richards [Comments by]; Lisbeth Sachs [Comments by]; Kaja Finkler [Comments by]. **Curr. Anthr.** 42:2 4:2001 pp.235-264.

2658   Kinship. David B. Kronenfeld; Per Hage; F.K. Lehman; Dwight W. Read; Thomas R. Trautmann. **Anth. Th.** 1:2 6:2001 pp.147-287. *Collection of 6 articles.*

2659   Kinship and corruption in contemporary Nigeria. Daniel Jordan Smith. **Ethnos** 66:3 2001 pp.344-364.

2660   Kinship ties of Mexican migrant women on the United States/Mexico border. Elena Bastida. **J. Comp. Fam. Stud.** XXXII:4 Autumn:2001 pp.549-570.

2661   *La familia*: methodological issues in the assessment of perinatal social support for *mexicanas* living in the United States. Lauren Clark. **Soc. Sci. Med.** 53:10 11:2001 pp.1303-1320.

2662   Le lien de parenté dans les jeunes générations suisses: lignées, structure et fonctions. *[In French]*; (Kinship relationships in the young Swiss generations: lineage, structure and function.) *[Summary]*; *[Summary in Spanish]*. R. Hammer; C. Burton-Jeangros; J. Kellerhals. **Population** 56:4 7-8:2001 pp.515-538.

2663   La mafia d'un village sicilien. *[In French]*; (The Mafia in a Sicilian village.) *[Summary]*; *[Summary in German]*. Anton Blok. **Ethn. Fr.** XXXI:1 1-3:2001 pp.61-67.

2664   Mahallah and kinship relations. A study on residential communal commitment structures in Central Asia of the 19th century. Paul Georg Geiss. **C. Asian Sur.** 20:1 3:2001 pp.97-106.

2665   La *maison* de Lévi-Strauss y la casa grande Wixarika. *[In Spanish]*; (Lévi-Strauss' *maison* and the Wixarika 'Great Houses'.) *[Summary]*; *[Summary in French]*. Johannes Neurath. **J. Soc. Amér.** 86 2000 pp.113-128.

2666   Le mariage qui dérange. Redéfinitions de l'identité nationale basque. *[In French]*; [The disturbing marriage: redifining the Basque national identity] *[Summary]*; *[Summary in German]*. Enric Porqueres Gené. **Ethn. Fr.** XXXI:3 7-9:2001 pp.527-536.

2667   The marking of sex distinctions in Polynesian kinship terminologies. Per Hage; Jeff Marck. **Oceanic Ling.** 40:1 6:2001 pp.156-166.

2668   Mothers, communities and the scale of difference. Stuart C. Aitken. **Soc. Cult. Geog.** 1:1 9:2000 pp.65-82.

2669   "Nisu dali gospodaru 'z ruk...". Starost u prigorskim i zagorskim selima između dva svjetska rata. *[In Croatian]*; ('They wouldn't let it out of the master's hand...'. Seniority in the Prigorje and Zagorje villages between the world wars.) Suzana Leček. **Etnoloska** 23:30 2000 pp.25-48.

2670   Oenpelli Kunwinjku kinship terminologies and marriage practices. Mark Harvey. **Oceania** 72:2 12:2001 pp.117-146.

2671   Of ships and saints: history, memory, and place in the making of *moreno* Mexican identity. Laura A. Lewis. **Cult. Anthro.** 16:1 2:2001 pp.62-82.

2672   On personhood: an anthropological perspective from Africa. John L. Comaroff; Jean Comaroff. **Soc. Ident.** 7:2 6:2001 pp.267-284.

2673   On the role of families and kinship networks in pre-industrial agricultural societies: an analysis of the 1698 Slavonian census. H.P. Kohler; E.A. Hammel. **J. Pop. Ec.** 14:1 2001 pp.21-50

2674   Professional constructions of family and kinship in medical genetics. Paul Atkınson; Evelyn Parsons; Katie Featherstone. **New Gen. & Soc.** 20:1 4:2001 pp.5-24.

2675   'Real men reawaken their fathers' homesteads, the educated leave them in ruins': the politics of domestic reproduction in post-apartheid rural South Africa. Zolani Ngwane. **J. Relig. Afr.** XXXI:4 2001 pp.402-426.

2676   A reconsideration of Chinese 'kinship': ethnography of a village in southwestern Taiwan. Wei-pin Lin. **B. Inst. Ethn. Ac. Sin.** 90 Autumn:2000 pp.1-38.

2677   (Reconstruction of 'blood tie': patrilineal descent and same surname associations in East Asia.); *[Text in Japanese]*. Kazuo Yoshihara; Masataka Suzuki; Michio Suenari. Tokyo: Fukyosha, 2000. 356p.

2678   (The remains of the matrilineal system in Li — with reference to the folklore on the lower Han River in Sui and C'hu.); *[Text in Japanese]*. Shigehiro Kubuki. **St. Ess. Beh. Sc. Phil.** 21 3:2001 pp.1-18.

2679   A remembrance of kinship studies past: a call for their rebirth. Susan Bedford. **Hist. Anthrop.** 12:4 2001 pp.315-341.

2680   Remuddling kinship: the state of the art. Harold W. Scheffler. **Z. Ethn.** 126:2 2001 pp.161-174.
2681   Rethinking western Motu descent groups. Michael Goddard. **Oceania** 71:4 6:2001 pp.313-334.
2682   Reviewing twinship in Africa. Elisha P. Renne; Misty L. Bastian; Susan Diduk; Adeline Masquelier. **Ethnology** XL:1 Winter:2001 pp.1-78. *Collection of 5 articles.*
2683   Romance, parenthood, and gender in a modern African society. Daniel Jordan Smith. **Ethnology** XL:2 Spring:2001 pp.129-151.
2684   Separation and reunion in modern China. Charles Lester Stafford. Cambridge: Cambridge University Press, 2000. viii, 202p. *ISBN: 0521780179, 0521784344. Includes bibliographical references (p. 192-199) and index.*
2685   Stolen children, invisible mothers and unspeakable stories: the experiences of non-aboriginal adoptive and foster mothers of aboriginal children. Denise Cuthbert. **Soc. Sem.** 11:2 8:2001 pp.139-154.
2686   Strengthening grandmother networks to improve community nutrition: experience from Senegal. Judi Aubel; Ibrahima Touré; Mamadou Diagne; Kalala Lazin; El Hadj Alioune Sène; Yirime Faye; Mouhamadou Tandia. **Gen. Dev.** 9:2 7:2001 pp.62-73.
2687   A study of East African kinship and marriage using a phylogenetically based comparative method. Monique Borgerhoff Mulder; Margaret George-Cramer; Jason Eshleman; Alessia Ortolani. **Am. Anthrop.** 103:4 12:2001 pp.1059-1082.
2688   The temporary migration of males and the power of females in a stem-family society: the case of nineteenth-century Auvergne. Rose Duroux. **Hist. Fam.** 6:1 2001 pp.33-49.
2689   Die Terminologie der Verwandtschaft. Zu mittelalterlichen Grundlagen von Wandel und Beharrung im europäischen Vergleich. *[In German]*; (The terminology of kinship. On the medieval foundations of change and continuity in Europe — a comparison.) Michael Mitterauer. **Eth. Balk.** 41 2000 pp.11-44.
2690   Tuvalılarda akrabalık sistemi. *[In Turkish]*; (The kinship system of Tuva people.) *[Summary]*. S.M. Biçe-Ool. **Bilig** 17 Spring:2001 pp.107-118.
2691   Understanding American Indian families. Walter T. Kawamoto; Michelle Christensen; Spero Manson; Jerry D. Stubben; Annmaria Rousey; Erich Longie; Luke Madrigal; Billy Rogers; David Baldridge; Tamara C. Cheshire. **Am. Behav. Sc.** 44:9 5:2001 pp.1445-1535. *Collection of 9 articles.*
2692   'Washing machines make lazy women' domestic appliances and the negotiation of women's propriety in Soweto. Helen Meintjes. **J. Mat. Cult.** 6:3 11:2001 pp.345-363.
2693   Whose mothers? Generational difference, war, and the Nazi cult of motherhood. Elizabeth D. Heineman. **J. Wom. Hist.** 12:4 Winter:2001 pp.139-163.
2694   Working mothers and the work of culture in a Papua New Guinea society. Kathleen Barlow. **Ethos** 29:1 3:2001 pp.78-107.

E.2.3:   **Life cycle**
          Cycle de vie

          Birth and childhood
          Naissance et enfance

2695   The acceptability of the female condom among US women at high risk from HIV. Lana D. Harrison; Tracy Bachman; Charles Freeman; James A. Inciardi. **Cult. Health. Sex.** 3:1 1-3:2001 pp.101-118.
2696   Adolescent parenthood: a costly mistake or a search for love?; *[Summary in Spanish]*; *[Summary in French]*. Barbara Hanna. **Reprod. Health Mat.** 9:17 5:2001 pp.101-107.
2697   The adventures of Peanut and Bo: summer camps and early-twentieth-century American girlhood. Leslie Paris. **J. Wom. Hist.** 12:4 Winter:2001 pp.47-76.

2698   Ambivalences in child training by the Semai of peninsular Malaysia and other peoples. Robert K. Dentan. **Crossroads** 15:1 2001 pp.89-132.

2699   A biocultural investigation of the weanling's dilemma in Kathmandu, Nepal: do universal recommendations for weaning practices make sense? Tina Moffat. **J. Biosoc. Sc.** 33:3 7:2001 pp.321-338.

2700   Birth customs, rituals and naming ceremonies' incantations among the Guidars of Cameroon. Babila J. Mutia. **B. Int. Com. Urg. Anthrop. Ethnol. R.** 40 1999-2000 pp.85-98.

2701   Care seeking in Sri Lanka: one possible explanation for low childhood mortality. M.W. Amarasiri de Silva; Ananda Wijekoon; Robert Hornik; Jose Martines. **Soc. Sci. Med.** 53:10 11:2001 pp.1363-1372.

2702   The challenges of meeting rural Bangladeshi women's needs in delivery care; *[Summary in Spanish]*; *[Summary in French]*. Kaosar Afsana; Sabina Faiz Rashid. **Reprod. Health Mat.** 9:18 11:2001 pp.79-89.

2703   De la culpabilité à la réparation. La responsabilité de la mère dans la pathologie de son enfant chez les Seereer Siin du Sénégal. *[In French]*; [From blame to reparation. Responsibility of the mother in the pathology of her child among the Seereer Siin in Senegal]. Simone Kalis. **Anthropos [St. Augustin]** 95:2 2000 pp.363-370.

2704   The effects of breastfeeding and birth spacing on infant and early childhood mortality in Ethiopia. David P. Lindstrom; Betemariam Berhanu. **Soc. Biol.** 47:1-2 Spring-Summer:2000 pp.1-17.

2705   Female genital mutilation and the moral status of abortion. Christopher Hughes Conn. **Publ. Aff. Q.** 15:1 1:2001 pp.1-15.

2706   Female-selective abortion in Asia: patterns, policies, and debates. Barbara D. Miller. **Am. Anthrop.** 103:4 12:2001 pp.1083-1095.

2707   From the forest to the clinic: changing birth practice among the Katang, Lao; *[Summary in French]*; *[Summary in Spanish]*. Seng-Amphone Chithtalath; Barbara Earth. **Reprod. Health Mat.** 9:18 11:2001 pp.99-104.

2708   Gap between preferred and actual birth intervals in sub-Saharan Africa: implications for fertility and child health. Hantamalala Rafalimanana; Charles F. Westoff. Calverton MD: ORC Macro, 2001. vii, 21p. *Includes bibliographical references (p. 20-21). (Series: DHS analytical studies - 2).*

2709   Giving birth in maternity hospitals in Benin: testimonies of women; *[Summary in Spanish]*; *[Summary in French]*. Françoise Grossmann-Kendall; Véronique Filippi; Maria De Koninck; Lydie Kanhonou. **Reprod. Health Mat.** 9:18 11:2001 pp.90-97.

2710   How do family planning workers' visits affect women's contraceptive behavior in Bangladesh? Mary Arends-Kuenning. **Demography** 38:4 11:2001 pp.481-496.

2711   Including expectant fathers in antenatal education programmes in Istanbul, Turkey; *[Summary in Spanish]*; *[Summary in French]*. Janet Molzan Turan; Hacer Nalbant; Ayşen Dulut; Yusuf Sahip. **Reprod. Health Mat.** 9:18 11:2001 pp 114-125.

2712   Infant care practices in New Zealand: a cross-cultural qualitative study. Sally Abel; Julie Park; David Tipene-Leach; Sitaleki Finau; Michele Lennan. **Soc. Sci. Med.** 53:9 11:2001 pp.1135-1148.

2713   Infant feeding in north east England: contested spaces of reproduction. Rachel Pain; Cathy Bailey; Graham Mowl. **Area** 33:3 9:2001 pp.261-272.

2714   'KB kills': political violence, birth control, and the Baliem Valley Dani. Leslie Butt. **Asia Pacific J. Anthr.** 2:1 4:2001 pp.63-88.

2715   'Like a white piece of paper'. Embodiment and the moral upbringing of Vietnamese children. Helle Rydstrøm. **Ethnos** 66:3 2001 pp.394-415.

2716   Mamki w Rzymie i w Państwie kościelnym w XVII i XVIII wieku. *[In Polish]*; (Wet-nurses in Rome and the papal state in the 17th and 18th centuries.) Marian Surdacki. **Kwart. Hist. Kult. Mater.** XLIX:4 2001 pp.327-344.

2717   Method-related experiences of Canadian women using Depo-Provera for contraception. Mary Rucklos Hampton; Barb McWatters; Bonnie Jeffery. **Canad. J. Human Sex.** 9:4 2000 pp.247-257.

2718   Perceptions médicales et populaires dans la prévention des difficultés maternelles en milieu rural peul guinéen. *[In French]*; [Medical and popular perceptions in the prevention of birthing difficulties among the rural Peul in Guinea] *[Summary]*. Mamadou Cellou Barry. **Afr. Stud. R.** 43:3 12:2000 pp.1-18.

2719   Practices of the pregnant self: compliance with and resistance to prenatal norms. Robin Root; C.H. Browner. **Cult. Medic. Psych.** 25:2 6:2001 pp.195-224.

2720   Risk factors and child mortality among the Miao in Yunnan, southwest China. Peter Foggin; Nagib Armijo-Hussein; Céline Marigaux; Hui Zhu; Zeyuan Liu. **Soc. Sci. Med.** 53:12 12:2001 pp.1683-1696.

2721   Safe motherhood in the time of AIDS: the illusion of reproductive 'choice'. Carolyn Baylies. **Gen. Dev.** 9:2 7:2001 pp.40-50.

2722   Sex selection in practice among Hong Kong Chinese. S.F. Wong; L.C. Ho. **Soc. Sci. Med.** 53:3 8:2001 pp.393-398.

2723   Sexual activity, contraceptive choice, and sexual and reproductive health indicators among single Canadian women aged 15-29: additional findings from the Canadian contraception study. William A. Fisher; Richard Boroditsky. **Canad. J. Human Sex.** 9:2 2000 pp.79-93.

2724   Situating women's reproductive activities. C.H. Browner. **Am. Anthrop.** 102:4 12:2000 pp.773-788.

2725   Some notes and reflections on sex-selective abortions in India. Dagmar Marková. **Arch. Orient.** 68:1 2:2000 pp.19-26.

2726   A study on knowledge of various family planning methods among rural populations of Andhra Pradesh. G.R. Varma; B.V. Babu; A. Rohini. **Man India** 80:3-4 7-12:2000 pp.331-336.

2727   Le *walthana hampi* ou la reconstruction du corps. Conception de la grossesse dans les Andes du sud du Pérou. *[In French]*; (The *walthana hampi* or the reconstruction of the body. Representations of pregnancy in the south Peruvian Andes.) *[Summary]*; *[Summary in Spanish]*. Palmira La Riva Gonzalez. **J. Soc. Amér.** 86 2000 pp.169-184.

2728   Women's rights and bioethics. Lorraine Dennerstein [Ed.]. Paris: UNESCO, 2000. 215p. *ISBN: 923103765X. Includes bibliographical references. (Series:* Ethics).

Adolescence
Adolescence

2729   The bush burnt, the stones remain: female initiation rites in urban Zambia. Thera Rasing. London: LIT-Verlag, 2001. x, 351p. *ISBN: 3825856119. Includes bibliographical references.*

2730   The Correll family and technological change in Australian agriculture. Lionel Frost. **Agr. Hist.** 75:2 Spring:2000 pp.217-243.

2731   Masks and madness. Ritual expressions of the transition to adulthood among Miskitu adolescents; *[Summary in French]*. Mark Jamieson. **Soc. Anthrop.** 9:3 10:2001 pp.257-272.

2732   Strangers or friends? The need for adults in the life of adolescents. Alice Schlegel. **Paideuma** 46 2000 pp.137-148.

2733   Tradition and health: the predicament of female adolescents among the Igbo. Clifford Obby Odigmegwu; Modupeola Ojo; Christian N. Okemgbo. **J. Cult. St.** 3:1 2001 pp.284-300.

Marriage
Mariage

2734   'Because it's our culture!' (re)negotiating the meaning of lobola in Southern African secondary schools. Nicola Ansell. **J. S. Afr. Stud.** 27:4 12:2001 pp.697-716.

2735   Changes in family and marriage in a Yangzi Delta farming community, 1930-1990. Eugene T. Murphy. **Ethnology** XL:3 Summer:2001 pp.213-236.

2736   Consequences of the dissolution of customary marriages; *[Summary in Afrikaans]*. L.P. Vorster; N. Dlamini-Ndandwe; M.J. Molapo. **S. Afr. J. Ethnol.** 24:2 2001 pp.62-66.

2737   Le corps à la lettre, ou les quatre femmes de Jacob. *[In French]*; (The body to the letter, or Jacob's four wives.) *[Summary]*. Claudine Vassas. **Homme** 160 10-12:2001 pp.11-40.

2738   Death by fire: *sati*, dowry death and female infanticide in modern India. Mala Sen. London: Weidenfeld & Nicolson, 2001. xiv, 270p. *ISBN: 0297607243*.

2739   Dissolution of customary marriages; *[Summary in Afrikaans]*. F.P. Van R. Whelpton; L.P. Vorster. **S. Afr. J. Ethnol.** 24:2 2001 pp.56-61.

2740   Fraternity and endogamy. The House of Rothschild; *[Summary in French]*. Adam Kuper. **Soc. Anthrop.** 9:3 10:2001 pp.273-288.

2741   Genesis of marriage among the Moso and empire-building in late imperial China. Chuan-Kang Shih. **J. Asian St.** 60:2 5:2001 pp.381-412.

2742   Interracial marriage and status exchange: a study of Pacific Islanders in Hawai'i from 1983 to 1994. Xuanning Fu. **Pac. Stud.** 22:1 3:1999 pp.51-76.

2743   'Many divorces and many spinsters': marriage as an invented tradition in southern Malawi, 1946-1999. Amy Kaler. **J. Fam. Hist.** 26:4 10:2001 pp.529-556.

2744   Marriage and bridewealth in a matrilineal society: the case of the Tonga of Southern Zambia, 1900-1996. Flexon M. Mizinga. **Afr. Econ. Hist.** 28 2000 pp.53-87.

2745   Marriage by abduction in twentieth century China. Anne E. McLaren. **Mod. Asian S.** 35:4 10:2001 pp.953-984.

2746   Marriage in Norwegian missionary practice and discourse in Norway and Madagascar, 1880-1910. Line Nyhagen Predelli. **J. Relig. Afr.** XXXI:1 2001 pp.4-48.

2747   Oenpelli Kunwinjku kinship terminologies and marriage practices. Mark Harvey. **Oceania** 72:2 12:2001 pp.117-146.

2748   Prophethood, marriageable consanguinity, and text: the problem of Abraham and Sarah's kinship relationship and the response of Jewish and Islamic exegesis. Reuven Firestone. **Jew. Q. Rev.** 83 1992-1993 pp.331-348.

2749   Regional standardization in the age at marriage: a comparative study of preindustrial Germany and Japan. Satoshi Murayama. **Hist. Fam.** 6:2 2001 pp.303-324.

2750   Requirements for validity of customary marriages; *[Summary in Afrikaans]*. J.C. Bekker. **S. Afr. J. Ethnol.** 24:2 2001 pp.41-47.

2751   Rethinking cousin marriage in rural China. Zhaoxiong Qin. **Ethnology** XL:4 Fall:2001 pp.347-360.

2752   Seasonality of marriages and ecological contexts in rural communities of central-southern Italy (Abruzzo), 1500-1871; *[Summary in Croatian]*. A. Coppa; L. Di Donato; F. Vecchi; M.E. Danubio. **Coll. Antrop.** 25:2 12:2001 pp.403-412.

2753   Sexual cleansing (*kusalazya*) and levirate marriage (*kunjilila mung'anda*) in the era of AIDS: changes in perceptions and practices in Zambia. J.R.S. Malungo. **Soc. Sci. Med.** 53:3 8:2001 pp.371-382.

2754   The suppression of mixed marriages among LMS missionaries in South Africa before 1820. Julia C. Wells. **S. Afr. Hist. J.** 44 2001 pp.1-20.

2755   Tambaram: the West African experience. Frieder Ludwig. **J. Relig. Afr.** XXXI:1 2001 pp.49-91.

2756   'To go and marry any man that you please': a study of the formulaic antecedents of the rabbinic writ of divorce. Shalom E. Holtz. **J. Near East.** 60:4 10:2001 pp.241-258.

2757   A uniform customary code? Marital breakdown and women's economic entitlements in rural Bijnor. Patricia Jeffery. **Contr. I. Soc.** 35:1 1-4:2001 pp.1-32.

2758   'We women worry a lot about our husbands': Ghanaian women talking about their health and their relationships with men. Joyce Yaa Avotri; Vivienne Walters. **J. Gender St.** 10:2 7:2001 pp.197-212.

2759   Who decides? Women's status and negotiation of sex in Uganda. Brent Wolff; Ann K. Blanc; Anastasia J. Gage. **Cult. Health. Sex.** 2:3 7-9:2000 pp.303-322.

2760   Women, domesticity and the family: recent feminist work in Irish cultural studies. Clair Wills. **Cult. St.** 15:1 1:2001 pp.33-57.

Ageing
Vieillissement

2761   'Aging': a problematic concept for women. Hilda L. Smith. **J. Wom. Hist.** 12:4 Winter:2001 pp.77-86.
2762   Aging and identity in dementia narratives. Joe Moran. **Cult. Val.** 5:2 4:2001 pp.245-260.
2763   Aging trends — making an invisible population visible: the elderly in Bangladesh. Zarina Nahar Kabir; Marta Szebehely; Carol Tishelman; Ahmed Mushtaque Raza Chowdhury; Bengt Höjer; Bengt Winblad. **J. Cr-Cult. Gerontol.** 13:4 1998 pp.361-378.
2764   El anciano en la sociedad prehispánica. Una perspectiva histórica. *[In Spanish]*; [The aged in pre-Hispanic society: an historical view] *[Summary]*. Héctor Luis Zarauz. **Acta Sociol. [Mexico]** 30 9-12:2000 pp.11-28.
2765   'Are women ... all minors?' Woman's rights and the politics of aging in the antebellum United States. Corinne T. Field. **J. Wom. Hist.** 12:4 Winter:2001 pp.113-137.
2766   The '*casser maison*' ritual: constructing the self by emptying the home. Jean-Sébastien Marcoux. **J. Mat. Cult.** 6:2 7:2001 pp.213-236.
2767   Farming, marketing, and changes in the authority of elders among pastoral Rendille and Ariaal. Kevin Smith. **J. Cr-Cult. Gerontol.** 13:4 1998 pp.309-332.
2768   Gender differences in the elderly population: different satisfaction levels in selected spheres of life; *[Summary in Italian]*; *[Summary in French]*. E. Aureli; B. Baldazzi. **Genus** LVII:2 4-6:2001 pp.103-122.
2769   Greying in the cloister: the Ursuline life course in eighteenth-century France. Sherri Klassen. **J. Wom. Hist.** 12:4 Winter:2001 pp.87-112.
2770   Intergenerational relationships in rural areas. G. Clare Wenger; Thomas Scharf; Vanessa Burholt; Dena Shenk; Sally Keeling; Anitha Kumari Bhat; Raj Dhruvarajan; I.N. Keasberry. **Age. Soc.** 21:5 9:2001 pp.537-665. *Collection of 6 articles.*
2771   Is feminism the province of old (or middle-aged) women? Leila J. Rupp. **J. Wom. Hist.** 12:4 Winter:2001 pp.164-173.
2772   Migration and old age: Japanese women growing older in British society. Misa Izuhara; Hiroshi Shibata. **J. Comp. Fam. Stud.** XXXII:4 Autumn:2001 pp.571-586.
2773   'No strength': sex and old age in a rural town in Ghana. Sjaak van der Geest. **Soc. Sci. Med.** 53:10 11:2001 pp.1383-1396.
2774   'The abandoned mother': ageing, old age and missionaries in early and mid-nineteenth century south-east Africa. Andreas Sagner. **J. Afr. Hist.** 42:2 2001 pp.173-198.
2775   Using an interactive framework of society and lifecourse to explain self-rated health in early adulthood. Clyde Hertzman; Chris Power; Sharon Matthews; Orly Manor. **Soc. Sci. Med.** 53:12 12:2001 pp.1575-1586.
2776   Wedding of calm and wedding of noise: aging performed and aging misquoted in Tuareg rites of passage. Susan J. Rasmussen. **J. Anthr. Res.** 57:3 Fall:2001 pp.277-304.
2777   *Yebisa Wo Fie* : growing old and building a house in the Akan culture of Ghana. Sjaak van der Geest. **J. Cr-Cult. Gerontol.** 13:4 1998 pp.333-360.

Death
Mort

2778   Are Jewish deathdates affected by the timing of important religious events? Peter Lee; Gary Smith. **Soc. Biol.** 47:1-2 Spring-Summer:2000 pp.127-134.
2779   At the margins of death: ritual space and the politics of location in an Indo-Himalayan border village. Ravina Aggarwal. **Am. Ethn.** 28:3 8:2001 pp.549-573.
2780   Bodies that don't matter: death and dereliction in Chicago. Eric Klinenberg. **Bod. Soc.** 7:2-3 6-9:2001 pp.121-136.
2781   'Buy me a bride': death and exchange in northern Japanese bride-doll marriage. Ellen Schattschneider. **Am. Ethn.** 28:4 11:2001 pp.854-880.

2782   The case of the disorderly graves: contemporary deathscapes in Guangzhou. Elizabeth Kenworthy Teather. **Soc. Cult. Geog.** 2:2 6:2001 pp.185-202.

2783   The cemetery at Waddilove Institute. John Clatworthy. **Herit. Zimb.** 10 1991 pp.89-92.

2784   'Crying the death.' Rituals of death among the Yamba (Cameroon). Hermann Gufler. **Anthropos [St. Augustin]** 95:2 2000 pp.349-362.

2785   Death by fire: *sati*, dowry death and female infanticide in modern India. Mala Sen. London: Weidenfeld & Nicolson, 2001. xiv, 270p. *ISBN: 0297607243.*

2786   Funerals for the living: conversations with elderly people in Kwahu, Ghana; *[Summary in French]*. Sjaak van der Geest. **Afr. Stud. R.** 43:3 12:2000 pp.103-130.

2787   Grief, mourning, and death ritual. Neil Small [Ed.]; Jennifer Lorna Hockey [Ed.]; Jeanne Katz [Ed.]. Philadelphia PA: Open University Press, 2001. *ISBN: 0335205011, 033520502X. Includes bibliographical references and index.* (*Series:* Facing death).

2788   Hindu death as reflected in Āśāpūrnā Debī's novel *The First Promise.* Hana Preinhaelterová. **Arch. Orient.** 68:3 8:2000 pp.419-432.

2789   The London way of death. Brian Parsons. Stroud: Sutton Publishing, 2001. 128p. *ISBN: 0750925396.*

2790   La mort dans les sociétés modernes: la thèse de Norbert Elias à l'épreuve. *[In French]*; [Death in modern societies: Norbert Elias's theory put to the test] *[Summary]*. Jean-Hugues Déchaux. **Ann. Sociol.** 51:1 2001 pp.161-184.

2791   La mort: perceptions et pratiques d'aujourd'hui. *[In French]*; (Death: beliefs and behaviour.) Jean-Pierre Hiernaux; Olivier Servais; Yves Lambert; Edmond Legros; Tony Walter; Helen Waterhouse; Hubert Knoblauch; Jean-Hugues Déchaux; Maria Clara Saraiva; Patrick Baudry; Étienne Bocquet. **Recher. Sociolog.** XXXII:2 2001 pp.1-140. *Collection of 10 articles.*

2792   Muti ritual murder in Natal: from chiefs to commoners (1900-1930). Rob Turrell. **S. Afr. Hist. J.** 44 2001 pp.21-39.

2793   Perpetual mourning: widowhood in rural India. Martha Alter Chen. Oxford: Oxford University Press, 2000. xxxiv, 436p. *ISBN: 0195648854. Includes bibliographical references and index.*

2794   Restless corpses: 'secondary burial' in the Babenberg and Habsburg dynasties. Estella Weiss-Krejci. **Antiquity** 75:290 12:2001 pp.769-780.

2795   Ritual killing, 419, and fast wealth: inequality and the popular imagination in southeastern Nigeria. Daniel Jordan Smith. **Am. Ethn.** 28:4 11:2001 pp.803-826.

2796   The social construction of gender. Female cannibalism in Papua New Guinea. Ilka Thiessen. **Anthropos [St. Augustin]** 96:1 2001 pp.141-156.

2797   Suicidal self-scorching in ancient India. Harry Falk. **Stud. Orient.** 94 2001 pp.131-146.

2798   Suicides in Guarani culture: the concept of acculturation in Egon Schaden's research. Maria de Lourdes Beldi de Alcântara; Sheila Maria Doula; Cristina Moreira Rocha. **B. Int. Com. Urg. Anthrop. Ethnol. R.** 40 1999-2000 pp.191-196.

2799   A survey of Jewish cemeteries in western Turkey. Minna Rozen. **Jew. Q. Rev.** 83 1992-1993 pp.71-126.

2800   The telegraphic abject: Buddhist meditation and the redemption of mechanical reproduction. Alan Klima. **Comp. Stud. S.** 43:3 7:2001 pp.552-582.

2801   Time out and worlds apart: tradition and modernity meet in the time-space of the gravesweeping festivals of Hong Kong. Elizabeth Kenworthy Teather. **Sing. J. Trop. Geogr.** 22:2 7:2001 pp.156-172.

2802   Wayward pastoral ghosts and regional xenophobia in a northern Madagascar town; *[Summary in French]*. Lesley A. Sharp. **Africa** 71:1 2001 pp.38-81.

E.2.4:   The body, gender and sexuality
           Le corps, genre et sexualité

Gender
Genre

2803   The adventures of Peanut and Bo: summer camps and early-twentieth-century American girlhood. Leslie Paris. **J. Wom. Hist.** 12:4 Winter:2001 pp.47-76.

2804   Age, gender, and knowledge revolutions in Africa and the United States. Claire C. Robertson. **J. Wom. Hist.** 12:4 Winter:2001 pp.174-183.

2805   Among the white moonfaces: memoirs of a Nyonya feminist. Shirley Lim. Singapore: Times Books International, 1996. 348p. *ISBN: 9812046607.*

2806   Appropriation of women's indigenous knowledge: the case of the matrilineal Lua in northern Thailand. Cholthira Satyawadhana. **Gen. Tech. Dev.** 5:1 1-4:2001 pp.91-111.

2807   'Biting your tongue': negotiating masculinities in contemporary Britain. Brendan Gough. **J. Gender St.** 10:2 7:2001 pp.169-186.

2808   *Bobolizan*, forests and gender relations in Sabah, Malaysia. Paul Porodong. **Gen. Tech. Dev.** 5:1 1-4:2001 pp.63-90.

2809   The complexities of acceptance: Thai student attitudes towards *kathoey*. Andrew Matzner. **Crossroads** 15:2 2001 pp.71-94.

2810   Constructing gendered bodies. Kathryn Backett-Milburn [Ed.]; Linda McKie [Ed.]. New York: Palgrave, 2001. 253p. *ISBN: 0333774620, 0333774612. Includes bibliographical references and index.* (*Series:* Explorations in sociology).

2811   Dcéry luny. Rituálne postavenie ženy v spoločnosti Mayov-Lacandóncov. *[In Slovak]*; [Daughters of the moon. Ritual status of woman in the community of Lacandon Maya] *[Summary]*. Tatiana Podolinská; Milan Kováč. **Slov. Národop.** 48:2 2000 pp.167-184.

2812   De la différence, de la hiérarchie et du jeu des sexes. Ethnographie des gestes et du langage dans un quartier de Naples. *[In French]*; [On difference, hierarchy and the game of the sexes: an ethnography of gestures and language in an area of Naples]. Patrick Ténoudji. **Temps Mod.** 56:615-616 9-11:2001 pp.240-256.

2813   Des mythes au féminin. Don Juan au Costa Rica. *[In French]*; [Feminine myths: Don Juan in Costa Rica]. Claire Pailler. **Caravelle** 76-77 12:2001 pp.537-547.

2814   Deszendenz, politische Macht und das Verhältnis der Geschlechter auf Yap, Westkarolinen. *[In German]*; [Descent, political power and gender relations in Yap, western Caroline Islands]. Corinna Erckenbrecht. **Anthropos [St. Augustin]** 96:1 2001 pp.119-140.

2815   Devenir des femmes Biliyan et dynamique familiale. *[In French]*; [The future of Biliyan women and family dynamics]. Odile Reveyrand-Coulon. **Stud. Afr.** 12 3:2001 pp.105-118.

2816   Duchowość i religijność kobiet dawniej i dziś. *[In Polish]*; (Women's spirituality and religiosity: past and present.) *[Summary]*. Elżbieta Pakszys [Ed.]; Liliana Sikorska [Ed.]. Poznan: Wydawnictwo Fundacji Humaniora, 2000. 150p. *ISBN: 8371121555.*

2817   Ecological feminism and Daoism. Sharon Rowe; James D. Sellmann. **Asian Cult. (Asian-Pac. Cult.) Q.** XXVIII:4 Winter:2000 pp.11-26.

2818   Empowerment and disempowerment of forest women in Uttarakhand, India. Madhu Sarin. **Gen. Tech. Dev.** 5:3 9-12:2001 pp.341-364.

2819   Enterpreneurs at home: secluded Muslim women and hidden economic activities in northern Nigeria. Zakaria Yakubu. **Nord. J. Afr. St.** 10:1 2001 pp.107-123.

2820   Envisioning (Black) male feminism: a cross-cultural perspective. Samuel Adu-Poku. **J. Gender St.** 10:2 7:2001 pp.157-168.

2821   Ethnography and prostitution in Peru. Lorraine Nencel. Sterling VA: Pluto Press, 2001. *ISBN: 074531662X.* (*Series:* Anthropology, culture, and society).

2822   Female entrepreneurship in the Caribbean: a multisite, pilot investigation of gender and work. Katherine E. Browne. **Human. Org.** 60:4 Winter:2001 pp.326-342.

2823   The fireplace: gender and culture among Yunnan nationalities. Yang Fuquan. **Gen. Tech. Dev.** 5:3 9-12:2001 pp.365-381.

2824   The food of elders, the 'ration' of women: brewing, gender, and domestic processes among the Samburu of northern Kenya. Jon Holtzman. **Am. Anthrop.** 103:4 12:2001 pp.1041-1058.

2825   From sea and garden to school and town: changing gender and household patterns among Pollap Atoll migrants. Juliana Flinn. **Pac. Stud.** 17:3 9:1994 pp.117-132.

2826   Gender ideology of Islam and women's public participation in North Africa. Masato Iizuka. **Senri Ethn. Stud.** 55 2001 pp.121-136.

2827   Gender in the 'contact zone'. Victoria Haskins; Alison Holland; Fiona Paisley; Katrina Schlunke; Hannah Robert; Amanda Nettelbeck; Jane Haggis; Sonja Kurtzer. **Aus. Fem. St.** 16:34 3:2001 pp.13-99. *Collection of 7 articles.*

2828   Gender relations in forest societies. Govind Kelkar; Dev Nathan; He Zhonghua; Paul Porodong; Cholthira Satyawadhana; K.S. Singh. **Gen. Tech. Dev.** 5:1 1-4:2001 pp.1-124. *Collection of 5 articles.*

2829   Gender relations in forest societies in Asia. Govind Kelkar; Dev Nathan. **Gen. Tech. Dev.** 5:1 1-4:2001 pp.1-31.

2830   Gender roles in history: women as hunters. K.S. Singh. **Gen. Tech. Dev.** 5:1 1-4:2001 pp.113-124.

2831   Gendered modernities: ethnographic perspectives. Dorothy Louise Hodgson [Ed.]. Palgrave, 2001. xiv, 271p. *ISBN: 0312238789. Includes bibliographical references and index.*

2832   Gendernaia lingvistika i istoricheskie nauki. *[In Russian]*; (Gender linguistics and historical sciences.) *[Summary]*. N.L. Pushkareva. **Etnograf. Oboz.** 2 3-4:2001 pp.31-40.

2833   "I will not eat stone": a women's history of colonial Asante. Jean Marie Allman; Victoria B. Tashjian. Portsmouth NH, Oxford: Heinemann, James Currey, 2000. xlvi, 255p. *ISBN: 0852556411, 0325070016, 0325070008, 0852556918. Includes bibliographical references and index.* (*Series:* Social history of Africa).

2834   Identity and gender in hunting and gathering societies. Ian Keen; Takako Yamada; Elena Glavatskaia; Christer Norström; Victor Shnirelman; Lisa Hiwasaki; Toshiaki Inoue; Will Karkavelas; Robin Ridington; Russell Taylor; Jean-Guy A. Goulet; Kaoru Imamura; Zubeeda Banu Quraishy; Sita Venkateswar; Elena G. Fedorova. **Senri Ethn. Stud.** 56 2001 pp.1-257. *Collection of 18 articles.*

2835   In search of a model: evolution of a feminist consciousness in Ukraine and Russia. Marian J. Rubchak. **Eur. J. Wom. Stud.** 8:2 5:2001 pp.149-160.

2836   Industrious women: resource use and gender norms among the Kalanguya of the Philippines. Bernadette P. Resurrección. **Gen. Tech. Dev.** 5:2 5-8:2001 pp.245-265.

2837   Kavkazskaia zhenshchina: mirovozzrencheskie predposylki obshchestvennogo statusa. *[In Russian]*; (Caucasian women: ideological prerequisites of social status.) *[Summary]*. Iu.Iu. Karpov. **Etnograf. Oboz.** 4 7-8:2000 pp.22-31.

2838   Kraljice u akademiji. *[In Croatian]*; (Kraljice [queens] in [the] academy.) *[Summary]*. Ivan Lozica. **Nar. Umjetn.** 37:2 2000 pp.67-86.

2839   Larger than Bengal: feminism in Rokeya Sakhawat Hossain's *Sultana's Dream* and *Global Modernities*. Sonita Sarker. **Arch. Orient.** 68:3 8:2000 pp.441-456.

2840   The man with two brains: hegemonic masculine subjectivity and the discursive construction of the unreasonable penis-self. Annie Potts. **J. Gender St.** 10:2 7:2001 pp.145-156.

2841   The masculinity studies reader. Rachel Adams [Ed.]; David Savran [Ed.]. Malden MA: Blackwell Publishers, 2001. 418p. *ISBN: 0631226605, 0631226591. Includes bibliographical references and index.* (*Series:* Keyworks in cultural studies - 5).

2842   Multiple voices, multiple selves: song style and north Indian women's identity. Amelia Maciszewski. **Asian Mus.** XXXII:2 Spring-Summer:2001 pp.1-40.

2843   Narratives of Embu rural women: gender roles and indigenous knowledges. Njoki Wane. **Gen. Tech. Dev.** 5:3 9-12:2001 pp.383-408.

2844   Naxi women: protection and management of forests in Lijiang, China. Yang Fuquan; Xi Yuhua. **Gen. Tech. Dev.** 5:2 5-8:2001 pp.199-222.

2845   Older women in academia: contemporary history and issues. Phyllis Bronstein. **J. Wom. Hist.** 12:4 Winter:2001 pp.184-201.

2846   Pakistani couples: different productive and reproductive realities? Zeba A. Sathar; Shahnaz Kazi; Arshad Mahmood [Comments by]. **Pak. Dev. R.** 39:4(II) Winter:2000 pp.891-912.

2847   Pig men and women, big men and women: gender and production in the New Guinea Highlands. Paul Sillitoe. **Ethnology** XL:3 Summer:2001 pp.171-192.

2848   Re-conceptualizing the role of men in the post-Cairo era. Axel I. Mundigo; Sonia Corrêa [Comments by]; Daniel C. Maguire [Comments by]; Juan-Guillermo Figueroa-Perea [Comments by]. **Cult. Health. Sex.** 2:3 7-9:2000 pp.323-351.

2849   Representing women: the politics of Minangkabau *Adat* writings. Evelyn Blackwood. **J. Asian St.** 60:1 2:2001 pp.125-150.

2850   Reproducing culture and society: women and the politics of gender, age, and social rank in Walāta; *[Summary in French]*. Timothy Cleaveland. **Can. J. Afr. St.** 34:2 2000 pp.189-217.

2851   Situating women's reproductive activities. C.H. Browner. **Am. Anthrop.** 102:4 12:2000 pp.773-788.

2852   The social construction of gender. Female cannibalism in Papua New Guinea. Ilka Thiessen. **Anthropos [St. Augustin]** 96:1 2001 pp.141-156.

2853   Toward historicizing gender in Polynesia: on Vilsoni Hereniko's *Woven Gods* and regional patterns. Jeannette Marie Mageo. **Pac. Stud.** 22:1 3:1999 pp.93-122.

2854   Towards gender balance: but will women physicians have an impact on medicine? E. Riska. **Soc. Sci. Med.** 52:2 1:2001 pp.179-188.

2855   (Troubling) spaces of mountains and men: New Zealand's Mount Cook and Hermitage Lodge. Karen M. Morin; Robyn Longhurst; Lynda Johnston. **Soc. Cult. Geog.** 2:2 6:2001 pp.117-140.

2856   A uniform customary code? Marital breakdown and women's economic entitlements in rural Bijnor. Patricia Jeffery. **Contr. I. Soc.** 35:1 1-4:2001 pp.1-32.

2857   Warring in America: encounters of gender and race. Gail D. Danvers; Rachel Van Duyvenbode; Liping Bu; Paul Christian Jones; Liese M. Perrin; David Monod; Peter Widdowson. **J. Am. Stud.** 35:2 8:2001 pp.187-335. *Collection of 7 articles.*

2858   Woman, sexual difference and the dance of undecidability in Nietzsche's *Thus Spoke Zarathustra*. Iva Popovicova. **Dialect. Anthrop.** 25:3-4 2000 pp.281-295.

2859   Women and forest: a study of the Warlis of western India. Indra Munshi. **Gen. Tech. Dev.** 5:2 5-8:2001 pp.177-198.

2860   Women and war: the role Kuwaiti women played during the Iraqi occupation. M. Juliá; H. Ridha. **J. Int. Dev.** 13:5 7:2001 pp.583-598.

2861   Women, domesticity and the family: recent feminist work in Irish cultural studies. Clair Wills. **Cult. St.** 15:1 1:2001 pp.33-57.

2862   Women's life-cycle transitions in world-historical perspective: comparing marriage in China and Europe. Mary Jo Maynes; Ann Waltner. **J. Wom. Hist.** 12:4 Winter:2001 pp.11-21.

2863   Women's rights and child rights. Wendy Harcourt; Judith L. Evans; Savitri Goonesekere; Julie Cupples; Janet Brown; Bernard Combes; Andrea Bosch; Joan French; Peggy Antrobus; Devaki Jain; Marilyn Thomson; Lena Karlsson; Jan Hammill; Susan Bissell; Berenice Nyland; Charlotte Johnson-Welch; Richard Strickland; George Kent; Nancy Salinas Ardaya; Claudia Schachinger; Richmond Tiemoko; Saliwe M. Kawewe; Sondra Seung Ja Doe. **Development** 44:2 6:2001 pp.3-116. *Collection of 20 articles.*

2864   Young women in France and England, 1050-1300. Fiona Harris Stoertz. **J. Wom. Hist.** 12:4 Winter:2001 pp.22-46.

Sexuality
Sexualité

2865   Addressing semen loss concerns: towards culturally appropriate HIV/AIDS interventions in Gujarat, India; *[Summary in Spanish]*; *[Summary in French]*. Aruna Lakhani; Ketan Gandhi; Martine Collumbien. **Reprod. Health Mat.** 9:18 11:2001 pp.49-59.

2866   Are younger German gay men more at risk from HIV? Results of a national survey in the gay press in Germany. Michael Bochow. **Cult. Health. Sex.** 2:2 4-6:2000 pp.183-195.

2867   Arousing suspicion and violating trust: the lived ideology of safe sex talk. Jeff Gavin. **Cult. Health. Sex.** 2:2 4-6:2000 pp.117-134.

2868   Breaking the speed of the sound of loneliness: sexual partner change and the fear of intimacy. Bente Træen; Dagfinn Sørensen. **Cult. Health. Sex.** 2:3 7-9:2000 pp.287-301.

2869   Common questions about sexual health education. Alexander McKay. **Canad. J. Human Sex.** 9:2 2000 pp.129-137.

2870   Community-based survey on female genital excision in Faranah district, Guinea; *[Summary in Spanish]*; *[Summary in French]*. Daman Keita; David Blankhart. **Reprod. Health Mat.** 9:18 11:2001 pp.135-142.

2871   Curing cut or ritual mutilation? Some remarks on the practice of female and male circumcision in Graeco-Roman Egypt. Mary Knight. **Isis** 92:2 6:2001 pp.317-350.

2872   De Clérambault's syndrome (erotomania) in an evolutionary perspective. Martin Brüne. **Evol. Hum. Behav.** 22:6 11:2001 pp.409-416.

2873   Discourses on women's (hetero)sexuality and desire in a South African local context. Tamara Shefer; Don Foster. **Cult. Health. Sex.** 3:4 10-12:2001 pp.375-390.

2874   Drug-using men who have sex with men: sexual behaviours and sexual identities. S. Deren; M. Stark; F. Rhodes; H. Siegel; L. Cottler; M. Wood; L. Kochems; R. Carlson; R. Falck; K. Rourke; R. Trotter; B. Weir; M.F. Goldstein; L. Wright-De Aguero. **Cult. Health. Sex.** 3:3 7-9:2001 pp.329-338.

2875   Ethiopian demons: male sexuality, the black-skinned other, and the monastic self. David Brakke. **J. Hist. Sexual.** 10:3-4 7-10:2001 pp.501-535.

2876   Ethnic variations in observance and rationale for postpartum sexual abstinence in Malawi. Eliya Msiyaphazi Zulu. **Demography** 38:4 11:2001 pp.467-479.

2877   An ethnography of silences: race, (homo)sexualities, and a discourse of Africa; *[Summary in French]*. Bill Stanford Pincheon. **Afr. Stud. R.** 43:3 12:2000 pp.39-58.

2878   An evaluation of the Choices and Changes student program: a grade four to seven sexual health education program based on the Canadian guidelines for sexual health education. Jeff Wackett; Lisa Evans. **Canad. J. Human Sex.** 9:4 2000 pp.265-273.

2879   Female education, adolescent sexuality and the risk of sexually transmitted infection in Ariaal Rendille culture. Eric A. Roth; Elliot M. Fratkin; Elizabeth N. Ngugi; Barry W. Glickman. **Cult. Health. Sex.** 3:1 1-3:2001 pp.35-47.

2880   Female genital cutting in Guinea: qualitative and quantitative research strategies. P. Stanley Yoder; Mary Mahy. Calverton MD: Measure DHS+, ORC Macro, 2001. 34p. (*Series:* DHS analytical studies - 5).

2881   Female genital mutilation and the moral status of abortion. Christopher Hughes Conn. **Publ. Aff. Q.** 15:1 1:2001 pp.1-15.

2882   Friendship patterns among lesbian and gay youth: an exploratory study. Margaret S. Schneider; Jennifer Jo Witherspoon. **Canad. J. Human Sex.** 9:4 2000 pp.239-246.

2883   Genital mutilation among female adolescents resident in Italy. P. Grassivaro Gallo; L. Araldi; F. Viviani. **Mankind Q.** XLII:2 Winter:2001 pp.155-168.

2884   Health care seeking behaviour for sexually transmitted diseases among commercial sex workers in Morogoro, Tanzania. Anne Outwater; Lucy Nkya; Eligius Lyamuya; George Lwihula; Edward C. Green; Jan Hogle; Susan E. Hassig; Gina Dallabetta. **Cult. Health. Sex.** 3:1 1-3:2001 pp.19-33.

2885   HIV and men who have sex with men: where is the Canadian epidemic headed? Jennifer A. Siushansian; Mai Nguyen; Chris P. Archibald. **Canad. J. Human Sex.** 9:4 2000 pp.219-237.

2886   Indian men, Afro-Creole women: 'casting' doubt on interracial sexual relationships in the late nineteenth-century Caribbean. Audra A. Diptee. **Imm. Minor.** 19:3 11:2000 pp.1-24.

2887   Law and persuasion in the elimination of female genital modification. Regina Smith Oboler. **Human. Org.** 60:4 Winter:2001 pp.311-318.

2888   Male circumcision and penis enhancement in Southeast Asia: matters of pain and pleasure; *[Summary in Spanish]*; *[Summary in French]*. Terence H. Hull; Meiwita Budiharsana. **Reprod. Health Mat.** 9:18 11:2001 pp.60-68.

2889   Male circumcision as an HIV control strategy: not a 'natural condom'; *[Summary in Spanish]*; *[Summary in French]*. Kate Bonner. **Reprod. Health Mat.** 9:18 11:2001 pp.143-155.

2890   Male complications of female genital mutilation. Lars Almroth; Vanja Almroth-Berggren; Osman Mahmoud Hassanein; Said Salah Eldin Al-Said; Sharif Siddiq Alamin Hasan; Ulla-Britt Lithell; Staffan Bergström. **Soc. Sci. Med.** 53:11 12:2001 pp.1455-1460.

2891   Mate choice trade-offs and women's preference for physically attractive men. David Waynforth. **Hum. Nature** 12:3 2001 pp.207-220.

2892   Men's attitudes to condoms and female controlled means of protection against HIV and STDs in south-western Uganda. Robert Pool; Graham Hart; Gillian Green; Susan Harrison; Stella Nyanzi; Jimmy Whitworth. **Cult. Health. Sex.** 2:2 4-6:2000 pp.197-211.

2893   Method-related experiences of Canadian women using Depo-Provera for contraception. Mary Rucklos Hampton; Barb McWatters; Bonnie Jeffery. **Canad. J. Human Sex.** 9:4 2000 pp.247-257.

2894   Missing men's messages: does the reproductive health approach respond to men's sexual health needs? Martine Collumbien; Sarah Hawkes. **Cult. Health. Sex.** 2:2 4-6:2000 pp.135-150.

2895   Moral argumentation in adolescents' commentaries about sex. Stephen L. Eyre; Eric W. Davis; Ben Peacock. **Cult. Health. Sex.** 3:1 1-3:2001 pp.1-17.

2896   Moral panic and the construction of national order: HIV/AIDS risk groups and moral boundaries in the creation of modern Thailand. Graham Fordham. **Crit. Anthr.** 21:3 9:2001 pp.259-316.

2897   My best informant's dress: the erotic equation in fieldwork. Esther Newton. **Cult. Anthro.** 8:1 2:1993 pp.3-23.

2898   'No strength': sex and old age in a rural town in Ghana. Sjaak van der Geest. **Soc. Sci. Med.** 53:10 11:2001 pp.1383-1396.

2899   The perils of love: magic and countermagic in Coptic Egypt. David Frankfurter. **J. Hist. Sexual.** 10:3-4 7-10:2001 pp.480-500.

2900   Queer pilgrimage: the San Francisco homeland and identity tourism. Alyssa Cymene Howe. **Cult. Anthro.** 16:1 2:2001 pp.35-61.

2901   Queer treasons: homosexuality and Irish national identity. Kathryn Conrad. **Cult. St.** 15:1 1:2001 pp.124-137.

2902   Refocusing HIV/AIDS interventions in Thailand: the case for male sex workers and other homosexually active men. Malcolm McCamish; Graeme Storer; Greg Carl. **Cult. Health. Sex.** 2:2 4-6:2000 pp.167-182.

2903   Sex research update. Alexander McKay [Comp.]. **Canad. J. Human Sex.** 9:2 2000 pp.121-127.

2904   Sexual abstinence among traditional peoples. Milan Kalous. **Arch. Orient.** 68:4 11:2000 pp.601-617.

2905   Sexual activity, contraceptive choice, and sexual and reproductive health indicators among single Canadian women aged 15-29: additional findings from the Canadian contraception study. William A. Fisher; Richard Boroditsky. **Canad. J. Human Sex.** 9:2 2000 pp.79-93.

2906   Sexual cleansing (*kusalazya*) and levirate marriage (*kunjilila mung'anda*) in the era of AIDS: changes in perceptions and practices in Zambia. J.R.S. Malungo. **Soc. Sci. Med.** 53:3 8:2001 pp.371-382.

2907   Sexual social scripts and the re-imaginings of community identity; *[Summary in French]*. Maria Fowler. **Ethnologies** 23:1 2001 pp.45-62.

2908   Sexuality, culture, and power in HIV/AIDS research. Richard Parker. **Ann. R. Anthr.** 30 2001 pp.163-179.

2909   Sexuality in late antiquity. Daniel Boyarin [Ed.]; Elizabeth A. Castelli [Ed.]; Dina Stein; Charlotte Elisheva Fonrobert; Jill Gorman; Virginia Burrus; David Frankfurter; David Brakke. **J. Hist. Sexual.** 10:3-4 7-10:2001 pp.357-535. *Collection of 7 articles.*

2910   Sexuality in Morocco: changing context and contested domain. Carla Makhlouf Obermeyer. **Cult. Health. Sex.** 2:3 7-9:2000 pp.239-254.

2911   Sexuality, masculinity and politics in Chinese culture: the case of the 'Sanguo' hero Guan Yu. Kam Louie. **Mod. Asian S.** 33:4 10:1999 pp.835-859.

2912   Social basis of deviant sexual behaviour: a historical perspective. Amarjeet Singh. **B. Ind. Inst. Hist. Med.** XXIX:1 1:1999 pp.51-62.

2913   Socializing influences and the value of sex: the experience of adolescent school girls in rural Masaka, Uganda. John Kinsman; Stella Nyanzi; Robert Pool. **Cult. Health. Sex.** 2:2 4-6:2000 pp.151-166.

2914   Socio-economic context and the sexual behaviour of Ugandan out of school youth. Lisa Bohmer; Edward K. Kirumira. **Cult. Health. Sex.** 2:3 7-9:2000 pp.269-285.

2915   Travestie und Transsexualität. Der ethnologische Beitrag zu einer interdisziplinären Debatte. *[In German]*; [Transvestism and transsexuality. The ethnological contribution to an interdisciplinary debate]. Susanne Schröter. **Paideuma** 47 2001 pp.61-82.

2916   Turkish university students' sexual behaviour, knowledge, attitudes and perceptions of risk related to HIV/AIDS. Figen Cok; Lizbeth Ann Gray; Hakan Ersever. **Cult. Health. Sex.** 3:1 1-3:2001 pp.81-99.

2917   Urban adolescents and sexual risk taking; *[Summary in Croatian]*. V. Hiršl-Hećej; A. Štulhofer. **Coll. Antrop.** 25:1 6:2001 pp.195-212.

2918   Who decides? Women's status and negotiation of sex in Uganda. Brent Wolff; Ann K. Blanc; Anastasia J. Gage. **Cult. Health. Sex.** 2:3 7-9:2000 pp.303-322.

2919   You don't eat Indian and Chinese food at the same meal: the bisexuality quandary. Moshe Shokeid. **Anthr. Quart.** 75:1 Winter:2001 pp.63-91.

The body
Le corps

2920   The alienation of body tissue and the biopolitics of immortalized cell lines. Margaret Lock. **Bod. Soc.** 7:2-3 6-9:2001 pp.63-92.

2921   The anthropological study of body decoration as art: collective representations and the somatization of affect. Ragnar Johnson. **Fash. Theory** 5:4 12:2001 pp.417-434.

2922   Behinderung und Kultur. *[In German]*; (Disability and culture.) *[Summary]*. Andreas Sagner. **Z. Ethn.** 126:2 2001 pp.175-207.

2923   Bodies for sale — whole or in parts. Nancy Scheper-Hughes. **Bod. Soc.** 7:2-3 6-9:2001 pp.1-8.

2924   Bodies that don't matter: death and dereliction in Chicago. Eric Klinenberg. **Bod. Soc.** 7:2-3 6-9:2001 pp.121-136.

2925   The body, culture, and society: an introduction. Philip Hancock; et al. Buckingham VA: Open University Press, 2000. x, 146p. *ISBN: 0335204139, 0335204147. Includes bibliographical references and index.*

2926   The body of one color: Indian wrestling, the Indian state, and Utopian somatics. Joseph S. Alter. **Cult. Anthro.** 8:1 2:1993 pp.49-72.

2927   The body of the nation: terrorism and the embodiment of nationalism in contemporary Israel. Meira Weiss. **Anthr. Quart.** 75:1 Winter:2001 pp.37-62.

2928   Clothes that matter: fashioning modernity in late Qing novels. Paola Zamperini. **Fash. Theory** 5:2 6:2001 pp.195-214.

2929   Commodified kin: death, mourning, and competing claims on the bodies of organ donors in the United States. Lesley A. Sharp. **Am. Anthrop.** 103:1 3:2001 pp.112-133.

2930   Commodity fetishism in organs trafficking. Nancy Scheper-Hughes. **Bod. Soc.** 7:2-3 6-9:2001 pp.31-62.

2931   Connotations of blood: reflections of adolescent school girls. Rajni Dhingra; S. Anandalakshmy. **Man India** 80:3-4 7-12:2000 pp.321-330.

2932   Constructing gendered bodies. Kathryn Backett-Milburn [Ed.]; Linda McKie [Ed.]. New York: Palgrave, 2001. 253p. *ISBN: 0333774620, 0333774612. Includes bibliographical references and index. (Series:* Explorations in sociology).

2933   The critical limits of embodiment: reflections on disability criticism. Carol A. Breckenridge; Candace Vogler; Eli Clare; Sharon L. Snyder; David T. Mitchell; W.J.T. Mitchell; Wu Hung; Kyeong-Hee Choi; Celeste Langan; Susan Schweik; Alexa Wright; Veena Das; Renu Addlakha; Rayna Rapp; Faye Ginsburg; Eva Feder Kittay. **Publ. Cult.** 13:3 Fall:2001 pp.349-579. *Collection of 12 articles.*

2934   Displaced persons: symbols of South Asian femininity and the returned gaze in U.S. media culture. Meenakshi Gigi Durham. **Commun. Theory** 11:2 5:2001 pp.201-217.

2935   Do you see what I see? Facial attractiveness and weight preoccupation in college women. Caroline Davis; Barbara Shuster; Michelle Dionne; Gordon Claridge. **J. Soc. Clin. Psychol.** 20:2 Summer:2001 pp.147-160.

2936   Dressing for the party: clothing, citizenship, and gender-formation in Mao's China. Tina Mai Chen. **Fash. Theory** 5:2 6:2001 pp.143-172.

2937   Essential marking: Maori tattooing and the properties of cultural identity. Stephen Pritchard. **Theory Cult. Soc.** 18:4 8:2001 pp.27-46.

2938   Gallo's body: decoration and damnation in the life of a Chicano gang member. Susan A. Phillips. **Ethnog.** 2:3 9:2001 pp.357-388.

2939   Geruch und Differenz. Körpergeruch als Kennzeichen konstruierter 'rassischer' Grenzen. *[In German]*; [Smell and difference. Body odour as a sign of constructed 'racial' borders]. Bettina Beer. **Paideuma** 46 2000 pp.207-230.

2940   Hair in African art and culture. Roy Sieber; Frank Herreman. **Afr. Arts** XXXIII:3 Autumn:2000 pp.54-69.

2941   Images of the body and the reproductive system among men and women living in shantytowns in Porto Alegre, Brazil; *[Summary in French]*; *[Summary in Spanish]*. Ceres G. Víctora; Daniela R. Knauth. **Reprod. Health Mat.** 9:18 11:2001 pp.22-33.

2942   Imperial bodies: the physical experience of the Raj, c.1800-1947. E.M. Collingham. Oxford: Polity, 2001. 256p. *ISBN: 0745623700, 0745623697.*

2943   Indumentaria en Murchante (Navarra). *[In Spanish]*; [Clothing in Murchante (Navarre)] *[Summary]*; *[Summary in French]*; *[Summary in Basque]*. Maria Carmen López Echarte. **An. Eusko. Folk.** 42 2000 pp.7-70.

2944   Japan's first cyborg? Miss Nippon, eugenics and wartime technologies of beauty, body and blood. Jennifer Robertson. **Bod. Soc.** 7:1 3:2001 pp.1-34.

2945   The laws of man and the laws of God: graphic patterns in Voltaic art. Christopher D. Roy. **Baes-A.** XLVII:2 6:2001 pp.223-258.

2946   Lo «stato barbarico delle donne» in Thorstein Bunde Veblen. *[In Italian]*; (The 'barbaric state of women' in Thorstein Bunde Veblen.) Umberto Marongiu. **Critica Sociol.** 136 Winter:2000-2001 pp.18-38.

2947   Mongolian representations of the body. Gaelle Lacaze. **Mon. St.** XXIII 2000 pp.43-68.

2948   No rules, only choices? Repositioning the self within the fashion system in relation to expertise and meaning: a case study of colour and image consultancy. Annie Grove-White. **J. Mat. Cult.** 6:2 7:2001 pp.193-212.

2949   Notes for a more sensuous history of twentieth-century Canada: the timely, the tacit, and the material body. Joy Parr. **Can. Hist. R.** 82:4 12:2001 pp.720-745.

2950   Nudity and framing: classifying art, pornography, information, and ambiguity. Beth A. Eck. **Sociol. For.** 16:4 12:2001 pp.603-632.

2951   Odzież i strój ludowy w Polsce. *[In Polish]*; (Folk clothes and costumes in Poland.) *[Summary]*. Barbara Bazielich. Wroclaw: Polskie Towarzystwo Ludoznawcze, 2000. 82p. *ISBN: 8387266450.*

2952   The other kidney: biopolitics beyond recognition. Lawrence Cohen. **Bod. Soc.** 7:2-3 6-9:2001 pp.9-30.

2953   The perfectible vagina: size matters. Virginia Braun; Celia Kitzinger. **Cult. Health. Sex.** 3:3 7-9:2001 pp.263-277.

2954   Property in the human body and its parts: reflections on self-determination in liberal society. Alexandra George; European University Institute. Law Department. Florence: European University Institute, 2001. 85p.

2955   Prostheses and cultural analysis. Diane M. Nelson; Melissa W. Wright; David Mills [Interviewer]. **Cult. Anthro.** 16:3 8:2001 pp.303-374. *Collection of 4 articles.*

2956   Semen as gift, semen as goods: reproductive workers and the market in altruism. Diane M. Tober. **Bod. Soc.** 7:2-3 6-9:2001 pp.137-160.

2957   Slimming the female body? Re-evaluating dress, corsets, and physical culture in France, 1890s-1930s. Mary Lynn Stewart; Nancy Janovicek. **Fash. Theory** 5:2 6:2001 pp.173-194.

2958   Somatic modes of attention. Thomas J. Csordas. **Cult. Anthro.** 8:2 5:1993 pp.135-156.

2959   Talking with/in pain: reflections of bodies under torture. Consuelo Rivera-Fuentes; Lynda Birke. **Wom. St. Inter. For.** 24:6 11-12:2001 pp.653-668.

2960   Tibetan army badges. Wolfgang Bertsch. **Tibet J.** XXVI:1 Spring:2001 pp.35-72.

2961   Whores, slaves and stallions: languages of exploitation and accommodation among professional boxers. Loïc Wacquant. **Bod. Soc.** 7:2-3 6-9:2001 pp.181-194.

2962   Young women and the body: a feminist sociology. Liz Frost. Basingstoke: Palgrave, 2001. x, 213p. *ISBN: 0333740890, 0333740904. Includes bibliographical references and index.*

E.3:   **Legal systems and moral codes**
       Systèmes juridiques et codifications morales

2963   Airborne *kula*: the appropriation of birds by Danish ornithologists. John Liep. **Anthr. Today** 17:5 10:2001 pp.10-15.

2964   Arguing with the KGB archives. Archival and narrative memory in post-Soviet Latvia. Vieda Skultans. **Ethnos** 66:3 2001 pp.320-343.

2965   Between diffidence and initiative: Ashkenazic legal decision-making in the late Middle Ages (1350-1500). Jeffrey R. Woolf. **J. Jew. Stud.** LII:1 Spring:2001 pp.85-97.

2966   The changing face of Catholic Ireland: conservatism and liberalism in the Ann Lovett and Kerry Babies scandals. Moira J. Maguire. **Fem. Stud.** 27:2 Summer:2001 pp.335-358.

2967   Civic virtue and religious reason: an Islamic counterpublic. Charles Hirschkind. **Cult. Anthro.** 16:1 2:2001 pp.3-34.

2968   Cocoa booms, the legalisation of land relations and politics in Cote d'Ivoire and Ghana: explaining farmers' responses. Richard C. Crook. **IDS Bull.** 32:1 1:2001 pp.35-45.

2969   Community justice and community policing in post-apartheid South Africa. Wilfried Schärf. **IDS Bull.** 32:1 1:2001 pp.74-82.

2970   Confucian ethics and virtue ethics. Wai-Ying Wong. **J. Ch. Philos.** 28:3 9:2001 pp.285-300.

2971   Corruption et justice. Adresse (1805) du gouverneur de Canton, Peling, à l'Empereur Jiaqing. *[In French]*; [Corruption and justice. An address (1805) by the Governor of Canton, Peling to Emperor Jiaqing]. George Staunton. **Péninsule** 40 2000 pp.159-166.

2972   Customary law in common law systems. Gordon R. Woodman. **IDS Bull.** 32:1 1:2001 pp.28-34.

2973   Dead monks and bad debts: some provisions of a Buddhist monastic inheritance law. Gregory Schopen. **Indo-Iran. J.** 44:2 2001 pp.99-148.

2974   Documentos legales en fuentes andalusíes. *[In Spanish]*; [Legal documents from Andalucia]. Maribel Fierro. **Al-Qantara** XXII:1 2001 pp.205-210.

2975   L'ethnologue et le juge. L'enquête de Giovanni Falcone sur la mafia en Sicile. *[In French]*; (The ethnologist and the judge: Giovanni Falcone's investigation of the Mafia in Sicily.)

[Summary]; *[Summary in German]*. Deborah Puccio. **Ethn. Fr.** XXXI:1 1-3:2001 pp.15-27.

2976   From law to custom: the shifting legal status of Muslim *originaires* in Kayes and Medine, 1903-13. Rebecca Shereikis. **J. Afr. Hist.** 42:2 2001 pp.261-284.

2977   Imjjat: genesis of a Rifian lineage, genesis of a Rifian vendetta. David M. Hart. **Morocco** 2 1997 pp.33-54.

2978   Introduction to making law matter. Richard C. Crook. **IDS Bull.** 32:1 1:2001 pp.1-7.

2979   Islam v sovremennoi Kabardino-Balkarii: pravovye aspekty. *[In Russian]*; (Islam in the modern Kabardin-Balkar Republic: legal aspects.) *[Summary]*. I.L. Babich. **Etnograf. Oboz.** 2 3-4:2001 pp.131-143.

2980   Land administration reforms and social differentiation: a case study of Ghana's Lands Commission. Kasim Kasanga. **IDS Bull.** 32:1 1:2001 pp.57-64.

2981   Law and colonial cultures: legal regimes in world history, 1400-1900. Lauren A. Benton. New York: Cambridge University Press, 2001. 285p. *ISBN: 052100926X, 0521804140. Includes bibliographical references and index.* (*Series:* Studies in comparative world history).

2982   Law and persuasion in the elimination of female genital modification. Regina Smith Oboler. **Human. Org.** 60:4 Winter:2001 pp.311-318.

2983   Legal and binding: time, change and long-term transactions; *[Summary in French]*. Catherine Alexander. **J. Royal Anth. Inst.** 7:3 9:2001 pp.467-486.

2984   Legal pluralism and social justice in economic and political development. Franz von Benda-Beckmann. **IDS Bull.** 32:1 1:2001 pp.46-56.

2985   Legalism from Kuan Chung to Shang Yang. Wong Yuk. **Chin. Cult.** XL:2 6:1999 pp.133-139.

2986   The Mediterranean family. Nimrod Hurvitz; Edward Fram; David S. Powers; Yossef Rapoport; Dror Ze'Evi; Bettina Dennerlein; Miriam Frenkel; Howard Tzvi Adelman. **Contin. Change** 16:2 8:2001 pp.169-319. *Collection of 7 articles.*

2987   Mots de plainte et mots de menace. Lettres au procureur de la République en Guadeloupe. *[In French]*; [Complaints and threats: letters to the state prosecutor in Guadeloupe]. Christiane Bougerol. **Homme** 160 10-12:2001 pp.117-136.

2988   Mythic prostitutes, AIDS and criminal law; *[Summary in French]*. Stephanie Kane. **Ethnologies** 23:1 2001 pp.255-288.

2989   Nationalité et citoyenneté en Afrique occidentale français: originaires et citoyens dans le Sénégal colonial. *[In French]*; [Nationality and citizenship in French West Africa: indigenous peoples and citizens in colonial Senegal] *[Summary]*. Catherine Coquery-Vidrovitch. **J. Afr. Hist.** 42:2 2001 pp.285-306.

2990   On the generification of culture: from blow fish to Melanesian; *[Summary in French]*. Frederick Errington; Deborah Gewertz. **J. Royal Anth. Inst.** 7:3 9:2001 pp.509-526.

2991   Ownership by birth: the *Mitāksarā* stand. Ludo Rocher; Rosane Rocher. **J. Ind. Phil.** 29:1-2 4:2001 pp.241-255.

2992   Penser le temps culturel du droit. Le destin anthropologique du concept de coutume. *[In French]*; (Thinking the cultural time of law: the anthropological destiny of the concept of custom.) *[Summary]*. Louis Assier-Andrieu. **Homme** 160 10-12:2001 pp.67-90.

2993   Le problème de la permanence des musulmans dans les territoires conquis par les chrétiens, du point de vue de la loi islamique. *[In French]*; [The problem of permanence among Muslims in territories conquered by Christians, from the perspective of Islamic law]. J.P. Molénat. **Arabica** XLVIII:3 7:2001 pp.392-400.

2994   The public prosecutor's office and legal change in Brazil. Maria Tereza Sadek. **IDS Bull.** 32:1 1:2001 pp.65-73.

2995   Reading Mesopotamian law cases, PBS 5 100: a question of filiation; *[Summary in French]*. Martha T. Roth. **J. Ec. Soc. Hist. O.** 44:3 8:2001 pp.243-292.

2996   Social justice and creative jurisprudence in late Bronze Age Syria; *[Summary in French]*. Raymond Westbrook. **J. Ec. Soc. Hist. O.** 44:1 2:2001 pp.22-43.

2997   Sri Guru Granth Sahib: a juristic person. An analysis of *SGPC* v. *SN Dass*. Kashmir Singh. **Sikh Rev.** 49:8(572) 8:2001 pp.47-53.

2998   Toleration and exclusion: al-Shāfi'ī and al-Ghazālī on the treatment of apostates. Frank Griffel. **B. Sch. Orient. Afr. Stud.** 64:3 2001 pp.339-354.

2999   Toward an anthropology of prisons. Lorna A. Rhodes. **Ann. R. Anthr.** 30 2001 pp.65-83.

3000   The truth and other irrelevant aspects of Nukulaelae gossip. Niko Besnier. **Pac. Stud.** 17:3 9:1994 pp.1-40.

3001   The underside of conflict management — in Africa and elsewhere. Laura Nader. **IDS Bull.** 32:1 1:2001 pp.19-27.

3002   The way of the Xunzi. Leo K.C. Cheung. **J. Ch. Philos.** 28:3 9:2001 pp.301-320.

3003   'We make the law and the law makes us': some ideas on a law in development research agenda. Peter P. Houtzager. **IDS Bull.** 32:1 1:2001 pp.8-18.

Crime
Crime

3004   AIDS and criminal justice. Stephanie Kane; Theresa Mason. **Ann. R. Anthr.** 30 2001 pp.457-480.

3005   Crime and punishment: narratives of order and disorder. Margaret Atack; David H. Walker; David Platten; Claire Gorrara; Amanda Crawley; Ann Miller; Charles Forsdick. **Fr. Cult. Stud.** 12(3):36 10:2001 pp.233-350. *Collection of 8 articles.*

3006   Korrekt optræden performative aspekter af politi og politiarbejde. *[In Danish]*; (Performative aspects of police and police work.) *[Summary]*. Camilla Kvist; Lars Holmberg. **Tids. Antrop.** 41 2000 pp.31-46.

3007   Muti ritual murder in Natal: from chiefs to commoners (1900-1930). Rob Turrell. **S. Afr. Hist. J.** 44 2001 pp.21-39.

3008   Princes as highway men. A consideration of the phenomenon of armed banditry in precolonial Borgu. Olayemi Akinwumi. **Cah. Ét. Afr.** XLI(2):162 2001 pp.333-350.

3009   The social relations and human nature in the prison. Mei-chih Li. **B. Inst. Ethn. Ac. Sin.** 90 Autumn:2000 pp.155-200.

Traditional and modern law
Loi traditionnelle et moderne

3010   Consequences of the dissolution of customary marriages; *[Summary in Afrikaans]*. L.P. Vorster; N. Dlamini-Ndandwe; M.J. Molapo. **S. Afr. J. Ethnol.** 24:2 2001 pp.62-66.

3011   A cost-benefit analysis of Hollow Waters community holistic circle healing process; Une analyse de rentabilité du processus holitique de guérison de la Première nation de Hollow Water. *[In French]*. Joseph E. Couture; Ted Parker; Ruth Couture; Patti Laboucane. Ottawa: Solicitor General Canada, 2001. viii, 147p. *ISBN: 0662300351. Includes bibliographical references (p. 145-147) Also available online. (Series:* Aboriginal peoples' collection - APC 20 CA).

3012   Dissolution of customary marriages; *[Summary in Afrikaans]*. F.P. Van R. Whelpton; L.P. Vorster. **S. Afr. J. Ethnol.** 24:2 2001 pp.56-61.

3013   Giving up homicide: Korowai experience of witches and police (West Papua). Rupert Stasch. **Oceania** 72:1 9:2001 pp.33-52.

3014   *Hadīth* and *fiqh*. G.H.A. Juynboll; Robert Gleave; Christopher Melchert; Susan Spectorsky. **Islam. Law Soc.** 8:3 10:2001 pp.303-431. *Collection of 4 articles.*

3015   Indigenous knowledge and customary law in South Africa; *[Summary in Afrikaans]*. L.P. Vorster. **S. Afr. J. Ethnol.** 24:2 2001 pp.51-55.

3016   Mixing bodies and beliefs: the predicament of tribes. L. Scott Gould. **Columb. Law R.** 101:4 5:2001 pp.702-772.

3017   Population growth and customary land law: the case of Cordillera villages in the Philippines. Lorelei Crisologo-Mendoza; Dirk Van de Gaer. **Econ. Dev. Cult. Change** 49:3 4:2001 pp.631-658.

3018   Prégnance du droit coutumier. *[In French]*; [The significance of customary law]. Geneviève Bédoucha; Gianni Albergoni; Anie Montigny; Andre Gingrich; Pierre Bonte; Négib Bouderbala; Gerhard Lichtenthäler; Stefan Kohler; Alain Mahé. **Rural Stud.** 155-156 7-12:2001 pp.11-214. *Collection of 10 articles.*

3019   Requirements for validity of customary marriages; *[Summary in Afrikaans]*. J.C. Bekker. **S. Afr. J. Ethnol.** 24:2 2001 pp.41-47.

3020   South African customary law and ethnicity: challenges for South Africa; *[Summary in Afrikaans]*. L.P. Vorster. **S. Afr. J. Ethnol.** 24:4 2001 pp.119-124.

Violence
Violence

3021   Antropologiia ekstremal'nykh grupp. Dominantnye otnosheniia sredi voenno-sluzhashchikh srochnoi Rossiiskoi Armii. *[In Russian]*; (Anthropology of extreme groups. Relations of dominance among the enlisted personnel of the Russian army.) *[Summary]*. K.L. Bannikov. **Etnograf. Oboz.** 1 1-2:2001 pp.112-141.

3022   Armiia glazami antropologa. K issledovaniiu ekstremal'nykh grupp. *[In Russian]*; (The army: the vision of an anthropologist. Towards the exploration of outlying groups.) *[Summary]*. K. Bannikov. **Mir Rossii** IX:4 2000 pp.125-134.

3023   Aryan destruction of Indus Valley civilization - myth or reality. M. Qasim Jan. **J. Pak. Hist. Soc.** XLIX:2 4-6:2001 pp.31-36.

3024   A bioarchaeological perspective on the history of violence. Phillip L. Walker. **Ann. R. Anthr.** 30 2001 pp.573-596.

3025   Cultural narratives, violence, and mother-son loyalty: an exploration into Gusii personification of evil. Justus M. Ogembo. **Ethos** 29:1 3:2001 pp.3-29.

3026   Culture, violence, and explanation. Nina Glick Schiller; B.G. Karlsson; Glenn Bowman; Matthew Frye Jacobson. **Identities** 8:1 3:2001 pp.1-104. *Collection of 4 articles.*

3027   Du danger et du terrain en Algérie. *[In French]*; (Danger and fieldwork in Algeria.) *[Summary]*; *[Summary in German]*. Abderrahmane Moussaoui. **Ethn. Fr.** XXXI:1 1-3:2001 pp.51-59.

3028   Gender-based violence: a critical US policy issue. F. Catherine Johnson. **Dev. Anthrop.** 18:1-2 Spring-Fall:2000 pp.25-33.

3029   Le génocide du Rwanda: l'adhésion populaire à la violence extrême, dimensions politique et culturelle. *[In French]*; [Genocide in Rwanda: popular support for extreme violence and political and cultural factors]. Jean-Pierre Chrétien. **Stud. Afr.** 12 3:2001 pp.53-68.

3030   Law and the pragmatics of inclusion: governing domestic violence in Trinidad and Tobago. Mindie Lazarus-Black. **Am. Ethn.** 28:2 5:2001 pp.388-416.

3031   Moçambique e as múltiplas formas da violência colonial. *[In Portuguese]*; [Mozambique and the many forms of colonial violence]. João Paulo Borges Coelho. **Stud. Afr.** 12 3:2001 pp.21-36.

3032   La résistance indienne au quotidien (El Quinche, 1755). *[In French]*; [Indigenous resistance on a daily basis (El Quinche, 1755)]. Bernard Lavallé. **Caravelle** 76-77 12:2001 pp.355-362.

3033   Sorcery, modernity and social transformation in Banyuwangi, East Java. Caroline Campbell; Linda H. Connor. **R. Ind. Malay. Aff.** 34:2 Summer:2000 pp.61-98.

3034   The underneath of things: violence, history, and the everyday in Sierra Leone. Mariane C. Ferme. Berkeley CA: University of California Press, 2001. xii, 287p. *ISBN: 0520225430, 0520225422. Includes bibliographical references (p. 253-280) and index.*

3035   Violencia y guerra. *[In Spanish]*; [Violence and war]. Javier Ordóñez. **Rev. de Human.** 11 Autumn:2001 pp.77-94.

3036   The war games victims. The impact of local and foreign military training exercises on the indigenous peoples of northern Kenya. J.O. Kaunga. **Indig. Aff.** 2 2001 pp.54-59.

E.4:   **Interethnic and intraethnic relations**
           Rapports interethniques et intraethniques

3037   Diagonales de la communication interculturelle. *[In French]*; [Cross currents of intercultural communication]. Martine Abdallah-Pretceille [Ed.]; Louis Porche [Ed.]. Paris: Anthropos, 1999. 228p. *ISBN: 2717837833. Includes bibliographical references.*

3038   Divining 'troubles', or 'divining' troubles? Emergent and conflictual dimensions of Bangladeshi divination. James M. Wilce. **Anthr. Quart.** 74:4 10:2001 pp.190-200.

3039   La marca de Marcos: ¿pueden hablar los indígenas mexicanos? *[In Spanish]*; [The mark of Marcos: do indigenous Mexicans have a voice?] Kristine Vanden Berghe. **Cuad. Am.** XV:3(87) 5-6:2001 pp.158-173.

3040   Natives with jackets and degrees. Othering, objectification and the role of Palestinians in the co-existence field in Israel; *[Summary in French]*; *[Summary in German]*; *[Summary in Spanish]*. Dan Rabinowitz. **Soc. Anthrop.** 9:1 2:2001 pp.65-80.

3041   New insights on relations between Russia and Africa. Irina Filatova. **S. Afr. Hist. J.** 42 2000 pp.341-364.

3042   North Africa, Islam and the Mediterranean world: from the Almoravids to the Algerian War. Julia Clancy-Smith; Amira K. Bennison; James A. Miller; Ronald A. Messier; Mohamed El Mansour; Dalenda Larguèche; Abdelhamid Larguèche; Edmund Burke, III; Jonathan G. Katz; James D. Le Sueur. **J. N. African Stud.** 6:1 Spring:2001 pp.1-186. *Collection of 10 articles.*

3043   Philosophical aspects of the 'AAA Statement on 'Race''. Naomi Zack; Lee D. Baker [Comments by]. **Anth. Th.** 1:4 12:2001 pp.445-472.

3044   The psychology of culture contact. Gerhard Kubik. **B. Int. Com. Urg. Anthrop. Ethnol. R.** 40 1999-2000 pp.149-156.

3045   The savage hits back or the White man through native eyes. Matthias Krings. **Paideuma** 47 2001 pp.223-236.

Africa
Afrique

3046   Anthropology and empire in post-Italian Ethiopia. Makonnen Desta and the imagination of an Ethiopian 'we-race'. Thomas Zitelmann. **Paideuma** 47 2001 pp.161-180.

3047   Le choc des cultures: plusieurs histoires coloniales et des conflits toujours en suspens. *[In French]*; [Culture shocks: numerous colonial histories and unresolved conflicts]. Mohamed Mohamed-Abdi. **Stud. Afr.** 12 3:2001 pp.7-20.

3048   Conflits, violences et ethnicités en République Islamique de Mauritanie: réflexions sur le rôle des propagandes à caractère raciste dans le déclenchement des violences collectives de 1989. *[In French]*; [Conflict, violence and ethnicity in the Islamic Republic of Mauritania: thoughts on the role of racist propaganda in causing the collective violence of 1989]. Mariella Villasante de Beauvais. **Stud. Afr.** 12 3:2001 pp.69-94.

3049   The contribution of the Ait Yusi tribe to Moroccan culture. Abdullah Bennesser Alaoui. **Morocco** 2 1997 pp.65-76.

3050   Le génocide du Rwanda: l'adhésion populaire à la violence extrême, dimensions politique et culturelle. *[In French]*; [Genocide in Rwanda: popular support for extreme violence and political and cultural factors]. Jean-Pierre Chrétien. **Stud. Afr.** 12 3:2001 pp.53-68.

3051   La guerre de 1940-45 vécue à Coquilhatville. *[In French]*; [The 1940-45 war as experienced in Coquilhatville] *[Summary]*. H. Vinck. **Ann. Æqua.** 22 2001 pp.21-102.

3052   In and out of culture: fieldwork in war-torn Uganda. Sverker Finnström. **Crit. Anthr.** 21:3 9:2001 pp.247-258.

3053   Indians and whites in the multicultural world of Rooke's *Ratoons*. J.A. Kearney. **Eng. Afr.** 26:2 10:1999 pp.89-112.

3054   Max Gluckman and the critique of segregation in South African anthropology, 1921-1940. Paul Cocks. **J. S. Afr. Stud.** 27:4 12:2001 pp.739-756.

3055   The question of cultural difference: anthropological perspectives in South Africa; *[Summary in Afrikaans]*. John Sharp. **S. Afr. J. Ethnol.** 24:3 2001 pp.67-74.

3056   Racism. Chandra Roy; Alberto Saldamando; Tarcila R. Zea; Peter Jull; Kathryn Bennett; Victoria Tauli-Corpuz; C.R. Bijo; Justin Kenrick; Jerome Lewis. **Indig. Aff.** 1 2001 pp.8-70. *Collection of 7 articles.*

3057   Soulèvement touareg et États: hiatus culturel ou démocratie absente? *[In French]*; [Tuareg uprising and the state: cultural hiatus or absent democracy?] Hélène Claudot-Hawad. **Stud. Afr.** 12 3:2001 pp.37-52.

3058   The suppression of mixed marriages among LMS missionaries in South Africa before 1820. Julia C. Wells. **S. Afr. Hist. J.** 44 2001 pp.1-20.

3059   The war games victims. The impact of local and foreign military training exercises on the indigenous peoples of northern Kenya. J.O. Kaunga. **Indig. Aff.** 2 2001 pp.54-59.

3060   Wayward pastoral ghosts and regional xenophobia in a northern Madagascar town; *[Summary in French]*. Lesley A. Sharp. **Africa** 71:1 2001 pp.38-81.

Americas
Amériques

3061   The anthropology of Afro-Latin America and the Caribbean: diasporic dimensions. Kevin A. Yelvington. **Ann. R. Anthr.** 30 2001 pp.227-260.

3062   Ataka zelenoi magii. Interkul'turnye protsessy v shamanizme shuarov (Ekvador). *[In Russian]*; (Attack of the green magic. Intercultural processes in the shamanism of Shuar (Ecuadorian Amazon region).) *[Summary]*. E. Mader. **Etnograf. Oboz.** 5 9-10:2000 pp.79-87.

3063   Autonomy in Chiapas, Mexico. IWGIA. **Indig. Aff.** 2 2001 pp.60-65.

3064   Color-full before color blind: the emergence of multiracial neighborhood politics in Queens, New York City. Roger Sanjek. **Am. Anthrop.** 102:4 12:2000 pp.762-772.

3065   Dancing with the devil: society and cultural poetics in Mexican-American south Texas. José E. Limón. Madison WI, London: University of Wisconsin Press, 1994. xii, 240p. *ISBN: 0299142248, 0299142205. (Series: New directions in anthropological writing).*

3066   The fall of the Bardados planter class: an interpretation of the 1980s crisis in the Barbados sugar industry. Robert Goddard. **Agr. Hist.** 75:3 Summer:2001 pp.329-351.

3067   Grupos tribais da Amazônia brasileira em processo de integracão à sociedade. Dois exemplos: os Makuxí e os Tenetehara. *[In Portuguese]*; [Tribal groups in the Brazilian Amazon in the process of integrating into society. The two examples of the Macushi and Tenetehara]. Edson Soares Diniz. **B. Int. Com. Urg. Anthrop. Ethnol. R.** 40 1999-2000 pp.185-190.

3068   'Like Nixon coming to China': finding common ground in a multi-ethnic coalition for environmental justice. Melissa Checker. **Anthr. Quart.** 74:3 7:2001 pp.135-146.

3069   Os Wapixána. Síntese de uma situação de contato interétnico. *[In Portuguese]*; [The Wapishana: an example of interethnic contact]. Orlando Sampaio Silva. **B. Int. Com. Urg. Anthrop. Ethnol. R.** 40 1999-2000 pp.171-184.

3070   'Pernicious aliens' and the mestizo nation: ethnicity and the shaping of collective identities in El Salvador before the Second World War. Jan Suter. **Imm. Minor.** 20:2 7:2001 pp.26-57.

3071   'Playing Indian': embracing or appropriating native cultural practices? Victoria Paraschak. **Kunapipi** XXIII:1 2001 pp.41-55.

3072   Plurietnicidade e intolerâncias no sul do Brasil. *[In Portuguese]*; [Multiethnic areas and intolerance in southern Brazil]. Ilka Boaventura Leite. **B. Int. Com. Urg. Anthrop. Ethnol. R.** 40 1999-2000 pp.197-204.

3073   Power in America: nationhood and ethnicity. Eileen Boris; Robert Garson; Rocío G. Davis; Priscilla Roberts; Bridget Kevane; Victor J. Viser. **J. Am. Stud.** 35:1 4:2001 pp.1-109. *Collection of 6 articles.*

3074   Public opinion on Canadian aboriginal issues, 1976-98: persistence, change, and cohort analysis. J. Rick Ponting. **Can. Ethn. Stud.** XXXII:3 2000 pp.44-75.

3075   Racism. Chandra Roy; Alberto Saldamando; Tarcila R. Zea; Peter Jull; Kathryn Bennett; Victoria Tauli-Corpuz; C.R. Bijo; Justin Kenrick; Jerome Lewis. **Indig. Aff.** 1 2001 pp.8-70. *Collection of 7 articles.*

3076   Warring in America: encounters of gender and race. Gail D. Danvers; Rachel Van Duyvenbode; Liping Bu; Paul Christian Jones; Liese M. Perrin; David Monod; Peter Widdowson. **J. Am. Stud.** 35:2 8:2001 pp.187-335. *Collection of 7 articles.*

3077   'Will the model minority please identify itself?' American ethnic identity and its discontents. Ruth Y. Hsu. **Diaspora** 5:1 Spring:1996 pp.37-64.

Asia
Asie

3078   Building cultural bridges: the Philippines and Japan in the 1930s. Lydia N. Yu-Jose. **Phil. Stud.** 49:3 2001 pp.399-416.

3079   Civilizations in contact: between East and West. Ynhui Park; Hyongtaek Lim; Young-bae Song; Woosung Huh; Won-shik Choi; Elaine H. Kim; Seung-hwan Lee; Seung-mi Han [Comments by]; Seok-choon Lew; Sang-in Jun [Comments by]; Hyun-key Kim Hogarth. **Korea J.** 41:3 Autumn:2001 pp.5-197. *Collection of 6 articles.*

3080   An interview with Subramani. Subramani; Vilsoni Hereniko [Interviewer]. **Cont. Pac.** 13:1 Spring:2001 pp.184-198.

3081   Listening patterns and identity of the Korean diaspora in the former USSR. Hae-Kyung Um. **Brit. J. Ethnomusic.** 9:2 2000 pp.121-142.

3082   The marginalization of a Dalit martial race in late nineteenth and early twentieth-century western India. Philip Constable. **J. Asian St.** 60:2 5:2001 pp.439-482.

3083   Natsional'no-kul'turnye ob"edineniia etnicheskikh men'shinstv Respubliki Buriatiia. *[In Russian]*; (Culture associations of the ethnic minorities of the Buryat Republic.) *[Summary]*. L.G. Iril'deeva. **Etnograf. Oboz.** 5 9-10:2000 pp.129-142.

3084   Savage imagery: (mis)representations of the Forest Tobelo of Indonesia. Christopher R. Duncan. **Asia Pacific J. Anthr.** 2:1 4:2001 pp.45-62.

3085   Un Tamoul, *syahbandar* de Samudera-Pasai au début du XVIᵉ siècle. *[In French]*; [A Tamil in Samudera-Pasai at the beginning of the sixteenth century]. Jorge Alves. **Archipel** 62 2001 pp.127-142.

3086   Women and war: the role Kuwaiti women played during the Iraqi occupation. M. Juliá; H. Ridha. **J. Int. Dev.** 13:5 7:2001 pp.583-598.

Europe
Europe

3087   Belaja-joen marit baškirian etnisessä mosaiikissa. *[In Finnish]*; [The Mari of the Belaja delta in the Bashkirian ethnic mosaic]. Tarmo Hakkarainen. **Suomal.-Ugril. Seur. Aikak.** 89 2001 pp.254-259.

3088   Between ethnic group and nation; *[Summary in Polish]*. Iwona Kabzińska. **Ethnol. Pol.** 21 2000 pp.7-26.

3089   Ephraim ben Jacob's compilation of twelfth-century persecutions. Robert Chazan. **Jew. Q. Rev.** 84 1993-1994 pp.397-485.

3090   Ethnic polarisation in an ethnically homogeneous town. Peter Salner. **Czech Soc. Rev.** IX:2 Fall:2001 pp.235-246.

3091   The Gypsy question and the Gypsy expert in Sweden. Norma Montesino. **Rom. Stud.** 11:1 6:2001 pp.1-24.

3092   O 'kolonial'nom politarizme', latinoamerikanskom 'feodalizme' i nekotorykh aspektakh otnosheniia k aborigenam v Russkoi Amerike. *[In Russian]*; (On 'colonial politarism',

Latin American 'feudalism' and some aspects of the attitude towards indigenous peoples in Russian America.) *[Summary]*. A.A. Istomin. **Etnograf. Oboz.** 3 5-6:2000 pp.89-108.

3093 Das Lob der Mischung, Reinheit als Gefahr: Nationalismus und Ethnizität in Gibraltar. *[In German]*; [Praise for mixing, purity as danger: nationalism and ethnicity in Gibraltar] *[Summary]*. Dieter Haller. **Z. Ethn.** 126:1 2001 pp.27-62.

3094 "Mint leveleket a vihar". Interetnikus kapcsolatok és helyi identitás egy vajdasági faluban. *[In Hungarian]*; ['As the storm through the leaves'. Interethnic relations and local identity awareness of Hungarians in a village in Voivodina, Yugoslavia] *[Summary]*. Virág Hajnal. **Regio** 12:3 2001 pp.119-140.

3095 A moldvai csángók magyar nyelvi oktatásának szükségességéről. *[In Hungarian]*; [About the Hungarian language teaching need of the Csángó minority] *[Summary]*. Attila Hegyeli. **Regio** 12:4 2001 pp.181-194.

3096 Natsional'no-kul'turnaia avtonomiia v kontekste sovershenstvovaniia zakonodatel'stva. *[In Russian]*; (National culture autonomies in the context of perfecting legislation.) *[Summary]*. V.R. Filippov; E.I. Filippova. **Etnograf. Oboz.** 3 5-6:2000 pp.46-59.

3097 Oświata a procesy asymilacyjne wśród mniejszości ukraińskiej. *[In Polish]*; (Education and assimilation processes among the Ukrainian minority.) Zofia Tracewicz. Toruń: Adam Marszałek, 2000. 227p. *ISBN: 8371745583.*

3098 Pluralizm kulturowy i etniczny a odrębność regionalna Kresów południowo-wschodnich w latach 1918-1939. *[In Polish]*; [Cultural and ethnic pluralism and the regional distinctiveness of the southeast borderlands between 1918 and 1939]. Łucja Kapralska. .

3099 The registration of Gypsies in National Socialism: responsibility in a German region. Ulrich F. Opfermann. **Rom. Stud.** 11:1 6:2001 pp.25-66.

3100 Russian-Jewish intellectuals confront the pogroms of 1881: the example of *Razsvet*. Steven Cassedy. **Jew. Q. Rev.** 84 1993-1994 pp.129-152.

3101 O sovremennoi etnicheskoi situatsii u Dolgan. *[In Russian]*; (On the modern ethnic situation of the Dolgans.) *[Summary]*. V.P. Krivonogov. **Etnograf. Oboz.** 5 9-10:2000 pp.106-116.

3102 A tiszaújlaki lakosság interetnikus kapcsolatai és lokális identitástudata egy állomásozó terepmunka nyomán. *[In Hungarian]*; (Interethnic relations and local identity awareness of the Hungarian inhabitants of Tiszaújlak in Ukraine in the light of fieldwork.) *[Summary]*. Zoltán Karmacsi. **Regio** 12:3 2001 pp.141-162.

3103 Zaginiony świat? Nazywają ich Łemkami. *[In Polish]*; [Missing world - the Łemko]. Jacek Nowak.

Oceania
Océanie

3104 Gender in the 'contact zone'. Victoria Haskins; Alison Holland; Fiona Paisley; Katrina Schlunke; Hannah Robert; Amanda Nettelbeck; Jane Haggis; Sonja Kurtzer. **Aus. Fem. St.** 16:34 3:2001 pp.13-99. *Collection of 7 articles.*

3105 Jean Martin and the exploration of (in)difference. Gillian Bottomley. **Asia Pacific J. Anthr.** 1:2 10:2000 pp.102-116.

3106 Of human bondage: the breaking in of stockmen in Northern Australia. Veronica Strang. **Oceania** 72:1 9:2001 pp.53-79.

3107 'Old contempt and new solicitude': race relations and Australian ethnography. Gillian Cowlishaw; Diane Austin-Broos; Toni Bauman; Judy Lattas; Barry Morris. **Oceania** 71:3 3:2001 pp.169-262. *Collection of 5 articles.*

3108 The politics of suffering: indigenous policy in Australia since the 1970s. Peter Sutton. **Anthro. forum** 11:2 11:2001 pp.125-173.

F.1: Cosmology and myth
Cosmologie et mythe

3109 An Amazonian myth and its history. Peter Gow. Oxford: Oxford University Press, 2001. xiii, 338p. *ISBN: 0199241961, 0199241953. Includes bibliographical references and index.* (*Series:* Oxford studies in social and cultural anthropology).

3110 Antenor and Vibhīshănă. Marcel A.J. Meulder. **J. Indo-Eur. S.** 28:3-4 Fall-Winter:2000 pp.399-406.

3111 The cosmic journey of Odysseus. Nanno Marinatos. **Numen** XLVIII:4 2001 pp.381-416.

3112 Defining moments and recurring myths: a reply. Seymour Martin Lipset; Edward Grabb [Comments by]; James Curtis [Comments by]; Douglas Baer [Comments by]. **Can. R. Soc. A.** 38:1 2:2001 pp.97-104.

3113 Des mythes au féminin. Don Juan au Costa Rica. *[In French]*; [Feminine myths: Don Juan in Costa Rica]. Claire Pailler. **Caravelle** 76-77 12:2001 pp.537-547.

3114 *El Negro,* El Niño, witchcraft and the absence of rain in Botswana. Jan-Bart Gewald. **Afr. Affairs** 100:401 10:2001 pp.555-580.

3115 The end of mythology: Hesiod's *Theogony* and the Indo-European myth of the final battle. Daniel Bray. **J. Indo-Eur. S.** 28:3-4 Fall-Winter:2000 pp.359-372.

3116 From Iranian myth to folk narrative: the legend of the dragon-slayer and the spinning maiden in the *Persian Book of the Kings.* Kinga Ilona Márkus-Takeshita. **Asian Folk. S.** LX:2 2001 pp.203-214.

3117 History and the genealogy of myth in Telefolmin. Dan Jorgensen. **Paideuma** 47 2001 pp.103-128.

3118 The illustration of *The Old Man of the Sea* and *The Story of Sindbad the Sailor*: its iconography and legendary background. Kazue Kobayashi. **Senri Ethn. Stud.** 55 2001 pp.101-120.

3119 Images de déesses ou prostituées? Les *ahuianime* de l'ancien Mexique central. *[In French]*; [Images of goddesses or prostitutes? The *ahuianime* of ancient central Mexico]. Guilhem Olivier. **Caravelle** 76-77 12:2001 pp.297-308.

3120 Die Legende von der Spaltung des Mondes. Ein koranisches Wunder in türkischem Kleid. *[In German]*; [The legend of the splitting of the moon. A wonder from the Koran in Turkish dress] *[Summary]*. Gisela Procházka-Eisl. **Arch. Orient.** 69:2 5:2001 pp.285-298.

3121 Montagnes mythiques: les Tumuc-Humac. *[In French]*; (Mythical mountains: Tumac-Humac.) *[Summary]*. J. Hurault. **Cah. Outre-mer** 53:212 10-12:2000 pp.367-392.

3122 Myth and masks in West Africa. Jack Goody. **Cam. Anthrop.** 22:2 2000 2001 pp.60-69.

3123 Die "Mythen" von den "Mystischen" Megalithen. Ein Diskussionsbeitrag zur Problematik der Realität. *[In German]*; ['Myths' of the 'mystical' megaliths. A contribution to the discussion on the problematic nature of reality]. Pia Maria Forster. **B. Int. Com. Urg. Anthrop. Ethnol. R.** 40 1999-2000 pp.215-231.

3124 Myths of the Czech Gypsies. Nina Pavelčík; Jiří Pavelčík. **Asian Folk. S.** LX:1 2001 pp.21-30.

3125 A new mythical theme in the saga of Hervör and King Heidrekr and the Armenian *Epic of Sasoon.* Stépan Ahyan. **J. Indo-Eur. S.** 28:3-4 Fall-Winter:2000 pp.373-384.

3126 Origen y uso del fuego, mito recogido entre los Tehuelches araucanizados de la Patagonia argentina. *[In Spanish]*; [Origin and use of fire - a myth taken up among the Araucanized Tehuelche of Argentinian Patagonia]. Ana Fernandez Garay; Graciela Hernandez. **Amerindia** 24 1999 pp.73-90.

3127 The origin of dragons. Robert Blust. **Anthropos [St. Augustin]** 95:2 2000 pp.519-541.

3128 El rastro de los pecaríes. Variaciones míticas, variaciones cosmológicas e identidades etnicas en la etnología pano. *[In Spanish]*; [The trail of the *pecaríes.* Mythical variations, cosmological variations and ethnic identities in the Pano ethnology]. Oscar Calavia Sáez. **J. Soc. Amér.** 87 2001 pp.161-176.

3129   The rebirth of myth? Nietzsche's *Eternal Recurrence* and its Romantic antecedents. Robert A. Yelle. **Numen** XLVII:2 2000 pp.175-202.

3130   Der Sexgeist und der Chusalungu. Überlegungen zum Mythos bei "postmodernen" Indianern. *[In German]*; [The sex spirit and Chusalungu. Reflections on myths among 'postmodern' Indians]. Bernhard Wörrle. **Anthropos [St. Augustin]** 95:2 2000 pp.542-547.

3131   Telling the facts of life: cosmology and the epic of evolution. Jon Turney. **Sci. Cult.** 10:2 6:2001 pp.225-248.

3132   A text that contains the truth on the origin of the Tibetans — an interpretation of the legendary genesis of the Tibetans from a macaque and a rock demon. Shi Shuo. **Soc. Sci. China** XXII:3 Autumn:2001 pp.162-172.

3133   La théomorphose de Huitzilopochtli. *[In French]*; [The theomorphosis of Huitzilopochli]. Marie-José Vabre. **Caravelle** 76-77 12:2001 pp.119-130.

3134   Über den chthonischen Ursprung des Isrâfîl. *[In German]*; [On the chthonic origins of Isrâfîl]. Dan Enok Sørensen. **Acta Orient.** 62 2001 pp.15-21.

3135   L'udová kozmovízia v bielych karpatoch. *[In Slovak]*; (The folk cosmovision in the White Carpathian mountains.) *[Summary]*. Milan Kováč. **Slov. Národop.** 47:2-3 1999 pp.173-181.

F.2:   **Major religions**
       Religions principales

3136   Ascetics and aesthetics in the *Analects*. Jeffrey L. Richey. **Numen** XLVII:2 2000 pp.161-174.

3137   'Asian values' and Confucian discourse. Seung-Hwan Lee; Seung-Mi Han [Comments by]. **Korea J.** 41:3 Autumn:2001 pp.198-212.

3138   Confucian ethics and virtue ethics. Wai-Ying Wong. **J. Ch. Philos.** 28:3 9:2001 pp.285-300.

3139   (Constructing belief: the actuality of the sociology of religion.); *[Text in Japanese]*. Eiichi Otani; Toshinori Kawamata; Hiroo Kikuchi. Tanashi: Harvest-sha, 2000. 185p.

3140   Duchowość i religijność kobiet dawniej i dziś. *[In Polish]*; (Women's spirituality and religiosity: past and present.) *[Summary]*. Elżbieta Pakszys [Ed.]; Liliana Sikorska [Ed.]. Poznan: Wydawnictwo Fundacji Humaniora, 2000. 150p. *ISBN: 8371121555*.

3141   Ecological feminism and Daoism. Sharon Rowe; James D. Sellmann. **Asian Cult. (Asian-Pac. Cult.) Q.** XXVIII:4 Winter:2000 pp.11-26.

3142   Ekologicheskaia funktsiia religii. *[In Russian]*; (Ecological function of religion.) *[Summary]*. V.L. Ogudin. **Etnograf. Oboz.** 1 1-2:2001 pp.23-38.

3143   Elements of Indian metaphysics. R.T. Vyas. **J. Orient. Inst.** XLVII:3-4(47) 3-6:1998 pp.215-226.

3144   The fractal self and the organization of nature: the Daoist sage and chaos theory. David Jones; John Culliney. **Asian Cult. (Asian-Pac. Cult.) Q.** XXVIII:3 Autumn:2000 pp.59-70.

3145   Hazor — a city state between the major powers. Christa Schäfer-Lichtenberger. **Scan. J. Old. Test.** 15:1 2001 pp.104-122.

3146   How critical is it to be historically critical? The case of the composition of the Book of Job. Douglas Lawrie. **J. N.W. Sem. Lang.** 27:1 2001 pp.121-146.

3147   'I will testify against them and challenge them': text and interpretation of Hosea 14:9. Jan A. Wagenaar. **J. N.W. Sem. Lang.** 26:2 2000 pp.127-134.

3148   The introductory part of the *Kiranāvalī*. Musashi Tachikawa. **J. Ind. Phil.** 29:1-2 4:2001 pp.275-291.

3149   Ken Wilber's spectrum model: identifying alternative soteriological perspectives. Leon Schlamm. **Religion** 31:1 1:2001 pp.19-39.

3150   On the Baltic theonyms: Baltic-Italic correspondences in divine-names. Václav Blažek. **J. Indo-Eur. S.** 29:3-4 Fall-Winter:2001 pp.351-366.

3151   On the translation of God. Suzuki Norihisa. **Jpn. Relig.** 26:2 7:2001 pp.131-148.

3152   Posviashcheniia glavnykh prestolov khramov na severo-vostoke Podmoskov'ia v XIV-nachale XX v. *[In Russian]*; (Main altar consecrations in the north-east of the Moscow region (14th—early 20th centuries).) *[Summary]*. V.A. Tkachenko. **Etnograf. Oboz.** 4 7-8:2000 pp.32-44.

3153   Reincarnation revisited rationally. Ashok Aklujkar. **J. Ind. Phil.** 29:1-2 4:2001 pp.3-15.

3154   Religijność a tolerancja. Obszary zależności. *[In Polish]*; (Religiousness and tolerance. Spheres of interdependence.) Ewa Wysocka. Krakow: Nomos, 2000. 294p. *ISBN: 8388508024.*

3155   Religion and ecology: can the climate change? Mary Evelyn Tucker; John A. Grim; George Rupp; Michael B. McElroy; Donald A. Brown; J. Baird Callicott; Hava Tirosh-Samuelson; Sallie McFague; S. Nomanul Haq; Vasudha Narayanan; Christopher Key Chapple; Donald K. Swearer; Tu Weiming; James Miller; Jack D. Forbes; Bill McKibben. **Dædalus** 130:4 Fall:2001 pp.1-307. *Collection of 15 articles.*

3156   Religion and modernity: ritual transformations and the reconstruction of space and time. Tong Chee Kiong; Lily Kong. **Soc. Cult. Geog.** 1:1 9:2000 pp.29-44.

3157   Religion in the Philippines. Ricardo G. Abad. **Phil. Stud.** 49:3 2001 pp.337-367.

3158   Religious affiliation and its manifestations in the system of cultural elements in Slovakia. Zuzana Beňušková. **Slov. Národop.** 47:2-3 1999 pp.211-222.

3159   Spirituality and well-being: an exploratory study of the patient perspective. Timothy P. Daaleman; Ann Kuckelman Cobb; Bruce B. Frey. **Soc. Sci. Med.** 53:11 12:2001 pp.1503-1512.

3160   A theology of national minorities. Joseph Pungur [Ed.]; Lóránt Hegedűs; Lajos Tóth; István Tőkés; Géza Boross; Judit Császár-Pungur; Gregory Baum; Robert J. Pátkai; László Tőkés; Botond Somogyi; Katalin Várady; Géza Erdélyi; Lajos Gulácsi; László Horkay; István Csete-Szemesi. Budapest: Angelus & Emmaus Publishers, 2000. 218p. *Includes bibliographical references.*

3161   A twice-told tale: the history of the history of religions' history. Jonathan Z. Smith. **Numen** XLVIII:2 2001 pp.131-146.

Buddhism
Bouddhisme

3162   The analytical method of Navya-Nyāya. Toshihiro Wada. **J. Ind. Phil.** 29:5-6 12:2001 pp.519-530.

3163   Another dialogue pattern concerning Buddhist ideas and practices: a case study of Bambusa Nana Luminary Study Group in Kaohsiung. Jen-yeh Shih. **B. Inst. Ethn. Ac. Sin.** 90 Autumn:2000 pp.111-154.

3164   The arrangement of the second *Śrutaskandha* of the *Āyāramga*. Herman Tieken. **J. Ind. Phil.** 29:5-6 12:2001 pp.575-588.

3165   Bhartrhari on A.1.1.68. Hideyo Ogawa. **J. Ind. Phil.** 29:5-6 12:2001 pp.531-544.

3166   Le bouddhisme en France: une tradition dans la modernité. *[In French]*; (Buddhism in France: a tradition in modernity.) *[Summary]*. Frédéric Lenoir. **Recher. Sociolog.** XXXII:3 2001 pp.97-107.

3167   Le bouddhisme médiéval japonais en question. *[In French]*; (Medieval Japanese Buddhism in question.) *[Summary]*. Frédéric Girard. **B. Éc. Fr. Ex.-Or.** 87:2 2000 pp.645-676.

3168   Bouddhismes en contact un zeste de Zen dans le bouddhisme thaï. *[In French]*; (Buddhist encounters: a touch of Zen in Thai Buddhism.) Louis Gabaude. **B. Éc. Fr. Ex.-Or.** 87:2 2000 pp.389-444.

3169   Buddhism; wisdom of SAARC: origin, development and modernisation. Mynak Tulku Rinpoche. **S. Asian Surv.** 8:2 7-12:2001 pp.195-202.

3170   Chinese *Tian Tai* (*T'ien-T'ai*) Buddhism and process philosophy. Chung-Ying Cheng; Gene Reeves; Steve Odin; Joseph Grange; Brook Ziporyn; Marjorie Hewitt Suchocki; Warren G. Frisina; Tao Jiang. **J. Ch. Philos.** 28:4 12:2001 pp.353-474. *Collection of 10 articles.*

3171   Contribution to the history of Buddhist ritualism: a Mahāyāna *Avadāna* on *Caitya* veneration from the Kathmandu Valley. Todd T. Lewis. **J. Asian Hist.** 28 1994 pp.1-58.

3172   Creative engagement: *Sujavanna Wua Luang* and its contribution to Buddhist literature. Justin McDaniel. **J. Siam Soc.** 88:1-2 2000 pp.156-177.

3173   Dead monks and bad debts: some provisions of a Buddhist monastic inheritance law. Gregory Schopen. **Indo-Iran. J.** 44:2 2001 pp.99-148.

3174   Emotions and ethics in Buddhist history: the *Sinhala Thupavamsa* and the work of virtue. Stephen C. Berkwitz. **Religion** 31:2 4:2001 pp.155-173.

3175   The enchanting spirit of Thai capitalism: the cult of Luang Phor Khoon and the post-modernization of Thai Buddhism. Peter A. Jackson. **S.E. Asia Res.** 7:1 3:1999 pp.5-60.

3176   Entering the temple: priests, peasants, and village contention in Tokugawa Japan. Alexander M. Vesey. **Jap. J. Relig. St.** 28:3-4 Fall:2001 pp.293-328.

3177   La face cachée du Soleil Levant. *[In French]*; (The hidden face of the Rising Sun.) *[Summary]*. Robert Duquenne. **B. Éc. Fr. Ex.-Or.** 87:2 2000 pp.629-644.

3178   Futile and false rejoinders, sophistical arguments and early Indian logic. Ernst Prets. **J. Ind. Phil.** 29:5-6 12:2001 pp.545-558.

3179   'Gāndhārī Hybrid Sanskrit': new sources for the study of the Sanskritization of Buddhist literature. Richard Salomon. **Indo-Iran. J.** 44:3 2001 pp.241-252.

3180   Imagining a place for Buddhism: literary culture and religious community in Tamil-speaking south India. Anne Elizabeth Monius. New York: Oxford University Press, 2001. 257p. *ISBN: 0195139992. Includes bibliographical references and index.*

3181   The intersection of the local and the translocal at a sacred site: the case of Osorezan in Tokugawa Japan. Miyazaki Fumiko; Duncan Williams. **Jap. J. Relig. St.** 28:3-4 Fall:2001 pp.399-440.

3182   Intrinsic validity reconsidered: a sympathetic study of the *Mīmāmsaka* inversion of Buddhist epistemology. Dan Arnold. **J. Ind. Phil.** 29:5-6 12:2001 pp.589-675.

3183   Jainism, Mahāvīra, Buddha and nirvāna. N.M. Kansara. **Jain J.** XXXVI:1 7:2001 pp.6-15.

3184   Klong rdol bla ma's list of 108 dharmas of *Prajñāpāramitā* and the commentary. Tsewang Bhuti. **Tibet J.** XXV:3 Autumn:2000 pp.48-68.

3185   The life and lineage of the Ninth Khalkha Jetsun Dampa Khutukhtu of Urga. F. Sanders. **Cent. Asia. J.** 45:2 2001 pp.273-303.

3186   Local society and the temple-parishioner relationship within the Bakufu's governance structure. Tamamuro Fumio. **Jap. J. Relig. St.** 28:3-4 Fall:2001 pp.261-292.

3187   Monks and charitable projects: the legacy of Gyōki Bosatsu. Jonathan Augustine. **Jpn. Relig.** 26:1 1:2001 pp.1-22.

3188   Naive sensualism. *Docta ignorantia*. Tibetan liberation through the senses. Joanna Tokarska-Bakir. **Numen** XLVII:1 2000 pp.69-112.

3189   New light on early Cambodian Buddhism. Nancy Dowling. **J. Siam Soc.** 88:1-2 2000 pp.122-155.

3190   A note on the date of Mahākassapa, author of the *Mohavicchedanī*. Kate Crosby; Andrew Skilton. **Bull. Ét. Indien.** 17-18 1999-2000 pp.173-180.

3191   Official monks and reclusive monks: focusing on the salvation of women. Matsuo Kenji. **B. Sch. Orient. Afr. Stud.** 64:3 2001 pp.369-380.

3192   On a previous birth story of Ma gcig Lab sgron ma. Adelheid Herrmann-Pfandt. **Tibet J.** XXV:3 Autumn:2000 pp.19-31.

3193   On the trail of two competing Buddhas from India to Korea: a study of the dynamics of cross-cultural assimilation. Cho Sungtaek. **Korea J.** 41:1 Spring:2001 pp.268-287.

3194   La place des communautés du Nord-Laos dans l'histoire du bouddhisme d'Asie du Sud-Est. *[In French]*; (The place of the communities of north Laos in the history of South-east Asian Buddhism.) *[Summary]*. François Bizot. **B. Éc. Fr. Ex.-Or.** 87:2 2000 pp.511-528.

3195   Poetic license in the Buddhist Sanskrit verses of the *Pālipariprcchā*. Karen C. Lang. **Indo-Iran. J.** 44:3 2001 pp.231-240.

3196 Pour mémoire d'un patrimoine sacré les manuscrits pāli du Cambodge à l'École française d'Extrême-Orient. *[In French]*; (Preserving a sacred inheritance: the Pali manuscripts of Cambodia at the EFEO.) *[Summary]*. Jacqueline Filliozat. **B. Éc. Fr. Ex.-Or.** 87:2 2000 pp.445-472.

3197 Quand les maîtres chinois s'éveillent au bouddhisme tibétain. *[In French]*; (When Chinese masters open themselves to Tibetan Buddhism.) *[Summary]*. Françoise Wang-Toutain. **B. Éc. Fr. Ex.-Or.** 87:2 2000 pp.707-728.

3198 Le rituel de la «grande probation annuelle» (*Mahāparivāsakamma*) des religieux du Cambodge. *[In French]*; (The ritual of the 'annual great probation' (*Mahāparivāsakamma*) among those in religious orders in Cambodia.) *[Summary]*. Olivier de Bernon. **B. Éc. Fr. Ex.-Or.** 87:2 2000 pp.473-510.

3199 The saffron army, violence, terror(ism): Buddhism, identity, and difference in Sri Lanka. Ananda Abeysekara. **Numen** XLVIII:1 2001 pp.1-46.

3200 Śankarācārya's preference to the readings from the Mādhyandina recension. M.L. Wadekar. **J. Orient. Inst.** XLVII:1-2(47) 9-12:1997 pp.61-64.

3201 *Satyadvaya* in Madhyamaka and Advaita. Mahesh Mehta. **J. Orient. Inst.** XLVII:1-2(47) 9-12:1997 pp.43-48.

3202 Das Seelenschiff im Lamaismus. *[In German]*; [Soul in Lamaism]. Siegbert Hummel. **Anthropos [St. Augustin]** 95:2 2000 pp.555-557.

3203 Some features of the language of the *Saddharmapundarīkasūtra*. Seishi Karashima. **Indo-Iran. J.** 44:3 2001 pp.207-230.

3204 Sources for the study of religion and society in the late Edo period. Helen Hardacre. **Jap. J. Relig. St.** 28:3-4 Fall:2001 pp.227-260.

3205 Sun and moon earrings: the teachings received by 'Jigs med Gling pa. Sam van Schaik. **Tibet J.** XXV:4 Winter:2000 pp.3-32.

3206 Sur les apocryphes bouddhiques chinois. *[In French]*; (On Chinese Buddhist apocrypha.) *[Summary]*. Kuo Liying. **B. Éc. Fr. Ex.-Or.** 87:2 2000 pp.677-706.

3207 The telegraphic abject: Buddhist meditation and the redemption of mechanical reproduction. Alan Klima. **Comp. Stud. S.** 43:3 7:2001 pp.552-582.

3208 The term 'true dream (*satya-svapna*)' in the Buddhist epistemological tradition. Keijin Hayashi. **J. Ind. Phil.** 29:5-6 12:2001 pp.559-574.

3209 Le *Tēvāram* au XXᵉ siècle. *[In French]*; (The *Tēvāram* in the twentieth century.) *[Summary]*. Jean-Luc Chevillard. **B. Éc. Fr. Ex.-Or.** 87:2 2000 pp.729-740.

3210 Theory of Apoha: its changing concepts in the Buddhist philosophy. Vijaya Rani. **J. Orient. Inst.** XLVII:1-2(47) 9-12:1997 pp.49-54.

3211 The twelve deeds of the Buddha: a 19th century Buriat translation of the hymn. Marta Kiripolská. **Mon. St.** XXIII 2000 pp.17-42.

3212 Two Siddhasenas and the authorship of the *Nyāyāvatāra* and the *Sammati-tarka-prakarana*. Piotr Balcerowicz. **J. Ind. Phil.** 29:3 4:2001 pp.351-378.

3213 The Vedic horse sacrifice and the changing use of the term *ahimsā*: an early insertion in TB 3.9.8? Jan E.M. Houben. **Stud. Orient.** 94 2001 pp.279-290.

3214 A visit to Brahmā the Heron. Richard Gombrich. **J. Ind. Phil.** 29:1-2 4:2001 pp.95-108.

Christianity
Christianisme

3215 Une anthropologie religieuse en Lorraine: hommage à Serge Bonnet. *[In French]*; [Religious anthropology in Lorraine: a tribute to Serge Bonnet]. Serge Bonnet [Dedicatee]; Serge Bonnet; Richard Lioger [Ed.]. Metz: Éditions Serpenoise, 2000. 292p. *ISBN: 2876924358. Papers presented at Une anthropologie religieuse en Lorraine?, Metz, September 1998. Includes bibliographical references.*

3216 Antonio Núñez de Miranda, confesor de Sor Juana, y las mujeres. *[In Spanish]*; [Antonio Núñez de Miranda, confessor to Sister Juana and her women]. María Águeda Méndez. **Caravelle** 76-77 12:2001 pp.411-420.

3217   Apparitions of the Virgin Mary in the late twentieth century: apocalyptic, representation, politics. E. Ann Matter. **Religion** 31:2 4:2001 pp.125-153.

3218   Bengali Bible translation. Alison Mukherjee. **Arch. Orient.** 68:3 8:2000 pp.407-418.

3219   Bishop Alfred Tucker and the establishment of a British protectorate in Uganda 1890-94. Tudor Griffiths. **J. Relig. Afr.** XXXI:1 2001 pp.92-114.

3220   Blessed Pedro Calungsod, martyr: an historian's comments on his Philippine background. John N. Schumacher. **Phil. Stud.** 49:3 2001 pp.287-336.

3221   Charismatic and Pentecostal Christianity in Oceania. Pamela J. Stewart; Andrew Strathern. **J. Rit. Stud.** 15:2 2001 pp.4-6.

3222   Christian base communities in Burkina Faso: between church and politics. Magloire Somé; Cecily Bennett [Tr.]. **J. Relig. Afr.** XXXI:3 2001 pp.275-304.

3223   (Christian culture and the African peasantry in the 20th century Western Kenya (2).); *[Text in Japanese]*. Nobuhiro Nakabayashi. **St. Ess. Beh. Sc. Phil.** 21 3:2001 pp.19-31.

3224   Colonial reformation in the highlands of Central Sulawesi, Indonesia, 1892-1995. Albert Schrauwers. Toronto: University of Toronto Press, 2000. xii, 279p. *ISBN: 080208303X, 0802047416. Includes bibliographical references and index.* (*Series:* Anthropological horizons - 14).

3225   The cremated Catholic: the ends of a deceased Guatemalan. Stanley Brandes. **Bod. Soc.** 7:2-3 6-9:2001 pp.111-120.

3226   The dynamics of language in cultural revolution and African spirituality: the case of *Ijo Orile-Ede Adulawo Ti Kristi* (National Church of Christ) in Nigeria. David O. Ogungbile. **Nord. J. Afr. St.** 10:1 2001 pp.66-79.

3227   L'étude de la Bible d'après l'exégète-sociologue J.H. Elliott. *[In French]*; (Biblical studies according to the sociologically-minded exegete, J.H. Elliott.) Albert Verdoodt. **Recher. Sociolog.** XXXII:1 2001 pp.143-150.

3228   Evangelical religion among Pacific Island migrants: new faiths or brief diversions? Cluny MacPherson; La'avasa MacPherson. **J. Rit. Stud.** 15:2 2001 pp.27-37.

3229   Formgeschichtliche und sprachliche Beobachtungen zu Psalm 57. *[In German]*; [Form and language criticism of Psalm 57] *[Summary]*. Beat Weber. **Scan. J. Old. Test.** 15:2 2001 pp.295-305.

3230   Frontiers of faith: religious exchange and the constitution of religious identities. 1400-1750. Eszter Andor [Ed.]; István György Tóth [Ed.]. Budapest: CEU - European Science Foundation, 2001. 295p. *Includes bibliographical references.* (*Series:* Cultural exchange in Europe, 1400-1750 - 1).

3231   Gender, power and ritual in cross-cultural perspective — essays in honour of Michael Allen. Mary Patterson; Robert Tonkinson; Michael Allen [Dedicatee]; Les Hiatt; Jeremy Beckett; Chris Eipper; Kenneth Maddock; Geoffrey Samuel; Vivienne Kondos. **Anthro. forum** 11:1 5:2001 pp.7-108. *Collection of 7 articles.*

3232   Global religions, Pacific Island transformations. Joel Robbins. **J. Rit. Stud.** 15:2 2001 pp.7-12.

3233   God is nothing but talk: modernity, language, and prayer in a Papua New Guinea society. Joel Robbins. **Am. Anthrop.** 103:4 12:2001 pp.901-912.

3234   The great exchange: *Moka* with God. Pamela J. Stewart; Andrew Strathern. **J. Rit. Stud.** 15:2 2001 pp.91-104.

3235   Heroism, spiritual development, and triadic bonds in Jain and Christian mendicancy and almsgiving. Stephen R. Munzer. **Numen** XLVIII:1 2001 pp.47-80.

3236   Islamic and Christian heterodox water cosmogonies from the Ottoman period — parallels and contrasts. Yuri Stoyanov. **B. Sch. Orient. Afr. Stud.** 64:1 2001 pp.19-33.

3237   Israel, America, and the ancestors: narratives of spiritual warfare in a Pentecostal denomination in Solomon Islands. Jolene Marie Stritecky. **J. Rit. Stud.** 15:2 2001 pp.62-78.

3238   Jeremiah's new covenant: Jer 31, 31-34. Bernard P. Robinson. **Scan. J. Old. Test.** 15:2 2001 pp.181-204.

3239   John Wesley slept here: American shrines and American Methodists. Thomas A. Tweed. **Numen** XLVII:1 2000 pp.41-68.

3240 Keltski tragovi u tradiciji sv. Martina i njihov odraz na hrvatskom prostoru. *[In Croatian]*; (Celtic traces in the tradition of St. Martin and their reflection in Croatian territories.) *[Summary]*. Antonija Zaradija Kiš. **Nar. Umjetn.** 37:2 2000 pp.109-120.

3241 Kościół Ewangelicznych Chrześcijan w Polsce jako kościół wyboru. Analiza etnologiczna wspólnoty religijnej. *[In Polish]*; (The Evangelical Christian Church in Poland as a church of choice: an ethnological analysis of a religious community.) Noemi Modncka. Krakow: Nomos, 343p. *ISBN: 8388508040. Includes bibliographical references.*

3242 Kotázke prelínania funkcií nebeských kl'učiarov v ruskom folklóre. *[In Slovak]*; (Some aspects of similarity of the images of saints with the attribute of a key in Russian folklore.) *[Summary]*. Tatiana Bužeková. **Slov. Národop.** 48:2 2000 pp.151-166.

3243 'Making all things new'? Remembering the ancestors in a Japanese Protestant family. Robert Enns. **Jpn. Relig.** 26:1 1:2001 pp.55-84.

3244 'More than seven sons': Ruth as example of the good son. Kristin Moen Saxegaard. **Scan. J. Old. Test.** 15:2 2001 pp.257-275.

3245 *Musemunuzhi*: Edwin Smith and the restoration and fulfillment of African society and religion. Paul Cocks. **Patt. Prej.** 35:2 4:2001 pp.19-32.

3246 Der Mythos der *Virgen de Guadalupe*. Audiovisuelle Veränderungen und neue politisch-religiöse Strategien im heutigen Mexiko. *[In German]*; [The myth of the Virgin of Guadalupe. Audiovisual changes and new political-religious strategies in modern Mexico]. Margarita Zires Roldán. **Anthropos [St. Augustin]** 95:2 2000 pp.445-462.

3247 New historical atlas of religion in America. Edwin S. Gaustad; Richard W. Dishno; Philip L. Barlow. Oxford: Oxford University Press, 2001. xxiii, 435p. *ISBN: 019509168X. Includes index.*

3248 On a new fragment of the Damascus Covenant. Menahem Kister. **Jew. Q. Rev.** 84 1993-1994 pp.249-252.

3249 The original form of the Turin shroud: the archaeology of the medieval religious mind. Paul M. Barford. **Fas. Arch. Hist.** XV 1999-2000 pp.37-46.

3250 Participation as resistance: the role of Pentecostal Christianity in maintaining identity for Marshallese migrants living in the midwestern United States. Linda Allen. **J. Rit. Stud.** 15:2 2001 pp.55-61.

3251 Philology as the handmaiden of philosophy in R. Saadia Gaon's interpretation of Genesis 1:1. Richard C. Steiner. **Is. Orient. Stud.** XIX 1999 pp.379-390.

3252 Protestant theories and anthropological knowledge: convergent models in the Ecuadorian Sierra. Kent Maynard. **Cult. Anthro.** 8:2 5:1993 pp.246-267.

3253 Pseudo-Kyrillos *In Mariam virginem. [In German]*; [Pseudo-Kyrillos *In Mariam virginem*]. St. Bombeck; Pierpont Morgan [Tr.]. **Orientalia** 70:1 2001 pp.40-88.

3254 Re-conceptualizing the role of men in the post-Cairo era. Axel I. Mundigo; Sonia Corrêa [Comments by]; Daniel C. Maguire [Comments by]; Juan-Guillermo Figueroa-Perea [Comments by]. **Cult. Health. Sex.** 2:3 7-9:2000 pp.323-351.

3255 La re-escritura de escrituras. *[In Spanish]*; [Rewriting the scriptures]. Gloria Prado. **Rev. de Human.** 10 Spring:2001 pp.85-94.

3256 Religious folk art and kitsch. The case of the Virgin Mary sanctuary at Licheń; *[Summary in Polish]*. Katarzyna Marciniak. **Ethnol. Pol.** 21 2000 pp.87-102.

3257 Sectarianism and the Miniafia people of Papua New Guinea. David C. Wakefield. **J. Rit. Stud.** 15:2 2001 pp.38-54.

3258 Un sermón de profesión de monjas del siglo XVII: la retórica de la perfección. *[In Spanish]*; [A 17th century sermon on nuns: the rhetoric of perfection]. María Dolores Bravo Arriaga. **Caravelle** 76-77 12:2001 pp.391-399.

3259 Signs of conversion, spirit of commitment: the Pentecostal Church in the Kingdom of Tonga. Ernest Olson. **J. Rit. Stud.** 15:2 2001 pp.13-26.

3260 The spirit of austerity and the materials of opulence: architectural sources of St. Casimir's Chapel in Vilnius. K. Paul Žygas. **J. Balt. St.** XXXI:1 Spring:2000 pp.5-43.

3261 St. John's Jesus and the Buddha. J.D.M. Derrett. **Arch. Orient.** 68:1 2:2000 pp.71-82.

3262   Suor Floriana e i Cenacoli Serafici: una ricerca etnografica nel sud del Lazio. *[In Italian]*;
        [Sister Floriana and the Seraphic Circles: ethnographic research in the south of Lazio].
        Lilli Romeo. **Critica Sociol.** 137 Spring:2001 pp.100-120.
3263   Sur la Sainte Montagne: le pèlerinage de la Salette dans la renaissance littéraire catholique.
        [In French]; [On the Holy Mountain: the *La Salette* pilgrimage in the renaissance of
        Catholic literature]. Jacques Marx. **R. Inst. Sociol.** 1-2 1998 pp.75-100.
3264   Über die Ursachen des Sieges des Christentums in Ägypten. *[In German]*; [On the causes
        of the Christian victories in Egypt]. Peter Hubai. **Numen** XLVIII:1 2001 pp.81-116.
3265   Whatever became of revival? From Charismatic movement to Charismatic Church in a
        Papua New Guinea society. Joel Robbins. **J. Rit. Stud.** 15:2 2001 pp.79-90.
3266   'White' Americans in 'Black' Africa: Black and White American Methodist missionaries in
        Liberia, 1820-1875. Eunjin Park. New York: Routledge, 2001. 244p. *ISBN: 0815340273.
        Includes bibliographical references and index.* (*Series:* Studies in African American
        history and culture).
3267   Why did Simeon and Levi rebuke their father in Genesis 34:31? Joseph Fleishman. **J.
        N.W. Sem. Lang.** 26:2 2000 pp.101-116.
3268   *Yā-btā l-lādī fī l-samāwāt...* Notas sobre antiguas versiones árabes del «Padre Nuestro».
        [In Spanish]; [Comments on ancient Arabic versions of The Lord's Prayer] *[Summary]*.
        Juan Pedro Monferrer Sala. **Al-Qantara** XXI:2 2000 pp.277-306.

Hinduism
Hindouisme

3269   12-letni cykl jowiszowy w wielkiej tradycji hinduizmu. Cykl świąt *Kumbha Mela*. *[In
        Polish]*; (The twelve year Jovian cycle in the great tradition of Hinduism. The ritual cycle
        of *Kumbha Mela*.) *[Summary]*. Dagnosław Demski. **Etn. Polska** XLV:1-2 2001 pp.117-
        134.
3270   'Alaksmīh' (the goddess of misfortune) as narrated in the Churning-myth. Gopinath Panda.
        J. Orient. Inst. XLVII:3-4(47) 3-6:1998 pp.259-262.
3271   *Apsaras* and hero. Minoru Hara. **J. Ind. Phil.** 29:1-2 4:2001 pp.135-153.
3272   *Āścaryakarman* and *prādurbhāva* in the *Harivamśa*. Horst Brinkhaus. **J. Ind. Phil.** 29:1-2
        4:2001 pp.25-41.
3273   Les Aśvin dans les énumérations divines du neuvième mandala de la *Rgvedasamhitā*. *[In
        French]*; [The Aśvin in the divine enumerations of the ninth mandala of the
        Rgvedasamhita]. É. Pirart. **Indo-Iran. J.** 44:4 Winter:2001 pp.329-353.
3274   Back to Śunahśepa: remarks on the gestation of the Indian literary narrative. Virpi
        Hämeen-Anttila. **Stud. Orient.** 94 2001 pp.181-214.
3275   Balancing *raudra* and *śānti*: rage and repose in states of possession. David M. Knipe.
        Stud. Orient. 94 2001 pp.343-358.
3276   Bhakti movement, its development in Orissa. Siba Prasad Nayak. **Oris. Hist. R. J.** XLV:1-
        4 2000 pp.6-13.
3277   The Brahman priest in the history of Vedic texts. Masato Fujii. **Stud. Orient.** 94 2001
        pp.147-160.
3278   Child in Prakrit poems. Veneemadhava Shastri. **J. Orient. Inst.** XLVII:1-2(47) 9-12:1997
        pp.101-112.
3279   Comic elements in the *Krsna-yātrās*. Bozena Sliwczynska. **Arch. Orient.** 68:3 8:2000
        pp.399-406.
3280   The concept of dream in *Kevalādvaita Vedānta*. Shuchita Y. Mehta. **J. Orient. Inst.**
        XLVII:3-4(47) 3-6:1998 pp.237-250.
3281   Contribution of Kalahandi district to Vaishnav tantra in Orissa. Jitamitra Prasad Singh
        Deo. **Oris. Hist. R. J.** XLV:1-4 2000 pp.45-55.
3282   Contribution to the functioning of *dvar-/dúr-* in the *Rgveda*. T.Y. Elizarenkova. **Stud.
        Orient.** 94 2001 pp.119-130.

3283   Cosmos encrusted: Śiva, Andhaka, Bhrngin, and the emptying of infinity. Don Handelman. **Stud. Orient.** 94 2001 pp.215-224.

3284   Le culte de la déesse de la fortune Laksmī chez les marchands Lohana. *[In French]*; [The cult of Laksmī, goddess of fortune, among Lohana merchants]. Pierre Lachaier. **B. Éc. Fr. Ex.-Or.** 87:2 2000 pp.787-808.

3285   Daksināmūrti. Hans Bakker. **Stud. Orient.** 94 2001 pp.41-54.

3286   Defending Hindu tradition: Sanatana Dharma as a symbol of orthodoxy in colonial India. John Zavos. **Religion** 31:2 4:2001 pp.109-123.

3287   Divine affairs: religion, pilgrimage and the state in colonial and postcolonial India. Ishita Banerjee Dube. Shimla: Indian Institute of Advanced Studies, 2001. 195p. *ISBN: 8185952884.*

3288   L'ethnographie contre l'idéologie. Le cas de l'hindouisme. *[In French]*; [Ethnography versus ideology: the case of Hinduism]. Robert Deliège. **Homme** 160 10-12:2001 pp.163-176.

3289   A first link between the Rgvedic Panjab and Mesopotamia: *śimbala/śalmali*, and ^{*GIŚ*} *gišimmar*? Michael Witzel. **Stud. Orient.** 94 2001 pp.497-508.

3290   From Visnu's deeds to Visnu's play, or observations on the word *avatāra* as a designation for the manifestations of Visnu. André Couture. **J. Ind. Phil.** 29:3 4:2001 pp.313-326.

3291   The Gaudapāda-*Kārikā* and *Śuddhādvaita*. N.M. Kansara. **J. Orient. Inst.** XLVII:3-4(47) 3-6:1998 pp.227-236.

3292   Holy cow! The apotheosis of Zebu, or why the cow is sacred in Hinduism. Frank J. Korom. **Asian Folk. S.** LIX:2 2000 pp.181-204.

3293   Husband or king? Yudhisthira's dilemma in the *Mahābhārata*. Mary Brockington. **Indo-Iran. J.** 44:3 2001 pp.253-268.

3294   Indo-European deities and the *Rgveda*. N.D. Kazanas. **J. Indo-Eur. S.** 29:3-4 Fall-Winter:2001 pp.257-294.

3295   Indra in the epics. John Brockington. **Stud. Orient.** 94 2001 pp.67-82.

3296   The interrupted sacrifice and the Sanskrit epics. Christopher Z. Minkowski. **J. Ind. Phil.** 29:1-2 4:2001 pp.169-186.

3297   *Jīvanmuktopanisad* — a study of a rare manuscript. Meena P. Pathak. **J. Orient. Inst.** XLVII:1-2(47) 9-12:1997 pp.73-86.

3298   Krsna concept in the Vedas: a reassessment — I. Rakesh Ranjan Pathak. **J. Orient. Inst.** XLVII:3-4(47) 3-6:1998 pp.203-214.

3299   Mantra, devatā, "mantradevatā": quelques observations sur les mantras tantriques. *[In French]*; [Mantra, devata, 'mantradevata': some observations on tantric mantras]. André Padoux. **Stud. Orient.** 94 2001 pp.397-404.

3300   The meaning and language of the *Rigveda*: Rigvedic *grávan* as a test case. Karen Thomson. **J. Indo-Eur. S.** 29:3-4 Fall-Winter:2001 pp.295-350.

3301   Le nom primitif de la rétribution rituelle en védique ancien. *[In French]*; [The primitive name for ritual retribution in ancient Vedic]. Georges-Jean Pinault. **Bull. Ét. Indien.** 17-18 1999-2000 pp.427-476.

3302   Observations sur trois des manifestations de Visnu dans le *Harivamśa*. *[In French]*; [Observations on three manifestations of Visnu in the *Harivamśa*. Marcelle Saindon. **Bull. Ét. Indien.** 17-18 1999-2000 pp.477-490.

3303   The origin of *Mīmāmsā* as a school of thought. Johannes Bronkhorst. **Stud. Orient.** 94 2001 pp.83-104.

3304   *Prācīna* Kauthuma traditions of south India: letters from L. S. Rajagopalan, 1985-1988. Wayne Howard. **Stud. Orient.** 94 2001 pp.291-302.

3305   Ranganātha's *Prakāśikā* on Kālidāsa's *Vikramorvaśīyam*. Joydev Kumar Saha. **J. Orient. Inst.** XLVII:1-2(47) 9-12:1997 pp.93-100.

3306   The recent history of Vedic ritual in Maharashtra. Frederick M. Smith. **Stud. Orient.** 94 2001 pp.443-464.

3307   The Rigvedic *svayamvara*? Formulaic evidence. Stephanie W. Jamison. **Stud. Orient.** 94 2001 pp.303-316.

3308   The *Samvargavidyā* and its context in two Sāmavedic texts. Henk Bodewitz. **Stud. Orient.** 94 2001 pp.55-66.

3309   The spiritual and Hindustani music. S.K. Saxena. **San. Nat.** 131-132 1999 pp.3-14.

3310   Studies in the Grhya Prayogas of the *Jaiminīya Sāmaveda*: 2. *Sthālīpāka*. Klaus Karttunen. **Stud. Orient.** 94 2001 pp.317-342.

3311   The supremacy of goddess Laksmī in *Viśistādvaita*. S.K. Pankaja. **J. Orient. Inst.** XLVII:3-4(47) 3-6:1998 pp.251-258.

3312   Swami Vivekananda and Rishi Bankimchandra as patriot and nationalist: a critical comparison. Narasingha P. Sil. **Asian Cult. (Asian-Pac. Cult.) Q.** XXVIII:3 Autumn:2000 pp.33-58.

3313   The system of teaching in the Principal Upanisads — a comparative study. Madhavi M. Pethe. **J. Orient. Inst.** XLVII:1-2(47) 9-12:1997 pp.65-72.

3314   The two versions of *Dūtavākya* and their sources. Anna Aurelia Esposito. **Bull. Ét. Indien.** 17-18 1999-2000 pp.551-562.

3315   Uddālaka's teaching in *Chāndogya* Upanisad 6, 8-16. H.W. Bodewitz. **Indo-Iran. J.** 44:4 Winter:2001 pp.289-298.

3316   Vedski obred u neohinduističkom kontekstu. *[In Croatian]*; (Vedic ritual in a neo-Hinduist context.) *[Summary]*. Zdravka Matišić. **Nar. Umjetn.** 37:2 2000 pp.121-132.

3317   A visit to Brahmā the Heron. Richard Gombrich. **J. Ind. Phil.** 29:1-2 4:2001 pp.95-108.

3318   Water and salt (II): 'material' causality and hylozoic thought in the Yājñavalkya-Maitreyī dialogue? W. Slaje. **Indo-Iran. J.** 44:4 Winter:2001 pp.299-327.

3319   Women one should not marry — some comments on *Manusmrti* 3.6-9, 11. Stella Sandahl. **Acta Orient.** 62 2001 pp.166-176.

Islam
Islam

3320   '*A l'ombre du Coran*' revisité: les lendemains possibles de la pensée de Sayyid Qutb et du 'Qutbisme'. *[In French]*; [*In the Shadow of the Koran* revisited: the consequences and potential of Sayyid Qutb's thought]. O. Carré. **Arabica** XLVII:1 1:2001 pp.81-111.

3321   *Adab*: poésie, prose, proverbes. *[In French]*; [*Adab*: poetry, prose, proverbs]. Toufic Fahd. **Is. Orient. Stud.** XIX 1999 pp.411-478.

3322   Amîr Temur and Sayyid Baraka. A. Muminov; B. Babadzhanov. **Cent. Asia. J.** 45:1 2001 pp.28-62.

3323   *Ansāb al-ašrāf* d'al-Balādurī, est-il un livre de *ta'rīh* ou d'*adab*? *[In French]*; [Al-Balādurī's *Ansāb al-ašrāf*: is this a *ta'rīh* or *adab* book?] Isaac Hasson. **Is. Orient. Stud.** XIX 1999 pp.479-494.

3324   L'assurance Islamique: fondements et perspectives. *[In French]*; [Islamic confidence: basics and perspectives]. Ali Meddeb. **Cah. Orient** 63 2001 pp.27-34.

3325   (Belief issues in the *hadeeth* of the branches of belief.) *[Summary]*; *[Text in Arabic]*. Shareef al-Khateeb. **Dirasat Ad. Sc.** 28:2 11:2001 pp.273-291.

3326   Beyond theology: toward an anthropology of 'fundamentalism'. Judith Nagata. **Am. Anthrop.** 103:2 6:2001 pp.481-498.

3327   Christians and Jews in the Ottoman Arab world: the roots of sectarianism. Bruce Alan Masters. New York: Cambridge University Press, 2001. 222p. *ISBN: 0521803330. Includes bibliographical references and index.* (*Series:* Cambridge studies in Islamic civilization).

3328   Civic virtue and religious reason: an Islamic counterpublic. Charles Hirschkind. **Cult. Anthro.** 16:1 2:2001 pp.3-34.

3329   The concept of *Hāl* in the *Kitāb al-muštamil* of Abū Farag Hārūn. Nasir Basal. **Is. Orient. Stud.** XIX 1999 pp.391-410.

3330   Le Coran. *[In French]*; [The Koran]. T. Nagel; S. Ory; Fr. Imbert; A.L. de Prémare; H. Toelle; P. Sander; P. Larcher; Cl. Fr. Audebert; U. Marzolph; Cl. Gilliot; P. Bachmann; D.

Gril; A. Al-Massri; Ch. Jones-Pauly; L. Berger. **Arabica** XLVII:3-4 7-10:2000 pp.329-561. *Collection of 15 articles.*

3331   *Dabistan-i-Mazahib*: a 17th century chronicle in Persian. Jasbir Singh Sarna. **Sikh Rev.** 49:8(572) 8:2001 pp.40-43.

3332   Different conceptions of religious practice, piety and God-man relations in the epistles of the *Ikhwān al-Safā'*. Carmela Baffioni. **Al-Qantara** XXI:2 2000 pp.381-386.

3333   Differing responses to an Ahmadi translation and exegesis : The Holy Qur'ân in Egypt and Indonesia. Moch Nur Ichwan. **Archipel** 62 2001 pp.143-162.

3334   (The dissemination of Islam in Bronai and the belief of its inhabitants.) *[Summary]*; *[Text in Arabic]*. H. Bani Khalid. **Dirasat Ad. Sc.** 28:2 11:2001 pp.243-252.

3335   Du syncrétisme philosophico-religieux au *Fasl al Maqal*. *[In French]*; [Philosophical-religious syncretism in *Fasl al Maqal*]. Abdelmajid El-Ghannouchi. **Cah. Tunis.** XLIX:178 1997 pp.61-90.

3336   Du texte de récitation au canon en passant par la liturgie. A propos de la genèse de la composition des sourates et de sa redissolution au cours de développement du culte islamique. *[In French]*; [Texts, liturgies and the development of Islamic cults]. A. Neuwirth. **Arabica** XLVII:2 4:2000 pp.194-229.

3337   The early *Šī'a* and Jerusalem. O. Livne-Kafri. **Arabica** XLVII:1 1:2001 pp.112-120.

3338   Experiencias religiosas y pertenencia a la comunidad. *[In Spanish]*; [Religious experience and a sense of belonging to the community]. Mercedes García-Arenal; Camilla Adang; David Waines; Leah Kinberg; Giovanna Calasso; Halima Ferhat; Manuela Marín; Nelly Amri. **Al-Qantara** XXI:2 2000 pp.389-510. *Collection of 8 articles.*

3339   Falsafa versus 'Arabiyya: al-Rāzī. Emilio Tornero. **Al-Qantara** XXI:1 2000 pp.3-16.

3340   Gender ideology of Islam and women's public participation in North Africa. Masato Iizuka. **Senri Ethn. Stud.** 55 2001 pp.121-136.

3341   *Hadīth* and *fiqh*. G.H.A. Juynboll; Robert Gleave; Christopher Melchert; Susan Spectorsky. **Islam. Law Soc.** 8:3 10:2001 pp.303-431. *Collection of 4 articles.*

3342   The *Hanābila* and the early Sufis. Ch. Melchert. **Arabica** XLVIII:3 7:2001 pp.352-367.

3343   Histoire des Alaouites (1268-1971). *[In French]*; [A history of the 'Alawites (1268-1971)]. Jacques Benoist-Méchin; Alain Decaux [Foreword]. Paris: Perrin, 1994. 285p. *ISBN: 226201597X.*

3344   (The holy religious verse of debt.) *[Summary]*; *[Text in Arabic]*. F. al-Salman. **Dirasat Ad. Sc.** 28:2 11:2001 pp.253-272.

3345   Hybrid identities: the Pomak community of Breznitza (southwest Bulgaria) in search of genealogy; *[Summary in German]*; *[Summary in French]*. Elka Agoston-Nikolova. **Fabula** 42:1-2 2001 pp.110-116.

3346   The imam's knowledge and the Quran according to al-Fadl b. Shādhān al-Nīsābūrī (d. 260 A.H./874 A.D.) Tamima Bayhom-Daou. **B. Sch. Orient. Afr. Stud.** 64:2 2001 pp.188-207.

3347   Islam i kul't sviatykh v Srednei Azii. *[In Russian]*; (Islam and the cult of saints in Central Asia.) S.N. Abashin. **Etnograf. Oboz.** 3 5-6:2001 pp.128-131.

3348   Islam in East Europe. Gyorgy Lederer. **C. Asian Sur.** 20:1 3:2001 pp.5-32.

3349   Islam v sovremennoi Kabardino-Balkarii: pravovye aspekty. *[In Russian]*; (Islam in the modern Kabardin-Balkar Republic: legal aspects.) *[Summary]*. I.L. Babich. **Etnograf. Oboz.** 2 3-4:2001 pp.131-143.

3350   Islamic and Christian heterodox water cosmogonies from the Ottoman period — parallels and contrasts. Yuri Stoyanov. **B. Sch. Orient. Afr. Stud.** 64:1 2001 pp.19-33.

3351   Die Legende von der Spaltung des Mondes. Ein koranisches Wunder in türkischem Kleid. *[In German]*; [The legend of the splitting of the moon. A wonder from the Koran in Turkish dress] *[Summary]*. Gisela Procházka-Eisl. **Arch. Orient.** 69:2 5:2001 pp.285-298.

3352   Mahallah and kinship relations. A study on residential communal commitment structures in Central Asia of the 19th century. Paul Georg Geiss. **C. Asian Sur.** 20:1 3:2001 pp.97-106.

3353   Morocco 2001: in memoriam — essays by David M. Hart. C.R. Pennell; David M. Hart. **J. N. African Stud.** 6:2 Summer:2001 pp.1-116. *Collection of 6 articles.*

3354   Motifs in *ādāb* and *fann*. Mohammed Arkoun; Rachel Milstein; Claude Gilliot; Gabriel M. Rosenbaum; Reuven Snir; Ulrich Marzolph; Joseph Sadan; Dominique Urvoy; Marie-

Thérèse Urvoy; Alber Arazi; David Wasserstein. **Is. Orient. Stud.** XIX 1999 pp.11-262. *Collection of 10 articles.*

3355   La nouvelle alliance dans la sourate *al-Mā'ida*. *[In French]*; [The new alliance in the *Al-Mā'ida* Sura]. V. Comerro. **Arabica** XLVIII:3 7:2001 pp.285-314.

3356   Opyt polevykh issledovanii islama na Severo-Zapadnom Kavkaze. *[In Russian]*; (Experience of Islamic field studies in the north-west Caucasus.) A.A. Iaarlykapov. **Etnograf. Oboz.** 3 5-6:2001 pp.132-135.

3357   The Qur'ân in Indonesian daily life: the public project of musical oratory. Anne K. Rasmussen. **Ethnomusicology** 45:1 Winter:2001 pp.30-57.

3358   Quranic description of gametes. Sikander Hussain. **B. Ind. Inst. Hist. Med.** XXIX:2 7:1999 pp.155-158.

3359   Le rasoir d'Occam et la tradition grammaticale arabe. *[In French]*; [Occam's razor and the Arabic grammatical tradition]. G. Bohas. **Arabica** XLVII:1 1:2001 pp.1-19.

3360   Rehearsed spontaneity and the conventionality of ritual: disciplines of *salāt*. Saba Mahmood. **Am. Ethn.** 28:4 11:2001 pp.827-853.

3361   Seminar «Perspektivy etnograficheskogo izucheniia islama v Srednei Azii i sopredel'nikh regionakh». *[In Russian]*; (Seminar on 'The prospects of ethnographic studies in the Islam of Central Asia and adjoining areas'.) S.N. Abashin; V.I. Bushkov. **Etnograf. Oboz.** 3 5-6:2001 pp.123-124.

3362   Sībawayhi's attitude to the language of the Quran. Aryeh Levin. **Is. Orient. Stud.** XIX 1999 pp.267-272.

3363   Sikh-Muslim bonds forged by Guru Ki Maseet. Anna Barry Bigellow. **Sikh Rev.** 49:9(573) 9:2001 pp.36-39.

3364   Sufism and the Indonesian Islamic revival. Julia Day Howell. **J. Asian St.** 60:3 8:2001 pp.701-729.

3365   [The use of religious heritage in the poetry of Haidar Mahmoud] *[Summary]*; *[Text in Arabic]*. Ibrahim Koufahi. **Dirasat Hum. Soc. Sc.** 28:1 2:2001 pp.225-251.

3366   Toleration and exclusion: al-Shāfi'ī and al-Ghazālī on the treatment of apostates. Frank Griffel. **B. Sch. Orient. Afr. Stud.** 64:3 2001 pp.339-354.

3367   Witnessing an Islamic rite of passage and a local/non-local articulation. Manuchehr Sanadjian. **Soc. Ident.** 7:2 6:2001 pp.203-220.

Jainism
Jaïnisme

3368   Bhagavān Mahāvīra: his life and doctrine. K.C. Lalwani. **Jain J.** XXXV:4 4:2001 pp.147-151.

3369   Chronological development of Jain literature. Satya Ranjan Banerjee. **Jain J.** XXXV:4 4:2001 pp.206-222.

3370   The date of Mahāvīra. Yogendra Mishra. **Jain J.** XXXV:4 4:2001 pp.152-169.

3371   Einige Aufgaben der Jinismus-Forschung zu Beginn des 3. Jahrtausends. *[In German]*; [Questions about Jainism research at the start of the third millenium]. Klaus Mylius. **Stud. Orient.** 94 2001 pp.387-396.

3372   The first cause: syncretic views of Haribhadra and others. Ramkrishna Bhattacharya. **Jain J.** XXXV:4 4:2001 pp.179-184.

3373   Haribhadra's views on *Svabhāvavāda* and the *Lokāyata*. Ramkrishna Bhattacharya. **Jain J.** XXXVI:1 7:2001 pp.46-52.

3374   Heroism, spiritual development, and triadic bonds in Jain and Christian mendicancy and almsgiving. Stephen R. Munzer. **Numen** XLVIII:1 2001 pp.47-80.

3375   Influence of Bhagavān Mahāvīra's teachings on Tamils. S. Thanya Kumar. **Jain J.** XXXVI:1 7:2001 pp.25-30.

3376   The intellectual formation of a Jain monk: a Śvetāmbara monastic curriculum. John E. Cort. **J. Ind. Phil.** 29:3 4:2001 pp.327-350.

3377   Jaina studies in Japan. Atsushi Uno. **Jain J.** XXXV:4 4:2001 pp.173-178.

3378   The Jaina way of life. Dulichand Jain. **Jain J.** XXXV:3 1:2001 pp.97-103.

3379   Jainism, Mahāvīra, Buddha and nirvāna. N.M. Kansara. **Jain J.** XXXVI:1 7:2001 pp.6-15.

3380   El Jainismo: doctrina heterodoxa de la India. Estudio sobre su contribución al desarrollo religioso y cultural de la India. *[In Spanish]*; [Jainism: heterodox doctrine of India. A study of its contribution to the religious and cultural development of India]. Roberto Marín. **Rev. de Human.** 11 Autumn:2001 pp.137-168.

3381   The logical structure of the *naya* method of the Jainas. Piotr Balcerowicz. **J. Ind. Phil.** 29:3 4:2001 pp.379-403.

3382   My rituals and my Gods: ritual exclusiveness in medieval India. Phyllis Granoff. **J. Ind. Phil.** 29:1-2 4:2001 pp.109-134.

3383   The notion of Dharma in Jainism: a comparative view. V.P. Jain. **Jain J.** XXXV:4 4:2001 pp.189-205.

3384   Polémiques autour du «voile buccal» des laïcs: la contribution de Vardhamānasūri. *[In French]*; [Polemics on the 'oral veil': the contribution of Vardhamānasūri]. Nalini Balbir. **Bull. Ét. Indien.** 17-18 1999-2000 pp.113-152.

3385   Relevance of Jain principles of Mahāvīra in modern context. Binod Kumar Tiwary. **Jain J.** XXXVI:1 7:2001 pp.31-36.

3386   The relevance of the teachings of Lord Mahāvīra in the modern age. Duli Chand Jain. **Jain J.** XXXVI:1 7:2001 pp.37-45.

3387   Rsabhadeva. Satya Ranjan Banerjee. **Jain J.** XXXV:4 4:2001 pp.185-188.

3388   Some reflections about Anekāntavāda. Maria Luisa Tornotti. **Jain J.** XXXVI:1 7:2001 pp.1-5.

3389   Some special aspects of Jaina philosophy as a school of Indian philosophy. Arvind Sharma. **Jain J.** XXXV:2 10:2000 pp.49-52.

3390   *Sumatisambhava* — a little-known Jaina *Mahākāvya*. Satya Vrat. **J. Orient. Inst.** XLVII:3-4(47) 3-6:1998 pp.273-282.

3391   The universal message of Jainism. Kalidas Nag. **Jain J.** XXXV:4 4:2001 pp.170-172.

Judaism
Judaïsme

3392   *Aggadat Bereshit* and the triennial lectionary cycle. Lieve Teugels. **J. Jew. Stud.** LI:1 Spring:2000 pp.117-132.

3393   Alternate renderings and additions in Yeshu'ah ben Yehudah's Arabic translation of the Pentateuch. Meira Polliack. **Jew. Q. Rev.** 84 1993-1994 pp.209-227.

3394   Between 'Ashkenazi' and Sepharad: an early modern German rabbinic response to religious pluralism in the Spanish-Portuguese community. Adam S. Ferziger. **St. Ros.** 35:1 2001 pp.7-22.

3395   Between diffidence and initiative: Ashkenazic legal decision-making in the late Middle Ages (1350-1500). Jeffrey R. Woolf. **J. Jew. Stud.** LII:1 Spring:2001 pp.85-97.

3396   Bild und Text. Mediale und historische Perspektiven auf das alttestamentliche Bilderverbot. *[In German]*; [Image and text - the Old Testament prohibition of cultic images] *[Summary]*. Thomas Podella. **Scan. J. Old. Test.** 15:2 2001 pp.205-256.

3397   Chinese perceptions of the Jews and Judaism: a history of the Youtai. Xun Zhou. Richmond: Curzon press, 2001. x, 202p. *ISBN: 0700712496. Includes bibliographical references and index.*

3398   Collegial interaction in the Babylonian Talmud. Richard Kalmin. **Jew. Q. Rev.** 82 1991-1992 pp.383-136.

3399   Le corps à la lettre, ou les quatre femmes de Jacob. *[In French]*; (The body to the letter, or Jacob's four wives.) *[Summary]*. Claudine Vassas. **Homme** 160 10-12:2001 pp.11-40.

3400   Cosmology in 1 Enoch. Peter Dubovský. **Arch. Orient.** 68:2 5:2000 pp.205-218.

3401   'Critical post-Judaism'; or, reinventing a Yiddish sensibility in a postmodern age. Noah Isenberg. **Diaspora** 6:1 Spring:1997 pp.85-96.

3402   The determination of Jewish identity below the Mason-Dixon line: crossing the boundary from Gentile to Jew in the nineteenth-century American South. Dana Evan Kaplan. **J. Jew. Stud.** LII:1 Spring:2001 pp.98-121.

3403   Did Maimonides' letter to Samuel Ibn Tibbon determine which philosophers would be studied by later Jewish thinkers? Steven Harvey. **Jew. Q. Rev.** 83 1992-1993 pp.51-71.

3404   Dynamics of inclusion and exclusion: comparing mental illness narratives of Haredi male patients and their rabbis. Yehuda Goodman. **Cult. Medic. Psych.** 25:2 6:2001 pp.169-194.

3405   The Elohistic Psalter: what, how and why? Laura Joffe. **Scan. J. Old. Test.** 15:1 2001 pp.142-166.

3406   Exarchon: an unsuspected Jewish liturgical title from ancient Rome. Margaret H. Williams. **J. Jew. Stud.** LI:1 Spring:2000 pp.77-87.

3407   The first date in *Megillat Ta'anit* in light of the Karaite commentary on the tabernacle dedication. Yoram Erder. **Jew. Q. Rev.** 82 1991-1992 pp.263-284.

3408   The first discovered leaves of *Sefer Hefes*. Neil Danzig. **Jew. Q. Rev.** 82 1991-1992 pp.51-262.

3409   Fistfights at the Moscow Choral Synagogue: ethnicity and ritual in post-Soviet Russia. Sascha L. Goluboff. **Anthr. Quart.** 74:2 4:2001 pp.55-71.

3410   For ourselves, our neighbours, our homelands: religion in Folklorama's Israel Pavilion; *[Summary in French]*. Paul Bramadat. **Ethnologies** 23:1 2001 pp.211-232.

3411   'For the vineyard of the Lord of hosts was the house of Israel': Cyprian of Carthage and the Jews. Charles A. Bobertz. **Jew. Q. Rev.** 82 1991-1992 pp.1-240.

3412   For which types of speech would a Jew have studied Greek rhetoric in seventeenth-century Amsterdam? Shlomo Berger. **St. Ros.** 34:2 2000 pp.153-167.

3413   Halakhah, Kabbalah, and heresy: a controversy in early eighteenth-century Amsterdam. Matt Goldish. **Jew. Q. Rev.** 84 1993-1994 pp.153-176.

3414   The identity of a mystic: the case of Sa'id Sarmad, a Jewish-yogi-sufi courtier of the Mughals. Nathan Katz. **Numen** XLVII:2 2000 pp.142-160.

3415   An inauguration in Suriname, 1804. Lies Kruijer-Poesiat. **St. Ros.** 34:2 2000 pp.194-197.

3416   The influence of Judaism among non-Jews in the imperial period. Wolf Liebeschuetz. **J. Jew. Stud.** LII:2 Autumn:2001 pp.235-252.

3417   Jewish and Christian astrology in late antiquity — a new approach. Kocku von Stuckrad. **Numen** XLVII:1 2000 pp.1-40.

3418   The Jewish view of natural law. Bernard S. Jackson. **J. Jew. Stud.** LII:1 Spring:2001 pp.136-145.

3419   Josephus' portrait of Moses. Louis H. Feldman. **Jew. Q. Rev.** 82 1991-1992 pp.285-328.

3420   Josephus' portrait of Moses: part three. Louis H. Feldman. **Jew. Q. Rev.** 83 1992-1993 pp.301-330.

3421   Josephus' portrait of Moses: part two. Louis H. Feldman. **Jew. Q. Rev.** 83 1992-1993 pp.7-51.

3422   Juggling identities among the Crypto-Jews of the American Southwest. Seth D. Kunin. **Religion** 31:1 1:2001 pp.41-61.

3423   Karaite *piyyut* in Southeastern Europe. Leon J. Weinberger. **Jew. Q. Rev.** 83 1992-1993 pp.145-166.

3424   King Manasseh and the Halakhah of the Sadducees. Aharon Shemesh. **J. Jew. Stud.** LII:1 Spring:2001 pp.27-39.

3425   The meaning in the Qumran wisdom texts. Matthew Morgenstern. **J. Jew. Stud.** LI:1 Spring:2000 pp.141-144.

3426   Meaninglessness, meaningfulness, and super-meaningfulness in scripture: an analysis of the controversy surrounding Dan 2:12 in the Middle Ages. Richard C. Steiner. **Jew. Q. Rev.** 82 1991-1992 pp.431-570.

3427   The messiah epithet in the Hebrew bible. Thomas L. Thompson. **Scan. J. Old. Test.** 15:1 2001 pp.57-82.

3428   Morton Smith on the Pharisees in Josephus. David S. Williams. **Jew. Q. Rev.** 84 1993-1994 pp.29-42.

3429   Moses Dar'ī, Karaite poet and physician. Leon J. Weinberger. **Jew. Q. Rev.** 84 1993-1994 pp.445-485.

3430   The mystical significance of Torah study in German pietism. Elliot R. Wolfson. **Jew. Q. Rev.** 84 1993-1994 pp.43-78.

3431   The mythic mind. N. Wyatt. **Scan. J. Old. Test.** 15:1 2001 pp.3-56.

3432   A new Qumran substitute for the divine name and *Mishnah Sukkah*. Joseph M. Baumgarten. **Jew. Q. Rev.** 83 1992-1993 pp.1-7.

3433   Notes on the language of 4QCant[b]. Ian Young. **J. Jew. Stud.** LII:1 Spring:2001 pp.122-131.

3434   On *Yerushalmi Baba Mesi'a* 6.1, 10d. Jerome A. Lund. **Jew. Q. Rev.** 84 1993-1994 pp.253-261.

3435   The opening of the psalter: a study in Jewish theology. J. Høgenhaven. **Scan. J. Old. Test.** 15:2 2001 pp.169-180.

3436   Physiological and philological notes to Psalm 137. Gary A. Rendsburg; Susan L. Rendsburg. **Jew. Q. Rev.** 83 1992-1993 pp.385-400.

3437   Polemic literary units in the classical Midrashim and Justin Martyr's *Dialogue with Trypho*. Marc Hirshman. **Jew. Q. Rev.** 83 1992-1993 pp.369-384.

3438   The Postzionism debates: knowledge and power in Israeli culture. Laurence J. Silberstein. New York, London: Routledge, 1999. x, 275p. *ISBN: 0415913152, 0415913160. Includes bibliographical references and index.*

3439   Praying king and sanctuary of prayer, part I: David and the temple's origins in Rabbinic psalms commentary (*Midrash Tehillim*). Esther M. Menn. **J. Jew. Stud.** LII:1 Spring:2001 pp.1-26.

3440   The preliminary edition of 5/6 Hev Psalms. Peter W. Flint. **J. Jew. Stud.** LI:1 Spring:2000 pp.19-41.

3441   The quadripartite division of the intellect in medieval Jewish thought. Dov Schwartz. **Jew. Q. Rev.** 84 1993-1994 pp.227-237.

3442   Rabbinic attitudes toward rabbis as a key to the dating of Talmudic sources. Richard Kalmin. **Jew. Q. Rev.** 84 1993-1994 pp.1-29.

3443   Religious oratory and the improvement of congregants: Dutch-Jewish preaching in the first half of the nineteenth century. Bart Wallet. **St. Ros.** 34:2 2000 pp.168-193.

3444   The rhetoric and substance of rebuke: social and religious criticism in the sermons of Hakham Saul Levi Morteira. Marc Saperstein. **St. Ros.** 34:2 2000 pp.131-152.

3445   The road to Jezreel. Primary history and the *Tel Dan* inscription. Jan-Wim Wesselius. **Scan. J. Old. Test.** 15:1 2001 pp.83-103.

3446   Rossiiskie evrei: konfessional'naia situatsiia v kontse XX v. *[In Russian]*; (Russian Jews: confessional situation in the late 20th century.) *[Summary]*. S.Ia. Kozlov. **Etnograf. Oboz.** 5 9-10:2000 pp.143-155.

3447   The Sadducees and the water libation. Jeffrey Rubenstein. **Jew. Q. Rev.** 84 1993-1994 pp.417-445.

3448   Sarah and Iscah: method and message in Midrashic tradition. Eliezer Segal. **Jew. Q. Rev.** 82 1991-1992 pp.417-430.

3449   Sarcasm, irony, wordplay, and humor in the Hebrew Bible: a response to Hershey Friedman. John Morreall. **Humor** 14:3 2001 pp.293-302.

3450   *Sefer HeHago*: the community and the book. Devora Steinmetz. **J. Jew. Stud.** LII:1 Spring:2001 pp.40-58.

3451   The silent women of Yehud: notes on Ezra 9-10. H. Zlotnick-Sivan. **J. Jew. Stud.** LI:1 Spring:2000 pp.3-18.

3452   Synagogi i domy modlitwy w Łodzi (do 1939 r.) *[In Polish]*; The synagogues and prayer houses of Łódź (until 1939). Jacek Walicki. Łódz: Ibidem, xxxiii, 94p. *ISBN: 8391240398.*

3453   *Targum Pseudo-Jonathan* to Genesis 27:31. Robert Hayward. **Jew. Q. Rev.** 84 1993-1994 pp.177-188.

3454   The temple experience of Jaddus in the *Antiquities* of Josephus: a report of Jewish dream incubation. Robert Gnuse. **Jew. Q. Rev.** 83 1992-1993 pp.349-368.

3455   Theology comes home: the role of theology in the academic study of religion and the role of theology of Judaism in the academic study of Judaism. Jacob Neusner. **Religion** 31:1 1:2001 pp.1-18.

3456   Three books on Jewish faith. Norman Solomon. **J. Jew. Stud.** LII:1 Spring:2001 pp.146-154.

3457   'To go and marry any man that you please': a study of the formulaic antecedents of the rabbinic writ of divorce. Shalom E. Holtz. **J. Near East.** 60:4 10:2001 pp.241-258.

3458   Two models of medieval Jewish marriage: a preliminary study. Michael S. Berger. **J. Jew. Stud.** LII:1 Spring:2001 pp.59-84.

3459   Will the real Targum please stand up? Translation and coordination in the ancient Aramaic versions of Job. David Shepherd. **J. Jew. Stud.** LI:1 Spring:2000 pp.88-116.

3460   'With a strong hand and an outstretched arm': the meaning of the expression. Karen Martens. **Scan. J. Old. Test.** 15:1 2001 pp.123-141.

Sikhism
Sikhisme

3461   Baba Budha Ji — child prodigy who became patriarch. Amar Singh. **Sikh Rev.** 49:8(572) 8:2001 pp.69-77.

3462   Basic questions every Sikh should know. Duncan Greenlees. **Sikh Rev.** 49:9(573) 9:2001 pp.6-10.

3463   Bhai Baldeep Singh and the *Kirtan Parampara*. Kunwar Ranvir Singh. **Sikh Rev.** 49:9(573) 9:2001 p.49.

3464   The blessed gift of *Sadh Sangat*. Inni Kaur Bawa Dhingra. **Sikh Rev.** 49:9(573) 9:2001 pp.56-67.

3465   Celestial *japji* — its universal appeal. Devinder Kaur Deep. **Sikh Rev.** 49:11(575) 11:2001 pp.7-8.

3466   Concept of God as creator in Sikhism. Debabrata Das. **Sikh Rev.** 49:8(572) 8:2001 pp.9-12.

3467   Crisis of character: a wake-up call. Bhagwant Singh Dalawari. **Sikh Rev.** 49:9(573) 9:2001 pp.18-23.

3468   *Dasvandh*: the law of sharing wealth. Preet Pal Singh Bumra. **Sikh Rev.** 49:11(575) 11:2001 pp.31-33.

3469   A discourse on the future of Sikhism. Harbans Singh Bhola. **Sikh Rev.** 49:9(573) 9:2001 pp.14-17.

3470   Early 20th century visions of Sikh religion and politics. N. Gerald Barrier. **Sikh Rev.** 49:8(572) 8:2001 pp.31-39.

3471   Elements of the education policy: a Sikh pespective. Amrik Singh. **Sikh Rev.** 49:7(571) 7:2001 pp.28-32.

3472   Glimpses of Bhagat Nam Devji. Rajinder Singh. **Sikh Rev.** 49:7(571) 7:2001 pp.24-27.

3473   The glorious Maharaja Ranjit Singh and the end of an era. Harwant Singh. **Sikh Rev.** 49:6(570) 6:2001 pp.26-30.

3474   *Gurmat Chetna Lehar*: new challenges, old responses. H.S. Gulati. **Sikh Rev.** 49:11(575) 11:2001 pp.49-52.

3475   Guru Har Krishan — beacon of hope for suffering humanity. Onkar Singh. **Sikh Rev.** 49:7(571) 7:2001 pp.15-16.

3476   Guru Hargobind Sahib's journey to Kashmir. A. Singh. **Sikh Rev.** 49:6(570) 6:2001 pp.8-20.

3477   Guru Nanak's mind and historical research. Sulakhan Singh Dhillon. **Sikh Rev.** 49:11(575) 11:2001 pp.9-18.

3478   The Guru, the Sikh and divine being. Guru Fatha Singh Khalsa. **Sikh Rev.** 49:7(571) 7:2001 pp.12-14.

3479   Gyani Ditt Singh and the great revival. Dalvinder Singh. **Sikh Rev.** 49:11(575) 11:2001 pp.36-43.

3480 Impact of Sikhism on Indian society. Hazara Singh. **Sikh Rev.** 49:6(570) 6:2001 pp.31-33.
3481 Interfaith dialogue. Dharam Singh. **Sikh Rev.** 49:8(572) 8:2001 pp.17-22.
3482 A journey of faith. Harbhajan Singh. **Sikh Rev.** 49:9(573) 9:2001 pp.34-35.
3483 Kesh: our link with Guru Nanak. Gurcharanjit Singh. **Sikh Rev.** 49:11(575) 11:2001 p.67.
3484 Khalsa as the divinely sanctioned order. Jasjit Singh Walia. **Sikh Rev.** 49:8(572) 8:2001 pp.23-30.
3485 The legacy of Guru Granth Sahib. Rajinder Singh Vidyarthi. **Sikh Rev.** 49:11(575) 11:2001 pp.19-24.
3486 Magic of meditational trance. Joginder Singh. **Sikh Rev.** 49:7(571) 7:2001 pp.6-8.
3487 A new challenge to Sikh identity. Jaspal Singh. **Sikh Rev.** 49:9(573) 9:2001 pp.40-42.
3488 Politics of religion: phony *sants* and *mahants*. Dalip Singh Wasan. **Sikh Rev.** 49:11(575) 11:2001 pp.60-66.
3489 Reclaiming Nanakpanthi Vanjaras: a challenge and opportunity. Mohinder Singh. **Sikh Rev.** 49:11(575) 11:2001 pp.53-58.
3490 Re-discovering the Sikh legacy: part IV. A.C. Katoch. **Sikh Rev.** 49:6(570) 6:2001 pp.21-25.
3491 Religion and science. David R. Peel. **Sikh Rev.** 49:6(570) 6:2001 pp.10-14.
3492 Satwant Kaur — an 18th century legend (part-XXX). Bhai Vir Singhji; Bimal Kaur [Tr.]. **Sikh Rev.** 49:6(570) 6:2001 pp.62-63.
3493 Satwant Kaur — an 18th century legend (part-XXXI). Bhai Vir Singhji; Bimal Kaur [Tr.]. **Sikh Rev.** 49:7(571) 7:2001 pp.60-62.
3494 Shabad Guru: a people's gospel. Mahindar Singh. **Sikh Rev.** 49:9(573) 9:2001 pp.11-13.
3495 A shrine in Ladakh: Gurdwara Pathar Sahib. Harbhajan Singh. **Sikh Rev.** 49:11(575) 11:2001 pp.34-35.
3496 *Siddha Goshth*: Guru Nanak redefines *Sahaj-Yog*. Hardev Singh Virk. **Sikh Rev.** 49:8(572) 8:2001 pp.13-16.
3497 Sikh spirituality and contribution of women. Shashi Bala. **Sikh Rev.** 49:11(575) 11:2001 pp.25-30.
3498 Sikh-Muslim bonds forged by Guru Ki Maseet. Anna Barry Bigellow. **Sikh Rev.** 49:9(573) 9:2001 pp.36-39.
3499 Soul and self: our link with the divine. Tarnindar Singh. **Sikh Rev.** 49:8(572) 8:2001 pp.6-8.
3500 Tagore's poetic celebration of Guru Gobind Singh. Rajat Dasgupta [Tr.]. **Sikh Rev.** 49:8(572) 8:2001 pp.54-56.
3501 This above all: a window on Sikh faith. Gurmit Singh. **Sikh Rev.** 49:6(570) 6:2001 pp.15-20.
3502 The tide turns: a saga of Sikh valour. Raj Bir Singh. **Sikh Rev.** 49:8(572) 8:2001 pp.44-46.
3503 Translating compassion into service. Raminder Singh. **Sikh Rev.** 49:7(571) 7:2001 pp.21-23.
3504 Universality of Sri Guru Granth Sahib Nanak Singh Nishter. **Sikh Rev.** 49:7(571) 7:2001 pp.17-20.
3505 Urbanization and the Sikhs. Hardyal Singh Paul. **Sikh Rev.** 49:9(573) 9:2001 pp.27-30.
3506 The way of life as propounded by gurus. Sahib Singh Arshi. **Sikh Rev.** 49:7(571) 7:2001 pp.9-11.
3507 Who is an apostate? Gurbaksh Singh; Bhai Harbans Lal. **Sikh Rev.** 49:9(573) 9:2001 pp.24-26.
3508 Youth and preachers: candid comment. Sharan Pal Singh Sandhu. **Sikh Rev.** 49:9(573) 9:2001 pp.52-55.

F.3:   **Local religions and rituals**
         Religions locales et rites

3509   Une absence remplie de présences. Herméneutiques de l'occultation chez les Shaykhiyya. *[In French]*; [An absence full of presence. Hermeneutics of occultation with the Shaykhiyya]. Mohammad Ali Amir-Moezzi. **B. Sch. Orient. Afr. Stud.** 64:1 2001 pp.1-18.

3510   Allusions to ancestral impropriety: understandings of arthritis and rheumatism in the contemporary Navajo world. Maureen Trudelle Schwarz. **Am. Ethn.** 28:3 8:2001 pp.650-678.

3511   Anthony's feast: the gift in Abelam aesthetics (Anthony Forge memorial lecture, Canberra 1999). Diane Losche. **Aus. J. Anth.** 12:2 8:2001 pp.155-165.

3512   Arguments and icons: divergent modes of religiosity. Harvey Whitehouse. Oxford: Oxford University Press, 2000. x, 204p. *ISBN: 0198234155, 0198234147. Includes bibliographical references and index.*

3513   Barong and Rangda in the context of Balinese religion. Michele Stephen. **R. Ind. Malay. Aff.** 35:1 Winter:2001 pp.137-194.

3514   Boundaries and passages: rule and ritual in Yupik Eskimo oral tradition. Ann Fienup-Riordan. Norman OK, London: University of Oklahoma Press, 1994. xxiv, 389p. *ISBN: 0806126469, 0806126043. Includes bibliographical references (p.371-379) and index.* (*Series:* The civilization of the American Indian series - 212).

3515   Le chichihualcuauhco, la résurrection et la renaissance dans la pensée aztèque. *[In French]*; (Chichihualcuauhco, resurrection and rebirth in the Aztecs' thought.) *[Summary]*; *[Summary in Spanish]*. Nathalie Ragot. **J. Soc. Amér.** 86 2000 pp.49-66.

3516   Conjeturas sobre la identidad de los santos tzeltales. *[In Spanish]*; (Conjectures about the identity of Tzeltal Saints.) *[Summary]*; *[Summary in French]*. Pedro Pitarch. **J. Soc. Amér.** 86 2000 pp.129-148.

3517   Dcéry luny. Rituálne postavenie ženy v spoločnosti Mayov-Lacandóncov. *[In Slovak]*; [Daughters of the moon. Ritual status of woman in the community of Lacandon Maya] *[Summary]*. Tatiana Podolinská; Milan Kováč. **Slov. Národop.** 48:2 2000 pp.167-184.

3518   Deux expressions modernes du rite chinois *rang* 'céder pour obtenir'. *[In]*; [Two modern expressions of the Chinese *rang* rite of 'handing over to obtain'] *[Summary in French]*; *[Summary in German]*; *[Summary in Spanish]*. Catherine Capdeville-Zeng. **Soc. Anthrop.** 9:2 6:2001 pp.193-206.

3519   Diversité ethnique et appropriation des cultes vodoun dans une population de réfugiés au Sud Bénin. *[In French]*; [Ethnic diversity and the appropriation of Vodun cults in the refugee population of southeast Benin] *[Summary]*. Roger Brand. **Rev. Fr. Hist. O.mer.** 1(330-331) 6:2001 pp.269-328.

3520   The exclusion of women in the Mithraic mysteries: ancient or modern? Jonathan David. **Numen** XLVII:2 2000 pp.121-141.

3521   Exclusions from the catechumenate: continuity or discontinuity with pagan cult? Matthew W. Dickie. **Numen** XLVIII:4 2001 pp.417-443.

3522   *Fandaano*: a vanishing socio-religious system of the Hadiyya in southern Ethiopia. Ulrich Braukämper. **B. Int. Com. Urg. Anthrop. Ethnol. R.** 40 1999-2000 pp.52-64.

3523   'Fractious statelets' and 'galactic polities': ideology, ritual practices and the rise and fall of classic Maya states. Jeanne Lopiparo. **Kroeber Anthr. Soc. Pap.** 85 2001 pp.49-67.

3524   Fragment d'un rituel de Walkui, prêtre de la déesse de la nuit (KBo XXXII 176 = Bo 83/902). *[In French]*; [Part of Walkui's ritual, priest of the goddess of the night (KBo XXXII 176 = Bo 83/902)]. René Lebrun. **Arch. Orient.** 67:4 11:1999 pp.601-608.

3525   Gender rituals of rebellion and patriarchy in Africa. Todd Sanders. London: London School of Economics and Political Science, Gender Institute, 2001. 38p. *Includes bibliographical references.* (*Series:* New working paper series, London School of Economics, Gender Institute - issue 3).

3526   The guardian of the forces. Anne-Laure Folly Reiman [Ed.]. London: Royal Anthropological Institute, 1991. *Video.*

3527   How monotheistic is Mani's dualism? Concetta Giuffré Scibona. **Numen** XLVIII:4 2001 pp.444-467.

3528   Hydraulic religion: 'great king' cults in the Ming and Qing. Randall Dodgen. **Mod. Asian S.** 33:4 10:1999 pp.815-833.

3529   The laws of man and the laws of God: graphic patterns in Voltaic art. Christopher D. Roy. **Baes-A.** XLVII:2 6:2001 pp.223-258.

3530   Local dynamics of renegotiating ritual space in Northern Vietnam: the case of the *dinh*. Kirsten W. Endres. **SOJOURN** 16:1 4:2001 pp.70-101.

3531   Local religion in Tokugawa history. Barbara Ambros; Duncan Williams. **Jap. J. Relig. St.** 28:3-4 Fall:2001 pp.209-226.

3532   Localized religious specialists in early modern Japan: the development of the Ōyama Oshi system. Barbara Ambros. **Jap. J. Relig. St.** 28:3-4 Fall:2001 pp.329-372.

3533   Missionaries, the phenomenology of religion and 're-presenting' nineteenth-century African religion: a case study of Peter McKenzie's *Hail Orisha*! James L. Cox. **J. Relig. Afr.** XXXI:3 2001 pp.336-353.

3534   Il New Age tra dislocazione sociale e ricomposizione del legame sociale. Il caso dell'Aumismo. *[In Italian]*; [The 'New Age': between social displacement and recomposition of social relations: the case of Aumism]. Fabio Perocco. **Critica Sociol.** 137 Spring:2001 pp.82-99.

3535   Nordic religions in the Viking age. Thomas A. DuBois. Philadelphia PA: University of Pennsylvania Press, 1999. 271p. *ISBN: 0812217144.*

3536   Ob odnom irrigatsionnom prazdnike shugnantsev doliny r. Shakhdary (Zapadnyi Pamir). *[In Russian]*; (One of the irrigation festivals of the Shugnans of the Shakhdara River (West Pamirs).) M.M. Alamshoev; T.S. Kalandarov. **Etnograf. Oboz.** 4 7-8:2000 pp.68-72.

3537   *Ocelocoatl*. De l'art secret de communiquer avec les dieux. *[In French]*; [*Ocelocoatl*: the secret art of communicating with the gods]. José Contel. **Caravelle** 76-77 12:2001 pp.153-164.

3538   Power, ideology and ritual: the practice of agriculture in the Inca Empire. Miriam Doutriaux. **Kroeber Anthr. Soc. Pap.** 85 2001 pp.91-108.

3539   Quelques chants du rituel abstenciel «ngunda» chez les Atetela. *[In French]*; [Songs from the *ngunda* abstinence ritual among the Atetela] *[Summary]*. O. Lowenga. **Ann. Æqua.** 22 2001 pp.153-162.

3540   Reinterpretando la religión en Loíza: un estudio antropológico de la experiencia de testificar de dos ancianos. *[In Spanish]*; [Reinterpreting religion in Loíza: an anthropological study of the use of witnessing by two elders] *[Summary]*; *[Summary in Spanish]*. Samiri Hernández Hiraldo. **Rev. Cien. Soc.** 10 1:2001 pp.105-139.

3541   Religion, agency, restitution. Roland Littlewood. Oxford: Oxford University Press, 2001. 175p. *ISBN: 0199246750, 019924197X. Includes bibliographical references and index.* (*Series:* Wilde lectures in natural religion 1999).

3542   Religion among the Lugbara. The triadic source of its meaning. Albert Titus Dalfovo. **Anthropos [St. Augustin]** 96:1 2001 pp.29-40.

3543   Religion and social crisis in Japan: understanding Japanese society through the Aum affair. Mark R. Mullins [Ed.]; Robert J. Kisala [Ed.]. Basingstoke, New York: Palgrave, 2001. viii, 227p. *ISBN: 0333772695. Includes bibliographical references (p. [211]-223) and index.*

3544   Religious consensus and secular dissent. Two alternative paths to survival for Utopian communes. Christoph Brumann. **Anthropos [St. Augustin]** 96:1 2001 pp.87-104.

3545   Religious issues in the *Alberta Elders' Cree Dictionary*. Earle H. Waugh. **Numen** XLVIII:4 2001 pp.468-490.

3546   Religious practices on the Miyako Islands in the 1920's: from the archives of Nikolai Nevsky. Alexander M. Kabanoff. **Jpn. Relig.** 26:1 1:2001 pp.23-40.

3547   Religious uses of alcohol among the woodland Indians of North America. Marin Trenk. **Anthropos [St. Augustin]** 96:1 2001 pp.73-86.

3548   Revisiting our indigenous shrines through *Mungiki*. Grace Nyatugah Wamue. **Afr. Affairs** 100:400 7:2001 pp.453-467.

3549   Ritual games for the goddess Pattini. Rohan Bastin. **Soc. Anal. [Adelaide]** 45(2) 10:2001 pp.120-142.

3550   Rituel interaktion og illusion en relationel tilgang. *[In Danish]*; (Ritual interaction and illusion: a relational approach.) *[Summary]*. Michael Houseman; Carlo Severi. **Tids. Antrop.** 41 2000 pp.83-110.

3551   Sexual exploitation of cult women: the challenges of problematizing harmful traditional practices in Africa from a doctrinalist approach. Kenneth Omeje. **Soc. Leg. Stud.** 10:1 3:2001 pp.45-60.

3552   Der Sinn der Rituale. Eine Antwort auf Bernhard Streck. *[In German]*; [The meaning of rituals: a reply to Bernhard Streck]. Thomas Hauschild. **Paideuma** 47 2001 pp.195-202. *This is a comment on Zur Kritik der rituellen Vernunft by Bernhard Streck which appeared in Paideuma 47, pp.181-194.*

3553   Soul and personality as a communal bond. Hermann Amborn. **Anthropos [St. Augustin]** 96:1 2001 pp.41-58.

3554   St. Wojciech (Adalbert), the patron saint of Europe and Poland. His image in Polish folk culture; *[Summary in Polish]*. Maria Paradowska. **Ethnol. Pol.** 21 2000 pp.103-118.

3555   Świat staroobrzędowców północnej Białorusi. Ciągłość i zmiana tradycyjnej kultury i obyczajowości. *[In Polish]*; (The world of the Old Believers in northern Belarus. Continuity and change of their traditional culture.) *[Summary]*. Zuzanna Grębecka. **Etn. Polska** XLV:1-2 2001 pp.195-214.

3556   Tambours de bronze et circumambulations cérémonielles. Notes à partir d'un rituel kantou (chaîne annamitique). *[In French]*; (Bronze drums and ceremonial circumambulations. Notes on a Kantou ritual (Annamitic Cordillera).) *[Summary]*. Yves Goudineau. **B. Éc. Fr. Ex.-Or.** 87:2 2000 pp.553-578.

3557   There are many Kongo worlds: particularities of magico-religious beliefs among the Vili and Yombe of Congo-Brazzaville; *[Summary in French]*. Dunja Hersak. **Africa** 71:4 2001 pp.614-640.

3558   Three sources of ritual blessings in traditional Indonesian societies. Reimar Schefold. **Bijdragen** 157:2 2001 pp.359-382.

3559   Tres dimensiones de la máscara ritual chané. *[In Spanish]*; [Three aspects of the Chane ritual mask]. Federico Bossert; Diego Villar. **Anthropos [St. Augustin]** 96:1 2001 pp.59-72.

3560   Universals, general terms and the comparative study of religion. Jeppe Sinding Jensen. **Numen** XLVIII:3 2001 pp.238-266.

3561   Universals revisited: human behaviors and cultural variations. William Paden. **Numen** XLVIII:3 2001 pp.276-289.

3562   Usages sociaux du religieux sur les hautes-terres malgaches: les ancêtres au quotidien. *[In French]*; [Social uses of religion in the Malagasy highlands: past and present]. Malanjaona M. Rakotomalala; Sophie Blanchy; Françoise Raison-Jourde. Paris: L'Harmattan, 2001. 529p. *ISBN: 2747500195. Includes bibliographical references (p. [503]-522) and index.*

3563   Why Waco? Cults and the battle for religious freedom in America. James D. Tabor; Eugene V. Gallagher. Berkeley CA, London: University of California Press, 1995. xiv,252 p,[8] p of platesp. *ISBN: 0520201868. Includes bibliographical references and index.*

3564   Zur Kritik der rituellen Vernunft. *[In German]*; [Criticism of ritual reason]. Bernhard Streck. **Paideuma** 47 2001 pp.181-194.

F.4:   Magic and sorcery
               Magie et sorcellerie

3565   Ataka zelenoi magii. Interkul'turnye protsessy v shamanizme shuarov (Ekvador). *[In Russian]*; (Attack of the green magic. Intercultural processes in the shamanism of Shuar (Ecuadorian Amazon region).) *[Summary]*. E. Mader. **Etnograf. Oboz.** 5 9-10:2000 pp.79-87.

3566   Contemporary shamanism — *vegetalismo* in the Peruvian Amazon; *[Summary in Portuguese]*; *[Summary in Spanish]*. Wynand Koch. **Unisa Lat.Am. Rep.** 16:2 2000 pp.42-58.

3567   Den magiske illusion? En kognitiv tilgang til magiske ritualer. *[In Danish]*; (The magic illusion: a cognitive approach to magic rituals.) *[Summary]*. Jesper Sørensen. **Tids. Antrop.** 41 2000 pp.65-82.

3568   Divining evil: the state and witchcraft in Bastar. Nandini Sundar. **Gen. Tech. Dev.** 5:3 9-12:2001 pp.425-448.

3569   Divining 'troubles', or 'divining' troubles? Emergent and conflictual dimensions of Bangladeshi divination. James M. Wilce. **Anthr. Quart.** 74:4 10:2001 pp.190-200.

3570   Du végétal au politique: étude des plantes à pouvoir chez les Indiens wayana du Haut-Maroni. *[In French]*; (From plants to politics: magical plants among the Wayana on the upper Maroni.) Jean Chapuis. **J. Soc. Amér.** 87 2001 pp.113-136.

3571   *El Negro*, El Niño, witchcraft and the absence of rain in Botswana. Jan-Bart Gewald. **Afr. Affairs** 100:401 10:2001 pp.555-580.

3572   Enfants, jeunes et politiques. *[In French]*; [Children, youth and politics]. Filip De Boeck; Alcinda Honwana; Tshikala K. Biaya; Ahmadou Kourouma; Jean Comaroff; John Comaroff; Michel Cahen; Jean-Pierre Chrétien; Jean-Pierre Olivier de Sardan; Abdoua Elhadji Dagobi; Pierre-Joseph Laurent. **Pol. Afr.** 80 12:2000 pp.5-110. *Collection of 5 articles.*

3573   Hitler and the occult: the magical thinking of Adolf Hitler. Raymond L. Sickinger. **J. Pop. Cult.** 34:2 Fall:2000 pp.107-126.

3574   Imagining the impossible: magical, scientific, and religious thinking in children. Paul L. Harris [Ed.]; Karl Sven Rosengren [Ed.]; Carl N. Johnson [Ed.]. Cambridge, New York: Cambridge University Press, 2000. xx, 418p. *ISBN: 0521665876, 0521593220. Includes bibliographical references and indexes.*

3575   In search of the magical flow: magic and market in contemporary Russia. Galina Lindquist. **Urban Anthro.** 29:4 Winter:2000 pp.315-358.

3576   Indo-Celtic connections: ethic, magic, and linguistic. Stefan Zimmer. **J. Indo-Eur. S.** 29:3-4 Fall-Winter:2001 pp.379-405.

3577   An innocent woman, unjustly accused? Charwe, medium of the Nehanda Mhondoro spirit, and the 1896-97 Central Shona rising in Zimbabwe. D.N. Beach. **Hist. Afr.** 25 1998 pp.27-54.

3578   Lure of the sinister: the unnatural history of Satanism. Gareth J. Medway. New York: New York University Press, 2001. ix, 465p. *ISBN: 081475645X. Includes bibliographical references (p. 425-442) and index.*

3579   Madumo, a man bewitched. Adam Ashforth. Chicago IL: University of Chicago Press, 2000. vii, 255p. *ISBN: 0226029719.*

3580   Mágia v živote kaukazských národov. *[In Slovak]*; (Magic in the life of nations in Caucasus.) *[Summary]*. Beata Čierniková. **Slov. Národop.** 47:1 1999 pp.33-41.

3581   Magiia v semeino-bytovoi obriadnosti shugnantsev. *[In Russian]*; (Magic in family daily life: rites and rituals of the Shugnans.) *[Summary]*. T.S. Kalandarov. **Etnograf. Oboz.** 1 1-2:2001 pp.39-52.

3582   The names and identities of the Boramey spirits possessing Cambodian mediums. Didier Bertrand. **Asian Folk. S.** LX:1 2001 pp.31-48.

3583   „Nowa antropologia" wobec dawniejszch koncepcji religii i magii. *[In Polish]*; ('New anthropology' in relation to former concepts of religion and magic.) Adam Szafrański. Krakow: Nomos, 2000. 126p. *ISBN: 8385527990.*

3584   Of spirit possession and structural adjustment programs: government downsizing, education and their enchantments in neo-liberal Kenya. James H. Smith. **J. Relig. Afr.** XXXI:4 2001 pp.427-456.

3585   On '*Ghost Dancing the Grand Canyon*'. Lynda D. McNeil; Carol Patterson; Richard W. Stoffle [Comments by]. **Curr. Anthr.** 42:2 4:2001 pp.277-280.

3586   Pain and 'progress': revisiting *Botol* sorcery in the southern highlands of Papua New Guinea. Michael Nihill. **Soc. Anal. [Adelaide]** 45(1) 4:2001 pp.103-121.

3587   Paraphernalia of the Selkup shaman: terms and their etymological explanations exhibiting metaphoric symbolism. Alexandra A. Kim. **Eur. Stud. Y.** 73 2001 pp.127-146.

3588   The Passamaquoddy 'witchcraft tales' of Newell S. Francis. Philip S. LeSourd. **Anthrop. Ling.** 42:4 Winter:2000 pp.441-498.

3589   Pokhishcheniia shamanskikh dukhov. *[In Russian]*; (Abduction of shaman spirits.) *[Summary]*. T.D. Bulgakova. **Etnograf. Oboz.** 3 5-6:2001 pp.32-41.

3590   Pouvoirs sorciers. *[In French]*; [Witchcraft and power]. Florence Bernault; Joseph Tonda; Peter Geschiere; Michael G. Schatzberg; Stephen Ellis; Luise White; Jane I. Guyer; Murray Last; Catherine Boudet. **Pol. Afr.** 79 10:2000 pp.5-164. *Collection of 9 articles.*

3591   Prophetes, visionnaires et guerisseurs de l'Afrique subsaharienne contemporaine. *[In French]*; (Prophets, visionaries and healers in contemporary sub-Saharan Africa.) André Mary; Pierre-Joseph Laurent; Christine Henry; Jean-Pierre Dozon; Marc-Éric Gruénais; Joseph Tonda; Sophie Bava; Cheikh Gueye. **Soc. Compass** 48:3 9:2001 pp.307-438. *Collection of 8 articles.*

3592   Relaciones de poder y apropiación del «otro» en relatos sobre iniciaciones shamánicas en el Chaco argentino. *[In Spanish]*; (Power relations and the incorporation of the 'other' in shamanic initiation accounts in the Argentine Chaco.) Florencia Carmen Tola. **J. Soc. Amér.** 87 2001 pp.197-210.

3593   Religion in Tuva: restoration or innovation? Philip Walters. **Relig. State Soc.** 29:1 3:2001 pp.23-38.

3594   Rethinking ancestors and colonial power in Madagascar; *[Summary in French]*. Jennifer Cole; Karen Middleton. **Africa** 71:1 2001 pp.1-37.

3595   Le retour des métapsychistes. *[In French]*; [The return of the psychics]. Giordana Charuty. **Homme** 158-159 4-9:2001 pp.353-364.

3596   Revisiting 'magical fright'. Bruce Lincoln. **Am. Ethn.** 28:4 11:2001 pp.778-802.

3597   Ritual killing, 419, and fast wealth: inequality and the popular imagination in southeastern Nigeria. Daniel Jordan Smith. **Am. Ethn.** 28:4 11:2001 pp.803-826.

3598   Sacred colors and shamanic vision among the Huichol Indians of Mexico. Hope MacLean. **J. Anthr. Res.** 57:3 Fall:2001 pp.305-324.

3599   Saints and spirits and their significance in Moroccan cultural beliefs and practices: an analysis of Westermarck's work. Mohamed Chtatou. **Morocco** 1 1996 pp.62-84.

3600   Schamanismus und Tourismus in der Mongolei. *[In German]*; (Shamanism and tourism in Mongolia.) *[Summary]*. Judith Schlehe; Helmut Weber. **Z. Ethn.** 126:1 2001 pp.93-116.

3601   Shamanism and hegemony: a Gramscian approach to the Chavin staff god. Sharon Small. **Kroeber Anthr. Soc. Pap.** 85 2001 pp.68-90.

3602   Shamanstvo i inye traditsionnye verovaniia i praktiki. *[In Russian]*; (Shamanism and other traditional beliefs and practices.) *[Summary]*. V.I. Kharitonova; V.M. Gatzak; E.V. Revunenkova; M. Harner. **Etnograf. Oboz.** 1 1-2:2000 pp.39-50.

3603   Sorcery, modernity and social transformation in Banyuwangi, East Java. Caroline Campbell; Linda H. Connor. **R. Ind. Malay. Aff.** 34:2 Summer:2000 pp.61-98.

3604   Die *Tabella defixionis* KAI 89 und die Magie des Fluches. *[In German]*; [The *Tabella defixionis* KAI 89 and the magic of curses]. H.P. Müller. **Orientalia** 69:4 2000 pp.393-406.

3605   O universo visual dos xamãs wauja (Alto Xingu). *[In Portuguese]*; (The visual universe of Wauja shamans (Upper Xingu).) Aristóteles Barcelos Neto. **J. Soc. Amér.** 87 2001 pp.137-160.

3606   The verbal art of Nenets' shamanism. Péter Simoncsics. **Eur. Stud. Y.** 73 2001 pp.43-126.

3607   Wayward pastoral ghosts and regional xenophobia in a northern Madagascar town; *[Summary in French]*. Lesley A. Sharp. **Africa** 71:1 2001 pp.38-81.

F.5: **Religious change**
Processus de changement religieux

3608 À la recherche de Voulet: sur les traces sanglantes de la Mission Afrique centrale, 1898-1899. *[In French]*; [In search of Voulet: on the bloody trail of the Central African Mission, 1898-1899]. Arsène Klobb; Octave Meynier; Chantal Ahounou; A. Maitrot de La Motte-Capron [Foreword]. Paris: Cosmopole, 2001. 229p. *ISBN: 284630002X. Includes bibliographical references (p. 224-226).*

3609 Afro-Cuban cults. Christine Ayorinde [Tr.]; Miguel Barnet. Princeton NJ: Markus Wiener Publishers, 2001. 160p. *ISBN: 1558762558, 155876254X. Includes bibliographical references.*

3610 Das „andere" Wachstumswunder. Protestantische Kirchen in Südkorea. *[In German]*; (The 'other' success story: Protestant churches in South Korea.) *[Summary]*. Thomas Kern. **Z. Soziol.** 30:5 10:2001 pp.341-361.

3611 Aum Shinrikyō in Russia. Alexander Kabanoff. **Jpn. Relig.** 26:2 7:2001 pp.149-170.

3612 Charisma and possession in Africa and Brazil. David Lehmann. **Theory Cult. Soc.** 18:5 10:2001 pp.45-74.

3613 Chinese perceptions of the Jews and Judaism: a history of the Youtai. Xun Zhou. Richmond: Curzon press, 2001. x, 202p. *ISBN: 0700712496. Includes bibliographical references and index.*

3614 Chokwe masks and Franciscan missionaries in Sandoa, Belgian Congo, ca.1948. Constantine Petridis. **Anthropos [St. Augustin]** 96:1 2001 pp.3-28.

3615 Christians among Muslims: the church missionary society in the northern Sudan. Heather J. Sharkey. **Espace Pop. Soc.** 43:1 2002 pp.51-75.

3616 De la religion chez les intellectuels africains en France. L'odyssée d'un référent identitaire. *[In French]*; (On religion among African intellectuals in France: the odyssey of a referent of identities.) *[Summary]*. Abdoulaye Gueye. **Cah. Ét. Afr.** XLI(2):162 2001 pp.267-291.

3617 Des rêveurs d'utopies dans l'Amérique espagnole du XVIᵉ siècle. Les convergences. *[In French]*; [Utopian dreamers in Spanish America during the 16ᵗʰ century]. Michel Bertrand. **Caravelle** 76-77 12:2001 pp.317-332.

3618 Dos figuras en la Utopía Franciscana de Nueva España: Fray Juan de Zumárraga y fray Martín de Valencia. *[In Spanish]*; [Two figures from New Spain's Franciscan Utopia: Fray Juan de Zumárraga and Fray Martín de Valencia]. Francisco Morales. **Caravelle** 76-77 12:2001 pp.333-344.

3619 Earth and nature-based spirituality (part II): from Earth First! and bioregionalism to scientific paganism and the new age. Bron Taylor. **Religion** 31:3 7:2001 pp.225-246.

3620 The ethical redemption of African imaginaire: Kä Mana's theology of reconstruction. Valentin Dedji. **J. Relig. Afr.** XXXI:3 2001 pp.254-274.

3621 The ethics of listening: cassette-sermon audition in contemporary Egypt. Charles Hirschkind. **Am. Ethn.** 28:3 8.2001 pp.623-649.

3622 From invisible Christians to Gothic theatre: the romance of the millennial in Melanesian anthropology. Bronwen Douglas. **Curr. Anthr.** 42:5 12:2001 pp.615-650.

3623 The *Iglesia ni Cristo*, 1914-2000: from obscure Philippine faith to global belief system. Robert R. Reed. **Bijdragen** 157:3 2001 pp.561-608.

3624 Indian altars of the spiritual church: Kongo echoes in New Orleans. Stephen C. Wehmeyer. **Afr. Arts** XXXIII:4 Winter:2000 pp.62-69.

3625 Indigenous expressions of world religions. John Gordon; Mark Mosko; Fiona Magowan; Sallie Anderson; Carolyn Brennan; Lynda Newland; Thomas Reuter; Philip Taylor; Arthur Saniotis. **Aus. J. Anth.** 12:3 12:2001 pp.253-366. *Collection of 9 articles.*

3626 La iniciación de un *tlamatqui* en la Sierra de Puebla. *[In Spanish]*; [the initiation of *tlamatqui* in Sierra de Puebla]. Olimpia Farfán Morales. **Rev. de Human.** 5 Autumn:1998 pp.135-152.

3627 Introduced writing and Christianity: differential access to religious knowledge among the Asabano. Roger Ivar Lohmann. **Ethnology** XL:2 Spring:2001 pp.93-111.

3628   K 100-letiiu pravoslaviia v Koree. *[In Russian]*; (To the centennial of orthodoxy in Korea.) T.M. Simbirtseva. **Etnograf. Oboz.** 5 9-10:2000 pp.42-56.

3629   Kartki z dziejów prawosławnej parafii św. Aleksandry w Stanisławowie koło Modlina. *[In Polish]*; (Some pages from the history of the St. Alexandra Russian Orthodox parish in Stanisławów near Modlin.) *[Summary]*. Andrzej Woźniak. **Etn. Polska** XLV:1-2 2001 pp.183-194.

3630   Krest'anské misie v Polynézii. *[In Slovak]*; (Christian missions in Polynesia.) Martina Bucková. **Slov. Národop.** 48:2 2000 pp.211-216.

3631   Mahikari: new religion and Japanese popular culture. William Sanborn Pfeiffer. **J. Pop. Cult.** 34:2 Fall:2000 pp.155-168.

3632   El manuscrito jesuita mesiánico de Andrés de Oviedo dirigido a Francisco de Borja (1550). *[In Spanish]*; [The Messianic Jesuit manuscript sent to Francisco de Borja by Andrés de Oviedo]. Alain Milhou. **Caravelle** 76-77 12:2001 pp.345-354.

3633   Las nuevas religiones en México como forma de identidad colectiva. *[In Spanish]*; [New religions in Mexico as a form of collective identity]. Yolotl Gonzalez Torres. **B. Int. Com. Urg. Anthrop. Ethnol. R.** 40 1999-2000 pp.163-170.

3634   Odbudowywanie pamięci. Przemiany religijne w Środkowo-Wschodniej Europie po upadku komunizmu. *[In Polish]*; (Rebuilding memory: religious changes in Central-East Europe after the fall of communism.) Irena Borowik. Krakow: Nomos, 2000. 86p. *ISBN: 8388508032.*

3635   Pacific Islander pastors and missionaries: some historiographical and analytical issues. Doug Munro; Andrew Thornley. **Pac. Stud.** 23:3-4 9-12:2000 pp.1-31.

3636   Pentecostalism: the world their parish. David Martin. Oxford: Blackwell Publishers, 2001. 197p. *ISBN: 0631231218.*

3637   Un prédicateur à Mexico au temps de Sor Juana Inés de la Cruz: le Père Juan Martínez de la Parra S. J. et son livre *Luz de verdades catolicas y exposicion de la Doctrina Christiana*. *[In French]*; [A preacher in Mexico during Sister Juana Inés de la Cruz's time: Father Juan Martínez de la Parra S.J. and his book *Luz de verdades católicas y exposición de la Doctrina Christiana*]. Marie-Cécile Benassy-Berling. **Caravelle** 76-77 12:2001 pp.401-409.

3638   Psychiatry treats heterodoxy: the 1995 Aum trial in Russia from a lawyer's perspective. Galina A. Krylova. **Jpn. Relig.** 26:2 7:2001 pp.171-190.

3639   Religiosidad popular. Anclajes locales de los imaginarios globales. *[In Spanish]*; [Popular religiosity: a local retreat for the world's imagination]. Renée De La Torre. **Metapolítica** 5:17 1-3:2001 pp.98-117.

3640   Religious feminism in an age of empire: CMS women missionaries in Iran, 1869-1934. Gulnar Eleanor Francis-Dehqani. Bristol: Centre for Comparative Studies in Religion and Gender, 2000. 251p. *ISBN: 0862924898. Includes bibliographical references.* (*Series:* CCSRG monograph series - 4).

3641   Rezente christliche Einflüsse in der Traumzeitvorstellung der australischen Aborigines. *[In German]*; [Recent Christian influences on the idea of Dreamtime among Australian Aborigines]. Stephan Krines. **Anthropos [St. Augustin]** 96:1 2001 pp.157-168.

3642   La saturación de eclesiásticos en la Lima barroca. *[In Spanish]*; [The profusion of religious buildings in Lima during the baroque period]. Ramón María Serrera. **Caravelle** 76-77 12:2001 pp.255-263.

3643   Secrecy and the sense of an ending: narrative, time, and everyday millenarianism in Papua New Guinea and in Christian fundamentalism. Joel Robbins. **Comp. Stud. S.** 43:3 7:2001 pp.525-551.

3644   Un sermón de profesión de monjas del siglo XVII: la retórica de la perfección. *[In Spanish]*; [A 17th century sermon on nuns: the rhetoric of perfection]. María Dolores Bravo Arriaga. **Caravelle** 76-77 12:2001 pp.391-399.

3645   Signs of conversion, spirit of commitment: the Pentecostal Church in the Kingdom of Tonga. Ernest Olson. **J. Rit. Stud.** 15:2 2001 pp.13-26.

3646   Sufism and the Indonesian Islamic revival. Julia Day Howell. **J. Asian St.** 60:3 8:2001 pp.701-729.

3647   Über die Ursachen des Sieges des Christentums in Ägypten. *[In German]*; [On the causes of the Christian victories in Egypt]. Peter Hubai. **Numen** XLVIII:1 2001 pp.81-116.

3648   'White' Americans in 'Black' Africa: Black and White American Methodist missionaries in Liberia, 1820-1875. Eunjin Park. New York: Routledge, 2001. 244p. *ISBN: 0815340273. Includes bibliographical references and index. (Series:* Studies in African American history and culture).

G: KNOWLEDGE, FOLK TRADITIONS, ARTS AND SCIENCE
CONNAISSANCE, TRADITIONS POPULAIRES, ARTS ET SCIENCE

G.1: Categories of thought and meaning
Catégories de la pensée et de la signification

3649 Bulgarie: voix d'hier, paroles d'aujourd'hui. *[In French]*; [Bulgaria: a voice from the past and present]. Stefana Stoykova; Stoyanka Boyadzhieva; Anna Ilieva; Anna Shtarbanova; Dimitrina Kaufman; Nikolai Kaufman; Ivanichka Georgieva; Elka Bakalova; Mila Santova; Iveta Todorova-Pirgova; Doroteya Dobreva; Petar Petrov; Haralan Aleksandrov; Ivaylo Ditchev; Frédéric Saumade. **Ethn. Fr.** XXXI:2 4-6:2001 pp.199-336. *Collection of 13 articles.*

3650 Cosmologies, cities, and cultural constructions of space: Oceanic enlargements of the world. Wolfgang Kempf. **Pac. Stud.** 22:2 6:1999 pp.97-114.

3651 Creating time and society. The annual cycle of the people of Langa in eastern Indonesia. Susanne Schröter. **Anthropos [St. Augustin]** 95:2 2000 pp.463-484.

3652 Culture in the world system: an interview with Immanuel Wallerstein. Immanuel Wallerstein; Anand Kumar [Interviewer]; Frank Welz [Interviewer]. **Soc. Ident.** 7:2 6:2001 pp.221-232.

3653 Danskhed. *[In Danish]*; [Danishness]. Ansa Lønstrup; Kusum Gopal; Tine Damsholt; Joel Leonard Katz; Evgenij Kluev; Inge Adriansen; Georg Brandes. **Tids. Antrop.** 42 2000 pp.7-104. *Collection of 7 articles.*

3654 De la mémoire communicative à la mémoire culturelle. Le passé dans les témoignages d'Arezzo et de Sienne (1177-1180). *[In French]*; (From communicative memory to cultural memory. The past in the testimonies of Arezzo and Siena (1177-1180).) *[Summary]*. Guy P. Marchal. **Annales** 56:3 5-6:2001 pp.563-590.

3655 The death of knowledge: ghosts on the plains. Te Maire Tau. **N.Z. J. Hist.** 35:2 10:2001 pp.131-152.

3656 Dresden: paradoxes of memory in history. Elizabeth A. Ten Dyke. London, New York: Routledge, 2001. xxiv, 316p. *ISBN: 0415270367. Includes bibliographical references (p. 273-307) and index.* (*Series:* Studies in anthropology and history - 28).

3657 Earth and nature-based spirituality (part 1): from deep ecology to radical environmentalism. Bron Taylor. **Religion** 31:2 4:2001 pp.175-193.

3658 Les échelles temporelles des oasis du Jérid tunisien. *[In French]*; [Timescales in the Tunisian Jerid oasis]. Vincent Battesti. **Anthropos [St. Augustin]** 95:2 2000 pp.419-432.

3659 Emplaced myth: space, narrative, and knowledge in Aboriginal Australia and Papua New Guinea. Alan. Rumsey [Ed.]; James F. Weiner [Ed.]. Honolulu HI: University of Hawaii Press, 2001. vii, 281p. *ISBN: 0824823893, 0824816633. Includes bibliographical references and index.*

3660 Espaces domestiques. *[In French]*; [Domestic space]. J.F. Staszak; X. Durang; B. Collignon; V. Gelézeau; J. Debanné. **Ann. Géogr.** 110:620 7-8:2001 pp.339-453. *Collection of 5 articles.*

3661 Etnopedagogicheskaia aforistika. *[In Russian]*; (Ethnopedagogical aphorisms.) *[Summary]*. Z.B. Tsallagova. **Etnograf. Oboz.** 5 9-10:2000 pp.70-78.

3662 Folkbiology. Douglas L. Medin [Ed.]; Scott Atran [Ed.]. Cambridge MA, London: MIT Press, 1999. ix, 504p. *ISBN: 026263192X, 0262133490. Includes bibliographical references and index.*

3663 The function and meaning of combs in the Newar culture (Nepal). Sushila Manandhar Fischer. **Contrib. Nepal. Stud.** 27:2 7:2000 pp.219-244.

3664 Ghosts in the cyber world. An analysis of folklore sites on the Internet; *[Summary in French]*; *[Summary in German]*. Larisa Fialkova; Maria N. Yelenevskaya. **Fabula** 42:1-2 2001 pp.64-89.

3665   *Hirbet Hizah*: between remembrance and forgetting. Anita Shapira. **Jew. Soc. Stud.** 7:1 Fall:2000 pp.1-62.

3666   Historical memory in Abraham Geiger's account of modern Jewish identity. Ken Koltun-Fromm. **Jew. Soc. Stud.** 7:1 Fall:2000 pp.109-126.

3667   Honduran folk entomology. Jeffery W. Bentley; Gonzalo Rodríguez. **Curr. Anthr.** 42:2 4:2001 pp.285-300.

3668   How not to explain the great divide. Diederick Raven. **Soc. Sci. Info.** 40:3 9:2001 pp.373-410.

3669   'How we know': Kwara'ae rural villagers doing indigenous epistemology. David Welchman Gegeo; Karen Ann Watson-Gegeo. **Cont. Pac.** 13:1 Spring:2001 pp.55-88.

3670   Inferring paradigms: referencing Andean and Mesoamerican texts. Claudette K. Columbus. **Semiotica** 135:1-4 2001 pp.157-174.

3671   Irruptions of the dreamings in post-colonial Australia. Basil Sansom. **Oceania** 72:1 9:2001 pp.1-32.

3672   Lire la langue des étoiles des prêtres mayas. *[In French]*; [Reading the language of the stars by Maya priests]. André Cauty. **Amerindia** 24 1999 pp.119-152.

3673   Le monument des martyrs de l'indépendance à Mbandaka. *[In French]*; [The monument to the martyrs of independence in Mbandaka] *[Summary]*. Lewono Lufungula. **Ann. Æqua.** 22 2001 pp.103-124.

3674   Mythology as an indicator of cultural change. Hunting and agriculture as reflected in North American traditions. Sonja Ross. **Anthropos [St. Augustin]** 95:2 2000 pp.433-444.

3675   Our own liberation: reflections on Hawaiian epistemology. Manulani Aluli Meyer; Subramani [Comments by]; Vilsoni Hereniko [Comments by]; Caroline Sinavaiana-Gabbard [Comments by]; David Welchman Gegeo [Comments by]. **Cont. Pac.** 13:1 Spring:2001 pp.124-182.

3676   Pansophy, wisdom, panharmony. Vladimír Zahradník. **Arch. Orient.** 68:1 2:2000 pp.27-30.

3677   Penser la connaissance de sens commun dans la modernité avancée. *[In French]*; [Common sense knowledge theory in advanced societies] *[Summary]*. Geneviève Daudelin. **Can. R. Soc. A.** 38:3 8:2001 pp.293-308.

3678   Podhale. Tradycja we współczesnej kulturze wsi. *[In Polish]*; (Podhale: tradition in contemporary folk culture.) *[Summary]*. Danuta Tylkowa [Ed.]. Krakow: Instytut Archeologii i Etnologii PAN, 2000. 455p. *Includes bibliographical references.*

3679   Pramene l'udových eschatologických legiend a povestí. *[In Slovak]*; (Sources of folk eschatological legends and stories.) *[Summary]*. Ján Komorovský. **Slov. Národop.** 47:2-3 1999 pp.141-158.

3680   Pratiques nautiques et cosmologie: l'*Odyssée* d'Homère revisitée. *[In French]*; (Nautical practices and cosmology: Homer's *Odyssey* revisited.) *[Summary]*; *[Summary in German]*. Jean Cuisenier. **Ethn. Fr.** XXXI:4 10-12:2001 pp.725-740.

3681   Religion and modernity: ritual transformations and the reconstruction of space and time. Tong Chee Kiong; Lily Kong. **Soc. Cult. Geog.** 1:1 9:2000 pp.29-44.

3682   (The remains of the matrilineal system in Li — with reference to the folklore on the lower Han River in Sui and C'hu.); *[Text in Japanese]*. Shigehiro Kubuki. **St. Ess. Beh. Sc. Phil.** 21 3:2001 pp.1-18.

3683   The rise and fall of *Varna-Vyavastha*. S.S. Gupta. **Indian J. Soc. W.** 62:2 4:2001 pp.169-179.

3684   Rola tradycji w kulturze wsi kujawskiej. *[In Polish]*; (The role of tradition in the folk culture of Kujawy.) Teresa Dunin-Karwicka. Toruń: Uniwersytet Mikołaja Kopernika, 2000. 127p. *ISBN: 8323111391.*

3685   Science et anthropologie. De la notion de l'âme en général et de sa conception singulière chez les Lyéla du Burkina Faso. *[In French]*; [Science and anthropology. The notion of soul in general and its singular meaning among the Lyela in Burkina Faso]. Pierre Bamony. **Anthropos [St. Augustin]** 95:2 2000 pp.548-554.

3686   The scouring of the shire: fairies, trolls and pixies in eco-protest culture. Andy Letcher. **Folklore** 112:2 10:2001 pp.147-162.

3687 Statist narratives and Maji Maji ellipses. Thaddeus Sunseri. **Int. J. Afr. H. S.** 33:3 2000 pp.567-584.

3688 *Strīrājya*: Indian accounts of kingdoms of women. William L. Smith. **Stud. Orient.** 94 2001 pp.465-478.

3689 Time out and worlds apart: tradition and modernity meet in the time-space of the gravesweeping festivals of Hong Kong. Elizabeth Kenworthy Teather. **Sing. J. Trop. Geogr.** 22:2 7:2001 pp.156-172.

3690 Totemism, animism and North Asian indigenous ontologies; *[Summary in French]*. Morten A. Pedersen. **J. Royal Anth. Inst.** 7:3 9:2001 pp.411-428.

3691 Tribal meditative consciousness and change of ethnonyms in the Tuva Republic area. N.V. Abayev. **Eur. Stud. Y.** 73 2001 pp.172-173.

3692 *Trifunctionalia redivivia*: a note on some Greek possibilities. Dean Miller. **J. Indo-Eur. S.** 29:1-2 Spring-Summer:2001 pp.173-184.

3693 Un(di)ing legacies: White matters of memory in portraits of 'our princess'. Ruby C. Tapia. **Cult. Val.** 5:2 4:2001 pp.261-287.

3694 Wierzenia, zwyczaje i obrzędy. Folklor pogranicza polsko-czeskiego. *[In Polish]*; [Beliefs, customs and rituals: the folklore of the Polish-Czech borderland]; *[Summary in German]*; *[Summary in Russian]*; *[Summary in Czech]*. Kornelia Lach. Wroclaw: Polskie Towarzystwo Ludoznawcze, 2000. 240p. *ISBN: 8387266353.*

3695 Worldviews and decision making: natural resource management of the Laka of Mapela in an anthropological perspective; *[Summary in Afrikaans]*. Britta Eckert; F.C. de Beer; L.P. Vorster. **S. Afr. J. Ethnol.** 24:3 2001 pp.88-98.

3696 *Yebisa Wo Fie* : growing old and building a house in the Akan culture of Ghana. Sjaak van der Geest. **J. Cr-Cult. Gerontol.** 13:4 1998 pp.333-360.

Invention of tradition
Invention de la tradition

3697 Archaeology and nationalism. Margarita Díaz-Andreu; Anthony D. Smith; Timothy Champion; Athena S. Leoussi; Neil Asher Silberman; John Hutchinson; D.A. Brading. **Nat. Nat.** 7:4 10:2001 pp.429-531. *Collection of 7 articles.*

3698 'Blame it on Maureen O'Hara': Ireland and the trope of authenticity. Colin Graham. **Cult. St.** 15:1 1:2001 pp.58-75.

3699 Consuming Ireland: Lucky Charms cereal, Irish Spring soap and 1-800-SHAMROCK. Diane Negra. **Cult. St.** 15:1 1:2001 pp.76-97.

3700 Crafting places through mobility: Chinese American 'roots-searching' in China. Andrea Louie. **Identities** 8:3 9:2001 pp.343-380.

3701 The creation of national treasures and monuments: the 1916 Japanese laws on the preservation of Korean remains and relics and their colonial legacies. Hyung Il Pai. **Kor. Stud.** 25:1 2001 pp.72-95.

3702 Exotiquement vôtres: les inventaires de la tradition en pays dogon. *[In French]*; (Exotically yours: inventories of tradition in Dogon country.) Gaetano Ciarcia. **Terrain** 37 9:2001 pp.105-122.

3703 Hungary after 1989: inscribing a new past on place. Kenneth E. Foote; Attila Tóth; Anett Árvay. **Geogr. Rev.** 90:3 7:2000 pp.301-334.

3704 'Many divorces and many spinsters': marriage as an invented tradition in southern Malawi, 1946-1999. Amy Kaler. **J. Fam. Hist.** 26:4 10:2001 pp.529-556.

3705 Perversion of history text books: judiciary to the rescue? M.S. Rahi. **Sikh Rev.** 49:7(571) 7:2001 pp.45-51.

3706 Religion and commercialization: the Shintō wedding ritual (*shinzenshiki*) as an 'invented tradition' in Japan. Klaus Antoni. **Jpn. Relig.** 26:1 1:2001 pp.41-54.

3707 The resurgence of tradition in a post-communist society: the role of the Mongolian *ger* as a vehicle for the maintenance of ideology and practice in the diachronic process of Mongolian society. Ch. Sauer. **Cent. Asia. J.** 45:1 2001 pp.63-127.

3708   Revival, invention or re-invention of traditions? The Mari diaspora. Paul Fryer. **Suomal.-
        Ugril. Seur. Aikak.** 89 2001 pp.21-32.
3709   Timeline history and the Anzac myth: settler narratives of local history in a north
        Australian town. Elizabeth Furniss. **Oceania** 71:4 6:2001 pp.279-297.
3710   'We don't know our descent': how the *gitanos* of Jarana manage the past; *[Summary in
        French]*. Paloma Gay y Blasco. **J. Royal Anth. Inst.** 7:4 12:2001 pp.631-648.

G.2:   **Symbolism**
        Symbolisme

3711   El águila real, símbolo del pueblo mexica. *[In Spanish]*; [The royal eagle, symbol of the
        Mexican people]. Mercedes de la Garza C. **Caravelle** 76-77 12:2001 pp.105-118.
3712   Car cultures. Daniel Miller [Ed.]. Oxford: Berg Publishers, 2001. xiv, 250p. *ISBN:
        1859734073, 185973412X. Includes bibliographical references and index. (Series:
        Materializing culture).*
3713   The comparative study on the rites of building traditional houses between King-men and
        Peng-hu. Yu-tung Chang; Min-fu Hsu. **B. Inst. Ethn. Ac. Sin.** 90 Autumn:2000 pp.39-110.
3714   'Crushing the pistachio': eroticism in Senegal and the art of Ousmane Ndiaye Dago. T.K.
        Biaya. **Publ. Cult.** 12:3 Fall:2000 pp.707-720.
3715   Des sacs chargés de mémoire. Du jeu des tambours à la résistance silencieuse des Wa de
        Xuelin (Yunnan). *[In French]*; (Bags laden with memories: from playing drums to silent
        resistence among the Wa of Xuelin (Yunnan).) *[Summary]*. Bernard Formoso. **Homme** 160
        10-12:2001 pp.41-66.
3716   The earliest Sikh coin: imprint of a saga. Surinder Singh. **Sikh Rev.** 49:7(571) 7:2001
        pp.33-39.
3717   La face cachée du Soleil Levant. *[In French]*; (The hidden face of the Rising Sun.)
        [Summary]. Robert Duquenne. **B. Éc. Fr. Ex.-Or.** 87:2 2000 pp.629-644.
3718   Fantastické predstavy vo výtvarnom a slovesnom prejave na Slovensku. *[In Slovak]*;
        (Imaginary images in visual and literary arts in Slovakia.) *[Summary]*. Soňa
        Kovačevičová. **Slov. Národop.** 47:2-3 1999 pp.159-172.
3719   La flûte pinkuyllu des provincias altas du Cuzco (Pérou): organologie et symbolique
        érotique d'un aérophone andin. *[In French]*; (The pinkuyllu flute of the high provinces of
        Cuzco (Peru): the organology and erotic symbolism of an Andean aerophone.) Raphaël
        Parejo-Coudert. **J. Soc. Amér.** 87 2001 pp.211-264.
3720   El fuego nuevo: interpretación de una «ofrenda contada» Tlapaneca (Guerrero, México).
        [In Spanish]; (The new fire: interpretation of a 'numerical offering' by the Tlapanecs
        (Guerrero, Mexico).) Danièle Dehouve. **J. Soc. Amér.** 87 2001 pp.89-112.
3721   Kotázke prelínania funkcií nebeských kl'učiarov v ruskom folklóre. *[In Slovak]*; (Some
        aspects of similarity of the images of saints with the attribute of a key in Russian folklore.)
        [Summary]. Tatiana Bužeková. **Slov. Národop.** 48:2 2000 pp.151-166.
3722   Masks and identity. The significance of masquerades in the symbolic cycle linking the
        living, the dead, and the Bush spirits among the Wawa (Cameroon). Quentin Gausset.
        Anthropos [St. Augustin] 96:1 2001 pp.193-199.
3723   *Mi les long yupela usim flag bilong mi*: symbols and identity in Papua New Guinea.
        Andrew J. Strathern; Pamela J. Stewart. **Pac. Stud.** 23:1-2 3-6:2000 pp.21-50.
3724   More than meets the eye and ear: gamelans and their meaning in a Central Javanese
        palace. Roger Vetter. **Asian Mus.** XXXII:2 Spring-Summer:2001 pp.41-92.
3725   Narciso e l'automobile: moderno e transmoderno. *[In Italian]*; [Narcissus and the car:
        modernism and postmodernism]. Giuseppe Prestipino. Naples: La città del sole, 2000.
        217p. *ISBN: 8882920461. Includes bibliographical references. Istituto italiano per gli studi
        filosofici.*
3726   Paraphernalia of the Selkup shaman: terms and their etymological explanations exhibiting
        metaphoric symbolism. Alexandra A. Kim. **Eur. Stud. Y.** 73 2001 pp.127-146.

3727   Pueblo mission churches as symbols of permanence and identity. Kevin S. Blake; Jeffrey S. Smith. **Geogr. Rev.** 90:3 7:2000 pp.359-380.

3728   Signs and light: illuminating paths in the semiotic web. Augusto Ponzio; Susan Petrilli; Floyd Merrell; Martin Krampen; Göran Sonesson; Julia Ponzio; Lucia Miccoli; Giuseppe Cascione; Joyce Cutler-Shaw; Domenico Silvestri; Marcel Danesi; Luigi Borzacchini; Vincent Colapietro; Cosimo Caputo; Laura Marchetti; Carmela Ferrandes; Silvano Petrosino; Traian D. Stănciulescu; Lisa Block de Behar; Roberto Baronti Marchiò; Antonio Prete; Maria Solimini; Luciano Ponzio; André Helbo; Pierre Dalla Vigna; Mario Valenti; Bella Golick; Gabriella Pranzo; Ugo Delle Grazie; Patrizia Calefato; Tiziana Villani; Michele Lomuto; Eero Tarasti. **Semiotica** 136:1-4 2001 pp.1-567. *Collection of 35 articles.*

3729   Symbolbildung und Symbolhandlungen. Ethnopsychologische Forschungen bei den Mpyemo (Zentralafrikanische Republik, 1966). *[In German]*; [Symbol formation and symbol action. Ethnopsychological research among the Mpyemo (Central African Republic, 1966)]. Gerhard Kubik. **Anthropos [St. Augustin]** 95:2 2000 pp.385-408.

3730   The symbolic capital of ignorance. Ilana Gershon; Dhooleka Sarhadi Raj; Philip C. Parnell; Michael W. Scott. **Soc. Anal. [Adelaide]** 44(2) 11:2000 pp.3-105. *Collection of 5 articles.*

3731   Le symbolique au cinéma. *[In French]*; (The symbolic in cinema.) *[Summary]*. Daniel Weyl. **Pensée** 325 1-3:2001 pp.79-88.

3732   The symbolism of *àrokò* and *ààlè* in Yoruba tradition. Eben Sheba. **Niger. F.** 66:2 10:2001 pp.137-144.

3733   The symbological project. Göran Aijmer. **Cult. Dyn.** 13:1 3:2001 pp.66-91.

3734   Symbols, stories, and practices: new empirical directions in the study of religious meaning. Don Sherman Grant, II. **Sociol. Q.** 42:2 Spring:2001 pp.233-252.

3735   Titres primordiaux et mémoire canonique en Méso-Amérique. *[In French]*; (Primordial titles and canonic memory in Mesoamerica.) Enrique Florescano. **Rural Stud.** 157-158 1-6:2001 pp.15-44.

3736   The track of the triangle: form and meaning in the Sepik, Papua New Guinea. Brigitta Hauser-Schäublin. **Pac. Stud.** 17:3 9:1994 pp.133-170.

3737   Die »Unbekleidete Frau« von Nasca: Eine Figurenplastik des Ethnologischen Museums, Berlin. *[In German]*; [The naked woman of Nazca: a ceramic figurine at the Ethnological Museum, Berlin] *[Summary]*. Christiane Clados. **Baes-A.** XLVIII:1 12:2001 pp.25-42.

3738   (The wolf as a symbol in the old Arabic poetry.) *[Summary]*; *[Text in Arabic]*. Y. Aiesh. **Dirasat Hum. Soc. Sc.** 28:1 2:2001 pp.26-48.

G.3:   **Anthropology of science and medicine**
        Anthropologie de la science et de la médecine

Anthropology of science
Anthropologie de la science

3739   Anthropology and/in/of science. Daniel A. Segal; Mei Zhan; Stacy Leigh Pigg; Vincanne Adams; Elizabeth L. Krause; Stefan Helmreich. **Cult. Anthro.** 16:4 11:2001 pp.451-627. *Collection of 6 articles.*

3740   But why the Kālacakra. David Gist. **Tibet J.** XXV:3 Autumn:2000 pp.32-38.

3741   Le calendrier non illustré du codex Ixtlilxochitl. Essai d'identification. *[In French]*; [Identifying the unillustrated *Codex Ixlilxochitl* calendar]. Jacqueline de Durand-Forest. **Caravelle** 76-77 12:2001 pp.37-46.

3742   A cladistic approach to comparative ethnobotany; *[Summary in Spanish]*; *[Summary in French]*. K.H. Hart; P.A. Cox. **J. Ethnobio.** 20:2 Winter:2000 pp.303-158.

3743   A comparative study of the paradigms between Dasan's philosophy and Matteo Ricci's *Tianzhu shiyi*. Young-bae Song. **Korea J.** 41:3 Autumn:2001 pp.57-99.

3744   Eastern Sumbanese bird classification; *[Summary in French]*; *[Summary in Spanish]*. G. Forth. **J. Ethnobio.** 20:2 Winter:2000 pp.161-196.

3745   Ecritures et lectures du *xiuhtlalpilli* ou ligature des années. *[In French]*; [Writings and lectures on *xiuhtlalpilli*]. Marc Thouvenot. **Amerindia** 24 1999 pp.153-228.

3746   Empire of the ants: H.G. Wells and tropical entomology. Charlotte Sleigh. **Sci. Cult.** 10:1 3:2001 pp.33-72.

3747   Evaluation of the cultural significance of wild food botanicals traditionally gathered in northwestern Tuscany, Italy; *[Summary in French]*; *[Summary in Spanish]*. A. Pieroni. **J. Ethnobio.** 21:1 Summer:2001 pp.89-106.

3748   The first date in *Megillat Ta'anit* in light of the Karaite commentary on the tabernacle dedication. Yoram Erder. **Jew. Q. Rev.** 82 1991-1992 pp.263-284.

3749   Gleanings from the travelogue of the traveller Nicholas Senn. P.K.J.P. Subhaktha. **B. Ind. Inst. Hist. Med.** XXIX:1 1:1999 pp.71-82.

3750   In the science zone: the Yanomami and the fight for representation. Michael J. Fischer. **Anthr. Today** 17:4 8:2001 pp.9-14.

3751   Knowing, gathering and eating: knowledge and attitudes about wild food in an Isan village in northeastern Thailand; *[Summary in Spanish]*; *[Summary in French]*. P. Somnasang; G. Moreno-Black. **J. Ethnobio.** 20:2 Winter:2000 pp.197-222.

3752   Lire la langue des étoiles des prêtres mayas. *[In French]*; [Reading the language of the stars by Maya priests]. André Cauty. **Amerindia** 24 1999 pp.119-152.

3753   Maya knowledge and 'science wars'; *[Summary in French]*; *[Summary in Spanish]*. E.N. Anderson. **J. Ethnobio.** 20:2 Winter:2000 pp.129-160.

3754   Pānini and Euclid: reflections on Indian geometry. Johannes Bronkhorst. **J. Ind. Phil.** 29:1-2 4:2001 pp.43-80.

3755   Scientific experiments in British India: scientists, indigo planters and the state, 1890-1930. Prakash Kumar. **Indian Ec. Soc. His. R.** XXXVIII:3 7-9:2001 pp.249-270.

3756   Semiokinesis — semiotic autopoiesis of the universe. Abir U. Igamberdiev. **Semiotica** 135:1-4 2001 pp.1-23.

3757   Traditional knowledge of Mexican continental algae; *[Summary in French]*; *[Summary in Spanish]*. J.L. Godínez; et al. **J. Ethnobio.** 21:1 Summer:2001 pp.57-88.

3758   The virtual nuclear weapons laboratory in the New World Order. Hugh Gusterson. **Am. Ethn.** 28:2 5:2001 pp.417-448.

3759   Weather types and traffic accidents; *[Summary in Croatian]*. Z. Bencetić Klaić. **Coll. Antrop.** 25:1 6:2001 pp.245-254.

Medical anthropology
Anthropologie de la médecine

3760   Against over-interpretation: the understanding of pain amongst Turkish and Kurdish speakers in London. Jale Yazar; Roland Littlewood. **Int. J. Soc. Psyc.** 47:2 Summer:2001 pp.20-33.

3761   AIDS in Africa: broadening the perspectives. Hansjörg Dilger; Michael Rabbow; Georgia A. Rakelmann; Johanna Offe; Matthias Rompel; Angelika Wolf. **Af. Spec.** 36:1 2001 pp.5-107. *Collection of 7 articles*.

3762   AIDS in Malawi: contemporary discourse and cultural continuities. Peter G. Forster. **Afr. Stud.** 60:2 12:2001 pp.245-261.

3763   AIDS. Studium antropologiczne. *[In Polish]*; (Aids: an anthropological study.) Violetta Krawczyk-Wasilewska. Lodz: Wydawnictwo Uniwersytetu Łódzkiego, 2000. 120p.

3764   Allusions to ancestral impropriety: understandings of arthritis and rheumatism in the contemporary Navajo world. Maureen Trudelle Schwarz. **Am. Ethn.** 28:3 8:2001 pp.650-678.

3765   Another complex step: a model of heroin experimentation. Michael H. Agar. **Fie. Meth.** 13:4 11:2001 pp.353-369.

3766   Aromatic drugs in Unani medicine with special reference to *Kitabul-Mia-Lil-Masihi*. K.A. Shafqat Azmi; Wasim Ahmed; M.K. Siddiqui. **B. Ind. Inst. Hist. Med.** XXIX:2 7:1999 pp.103-112.

3767   Attory - aptekari narodnoi meditsiny musul'manskogo Vostoka. *[In Russian]*; (Folk medicine apothecaries of the Muslim orient.) *[Summary]*. V.L. Ogudin. **Etnograf. Oboz.** 2 3-4:2001 pp.112-130.

3768   Ayurvedic literature in Urdu (part — II). S.A. Husain Vinod Kumar Bhatnagar; Momin Ali. **B. Ind. Inst. Hist. Med.** XXIX:2 7:1999 pp.149-154.

3769   Beliefs matter: cultural beliefs and the use of cervical cancer-screening tests. Leo R. Chavez; Juliet M. McMullin; Shiraz I. Mishra; F. Allan Hubbell. **Am. Anthrop.** 103:4 12:2001 pp.1114-1129.

3770   Biological, epidemiological and clinical basis of understanding human immunodeficiency virus infection; *[Summary in Croatian]*. J. Begovac; S. Židovec Lepej; T. Kniewald; M. Lisić. **Coll. Antrop.** 25:1 6:2001 pp.111-126.

3771   The biology and evolution of HIV. Janis Faye Hutchinson. **Ann. R. Anthr.** 30 2001 pp.85-108.

3772   Blood pressure and its biocultural correlates among the Lepchas of Sikkim, India: a microlevel epidemiological study; *[Summary in Croatian]*. B. Mukhopadhyay; S. Mukhopadhyay. **Coll. Antrop.** 25:1 6:2001 pp.97-110.

3773   'Break the silence' art and HIV/AIDS in KwaZulu-Natal. Allen F. Roberts. **Afr. Arts** XXXIV:1 Spring:1999 pp.36-49.

3774   Care seeking in Sri Lanka: one possible explanation for low childhood mortality. M.W. Amarasiri de Silva; Ananda Wijekoon; Robert Hornik; Jose Martines. **Soc. Sci. Med.** 53:10 11:2001 pp.1363-1372.

3775   The challenges of meeting rural Bangladeshi women's needs in delivery care; *[Summary in Spanish]*; *[Summary in French]*. Kaosar Afsana; Sabina Faiz Rashid. **Reprod. Health Mat.** 9:18 11:2001 pp.79-89.

3776   Changing power and positions of Mo Muang in Northern Thai healing rituals. Anan Ganjanapan. **J. Siam Soc.** 88:1-2 2000 pp.58-71.

3777   Chronicity. Els van Dongen; Ria Reis; Lisbeth Sachs; Marja-Liisa Honkasalo; Sue E. Estroff. **Med. Anthrop.** 19:4 2001 pp.293-413. *Collection of 6 articles.*

3778   De l'usage de l'*ololiuhqui* dans le Mexique colonial. *[In French]*; [The use of *ololiuhqui* in colonial Mexico]. Placer Marey-Thibon. **Caravelle** 76-77 12:2001 pp.289-294.

3779   Definition of *Nidana Pancaka* (first chapter of *Madhavanidana*). Momin Ali. **B. Ind. Inst. Hist. Med.** XXIX:1 1:1999 pp.1-14.

3780   Determinants of HIV risk among Indian truck drivers. Angela D. Bryan; Jeffrey D. Fisher; T. Joseph Benziger. **Soc. Sci. Med.** 53:11 12:2001 pp.1413-1426.

3781   The doctor-nurse relationship: how easy is it to be a female doctor co-operating with a female nurse? E. Gjerberg; L. Kjølsrød. **Soc. Sci. Med.** 52:2 1:2001 pp.189-202.

3782   Drug-using men who have sex with men: sexual behaviours and sexual identities. S. Deren; M. Stark; F. Rhodes; H. Siegel; L. Cottler; M. Wood; L. Kochems; R. Carlson; R. Falck; K. Rourke; R. Trotter; B. Weir; M.F. Goldstein; L. Wright-De Aguero. **Cult. Health. Sex.** 3:3 7-9:2001 pp.329-338.

3783   Du végétal au politique: étude des plantes à pouvoir chez les Indiens wayana du Haut-Maroni. *[In French]*; (From plants to politics: magical plants among the Wayana on the upper Maroni.) Jean Chapuis. **J. Soc. Amér.** 87 2001 pp.113-136.

3784   Épidémies, médecine et politique dans l'Iran du XIXe siècle. *[In French]*; [Epidemics, medicine and politics in 19th century Iran] *[Summary]*. H. Ebrahimnejad. **Stud. Iran.** 30:1 2001 pp.105-136.

3785   Ethnobiology in Mizoram state: folklore medico-zoology. H. Lalramnghinglova. **B. Ind. Inst. Hist. Med.** XXIX:2 7:1999 pp.123-148.

3786   Ethnozoology of fishing communities from Ilha Grande (Atlantic forest coast, Brazil); *[Summary in French]*; *[Summary in Spanish]*. C.S. Seixas; A. Begossi. **J. Ethnobio.** 21:1 Summer:2001 pp.107-135.

3787   European alchemy: some traditional beliefs. Vladimir Karpenko. **B. Ind. Inst. Hist. Med.** XXIX:1 1:1999 pp.63-70.

3788   An evaluation of the Choices and Changes student program: a grade four to seven sexual health education program based on the Canadian guidelines for sexual health education. Jeff Wackett; Lisa Evans. **Canad. J. Human Sex.** 9:4 2000 pp.265-273.

3789   Event-related potentials in medical workers with long-term exposure to xylene; *[Summary in Croatian].* R.M. Liščić; Lj. Skender; J. Jakić-Razumović; D. Šimić; S. Milković-Kraus. **Coll. Antrop.** 25:1 6:2001 pp.357-362.

3790   The fragility of healing. Cheryl Mattingly; Mary Lawlor. **Ethos** 29:1 3:2001 pp.30-57.

3791   From rights to recognition: mental health and spiritual healing among older Pakistanis. Lynn Froggett. **Psych. St.** 3:2 6:2001 pp.177-186.

3792   General subjective health status or age-related subjective health status: does it make a difference? Orna Baron-Epel; Giora Kaplan. **Soc. Sci. Med.** 53:10 11:2001 pp.1373-1382.

3793   Genetic optimism: framing genes and mental illness in the news. Peter Conrad. **Cult. Medic. Psych.** 25:2 6:2001 pp.225-247.

3794   Harmony or hegemony? The rise and fall of the Native Medical Institution, Calcutta; 1822-35. Zhaleh Khaleeli. **S. Asia R.** 21:1 Autumn:2001 pp.77-104.

3795   Health behaviour, risk awareness and emotional well-being in students from Eastern Europe and Western Europe. Andrew Steptoe; Jane Wardle. **Soc. Sci. Med.** 53:12 12:2001 pp.1621-1630.

3796   Health care seeking behaviour for sexually transmitted diseases among commercial sex workers in Morogoro, Tanzania. Anne Outwater; Lucy Nkya; Eligius Lyamuya; George Lwihula; Edward C. Green; Jan Hogle; Susan E. Hassig; Gina Dallabetta. **Cult. Health. Sex.** 3:1 1-3:2001 pp.19-33.

3797   Health in Goa in the 17th century: the reports of some French travellers. Francoise De Valence. **B. Ind. Inst. Hist. Med.** XXIX:2 7:1999 pp.113-122.

3798   Health needs of the Roma population in the Czech and Slovak republics. Ilona Koupilová; Helen Epstein; Jan Holčík; Steve Hajioff; Martin McKee. **Soc. Sci. Med.** 53:9 11:2001 pp.1191-1204.

3799   Hommage a Paul Broca (1824-1880) Sainte-Foy-la-Grande (Gironde), 2 et 3 février 2001. *[In French]*; [A tribute to Paul Broca (1824-1880), Sainte-Foy-la-Grande (Gironde), 2-3 February 2001]. P. Monod-Broca; Cl. Massé; J.Cl. Drouin; F. Boller; P. Marcie; T. Hamanaka; E.A. Cabanis; M.T. Iba-Zizen; R. Saban; C.L. Hamonet. **Bio. Hum. Anthrop.** 19:3-4 7-12:2001 pp.127-188. *Collection of 8 articles.*

3800   Implications of health care provision on acute lower respiratory infection mortality in Bangladeshi children. M. Ali; M. Emch; F. Tofail; A.H. Baqui. **Soc. Sci. Med.** 52:2 1:2001 pp.267-278.

3801   International AIDS research in anthropology: taking a critical perspective on the crisis. Brooke G. Schoepf. **Ann. R. Anthr.** 30 2001 pp.335-362.

3802   Islamic medical ethics with special reference to *Moalejat-E-Buqratiya.* K.A. Shafqat Azmi; M.K. Siddiqui. **B. Ind. Inst. Hist. Med.** XXIX:1 1:1999 pp.15-28.

3803   Kuru, prions, and human affairs: thinking about epidemics. Shirley Lindenbaum. **Ann. Anthr.** 30 2001 pp.363-456.

3804   A large cross-sectional study of health attitudes, knowledge, behaviour and risks in the post-war Croatian population (the first Croatian health project); *[Summary in Croatian].* S. Turek; I. Rudan; N. Smolej-Narančić; L. Szirovicza; M. Čubrilo-Turek; V. Žerjavić-Hrabak; A. Rak-Kaić; D. Vrhovski-Hebrang; Ž. Prebeg; M. Ljubičić; B. Janićijević; P. Rudan. **Coll. Antrop.** 25:1 6:2001 pp.77-96.

3805   Life disruption and generic complexity: a social linguistic analysis of narratives of cancer illness. Christopher F.C. Jordens; Miles Little; Kim Paul; Emma-Jane Sayers. **Soc. Sci. Med.** 53:9 11:2001 pp.1227-1236.

3806   Maternal health practices among the Maasai of Namalulu, northern Tanzania. Fouad Ibrahim; Barbara Ibrahim. **B. Int. Com. Urg. Anthrop. Ethnol. R.** 40 1999-2000 pp.75-84.

3807 Les médecines touarègues traditionnelles: approche ethnologique. *[In French]*; [Traditional Tuareg medicines: an ethnological approach]. Jacques Hureiki; André Bourgeot [Foreword]. Paris: Karthala, 2000. 188p. *ISBN: 2845860404. Includes bibliographical references (p. 179-186).*

3808 Medical anthropology, subaltern traces, and the making and meaning of Western medicine in South Africa: 1895-1899. Premesh Lalu. **Hist. Afr.** 25 1998 pp.133-160.

3809 Medical magic and medicinal cure: manipulating meanings with ease of disease. Laurence Marshall Carucci. **Cult. Anthro.** 8:2 5:1993 pp.157-168.

3810 Men's attitudes to condoms and female controlled means of protection against HIV and STDs in south-western Uganda. Robert Pool; Graham Hart; Gillian Green; Susan Harrison; Stella Nyanzi; Jimmy Whitworth. **Cult. Health. Sex.** 2:2 4-6:2000 pp.197-211.

3811 *Mot Luuk* problems in northeast Thailand: why women's own health concerns matter as much as disease rates. Pimpawun Boonmongkon; Mark Nichter; Jen Pylypa. **Soc. Sci. Med.** 53:8 10:2001 pp.1095-1112.

3812 Orakel und Heiler in Westtibet. Die Initiation und ihre Verweigerung. *[In German]*; (Oracle and healer in western Tibet: initiation and rejection.) *[Summary]*. Amélie Schenk. **Z. Ethn.** 126:1 2001 pp.63-92.

3813 Palawan attitudes towards illness. Dario Novellino. **Phil. Stud.** 49:1 2001 pp.78-93.

3814 Perceptions médicales et populaires dans la prévention des difficultés maternelles en milieu rural peul guinéen. *[In French]*; [Medical and popular perceptions in the prevention of birthing difficulties among the rural Peul in Guinea] *[Summary]*. Mamadou Cellou Barry. **Afr. Stud. R.** 43:3 12:2000 pp.1-18.

3815 Plant-based medicines of the Dikgale of the Northern Province; *[Summary in Afrikaans]*. S.A. Rankoana. **S. Afr. J. Ethnol.** 24:3 2001 pp.99-104.

3816 Plants and the concept of *maatla* among the northern Sotho; *[Summary in Afrikaans]*. L.P. Vorster. **S. Afr. J. Ethnol.** 24:3 2001 pp.75-80.

3817 Practices of the pregnant self: compliance with and resistance to prenatal norms. Robin Root; C.H. Browner. **Cult. Medic. Psych.** 25:2 6:2001 pp.195-224.

3818 Preservation of the Tibetan medical system as an integral part of Tibetan culture in the prevailing Himalayan environment. Nupur Pathak. **Tibet J.** XXVI:2 Summer:2001 pp.56-59.

3819 Prevention and cure from around the home: homestead forests and primary health care in rural Bangladesh. Khondoker Mokaddem Hossain; Srikanta Chatterjee. **J. Interd. Ec.** 12:2 2001 pp.139-158.

3820 Prevention of sexually transmitted infections in different populations: a review of behaviourally effective and cost-effective interventions. Alexander McKay. **Canad. J. Human Sex.** 9:2 2000 pp.95-120.

3821 Promoting travel clinic referrals: exploring partnerships for healthier travel. Laura MacDougall; Theresa Gyorkos. **Soc. Sci. Med.** 53:11 12:2001 pp.1461-1468.

3822 Prophetes, visionnaires et guerisseurs de l'Afrique subsaharienne contemporaine. *[In French]*; (Prophets, visionaries and healers in contemporary sub-Saharan Africa.) André Mary; Pierre-Joseph Laurent; Christine Henry; Jean-Pierre Dozon; Marc-Éric Gruénais; Joseph Tonda; Sophie Bava; Cheikh Gueye. **Soc. Compass** 48:3 9:2001 pp.307-438. *Collection of 8 articles.*

3823 Representations of HIV and AIDS: visibility blue/s. Gabriele Griffin. Manchester: Manchester University Press, 2000. 216p. *ISBN: 0719047110, 0719047102. Includes bibliographical references and index.*

3824 Reproductive health and culture among the Mapuche and Tehuelche of South America. Maria Christina Chiriguini; Maria Elina Vitello. **Mankind Q.** XLII:2 Winter:2001 pp.117-132.

3825 Slovenska etnologija med ljudsko in alternativno medicino. *[In Slovene]*; (Slovene ethnology between popular and alternative medicine.) *[Summary]*. Nena Židov. **Bull. Slov. Ethno. Soc.** 41:1-2 2001 pp.134-137.

3826   Some Sri Lankan medical manuscripts of importance for the history of South Asian traditional medicine. Jinadasa Liyanaratne. **B. Sch. Orient. Afr. Stud.** 64:3 2001 pp.392-400.

3827   Staying healthy: the salience and meaning of health maintenance behaviors among rural older adults in North Carolina. Thomas A. Arcury; Sara A. Quandt; Ronny A. Bell. **Soc. Sci. Med.** 53:11 12:2001 pp.1541-1556.

3828   The strange death of Margarita Marcellini: *male*, signs, and the everyday world of pre-modern medicine. Guido Ruggiero. **Am. Hist. Rev.** 106:4 10:2001 pp.1141-1158.

3829   A sword of empire? Medicine and colonialism in King William's Town, Xhosaland, 1856-1891. David Gordon. **Afr. Stud.** 60:2 12:2001 pp.165-184.

3830   Transforming signs. Iconicity and indexicality in Russian healing and magic. Galina Lindquist. **Ethnos** 66:2 2001 pp.181-206.

3831   Turkish university students' sexual behaviour, knowledge, attitudes and perceptions of risk related to HIV/AIDS. Figen Cok; Lizbeth Ann Gray; Hakan Ersever. **Cult. Health. Sex.** 3:1 1-3:2001 pp.81-99.

3832   Using an interactive framework of society and lifecourse to explain self-rated health in early adulthood. Clyde Hertzman; Chris Power; Sharon Matthews; Orly Manor. **Soc. Sci. Med.** 53:12 12:2001 pp.1575-1586.

3833   *Vegetalismo*, consciousness and the new sciences; *[Summary in Spanish]*; *[Summary in Portuguese]*. Wynand Koch. **Unisa Lat.Am. Rep.** 17:1 2001 pp.16-28.

3834   Voluntary counseling and testing for couples: a high-leverage intervention for HIV/AIDS prevention in sub-Saharan Africa. Thomas M. Painter. **Soc. Sci. Med.** 53:11 12:2001 pp.1397-1412.

3835   Water and healing — experiences from the traditional healers in Ile-Ife, Nigeria. Eva-Marita Rinne. **Nord. J. Afr. St.** 10:1 2001 pp.41-65.

3836   Yugi's *pramegam* and *Diabetes mellitus* — an analogue. S. Rajalakshmi; G. Veluchamy. **B. Ind. Inst. Hist. Med.** XXIX:1 1:1999 pp.83-88.

G.4:   **Creative expression**
           Expressions créatrices

Architecture
Architecture

3837   The Amoghapāśa-Lokeśvara in Orissa. Adalbert J. Gail. **Stud. Orient.** 94 2001 pp.161-166.

3838   Architecture in a changing world: the new rhetoric of form. Gerald Gutenschwager. **Ekistics** 65:391-393 7-12:1998 pp.262-271.

3839   Architekturdekor aus dem Panjab: Die Sammlung des Linden-Museums Stuttgart, III: Baukeramik/Fliesen. *[In German]*; [Architectural decoration from the Punjab: the Linden Museum Stuttgart's collection, III: ceramics and tiles]. Margareta Pavaloi. **Tribus** 50 12:2001 pp.107-134.

3840   The art of architectural decoration in the traditional houses of Al-Alkhalaf, Saudi Arabia. Tawfiq M. Abu- Ghazzeh. **J. Arch. Plan. Res.** 18:2 Summer:2001 pp.156-177.

3841   Baba Wagué Diakité. Victoria Rovine. **Afr. Arts** XXXIV:2 Summer:2001 pp.64-71.

3842   Decorating Cantonese Huaqiao houses: remote worlds in the Chinese mind. Laura Lin Luo. **Ekistics** 65:391-393 7-12:1998 pp.303-315.

3843   From garden suburb to olde city ward a longitudinal study of social process and incremental architecture in Jaipur, India. R. Thomas Rosin. **J. Mat. Cult.** 6:2 7:2001 pp.165-192.

3844   The Ile Nla a colonial town hall in Ile-Ife, Nigeria. Cordelia O. Osasona. **Afr. Arts** XXXIV:1 Spring:1999 pp.78-85.

3845   Landscape, violence and social bodies: ritualized architecture in a Solomon Islands society; *[Summary in French]*. Tim Thomas; Peter Sheppard; Richard Walter. **J. Royal Anth. Inst.** 7:3 9:2001 pp.545-572.

3846   Libertarian themes in the work of Giancarlo De Carlo. P.G. Raman. **Ekistics** 65:391-393 7-12:1998 pp.192-206.

3847   Minimal design constructions for remote coastal sites on islands. Mit Mitropoulos. **Ekistics** 65:391-393 7-12:1998 pp.185-191.

3848   Mosque at Ait Isman: Todra Gorge, Morocco. Lealan Swanson. **J. N. African Stud.** 5:1 Spring:2000 pp.147-164.

3849   The mosque at al-Qastal: report from al-Qastal conservation and development project, 1999-2000. Erin Addison. **A. Dept. Antiq. Jordan** XLIV 2000 pp.477-492.

3850   New Moscow monuments, or, states of innocence. Bruce Grant. **Am. Ethn.** 28:2 5:2001 pp.332-362.

3851   A note on some typical architectural designs of western Nepal. Dilli Raj Sharma. **Contrib. Nepal. Stud.** 27:2 7:2000 pp.201-218.

3852   El palacio de Ruy López Dávalos y sus bocetos inéditos en la Sinagoga del tránsito: estudio de sus yeserías en el contexto artístico de 1361 (II). *[In Spanish]*; [The design and decoration of the Palace of Ruy López Dávalos in the context of the 14th century artistic tradition]. Carmen Rallo Gruss; Juan Carlos Ruiz Souza. **Al-Qantara** XXI:1 2000 pp.143-154.

3853   Un palais islamique du VIIIe siècle à Samarkand. *[In French]*; [An 8th century Islamic palace in Samarkand] *[Summary]*. Y. Karev. **Stud. Iran.** 29:2 2000 pp.273-298.

3854   Saivite monuments in the undivided district of Balasore. Bhagabat Tripathy. **Oris. Hist. R. J.** XLV:1-4 2000 pp.100-106.

3855   A Sikh pioneers earthquake-proof buildings: Avtar Singh Pali. Bhupinder Singh Mahal. **Sikh Rev.** 49:8(572) 8:2001 pp.67-68.

3856   The spirit of austerity and the materials of opulence: architectural sources of St. Casimir's Chapel in Vilnius. K. Paul Žygas. **J. Balt. St.** XXXI:1 Spring:2000 pp.5-43.

3857   Squares and oblongs in the Veda. Frits Staal. **J. Ind. Phil.** 29:1-2 4:2001 pp.257-273.

3858   Tradicijsko pučko graditeljstvo na Baniji. *[In Croatian]*; (Traditional rural architecture of Banija.) Branko Đaković; Manda Horvat. **Etnoloska** 23:30 2000 pp.113-130.

3859   Two forts on the medieval Hajj route in Jordan. A.D. Petersen. **A. Dept. Antiq. Jordan** XXXV 1991 pp.347-360.

3860   The 'Vajra temple' of gTer ston Zhig po gling pa and the politics of flood control in 16th century lHa sa. Matthew Akester. **Tibet J.** XXVI:1 Spring:2001 pp.3-24.

3861   Vernacular architectural form and the planning paradox: a study of actual and perceived rural building tradition. H. Martin Edge; Robert Pearson. **J. Arch. Plan. Res.** 18:2 Summer:2001 pp.91-109.

Dance and theatre
Danse et théâtre

3862   Alfonso Reyes: el hombre y la naturaleza en el monólogo de Segismundo. *[In Spanish]*; [Alfonso Reyes: man and nature in the monologue of Segismundo]. María Andueza. **Cuad. Am.** XV:3(87) 5-6:2001 pp.16-23.

3863   *Al-Gēs*: women's festival and drama in Mecca. Ahmad A. Nasr; Abu Bakar A. Bagader. **J. Folk. Res.** 38:3 9-12:2001 pp.243-262.

3864   *Avimārakam* — an enigma. Vijay Pandya. **J. Orient. Inst.** XLVII:3-4(47) 3-6:1998 pp.269-272.

3865   Bhāsa problem — a probable theory. Laxmi Warier. **J. Orient. Inst.** XLVII:1-2(47) 9-12:1997 pp.87-92.

3866   *Ch'anggūk* opera and the category of the 'traditionesque'. Andrew P. Killick. **Kor. Stud.** 25:1 2001 pp.51-71.

3867   The Chhau dance of Mayurbhanj: III. D.N. Patnaik. **San. Nat.** 131-132 1999 pp.21-43.

3868   Dance in Mesopotamia. Marie Matoušová-Rajmová. **Arch. Orient.** 69:1 2:2001 pp.21-32.

3869   Demoke's totem: the role of the artist in Soyinka's *A Dance of the Forest*. Moteane John Melamu. **J. Cult. St.** 3:1 2001 pp.259-276.

3870   Gabriel Martínez. *[In French]*; [Gabriel Martínez]. Antoinette Molinié. **J. Soc. Amér.** 86 2000 pp.225-228.

3871   Gender performance in a Finnish dance restaurant: reflections on a multicultural fieldwork experiment. Pirkko Moisala. **Nar. Umjetn.** 38:1 2001 pp.7-20.

3872   Illusion et réalité: le contact ou de la théâtralité en 1595. *[In French]*; [Illusion and reality: contact or dramatic quality in 1595]. Jean-François Durban. **Soc. Ét. Océan.** 288 3:2001 pp.64-125.

3873   The labyrinthine madness of Švankmajer's *Faust*. Peta Allen Shera. **J. Gender St.** 10:2 7:2001 pp.127-144.

3874   Language and style in dramatic discourse: a phonostylistic analysis of Athol Fugard's *The Island*. A. Lekan Dairo. **J. Cult. St.** 3:1 2001 pp.277-283.

3875   *Mantrānkam*. The third act of *Pratijñāyaugandharāyanam* in Kūtiyāttam. Heike Moser-Achuthat. **Bull. Ét. Indien.** 17-18 1999-2000 pp.563-584.

3876   Manuscripts and performance traditions of the so-called 'Trivandrum plays' ascribed to Bhāsa — a report on work in progress. Heidrun Brückner. **Bull. Ét. Indien.** 17-18 1999-2000 pp.501-550.

3877   Masochism, spectacle, and the 'broken mirror' clown *entrée*: a note on the anthropology of performance in postmodern culture. Kenneth Little. **Cult. Anthro.** 8:1 2:1993 pp.117-129.

3878   Menneskelig handling illusionen som dramatisk grundvilkår. *[In Danish]*; (Human action: illusion as its dramatic condition.) Kirsten Hastrup. **Tids. Antrop.** 41 2000 pp.5-24.

3879   My dance-odyssey. Ritha Devi. **San. Nat.** XXXVI:1 2001 pp.44-56.

3880   On the origin of the Komedie Stamboel popular culture, colonial society, and the Parsi theatre movement. Matthew Isaac Cohen. **Bijdragen** 157:2 2001 pp.313-358.

3881   The originality variations in contemporary performing art the case of Kenya. B.S. Onyango. **B. Int. Com. Urg. Anthrop. Ethnol. R.** 40 1999-2000 pp.99-112.

3882   The Parsi theatre: its origins and development (1). Somnath Gupt; Kathryn Hansen [Tr.]. **San. Nat.** XXXVI:1 2001 pp.3-31.

3883   *Performance*. Braves Theater oder Ausbruch des Nicht-Meßbaren? *[In German]*; [Performance. Good theatre or an outburst of the immeasurable?] Mark Münzel. **Paideuma** 46 2000 pp.301-312.

3884   Performers and professionalization in Java: between leisure and livelihood. Felicia Hughes-Freeland. **S.E. Asia Res.** 9:2 7:2001 pp.213-233.

3885   The place of the Mālavikāgnimitra within Kālidāsa's *oeuvre*. Herman Tieken. **Indo-Iran. J.** 44:2 2001 pp.149-166.

3886   The politics of dance: changing representations of the nation in Ghana. Katharina Schramm. **Af. Spec.** 35:3 2000 pp.339-358.

3887   El problema de la nominación en el teatro de evangelización: un acercamiento ideológico. *[In Spanish]*; [The problem of naming in evangelical theatre: an ideological approach]. Blanca López de Mariscal. **Caravelle** 76-77 12:2001 pp.205-212.

3888   Some Egyptianizing theatre decorations at the stage of the National Theatre in Prague, 1883-1900. Hana Navrátilová. **Arch. Orient.** 69:3 8:2001 pp.419-426.

3889   The Swadeshi movement and Bengali theatre. Minoti Chatterjee. **San. Nat.** 133-134 1999 pp.33-56.

3890   Tanz in der sudanesischen Bruderschaft Tarīqa Burhānīya — Beschreibung einer Hadra. *[In German]*; [Dance in the Sudanese brotherhood Tarīqa Burhānīya - a description of a hadra]. Eva-Maria Glasbrenner. **Acta Orient.** 62 2001 pp.81-91.

3891   *Teatro abierto* comme expression de l'identité argentine. *[In French]*; [*Teatro abierto* as an expression of Argentinian identity]. Isabelle Clerc. **Caravelle** 76-77 12:2001 pp.631-641.

3892   Tradition and innovation in Yaksagana: Kota Shivarama Karanth and Keremane Shambhu Hegde. Guru Rao Bapat. **San. Nat.** 133-134 1999 pp.3-15.

3893   *Yellowface*: the racial branding of the Chinese in American theatre and media. Anthony B. Chan. **Asian Prof.** 29:2 4:2001 pp.159-178.

Music and songs
Musique et chanson

3894 The *abhoga* and its 'signature'. Vijaya Chandorkar. **San. Nat.** 133-134 1999 pp.57-60.

3895 All that is not given is lost: Irish traditional music, copyright, and common property. Anthony McCann. **Ethnomusicology** 45:1 Winter:2001 pp.89-106.

3896 An ancient name of the lyre. Vjačeslav V. Ivanov. **Arch. Orient.** 67:4 11:1999 pp.585-600.

3897 The Andean anacrusis? Rhythmic structure and perception in Easter songs of northern Potosí, Bolivia. Henry Stobart; Ian Cross. **Brit. J. Ethnomusic.** 9:2 2000 pp.63-92.

3898 Architecture in modern Hindustani music. Deepak S. Raja. **San. Nat.** XXXVI:1 2001 pp.32-40.

3899 The Bible, prayer, and *maqām*: extra-musical associations of Syrian Jews. Mark Kligman. **Ethnomusicology** 45:3 Fall:2001 pp.443-479.

3900 Blackness and the politics of memory in the New Orleans second line. Helen A. Regis. **Am. Ethn.** 28:4 11:2001 pp.752-777.

3901 *Catuṣṣruti-jāti* Rāgas: an amateur's investigation. H.V. Sharma. **San. Nat.** 135-136 2000 pp.63-69.

3902 Chant de Teanatzin: traditions préhispaniques acolhua et chroniques coloniales. *[In French]*; [Teanatzin's song: pre-Hispanic Acolhua tradition and colonial chronicles]. Patrick Lesbre. **Caravelle** 76-77 12:2001 pp.213-222.

3903 Chindonya today: Japanese street performers in commercial advertising. Ingrid Fritsch. **Asian Folk. S.** LX:1 2001 pp.49-78.

3904 Chou Wen-Chung's cross cultural experience and his musical synthesis: the concept of syncretism revisited. Peter Chang. **Asian Mus.** XXXII:2 Spring-Summer:2001 pp.93-118.

3905 The classification of musical instruments: changing trends in research from the late nineteenth century, with special reference to the 1990s. Margaret Kartomi. **Ethnomusicology** 45:2 Spring-Summer:2001 pp.283-314.

3906 A comparative study of Peking Opera. Yao-Kun Liu. **Asian Cult. (Asian-Pac. Cult.) Q.** XXVIII:3 Autumn:2000 pp.21-32.

3907 Competition and conflict as a framework for understanding performance culture among the urban Anlo-Ewe. Daniel Avorgbedor. **Ethnomusicology** 45:2 Spring-Summer:2001 pp.260-282.

3908 Dancing towards dictatorship: political songs and popular culture in Malawi. W.C. Chirwa. **Nord. J. Afr. St.** 10:1 2001 pp.1-27.

3909 Divine decadence, darling! The sixty-year history of the Kit Kat Klub. Linda K. Brengle. **J. Pop. Cult.** 34:2 Fall:2000 pp.147-154.

3910 Emotional dimensions of ritual music among the Kotas, a South Indian tribe. Richard K. Wolf. **Ethnomusicology** 45:3 Fall:2001 pp.379-422.

3911 Entre kenas et pututus: la représentation de 'l'autre' dans la littérature des pays andins. *[In French]*; [Between kenas and pututus: representing the 'other' in Andean literature]. Gérard Borras. **Caravelle** 76-77 12:2001 pp.527-536.

3912 Ethics in the sung duels of north-eastern Brazil: collective memory and contemporary practice. Elizabeth Travassos. **Brit. J. Ethnomusic.** 9:1 2000 pp.61-94.

3913 Etymological and technical definitions of musical terms. Hema Ramanathan; N. Ramanathan. **San. Nat.** 133-134 1999 pp.25-32.

3914 The experimental music of Hermeto Paschoal *e grupo* (1981-93): a musical system in the making. Luiz Costa Lima Neto. **Brit. J. Ethnomusic.** 9:1 2000 pp.119-142.

3915 'From here on, I will be praying to you': Indian churches, Kiowa hymns, and Native American Christianity in southwestern Oklahoma. Luke Eric Lassiter. **Ethnomusicology** 45:2 Spring-Summer:2001 pp.338-352.

3916 Gagaku in the provinces: imperial court music at the Ikeda Fief at Bizen. Larry V. Shumway. **Asian Mus.** XXXII:2 Spring-Summer:2001 pp.119-142.

3917 Gaucho musical regionalism. Maria Elizabeth Lucas. **Brit. J. Ethnomusic.** 9:1 2000 pp.41-60.

3918   How it was sung in Odessa: at the intersection of Russian and Yiddish folk culture. Robert A. Rothstein. **Slavic R.** 60:4 Winter:2001 pp.781-801.

3919   How Mohan Upreti found his guru: the Rithagarh episode. P.C. Joshi. **San. Nat.** 135-136 2000 pp.27-46.

3920   A hymn glorifying Ashurnasirpal II. Jiří Prosecký. **Arch. Orient.** 69:3 8:2001 pp.427-436.

3921   Hypermedia and ethnomusicology. Barbara Rose Lange. **Ethnomusicology** 45:1 Winter:2001 pp.132-149.

3922   The importance of being a *jali muso*: some aspects of the role and status of women in the musical life of today's Gambia. Mojca Piškor. **Nar. Umjetn.** 38:1 2001 pp.41-66.

3923   In between ethnomusicological and social canons: historical sources on women players of folk music instruments in Croatia. Naila Ceribašić. **Nar. Umjetn.** 38:1 2001 pp.21-40.

3924   Indeterminancy in Rabīndrasangīt. William Radice. **Arch. Orient.** 68:3 8:2000 pp.477-506.

3925   Instruments of power: Sundanese 'multi-laras' Gamelan in new order Indonesia. Andrew N. Weintraub. **Ethnomusicology** 45:2 Spring-Summer:2001 pp.197-227.

3926   Intercultural contact and the evolution of the Baltic psaltery. Ain Haas. **J. Balt. St.** XXXII:3 Fall:2001 pp.209-250.

3927   Inventing Brajabuli. William L. Smith. **Arch. Orient.** 68:3 8:2000 pp.387-398.

3928   Invitation au chant. *[In French]*; [Invitation to sing]. Patrick Saurin. **Caravelle** 76-77 12:2001 pp.145-152.

3929   Jazz et anthropologie. *[In French]*; [Jazz and anthropology]. Jean Jamin; Lucien Malson; Anne-Marie Mercier-Faivre; Yannick Seité; Pascal Colard; Jean-Luc Jamard; Claude Macherel; Jean-François Baré; Francis Marmande; Denis Laborde; Patrick Williams; Xavier Daverat; Alexandre Pierrepont; Francis Hofstein; Olivier Roueff; Denis-Constant Martin; Michel Naepels. **Homme** 158-159 4-9:2001 pp.7-300. *Collection of 17 articles.*

3930   Juegos y canciones infantiles de la tierra de Estella (Navarra). *[In Spanish]*; [Children's games and songs of the earth in Estella (Navarre)] *[Summary]*; *[Summary in French]*; *[Summary in Basque]*. José Manuel Pedrosa. **An. Eusko. Folk.** 42 2000 pp.137-164.

3931   Kenneth Howard Peacock 1922-2000. Anna K. Guigné. **Ethnologies** 22:2 2000 pp.289-294.

3932   K.R. Kumaraswamy and his times. Vijaya Ramaswamy. **San. Nat.** 135-136 2000 pp.19-26.

3933   The landscape of African music. F. Abiola Irele; Kofi Agawu; Daniel K. Avorgbedor; Tanure Ojaide; Tejumola Olaniyan; Meki Nzewi; Israel Anyahuru; Tom Ohiaraumunna; Luke Eyoh; Akin Euba; Carol Muller; Bode Omojola; Nick Nesbitt. **R. African Lit.** 32:2 Summer:2001 pp.1-186. *Collection of 12 articles.*

3934   *Las caleñas son como las flores*: the rise of all-women salsa bands. Lise Waxer. **Ethnomusicology** 45:2 Spring-Summer:2001 pp.228-259.

3935   La Macédoine en fanfare. *[In French]*; (Brass bands in Macedonia.) *[Summary]*; *[Summary in German]*. Nicolas Prévôt. **Ethn. Fr.** XXXI:4 10-12:2001 pp.695-706.

3936   Módulos de afinación prehispanos. *[In Spanish]*; [Prehispanic tuning modules] *[Summary]*. Mónica Gudemos. **Baes-A.** XLVIII:1 12:2001 pp.43-105.

3937   More than meets the eye and ear: gamelans and their meaning in a Central Javanese palace. Roger Vetter. **Asian Mus.** XXXII:2 Spring-Summer:2001 pp.41-92.

3938   Multiple voices, multiple selves: song style and north Indian women's identity. Amelia Maciszewski. **Asian Mus.** XXXII:2 Spring-Summer:2001 pp.1-40.

3939   Music and ritual of pre-twentieth century origins in Manggarai, West Flores. Margaret Kartomi. **R. Ind. Malay. Aff.** 35:1 Winter:2001 pp.79-136.

3940   *Música romântica* in Montes Claros: inter-gender relations in Brazilian popular song. Martha Tupinambá de Ulhôa. **Brit. J. Ethnomusic.** 9:1 2000 pp.11-40.

3941   Musical behaviour and the archaeology of the mind. Ezra Zubrow; Ian Cross; Frank Cowan. **Archaeol. Polona** 39 2001 pp.111-126.

3942   Musical time organization and space concept: a model of cross-cultural analogy. Amatzia Bar-Yosef. **Ethnomusicology** 45:3 Fall:2001 pp.423-442.

3943   Music-halls and the assimilation of jazz in 1920s Paris. Jeffrey H. Jackson. **J. Pop. Cult.** 34:2 Fall:2000 pp.69-82.

3944 Musique et évolution politique en R.D.Congo. *[In French]*; [Music and political change in the Democratic Republic of Congo] *[Summary]*. Onyumbe Tshonga. **Ann. Æqua.** 22 2001 pp.7-20.

3945 Muzykal'nyi instrument v kalmytskoi kul'ture. *[In Russian]*; (Musical instruments in the Kalmyk culture.) *[Summary]*. G.Iu. Badmaeva. **Etnograf. Oboz.** 4 7-8:2000 pp.59-67.

3946 Narcocorridos: an emerging micromusic of Nuevo L.A. Helena Simonett. **Ethnomusicology** 45:2 Spring-Summer:2001 pp.315-337.

3947 No nonsense: the logic and power of acoustic-iconic mnemonic systems. David W. Hughes. **Brit. J. Ethnomusic.** 9:2 2000 pp.93-120.

3948 On some relations between *kokles* styles and contexts in the twentieth century. Valdis Muktupāvels. **J. Balt. St.** XXXI:4 Winter:2000 pp.388-405.

3949 Protesting politics of 'death and darkness' in Malawi. Reuben Makayiko Chirambo. **J. Folk. Res.** 38:3 9-12:2001 pp.205-228.

3950 Quelques chants du rituel abstenciel «ngunda» chez les Atetela. *[In French]*; [Songs from the *ngunda* abstinence ritual among the Atetela] *[Summary]*. O. Lowenga. **Ann. Æqua.** 22 2001 pp.153-162.

3951 The Qur'ân in Indonesian daily life: the public project of musical oratory. Anne K. Rasmussen. **Ethnomusicology** 45:1 Winter:2001 pp.30-57.

3952 Reading Indian music: the interpretation of seventeenth-century European travel-writing in the (re)construction of Indian music history. Katherine Brown. **Brit. J. Ethnomusic.** 9:2 2000 pp.1-34.

3953 Reflections on musical categorization. Emmanuelle Olivier; Hervé Rivière. **Ethnomusicology** 45:3 Fall:2001 pp.480-488.

3954 The *sāqiya*, the *Ilyre*, and the *qasīda*: a sketch of the Egyptian soundscape. Nobuo Mizuno. **Senri Ethn. Stud.** 55 2001 pp.1-12.

3955 Shadows of song: exploring research and performance strategies in Yolngu women's crying-songs. Fiona Magowan. **Oceania** 72:2 12:2001 pp.89-104.

3956 Singing contests in the ethnic enclosure of the postwar Japanese-Brazilian community. Shuhei Hosokawa. **Brit. J. Ethnomusic.** 9:1 2000 pp.95-118.

3957 The situation of music in Iran since the revolution: the role of official organizations. Ameneh Youssefzadeh. **Brit. J. Ethnomusic.** 9:2 2000 pp.35-62.

3958 The sonic dimensions of nationalism in modern China: musical representation and transformation. Sue Tuohy. **Ethnomusicology** 45:1 Winter:2001 pp.107-131.

3959 Sound, pitch, and scale: from 'tone measurements' to sonological analysis in ethnomusicology. Albrecht Schneider. **Ethnomusicology** 45:3 Fall:2001 pp.489-520.

3960 Sound systems, world beat, and diasporan identity in Cartagena, Colombia. Deborah Pacini Hernandez. **Diaspora** 5:3 Winter:1996 pp.429-466.

3961 Space and the Irish cultural imagination. Gerry Smyth. Basingstoke, New York: Palgrave, 2001. 228p. *ISBN: 0333794079. Includes bibliographical references and index.*

3962 The spiritual and Hindustani music. S.K. Saxena. **San. Nat.** 131-132 1999 pp.3-14.

3963 The structure of principal court musics of East and Southeast Asia. José Maceda. **Asian Mus.** XXXII:2 Spring-Summer:2001 pp.143-178.

3964 Synthesizing Carnatic music with a computer. M. Subramanian. **San. Nat.** 133-134 1999 pp.16-24.

3965 Toward an ethnomusicology of the early music movement: thoughts on bridging disciplines and musical worlds. Kay Kaufman Shelemay. **Ethnomusicology** 45:1 Winter:2001 pp.1-29.

3966 Traditsionnye i novye ballady ob intseste. *[In Russian]*; (Traditional and new ballads about incest.) A.Yu. Neshina. **Vest. Mosk. Univ. Ser. 9 Filol.** 3 2001 pp.135-146.

3967 Tribal music of India. Roderic Knight; Carol Babiracki; David Roche; Roderic Knight; Richard Kent Wolf. **Asian Mus.** XXXII:1 Fall-Winter:2000-2001 pp.1-184. *Collection of 6 articles.*

3968 Trois récits communistes. De l'usage de la poésie populaire chantée en pays télougou. *[In French]*; [Three communist stories. The use of popular sung poetry in Telugu speaking countries]. Daniel Negers. **Bull. Ét. Indien.** 17-18 1999-2000 pp.295-426.

3969   Uchinaa pop: place and identity in contemporary Okinawan popular music. James E. Roberson. **Crit. Asian St.** 33:2 6:2001 pp.211-242.

3970   Varyiantnasts' u belaruskim pesennym fal'klory. *[In Belorussian]*; (Variations in Belarussian song folklore.) *[Summary]*; *[Summary in Russian]*. N.G. Mazuryna. **V. Aka. Belarusi** 2 1999 pp.95-100.

3971   The Yinyang theory's numbers and their influence on Chinese traditional music. Yaxiong Du. **Eur. Stud. Y.** 73 2001 pp.135-126.

Oral tradition
Tradition orale

3972   The appeal of *Kaidan*, tales of the strange. Noriko T. Reider. **Asian Folk. S.** LIX:2 2000 pp.265-284.

3973   The archeology of oral communication. In search of spoken language in the Bible. Andreas Wagner. **J. N.W. Sem. Lang.** 26:2 2000 pp.117-126.

3974   Baltazar Adam Krčelić: chronicler of everyday life. Ljiljana Marks. **Nar. Umjetn.** 38:1 2001 pp.135-152.

3975   Chernobyl stories and anthropological shock in Hungary. Krista M. Harper. **Anthr. Quart.** 74:3 7:2001 pp.114-123.

3976   Chernobyl's folklore: vernacular commentary on nuclear disaster. Larisa Fialkova. **J. Folk. Res.** 38:3 9-12:2001 pp.181-204.

3977   Cinematically speaking: the impact of orality on Indian popular film. Sheila J. Nayar. **Vis. Anthrop.** 14:2 2001 pp.121-153.

3978   Constructing narratives of monition and guile: the politics of interpretation. A. Afsaruddin. **Arabica** XLVIII:3 7:2001 pp.315-351.

3979   Le conte et la théorie. *[In French]*; [The theory of storytelling]. Harold Neemann. **Fabula** 42:3-4 2001 pp.297-303.

3980   Creolist mystification: oral writing in the works of Patrick Chamoiseau and Simone Schwarz-Bart. Alexie Tcheuyap. **R. African Lit.** 32:4 Winter:2001 pp.44-60.

3981   Los cuentos negros de Cuba de Lydia Cabrera: desde la tradición hasta la criollización. *[In Spanish]*; [Lydia Cabrera's *Cuentos Negros*: from tradition to creolization]. Michèle Guicharnaud-Tollis. **Caravelle** 76-77 12:2001 pp.549-558.

3982   A description of *Jiangjing* (telling scriptures) services in Jingjiang, China. Mark Bender. **Asian Folk. S.** LX:1 2001 pp.101-134.

3983   Description of structure of the folktale: using a bioinformatics multiple alignment program. Jun'ichi Oda. **Senri Ethn. Stud.** 55 2001 pp.153-174.

3984   Descriptividad en el corrido tradicional. *[In Spanish]*; [The use of description in traditional *corridos*]. Aurelio González. **Caravelle** 76-77 12:2001 pp.495-505.

3985   Donald Moodie: South Africa's pioneer oral historian. V.C. Malherbe. **Hist. Afr.** 25 1998 pp.171-198.

3986   'Dust to dust': oral testimonies of asbestos-related disease on Clydeside, c.1930 to the present. Ronald Johnston; Arthur McIvor. **Oral Hist.** 29:2 Autumn:2001 pp.48-61.

3987   The emergence of *kaidan-shū*: the collection of tales of the strange and mysterious in the Edo period. Noriko T. Reider. **Asian Folk. S.** LX:1 2001 pp.79-100.

3988   Erzählungen über das sozialistische Dorf. Zur erzählerischen Bewältigung der Vergangenheit und der Gegenwart in Bulgarien. *[In German]*; [Tales about a socialist village: narratives on coping with past and present in Bulgaria]; *[Summary in French]*; *[Summary in German]*. Doroteja Dobreva. **Fabula** 42:1-2 2001 pp.90-109.

3989   Event and story schemas in Australian Aboriginal English discourse. Ian G. Malcolm; Judith Rochecouste. **Eng. Wor.-wide** 21:2 2000 pp.261-289.

3990   Fairy tales as a forerunner of European children's literature: cross-border fairy tale materials and fairy tale motifs. Hans-Jörg Uther. **Nar. Umjetn.** 38:1 2001 pp.121-134.

3991   Folklore of the Iranian region. John R. Perry; Kinga Ilona Márkus-Takeshita; Ulrich Marzolph; Margaret A. Mills; Mahmoud Omidsalar; Ravšan Rahmonī; Judith M. Wilks;

Victoria Arakelova; Almuth Degener. **Asian Folk. S.** LX:2 2001 pp.191-344. *Collection of 9 articles.*

3992 Food, foragers, and folklore: the role of narrative in human subsistence. Michelle Scalise Sugiyama. **Evol. Hum. Behav.** 22:4 7:2001 pp.221-240.

3993 From Iranian myth to folk narrative: the legend of the dragon-slayer and the spinning maiden in the *Persian Book of the Kings*. Kinga Ilona Márkus-Takeshita. **Asian Folk. S.** LX:2 2001 pp.203-214.

3994 Gender and disguise in the Arabic *Cinderella*: a study in the cultural dynamics of representation. Ibrahim Muhawi. **Fabula** 42:3-4 2001 pp.263-283.

3995 The gender of the trick: female tricksters and male narrators. Margaret A. Mills. **Asian Folk. S.** LX:2 2001 pp.237-258.

3996 Govorni žanrovi u Gjalskijevu djeiu *Pod Starim Krovovima* u kontekstu povijesnih, političkih i ekonomskih zbivanja. *[In Croatian]*; (The language genres in *Pod Starim Krovovima* [*Under the Ancient Roofs*] by Gjalski in historical, political and economic context.) *[Summary]*. Vilko Endstrasser. **Nar. Umjetn.** 37:2 2000 pp.163-180.

3997 How one becomes a perfect *ṣaddik*. A comparative study of *Nathan of the Radiance* and *The Story of Joseph the Gardener of Ashkelon and his Wife*. Avidov Lipsker. **Fabula** 42:3-4 2001 pp.243-262.

3998 Hunters' lore in Nuristan. Almuth Degener. **Asian Folk. S.** LX:2 2001 pp.329-344.

3999 The illustration of *The Old Man of the Sea* and *The Story of Sindbad the Sailor*: its iconography and legendary background. Kazue Kobayashi. **Senri Ethn. Stud.** 55 2001 pp.101-120.

4000 Irruptions of the dreamings in post-colonial Australia. Basil Sansom. **Oceania** 72:1 9:2001 pp.1-32.

4001 Der Jäger, die Ziegen und der Erdschrein. Politik mit oralen Traditionen zur Siedlungsgeschichte in Nordghana. *[In German]*; [The hunter, the goats and the shrine: politics and oral narratives of settlement histories in northern Ghana] *[Summary]*. Carola Lentz. **Z. Ethn.** 125:2 2000 pp.281-304.

4002 The Jew and the king's cup-bearer: a tale of Jewish life in medieval Europe. Esther Zago; Janice Owen; Michael Serwatka. **Fabula** 42:3-4 2001 pp.213-242.

4003 Killer *khilats*, part 2: imperial collecting of poison dress legends in India. Michelle Maskiell; Adrienne Mayor. **Folklore** 112:2 10:2001 pp.163-182.

4004 'Les contes, il faut avoir le temps de les rêver'. *[In French]*; ['Stories - you must have time to dream them']. Margarita Xanthakou. **Homme** 158-159 4-9:2001 pp.365-376.

4005 Leyendas coloniales y tradicionales: una relectura desde el género. *[In Spanish]*; [Colonial and traditional legends: a rereading from a gender perspective]. Anna M. Fernández Poncela. **Cuad. Am.** XV:1(85) 1-2:2001 pp.208-225.

4006 Luck and three Gypsy folktales. Carol Miller. **J. Folk. Res.** 38:3 9-12:2001 pp.263-284.

4007 Ludewig Ferdinand Römer's *Nachrichten von der Küste Guinea*, (mid-18th century) as a source on the Benin kingdom history and culture. Peter M. Roese; Dmitri M. Bondarenko; Tobias M.L. Roese. **Tribus** 50 12:2001 pp.135-150.

4008 La mafia d'un village sicilien. *[In French]*; (The Mafia in a Sicilian village.) *[Summary]*; *[Summary in German]*. Anton Blok. **Ethn. Fr.** XXXI:1 1-3:2001 pp.61-67.

4009 Making history, creating gender: some methodological and interpretive questions in the writing of Oyo oral traditions. Oyeronke Oyewumi. **Hist. Afr.** 25 1998 pp.263-306.

4010 »Mga Dili Ingon Nato« (<Die nicht wie wir sind>): Weisse Geister und fremde Menschen auf den Philippinen. *[In German]*; ['That which we are not': White ghosts and foreigners in the Philippines] *[Summary]*. Bettina Beer. **Baes-A.** XLVII:2 6:2001 pp.299-322.

4011 The oral and ritual culture of Chinese women: bridal lamentations of Nanhui. Anne McLaren; Qinjian Chen. **Asian Folk. S.** LIX:2 2000 pp.205-238.

4012 Oral history in the Western Cape. Vivian Bickford-Smith; Sean Field; Clive Glaser; Albert Thomas; Karen Daniels; Wiesahl Taliep; Lisa Baxter; Msokoli Qotole; Silke Heiss. **Afr. Stud.** 60:1 7:2001 pp.5-158. *Collection of 8 articles.*

4013 Oral tradition in changing political contexts: the Kisra legend in northern Borgu. Olayemi Akinwumi. **Hist. Afr.** 25 1998 pp.1-8.

4014   Patrimonio oral: la experiencia de Marraquech. *[In Spanish]*; [Oral heritage: the experience of Marrakesh]. Juan Goytisolo. **Rev. de Human.** 11 Autumn:2001 pp.69-76.

4015   The Persianization of Köroğlu: banditry and royalty in three versions of the Köroğlu *destan*. Judith M. Wilks. **Asian Folk. S.** LX:2 2001 pp.305-318.

4016   Perspectives on the Jack tales and other North American *Märchen*. Samuel Harmon; Carl Lindahl; Jane Muncy Fugate; Glen Muncy Anderson; James Taylor Adams; Richard Chase; Polly Johnson; Louise Fontaine Mann; Charles L. Perdue, Jr.; Alice Lannon; Martin Lovelace. **J. Folk. Res.** 38:1-2 1-8:2001 pp.1-170. *Collection of 10 articles.*

4017   Prechodové rituály v slovenskej čarodejnej rozprávke. *[In Slovak]*; (Rites of passage in Slovak magic fairy tales.) *[Summary]*. Martina Bocánová. **Slov. Národop.** 48:2 2000 pp.195-205.

4018   Proverbs in Zimbabwean advertisements. Liveson Tatira. **J. Folk. Res.** 38:3 9-12:2001 pp.229-242.

4019   The psychological foundations of the hero-ogre story. A cross-cultural study. Ian Jobling. **Hum. Nature** 12:3 2001 pp.247-275.

4020   Reflections of Hindu mythology in Tamil folktales. Gabriella Eichinger Ferro-Luzzi. **Stud. Orient.** 94 2001 pp.105-118.

4021   Regionalne crte usmene hrvatske književnosti. *[In Croatian]*; (Regional features of Croatian oral literature.) *[Summary]*. Maja Bošković-Stulli. **Nar. Umjetn.** 37:2 2000 pp.151-162.

4022   Rostam's seven trials and the logic of epic narrative in the *Shahnama*. Mahmoud Omidsalar. **Asian Folk. S.** LX:2 2001 pp.259-294.

4023   Sangalan oral traditions as philosophy and ideologies. Mohamed Saidou N'Daou. **Hist. Afr.** 26 1999 pp.239-268.

4024   Siedlungsgeschichten bei den Kassena: orale Traditionen und Lokalität. *[In German]*; [Settlement narratives among the Kasena: oral traditions and locality] *[Summary]*. Hans Peter Hahn. **Z. Ethn.** 125:2 2000 pp.241-263.

4025   Some geser motifs in a khalkha narrative. Marta Kiripolská. **Acta Orient.** 62 2001 pp.177-192.

4026   Some remarks about the Sibyl(s) in Maltese legends; *[Summary in French]*; *[Summary in German]*. Micheline Galley. **Fabula** 42:1-2 2001 pp.22-31.

4027   The *Sunjata* epic — the ultimate version. Jan Jansen. **R. African Lit.** 32:1 Spring:2001 pp.14-46.

4028   Tales of the white lady in the Chamoru folklore. Peter R. Onedera. **Asian Cult. (Asian-Pac. Cult.) Q.** XXVIII:4 Winter:2000 pp.1-10.

4029   The teaching of the ancestors. Nicole Revel. **Phil. Stud.** 49:3 2001 pp.417-428.

4030   Telling stories in the era of global communication: Black writing — oraliture. Susan Petrilli; Augusto Ponzio. **R. African Lit.** 32:1 Spring:2001 pp.98-109.

4031   Topoi in oralen Traditionen über Siedlungsgründungen in Borno (Nigeria). *[In German]*; [Topoi in oral settlement narratives in Borno state, Nigeria] *[Summary]*. Editha Platte; Holger Kirscht. **Z. Ethn.** 125:2 2000 pp.215-240.

4032   Two patterns of an international tale: the lawyer's letter opened; *[Summary in French]*; *[Summary in German]*. Herbert Halpert; Gerald Thomas. **Fabula** 42:1-2 2001 pp.32-63.

4033   Why the fish laughed, and other matters relating to (the Indian sense of) 'humor'. Edwin Gerow. **Stud. Orient.** 94 2001 pp.167-180.

4034   The *Yokobue-sōshi*: conflicts between social convention, human love and religious renunciation. Yoshiko Dykstra; Yuko Kurata. **Jpn. Relig.** 26:2 7:2001 pp.117-130.

Poetry
Poésie

4035   The allegorical landscape: Peire Vidal's '*ric thesaur*'. Matthew Bardell. **Fr. Stud.** LV:2 4:2001 pp.151-166.

4036   ('*Al-Tibaq*' in Al-Akhtal's poetry.) *[Summary]*; *[Text in Arabic]*. I. al-Alim. **Dirasat Hum. Soc. Sc.** 28:2 8:2001 pp.361-376.

4037   Amazigh poetry of the resistance period (central Morocco). Michael Peyron. **J. N. African Stud.** 5:1 Spring:2000 pp.109-120.

4038   'And brewsters pay for smiles': Ray Bagley's alienated verse. George W. Lyon. **Ethnologies** 22:2 2000 pp.237-254.

4039   And unafraid of the Gorgon on the breastplate, the stones speak: the anguished drama of return in M. Nourbese Philip's *Discourse on the Logic of Language*. Coomi S. Vevaina. **Kunapipi** XXIII:2 2001 pp.103-120.

4040   Back from oblivion: the nature of 'word' in Yona Wallach's poetry. Zafrira Lidovsky Cohen. **Heb. St.** XLI 2000 pp.99-148.

4041   Barbara Guest: this art. Catherine Kasper; Sara Lundquist; Robert Bennett; Mei-Mei Berssenbrugge; Terence Diggory; Anna Rabinowitz; Arielle Greenberg; Garrett Caples. **Wom. Stud.** 30:1 2001 pp.1-129. *Collection of 7 articles*.

4042   Bing Xin and her reception in Bohemia and Slovakia. Marián Gálik. **Arch. Orient.** 68:1 2:2000 pp.41-52.

4043   The celebration of failure as dissent in Urdu *ghazal*. Harbans Mukhia. **Mod. Asian S.** 33:4 10:1999 pp.861-881.

4044   Chinese and indigenous influences in Vietnamese verse romances of the 19ᵗʰ century. Eric Henry. **Crossroads** 15:2 2001 pp.1-40.

4045   (Conflict between reality and idealism in pre-Islamic poetry: blaming woman as an example.) *[Summary]*; *[Text in Arabic]*. Hamdi Mansour. **Dirasat Hum. Soc. Sc.** 28:Supp. 2001 pp.46-66.

4046   The desert as a realm of unbound passion: love and madness in the *Tale of Laylā and Majnūn*. Yuriko Yamanaka. **Senri Ethn. Stud.** 55 2001 pp.147-152.

4047   (Eagerness to life in Al-Maa'ri's poetry.) *[Summary]*; *[Text in Arabic]*. Sameeh M. Ismael. **Dirasat Hum. Soc. Sc.** 28:2 8:2001 pp.317-340.

4048   Esculpiendo el mito: Sarmiento, Lincoln y la traducción de un poema escocés. *[In Spanish]*; [Sculpting myth: Sarmiento, Lincoln and the translation of a Scottish poem]. Barry L. Velleman. **Cuad. Am.** XV:3(87) 5-6:2001 pp.91-108.

4049   Eternal present: poetic figuration and cultural memory in the poetry of Yehuda Amichai, Dan Pagis, and Tuvia Rübner. Amir Eshel. **Jew. Soc. Stud.** 7:1 Fall:2000 pp.141-166.

4050   First grammarian, first poet: a south Indian vision of cultural origins. David Shulman. **Indian Ec. Soc. His. R.** XXXVIII:4 10-12:2001 pp.353-374.

4051   Fujiwara Kintō's dual poetical taste in *Wakanrōeishū*. Zdenka Švarcová. **Arch. Orient.** 69:3 8:2001 pp.485-494.

4052   Gender politics and the Urdu ghazal: exploratory observations on *Rekhta* versus *Rekhtī*. Carla Petievich. **Indian Ec. Soc. His. R.** XXXVIII:3 7-9:2001 pp.223-248.

4053   El grupo de Martín Fierro y los poetas de *Contemporáneos*. *[In Spanish]*; [The *martinferristas* and the *contemporaneos* poets]. Rose Corral. **Caravelle** 76-77 12:2001 pp.517-525.

4054   Hebrew style in the liturgical poetry of Shemu'el HaShelishi. Naoya Katsumata. **J. Jew. Stud.** LII:2 Autumn:2001 pp.308-322.

4055   Indonesian poetry about time. Eva Vaníčková. **Arch. Orient.** 68:2 5:2000 pp.171-190.

4056   The Japanization of Tu Fu, Li Po and others: on problems of translating classical poetry. Anthony V. Liman; Wayne Schlepp. **Arch. Orient.** 69:1 2:2001 pp.33-50.

4057   The *Kathakautuka* — a Persian love poem in Sanskrit garb. Rani Majumdar. **J. Orient. Inst.** XLVII:3-4(47) 3-6:1998 pp.283-288.

4058   *Kimondo*, satire, and political dialogue: electioneering through versification. Kimani Njogu. **R. African Lit.** 32:1 Spring:2001 pp.1-13.

4059   The landscape of African music. F. Abiola Irele; Kofi Agawu; Daniel K. Avorgbedor; Tanure Ojaide; Tejumola Olaniyan; Meki Nzewi; Israel Anyahuru; Tom Ohiaraumunna; Luke Eyoh; Akin Euba; Carol Muller; Bode Omojola; Nick Nesbitt. **R. African Lit.** 32:2 Summer:2001 pp.1-186. *Collection of 12 articles*.

4060   Love poems in modern Thai *Nirat*. Suchitra Chongstitvatana. **J. Siam Soc.** 88:1-2 2000 pp.15-20.

4061   Lyric epiphany. Paul Friedrich. **Lang. Soc.** 30:2 6:2001 pp.217-247.

4062   Mahmoud Darwich: Rita et la poétique du couple. *[In French]*; [Mahmoud Darwich: Rita and the romantic relationship]. Elias Khoury. **R. Et. Palest.** 81 Autumn:2001 pp.58-69.

4063   Onitsura's *makoto* and the Daoist concept of the natural. Peipei Qiu. **Philos. E.W.** 51:2 4:2001 pp.232-246.

4064   Pandnāma — Kritische Textausgabe und Übersetzung der Urduinterpretation des klassischen persischen Lehrgedichtes Pandnāma. *[In German]*; [Pandnāma - critical edition and translation of the Urdu interpretation of the classical Persian didactic poem]. Kandida Zweng. **Acta Orient.** 61 2000 pp.23-144.

4065   Le patio du poète nahua. *[In French]*; [The courtyard in Nahuatl poetry]. Marie Sautron. **Caravelle** 76-77 12:2001 pp.131-143.

4066   Poètes grecs et princes mexicains: comparaison entre la poésie grecque ancienne et la poésie nahuatl précolombienne. *[In French]*; [Greek poets and Mexican princes: a comparison between ancient Greek poetry and pre-Columbian Nahuatl poetry]. Philippe Yziquel. **Caravelle** 76-77 12:2001 pp.165-174.

4067   The poetics of distortive talk: plot and character in Ratnākara's *Fifty Verbal Perversions* (Vakroktipañcāśikā). Yigal Bronner; Lawrence McCrea. **J. Ind. Phil.** 29:4 8:2001 pp.435-464.

4068   Premodernity and (post)modernity: superposition, montage, and dialectics in *haiku*, Pound, Eisenstein, and Benjamin. Takao Hagiwara. **Arch. Orient.** 68:4 11:2000 pp.549-570.

4069   The private 'I' in the works of Nina Berberova. Nadya L. Peterson. **Slavic R.** 60:3 Fall:2001 pp.491-512.

4070   A proverb poem by Refiki. A.L. MacFie; F. MacFie. **Asian Folk. S.** LX:1 2001 pp.5-20.

4071   Rivai Apin and the modernist aesthetic in Indonesian poetry. Keith Foulcher. **Bijdragen** 157:4 2001 pp.771-798.

4072   The role of woman in the poetry of two Bengali modernists. Blanka Knotková-Čapková. **Arch. Orient.** 68:3 8:2000 pp.433-440.

4073   Scared into selfhood: the poetry of Inna Lisnianskaia, Elena Shvarts, Olga Sedakova. Stephanie Sandler. **Slavic R.** 60:3 Fall:2001 pp.473-490.

4074   Şiir mecmuaları ve metin teşkilinde mecmuaların rolü. *[In Turkish]*; (*Mecmua* of poetry and the role of *mecmua* in the composition of a text.) Yaşar Aydemir. **Bilig** 19 Autumn:2001 pp.147-155.

4075   (The social tendency in the poetry of Ibn Danial Al-Mouseli.) *[Summary]*; *[Text in Arabic]*. Shafiq Al-Raqab. **Dirasat Hum. Soc. Sc.** 28:1 2:2001 pp.187-194.

4076   Studies of traditional Chinese poetry in the U.S., 1962-1996 (part II). William H. Nienhauser, Jr. **Chin. Cult.** XL:2 6:1999 pp.45-72.

4077   (Subjectivity and objectivity in the poetry of Ibn Qais Al-Ruqayyat.) *[Summary]*; *[Text in Arabic]*. Amal T. Nusair. **Dirasat Hum. Soc. Sc.** 28:1 2:2001 pp.252-280.

4078   Tagore's poetic celebration of Guru Gobind Singh. Rajat Dasgupta [Tr.]. **Sikh Rev.** 49:8(572) 8:2001 pp.54-56.

4079   'The raw and the cooked': Arthur Kenneth Nortje, Canada, and a comprehensive bibliography. Craig W. McLuckie; Ross Tyner. **Eng. Afr.** 26:2 10:1999 pp.1-54.

4080   [The use of religious heritage in the poetry of Haidar Mahmoud] *[Summary]*; *[Text in Arabic]*. Ibrahim Koufahi. **Dirasat Hum. Soc. Sc.** 28:1 2:2001 pp.225-251.

4081   'This will (not) be handled by the press:' problems — and their solution — in preparing camera-ready copy for the collected works of Nana Asma'u, 1793-1864. Beverly Mack. **Hist. Afr.** 25 1998 pp.161-170.

4082   Thomas Pringle and the 'Xhosa'. Matthew Shum. **Eng. Afr.** 27:2 10:2000 pp.1-28.

4083   (Tragedy manifestation in the poetry of Deek Al-Jin Al-Humsi.); *[Text in Arabic]*. Abd al-Fattah Nafi'. **Dirasat Hum. Soc. Sc.** 28:2 8:2001 pp.377-390.

4084   (Tribe and politics in Al-A'sha poetry.) *[Summary]*; *[Text in Arabic]*. Irsan Ramini. **Dirasat Hum. Soc. Sc.** 28:1 2:2001 pp.281-282.

4085   Türkçe mesnevilerin tertip özellikleri. *[In Turkish]*; (Composition characteristics of Turkish *mesnevîs.*) Ahmet Kartal. **Bilig** 19 Autumn:2001 pp.69-122.

4086   'Will come forth in tongues and fury': relocating Irish cultural studies. Katie Kane. **Cult. St.** 15:1 1:2001 pp.98-123.

4087   (The wolf as a symbol in the old Arabic poetry.) *[Summary]*; *[Text in Arabic]*. Y. Aiesh. **Dirasat Hum. Soc. Sc.** 28:1 2:2001 pp.26-48.

4088   (The woman in Ibn Al-Farid's poetry: a study in the poetic symbol.) *[Summary]*; *[Text in Arabic]*. Rushdi Ali Hassan. **Dirasat Hum. Soc. Sc.** 28:1 2:2001 pp.98-117.

4089   Wu Zhen's poetic inscriptions on paintings. Tzi-Cheng Wang. **B. Sch. Orient. Afr. Stud.** 64:2 2001 pp.208-239.

4090   The Yorùbá royal bards: their work and relevance in the society. Akintunde Akinyemi. **Nord. J. Afr. St.** 10:1 2001 pp.98-106.

Visual arts
Arts visuels

4091   African art at the Nelson-Atkins museum of art. Joyce M. Youmans. **Afr. Arts** XXXIII:4 Winter:2000 pp.40-61.

4092   African art in the Ethnologisches Museum in Berlin. Paola Ivanov. **Afr. Arts** XXXIII:3 Autumn:2000 pp.18-39.

4093   Andy Warhol: his Kafka and 'Jewish geniuses'. Bluma Goldstein. **Jew. Soc. Stud.** 7:1 Fall:2000 pp.127-140.

4094   El arte de la fotografía. Hacia una nueva mirada aristocrática. *[In Spanish]*; (The art of photography: towards an aristocratic vision.) Jorge Latorre. **Com. y. Soc.** XIII:2 12:2000 pp.117-139.

4095   The artistic exchanges among three countries: Korea, China, and Japan. Sun-pyo Hong; Songeun Choe; Junghee Han; Pyong-mo Chong. **Korea J.** 40:4 Winter:2000 pp.5-166. *Collection of 4 articles.*

4096   Bad Aboriginal art: tradition, media, and technological horizons. Eric Michaels; Dick Hebdige [Foreword]; Marcia Langton [Intro.]. Minneapolis MN: University of Minnesota Press, 1994. xlix, 203p. *ISBN: 0816623414. Volume 3. (Series:* Theory out of bounds).

4097   Bosch dans les Andes: le millénium pictural de Marcelo Suaznábar. *[In French]*; [Bosch in the Andes: Marcelo Suaznábar's pictoral millenium]. Gérard Teulière. **Caravelle** 76-77 12:2001 pp.677-692.

4098   Les contenus subliminaux de l'image chez Felipe Guaman Poma de Ayala. *[In French]*; (Subliminal contents of Guaman Poma's images.) *[Summary]*; *[Summary in Spanish]*. Michel Graulich; Serge Núñez Tolin. **J. Soc. Amér.** 86 2000 pp.67-112.

4099   La creatividad en la producción cinematográfica. *[In Spanish]*; (Creativity in film production: the film producer as a creative force.) Alejandro Pardo. **Com. y. Soc.** XIII:2 12:2000 pp.227-249.

4100   Cyborg violence: bursting borders and bodies with queer machines. Anne Allison. **Cult. Anthro.** 16:2 5:2001 pp.237-265.

4101   Development of modern painting in the Mashriq within its socio-political context; *[Summary in Arabic]*. Wijdan Ali [Princess]. **Dirasat Hum. Soc. Sc.** 28:1 2:2001 pp.302-316.

4102   Exhibiting Ghana: display, documentary, and 'national' art in the Nkrumah era; *[Summary in French]*. Janet Hess. **Afr. Stud. R.** 44:1 4:2001 pp.59-77.

4103   Expeditionary art: an appraisal. Roger Balm. **Geogr. Rev.** 90:4 10:2000 pp.585-602.

4104   'Feeling global' the Likoni ferry photographers of Mombasa, Kenya. Heike Behrend. **Afr. Arts** XXXIII:3 Autumn:2000 pp.70-76.

4105   Filmer le social filmer l'histoire. *[In French]*; [Filming social reality, filming history]. Larry Portis; Gérard Althabe; Jean-Pierre Durand; Laurent Cholet; Jean-Pierre Garnier; Pascal Dupuy; Peter Watkins; L'Homme et la Société [Interviewer]; Gérard Raynal;

Richard Prost; Frederick Wiseman; L. Mīkles [Interviewer]; Christiane Passevant. **Hom. Soc.** 142(4) 10-12:2001 pp.3-175. *Collection of 11 articles.*

4106 Folk art at the crossroads of tradition and modernity: a study of patta painting in Orissa. Mamata Tripathy. **J. Anthrop. Soc. Oxford** XXIX:3 1998 pp.197-211.

4107 Fotografie In Afrika Voraussetzungen Ihrer Rezeption. *[In German]*; [Photography in Africa: prerequisites for its reception] *[Summary]*. Peter Stepan. **Baes-A.** XLVII:2 6:2001 pp.277-298.

4108 Framing the framed self: a reading of Victor Nunez's *Ruby in Paradise*. Kathleen J. Waites. **Biography** 24:2 Spring:2001 pp.425-441.

4109 George Hughes (portfolio). Doran H. Ross. **Afr. Arts** XXXIV:1 Spring:1999 pp.50-57.

4110 Hair in African art and culture. Roy Sieber; Frank Herreman. **Afr. Arts** XXXIII:3 Autumn:2000 pp.54-69.

4111 Home is where the art is: six South African rural artists. Anitra Nettleton. **Afr. Arts** XXXIII:4 Winter:2000 pp.26-39.

4112 The illustrators of the *Printemps parfumé*. Zdenka Klöslová. **Arch. Orient.** 69:3 8:2001 pp.465-474.

4113 A journey into pictorial space: poetics of frame and field in Maithil painting. Mani Shekhar Singh. **Contr. I. Soc.** 34:3 9-12:2000 pp.409-442.

4114 Katekesbonaden från Knäred. *[In Swedish]*; [Catechism tapestries from Knäred] *[Summary]*. Nils-Arvid Bringéus. **Rig** 2 2001 pp.92-104.

4115 El lazo 6 de la Alcudia (Elche), el primer ejemplo conocido de Occidente. Las tramas hexagonales en el arte árabe. *[In Spanish]*; [The first known example of the *lazo de 6* in the Western world. Hexagonal patterns in Islamic art]. Basilio Pavón Maldonado. **Al-Qantara** XXII:1 2001 pp.171-204.

4116 Lo «stato barbarico delle donne» in Thorstein Bunde Veblen. *[In Italian]*; (The 'barbaric state of women' in Thorstein Bunde Veblen.) Umberto Marongiu. **Critica Sociol.** 136 Winter:2000-2001 pp.18-38.

4117 Mahāvīra in sculptural art - Tamil Nadu. A. Ekambaranathan. **Jain J.** XXXVI:1 7:2001 pp.16-24.

4118 More than the human figure the Marc and Denyse Ginzberg collection of African art. Elisabeth L. Cameron. **Afr. Arts** XXXIV:2 Summer:2001 pp.50-63.

4119 Music videos and the effeminate vices of urban culture in Mali; *[Summary in French]*. Dorothea E. Schulz. **Africa** 71:3 2001 pp.345-372.

4120 Nation and anti-nation: concepts of national cinema in the 'new' media era. Philip Rosen. **Diaspora** 5:3 Winter:1996 pp.375-402.

4121 A note: getting the invitation. Judith Clark. **Fash. Theory** 5:3 9:2001 pp.343-354.

4122 A note: performance art lives. Michael Rush. **Fash. Theory** 5:3 9:2001 pp.331-342.

4123 Palo Monte Mayombe and its influence on Cuban contemporary art. Judith Bettelheim. **Afr. Arts** XXXIV:2 Summer:2001 pp.36-49.

4124 Palo Verde: un centro secundario en la zona de Cotzumalguapa, Guatemala. *[In Spanish]*; [Palo Verde: a secondary capital in the Cotzumalguapa zone, Guatemala]. Oswaldo Chinchilla Mazariegos; Sébastien Perrot-Minnot; José Vicente Genovez. **J. Soc. Amér.** 87 2001 pp.303-324.

4125 A personal journey: Central African art from the Lawrence Gussman collection. Christa Clarke. **Afr. Arts** XXXIV:1 Spring:1999 pp.16-35.

4126 Photographies and modernities in Africa. Paul Hockings; Guy Hersant; Jean-François Werner; Tobias Wendl; Erika Nimis; Heike Behrend; Charles D. Gore. **Vis. Anthrop.** 14:3 2001 pp.241-342. *Collection of 7 articles.*

4127 Photographing in the Cameroon grassfields, 1970 to 1984. Christraud M. Geary. **Afr. Arts** XXXIII:4 Winter:2000 pp.70-77.

4128 Pierre-Toussaint-Frédéric Mialhe, un lithographe gascon à Cuba (1838-1854). *[In French]*; [Pierre-Toussaint-Frédéric Mialhe, a Gascon lithographer in Cuba (1838-1854)]. Sylvie Mégevand. **Caravelle** 76-77 12:2001 pp.443-453.

4129 The politics and ecology of indigenous folk art in Mexico. David V. Carruthers. **Human. Org.** 60:4 Winter:2001 pp.356-366.

4130　The recovery of the Tang dynasty painting: Master Wang Wei's ink-wash creation *On the Wangchuan river*. Kwong Lum; Jia Chen. **Int. J. Pol. C. S.** 11:3 Spring:1998 pp.439-450.

4131　Religious folk art and kitsch. The case of the Virgin Mary sanctuary at Licheń; *[Summary in Polish]*. Katarzyna Marciniak. **Ethnol. Pol.** 21 2000 pp.87-102.

4132　Revealing the *Mbusa* as art: women artists in Zambia. Deborah A. Hoover. **Afr. Arts** XXXIII:3 Autumn:2000 pp.40-53.

4133　Revisiting PWO. Manuel Jordán. **Afr. Arts** XXXIII:4 Winter:2000 pp.16-25.

4134　The role of craft and the significance of community public art in the work of Haida artist Bernie Williams. Lycia Danielle Trouton. **Kunapipi** XXIII:2 2001 pp.63-102.

4135　Rural artists colonies in Europe, 1870-1910. Nina Lübbren. Manchester: Manchester University Press, 2001. 280p. *ISBN: 0719058678, 071905866X. Includes bibliographical references.*

4136　The semiotics of anthropological authenticity: the film apparatus and cultural accommodation. Keyan G. Tomaselli. **Vis. Anthrop.** 14:2 2001 pp.173-183.

4137　Some thoughts on style in Tibetan art. Deborah Klimburg-Salter. **Tibet J.** XXV:4 Winter:2000 pp.83-90.

4138　Sòmonò puppet masquerades in Kirango, Mali (photo essay). Susan Vogel; Mary Jo Arnoldi. **Afr. Arts** XXXIV:1 Spring:1999 pp.72-77.

4139　Sözcük sanatı edebiyattan görüntü sanatı sinemaya sevginin aktarılışı. *[In Turkish]*; (The transformation of love from literature to cinema.) H. Hale Künüçen. **Bilig** 19 Autumn:2001 pp.33-52.

4140　A study of the Mahisamardini images from Jajpur. Harihar Routray. **Oris. Hist. R. J.** XLV:1-4 2000 pp.82-86.

4141　Symbols of Jewish sepulchral art. Klára Břeňová. **Arch. Orient.** 68:2 5:2000 pp.191-204.

4142　'Technical sciences and fine arts'. Siddharth Yeshwant Wakankar. **J. Orient. Inst.** XLVII:3-4(47) 3-6:1998 pp.189-202.

4143　'The day the world took off'; reflections on the experience of working on a television series. Alan MacFarlane. **Cam. Anthrop.** 22:1 2000-2001 pp.67-77.

4144　Tonkin wood-prints in the late 20th century. Petra Müllerová. **Arch. Orient.** 69:1 2:2001 pp.61-66.

4145　Urgent tasks in music and art: Tingatinga and Makonde art of southern Tanzania. J.A.R. Wembah-Rashid. **B. Int. Com. Urg. Anthrop. Ethnol. R.** 40 1999-2000 pp.65-74.

Written materials
Matériaux écrits

4146　African popular fiction: consideration of a category. Michael Chapman. **Eng. Afr.** 26:2 10:1999 pp.113-124.

4147　L'air du temps dans un conte de Silvina Ocampo. *[In French]*; [The tune of time in a tale by Silvina Ocampo]. Annick Mangin. **Caravelle** 76-77 12:2001 pp.559-568.

4148　Altanatolien und das mykenische Pylos: Einige Überlegungen zum Nestorbecher der *Ilias*. *[In German]*; [Old Anatolia and Mycenæan Pylos: reflections on Nestor in the *Iliad*]. Erich Neu. **Arch. Orient.** 67:4 11:1999 pp.619-628.

4149　Ambiguous narratives. Thomas Lyons. **Cult. Anthro.** 16:2 5:2001 pp.183-201.

4150　Among head-hunters and cannibals: Spenser St. John in Borneo and Haiti. Helen Tiffin. **Kunapipi** XXIII:2 2001 pp.18-30.

4151　André Brink's magical history tour: postmodern and postcolonial influences in *The First Life Of Adamastor*. Jochen Petzold. **Eng. Afr.** 27:2 10:2000 pp.45-58.

4152　Anomy and agony in a nation in crisis: Soyinka's *Season of Anomy*. Annie Gagiano. **Eng. Afr.** 26:2 10:1999 pp.125-140.

4153　Une approche littéraire du Champa: le conte *Madame Ivoire*. *[In French]*; [A Champa literary approach: the tale *Madame Ivoire*]. Vanthana Hang Minh Kim. **Péninsule** 40 2000 pp.105-110.

4154   *Arabian Nights* in England and America. Muhammed A. Al Da'mi. **Asian Cult. (Asian-Pac. Cult.) Q.** XXVIII:4 Winter:2000 pp.27-46.

4155   Arabic works shown to the Qianlong emperor in 1782. D.D. Leslie; Yang Daye; Ahmed Youssef. **Cent. Asia. J.** 45:1 2001 pp.7-27.

4156   *Ayedawbon Kyan*, an important Myanmar literary genre recording historical events. U. Thaw Kaung. **J. Siam Soc.** 88:1-2 2000 pp.21-33.

4157   Un balance de *Ariel* en su centenario. *[In Spanish]*; [A hundred years of *Ariel*]. Gonzalo Varela Petito. **Cuad. Am.** XV:4(88) 7-8:2001 pp.174-198.

4158   Beyond the curtains: unveiling Afro-Brazilian women writers. Niyi Afolabi. **R. African Lit.** 32:4 Winter:2001 pp.117-135.

4159   The 'Césaire effect,' or how to cultivate one's nation. Mireille Rosello. **R. African Lit.** 32:4 Winter:2001 pp.77-91.

4160   Christ as Creole: hybridity and the revision of colonial imagery in the works of Bessie Head. Lauren Smith. **Eng. Afr.** 26:1 5:1999 pp.61-80.

4161   Chronological problems in C.G. Okojie's Esan narrative traditions. James B. Webster; Onaiwu W. Ogbomo. **Hist. Afr.** 24 1997 pp.345-362.

4162   Clairière de soleil — figures de la Polynésie dans l'oeuvre de Melville. *[In French]*; [Polynesian characters in Melville's works]. Ricardo Pineri. **Soc. Ét. Océan.** 288 3:2001 pp.44-63.

4163   Classicism in Shaaban Robert's utopian novel, *Kusadikika*. Said A.M. Khamis. **R. African Lit.** 32:1 Spring:2001 pp.47-65.

4164   Clothes that matter: fashioning modernity in late Qing novels. Paola Zamperini. **Fash. Theory** 5:2 6:2001 pp.195-214.

4165   A comparison of Jacob Egharevba's *Ekhere Vb Itan Edo* and the four editions of its English translation, *A Short History of Benin*. Uyilawa Usuanlele; Toyin Falola. **Hist. Afr.** 25 1998 pp.361-386.

4166   Contradictions and misunderstandings in the literary response to colonial culture in nineteenth century Gujarat. Françoise Mallison. **S. Asia R.** 20:2 Spring:2000 pp.119-132.

4167   Contribución al estudio de la difusión de *La Cosmografía* de Julio Honorio en la península Ibérica. *[In Spanish]*; [The spread of Iulius Honorius's *Cosmography* through the Iberian Peninsula] *[Summary]*. Mayte Penelas. **Al-Qantara** XXII:1 2001 pp.1-18.

4168   Contribution of Bhavnagar to Sanskrit literature. Arun Joshi. **J. Orient. Inst.** XLVII:1-2(47) 9-12:1997 pp.113-118.

4169   A contribution to a better understanding of M.A. Jamālzāde. Jiří Bečka. **Arch. Orient.** 68:1 2:2000 pp.11-18.

4170   Crossover texts/Creole tongues: a conversation with Maryse Condé. Emily Apter [Interviewer]; Maryse Condé. **Publ. Cult.** 13:1 Winter:2001 pp.89-96.

4171   Decolonizing geographies of travel: reading James/Jan Morris. Richard Phillips. **Soc. Cult. Geog.** 2:1 3:2001 pp.5-24.

4172   Deux pages inédites d'une instruction d'Horièse sur les amitiés particulières. *[In French]*; [Two inedited pages of a lesson from Horace on special friendships]. F. Lucchesi. **Orientalia** 70:2 2001 pp.183-192.

4173   'Dirty' Hindi literature: contests about obscenity in late colonial north India. Charu Gupta. **S. Asia R.** 20:2 Spring:2000 pp.89-118.

4174   Doctors in literature. Sisir K. Majumdar. **B. Ind. Inst. Hist. Med.** XXIX:1 1:1999 pp.29-50.

4175   The doll's house or the house of the father? Maja Kriel's interrogation of the 'maid'/'madam' theme in *Original Sin and Other Stories*. Sue Marais. **Eng. Afr.** 26:1 5:1999 pp.81-106.

4176   Dr. Johnson and the Pandits: imagining the perfect dictionary in colonial Madras. Thomas R. Trautmann. **Indian Ec. Soc. His. R.** XXXVIII:4 10-12:2001 pp.375-398.

4177   A dream shattered: Lloyd Fernando's literary vision of Malaysia. Peter Wicks. **Asian Cult. (Asian-Pac. Cult.) Q.** XXVIII:2 Summer:2000 pp.49-54.

4178   Drohbriefe der Karo-Batak. *[In German]*; [Threatening letters of the Karo Batak]. Uli Kozok. **Tribus** 50 12:2001 pp.101-106.

4179   L'écrivain voyageur: le pèlerinage littéraire. *[In French]*; [The travel writer: the literary pilgrimage]. Roland Mortier; François Moureau; Claude Reichler; Jacques Huré; Raymond Trousson; Jacques Marx; Sophie-Jenny Linon-Chipon; Sarga Moussa; Claude Javeau; Georges Tolias; Manuel Couvreur. **R. Inst. Sociol.** 1-2 1998 pp.9-196. *Collection of 13 articles.*

4180   Edition und Interpretation von Texten: Aneignung, Enteignung und Zuneigung. Über den Umgang mit schriftlichen Quellen des Südens von Afrika. *[In German]*; [Editing and interpreting texts: appropriation, expropriation and fondness. Contact with written materials from Southern Africa]. Walter Schicho. **B. Int. Com. Urg. Anthrop. Ethnol. R.** 40 1999-2000 pp.121-132.

4181   Effects of writing about traumatic experiences: the necessity for narrative structuring. Joshua Smyth; Nicole True; Joy Souto. **J. Soc. Clin. Psychol.** 20:2 Summer:2001 pp.161-172.

4182   An empire of good sports: Roger Casement, the Boer War and James Joyces' *Ulysses*. Marilyn Reizbaum. **Kunapipi** XXIII:1 2001 pp.83-96.

4183   Eine erstaunliche Entdeckung in einer kolonialzeitlichen Maya-Handschrift. *[In German]*; [An astounding discovery in a Maya manuscript from the colonial period] *[Summary]*. Helga-Maria Miram. **Baes-A.** XLVII:2 6:2001 pp.345-360.

4184   Finding creative identities: Mennonite writers in Winnipeg; *[Summary in French]*. Leo Driedger; Diane Driedger. **Can. Ethn. Stud.** XXXII:2 2000 pp.75-94.

4185   From Adam to Abaqa: Qāḍī Baidawī's rearrangement of history; *[Summary in French]*. Ch. Melville. **Stud. Iran.** 30:1 2001 pp.67-86.

4186   The geographical data of the *Kāśyapa Samhitā*. Jyotir Mitra. **B. Ind. Inst. Hist. Med.** XXIX:2 7:1999 pp.93-102.

4187   Glissant's Africas: from departmentalization to the poetics of relation. Cilas Kemedjio. **R. African Lit.** 32:4 Winter:2001 pp.92-116.

4188   The golden image of the Akan negated: a reading of Ayi Kwei Armah's *The Healers*. Kwame Ayivor. **Eng. Afr.** 27:2 10:2000 pp.59-84.

4189   Hindu death as reflected in Āśāpūrnā Debī's novel *The First Promise*. Hana Preinhaelterová. **Arch. Orient.** 68:3 8:2000 pp.419-432.

4190   Historical writings, historical novels and period movies and dramas: an observation concerning Burma in Thai perception and understanding. Sunait Chutintharanon. **J. Siam Soc.** 88:1-2 2000 pp.53-57.

4191   Homenaje a José Enrique Rodó. *[In Spanish]*; [Homage to José Enrique Rodó]. Leopoldo Zea; Fernando Ainsa; María Andueza; Ricardo Melgar Bao; Liliana Weinberg. **Cuad. Am.** XV:1(85) 1-2:2001 pp.11-81. *Collection of 5 articles.*

4192   Homenaje a Mariano Picón Salas. *[In Spanish]*; [Homage to Mariano Picón Salas]. Domingo Miliani; Luis Rubilar Solis; Nelson Osorio Tejada; Luis Navarrete Orta; Jaime Valdivieso B.; Gregory Zambrano; Alexander Betancourt Mendieta. **Cuad. Am.** XV:4(88) 7-8:2001 pp.13-121. *Collection of 7 articles.*

4193   'How sisters should behave to sisters': women's culture and Igbo society in Flora Nwapa's *Efuru*. Patrick Colm Hogan. **Eng. Afr.** 26:1 5:1999 pp.45-60.

4194   Humour, satire and parody in Zhang Tianyi's writing. Yifeng Sun. **Chin. Cult.** XL:2 6:1999 pp.1-44.

4195   Images of America in Paz Marquez Benitez. Jennifer M. McMahon. **Phil. Stud.** 49:2 2001 pp.203-214.

4196   *In toyolnonotzaliz itechpa in axcan nahuatlahtoltlatlalilli. Algunas reflexiones sobre la literatura náhuatl actual. [In Spanish]*; [*In toyolnonotzaliz itechpa in axcan nahuatlahtoltlatlalilli.* Reflections on contemporary Nahuatl literature]. Librado Silva Galeana. **Caravelle** 76-77 12:2001 pp.623-629.

4197   Indian and international: some examples of Marathi science fiction writing. Hans Harder. **S. Asia R.** 21:1 Autumn:2001 pp.105-120.

4198   Inferring paradigms: referencing Andean and Mesoamerican texts. Claudette K. Columbus. **Semiotica** 135:1-4 2001 pp.157-174.

4199   The initiation archetype in fiction: a reading of Hemingway's '*Indian Camp*' and Yuson's '*Voice in the Hills*'. Jerry R. Yapo. **Phil. Stud.** 49:2 2001 pp.265-272.

4200   The island writes back: discourse/power and marginality in Wole Soyinka's *The swamp dwellers*, Derek Walcott's *The sea at Dauphin*, and Athol Fugard's *The Island*. Harry Garuba. **R. African Lit.** 32:4 Winter:2001 pp.61-76.

4201   Itinéraires d'un passeur: Jesús Morales Bermúdez, romancier chiapanèque. *[In French]*; [A smuggler's journey: Jesús Morales Bermúdez, Chiapan novelist]. Martine Dauzier. **Caravelle** 76-77 12:2001 pp.657-666.

4202   Juan Goytisolo por los discursos de la escritura. *[In Spanish]*; [Juan Goytisolo in the discourse of writing]. Fidel Chávez Pérez. **Rev. de Human.** 11 Autumn:2001 pp.63-68.

4203   *Jus gentium sinense*. The earliest Chinese translation of international law with some considerations regarding the compilation of Haiguo tuzhi. Rune Svarverud. **Acta Orient.** 61 2000 pp.202-238.

4204   Kita Morio's *Nireke no hitobito* and the saga-novel genre in Japanese literature. Vlasta Winkelhöferová. **Arch. Orient.** 68:4 11:2000 pp.539-548.

4205   Lebanese women's fiction: urban identity and the tyranny of the past. Samira Aghacy. **Int. J. M. E. Stud.** 33:4 11:2001 pp.503-523.

4206   Lecture actentielle dans *Trop C'est Trop* de Protais Asseng. *[In French]*; [Actor reading in Protais Asseng's *Trop C'est Trop*] *[Summary]*. P. Ikanga. **Ann. Æqua.** 22 2001 pp.137-152.

4207   Letting a text speak: some remarks on the sādhanapāda of the yogasūtra and the yogabhāsya I. The wording of yogasūtra 2.22. Albrecht Wezler. **J. Ind. Phil.** 29:1-2 4:2001 pp.293-304.

4208   The literary legacy of Frederick Courteney Selous. E. Mandiringana; T.J. Stapleton. **Hist. Afr.** 25 1998 pp.199-218.

4209   The literary structure of the chunqiu and zuo zhuan. Zbigniew Słupski. **Arch. Orient.** 69:1 2:2001 pp.51-60.

4210   Literatura y sociedad: dos ámbitos de aplicación del ensayismo romántico-social latinoamericano en los textos juveniles de Sarmiento y Alberdi. *[In Spanish]*; [Literature and society: two examples of Latin American socio-romantic essayism in Sarmiento and Alberdi's early texts]. Estela Fernández Nadal. **Cuad. Am.** XV:3(87) 5-6:2001 pp.66-90.

4211   Lovesick: illness, romance and the portrayal of women in Low Malay novels from the Dutch East Indies. Helen Pausacker; Charles A. Coppel. **R. Ind. Malay. Aff.** 35:1 Winter:2001 pp.43-77.

4212   Der Löwe und der Fuchs in dem Brief KBo 1.14. *[In German]*; [The lion and the fox in KBo 1.14]. M. Giorgieri. **Orientalia** 70:1 2001 pp.89-96.

4213   Making it new: Pudumaippittan and the Tamil short story, 1934-48. Lakshmi Holmström. **S. Asia R.** 20:2 Spring:2000 pp.133-146.

4214   Manuscripts on *Gitagovinda* found in Orissa. Karunakar Bisoi. **Oris. Hist. R. J.** XLV:1-4 2000 pp.77-81.

4215   Manuscrits, textes et «malaïté». *[In French]*; [Manuscripts, texts and 'Malayness']. Léonard Andaya; Ian Proudfoot; Lioubov Goriaeva; Roger Tol; C.C. MacKnight; I.A. Caldwell. **Archipel** 61 2001 pp.29-154. *Collection of 5 articles.*

4216   Maurice G. Dantec sur tous les fronts. À propos du *Théâtre des opérations*. *[In French]*; [Maurice G. Dantec on all fronts. Foreword to *Théâtre des opérations*. Paul Garapon. **Esprit** 279 11:2001 pp.118-134.

4217   Memoirs of the Orient. Anne Allison. **J. Jpn. Stud.** 27:2 Summer:2001 pp.381-398.

4218   Michel Houellebecq: *Plateforme* pour l'échange des misères mondiales. *[In French]*; [Michel Houllebecq: *Plateforme* for changing world poverty]. Pierre Varrod. **Esprit** 279 11:2001 pp.96-117.

4219   Mirror for princes or vizor for viziers: the twelfth-century Arabic popular encyclopedia Mufīd al-'ulūm and its relationship with the anonymous Persian Bahr al-fawā'id. Geert Jan Van Gelder. **B. Sch. Orient. Afr. Stud.** 64:3 2001 pp.313-338.

4220   Le monde précolombien dans l'œuvre d'Octavio Paz. *[In French]*; [The pre-Columbian world in the work of Octavio Paz]. Marcel Nérée. **Caravelle** 76-77 12:2001 pp.569-584.

4221   Myth and national identity in nineteenth-century Britain: the legends of King Arthur and Robin Hood. Stephanie L. Barczewski. Oxford, New York: Oxford University Press, 2000. viii, 274p. *ISBN: 019820728X. Includes bibliographical references (p. [247]-267) and index.*

4222   Le nahualisme dans *Hombres de maíz* de M.Á. Asturias. *[In French]*; [Nahualism in *Hombres de maíz* by M.Á Asturias]. Marie-Louise Ollé. **Caravelle** 76-77 12:2001 pp.593-602.

4223   Nasr al-Soltāni, Nasir al-Din Mozahheb et la bibliothèque d'Ebrāhim Soltān à Širāz. *[In French]*; [Nasr al-Soltāni, Nasir al-Din Mozahheb and Ebrāhim Soltān's library in Širāz] *[Summary]*. F. Richard. **Stud. Iran.** 30:1 2001 pp.87-104.

4224   Neologisms in the Septuagint of Ezekiel. Katrin Hauspie. **J. N.W. Sem. Lang.** 27:1 2001 pp.17-38.

4225   Nerval et la tombe de J.-J. Rousseau. *[In French]*; [Nerval and Rousseau's tomb]. Sarga Moussa. **R. Inst. Sociol.** 1-2 1998 pp.119-132.

4226   New and old worlds: *The Tempest* and early colonial discourse. John Wylie. **Soc. Cult. Geog.** 1:1 9:2000 pp.45-64.

4227   New data on an old manuscript: an Andalusian version of the work entitled Futūh al-Shām. Ella Landau-Tasseron. **Al-Qantara** XXI:2 2000 pp.361-380.

4228   New writings from Pacific islands. Agatha Ferei; Akanette Ta'ai. **Asian Cult. (Asian-Pac. Cult.) Q.** XXVIII:2 Summer:2000 pp.1-12.

4229   The N'ko alphabet as a vehicle of indigenous historiography. Dianne White Oyler. **Hist. Afr.** 24 1997 pp.239-256.

4230   Un nouveau réactionnaire: M. Philippe Muray. *[In French]*; [M. Philippe Muray: a neo-reactionary]. Joël Roman. **Esprit** 279 11:2001 pp.135-142.

4231   Old Javanese texts and culture. Helen Creese; Stuart Robson; I. Kuntara Wiryamartana; W. Van Der Molen; Thomas M. Hunter, Jr.; Jan Van Den Veerdonk; S. Supomo. **Bijdragen** 157:1 2001 pp.3-166. *Collection of 7 articles.*

4232   Oral v. written transmission: the case of Tabarī and Ibn Sa'd. Gh. Osman. **Arabica** XLVII:1 1:2001 pp.66-80.

4233   The *Oyun tülkigür* or *Key to Wisdom*: text and translation based on the MSS in the Institute for Oriental Studies at St. Petersburg. N.S. Yakhontova. **Mon. St.** XXIII 2000 pp.69-138.

4234   El Padre Las Casas entre los modernistas. *[In Spanish]*; [Father Las Casas and the modernists]. Ana Vigne Pacheco. **Caravelle** 76-77 12:2001 pp.475-483.

4235   Le peintre et les lettrés. Alejandro Obregón la plume à la main (1948). *[In French]*; [Painter and writers: Alejandro Obregón, pen in hand (1948)]. Jacques Gilard. **Caravelle** 76-77 12:2001 pp.585-592.

4236   Le pèlerinage istanbouliote de Pierre Loti. *[In French]*; [The Istanbul pilgrimage of Pierre Loti]. Jacques Huré. **R. Inst. Sociol.** 1-2 1998 pp.41-52.

4237   Le pèlerinage littéraire dans les Mascareignes aux XIXe et XXe siècles. *[In French]*; [The literary pilgrimage in the Mascareignes in the nineteenth and twentieth centuries]. Sophie-Jenny Linon-Chipon. **R. Inst. Sociol.** 1-2 1998 pp.101-118.

4238   Penser notre humanité comme une énigme. Autour d'*Une voix vient de l'autre rive*, d'Alain Finkielkraut. *[In French]*; [Humanity as an enigma: *Une voix vient de l'autre rive* by Alain Finkielkraut]. Robert Legros. **Esprit** 279 11:2001 pp.171-181.

4239   El perfil anímico y existencial de la mujer en la obra de María Luisa Bombal. *[In Spanish]*; [A mental and existential profile of the woman in the work of María Luisa Bombal] *[Summary]*. Dolores Rangel. **Rev. de Human.** 11 Autumn:2001 pp.33-48.

4240   Persian popular literature in the Qajar period. Ulrich Marzolph. **Asian Folk. S.** LX:2 2001 pp.215-236.

4241   Petra Papyri. T. Gagos; J. Frösén. **A. Dept. Antiq. Jordan** XLII 1998 pp.473-482.

4242   Poètes du monde aztèque, Tenochtitlan, Mexico et le premier roman multimédia. *[In French]*; [Aztec poets, Tenochtitlan, Mexico and the first multimedia novel]. Carla Fernandes. **Caravelle** 76-77 12:2001 pp.667-675.

4243   Politische Witze im *Simplicissimus* (1897-1933). *[In German]*; [Political jokes in *Simplicissimus* (1897-1933)]. Ines Mayer. **Fabula** 42:3-4 2001 pp.284-296.

4244   Postcolonial children and parents: Pauline Smith's *Platkops Children*. Margaret Lenta. **Eng. Afr.** 27:2 10:2000 pp.29-44.

4245   Posturas 'testimoniales' en *Historia verdadera de la conquista de la Nueva España*. *[In Spanish]*; ['Witness' accounts in the *Conquest of New Spain*]. Gustavo V. García. **Rev. de Human.** 10 Spring:2001 pp.65-84.

4246   Pour décrire un commentaire traditionnel sur une œuvre littéraire sanskrite. *[In French]*; [A traditional commentary on a Sanskrit literary work]. François Grimal. **B. Éc. Fr. Ex.-Or.** 87:2 2000 pp.765-786.

4247   Pratiques d'écriture. *[In French]*; [Writing practices]. Roger Chartier; Antonio Castillo Gómez; Marta Madero; Guglielmo Cavallo; István György Tóth; Christine Métayer; Marina Roggero; Martyn Lyons; Gábor Klaniczay; Ildikó Kristóf. **Ann.** 56:4-5 7-10:2001 pp.783-997. *Collection of 10 articles.*

4248   A propos de l'*airiiana vaējah*. *[In French]*; [On the *airiiana vaējah*] *[Summary]*. Ph. Gignoux. **Stud. Iran.** 29:2 2000 pp.163-166.

4249   Radical democracy and literary form: Alan Paton's *Ah, but your Land is Beautiful*. Jean-Philippe Wade. **Eng. Afr.** 28:1 5:2001 pp.91-104.

4250   Report on decipherment of Petra Papyri (1996/97). M. Kaimio; L. Koenen. **A. Dept. Antiq. Jordan** XLI 1997 pp.459-462.

4251   Resisting silence in Arab women's autobiographies. Magda M. al-Nowaihi. **Int. J. M. E. Stud.** 33:4 11:2001 pp.477-502.

4252   Rhythm as a stylistic device in Chinese literary texts. N. Speshnev. **Arch. Orient.** 68:1 2:2000 pp.31-40.

4253   The saga of an epic: Gilgamesh and the constitution of Uruk. R.T. Ridley. **Orientalia** 69:4 2000 pp.341-367.

4254   Saikaku and the narrative turnabout. Jeffrey Johnson. **J. Jpn. Stud.** 27:2 Summer:2001 pp.323-345.

4255   Schriftliche Folklore im 17. Jahrhundert. *[In German]*; [Written folklore in the 17th century] *[Summary]*; *[Summary in French]*. Gábor Tüskés. **Fabula** 42:1-2 2001 pp.1-21.

4256   The scorpion spell from Wadi Hammamat: another Aramaic text in demotic script. Richard C. Steiner. **J. Near East.** 60:4 10:2001 pp.259-268.

4257   Secular and sacred legitimation in Bharatcandra Ray's *Annada-mangal*. Clinton B. Seely. **Arch. Orient.** 68:3 8:2000 pp.327-358.

4258   Seven onomastic problems in Josephus' *Bellum Judaicum*. Tal Ilan; Jonathan J. Price. **Jew. Q. Rev.** 84 1993-1994 pp.189-209.

4259   Sinister fluids: the evil juices of love, writing and religion. Fabrizia Baldissera. **Bull. Ét. Indien.** 17-18 1999-2000 pp.153-172.

4260   Sistemas de emergencia del pasado en la literatura del siglo XX. *[In Spanish]*; [Ways of writing about the past in 20th century literature]. José Carlos Rovira. **Caravelle** 76-77 12:2001 pp.507-516.

4261   The social aesthetic and Sanskrit literary theory. Sheldon Pollock. **J. Ind. Phil.** 29:1-2 4:2001 pp.197-230.

4262   Stylizing the mundane: Bernice Morgan's random passage; *[Summary in French]*. Tracy Whalen. **Ethnologies** 23:1 2001 pp.23-44.

4263   Supplément au *Mariage de Loti*. *[In French]*; [Supplement to the *Marriage of Loti*]. Daniel Margueron; Robert Koenig; Alain Quella-Villéger; Philippe Blay; Bruno Vercier; Pierre Loti; Jean-Paul Berlier; Yannick Fer; Christian Beslu; Francis Cheung; Henri Blondin; Albert t'Serstevens; Henry Fouquier; Philippe Draperi; Patricia Roman; Jean-Jo Scemla; Paul Reboux; F. Devatine; S. Drollet; L. Peltzer; W. Pukoki; L. Sanford; Ch.T. Spitz; Pierre Bazantay; Francine Besson; Pierre Boixière; Alain Collard; Alain Deviègre. **Soc. Ét. Océan.** 285-287 4-9:2000 pp.4-251. *Collection of 30 articles.*

4264   Sur les pas de Laure et de Pétrarque. Le pèlerinage à la fontaine de Vaucluse aux XVIIᵉ et XVIIIᵉ siècles. *[In French]*; [In the footsteps of Laure and Pétrarque. The pilgrimage to the fountain at Vaucluse in the 17th and 18th centuries]. Manuel Couvreur. **R. Inst. Sociol.** 1-2 1998 pp.165-184.

4265   'Tableaux of queerness': the ethnographic novels of John White. John O'Leary. **Kunapipi** XXIII:2 2001 pp.7-17.

4266   Tadano Makuzu and her '*Hitori Kangae*'. Bettina Gramlich-Oka. **Monu. Nippon.** 56:1 Spring:2001 pp.1-20.

4267   El *Tahdīb de al-Barādī'ī* en al-Andalus: a propósito de un manuscrito aljamiado de la Real Academia de la Historia. *[In Spanish]*; [Spanish texts in Arabic characters and the *Real Academia de la Historia*]. Maribel Fierro. **Al-Qantara** XXI:1 2000 pp.227-236.

4268   A tale of two helmets: the Negau A and B inscriptions. Tom Markey. **J. Indo-Eur. S.** 29:1-2 Spring-Summer:2001 pp.69-172.

4269   Text and lineage in early Sikh history: issues in the study of the Adi Granth. Jeevan Singh Deol. **B. Sch. Orient. Afr. Stud.** 64:1 2001 pp.34-58.

4270   El texto castellano del *Códice florentino*: traducción, paráfrasis o interpolación. *[In Spanish]*; [The Castillian text of the *Codex florentino*: translation, paraphrase or interpolation]. Pilar Máynez. **Caravelle** 76-77 12:2001 pp.197-204.

4271   Topografía insospechada de la luna. Las *Memorias de infancia* de José Luis González. *[In Spanish]*; [The Moon's unexpected topography: the *Childhood Memoirs* of José Luis González]. Fatima Rodriguez. **Caravelle** 76-77 12:2001 pp.643-655.

4272   Trade and commerce in Balasore from the literary works of Fakir Mohan Senapati. Brajabandhu Bhatta. **Oris. Hist. R. J.** XLV:1-4 2000 pp.56-67.

4273   Traversing the abyss: Moses Isegawa — an interview and commentary. Jacqui Jones [Interviewer]; Moses Isegawa. **Eng. Afr.** 27:2 10:2000 pp.85-102.

4274   The tree that set forth. Rabindranath Tagore's reception in Hungary. Imre Bangha. **Arch. Orient.** 68:3 8:2000 pp.457-476.

4275   *Triunfo Partenico*: jeroglífico barroco. *[In Spanish]*; [The *Triunfo Partenico*: baroque hieroglyphics]. José Pascual Buxó. **Caravelle** 76-77 12:2001 pp.421-436.

4276   Trois *Maqālāt* au sujet des épidémies de peste en Andalousie et au Maghreb. *[In French]*; [Three *Maqālāt* on the subject of plagues in Andalusia and Maghreb]. S. Gigandet. **Arabica** XLVIII:3 7:2001 pp.401-407.

4277   ¿Una futura resurrección? El *Diario* de Vargas Vila. *[In Spanish]*; [A future resurrection? The diary of Vargas Vila]. Efrin Knight. **Rev. de Human.** 11 Autumn:2001 pp.21-32.

4278   Unmasking Mudrooroo. Maureen Clark. **Kunapipi** XXIII:2 2001 pp.48-62.

4279   The use(s) of genre in Mesopotamian literature. An afterthought. Herman L.J. Vanstiphout. **Arch. Orient.** 67:4 11:1999 pp.703-717.

4280   'Våld mot huvudet' om kriminaljournalistikens text och kontext. *[In Swedish]*; (Blows to the head — text and context in the journalism of crime.) *[Summary]*. Simon Lindgren. **Rig** 3 2001 pp.129-140.

4281   A view of the Hindu family presented in Śivānī's short stories published in the 1980-1990s. Dagmar Marková. **Arch. Orient.** 69:3 8:2001 pp.475-484.

4282   Waldo Frank: el sueño de dos escritores para América. *[In Spanish]*; [Alfonso Reyes and Waldo Frank: two writers' dream of America]. Eugenia Houvenaghel. **Cuad. Am.** XV:3(87) 5-6:2001 pp.24-36.

4283   'Wandering about' as a Utopos of depression in ancient near eastern literature and in the Bible. Michael L. Barré. **J. Near East.** 60:3 7:2001 pp.177-188.

4284   What is in *Kim*? Rudyard Kipling and Tibetan Buddhist traditions. Janice Leoshko. **S. Asia R.** 21:1 Autumn:2001 pp.51-76.

4285   'Where there is no novelty, there can be no curiosity': reading Imoinda's body in Aphra Behn's *Oronooko Or, The Royal Slave*. Pumla Dineo Gqola. **Eng. Afr.** 28:1 5:2001 pp.105-117.

4286   Wisdom — woman or angel in Sirach 24? Jessie Rogers. **J. N.W. Sem. Lang.** 27:1 2001 pp.71-80.

4287   Wise spirits: the limits of modernity in Suwarsih Dojopuspito's *Siluman Karangkobar*. Julie Shackford-Bradley. **R. Ind. Malay. Aff.** 35:1 Winter:2001 pp.1-41.

4288   Years of silence came to an end. Shashi Deshpande; Joel Kuortti [Interviewer]. **Kunapipi** XXIII:2 2001 pp.145-166.

4289   Yoruba writers and the construction of heroes. Toyin Falola. **Hist. Afr.** 24 1997 pp.157-176.

G.5:   **Games, leisure and tourism**
        Jeux, loisirs et tourisme

4290   À la recherche d'Homère. Les aventures de la géographie homérique au XVIIIᵉ siècle. *[In French]*; [In search of Homer. The adventures of Homeric geography in the 18th century]. Georges Tolias. **R. Inst. Sociol.** 1-2 1998 pp.153-164.

4291   Agroturismo: ¿Una alternativa real para la ruralidad mexicana? *[In Spanish]*; [Is agri-tourism a real alternative for rural Mexico?] *[Summary]*. Rosa María Larroa Torres. **Acta Sociol. [Mexico]** 31 1-4:2001 pp.95-122.

4292   Un Allemand découvre le Paris de 1850. *[In French]*; [A German discovers the Paris of 1850]. Roland Mortier. **R. Inst. Sociol.** 1-2 1998 pp.185-196.

4293   'Almost the same, but not quite... Almost the same, but not white': Maori and Aotearoa/New Zealand's 1981 Springbok tour. Malcolm MacLean. **Kunapipi** XXIII:1 2001 pp.69-82.

4294   Anthropology of tourism: forging new ground for ecotourism and other alternatives. Amanda Stronza. **Ann. R. Anthr.** 30 2001 pp.261-284.

4295   The big Koori sports carnival: they called it 'The Olympics'. Wendy Brady. **Kunapipi** XXIII:1 2001 pp.56-62.

4296   Błazen. Maski i metafory. *[In Polish]*; (Jesters: masks and metaphors.) Monika Sznajderman. Gdansk: Słowo Obraz Terytoria, 2000. 267p. *ISBN: 8388560859.*

4297   The body of one color: Indian wrestling, the Indian state, and Utopian somatics. Joseph S. Alter. **Cult. Anthro.** 8:1 2:1993 pp.49-72.

4298   The body of the imperial mother: women, exercise and the future of 'the race' in Britain, 1870-1914. Mandy Treagus. **Kunapipi** XXIII:1 2001 pp.138-150.

4299   The city's many uses: cultural tourism, the sacred monarchy and the preservation of Fez's Medina. Geoffrey D. Porter. **J. N. African Stud.** 5:2 Summer:2000 pp.59-88.

4300   Conceptualising state-controlled resort islands for an environment-friendly development of tourism: the Maldivian experience. Manfred Domroes. **Sing. J. Trop. Geogr.** 22:2 7:2001 pp.122-137.

4301   Contrasting models of land use regulation: community, government and tourism development. Anthony van Fossen; George Lafferty. **Comm. Dev. J.** 36:3 7:2001 pp.198-211.

4302   Coping with marginality: tourism and the projection of Grahamstown, 1870-1955. Jim Davidson. **S. Afr. Hist. J.** 42 2000 pp.176-190.

4303   Cricket — 'passing the test'? Analysis of an interview with David 'Syd' Lawrence. Patrick Ismond. **J. Pop. Cult.** 34:2 Fall:2000 pp.127-146.

4304   The cricketing wonder from Jalandhar. Kushanava Choudhury. **Sikh Rev.** 49:6(570) 6:2001 pp.64-74.

4305   Des taureaux et des hommes: tauromachie et société dans le monde ibérique et ibéro-américain. *[In French]*; [Of bulls and men: the study of bull-fighting and society in the Spanish and Spanish-American world]. Jean-Paul Duviols; Araceli Guillaume-Alonso; Annie Molinié-Bertrand. Paris: Presses de l'Université de Paris-Sorbonne, 1999. 401p. *ISBN: 2840501481. Papers presented at a conference on psychologies and representations in the Spanish and Spanish-American world, Université de Paris IV - Sorbonne, February 1999. Includes bibliographical references.*

4306   Dzitsiachy gul'niovy fal'klor uskhodnikh slavian (ruskaia historyiagrafiia 1917-1941 gg.) *[In Belorussian]*; (Children's games folklore of the eastern Slavs (Russian historiography 1917-1941).) *[Summary]*; *[Summary in Russian]*. A.U. Marozau. **V. Aka. Belarusi** 2 1999 pp.78-83.

4307   Expert model of decision-making system for efficient orientation of basketball players to positions and roles in the game — empirical verification; *[Summary in Croatian]*. B. Dežman; S. Trninić; D. Dizdar. **Coll. Antrop.** 25:1 6:2001 pp.141-152.

4308   Food, time, and heritage tourism in Languedoc, France. Matt Hodges. **Hist. Anthrop.** 12:2 2001 pp.179-212.

4309   Football et représentation territoriale: un club amateur dans un village ouvrier. *[In French]*; (Football and territorial representation: an amateur club in a workers' village.) *[Summary]*; *[Summary in German]*. Nicolas Renahy. **Ethn. Fr.** XXXI:4 10-12:2001 pp.707-716.

4310   Habiter la nature? Le camping. *[In French]*; [Camping - living in nature?] Olivier Sirost; Bernard Kalaora; André Rauch; Arnaud Baubérot; Catherine Bertho Lavenir; Aude Tissandier; Jean Griffet; Martin de La Soudière; Gilles Raveneau; Sergio Dalla Bernardina. **Ethn. Fr.** XXXI:4 10-12:2001 pp.581-694. *Collection of 11 articles.*

4311   L'île-hôtel symbole du tourisme maldivien. *[In French]*; (The island-hotel: tourism's emblem in the Maldives.) *[Summary]*. Jean-Christophe Gay. **Cah. Outre-mer** 54:213 1-3:2001 pp.27-52.

4312   Imaginative sports and African athleticism: colonial representations of Rwandan corporeality. John Bale. **Kunapipi** XXIII:1 2001 pp.11-26.

4313   Is the 'world game' an 'ethnic game' or an 'Aussie game'? Narrating the nation in Australian soccer. Loring M. Danforth. **Am. Ethn.** 28:2 5:2001 pp.363-387.

4314   Jeux et sport en Polynésie ancienne. *[In French]*; [Games and sport in ancient Polynesia]. Douglas Oliver. **Soc. Ét. Océan.** 288 3:2001 pp.2-15.

4315   El juego mapuche en el proceso de globalización humana. *[In Spanish]*; [The Mapuche game and the process of human globalization]. Stela Maris Ferrarese Capettini. **B. Int. Com. Urg. Anthrop. Ethnol. R.** 40 1999-2000 pp.205-214.

4316   The Maasai and the Lion King: authenticity, nationalism, and globalization in African tourism. Edward M. Bruner. **Am. Ethn.** 28:4 11:2001 pp.881-923.

4317   Management of historic centres. Rob Pickard [Ed.]. London: E & FN Spon, 2000. 256p. *ISBN: 0419232907. Includes index.*

4318   Mashonaland branch outing to the Rusape area. Vivienne Somerville. **Herit. Zimb.** 10 1991 pp.99-101.

4319   Obnova hiše čigoć 26, naravni park Lonjsko polje. *[In Slovene]*; (Renovation of the house at 26 Čigoć. The Lonjsko Polje nature reserve.) Ana Mlinar. **Bull. Slov. Ethno. Soc.** 41:3-4 2001 pp.79-83.

4320   Pampang culture village and international tourism in East Kalimantan, Indonesian Borneo. Anne Schiller. **Human. Org.** 60:4 Winter:2001 pp.414-422.

4321   Pèlerinage à Marie: Lorette dans la littérature de voyage. *[In French]*; [Pilgrimage to Marie: Lorette in travel literature]. François Moureau. **R. Inst. Sociol.** 1-2 1998 pp.11-28.

4322   Le pèlerinage istanbouliote de Pierre Loti. *[In French]*; [The Istanbul pilgrimage of Pierre Loti]. Jacques Huré. **R. Inst. Sociol.** 1-2 1998 pp.41-52.

4323   Le pèlerinage littéraire dans les Mascareignes aux XIXe et XXe siècles. *[In French]*; [The literary pilgrimage in the Mascareignes in the nineteenth and twentieth centuries]. Sophie-Jenny Linon-Chipon. **R. Inst. Sociol.** 1-2 1998 pp.101-118.

4324   The Pieter Lourens Van Der Byl trek. J.W. Bousfield. **Herit. Zimb.** 10 1991 pp.102-104.

4325   Poti dediščine — na obeh straneh reke Kolpe. *[In Slovene]*; (Heritage trails — on both sides of the River Kolpa.) *[Summary]*. Tihana Stepinac Fabijanić. **Bull. Slov. Ethno. Soc.** 41:3-4 2001 pp.70-74.

4326   Problematika stanja in varstva nepremične etnološke dediščine v Republiki Sloveniji. *[In Slovene]*; (Outlines for professional groundwork on planning regulations in heritage protection.) *[Summary]*. Zvezda Delak Koželj. **Bull. Slov. Ethno. Soc.** 41:3-4 2001 pp.60-64.

4327   A program to develop a national register of cultural heritage properties for Jordan. Julia G. Costello; Gaetano Palumbo [Contrib.]. **A. Dept. Antiq. Jordan** XXXIX 1995 pp.541-552.

4328   Promoting travel clinic referrals: exploring partnerships for healthier travel. Laura MacDougall; Theresa Gyorkos. **Soc. Sci. Med.** 53:11 12:2001 pp.1461-1468.

4329   Qal'at el-Mishnaqa: restoration and tourist development. Luigi Marino. **A. Dept. Antiq. Jordan** XXXVII 1993 pp.397-406.

4330   Queer pilgrimage: the San Francisco homeland and identity tourism. Alyssa Cymene Howe. **Cult. Anthro.** 16:1 2:2001 pp.35-61.

4331   La route du poisson. Le sport au service du patrimoine. *[In French]*; (Sports in the service of cultural heritage.) *[Summary]*; *[Summary in German]*. Olivier Pégard; Jérôme Pruneau. **Ethn. Fr.** XXXI:1 1-3:2001 pp.161-168.

4332   La sacralisation du paysage dans le voyage en Suisse au début du XIXe siècle. *[In French]*; [The sacralisation of the countryside in Swiss journies at the start of the 19th century]. Claude Reichler. **R. Inst. Sociol.** 1-2 1998 pp.29-40.

4333   Schach im Iran. *[In German]*; [Chess in Iran]. M. Abka'I-Khavari. **Iran. Ant.** XXXVI 2001 pp.329-360.

4334   Schamanismus und Tourismus in der Mongolei. *[In German]*; (Shamanism and tourism in Mongolia.) *[Summary]*. Judith Schlehe; Helmut Weber. **Z. Ethn.** 126:1 2001 pp.93-116.

4335   Spectacular quetzals, ecotourism, and environmental futures in Monte Verde, Costa Rica. Luis A. Vivanco. **Ethnology** XL:2 Spring:2001 pp.79-92.

4336   Sport in Latin American society: past and present. J.A. Mangan; Joseph L. Arbena; Cesar R. Torres; Vic Duke; Liz Crolley; Thomas Carter; Cesar Gordon; Ronaldo Helal; Robert Chappell; Lamartine P. DaCosta. **Int. J. Hist. Sport** 18:3 9:2001 pp.1-196. *Collection of 9 articles.*

4337   Sports, gambling, and government: America's first social compact? Warren D. Hill; John E. Clark. **Am. Anthrop.** 103:2 6:2001 pp.331-345.

4338   Structural adjustment programmes and the international tourism trade in Ghana, 1983-99: some socio-spatial implications; *[Summary in French]*. Kwadwo Konadu-Agyemang. **Tour. Geog.** 3:2 5:2001 pp.187-206.

4339   Tourism and spatial development initiatives: the case of the Maputo development corridor. Christian M. Rogerson. **S. Afr. Geogr. J.** 83:2 2001 pp.124-136.

4340   Tourism satellite account: recommended methodological framework. Statistical Office of the European Communities. Luxembourg; New York: Commission of the European Communities; Eurostat; United Nations - United Nations (Publications), 2001. xii, 138p. *ISBN: 9264176969, 9211614384, 9284404371. Includes bibliographical references (p. 132-133) and index.*

4341   Tourisme et voyage littéraire. *[In French]*; [Tourism and the literary journey]. Claude Javeau. **R. Inst. Sociol.** 1-2 1998 pp.133-140.

4342   (Troubling) spaces of mountains and men: New Zealand's Mount Cook and Hermitage Lodge. Karen M. Morin; Robyn Longhurst; Lynda Johnston. **Soc. Cult. Geog.** 2:2 6:2001 pp.117-140.

4343   Unpacking the canoe: alternative perspectives on the canoe as a national symbol. Susan Knabe; Wendy Pearson. **Kunapipi** XXIII:1 2001 pp.114-129.

4344   Varstvo etnografske dediščine na prehodu stoletja. *[In Slovene]*; [Protection of ethnographic heritage in the new century]. Nada Duić Kowalsky. **Bull. Slov. Ethno. Soc.** 41:3-4 2001 pp.65-69.

4345   Vas Blaževci ob kolpi v Gorskem Kotarju — stanje ljudskega stavbarstva in možnosti ohranitve. *[In Slovene]*; (The village of Blaževci by the River Kolpa in Gorski Kotar - the situation of rural architecture and prospects for preservation.) *[Summary]*. Manja Horvat; Ksenija Marković; Zdravko Živković. **Bull. Slov. Ethno. Soc.** 41:3-4 2001 pp.84-88.

4346   The *Via Nova Traiana* in northern Jordan: a cultural resource under threat. David Kennedy. **A. Dept. Antiq. Jordan** XXXIX 1995 pp.221-228.

4347   Viajeros alemanes a Venezuela en el siglo XIX. *[In Spanish]*; [German travellers in Venezuela during the 19th century] *[Summary]*. José Ángel Rodríguez. **Jahrb. Ges. Lat.am.** 38 2001 pp.233-244.

4348   The White man's body: Danish gymnasts in South Africa, 1939. Hans Bonde. **S. Afr. Hist. J.** 44 2001 pp.143-162.

G.6:   **Food and festivals**
         Nourriture et fêtes

4349   *Al-Gēs*: women's festival and drama in Mecca. Ahmad A. Nasr; Abu Bakar A. Bagader. **J. Folk. Res.** 38:3 9-12:2001 pp.243-262.

4350   America's public holidays, 1865-1920. Ellen M. Litwicki. Washington DC: Smithsonian Institution Press, 2000. ix, 293p. *ISBN: 1560988630. Includes bibliographical references (p. 249-286) and index.*

4351   A calendar of days: the Pécs International Folk Days; *[Summary in French]*. Andrew C. Rouse. **Ethnologies** 23:1 2001 pp.147-166.

4352   Celebrating ethnicity and nation: American festive culture from the Revolution to the early twentieth century. Kai Dreisbach [Ed.]; Geneviève Fabre [Ed.]; European Association for American Studies; Jürgen Heideking [Ed.]. New York, Oxford: Berghahn Books, 2000. vi, 308p. *ISBN: 1571812377. (Series:* European studies in American history).

4353   Celebrations as social investments: festival expenditures, unit price variation and social status in rural India. Vijayendra Rao. **J. Dev. Stud.** 38:1 10:2001 pp.71-97.

4354   Chleb nasz powszedni. O pieczywie w obrzędach, magii, literackich obrazach i opiniach dietetyków. *[In Polish]*; [Our daily bread: about bread in rituals, magic, literary representation and the opinions of dieticians]. Piotr Kowalski. Wroclaw: Towarzystwo Przyjaciół Ossolineum, 2000. 252p. *ISBN: 8370950426.*

4355   Coordinates of power and performance festivals as sites of (re)presentation and reclamation in Sardinia; *[Summary in French]*. Sabina Magliocco. **Ethnologies** 23:1 2001 pp.167-188.

4356   Cultural performance, subjectivity and space: Osaka's Korean festival. L.H. Lee. **Geogr. Rev. Jpn.** 74:1 2001 pp.78-91.

4357   Festivity and popular memory in southern India. Mary Hancock. **S. Asia R.** 21:1 Autumn:2001 pp.1-22.

4358   Food for health, food for wealth: the performance of ethnic and gender identities by Iranian settlers in Britain. Lynn Harbottle. New York: Berghahn Books, 2000. vii, 184p. *ISBN: 1571817409. Includes bibliographical references (p. [171]-181) and index. (Series:* The anthropology of food and nutrition - 3).

4359   For ourselves, our neighbours, our homelands: religion in Folklorama's Israel Pavilion; *[Summary in French]*. Paul Bramadat. **Ethnologies** 23:1 2001 pp.211-232.

4360   The Gangneung Dano festival: the folklorization of the Korean shamanistic heritage. Hyun-key Kim Hogarth. **Korea J.** 41:3 Autumn:2001 pp.254-284.

4361   Introduction. Pauline Greenhill. **Ethnologies** 23:1 2001 pp.5-22. *Article in English and French.*

4362   'Like king and queen, like Balinese and Sasak' musical narratives at the Lingsar temple festival in Lombok, Indonesia; *[Summary in French]*. David Harnish. **Ethnologies** 23:1 2001 pp.63-88.

4363   Parade zouloue et carnaval indien, un Mardi Gras différent à la Nouvelle-Orléans. *[In French]*; [Zulu parade and Indian carnival: a different Mardi Gras from New Orleans] *[Summary]*. Martine Geronimi. **Ethnologies** 23:1 2001 pp.89-122.

4364   Producing locality: space, houses and public culture in a Hindu festival in Malaysia. Yeoh Seng Guan. **Contr. I. Soc.** 35:1 1-4:2001 pp.33-64.

4365   Putting a price on culture ethnic organisations, volunteers, and the marketing of multicultural festivals; *[Summary in French]*. Cynthia Thoroski; Pauline Greenhill. **Ethnologies** 23:1 2001 pp.189-210.

4366   Realities of the carnival expressed by ethnographic film. Sanja Puljar D'Alessio. **Nar. Umjetn.** 38:1 2001 pp.67-88.

4367   Repulsion to ritual interpreting folk festivals in the Polish Tatras; *[Summary in French]*. Timothy J. Cooley. **Ethnologies** 23:1 2001 pp.233-254.

4368   Rethinking the public sphere: the Ganapati festival and media competitions in Mumbai. Raminder Kaur. **S. Asia R.** 21:1 Autumn:2001 pp.23-50.

4369   Septiembre: mes de la patria en la Ciudad de México y poblaciones aledañas en el siglo XIX (Parte primera). *[In Spanish]*; [September: *mes de la patria* in Mexico City and surrounding villages during the 19th century (part 1)] *[Summary]*. Verónica Zárate Toscano. **Jahrb. Ges. Lat.am.** 38 2001 pp.183-206.

4370   Sikhs on march: the 14th Annual Sikh Day Parade in New York. I.J. Singh. **Sikh Rev.** 49:7(571) 7:2001 pp.42-44.

4371   Święto i zabawa. Odpusty parafialne na Górnym Śląsku. *[In Polish]*; (Piety and revelry: parish church fetes in the region of Upper Silesia.) *[Summary]*. Dorota Świtała-Trybek. Wroclaw: Polskie Towarzystwo Ludoznawcze, 2000. 172p. *ISBN: 8387266507.*

4372   The traditional craft of Christmas form letters. Diane Tye. **Fabula** 42:3-4 2001 pp.201-212.

4373   L'udová zábava v obrade. *[In Slovak]*; (Popular entertainment in ceremonies.) *[Summary]*. Malgorzata Maj. **Slov. Národop.** 47:2-3 1999 pp.205-210.

Food and drink
Alimentation

4374   'Beer used to belong to older men': drink and authority among the Nyakusa of Tanzania; *[Summary in French]*. Justin Willis. **Africa** 71:3 2001 pp.373-390.

4375   Between fasting and feasting: the literary and archaeobotanical evidence for monastic diet in Late Antique Egypt. Mary Harlow; Wendy Smith. **Antiquity** 75:290 12:2001 pp.758-768.

4376   Le cari partagé: anthropologie de l'alimentation à l'île de la Réunion. *[In French]*; [Shared curry: the anthropology of food on the island of Réunion]. Patrice Cohen; Françoise Loux [Foreword]. Paris: Karthala, 2000. 358p. *ISBN: 284586017X. Includes bibliographical references (p. [337]-352).*

4377   Ethnobotany of ku-nu-che: Cherokee hickory nut soup. Gayle J. Fritz; et al. **J. Ethnobio.** 21:2 Winter:2001 pp.1-28.

4378   Food and education. Martin Bruegel; Séverine Gojard; Blandine Bril; Estelle Hombessa-Nkounkou; Jean-François Bouville; Célina Ocampo; Séverine Gojard; Karola Elwert-Kretschmer; Lucy M. Long. **Food Food.** 9:3-4 2001 pp.149-259. *Collection of 5 articles.*

4379   Food, drink and identity: cooking, eating and drinking in Europe since the Middle Ages. Peter Scholliers [Ed.]. Oxford: Berg Publishers, 2001. 221p. *ISBN: 1859734618, 1859734561. Includes index.*

4380   From Minnesota fat to Seoul food: spam in America and the Pacific Rim. George H. Lewis. **J. Pop. Cult.** 34:2 Fall:2000 pp.83-106.

4381   The giving of leftovers in medieval England. Maria A. Moisà. **Food Food.** 9:2 2001 pp.81-94.

4382   *In imago veritas.* Images souhaitées, images produites. *[In French]*; (*In imago veritas.* Images wished, images produced.) *[Summary]*; *[Summary in German]*. Philippe Chaudat. **Ethn. Fr.** XXXI:4 10-12:2001 pp.717-724.

4383   L'interprétation symbolique des lois alimentaires dans la lettre d'Aristée: une influence pythagoricienne. *[In French]*; [Sybolic interpretation of dietry rules in Aristée: a pythagoras influence]. Katell Berthelot. **J. Jew. Stud.** LII:2 Autumn:2001 pp.253-268.

4384   Jewish cuisine. David Apfelbaum. **Ethnology** XL:2 Spring:2001 pp.165-169.

4385   Knowing, gathering and eating: knowledge and attitudes about wild food in an Isan village in northeastern Thailand; *[Summary in Spanish]*; *[Summary in French]*. P. Somnasang; G. Moreno-Black. **J. Ethnobio.** 20:2 Winter:2000 pp.197-222.

4386   Kul't pishchi i pishchevoi animatizm. *[In Russian]*; (Cult of food and food animatism.) *[Summary]*. B.Kh. Bgazhnokov. **Etnograf. Oboz.** 2 3-4:2001 pp.103-111.

4387   Like water for chocolate: feasting and political ritual among the late classic Maya at Xunantunich, Belize. Lisa J. LeCount. **Am. Anthrop.** 103:4 12:2001 pp.935-953.

4388   Loss and recovery: patrimonial food of Andalusia. Isabel González Turmo. **Food Food.** 9:2 2001 pp.95-114.

4389   Not feasting with friends: the meaning of meat in Anganen. Michael Nihill. **Oceania** 71:4 6:2001 pp.265-278.

4390   The place of drink: temperance and the public, 1856-1914. James Kneale. **Soc. Cult. Geog.** 2:1 3:2001 pp.43-60.

4391   Produits carnés, sensibilité animalière et tradition. Les bœufs festifs de Barjols (Var). *[In French]*; (Meat products, sensitivity to animals and tradition: festive cattle in Barjols (France).) Danièle Dossetto. **Rural Stud.** :157-158 1-6:2001 pp.141-158.

4392   Un regard sur la tradition alimentaire vietnamienne à travers le parler populaire. *[In French]*; [A look at Vietnamese dietary tradition through popular speech]. Xuân Hiên Nguyen. **Péninsule** 40 2000 pp.111-154.

4393   Reservation food sharing among the ache of Paraguay. Michael Gurven; Wesley Allen-Arave; Kim Hill; A. Magdalena Hurtado. **Hum. Nature** 12:4 2001 pp.273-298.

4394   Sharing, consumption, and patch choice on Ifaluk Atoll. Evaluating an explanatory hypothesis. Richard Sosis. **Hum. Nature** 12:3 2001 pp.221-246.

4395   Views about food prejudice and stereotypes. Igor de Garine. **Soc. Sci. Info.** 40:3 9:2001 pp.487-505.

4396   Why vegetable recipes are not very spicy. Paul W. Sherman; Geoffrey A. Hash. **Evol. Hum. Behav.** 22:3 5:2001 pp.147-163.

4397   Wine makes good blood: wine culture among Toronto Italians. Luisa Del Giudice. **Ethnologies** 22:2 2000 pp.209-236.

CULTURE, PERSONALITY, IDENTITY
CULTURE, PERSONNALITÉ, IDENTITÉ

Ethnicity
Ethnicité

4398   A case of mistaken identity: why British 'African Asians' are not an 'ethnic' community. John Mattausch. **S. Asia R.** 20:2 Spring:2000 pp.171-182.

4399   The contested role of heterogeneity in collective action: some evidence from community forestry in Nepal. G. Varughese; E. Ostrom. **World Dev.** 29:5 5:2001 pp.747-765.

4400   Convergence and divergence: interfaces between ethnicity and organisational culture; *[Summary in Afrikaans]*. Stephné Herselman. **S. Afr. J. Ethnol.** 24:4 2001 pp.125-130.

4401   Do the ties still bind: reflections on Pan-African consciousness and identity in the twentieth century. William Ackah. **Afr. Q.** 41:1-2 1-6:2001 pp.19-40.

4402   Fistfights at the Moscow Choral Synagogue: ethnicity and ritual in post-Soviet Russia. Sascha L. Goluboff. **Anthr. Quart.** 74:2 4:2001 pp.55-71.

4403   Food for health, food for wealth: the performance of ethnic and gender identities by Iranian settlers in Britain. Lynn Harbottle. New York: Berghahn Books, 2000. vii, 184p. *ISBN: 1571817409. Includes bibliographical references (p. [171]-181) and index. (Series:* The anthropology of food and nutrition - 3).

4404   Hrvatske etničke zajednice u Europi. Prilog za bibliografiju. *[In Croatian]*; (Croatian ethnic communities in Europe. Contribution to the bibliography.) Jelica Leščić. **Etnoloska** 23:30 2000 pp.135-156.

4405   Identité et territoire chez les Kali'na. À propos d'un récit du retour des morts. *[In French]*; (Identity and territory among the Kali'na. From a narrative of the return of the dead.) *[Summary]*; *[Summary in Spanish]*. Gérard Collomb. **J. Soc. Amér.** 86 2000 pp.149-168.

4406   Identity and gender in hunting and gathering societies. Ian Keen; Takako Yamada; Elena Glavatskaia; Christer Norström; Victor Shnirelman; Lisa Hiwasaki; Toshiaki Inoue; Will Karkavelas; Robin Ridington; Russell Taylor; Jean-Guy A. Goulet; Kaoru Imamura; Zubeeda Banu Quraishy; Sita Venkateswar; Elena G. Fedorova. **Senri Ethn. Stud.** 56 2001 pp.1-257. *Collection of 18 articles.*

4407   L'implosion de la modernité: un nouveau tribalisme. *[In French]*; (The implosion of modernity: a new tribalism.) *[Summary]*. Johnathan Friedman. **Pensée** 325 1-3:2001 pp.21-34.

4408   Índios e antropologia: reflexões sobre cultura, etnicidade e situação de contato. *[In Portuguese]*; [Indians and anthropology: reflections on culture, ethnicity and contact situations] *[Summary]*. Rinaldo Sérgio Vieira Arruda. **Bol. Mus. Par. Emílio Goeldi** 15:1 7:1999 pp.33-90.

4409   Interlingual variables in measuring and interpreting the degree of ethnicity in speech. Margaret Jepkirui Muthwii. **S. Afr. J. Afr. Lang.** 20:4 2000 pp.353-369.

4410   Kalmyki v S.SH.A.: kaleidoskop identichnostei. *[In Russian]*; (Kalmyks in the U.S.A. - a kaleidoscope of identities.) *[Summary]*. E.B.M. Guchinova. **Etnograf. Oboz.** 4 7-8:2000 pp.108-118.

4411   Kazakhskaia diaspora v Rossii: etnicheskoe samosoznanie i migratsionnoe povedenie. *[In Russian]*; (Kazakh diaspora in Russia: ethnic identity and migratory behaviour.) O.B. Naumova. **Etnograf. Oboz.** 3 5-6:2000 pp.60-73.

4412   Korni i krona (mistika i metafizika v konstruirovanii statusa 'korennykh narodov'). *[In Russian]*; (The roots and the crown (mysticism and metaphysics in indigenous peoples' status construction).) *[Summary]*. S.V. Sokolovskii. **Etnograf. Oboz.** 3 5-6:2000 pp.3-8.

4413   Das Lob der Mischung, Reinheit als Gefahr: Nationalismus und Ethnizität in Gibraltar. *[In German]*; [Praise for mixing, purity as danger: nationalism and ethnicity in Gibraltar] *[Summary]*. Dieter Haller. **Z. Ethn.** 126:1 2001 pp.27-62.

4414   Narrations of shifting Maya identities. Peter Hervik. **B. Lat. Am. Res.** 20:3 7:2001 pp.342-359.

4415   Negotiated and mediated meanings: ethnicity and politics in Israeli newspapers. Daniel Lefkowitz. **Anthr. Quart.** 74:4 10:2001 pp.179-189.

4416   Reconstructing ethnicity: recorded and remembered identity in Taiwan. Melissa J. Brown. **Ethnology** XL:2 Spring:2001 pp.153-164.

4417   Rethinking diaspora(s): stateless power in the transnational moment. Khachig Tölölyan. **Diaspora** 5:1 Spring:1996 pp.3-36.

4418   South African customary law and ethnicity: challenges for South Africa; *[Summary in Afrikaans]*. L.P. Vorster. **S. Afr. J. Ethnol.** 24:4 2001 pp.119-124.

4419   'This guy is Japanese stuck in a white man's body': a discussion of meaning making, identity slippage, and cross-cultural adaptation. William S. Armour. **J. Multiling.** 22:1 2001 pp.1-18.

4420   Una mirada sobre la etnicidad en el Perú. *[In Portuguese]*; [A look at ethnicity in Peru] *[Summary]*. Ladislao Landa Vásquez. **Bol. Mus. Par. Emílio Goeldi** 15:1 7:1999 pp.91-124.

4421   'Will the model minority please identify itself?' American ethnic identity and its discontents. Ruth Y. Hsu. **Diaspora** 5:1 Spring:1996 pp.37-64.

Identity
Identité

4422   Aboriginality, identity and belonging in South Africa and beyond. Duncan Brown. **Eng. Afr.** 28:1 5:2001 pp.67-90.

4423   Ambivalent Europeans: ritual, memory, and the public sphere in Malta. Jon P. Mitchell. New York, London: Routledge, 2001. 275p. *ISBN: 0415271525. Includes bibliographical references and index.*

4424   Anthropological methods of studying Jewish identity in Hungary and Wales; *[Summary in Polish]*. Leonard Mars. **Ethnol. Pol.** 21 2000 pp.53-64.

4425   Australian (alter)natives: cultural drama and indigeneity. Graham St. John. **Soc. Anal.** [Adelaide] 45(1) 4:2001 pp.122-140.

4426   Between worlds of exchange: ethnicity among Peruvian market women. Linda J. Seligmann. **Cult. Anthro.** 8:2 5:1993 pp.187-213.

4427   Blind spots in portraiture: on Oz Almog's *Ha-tsabar—Dyokan, sabra*: the creation of the new Jew. Yael Ben-Zvi. **Jew. Soc. Stud.** 7:1 Fall:2000 pp.167-174.

4428   Bulgarie: voix d'hier, paroles d'aujourd'hui. *[In French]*; [Bulgaria: a voice from the past and present]. Stefana Stoykova; Stoyanka Boyadzhieva; Anna Ilieva; Anna Shtarbanova; Dimitrina Kaufman; Nikolai Kaufman; Ivanichka Georgieva; Elka Bakalova; Mila Santova; Iveta Todorova-Pirgova; Doroteya Dobreva; Petar Petrov; Haralan Aleksandrov; Ivaylo Ditchev; Frédéric Saumade. **Ethn. Fr.** XXXI:2 4-6:2001 pp.199-336. *Collection of 13 articles.*

4429   The Citadel — a metaphor for the study of the European Union identity? Monica Heintz. **Cam. Anthrop.** 22:2 2000-2001 pp.37-49.

4430   Constructing identity through ceremonial language in rural Fiji. Karen J. Brison. **Ethnology** XL:4 Fall:2001 pp.309-328.

4431   Constructions of community and identity among Indians in colonial Natal, 1860-1910: the role of the *Muharram* festival. Goolam Vahed. **Espace Pop. Soc.** 43:1 2002 pp.77-93.

4432   Contesting traditional culture in post-colonial Maori society. On the tension between culture and identity. Toon van Meijl. **Paideuma** 47 2001 pp.129-146.

4433   The cultural identity of minority children in the multicultural environment of eastern Poland; *[Summary in Polish]*. Dorota Misiejuk. **Ethnol. Pol.** 21 2000 pp.75-86.

4434   Cultural studies and discourse analysis: a dialogue on language and identity. Chris Barker; Dariusz Galasiński. London: Sage Publications, 2001. viii, 192p. *ISBN: 0761963847, 0761963839. Includes bibliographical references and index.*

4435   Desde abajo: la transformación de las identidades sociales. *[In Spanish]*; [Coming from below: the transformation of social identity]. Maristella. Svampa [Ed.]; Javier. Auyero; et al, San Miguel: Universidad Nacional de General Sarmiento, 2000. 252p. *ISBN: 9507862676. Includes bibliographical references (p. 243-250).*

4436   Difference, identity, and access to official discourses. Haillom, 'Bushmen,' and a recent Namibian ethnography. Sian Sullivan. **Anthropos [St. Augustin]** 96:1 2001 pp.179-192.

4437   Entextualizing famine, reconstituting self: testimonial narratives from Ireland. Eileen Moore Quinn. **Anthr. Quart.** 74:2 4:2001 pp.72-88.

4438   Essential marking: Maori tattooing and the properties of cultural identity. Stephen Pritchard. **Theory Cult. Soc.** 18:4 8:2001 pp.27-46.

4439   Eternal present: poetic figuration and cultural memory in the poetry of Yehuda Amichai, Dan Pagis, and Tuvia Rübner. Amir Eshel. **Jew. Soc. Stud.** 7:1 Fall:2000 pp.141-166.

4440   The fatal splitting. Symbolizing anxiety in post-Soviet Russia. Serguei A. Oushakine. **Ethnos** 66:3 2001 pp.291-319.

4441   Frontiers of faith: religious exchange and the constitution of religious identities. 1400-1750. Eszter Andor [Ed.]; István György Tóth [Ed.]. Budapest: CEU - European Science Foundation, 2001. 295p. *Includes bibliographical references.* (*Series:* Cultural exchange in Europe, 1400-1750 - 1).

4442   Globalization and the cultivation of peripheral vision. June Nash. **Anthr. Today** 17:4 8:2001 pp.15-22.

4443   Graves, groves and gardens: place and identity — Central Maluku, Indonesia. Phillip Winn. **Asia Pacific J. Anthr.** 2:1 4:2001 pp.24-44.

4444   H. N. Bialik and the quest for ethical identity. Dan Miron. **Heb. St.** XLI 2000 pp.189-208.

4445   Historical memory in Abraham Geiger's account of modern Jewish identity. Ken Koltun-Fromm. **Jew. Soc. Stud.** 7:1 Fall:2000 pp.109-126.

4446   L'identità culturale degli italiani. *[In Italian]*; (On the cultural identity of the Italians.) Roberto Cipriani. **Critica Sociol.** 136 Winter:2000-2001 pp.1-17.

4447   Identity constructions among the Mande. Dorothea Schulz; Allen M. Howard; Alice Bellagama; Robert Launay; Marie Miran; Marie Nathalie LeBlanc. **Paideuma** 46 2000 pp.7-136. *Collection of 6 articles.*

4448   Identity in a post-communist Balkan state: an Albanian village study. Douglas Saltmarshe. Aldershot: Ashgate, 2001. 237p. *ISBN: 0754617270. Includes bibliographical references.*

4449   Identity in the globalising world; *[Summary in French]*; *[Summary in German]*; *[Summary in Spanish]*. Zygmunt Bauman. **Soc. Anthrop.** 9:2 6:2001 pp.121-130.

4450   Indian giver or Nobel savage: duping, assumptions of identity, and other double entendres in Rigoberta Menchú Tum's Stoll/en past. Diane M. Nelson. **Am. Ethn.** 28:2 5:2001 pp.303-331.

4451   The Jewish community of Kaifeng in China. Y. Du. **Eur. Stud. Y.** 73 2001 pp.176-177.

4452   Journey to the center of the earth: the Caribbean as master symbol. Aisha Khan. **Cult. Anthro.** 16:3 8:2001 pp.271-302.

4453   Know who you are and where you come from. Debra Sparrow; Lycia Danielle Trouton [Interviewer]. **Kunapipi** XXIII:2 2001 pp.79-93.

4454   Kulturna identiteta in etnologija v okviru moderne globalizacije. *[In Slovene]*; (Cultural identity and ethnology within the framework of modern globalisation.) *[Summary]*. Inga Miklavčič Brezigar. **Bull. Slov. Ethno. Soc.** 41:1-2 2001 pp.34-40.

4455   Listening patterns and identity of the Korean diaspora in the former USSR. Hae-Kyung Um. **Brit. J. Ethnomusic.** 9:2 2000 pp.121-142.

4456   *Mi les long yupela usim flag bilong mi*: symbols and identity in Papua New Guinea. Andrew J. Strathern; Pamela J. Stewart. **Pac. Stud.** 23:1-2 3-6:2000 pp.21-50.

4457   Native Pacific cultural studies on the edge. Margaret Jolly; Geoffrey M. White; Ty Kāwika Tengan; Jonathan Kamakawiwo'ole Osorio; Teresia K. Teaiwa; Vicente M. Diaz; J. Kēhaulani Kauanui; James Clifford; David Welchman Gegeo; Karin von Strokirch; David A. Chappell; John Moffat Fugui; Anita Jowitt; Sandra Tarte. **Cont. Pac.** 13:2 Fall:2001 pp.315-563. *Collection of 9 articles.*

4458 Northern lights: the making and unmaking of Karafuto identity. Tessa Morris-Suzuki. **J. Asian St.** 60:3 8:2001 pp.645-672.

4459 Las nuevas religiones en México como forma de identidad colectiva. *[In Spanish]*; [New religions in Mexico as a form of collective identity]. Yolotl Gonzalez Torres. **B. Int. Com. Urg. Anthrop. Ethnol. R.** 40 1999-2000 pp.163-170.

4460 Of ships and saints: history, memory, and place in the making of *moreno* Mexican identity. Laura A. Lewis. **Cult. Anthro.** 16:1 2:2001 pp.62-82.

4461 On stoves, sex, and slave-girls: rabbinic orthodoxy and the definition of Jewish identity. Daniel Boyarin. **Heb. St.** XLI 2000 pp.169-188.

4462 Participation as resistance: the role of Pentecostal Christianity in maintaining identity for Marshallese migrants living in the midwestern United States. Linda Allen. **J. Rit. Stud.** 15:2 2001 pp.55-61.

4463 Peoples of the gourd: imagined ethnicities in highland Southeast Asia. Frank Proschan. **J. Asian St.** 60:4 11:2001 pp.999-1032.

4464 Popculture China. Chua Beng-Huat. **Sing. J. Trop. Geogr.** 22:2 7:2001 pp.113-121.

4465 Powwows and identity on the Piedmont and coastal plains of North Carolina. Chris Goertzen. **Ethnomusicology** 45:1 Winter:2001 pp.58-88.

4466 Pre-judice and identity. Heidrun Friese. **Patt. Prej.** 35:2 4:2001 pp.63-80.

4467 The Rab Šāqēh at the wall of Jerusalem: Israelite identity in the face of the Assyrian 'other'. Peter Machinist. **Heb. St.** XLI 2000 pp.151-168.

4468 'Race places': changing locations of Jewish identities. Sascha L. Goluboff; Gelya Frank; Katya Gibel Azoulay; Jeffrey D. Feldman. **Identities** 8:2 6:2001 pp.163-312. *Collection of 5 articles.*

4469 Random mind: towards an appreciation of openness in individual, society and anthropology. Nigel Rapport. **Aus. J. Anth.** 12:2 8:2001 pp.190-208.

4470 Riverine crossings: gender, identity and the reconstruction of national mythic narrative in *The Crying Game*. Margot Gaylor Backus; James Doan. **Cult. St.** 15:1 1:2001 pp.173-191.

4471 The saffron army, violence, terror(ism): Buddhism, identity, and difference in Sri Lanka. Ananda Abeysekara. **Numen** XLVIII:1 2001 pp.1-46.

4472 Savoir colonial, missions chrétiennes et nationalisme en Angola. *[In French]*; (Colonial knowledge, Christian missions and nationalism in Angola.) *[Summary]*. Didier Péclard. **Genèses** 45 12:2001 pp.114-133.

4473 Triangulation and confirmation in the study of Welsh concepts of personhood. Carol Trosset; Douglas Caulkins. **J. Anthr. Res.** 57:1 Spring:2001 pp.61-81.

4474 Tribals: the politics of identity construction. Fernando Franco; Suguna Ramanathan; Sarvar V. Sherry Chand. **Ind. Soc. Sci. R.** 3:1 1-6:2001 pp.145-174.

4475 The 'true *nzema*': a layered identity; *[Summary in French]*. Pierluigi Valsecchi. **Africa** 71:3 2001 pp.391-425.

4476 Utopijna idea słowiańskiej jedności w świetle podziałów w łonie katolicyzmu i prawosławia oraz konfliktów między „siostrzanymi kościołami" (przykład Słowian wschodnich i zachodnich). *[In Polish]*; (The Utopian idea of Slavonic unity in the light of religious divisions within Roman Catholicism and the Russian Orthodox Church and the conflict of 'sister churches'. The case of the Eastern and Western Slavs.) *[Summary]*. Iwona Kabzińska. **Etn. Polska** XLV:1-2 2001 pp.99-116.

4477 Verbalno nasilje i (raz)gradnja kolektivnih identiteta u iskazima ratnih zarobljenika i političkih zatvorenika (1945-1995). *[In Croatian]*; (Verbal violence and (de)construction of collective identities in the accounts of war and political prisoners (1945-1995).) *[Summary]*. Renata Jambrešić Kirin. **Nar. Umjetn.** 37:2 2000 pp.181-237.

4478 Why insist on an Asian flavor? Fernando N. Zialcita. **Phil. Stud.** 48:4 2000 pp.523-571.

4479 Yugoslav Jewry: aspect of post-World War II and post-Yugoslav developments. Ari Kerkkänen. **Stud. Orient.** 93 2001 pp.3-237.

4480 The Yugur nationality of China. Y. Du. **Eur. Stud. Y.** 73 2001 pp.174-176.

National identity
Identité nationale

4481 'Archipelagic culture' as an exclusionary government discourse in Indonesia. Greg Acciaioli. **Asia Pacific J. Anthr.** 2:1 4:2001 pp.1-23.

4482 The body of the nation: terrorism and the embodiment of nationalism in contemporary Israel. Meira Weiss. **Anthr. Quart.** 75:1 Winter:2001 pp.37-62.

4483 Brazilians in Portugal, Portuguese in Brazil: constructions of sameness and difference. Bela Feldman-Bianco. **Identities** 8:4 12:2001 pp.607-650.

4484 Danskhed. *[In Danish]*; [Danishness]. Ansa Lønstrup; Kusum Gopal; Tine Damsholt; Joel Leonard Katz; Evgenij Kluev; Inge Adriansen; Georg Brandes. **Tids. Antrop.** 42 2000 pp.7-104. *Collection of 7 articles.*

4485 The erroneous zones in the Western classical theory of nationalism and the contemporary development of inter-ethno-national political thinking. Zhu Lun. **Soc. Sci. China** XXV:4 Winter:2001 pp.128-139.

4486 Est' li budushchee u russkoi idei? *[In Russian]*; (Does the Russian idea have a future?) *[Summary]*. O.D. Volkogonova. **Mir Rossii** IX:2 2000 pp.28-52.

4487 Expo.02: exhibiting Swiss identity. Ola Söderström. **Ecumene** 8:4 10:2001 pp.497-502.

4488 Górale dwóch narodów? O warunkach i konsekwencjach polsko-słowackiego rozbratu we wsiach Bukowiny rumuńskiej. *[In Polish]*; (The highlanders of two nations? Circumstances and consequences of the Polish-Slovakian breach in the villages of the Romanian Bucovina.) *[Summary]*. Eugeniusz Kłosek. **Etn. Polska** XLV:1-2 2001 pp.135-154.

4489 Identités et identifications dans la pensée et la praxis allemandes. *[In French]*; [Identity and identification in German thought and practice]. Mohamed Turki. **Cah. Tunis.** XLIX:177 1997 pp.77-88.

4490 *Imagined Communities* reconsidered: is print-capitalism what we think it is? Peter Wogan. **Anth. Th.** 1:4 12:2001 pp.403-418.

4491 Introduction: towards an Irish cultural studies. Spurgeon Thompson. **Cult. St.** 15:1 1:2001 pp.1-11.

4492 Is the 'world game' an 'ethnic game' or an 'Aussie game'? Narrating the nation in Australian soccer. Loring M. Danforth. **Am. Ethn.** 28:2 5:2001 pp.363-387.

4493 Le mariage qui dérange. Redéfinitions de l'identité nationale basque. *[In French]*; [The disturbing marriage: redifining the Basque national identity] *[Summary]*; *[Summary in German]*. Enric Porqueres Gené. **Ethn. Fr.** XXXI:3 7-9:2001 pp.527-536.

4494 National belonging and cultural difference: South Africa and the global imaginary. Duncan Brown. **J. S. Afr. Stud.** 27:4 12:2001 pp.757-770.

4495 Nationalism and resistance: the two faces of everyday activism in Palestine during the Intifada. Iris Jean-Klein. **Cult. Anthro.** 16:1 2:2001 pp.83-126.

4496 Odjeci dekapitacije vola u pupnatu na otoku Korčuli: hrvati između tradicionalizma i modernizma. *[In Croatian]*; (Echoes of the decapitation of an ox in the village of Pupnat on the island of Korčula: the Croats between tradition and modernity.) *[Summary]*. Jasna Čapo Žmegač. **Nar. Umjetn.** 37:2 2000 pp.9-26.

4497 Overseas Chinese merchants and multiple nationality: a means for reducing commercial risk (1895-1935). Man-Houng Lin. **Mod. Asian S.** 35:4 10:2001 pp.985-1009.

4498 Prostor na gala plesu in bojnem polju etnične, narodne ter nacionalne identitete: izbrani teoretski vidik. *[In Slovene]*; (The role of space in the formation and preservation of ethnic, national and statehood identity.) *[Summary]*. Jernej Mlekuz. **Bull. Slov. Ethno. Soc.** 41:1-2 2001 pp.55-61.

4499 Queer treasons: homosexuality and Irish national identity. Kathryn Conrad. **Cult. St.** 15:1 1:2001 pp.124-137.

4500 Regarding Ireland in a post-colonial frame. David Lloyd. **Cult. St.** 15:1 1:2001 pp.12-32.

4501 Remains of the race: archaeology, nationalism, and the yearning for civilisation in the Indus Aalley. Sumathi Ramaswamy. **Indian Ec. Soc. His. R.** XXXVIII:2 4-6:2001 pp.105-145.

4502   The 'spirit of the Alps' and the making of political and economic modernity in Switzerland; *[Summary in French]*; *[Summary in German]*; *[Summary in Spanish]*. Gérald Berthoud. **Soc. Anthrop.** 9:1 2:2001 pp.81-94.

4503   Symposium on the role of Hebrew literature in the formation of Jewish national identity: a note of introduction. Michael V. Fox. **Heb. St.** XLI 2000 pp.149-150.

4504   To what can late eighteenth-century French, British, and American anxieties be compared? Comment on three papers. Benedict Anderson. **Am. Hist. Rev.** 106:4 10:2001 pp.1281-1289.

4505   Women playing the bandura: challenging discourses of nationhood; *[Summary in French]*. Marcia Ostashewski. **Ethnologies** 23:1 2001 pp.123-146.

Psychology
Psychologie

4506   Agency and appropriation of voice — cultural differences in parental ideas about young children's talk. V.G. Aukrust. **Hum. Dev.** 44:5 9-10:2001 pp.235-249.

4507   Are we all natural dualists? A cognitive developmental approach; *[Summary in French]*. Rita Astuti. **J. Royal Anth. Inst.** 7:3 9:2001 pp.429-448.

4508   Authenticity and memory at Dachau. Jenny Edkins. **Cult. Val.** 5:4 10:2001 pp.405-420.

4509   Bereavement research and theory: retrospective and prospective. Margaret S. Stroebe. **Am. Behav. Sc.** 44:5 1:2001 pp.854-865.

4510   The category of the person in rural Punjab; *[Summary in French]*; *[Summary in German]*; *[Summary in Spanish]*. Anjum Alvi. **Soc. Anthrop.** 9:1 2:2001 pp.45-63.

4511   Commemoration and the healing of memories in Alcoholics Anonymous. Maria Gabrielle Swora. **Ethos** 29:1 3:2001 pp.58-77.

4512   Continuing bonds in the resolution of grief in Japan and North America. Dennis Klass. **Am. Behav. Sc.** 44:5 1:2001 pp.742-763.

4513   Cultural determinism, cultural relativism, and the comparative study of psychopathology. Melford E. Spiro. **Ethos** 29:2 6:2001 pp.218-234.

4514   Dream play and discovering cultural psychology. Jeanette Marie Mageo. **Ethos** 29:2 6:2001 pp.187-217.

4515   Dynamics of inclusion and exclusion: comparing mental illness narratives of Haredi male patients and their rabbis. Yehuda Goodman. **Cult. Medic. Psych.** 25:2 6:2001 pp.169-194.

4516   Encounter images in the meetings between Africa and Europe. Mai Palmberg [Ed.]. Uppsala: Nordiska Afrikainstitutet, 2001. 278p. *ISBN: 9171064788.*

4517   Ethnography or self-cultural anthropology? Reflections on writing about ourselves. Sonia Ryang. **Dialect. Anthrop.** 25:3-4 2000 pp.297-320.

4518   Examining the delayed grief hypothesis across 5 years of bereavement. George A. Bonanno; Nigel P. Field. **Am. Behav. Sc.** 44:5 1:2001 pp.798-816.

4519   Fantasy and reality: the dialectic of work and play in Kwara'ae children's lives. Karen Ann Watson-Gegeo. **Ethos** 29:2 6:2001 pp.138-158.

4520   Father absence and male aggression: a re-examination of the comparative evidence. Carol R. Ember; Melvin Ember. **Ethos** 29:3 9:2001 pp.296-314.

4521   Father absence, social structure, and attention allocation in children: a four-culture comparison. Robert L. Munroe. **Ethos** 29:3 9:2001 pp.315-328.

4522   Festivity and popular memory in southern India. Mary Hancock. **S. Asia R.** 21:1 Autumn:2001 pp.1-22.

4523   Filmer le social filmer l'histoire. *[In French]*; [Filming social reality, filming history]. Larry Portis; Gérard Althabe; Jean-Pierre Durand; Laurent Cholet; Jean-Pierre Garnier; Pascal Dupuy; Peter Watkins; L'Homme et la Société [Interviewer]; Gérard Raynal; Richard Prost; Frederick Wiseman; L. Mîkles [Interviewer]; Christiane Passevant. **Hom. Soc.** 142(4) 10-12:2001 pp.3-175. *Collection of 11 articles.*

4524   Freud in the field. Beatrice B. Whiting. **Ethos** 29:3 9:2001 pp.247-258.

4525   From causation to correlation: the story of *Psychosomatic Medicine* 1939-1979. Nissim
        Mizrachi; Gary S. Belkin [Comments by]. **Cult. Medic. Psych.** 25:3 9:2001 pp.317-343.

4526   Guilt as a cause of sickness. Yolotl Gonzalez Torres. **B. Int. Com. Urg. Anthrop. Ethnol.
        R.** 40 1999-2000 pp.157-162.

4527   Intelligence in Russia. Richard Lynn. **Mankind Q.** XLII:2 Winter:2001 pp.151-154.

4528   Intercultural perception and social change as seen in human figure drawings by school
        children in Jordan. Helga Unger-Heitsch. **Z. Ethn.** 126:2 2001 pp.269-291.

4529   Introduction: new directions in bereavement research and theory. George A. Bonanno. **Am.
        Behav. Sc.** 44:5 1:2001 pp.718-725.

4530   Knowing our own minds. Cynthia Macdonald; Crispin Wright [Ed.]; Barry Smith; Mind
        Association. Oxford: Clarendon Press, 2000. 450p. *ISBN: 0199241406. Includes
        bibliographical references and index.*

4531   Legal abortion: a painful necessity. A. Kero; U. Högberg; L. Jacobsson; A. Lalos. **Soc. Sci.
        Med.** 53:11 12:2001 pp.1481-1490.

4532   Loss and meaning: how do people make sense of loss? Christopher G. Davis; Susan Nolen-
        Hoeksema. **Am. Behav. Sc.** 44:5 1:2001 pp.726-741.

4533   Memory and external reference points among Fijians in (urban) Fiji. Solrun Williksen-
        Bakker. **Bijdragen** 157:2 2001 pp.383-402.

4534   Narrating transgressions in Longwood: the discourses, meanings, and paradoxes of an
        American socializing practice. Peggy J. Miller; Todd L. Sandel; Chung-Hui Liang; Heidi
        Fung. **Ethos** 29:2 6:2001 pp.159-186.

4535   Other worlds: notions of self and emotion among the Lohorung Rai. Charlotte Hardman.
        Oxford: Berg Publishers, 2000. 315p. *ISBN: 1859731503, 1859731554.*

4536   Perceptions of poverty among poor livestock keepers in Kenya: a discourse analysis
        approach. F. Misturelli; C. Heffernan. **J. Int. Dev.** 13:7 10:2001 pp.863-875.

4537   Probleme und Grenzen der Anwendung psychoanalytischer Begriffe in der
        Religionswissenschaft. *[In German]*; [Problems with and limits to the use of
        psychoanalytical concepts in religious studies]. Hartmut Zinser. **Paideuma** 46 2000
        pp.189-206.

4538   Psychological outcomes associated with traumatic loss in a sample of young women.
        Bonnie L. Green; Janice L. Krupnick; Patricia Stockton; Lisa Goodman; Carole Corcoran;
        Rachel Petty. **Am. Behav. Sc.** 44:5 1:2001 pp.817-837.

4539   The psychology of loss as a lens to a positive psychology. John H. Harvey. **Am. Behav.
        Sc.** 44:5 1:2001 pp.838-853.

4540   Remodeling concepts of the self: an Ijo example. Marida Hollos; Philip E. Leis. **Ethos**
        29:3 9:2001 pp.371-387.

4541   The role of blame in adaptation in the first 5 years following the death of a spouse. Nigel P.
        Field; George A. Bonanno. **Am. Behav. Sc.** 44:5 1:2001 pp.764-781.

4542   The schooling of women: maternal behavior and child environments. Robert A. LeVine;
        Sarah E. LeVine **Ethos** 29:3 9:2001 pp.259-270.

4543   The search for meaning: eventfulness in the lives of homeless mentally ill persons in the
        Skid Row district of Los Angeles. Alex Cohen. **Cult. Medic. Psych.** 25:3 9:2001 pp.277-
        296.

4544   Selective memory and collective forgetting: historiography and the Philippine centennial
        of 1898. Greg Bankoff. **Bijdragen** 157:3 2001 pp.539-560.

4545   Self and illness: changing relationships in response to life in the community following
        prolonged institutionalisation. Liz Newton. **Aus. J. Anth.** 12:2 8:2001 pp.166-181.

4546   Treatment of the depressions of bereavement. Sidney Zisook; Stephen R. Shuchter. **Am.
        Behav. Sc.** 44:5 1:2001 pp.782-797.

4547   A unique panic-disorder presentation among Khmer refugees: the sore-neck syndrome.
        Devon Hinton; Khin Um; Phalnarith Ba. **Cult. Medic. Psych.** 25:3 9:2001 pp.297-316.

H.1: **Educational systems**
Systèmes d'enseignement

4548 Africa and the politics of knowledge. Wambui Mwangi; Elisa von Joeden-Forgey; Sulaiman Adebowale; Adams B. Bodomo; Isaiah Munang Ayafor; Kwabena Akurang-Parry; David Aworawo; Jide Osuntokun; Gampi Matheba; Dominic Milazi; Gerd Bayer; Uduopegeme J. Yakubu. **J. Cult. St.** 3:1 2001 pp.1-167. *Collection of 11 articles.*

4549 Chinese conceptualization of learning. Jin Li. **Ethos** 29:2 6:2001 pp.111-137.

4550 Early days at charter estate. D.K. Worthington. **Herit. Zimb.** 10 1991 pp.93-98.

4551 Education in the Indo-Muslim society. N.A. Baloch. **J. Pak. Hist. Soc.** XLIX:3 7-9:2001 pp.5-14.

4552 History of Muslim women's education in Sri Lanka. M.N.M. Kamil Asad. **J. Pak. Hist. Soc.** XLIX:3 7-9:2001 pp.15-20.

4553 A moldvai csángók magyar nyelvi oktatásának szükségességéröl. *[In Hungarian]*; [About the Hungarian language teaching need of the Csángó minority] *[Summary]*. Attila Hegyeli. **Regio** 12:4 2001 pp.181-194.

4554 Primary education quality in Francophone sub-Saharan Africa: determinants of learning achievement and efficiency considerations. K. Michaelowa. **World Dev.** 29:10 10:2001 pp.1699-1716.

4555 Problématique de la scolarisation des Pygmées dans le territoire de mambasa en République Démocratique du Congo. *[In French]*; [Problems in the schooling of Pygmies in the Mambasa area of the Democratic Republic of Congo]. Gratien Mokonzi Bambanota; Paul Vitamara Masimango; Flory Kakule Mupopolo. **B. Int. Com. Urg. Anthrop. Ethnol. R.** 40 1999-2000 pp.113-120.

4556 Realism in Philippine values education. Niels Mulder. **Phil. Stud.** 49:3 2001 pp.429-444.

4557 Scottish life and society. A compendium of Scottish ethnology: institutions of Scotland education. European Ethnological Research Centre; Heather Holmes [Ed.]. East Linton: Tuckwell Press, 2000. xviii, 558p. *ISBN: 1862321868. Volume 11. Includes bibliographical references and index. European Ethnological Research Centre.*

4558 The spread of Muslim education in Assam (1905-1916). Abdullah Al-Masum. **J. Pak. Hist. Soc.** XLIX:3 7-9:2001 pp.27-34.

4559 Teaching elsewhere: anthropological pedagogy, racism and indifference in a Hong Kong classroom. Rozanna Lilley. **Aus. J. Anth.** 12:2 8:2001 pp.127-154.

4560 'Walking the walk and talking the talk': bodies, conversation, gender and power in higher education in England. Tom Delph-Janiurek. **Soc. Cult. Geog.** 1:1 9:2000 pp.83-100.

H.2: **Biographical material**
Matériaux biographiques

4561 Among the white moonfaces: memoirs of a Nyonya feminist. Shirley Lim. Singapore: Times Books International, 1996. 348p. *ISBN: 9812046607.*

4562 Autobiographical desires: repetition and rectification in Serge Doubrovsky's '*Laissé Pour Conte*'. Alex Hughes. **Fr. Stud.** LV:2 4:2001 pp.179-194.

4563 Biography as promotional discourse: the case of Maud Gonne. Karen Steele. **Cult. St.** 15:1 1:2001 pp.138-160.

4564 Biography writing in Swahili. Farouk Topan. **Hist. Afr.** 24 1997 pp.299-308.

4565 Black lambs and grey falcons: women travellers in the Balkans. John B. Allcock [Ed.]; Antonia Young [Ed.]. New York, Oxford: Berghahn Books, 2000 |e r. xxxiii, 274p. *ISBN: 1571817441. Includes bibliographical references and index.*

4566 'Blurbing' biographical: authorship and autobiography. Kate Douglas. **Biography** 24:4 Fall:2001 pp.806-916.

4567 Coordinated lives: between autobiography and scholarship. Jeremy D. Popkin. **Biography** 24:4 Fall:2001 pp.781-805.

4568   Disarming testimony: speakers' resistance to readers' defenses in Latin American *testimonio*. Kimberly Nance. **Biography** 24:3 Summer:2001 pp.570-588.

4569   Empowered speech: social fields, *testimonio*, and the Stoll-Menchú debate. Leigh Binford. **Identities** 8:1 3:2001 pp.105-134.

4570   Estafeta pamiati. *[In Russian]*; (Memory torch.) *[Summary]*. A. Alexeev. **Mir Rossii** IX:4 2000 pp.170-175.

4571   Homeless in Gujarat and India: on the curious love of Indulal Yagnik. Ajay Skaria. **Indian Ec. Soc. His. R.** XXXVIII:3 7-9:2001 pp.271-298.

4572   Iz dievnika kavkazoveda. I. Nachalo puti. *[In Russian]*; (From the diary of a student of Caucasus I. At the beginning of the road.) *[Summary]*. B.A. Kaloev. **Etnograf. Oboz.** 4 7-8:2000 pp.119-145.

4573   *La mietitura*: video between imagined community and auto-ethnography. Francesco Marano. **Vis. Anthrop.** 14:2 2001 pp.185-202.

4574   The legend of Reg 'Snowy' Baker: an Australian story with a Hollywood ending. David Headon. **Kunapipi** XXIII:1 2001 pp.27-40.

4575   Life markers in biographical narratives of people from three cohorts: a life span perspective in its historical context. A. Grob; F. Krings; A. Bangerter. **Hum. Dev.** 44:4 7-8:2001 pp.171-190.

4576   Native American women: a biographical dictionary. Gretchen M. Bataille [Ed.]; Lisa Laurie [Ed.]. New York, London: Routledge, 2001 |e r. 384p. *ISBN: 0415930200*.

4577   A prismatic presence: the multiple iconisation of Dr Anandibai Joshee and the politics of life-writing. Meera Kosambi. **Aus. Fem. St.** 16:35 7:2001 pp.157-173.

4578   The private 'I' in the works of Nina Berberova. Nadya L. Peterson. **Slavic R.** 60:3 Fall:2001 pp.491-512.

4579   A shepherd remembers: reminiscences of a border shepherd. Andrew Purves. East Linton: Tuckwell Press, 2001. 280p. *ISBN: 1862321574. European Ethnological Research Centre. (Series:* Flashbacks - 13).

4580   Ville réelle et ville idéale à la fin du Moyen Âge: une géographie au prisme des témoignages autobiographiques allemands. *[In French]*; (Real city and ideal city at the end of the Middle Ages: a geography revealed by German autobiographical sources.) *[Summary]*. Pierre Monnet. **Annales** 56:3 5-6:2001 pp.591-624.

4581   Willem van Leer: businessman by profession, writer by vocation. Marcel Poorthuis. **St. Ros.** 35:1 2001 pp.48-66.

4582   Antropologiia rossiiskikh transformatsii. *[In Russian]*; (Anthropology of Russia's transformations.) *[Summary]*. V.A. Tishkov. **Etnograf. Oboz.** 1 1-2:2000 pp.3-18.

4583   Arabs under Japanese occupation: a preliminary overview. Kazuhiro Arai. **Senri Ethn. Stud.** 55 2001 pp.41-54.

4584   Bidayuh housewives in a changing world: Sarawak, Malaysia. Hew Cheng Sim. **J. Anthr. Res.** 57:2 Summer:2001 pp.151-166.

4585   Cultural change in the Arab world. Tetsuo Nishio [Ed.]. Osaka: National Museum of Ethnology, 2001. ii, 174p. *Includes bibliographical references.* (*Series:* Senri ethnological studies - 55).

4586   Culture acquisition: old moulds, new challenges; *[Summary in Afrikaans]*. Petro Esterhuyse. **S. Afr. J. Ethnol.** 24:4 2001 pp.162-171.

4587   Culture in the world system: an interview with Immanuel Wallerstein. Immanuel Wallerstein; Anand Kumar [Interviewer]; Frank Welz [Interviewer]. **Soc. Ident.** 7:2 6:2001 pp.221-232.

4588   Democratisation: a global concept within a particular context. A case study of South Africa. Jan K. Coetzee. **Arch. Orient.** 68:1 2:2000 pp.53-70.

4589   Une évolution lente et des perspectives contrastées. *[In French]*; [Contrasting perspectives of a slow evolution]. Farid Benbouzid. **Cah. Orient** 63 2001 pp.39-52.

4590   Índios e antropologia: reflexões sobre cultura, etnicidade e situação de contato. *[In Portuguese]*; [Indians and anthropology: reflections on culture, ethnicity and contact situations] *[Summary]*. Rinaldo Sérgio Vieira Arruda. **Bol. Mus. Par. Emílio Goeldi** 15:1 7:1999 pp.33-90.

4591   Intercultural perception and social change as seen in human figure drawings by school children in Jordan. Helga Unger-Heitsch. **Z. Ethn.** 126:2 2001 pp.269-291.

4592   Italy: the enduring culture. Jonathan Charles White. New York: Leicester University Press, 2001. *ISBN: 0718502582, 0718502574. Includes bibliographical references and index.*

4593   Locating cultural creativity. John Liep [Ed.]. London: Pluto Press, 2001. vii, 181p. *ISBN: 0745317030, 0745317022. Papers presented at a workshop organized by the Institute of Anthropology, University of Copenhagen, 1994. Includes bibliographical references and index.* (*Series:* Anthropology, culture, and society).

4594   Moved, left no address: dam construction, displacement and issue salience. H. Sims. **Publ. Adm. D.** 21:3 8:2001 pp.187-200.

4595   Mythology as an indicator of cultural change. Hunting and agriculture as reflected in North American traditions. Sonja Ross. **Anthropos [St. Augustin]** 95:2 2000 pp.433-444.

4596   Nepal's quest for modernity. C.K. Lal. **S. Asian Surv.** 8:2 7-12:2001 pp.249-260.

4597   Oświata a procesy asymilacyjne wśród mniejszości ukraińskiej. *[In Polish]*; (Education and assimilation processes among the Ukrainian minority.) Zofia Tracewicz. Toruń: Adam Marszałek, 2000. 227p. *ISBN: 8371745583.*

4598   Pampang culture village and international tourism in East Kalimantan, Indonesian Borneo. Anne Schiller. **Human. Org.** 60:4 Winter:2001 pp.414-422.

4599   The place of the '*imaginaire religieux*' in social change and political recomposition in sub-Saharan Africa. Patrick Claffey. **Anthropos [St. Augustin]** 96:1 2001 pp.200-205.

4600   *Ubuntu* and nation building in South Africa; *[Summary in Afrikaans]*. R.D. Coertze. **S. Afr. J. Ethnol.** 24:4 2001 pp.113-118.

4601   Wandel einer Megalithkultur im 20. Jahrhundert (Nias/Indonesien). *[In German]*; [Changes in a 20th century megalithic culture in the 20th century (Nias, Indonesia)]. Dominik Bonatz. **Anthropos [St. Augustin]** 96:1 2001 pp.105-118.

4602   When was modernity in Melanesia?; *[Summary in French]*; *[Summary in German]*; *[Summary in Spanish]*. Eric Hirsch. **Soc. Anthrop.** 9:2 6:2001 pp.131-146.

4603   'Why don't you just teach the Turks right from the start?!' Culturalisation and conflict dynamics in teaching practices at a multi-ethnic comprehensive school in Berlin. Sabine Mannitz. **Z. Ethn.** 126:2 2001 pp.293-312.

Globalization and localization
Mondialisation et localisation

4604   Bâb al-Nayrab, un faubourg d'Alep, hors la ville et dans la cité. *[In French]*; (Bâb al-Nayrab: outside, but a part of the city of Aleppo.) *[Summary]*. Jacques Hivernel. **Rural Stud.** 155-156 7-12:2001 pp.215-238.

4605   China's minority cultures at the turn of the century: issues of modernization and globalization. Colin MacKerras. **Arch. Orient.** 69:3 8:2001 pp.447-464.

4606   A clash of vulnerabilities: citizenship, labor, and expatriacy in the Cayman Islands. Vered Amit. **Am. Ethn.** 28:3 8:2001 pp.574-594.

4607   Contrasting models of land use regulation: community, government and tourism development. Anthony van Fossen; George Lafferty. **Comm. Dev. J.** 36:3 7:2001 pp.198-211.

4608   De l'enclavement à la globalisation. Une ouverture risquée pour la Bolivie. *[In French]*; (From enclosure to economic globalization: a risky developmental opportunity for Bolivia.) *[Summary]*; *[Summary in Spanish]*. J.C. Roux. **Cah. Outre-mer** 53:212 10-12:2000 pp.317-342.

4609   Disparités régionales et globalisation, organisations paysannes et marchés… *[In French]*; (Regional disparities and globalisation, peasant organisations and markets…). Hartmut Elsenhans; Pierre Salama; Mikael Petitjean; Pierre Janin; Sylvain Fauroux; Éric Léonard; Horacio MacKinlay; Marie-José Nadal; Paul Hoebink; Miloud Kaddar; Friedeger Stierle; Bergis Schmidt-Ehry; Anastase Tchicaya. **R. T. Monde** XLI:164 10-12:2000 pp.729-884. *Collection of 7 articles.*

4610   L'enseignement des arts plastiques face aux défis de la mondialisation. *[In French]*; [Teaching plastic arts facing the challenge of globalization]. Sami Ben Ameur. **Cah. Tunis.** XLIX:177 1997 pp.89-104.

4611   Global capitalism, neoliberal policy and poverty. Jeff Maskovsky; Catherine Kingfisher; John Gledhill; Sarah Hill; Lynn Stephen; Ananthakrishnan Aiyer. **Urban Anthro.** 30:2-3 Summer-Fall:2001 pp.105-268. *Collection of 6 articles.*

4612   Global ethnography. Michael Burawoy; Sally Falk Moore; Michael Goldman; Gay W. Seidman; Millie Thayer; Maxine Molyneux; Michael Watts. **Ethnog.** 2:2 6:2001 pp.147-320. *Collection of 7 articles.*

4613   Globalisation: human rights amidst risk and regression. Upendra Baxi. **IDS Bull.** 32:1 1:2001 pp.94-102.

4614   Globalization and its effects on South Asia. Saira Bano Orakzai. **J. Pak. Hist. Soc.** XLIX:3 7-9:2001 pp.77-86.

4615   Globalization, governance and Islam in the new millennium. Sohail Mahmood. **J. Res. Soc. Pakist.** XXXVII:3 7:2001 pp.31-48.

4616   Governance, decentralisation, and poverty: the case of Pakistan. Zafar H. Ismail; Sehar Rizvi; Akhtar Mahmood [Comments by]. **Pak. Dev. R.** 39:4(II) Winter:2000 pp.1013-1030.

4617   Lost worlds: environmental disaster, 'culture loss,' and the law. Stuart Kirsch; Gary M. Biery-Hamilton [Comments by]; Michael F. Brown [Comments by]; Stephen B. Brush [Comments by]; David A. Cleveland [Comments by]; Arif Dirlik [Comments by]; Virginia Dominguez [Comments by]; Arturo Escobar [Comments by]; Ben Finney [Comments by]; Tamara Giles-Vernick [Comments by]; B.G. Karlsson [Comments by]; Francesca Merlan [Comments by]; Alcida Rita Ramos [Comments by]; Lawrence Rosen [Comments by]; Madhavi Sunder [Comments by]; Edith Turner [Comments by]; Toon van Meijl

[Comments by]; Shinji Yamashita [Comments by]; Stuart Kirsch [Comments by]. **Curr. Anthr.** 42:2 4:2001 pp.167-198.

4618   Mondialisation et diversité. *[In French]*; [Globalization and diversity]. P.J. Thumerelle; J.R. Pitte; A. Miossec; O. Sevin; M. Droulers; F.M. Le Tourneau. **Ann. Géogr.** 110:621 9-10:2001 pp.468-570. *Collection of 5 articles.*

4619   New boundaries of influence in highland Papua: 'culture', mining and ritual conversions. Eric Hirsch. **Oceania** 71:4 6:2001 pp.298-312.

4620   On the generification of culture: from blow fish to Melanesian; *[Summary in French]*. Frederick Errington; Deborah Gewertz. **J. Royal Anth. Inst.** 7:3 9:2001 pp.509-526.

4621   Pro-poor growth in a globalized economy. H. White. **J. Int. Dev.** 13:5 7:2001 pp.549-569.

4622   The Senegalese murid trade diaspora and the making of a vernacular cosmopolitanism. Mamadou Diouf. **Publ. Cult.** 12:3 Fall:2000 pp.679-702.

J: APPLIED ANTHROPOLOGY
ANTHROPOLOGIE APPLIQUÉE

J.1: **Borders and rights**
Frontières et droits

4623 Dialogue paper by indigenous peoples. CSD Indigenous Peoples' Caucus. **Indig. Aff.** :4 2001 pp.12-25.

4624 Encountering different territorialities: political fragmentation of the Sami homeland. Kristiina Karppi. **J. Econ. Soc. Geogr.** 92:4 2001 pp.394-404.

4625 From skepticism to embrace: human rights and the American Anthropological Association from 1947-1999. Karen Engle. **Hum. Rights Q.** 23:3 8:2001 pp.536-559.

4626 Frontiers, borders, edges: liminal challenges to the hegemony of exclusion. Richie Howitt. **Aust. Geogr. Stud.** 39:2 7:2001 pp.233-245.

4627 Krizis doktriny samoopredeleniia. *[In Russian]*; [Crisis of the doctrine of self-determination] *[Summary]*. S.V. Cheshko. **Etnograf. Oboz.** 2 3-4:2001 pp.3-16.

4628 Pluralizm kulturowy i etniczny a odrębność regionalna Kresów południowo-wschodnich w latach 1918-1939. *[In Polish]*; [Cultural and ethnic pluralism and the regional distinctiveness of the southeast borderlands between 1918 and 1939]. Łucja Kapralska..

4629 Self-determination and *uti possidetis*: the Western Sahara and the 'lost provinces'. George Joffé. **Morocco** 1 1996 pp.97-115.

4630 Tenure rights and ancestral domains in the Philippines: a study of the roots of conflict. Ben S. Malayang, III. **Bijdragen** 157:3 2001 pp.661-676.

4631 The unincorporated, unorganized U.S. territory of American Samoa: Samoan traditionalism v. U.S. constitutionalism. E. Robert Statham, Jr. **Asian Cult. (Asian-Pac. Cult.) Q.** XXVIII:4 Winter:2000 pp.65-81.

4632 The U.S.-Mexico borderlands in 2001: a postnational work in progress. Robert R. Alvarez; Thomas Weaver; Josiah McC. Heyman; Thomas E. Sheridan; Robert A. Hackenberg; Nick Benequista; Douglas H. Keare; Mark Moberg; Mike Mathambo Mtika; Lyla Mehta. **Human. Org.** 60:2 Summer:2001 pp.95-165. *Collection of 8 articles.*

Indigenous rights
Droits indigènes

4633 Anthropology and global capital: rediscovering the noble savage. Sangeeta Kamat. **Cult. Dyn.** 13:1 3:2001 pp.29-52.

4634 Autonomy in Chiapas, Mexico. IWGIA. **Indig. Aff.** 2 2001 pp.60-65.

4635 The battlefield of water rights: rule making amidst conflicting normative frameworks in the Ecuadorian highlands. Rutgerd Boelens; Bernita Doornbos. **Human. Org.** 60:4 Winter:2001 pp.343-355.

4636 Biodiversity prospecting: lessons and prospects. Katy Moran; Steven R. King; Thomas J. Carlson. **Ann. R. Anthr.** 30 2001 pp.505-526.

4637 Bioprospecting and its discontents: indigenous resistances as legitimate politics. Chikako Takeshita. **Alternatives** 26:3 7-9:2001 pp.259-282.

4638 The Bushmen of Southern Africa: slaughter of the innocent. Sandy Gall. London: Chatto & Windus, 2001. xxxix, 264p. *ISBN: 0701169060. Includes index.*

4639 Children of colonialism: Anglo-Indians in a postcolonial world. Lionel Caplan. Oxford, New York: Berg Publishers, 2001. x, 260p. *ISBN: 1859735312. Includes bibliographical references and index.*

4640 Chinyanja and the language of rights. Harri Englund. **Nord. J. Afr. St.** 10:3 2001 pp.299-319.

4641   Culture and rights: anthropological perspectives. Richard Wilson [Ed.]; Jane K. Cowan [Ed.]; Marie-Bénédicte Dembour [Ed.]. Cambridge: Cambridge University Press, 2001. xiv, 258p. *ISBN: 0521797357, 0521793394. Includes bibliographical references and index.*

4642   Estado, legislación y resurgimiento indígena mapuche en Chile. *[In Spanish]*; [State, legislation and the indigenous mapuche revival in Chile]. Gilda Waldman M. **Cuad. Am.** XV:5(89) 9-10:2001 pp.172-187.

4643   From sovereignty to freedom: towards an indigenous political discourse. T. Alfred. **Indig. Aff.** 3 2001 pp.22-35.

4644   The human rights situation of the indigenous people in the Americas. Inter-American Commission on Human Rights; Organization of American States, General Secretariat. Washington DC: General Secretariat, Organization of American States, 2000. 371p. *ISBN: 0827042167. (Series: OAS official records - OEA/Ser.L/V/II.108).*

4645   If gender mattered: a case study of Inuit women, land claims and the Voiseys Bay Nickel Project. Linda Archibald; Mary Crnkovich. Ottawa: Status of Women Canada, 1999. *ISBN: 0662280024. Text in English and French. Includes bibliographical references.*

4646   Implementation of the right of self-determination of indigenous peoples. J.B. Henriksen. **Indig. Aff.** 3 2001 pp.6-21.

4647   Indigenous Australians: a national commitment. Department of Reconciliation and Aboriginal and Torres Strait Islander Affairs. Canberra, 2001. 31p. *ISBN: 0957940904.*

4648   Indigenous peoples and the World Summit for Sustainable Development (WSSD). Joji Cariño. **Indig. Aff.** :4 2001 pp.4-6.

4649   Indigenous peoples' self-determination in northeast India. C. Emi. **Indig. Aff.** 3 2001 pp.56-66.

4650   Land and freedom: law, property rights and the British diaspora. A.R. Buck [Ed.]; John McLaren [Ed.]; Nancy E. Wright [Ed.]. Aldershot: Ashgate, 2001. xvii, 201p. *ISBN: 0754622096. Includes bibliographical references and index.*

4651   Lost worlds: environmental disaster, 'culture loss,' and the law. Stuart Kirsch; Gary M. Biery-Hamilton [Comments by]; Michael F. Brown [Comments by]; Stephen B. Brush [Comments by]; David A. Cleveland [Comments by]; Arif Dirlik [Comments by]; Virginia Dominguez [Comments by]; Arturo Escobar [Comments by]; Ben Finney [Comments by]; Tamara Giles-Vernick [Comments by]; B.G. Karlsson [Comments by]; Francesca Merlan [Comments by]; Alcida Rita Ramos [Comments by]; Lawrence Rosen [Comments by]; Madhavi Sunder [Comments by]; Edith Turner [Comments by]; Toon van Meijl [Comments by]; Shinji Yamashita [Comments by]; Stuart Kirsch [Comments by]. **Curr. Anthr.** 42:2 4:2001 pp.167-198.

4652   La marca de Marcos: ¿pueden hablar los indígenas mexicanos? *[In Spanish]*; [The mark of Marcos: do indigenous Mexicans have a voice?] Kristine Vanden Berghe. **Cuad. Am.** XV:3(87) 5-6:2001 pp.158-173.

4653   Militarization and human rights violations. M. Jensen. **Indig. Aff.** 2 2001 pp.4-7.

4654   Native 'land claims', Russian style. Gail Fondahl; Olga Lazebnik; Greg Poelzer; Vasily Robbek. **Can. Geogr.** 45:4 Winter:2001 pp.545-561.

4655   A política indigenista em três estados nacionais de colonização Européia: Brasil, Austrália e Canadá. *[In Portuguese]*; [On indigenist policy in three nation states colonized by Europeans: Brazil, Australia and Canada] *[Summary]*. Stephen G. Baines. **Bol. Mus. Par. Emílio Goeldi** 15:1 7:1999 pp.7-32.

4656   Problemy somoopredeleniia korennykh narodov (obzor). *[In Russian]*; (Self-determination and self-government problems of aboriginal peoples.) *[Summary]*. S.V. Sokolovskii. **Etnograf. Oboz.** 2 3-4:2001 pp.17-30.

4657   The Tiwi: from isolation to cultural change. John Morris. Darwin: Northern University Press, 2001. 160p. *ISBN: 1876248602.*

4658   Towards the World Summit on Sustainable Development - a brief introduction. Birgitte Feiring. **Indig. Aff.** :4 2001 pp.7-11.

4659   Tribal land rights in central Morocco: a call for comparative research. Wolfgang Kraus. **Morocco** 2 1997 pp.16-32.

4660   Working towards regional agreements: recent developments in co-operative resource management in Canada's British Columbia. Cathy Robinson. **Aust. Geogr. Stud.** 39:2 7:2001 pp.183-197.

J.2:   **Social development and welfare**
        Développement et bien-être social

4661   Adapting to adjustment: smallholder livelihood strategies in southern Malawi. A. Orr; B. Mwale. **World Dev.** 29:8 8:2001 pp.1325-1343.

4662   El ajuste estructural en América Latina: costos sociales y alternativas. *[In Spanish]*; [Structural adjustment in Latin America: social costs and alternatives]. Emir Sader; Irma Manrique [Comp.]. Buenos Aires: Consejo Latinoamericano de Ciencias Sociales (CLASO), 2001. 287p. *ISBN: 9509231568. Text in Spanish and Portuguese. Includes bibliographical references.*

4663   Anthropologie du développement, fiscalité, géographie industrielle, éducation... *[In French]*; [Anthropology of development, fiscality, industrial geography, education...]. J.P. Olivier de Sardan; Emmanuel Kamdem; Catherine Araujo-Bonjean; Gérard Chambas; Alain Karsenty; Jean-François Gautier; Faly Rakotomanana; François Roubaud; Claudio Jedlicki; Jean-Yves Chamboux-Leroux; Hadj Saadi; Éric Mulot; Claude Carpentier; Bernard Gazier; Rémy Herrera. **R. T. Monde** XLII:168 10-12:2001 pp.729-946. *Collection of 11 articles.*

4664   Etnologija razvoja/etnologija, regionalne kulture in razvoj. *[In Slovene]*; (Ethnology, regional cultures and development.) *[Summary]*. Aleš Gačnik. **Bull. Slov. Ethno. Soc.** 41:1-2 2001 pp.44-51.

4665   Gestión pública de necesidades básicas y actores sociales locales en la época del ajuste estructural: una reflexión sobre México. *[In Spanish]*; [Public management of basic needs and local social actors in the era of structural adjustment: a reflection on Mexico] *[Summary]*. Jesús Aurelio Cuevas Díaz. **Acta Sociol. [Mexico]** 31 1-4:2001 pp.139-166.

4666   Global human responsibilities human ecology, sustainable development and global partnerships. Zena Daysh [Speech by]; Anna Kajumulo Tibaijuka; Jagmohan S. Maini; Kamla Chowdhry; Clive L. Spash; Ian Douglas; Aubrey Meyer; Alex Evans; Michael Mutter; Anwar Hossain; Salvino Busuttil; Margaret Evans. **Human ecology** 18-19 10:2001 pp.4-39. *Collection of 11 articles.*

4667   IMF and World Bank sponsored structural adjustment programs in Africa: Ghana's experience, 1983-1999. Kwadwo Konadu-Agyemang [Ed.]. Aldershot: Ashgate, 2001. 444p. *ISBN: 0754613968. Includes bibliographical references and index. (Series: University of North London voices in development management).*

4668   The impact of structural adjustment programme on the acceptance of family planning programmes in Nigeria. P. Kassey Garba. **Ind. J. Eco.** LXXXI:322 1:2001 pp.291-306.

4669   Land reform under structural adjustment in Zimbabwe: land use change in the Machonaland provinces. Sam Moyo. Uppsala: Nordiska Afrikainstitutet, 2000. 177p. *ISBN: 9171064575.*

4670   Legal pluralism and social justice in economic and political development. Franz von Benda-Beckmann. **IDS Bull.** 32:1 1:2001 pp.46-56.

4671   La libéralisation économique en Inde: inflexion ou rupture? *[In French]*; (Economic liberalization in India: change or break?) Frédéric Landy; Basudeb Chaudhuri; Gérard Heuzé; Jayati Sarkar; Subrata Sarkar; Joël Ruet; Loraine Kennedy; S.S. Acharya; Véronique Alary; Emmanuel Hache; Isabelle Milbert; Véronique Dupont. **R. T. Monde** XLII:165 1-3:2001 pp.9-211. *Collection of 10 articles.*

4672   Looking ahead: areas of future research in human development. Paul Streeten. **J. Hum. Dev.** 1:1 2:2000 pp.25-48.

4673   Non-economic factors in development. Najamul Saqib Khan. **Pak. Dev. R.** 39:4(II) Winter:2000 pp.715-728.

4674   Of spirit possession and structural adjustment programs: government downsizing, education and their enchantments in neo-liberal Kenya. James H. Smith. **J. Relig. Afr.** XXXI:4 2001 pp.427-456.

4675   Participatory developmental research: a working model. F.J. Coughlan; K.J. Collins. **Int. Soc. Work** 44:4 10:2001 pp.505-518.

4676   Participatory rural appraisal as qualitative research: distinguishing methodological issues from participatory claims. John R. Campbell. **Human. Org.** 60:4 Winter:2001 pp.380-389.

4677   Poverty and structural adjustment: some remarks on tradeoffs between equity and growth. Rolph van der Hoeven. Geneva: International Labour Office, 2000. 25p. *ISBN: 9221120716. Includes bibliographical references. (Series:* Employment papers - 2000/4).

4678   Spatial integration, adjustment, and structural transformation in sub-Saharan Africa: some linkage pattern changes in Ghana. J. Henry Owusu. **Prof. Geogr.** 53:2 5:2001 pp.230-247.

4679   The state in development theory: the Philippines under Marcos. M.D. Litonjua. **Phil. Stud.** 49:3 2001 pp.368-398.

4680   Structural adjustment programmes and the international tourism trade in Ghana, 1983-99: some socio-spatial implications; *[Summary in French].* Kwadwo Konadu-Agyemang. **Tour. Geog.** 3:2 5:2001 pp.187-206.

4681   Structural adjustment programs and housing affordability in Accra, Ghana. Kwadwo Konadu-Agyemang. **Can. Geogr.** 45:4 Winter:2001 pp.528-544.

4682   Tensions brésiliennes. *[In French]*; [Brazilian tensions]. José Luis Fiori; Brasilio Sallum, Jr.; Angelina Peralva; Jaime Marques-Pereira; Claudio Salvadori Dedecca; Pierre Salama; Blandine Destremau; Marcel Bursztyn; Ademar Ribeiro Romeiro; Maria D. Vasconcellos; Martine Droulers; Céline Broggio; Alain Karsenty. **R. T. Monde** XLII:167 7-9:2001 pp.493-688. *Collection of 10 articles.*

4683   Tourism and spatial development initiatives: the case of the Maputo development corridor. Christian M. Rogerson. **S. Afr. Geogr. J.** 83:2 2001 pp.124-136.

4684   Transforming cultural villages in the spatial development initiatives of South Africa. Elizabeth Jansen Van Veuren. **S. Afr. Geogr. J.** 83:2 2001 pp.137-148.

4685   Unveiling Muslim women: a trajectory of post-colonial culture. Reza Rahbari. **Dialect. Anthrop.** 25:3-4 2000 pp.321-332.

Agricultural development
Développement agricole

4686   Agricultural implements used by women farmers in Africa. Japan Official Development Assistance; Food and Agriculture Organization of the United Nations. Rome: International Fund for Agricultural Development, 1998. xiv, 129p. *ISBN: 9290720085. Includes bibliographical references.*

4687   Agriculture et «développement durable» en Asie du Sud-Est. *[In French]*; (Agriculture and 'sustainable development' in South-East Asia.) *[Summary].* Marc Dufumier. **R. T. Monde** XLI:162 4-6:2000 pp.257-276.

4688   Des périmètres irrigués saheliens à la recherche d'une nécessaire intégration régionale: exemple du Macina (office du Niger, Mali). *[In French]*; (From the irrigated Sahelian perimeters to searching for necessary regional integration; the example of Macina, *Office du Niger*, Mali.) *[Summary].* Florence Brondeau. **Cah. Outre-mer** 54:215 7-9:2001 pp.249-282.

4689   Development and tribal agricultural economy in a Yao mountain village in northern Thailand. Li Jian. **Human. Org.** 60:1 Spring:2001 pp.80-94.

4690   Facilitating the wider use of agroforestry for development in Southern Africa. Andreas Böhringer. **Develop. Pract.** 11:4 8:2001 pp.434-448.

4691   Farmer adaptation, change and 'crisis' in the Sahel. Michael J. Mortimore; William M. Adams. **Glo. Environ. Chan.** 11:1 4:2001 pp.49-57.

4692   From farmer to planner and back: harvesting best practices. Food and Agriculture Organization of the United Nations. Rome: Food and Agriculture Organization of the

United Nations, 2001. *ISBN: 9251045720. 5 volumes. Papers presented at From Farmer to Planner and Back: Harvesting Best Practices, Rome, December 1997. Includes bibliographical references.*

4693 Les grands types de rizicultures en Asie du Sud-Est: transformations récentes, enjeux actuels et perspectives d'évolution. *[In French]*; [Large rice farms in South-East Asia: recent changes, current issues and development perspectives] *[Summary]*. Guy Trébuil; Mahabub Hossain. **R. T. Monde** XLI:162 4-6:2000 pp.277-300.

4694 The landcare experience in the Philippines: technical and institutional innovations for conservation farming. Agustin R. Mercado, Jr.; Marcelino Patindol; Dennis P. Garrity. **Develop. Pract.** 11:4 8:2001 pp.495-508.

4695 Livelihoods and sustainability at the agrarian frontier: the evolution of the frontier in southeastern Nicaragua. Matilde Mordt. Gothenburg: Department of Human and Economic Geography, Gothenburg University, 2001. 321p. *ISBN: 9186472380.*

4696 Participatory design of agroforestry systems: developing farmer participatory research methods in Mexico. Jeremy Haggar; Alejandro Ayala; Blanca Díaz; Carlos Uc Reyes. **Develop. Pract.** 11:4 8:2001 pp.417-424.

4697 Participatory domestication of agroforestry trees: an example from the Peruvian Amazon. John C. Weber; Carmen Sotelo Montes; Héctor Vidaurre; Ian K. Dawson; Anthony J. Simons. **Develop. Pract.** 11:4 8:2001 pp.425-433.

4698 Productivity growth and sustainability in post-green revolution agriculture: the case of the Indian and Pakistan punjabs. Rinku Murgai; Mubarik Ali; Derek Byerlee. **World Bank Res. Obser.** 16:2 Fall:2001 pp.199-218.

4699 Realising the potential of agroforestry: integrating research and development to achieve greater impact. Glenn L. Denning. **Develop. Pract.** 11:4 8:2001 pp.407-416.

4700 Reconfiguring the countryside: power, control, and the (re)organization of farmers in west Mexico. James H. McDonald. **Human. Org.** 60:3 Fall:2001 pp.247-258.

4701 Recursos humanos en el desarrollo agrícola y rural. *[In Spanish]*; Ressources humaines pour le développement agricole et rural. *[In French]*; Human resources in agricultural and rural development. Food and Agriculture Organization of the United Nations. Rome, 2000. xii, 173p. *ISBN: 9250044690. Text in English, French, Spanish and Arabic. United Nations Extension, Education, and Communication Service.*

4702 Scaling up participatory agroforestry extension in Kenya: from pilot projects to extension policy. T.M. Anyonge; Christine Holding; K.K. Kareko; J.W. Kimani. **Develop. Pract.** 11:4 8:2001 pp.449-459.

4703 Scaling up the benefits of agroforestry research: lessons learned and research challenges. Steven Franzel; Peter Cooper; Glenn L. Denning. **Develop. Pract.** 11:4 8:2001 pp.524-534.

4704 Structural adjustment and the agricultural sector in Latin America and the Caribbean. John Weeks [Ed.]. New York: St. Martin's Press, 1995. xv, 297p. *ISBN: 0312126794. Includes bibliographical references (p. [265]-288) and index. Institute of Latin American Studies, University of London. (Series: Institute of Latin American Studies).*

Development policy, aid and management
Politique, aide et gestion du développement

4705 Aid policies and growth: in search of the holy grail. J. Hudson; P. Mosley. **J. Int. Dev.** 13:7 10:2001 pp.1023-1038.

4706 Associating development projects with military operations: lessons from NATO's first year in BiH. Adam B. Siegel. **Int. Peace.** 8:3 Autumn:2001 pp.99-114.

4707 Can the world cut poverty in half? How policy reform and effective aid can meet international development goals. P. Collier; D. Dollar. **World Dev.** 29:11 11:2001 pp.1787-1802.

4708 Child sponsorship, evangelism, and belonging in the work of World Vision Zimbabwe. Erica Bornstein. **Am. Ethn.** 28:3 8:2001 pp.595-622.

4709   Community auditing as community development. Carol Packham. **Comm. Dev. J.** 33:3 7:1998 pp.249-259.

4710   A comparative study of water user associations in Tunisia. Andrew W. Wolfe. **Dev. Anthrop.** 18:1-2 Spring-Fall:2000 pp.17-24.

4711   Costa Rica's development strategy based on human capital and technology: how it got there, the impact of Intel, and lessons for other countries. Andrés Rodríguez-Clare. **J. Hum. Dev.** 2:2 7:2001 pp.311-324.

4712   Dag Hammarskjöld and the 21st century. Kofi Annan; Manuel Fröhlich; Marie-Noëlle Little; Bengt Thelin. **Dev. Dialog.** 1 2001 pp.3-90. *Collection of 4 articles.*

4713   Development and management: selected essays from Development in practice. Tina Wallace [Intro.]; Open University. Oxford: Oxfam, 2000. 326p. *ISBN: 0855984295. Includes bibliographical references. The Open University. (Series:* Development in practice readers).

4714   Displacement for development? The impact of changing state-society relations. L.A. Brand. **World Dev.** 29:6 6:2001 pp.961-976.

4715   L'espace public dans une ville émergente d'Afrique de l'Ouest. Aux frontières de la théorie des conventions, l'anthropologie prospective? *[In French]*; [Public space in a West African village: prospective anthropology at the threshhold of the theory of conventions?] Pierre-Joseph Laurent. **Recher. Sociolog.** XXXII:1 2001 pp.101-126.

4716   Experiences of participation in integrated watershed development project in Himachal Pradesh. S.S. Negi. **Indian J. Publ. Admin.** XLVII:1 1-3:2001 pp.26-37.

4717   The genealogy of South Africa's integrated development plan. Philip Harrison. **Third World Plan. R.** 23:2 5:2001 pp.175-193.

4718   La gestion communautaire sert-elle l'intérêt public? Le cas de l'hydraulique villageoise au Niger. *[In French]*; (Does community management serve the public interest? The case of village water projects in Niger.) *[Summary]*. Jean-Pierre Olivier de Sardan; Abdoua Elhadji Dagobi. **Pol. Afr.** 80 12:2000 pp.153-168.

4719   Getting the scale right: a comparison of analytical methods for vulnerability assessment and household-level targeting. Linda Stephen; Thomas E. Downing. **Disasters** 25:2 6:2001 pp.113-135.

4720   Les hautes terres du nord de la Thaïlande en transition. Développement, courtage et construction nationale. *[In French]*; [The highlands of northern Thailand in transition: development, brokerage and national construction] *[Summary]*. Pierre-Yves Le Meur. **R. T. Monde** XLI:162 4-6:2000 pp.365-388.

4721   Human development challenges in South Asia. Khadija Haq. **J. Hum. Dev.** 1:1 2:2000 pp.71-82.

4722   Involving young people in development. Pamela Thomas; Richard Curtain; Julie Ballington; Rachel Ingwersen; Dianne Proctor; Helen Hill; Meg Keen; Tess Newton Cain; Tangata Vainerere; Edward D. Lowe; Laitia Tamata; Christopher Chevalier; Sally Gibson; Sharon Bhagwan Rolls; Patrick Vakaoti; Peter Walker; Jo Dorrit; Anita Jowitt; Michael Morgan; Teorongonui Josie Keelan; Victoria White; David Maunders; Lincoln K. Ndogoni; Sarah Lendon; Akiko Fraval; Robert Bennoun; Prudence Borthwick; Karl Dorning; Tim O'Shaughnessy. **Dev. Bul.** 56 10:2001 pp.4-89. *Collection of 24 articles.*

4723   The Malawi Social Action Fund and community development. Paul Kishindo. **Comm. Dev. J.** 36:4 10:2001 pp.303-311.

4724   Marine Col. Sukhvinder Singh of Singapore. Dharmesh Thakkar. **Sikh Rev.** 49:9(573) 9:2001 pp.50-51.

4725   Mouvements forcés de population et aide humanitaire dans la North Eastern Province. *[In French]*; [Forced population movements and humanitarian aid in the North Eastern Province]. Olivier Damourette. **IFRA** 15 1-2:1999 pp.17-32.

4726   Moving from the stock of social capital to the flow of benefits: the role of agency. A. Krishna. **World Dev.** 29:6 6:2001 pp.925-944.

4727   NGOs and dryland development in Anantapur district, Andhra Pradesh. A.J. Dietz; M. Put. **Ind. Geograph. J.** 73:1 6:1998 pp.1-15.

4728 Nongovernmental organizations, 'grassroots', and the politics of virtue. Deborah Mindry. **Signs** 26:4 Summer:2001 pp.1187-1211.

4729 A people in travail II: 'livelihood projects', slapstick 'development', and development irony among veteran *Muro-Ami* fisherfolk of southern Cebu. Harold Olofson; Bernie Cañizares; Farah de Jose. **Phil. Q. Cult. Soc.** 28:3 9:2000 pp.317-354.

4730 People's development with people's money: the mobilisation-organisation-finance nexus. Reidar Dale. **Develop. Pract.** 11:5 11:2001 pp.606-621.

4731 Planning without plans and the neoliberal state: the case of St. Lucia, West Indies. Robert B. Potter; Jonathan Pugh. **Third World Plan. R.** 23:3 8:2001 pp.323-340.

4732 Poverty alleviation through community participation: realism or idealism?; *[Summary in Afrikaans]*. Inge Wassermann. **S. Afr. J. Ethnol.** 24:4 2001 pp.172-178.

4733 Rebuilding Sierra Leone: a report on work with young people. Saidu Sesay. **Comm. Dev. J.** 36:2 4:2001 pp.154-158.

4734 Review of implementation of the programme of action for the least developed countries for the 1990s: subregional studies. Economic and Social Commission for Asia and the Pacific. New York: United Nations - United Nations (Publications), 2001. 260p. *ISBN: 9211200156. Includes bibliographical references. (Series:* Least developed countries - 5).

4735 The role of geographical information systems in development planning in South Africa. T.R. Hill; D. McConnachie. **Third World Plan. R.** 23:3 8:2001 pp.289-299.

4736 The Sahel in West Africa: countries in transition to a full market economy. Jean Marie Cour. **Glo. Environ. Chan.** 11:1 4:2001 pp.31-48.

4737 Some thoughts on the effectiveness of aid, non-aid development finance and technical assistance. D. Dollar. **J. Int. Dev.** 13:7 10:2001 pp.1039-1055.

4738 Strategies for success in human development. Gustav Ranis; Frances Stewart. **J. Hum. Dev.** 1:1 2:2000 pp.49-70.

4739 Study of the incidence and nature of chronic poverty and development policy in South Africa: an overview. Michael Aliber. Manchester: Chronic Poverty Research Centre, 2001. vi, 70p. *ISBN: 1904049028.* (*Series:* CPRC working paper - 3).

4740 The sustainability of the *Botika-Binhi* Program. Virginia G. Abiad; Romel Del Mundo; Napoleon Y. Navarro; Victor S. Venida; Arleen Ramirez-Villoria. **Phil. Stud.** 49:2 2001 pp.176-202.

4741 Towards participatory communal appraisal. Joseph G. Bock. **Comm. Dev. J.** 36:2 4:2001 pp.146-153.

4742 We decide, they decide for us: popular participation as an issue in two Nigerian women's development programmes; *[Summary in French]*. Emma T. Lucas. **Afr. Devel.** XXV:1-2 2000 pp.75-98.

4743 Why research partnerships really matter: innovation theory, institutional arrangements and implications for developing new technology for the poor. A. Hall; G. Bockett; S. Taylor; M.V.K. Sivamohan; N. Clark. **World Dev.** 29:5 5:2001 pp.783-797.

4744 Will the new aid agenda help promote poverty reduction? H. White. **J. Int. Dev.** 13:7 10:2001 pp.1057-1070.

4745 The wolf-man and the Third World: exploring parallels between psychoanalysis and 'Third World' development. Emily Hinshelwood. **Psych. St.** 3:2 6:2001 pp.161-176.

4746 The World Development Report and the global development network. L. Squire. **J. Int. Dev.** 13:7 10:2001 pp.813-821.

4747 Zimbabwe human development report, 1998. Yash Tandon. Harare: United Nations Development Programme, Poverty Reduction Forum, Institute of Development Studies, 1999. 119p. *Includes bibliographical references (p. 115-119).*

Education
Éducation

4748　Academic paths, ageing and the living conditions of students in the late 20th century; *[Summary in French]*. Arnaud Sales; Réjean Drolet; Isabelle Bonneau. **Can. R. Soc. A.** 38:2 5:2001 pp.167-188.

4749　An architecture for learning. Christopher C. Benninger. **Ekistics** 65:391-393 7-12:1998 pp.207-238.

4750　Assessing directions for educational development assistance. David W. Chapman. **Int. R. Educat.** 47:5 9:2001 pp.459-476.

4751　Biros, books and big-men: literacy and the transformation of leadership in Simbu, Papua New Guinea. Eamonn McKeown. **Oceania** 72:2 12:2001 pp.105-116.

4752　Can 28 days make a difference? A case study of Community Aid Abroad's community leadership program. Cathryn E. Ollif. **Aust. Geogr. Stud.** 39:3 11:2001 pp.353-372.

4753　Enhancing female education in the Northern States of Nigeria. S.U. Balogun. **J. Pak. Hist. Soc.** XLIX:3 7-9:2001 pp.21-26.

4754　Food and education. Martin Bruegel; Séverine Gojard; Blandine Bril; Estelle Hombessa-Nkounkou; Jean-François Bouville; Célina Ocampo; Karola Elwert-Kretschmer; Lucy M. Long. **Food Food.** 9:3-4 2001 pp.149-259. *Collection of 5 articles.*

4755　Human resources, poverty, and regional development. Gavin W. Jones; Mark R. Rosenzweig [Comments by]; Zeba A. Sathar [Comments by]. **Pak. Dev. R.** 39:4(I) Winter:2000 pp.389-413.

4756　Literacy without formal education: the case of Pakistan. S. Nazli. **J. Int. Dev.** 13:5 7:2001 pp.535-548.

4757　Pre-application considerations for total quality management in a rural school in Peru; *[Summary in Spanish]*; *[Summary in Portuguese]*. Luis Andrés Lancho. **Unisa Lat.Am. Rep.** 17:1 2001 pp.29-37.

4758　Reflexiones acerca de algunos rituales escolares: las efemérides y los actos. *[In Spanish]*; [Reflections on a number of school rituals: events and actions]. Graciela G. Gómez; María Elena Pensiero. **Cuad. Am.** XV:3(87) 5-6:2001 pp.111-127.

4759　The role of universities in capacity building for better human settlements in South Africa. S. Krige. **S. Afr. Geogr. J.** 83:1 2001 pp.8-17.

4760　Skill training opportunities for rural women: problems and prospects. Shafiqul Islam; Ranjan Kumar Guha; Begum Nurun Naher. Kotbari: Bangladesh Academy for Rural Development, 2000. 109p. *ISBN: 9895591175.*

4761　'Why don't you just teach the Turks right from the start?!' Culturalisation and conflict dynamics in teaching practices at a multi-ethnic comprehensive school in Berlin. Sabine Mannitz. **Z. Ethn.** 126:2 2001 pp.293-312.

Environment and development
Environnement et développement

4762　Access to environmental justice? Litigation against TNCs in the South. Peter Newell. **IDS Bull.** 32:1 1:2001 pp.83-93.

4763　Adapting to climate change in Pacific Island countries: the problem of uncertainty. J. Barnett. **World Dev.** 29:6 6:2001 pp.977-994.

4764　The African Sahel 25 years after the great drought: assessing progress and moving towards new agendas and approaches. Simon Batterbury; Andrew Warren. **Glo. Environ. Chan.** 11:1 4:2001 pp.1-8.

4765　Alternative perspectives on livelihoods, agriculture and air pollution: agriculture in urban and peri-urban areas in a developing country. Neela Mukherjee; Meera Jayaswal; et al. Aldershot: Ashgate, 2001. xxvii, 205p. *ISBN: 0754616959. Includes bibliographical references and index. University of London. School of Oriental and African Studies.* (*Series:* SOAS studies in development geography).

4766   Artificial drainage induced erosion: the care of railway culverts on the Kewzana Ridge, near Alice, Eastern Cape. V. Kakembo. **S. Afr. Geogr. J.** 82:3 2000 pp.149-153.

4767   Biodiversity conservation through agrodiversity. Luohui Liang; Michael Stocking; Harold Brookfield; Libor Jansky. **Glo. Environ. Chan.** 11:1 4:2001 pp.97-101.

4768   Conceptualising state-controlled resort islands for an environment-friendly development of tourism: the Maldivian experience. Manfred Domroes. **Sing. J. Trop. Geogr.** 22:2 7:2001 pp.122-137.

4769   Coping with change: a study of local irrigation institutions in Taiwan. W.F. Lam. **World Dev.** 29:9 9:2001 pp.1569-1592.

4770   Culture, politics, and toxic dinoflagellate blooms: the anthropology of *Pfiesteria*. Michael Paolisso; Erve Chambers. **Human. Org.** 60:1 Spring:2001 pp.1-12.

4771   Deforestation and declining irrigation in Bohol. Peter B. Urich. **Phil. Q. Cult. Soc.** 28:4 12:2000 pp.476-497.

4772   Deforestation and Mangyan in Mindoro. Volker Schult. **Phil. Stud.** 49:2 2001 pp.151-175.

4773   Degradation debates and data deficiencies: the Mkomazi game reserve, Tanzania; *[Summary in French]*. Dan Brockington; Katherine Homewood. **Africa** 71:3 2001 pp.449-480.

4774   Documenting the effects of veld burning on soil and vegetation characteristics in Giant's Castle Game Reserve, Kwazulu-Natal Drakensberg. H.J. Bijker; P.D. Sumner; K.J. Meiklejohn; G.J. Bredenkamp. **S. Afr. Geogr. J.** 83:1 2001 pp.28-33.

4775   Encounters with the super-citizen: neoliberalism, environmental activism, and the American Heritage Rivers Intitiative. Thaddeus Countway Guldbrandsen; Dorothy C. Holland. **Anthr. Quart.** 74:3 7:2001 pp.124-134.

4776   The Environment Program: challenges and changes at the dawn of the new millennium. Asian Development Bank. Manila: Asian Development Bank, 2001. 50p. *ISBN: 9715613608.*

4777   Evolution de la gestion de l'eau dans un village périurbain de Ouagadougou, Basséko 4 ans après. *[In French]*; (Progress in the management of water in a neighbouring village of Ouagadougou — Basséko — in Burkina Faso, four years later.) *[Summary]*. Laurence Meï. **Cah. Outre-mer** 54:215 7-9:2001 pp.227-248.

4778   Explaining state-environmental NGO relations in the Philippines and Indonesia. Raymond L. Bryant. **Sing. J. Trop. Geogr.** 22:1 3:2001 pp.15-37.

4779   From users to custodians: changing relations between people and the state in forest management in Tanzania. Liz Wily; Peter A. Dewees. Washington DC: World Bank, Africa Technical Families, Environment and Social Development Unit, 2001. 31p. *Includes bibliographical references (p. 29-31). Also available online.* (*Series:* Policy research working paper - 2569).

4780   Gender and community rights in natural resource management. Sumi Krishna; Sagari R. Ramdas; Anthra Team; Yakshi Team; Girijana Deepika Team; P. Thamizoli; MSSRF Team; Ratna M. Sudarshan; Chhaya Datar; Aseem Prakash; Smita Gate; Neera M. Singh; Nitya Rao; Praveena Kodoth. **Ind. J. Gend. Stud.** 8:2 7-12:2001 pp.151-321. *Collection of 9 articles.*

4781   Green aid in India and Zimbabwe — conserving whose community? Z. Young; G. Makoni; S. Boehmer-Christiansen. **Geoforum** 32:3 8:2001 pp.299-318.

4782   Hunting for conservation in the Papua New Guinea highlands. Paul Sillitoe. **Ethnos** 66:3 2001 pp.365-393.

4783   Impacts of irrigation and drainage development projects in Pakistan: farmers' perceptions. Waheed-uz-Zaman. **Pak. Dev. R.** 39:2 Summer:2000 pp.131-152.

4784   Including herders in conservation management: reflections from both sides. Mary Ellen Zuppan. **Dev. Anthrop.** 18:1-2 Spring-Fall:2000 pp.3-16.

4785   Indigenous peoples and climate change research in the Arctic. Mark Nuttall. **Indig. Aff.** :4 2001 pp.26-33.

4786   Institutionalising the concept of environmental planning and management (EPM): successes and challenges in Dar es Salaam; *[Summary in French]*; *[Summary in Spanish]*; *[Summary in Portuguese]*. Wilbard J. Kombe. **Develop. Pract.** 11:2-3 5:2001 pp.190-207.

4787   Institutions and the environmental Kuznets Curve for deforestation: a crosscountry analysis for Latin America, Africa and Asia. M. Bhattarai; M. Hammig. **World Dev.** 29:6 6:2001 pp.995-1010.

4788   Integrated impact assessment for sustainable development: a case study approach. R. Bond; J. Curran; C. Kirkpatrick; N. Lee; P. Francis. **World Dev.** 29:6 6:2001 pp.1011-1024.

4789   Ist nachhaltige Entwicklung möglich? *[In German]*; (Is sustainable development possible?) *[Summary]*. Manuel Flury. **Geogr. Rund.** 53:9 9:2001 pp.57-62.

4790   It's traditional to change: a case study of strategic decision-making. Barbara Bodenhorn. **Cam. Anthrop.** 22:1 2000-2001 pp.24-51.

4791   The Karen response to Thai conservation policies. Chumpol Maniratanavongsiri. **Indig. Aff.** :4 2001 pp.58-70.

4792   A land renewed. Roger Hamilton. **Unisa Lat.Am. Rep.** 17:1 2001 pp.43-48.

4793   Local-level responses to environmental degradation in northwestern Mexico. María L. Cruz-Torres. **J. Anthr. Res.** 57:2 Summer:2001 pp.111-136.

4794   Mondialisation et diversité. *[In French]*; [Globalization and diversity]. P.J. Thumerelle; J.R. Pitte; A. Miossec; O. Sevin; M. Droulers; F.M. Le Tourneau. **Ann. Géogr.** 110:621 9-10:2001 pp.468-570. *Collection of 5 articles.*

4795   Power to the people: community-led wind energy — obstacles and opportunities in a South Wales valley. Emily Hinshelwood. **Comm. Dev. J.** 36:2 4:2001 pp.95-110.

4796   Le projet Natura 2000 et la protection du patrimoine naturel. L'exemple des sites expérimentaux pyrénéens. *[In French]*; (Natura 2000 and the protection of our natural heritage at experimental sites in the Pyrenees.) Johan Milian. **Rural Stud.** 157-158 1-6:2001 pp.173-194.

4797   The question of development and environment in geography in the era of globalisation. Leo J. De Haan. **Geojournal** 50:4 2000 pp.359-368.

4798   Quitovac oasis: a sense of home place and the development of water resources. Daniel R. Weir; Irisita Azary. **Prof. Geogr.** 53:1 2:2001 pp.45-55.

4799   Re-sourcing community: case studies from the Asia-Pacific. Andrew Walker; Flip Vanhelden; Simon Foale; Leontine E. Visser; Andrew McWilliam; Craig Johnson; Chun-Chieh Chi. **Asia Pacific J. Anthr.** 2:2 10:2001 pp.1-153. *Collection of 7 articles.*

4800   Responding to deforestation: productive conservation, the World Bank, and beekeeping in Rondônia, Brazil. J. Christopher Brown. **Prof. Geogr.** 53:1 2:2001 pp.106-118.

4801   Rethinking resource management: justice, sustainability and indigenous peoples. Richard Howitt. London: Routledge, 2001. 446p. *ISBN: 041512333X, 0415123321.*

4802   Rethinking sustainable development: indigenous peoples and resource use relations in the Philippines. Levita Duhaylungsod. **Bijdragen** 157:3 2001 pp.609-628.

4803   Sustainability and Sahelian soils: evidence from Niger. Andrew Warren; Simon Batterbury; Henny Osbahr. **Geogr. J.** 167:4 12:2001 pp.324-341.

4804   Sustainability in the small island states of the Pacific. Charles J. Stevens; Michael D. Lieber; Michèle D. Dominy; Karen L. Nero; Jim Hess; Mike Evans; Paul Shankman. **Pac. Stud.** 22:3-4 9-12:1999 pp.1-219. *Collection of 8 articles.*

4805   Understanding the links between conservation and development in the Bamenda highlands, Cameroon. J.I.O. Abbot; D.H.L. Thomas; A.A. Gardner; S.E. Neba; M.W. Khen. **World Dev.** 29:7 7:2001 pp.1115-1136.

4806   Urban sustainability under threat: the restructuring of the fishing industry in Mar del Plata, Argentina; *[Summary in French]*; *[Summary in Spanish]*; *[Summary in Portuguese]*. Adriana Allen. **Develop. Pract.** 11:2-3 5:2001 pp.152-173.

Food supply and nutrition
Approvisionnement alimentaire et nutrition

4807   Agronomy, environment and food security for 21st century. Panjab Singh [Ed.]; Rajenda Prasad [Ed.]; I.P.S. Ahlawat [Ed.]. New Delhi: Indian Society of Agronomy, 2000. 488p.

Includes bibliographical references. Conference papers. Indian Council of Agricultural Research.

4808 The AIDS epidemic in Malawi and its threat to household food security. Mike Mathambo Mtika. **Human. Org.** 60:2 Summer:2001 pp.178-188.

4809 Bean-curd consumption in Hong Kong. Sidney W. Mintz; Chee Beng Tan. **Ethnology** XL:2 Spring:2001 pp.113-128.

4810 Confronting dietary energy supply with anthropometry in the assessment of undernutrition prevalence at the level of countries. M. Nubé. **World Dev.** 29:7 7:2001 pp.1275-1289.

4811 Evolution de la nutrition et de la sécurité alimentaire dans deux collectivités inuites entre 1992 et 1997. *[In French]*; Change in nutrition and food security in two Inuit communities, 1992 to 1997. Judith Lawn; Dan Harvey. Ottawa: Department of Indian and Northern Affairs, Canada, 2001. xvii, 108p. *ISBN: 0662311450. Includes bibliographical references (p. 105-108). Government of Canada Depository Services Program.*

4812 Famine in North Korea: causes and cures. Marcus Noland; Sherman Robinson; Tao Wang. **Econ. Dev. Cult. Change** 49:4 7:2001 pp.741-767.

4813 Food into cities: selected papers. Olivio Argenti [Ed.]. Rome: Food and Agriculture Organization of the United Nations, 2000. *ISBN: 9251044783. (Series:* FAO agricultural services bulletin - 143).

4814 Food security and food policy in Papua New Guinea. John Gibson. Port Moresby: Institute of National Affairs, 2001. 71p. *ISBN: 9980774320. (Series:* Discussion Paper - 83).

4815 Food security in sub-Saharan Africa. Simon Maxwell [Ed.]; Stephen Devereux [Ed.]. London: ITDG, 2001. xviii, 350p. *ISBN: 1853395234. Includes bibliographical references and index. University of Sussex, Institute of Development Studies.*

4816 From policy to practice: challenges in infant feeding in emergencies during the Balkan crisis. Annalies Borrel; Anna Taylor; Marie McGrath; Andrew Seal; Elizabeth Hormann; Laura Phelps; Frances Mason. **Disasters** 25:2 6:2001 pp.149-163.

4817 Giving to the poor? Targeting of food aid in rural Ethiopia. T.S. Jayne; J. Strauss; T. Yamano; D. Molla. **World Dev.** 29:5 5:2001 pp.887-910.

4818 'I am because we are': rethinking qualitative research for food security in Africa's rural communities. Cornelius B. Pratt; Charles Okigbo. **Development** 44:4 12:2001 pp.108-113.

4819 Land resources information systems for food security in SADC countries. Food and Agriculture Organization of the United Nations. Rome: Food and Agriculture Organization of the United Nations, 2000. 76p. *ISBN: 9251044279. Selected papers from a subregional workshop, Harare, November 1999. (Series:* World soil resources report - 89).

4820 Local/global encounters: community innovations against hunger. Stuart J. Clark; C. Stuart Taylor; Karim Hussein; Binayak Rajbhandari; Shahid Zia; Mushtaq Gadi; Roy Prosterman; Marjan Leneman; Robin S. Reid; Vanita Viswanath; Lenard Milich. **Development** 44:4 12:2001 pp.57-97. *Collection of 8 articles.*

4821 Mortality responses to rice price fluctuations and household factors in a farming village in central Tokugawa, Japan. Noriko O. Tsuya; Kiyoshi Hamano. **Hist. Fam.** 6:1 2001 pp.1-31.

4822 Parental investment and child health in a Yanomamö village suffering short-term food stress. Edward H. Hagen; Raymond B. Hames; Nathan M. Craig; Matthew T. Lauer; Michael E. Price. **J. Biosoc. Sc.** 33:4 10:2001 pp.503-528.

4823 Poverty and undernutrition: theory, measurement, and policy. Peter Svedberg. Oxford: Oxford University Press, 2000. 348p. *ISBN: 0198292686. Includes bibliographical references. World Institute for Development Economics Research of the United Nations University. (Series:* Studies in development economics).

4824 Review of policies and guidelines on infant feeding in emergencies: common ground and gaps. Andrew Seal; Anna Taylor; Lola Gostelow; Marie McGrath. **Disasters** 25:2 6:2001 pp.136-148.

4825 Reviving global poverty reduction: what role for genetically modified plants? M. Lipton. **J. Int. Dev.** 13:7 10:2001 pp.823-846.

4826 Security of movement, security of livelihood: combating trafficking in women and children and ensuring food security. South Asia Network on Food, Ecology and Culture.

Dhaka: UBINIG, 2000. 64p. *ISBN: 9848113053. Papers presented at the South Asian Association of the Regional Co-operation Peoples Forum Colombo seminar, Dhaka, 1998. SANFEC. Resistance Network.*

4827   Social protection via rice: the OPK rice subsidy program in Indonesia. Steven R. Tabor; M. Husein Sawit. **Develop. Eco.** XXXIX:3 9:2001 pp.267-294.

Gender and development
Genre et développement

4828   Analysis of non-conventional indicators of gender relations: evidence from Pakistan. Rehana Siddiqui; Shahnaz Hamid; Rizwana Siddiqui. **Pak. Dev. R.** 39:4(II) Winter:2000 pp.913-932.

4829   The challenge of gender equity and human rights on the threshold of the twenty-first century. United Nations, Economic Commission for Latin America and the Caribbean, Women and Development Unit. Santiago: United Nations, CEPAL, ECLAC, Women and Development Unit, 2000. 68p. *ISBN: 9211212677. Papers presented at the 8th Regional Conference on Women in Latin America and the Caribbean, Lima, 2000. Includes bibliographical references (p. 61-66). (Series: Mujer y desarrollo - 27).*

4830   Civic society and the new economy in patriarchal Singapore: emasculating the political, feminizing the public. Kenneth Paul Andrew Sze Sian Tan. **Crossroads** 15:2 2001 pp.95-124.

4831   Class, gender and ecology in spatial development initiatives: the case of the Maputo Development Corridor. Ian Taylor. Bellville: Centre for Southern African Studies, School of Government, University of the Western Cape, 2000. 23p. *ISBN: 1868084566. Includes bibliographical references. (Series: Southern African Perspectives - 82).*

4832   Community programs and women's participation: the Chinese experience. David Coady; Xinyl Dai; Limin Wang; World Bank Development Research Group. Washington DC: World Bank, 2001. 37p. *(Series: Policy research working paper - 2622).*

4833   Empowering women in agricultural education for sustainable rural development. George M.M. Ugbomeh. **Comm. Dev. J.** 36:4 10:2001 pp.289-302.

4834   Empowering women through cash relief in humanitarian contexts. Hisham Khogali; Parmjit Takhar. **Gen. Dev.** 9:3 11:2001 pp.40-49.

4835   Endangered daughters: discrimination and development in Asia. Elisabeth Croll. London: Routledge, 2000. 207p. *ISBN: 0415247659, 0415247640.*

4836   Fostering women's participation in development through non-governmental efforts in Cameroon. Lotsmart Fonjong. **Geogr. J.** 167:3 9:2001 pp.223-234.

4837   Gender checklist: agriculture. Asian Development Bank. Manila: Asian Development Bank, 2001. 54p. *Includes bibliographical references.*

4838   Gender checklist: urban development and housing. Asian Development Bank. Manila: Asian Development Bank, 2001. 37p. *Includes bibliographical references.*

4839   Gender, development and humanitarian work. Caroline Sweetman [Ed.]. Oxford: Oxfam, 2001. 97p. *ISBN: 0855984570.*

4840   Gender dimensions of population and development in South-east Asia. Economic and Social Commission for Asia and the Pacific; United Nations. New York: United Nations - United Nations (Publications), 1999. x, 134p. *ISBN: 9211199271. Includes bibliographical references. (Series: Asian population studies - 150).*

4841   Gender issues in poverty alleviation: recent experiences with demand-based programs in Latin America, Africa and Eastern Europe. Carol Graham. Geneva: International Labour Office, Development and Technical Cooperation Department, 1996. vii, 26p. *ISBN: 9221100987. Includes bibliographical references (p. 23). (Series: Issues in development discussion paper - 11).*

4842   Gender, poverty, and sustainable development: towards a holistic framework of understanding and action. Vivienne Wee; Noeleen Heyzer; Aileen Kwa [Ed.]; et al.

Engender, UNDP, 1995. xvi, 168p. *ISBN: 9810069936. Includes bibliographical references (p. 159-168).*

4843   The genre of women leaders in local bodies: experience from Tamil Nadu. G. Palanithurai. **Indian J. Publ. Admin.** XLVII:1 1-3:2001 pp.38-50.

4844   Including expectant fathers in antenatal education programmes in Istanbul, Turkey; *[Summary in Spanish]*; *[Summary in French].* Janet Molzan Turan; Hacer Nalbant; Ayşen Bulut; Yusuf Sahip. **Reprod. Health Mat.** 9:18 11:2001 pp.114-125.

4845   Men's involvement in gender and development policy and practice: beyond rhetoric. Caroline Sweetman [Ed.]. Oxford: Oxfam, 2001. 80p. *ISBN: 085598466X.*

4846   Micro-credit and emotional well-being: experience of poor rural women from Matlab, Bangladesh. S.M. Ahmed; M. Chowdhury; A. Bhuiya. **World Dev.** 29:11 11:2001 pp.1957-1966.

4847   Microenterprise lending to female entrepreneurs: sacrificing economic growth for poverty alleviation? M. Kevane; B. Wydick. **World Dev.** 29:7 7:2001 pp.1225-1236.

4848   Operationalizing microfinance: women and craftwork in Ifugao, upland Philippines. B. Lynne Milgram. **Human. Org.** 60:3 Fall:2001 pp.212-224.

4849   Purity and communal boundaries: women and social change in a Bangladeshi village. Santi Rozario. Dhaka: University Press Limited, 2001. 200p. *ISBN: 9840516118.*

4850   Sisterhood and seine-nets: engendering development and conservation in Ghana's marine fishery. Barbara Louise Endemaño Walker. **Prof. Geogr.** 53:2 5:2001 pp.160-177.

4851   Targeting women in micro-finance schemes: objectives and outcomes. Soofia Mumtaz. **Pak. Dev. R.** 39:4(II) Winter:2000 pp.877-890.

4852   Village experts and development discourse: 'progress' in a Philippine Igorot village. Dorothea Hilhorst. **Human. Org.** 60:4 Winter:2001 pp.401-413.

4853   'Washing machines make lazy women' domestic appliances and the negotiation of women's propriety in Soweto. Helen Meintjes. **J. Mat. Cult.** 6:3 11:2001 pp.345-363.

4854   What is 'the local' in women's participation? The contexts of two development programs in Samoa. M. Kuramitsu. **Geogr. Rev. Jpn.** 74:1 2001 pp.15-32.

4855   Women development workers: implementing rural credit programmes in Bangladesh. Anne Marie Goetz. Dhaka: University Press Limited, 2001. 443p. *ISBN: 9840516108.*

4856   Women in post-independence Sri Lanka. Swarna Jayaweera [Ed.]. Thousand Oaks CA: Sage Publications, 2001. *ISBN: 0761995048, 076199503X. Includes bibliographical references and index.*

4857   Women in the Republic of Uzbekistan. Wendy Mee. Manila: Asian Development Bank, 2001. 69p. *Asian Development Bank, Office of Environment and Social Development.* (*Series:* Country briefing paper).

4858   Women's autonomy in the context of rural Pakistan. Zeba Ayesha Sathar; Shahnaz Kazi. **Pak. Dev. R.** 39:2 Summer:2000 pp.89-110.

4859   Women's development and empowerment in Tamil Nadu: a performance appraisal. S. Sundari; N. Geetha. **Ind. J. Eco.** LXXXII:324 7:2001 pp.25-44.

4860   Women's participation projects: a rights approach to social exclusion. Gil Long; Kate Phillips. Glasgow: Active Learning Centre, Glasgow Caledonian University, 2000. 50p. *ISBN: 190124895X.*

4861   The Women's Reservation Bill: a crisis of identity. Roopa Sharma. **Indian J. Publ. Admin.** XLVII:1 1-3:2001 pp.51-66.

4862   Yoruba rural women and alley farming. Elizabeth A. Ogunlana. **Gen. Tech. Dev.** 5:3 9-12:2001 pp.409-424.

Health
Santé

4863   Aids and development in Africa. S. Dixon; S. McDonald; J. Roberts; G.P. Garnett; N.C. Grassly; S. Gregson; C. Arndt; J.D. Lewis; L. Kumaranayake; C. Watts; H. Waddell; S.

Chandiwana; L. Haddad; S. Gillespie; J.L. Lamboray; S.M. Skevington. **J. Int. Dev.** 13:4 5:2001 pp.381-521. *Collection of 8 articles.*

4864 AIDS in Swaziland: the battle from within; *[Summary in French]*. John L. Daly. **Afr. Stud. R.** 44:1 4:2001 pp.21-35.

4865 Becoming poverty focused: implications for health actors. Eleanor Fisher; Jeremy Holland; Sarah James. **Development** 44:1 3:2001 pp.22-30.

4866 Capacity building to improve women's health in rural China. V.C. Li; W. Shaoxian; W. Kunyi; Z. Wentao; O. Buchthal; G.C. Wong; M.A. Burris. **Soc. Sci. Med.** 52:2 1:2001 pp.279-292.

4867 Chronic disease and disability of the poor: tackling the challenge. Derek Yach. **Development** 44:1 3:2001 pp.59-65.

4868 Collaboration in community development and health by non- government and government organizations in Bogra district (1996-2000). Integrated Community Family Health Development Program, 2000.

4869 Common questions about sexual health education. Alexander McKay. **Canad. J. Human Sex.** 9:2 2000 pp.129-137.

4870 Communicable disease and disability of the poor. Sergio Spinaci; David Heymann. **Development** 44:1 3:2001 pp.66-72.

4871 Community participatory approaches to dengue prevention in Sarawak, Malaysia. Sara Ashencaen Crabtree; Christina M. Wong; Faizah Mas'ud. **Human. Org.** 60:3 Fall:2001 pp.281-287.

4872 'Consultations with the poor' from a health perspective. Deepa Narayan. **Development** 44:1 3:2001 pp.15-21.

4873 Danger and opportunity: responding to HIV with vision. Kate Butcher; Alice Welbourn. **Gen. Dev.** 9:2 7:2001 pp.51-61.

4874 Decentralization and public health in the Philippines. Xavier Furtado. **Development** 44:1 3:2001 pp.108-116.

4875 Economic dynamics and health: lessons from Thailand. Suwit Wibulpolprasert; Paichit Pengpaiboon. **Development** 44:1 3:2001 pp.99-107.

4876 Enhancing gender equity in health programmes: monitoring and evaluation. Mohga Kamal Smith. **Gen. Dev.** 9:2 7:2001 pp.95-105.

4877 An evaluation of the Choices and Changes student program: a grade four to seven sexual health education program based on the Canadian guidelines for sexual health education. Jeff Wackett; Lisa Evans. **Canad. J. Human Sex.** 9:4 2000 pp.265-273.

4878 Female education, adolescent sexuality and the risk of sexually transmitted infection in Ariaal Rendille culture. Eric A. Roth; Elliot M. Fratkin; Elizabeth N. Ngugi; Barry W. Glickman. **Cult. Health. Sex.** 3:1 1-3:2001 pp.35-47.

4879 Gender and health care utilisation in Pakistan. Syed Mubashir Ali. **Pak. Dev. R.** 39:3 Autumn:2000 pp.213-234.

4880 Global public goods and the poor. Inge Kaul. **Development** 44:1 3:2001 pp.77-84.

4881 Health and development in South Africa: from principles to practice. Desmond Johns. **Development** 44:1 3:2001 pp.122-128.

4882 Health policy, and health care delivery in Africa. Ellen E. Foley; L. Carlin; T. Aspray; R. Edwards; L. Hayes; H. Kitange; N. Unwin; Hanne Mogensen; Thabale J. Ngulube. **Urban Anthro.** 30:1 Spring:2001 pp.1-104. *Collection of 3 articles.*

4883 Health, poverty and dignified living. Charles Omondi Oyaya; Dan C.O. Kaseje. **Development** 44:1 3:2001 pp.51-57.

4884 Immunization status and child survival in rural Ghana. Philomena Nyarko; Brian Pence; Cornelius Debpuur. New York: Population Council, 2001. 29p. *Includes bibliographical references (p. 28-29). (Series:* Policy Research Division working papers - 147).

4885 Integration of an essential services package (ESP) in child and reproductive health and family planning with a micro-credit program for poor women: experience from a pilot project in rural Bangladesh. R. Amin; M. St. Pierre; A. Ahmed; R. Haq. **World Dev.** 29:9 9:2001 pp.1611-1621.

AUTHOR INDEX
INDEX DES AUTEURS

Aarts, F. 1923
Abad, R. 3157
Abadie-Reynal, C. 458
Abakerli, S. 2222
Abashin, S. 202, 3347, 3361
Abayev, N. 1876, 3691
Abbadi, A. 1122
Abbot, J. 4805
Abboud-Haggar, S. 1862
Abdallah-Pretceille, M. 3037
Abdo, K. 831
Abel, S. 2712
Abeysekara, A. 3199, 4471
Abiad, V. 4740
Abileh, M. 1278
Abileh, M. Abu 1315
Abka'I-Khavari, M. 4333
Aboshi, H. 1482
Abreu, M. 2222
Abu-Dalu, R. 1318
Acciaioli, G. 4481
Acharya, S. 4671
Acioly, Jr., C. 2222
Ackah, W. 4401
Adams, J. 1616, 4016
Adams, N. 518
Adams, R. 456, 2841
Adams, V. 3739
Adams, W. 2338, 4691
Adang, C. 324, 3338
Addison, E. 3849
Addlakha, R. 2933
Adebowale, S. 4548
Adelman, H. 606, 2986
Adenaike, C. 231
Adetoro, S. 2252
Adler, A. 2579
Adriansen, I. 3653, 4484
Adu-Poku, S. 2820
Afigbo, A. 532
Afolabi, N. 4158
Afsana, K. 2702, 3775
Afsaruddin, A. 3978
Agar, M. 3765
Agawu, K. 3933, 4059

Agboola, C. 573
Agetsuma, N. 1653
Aggarwal, R. 383, 2779
Aghacy, S. 4205
Aghali Zakara, M. 122, 600
Agoston-Nikolova, E. 2652, 3345
Agueda Castro, M. 1375
Águeda Méndez, M. 3216
Aguilar, M. 675
Aguilar, S. 1978
Aguirre, E. 1379
Agusta-Boularot, S. 1418, 1419
Ahearn, L. 248
Ahiadeke, C. 1548
Ahlawat, I. 4807
Ahluwalia, J. 2511
Ahmed, A. 4885
Ahmed, S. 4846
Ahmed, W. 3766
Ahounou, C. 3608
Ahyan, S. 3125
Ai, G. 632, 2580
Aidoo, J. 2427
Aiesh, Y. 3738, 4087
Aijmer, G. 3733
Ainley, J. 2298
Ainsa, F. 4191
Aitken, S. 291, 2668
Aiyer, A. 4611
Akester, M. 3860
Akinwumi, O. 633, 3008, 4013
Akinyele, R. 2504
Akinyemi, A. 2584, 4090
Aklujkar, A. 3153
Aksenov, M. 819
Akurang-Parry, K. 4548
Alamshoev, M. 3536
Alaoui, A. 3049
Alary, V. 4671
Alatriste Guzmán, Ó. 1428
Alber, E. 697
Albera, D. 426
Albergoni, G. 2417, 3018
Albers, I. 49, 311
Alberts, S. 1659

Albore-Livadie, C. 1376
Albrecht, G. 827
Albuquerque, A. 1606
Alcântara, M. de 2798
Alcaraz, F. 2317
Alcina Franch, J. 1005
Alcock, S. 984
Aldazabal, V. 1375
Aldhouse Green, M. 828
Aldhouse-Green, S. 873
Aleixandre, T. 839
Aleksandrov, H. 166, 3649, 4428
Alessio, S. D' 4366
Alexaki, N. 2210
Alexander, C. 2983
Alexeev, A. 4570
Alfred, T. 4643
Algaze, G. 2358
Ali, K. 2455
Ali, M. 2138, 3768, 3779, 3800, 4698
Ali, S. 4879
Aliber, M. 4739
Alilović, M. 1575
Alim, I. al- 4036
Alisherov, A. 1504
Alivelu, C. 1490
Allan, N. 291
Allart, M. 2269
Allason-Jones, L. 1396
Allcock, J. 4565
Allen, A. 4806
Allen, G. 589
Allen, L. 3250, 4462
Allen, N. 223
Allen-Arave, W. 4393
Alleton, V. 2019
Allison, A. 4100, 4217
Allman, J. 2833
Almagro, A. 1015, 1021, 1099, 1166
Almeida, F. 1953
Almeida, M. de 735
Almeyda, A. 2404
Almroth, L. 2890
Almroth-Berggren, V. 2890
Alonso, S. 1522
Alpern, S. 354, 724, 790
Alter, J. 2926, 4297
Althabe, G. 4105, 4523
Altmann, J. 1659
Alvard, M. 2433
Alvarez, R. 4632
Alves, J. 3085
Alvi, A. 4510
Amabe, F. 470, 2567
Amali, O. 2137

Amanor, K. 2411
Amaral, I. do 323, 707, 721, 806
Amborn, H. 3553
Ambros, B. 3531, 3532
Amédégnato, S. 1749
Ames, G. 215
Ameur, S. 4610
Ami, D. Ben- 928
Amiet, P. 1086
Amin, R. 4885
Amir-Moezzi, M. 3509
Amis, P. 4937
Amit, D. 1399
Amit, V. 4606
Ammerman, A. 948
Amor, H. 1540, 1552
'Amr, K. 952, 1075, 1151, 1162, 1187, 1202,
     1204, 1206, 1209, 1211, 1239, 1273, 1275,
     1380, 1388
Amri, N. 3338
Amubode, A. 2252
Anandalakshmy, S. 2931
Ananthanarayana, H. 1907
Anckar, D. 2559
Andaya, L. 4215
Andersen, H. 371
Anderson, A. 623, 931, 1290
Anderson, B. 4504
Anderson, E. 3753
Anderson, G. 4016
Anderson, M. 1719
Anderson, S. 3625
Andersson, J. 684, 2120, 2179
Andor, E. 3230, 4441
Andrea, A. D' 900
Andrews, P. 822
Andreyev, A. 762
Andueza, M. 3862, 4191
Anetshofer, H. 117
Anezaki, T. 1464
Angleviel, F. 326
Anignikin, S. 2475
Annan, K. 4712
Anping, P. 2304
Ansari, G. 2220
Ansell, N. 2734
Anthra Team 4780
Antoljak, N. 1570
Antón, S. 1521
Antoni, K. 181, 3706
Antrobus, P. 2496, 2863
Antunes, R. 2222
Anyahuru, I. 3933, 4059
Anyonge, T. 4702
Aoki, K. 246, 2135

Aoyama, K. 1372
Apâvàloae, L. 1566
Apfelbaum, D. 4384
Appadurai, A. 178, 2210
Applbaum, K. 2363
Apter, E. 4170
Arab, G. 2404
Arai, K. 4583
Arakelova, V. 3991
Araldi, L. 2883
Aranguren, B. 850
Araujo-Bonjean, C. 4663
Arazi, A. 3354
Arbena, J. 4336
Archi, A. 2261
Archibald, C. 2885
Archibald, L. 4645
Arcury, T. 3827
Ardaya, N. 2863
Ardener, S. 7
Ardèvol, J. 841
Aréchiga, J. 1593
Arenas Monreal, R. 546
Arends-Kuenning, M. 2710
Argenti, O. 4813
Arkoun, M. 3354
Armijo-Hussein, N. 2149, 2720
Armour, W. 4419
Armstrong, D. 988
Armstrong, R. 1546
Arnaud, V. 768
Arndt, C. 4863
Arnold, B. 991
Arnold, D. 3182
Arnold, K. 1681, 1682
Arnoldi, M. 368, 4138
Aron, A. 122, 600
Arpi, C. 661
Arreola, D. 291
Arrif, A. 2214
Arruda, R. 4408, 4590
Arshi, S. 3506
Arsuaga, J. 460, 824, 899, 1458, 1534
Artemova, O. 1554
Arvaniti, A. 1922, 1959
Árvay, A. 3703
Arvidsson, A. 2326
Asad, M. 4552
Asagiri, K. 787
Ashforth, A. 3579
Ashkaba, J. 2010
Ashley, S. 628
Asian Coalition for Housing Rights 2210
Asian Development Bank 4776, 4837, 4838
Asian Productivity Organization 4920

Aslan, Z. 1010, 1064
Asombang, R. 968
Aspray, T. 4882
Assier-Andrieu, L. 262, 2992
Aston, M. 938
Astuti, R. 4507
Atack, M. 3005
Athens, J. 857
Atherton, M. 40
Atkinson, A. 4933
Atkinson, P. 28, 72, 406, 1505, 2674
Atran, S. 2080, 3662
'Attiyat, T. 1150
Atwood Mason, M. 368
Aubel, J. 2686
Aubriot, O. 2289
Audebert, C. 3330
Aufreiter, S. 1601, 1651
Augustine, J. 3187
Aujard, F. 1634, 1695
Aukrust, V. 4506
Aung-Thwin, M. 906
Aureli, E. 2768
Aureli, F. 1636
Ausec, M. 504, 2530
Austen, R. 575
Austin-Broos, D. 3107
Auyero, J. 4435
Auzanneau, M. 1749
Avellino, E. 1278
Avenne, C. Van Den 1749
Avorgbedor, D. 3907, 3933, 4059
Avotri, J. 2758
Avruch, K. 395
Awe, J. 499, 2240, 2444
Aworawo, D. 4548
Axthelm, M. 1500
Ayafor, I. 4548
Ayala, A. 4696
Aydemir, Y. 4074
Ayivor, K. 4188
Ayyankeril, D. 291
Azary, I. 4798
Aziz, F. 1137
Azmi, K. 3766, 3802
Azoulay, K. 4468
Ba, P. 4547
Baali, A. 1540, 1552
Babadzhanov, B. 3322
Babich, I. 2979, 3349
Babin, J. 1559
Babiracki, C. 3967
Babo, R. 1626
Babu, B. 2726
Babyonyshev, M. 1936

Bachman, T. 2695
Bachmann, P. 3330
Backett-Milburn, K. 2810, 2932
Backus, M. 4470
Baczyńska, B. 871
Badmaeva, G. 3945
Baer, A. 434
Baer, D. 3112
Baer, R. 313
Baffioni, C. 3332
Bagader, A. 3863, 4349
Bahain, J. 460
Bahn, P. 1023
Bailey, C. 2713
Baillie, I. 2313
Baines, S. 4655
Baird, D. 1219
Bakalova, E. 166, 3649, 4428
Bakamba, M. 1993
Baker, A. 1708
Baker, F. 1310
Baker, L. 263, 3043
Baker, P. 1789
Bækken, B. 1948
Bakker, H. 3285
Bakri, J. al- 2287
Bala, S. 3497
Balakrishna, N. 1568
Balandine, S. 2148
Balard, M. 326
Balbir, N. 3384
Balcerowicz, P. 3212, 3381
Baldazzi, B. 2768
Baldi, P. 1920
Baldissera, F. 4259
Baldridge, D. 2691
Baldwin, M. 694
Bale, J. 4312
Bales, K. 1708
Balgir, R. 1495
Ballard, C. 809
Ballesté, P. 841
Ballinger, D. 929
Ballington, J. 4722
Balm, R. 4103
Baloch, N. 446, 4551
Balogun, S. 4753
Balqar, S. 990
Balutet, N. 1810
Bambanota, G. 4555
Bamony, P. 3685
Banek, L. 1555
Banerjee, S. 3369, 3387
Bangerter, A. 4575
Bangha, I. 4274

Bankoff, G. 2443, 4544
Bannerjee, K. 4937
Bannikov, K. 3021, 3022
Banning, E. 891, 1112
Bapat, G. 3892
Baqui, A. 2138, 3800
Barbash, I. 133, 439
Barbetti, M. 906
Barclay, G. 1029
Barczewski, S. 4221
Bardell, M. 4035
Bardi, M. 1658, 1675
Baré, J. 3929
Barello, A. 296
Barford, P. 1001, 3249
Bargh, J. 2555
Barker, C. 4434
Barker, J. 215, 2650
Barlow, K. 2694
Barlow, P. 3247
Barman, B. 2452
Barnes, J. 2045
Barnes, R. 688, 1197
Barnet, M. 3609
Barnett, J. 4763
Baroin, C. 2586
Baron-Epel, O. 3792
Baronti Marchiò, R. 3728
Barré, M. 4283
Barreteau, D. 113, 1802
Barreto, M. 4937
Barrett, C. 1563
Barrett, J. 888
Barrett, K. 1265
Barrett, S. 98, 2503
Barrett, T. 2253
Barrientos, S. 2469
Barrier, N. 3470
Barriga Villanueva, R. 1787
Barros, F. 4937
Barry, M. 2718, 3814
Barth, F. 213
Barton, A. 598
Barton, G. 360, 2311
Barton, R. 1618, 1681, 1682
Bartosiewicz, L. 454, 974, 1367
Baruah, K. 2592
Bar-Yosef, A. 3942
Bar-Yosef, O. 1384
Basal, N. 3329
Bašić, V. 1591
Basile, J. 1051, 1078
Bassett, T. 4912
Bastert, K. 1139, 1140, 1155
Bastian, M. 2682

Bastida, E. 2169, 2660
Bastin, R. 3549
Bastin, Y. 1990
Bastos, C. 729
Bataille, G. 4576
Batayneh, T. 1355
Bate, R. 4888
Batibo, H. 1990
Batteau, A. 255, 2369
Batterbury, S. 2106, 2207, 2446, 4764, 4803
Battesti, V. 3658
Baubérot, A. 2085, 4310
Baučić, I. 1474
Baudry, P. 2791
Bauer, H. 1249
Baum, G. 3160
Bauman, T. 3107
Bauman, Z. 2322, 2516, 4449
Baumann, T. 2210
Baumer, U. 845
Baumgarten, J. 3432
Bausinger, H. 141
Bava, S. 3591, 3822
Baxi, U. 4613
Baxter, L. 4012
Bayer, G. 4548
Bayhom-Daou, T. 3346
Baylies, C. 2721
Bayliss, A. 868
Bazantay, P. 4263
Bazielich, B. 2951
Beach, D. 767, 3577
Beaglehole, J. 594
Beall, C. 1514
Beard, V. 2221
Beauvais, M. de 3048
Beaver, J. 1249
Bebbington, A. 2207
Becerra, H. 2210
Becerra, M. 265
Bech, K. 1951
Bechhofer, F. 2600
Bechtel, F. 1376
Beck, B. 1711
Bečka, J. 4169
Becker, H. 107, 405
Beckett, J. 105, 3231
Becquelin, P. 942
Bedal, L. 1073
Bedaux, R. 968
Bedell, J. 982
Bedford, S. 198, 2679
Bédoucha, G. 2417, 3018
Beek, W. van 270, 2537
Beekman, C. 789

Beer, B. 2939, 4010
Beer, F. de 2116, 2523, 3695
Begemann, F. 912
Begossi, A. 3786
Begovac, J. 3770
Behrend, H. 674, 4104, 4126
Beialy, S. el 1185
Beisembiev, T. 741
Bekić, A. 1575
Bekker, J. 2750, 3019
Belanger, F. 2148
Belcastro, M. 1280
Belfer-Cohen, A. 1384
Belkeziz, N. 1540
Belkin, G. 4525
Bell, R. 3827
Bellagama, A. 4447
Bellamy, E. 2092
Bellier, I. 2486
Bellon, M. 2312
Bellwald, U. 1251
Bellwood, P. 830
Benali, A. 2289
Benassy-Berling, M. 3637
Benbouzid, F. 2506, 4589
Benda-Beckmann, F. von 2984, 4670
Bender, B. 2170
Bender, M. 3982
Bendjaballah, S. 1854
Bénéfice, E. 1557
Bénéï, V. 801
Benequista, N. 4632
Beng-Huat, C. 4464
Benitah, R. 1460
Benito, A. 839
Benjamin, J. 228
Bennardo, G. 1880
Bennett, C. 1597
Bennett, K. 3056, 3075
Bennett, L. 215
Bennett, N. 1582
Bennett, R. 4041
Bennett, S. 1511
Benninger, C. 4749
Bennion, L. 291
Bennis, S. 1749
Bennison, A. 611, 3042
Bennoun, R. 4722
Benoist-Méchin, J. 571, 3343
Bentaher, F. 1089
Bentley, J. 2088, 3667
Bentley, R. 877, 2177
Bentley-Condit, V. 1603
Benton, L. 771, 2981
Beňušková, Z. 3158

Benziger, T. 3780
Berard, J. 1564
Berdimuradov, A. 1072
Berezhnova, M. 211, 430
Berg, G. 800, 818
Berg, J. 2231
Berge, C. 121, 408, 1610
Berger, L. 3330
Berger, M. 666, 3458
Berger, S. 560, 3412
Bergeret, P. 2318
Bergström, S. 2890
Berhane, Y. 4902
Berhanu, B. 2129, 2704
Berkwitz, S. 3174
Berlage, N. 2294
Berlier, J. 4263
Berman, C. 1614
Berman, R. 1840
Bernacky, B. 1625
Bernand, C. 2336
Bernard, H. 286, 2124
Bernardina, S. 2085, 4310
Bernault, F. 2532, 3590
Bernbeck, R. 1108
Berner, E. 4934
Bernier, H. 475
Bernon, O. de 3198
Bernstein, I. 1661, 1686
Bernsten, J. 1797
Berssenbrugge, M. 4041
Bertacca, A. 1801
Berthelot, K. 4383
Berthoud, G. 4502
Bertocci, S. 953
Bertolani, G. 1063
Bertrand, D. 3582
Bertrand, M. 3617
Bertsch, W. 2389, 2960
Bescos, G. 884
Beslu, C. 4263
Besnier, N. 3000
Bessant, L. 333, 547
Bessell, N. 1968
Besson, F. 4263
Bestock, L. 1417
Betancourt Mendieta, A. 4192
Bettelheim, J. 4123
Bettinger, R. 1378
Betts, A. 1152
Beydoun, M. 2141
Bgazhnokov, B. 4386
Bhat, A. 2655, 2770
Bhatnagar, S. 3768
Bhatt, R. 1815

Bhatta, B. 4272
Bhattacharya, F. 2624
Bhattacharya, R. 3372, 3373
Bhattacharya, S. 1906
Bhattacharyya, S. 2399
Bhattarai, M. 4787
Bhola, H. 3469
Bhuiya, A. 4846
Bhuti, T. 3184
Bialystok, E. 1790
Bianchi, S. 1232
Bianco, L. 2188
Biaya, T. 2502, 3572, 3714
Biçe-Ool, S. 2690
Bickel, B. 2037
Bickford-Smith, V. 4012
Bidet, A. 2471
Bidi, J. 2070
Bielmeier, R. 2037
Bienert, H. 1139, 1140, 1155
Bienfait, H. 270, 2537
Bienkowski, P. 895
Biermann, F. 951
Biery-Hamilton, G. 4617, 4651
Biewers, M. 1278
Bigellow, A. 3363, 3498
Bijker, H. 2272, 4774
Bijo, C. 3056, 3075
Bik, K. Van 2030
Bikai, P. 1022, 1085, 1189, 1271, 1351, 1435
Bilewicz-Wyrozumska, T. 1572
Bilik, N. 41, 189, 190
Bill, C. 499, 2240
Billari, F. 1558
Bilmes, L. 1747
Binford, L. 4569
Bini, M. 953
Binsted, K. 1767
Biondi, G. 1822
Bird Rose, D. 2403
Birke, L. 2959
Bischof, H. 99
Bischoff, J. 460
Bisheh, G. 112, 1082, 1144
Bishnoi, I. 1541
Bishop, L. 968
Bisoi, K. 4214
Bissell, S. 2863
Bissiri, A. 1749
Biswas, J. 1686, 1712
Bitetti, M. Di 1698
Bizot, F. 3194
Black, E. 471
Blackwell, C. 2481
Blackwood, E. 2849

Blais, H. 691, 1820
Blake, J. 342
Blake, K. 3727
Blakey, M. 538
Blanc, A. 2759, 2918
Blanchy, S. 3562
Blankhart, D. 285, 2870
Blau, S. 1296
Blay, P. 4263
Blažek, V. 1941, 3150
Blažić-Čop, N. 1591
Blim, M. 2644
Bloch, E. 2205, 2423
Bloch, M. 2205, 2423
Block de Behar, L. 3728
Blok, A. 2663, 4008
Blommaert, J. 230, 1736
Blondin, H. 4263
Bloom, D. 4894
Blumberg, R. 2644
Blümmel, M. 181
Blurton Jones, N. 2651
Blust, R. 1889, 3127
Boado, F. 996, 1226
Boardman, J. 449
Bobbio, L. 277
Bobertz, C. 473, 3411
Bocánová, M. 4017
Bochow, M. 2866
Bock, J. 4741
Bockett, G. 4743
Bocquet, É. 2791
Bocquet-Appel, J. 1516
Bodenhorn, B. 4790
Bodeux, F. 265
Bodewitz, H. 3308, 3315
Bodó, I. 2445
Bodomo, A. 4548
Boeck, F. De 2502, 3572
Boěda, E. 1406
Boehmer-Christiansen, S. 4781
Boelens, R. 2062, 4635
Boesch, C. 1716
Boëtsch, G. 1552
Bogaard, A. 1132
Bohas, G. 1863, 3359
Bohmer, L. 2914
Böhringer, A. 4690
Boinski, S. 1715
Boixière, P. 4263
Boldrick, L. 1616
Boller, F. 110, 3799
Bolnick, J. 2210
Bolozky, S. 1866
Bolten, J. 74

Bolton, L. 284
Bombeck, S. 3253
Bon, E. 2289
Bonacin, D. 1559
Bonani, G. 825
Bonanno, G. 38, 4518, 4529, 4541
Bonasera, M. 909, 2208
Bonatz, D. 4601
Bončina, J. 301
Bond, R. 4788
Bondarenko, D. 4007
Bonde, H. 4348
Bonnain-Dulon, R. 2346
Bonneau, I. 4748
Bonner, K. 2889, 4889
Bonnet, S. 86, 3215
Bonte, P. 2417, 2554, 3018
Boomert, A. 1827
Boon, R. 2210
Boonmongkon, P. 3811
Boonyabancha, S. 2210
Bordigoni, M. 425
Boretzky, N. 1938
Borgognini-Tarli, S. 21, 1595, 1658
Boris, E. 2533, 3073
Borja, P. 4937
Bornstein, A. 395, 2456
Bornstein, E. 4708
Boroditsky, R. 2723, 2905
Borofsky, R. 213
Boross, G. 3160
Borowik, I. 3634
Borras, G. 3911
Borrel, A. 4816
Borries, C. 1707
Borthwick, P. 4722
Borzacchini, L. 3728
Bosch, A. 2863
Bosch, F. van der 1079
Bošković-Stulli, M. 4021
Bossert, F. 3559
Bossong, B. 2645
Botha, C. 797
Bottomley, G. 3105
Bouchard, M. 1545, 1564
Boucharlat, R. 823
Bouderbala, N. 2417, 3018
Boudet, C. 2532, 3590
Boudreau, B. 1664
Bougchiche, L. 122, 600
Bougerol, C. 2987
Bouju, S. 288
Boulagnon, P. 566
Bourgeot, A. 3807
Bourke, S. 1164, 1176, 1225, 1242

Bousfield, J. 4324
Bouville, J. 4378, 4754
Bowers, P. 2338
Bowman, G. 2549, 3026
Boyadzhieva, S. 166, 3649, 4428
Boyarin, D. 514, 2909, 4461
Boyd, W. 826
Boyer, P. 224
Božin-Juračić, J. 1589
Brading, D. 1361, 3697
Bradley, D. 2022
Bradshaw, A. 955
Brady, S. 2084
Brady, W. 4295
Brakke, D. 514, 2875, 2909
Bramadat, P. 3410, 4359
Brand, L. 4714
Brand, R. 3519
Brandes, G. 3653, 4484
Brandes, S. 3225
Brandl, B. 1097
Branigan, P. 290
Brannstrom, C. 2418
Brantingham, P. 849, 1378, 1408
Brashler, J. 1279
Brasme, P. 2147
Brass, T. 2198
Braukämper, U. 58, 3522
Braun, V. 2953
Brauner, R. 1553
Bravo Arriaga, M. 3258, 3644
Bravo, G. 2476
Bray, D. 3115
Brayer, J. 1105
Breckenridge, C. 2933
Bredenkamp, G. 2272, 4774
Breen, C. 968
Breman, H. 2303
Brengle, L. 3909
Brenk, B. 1018, 1046, 1070, 1092
Brennan, C. 3625
Břeňová, K. 4141
Brentjes, B. 1102, 2358
Breton, R. 1915
Breusers, M. 2420
Brewer, J. 394
Brewer, T. 2287
Brezigar, I. 4454
Bricker, V. 1970
Briggs, C. 135, 416
Brighton, S. 909, 2208
Bril, B. 4378, 4754
Bringéus, N. 4114
Brink, E. van den 825
Brinkhaus, H. 3272

Brison, K. 1733, 4430
Britain, D. 1814
Britt, D. 388
Broadway, M. 2224
Brocheux, P. 726
Brockett, R. 1705
Brockington, D. 4773
Brockington, J. 3295
Brockington, M. 3293
Broggio, C. 4682
Brogli, R. 1252
Brondeau, F. 4688
Bronkhorst, J. 1738, 3303, 3754
Bronner, Y. 4067
Bronstein, P. 2845
Brook, M. 2283
Brookfield, H. 4767
Brooks, A. 1359
Brosman, P. 1943
Brown, A. 1236, 4930
Brown, D. 2099, 3155, 4422, 4494
Brown, J. 2863, 4800
Brown, K. 2284, 2553, 3952
Brown, M. 4416, 4617, 4651
Brown, V. 2148
Browne, G. 1349, 2000
Browne, K. 2822
Browner, C. 2719, 2724, 2851, 3817
Brownlow, A. 1709
Brück, J. 1066
Brückner, H. 1147, 3876
Bruegel, M. 4378, 4754
Bruguier, B. 1076
Bruijn, M. de 2073
Brumann, C. 3544
Brumen, B. 197
Brun, B. 1699
Brüne, M. 2872
Bruner, E. 4316
Brusasco, P. 2642
Brush, S. 4617, 4651
Brutti, L. 158
Bryan, A. 3780
Bryant, R. 4778
Bu, L. 2857, 3076
Buchan, B. 810
Bucholtz, M. 196, 235
Buchthal, O. 4866
Buck, A. 2408, 4650
Buckland, P. 507
Bucková, M. 3630
Budiharsana, M. 2888
Budina, O. 2217
Buggenhagen, B. 2375, 2605
Bühnen, S. 2488

Buijtenhuijs, R. 2491
Bujarbarua, P. 1712
Bujard, J. 1038, 1100
Bukraba-Rylska, I. 2601
Bulbeck, D. 543
Bulgakova, T. 3589
Bullo, S. 461
Bulmer, M. 1537
Bulut, A. 2711, 4844
Bumra, P. 3468
Bunimovitz, S. 387, 1057
Burawoy, M. 4612
Burholt, V. 2655, 2770
Burjachs, F. 1535
Burke, III, E. 611, 3042
Burke, J. 98, 2503
Burley, D. 598
Burling, R. 2039, 2048
Burnham, G. 2119
Burov, V. 1088
Burra, S. 2210
Burrett, R. 791
Burris, M. 4866
Burrus, V. 514, 2909
Bursztyn, M. 4682
Burt, D. 1494
Burton, A. 2223
Burton, M. 2158, 2633
Burton-Jeangros, C. 2662
Burykin, A. 1825
Bushkov, V. 202, 3361
Busuttil, S. 4666
Butcher, K. 4873
Butovskaia, M. 1554
Butt, L. 2629, 2714
Buzarbarua, P. 1686
Bužeková, T. 3242, 3721
Byerlee, D. 4698
Cabanas Díaz, A. 4937
Cabanis, E. 110, 310, 3799
Cabral, I. 323, 707
Cabrera, V. 894
Cadet, X. 326
Cadogan, G. 445
Cahen, M. 2502, 3572
Cain, T. 4722
Cal, C. 816
Calasso, G. 3338
Calavia Sáez, O. 3128
Caldwell, I. 4215
Calefato, P. 3728
Callaghan, R. 455, 2225
Callender, V. 495
Callicott, J. 2099, 3155
Camara, R. 2448

Camargo, E. 1977
Cameron, D. 1480
Cameron, E. 4118
Campbell, C. 1640, 2460, 3033, 3603
Campbell, E. 669
Campbell, J. 306, 4676
Canals, A. 1535
Cañete, A. 341, 1527, 2436
Čanić, R. 1555
Cañizares, B. 2440, 2467, 4729
Canning, D. 4894
Cantin, S. 2232
Cantó, M. 1593
Canudo, J. 884
Canut, C. 1749
Capdeville-Zeng, C. 3518
Caplan, L. 4639
Caples, G. 4041
Caputo, C. 3728
Carbonell, E. 460, 839, 842, 846, 890, 1535
Cardano, M. 241
Cariño, J. 4648
Carl, G. 2902, 4898
Carlin, L. 4882
Carling, J. 2578
Carlson, R. 2874, 3782
Carlson, T. 4636
Carme, B. 1657
Carmenate, M. 1593
Carmona, A. 1865
Carpentier, C. 4663
Carré, O. 3320
Carretero, J. 1534
Carrier, J. 276
Carroll, R. 1671
Carruba, O. 1930
Carruthers, D. 4129
Carter, M. 1852
Carter, R. 70
Carter, S. 1597
Carter, T. 4336
Carucci, L. 3809
Casajus, D. 122, 600
Cascione, G. 3728
Casey, J. 900
Cashdan, E. 2077
Casino, Jr., V. Del 291
Casinos, A. 1610
Cass, P. 2018
Cassano, F. 2092
Cassedy, S. 3100
Castelli, E. 514, 2909
Castillo Gómez, A. 4247
Castro, J. de 460, 898, 1467
Caton, J. 1701

Caubet, D. 1749
Caulkins, D. 4473
Cauquelin, J. 54
Cauty, A. 3672, 3752
Cavallari, W. 1563
Cavallo, G. 4247
Čavčić, J. 1555
Cech, P. 1924
Ćelić, R. 1474
Ceribašić, N. 3923
Cessford, C. 935
Chadefaud, C. 1818, 2063
Chadwick, A. 352
Chadwick, R. 1178
Chakrabarti, P. 4941
Chakrabarty, G. 2620
Chakraborty, S. 2359
Chakravarty, M. 1486, 2118
Chaline, J. 1465
Chambas, G. 4663
Chambers, E. 4770
Chamboux-Leroux, J. 4663
Chamoux, M. 1973
Champion, T. 1361, 3697
Chan, A. 3893
Chan, S. 2421
Chand, S. 4474
Chandiwana, S. 4863
Chandorkar, V. 3894
Chandramathi, P. 1895
Chang, P. 3904
Chang, Y. 3713
Chanthourn, T. 827
Chapais, B. 1685
Chapdelaine, C. 475
Chapman, D. 4750
Chapman, M. 4146
Chappell, D. 254, 4457
Chappell, R. 4336
Chapple, C. 2099, 3155
Chapuis, J. 3570, 3783
Charles, M. 1132
Charney, M. 678
Chartier, R. 4247
Charuty, G. 3595
Charvát, P. 2358
Chase, R. 4016
Chatterjee, M. 3889
Chatterjee, P. 717, 2522
Chatterjee, S. 3819
Chaudat, P. 4382
Chaudhuri, B. 4671
Chavez, L. 3769
Chawla, L. 4937
Chazan, M. 1215

Chazan, R. 3089
Checker, M. 2218, 3068
Chen, F. 2654
Chen, H. 1616
Chen, J. 4130
Chen, L. 4903
Chen, M. 2793
Chen, Q. 4011
Chen, T. 2936
Chen, Y. 1667
Chenevix-Trench, H. 2402
Cheng, C. 3170
Cheshire, T. 2691
Cheshko, S. 309, 2146, 4627
Chesson, M. 926
Cheung, F. 4263
Cheung, L. 3002
Chevalier, C. 4722
Cheverud, J. 1509
Chevillard, J. 3209
Cheyney, M. 1321
Chi, C. 4799
Chiarello, A. 1687
Childs, G. 307, 2127
Chilver, E. 43
Chirambo, R. 3949
Chiriguini, M. 1586, 3824
Chirwa, W. 3908
Chitekwe, B. 2210
Chithtalath, S. 2707
Chittagong Hill Tracts Commission 2414
Choat, M. 1265
Choe, S. 4095
Choi, K. 2933
Choi, W. 3079
Cholet, L. 4105, 4523
Chong, G. 41, 190
Chong, P. 4095
Chongstitvatana, S. 4060
Chopra, K. 62
Chopra, P. 585
Chotel, F. 1564
Choubey, R. 2153
Choudhury, K. 4304
Chouvy, P. 2296
Chowdhry, K. 4666
Chowdhury, A. 2763
Chowdhury, M. 4846
Chrétien, J. 2502, 3029, 3050, 3572
Christensen, K. 1488
Christensen, M. 2691
Christin, A. 545
Chtatou, M. 142, 3599
Chun, R. 1616
Chutintharanon, S. 4190

Chutiwongs, N. 937
Chvyr', L. 413
Ciarcia, G. 1033, 3702
Cid Vargas, P. del 4937
Čierniková, B. 3580
Cieza de León, P. de 728
Cioffi-Revilla, C. 2358
Cipriani, R. 4446
Ciudad Ruiz, A. 657, 2547
Clados, C. 378, 3737
Claffey, P. 4599
Clahsen, H. 1751
Clancey, W. 33
Clancy-Smith, J. 611, 3042
Clare, E. 2933
Claridge, G. 1449, 2935
Clark, C. 1700
Clark, D. 1191, 1192, 1194
Clark, G. 623, 931, 1248, 1273, 1298
Clark, J. 4, 165, 809, 4121, 4337
Clark, L. 443, 2661
Clark, M. 4278
Clark, N. 4743
Clark, S. 4820
Clark, W. 1487
Clarke, A. 494
Clarke, C. 4125
Clarke, D. 981
Clatworthy, J. 2783
Claudot-Hawad, H. 3057
Clausen, T. 831
Claxton, M. 2070
Cleal, B. 371
Cleary, D. 893, 2110
Cleaveland, T. 2535, 2850
Cleaver, F. 2404
Cleland, C. 988
Clement, J. 97
Clerc, I. 3891
Cleveland, D. 4617, 4651
Clifford, J. 254, 4457
Coady, D. 4832
Cobb, A. 3159
Cobos, J. 653
Cocks, P. 126, 3054, 3245
Coe, C. 407
Coelho, J. 780, 3031
Coen Flynn, K. 2316, 4940
Coertze, R. 4600
Coetzee, F. 950
Coetzee, J. 4588
Coffey, A. 28
Cohen, A. 4543
Cohen, D. 510, 2536
Cohen, J. 2185, 2202

Cohen, L. 2952
Cohen, M. 214, 3880, 4937
Cohen, P. 4376
Cohen, Z. 323, 707, 4040
Coimbra, O. 71
Coinman, N. 831
Cok, F. 2916, 3831
Colaneri, M. 910
Colapietro, V. 3728
Colard, P. 3929
Cole, J. 804, 3594
Coleman, J. 1858
Collard, A. 4263
Collier, P. 704, 705, 2333, 4707
Collignon, B. 3660
Collingham, E. 760, 2942
Collins, C. 1726
Collins, J. 235, 1736
Collins, K. 305, 4675
Collins, R. 73
Collins, S. 1277
Collomb, G. 4405
Collumbien, M. 2865, 2894, 4891
Colombel, V. de 2002
Colombo, E. 240, 397
Columbus, C. 3670, 4198
Comaroff, J. 278, 2502, 2672, 3572
Combes, B. 2863
Comerro, V. 3355
Comfort, A. 458
Comrie, B. 1741
Conati, C. 1278
Conceição, M. Da 323, 707
Condé, K. 288
Condé, M. 4170
Conklin, H. 102, 1799
Conley, D. 1582
Conn, C. 2705, 2881
Connor, L. 3033, 3603
Connor, M. 970
Conrad, K. 2901, 4499
Conrad, P. 1781, 3793
Constable, P. 3082
Conte, É. 2628
Contel, J. 3537
Cook, A. 728
Cook, J. 594, 1850
Cook, N. 728
Cooley, T. 4367
Cooper, E. 2256
Cooper, J. 831
Cooper, M. 1661
Cooper, P. 2308, 4703
Coover, R. 151, 444
Cope, D. 1528

Copeland, P. 1499, 1507
Coppa, A. 646, 2752
Coppel, C. 4211
Coquery-Vidrovitch, C. 784, 2989
Corcoran, C. 4538
Coronel-Molina, S. 1983
Coronil, F. 135, 416
Corral, R. 4053
Corrêa, S. 2848, 3254
Correia, C. 323, 707
Corruccini, R. 1620
Cort, J. 3376
Cort, L. 2233
Corteel, D. 2453
Coss, R. 1713
Costa, A. Da 323, 707
Costello, J. 4327
Cottam, G. 363
Cottler, L. 2874, 3782
Coughlan, F. 305, 4675
Coulombier, D. 2148
Coulon, F. 326
Cour, J. 2380, 4736
Courant, F. 1465
Courty, M. 1535
Cousins, B. 2404
Couture, A. 3290
Couture, J. 3011
Couture, R. 3011
Couvreur, M. 4179, 4264
Cowan, F. 3941
Cowan, J. 4641
Cowlishaw, G. 3107
Cox, J. 3533
Cox, P. 3742
Coy, P. 395
Crabtree, P. 909, 2208
Crabtree, S. 4871
Craig, C. 4918
Craig, N. 1577, 4822
Craviari, T. 1564
Crawford, G. 2304
Crawley, A. 3005
Creese, H. 4231
Crégut-Bonnoure, É. 1533
Cremaschi, M. 847, 968, 1063
Crisologo-Mendoza, L. 2416, 3017
Crist, J. 395
Crist, T. 970
Crnčević-Urek, M. 1585
Crnkovich, M. 4645
Crognier, E. 1552
Croll, E. 4835
Crolley, L. 4336
Crook, R. 2400, 2968, 2978

Crosby, K. 3190
Cross, F. 1337
Cross, I. 3897, 3941
Crossland, Z. 968
Crothers, A. 687, 2254
Crouau-Roy, B. 1510
Crouwel, J. 1383
Crow, B. 2196
Crowley, T. 597, 1744
Crown, A. 509
Crown, P. 1405, 2236
Cruz, C. 323, 707
Cruz, C. D' 2210
Cruz, V. 1007
Cruz-Torres, M. 4793
Császár-Pungur, J. 3160
CSD Indigenous Peoples' Caucus 4623
Csete-Szemesi, I. 3160
Csordas, T. 2958
Čubrilo-Turek, M. 1585, 3804
Cuenca-Bescós, G. 842
Cuevas Díaz, J. 4665
Cuisenier, J. 3680
Čukan, J. 303
Cullen, T. 1304
Culliney, J. 3144
Cumbe, C. 1749
Cunzo, L. de 988
Cupples, J. 2863
Curley, D. 2282, 2575
Curran, J. 4788
Current Anthropology 1298
Curta, F. 1426
Curtain, R. 4722
Curtin, P. 2173
Curtis, J. 3112
Curtis, M. 968
Curtis, V. 1423
Cuthbert, D. 2685
Cutler-Shaw, J. 3728
Czekaj-Zastawny, A. 854, 1300
Daaleman, T. 3159
DaCosta, L. 4336
Daegling, D. 1641
Daems, A. 1055
Dafeng, Q. 2526
Dafinger, A. 2509
Dagobi, A. 2502, 3572, 4718
Dagosto, M. 1680
Dahl, J. 2540
Dai, X. 4832
Dairo, A. 3874
Ðaković, B. 3858
Dalai, U. 1901
Dalawari, B. 3467

Dale, R. 4730
Dalfovo, A. 3542
Dallabetta, G. 2884, 3796
Dalley, S. 1087
Daly, J. 4864
Da'mi, M. Al 4154
Daming, Z. 41, 189, 190
Damon, F. 2349, 2593
Damourette, O. 4725
Damsholt, T. 3653, 4484
Dandamayev, M. 493
Danesi, M. 3728
Danforth, L. 4313, 4492
Daniels, K. 4012
Dankovičová, J. 1764
Danubio, M. 646, 2752
Danvers, G. 2857, 3076
Danzig, N. 472, 3408
Darbyshire, G. 922
Dart, S. 1891
Dartigues, L. 326
Das, B. 62, 1541
Das, D. 3466
Das Gupta, M. 4903
Das, J. 1686, 1712
Das, L. 1541
Das, P. 1491
Das, S. 1453
Das, V. 2933
DasGupta, S. 876
Dash, S. 2528
Datar, C. 4780
Dattamajumdar, S. 1899
Daudelin, G. 261, 3677
Dauzier, M. 4201
Davenport, G. 970
Daverat, X. 3929
Davey, W. 1829
Daviau, P. 934, 1173, 1174, 1178, 1207, 1210, 1213
David, B. 1105
David, J. 3520
Davids, L. 1816
Davidson, A. 116
Davidson, B. 1809
Davidson, D. 1029
Davidson, J. 4302
Davies, G. 915
Davies, K. 1511
Davies, P. 858
Davies, V. 68
Davis, C. 1449, 2935, 4532
Davis, D. 291
Davis, E. 2895
Davis, L. 647

Davis, R. 2533, 3073
Dawod, H. 2552
Dawson, I. 4697
Daye, Y. 4155
Daysh, Z. 4666
Dayyah, A. 1149
Dean, C. 766, 1472
Dean, E. 911
Debanné, J. 3660
Debpuur, C. 4884
Decaillot, M. 2342
Decaux, A. 571, 3343
Déchaux, J. 2790, 2791
Decker, M. 463, 2343
DeCorse, C. 961
Décsy, G. 2026
Dedecca, C. 4682
Dedji, V. 3620
Deep, D. 3465
Defleur, A. 1533
Degener, A. 3991, 3998
Dehouve, D. 3720
Deka, U. 1491
Delamont, S. 28
Deler, J. 2385
Deleu, R. 1692
Delgado, E. 1581
Deliège, R. 3288
Delisle, P. 732
Delneuf, M. 968
Deloison, Y. 310
Delph-Janiurek, T. 4560
Demarchi, D. 1502
Demarin, V. 1591
Demars, P. 1516
Dematteo, L. 2514
Dembélé, A. 326
Dembour, M. 4641
Demeter, F. 870
Demkin, V. 1324
Demkina, T. 1324
Demolin, D. 2008
Demski, D. 3269
Denbow, J. 1990
Dening, G. 660
Denisova, I. 2243
Dennerlein, B. 606, 2986
Dennerstein, L. 2728
Denning, G. 2308, 4699, 4703
Dentan, R. 2698
Deo, J. 3281
Deol, J. 4269
Department for International Development,
    House of Commons, UK 4936

Department of Reconciliation and Aboriginal
   and Torres Strait Islanders 4647
Deputte, B. 19, 1594
Deren, S. 2874, 3782
Derèze, G. 411
Dergachev, V. 2175
Derrett, J. 3261
Desai, P. 4928
Desclaux, E. 1533
Deshpande, S. 4288
Desideri, A. 1146
Desramaut, E. 326
Desrayaud, G. 1369
Destremau, B. 4682
Deus Ferreira, T. De 323, 707
Deutcher, G. 1807
Devatine, F. 4263
Devereux, S. 4815
Devi, R. 3879
Deviègre, A. 4263
Devinney, B. 1614
Dewees, P. 4779
Dežman, B. 4307
Dhansay, M. 1688
Dhillon, S. 3477
Dhingra, I. 3464
Dhingra, R. 2931
Dhruvarajan, R. 2655, 2770
Dhupelia-Mesthrie, U. 613
Diagne, M. 2686
Dias, N. 31
Díaz, B. 4696
Diaz, V. 254, 4457
Díaz Vázquez, J. 2424
Díaz-Andreu, M. 1361, 3697
Díaz de Ovando, C. 106, 752
Dickie, M. 3521
Dickinson, W. 598
Dickson, J. 896
Diduk, S. 2682
Diego Espinel, A. 1335
Diensberg, B. 1927
Dierenfeld, E. 1671
Diessel, H. 1756
Dietz, A. 4727
Dietz, J. 1708
Diggory, T. 4041
Dijk, H. Van 2073
Dilger, H. 3761
Diniz, E. 3067
Diome, F. 2070
Dionne, M. 1449, 2935
Diop-Wane, M. 2070
Diouf, L. 2210
Diouf, M. 2182, 4622

DiPaolo Loren, D. 991
Diptee, A. 2621, 2886
Dirjec, J. 454, 1367
Dirksen, P. 1838
Dirlik, A. 4617, 4651
Dishno, R. 3247
Ditchev, I. 166, 3649, 4428
Ditchfield, P. 968
Dittman, R. 2358
Divay, S. 2458
Dixon, S. 4863
Dixon, T. 896
Dizdar, D. 4307
Djlelati, R. 1699
Dlamini-Ndandwe, N. 2736, 3010
Doan, J. 4470
Doboszyńska, J. 2154
Dobreva, D. 166, 3649, 3988, 4428
Dobson, J. 291
Dodgen, R. 3528
Dodo, Y. 1459, 1461, 1462
Dods, R. 891
Dodson, J. 913
Doe, S. 2863
Doelman, T. 2107
Doi, N. 1462
Dolgin, J. 1498, 2657
Dolino, C. 1680
Dollar, D. 4707, 4737
Dollfus, G. 941
Dolo, J. 460
Domanski, M. 2107
Domett, K. 1285
Dominguez, V. 4617, 4651
Dominy, M. 4804
Dominy, N. 1703
Domroes, M. 4300, 4768
Donaghey, S. 494
Donato, L. Di 646, 2752
Donet-Vincent, D. 698
Dongen, E. van 3777
Donham, D. 278
Doniger, W. 1945
Donohue, M. 1765
Doolittle, W. 291
Doornbos, B. 2062, 4635
Doorslaer, E. van 4895
Dorning, K. 4722
Dorrit, J. 4722
Dortch, C. 298, 2134
Dossetto, D. 4391
Douglas, B. 3622
Douglas, I. 4666
Douglas, K. 4566
Doula, S. 2798

Doutreloux, A. 157
Doutriaux, M. 3538
Dowler, L. 291
Dowling, N. 3189
Downing, T. 4719
Dozon, J. 3591, 3822
Dragomirescu, L. 1566
Draperi, P. 4263
Drees, W. 1519
Dreisbach, K. 4352
Drennon, C. 291
Drescher, S. 807
Drexler, J. 2260
Dreyer, J. 1282
Dreyfus, M. 1749
Driedger, D. 4184
Driedger, L. 4184
Driessen, C. 1942
Driskell, D. 4937
Drolet, R. 4748
Drollet, S. 4263
Drouin, J. 110, 122, 600, 3799
Droulers, M. 4618, 4682, 4794
Drucker-Brown, S. 9, 108, 2594
Du, Y. 3971, 4451, 4480
Dube, I. 3287
Dubis, E. 1205
Dubois, M. 1710
DuBois, T. 3535
Dubova, N. 179
Dubovský, P. 3400
Ducas, S. 326
Ducke, B. 840
Dufumier, M. 2255, 2280, 4687
Duhaylungsod, L. 4802
Duhin, A. 2453
Duke, V. 4336
Dukić, W. 1475
Dulichand Jain 3378
Dulinicz, M. 951
Dumestre, G. 1818, 2063
Dunbar, R. 1539
Duncan, C. 3084
Duncan, J. 291
Duncan, N. 291
Dunfu, Z. 41, 190
Dunin-Karwicka, T. 3684
Dunn, E. 4911
Dunn, M. 1732
Dupaigne, B. 326
Duplan, S. 723
Dupont, V. 4671
Dupuy, P. 4105, 4523
Duquenne, R. 3177, 3717
Durand, J. 390, 4105, 4523

Durand-Forest, J. de 214, 3741
Durang, X. 3660
Duranti, A. 428
Durban, J. 3872
Durham, M. 1777, 2934
Durotoye, B. 2061
Duroux, R. 2183, 2688
Durrenberger, E. 2618
Duvert, M. 2187
Duviols, J. 4305
Duvnjak, M. 1570
Duyvenbode, R. Van 2857, 3076
Dyczek, P. 1200
Dyke, B. 1625
Dyke, E. 3656
Dykstra, Y. 4034
Eames, S. 1152
Earth, B. 2707
Eber, C. 215
Ebong, G. 2288
Ebrahimnejad, H. 3784
Eck, B. 2950
Eckert, B. 2116, 3695
Economic and Social Commission for Asia and
     the Pacific 4734, 4840, 4914
Edge, H. 3861
Edkins, J. 4508
Edmonson, M. 1970, 1979
Edwards, D. 907
Edwards, E. 367
Edwards, K. 1185
Edwards, M. 2210
Edwards, P. 594, 834, 1164
Edwards, R. 4882
Egan, J. 2633
Egbokharé, F. 1991
Eggler, J. 1435
Ehmer, J. 2644
Ehresmann, P. 1621
Ehret, C. 1988, 1990
Eichmann, R. 1147
Eighmey, J. 1248
Eiji, K. 595
Eijk, J. van 1837
Eipper, C. 105, 3231
Eiras, V. 2055
Eisenbeiss, S. 1751
Eisenhofer, S. 537
Ekambaranathan, A. 4117
Ekholm Friedman, K. 2358
Elder, C. 1629
Eley, T. 291
Elias, M. 2297
Elizarenkova, T. 3282
Ellis, S. 2532, 3590

Elsenhans, H. 4609
Elston, R. 1378
Elwert-Kretschmer, K. 4378, 4754
Ember, C. 4520
Ember, M. 4520
Emch, M. 2138, 3800
Emi, C. 4649
Emmelin, M. 4902
Endemaño Walker, B. 4850
Endres, K. 3530
Endstrasser, V. 3996
Engel, G. 1626
Engelking, A. 15, 136
Engerman, S. 807
Engle, K. 4625
Englund, H. 4640
Enns, R. 3243
Entwisle, B. 2654
Epprecht, M. 562
Epstein, H. 3798
Epstein, L. 1556
Erckenbrecht, C. 2498, 2814
Erdélyi, G. 3160
Erder, Y. 3407, 3748
Erdtsieck, I. 592, 2573
Ergeç, R. 458
Ericsson, T. 2644
Eriksen, T. 11, 205
Eriksson, M. 968
Errico, F. d' 1042
Errington, F. 2370, 2990, 4620
Errington, J. 1792
Ersever, H. 2916, 3831
Ertel, R. 1965
Ertug, F. 488
Eržen, T. 32
Escobar, A. 1794, 1915, 4617, 4651
Escobar Ohmstede, A. 2197
Escutenaire, C. 836
Eshed, V. 1327
Eshel, A. 4049, 4439
Eshel, H. 897
Eshleman, J. 2687
Esoavelomandroso, M. 2558
Esposito, A. 3314
Esterhuyse, P. 4586
Estrada, A. 946
Estroff, S. 3777
Estudillo, J. 2350
Euba, A. 3933, 4059
European Association for American Studies
    4352
European Ethnological Research Centre 645,
    4557

European University Institute. Law
    Department 2954
Evangelista, P. 2313
Evans, A. 4666
Evans, B. 1879
Evans, J. 1498, 2657, 2863
Evans, L. 2878, 3788, 4877
Evans, M. 4666, 4804
Evans, S. 1637
Everling, J. 332, 1332
Évora, J. 323, 707
Eyoh, L. 3933, 4059
Eyre, S. 2895
Fabijanić, T. 4325
Fabre, G. 4352
Fabre, M. 1699
Facchini, F. 1280
Faggella, F. 1232
Fahd, T. 3321
Fajer, M. 959
Falahat, H. 1202
Falck, R. 2874, 3782
Falguères, C. 460
Falk, H. 2797
Falola, T. 4165, 4289
Faminow, M. 2292
Fantalkin, A. 1238
Farajat, S. 1144, 1202, 1203
Farès-Drappeau, S. 1340
Farfán Morales, O. 3626
Faria Galvão, O. de 1710
Farnell, R. 4931
Fashing, P. 1599, 1642
Fassberg, S. 1839
Fatihi, A. 1776
Fattah Nafi', A. al- 4083
Faure-Rouesnel, L. 175
Fauroux, S. 4609
Fausser, J. 1650
Faust, A. 387, 1036
Fauve-Chamoux, A. 2644
Faye, Y. 2686
Fayez, A. Al- 2139
Featherstone, K. 1505, 2674
Feckoua, L. 2070
Fedigan, L. 1662, 1669
Fedorov, M. 150, 382, 1433
Fedorova, E. 2834, 4406
Feiring, B. 4658
Feistner, A. 1646
Feldman, J. 4468
Feldman, L. 3419-3421
Feldman-Bianco, B. 716, 4483
Fellman, J. 1845
Feng, Z. 1666

Fenske, S. 811
Fer, Y. 4263
Ferei, A. 4228
Ferhat, H. 3338
Ferme, M. 3034
Fernandes, A. 2222
Fernandes, C. 4242
Fernandes, E. 2222
Fernandez, E. 1362
Fernández Nadal, E. 4210
Fernández Poncela, A. 4005
Fernández-Jalvo, Y. 822
Fernàndez-Lomana, C. 841
Ferrandes, C. 3728
Ferrarese Capettini, S. 4315
Ferrari, S. 1677
Ferraro, J. 968
Ferraz Torrão, M. 323, 707
Ferreira Gonçalves, P. 323, 707
Ferrie, H. 851
Ferro-Luzzi, G. 4020
Ferziger, A. 3394
Fetter, B. 580
Fewster, K. 888
Fezas, J. 2519
Fialkova, L. 1782, 3664, 3976
Ficquet, É. 1749
Fiddian, R. 799
Field, C. 2765
Field, J. 891, 1190
Field, N. 4518, 4541
Field, S. 4012
Fields, L. 481
Fiema, Z. 484, 513, 1075, 1126, 1129, 1175
Fienup-Riordan, A. 3514
Fierro, M. 2974, 4267
Fife, W. 722
Figueroa-Perea, J. 2848, 3254
Filatova, I. 116, 3041
Filho, J. 323, 707
Filipovich, J. 727, 2270
Filippi, V. 2709
Filippov, V. 3096
Filippova, E. 3096
Filliozat, J. 3196
Finau, S. 2712
Fincke, J. 450
Fine, S. 1308
Finkelstein, D. 785
Finkelstein, I. 924
Finkler, K. 1498, 2657
Finlayson, B. 1160
Finney, B. 4617, 4651
Finnström, S. 299, 3052
Fiore, A. Di 1717

Fiori, J. 2222, 4682
Firestone, R. 2748
Fischer, H. 8
Fischer, M. 236, 3750
Fischer, P. 1257-1259, 1261-1263
Fischer, S. 1881, 3663
Fisher, E. 4865
Fisher, H. 612
Fisher, J. 3780
Fisher, K. 2113
Fisher, W. 2723, 2905
Fitts, R. 909, 2208
Fitzgerald, B. 1022
Fitzhugh, B. 879
Fitzner, B. 1030, 1043, 1062
Fitzpatrick, S. 1143
Fix, A. 135, 416
Flanagan, J. 1208, 1260, 1264, 1438
Fleck, D. 1971
Fleishman, J. 3267
Flinn, J. 2163, 2825
Flint, P. 3440
Florek, M. 1325
Flores Farfan, J. 1985
Florescano, E. 3735
Floris, G. 1576
Flury, M. 4789
Foale, S. 4799
Foggin, P. 2149, 2720
Foley, E. 4882
Foley, J. 2155
Foley, L. 1207
Folly Reiman, A. 3526
Foltyn, E. 959
Fonda, R. 1515
Fondahl, G. 4654
Fonjong, L. 4836
Fonrobert, C. 514, 2909
Food and Agriculture Organization of the
    United Nations 4686, 4692, 4701, 4819
Foote, K. 3703
Foote, R. 1187, 1209, 1211
Forbes, J. 2099, 3155
Ford, C. 746
Ford, J. 668, 2556
Ford, L. 291
Fordham, G. 2896, 4893
Forenbaher, S. 820
Formoso, B. 3715
Forsdick, C. 3005
Forshee, J. 2245
Forster, P. 3123, 3762
Forsythe, W. 968
Forth, G. 2474, 3744
Fortier, J. 2382

Fossen, A. van 4301, 4607
Foster, D. 2873
Foulcher, K. 4071
Fouquier, H. 4263
Fournier, P. 2454
Fournier-Chambrillon, C. 1598
Fouts, H. 1584
Fowler, C. 874, 2604
Fowler, M. 2907
Fowler, P. 932
Fox, J. 37, 114, 831
Fox, M. 4503
Foxen, P. 2165
Fragaszy, D. 46, 1661, 1689
Fraiser, D. 2409
Fram, E. 606, 2986
Francis, D. 2529
Francis, P. 4788
Francis-Dehqani, G. 3640
Franco, F. 4474
Francq, B. 265
Frank, G. 4468
Frank, R. 1583
Frankfurter, D. 502, 514, 2899, 2909
Franklin, M. 978
Franklin, S. 1498, 2310, 2657
Franzel, S. 2308, 2309, 4703
Fratkin, E. 2879, 4878
Fraval, A. 4722
Freeman, C. 2695
Freemantle, B. 380
French, E. 1098
French, J. 2863
Frenkel, M. 606, 2986
Fretheim, T. 1921
Frey, B. 3159
Friedman, J. 2358, 4407
Friedrich, P. 4061
Friese, H. 4466
Friesen, G. 2078
Frisbie, W. 1583
Frisina, W. 3170
Fritsch, I. 3903
Fritz, G. 4377
Froehlich, J. 1626
Froggett, L. 3791
Fröhlich, M. 4712
Frösén, J. 1126, 1129, 1175, 4241
Frost, L. 2265, 2730, 2962
Fryer, P. 3708
Fu, X. 2742
Fubini, E. 296
Fugate, J. 4016
Fugui, J. 254, 4457
Fujii, M. 3277

Fujii, S. 1227, 1228
Fujita, S. 1658, 1665
Fujitani, N. 1503
Fuks, G. 447
Fukui, K. 2610
Fukui, S. 2285
Fullagar, R. 1190
Fumiko, M. 3181
Fumio, T. 3186
Funakoshi, M. 1672
Funder, T. 371
Fung, H. 4534
Funk, D. 2477
Funtecha, H. 1395
Fuquan, Y. 2823, 2844
Furniss, E. 662, 3709
Furtado, X. 4874
Furuichi, T. 1638, 1648, 1720
Fusek, G. 943
Gabaude, L. 3168
Gabbert, W. 808
Gabunia, L. 1521
Gačnik, A. 4664
Gade, D. 291
Gadgil, M. 2111
Gadi, M. 4820
Gaer, D. Van de 2416, 3017
Gage, A. 2759, 2918
Gagiano, A. 4152
Gagos, T. 4241
Gail, A. 3837
Gajewska, H. 1325
Gajewski, L. 1288, 1325
Galand, L. 122, 600
Galand-Pernet, P. 122, 600
Galasiński, D. 4434
Galaverna, S. 296
Gale, N. 908
Gálik, M. 4042
Gall, S. 2398, 4638
Gallagher, E. 3563
Gallego, M. 653
Galley, M. 4026
Gallo, P. 2883
Galpin, J. 1697
Galtier, G. 2004
Gamonet, M. 1081
Gandhi, K. 2865
Ganger, J. 1936
Ganjanapan, A. 3776
Garapon, P. 4216
Garay, A. 3126
Garba, P. 4668
Garbacz, K. 855
Garber, P. 1678

Garcia, A. 526
García, G. 4245
Garcia, N. 824
García Sanjuán, L. 835, 2590
García-Arenal, M. 3338
Gardner, A. 4805
Gardner, R. 133, 439
Garine, I. de 4395
Garland, G. 2079
Garnett, G. 4863
Garnier, D. 1557
Garnier, J. 4105, 4523
Garrity, D. 4694
Garson, R. 2533, 3073
Garuba, H. 4200
Garza C., M. de la 3711
Gate, S. 4780
Gatzak, V. 3602
Gausset, Q. 2510, 3722
Gaustad, E. 3247
Gautier, J. 4663
Gautier-Hion, A. 1510
Gavin, J. 2867
Gavrilescu, D. 2315
Gay, J. 4311
Gay y Blasco, P. 3710
Gaye, M. 2210
Gazier, B. 4663
Geary, C. 4127
Gebel, H. 1230
Gebo, D. 1680
Geertz, C. 148
Geest, S. van der 2773, 2777, 2786, 2898, 3696
Geetha, N. 4859
Geethakumary, V. 1896
Gegeo, D. 254, 3669, 3675, 4457
Geiss, P. 2664, 3352
Gelder, G. Van 4219
Gelderen, E. van 1961
Gelézeau, V. 3660
Gellner, D. 275, 2539
Geneste, J. 1406
Gengenbach, H. 1828
Genovez, J. 4124
Gente, M. 557, 2639
Gentil, D. 288
George, A. 2954
George, T. 4916
George-Cramer, M. 2687
Georgieva, I. 166, 3649, 4428
Gérard, F. 2268
Gerard, J. 1710
Geraty, L. 1191, 1192, 1194-1196
Gerber, Y. 1129, 1251, 1255, 1416

Geronimi, M. 4363
Gerow, E. 4033
Gershon, I. 3730
Geschiere, P. 2532, 3590
Gessain, M. 326
Gewald, J. 3114, 3571
Gewertz, D. 2370, 2990, 4620
Geyer, P. 918
Ghannouchi, A. El- 3335
Ghate, P. 4911
Ghazzeh, T. Abu- 3840
Giacometti, J. 718
Gibb, R. 115
Gibson, J. 4814
Gibson, S. 4722
Giessen, H. 2379
Gigandet, S. 4276
Gignoux, P. 4248
Gil Lozano, F. 755
Gilard, J. 4235
Gilberg, R. 371
Giles-Vernick, T. 4617, 4651
Gill, B. 2357
Gill, D. 85, 967
Gillespie, S. 4863
Gilliot, C. 3330, 3354
Gil-White, F. 2589
Gimeno Prats, J. 2490
Gindin, C. 2229
Gingrich, A. 2417, 3018
Ginsburg, F. 2933
Ginter, B. 836
Giorgadze, G. 479
Giorgieri, M. 4212
Girard, F. 3167
Giraud, P. 2453
Girijana Deepika Team 4780
Gist, D. 3740
Giudice, L. Del 4397
Gjerberg, E. 3781
Glasbrenner, E. 3890
Glaser, C. 4012
Glatston, A. 1696
Glatt-Gilad, D. 1831
Glavatskaia, E. 2834, 4406
Glavce, C. 1566
Glavina, D. 1475, 1476
Gleave, R. 3014, 3341
Gledhill, J. 95, 234, 4611
Glickman, B. 2879, 4878
Glover, I. 906
Gnuse, R. 3454
Goddard, M. 2681
Goddard, R. 2619, 3066
Godelier, M. 2568

Godínez, J. 3757
Goebel, T. 819, 862
Goertzen, C. 4465
Goetz, A. 4855
Gogte, V. 503, 2372
Goguel, A. 1087
Goin, P. 291
Gojard, S. 4378, 4754
Goldey, P. 2441
Goldish, M. 568, 3413
Goldlust, J. 1773
Goldman, M. 2505, 4612
Goldschmidt, H. 253
Goldschmidt, W. 193, 249
Goldstein, B. 4093
Goldstein, J. 2330
Goldstein, M. 2874, 3782
Golick, B. 3728
Goluboff, S. 3409, 4402, 4468
Gombrich, R. 3214, 3317
Gomes, A. 1773
Gómez, G. 4758
Gómez Mendoza, J. 291
González, A. 3984
Gonzalez Torres, Y. 3633, 4459, 4526
González Turmo, I. 4388
Good, I. 1360
Goodman, L. 4538
Goodman, Y. 3404, 4515
Goody, J. 3122
Goonesekere, S. 2863
Goos, L. 1496
Goovaerts, E. 265
Gopal, K. 3653, 4484
Gordon, A. 4918
Gordon, C. 4336
Gordon, D. 3829
Gordon, J. 3625
Gore, C. 4126
Gorer, G. 2480
Gorgerat, L. 1256
Goriaeva, L. 4215
Gorman, J. 514, 2909
Górniak, M. 1205
Gorrara, C. 3005
Görsdorf, J. 1147
Goscha, C. 326
Gosden, C. 714
Gossaye, Y. 4902
Gosset, D. 1639
Gostelow, L. 4824
Goswami, K. 2097
Goudineau, Y. 3556
Gough, B. 2807
Gouglas, S. 2267

Gould, L. 3016
Gould, S. 1463
Goulet, J. 2834, 4406
Govindaiah, V. 1506
Gow, H. 2315
Gow, P. 2472, 3109
Goytisolo, J. 1758, 4014
Gqola, P. 4285
Grabb, E. 3112
Gracia, A. 899, 1458
Graham, C. 3698, 4841
Graham, S. 252, 2013
Gramain, A. 172
Gramlich-Oka, B. 4266
Granat, J. 1468, 1469, 1477
Granda, G. de 1915, 1952
Grange, J. 3170
Granoff, P. 3382
Grant, B. 3850
Grant, E. 4937
Grant, II, D. 3734
Grassly, N. 4863
Graulich, M. 4098
Grave, P. 906
Gravett, M. 1500
Grawehr, M. 1256
Gray, D. 352
Gray, J. 599
Gray, L. 2916, 3831
Gray, S. 608
Grazie, U. 3728
Grbeša, Đ. 1555
Greatrex, G. 467
Grębecka, Z. 3555
Green, B. 4538
Green, E. 2884, 3796
Green, G. 2892, 3810
Green, N. 2462
Green, R. 2649
Greenberg, A. 4041
Greene, J. 1149, 1162
Greene, P. 436
Greenhill, P. 4361, 4365
Greenlees, D. 3462
Greenwood, R. 988
Gregorace, A. 21, 1595
Gregson, S. 4863
Grellet, G. 2289
Grenet, F. 1072
Grey, T. 1265
Grgurić, J. 1574
Griffel, F. 2998, 3366
Griffet, J. 2085, 4310
Griffin, D. 2066
Griffin, G. 3823

Griffiths, T. 700, 3219
Griggo, C. 1406
Griggs, H. 909, 2208
Gril, D. 3330
Grim, J. 2099, 3155
Grimal, F. 1950, 4246
Grimshaw, A. 55, 293, 442
Grinev, A. 2391
Grischow, J. 770
Griswold, W. 1009
Groark, K. 2109
Grob, A. 4575
Groce, N. 1652
Groes-Green, C. 180
Gronenborn, D. 877, 2177
Groot, J. 2303
Groover, M. 1407
Gropper, R. 399
Grossmann-Kendall, F. 2709
Groves, C. 1721
Grove-White, A. 2948
Grubišić-Greblo, H. 1589
Gruénais, M. 3591, 3822
Grunau, T. 1631
Grünberger, H. 561
Grunstein, M. 1487
Guan, Y. 2212, 4364
Guanqiong, R. 189
Guatelli-Steinberg, D. 1485
Guchinova, E. 4410
Gudeman, S. 2331, 2332
Gudemos, M. 3936
Guen, T. Le 2271
Gueye, A. 3616
Gueye, C. 3591, 3822
Gufler, H. 2784
Guha, M. 1486, 2118
Guha, R. 2111, 4760
Guibert, P. 1376
Guicharnaud-Tollis, M. 3981
Guigné, A. 118, 3931
Guilhem, C. 1710
Guillaume-Alonso, A. 4305
Guillet, D. 2376
Guimarães, C. 734
Guimarães, G. 323, 707
Guimarães, V. 1602
Guinée, R. 1045, 1079, 1217
Gulácsi, L. 3160
Gulati, H. 3474
Guldin, G. 41, 190
Guma, M. 1821
Gunsam, E. 958
Guo, J. 1497
Guo, Z. 1497

Guoqing, M. 41, 190
Gupt, S. 3882
Gupta, A. 2359
Gupta, C. 4173
Gupta, D. 2520
Gupta, S. 2623, 3683
Gurven, M. 4393
Gussenhoven, C. 1923
Gusterson, H. 1498, 2657, 3758
Gutenschwager, G. 3838
Gutman, P. 906
Guy, J. 817
Guyer, J. 2532, 3590
Gyorkos, T. 3821, 4328
Gyselen, R. 366, 2497
Gysens, J. 1165, 1214
Haan, G. de 1964
Haan, L. De 4797
Haas, A. 3926
Haas, H. de 1241
Haberkorn, J. 1155
Habu, J. 2235
Hache, E. 4671
Hackenberg, R. 4632
Hadamik, C. 1446
Haddad, L. 4863
Hadfield, R. 1511
Hadidi, S. 1421
Hadjisavvas, S. 445
Hadler, M. 1751
Hadler, N. 1498, 2657
Hadžihalilović, J. 1569
Hadžiselimović, R. 1569
Hafen, T. 1617
Hagberg, S. 2191
Hage, P. 1882, 1900, 2638, 2658, 2667
Hagen, E. 1577, 4822
Hagens, G. 523
Haggar, J. 4696
Haggis, J. 2827, 3104
Haggrén, H. 1175
Hagiwara, T. 4068
Haglund, W. 970
Hagström, C. 1817
Hahn, H. 2103, 4024
Haidle, M. 827
Hair, P. 553, 574, 696, 821
Hajdú, P. 139
Hajek, J. 2001
Hajioff, S. 3798
Hajnal, V. 3094
Hakkarainen, T. 3087
Haldimann, M. 483
Hale, A. 2622
Hall, A. 4743

Hall, M. 1432, 2235
Haller, D. 3093, 4413
Haller, F. 2037
Halperin, C. 607
Halpert, H. 4032
Halstead, N. 237, 392
Haluska, G. 1500
Hama, A. 1492
Hamanaka, T. 110, 3799
Hamano, K. 2142, 4821
Hamari, A. 2053
Hamdan, K. 1151
Hameau, P. 1007, 1013
Hämeen-Anttila, V. 3274
Hamel, J. 2457
Hamer, D. 1499, 1507
Hames, R. 135, 416, 1577, 4822
Hamid, S. 4828
Hamilton, R. 4792
Hamilton, S. 1053
Hammad, M. 451
Hammel, E. 2143, 2673
Hammer, R. 2662
Hammig, M. 4787
Hammill, J. 2863
Hammond, N. 494
Hammond, P. 1068, 1134
Hamonet, C. 110, 3799
Hampton, M. 2717, 2893
Han, B. 649
Han, J. 4095
Han, S. 2581, 3079, 3137
Hanamura, H. 1473, 1483
Hancock, M. 4357, 4522
Hancock, P. 2925
Hancock, R. 1601, 1651
Handelman, D. 3283
Hang Minh Kim, V. 4153
Hann, C. 138
Hanna, B. 2696
Hannoum, A. 329
Hansen, J. 371
Hao, S. 1382
Hapke, H. 291
Haq, K. 4721
Haq, R. 4885
Haq, S. 2099, 3155
Hara, M. 1503, 1939, 3271
Harbottle, L. 4358, 4403
Harcourt, W. 2863, 4904
Hardacre, H. 3204
Harder, H. 4197
Hardesty, D. 988
Harding, D. 859
Hardman, C. 4535

Hardwick, S. 291
Hareven, T. 2644
Harithy, H. Al 1387
Harkness, S. 2611
Harland, M. 68
Harlow, M. 452, 4375
Harmon, S. 4016
Harner, M. 3602
Harnish, D. 4362
Harper, K. 3975
Harrell, S. 3
Harris, C. 291, 4899
Harris, M. 2194
Harris, P. 3574
Harrison, L. 2695
Harrison, P. 4717
Harrison, R. 1363
Harrison, S. 621, 2892, 3810
Harrison, T. 1272, 1431
Harrow, K. 89
Hart, D. 1830, 2653, 2977, 3353
Hart, G. 2892, 3810
Hart, J. 291
Hart, K. 247, 2596, 3742
Harts-Broekhuis, A. 2419
Harvey, D. 4811
Harvey, J. 4539
Harvey, M. 2670, 2747
Harvey, S. 3403
Harwich, N. 2275
Hasan, S. 2890
Hash, G. 4396
Hashimoto, C. 1638, 1648, 1720
Haskins, V. 2827, 3104
Häsler, K. 2024
Hassan, I. 1149
Hassan, R. 4088
Hassanein, O. 2890
Hassig, S. 2884, 3796
Hasson, I. 3323
Hastorf, C. 656, 2266
Hastrup, K. 3878
Hatamleh, M. 1276
Hatav, G. 1846
Hatvany, M. 2426
Hauptmann, A. 1147, 1414
Hauschild, T. 131, 3552
Hauser, M. 1612, 1693
Hauser-Schäublin, B. 3736
Hauspie, K. 4224
Hawkes, K. 2352, 2651
Hawkes, S. 2894, 4891
Hayajneh, H. 1331
Hayami, Y. 4908
Hayashi, K. 3208

Hayden, B. 2340
Hayem, J. 2453
Hayes, L. 4882
Hays-Mitchell, M. 291
Hayward, R. 2010, 3453
Hazout, I. 1860
He, Y. 1613
Head, M. 834
Headland, T. 119
Headon, D. 4574
Heald, A. 1402
Healy, P. 499, 2240, 2444
Hearn, R. 2250
Heatherington, T. 2190
Hebdige, D. 4096
Hedges, R. 867, 868
Heerden, E. van 380
Heesterman, J. 2351
Heffernan, C. 2189, 4536
Hegedűs, L. 3160
Hegyeli, A. 3095, 4553
Heideking, J. 4352
Heim, I. 2133
Heim, J. 1468, 1469
Hein, V. 2040
Heine, B. 1990
Heineman, E. 2693
Heinhold-Krahmer, S. 976
Heinrichs, K. 1030, 1043, 1062
Heinschink, M. 1924
Heintz, M. 4429
Heintze, B. 391
Heinz, B. 1798
Heiss, S. 4012
Helal, R. 4336
Helbo, A. 3728
Heller, M. 235, 1736
Helmersson, H. 435
Helmreich, S. 3739
Helms, S. 1151
Hémery, D. 765
Hendrix, K. 1297
Hendry, J. 1772
Henige, D. 312, 536
Henke, H. 2496
Henningsen, P. 2371
Henrich, J. 2588, 2589
Henrickson, R. 921
Henriksen, J. 4646
Henry, C. 3591, 3822
Henry, D. 1249
Henry, E. 4044
Hensel, W. 1381
Henshilwood, C. 1042
Hérard, M. 2453

Herbert, S. 291
Herbinger, I. 1716
Hereniko, V. 3080, 3675
Herling, L. 1139, 1140, 1147
Heřmanová, Z. 1800
Hernandez, D. 3960
Hernandez, G. 3126
Hernández Hiraldo, S. 3540
Hernandez, R. 2207
Hernández de León-Portilla, A. 745
Herr, L. 955, 1106, 1191, 1192, 1194-1196,
    1442
Herreman, F. 2940, 4110
Herrera, R. 4663
Herrera Z., E. 1967
Herrmann-Pfandt, A. 3192
Herrold, M. 291
Hersak, D. 3557
Hersant, G. 4126
Herselman, S. 2468, 4400
Hertzman, C. 2775, 3832
Hervik, P. 4414
Herzfeld, M. 415
Hespanha, A. 774
Hess, J. 2158, 4102, 4804
Hesse, B. 1272
Heuzé, G. 4671
Hewitt, G. 1734
Hewlett, B. 1584, 2431
Heyden, U. van der 25
Heyman, J. 4632
Heymann, D. 4870
Heyzer, N. 4842
Hiatt, L. 105, 3231
Hickey, R. 962
Hidalgo, M. 1915, 1946, 1955
Hidouci, M. 2453
Hiernaux, J. 2791
Higham, C. 906, 2304
Higham, T. 1290
Hilhorst, D. 4852
Hill, A. 2616
Hill, H. 4722
Hill, J. 1183, 2302
Hill, K. 4393
Hill, S. 4611
Hill, T. 4735, 4910
Hill, W. 4337
Hiltebeitel, A. 61
Hincape, L. 742
Hindawi, N. 1155
Hinshelwood, E. 4745, 4795
Hinton, D. 4547
Hirata, J. 2204
Hiroki, N. 595

Hirsch, E. 4602, 4619
Hirschfeld, Y. 905
Hirschkind, C. 2967, 3328, 3621
Hirshman, M. 3437
Hiršl-Hećej, V. 2917
Hitchcock, R. 2067
Hivernel, J. 4604
Hiwasaki, L. 2834, 4406
Hladik, C. 4923
Hlusko, L. 1479
Ho, L. 2722
Hobbs, D. 1137
Hobbs, J. 291
Hockey, J. 2787
Hockings, P. 4126
Hodeir, C. 753
Hodges, M. 4308
Hodgson, D. 2831
Hoebink, P. 4609
Hoehnle, P. 2259
Hoeven, R. van der 4677
Hoff, M. 1656
Hoffmann, A. 1180
Hofstein, F. 3929
Hogan, L. 1877, 2021
Hogan, P. 4193
Hogarth, H. 3079, 4360
Hogberg, U. 4531, 4902
Høgenhaven, J. 3435
Hogle, J. 2884, 3796
Höjer, B. 2763
Holčik, J. 3798
Holding, C. 4702
Holland, A. 2827, 3104
Holland, D. 4775
Holland, J. 4865
Hollos, M. 4540
Holmberg, L. 371, 3006
Holmes, H. 645, 4557
Holmgren, R. 1120, 1126, 1129
Holmstedt, R. 1742
Holmström, L. 4213
Holst, J. 2051
Holtz, S. 2756, 3457
Holtzman, J. 2824
Hombessa-Nkounkou, E. 4378, 4754
Homewood, K. 4773
Hong, H. 827
Hong, S. 4095
Honkasalo, M. 3777
Honwana, A. 2502, 3572
Hooff, J. van 46, 1689
Hoop, R. de 1844
Hoover, D. 4132
Hopkins, W. 1636

Hoppan, J. 1370
Horen, B. van 4937
Horiuchi, M. 2473
Horkay, L. 3160
Hormann, E. 4816
Hornborg, A. 2387
Hornik, R. 2701, 3774
Horowitz, L. 2096
Horst, O. 787
Horstmanshof, M. 1266
Horton, M. 2386
Horvat, M. 3858, 4345
Horwich, R. 1705
Hosokawa, S. 3956
Hossain, A. 4666
Hossain, K. 3819
Hossain, M. 4693
Houben, J. 3213
Hourani, F. 1277
Houseman, M. 3550
Housley, R. 948
Houtzager, P. 59, 3003
Houvenaghel, E. 4282
Hovelsrud-Broda, G. 2449
Howard, A. 4447
Howard, W. 3304
Howe, A. 2900, 4330
Howell, J. 3364, 3646
Howell, S. 253
Howitt, R. 4626, 4801
Howland, D. 2625
Howman, R. 706
Hoxie, F. 531
Hromadko, M. 2133
Hsiao, S. 2492
Hsu, M. 3713
Hsu, R. 3077, 4421
Huayhua Pari, F. 1975
Hubai, P. 3264, 3647
Hubbell, F. 3769
Huber, B. 2037
Huber, J. 1450
Huber, M. 1789
Hübl, H. 1058
Hübl, J. 492, 927
Hübner, U. 492, 1181
Hudelja, M. 438
Hudson, B. 906
Hudson, J. 4705
Hue, L. Van 2404
Huffman, M. 1601, 1658, 1701
Hughes, A. 4562
Hughes, D. 3947
Hughes-Freeland, F. 3884
Huguet, R. 842

Huh, W. 3079
Huisman, H. 2419
Hulin, L. 1411
Hull, T. 2888
Hulme, M. 2065
Hulsebosch, J. 4924
Hulstaert, G. 1992
Humbert, A. 291
Humbert, J. 1122, 1133, 1293
Hume, D. 1493
Humery-Dieng, M. 1749
Humle, T. 1608
Hummel, S. 1104, 2248, 2295, 3202
Humphrey, C. 247, 2596
Hung, W. 2933
Hunt, G. 215
Hunter, A. 2466
Hunter, Jr., T. 4231
Huntsinger, L. 291
Hurault, J. 3121
Huré, J. 4179, 4236, 4322
Hureiki, J. 3807
Hurt, R. 2276
Hurtado, A. 4393
Hurvitz, N. 606, 2986
Husan, A. al 1152
Hussain, S. 3358
Hussein, K. 4820
Hutchinson, D. 1289
Hutchinson, J. 1361, 3697, 3771
Hutson, S. 2334
Hvoslef, E. 1834
Hyatt, C. 1636
Hyndman, J. 291
Iaarlykapov, A. 191, 3356
Iannone, G. 499, 2240
Iba-Zizen, M. 110, 3799
Ibrahim, B. 3806
Ibrahim, F. 3806
Ibrahim, M. 1172
Ibrahim, R. 1035
Ibrahimagić, L. 1549
Ichwan, M. 3333
Iedema, R. 1763
Igamberdiev, A. 3756
Igarashi, Y. 1482
Igboanusi, H. 2005
Ignazi, G. 310
Iizuka, M. 2826, 3340
Ikanga, P. 4206
Ilahiane, H. 2609
Ilan, T. 343, 486, 4258
Ilieva, A. 166, 3649, 4428
Iljic, R. 2036
Ilyasov, J. 322

Imam, M. 4911
Imamura, K. 2834, 4406
Imbert, F. 3330
Inada, Y. 1670
Inciardi, J. 2695
Inciong, N. 2313
Ingemarsdotter, H. 1258
Ingwersen, R. 4722
Ini, M. 755
Inoue, H. 2643
Inoue, T. 2834, 4406
Insoll, T. 1366
Integrated Community Family Health
    Development Program 4868
Inter-American Commission on Human Rights
    4644
International Fund for Agricultural
    Development 4919
Ippolitova, A. 345
Irani, A. 480
Irele, F. 3933, 4059
Iril'deeva, L. 3083
Isaac, G. 1928
Isegawa, M. 4273
Isenberg, N. 3401
Ishida, H. 1464
Ishii, H. 1670
Islam, S. 4760
İşler, E. 1874
Ismael, S. 4047
Ismail, Z. 4616
Ismond, P. 4303
Istomin, A. 3092
Itier, C. 1974
Itoh, N. 1605
Ivanković, D. 2132, 2646
Ivanov, P. 315, 4092
Ivanov, V. 3896
Ivanova, I. 2394
Ivanova, I. 365
Ivičević, A. 1575
Ivković, V. 301
Iwanaga, S. 1677
Iwańczak, W. 624
Iyenda, G. 2210
Izagirre, N. 1522
Izuhara, M. 2174, 2772
Jabłonowska-Taracha, J. 1364
Jack, K. 1635, 1669
Jacka, J. 2337
Jackson, A. 938
Jackson, B. 3418
Jackson, J. 3943
Jackson, P. 2345, 3175
Jacob, J. 2595

Jacobs, J. 1989
Jacobson, M. 3026
Jacobsson, L. 4531
Jacoby, R. 1047
Jacomb, C. 1290
Jacquat, C. 1251
Jacquesson, F. 2038
Jacquier, G. 2148
Jaffal, M. 1869
Jäggi, C. 1018, 1046, 1070, 1092
Jaglin, S. 2289
Jain, D. 2153, 2863, 3386
Jain, V. 3383
Jakeman, V. 63
Jakić-Razumović, J. 3789
Jalla, B. 326
Jama, B. 2307
Jamard, J. 3929
James, S. 4865
Jamieson, M. 2731
Jamieson, R. 738
Jamin, J. 3929
Jamison, S. 3307
Jamzadeh, P. 1083
Jan, M. 535, 3023
Janetski, J. 1215
Janićijević, B. 3804
Janin, P. 4609
Janovicek, N. 2957
Jansen, J. 575, 629, 641, 2531, 2608, 4027
Jansen, M. 214
Jansen-Winkeln, K. 521
Jansky, L. 4767
Janson, C. 1698
Janvry, A. de 2285, 2396, 4905
Japan Official Development Assistance 4686
Jaradat, M. 1184
Jarosz, P. 1391
Javeau, C. 4179, 4341
Jayaswal, M. 4765
Jayaweera, S. 4856
Jayne, T. 4817
Jean-Klein, I. 4495
Jedlicki, C. 4663
Jeffery, B. 2717, 2893
Jeffery, P. 2757, 2856
Jeganathan, P. 717
Jelks, E. 979
Jenkins, C. 155, 530, 969
Jenkins, D. 13, 2597
Jenkins, P. 441
Jenni, H. 1416
Jennings, L. 693
Jensen, J. 209, 3560
Jensen, M. 4653

Jerardino, A. 968
Ježek, D. 1555
Jha, H. 2200
Ji, C. 940, 1127, 1148, 1150, 1158, 1220, 1222, 1312
Ji, W. 1613
Jian, L. 4689
Jiang, T. 3170
Jianmin, W. 41, 190
Jidoi, K. 1459
Jieshun, X. 189
Jihad, M. El 2274
Jiménez, P. 1099, 1166
Jimeno, M. 2583
Jing, Z. 41, 190
Jingzen, L. 1378
Jinzeng, L. 849
Jироušková, J. 336
Jobling, I. 4019
Joeden-Forgey, E. von 4548
Joffé, G. 4629
Joffe, L. 3405
Johansson, P. 542
Johns, D. 4881
Johnsen, E. 286, 2124
Johnson, C. 3574, 4799
Johnson, D. 1134, 1215
Johnson, F. 3028
Johnson, J. 4254
Johnson, P. 4016
Johnson, R. 2921
Johnson-Welch, C. 2863
Johnsson, R. 2289
Johnston, K. 453, 2562
Johnston, L. 2855, 4342
Johnston, R. 526, 3986
Jolly, M. 254, 4457
Jones, B. 1494
Jones, D. 3144
Jones, G. 4755
Jones, J. 1396, 4273
Jones, N. 2352
Jones, P. 2857, 3076
Jones, R. 956
Jones, T. 291
Jones-Engel, L. 1626
Jones-Pauly, C. 3330
Jongbloet, P. 2131
Jonjić, A. 1589
Jordán, M. 4133
Jordens, C. 3805
Jorgaqi, K. 1932
Jorgensen, D. 3117
Jørgensen, K. 371
Jose, F. de 2440, 2467, 4729

Joseph, J. 4938
Joshel, S. 528
Joshi, A. 4168
Joshi, L. 457
Joshi, P. 50, 51, 3919
Joshi, S. 1960
Jouffroy, F. 1610
Joukowsky, M. 1116, 1118, 1121, 1156, 1157
Jovanović, V. 301
Jowitt, A. 254, 4457, 4722
Juillard, C. 1749
Jules-Rosette, B. 253
Juliá, M. 2860, 3086
Jull, P. 2524, 3056, 3075
Jun, S. 3079
Jurić, H. 1475, 1476
Just, R. 2647
Justus, A. 1521
Juynboll, G. 3014, 3341
Juzhong, Z. 2304
Kaarma, H. 1542
Kaba, L. 695
Kabanoff, A. 3546, 3611
Kabeer, N. 2136
Kabir, M. 2640
Kabir, Z. 2763
Kabzińska, I. 3088, 4476
Kada, S. 827
Kaddar, M. 4609
Kaddouri, S. 578
Kafafi, Z. 941, 1114, 1117, 1119, 1123, 1125,
    1184, 1276
Kahn, D. 1341
Kahn, J. 216
Kaifu, Y. 1484
Kaimio, M. 4250
Kaiser, T. 820
Kajzer, L. 1412
Kakembo, V. 4766
Kalandarov, T. 3536, 3581
Kalaora, B. 2085, 4310
Kaler, A. 776, 2743, 3704
Kaliff, A. 1120
Kalis, S. 2703
Kallweit, H. 1147
Kalmin, R. 3398, 3442
Kaloev, B. 128, 4572
Kalous, M. 2904
Kamalov, A. 522
Kamanda, M. 2529
Kamat, S. 4633
Kamdem, E. 4663
Kamete, A. 4937
Kamiński, K. 1422
Kamp, K. 1427

Kämpf, H. 281
Kana'an, R. 1197, 1278
Kanazawa, E. 1473, 1478, 1482
Kane, K. 4086
Kane, N. 2070
Kane, S. 2988, 3004
Kanhonou, L. 2709
Kanovský, M. 162
Kansara, N. 3183, 3291, 3379
Kanya-Forstner, A. 552
Kapferer, B. 275, 2539
Kapica, M. 1205
Kaplan, D. 3402
Kaplan, G. 3792
Kaplin, B. 1690
Kapralska, Ł. 3098, 4628
Kapur, P. 2515
Karageorghis, V. 1017
Karanja, G. 2309
Karashima, S. 3203
Karasneh, W. 1167, 1355
Karczewski, M. 997
Kareem, J. 1136, 1319, 1344
Kareko, K. 4702
Karev, Y. 3853
Karkavelas, W. 2834, 4406
Karlov, V. 123, 173, 243
Karlsson, B. 3026, 4617, 4651
Karlsson, L. 2863
Karmacsi, Z. 3102
Karmakar, B. 1508
Karnaukh, V. 56, 207
Karpenko, V. 3787
Karpov, I. 2656, 2837
Karppi, K. 4624
Karsenty, A. 4663, 4682
Karsgaard, P. 1265
Karsten, P. 892
Kartal, A. 4085
Kartomi, M. 3905, 3939
Karttunen, K. 3310
Kasai, K. 1482
Kasanga, K. 2407, 2980
Kaseje, D. 4883
Kasmel, J. 1542
Kasper, C. 4041
Kassapi, A. 2453
Kassasbeh, H. 485, 2361
Kassim, D. Al- 2641
Katić, R. 1559
Katoch, A. 3490
Katsumata, N. 4054
Katz, J. 403, 611, 2787, 3042, 3653, 4484
Katz, N. 3414
Katz, R. 2160

Kauanui, J. 254, 4457
Kaučič, M. 188
Kaufman, D. 166, 865, 914, 1518, 3649, 4428
Kaufman, N. 166, 3649, 4428
Kaufmann, J. 317, 2507
Kaul, I. 4880
Kaung, U. 4156
Kaunga, J. 3036, 3059
Kaur, R. 4368
Kavitskaya, D. 2043
Kawamata, T. 168, 3139
Kawamoto, W. 2691
Kawamoto, Y. 1649
Kawasaki, Y. 1482
Kawatoko, M. 356, 617
Kawewe, S. 2863
Kazanas, N. 3294
Kazanji, M. 1657
Kazi, S. 2846, 4858
Ke, F. 41, 190
Keare, D. 4632
Kearney, J. 3053
Keasberry, I. 2655, 2770
Keating, D. 1011
Keelan, T. 4722
Keeling, M. 1625
Keeling, S. 2655, 2770
Keen, I. 2834, 4406
Keen, M. 4722
Keenan, E. 1885
Keenan, J. 2102
Kehrberg, I. 1070, 1092
Keim, C. 36, 339
Keita, D. 285, 2870
Keita, M. 228
Kelkar, G. 2828, 2829
Keller, D. 1252, 1253
Keller, N. 2210
Keller, O. 832
Keller, R. 775
Kellerhals, J. 2662
Kelly, J. 1679
Kelly, S. 1539
Kemedjio, C. 4187
Kemnitz, J. 1511
Kempf, W. 3650
Kempisty, A. 1299
Kenji, M. 3191
Kennedy, D. 524, 923, 4346
Kennedy, J. 923
Kennedy, L. 4671
Kennedy, M. 709, 2335
Kennedy, S. 1511
Kenrick, J. 3056, 3075
Kent, G. 2863

Kenworthy Teather, E. 2782
Kerans, D. 2286
Kerkkänen, A. 4479
Kermel-Torrès, D. 2279
Kern, J. 2132, 2646
Kern, T. 3610
Kerner, S. 1108, 1147, 1180, 1269, 1275
Kero, A. 4531
Kerry, K. 1249
Keršič, I. 346
Keulen, H. van 2303
Kevane, B. 2533, 3073
Kevane, M. 4847
Key, C. 985, 2591
Khadija, L. 1034
Khaldi, F. 1565
Khaleeli, Z. 3794
Khalid, H. 3334
Khalil, L. 1147, 1243, 1270
Khalily, M. 4911
Khalsa, G. 3478
Khamis, E. 1357
Khamis, S. 4163
Khan, A. 4452
Khan, N. 4673
Khan, S. 4911
Khandker, S. 4911
Kharitonova, V. 3602
Khateeb, S. al- 3325
Khen, M. 4805
Khenrap, K. 642
Khogali, H. 4834
Khoury, E. 4062
Khraysheh, F. al- 1214
Kian, J. 1096
Kido, A. 1503
Kiely, R. 2600
Kikuchi, H. 168, 3139
Kikusawa, R. 1887
Kiliánová, G. 140
Killick, A. 3866
Killworth, P. 286, 2124
Kim, A. 42, 3587, 3726
Kim, E. 3079
Kimani, J. 4702
Kimberley, M. 792
Kimura, H. 1503
Kimura, M. 2263
Kimura, T. 1457
Kinberg, L. 3338
King, A. 76, 355
King, J. 2020
King, L. 228
King, M. 1303
King, S. 4636

Kingfisher, C. 4611
Kingsley, S. 463, 2343
Kinoshita, N. 338
Kinsman, J. 2913
Kiong, T. 3156, 3681
Kirch, P. 2649
Kirchengast, S. 1450, 1544, 1588
Kirin, R. 4477
Kiripolská, M. 3211, 4025
Kirkpatrick, C. 4788
Kirsch, S. 2373, 4617, 4651
Kirscht, H. 2184, 4031
Kirumira, E. 2914
Kiš, A. 3240
Kisala, R. 3543
Kish, J. 1911
Kishigami, N. 2449
Kishindo, P. 4723
Kister, M. 3248
Kitaev, M. 1504
Kitamura, T. 1497
Kitange, H. 4882
Kitchen, W. 986
Kittay, E. 2933
Kitzinger, C. 2953
Kiyaga-Nsubuga, J. 4937
Kjølsrød, L. 3781
Klaić, Z. 3759
Klaniczay, G. 4247
Klass, D. 4512
Klassen, S. 565, 2769
Klee, M. 900
Klein, I. 2128
Klein, K. 2292
Klein, R. 1536
Kleinitz, C. 968
Klieman, K. 1990
Kligman, M. 3899
Klima, A. 2800, 3207
Klimburg-Salter, D. 4137
Klinenberg, E. 2780, 2924
Kling, B. 445
Klinger, S. 1093
Klink, J. 2222
Klobb, A. 3608
Kłosek, E. 4488
Klöslová, Z. 4112
Kluev, E. 3653, 4484
Knabe, S. 4343
Knapp, A. 2358
Knarrström, B. 892
Knauf, E. 927, 1037, 1058
Knauth, D. 2941
Kneale, J. 4390
Kniewald, T. 3770

Knight, E. 4277
Knight, G. 708, 812
Knight, M. 459, 2871
Knight, R. 3967
Knipe, D. 3275
Knoblauch, H. 2791
Knotková-Čapková, B. 4072
Knowles, C. 714
Ko, D. 2339
Kobayashi, K. 1482, 3118, 3999
Kobyliansky, E. 1508
Koch, W. 3566, 3833
Kochems, L. 2874, 3782
Kochnev, B. 2366
Kodoth, P. 4780
Koehl, C. 1699
Koenen, L. 4250
Koenig, A. 1707
Koenig, R. 4263
Koerner, F. 803
Kogbe, C. 2070
Kohler, H. 1488, 2143, 2673
Kohler, S. 2417, 3018
Kohn, L. 1509
Koistinen, K. 1126, 1129, 1175
Koivulehto, J. 2059
Kojan, D. 911
Kojima, M. 1670
Kojima, S. 1653
Kolb, B. 1212, 1251-1253, 1255, 1256
Kolendo, J. 1358
Kolig, E. 2525
Koller, J. 845
Koltun-Fromm, K. 3666, 4445
Kombe, W. 4786
Kominiak, T. 2207
Komorovský, J. 3679
Konadu-Agyemang, K. 4338, 4680, 4681,
    4667
Konaka, S. 2447
Kondo, O. 1462
Kondo, S. 1473, 1478, 1483
Kondos, V. 105, 3231
Kong, L. 3156, 3681
Koninck, M. De 2213, 2709
Koninck, R. de 2273
Kontošić, I. 1589
Konwar, A. 2042
Kooij, G. van der 1172
Koontz, F. 1705
Korom, F. 3292
Korusenko, S. 211, 430
Kosambi, M. 4577
Kosarev, M. 2052
Köstlin, K. 140

Kostyrko, T. 2193
Kothandaraman, R. 1908
Kotorova, E. 1768
Kottsieper, I. 489
Koufahi, I. 3365, 4080
Kouloughli, D. 1867
Koumouzelis, M. 836
Koupilová, I. 3798
Kourouma, A. 2502, 3572
Kováč, M. 1320, 2811, 3135, 3517
Kovačevičová, S. 3718
Koven, M. 1793
Kowalski, P. 4354
Kowalsky, N. 4344
Koželj, Z. 4326
Kozlov, S. 3446
Kozłowski, J. 836, 959
Kozok, U. 334, 4178
Krampen, M. 3728
Kraus, W. 2425, 4659
Krause, E. 3739
Krawczyk-Wasilewska, V. 3763
Krech, III, S. 2072
Krige, S. 4759
Kriger, C. 351, 610
Krines, S. 3641
Krings, F. 4575
Krings, M. 3045
Krishna, A. 4726
Krishna, D. 1568
Krishna, S. 4780
Krishnamani, R. 1651
Krishnan, T. 4903
Kristjanson, P. 2434
Kristóf, I. 4247
Krivonogov, V. 3101
Krivoshapkin, A. 849
Križnar, N. 427
Krohn-Hansen, C. 2551
Kronenfeld, D. 2658
Kros, C. 613
Kruger, P. 1855
Kruijer-Poesiat, L. 3415
Krupnick, J. 4538
Krykin, S. 829
Krylova, G. 3638
Kubica-Kabacińska, E. 1424
Kubik, G. 3044, 3729
Kubo, S. 983
Kubuki, S. 2678, 3682
Kuchmezov, B. 2321
Kuczyński, A. 92
Kuester, J. 1631
Kuhlmann, M. 2453
Kuijt, I. 926

Kujit, I. 891
Kumakura, I. 374
Kumar, A. 3652, 4587
Kumar, P. 3755
Kumar, S. 3375
Kumara, K. 2397
Kumaranayake, L. 4863
Kundid, L. 2453
Kundu, A. 4932
Kuniholm, P. 445
Kunin, S. 3422
Künnap, A. 57
Künüçen, H. 4139
Kunyi, W. 4866
Kuortti, J. 4288
Kuper, A. 2, 115, 2740
Kuper, R. 968
Kuramitsu, M. 4854
Kurata, Y. 4034
Kurotori, H. 1667
Kurtzer, S. 2827, 3104
Kushner, T. 357
Kuteva, T. 1987, 2007
Kutukeev, T. 1504
Kuzman, K. 88
Kuzmina, E. 559, 2162
Kuz'minych, S. 2052
Kuznar, L. 294, 393, 2433, 2435
Kvist, C. 3006
Kwa, A. 4842
Kyes, R. 1649
Kyvik, K. 1488
Labaere, H. 1996
Labanda, E. de 910
Labastida, J. 1925
LaBianca, O. 1191-1196
Laborde, D. 3929
Laboucane, P. 3011
Labrousse, P. 759
Lacadena García-Gallo, A. 657, 2547
Lacaze, G. 2947
Lacerenza, G. 1346
Lach, K. 3694
Lachaier, P. 3284
Lacombe, P. 2428
Lafferty, G. 4301, 4607
Lafont, J. 747
LaGro, H. 1241
Lakhani, A. 2865
Lal, B. 3507
Lal, C. 4596
Lal, S. 22
Laland, K. 1684
Lalos, A. 4531
Lalramnghinglova, H. 3785

Lalu, P. 605, 3808
Lalwani, K. 3368
Lam, W. 4769
Lamb, M. 1584
Lamb, W. 85, 967
Lambek, M. 2392
Lamberg-Karlovsky, C. 2358
Lambert, J. 1694
Lambert, Y. 2791
Lamboray, J. 4863
Lamont, M. 2327
Lamprichs, R. 1108, 1155
Lancho, L. 4757
Landa Vásquez, L. 4420
Landau-Tasseron, E. 4227
Landy, F. 4671
Landzelius, K. 2632
Lane, P. 968
Lang, H. 272
Lang, K. 3195
Langan, C. 2933
Lange, B. 3921
Lange, D. 2493
Lange, K. 1813
Langton, L. 1509
Langton, M. 4096
Lannon, A. 4016
Laplana, C. 842, 884
Lapp, E. 1365
Lapuyade, S. 2284
Lara, V. 841
Larcher, P. 1856, 3330
Larguèche, A. 611, 3042
Larguèche, D. 611, 3042
Larner, J. 779
LaRoche, C. 909, 2208
Larroa Torres, R. 4291, 4906
Larsen, U. 2122
Larsson, L. 1000
Lashuk, L. 137, 267, 631, 1760
Lasley, B. 1640
Lassiter, L. 404, 3915
Last, M. 2532, 3590
Lather, P. 264, 419
Lathuillière, M. 1510
Latorre, J. 4094
Latour, C. de 169
Lattas, J. 3107
Lauer, M. 1577, 4822
Launay, R. 228, 4447
Laurencich-Minelli, L. 1101
Laurent, P. 2502, 3572, 3591, 3822, 4715
Laurie, L. 4576
Laval, E. 1007
Lavallé, B. 3032

Lavenir, C. 2085, 4310
Lavento, M. 1126, 1129, 1175
Law, R. 554
Lawler, R. 1615
Lawlor, J. 1132
Lawlor, M. 3790
Lawn, J. 4811
Lawrance, B. 1749
Lawrence, S. 744
Lawrie, D. 3146
Laychour, V. 827
Lazar, D. 825
Lazarus, S. 2453
Lazarus-Black, M. 3030
Lazebnik, O. 4654
Lazin, K. 2686
Leach, M. 2404
Leache, T. 2438
Leavens, D. 1636
LeBlanc, M. 4447
Lebrun, R. 3524
Leček, S. 2669
Lech, J. 1403
Lecker, M. 527, 2395
Leclant, J. 1177
LeCount, L. 4387
Lederer, G. 3348
Lederman, Z. 1057
Ledovski, A. 658
Lee, D. 2234
Lee, J. 940, 1127, 1222, 2460
Lee, K. 14
Lee, L. 1644, 4356
Lee, N. 2324, 4788
Lee, P. 2778
Lee, S. 3079, 3137
Lee-Chai, A. 2555
Lee-Parritz, D. 1675
Lefebvre, C. 2014, 2016
Lefferts, L. 2233
Lefkowitz, D. 4415
Légaré, J. 2636
Legros, D. 2148
Legros, E. 2791
Legros, H. 36, 339
Legros, R. 4238
Lehman, F. 2658
Lehmann, D. 3612
Lehmann, G. 1108
Leicht, R. 476
Leigh Pigg, S. 3739
Leigh, S. 1567, 1678
Leighty, K. 46, 1689
Leinfelder, I. 1692
Leinonen, M. 2054

Leis, P. 4540
Leite, I. 71, 3072
Leite, J. 764
Leiverkus, P. 1184
Lelana, R. 1649
Lello, A. Di 543
Leloup, X. 265
Lemordant, D. 1818, 2063
Lendon, S. 4722
Leneman, M. 4820
Lennan, M. 2712
Lenoir, F. 3166
Lenta, M. 4244
Lentz, C. 418, 2104, 2512, 4001
Léonard, É. 4609
Leonard, K. 253
Leonard, S. 1597
León-Portilla, M. 783
Leontis, A. 2092
Leopold, J. 1095
Leoshko, J. 4284
Leoussi, A. 1361, 3697
Lepej, S. 3770
Lepoutre, D. 417
Lernia, S. di 968, 1063
Léry, J. de 756
Lesbre, P. 214, 3902
Leščić, J. 4404
Leslie, D. 4155
LeSourd, P. 3588
Letcher, A. 3686
Létolle, R. 2086
Lettow-Vorbeck, C. von 462
Levin, A. 3362
LeVine, R. 4542
LeVine, S. 4542
Levitt, S. 1956
Levy, A. 253
Lew, S. 3079
Lewis, G. 4380
Lewis, H. 134
Lewis, J. 3056, 3075, 4863
Lewis, L. 2671, 4460
Lewis, T. 2151, 2306, 3171
L'Homme et la Société 4105, 4523
Li, D. 1803
Li, H. 1796
Li, J. 4549
Li, M. 1666, 3009
Li, T. 2404
Li, V. 4866
Liang, B. 1666
Liang, C. 4534
Liang, L. 4767
Lichtenthäler, G. 2417, 3018

Lieber, M. 4804
Lieberman, M. 170
Liebeschuetz, W. 3416
Liep, J. 2328, 2963, 4593
Lilley, R. 4559
Lim, H. 3079
Lim, S. 2805, 4561
Lima, A. 323, 707
Lima, J. 2222
Lima, W. 2070
Liman, A. 4056
Limón, J. 3065
Lin, C. 2164
Lin, M. 4497
Lin, W. 2676
Lincoln, B. 3596
Lindahl, C. 4016
Lindee, S. 135, 416
Lindemann, G. 638
Lindenbaum, S. 3803
Lindgren, S. 4280
Lindner, M. 492, 927, 954, 958, 1037, 1058, 1061
Lindquist, G. 3575, 3830
Lindstrom, D. 2129, 2704
Linebaugh, P. 778
Linon-Chipon, S. 4179, 4237, 4323
Lioger, R. 86, 3215
Liphschitz, N. 825
Lippmann, E. 1184
Lipschitz, D. 1697
Lipset, S. 3112
Lipsker, A. 3997
Lipton, M. 4825
Lirola Delgado, J. 344, 586, 1339
Lis, V. 1306
Liščić, R. 3789
Lisić, M. 3770
List, D. 287
Lithell, U. 2890
Litonjua, M. 4679
Littauer, M. 1383
Little, A. 1494
Little, K. 3877
Little, M. 3805, 4712
Littlewood, R. 3541, 3760
Litwicki, E. 4350
Liu, J. 588
Liu, W. 1479
Liu, Y. 3906
Liu, Z. 2149, 2720
Livne-Kafri, O. 3337
Liyanaratne, J. 3826
Liying, K. 3206
Ljubičić, M. 3804

Llorens, L. 1610
Lloret, M. 894
Lloyd, D. 4500
Lloyd, F. 201
Lobligeois, M. 326
Lobo de Carvalho, J. 323, 707
Lock, G. 1002
Lock, M. 1448, 2920
Locke, P. 2242, 2378
Lockhart, J. 584
Lockyer, A. 347
Loftsdóttir, K. 2064
Loftus, A. 2210
Logan, J. 1209
Loh, C. 1220, 1312
Lohmann, R. 2598, 3627
Lombard, P. 823
Lomuto, M. 3728
Long, G. 4860
Long, Jr., J. 1141
Long, L. 4378, 4754
Longchari, A. 2582
Longhurst, R. 2855, 4342
Longie, E. 2691
Longo, A. 84
Longstaffe, F. 2444
Longworth, I. 1403
Lønstrup, A. 3653, 4484
Looman, C. 2150
Loosová, L. 336
Lopašić, A. 2478
López Austin, A. 1024
López Echarte, M. 2943
López Lujan, L. 1024
Lòpez, N. 841
López de Mariscal, B. 3887
Lopiparo, J. 3523
Lord, G. 1190
Lordkipanidze, D. 1521
Loreille, J. 1470
Lorenzo, C. 1534
Losche, D. 3511
Loti, P. 4263
Louie, A. 3700
Louie, K. 2911
Lourd, P. Le 2289
Louwrens, L. 1832
Loux, F. 4376
Lovejoy, P. 552
Lovelace, M. 4016
Lovell, J. 1176, 1242
Lovell, W. 291
Lowe, E. 4722
Lowe, K. 1944
Lowenga, O. 3539, 3950

Lozica, I. 2838
Lu, T. 2304
Lübbren, N. 4135
Lucas, E. 4742
Lucas, M. 3917
Lucas, P. 1703
Lucchesi, E. 4172
Łuczkiewicz, P. 1443
Ludvico, L. 1625
Ludwig, F. 2755
Ludykova, V. 2054
Luetjens, C. 1500
Lufungula, L. 609, 3673
Lulić-Dukić, O. 1475, 1476
Lum, K. 4130
Lun, Z. 4485
Lund, C. 2404
Lund, J. 3434
Lundberg, A. 222, 384
Lundquist, S. 4041
Lüning, J. 877, 2177
Luo, L. 3842
Lupo, K. 1281
Luzzadder-Beach, S. 525, 2112
IWGIA 3063, 4634
Lwihula, G. 2884, 3796
Lwin, N. 906
Lyamuya, E. 2884, 3796
Lynch, J. 1725, 1888
Lynch, O. 2627
Lynn, R. 4527
Lyon, G. 4038
Lyons, M. 4247, 4929
Lyons, T. 4149
Ma, X. 1382
Maamoe, M. 77, 359
Ma'ani, S. al- 1136, 1347
Mabry, J. 1278
McCall, D. 569
McCall, G. 1526
McCamish, M. 2902, 4898
McCann, A. 3895
McCarthy, J. 2479
McCarthy, M. 70
McCarty, C. 286, 2124
McClenaghan, S. 2469
McClennen, C. 948
McConkey, R. 968
McConnachie, D. 4735
McCook, S. 2300
McCorriston, J. 891, 2358
McCrea, L. 4067
McCreery, D. 1208, 1240, 1260, 1264, 1275, 1438
McCrone, D. 2600

McDade, T. 1584
McDaniel, J. 3172
MacDonald, B. 955, 1247, 1273
Macdonald, C. 4530
McDonald, D. 2210
McDonald, J. 4700
MacDonald, K. 968
McDonald Pavelka, M. 1662
McDonald, S. 4863
MacDougall, D. 440
MacDougall, L. 3821, 4328
McDowell, C. 63
McDowell, L. 291
MacEachern, S. 968, 1990
Maceda, J. 3963
McElroy, M. 2099, 3155
McErlean, T. 968
McEwan, B. 155, 530, 969
McFague, S. 2099, 3155
MacFarlane, A. 4143
MacFie, A. 4070
MacFie, F. 4070
McGillivray, J. 2075
McGowan, G. 909, 2208
McGrath, M. 4816, 4824
McGrath, R. 826
McGraw, W. 1641
McGregor, A. 2494
McGrew, W. 1604
McGuire, J. 2152
Macherel, C. 3929
Machida, T. 1667
Machinist, P. 4467
Macho, G. 1481
Macias, A. 1500
McIntyre, B. 66
MacIntyre, M. 158
Maciszewski, A. 2842, 3938
McIvor, A. 3986
Mack, B. 4081
McKay, A. 44, 1580, 2869, 2903, 3820, 4869
McKee, M. 3798
Mackenbach, J. 2150
McKeown, E. 2561, 4751
MacKerras, C. 4605
McKibben, B. 2099, 3155
McKie, L. 2810, 2932
MacKinlay, H. 4609
MacKinnon, J. 985, 2591
MacKinnon, R. 1829
McKivigan, J. 680
MacKnight, C. 4215
McLaren, A. 2745, 4011
McLaren, J. 2408, 4650
MacLean, H. 3598

MacLean, M. 4293
McLuckie, C. 4079
McMahon, J. 4195
McMullin, J. 3769
McNeil, L. 3585
MacNeish, R. 851
McNiven, I. 1105
McOrec, J. 1826
McPeak, J. 2434
MacPherson, C. 2290, 2630, 2631, 3228
MacPherson, L. 3228
Macumber, P. 834, 1164
McWatters, B. 2717, 2893
McWilliam, A. 4799
Maddieson, I. 1968
Maddin, R. 1414
Maddock, K. 105, 3231
Made, J. van der 842, 872
Madeira Santos, M. 323, 707
Mader, E. 3062, 3565
Madero, M. 4247
Madgearu, A. 917
Madhavan, B. 983
Madhavilatha, K. 1578
Madrid, C. 1460
Madrigal, L. 2691
Madsen, D. 1378
Maestri, E. 326
Mageo, J. 663, 2853, 4514
Magistro, M. 1006
Magliocco, S. 4355
Magness, J. 1328
Magniez-Jannin, F. 1465
Magowan, F. 3625, 3955
Maguire, D. 2848, 3254
Maguire, M. 2966
Magyezi, R. 4937
Mahadevan, I. 1056
Mahadevia, D. 4939
Mahal, B. 3855
Mahaney, W. 1601, 1651
Mahar, C. 2215
Mahé, A. 2417, 3018
Mahmood, A. 2846, 4616
Mahmood, C. 395
Mahmood, S. 245, 3360, 4615
Mahmoudi, A. el 1185
Mahmud, S. 4911
Mahy, M. 2880
Maillo, J. 894
Maines, D. 388
Maini, J. 4666
Mairs, L. 1176, 1225, 1242
Maitrot de La Motte-Capron, A. 3608
Maj, M. 4373

Majima, A. 1482
Majoral, M. 1610
Majstorović, M. 1476
Majumdar, R. 4057
Majumdar, S. 1910, 4174
Makihara, M. 1806
Makoni, G. 4781
Makowicz-Poliszot, D. 966
Maksimov, S. 2056
Malaret, L. 2207
Malayang, III, B. 4630
Malcolm, I. 3989
Malcolm, S. 2186
Malherbe, V. 96, 3985
Malhotra, K. 1502
Malik, N. 1512
Malina, R. 1557
Malinowski, B. 91, 386
Malinowski, T. 881
Mallison, F. 4166
Malone, C. 867
Malson, L. 3929
Malungo, J. 2753, 2906
Malville, N. 861
Maman, A. 1857
Mammini, S. 1278
Mancall, P. 531
Mandal, B. 1455
Mandal, M. 2293
Mandić, N. 2606
Mandiringana, E. 4208
Mangan, J. 4336
Mangin, A. 4147
Mania, D. 845
Maniratanavongsiri, C. 4791
Manjali, F. 250, 1750
Manley, J. 1053
Mann, G. 335
Mann, L. 4016
Mann, M. 1990
Manning, H. 1753
Manning, S. 445
Mannitz, S. 4603, 4761
Mannu, M. 1702
Manoharan, S. 1898
Manor, O. 2775, 3832
Manorohanta, C. 1885
Manrique, I. 4662
Manson, S. 2691
Mansour, A. 1565
Mansour, H. 4045
Mansour, M. El 611, 3042
Manzi, F. 1063
Maple, T. 1656
Mapunda, B. 968

Marais, S. 4175
Marano, F. 4573
Marchal, G. 544, 3654
Marchand, D. 1465
Marchand, T. 2227
Marchetti, L. 3728
Marcie, P. 110, 3799
Marciniak, A. 947, 971
Marciniak, K. 3256, 4131
Marcinkowski, M. 626, 2566
Marck, J. 1882, 2667
Marcoux, J. 2766
Mare, W. 1014, 1107, 1110, 1115, 1124, 1128
Marey-Thibon, P. 3778
Margueron, D. 4263
Marigaux, C. 2149, 2720
Marín, M. 3338
Marín, R. 3380
Marinatos, N. 3111
Marino, L. 1165, 4329
Mariscal Hay, B. 733
Marjanić, S. 147, 1323
Mark, P. 798
Markey, T. 4268
Marková, D. 2725, 4281
Marković, K. 4345
Markovits, C. 2356
Marks, J. 1652
Marks, L. 3974
Márkus-Takeshita, K. 3116, 3991, 3993
Marmande, F. 3929
Marongiu, U. 2946, 4116
Marozau, A. 4306
Marques, J. 692
Marques-Pereira, J. 4682
Márquez, B. 875
Mars, L. 4424
Marsh, B. 291
Marshak, B. 1072
Marshall, J. 1773
Marshall, M. 215
Martens, J. 719
Martens, K. 3460
Martin, D. 3636, 3929
Martin, L. 227
Martin, M. 938
Martines, J. 2701, 3774
Martinez, D. 526
Martínez, G. 837
Martínez, I. 47, 421, 899, 1458
Martínez Núñez, M. 1336
Martins, L. 2222
Marx, J. 3263, 4179
Mary, A. 3591, 3822
Marzano, M. 242, 398

Marzolph, U. 3330, 3354, 3991, 4240
Masaru, O. 1926
Masimango, P. 4555
Masipiqueña, A. 29
Maskiell, M. 4003
Maskovsky, J. 4611
Mason, F. 4816
Mason, T. 3004
Masonen, P. 612
Masquelier, A. 2682
Massé, C. 110, 3799
Massey, K. 1625
Massri, A. Al- 3330
Masters, B. 3327
Mas'ud, F. 4871
Masum, A. Al- 4558
Matararaba, S. 931
Matheba, G. 4548
Matheson, J. 291
Mathewson, K. 291
Mathieu, P. 2289
Mathijs, E. 2315
Matias, C. 323, 707
Matin, I. 4911
Matišić, Z. 3316
Matos Moctezuma, E. 802
Matoušová-Rajmová, M. 3868
Matsubara, M. 1672
Matsumura, H. 1464
Matsumura, S. 1655
Matsumuro, M. 1668
Matsuno, M. 1482
Matsuzawa, T. 1608
Mattausch, J. 4398
Matter, E. 3217
Matthews, S. 2775, 3832
Mattingley, D. 1236
Mattingly, C. 3790
Mattingly, G. 960, 1131, 1132
Mattsson, J. 435
Matzner, A. 2809
Maunders, D. 4722
Maver, H. 2133
Mawkanuli, T. 1746
Maxwell, G. 1029
Maxwell, S. 4815
Mayer, D. 4886
Mayer, H. 1729
Mayer, I. 4243
Mayer, K. 1016
Mayer, V. 432
Maylam, P. 613
Maynard, K. 3252
Maynes, M. 2862
Máynez, P. 4270

Mayor, A. 4003
Mays, S. 1283
Mayuri, K. 1578
Mazariegos, O. 4124
Mazuryna, N. 3970
Mbiba, B. 2401
Mburu, N. 558, 2508
Mead, D. 1884
Mead, M. 2480
Meadow, R. 1215
Meadows, A. 491, 2365
Meadows, I. 1236
Meadows, J. 1139, 1242
Meddeb, A. 3324
Medin, D. 2080, 3662
Medway, G. 3578
Mee, W. 4857
Meenakshi, K. 1902
Meeuwis, M. 109, 1995
Mégevand, S. 4128
Mehta, L. 2404, 4632
Mehta, M. 3201
Mehta, S. 3280
Meï, L. 4777
Meier, H. 1018, 1046, 1070, 1092
Meijl, T. van 4432, 4617, 4651
Meiklejohn, K. 2272, 4774
Meintjes, H. 2692, 4853
Meinzen-Dick, R. 2404
Melamu, M. 3869
Melchert, C. 3014, 3341, 3342
Melgar Bao, R. 4191
Melhim, I. 111, 1168, 1421
Melhuus, M. 1498, 2657
Melkawi, A. 1388
Mellott-Khan, T. 1068
Melnik, N. 2041, 2046
Melo, F. de 1687
Meloy, J. 944
Melville, C. 4185
Ménard, C. 2289
Ménard, N. 1510
Mendes, S. 1718
Menn, E. 3439
Menotti, F. 995
Menu, M. 1007
Menzel, C. 1629
Mercader, J. 1359
Mercado, Jr., A. 4694
Mercier, N. 1406
Mercier-Faivre, A. 3929
Merighi, F. 1063
Merino, M. 839
Mériot, C. 326
Merlan, F. 4617, 4651

Merrell, F. 3728
Merrell, J. 531
Merwe, C. van der 1843
Mesaroš-Kanjski, E. 1589
Meshcherin, M. 862
Meskell, L. 34, 987
Messeiller, G. 630
Messenger, Jr., J. 409
Messier, R. 611, 3042
Métayer, C. 4247
Metcalf, B. 541
Metcalf, P. 177
Metcalf, T. 541
Meublat, G. 2289
Meulder, M. 3110
Meur, P. Le 4720
Meyer, A. 4666
Meyer, C. 282
Meyer, D. 1697
Meyer, M. 3675
Meyer, R. 4911
Meyerhoff, M. 1724
Meynier, O. 3608
Meza, A. 1039, 1040
Mguni, S. 968
Miccoli, L. 3728
Michaelowa, K. 4554
Michaels, E. 4096
Michailovsky, B. 2032, 2035
Michalove, P. 2058
Michelet, D. 533
Middleton, J. 2386
Middleton, K. 804, 3594
Mierzwiński, A. 965
Migeon, G. 533
Mignolo, W. 777
Mīkles, L. 4105, 4523
Miksic, J. 906
Mikulandra, F. 1574
Milazi, D. 4548
Milbert, I. 4671
Milčić, D. 1549
Milgram, B. 4848
Milhou, A. 3632
Milian, J. 4796
Miliani, D. 4192
Milich, L. 4820
Milković-Kraus, S. 3789
Millard, A. 1377
Miller, A. 3005
Miller, B. 2706
Miller, C. 399, 4006
Miller, D. 2612, 3692, 3712
Miller, J. 611, 896, 2099, 3042, 3155
Miller, P. 4534

Millet, J. 1465
Millett, M. 512
Mills, D. 115, 2955
Mills, M. 3991, 3995
Mills, R. 2338
Milne, C. 909, 2208
Milner, M. 1651
Milner, N. 1348
Milroy, C. 4937
Milstein, R. 3354
Milton, G. 699
Min, M. De 948
Minar, C. 1415, 2236
Minault-Gout, A. 1177
Mind Association 4530
Mindry, D. 4728
Mindzie, C. 968
Minelli, A. 1101
Minkowski, C. 3296
Minta-Tworzowska, D. 998
Mintz, S. 4809
Miossec, A. 4618, 4794
Miqdadi, R. 1147
Miram, H. 4183
Miran, M. 4447
Miron, D. 4444
Mishra, S. 3769
Mishra, U. 4901
Mishra, Y. 3370
Misiejuk, D. 4433
Misturelli, F. 4536
Mitchell, D. 2933
Mitchell, J. 4423
Mitchell, K. 290
Mitchell, S. 467, 922
Mitchell, W. 2933
Mitchem, J. 1289
Mitford, T. 520
Mithen, S. 1160
Mitlin, D. 2210
Mitra, J. 4186
Mitropoulos, M. 3847
Mitsunaga, F. 1665
Mitterauer, M. 2689
Mittmann, S. 2550
Miyamoto, S. 1667, 1668
Mizinga, F. 2744
Mizoguchi, Y. 1461
Mizrachi, N. 4525
Mizuno, N. 3954
Mladenova, O. 1752
Mlekuz, J. 4498
Mlinar, A. 4319
Moberg, M. 2587, 4632
Moblo, P. 739

Moctezuma, P. 2210
Modncka, N. 3241
Moffat, T. 2699
Mogensen, H. 4882
Mohamadieh, L. 1151
Mohamed, C. 1625
Mohamed-Abdi, M. 712, 3047
Mohanta, B. 904
Mohanty, B. 1491
Mohanty, P. 1048
Mohnot, S. 1686
Moisà, M. 4381
Moisala, P. 3871
Moitt, B. 749
Molapo, M. 2736, 3010
Molen, W. Van Der 4231
Molénat, J. 2993
Molinié, A. 103, 3870
Molinié-Bertrand, A. 4305
Molla, D. 4817
Mollat, H. 2329
Molle, F. 2314
Mollenhauer, A. 1054
Moller, J. 2614
Molnár, V. 2327
Moloney, L. 2238
Molyneux, M. 4612
Momani, A. 1266
Momani, A. al- 952, 1202, 1380
Monferrer Sala, J. 1871, 3268
Mongne, P. 326
Monius, A. 3180
Monjaret, A. 401
Monnet, P. 4580
Monod, D. 2857, 3076
Monod-Broca, P. 110, 3799
Monteiro, R. 323, 707
Montes, C. 4697
Montesino, N. 10, 3091
Montgomerie, R. 1493
Montiel, L. 903
Montigny, A. 2417, 3018
Mooney, S. 913
Moore, E. 906
Moore, J. 295, 2130
Moore, S. 4612
Moore, T. 1603
Moraïs, L. De 2271
Morales, F. 3618
Morales, M. 2165
Morales Muñiz, A. 462
Moran, J. 2762
Moran, K. 4636
Mordt, M. 4695
Moreau, M. 1749

Moreno-Black, G. 3751, 4385
Morgan, K. 2383
Morgan, M. 4722
Morgenstern, M. 3425
Morin, K. 2855, 4342
Morin, T. 1082, 1091, 1311
Moro, M. 1670
Morreall, J. 1864, 3449
Morrell, E. 2325
Morris, B. 3107
Morris, J. 4657
Morris-Suzuki, T. 4458
Morrobel, J. 2207
Mortier, R. 4179, 4292
Mortimore, M. 4691
Morton, H. 1773
Morwood, M. 1137
Moser-Achuthat, H. 3875
Mosko, M. 3625
Mosley, P. 4705
Mosman, K. 1625
Mosquera, M. 890
Mota, S. 323, 707
Motingea, M. 1994, 1999, 2009
Moto, F. 1748
Motteux, N. 4910
Moucharik, S. 2453
Moureau, F. 4179, 4321
Mousavi, A. 878
Mouser, B. 679
Moussa, S. 4179, 4225
Moussaoui, A. 292, 3027
Mowl, G. 2713
Mowry, C. 1671
Moyo, S. 4669
Możejko, B. 581
MSSRF Team 4780
Mtika, M. 4632, 4808
Muazzam Hussain, A. 4913
Muchanga, A. 1749
Mudry, M. 1501
Muftić, O. 1549
Muhawi, I. 3994
Muheisen, M. 1230
Muheisen, Z. al- 964, 1155
Muhesen, S. 1406
Muhly, J. 445
Muhs, B. 490
Muijzenberg, O. van den 793
Mukherjee, A. 1893, 3218
Mukherjee, J. 1486, 2118
Mukherjee, N. 4765
Mukhia, H. 4043
Mukhopadhyay, B. 3772
Mukhopadhyay, S. 3772

Muktupāvels, V. 3948
Mulder, M. 279, 2687
Mulder, N. 1045, 1079, 1217, 4556
Mulder-Hymans, N. 1207
Mullen Kreamer, C. 368
Müller, A. 23, 1596
Muller, C. 2277, 2484, 3933, 4059
Müller, H. 1317, 3604
Muller, J. 844, 2571
Müller-Neuhof, B. 1155
Müllerová, P. 4144
Müller-Scheeßel, N. 1390
Mullins, M. 3543
Mulot, É. 4663
Muminov, A. 3322
Mumtaz, S. 4851
Mundigo, A. 2848, 3254
Mundo, R. Del 4740
Mundy, N. 1679
Munro, D. 616, 3635
Munro, R. 2324
Munroe, R. 4521
Munshi, I. 2115, 2859
Münzel, M. 3883
Munzer, S. 3235, 3374
Munzi, M. 1277
Mupopolo, F. 4555
Muraj, A. 101
Murayama, S. 2749
Murgai, R. 4698
Murià, J. 701
Murnaghan, S. 528
Muroyama, Y. 1668
Murphy, E. 2735
Murphy, L. 2430
Murphy, P. 2092
Murshed, S. 2293
Murshid, K. 2196
Muršič, R. 204
Mursy, A. 1766
Musa, A. 1239
Musiime, J. 2288
Musil, J. 138
Musisi, N. 627
Muthumohan, N. 2485
Muthwii, M. 4409
Mutia, B. 2700
Mutter, M. 4666
Mwale, B. 4661
Mwangi, W. 4548
Myers, D. 2047
Myers, G. 291
Myers-Scotton, C. 2012
Mylius, K. 3371
Myszka, M. 1326

Myszka, R. 1326
Na'aman, N. 1330
Nabulsi, A. 1122, 1287, 1293
Nadal, M. 4609
Nader, L. 155, 219, 530, 969, 3001
Naepels, M. 3929
Naerssen, T. van 2216
Nag, K. 3391
Naga, S. 2023
Nagar, Y. 1327
Nagarajan, G. 4911
Nagata, J. 3326
Nagel, T. 3330
Naghawai, A. 990
Naglič, K. 78
Nagothu, U. 2083
Nahar, M. al- 831
Naher, B. 4760
Naidu, G. 1490
Naiqun, W. 189
Nair, S. 1894
Najjar, M. 1275, 1307
Najjar, M. el- 1237
Nakabayashi, N. 3223
Nakamichi, M. 1607
Nakayama, M. 1473
Nalbant, H. 2711, 4844
Nance, K. 4568
Nanoglou, S. 886
Nanri, K. 1875
Napon, A. 1749
Nara, T. 1459
Narayan, D. 4872
Narayanan, V. 2099, 3155
Narrog, H. 1872
Nascimento, O. Do 323, 707
Nash, J. 4442
Nasr, A. 3863, 4349
Nasruddin 1137
Nast, H. 291
Nastri, J. 1385
Nathan, D. 2828, 2829
Nattapoolwat, S. 4909
Naud, J. 2636
Naumova, O. 4411
Navarini, G. 239, 396
Navarrete Orta, L. 4192
Navarro, J. 1166
Navarro, L. 4937
Navarro, N. 4740
Naveh, J. 1338
Navrátilová, H. 3888
Nawafleh, N. al- 952
Nawafleh, S. al- 952, 1206
Nawata, H. 2429

Nawotka, K. 349
Nayak, P. 1350
Nayak, S. 3276
Nayar, S. 3977
Nazli, S. 4756
N'Daou, M. 4023
Ndogoni, L. 4722
Nduma, I. 2434
Neba, S. 4805
Neef, R. 1147
Neeley, M. 949, 955, 1273
Neemann, H. 229, 3979
Negers, D. 3968
Negi, S. 4716
Negra, D. 1774, 3699
Negreiros, R. 2222
Nehring, G. 1913
Nekaris, K. 1600
Nel, C. 1025
Nel, E. 4910
Nel, P. 2544
Nelissen, M. 1692
Nelkin, D. 1498, 2657
Nelson, D. 2955, 4450
Nemysova, E. 2057
Nencel, L. 2821
Nepote, J. 1081
Nérée, M. 4220
Nero, K. 2158, 2633, 4804
Nesbitt, N. 3933, 4059
Neshina, A. 3966
Neto, A. 3605
Neto, L. 3914
Nettelbeck, A. 2827, 3104
Nettleton, A. 4111
Neu, E. 4148
Neumann, R. 685
Neumayer, E. 1571
Neurath, J. 2602, 2665
Neusner, J. 208, 3455
Neuwirth, A. 3336
Newell, P. 4762
Newland, L. 3625
Newton, E. 304, 2897
Newton, L. 4545
Ngaido, T. 2404
N'Gouah-Beaud, P. 2070
Ngugi, E. 2879, 4878
Ngulube, T. 4882
Nguyen, M. 2885
Nguyen, X. 4392
Ngwane, Z. 2675
Niang, A. 2307, 4927
Nicastro, N. 1525
Nicholson, H. 214

Nicholson, P. 1003
Nicholson, R. 994
Nichter, M. 3811
Nicolaï, R. 1749
Nicolle, C. 1133
Nielsen, F. 11
Niemeier, W. 448
Niemi, T. 945
Nienhauser, Jr., W. 206, 4076
Nietschmann, B. 291
Nihalani, P. 1891
Nihill, M. 809, 3586, 4389
Nikishenkov, A. 45
Nikulin, N. 1833
Nilssen, P. 1042
Nimis, E. 4126
Niño-Murcia, M. 1785, 1915
Ninow, F. 1216, 1223, 1224
Niranjana, T. 650
Nishida, T. 1605
Nishino, Y. 337
Nishio, T. 4585
Nishter, N. 3504
Nissen, H. 1230
Nisson, H. 2358
Njie, A. 4896
Njogu, K. 4058
Nkaké, L. 2070
Nkya, L. 2884, 3796
Noboru, H. 595
Nobuya, W. 983
Noel, J. 2617
Noiret, P. 1413
Nolan, F. 1764
Nolan, J. 2201
Noland, M. 4812
Nolen-Hoeksema, S. 4532
Noordin, Q. 2307
Noort, R. Van de 868
Norbu, D. 2178
Norihisa, S. 1755, 3151
Norio, M. 501
Norrick, N. 1754
Norström, C. 2834, 4406
Northon, C. 291
Norton, R. 2564
Noss, A. 2431
Novellino, D. 3813
Novy, M. 1500
Nowaihi, M. al- 4251
Nowak, J. 3103
Nowak, M. 883
Nowicka, M. 1077
Nubé, M. 4810
Nugent, S. 24

Nunn, C. 1618
Nurse, D. 1990
Nusair, A. 4077
Nuttall, M. 4785
Nuttall, T. 613
Nyanzi, S. 2892, 2913, 3810
Nyarko, P. 4884
Nyasimi, M. 2307
Nyland, B. 2863
Nzewi, M. 3933, 4059
Oates, J. 2358
Obermeyer, C. 2910
Obiedat, N. 1868
Oboler, R. 2887, 2982
O'Brien, C. 201
O'Brien, S. 4937
Ocampo, C. 4378, 4754
Ochalla, N. 2570
Ochsner, K. 170
O'Connell, J. 2352, 2651
O'Connor, T. 994
Oda, J. 289, 3983
Odigmegwu, C. 2733
Odin, S. 3170
Offe, J. 3761
Ogawa, H. 3165
Ogbomo, O. 4161
Ogembo, J. 2635, 3025
Ogiue-Ikeda, M. 1457
Ogudin, V. 3142, 3767
Ogungbile, D. 3226
Ogunlana, E. 2320, 4862
Ogura, M. 1730, 1947
Ohashi, J. 1504
O'Herron, M. 1708
Ohiaraumunna, T. 3933, 4059
Ohkado, M. 1940, 1949
Ohnuki-Tierney, E. 572
Ohsako, M. 1590
Ohta, I. 2367
Ojaide, T. 3933, 4059
Ojo, M. 2733
Okamoto, K. 1653, 1655
Okayasu, N. 1622
Oke, S. 2246
Okemgbo, C. 2733
Okigbo, C. 4818
Olaniyan, T. 3933, 4059
O'Leary, J. 4265
Oleson, J. 1187, 1209, 1211
Oliveira Ramos, M. De 323, 707
Oliver, D. 4314
Oliver, R. 1990
Olivier, E. 3953
Olivier, G. 3119

Ollé, A. 875, 890
Ollé, M. 4222
Ollif, C. 4752
Olofson, H. 2440, 2467, 4729
Olsen, J. 1408
Olson, E. 3259, 3645
Olson, K. 2001
Olszewski, D. 831, 1248
Olszewski, M. 1044
Olupot, W. 1623
Omar, A. 968
Omeje, K. 3551
Omeonga, B. 1989
Omidsalar, M. 3991, 4022
Omojola, B. 3933, 4059
Onedera, P. 4028
Onyango, B. 3881
Oonk, G. 2368
Open University 4713
Opfermann, U. 3099
Orakzai, S. 4614
Ordóñez, J. 3035
O'Reilly, D. 838
Organisation for Economic Co-operation and
    Development 4925
Organization of American States, General
    Secretariat 4644
Ornan, T. 1020
Oro, I. de 841
Orozco Köhler, T. 1363
Orr, A. 4661
Orser, Jr., C. 155, 530, 969
Orsini, C. 1101
Ortega, A. 839, 846
Ortiz Vadillo, J. 2437
Ortner, S. 244, 991
Ortolani, A. 2687
Orton, L. 2469
Ory, S. 3330
Osasona, C. 3844
Osbahr, H. 2106, 4803
Osborne, E. 66
Osenton, C. 863
O'Shaughnessy, T. 4722
Osman, G. 4232
Osorio, D. 1703
Osorio, J. 254, 4457
Osorio Tejada, N. 4192
Ostapirat, W. 2044
Ostapkowicz, J. 1322
Ostashewski, M. 4505
Ostrasz, A. 469, 1028
Ostro, L. 1705
Ostrom, E. 2264, 4399
Osu, S. 1998

O'Sullivan, P. 1137
Osuntokun, J. 4548
Otani, E. 168, 3139
Otani, Y. 1769, 1770
Otsuka, K. 2350, 2410, 2413, 2427
Ottaway, B. 1397
Otte, M. 1413
Ottenheimer, M. 138
Otto, L. 371
Otto Parrodi, E. 2262
Ottoni, E. 1702
Oushakine, S. 4440
Outa, G. 2499
Outwater, A. 2884, 3796
Owen, J. 1429, 4002
Owens, J. 1842, 1847
Owsley, D. 970
Owusu, J. 4678
Oya, M. 1503
Oyaya, C. 4883
Oyewumi, O. 4009
Oyler, D. 4229
Ozanne-Rivierre, F. 1888
Özyetgin, M. 1836
Paaske, J. 371
Pace, J. 960, 1027, 1132, 1371
Packham, C. 4709
Pacquement, J. 124, 1805
Paden, W. 210, 3561
Padhi, M. 62
Padoux, A. 3299
Page, S. 4897
Pai, H. Il 3701
Paice, E. 773
Pailler, C. 2813, 3113
Pain, R. 2713
Painter, T. 3834
Paisley, F. 2827, 3104
Pakszys, E. 2816, 3140
Palacios, E. 1691
Palagi, E. 21, 1595
Palanithurai, G. 2569, 4843
Paley, J. 2518
Palmas, L. 1576
Palmberg, M. 4516
Palmer, C. 1094
Palumbo, B. 373
Palumbo, G. 1109, 1144, 1239, 1276-1278,
    1292, 1314, 1315, 4327
Pàmies, R. 841
Panagiotakopulu, E. 507
Panagiotopoulos, D. 1060
Panda, G. 3270
Pandey, G. 2153
Pandey, P. 2153

Pandya, V. 3864
Paniagua Pérez, J. 758
Pankaja, S. 3311
Paolisso, M. 4770
Papaloizou, G. 4910
Papasavvas, G. 1017
Papin, P. 474
Paquette, R. 807
Paradise, T. 1008
Paradowska, M. 3554
Parapetti, R. 1035, 1069
Paraschak, V. 3071
Pardo, A. 4099
Paré, L. 2415
Parejo-Coudert, R. 3719
Parenti, F. 1276
Parés, J. 839, 842
Parezo, N. 120
Paris, L. 2697, 2803
Park, E. 2521, 3266, 3648
Park, J. 2712
Park, Y. 3079
Parker, G. 2092
Parker, K. 291
Parker, R. 52, 2908
Parker, S. 1233-1235, 1302
Parker, T. 3011
Parkvall, M. 2014
Parnell, P. 3730
Parodi, C. 1795, 1915
Parr, H. 291
Parr, J. 2949
Parsons, B. 2789
Parsons, E. 1505, 2674
Pascual Buxó, J. 4275
Pasqua, M. 543
Passevant, C. 4105, 4523
Patacsil, P. 2384
Patel, K. 2541
Patel, S. 2210
Patent, J. 2031, 2049
Pathak, M. 3297
Pathak, N. 62, 3818
Pathak, R. 3298
Pati, B. 651
Patindol, M. 4694
Pátkai, R. 3160
Patnaik, D. 3867
Patole-Edoumba, E. 326
Patte, M. 1980, 1982
Patterson, C. 3585
Patterson, M. 105, 3231
Patterson, T. 18
Pauk, P. 906
Pauk, U. 1285

Paul, H. 3505
Paul, K. 3805
Pausacker, H. 4211
Pavaloi, M. 316, 322, 3839
Pavelčík, J. 3124
Pavelčík, N. 3124
Pavia, C. 1545
Pavlović, S. 220, 2585
Pavón Maldonado, B. 1032, 4115
Pawley, A. 1878
Pawlikowski, M. 1445
Payne, G. 4935
Payne, R. 228
Payongayong, E. 2427
PCRC 2576
Peace, A. 2068
Peacock, B. 2895
Peacock, D. 500
Peacocke, N. 2496
Pearson, M. 637
Pearson, R. 3861
Pearson, W. 4343
Pearthree, E. 2393
Peatrik, A. 2613
Pecha, L. 482, 2354
Péclard, D. 4472
Pedersen, M. 3690
Pedersen, S. 694
Pedrosa, J. 3930
Peel, D. 3491
Peers, D. 785
Pégard, O. 4331
Pei, Y. 1613
Peirano, M. 182
Peláez, F. 1630, 1654
Peled, Y. 129, 1853
Pelras, C. 328
Pels, P. 135, 416
Peltzer, L. 4263
Peña, L. de la 2117
Pence, B. 4884
Penelas, M. 4167
Peng, L. 1997
Pengpaiboon, P. 4875
Pennell, C. 2362, 3353
Pensiero, M. 4758
Penton-Voak, I. 1494
Peralva, A. 4682
Perdue, Jr., C. 4016
Peregrine, P. 980
Pereira, G. 533
Peresani, M. 864
Pérez, F. 4202
Pérez-González, A. 839, 842
Perinbam, B. 643

Periša, M. 1574
Periwal, S. 138
Perks, R. 375
Perlman, J. 1664
Perminow, A. 2563
Pernicka, E. 912
Perocco, F. 3534
Peroš-Golubičić, T. 1575
Pérouse de Montclos, M. 2159
Perramond, E. 291
Perreault, T. 2207
Perret, D. 1316
Perret, M. 1695, 1818, 2063
Perrett, D. 1494
Perrin, L. 2857, 3076
Perrot, C. 326
Perrot-Minnot, S. 4124
Perry, J. 3991
Person, A. 968
Persoon, G. 29, 184
Peruzzetto, A. 1277
Perwitasari-Farajallah, D. 1649
Pesetsky, D. 1936
Pesteil, P. 2257
Peterman, G. 1065, 1175
Petersen, A. 3859
Petersen, V. 371
Peterson, D. 540, 2034
Peterson, J. 1542, 2037
Peterson, N. 4069, 4578
Pethe, M. 3313
Petievich, C. 4052
Petit, L. 1393
Petitjean, M. 4609
Petrić, K. 667
Petridis, C. 3614
Petrilli, S. 3728, 4030
Petrosino, S. 3728
Petrov, P. 166, 3649, 4428
Pettitt, P. 873, 1516
Petto, A. 1675
Petty, R. 4538
Petzold, J. 4151
Peyre, E. 1477
Peyron, M. 4037
Pezerović, D. 1555
Pezerović-Panijan, R. 1555
Pfeiffer, W. 3631
Pfister, U. 2644
Pflegerl, J. 2171
Pflüger, F. 901
Phélinas, P. 2305
Phelps, L. 4816
Philander, D. 4917
Philip, G. 1219

Philip, L. 2402
Phillips, K. 4860
Phillips, R. 4171
Phillips, S. 2938
Phom, L. 2039
Photos-Jones, E. 956
Piazza, A. Di 2393
Picard, M. 1981
Piccirillo, M. 1026, 1038
Pickard, R. 4317
Pierart, J. 265
Pieroni, A. 3747
Pierrepont, A. 3929
Pika, S. 1704
Pike, A. 1516
Pimentel, V. 475
Pina-Cabral, J. De 275, 751, 2539
Pinault, G. 3301
Pincheon, B. 2877
Pineau, J. 310
Pinedo, D. 2404
Pineri, R. 4162
Ping, H. 648
Pink, S. 389
Pint, J. 789
Piontek, J. 2144
Pirart, É. 3273
Pirie, A. 1160
Pirta, R. 2097
Pishwa, H. 1918
Piškor, M. 3922
Pistorius, J. 936
Pita, V. 755
Pitarch, P. 3516
Pitt, M. 4911
Pitte, J. 4618, 4794
Pitti, L. 2453
Pitts, R. 909, 2208
Place, F. 2413
Plag, I. 2015
Plakans, A. 2644
Platte, E. 2184, 4031
Platten, D. 3005
Plattner, S. 2353
Plavcan, J. 1528
Plewczyński, M. 563
Ploeg, A. 2199
Ploog, K. 1749
Pluciennik, M. 164, 972
Plug, I. 920
Plummer, T. 968
Plumptre, A. 1709
Pobutsky, A. 2637
Pochron, S. 1611
Pocius, G. 152, 153

Podella, T. 3396
Podolinská, T. 2811, 3517
Poelzer, G. 4654
Pogoson, O. 1071
Pogue, D. 664
Poiatti-Haldimann, M. 1038
Polet, J. 968
Politis, G. 258
Politis, K. 956, 1111, 1169-1171, 1313, 1436
Pollard, A. 60
Polliack, M. 3393
Pollock, S. 4261
Pondopoulo, A. 582
Pons, V. 2156
Ponting, J. 3074
Ponzio, A. 3728, 4030
Ponzio, J. 3728
Ponzio, L. 3728
Pool, R. 2892, 2913, 3810
Poorthuis, M. 4581
Popkin, J. 4567
Popovicova, I. 280, 2858
Poppel, F. van 2150
Porche, L. 3037
Porodong, P. 2808, 2828
Porqueres Gené, E. 2666, 4493
Porter, G. 4299
Porter, L. 1609, 1627, 1706
Portis, L. 4105, 4523
Posthumus, L. 2006
Potapov, L. 487
Potter, R. 4731
Potter, S. 1737
Potts, A. 2840
Potts, D. 350, 1410
Potts, R. 968
Pouliquen, J. 1657
Poulsen, J. 1700
Poussa, P. 1954
Pouwels, R. 622
Power, C. 2775, 3832
Powers, D. 606, 2986
Powis, T. 2444
Pradhan, R. 2404
Prado, C. 1593
Prado, G. 3255
Prado-Martinez, C. 1551, 1581
Praetzellis, A. 155, 530, 969
Praetzellis, M. 155, 530, 969
Prakash, A. 4780
Prakash, J. 1437
Prakash, P. 1895
Pranzo, G. 3728
Prasad, R. 4807
Pratt, C. 4818

Pratt, S. 402
Prebeg, Ž. 3804
Predelli, L. 2746
Preinhaelterová, H. 2788, 4189
Prémare, A. de 3330
Prestholdt, J. 228
Prestipino, G. 3725
Prete, A. 3728
Pretorius, J. 920
Prets, E. 3178
Prévôt, N. 3935
Prica, I. 194, 412, 420
Price, E. 1646
Price, J. 4258
Price, M. 291, 1577, 4822
Price, T. 877, 2177
Prignitz, G. 1749
Primavera, J. 2117
Prince, J. 1456
Prinsloo, D. 1778, 1779
Prinsloo, H. 950
Pritchard, S. 2937, 4438
Procházka-Eisl, G. 3120, 3351
Procida, M. 694
Proctor, D. 4722
Project Operations Unit 2292
Proschan, F. 4463
Prosecký, J. 3920
Prossinger, H. 1466
Prost, R. 4105, 4523
Prosterman, R. 4820
Proudfoot, I. 4215
Provençal, P. 1819
Pruneau, J. 4331
Prynn, B. 2648
Puccio, D. 2975
Pugh, J. 4731
Pukoki, W. 4263
Pullen, J. 1511
Pullum, S. 1583
Pullum, T. 2634
Pulsipher, L. 291
Pungur, J. 3160
Puplampu, K. 53
Purves, A. 4579
Pury, S. de 1986
Pushkareva, N. 1740, 2832
Put, M. 4727
Pylypa, J. 3811
Qin, Z. 2751
Qiu, P. 4063
Qotole, M. 4012
Qrarhi, H. 1206
Quaintance, S. 955
Quandt, S. 3827

Quatrone, R. 1715
Quayson, A. 187
Quella-Villéger, A. 4263
Quemeneur, T. 326
Quéré, A. 1916
Quesada, J. 1984
Quigley, D. 159, 217
Quinn, E. 4437
Quinn, R. 968
Quiñones Keber, E. 214
Quiros, F. de 894
Quisumbing, A. 2350, 2410, 2427
Quraishy, Z. 2834, 4406
R. Whelpton, F. Van 2739, 3012
Raahauge, K. 371
Rabbow, M. 3761
Rabinowitz, A. 4041
Rabinowitz, D. 3040
Rączkowski, W. 273, 971, 999
Radav, S. 761
Radding, C. 750, 2082
Radespiel, U. 1619, 1621, 1632, 1643
Radice, W. 3924
Rafalimanana, H. 2708
Ragot, N. 3515
Rahbari, R. 4685
Rahi, M. 3705
Rahimi, D. 1112
Rahman, M. 2293
Rahmonī, R. 3991
Rahn, I. 1501
Rainey, A. 1343
Raison-Jourde, F. 3562
Raitz, K. 291
Raj, D. 3730
Raja, D. 3898
Rajah, A. 35, 104
Rajak, T. 593
Rajalakshmi, S. 3836
Rajbhandari, B. 4820
Rakelmann, G. 3761
Rak-Kaić, A. 3804
Rakotomalala, M. 3562
Rakotomanana, F. 4663
Rakuts, N. 1784
Rallo Gruss, C. 3852
Ramakrishnan, U. 1713
Raman, P. 3846
Ramanathan, B. 1562
Ramanathan, H. 3913
Ramanathan, N. 3913
Ramanathan, S. 4474
Ramaswamy, S. 4501
Ramaswamy, V. 3932
Ramdas, S. 4780

Ramesh, M. 1506
Ramini, I. 4084
Ramírez, J. 2465
Ramirez, R. 2222
Ramirez-Villoria, A. 4740
Ramløv, K. 371
Ramos, A. 135, 416, 4617, 4651
Rampton, B. 1735, 1736
Ramson, W. 1723
Randolph, K. 1389
Ranganayakamma, M. 2461
Rangel, D. 4239
Rani, V. 3210
Ranis, G. 4738
Rankoana, S. 3815
Rao, I. 1506
Rao, J. 1909
Rao, K. 1568
Rao, N. 4780
Rao, P. 82, 370
Rao, S. 2247
Rao, V. 4353
Rapaport, L. 1647
Rapoport, Y. 606, 2986
Rapp, R. 2933
Rapport, N. 4469
Rapuano, Y. 1050
Raqab, S. Al- 596, 4075
Rashid, S. 2702, 3775
Rasing, T. 2729
Rasmussen, A. 3357, 3951
Rasmussen, K. 1614
Rasmussen, M. 371
Rasmussen, S. 2776
Rassinier, G. 326
Rasson, A. 1295
Rasson-Seigne, A. 496, 1418, 1419, 2228
Rasson-Seigne, M. 1239
Rastogi, K. 1904
Ratliff, M. 2028
Rauch, A. 2085, 4310
Raussen, T. 2288
Ravaoarimanana, B. 1650
Raven, D. 1743, 3668
Raveneau, G. 2085, 4310
Ravid, D. 1840, 1870
Ravindran, T. 4901
Ray, I. 2355
Ray, Jr., P. 1193
Raya, R. 910
Raymer, L. 909, 2208
Raymond, C. 2278
Raynal, G. 4105, 4523
Raynaut, C. 2105
Raynor, H. 1556

Raza, A. 1137
Razarihelisoa, M. 1818, 2063
Razmjou, S. 1334
Read, D. 2658
Reade, J. 1284
Reader, S. 1684
Real Academia Española 67
Rebato, E. 1587
Reboux, P. 4263
Reckner, P. 909, 2208
Reddy, B. 1502, 1897
Reddy, V. 1490
Rediker, M. 778
Redmond, E. 993
Reed, R. 3623
Rees, A. 1683
Reeves, G. 3170
Reeves, M. 1209
Regis, H. 3900
Reich, S. 1601
Reichler, C. 4179, 4332
Reid, A. 968
Reid, D. 1472
Reid, R. 639, 4820
Reider, N. 3972, 3987
Reikat, A. 2517
Reimann, M. 69, 83
Reis, R. 3777
Reiss, T. 2092
Reizbaum, M. 4182
Remis, M. 1671
Renahy, N. 4309
Rendsburg, G. 1859, 3436
Rendsburg, S. 1859, 3436
Renfrew, C. 34, 325, 987
Renne, E. 2682
Reshetov, A. 145
Resta, G. 277
Resurrección, B. 2089, 2836
Reuck, J. De 654
Reuter, T. 3625
Revel, N. 4029
Reverdin, A. 850
Reveyrand-Coulon, O. 2815
Revunenkova, E. 3602
Rey, A. 75
Rey-Debove, J. 75
Reyes, C. 4696
Reynes, J. 1657
Reyniers, A. 238
Reynolds, V. 1663, 1709
Reyss, J. 1406
Rhodes, F. 2874, 3782
Rhodes, L. 2999
Riabchikova, Z. 2057

Ribeiro Romeiro, A. 4682
Richard, A. 1615
Richard, F. 4223
Richard, J. 1633
Richard, S. 1141
Richard-Hansen, C. 1598
Richards, M. 867, 1291, 1498, 2657
Richardson, A. 498
Richey, E. 831
Richey, J. 3136
Richter, R. 2171
Richter, T. 1861
Ricklefs, M. 1186
Ricklefs, N. 1186
Rickman, J. 2480
Ricks, T. 228
Rida, N. 1248
Ridha, H. 2860, 3086
Ridington, R. 2834, 4406
Ridley, R. 4253
Rielly, K. 1275
Riel-Salvatore, J. 1298
Riese, B. 214, 1345
Rieth, E. 326
Rigg, J. 4909
Riley, C. 2281
Riley, E. 2222
Riley, M. 1615
Riney-Kehrberg, P. 2463
Rinne, E. 3835
Rinpoche, M. 3169
Riquelme, J. 462
Riska, E. 2470, 2854
Risopoulos, J. 2312
Ritchie, G. 1767
Rius, M. 652
Riva Gonzalez, P. La 2727
Rival, L. 90, 385
Rivallain, J. 326
Rivera-Fuentes, C. 2959
Riverso, E. 529
Riviale, P. 326
Rivière, H. 3953
Rizov, M. 2315
Rizvi, S. 4616
Rob, U. 2640
Robb, J. 852
Robbek, V. 4654
Robbins, J. 271, 3232, 3233, 3265, 3643
Roberson, J. 3969
Robert, H. 2827, 3104
Robert, P. 75
Roberts, A. 3773
Roberts, J. 4863
Roberts, M. 2489

Roberts, P. 2533, 3073
Robertson, C. 2804
Robertson, J. 769, 2944
Robillard, D. de 1749
Robin, C. 1342
Robinson, B. 3238
Robinson, C. 218, 4660
Robinson, S. 4812
Robotham, D. 2496
Robson, S. 4231
Rocha, C. 2798
Rocha, J. 429
Roche, D. 3967
Rochecouste, J. 3989
Rocheleau, D. 2207, 2404
Rocher, L. 2991
Rocher, R. 2991
Rodgers, J. 1488
Rodman, P. 1717
Rodrigues, A. 323, 707
Rodriguez, A. 1691
Rodriguez, F. 4271
Rodríguez, G. 2088, 3667
Rodríguez, J. 889, 4347
Rodríguez, M. 1333
Rodríguez, X. 846, 890
Rodríguez-Clare, A. 4711
Rodríguez-Pose, A. 2222
Rodseth, L. 213
Roeder, J. 1639
Roengpitya, R. 2027
Roese, P. 4007
Roese, T. 4007
Rogers, B. 2691
Rogers, J. 4286
Rogers, S. 160
Rogerson, C. 2244, 4339, 4683, 4917
Roggero, M. 4247
Rohatynskyj, M. 158
Rohde, J. 291
Rohini, A. 2726
Röhm, J. 372
Rokicki, W. 1572
Rollefson, G. 1114, 1117, 1119, 1123, 1125
Rolls, S. 4722
Rolnik, R. 2222
Roman, J. 4230
Roman, P. 4263
Romeo, L. 3262
Römer, M. 517
Romero Galván, J. 214
Romero-Marin, J. 2644
Rompel, M. 3761
Room, R. 215
Roopnarine, L. 2167

Root, R. 2719, 3817
Ropac, D. 1559
Roś, J. 1444
Rosas, A. 842
Röschenthaler, U. 2195
Rose, D. 2074
Rose, J. 1237
Rosello, M. 4159
Rosen, J. 1531
Rosen, L. 4617, 4651
Rosen, P. 4120
Rosen, V. 1560
Rosenbaum, G. 3354
Rosengren, K. 3574
Rosenzweig, M. 4755
Rosin, R. 2114, 3843
Rosina, A. 1558
Rosique, J. 1587
Rosman, A. 327
Ross, C. 1676
Ross, D. 4109
Ross, L. 2207
Ross, M. 1041, 1879
Ross, S. 3674, 4595
Roşu, A. 6, 94, 2071
Rotermund, H. 1489
Roth, C. 1835
Roth, E. 2126, 2879, 4878
Roth, G. 1547
Roth, M. 508, 2500, 2995
Rothe, H. 1716
Rothstein, R. 3918
Rouaud, A. 1818, 2063
Roubaud, F. 4663
Roueff, O. 3929
Rouiller, F. 1749
Rourke, K. 2874, 3782
Rouse, A. 4351
Rousey, A. 2691
Rousseau, C. 2165
Routledge, B. 1142
Routledge, P. 291
Routray, H. 4140
Rouveroy van Nieuwaal, E. van 2565
Roux, J. 4608
Rova, E. 1440
Rovillé-Sausse, F. 1540, 1551, 1552
Rovine, V. 3841
Rovira, J. 4260
Rowe, S. 2817, 3141
Rowlands, M. 968
Rowley-Conwy, P. 274
Roy, C. 2577, 2945, 3056, 3075, 3529
Roy Ladurie, E. Le 2205, 2423
Rozario, S. 4849

Rozen, M. 2799
Rozmus, D. 1444
Rúa, C. de la 1522
Rubchak, M. 2835
Rubel, P. 327
Ruben, I. 1155, 1197
Rubenstein, J. 3447
Rubilar Solis, L. 4192
Rudan, I. 3804
Rudan, P. 3804
Rudolphi, W. 1374
Ruet, J. 4671
Ruf, F. 2258
Ruggiero, G. 3828
Ruhnau, E. 214
Ruiz Medrano, E. 214
Ruiz Souza, J. 620, 3852
Rumpler, Y. 1650, 1699
Rumsey, A. 3659
Rupp, G. 2099, 3155
Rupp, L. 2771
Rush, M. 4122
Russel, S. 1601
Russell, D. 40
Russell, K. 555, 1094
Russow, F. 2079
Rutten, R. 2557
Rutter, L. 1886
Ryan, F. 843
Ryan, M. 970
Ryang, S. 4517
Ryba, T. 5, 226
Rybakov, S. 146, 410
Rydstrøm, H. 2715
Rygiel, J. 2251
Ryzhakova, S. 39
Saadi, H. 4663
Saage, R. 100, 740
Saban, R. 110, 3799
Sacchi, M. 755
Sachs, L. 1498, 2657, 3777
Sadan, J. 3354
Sadek, M. 2994
Sader, E. 4662
Sadoulet, E. 2285
Sadowsky, D. 1500
Saele, L. 831
Sáez De Albéniz, M. 2438
Sagner, A. 813, 2774, 2922
Saha, J. 3305
Sahip, Y. 2711, 4844
Sahnouni, M. 890
Said, S. Al- 2890
Saidel, B. 939
Saïdi, F. 2289

Saindon, M. 3302
St. John, G. 4425
San Juan, Jr., E. 2161
San Martin, L. 1587
St. Pierre, M. 4885
St. Pierre, P. 689
Sainz, F. 1012
Sajbin Velásquez, V. 4937
Sajuthi, D. 1649
Sakamaki, T. 1605
Sakurai, A. 297
Sala, R. 875, 890
Salama, P. 4609, 4682
Salces, I. 1587
Saldamando, A. 3056, 3075
Saler, B. 167
Sales, A. 4748
Salgado López, H. 251
Salinas, A. 1811
Sallum, Jr., B. 4682
Salman, F. al- 3344
Salmon, C. 649
Salner, P. 138, 3090
Salomon, R. 3179
Salter, C. 291
Saltmarshe, D. 4448
Salzman, P. 2626
Samarin, W. 2017
Samibaev, M. 1072
Sampaio, E. 1710
Sampaio, J. 66
Sampiev, I. 2538
Samson, J. 703
Samuel, G. 105, 3231
Samuels, D. 1824
Sanabria, H. 1823
Sanadjian, M. 3367
Sánchez, A. 84, 842
Sanchez, J. 713
Sánchez-Moreno, E. 916
Sand, C. 556
Sandahl, S. 3319
Sandel, T. 4534
Sander, P. 3330
Sanders, F. 3185
Sanders, T. 3525
Sandhu, S. 3508
Sandler, S. 4073
Sanford, L. 4263
Sangarasivam, Y. 291
Saniotis, A. 3625
Sanjek, R. 3064
Sankai, T. 1667, 1668
Sanna, E. 1576
Sanogo, K. 968

Sansom, B. 3671, 4000
Šantek, G. 2344
Santos Cruz, A. Dos 323, 707
Santos, H. 1606
Santos, L. 1693
Santos, R. 1718
Santova, M. 166, 3649, 4428
Santucci, E. 1276
Saperstein, M. 3444
Saraiva, M. 2791
Sardan, J. de 2502, 3572, 4663, 4718
Sardica, J. 815
Sari, S. 1237
Sarianidi, V. 925
Sarin, M. 2818
Sarkar, J. 4671
Sarkar, P. 1686
Sarkar, S. 4671
Sarker, S. 2839
Sarmiento, S. 898, 1467
Sarna, J. 3331
Sarnowski, T. 1199
Sassaman, K. 1374
Sathar, Z. 2846, 4755, 4858
Sattayanurak, A. 587, 2572
Satterthwaite, D. 2210, 4937
Satyawadhana, C. 2806, 2828
Sauer, C. 2100, 3707
Saumade, F. 166, 730, 3649, 4428
Saunders, R. 291
Saurin, P. 3928
Sautman, B. 1532
Sautron, M. 4065
Savage, S. 1272
Savin, I. 1745
Savran, D. 2841
Sawicka, I. 1937
Sawit, M. 4827
Saxegaard, K. 3244
Saxena, S. 3309, 3962
Sayers, E. 3805
Sbacchi, A. 318
Scaglion, R. 158
Scarre, C. 866
Scemla, J. 4263
Schachinger, C. 2863
Schachner, G. 880
Schäfer-Lichtenberger, C. 3145
Schaffer, S. 16
Schaik, C. van 1674
Schaik, S. van 3205
Schaller, G. 1408
Schaller, H. 1914
Schamiloglu, U. 27
Schapiro, S. 1664

Schar, P. 2279
Scharf, T. 2655, 2770
Schärf, W. 2969
Schattschneider, E. 2781
Schatzberg, M. 2532, 3590
Scheffler, H. 2680
Scheffrahn, W. 23, 1596
Schefold, R. 3558
Schely-Newman, E. 1762
Schendler, R. 2548
Schenk, A. 3812
Scheper-Hughes, N. 2923, 2930
Schiavo, F. Lo 912
Schicho, W. 4180
Schick, R. 1065, 1075, 1080, 1187, 1209,
     1211
Schillaci, M. 1626
Schiller, A. 4320, 4598
Schiller, N. 2496, 3026
Schilling, A. 1633
Schindlbeck, M. 348
Schlamm, L. 186, 3149
Schlegel, A. 2732
Schlehe, J. 3600, 4334
Schlepp, W. 4056
Schlunke, K. 2827, 3104
Schluntz, E. 1116
Schmalstieg, W. 1935
Schmid, J. 1624
Schmid, S. 511, 1188, 1251, 1255
Schmidt, A. 968
Schmidt, E. 320, 2057
Schmidt, N. 681
Schmidt, P. 968
Schmidt-Ehry, B. 4609
Schmidt-Nowara, C. 720
Schmitt-Strecker, S. 912
Schneider, A. 3959
Schneider, M. 2882
Schniedewind, W. 1352
Schnurrenberger, D. 1272
Schoenbrun, D. 1990, 2003
Schoepf, B. 183, 3801
Scholliers, P. 4379
Schopen, G. 2973, 3173
Schortman, E. 504, 2530
Schramm, K. 3886
Schrauwers, A. 3224
Schrire, C. 1546
Schroder, M. 1152
Schröter, S. 2915, 3651
Schryer, F. 2603
Schryver, G. de 1778, 1779
Schuldenrein, J. 1248, 1273
Schülke, O. 1628

Schult, V. 4772
Schulting, R. 1291
Schultz, K. 814
Schultz, W. 321
Schulz, D. 4119, 4447
Schumacher, J. 3220
Schumann, M. 2453
Schütz, A. 1890
Schuyler, R. 979
Schvoerer, M. 1376
Schwartz, B. 1637
Schwartz, D. 634, 3441
Schwartz, G. 1472, 1958
Schwarz, M. 3510, 3764
Schweik, S. 2933
Schwidder, E. 340
Scibona, C. 3527
Sciulli, P. 1563
Scoones, I. 2404
Scott, D. 970
Scott, E. 155, 530, 969
Scott, M. 3730
Scott, R. 1513, 1561
Screech, T. 361
Ščukovt, A. 1386
S.E. Silva, I. De 323, 707
Seal, A. 4816, 4824
Sealy, J. 1546
Sear, F. 1090
Seaton, E. 130, 353
Seaton, P. 1176, 1242
Sebestyén, E. 690
Seely, C. 4257
Segal, D. 395, 3739
Segal, E. 3448
Segal, R. 300
Segert, S. 87, 975
Seidman, G. 4612
Seier, J. 1688
Seigne, J. 496, 1059, 1161, 1295, 1311, 1418,
     1419, 2228
Seité, Y. 3929
Seitz, S. 2432
Seixas, C. 3786
Seki, K. 2451
Seki, Y. 2090
Seligmann, L. 4426
Sellen, D. 1584
Sellmann, J. 2817, 3141
Sempé, M. 1545, 1564
Sen, M. 2738, 2785
Sène, E. 2686
Sengupta, K. 2542
Šerić, V. 1591
Serrera, R. 3642

Serstevens, A. t' 4263
Servais, O. 238, 2791
Servière, J. 1633
Serwatka, M. 4002
Sesay, S. 4733
Severi, C. 3550
Sevin, O. 4618, 4794
Sewell, D. 445
Sexton, P. 1607
Shackel, P. 155, 530, 969
Shackford-Bradley, J. 4287
Shackley, M. 887
Shaer, M. 1010, 1022, 1064
Shakoori, A. 4921
Shankman, P. 4804
Shanmugam, S. 1892
Shaoxian, W. 4866
Shapira, A. 3665
Sharkey, H. 3615
Sharma, A. 3389
Sharma, D. 3851
Sharma, H. 3901
Sharma, K. 1455
Sharma, M. 82, 370
Sharma, R. 4861
Sharp, J. 269, 3055
Sharp Joukowsky, M. 1113
Sharp, L. 2802, 2929, 3060, 3607
Shastri, V. 3278
Shavit, A. 885
Shea, J. 1153
Sheba, E. 3732
Shefer, T. 2873
Sheik, M. 2119
Shelat, B. 1401
Sheldon, K. 1761
Sheldrake, M. 4937
Shelemay, K. 3965
Shelley, G. 286, 2124
Shemesh, A. 3424
Shen, C. 2304
Shenk, D. 2655, 2770
Shennan, S. 2226
Shepard, G. 2098
Shepherd, D. 3459
Sheppard, P. 3845
Shera, P. 3873
Shereikis, R. 748, 2976
Sheridan, T. 4632
Sherman, P. 4396
Shetty, S. 2092
Shibata, H. 2174, 2772
Shideler, S. 1640
Shields, K. 1929
Shih, C. 2741

Shih, J. 3163
Shimizu, K. 1658, 1665
Shindo, Y. 1373
Shintani, T. 127
Shipton, K. 491, 2365
Shirahata, Y. 362
Shirono, Y. 1473
Shishlina, N. 882
Shiyab, A. al- 1276
Shlesinger, Y. 1870
Shnirelman, V. 2834, 4406
Shoemaker, N. 225, 539
Shokeid, M. 2919
Shomo, F. 2404
Short, S. 2654
Shortall, S. 4915
Shtarbanova, A. 166, 3649, 4428
Shuchter, S. 4546
Shucksmith, M. 4915
Shukla, S. 2172
Shulman, D. 4050
Shum, M. 4082
Shumway, L. 3916
Shunnaq, M. 1276
Shuo, S. 659, 3132
Shuping, H. 41, 190
Shuster, B. 1449, 2935
Shutler, Jr., R. 598
Shutt, A. 795, 2299
Shweder, R. 213
Sickinger, R. 576, 3573
Siddiqui, M. 3766, 3802
Siddiqui, R. 4828
Sidibé, S. 968
Sieber, R. 2940, 4110
Siegel, A. 4706
Siegel, H. 2874, 3782
Siggers, J. 891, 1112
Sikh Review 2483
Sikod, F. 4937
Sikorska, L. 2816, 3140
Sil, N. 3312
Silberman, N. 1361, 3697
Silberstein, L. 3438
Sillanpää, L. 2477
Silldorff, A. 1607
Silliman, S. 991
Sillitoe, P. 2442, 2847, 4782
Silva Galeana, L. 4196
Silva Horta, J. da 625
Silva, M. de 2701, 3774
Silva, O. 3069
Silver, S. 1705
Silverman, I. 1496
Silvestri, D. 3728

Sim, H. 4584
Simard, P. 2213
Simbirtseva, T. 3628
Šimić, D. 3789
Simoncsics, P. 1771, 3606
Simondon, K. 1557
Simonett, H. 3946
Simonin, M. 214
Simons, A. 4697
Simpson, C. 1207
Simpson, I. 1029
Simpson, J. 143
Sims, H. 4594
Sinavaiana-Gabbard, C. 3675
Sinclair-Loutit, K. 2209
Singer, I. 1394
Singer, M. 215
Singh, A. 2912, 3461, 3471, 3476
Singh, C. 2029
Singh, D. 1560, 3479, 3481
Singh, G. 3483, 3501, 3507
Singh, H. 3473, 3480, 3482, 3495
Singh, I. 4370
Singh, J. 3486, 3487
Singh, K. 564, 2828, 2830, 2997, 3463
Singh, L. 1579
Singh, M. 3489, 3494, 4113
Singh, N. 4780
Singh, O. 3475
Singh, P. 577, 2495, 4807
Singh, R. 3472, 3502, 3503
Singh, S. 3716
Singh, T. 1579, 3499
Singh, U. 1454
Singhji, B. 3492, 3493
Singleton, I. 1674
Singleton, M. 232
Singy, P. 1749
Sinha, D. 2359
Sinha, M. 694
Siniarska, A. 1543
Sirost, O. 2085, 4310
Sissao, A. 1749
Sithole, P. 2244
Sitlivy, V. 836
Sittert, L. van 757, 2406
Siushansian, J. 2885
Sivakumar, M. 2121
Sivamohan, M. 4743
Sivanna, N. 4907
Sivleng, C. 827
Sjørslev, I. 371
Škafar, B. 346
Skaria, A. 4571
Skender, L. 3789

Sketelj, P. 346
Skevington, S. 4863
Skierska, A. 1572
Skilton, A. 3190
Skotarczak, D. 2482
Skultans, V. 319, 2964
Slaje, W. 3318
Sleigh, C. 3746
Slembrouck, S. 1736, 1780
Slifer, S. 1625
Slingerland, D. 519
Sliwczynska, B. 3279
Słupski, Z. 4209
Smadeh, M. 1295
Small, N. 2787
Small, S. 3601
Smay, D. 1584
Smit, R. 2166
Smith, A. 991, 1361, 3697
Smith, B. 4530
Smith, C. 1968
Smith, D. 2513, 2659, 2683, 2795, 3597
Smith, E. 1603
Smith, F. 3306
Smith, G. 2778
Smith, H. 2761
Smith, II, A. 945
Smith, J. 3161, 3584, 3727, 4674
Smith, K. 2767
Smith, L. 4160
Smith, M. 298, 464, 903, 973, 2134, 2390,
    4876
Smith, R. 2404
Smith Stark, T. 1812
Smith, T. 1700, 2033
Smith, W. 452, 2546, 3688, 3927, 4375
Smits, L. 2131
Smojver-Ježek, S. 1575
Smoláriková, K. 1049
Smolej-Narančić, N. 3804
Smuts, C. 4929
Smyth, G. 3961
Smyth, I. 4899
Smyth, J. 4181
Smythe, K. 381, 672
Snelder, D. 29
Snir, R. 3354
Snodgrass, J. 2615
Snyder, K. 2487
Snyder, S. 2933
Soares, M. 323, 707
Sobczyk, K. 836
Sobolev, A. 1917
Soda, R. 2181
Söderström, O. 4487

Sodhi, R. 1601
Sokolovskii, S. 308, 2145, 2538, 4412, 4656
Solang, B. 2578
Solari, A. 1501
Solimini, M. 3728
Solomon, N. 3456
Solórzano Fonseca, J. 763
Solovei, T. 12
Somé, M. 3222
Someaphyvath, M. 827
Somerville, V. 4318
Sommer, U. 991
Somnasang, P. 3751, 4385
Somogyi, B. 3160
Somogyi-Csizmazia, J. 1187
Sonderman, R. 970
Sonesson, G. 3728
Song, Y. 3079, 3743
Sonnenstuhl, I. 1751
Sophady, H. 827
Sophal, S. 827
Soquet, A. 2008
Sørensen, D. 2868, 3134
Sørensen, J. 233, 3567
Sørensen, N. 2176
Sosis, R. 4394
Soto-Heim, P. 1550
Soudière, M. de La 2085, 4310
Soulliere, D. 388
Sousa, M. 1606
Sousa Maia, F. 323, 707
South, A. 445
South Asia Network on Food, Ecology and
    Culture 4826
Southern, M. 1791
Southon, J. 1382
Souto, J. 1333, 4181
Souza, C. 4937
Souza, F. de 2222
Souza, M. de 2222
Sow, S. 1749
Sowada, K. 1225
Sparks, R. 1176, 1225, 1242
Sparrow, D. 4453
Spash, C. 4666
Spear, T. 550, 1990
Spectorsky, S. 3014, 3341
Spelke, E. 1693
Spence, M. 833
Spencer, C. 993
Speshnev, N. 4252
Spicer, P. 215
Spiegel, P. 2119
Spinaci, S. 4870
Spiro, M. 4513

Spitler, S. 214
Spittler, G. 424
Spitz, C. 4263
Spriggs, M. 1130
Spurr, D. 805
Squire, L. 4746
Srijantr, T. 2314
Srikanth, N. 62
Srivastava, A. 1686, 1712
Staal, F. 3857
Stafford, C. 2684
Stagl, J. 26, 93
Stahl, A. 992
Stan, S. 2450
Stanchly, N. 2444
Stănciulescu, T. 3728
Stanford, C. 1714
Stanish, C. 2358, 2527
Stanonik, M. 163
Stapleton, T. 77, 359, 686, 4208
Stark, M. 906, 2874, 3782
Starrs, C. 291
Starrs, G. 291
Starrs, P. 291
Stasch, R. 3013
Staszak, J. 3660
Statham, Jr., E. 4631
Statistical Office of the European Communities
    4340
Staunton, G. 2971
Stavenow-Hidemark, E. 2231
Steckel, R. 1456
Steele, K. 4563
Steen, E. van der 895, 1398, 1425
Štefanková, M. 2239
Stefano, P. De 736
Steichen, R. 221
Steimer, T. 1133
Stein, A. 4937
Stein, D. 514, 2909
Stein, M. 149
Steiner, M. 934, 1178, 1241
Steiner, R. 604, 1722, 3251, 3426, 4256
Steiner, V. 1588
Steinmetz, D. 3450
Steins, N. 2404
Stelzig, C. 372
Stemper, D. 251
Stepan, P. 4107
Štepec, D. 2203
Stephen, L. 4611, 4719
Stephen, M. 3513
Stephens, A. 4929
Stephenson, R. 120, 960
Stepputat, F. 2176

Steptoe, A. 3795
Stevens, C. 4804
Stevens, S. 291
Stewart, C. 275, 2539
Stewart, F. 4738
Stewart, M. 2957
Stewart, P. 158, 3221, 3234, 3723, 4456
Stewart, R. 2600
Stierle, F. 4609
Stilborg, O. 1439
Stobart, H. 3897
Stocking, M. 4767
Stockton, P. 4538
Stoczkowski, W. 199
Stoddart, S. 867
Stoertz, F. 676, 2864
Stoffle, R. 3585
Stoinski, T. 1656, 1711
Stokholm, S. 98, 2503
Stoličná, R. 20
Stolzenberg, N. 213
Stomper, J. 929
Stone, W. 1625
Storer, G. 2902, 4898
Storm, P. 1524
Stover, E. 970
Stoyanov, Y. 3236, 3350
Stoykova, S. 166, 3649, 4428
Strang, V. 3106
Strathern, A. 158, 3221, 3234, 3723, 4456
Strathern, M. 212, 431, 2241, 2374
Straus, S. 192, 618
Strauss, J. 4817
Streck, B. 3564
Streck, M. 477
Street, M. 856
Streeten, P. 4672
Strickland, R. 2863
Strier, K. 1602, 1718
Stritecky, J. 3237
Stroebe, M. 4509
Strokirch, K. von 254, 4457
Stronza, A. 4294
Strunin, L. 215
Stuart, A. 788
Stubben, J. 2691
Stuckrad, K. von 591, 3417
Stucky, R. 1212, 1250, 1251, 1254, 1255
Štulhofer, A. 2917
Stull, D. 2224
Su, H. 1644
Subhaktha, P. 3749
Sublet, J. 30
Subrahmanyam, S. 671
Subramani 3080, 3675

Subramanian, M. 3964
Šubrt, J. 138
Suchocki, M. 3170
Suda, Z. 138
Sudarshan, R. 4780
Suder, W. 1309
Suenari, M. 2677
Sueur, J. Le 611, 3042
Suggs, D. 215
Sugimoto, C. 1497
Sugiura, H. 1665
Sugiyama, M. 3992
Suleiman, E. 1080, 1149, 1244
Sulima, R. 161
Sulkowski, G. 1612
Sullivan, S. 4436
Summerhayes, G. 919, 1404
Summers, G. 933
Summers, P. 2404
Sumner, P. 2272, 4774
Sumsky, V. 2534
Sun, Y. 4194
Sundar, N. 3568
Sundari, S. 4859
Sunder, M. 4617, 4651
Sungtaek, C. 3193
Sunseri, T. 601, 781, 3687
Super, C. 2611
Supomo, S. 4231
Surdacki, M. 603, 2716
Susanne, C. 1587
Susukida, R. 1503
Suter, J. 3070
Sutrop, U. 302
Sutton, P. 3108
Suwal, J. 2140
Suzuki, M. 2677
Svampa, M. 4435
Švarcová, Z. 4051
Svarverud, R. 4203
Svedberg, P. 4823
Svensson, J. 1120
Swanson, L. 3848
Swanton, M. 214
Swart, S. 548
Swartz, H. 1715
Swearer, D. 2099, 3155
Sweet, C. 1616
Sweetman, C. 4839, 4845
Swindler, D. 1471
Swinnen, J. 2315
Swisher, III, C. 1521
Świtała-Trybek, D. 4371
Swora, M. 4511
Symanski, R. 291

Syversen, U. 1283
Szafrański, A. 256, 3583
Szalek, B. 497, 1934
Szczepanek, A. 1391
Szebehely, M. 2763
Szirovicza, L. 3804
Sznajderman, M. 4296
Szyfer, A. 2192
Szymczak, J. 534
Ta'ai, A. 4228
Taani, H. 891
Ta'ani, H. 1112
Tabor, J. 3563
Tabor, S. 4827
Tacelosky, K. 1969
Tachikawa, M. 3148
Taddia, I. 80, 369
Tadin, I. 1574
Taha, A. 1406
Taher, H. al- 1221
Taher, N. 4937
Takahashi, H. 1660
Takaoglu, T. 1052
Takasaka, T. 1497
Takenoshita, Y. 1668
Takeshita, C. 4637
Takhar, P. 4834
Taliep, W. 4012
Tamata, L. 4722
Tamate, H. 1666
Tan, C. 4809
Tan, K. 4830
Tandia, M. 2686
Tandon, Y. 4747
Tanioka, Y. 1670
Tanpawady, W. 906
Tanser, T. 711, 794
Taomia, J. 848
Tapia, R. 3693
Tapp, N. 2323
Tarasenko, O. 1504
Tarasti, E. 3728
Tarte, S. 254, 4457
Tashiro, Y. 1638, 1648, 1668, 1720
Tashjian, V. 2833
Tatira, L. 1788, 4018
Tau, T. 3655
Tauber, M. 1460
Tauli-Corpuz, V. 3056, 3075
Tavernier, J. 1329, 1966
Tavkul, U. 1873
Tayles, N. 1285
Taylor, A. 4816, 4824
Taylor, B. 2069, 3619, 3657
Taylor, C. 4820

Taylor, G. 796
Taylor, I. 4831
Taylor, J. 2287, 2360
Taylor, P. 3625
Taylor, R. 2834, 4406
Taylor, S. 4743
Tcheuyap, A. 3980
Tchicaya, A. 4609
Teaiwa, T. 254, 4457
Teather, E. 2801, 3689
Tedesco, N. 1576
Tekavec-Trkanjec, J. 1575
Teles, L. 2459
Temu, A. 613, 614
Tengan, T. 254, 4457
Ténoudji, P. 1775, 2812
Tent, J. 1808
Terberger, T. 856
Terrell, J. 156
Terry, A. 4926
Tertrais, H. 551
Testart, A. 2341
Tettey, W. 53
Teugels, L. 3392
Teulière, G. 4097
Countway Guldbrandsen, T. 4775
Thakkar, D. 4724
Thakur, S. 2441
Thaller, N. 1591
Thalmann, U. 1645
Thamizoli, P. 4780
Than, H. 827
Thapar, R. 2095
Thayer, B. 1517
Thayer, M. 4612
Thébaud, B. 2446
Thelin, B. 4712
Thiessen, I. 2796, 2852
Thinon, M. 1533
Thoisy, D. de 1657
Thomas, A. 4012
Thomas, D. 4805
Thomas, G. 81, 4032
Thomas, J. 986
Thomas, P. 4722
Thomas, T. 3845
Thomason, A. 1084
Thompson, J. 1673
Thompson, K. 1773
Thompson, M. 325
Thompson, S. 4491
Thompson, T. 3427
Thomson, K. 3300
Thomson, M. 2863
Thorbjørnsrud, B. 154

Thorley, P. 957
Thornhill, P. 1912
Thornley, A. 3635
Thornton, J. 619
Thoroski, C. 4365
Thouvenot, M. 214, 1972, 3745
Thumerelle, P. 4618, 4794
Tibaijuka, A. 4666
Tiddeman, B. 1494
Tidmarsh, J. 1201
Tidsskriftet antropologi 371
Tieken, H. 3164, 3885
Tiemoko, R. 2863
Tiffin, H. 4150
Tikkanen, B. 1731
Tiljak, H. 2132, 2646
Tiljak, M. 2132, 2646
Till, K. 291
Tillotson, J. 1957
Tilly, C. 247, 2596
Timura, C. 2076
Tipene-Leach, D. 2712
Tirosh-Samuelson, H. 2099, 3155
Tischler, J. 478
Tishelman, C. 2763
Tishkov, V. 4582
Tisnerat-Laborde, N. 836
Tissandier, A. 2085, 4310
Tiwary, B. 3385
Tiwary, R. 2153
Tkachenko, V. 3152
Tober, D. 2381, 2956
Todd, H. 1640
Todes, A. 2219
Todorov, T. 725
Todorova-Pirgova, I. 166, 3649, 4428
Toelle, H. 3330
Tofail, F. 2138, 3800
Toit, M. du 613
Tokarska-Bakir, J. 257, 3188
Tőkés, I. 3160
Tőkés, L. 3160
Tokunaga, K. 1504
Tol, R. 4215
Tola, F. 3592
Tolias, G. 4179, 4290
Tolin, S. 4098
Tölölyan, K. 253, 4417
Tomaney, J. 2222
Tomaselli, K. 4136
Tomasello, A. 1031
Tomasello, M. 1704
Tomášková, S. 1245
Tomczak, E. 930
Tomilov, N. 48, 200, 211, 376, 430

Tompsett, G. 956
Tonda, J. 2532, 3590, 3591, 3822
Tonkinson, R. 105, 3231
Toops, G. 1933
Topan, F. 4564
Topić, E. 1570
Torii, R. 1670
Torkler, F. 1630, 1654
Tornero, E. 3339
Tornotti, M. 3388
Torre, R. De La 3639
Torres, C. 4336
Toscano, V. 2211
Tosco, M. 1849
Tóth, A. 3703
Tóth, I. 3230, 4247, 4441
Tóth, L. 3160
Toufique, K. 4922
Tounouga, C. 2070
Touré, I. 2686
Tournadre, N. 2025
Tourneau, F. Le 4618, 4794
Tourshan, N. 1237
Tourtellot, G. 494
Trabulse, E. 132, 437
Tracewicz, Z. 3097, 4597
Tracy, S. 1354
Træen, B. 2868
Traill, D. 505
Traimond, B. 1919
Tranchant, A. 2180
Trautmann, T. 2658, 4176
Travassos, E. 3912
Trawick, P. 2093
Treagus, M. 4298
Trébuil, G. 4693
Treil, J. 1460
Tren, R. 4888
Trenk, M. 3547
Trepavlov, V. 283, 2123
Tresch, J. 259, 414
Trevathan, W. 341, 1527
Treyer, S. 2289
Triggs, J. 891
Trillen, W. 1100
Tripathy, B. 3854
Tripathy, M. 4106
Tripathy, S. 358
Trninić, S. 4307
Trosset, C. 4473
Trotter, J. 1103
Trotter, R. 2874, 3782
Trousson, R. 4179
Trouton, L. 4134, 4453
True, N. 4181

Tsallagova, Z. 3661
Tseëlon, E. 174
Tserendagva, Y. 849
Tshonga, O. 3944
Tsujii, H. 1670
Tsuya, N. 2142, 4821
Tuan, Y. 291
Tubb, J. 1218
Tubiana, J. 326
Tucker, M. 2099, 3155
Tuggle, H. 1130
Tuljapurkar, S. 246, 2135
Tuma, M. 155, 530, 969
Tuohy, S. 3958
Tur Donatti, C. 2405
Turan, J. 2711, 4844
Turek, S. 3804
Turgeon, L. 1392
Turki, M. 4489
Turner, B. 260
Turner, E. 4617, 4651
Turner, G. 40
Turner, S. 1236
Turner-Walker, G. 1283
Turney, J. 3131
Turrell, R. 2792, 3007
Tüskés, G. 4255
Tuttle, R. 144
Tuwei, P. 2309
Twaddle, M. 677
Twardzisz, P. 1963
Tweed, T. 3239
Twiss, K. 1430
Twohig, P. 2464
Tye, D. 4372
Tyler, W. 2422
Tylkowa, D. 3678
Tyner, R. 4079
Tyurebaeva, B. 1504
Ucko, P. 379
Uehling, G. 2125
Ugbomeh, G. 4833
Ugrynovich-Kaminskaia, V. 2249
Uherek, Z. 138
Ulhôa, M. de 3940
Um, H. 3081, 4455
Um, K. 4547
Umeh, E. 2137
Umeh, J. 2137
Umesao, T. 330
UNESCO 4923
Unger-Heitsch, H. 4528, 4591
United Nations 4840
United Nations, Economic and Social
    Commission for Asia and the Pacific 4892

United Nations, Economic Commission for
    Latin America and the Caribbean, 4829
Uno, A. 185, 3377
Unwin, N. 4882
Urban, P. 504, 2530
Urban Resource Centre 4937
Urek, R. 1585
Urich, P. 2113, 4771
Urlić, I. 220, 2585
Urvoy, D. 3354
Urvoy, M. 3354
Uscatescu, A. 1400
Ussishkin, D. 1159
Usuanlele, U. 4165
Uther, H. 3990
Vaaben, N. 371
Vabre, M. 3133
Vacher, M. 371
Vahed, G. 782, 4431
Vail, D. 422
Vainerere, T. 4722
Vakaoti, P. 4722
Valadez Moreno, M. 1294
Valdivieso B., J. 4192
Valença, M. 2222
Valence, F. De 3797
Valente, V. 754
Valenti, M. 3728
Valentin, C. 1566
Valladas, H. 836, 1406
Valle, P. 214
Vallverdú, J. 1535
Valsecchi, P. 4475
Vandemoortele, J. 4900
Vanden Berghe, K. 3039, 4652
Vanhelden, F. 4799
Vaníčková, E. 4055
Vannini, G. 1146
Vansina, J. 549, 635, 655, 690, 1990, 2168
Vanstiphout, H. 4279
Vaquero, J. 653
Várady, K. 3160
Vardar, L. 922
Varela Petito, G. 4157
Varma, G. 2726
Varma, S. 2441
Varrod, P. 4218
Vartanian, E. 1376
Varughese, G. 2264, 4399
Vasconcellos, M. 4682
Vasconcelos, J. 171
Vasil'ev, M. 2230
Vásquez-Bronfman, A. 47, 421
Vassas, C. 2737, 3399
Vasseur, F. 1634

Vassilkov, Y. 1931
Vaughan, A. 786
Vaysse, F. 1460
Veber, H. 371
Vecchi, F. 646, 2752
Veeck, G. 291
Veerdonk, J. Van Den 4231
Veit, U. 1004
Vekua, A. 1521
Veldre, G. 1542
Velleman, B. 4048
Veluchamy, G. 3836
Veney, C. 228
Venida, V. 4740
Venkateswar, S. 2834, 4406
Venturini, L. 277
Vercauteren, M. 1551, 1592
Vercier, B. 4263
Verdery, K. 247, 2596
Verdoodt, A. 3227
Vergès, J. 875, 890
Verkhovin, V. 2364
Vermeij, E. 340
Verner, M. 902
Verschueren, J. 266, 1736
Versteegh, K. 1804, 1841, 1851
Vesey, A. 3176
Vetter, E. 1759
Vetter, R. 3724, 3937
Veuren, E. Van 4684
Vevaina, C. 4039
Vibert-Guigue, C. 1074, 1082, 1091
Víctora, C. 2941
Vidaurre, H. 4697
Videan, E. 1604
Vidyarthi, R. 2543, 3485
Vié, J. 1598, 1657
Vienna, A. 1822
Vieweger, D. 1139, 1140, 1155, 1184
Vigilante, T. 2060
Vigna, P. 3728
Vignaud, C. 1007
Vigne Pacheco, A. 4234
Viguier, B. 1465
Viljoen, R. 682
Villani, T. 3728
Villar, D. 3559
Ville, J. 1818, 2063
Villiers, C. de 1688
Vinagre, A. 1587
Vincentian Missionaries Social Development
    Foundation Incorporated 2210
Vinck, H. 567, 772, 3051
Virk, H. 3496
Viser, V. 2533, 3073

Visser, L. 4799
Visser, W. 2545
Viswanath, V. 4820
Vitello, M. 1586, 3824
Vitez, Z. 2291
Vittinghoff, H. 79
Vivanco, L. 2108, 4335
Viviani, F. 2883
Vlastelica, M. 220, 2585
Vogel, I. 1657
Vogel, S. 4138
Vogler, C. 2933
Voigt, M. 921
Voisin, J. 1523
Volkart, M. 2037
Volkogonova, O. 4486
Voros, J. 1651
Vorster, L. 2116, 2736, 2739, 3010, 3012,
    3015, 3020, 3695, 3816, 4418
Vos, K. 331
Vrat, S. 3390
Vrhovski-Hebrang, D. 3804
Vries, B. de 1267, 1268
Vries, H. de 1692
Vriezen, K. 1045, 1079, 1217
Vrkić, N. 1570
Vukelić, M. 1589
Vukšić-Mihaljević, Ž. 2606
Vuletić, S. 2132, 2133, 2646
Vyas, R. 3143
Waal, F. de 1661
Wackett, J. 2878, 3788, 4877
Wacquant, L. 2961
Wada, T. 3162
Waddell, H. 4863
Wade, J. 4249
Wadekar, M. 3200
Wagenaar, J. 3147
Wagner, A. 3973
Wagner, C. 1059
Wagner, J. 158
Wagner-Lux, U. 1079, 1217
Wagnon, E. 960
Wagstaff, A. 4895
Waheeb, M. 1135, 1138, 1144, 1145, 1163,
    1198, 1229, 1231, 1274, 1292, 1305, 1314,
    1315
Waheed-uz-Zaman 4783
Wahl, J. 877, 2177
Wæhle, E. 371
Waines, D. 3338
Waites, K. 4108
Wakankar, S. 4142
Wakefield, D. 3257
Wakibara, J. 1601

Waldman M., G. 4642
Waldren, W. 869
Walia, J. 3484
Walicki, J. 3452
Walker, A. 4799
Walker, B. 1301
Walker, D. 3005
Walker, K. 2087
Walker, P. 579, 977, 3024, 4722
Walker, R. 1976
Wall, D. 909, 2208
Wallace, T. 4713
Wallach, B. 291
Wallaert-Pêtre, H. 2237
Waller, J. 1663
Wallerstein, I. 3652, 4587
Wallet, B. 640, 3443
Wallman, S. 2156
Walmsley, A. 1164, 1186, 1259, 1265
Walter, R. 3845
Walter, T. 2791
Walters, P. 3593
Walters, V. 2758
Waltner, A. 2862
Walton, I. 867
Wambugu, C. 2309
Wamue, G. 3548
Wane, M. 2070
Wane, N. 2094, 2843
Wang, L. 4832
Wang, T. 4089, 4812
Wang, Y. 1497
Wangsu, M. 2048
Wang-Toutain, F. 3197
Ward, J. 857
Ward, R. 1709
Ward, S. 702
Wardle, J. 3795
Warier, L. 3865
Warren, A. 2106, 4764, 4803
Wasan, D. 3488
Waselkov, G. 988
Waser, P. 1623
Wassermann, I. 4732
Wasserstein, D. 615, 2501, 3354
Wastell, S. 235, 268
Watanabe, N. 4895
Watchman, A. 1105
WaterAid 4887
Waterhouse, H. 2791
Waters, M. 862
Watkins, P. 4105, 4523
Watson, A. 1011
Watson, C. 1772
Watson, D. 968

Watson, H. 2412
Watson, P. 1164, 1201
Watson-Gegeo, K. 3669, 4519
Watt, D. 1957
Watts, C. 4863
Watts, M. 4612
Waugh, E. 3545
Waxer, L. 3934
Waynforth, D. 1452, 2891
Weaver, T. 4632
Webb, J. 1409, 2107
Weber, B. 3229
Weber, F. 172, 203, 423
Weber, H. 3600, 4334
Weber, J. 4697
Weber, T. 989, 1181, 1182, 1355
Webster, J. 4161
Webster, W. 694
Wee, V. 4842
Weeks, D. 1511
Weeks, J. 4704
Wehmeyer, S. 3624
Weigand, P. 789
Weik, S. 360
Weiming, T. 2099, 3155
Weinberg, L. 4191
Weinberger, L. 3423, 3429
Weiner, J. 3659
Weintraub, A. 3925
Weir, B. 2874, 3782
Weir, D. 4798
Weisgerber, G. 1414
Weisler, M. 860, 1471
Weiss, K. 1538
Weiss, M. 433, 2927, 4482
Weiss-Krejci, E. 2794
Welbourn, A. 4873
Weller, S. 313
Wellings, K. 290
Wells, J. 644, 2754, 3058
Welz, F. 3652, 4587
Wembah-Rashid, J. 4145
Wendl, T. 4126
Wenger, G. 2655, 2770
Wengrow, D. 2206
Weninger, B. 445
Wenk, K. 1420
Wentao, Z. 4866
Wenzel, G. 2449
Werbner, P. 253
Werner, J. 4126
Werner, O. 294, 393
Werthmann, K. 2439
Wesselius, J. 1353, 3445
West, F. 715

West, P. 158
Westbrook, R. 516, 2996
Westermark, G. 636
Westoff, C. 2708
Wexler, K. 1936
Weyl, D. 3731
Wezel, A. 2319
Wezler, A. 4207
Whalen, T. 4262
Whatley, J. 756
Whitcomb, D. 1179, 1246, 1388
White, C. 2444
White, G. 254, 4457
White, H. 2388, 4621, 4744
White, J. 1249, 4592
White, L. 613, 2532, 3590
White, V. 4722
Whitehead, N. 90, 385
Whitehouse, H. 1520, 3512
Whiting, B. 176, 4524
Whitlam, J. 68
Whitlock, C. 291
Whittaker, J. 1441, 1526
Whitworth, J. 2892, 3810
Wibulpolprasert, S. 4875
Wicks, P. 4177
Widdowson, P. 2857, 3076
Widlok, T. 2377
Wieczorek-Szmal, M. 1391
Wierzbicka, A. 1728
Wiese, B. 910
Wijdan Ali [Princess] 4101
Wijekoon, A. 2701, 3774
Wilce, J. 3038, 3569
Wilk, J. 2091
Wilkie, L. 991
Wilkinson, R. 1529
Wilkinson, T. 2358
Wilks, J. 3991, 4015
Williams, B. 968, 2101
Williams, D. 3181, 3428, 3531
Williams, J. 2011
Williams, M. 468, 3406
Williams, P. 3929
Williksen-Bakker, S. 4533
Willis, J. 665, 2560, 4374
Wills, C. 2760, 2861
Wilson, C. 2607
Wilson, J. 1766
Wilson, M. 1276, 1277
Wilson, R. 4641
Wilson, T. 2486
Wily, L. 4779
Winblad, B. 2763
Wineland, J. 1132

Wink, M. 1601
Winkelhöferová, V. 4204
Winn, P. 4443
Winters, C. 1903, 2301
Wiryamartana, I. 4231
Wiseman, F. 4105, 4523
Witcher, S. 1215
Witherspoon, J. 2882
Witzel, M. 1905, 3289
Włodarczak, P. 1299
Wogan, P. 4490
Wojtal, P. 836
Wolański, N. 1543
Wolf, A. 3761
Wolf, D. 2634
Wolf, R. 3910, 3967
Wolfe, A. 4710
Wolfensohn, S. 1511
Wolff, B. 2759, 2918
Wolfson, E. 3430
Wolleswinkel-van den Bosch, J. 2150
Wolski, C. 858
Wolters, W. 743, 2348
Wolverton, S. 1368
Wong, C. 4871
Wong, G. 4866
Wong, S. 1500, 2722
Wong, W. 2970, 3138
Woobang, K. 1019
Wood, G. 1573
Wood, M. 2874, 3782
Wood, R. 710
Wood, S. 214
Woodhouse, J. 968
Woodman, G. 2972
Woodruff, B. 2119
Woolf, J. 2965, 3395
World Bank Development Research Group. 4832
Wörrle, B. 3130
Worschech, U. 1216, 1223, 1224, 1286
Worthington, D. 4550
Woźniak, A. 2599, 3629
Woźniak, Z. 963, 1288
Woźny, J. 1447
Wright, A. 2933
Wright, C. 4530
Wright, D. 670
Wright, E. 868
Wright, G. 1434
Wright, J. 125, 291, 602, 613
Wright, M. 2955
Wright, N. 2408, 4650
Wright-De Aguero, L. 2874, 3782
Wrogemann, D. 1619

Wullimann, M. 1547
Wurm, S. 1727
Wyatt, N. 3431
Wydick, B. 4847
Wylie, J. 4226
Wysocka, E. 3154
Xanthakou, M. 4004
Xiangkun, W. 2304
Xiaotong, F. 189
Xing, G. 1378
Yach, D. 4867
Yakhontova, N. 4233
Yakovenko, K. 1508
Yakshi Team 4780
Yakubu, U. 4548
Yakubu, Z. 2347, 2819
Yalçin-Heckmann, L. 275, 2539
Yamada, H. 1473, 1478, 1483, 1786
Yamada, T. 2834, 4406
Yamanaka, Y. 4046
Yamano, T. 4817
Yamashita, N. 1703
Yamashita, S. 4617, 4651
Yamin, R. 909, 2208
Yan, S. 2122
Yapo, J. 4199
Yarak, L. 731
Yassine, K. 1208, 1260, 1264, 1438
Yazar, J. 3760
Yelenevskaya, M. 1782, 3664
Yelle, R. 3129
Yelvington, K. 2157, 3061
Yeon, J. 1962
Yezerski, I. 1399
Yi, T. 2574
Yigael, Y. 1739
Ylikoski, J. 2050
Yochim, M. 1
Yoder, P. 2880
Yogo, Y. 1497
Yokoyama, Y. 460
Yoneyama, L. 364
Yoshida, K. 377
Yoshida, T. 1667, 1668
Yoshihara, K. 2677
Yoshii, H. 297
Youé, C. 686
Youmans, J. 314, 4091
Young, A. 155, 530, 969, 4565
Young, I. 3433
Young, Z. 4781
Youngs, T. 673
Younker, R. 1191, 1192, 1196
Younker, W. 1195
Youssef, A. 4155

Youssefzadeh, A. 3957
Yuan, S. 1382
Yuhua, X. 2844
Yu-Jose, L. 3078
Yuk, W. 2985
Yunus, M. 4911
Yziquel, P. 4066
Zabin, I. az- 1221
Zack, N. 263, 3043
Zadok, R. 1330
Žagar, J. 346
Zago, E. 4002
Zahorka, H. 1067
Zahradník, V. 3676
Zakanj, Z. 1574
Zambrano, G. 4192
Zamperini, P. 2928, 4164
Zárate Toscano, V. 4369
Zarauz, H. 2764
Zarman, M. 683
Zastawny, A. 853
Zavos, J. 3286
Zayadine, F. 466, 1154, 1203, 1356
Zea, L. 4191
Zea, T. 3056, 3075
Ze'Evi, D. 606, 2986
Zeisler, B. 2037
Zeitler, J. 927, 1037, 1058
Zeitoun, E. 1883
Żelazowski, J. 1031
Zelinsky, W. 291
Zenko, A. 2477
Žerjavić-Hrabak, V. 3804
Zerwick, L. 1783
Zewde, B. 570
Zewi, T. 1843, 1848
Zgółka, T. 2193
Zhan, M. 3739
Zheng, H. 1497
Zheng, L. 1479
Zheng, S. 1497
Zhigunova, M. 590
Zhijun, Z. 2304
Zhiming, B. 1757
Zhonghua, H. 2081, 2828
Zhou, X. 3397, 3613
Zhu, H. 2149, 2720
Zia, S. 4820
Zialcita, F. 4478
Zibda, A. al- 1167
Židov, N. 17, 3825
Ziegler, T. 1606
Zielhuis, G. 2131
Zimmer, L. 443
Zimmer, S. 3576

Zimmermann, E. 1617, 1619, 1621, 1632, 1643
Zinner, D. 1630, 1654
Zinser, H. 195, 4537
Ziporyn, B. 3170
Zires Roldán, M. 3246
Zisook, S. 4546
Zitelmann, T. 3046
Živković, Z. 4345
Zlatarić, D. 1474
Zlotnick-Sivan, H. 515, 3451
Žmegač, J. 400, 4496
Zolotova, T. 590
Zou, R. 1613
Zournatzi, A. 506
Zu'bi, Z. 1229
Zubov, A. 1530
Zubrow, E. 3941
Zuckerman, B. 1352
Zuleta Alvarez, E. 737
Zulu, E. 2876
Žuntar, I. 1570
Zuppan, M. 4784
Zurayk, H. 4890
Zuss, M. 1451
Zvi, Y. Ben- 4427
Zweng, K. 4064
Žygas, K. 3260, 3856
Żyromski, M. 465

PLACENAME INDEX

INDEX DES ENDROITS

Afghanistan 322, 3991, 3995, 3998
Africa 9, 73, 88, 89, 108, 113, 183, 192, 228,
    231, 314, 351, 356, 372, 441, 461, 549,
    552, 553, 610, 612, 617, 618, 625, 655,
    665, 670, 685, 686, 695, 700, 712, 727,
    748, 782, 784, 788, 799, 804, 817, 818,
    968, 1025, 1366, 1515, 1536, 1657, 1701,
    1719, 1749, 1778, 1779, 1802, 1818,
    1988, 1990, 1991, 1998, 2001-2003, 2008,
    2063-2065, 2070, 2073, 2094, 2105, 2106,
    2148, 2156, 2179, 2210, 2213, 2223,
    2270, 2283, 2289, 2303, 2316, 2341,
    2375, 2380, 2388, 2413, 2420, 2446,
    2475, 2487, 2491, 2502, 2504, 2532,
    2560, 2571, 2579, 2584, 2595, 2605,
    2672, 2686, 2746, 2758, 2767, 2777,
    2802, 2804, 2826, 2843, 2863, 2877,
    2922, 2945, 2972, 2976, 2989, 3001,
    3047, 3056, 3060, 3075, 3114, 3219, 3222,
    3245, 3340, 3525, 3529, 3533, 3548,
    3551, 3557, 3571, 3572, 3584, 3590,
    3591, 3594, 3607, 3608, 3612, 3616,
    3620, 3624, 3696, 3746, 3761, 3773,
    3801, 3822, 3835, 3841, 3869, 3874,
    3929, 3933, 3954, 3980, 3981, 4030,
    4058, 4059, 4090, 4091, 4102, 4107, 4118,
    4126, 4133, 4146, 4158, 4159, 4161,
    4163, 4187, 4200, 4374, 4401, 4516,
    4548, 4564, 4612, 4640, 4661, 4666,
    4674, 4690, 4692, 4736, 4764, 4767, 4779,
    4786, 4787, 4818, 4820, 4823, 4860,
    4863, 4864, 4882, 4930, 4937, 4940
    see also: Central Africa, East Africa,
    North Africa, Sahara, Sahel, Southern
    Africa, Sub-Saharan Africa, West Africa
Alabama 2587
Alaska 130, 353, 879, 1968, 2338, 2834, 3514,
    4406
Albania 247, 1913, 2596, 4448
Alberta 3545, 4038
Algeria 122, 292, 329, 470, 600, 606, 611,
    683, 1854, 2289, 2567, 2986, 3027, 3042
Alps 995
Amazon 90, 148, 385, 857, 893, 1597, 1677,
    1691, 1715, 1969, 1971, 2098, 2110, 2194,

2404, 2472, 3062, 3067, 3109, 3565,
    3566, 4697, 4800
American Samoa 4631
Americas 33, 99, 102, 119, 538, 699, 701,
    713, 725, 733, 745, 758, 768, 783, 796,
    802, 814, 833, 929, 1016, 1370, 1385,
    1609, 1678, 1702, 1706, 1708, 1711, 1717,
    1718, 1795, 1799, 1812, 1915, 1925,
    1972-1975, 1977, 1978, 1980, 1982-1986,
    2084, 2098, 2099, 2165, 2297, 2341,
    2430, 2435, 2597, 2671, 2834, 2857,
    3030, 3032, 3056, 3075, 3076, 3126,
    3155, 3216, 3617, 3618, 3632, 3672,
    3742, 3745, 3752, 3753, 3757, 3786,
    3887, 3902, 3960, 4183, 4222, 4234,
    4260, 4275, 4406, 4450, 4460, 4504,
    4612, 4806
    see also: Central America, Latin America,
    North America, South America
Andes 258, 911, 1514, 1823, 1952, 2062,
    2093, 2207, 2336, 2405, 2527, 2727,
    3252, 3538, 3670, 3719, 3911, 4097, 4198,
    4635
Andhra Pradesh 1490, 1506, 1578, 2726, 4727
Angola 690, 692, 721, 754, 806, 4472
Arctic Region 33, 1825, 4785, 4790
Argentina 737, 755, 837, 910, 970, 1375,
    1385, 1550, 1698, 3126, 3559, 3592,
    3891, 3917, 4053, 4147, 4435, 4758
Arizona 1824
Armenia 3125, 3991
Arunachal Pradesh 2048
Asia 27, 192, 340, 441, 448, 481, 559, 618,
    678, 741, 761, 779, 788, 849, 914, 1430,
    1518, 1532, 1707, 1803, 1935, 1956,
    2148, 2162, 2175, 2210, 2212, 2245,
    2323, 2325, 2350, 2358, 2413, 2416,
    2479, 2481, 2627, 2686, 2690, 2706,
    2738, 2763, 2785, 2828, 2834, 2849,
    2863, 3017, 3056, 3075, 3110, 3115, 3137,
    3156, 3171, 3292, 3322, 3347, 3397,
    3530, 3613, 3681, 3690, 3744, 3751,
    3767, 3772, 3843, 3968, 4010, 4011, 4362,
    4385, 4406, 4478, 4510, 4612, 4689,
    4692, 4721, 4776, 4787, 4807, 4809,

4820, 4835, 4837, 4842, 4892, 4909,
4914, 4920, 4932, 4934, 4937, 4939, 4941
see also: Central Asia, East Asia,
Himalayas, Indochina, South Asia,
Southeast Asia
Assam 1686, 1712, 4558
Atlantic Ocean 961
Australia 105, 662, 744, 810, 833, 957, 1105,
1190, 1723, 1728, 1773, 2068, 2074, 2265,
2403, 2408, 2670, 2685, 2696, 2730,
2747, 2827, 2863, 3056, 3075, 3104-3108,
3231, 3625, 3641, 3659, 3671, 3709,
3955, 3989, 4000, 4096, 4278, 4295,
4313, 4425, 4492, 4545, 4574, 4626,
4647, 4650, 4655, 4657, 4660, 4722, 4752
see also: New South Wales, Queensland,
Tasmania, Victoria, Western Australia
Austria 1588, 2171, 2644, 2794
Bahamas 455, 2225
Bahia 2505
Bali 3513, 4231, 4287
Baltic Sea 39
Baltic states 3926, 3948
Bangladesh 1503, 1573, 2029, 2136, 2138,
2293, 2414, 2452, 2577, 2702, 2710,
2763, 2894, 3312, 3775, 3800, 3819,
4722, 4760, 4826, 4846, 4849, 4855,
4868, 4885, 4891, 4911, 4913, 4922
Barbados 2619, 3066
Basque Country 1522, 1587, 2187, 2437
Belarus 2249, 3555, 3970
Belgium 36, 339, 366, 1551, 1592, 1923
Belize 494, 499, 2240, 2444, 4387
Benin 537, 724, 790, 1071, 2475, 2709, 3519,
4007, 4165, 4378, 4754, 4784
Berlin 372
Bihar 1454
Bolivia 103, 750, 1627, 1823, 2082, 2207,
3870, 3897, 4097, 4608
Borneo 4150, 4320, 4598
see also: Brunei, Kalimantan, Sabah
Bosnia and Herzegovina 4479, 4706
Botswana 215, 1726, 3114, 3571, 3761
Brazil 24, 66, 371, 734, 756, 783, 1606, 1687,
1718, 1971, 2194, 2222, 2289, 2418,
2505, 2798, 2941, 2994, 3069, 3072,
3121, 3605, 3612, 3786, 3912, 3914,
3940, 3956, 4158, 4408, 4483, 4590,
4612, 4618, 4655, 4682, 4794
see also: Bahia, Espírito Santo, Mato
Grosso, Minas Gerais, Pernambuco, Rio
de Janeiro, Rio Grande do Sul, Rondônia,
Roraima, São Paulo
British Columbia 1835, 4660
Brunei 3334

Bulgaria 166, 1917, 2652, 3345, 3649, 3988,
4428
Burkina Faso 582, 1749, 2004, 2103, 2191,
2415, 2439, 2517, 2595, 2945, 3222,
3529, 3685, 4024, 4777, 4784
Burma 678, 906, 1285, 2029, 4156, 4190,
4722
California 887, 991, 2668, 2719, 2778, 3790,
3817, 3946
Cambodia 192, 618, 765, 827, 983, 1076,
1081, 3189, 3196, 3198, 3582, 4547
Cameroon 81, 2002, 2195, 2284, 2510, 2700,
2784, 3660, 3722, 4127, 4548, 4805, 4836
Canada 102, 152, 153, 1322, 1799, 1816,
1835, 2075, 2078, 2122, 2151, 2306,
2408, 2524, 2717, 2723, 2834, 2869,
2878, 2885, 2893, 2905, 2949, 3074,
3107, 3112, 3660, 3788, 4016, 4079, 4134,
4184, 4321, 4343, 4406, 4643, 4645,
4646, 4650, 4654-4656, 4748, 4869, 4877
see also: Alberta, British Columbia,
Manitoba, New Brunswick, Northwest
Territories, Nova Scotia, Ontario, Prince
Edward Island, Quebec
Cape Verde 323, 707
Caribbean 455, 723, 732, 778, 978, 1791,
1827, 2157, 2167, 2173, 2225, 2496,
2559, 2621, 2822, 2863, 2886, 3061,
4170, 4179, 4452, 4704, 4731, 4829
Cayman Islands 4606
Central Africa 391, 580, 1584, 1714, 2168,
2431, 2682, 3608, 4125, 4805
Central African Republic 1671, 2431, 3729
Central America 504, 657, 763, 1024, 1715,
1946, 1955, 1979, 2530, 2547, 3133, 3711,
4065, 4066, 4270
Central Asia 145, 150, 202, 382, 487, 1746,
2086, 2125, 2664, 3352, 3361
Central Europe 856, 877, 959, 2177, 3098,
3160, 3634, 3679, 4628
Chad 584, 2491, 2579
Chile 103, 1550, 1806, 2518, 3870, 4315,
4642
China 3, 41, 79, 145, 189, 190, 522, 545, 588,
632, 648, 659, 1378, 1382, 1479, 1480,
1497, 1532, 1666, 1746, 1800, 2019,
2036, 2047, 2081, 2099, 2149, 2188,
2253, 2256, 2304, 2460, 2492, 2580,
2616, 2654, 2678, 2684, 2720, 2735,
2741, 2745, 2751, 2782, 2823, 2828,
2844, 2862, 2911, 2928, 2936, 2970, 2971,
3002, 3132, 3138, 3155, 3170, 3197,
3206, 3397, 3518, 3528, 3613, 3682,
3700, 3715, 3842, 3893, 3904, 3958,
3982, 4011, 4056, 4095, 4130, 4155, 4164,

4451, 4464, 4480, 4497, 4549, 4594, 4605, 4832, 4866

Colombia 251, 1691, 1785, 2260, 2300, 2583, 2724, 2851, 3934, 4235, 4277

Connecticut 313

Cook Islands 848, 1483, 2290

Costa Rica 1369, 1669, 2108, 2813, 3113, 4335, 4711

Côte d'Ivoire 1608, 1716, 1749, 2271, 2400, 2968, 4378, 4447, 4475, 4754, 4912

Croatia 101, 147, 220, 400, 412, 970, 986, 1323, 1476, 1574, 1591, 2132, 2133, 2203, 2291, 2344, 2585, 2646, 2838, 2917, 3240, 3759, 3770, 3789, 3804, 3858, 3923, 3974, 3996, 4021, 4307, 4325, 4345, 4366, 4404, 4477, 4479, 4496

Cuba 720, 742, 1593, 2424, 3609, 3981, 4123, 4128

Cyprus 445, 1017, 1409, 1922

Czech Republic 336, 1245, 2548, 3694, 3798, 3888, 4112

Czechoslovakia 624, 3124, 4042
see also: Slovakia

Delaware 982

Delhi 3730

Democratic Republic of Congo 371, 609, 1989, 1993, 1994, 1999, 2001, 2009, 2502, 3542, 3550, 3572, 3673, 3944, 4555

Denmark 371, 1488, 2371, 2470, 2540, 2854, 3653, 4484

Dominican Republic 787, 2207, 2551

East Africa 550, 622, 673, 677, 1987, 2007, 2386, 2687

East Asia 870, 2152, 2304, 2677, 3963

East Timor 735

Eastern Europe 1320, 1569, 1589, 2644, 3135, 3348, 3634, 3795, 4476

Ecuador 857, 2062, 2207, 3032, 3062, 3130, 3252, 3565, 4635

Egypt 245, 356, 452, 490, 495, 502, 507, 523, 545, 606, 611, 617, 902, 1060, 1077, 1177, 1185, 1335, 1343, 1364, 1766, 2494, 2899, 2967, 2986, 3042, 3264, 3328, 3333, 3360, 3621, 3647, 3954, 4075, 4256, 4375

El Salvador 3070

England 361, 599, 668, 674, 676, 699, 704, 761, 1053, 1066, 1283, 1396, 1735, 1944, 1953, 2085, 2333, 2360, 2362, 2556, 2713, 2789, 2864, 4154, 4310, 4381, 4504, 4579

Eritrea 80, 369, 1630, 1654, 2010

Espírito Santo 1687

Estonia 42, 57, 1542, 2051, 2052

Ethiopia 326, 1845, 1849, 2129, 2502, 2570, 2610, 2704, 2875, 3046, 3522, 3572, 4719, 4817, 4902

Europe 16, 47, 141, 220, 253, 291, 421, 460, 462, 500, 559, 561, 774, 809, 822, 824, 839, 841, 842, 846, 872, 874, 875, 881, 883, 884, 889, 890, 898, 899, 908, 912, 917, 943, 965, 972, 991, 1362, 1379, 1403, 1443, 1458, 1467, 1474-1476, 1534, 1535, 1569, 1570, 1574, 1588, 1589, 1591, 1800, 1822, 1935, 1956, 2133, 2162, 2175, 2226, 2340, 2374, 2478, 2479, 2486, 2585, 2604, 2689, 2791, 2862, 2887, 2917, 2922, 2982, 3089, 3110, 3115, 3124, 3230, 3256, 3554, 3746, 3747, 3759, 3760, 3770, 3787, 3789, 3803, 3804, 3830, 3850, 3990, 4002, 4131, 4135, 4179, 4247, 4255, 4307, 4308, 4317, 4340, 4367, 4379, 4404, 4423, 4424, 4429, 4433, 4441, 4502, 4505, 4516, 4560
see also: Baltic states, Central Europe, Eastern Europe, Northern Europe, Scandinavia, Southeast Europe, Western Europe

Falkland Islands 768

Fiji 623, 931, 1733, 1808, 1887, 2564, 4430, 4533, 4722

Finland 2052, 2470, 2854, 3535, 3871, 4624

Florida 1289, 2087

France 6, 19, 31, 86, 94, 106, 107, 110, 121, 160, 214, 253, 326, 329, 332, 337, 401, 405, 408, 551, 565, 661, 676, 681, 686, 718, 752, 753, 759, 765, 775, 783, 803, 866, 932, 1007, 1013, 1095, 1291, 1332, 1390, 1392, 1469, 1522, 1533, 1551, 1594, 1759, 1916, 2085, 2147, 2183, 2205, 2257, 2269, 2362, 2423, 2453, 2507, 2644, 2666, 2688, 2769, 2791, 2864, 2957, 3005, 3166, 3215, 3249, 3534, 3608, 3616, 3799, 3929, 3943, 4105, 4215, 4218, 4225, 4230, 4247, 4264, 4292, 4308-4310, 4331, 4378, 4382, 4391, 4493, 4504, 4523, 4754, 4796

French Guiana 693, 698, 1598, 1657, 3121, 4405

French Polynesia 365, 566, 630, 4162, 4263

Gabon 1749, 3591, 3822

Gambia 3922, 4023, 4447

Georgia 1521, 2154

Georgia (U.S.A.) 2466

Germany 25, 58, 117, 315, 316, 322, 332, 334, 348, 360, 372, 391, 563, 576, 581, 845, 1332, 1530, 1914, 1923, 1933, 2453, 2655, 2693, 2749, 2770, 2791, 2794,

2866, 3099, 3430, 3573, 3656, 3839,
4092, 4178, 4243, 4347, 4489, 4508,
4580, 4603, 4761
see also: Berlin
Germany (East) 781, 3656
Germany (West) 3656
Ghana 326, 407, 611, 612, 992, 2400, 2407,
2411, 2427, 2493, 2512, 2594, 2758, 2773,
2777, 2786, 2833, 2898, 2968, 2980,
3042, 3696, 3886, 3907, 3933, 4001,
4007, 4059, 4102, 4126, 4188, 4338,
4548, 4667, 4678, 4680, 4681, 4850, 4884
Gibraltar 3093, 4413
Goa 1773, 3797
Greece 415, 491, 511, 528, 836, 886, 1047,
1304, 1361, 1738, 1959, 2365, 2453,
2612, 2647, 3110, 3115, 3692, 3697, 3847,
4066, 4148
Greenland 2540, 4646
Guadeloupe 2987
Guam 2637, 4028
Guatemala 95, 234, 313, 970, 2165, 3225,
3596, 4124, 4414, 4442, 4569, 4663, 4847
Guinea 285, 288, 326, 574, 679, 696, 798,
1608, 2269, 2718, 2870, 2880, 3814, 4229
Guinea Bissau 323, 707
Gujarat 480, 1401, 2865, 4166, 4168, 4474,
4571, 4724
Guyana 237, 392, 2167, 2297
Haiti 2490, 4150
Haryana 2441
Hawaii 120, 254, 739, 1130, 2533, 2649,
2742, 3073, 3675, 4301, 4457, 4607
Himachal Pradesh 4716
Himalayas 383, 2614, 2779, 3818
Holland
see: Netherlands
Honduras 504, 929, 1372, 2084, 2088, 2530,
2731, 3667
Hong Kong 1803, 2421, 2722, 2801, 3689,
4559, 4809
Hungary 139, 379, 2052, 2445, 2778, 3703,
3975, 4247, 4274, 4424
Iceland 3125
Illinois 2780, 2924, 2961, 3790
India 14, 326, 457, 535, 541, 564, 577, 585,
651, 671, 677, 694, 717, 729, 741, 747,
760, 761, 785, 1480, 1495, 1502, 1600,
1614, 1625, 1651, 1707, 1712, 1713,
1731, 1738, 1891, 1898, 1956, 2029,
2038, 2039, 2042, 2071, 2095, 2099, 2111,
2114, 2115, 2128, 2200, 2289, 2292,
2355-2357, 2368, 2441, 2483, 2485, 2495,
2511, 2515, 2522, 2543, 2546, 2582, 2614,
2615, 2623, 2627, 2655, 2725, 2738,

2755, 2757, 2770, 2785, 2793, 2797,
2818, 2830, 2834, 2842, 2856, 2859,
2865, 2894, 2926, 2942, 2952, 2973,
3023, 3026, 3082, 3110, 3143, 3148, 3155,
3162, 3169, 3173, 3178, 3180, 3193,
3269, 3284, 3286-3289, 3292, 3304, 3309,
3312, 3318, 3331, 3376, 3380, 3382,
3389, 3414, 3468, 3476, 3479, 3480,
3483-3485, 3488, 3495, 3502, 3568, 3625,
3683, 3688, 3749, 3755, 3780, 3843,
3867, 3875, 3876, 3879, 3882, 3889,
3892, 3894, 3898, 3910, 3919, 3932,
3938, 3952, 3962, 3964, 3967, 3977,
4003, 4033, 4043, 4050, 4052, 4106, 4113,
4186, 4197, 4207, 4261, 4288, 4297,
4353, 4357, 4406, 4501, 4510, 4522,
4571, 4577, 4594, 4633, 4639, 4649,
4671, 4698, 4716, 4726, 4727, 4743,
4765, 4780, 4781, 4861, 4891, 4901,
4903, 4916, 4928, 4932
see also: Andhra Pradesh, Arunachal
Pradesh, Assam, Bihar, Delhi, Goa,
Gujarat, Haryana, Himachal Pradesh,
Karnataka, Kerala, Madhya Pradesh,
Maharashtra, Manipur, Mizoram,
Nagaland, Orissa, Punjab, Rajasthan,
Tamil Nadu, Uttar Pradesh, West Bengal
Indian Ocean 2092
Indochina 551, 698, 718, 753
Indonesia 37, 114, 340, 688, 759, 1067, 1137,
1649, 2221, 2245, 2258, 2268, 2289,
2325, 2474, 2629, 2655, 2714, 2770,
2849, 2888, 3033, 3084, 3085, 3224,
3333, 3357, 3364, 3513, 3558, 3603,
3646, 3651, 3880, 3925, 3939, 3951,
4055, 4071, 4211, 4287, 4362, 4443, 4481,
4601, 4618, 4653, 4778, 4794, 4827
see also: Bali, East Timor, Irian Jaya,
Java, Sulawesi, Sumatra
Iowa 4038
Iran 322, 366, 559, 878, 1055, 1083, 1096,
1334, 1423, 1433, 2162, 2566, 3116, 3640,
3784, 3957, 3991, 3993, 4015, 4022,
4169, 4240, 4248, 4333, 4358, 4403, 4921
Iraq 450, 1035, 1102, 1341
Ireland 105, 352, 409, 628, 647, 669, 1361,
1402, 1774, 2622, 2760, 2861, 2901,
2966, 3231, 3697-3699, 3895, 3961, 4086,
4437, 4470, 4491, 4499, 4500, 4563
Irian Jaya 2714, 4799
Israel 324, 343, 395, 433, 825, 885, 918, 924,
928, 1020, 1036, 1050, 1057, 1093, 1097,
1103, 1159, 1308, 1327, 1330, 1337, 1338,
1343, 1352, 1357, 1361, 1377, 1384,
1399, 1762, 1840, 1866, 2160, 2456,

2756, 2927, 3040, 3237, 3337, 3392,
    3404, 3428, 3432, 3438, 3457, 3665,
    3697, 3849, 4258, 4415, 4467, 4482, 4515
Italy 21, 296, 349, 373, 415, 465, 467, 468,
    471, 528, 529, 544, 603, 606, 646, 864,
    912, 948, 1031, 1199, 1200, 1280, 1358,
    1376, 1576, 1595, 1775, 2085, 2190,
    2326, 2476, 2514, 2644, 2663, 2716,
    2752, 2812, 2883, 2975, 2986, 3262,
    3406, 3654, 3747, 3828, 4008, 4268,
    4310, 4355, 4446, 4468, 4573, 4592
Ivory Coast
    see: Côte d'Ivoire
Jamaica 2496
Japan 110, 127, 168, 185, 246, 330, 338, 347,
    361, 362, 364, 374, 377, 501, 585, 595,
    1461, 1462, 1464, 1478, 1489, 1590,
    1601, 1622, 1653, 1660, 1662, 1737,
    1786, 1875, 2135, 2142, 2174, 2204,
    2235, 2625, 2749, 2772, 2781, 3078,
    3139, 3167, 3176, 3177, 3181, 3186,
    3187, 3204, 3243, 3377, 3531, 3532,
    3543, 3546, 3631, 3701, 3706, 3717,
    3799, 3903, 3916, 3969, 3972, 3987,
    4056, 4095, 4100, 4204, 4217, 4254,
    4266, 4356, 4458, 4512, 4821
Java 37, 114, 708, 812, 1524, 3033, 3603,
    3625, 3724, 3884, 3937, 4231
Jordan 112, 466, 469, 483, 484, 492, 496, 503,
    513, 524, 555, 831, 834, 891, 895, 901,
    923, 926, 927, 934, 939, 940, 944, 945,
    952-956, 958, 960, 964, 989, 1008, 1010,
    1014, 1018, 1021, 1022, 1026-1028, 1030,
    1034, 1037-1040, 1045, 1046, 1051, 1054,
    1058, 1059, 1061, 1062, 1064, 1065,
    1068-1070, 1073, 1074, 1078, 1080, 1082,
    1085, 1087, 1090-1092, 1094, 1098-1100,
    1106-1129, 1131-1135, 1138-1142, 1144-
    1158, 1160-1162, 1164-1176, 1178-1184,
    1186-1189, 1191, 1193-1198, 1201-1225,
    1227-1235, 1237, 1239-1244, 1246, 1247,
    1249-1261, 1263-1274, 1276-1279, 1286,
    1287, 1292, 1293, 1295, 1297, 1301,
    1302, 1305, 1307, 1311-1315, 1318, 1319,
    1321, 1340, 1344, 1346, 1351, 1354-1356,
    1365, 1371, 1380, 1388, 1393, 1398,
    1400, 1414, 1416-1419, 1421, 1425, 1431,
    1435, 1436, 1442, 2139, 2228, 2287,
    2372, 3859, 4241, 4250, 4327, 4329,
    4346, 4528, 4591, 4714
Kalimantan 1067, 4320, 4598
Kansas 2224, 2259
Karnataka 4907
Kazakhstan 283, 1745, 1874, 2123, 4411

Kenya 540, 558, 675, 773, 1599, 1642, 1659,
    1997, 2126, 2159, 2180, 2189, 2307,
    2309, 2367, 2434, 2447, 2499, 2508, 2611,
    2613, 2635, 2767, 2824, 2879, 3025,
    3036, 3059, 3223, 3584, 3881, 4058,
    4104, 4316, 4409, 4536, 4674, 4702,
    4725, 4878
Kerala 1891, 2121, 3875, 3876
Korea 595, 1019, 1962, 2155, 2339, 2521,
    2574, 2581, 2678, 3079, 3193, 3628,
    3682, 3701, 3866, 4095, 4360
    see also: North Korea, South Korea
Kurdistan 970
Kuwait 2860, 3086
Kyrgyzstan 1504
Laos 2707, 3194, 3556, 4612
Latin America 214, 441, 737, 799, 851, 2152,
    2157, 2173, 2197, 2210, 2334, 2385,
    2448, 2686, 2724, 2851, 2863, 3061,
    3062, 3121, 3565, 3566, 3670, 3735,
    3833, 3862, 4005, 4048, 4157, 4191,
    4192, 4198, 4210, 4282, 4305, 4336,
    4414, 4608, 4609, 4642, 4644, 4662,
    4692, 4704, 4757, 4787, 4792, 4829,
    4886, 4937
Latvia 319, 2964
Lebanon 2141, 4205
Liberia 3266, 3648
Libya 518, 569, 843, 847, 907, 1063, 1089,
    1411
Lithuania 3260, 3856
Louisiana 3900, 4363
Macedonia 3935, 4479
Madagascar 317, 326, 637, 800, 803, 804,
    1615, 1617, 1621, 1624, 1650, 1818,
    1841, 1885, 2063, 2392, 2507, 2558,
    3562, 3594, 4507
Madhya Pradesh 1486, 1512, 2118, 2153
Maharashtra 801, 1826, 2368, 3306, 4368,
    4928
Maine 3588
Malawi 776, 1748, 2743, 2876, 3704, 3762,
    3908, 3949, 4661, 4723, 4808
Malaysia 1316, 2164, 2273, 2698, 2805, 2808,
    2828, 3326, 3513, 3939, 4177, 4211, 4215,
    4287, 4364, 4561, 4584, 4871
    see also: Sarawak
Maldives 4300, 4311, 4768
Mali 335, 575, 629, 641, 643, 727, 1366,
    1749, 2004, 2073, 2213, 2270, 2488,
    2531, 2608, 3702, 3807, 4027, 4119, 4138,
    4378, 4447, 4688, 4754, 4788, 4924
Malta 852, 4026, 4423
Manipur 1579
Manitoba 3011, 3410, 4184, 4359

Marshall Islands 860, 1471, 2576, 3250, 3809, 4462, 4617, 4651, 4804
Martinique 723, 4187
Mato Grosso 942
Mauritania 1749, 2417, 3018, 3048
Mediterranean Region 448, 449, 463, 1006, 1363, 2092, 2343, 4290
Melanesia 271, 556, 621, 1900, 2337, 2341, 2373, 2638, 3257, 3265, 3512, 3622, 3659, 3845, 4389, 4602
Mexico 106, 132, 214, 215, 291, 313, 437, 533, 542, 546, 730, 750, 752, 789, 903, 946, 993, 1005, 1016, 1044, 1294, 1361, 1415, 1428, 1543, 1593, 1787, 1970, 2082, 2169, 2185, 2197, 2202, 2211, 2215, 2262, 2289, 2302, 2312, 2602, 2660, 2665, 2724, 2764, 2811, 2851, 3039, 3063, 3119, 3246, 3515-3517, 3537, 3598, 3626, 3637, 3639, 3697, 3720, 3741, 3753, 3757, 3778, 3928, 3984, 4053, 4129, 4183, 4196, 4201, 4220, 4242, 4245, 4291, 4337, 4369, 4414, 4442, 4632, 4634, 4652, 4663, 4665, 4696, 4700, 4793, 4798, 4906
Michigan 2907, 3660
Micronesia 1471, 2384, 2498, 2814, 4394, 4763, 4804
Middle East 129, 321, 447, 472, 509, 527, 593, 897, 905, 1136, 1342, 1373, 1851, 1853, 1857, 1871, 2261, 2395, 2417, 2473, 2506, 2544, 2549, 3018, 3268, 3321, 3323, 3324, 3329, 3354, 3362, 3367, 3398, 3404, 3408, 3440, 3459, 3767, 3994, 4046, 4084, 4179, 4205, 4251, 4283, 4495, 4515, 4583, 4585, 4589, 4692, 4714, 4890
Minas Gerais 1602, 1718
Minnesota 215, 2655, 2770, 4380
Mississippi 991
Missouri 2201, 2353
Mizoram 3785
Moldova 3095, 4553
Mongolia 607, 2100, 2947, 3185, 3211, 3600, 3707, 4025, 4233, 4334
Montserrat 291
Morocco 142, 571, 611, 658, 704, 705, 1540, 1552, 1749, 1758, 2209, 2214, 2274, 2289, 2333, 2362, 2425, 2553, 2609, 2653, 2910, 2977, 3042, 3049, 3343, 3353, 3599, 3848, 4014, 4037, 4299, 4629, 4659
Mozambique 764, 780, 1749, 1761, 1828, 3031, 4339, 4683, 4831, 4888
Myanmar
    see: Burma

Nagaland 2292
Namibia 2377, 3761, 4436
Nepal 105, 861, 2127, 2140, 2264, 2519, 2699, 3171, 3231, 3663, 3851, 4399, 4535, 4596
Netherlands 29, 331, 560, 568, 592, 640, 793, 1923, 2131, 2150, 2573, 3412, 3413, 3443, 3444, 3777, 4581
New Brunswick 2151, 2251, 2306
New Caledonia 556, 2096
New Guinea 2442, 2568, 2847
New Mexico 973, 2302, 3422, 3727, 4103
New South Wales 350, 1410, 2107, 3107
New York 909, 1009, 2208, 2778, 2919, 3064, 4041, 4370
New Zealand 1290, 1814, 2408, 2463, 2525, 2655, 2712, 2770, 2855, 3228, 3655, 4215, 4293, 4342, 4432, 4650, 4722, 4804
Nicaragua 1369, 2731, 4695, 4792
Niger 402, 582, 2106, 2207, 2404, 2446, 2776, 4718, 4784, 4789, 4803
Nigeria 532, 573, 962, 1548, 1749, 1847, 1991, 1998, 2002, 2005, 2061, 2137, 2184, 2238, 2246, 2252, 2320, 2347, 2504, 2513, 2659, 2683, 2733, 2795, 2819, 3226, 3591, 3597, 3732, 3822, 3835, 3844, 3933, 4009, 4031, 4059, 4126, 4152, 4193, 4289, 4540, 4668, 4742, 4753, 4833, 4862
North Africa 329, 473, 611, 753, 765, 1830, 1856, 2417, 2535, 2737, 2850, 3018, 3042, 3399, 3411, 4276, 4299
North America 47, 421, 2072, 2408, 3547, 3674, 4016, 4576, 4595, 4643, 4650
North Carolina 3827, 4465
North Korea 2263, 4812
Northern Europe 4624
Northern Ireland 3961, 4915
Northwest Territories 4811
Norway 282, 371, 1283, 2470, 2746, 2854, 4506, 4624
Nova Scotia 1429, 1829, 2464
Oceania 594, 636, 714, 809, 1404, 1473, 1725, 1820, 1878, 1879, 1881, 1884-1888, 1900, 2163, 2349, 2393, 2593, 2631, 2638, 2650, 2825, 3000, 3056, 3075, 3105, 3107, 3221, 3228, 3232, 3234, 3250, 3257, 3259, 3265, 3645, 3650, 3736, 4311, 4313, 4462, 4492
Oklahoma 3915
Oman 823, 1296
Ontario 118, 1816, 2267, 2607, 3931, 4397
Orissa 358, 651, 876, 904, 1048, 1350, 1437, 1491, 2528, 3276, 3281, 3837, 3854, 4140, 4214, 4272

Pacific Ocean 691
Pacific Region 254, 636, 811, 1473, 2158, 2199, 2559, 2630, 3000, 3080, 3635, 3669, 3675, 4228, 4380, 4457, 4722, 4763, 4892, 4920
   see also: Melanesia, Micronesia, Polynesia
Pakistan 82, 370, 446, 497, 577, 1731, 2455, 2495, 2541, 2846, 3330, 3476, 3479, 3791, 4551, 4616, 4698, 4755, 4756, 4783, 4828, 4851, 4858, 4879, 4934
Palau 1143
Palestinian Authority 291, 395, 1840, 2456, 3026
Panama 3550
Papua New Guinea 158, 284, 360, 714, 722, 736, 809, 919, 1482, 1765, 2018, 2199, 2241, 2337, 2370, 2373, 2374, 2561, 2598, 2681, 2694, 2796, 2852, 2990, 3013, 3117, 3233, 3234, 3257, 3265, 3511, 3550, 3586, 3625, 3627, 3643, 3659, 3723, 3803, 4389, 4456, 4602, 4619, 4620, 4751, 4782, 4799, 4814
Paraguay 1976, 4393
Pennsylvania 709, 2335
Pernambuco 2459
Peru 99, 378, 475, 728, 766, 1101, 1597, 1784, 1794, 1969, 1971, 1975, 1983, 2093, 2098, 2207, 2336, 2727, 2821, 3566, 3642, 3719, 3737, 3833, 3936, 4098, 4378, 4420, 4426, 4697, 4754, 4757
Philippines 29, 184, 341, 743, 793, 1395, 1527, 1680, 2089, 2090, 2113, 2117, 2161, 2216, 2285, 2313, 2348, 2409, 2416, 2432, 2436, 2440, 2443, 2451, 2467, 2492, 2534, 2557, 2578, 2592, 2836, 3017, 3078, 3157, 3220, 3623, 3730, 3813, 4010, 4195, 4500, 4544, 4556, 4630, 4679, 4694, 4740, 4771, 4772, 4778, 4802, 4848, 4852, 4934
Poland 15, 136, 534, 581, 840, 853-855, 871, 881, 930, 951, 959, 963, 966, 1001, 1288, 1299, 1300, 1306, 1309, 1325, 1326, 1381, 1391, 1412, 1422, 1424, 1444-1447, 1543, 1572, 2154, 2192, 2482, 2599, 2951, 3097, 3098, 3103, 3241, 3256, 3452, 3554, 3629, 3678, 3684, 3694, 4131, 4367, 4371, 4433, 4597, 4628
Polynesia 630, 663, 691, 848, 1290, 1882, 1900, 2638, 2649, 2667, 2853, 3630, 4314, 4763
Portugal 171, 323, 354, 692, 707, 716, 721, 729, 735, 751, 754, 798, 814, 815, 1023, 2281, 2791, 4483
Prince Edward Island 2426

Puerto Rico 720, 2300, 3540, 4271
Punjab 316, 2520, 2997, 3470, 3473, 3493, 3496, 3716, 3839, 3855, 4510
Qatar 2417, 3018
Quebec 1816, 2617, 2636, 2766, 4748
Queensland 4301, 4607
Rajasthan 2083, 2615, 3967
Republic of Congo 619, 1359, 3557, 3591, 3614, 3620, 3822
Réunion 732, 1749, 4237, 4323, 4376
Rio de Janeiro 756, 814
Rio Grande do Sul 2941
Romania 247, 1566, 2239, 2315, 2450, 2596, 3095, 4553
Rondônia 4800
Roraima 3067
Russia 12, 123, 179, 247, 376, 590, 658, 762, 882, 1088, 1554, 1936, 2230, 2243, 2286, 2321, 2364, 2391, 2477, 2480, 2596, 2599, 2835, 3021, 3087, 3092, 3096, 3152, 3242, 3575, 3611, 3629, 3638, 3721, 3830, 3850, 3966, 4411, 4412, 4440, 4468, 4527, 4624, 4654
Russian Federation 308, 309, 1732, 2054, 2057, 2145, 2146, 2979, 3022, 3081, 3349, 3446, 3589, 3593, 3708, 4455, 4486, 4570, 4582, 4656
Rwanda 192, 618, 970, 1690, 2277, 3029, 3050, 4312
Sabah 2273, 2808
Sahara 122, 600, 2102, 2586, 2609, 3057, 3658, 4629
Sahel 2065, 2105, 2303, 2380, 2446, 4688, 4691, 4736, 4764, 4767, 4789
Saint Lucia 4731
Samoa 1503, 3730, 4514, 4804, 4854
   see also: American Samoa, Western Samoa
São Paulo 2418
São Tomé and Príncipe 323, 354, 635, 707
Sarawak 2181, 2273, 4871
Saudi Arabia 1331, 2417, 3018, 3840, 3863, 4349
Scandinavia 892, 1439, 2371, 3535, 4656
Scotland 599, 645, 669, 859, 896, 1029, 2402, 2600, 3986, 4557, 4579, 4915
Senegal 326, 748, 749, 784, 1557, 1749, 2182, 2375, 2502, 2605, 2703, 2976, 2989, 3572, 3591, 3714, 3822, 4622, 4882, 4927
Serbia 147, 1323, 2838, 4479
Siberia 48, 200, 376, 819, 862, 1741, 1768, 1771, 1876, 3083, 3101, 3587, 3606, 3691, 3726
Sierra Leone 821, 2529, 3034, 4447, 4733
Singapore 3156, 3681, 4724, 4830

Slovakia 943, 3090, 3158, 3718, 3798, 4017, 4042
Slovenia 17, 32, 78, 188, 197, 204, 303, 427, 438, 454, 667, 1367, 1386, 1924, 2203, 3825, 4319, 4325, 4326, 4344, 4345, 4454, 4479, 4664
Solomon Islands 3237, 3669, 3730, 3845, 4519, 4799
South Africa 77, 96, 116, 125, 269, 305, 359, 380, 548, 589, 602, 605, 608, 613, 614, 644, 654, 682, 710, 719, 757, 782, 797, 813, 817, 920, 936, 950, 986, 1042, 1282, 1432, 1503, 1783, 1797, 1821, 2067, 2079, 2116, 2166, 2219, 2244, 2272, 2388, 2404, 2406, 2412, 2453, 2468, 2469, 2500, 2523, 2545, 2675, 2692, 2739, 2750, 2754, 2774, 2792, 2873, 2969, 3007, 3012, 3015, 3019, 3020, 3041, 3055, 3058, 3579, 3695, 3808, 3815, 3816, 3829, 3985, 4012, 4079, 4082, 4111, 4151, 4160, 4244, 4249, 4302, 4339, 4348, 4400, 4418, 4422, 4431, 4494, 4548, 4586, 4588, 4600, 4648, 4675, 4683, 4684, 4717, 4728, 4735, 4739, 4759, 4766, 4774, 4831, 4853, 4910, 4917, 4929
South America 258, 1586, 1597, 1946, 2266, 2527, 3128, 3570, 3601, 3746, 3750, 3783, 3824, 4277
see also: Amazon, Andes
South Asia 1573, 2172, 2196, 2382, 2829, 3169, 3826, 4166, 4173, 4213, 4596, 4614, 4726
South Korea 3610, 3660, 4663
Southeast Asia 626, 648, 1649, 2233, 2255, 2258, 2268, 2273, 2279, 2280, 2304, 2305, 2314, 2318, 2340, 2345, 2829, 2888, 3175, 3194, 3744, 3884, 3963, 4231, 4463, 4687, 4693, 4720, 4840, 4908
Southeast Europe 829, 1413, 1752, 1913, 1914, 1917, 1932, 1937, 1938, 2394, 3423, 4565
Southern Africa 126, 710, 1832, 2398, 2734, 3054, 3761, 4180, 4208, 4494, 4638, 4690, 4819, 4831, 4897
Spain 344, 460, 462, 586, 611, 620, 737, 758, 793, 816, 822, 824, 835, 839, 841, 842, 846, 869, 872, 875, 884, 889, 890, 894, 898, 899, 916, 1012, 1015, 1032, 1333, 1336, 1339, 1363, 1379, 1458, 1467, 1522, 1534, 1535, 1551, 1581, 1587, 1593, 1862, 1925, 2183, 2362, 2376, 2438, 2484, 2501, 2590, 2644, 2666, 2688, 2943, 2974, 3042, 3338, 3394,

3710, 3852, 4105, 4115, 4167, 4245, 4247, 4267, 4276, 4305, 4388, 4493, 4523
Sri Lanka 35, 104, 326, 395, 2397, 2489, 2701, 3174, 3199, 3549, 3774, 3826, 4471, 4552, 4788, 4856
Sub-Saharan Africa 686, 774, 1667, 1673, 2173, 2490, 2682, 2708, 2876, 3591, 3822, 3834, 4338, 4554, 4599, 4663, 4678, 4680, 4686, 4739, 4815, 4819, 4823, 4918
Sudan 88, 611, 1177, 2008, 2429, 2494, 2890, 3042, 3615, 3890
Sulawesi 543, 1626, 2258, 3224
Sumatra 334, 1674, 2410, 4178
Suriname 1715, 1982, 3415, 4285, 4405
Swaziland 4864, 4926
Sweden 10, 352, 435, 892, 1817, 2231, 2470, 2854, 2868, 3091, 4114, 4280, 4531, 4624, 4712
Switzerland 23, 1596, 2644, 2662, 4332, 4487
Syria 449, 516, 523, 596, 1084, 1406, 2404, 2996, 3899, 4604
Tadzhikistan 3536, 3581
Taiwan 54, 1644, 1883, 1889, 2676, 2684, 3009, 3163, 4416, 4534, 4769, 4799
Tamil Nadu 2569, 3180, 4117, 4176, 4639, 4843, 4859
Tanzania 381, 601, 672, 685, 808, 1605, 1611, 2223, 2298, 2316, 2352, 2404, 2487, 2560, 2651, 2884, 3687, 3796, 3806, 4145, 4163, 4374, 4773, 4779, 4786, 4882, 4940
Tasmania 744
Tennessee 1407
Texas 193, 313, 3065, 3563
Thailand 35, 104, 415, 626, 826, 838, 937, 1389, 1420, 2250, 2279, 2305, 2314, 2345, 2806, 2809, 2828, 2896, 2902, 3168, 3175, 3776, 3811, 4060, 4190, 4218, 4720, 4791, 4799, 4875, 4893, 4898, 4909
Tibet 307, 642, 659, 661, 762, 1104, 1408, 1503, 1514, 2023-2025, 2040, 2097, 2178, 2248, 2295, 2357, 2389, 2960, 3132, 3184, 3188, 3192, 3202, 3205, 3740, 3812, 3818, 3860, 4137
Togo 1749, 2565, 3526, 4126
Tonga 598, 1773, 1880, 2563, 2744, 3259, 3645, 4804
Transcaucasia 128, 191, 1873, 2656, 2837, 2979, 3349, 3356, 3580, 4572
Trinidad and Tobago 732, 1827
Tunisia 470, 529, 611, 1565, 1762, 2289, 2567, 3042, 3658, 4710
Turkey 85, 117, 342, 458, 464, 488, 505, 520, 915, 921, 922, 933, 935, 967, 1052, 1348,

1434, 1836, 1873, 2479, 2690, 2711, 2799, 2916, 3120, 3327, 3351, 3831, 4015, 4070, 4074, 4085, 4236, 4322, 4844

Turkmenistan 925, 2481

Tuvalu 616, 3000

U.S.A. 1, 13, 18, 45, 100, 102, 115, 130, 144, 206, 215, 235, 253, 291, 327, 353, 422, 432, 443, 531, 664, 680, 687, 740, 778, 786, 861, 880, 970, 978, 979, 1374, 1392, 1405, 1427, 1498, 1550, 1777, 1798, 1799, 1824, 1967, 2087, 2099, 2158, 2161, 2169, 2218, 2254, 2259, 2276, 2294, 2327, 2330, 2374, 2391, 2463, 2533, 2549, 2576, 2618, 2622, 2655, 2657, 2660, 2661, 2668, 2691, 2695, 2697, 2724, 2765, 2770, 2771, 2791, 2803, 2804, 2834, 2845, 2851, 2857, 2874, 2887, 2900, 2907, 2919, 2929, 2934, 2982, 2988, 2999, 3016, 3026, 3068, 3071, 3073, 3076, 3077, 3092, 3112, 3155, 3159, 3225, 3237, 3239, 3247, 3250, 3401, 3402, 3410, 3422, 3510, 3563, 3585, 3588, 3693, 3700, 3749, 3758, 3764, 3782, 3809, 3893, 3900, 3929, 4006, 4016, 4041, 4048, 4076, 4086, 4100, 4154, 4195, 4217, 4262, 4282, 4330, 4350, 4352, 4359, 4363, 4372, 4380, 4406, 4410, 4421, 4462, 4468, 4512, 4534, 4543, 4594, 4612, 4631, 4632, 4656, 4937
see also: Alabama, Alaska, Arizona, California, Connecticut, Delaware, Florida, Georgia (U.S.A.), Hawaii, Illinois, Iowa, Kansas, Louisiana, Maine, Michigan, Minnesota, Mississippi, Missouri, New Mexico, New York, North Carolina, Oklahoma, Pennsylvania, Tennessee, Texas, Virginia, Washington

U.S.S.R. 345, 658, 2125, 2160, 2480, 3021, 3409, 4069, 4073, 4402, 4578
see also: Armenia, Belarus, Estonia, Georgia, Kazakhstan, Kyrgyzstan, Latvia, Lithuania, Moldova, Russia, Tadzhikistan, Turkmenistan, Ukraine, Uzbekistan

Uganda 299, 583, 627, 639, 674, 1638, 1648, 1663, 1709, 1720, 2156, 2288, 2759, 2892, 2913, 2914, 2918, 3052, 3542, 3810, 4126, 4273, 4896

Ukraine 2835, 3102, 3103, 3918, 3976, 4505

United Kingdom 34, 40, 45, 115, 325, 352, 357, 375, 471, 498, 557, 686, 694, 702, 703, 714, 762, 775, 778, 785, 788, 828, 858, 868, 873, 874, 888, 938, 987, 1011, 1236, 1303, 1361, 1402, 1403, 1429, 1505, 1957, 2174, 2186, 2298, 2310, 2311,

2383, 2408, 2469, 2542, 2604, 2639, 2648, 2674, 2772, 3686, 3697, 3760, 4086, 4182, 4221, 4298, 4358, 4390, 4398, 4403, 4470, 4560, 4650, 4709, 4931, 4936, 4937
see also: England, Northern Ireland, Scotland, Wales

Uttar Pradesh 1541, 2620, 3967

Uzbekistan 741, 3853, 3991, 4857

Vanuatu 105, 284, 597, 1724, 1744, 3231, 4722

Venezuela 135, 416, 816, 1577, 4347, 4822

Victoria 913

Vietnam 54, 326, 474, 551, 726, 765, 827, 1480, 1833, 2318, 2319, 2404, 2715, 3556, 4044, 4144, 4153, 4392, 4895

Virginia 687, 2254

Wales 2655, 2770, 4171, 4424, 4473, 4788, 4795

Washington 2101

West Africa 252, 391, 554, 633, 697, 770, 900, 961, 1641, 1818, 2013, 2063, 2104, 2682, 2776, 3008, 3122, 4013, 4447, 4548, 4715

West Bengal 1455, 1906, 2282, 2399, 2575, 3794, 3889

Western Australia 298, 2060, 2134

Western Europe 828, 3795

Western Samoa 2630

Yemen 2227, 2417, 3018, 3848

Yugoslavia 970, 3094, 4477, 4479
see also: Bosnia and Herzegovina, Croatia, Macedonia, Serbia, Slovenia

Zambia 2509, 2721, 2729, 2744, 2753, 2906, 4132, 4882

Zimbabwe 76, 333, 355, 547, 562, 684, 711, 767, 791, 795, 1788, 2120, 2179, 2299, 2378, 2401, 2419, 2783, 3577, 4018, 4318, 4550, 4669, 4708, 4747, 4781

SUBJECT INDEX

INDEX DES MATIÈRES EN ANGLAIS

'Alawi 571, 3343
A'sha Al- 4084
Abdulkadir Munsyi, Abdullah bin 4215
Abelam 158, 3511
Ability 1463, 4593
Abolitionism 680, 681, 692, 2857, 3076
Aborigines 298, 662, 706, 2060, 2074, 2078,
    2134, 2403, 2408, 2685, 2827, 3056,
    3074, 3075, 3104, 3106, 3107, 3625,
    3641, 3659, 3671, 3709, 3989, 4000,
    4096, 4278, 4626, 4647, 4650, 4656, 4657
Abortion 2705, 2706, 2722, 2724, 2725, 2851,
    2881, 2966, 4531
Abraham 2748
Abramzon, S.M. 145
Academic achievement 4554
Academic discipline 3, 4, 11, 24, 32, 41, 53,
    115, 146, 152, 160, 165, 178, 180, 189,
    190, 193, 198, 213, 215, 399, 996, 1004,
    1226, 1914, 2679, 3142, 3288, 4745
Academic freedom 4748
Academic profession 2845
Accent 1844, 1957
Access to culture 4329
Access to education 4748
Access to health care 1529, 2138, 2863, 3800,
    4609
Access to information 4820
Accountability 158
Acculturation 259, 414, 637, 708, 887, 2409,
    2616, 2661, 2798, 3098, 4479, 4600, 4628
Ache 4393
Achievement motivation
    see: Academic achievement
Activism 2108, 2827, 3104, 3758, 4335, 4495,
    4775
Activists 2218, 3068
Actors 3040, 3878, 4206
Adaptation to change 1601, 4010
Addiction 1591, 2322
    see also: Drug addiction
Administration 125, 482, 602, 2354, 2484,
    2504
    see also: Development administration,
    Public administration

Administrative organization 2528
Adolescence 1553, 1557, 1592, 2731, 2732,
    2962
Adolescents 1466, 1477, 1578, 2223, 2696,
    2732, 2733, 2879, 2883, 2895, 2913,
    2931, 2962, 4878
Adornments 1373, 1777, 2934
Adorno, Theodor W. 3698
Adulthood 676, 2731, 2775, 2864, 3832
Adults 1602, 1654, 1693, 2662, 2732
Adverbs 1756, 1769, 2017, 2050
Advertising 1774, 1788, 2317, 2326, 2327,
    2950, 3698, 3699, 3903, 4018, 4388
Aerial archaeology 932, 983
Aesthetics 171, 253, 314, 368, 2571, 3136,
    3256, 3660, 3773, 3844, 3850, 4071,
    4091, 4109, 4111, 4118, 4125, 4131, 4133,
    4261, 4469
Aeta 2432
Affiliation 1653, 2791
Afforestation 2448
African National Congress 77, 359, 2523
African studies 53, 116, 187, 558, 619, 695,
    1748, 1821, 1988, 1990, 2003, 2064,
    2347, 2494, 2499, 2508, 2584, 2819,
    3226, 3835, 3908, 4012, 4090, 4126,
    4160, 4175, 4193, 4548, 4640
African-Americans 215, 538, 680, 978, 1582,
    2327, 2466, 2533, 2622, 2857, 3073,
    3076, 3900, 3929, 4363
Africans 253, 279, 567, 692, 774, 806, 1536,
    2070, 2173, 2535, 2755, 2820, 2850,
    2883, 3051, 3616, 3929, 4107, 4398
Afro-Brazilian 4158
Age 565, 676, 1466, 1468, 1469, 1474, 1477,
    1515, 1544, 1558, 1574, 1633, 1684,
    1752, 2142, 2156, 2535, 2560, 2603,
    2613, 2645, 2655, 2669, 2697, 2731,
    2761, 2765, 2768-2771, 2803, 2804, 2845,
    2850, 2862, 2864, 2950, 3751, 3772,
    3792, 4374, 4385, 4542, 4748, 4821
    see also: Old age
Age at marriage 2139, 2153, 2726, 2749
Age difference 1283, 2594, 4748
Age distribution 4750

Age groups 1327, 1477, 2121, 2122, 2139
Aged 2133, 2650, 2763, 2764, 2768, 2773,
    2777, 2786, 2824, 2898, 3540, 3545,
    3696, 3777, 3791, 3792, 3827, 4573
    see also: Care of the aged
Ageing 565, 813, 1545, 1564, 1633, 2174,
    2655, 2761-2763, 2765-2767, 2769-2772,
    2774, 2776, 2804, 2845, 2925, 3540
Agency 95, 234, 248, 276, 686, 991, 1777,
    2241, 2502, 2934, 3030, 3170, 3510,
    3541, 3572, 3625, 3764, 3843, 3878,
    4506, 4726
Aggression 1614, 1631, 1653, 3062, 3565
Agrarian reform 2405, 4682
Agrarian society 633, 830, 2143, 2198, 2399,
    2673, 3008, 4909
Agricultural and food market 709, 2335, 4693
Agricultural development 830, 2267, 2274,
    2280, 2300, 2315, 4618, 4692, 4694,
    4700, 4701, 4743, 4794, 4798, 4802, 4919
    see also: Green Revolution
Agricultural economics 2285, 2316, 2424,
    4704, 4807, 4888, 4940
Agricultural education 4, 165, 4701, 4833
Agricultural enterprises 2277
Agricultural equipment
    see: Fertilizers
Agricultural exports 727, 743, 2270, 2273,
    2300, 2348
Agricultural extension 4701
Agricultural history 4, 165, 323, 682, 707,
    727, 857, 2259, 2261, 2265, 2267, 2270,
    2276, 2281, 2282, 2286, 2294, 2300,
    2304, 2405, 2418, 2424, 2575, 2619,
    2730, 3066
Agricultural implements 4686
Agricultural industry 2279
Agricultural innovations 2255, 2273, 2280,
    2308, 4687, 4694, 4703
Agricultural intensification 2314
Agricultural labour 2286, 4686, 4692, 4701,
    4837
Agricultural management 4692, 4767, 4780
Agricultural planning 4692
Agricultural policy 249, 2273, 2305, 2310,
    2315, 4671, 4767
Agricultural prices 2142, 4821
Agricultural production 709, 1454, 2255,
    2258, 2262, 2263, 2278, 2280, 2293,
    2305, 2312, 2314, 2335, 2419, 3678,
    4687, 4688, 4693, 4727, 4793
Agricultural productivity 2303, 2358, 4663
Agricultural products 4443
Agricultural research 4, 165, 4825
Agricultural sector 2279, 4704

Agricultural systems 2262, 2263, 2278, 2314,
    2404, 2419, 2426, 4609, 4691, 4692, 4692
Agricultural techniques 687, 2254
Agricultural technology 2265, 2730, 4820
Agricultural trade 749
Agricultural workers 1490, 2269, 4701, 4765,
    4837
Agriculture 24, 488, 525, 596, 687, 709, 726,
    757, 851, 857, 867, 1236, 1446, 1550,
    1903, 2070, 2105, 2106, 2112, 2199, 2205,
    2206, 2254-2259, 2263, 2266-2268, 2271,
    2273, 2276, 2278-2281, 2283, 2285, 2286,
    2288, 2290, 2292, 2294, 2297, 2298,
    2301, 2303-2305, 2307-2309, 2314, 2316-
    2319, 2335, 2397, 2400, 2405, 2406,
    2423, 2430, 2441, 2463, 2619, 2968,
    3066, 3538, 3674, 3678, 4291, 4595,
    4609, 4686, 4687, 4689, 4690, 4692-4695,
    4697-4700, 4702-4704, 4720, 4764, 4765,
    4767, 4780, 4803, 4804, 4812, 4837,
    4906, 4909, 4911, 4924, 4940
    see also: Agricultural systems, Prehistoric
    agriculture, Sharecropping
Agrofood industry 4784
Agronomy 4807
Aid 4705, 4708, 4737, 4744, 4747, 4812,
    4834, 4839, 4937
    see also: Development aid, Economic aid,
    Food aid, Foreign aid
Aid evaluation 4744
Aid institutions 4750
AIDS 52, 183, 264, 419, 2156, 2721, 2753,
    2865, 2867, 2879, 2884, 2896, 2902,
    2906, 2908, 2916, 2988, 3004, 3739,
    3761-3763, 3770, 3771, 3773, 3796, 3801,
    3823, 3831, 3834, 4666, 4808, 4863,
    4864, 4870, 4878, 4880, 4893, 4897, 4898
Ainley, John 2298
Ainu 92
Air 1514, 4765
Air force 3463
Air pollution 2210, 4765
Airports 4311
Ait Youssi 3049
Aka 2431
Akan 2329, 2777, 2786, 3696, 4188
Akhtal al- 4036
Aklan 2592
Albanian language 1913, 1932, 1938
Alberdi, Juan Bautista 4210
Alchemy 643, 3787
Alcohol 215, 719, 2824, 3547
Alcoholic beverages 215, 490, 4390
    see also: Beer, Wine
Alcoholism 215, 1570, 4511

Alienation 1448, 2920, 4038
 see also: Cultural alienation
Alliances 470, 688, 1646, 1900, 2210, 2474,
 2567, 2638, 2658, 2983, 3355, 3502
Alphabet 545, 1913, 1996, 2019, 4229
Alternation 1962
Alternative medicine 17, 3825
Altruism 220, 1539, 2585, 3468
American Civil War 982
Americans 743, 2348, 2533, 3073
Amerindians 102, 119, 404, 774, 783, 1799,
 2099, 2691, 2834, 3155, 3550, 3617,
 3915, 4406
 see also: North Amerindians, South
 Amerindians
Amichai, Yehuda 4049, 4439
Amuzgo 1967
An, Lu-shan 522
Anatomy 110, 1464, 1465, 1469, 1523, 1531,
 1590, 1593, 1610, 1620, 1678, 3779, 3799
Ancestor cults 804, 3594
Ancestry 649, 804, 813, 2337, 2421, 2551,
 2643, 2649, 2774, 2801, 2997, 3078,
 3243, 3558, 3562, 3594, 3689, 3690,
 4013, 4029, 4248, 4572, 4630
Ancien Régime 2205, 2423
Ancient architecture 469, 989, 1008, 1010,
 1016, 1018, 1021, 1022, 1025, 1027,
 1028, 1031, 1032, 1038, 1045, 1049,
 1059, 1065, 1073, 1076, 1083, 1085,
 1090, 1099, 1102-1104, 1106, 1113, 1116,
 1118, 1121, 1156, 1157, 1199, 1200, 1217,
 1229, 1311, 1318, 1321, 1351, 1371, 1416
Ancient art 1040, 1055, 1056, 1072, 1081,
 1096, 1102
Ancient civilization 73, 214, 343, 349, 356,
 366, 446, 447, 449-453, 455-457, 462,
 465, 467, 474, 477-481, 483, 486, 487,
 489, 491, 493, 494, 496, 497, 499, 500,
 503, 510, 515, 517, 521, 523, 524, 526,
 535, 541, 617, 632, 669, 802, 881, 903,
 925, 942, 984, 1005, 1024, 1036, 1049,
 1083, 1106, 1224, 1294, 1317, 1329,
 1341-1343, 1352, 1370, 1373, 1377, 1495,
 1738, 2092, 2225, 2228, 2240, 2261,
 2358, 2365, 2366, 2372, 2378, 2444,
 2536, 2544, 2546, 2550, 2562, 2580,
 2642, 2797, 3023, 3119, 3301, 3387, 3398,
 3451, 3604, 3680, 3688, 3896, 3920,
 3928, 3973, 4066, 4253, 4279, 4314,
 4346, 4375, 4548
Ancient cultures 356, 617, 1373, 1437, 3991
Ancient economies 356, 482, 488, 503, 517,
 527, 617, 897, 2354, 2372, 2395

Ancient Egypt 387, 452, 459, 490, 507, 517,
 902, 1335, 1818, 1928, 2063, 2871, 4375
Ancient funeral art 1311, 1317, 1318, 1321,
 1385, 3604
Ancient funeral rites 874, 2604
Ancient Greece 448, 449, 490, 491, 496, 510,
 521, 1044, 1738, 2228, 2324, 2365, 2536,
 2612, 3692, 3754, 3756, 4066, 4148, 4290
Ancient history 73, 214, 446, 447, 457-459,
 462, 465, 468, 473, 478, 480-482, 486,
 491, 493-495, 499, 508-510, 520, 523,
 525, 528, 535, 559, 632, 918, 925, 933,
 1004, 1005, 1024, 1036, 1047, 1055,
 1060, 1093, 1103, 1308, 1329, 1338, 1343,
 1353, 2112, 2162, 2240, 2354, 2365, 2444,
 2536, 2580, 2871, 2995, 3023, 3119, 3145,
 3398, 3406, 3411, 3419, 3440, 3445, 3459,
 3753, 3928, 4066, 4209, 4241, 4258, 4268
Ancient mortuary customs 343, 859, 906, 991,
 1074, 1280, 1292, 1294, 1298, 1302-1304,
 1308, 1322, 1327
Ancient religions 1025, 3515
Ancient Rome 454, 490, 512, 528, 1031,
 1200, 1364, 1367
Ancient scripts 1331, 1349, 2000
Androgyny 2838
Anikulapo-Kuti, Fela 3933, 4059
Animal domestication 966, 2310
Animal ecology 46, 1510, 1597, 1599, 1600,
 1611, 1623, 1624, 1627, 1638, 1641, 1642,
 1646, 1648, 1657, 1658, 1661, 1664,
 1671, 1674, 1676, 1677, 1682, 1683,
 1689, 1690, 1698, 1700, 1710, 1720, 2109
Animal feeding 1700
Animal husbandry 757, 2406, 2433, 2441,
 2443, 2445, 2450
Animal rights 1652
Animals 46, 462, 638, 730, 749, 824, 872,
 884, 889, 929, 947, 1020, 1366, 1501,
 1620, 1624, 1657, 1678, 1679, 1689,
 1696, 1700, 2068, 2189, 2291, 2445,
 3998, 4212, 4391, 4496
 see also: Domestic animals, Mythical
 animals, Oxen, Sheep
Animism 3609, 3690, 3702, 3939
Ankutshu 1996
Anomie 4152
Anthologies 4074
Anthropocentrism 167
Anthropological analysis 177, 212, 213, 431
Anthropological methodology 126, 158, 174,
 177, 179, 197, 212, 232, 240-242, 259,
 275, 277, 346, 397, 398, 403, 414, 424,
 431, 440, 1564, 2539, 3054
 see also: Participant observation

Anthropological research 1, 2, 6, 7, 9, 24, 26, 28, 35, 37, 41, 45-47, 49-52, 55, 56, 58, 93, 94, 104, 105, 108, 114, 135, 142, 147, 148, 157, 158, 160, 169, 174, 177, 183, 189, 190, 207, 212, 215, 219, 232, 238, 240, 242, 253, 265, 288, 292, 297, 301, 302, 304, 311, 312, 317, 333, 341, 354, 367, 381, 390, 397, 398, 400, 404, 411, 413, 416, 421, 424, 431, 440, 442, 547, 552, 562, 574, 595, 655, 672, 793, 961, 1323, 1359, 1514, 1527, 1689, 1823, 2157, 2214, 2344, 2458, 2568, 2597, 2680, 2751, 2777, 2798, 2897, 2908, 2910, 2941, 3022, 3027, 3061, 3231, 3245, 3540, 3558, 3599, 3656, 3696, 3729, 3765, 3801, 3804, 4105, 4182, 4295, 4312, 4364, 4378, 4408, 4410, 4420, 4473, 4495, 4523, 4584, 4590, 4641, 4655, 4715, 4754, 4793, 4799
Anthropological theory 9, 12, 58, 108, 121, 123, 126, 127, 133, 137, 138, 146, 157, 158, 161, 164, 174, 179, 180, 203, 204, 212, 215, 216, 218, 219, 221-223, 228, 232, 233, 235, 238, 240-242, 244, 247, 249, 254-256, 263, 265, 267, 268, 270-272, 275, 277-279, 284, 384, 395, 397, 398, 403, 408, 411, 415, 423, 426, 431, 439, 638, 911, 1584, 1772, 2369, 2387, 2527, 2537, 2539, 2552, 2596, 2612, 2658, 2680, 2751, 3022, 3043, 3054, 3567, 3583, 3622, 3653, 3692, 4378, 4414, 4457, 4484, 4485, 4490, 4715, 4754
Anthropologists 1, 6, 9, 18, 24, 26, 35, 37, 41, 91, 93, 94, 102-105, 108, 110, 113-115, 120, 123, 128, 134, 138, 143, 144, 148, 157, 169, 180, 190, 193, 214, 223, 244, 304, 386, 404, 1799, 1802, 2170, 2658, 2798, 2834, 2897, 3231, 3799, 3870, 4406, 4408, 4590, 4625, 4804
Anthropology 2, 3, 6-9, 11, 13, 16, 18, 26, 29, 31, 35, 37, 41, 43, 48-52, 56, 76, 77, 80-82, 90, 93-98, 100, 104, 108, 110, 114, 115, 119-121, 127, 131, 133, 134, 137, 151, 155-157, 159-164, 169, 171, 175, 176, 180, 182-184, 187, 189, 190, 192, 193, 195, 198-200, 202, 207, 212-214, 216, 217, 219, 221, 223, 224, 232-234, 237, 238, 241, 244, 246-248, 256, 262, 267, 269-272, 275, 276, 279-281, 291, 293, 295-297, 299, 301, 303, 304, 310-312, 317, 318, 328, 341, 348, 354, 355, 359, 365, 369-371, 385, 391, 392, 402, 408, 410-413, 418, 424, 428, 431, 439, 444, 456, 482, 504, 521, 530, 532, 533, 538, 545, 549, 552, 561, 572-574, 587, 590, 597, 605, 614, 618, 621, 626, 636, 638, 648, 655, 657, 660, 665, 674, 677, 679, 688, 689, 697, 736, 740, 742, 743, 745, 767, 774, 790, 793, 796, 800, 821, 830, 832, 836, 849, 850, 866, 870, 876, 879, 903, 937, 969, 974, 977, 980, 985, 992, 993, 1007, 1095, 1101, 1280, 1291, 1345, 1357, 1360, 1369, 1370, 1372, 1374, 1387, 1389, 1420, 1450, 1451, 1457, 1459-1465, 1468, 1469, 1471, 1473, 1477, 1478, 1482-1484, 1492, 1495, 1497, 1502-1504, 1512-1515, 1520, 1521, 1523-1528, 1538, 1542, 1545, 1550, 1552, 1561, 1566, 1567, 1572, 1576, 1584, 1586, 1590, 1592, 1593, 1622, 1662, 1703, 1721, 1752, 1753, 1761, 1772, 1773, 1792, 1800, 1809, 1815, 1823, 1827, 1830, 1837, 1841, 1845, 1880, 1912, 1962, 1967, 1968, 1971-1975, 1977, 1978, 1980, 1982-1986, 2018, 2022, 2036, 2052, 2068, 2070, 2071, 2076, 2077, 2093, 2101, 2116, 2126, 2127, 2130, 2135, 2157, 2168, 2170, 2172, 2185, 2190, 2194, 2198, 2216, 2218, 2220, 2224, 2233, 2235, 2247, 2250, 2253, 2302, 2328, 2334, 2348, 2354, 2367, 2373, 2379, 2387, 2428, 2429, 2431, 2433, 2447, 2450, 2475, 2488, 2498, 2503, 2505, 2507, 2510, 2516, 2517, 2519, 2525, 2527, 2530, 2537, 2539, 2547, 2549, 2551, 2557, 2561, 2563, 2571, 2572, 2583, 2588, 2591, 2596, 2609-2611, 2623, 2633, 2647, 2670, 2679, 2687, 2689, 2700, 2703, 2706, 2714, 2731, 2732, 2737, 2740, 2747, 2751, 2776, 2784, 2796, 2798, 2814, 2824, 2842, 2852, 2858, 2883, 2896, 2897, 2908, 2915, 2919, 2926, 2927, 2929, 2939, 2955, 2958, 2963, 2987, 2992, 2998, 2999, 3004, 3021, 3024, 3038, 3044-3046, 3052, 3055, 3061, 3067-3069, 3071, 3072, 3084, 3108, 3117, 3122, 3123, 3126-3128, 3130, 3172, 3189-3191, 3202, 3233, 3235, 3236, 3245, 3246, 3252, 3264, 3288, 3292, 3301, 3302, 3309, 3314, 3326, 3346, 3347, 3350, 3361, 3366, 3374, 3384, 3399, 3409, 3509, 3511, 3518, 3522, 3540, 3542, 3544, 3547, 3552, 3553, 3558, 3559, 3564, 3567, 3569, 3570, 3577, 3583, 3588, 3592, 3598, 3605, 3614, 3622, 3623, 3630, 3633, 3641, 3647, 3651, 3653, 3658, 3672, 3674, 3683, 3685, 3686, 3695, 3710, 3715, 3719, 3720, 3722, 3724, 3729, 3739, 3741, 3745, 3747, 3752, 3763, 3769,

3771, 3776, 3777, 3783, 3799, 3801,
3803, 3806, 3808, 3809, 3824, 3826,
3851, 3867, 3868, 3875-3877, 3879-3883,
3889, 3892, 3894, 3898, 3901, 3904,
3905, 3913, 3916, 3919, 3929, 3932,
3937, 3938, 3955, 3962-3964, 3967, 3968,
3975, 3981, 3985, 4003, 4004, 4009,
4013, 4039, 4056, 4060, 4071, 4081,
4089, 4105, 4109, 4111, 4124, 4125, 4134,
4143-4145, 4150, 4156, 4165, 4172, 4180,
4182, 4190, 4208, 4209, 4219, 4259,
4265, 4269, 4278, 4288, 4293-4295, 4297,
4298, 4312, 4315, 4337, 4343, 4381,
4387, 4388, 4402, 4415, 4424, 4426,
4429, 4432, 4436, 4437, 4443, 4447,
4449, 4452, 4453, 4459, 4466, 4468,
4469, 4481, 4482, 4484, 4489, 4490,
4513, 4514, 4517, 4519-4521, 4523, 4524,
4526, 4527, 4533, 4534, 4537, 4540,
4542, 4544, 4545, 4549, 4555, 4559,
4566-4568, 4574, 4582, 4595, 4599, 4601,
4602, 4611, 4630, 4633, 4636, 4641, 4685,
4751, 4775, 4790, 4799, 4802, 4804, 4893
see also: Applied anthropology, Criminal
anthropology, Cultural anthropology,
Development anthropology, Economic
anthropology, Forensic anthropology,
Historical anthropology, History of
anthropology, Linguistic anthropology,
Maritime anthropology, Medical
anthropology, Nutritional anthropology,
Paleoanthropology, Philosophical
anthropology, Physical anthropology,
Political anthropology, Rural
anthropology, Social anthropology,
Sociological anthropology, Urban
anthropology, Visual anthropology
Anthropology of art 4149
Anthropology of dance 3890
Anthropology of education 47, 421
Anthropology of food 4354, 4376-4379, 4386,
4395, 4754, 4809
Anthropology of knowledge 199, 3655
Anthropology of law 59, 262, 2400, 2407,
2968, 2972, 2978, 2980, 2984, 2991,
2992, 3003, 3016, 4670
Anthropology of religion 86, 105, 191, 202,
208, 256, 275, 413, 869, 1353, 2539,
3145, 3215, 3221, 3227, 3228, 3231,
3232, 3234, 3237, 3250, 3257, 3259,
3265, 3326, 3347, 3356, 3361, 3405,
3422, 3427, 3431, 3445, 3455, 3460,
3583, 3645, 4462
Anthropology of science 3739, 3750, 3758,
3759

Anthropology of sport 1559
Anthropology of the body 1448, 1459, 1483,
2715, 2780, 2920, 2921, 2923, 2924,
2927, 2929, 2930, 2938, 2947, 2950,
2952, 2958, 2961, 3338, 4482
Anthropology of work 2453, 2468, 2471
Anthropometry 296, 310, 628, 898, 1455,
1456, 1467, 1531, 1541, 1542, 1549,
1557, 1566, 1576, 1587, 1589, 3772,
3804, 4307, 4810
Anthropomorphism 828, 1067, 1430, 3601,
4386
Anthropophagy 751, 822, 977, 2796, 2852,
3024, 3588
Anti-clericalism 4277
Anti-colonialism 4544
Anti-Semitism 4479
Antiquity 342, 379, 445, 453, 454, 462, 463,
467, 475, 514, 526, 591, 669, 826, 863,
900, 961, 1003, 1042, 1044, 1086, 1096,
1097, 1285, 1358, 1367, 1390, 1408,
1423, 1433, 1441, 1516, 2093, 2343,
2562, 2875, 2909, 3417, 3454, 3680, 3701
see also: Ancient Egypt, Ancient Greece,
Ancient Rome
Anxiety 4504
Apaches 1824
Apartheid 126, 269, 613, 2219, 2969, 3054,
3055, 4012, 4293, 4548, 4663, 4881
see also: Post-apartheid society
Apiculture 4800
Apin, Rivai 4071
Apostasy 2998, 3366
Applied anthropology 41, 45, 190, 249, 401,
2587, 4632, 4808
Apprentices 2227
Apprenticeship 424, 2237
Appropriate technology 1001
Aquaculture 2117, 2452
Arab countries 1342, 2417, 2554, 3018, 3327,
3339, 4101
Arab-Israeli conflict 4495
Arabic language 129, 324, 344, 586, 1136,
1339, 1347, 1356, 1762, 1804, 1819,
1840-1842, 1847, 1851-1853, 1860, 1862,
1863, 1865, 1867-1869, 1871, 1874, 3268,
3354, 3359, 3393, 3738, 4087, 4155,
4167, 4267
Arabs 253, 484, 555, 579, 1830, 1856, 2422,
2628, 3848, 3954, 4084, 4583, 4585
Aragão, Baltasar Rebelo de 806
Araucana 3126
Araucanian 3126
Arawak 1982

Archaeobotany 452, 858, 896, 900, 2296, 2304, 4375

Archaeological artifacts 325, 342, 356, 460, 499, 507, 617, 837, 839, 846, 860, 890, 912, 943, 951, 968, 973, 1016, 1042, 1236, 1306, 1363, 1366, 1368, 1373, 1378, 1379, 1382, 1384, 1390, 1392, 1402-1404, 1407, 1412, 1422, 1429, 1440, 1441, 1443, 1447, 1536, 2240, 2360, 4268

Archaeological collections 325, 330, 342, 959

Archaeological dating 34, 523, 819, 839, 869, 902, 948, 951, 987, 1130, 1290, 1291, 1316, 1378, 1422

Archaeological discoveries 322, 332, 448, 469, 872, 904, 925, 944, 952, 959, 961, 1014, 1016, 1034, 1080, 1107, 1115, 1117, 1119, 1126, 1133, 1138, 1146, 1161, 1162, 1171, 1178, 1182, 1195, 1199-1201, 1204, 1205, 1207, 1208, 1210, 1216, 1218, 1220, 1250, 1253, 1259, 1260, 1272, 1279, 1306, 1307, 1312, 1316, 1317, 1332, 1365, 1372, 1380, 1393, 1401, 1412, 1414, 1417, 1422, 1443, 1530, 2378, 3604

Archaeological excavation 85, 356, 445, 452, 454, 460, 469, 494, 498, 499, 507, 512, 513, 556, 598, 617, 623, 744, 819, 820, 822-826, 831, 837, 839, 840, 842, 856, 859, 860, 865, 868, 872, 873, 883, 884, 888, 889, 891, 899, 900, 906, 911, 915, 917, 918, 922, 925, 927-929, 931, 935, 938, 941, 943, 944, 948, 950, 954, 956, 958, 959, 961, 964, 967, 968, 970, 973, 976, 979, 981, 982, 1009, 1010, 1014, 1018, 1020, 1023, 1026-1028, 1034-1036, 1038, 1042, 1050, 1057, 1068, 1070, 1072, 1073, 1075, 1078-1080, 1082, 1085, 1087, 1092, 1100, 1107-1112, 1114-1122, 1124-1129, 1131-1136, 1138-1145, 1147, 1150-1154, 1156-1162, 1164-1171, 1174-1176, 1178-1182, 1185-1187, 1189-1195, 1198, 1200-1213, 1215-1222, 1224, 1227-1232, 1234, 1236, 1237, 1239, 1241-1247, 1250-1254, 1256-1262, 1265-1270, 1272-1275, 1277-1279, 1285, 1293, 1295-1297, 1307, 1312-1314, 1318, 1326-1328, 1330, 1337, 1344, 1363-1367, 1371, 1378, 1379, 1381, 1382, 1384, 1390, 1398, 1400, 1402-1404, 1407-1409, 1416, 1417, 1419, 1429, 1433, 1440-1442, 1458, 1461, 1464, 1471, 1535, 2240, 2304, 2360, 2393, 2444, 3853, 4007, 4375

Archaeological expeditions 1199, 1257

Archaeological methodology 60, 258, 458, 923, 938, 941, 945, 953, 970, 980, 983, 988, 996, 997, 1002, 1010, 1046, 1054, 1064, 1074, 1075, 1079, 1082, 1110, 1111, 1113, 1120, 1123, 1124, 1134, 1144, 1145, 1148, 1150, 1154, 1163, 1164, 1169, 1172, 1179, 1180, 1186, 1187, 1189, 1192, 1197, 1206, 1212, 1213, 1221, 1225, 1226, 1231, 1232, 1237, 1239, 1252, 1255, 1258, 1262, 1268, 1269, 1271, 1274-1276, 1278, 1305, 1310, 1360, 1407, 1418, 1419, 1436, 2144

Archaeological research 34, 60, 87, 155, 162, 211, 251, 273, 274, 430, 445, 450, 454, 469, 475, 492, 513, 520, 526, 530, 550, 556, 598, 623, 664, 669, 789, 819, 820, 825-827, 831, 834, 837, 846, 858-860, 862, 863, 865, 883, 891, 893, 897, 900, 901, 903, 904, 906, 908, 910, 918, 922, 923, 925, 928, 930, 931, 935, 939-942, 944, 948-950, 952, 954-956, 958, 960, 961, 964, 968-970, 972, 975-979, 981, 983, 984, 986, 987, 989, 995-997, 999, 1002, 1003, 1018, 1020, 1031, 1038, 1041, 1042, 1050, 1057, 1059, 1068, 1069, 1073-1075, 1077, 1079, 1080, 1092, 1107-1112, 1114, 1116, 1117, 1119, 1121-1129, 1131-1135, 1137-1152, 1154-1157, 1160-1162, 1164, 1168, 1170, 1171, 1174-1176, 1179, 1180, 1182-1189, 1191, 1193-1195, 1198-1204, 1206, 1208-1216, 1218, 1219, 1222, 1224, 1226-1228, 1230, 1232-1235, 1237, 1239, 1241-1247, 1250, 1251, 1253, 1254, 1256, 1257, 1259, 1261, 1262, 1265-1268, 1270, 1273-1275, 1277-1279, 1282, 1285-1287, 1289, 1294, 1296, 1297, 1307, 1329, 1343, 1351, 1352, 1360, 1367, 1375, 1377, 1380, 1390, 1393, 1398-1400, 1404, 1407, 1408, 1414, 1416, 1418, 1421, 1434, 1436, 1441, 1442, 1516, 1546, 2110, 2144, 2296, 2393, 2794, 3024, 3520, 3859, 3941, 4215, 4241, 4256

Archaeological sites 85, 251, 458, 469, 475, 488, 497, 518, 543, 822, 824, 827, 842, 843, 847, 856, 862, 873, 888, 891, 900, 907, 913, 915, 919, 922, 931, 933, 936, 938, 942, 944, 950, 951, 954, 958, 964, 967, 968, 973, 981-983, 989, 997, 1011, 1018, 1021, 1026, 1034, 1037, 1038, 1053, 1059, 1063, 1073, 1080, 1085, 1089, 1091, 1106-1110, 1112, 1115-1119, 1123, 1125, 1127, 1128, 1130-1133, 1139-1143, 1146, 1147, 1149, 1151-1153, 1155, 1156, 1160, 1162, 1170, 1171, 1174, 1177, 1182, 1185, 1191, 1193-1195, 1198, 1203, 1204, 1208-1211, 1214-1216, 1218, 1219,

1224, 1229, 1230, 1233, 1241, 1243-1247,
1249-1251, 1254, 1256, 1259, 1261, 1265-
1267, 1273, 1279, 1281, 1284-1286, 1295,
1304, 1306, 1307, 1318, 1348, 1359,
1365, 1378, 1380, 1381, 1384, 1393,
1398, 1400, 1401, 1409, 1411, 1412, 1414,
1416, 1417, 1429, 1442, 1536, 2235,
2378, 2393, 3859
Archaeological techniques 60, 819, 865, 868,
932, 935, 938, 963, 988, 997, 1001, 1059,
1105, 1162, 1290, 1295, 2304
Archaeological theory 34, 85, 155, 164, 251,
274, 520, 530, 844, 865, 933, 965, 967,
969, 971, 978, 980-982, 987, 988, 991,
995, 996, 1002, 1135, 1221, 1226, 1239,
1361, 3697
Archaeologists 60, 85, 87, 111, 112, 851, 967,
972, 975, 976, 979, 989, 990, 4326
Archaeology 34, 60, 85, 111, 112, 117, 150,
155, 162, 164, 178, 211, 246, 251, 258,
260, 273, 274, 298, 325, 326, 332, 342,
343, 363, 382, 409, 430, 445, 448, 452-
454, 456, 458, 459, 462-464, 466, 469,
471, 475, 483, 484, 488, 492, 494, 496-
500, 503-505, 507, 511-513, 518, 520,
522-524, 526, 530, 533, 538, 543, 545,
550, 555, 556, 595, 598, 619, 623, 631,
646, 656, 657, 664, 669, 744, 762, 789,
819, 820, 823, 825-827, 829, 831, 832,
834-838, 840, 843, 844, 846-848, 850,
851, 853-863, 865, 866, 868, 869, 871,
873, 874, 877, 879-883, 885, 888, 891,
894, 896, 898, 900-910, 912, 914-918,
924, 926-933, 935, 937-941, 943-960,
962-974, 977-983, 985-992, 994-1003,
1008-1014, 1017, 1018, 1020-1023, 1026-
1030, 1034-1043, 1045-1047, 1050-1054,
1057-1065, 1068-1071, 1073-1075, 1078-
1080, 1082, 1085, 1087, 1089-1094, 1098-
1101, 1105-1198, 1201-1204, 1206-1282,
1284-1293, 1295, 1297-1300, 1302, 1304-
1307, 1309-1315, 1317, 1318, 1320-1322,
1325-1328, 1330-1332, 1337, 1338, 1340,
1343, 1344, 1346, 1348, 1351, 1352,
1354-1356, 1360, 1362, 1363, 1365-1369,
1371, 1376-1378, 1380-1384, 1388-1393,
1396-1402, 1404, 1406-1409, 1411, 1412,
1414-1419, 1421, 1424-1427, 1429, 1431-
1436, 1438, 1440-1447, 1461, 1464, 1467,
1471, 1479, 1516, 1518, 1532, 1533,
1546, 1760, 2087, 2100, 2107, 2134,
2135, 2144, 2170, 2175, 2177, 2206,
2208, 2226, 2228, 2230, 2240, 2266,
2304, 2321, 2338, 2340, 2343, 2360,
2372, 2393, 2444, 2526, 2530, 2547,
2562, 2590, 2591, 2604, 2642, 2752,
2794, 2871, 3024, 3135, 3185, 3322,
3604, 3707, 3849, 3859, 3973, 4155,
4241, 4250, 4256, 4327, 4329, 4346,
4375, 4501
see also: Aerial archaeology, Biblical
archaeology, Classical archaeology,
Experimental archaeology, Field
archaeology, Historical archaeology,
History of archaeology, Rescue
archaeology, Settlement archaeology,
Urban archaeology
Archaeozoology 824, 841, 842, 872, 884, 889,
929, 947, 974
Architects 1009, 1763, 3660, 3846, 3853
Architecture 316, 323, 343, 512, 620, 707,
798, 825, 880, 906, 918, 995, 1009-1012,
1015, 1019, 1021, 1022, 1025, 1032,
1035, 1043, 1045, 1047, 1048, 1050,
1052, 1054, 1057, 1063, 1069, 1070,
1075, 1079, 1082, 1089, 1091, 1092, 1100,
1110, 1113, 1121, 1165-1167, 1181, 1188,
1217, 1246, 1296, 1333, 1337, 1343,
1346, 1357, 1364, 1420, 1763, 2092,
2227, 2459, 3260, 3354, 3452, 3660,
3678, 3838, 3839, 3842-3844, 3846-3848,
3851-3853, 3856-3861, 3898, 4124, 4345,
4749
see also: Ancient architecture, Domestic
architecture, Traditional architecture
Archives 25, 36, 61, 76, 77, 80, 81, 89, 150,
283, 291, 317, 318, 320, 323, 329, 333,
335, 339, 340, 354, 355, 359, 369, 372,
375, 381, 382, 547, 672, 707, 753, 781,
902, 1745, 1825, 2123, 2642, 3546, 3929
see also: National archives
Area studies 27, 39, 82, 184, 370, 559, 1342,
1941, 1942, 2099, 2162, 2612, 2677,
3087, 3150, 3155, 3692, 4268, 4506
Arid zones 957
Aristocracy 557, 624, 2639, 4094
Armah, Ayi Kwei 4188
Armament 534, 581
Armed forces 2577, 2578, 4653
Armenians 253
Armies 283, 299, 498, 624, 1029, 1076, 2123,
2483, 2526, 2542, 2577, 2960, 3021,
3022, 3052, 3502, 3716
Armstrong, Hamilton F. 2533, 3073
Arrest 2570
Art 133, 151, 174, 201, 273, 314, 327, 330,
337, 338, 343, 368, 439, 444, 759, 828,
894, 937, 999, 1005, 1007, 1012-1014,
1016, 1017, 1020, 1039, 1048, 1051,
1068, 1071, 1074, 1084, 1087, 1094,

1097, 1098, 1102, 1110, 1114, 1337, 1343,
  1352, 1384, 1387, 1391, 1420, 2234,
  2245, 2250, 2253, 2324, 2353, 2453,
  2921, 2933, 2945, 2950, 3354, 3529,
  3598, 3624, 3714, 3731, 3736, 3773,
  3838, 3841, 3850, 3852, 3866, 3906,
  4041, 4091, 4093-4095, 4097, 4101-4103,
  4106, 4109, 4111-4113, 4115, 4121-4123,
  4125, 4127, 4128, 4130, 4133-4135, 4137,
  4139, 4141, 4144, 4145, 4223, 4235,
  4247, 4453
  see also: Ancient art, Anthropology of art,
  Buddhist art, Contemporary art, Dramatic
  art, Figurative art, Fine arts, Folk art,
  Funeral art, Graphic arts, History of art,
  Islamic art, Martial arts, Medieval art,
  Native art, Performing arts, Philosophy of
  art, Plastic arts, Prehistoric art, Primitive
  art, Religious art, Rock art, Traditional art,
  Tribal art, Visual arts, Works of art,
  Zoomorphic arts
Art collections 315, 327, 330, 337, 347, 379,
  380, 2346, 2353, 4092, 4118, 4125
Art market 2353
Art metalwork 1017
Art museums 314, 366, 374, 4091
Art style 1048, 3212, 3848, 4016, 4101, 4130,
  4137, 4145
Artifacts 130, 330, 331, 353, 379, 380, 505,
  869, 981, 1039, 1040, 1071, 1098, 1299,
  1322, 1372, 1396, 1418, 1421, 1424,
  1431, 1434, 1436, 1438, 3580, 4241
Artisans 1425, 2644
Artistic creation 1033
Artistic tradition 1031, 3714
Artists 1094, 3841, 3869, 4093, 4103, 4109,
  4111, 4123, 4128, 4132, 4135, 4223, 4235
Arts 314, 315, 368, 1033, 1047, 1081, 1093,
  1094, 1331, 1357, 1819, 2325, 2571,
  2842, 2940, 3134, 3319, 3624, 3724,
  3749, 3768, 3773, 3823, 3841, 3844,
  3882, 3884, 3890, 3904, 3916, 3937,
  3938, 3963, 3967, 4025, 4064, 4091,
  4092, 4104, 4108-4111, 4118, 4123, 4125,
  4127, 4132, 4133, 4138, 4203, 4610, 4712
Asbestos 3986
Asceticism 2085, 3136, 4310
Ashanti 2833
Ashkenazi 2965, 3394, 3395, 3997
Ashurnasirpal, II [King] 3920
Asian and Pacific languages 1725, 1744, 1883
Asian studies 27, 1746, 3364, 3646, 4458
Asian-Americans 2161, 2533, 3073, 3700
Asians 253, 4398, 4478
Asma'u, Nana 4081

Asseng, Protais 4206
Assets 3344
Assistance 1571
Associations 693, 4927
Assyrians 450, 489, 1102, 1284, 1330, 1341,
  1839, 3920
Astrology 591, 3417
Astronomy 652, 653, 3269, 3672, 3740, 3752,
  4095
Asturias, Miguel Ángel 4222
Asylum 2186
Atheism 3131
Athletes 4307, 4312, 4336, 4574
Ati 2592
Atlas
  see: Ethnographic atlases, Linguistic
  atlases
Atlases 1727, 3247
Attitude change 3074, 3813
Attitudes 45, 53, 399, 625, 1748, 2047, 2097,
  2443, 2502, 2791, 2802, 2809, 2892,
  2910, 2931, 2933, 2988, 3060, 3078,
  3092, 3442, 3572, 3607, 3810, 3811, 3813,
  3893, 4668, 4722, 4805
  see also: Collective attitudes, Cultural
  attitudes, Racial attitudes
Auctions 2346
Audience 660
Auditing 4709
Austerlitz, Robert 139
Australians 1723, 1728
Autarchy 2507
Authoritarianism 4778
Authority 563, 2176, 2324, 2480, 2528, 2560,
  2583, 2598, 2669, 3627, 3803, 4374, 4560
  see also: Political authority, Religious
  authorities
Authors 799, 1833, 2998, 3190, 3212, 3331,
  3366, 3876, 3895, 4162, 4170, 4194,
  4202, 4239, 4258, 4263, 4266, 4272,
  4277, 4278, 4566
Autobiography 1740, 2832, 3988, 4062, 4069,
  4171, 4215, 4251, 4511, 4517, 4562,
  4566-4568, 4570, 4571, 4575, 4578-4580
Automobile industry 4671
Automobiles 161, 697, 3712
Autonomy 739, 2417, 2524, 2540, 2614, 2672,
  2834, 2933, 3018, 3063, 3967, 4406,
  4480, 4634, 4858, 4902
Ávila, António José de 815
Aztec 98, 214, 802, 1005, 1024, 2302, 2503,
  3515, 4242
Bablot, Alfredo J. 106, 752
Baga 574
Bagley, Ray 4038

Baidawī, Qāḍī 4185
Baker, Reginald 4574
Bakgatla 215
Balādurī, Ahmad Ibn Yahya al 3323
Balance of power 228, 612, 2488, 3925
Baldeep Singh, Bhai 3463
Balkar 2321, 2979, 3349
Ball games 4304, 4336, 4337
Bambara 1818, 2063
Bananas 723
Banditry 633, 3008, 3991, 4015, 4500
Bankimchandra, Rishi 3312
Banking 380, 734, 4671
Banks 734, 4911
     see also: Development banks,
     International banks, World Bank
Bantu 1987, 1988, 1990, 1996, 1997, 1999,
     2003, 2007
Baptism 4183
Baraka, Sayyid 3322
Bargaining 2446, 2681, 2759, 2918, 3354
Bargaining power 2983
Baseball 4336
Basic needs 2640, 2863, 4665
Basotho 1821
Basques 1522, 2187, 2666, 4493
Baudelaire, Charles 3728
Baudot, Georges 106, 752
Baudrillard, Jean 3698
Bazié, Jean-Hubert 1749
Beads 1392
Bears 1368
Beaud, Stéphane 2453
Bedouin 555, 939, 1301, 2287, 2417, 2473,
     3018, 4604
Beer 2277, 2824
Behavioural sciences 1487, 1606, 1623, 1662,
     1683, 1694, 1698, 2691
Behn, Aphra 4285
Beliefs 143, 191, 199, 468, 487, 544, 790,
     804, 828, 1308, 1320, 1586, 1863, 2727,
     2791, 2808, 2823, 2828, 3006, 3015,
     3016, 3135, 3148, 3153, 3156, 3225,
     3300, 3318, 3325, 3334, 3356, 3359,
     3382, 3406, 3440, 3465, 3479, 3483,
     3485, 3509, 3536, 3553, 3557, 3589,
     3591, 3594, 3602, 3616, 3620, 3622,
     3654, 3681, 3690, 3736, 3739, 3769,
     3787, 3822, 3824, 3830, 4535
     see also: Folk beliefs, Food beliefs,
     Medical beliefs, Religious beliefs
Bemba 2729
Bengali 1893, 1906, 2282, 2575, 3218, 4072
Benjamin, Sathima Bea 3933, 4059
Benjamin, Walter 4068

Berber 122, 470, 600, 1830, 1854, 1858, 2274,
     2417, 2567, 2653, 2977, 3018, 4037
Berberova, Nina 4069, 4578
Bereavement 38, 2787, 4509, 4512, 4518,
     4529, 4532, 4541, 4546
Berenicianus, Alexander 486
Beverages
     see: Alcoholic beverages
Bhagat Nam Devji [Saint] 3472
Bhangi 1455
Bhāsa 3314, 3865, 3875, 3876
Bialik, H.N. 4444
Bias 228, 241, 258, 635, 1548, 2588, 4415,
     4879
Bible 87, 506, 604, 975, 1353, 1831, 1838,
     1843, 1846, 1848, 1850, 1855, 1859,
     1861, 1864, 1893, 2310, 2598, 2737,
     2748, 3146, 3147, 3218, 3227, 3229,
     3237, 3238, 3244, 3251, 3255, 3267,
     3337, 3392, 3393, 3396, 3399, 3400,
     3405, 3420, 3421, 3426, 3427, 3431,
     3434-3436, 3445, 3447, 3449, 3453, 3459,
     3460, 3627, 3899, 3973, 4026, 4114, 4224,
     4283
Biblical archaeology 87, 506, 897, 975, 976,
     1027, 1129, 1131, 1371, 3145, 3973
Bibliographers 3206
Bibliographies 79, 109, 340, 1995, 4079, 4404
Biculturalism 2525
Bidayuh 4584
Big Man 2199
Biggs, Bruce 1878
Bilateral economic relations 4632
Bilateral relations 4632
Bilingual education 1969
Bilingualism 1770, 1790, 1793, 1798, 1803,
     1895, 1969, 1985, 2005, 3989, 4548
Bills
     see: Parliamentary bills
Bini 4007
Biodiversity 2105, 2272, 2445, 4636, 4658,
     4767, 4774, 4781, 4820
Bioethics 2728
Biographies 88, 92, 99, 106, 111, 123, 128,
     181, 371, 433, 570, 615, 627, 675, 752,
     773, 817, 979, 990, 1878, 2281, 2298,
     2465, 3841, 4192, 4271, 4477, 4563-4568,
     4574-4577, 4579, 4712
Biological anthropology 1465, 1472, 1502,
     1522, 1523, 1545, 1564, 1581, 1593,
     1610, 1635, 2699
Biological evolution 1485
Biology 46, 263, 279, 910, 1465, 1500, 1501,
     1504, 1508, 1519, 1520, 1537, 1538,
     1593, 1616, 1618, 1632, 1634, 1640,

1689, 1695, 3043, 4507, 4770
see also: Human biology, Social biology
Biomechanics 1549, 1610
Biomedicine 1498, 2657, 2719, 2959, 3817
Biometrics 1553, 1564, 1566, 1572, 1581, 1592
Biopolitics 1448, 2920
Biotechnology 2930
Birds 360, 371, 1818, 1819, 2063, 2064, 2108, 2445, 3744, 3753, 4335
Birth 378, 1500, 1544, 1566, 1582, 1583, 1614, 1708, 1718, 2121, 2122, 2632, 2702, 2707, 2709, 2711, 2718, 2727, 3192, 3581, 3737, 3775, 3814, 4844
Birth control 2122, 2131, 2714
Birth customs 2700
Birth intervals 2131, 2708
Birth rate 3739
Birth spacing 2129, 2704
Bisa 2509
Bisexuality 1454, 2874, 2919, 3782
Bislama 1724, 2018
Black politics 3929
Blacks 562, 695, 774, 978, 1503, 1582, 2173, 2327, 2505, 2671, 2875, 3266, 3609, 3648, 4012, 4030, 4401, 4460, 4468
Blindness
see: Colour blindness
Bloch, Jules 124, 1805
Blood 769, 1490, 1510, 1626, 1699, 2931, 2944, 3510, 3764
Blood groups 1486, 1490, 1491, 2118
Boas, Franz 134
Boats 868, 1395, 2248, 3680
Bodi 2610
Body mutilations 2921
Body symbolism 2938, 2947
Body techniques
see: Tattooing
Boeck, Egide De 109, 1995
Boer War 654, 1282, 4182
Bombal, María Luisa 4239
Bonaventure [Saint] 3728
Bonds 2983
Books 124, 593, 796, 1044, 1761, 1805, 1865, 3164, 3209, 3323, 3485, 3766, 3768, 4154, 4165, 4186, 4200, 4223, 4244, 4247, 4249
Border conflicts 611, 3042
Border regions 291, 599, 2192, 2495, 3098, 3121, 3694, 4488, 4628, 4632, 4695
Borders 383, 599, 641, 670, 750, 763, 777, 2082, 2092, 2125, 2456, 2608, 2779, 2827, 3085, 3098, 3104, 4619, 4624,

4626, 4628, 4632
see also: Maritime borders
Borrowing 4911
Boruca 1984
Bosatsu, Gyōki 3187
Bosch, Hieronymous 4097
Botany 900, 1722, 2066, 2201, 2297
see also: Archaeobotany
Bourdieu, Pierre 2609
Boys 1579
Brahmans 3277
Brain 110, 170, 1481, 1496, 1547, 1561, 1567, 1612, 1730, 3799
Brain drain 4875
Branco, Garcia Mendes Castelo 806
Brands 2363, 3893
Bread 1398, 4354
Breast-feeding 1540, 1548, 1551, 1584, 2129, 2699, 2704, 2713, 2863, 4816, 4824
Brides 2744
Bridewealth 2734
Bridges 1076
Brink, André 4151
British Empire 694, 696, 702, 703, 710, 717, 762, 791, 792, 3755, 4215, 4336
Broadcasting 375, 1786
see also: Religious broadcasting
Broca, Paul 110, 3799
Brong 992
Bronze 322, 912, 1017, 1067, 1199, 3556
Bronze Age 445, 449, 516, 820, 835, 838, 840, 868, 881, 882, 885, 906, 908, 912, 924, 965, 991, 995, 1000, 1017, 1052, 1053, 1158, 1184, 1205, 1263, 1285, 1292, 1305, 1307, 1309, 1314, 1315, 1324, 1366, 1391, 1397, 1409, 2226, 2590, 2996
Brotherhoods 2182, 2485, 2628, 4622
Brothers 3125
Buck, Pearl S. 3079
Buddhism 105, 2099, 2345, 2800, 2973, 3079, 3155, 3162-3164, 3166-3177, 3180-3195, 3197-3208, 3210-3214, 3231, 3261, 3291, 3297, 3313, 3317, 3379, 3496, 3531, 3532, 3549, 3593, 3717, 3826, 3860, 4095, 4284, 4471
Buddhist art 3211
Budgeting 4937
Budha, Baba 3461
Buildings 667, 906, 965, 1015, 1016, 1021, 1022, 1046, 1053, 1069, 1091, 1102, 1166, 1167, 1181, 1207, 1420, 2227, 3354, 3840, 3842-3844, 3855, 3861, 4148, 4319, 4345, 4749
Bulgarian language 1917
Bullfighting 4305

Bunting, Edward 647
Bureaucracy 818, 2625, 3107, 4365
Burgh, James 713
Burial 147, 258, 365, 475, 838, 869, 873, 874, 878, 970, 991, 1129, 1205, 1220, 1240, 1267, 1279, 1282, 1284-1287, 1291, 1293, 1296, 1298, 1300, 1301, 1304, 1307, 1308, 1311, 1312, 1317, 1318, 1320, 1321, 1323, 1325, 1327, 1328, 1464, 2494, 2604, 2783, 2794, 2799, 2801, 3135, 3604, 3689
Burton, Richard F. 291
Bushmen 2398, 4436, 4638
Business 74, 1926, 2257, 2644, 2740
Business history 2368
Business partnership 2269, 4648, 4671, 4759, 4786
Butchering 1281
Butler, William 97
Bwa 2945, 3529
Byzantine civilization 484, 1021, 1022, 1122, 1205, 1287, 1293, 1365, 1434, 1438, 1722, 4247
Byzantine Empire 529
Cabanis, Pierre-Jean-Georges 3728
Cabrera, Lydia 3981
Cadornega, António de Oliveira de 806
Calderón de la Barca, Pedro 3862
Caldwell, Robert 1894
Calendars 166, 1979, 2256, 3407, 3649, 3740, 3741, 3745, 3748, 4095, 4428
Calligraphy 3330, 4223
Calungsod, Pedro 3220
Camels 454, 462, 1367, 2429
Camping 2085, 4310
Camps 498, 698, 1282, 2119, 2148, 2697, 2803
Camus, Albert 3728
Canadians 1796, 2122
Cancer 3769, 3805
Canoes 360, 1375, 4343
Canto, José do 2281
Capital 2068, 2293, 2456, 4932
    see also: Human capital
Capital cities 450, 466, 521, 2154
Capital market 4671
Capital punishment 3013
Capitalism 777, 778, 2229, 2290, 2323, 2325, 2332, 2345, 2363, 2385, 2399, 2459, 2955, 3175, 3409, 3895, 4218, 4351, 4402, 4483
Capitalist development 2337
Capitalist economy 2290
Capitalist society 3534
Cardew, Michael 2238

Care of the aged 2655, 2770
Cargo cults 3512
Caring 2762
Carlos de Chelmichi, José Conrado 323, 707
Carnivals 2334, 3877, 4363, 4366
Carpo, Arsénio Pompílio Pompeu de 692
Cartoons 4100
Casas, Bartolomé de las 4234
Case studies 98, 159, 217, 282, 352, 508, 910, 1568, 1786, 1897, 1904, 1909, 2115, 2164, 2189, 2213, 2244, 2292, 2308, 2309, 2312, 2402, 2441, 2446, 2455, 2503, 2504, 2527, 2859, 2874, 2876, 2995, 3163, 3579, 3782, 4339, 4353, 4472, 4497, 4545, 4588, 4645, 4683, 4692, 4698, 4703, 4706, 4716, 4719, 4730, 4731, 4740, 4743, 4752, 4756, 4769, 4783, 4788, 4849, 4871, 4879, 4912, 4916, 4924, 4926, 4928, 4937
Casement, Roger 4182
Cash crops 2207, 4689
Cassava 2297
Caste 1506, 1508, 2197, 2569, 2614, 2615, 2617, 2620, 2623, 2624, 2627, 3056, 3075, 3082, 3284, 3288, 3683, 4106, 4596, 4843
Catholic Church 110, 122, 567, 600, 766, 2760, 2861, 3051, 3246, 3634, 3799, 4371, 4476
Catholicism 105, 565, 732, 736, 2617, 2729, 2769, 2966, 3217, 3225, 3230, 3231, 3256, 3263, 3637, 4131, 4441
Catholics 754, 3230, 4441
Cattle 2430, 2437, 2438, 2445, 3917
Cattle breeding 101, 2437, 2438, 2690
Cattle production 2437, 2438
Cattle-breeders 4038
Causal inference 224
Causality 1567, 1872, 2137, 2490, 2532, 3590
Cause 4812
Celibacy 2127, 2904
Cells 1699, 3728
Celts 916, 1361, 1928, 3240, 3697
Censorship 3714
Censuses 308, 2143, 2145, 2673
    see also: Population censuses
Centre-periphery relations 2511
Ceramics 316, 378, 838, 909, 951, 1324, 1369, 1370, 1374, 1376, 1388, 1404, 1415, 1424, 1425, 1427, 1431, 1439, 1440, 1445, 2208, 2249, 2250, 3737, 3839
Cereals 900, 2261, 4671
Ceremonies 285, 374, 911, 2252, 2563, 2579, 2602, 2665, 2700, 2870, 2943, 3307, 3514, 3525, 3556, 3778, 4011, 4373, 4602

Césaire, Aimée 4159
Cœuroy, André 3929
Ch'ien-lung [Emperor] 4155
Chalcolithic Age 825, 1158, 1243, 1440
Chalukya Bhima [II] 1437
Cham 4153
Chambri 2370, 2990, 4620
Chamoiseau, Patrick 3980
Chamorro 120, 2637, 4028
Chane 3559
Chanoine, Julien 3608
Chantepie de la Saussaye, P.D. 5, 226
Chaos theory 3144
Character 3110, 3467, 3878, 3991, 3995, 4162
    see also: National character
Charisma 3221, 3265
Charismatic leaders 3262
Charity 3163, 3187, 3468, 3693, 4381, 4708
Charwe 767, 3577
Chavin 3601
Chemicals 912, 2235, 3789
Chemistry 60
Cherokee 2330
Chess 4333
Chiefdom 2073, 2488, 2565
Chiefs 711, 733, 2195, 2564, 2792, 3007
Chieftaincy 2568
Child abuse 4722
Child adoption 2648, 2685, 4416
Child care 603, 2648, 2654, 2668, 2701, 2712,
    2716, 2863, 3774
Child custody 2736, 3010
Child development 1405, 1460, 1469, 1470,
    1540, 1550-1554, 1557, 1559, 1569, 1576,
    1790, 1936, 2698, 2715, 2775, 3832,
    4378, 4506, 4542, 4754
Child fostering 2648, 2685
Child health 443, 1544, 1548, 1572, 1577,
    1582, 1584, 2686, 2703, 2708, 2711, 4822,
    4844, 4885
Child labour 2463, 2863, 4668
Child mortality 2129, 2149, 2701, 2704, 2720,
    3774
Child protection 4722
Child rearing 603, 1584, 1603, 1706, 2633,
    2698, 2716, 4528, 4591
Child welfare 2648
Childhood 1541, 2697, 2803, 2805, 4271,
    4561
Children 557, 1327, 1427, 1460, 1466, 1475,
    1540, 1541, 1554, 1561, 1565, 1568,
    1572, 1576, 1588, 1592, 1783, 1790,
    1936, 2085, 2119, 2138, 2463, 2502, 2633,
    2639, 2645, 2648, 2698, 2703, 2708,
    3278, 3572, 3574, 3800, 3930, 3982,

3990, 4004, 4244, 4306, 4310, 4433,
    4519, 4521, 4586, 4826, 4879, 4884
    see also: Infants
Children's rights 2863, 4722
Chimalpahin, Domingo 214
Chimpanzees 1604, 1605, 1608, 1636, 1638,
    1648, 1653, 1663, 1673, 1701, 1709,
    1716, 1720, 3771
Chin 2044, 2045
Chinese 642, 1796, 1803, 1877, 2021, 2036,
    2722, 3156, 3397, 3613, 3681, 3700,
    4203, 4451
Chinese languages 54, 2019, 2026, 2047
Chokwe 3614
Chokye Gyaltsen, Jampal Namdol 3185
Chongjo [King] 2339, 2574, 2581
Choreography 3867
Christian churches 3226, 3241, 4371
    see also: Catholic Church, Coptic Church,
    Denominationalism, Hutterites,
    Lutheranism, Mennonites, Methodist
    churches, Orthodox Church, Pietism,
    Protestant churches, Russian Orthodox
    Church, Uniate churches
Christian orders
    see: Franciscans, Jesuits
Christianity 86, 119, 329, 451, 473, 514, 591,
    611, 644, 722, 732, 777, 796, 808, 1046,
    1070, 1092, 1871, 2099, 2232, 2598,
    2682, 2755, 2875, 2909, 3042, 3155,
    3160, 3215, 3217, 3221-3223, 3227, 3228,
    3232, 3236-3238, 3242, 3245, 3248-3250,
    3253, 3259-3261, 3264-3266, 3268, 3350,
    3400, 3411, 3417, 3435, 3437, 3460, 3521,
    3535, 3554, 3580, 3591, 3593, 3622,
    3625, 3627, 3635, 3636, 3640, 3641,
    3645, 3647, 3648, 3721, 3822, 3856,
    3915, 4114, 4183, 4264, 4462, 4472
    see also: Catholicism, Pentecostalism
Christianization 3233, 3622
Christians 451, 473, 1454, 2121, 2993, 3026,
    3089, 3223, 3235, 3239, 3327, 3374, 3411,
    3615, 3630
Christmas 4372
Chromosomes 1500, 1501, 1721
Chronology 387, 445, 460, 475, 523, 537, 575,
    824, 826, 839, 842, 884, 889, 902, 912,
    926, 943, 951, 1016, 1248, 1290, 1324,
    1340, 1341, 1352, 1373, 1376, 1403,
    1430, 1443, 1468, 1516, 1535, 2302,
    3369, 4161
Chukchee 1732, 1825
Chung, Kuan 2985
Church and state 3186, 3287, 3610

Church history 86, 3215, 3224, 3247, 3266, 3648

Churches 81, 323, 700, 707, 1012, 1018, 1022, 1026, 1038, 1046, 1070, 1075, 1080, 1085, 1092, 1167, 1351, 1381, 2018, 2755, 3152, 3219, 3241, 3256, 3260, 3591, 3610, 3623, 3631, 3636, 3642, 3727, 3822, 3856, 3915, 4131

Cinema 55, 442, 3731, 3977, 4099, 4105, 4136, 4139, 4523, 4574

Circumcision 2888, 2889, 3267, 4889

Circus 3877

Cities 450, 496, 563, 906, 989, 1083, 1090, 1099, 1102, 1106, 1115, 1116, 1149, 1203, 1204, 1229, 1250, 1942, 2092, 2209, 2211, 2212, 2217, 2224, 2228, 2789, 3145, 3650, 3656, 3853, 3918, 4124, 4168, 4186, 4317, 4580, 4604, 4759, 4806, 4813, 4934, 4937, 4939
see also: Capital cities, Megacities

Citizen participation 2826, 2834, 3340, 4406, 4742

Citizens 748, 2457, 2967, 2976, 3006, 3328

Citizenship 784, 2457, 2516, 2933, 2936, 2989, 4606

Civil rights 680, 4465, 4627, 4791

Civil society 694, 2210, 2491, 2775, 3832, 3975, 4665, 4721, 4820, 4830

Civil war 2532, 3590, 4792

Civilization 148, 371, 467, 596, 638, 702, 737, 799, 2476, 2480, 2647, 3035, 3079, 3137, 3199, 3656, 3743, 4221, 4471, 4501, 4592
see also: Ancient civilization, Classical civilizations, Eastern civilization, History of civilization, Medieval civilization, Modern civilization, Western civilization

Clans 41, 190, 470, 1834, 2509, 2567, 2597, 2681

Clapperton, Hugh 584

Clark-Bekederemo, J.P. 3933, 4059

Class 247, 563, 629, 760, 909, 1529, 1540, 1735, 1817, 1989, 2196, 2208, 2496, 2531, 2596, 2618, 2619, 2622, 2625, 2626, 2746, 2942, 2955, 3066, 3105, 3843, 4266, 4298, 4378, 4414, 4435, 4468, 4754, 4831, 4858, 4895
see also: Aristocracy, Middle class, Working class

Class differentiation 4748

Class relations 563

Classical archaeology 464, 505, 513, 520, 569, 915, 1069, 1161, 1234, 1297, 1348

Classical civilizations 451, 459, 463, 464, 471, 505, 513, 520, 528, 569, 905, 915, 1014, 1047, 1069, 1093, 1098, 1110, 1113, 1134,

1161, 1165, 1173, 1225, 1234, 1252, 1255, 1297, 1348, 1361, 2343, 2871, 3697, 4592

Classical literature 1819, 4215, 4231

Classical music 118, 3894, 3931, 3964

Classification 223, 270, 284, 310, 910, 1062, 1373, 1385, 1719, 1729, 1741, 1752, 1996, 1999, 2022, 2098, 2537, 2950, 2999, 3753, 3757, 3905, 3953

Clause 1756, 1848, 1992

Clay 349, 2206

Clergy 3618, 3637, 3642

Clientelism 2558

Climate 455, 857, 1382, 1533, 2065, 2225, 2271, 2283, 4772
see also: Meteorology, Weather

Climate change 833, 847, 857, 1190, 4666, 4763, 4785

Clinical psychology 221, 4525, 4543, 4546, 4547

Clinton, Bill 4548

Cloning 1616

Clothes 174, 760, 1360, 1423, 2928, 2936, 2942, 2943, 2951, 2957, 2960, 4003, 4121, 4164

Clothing industry 2456

Clubs 2085, 2586, 3909, 4309, 4310

Cluster analysis 943

Co-operatives 2440, 4609
see also: Fishery co-operatives

Coal 1829

Coal industry 1829

Coal mining 1829

Coalitions 2218, 2587, 3068

Coast Salish 1322

Coastal areas 298, 806, 1151, 1246, 1825, 2079, 2117, 2134, 2260, 2313, 2362, 3084, 4618, 4794

Coasts 251, 2429

Cocaine 3004

Cocoa 2258, 2275, 2400, 2968

Coffee 738

Cognition 38, 170, 224, 302, 438, 542, 1004, 1405, 1520, 1547, 1612, 1636, 1693, 1730, 1790, 1832, 1921, 1973, 2080, 2201, 2895, 3512, 3574, 3662, 3789, 3842, 3941, 4507, 4529
see also: Social cognition

Cognitive development 1547, 4506, 4507

Cohabitation 2160

Cohort analysis 2121, 2131, 3074, 4575

Cold War 658, 2857, 3076, 3975

Colenso, Harriette 817

Collaboration 53, 291, 404, 3005, 4548

Collective action 2264, 4399

Collective attitudes 3074

Collective behaviour 3048, 3633, 4459
Collective consciousness 3074
Collective memory 155, 373, 530, 544, 969,
    1782, 1828, 2165, 3654, 3656, 3664-3666,
    3687, 3735, 3912, 4012, 4105, 4357,
    4445, 4477, 4498, 4522, 4523, 4544
Collective security 4746
Collectivism 2376
Collectivization 2278
Colonial government 125, 323, 592, 602, 636,
    681, 682, 684-686, 688, 703, 705, 707,
    715, 721, 727, 731, 748, 770, 771, 773,
    780, 785, 788, 805, 816-818, 2120, 2270,
    2362, 2573, 2828, 2829, 2976, 2981,
    3031, 3057, 4215
Colonial history 43, 97, 100, 106, 125, 132,
    155, 184, 228, 254, 317, 318, 323, 326,
    335, 348, 391, 437, 530, 532, 540, 548,
    551, 553, 558, 575, 580, 583, 584, 592,
    601, 602, 613, 614, 616, 619, 622, 627,
    636, 637, 641, 643, 644, 650, 651, 658,
    664, 673, 675, 678, 681-686, 688-690,
    692-694, 696, 697, 699, 701-703, 705-
    707, 710-715, 717-721, 725, 726, 728,
    730, 731, 733, 734, 736, 737, 739-742,
    745-748, 750, 752, 754, 760-763, 766,
    768, 770-773, 775, 780-783, 786, 789-
    791, 793-798, 800-803, 806, 808, 810-
    814, 816-818, 893, 969, 991, 1289, 1392,
    1428, 1429, 1761, 1792, 1794, 1915,
    2078, 2082, 2110, 2120, 2128, 2223, 2262,
    2274, 2298, 2299, 2336, 2355, 2362,
    2368, 2383, 2385, 2401, 2424, 2443,
    2500, 2507, 2508, 2510, 2522, 2553,
    2559, 2573, 2608, 2617, 2630, 2744,
    2754, 2774, 2827, 2833, 2933, 2942,
    2976, 2981, 2993, 3031, 3032, 3047,
    3057, 3058, 3104, 3216, 3224, 3286,
    3287, 3353, 3402, 3415, 3533, 3608,
    3614, 3617, 3618, 3630, 3637, 3701,
    3735, 3755, 3778, 3829, 3844, 3880,
    4005, 4007, 4098, 4128, 4134, 4150,
    4166, 4173, 4176, 4182, 4183, 4187,
    4191, 4215, 4234, 4245, 4260, 4270,
    4275, 4285, 4298, 4302, 4312, 4431,
    4437, 4457, 4458, 4501, 4608, 4657
    see also: Precolonial history
Colonial policy 636, 684, 784, 2120, 2989,
    3746, 4195
Colonialism 2, 14, 43, 97, 125, 155, 326, 328,
    329, 530, 532, 540, 553, 580, 583, 602,
    611, 622, 637, 641, 643, 647, 650, 651,
    662, 665, 670, 673, 675, 683, 689, 690,
    693, 694, 698, 700, 708-710, 715, 716,
    718, 720, 722, 726, 729, 731, 732, 735,
    736, 738, 746, 747, 750, 751, 753, 754,
    759, 764, 765, 770, 772, 775, 777, 780,
    787, 793, 794, 797-799, 801, 803, 804,
    808, 810, 812, 818, 969, 1432, 2082,
    2179, 2199, 2223, 2335, 2359, 2397,
    2507, 2534, 2608, 2671, 2682, 2808,
    2828, 3031, 3042, 3219, 3245, 3353,
    3594, 3596, 3624, 3709, 3829, 3844,
    4037, 4086, 4160, 4166, 4173, 4187,
    4213, 4226, 4293, 4299, 4312, 4336,
    4460, 4639, 4657, 4679, 4772
Colonies 348, 360, 493, 592, 681, 686, 697-
    699, 706, 710, 714, 721, 727, 728, 739,
    743, 746, 764, 780, 784, 787, 788, 794,
    795, 809, 811, 812, 814, 816, 817, 1617,
    1625, 1955, 2078, 2222, 2270, 2298,
    2299, 2348, 2408, 2424, 2559, 2573,
    2989, 3031, 3415, 3608, 3746, 4135,
    4166, 4173, 4458, 4472, 4650
Colonization 295, 329, 391, 449, 567, 583,
    584, 598, 608, 623, 690, 691, 696, 713,
    715, 725, 728, 759, 761, 781, 787, 797,
    803, 806, 809, 814, 1130, 1137, 1289,
    1290, 1413, 1497, 2130, 2161, 2385,
    2448, 2507, 3032, 3051, 3078, 3608,
    3746, 4195, 4215, 4630, 4639, 4643, 4655
Colour 1912, 3598, 3728, 3840
Colour blindness 1506
Columbus, Christopher 2551
Combs 3663
Comedy 1754, 3279, 4254
Commerce 529, 709, 734, 764, 2256, 2335,
    2339, 2386, 3575, 4272
Commercial law 734
Commercial policy 2339
Commercialization 3706
Commodification 738, 1448, 2325, 2363,
    2381, 2780, 2920, 2923, 2924, 2929,
    2952, 2956, 2961, 3895, 3921
Commodities 2323
Commodity prices 4663
Common law 2656, 2837, 2972
Commonwealth 43, 616
Communalism 2408, 4650
Communes 3544, 4105, 4523
Communication 148, 182, 271, 526, 544, 991,
    1362, 1525, 1743, 1754, 1762, 1771-1773,
    1798, 1803, 1809, 1811, 1921, 1925, 2453,
    2955, 3015, 3537, 3598, 3606, 3654,
    3668, 4030, 4094, 4096, 4099, 4119, 4143,
    4202, 4434
    see also: Intercultural communication,
    Interpersonal communication, Non-verbal
    communication, Oral communication,

Political communication, Verbal communication, Visual communication
Communications technology 1782, 2800, 3207, 3664
Communism 218, 319, 2480, 2500, 2964, 3968, 3988
Communist parties 2500
Communists 2557
Community 3, 253, 307, 425, 717, 937, 1361, 1426, 1623, 1716, 1773, 1786, 2067, 2075, 2078, 2089, 2103, 2104, 2154, 2158, 2164, 2165, 2184, 2201, 2202, 2204, 2210, 2264, 2284, 2294, 2307, 2324, 2331, 2332, 2359, 2487, 2509, 2557, 2592, 2599, 2602, 2647, 2664, 2665, 2668, 2672, 2686, 2818, 2828, 2829, 2836, 2844, 2907, 3011, 3026, 3105, 3352, 3450, 3483, 3530, 3558, 3629, 3697, 3710, 3720, 3723, 3739, 3847, 3886, 4024, 4031, 4075, 4134, 4184, 4262, 4337, 4353, 4355, 4399, 4431, 4451, 4456, 4475, 4478, 4479, 4498, 4536, 4545, 4573, 4611, 4654, 4752, 4780, 4799, 4804, 4820, 4871, 4882, 4938
see also: Ethnic communities, International community, Local communities, Religious communities, Rural communities, Scientific communities, Urban communities
Community care 285, 2870
Community development 32, 2210, 4709, 4723, 4726, 4733, 4741, 4795, 4832, 4833, 4866, 4868, 4873, 4915, 4929, 4931
Community organization 2210, 4442, 4924
Community participation 2309, 2402, 4714, 4732, 4795, 4832, 4927, 4937
Community power 4301, 4607
Comparative advantage 2226
Comparative analysis 286, 330, 415, 663, 733, 984, 1283, 1424, 1445, 1455, 1471, 1479, 1618, 1743, 1909, 1932, 2002, 2124, 2413, 2425, 2499, 2527, 2687, 2689, 2853, 3092, 3110, 3112, 3115, 3125, 3313, 3383, 3661, 3668, 3713, 3743, 3848, 3906, 4048, 4167, 4219, 4270, 4282, 4513, 4656, 4659, 4710
Comparative linguistics 1847, 1885, 1896, 1920, 2002
Comparative religion 5, 105, 167, 209, 210, 226, 227, 300, 3231, 3235, 3294, 3374, 3527, 3560, 3561
Compensation 2373
Competition 1621, 2334, 2436, 3907, 3956, 4320, 4368, 4447, 4598, 4750
Competitiveness 718, 4671

Complex societies 456, 1372, 2358, 4649
Composers 118, 3904, 3919, 3924, 3931, 3933, 4059, 4263
Computers 30, 436, 1629, 1773, 1778, 1779, 1782, 2019, 3664, 3964
Concentration camps 654, 4508
Conceptualization 56, 98, 154, 167, 195, 207, 213, 233, 262, 272, 320, 388, 435, 436, 634, 1751, 1855, 2490, 2503, 2992, 3062, 3111, 3162, 3199, 3280, 3298, 3431, 3441, 3466, 3565, 3567, 3685, 3728, 3816, 3942, 4107, 4463, 4471, 4537, 4549
Condé, Maryse 4170
Conflict 329, 395, 641, 654, 705, 712, 719, 993, 1496, 1643, 1681, 1682, 2076, 2127, 2188, 2202, 2221, 2278, 2289, 2409, 2436, 2456, 2529, 2532, 2550, 2583, 2608, 2653, 2724, 2782, 2851, 2977, 2987, 3035, 3038, 3040, 3047, 3048, 3057, 3115, 3267, 3470, 3492, 3569, 3570, 3590, 3783, 3907, 4032, 4034, 4475, 4630, 4706, 4799, 4820
see also: Border conflicts, Generation conflicts, Interethnic conflict, International conflicts, Linguistic conflict, Marital conflict, Political conflicts, Regional conflicts, Religious conflicts
Conflict resolution 395, 1681, 1682, 2446, 2529, 3001, 3038, 3176, 3569
see also: Third-party intervention
Confucianism 79, 2099, 2574, 2970, 3136-3138, 3155, 3518
Congenital deformities 1663
Congregations 640, 3230, 3443, 3461, 3464, 3623, 4441
Consanguineous marriage 2748
Consanguinity 2748
Consciousness 173, 186, 243, 303, 660, 1739, 1876, 2840, 3079, 3143, 3149, 3291, 3481, 3494, 3499, 3691, 3728, 3761, 3821, 3833, 4328, 4450, 4668
Consensus 2724, 2851, 3544, 4824
Conservation 158, 564, 667, 909, 1028, 1064, 1510, 1626, 1669, 2084, 2203, 2208, 2311, 2402, 2830, 2844, 3849, 4294, 4319, 4344, 4345, 4671, 4694, 4773, 4782, 4799, 4805, 4850
see also: Nature conservation, Soil conservation
Conservation of monuments 1358
Conservatism 754
Conservatives 754
Consonants 1858, 1922, 1989, 1991, 2058
Constitution 2511, 2523, 2540, 3036, 3059, 4253, 4629, 4643

Constitutional history 2511
Constitutional reform 2511, 3020, 4418
Constitutionalism 815, 4631
Construction activity 1012, 1104, 1375, 1838,
  2394, 3855, 4594
Construction industry 2456
Constructivism 56, 168, 207, 244, 3139, 3708,
  3739, 4289, 4412
Consulates 658, 721
Consumer behaviour 1409
Consumer culture 2322, 2326, 2462
Consumer society 664, 2322
Consumers 2189, 2390, 4388, 4610, 4618,
  4794
Consumption 175, 1407, 2323, 2324, 2327,
  2328, 2390, 2401, 2450, 2462, 2923,
  2946, 2948, 2963, 3256, 3725, 4116, 4131,
  4382, 4389, 4391, 4394, 4397, 4440, 4809
  see also: Food consumption, Mass
  consumption
Contemporary art 3881, 4107
Contemporary music 3969
Content analysis 331, 1921
Contextual analysis 212, 230, 415, 431, 1753,
  1780
Contraception 2640, 2695, 2710, 2717, 2723,
  2857, 2869, 2889, 2892, 2893, 2903,
  2905, 3076, 3810, 4869, 4889, 4901
Contraceptive methods 2695, 2723, 2726,
  2892, 2903, 2905, 3810
Contracts 2983
Convergence 1791, 4400
Cooking 1398, 4376, 4379, 4396
Cooperation 172, 2093, 2285, 2352, 4393,
  4660
Coopers 1401
Copper 358, 908, 912, 1397, 2226
Copper Age 820, 1376, 1397
Copper mines 580
Coptic Church 502, 1861, 2899
Copyright 3895, 3921
Corporate culture 380
Correlation 283, 1449, 1457, 1481, 1542,
  2123, 2634, 2687, 2935, 3028, 3142, 3780
Correll family 2265, 2730
Correspondence 110, 122, 334, 600, 721,
  1926, 2259, 2987, 3304, 3403, 3799,
  3945, 4178, 4372
Corruption 2258, 2278, 2513, 2555, 2659,
  2971
  see also: Political corruption
Cortés, Hernán 802
Cosmogony 3124, 3236, 3350, 3711
Cosmology 105, 214, 299, 588, 652, 828, 852,
  1036, 1320, 1837, 2069, 2099, 2544,

2551, 2602, 2665, 3052, 3111, 3128, 3131,
  3135, 3155, 3168, 3231, 3400, 3510,
  3605, 3650, 3653, 3657, 3659, 3672,
  3680, 3730, 3752, 3764, 4035, 4098,
  4397, 4484
Cosmopolitanism 777, 2182, 4622
Cost of living 2455
Cost-benefit analysis 2588
Cost-effectiveness 3011, 4870
Costs 2226, 3011, 4804
  see also: Distribution costs, Labour costs,
  Production costs, Social costs, Transaction
  costs
Cotton 727, 2270, 4912
Cotton production 2415
Couceiro, Henrique Mitchel Paiva 754
Council of Europe 972
Counselling 2717, 2893, 3834
Counterculture 3619
Countries
  see: Arab countries, Eastern countries
Countryside 2198, 2578, 4332, 4796
Coup d'État 4533
Courts 516, 2996, 3330, 3724, 3916, 3937,
  3963
  see also: Supreme Court
Courtship 2683
Craft 322, 1365, 1400, 1405, 1423, 1439,
  2233, 2234, 2236-2239, 2242, 2243, 2246,
  2247, 2249, 2250, 2253, 2644, 4129,
  4453, 4848
Craft workers 1441, 2246, 4848
Craniology 899, 1458, 1460-1462, 1464-1466,
  1509, 1524
Craniometry 628, 1460, 1462, 1463
Creation myths 3124, 3131, 3133, 3625
Creativity 1033, 3170, 3255, 3354, 3731,
  3841, 3886, 3929, 3958, 3965, 4039,
  4099, 4111, 4123, 4126, 4133, 4184, 4265,
  4465, 4593, 4610
Credit 4851, 4897, 4911
  see also: Microfinance, Rural credit
Credit market 4911
Credit policy 4847
Cree 1981, 3545
Cremation 147, 1323, 3225
Creole languages 252, 1724, 1749, 1757,
  1789, 1791, 2011-2017, 4170
Creoles 252, 821, 1791, 2013, 2621, 2886,
  3980, 4452
Creolization 2157, 2312, 3061, 3981
Crime 599, 970, 2738, 2785, 3005, 3006, 4280
  see also: War crimes
Criminal anthropology 633, 3008
Criminal jurisdiction 3011

Criminal justice 3004, 3011
Criminal law 2988
Criminality 3005
Criminology 3005
Crisis management 2549
Crispina, Julia 486
Critical theory 183, 1777, 2934, 3801, 4494
Criticism 180, 230, 266, 514, 1723, 1735,
    1736, 1780, 2570, 2909, 2955, 3229,
    3238, 3444
    see also: Literary criticism
Crop diversification 2258, 2277, 2314
Crop rotation 2276
Crops 2261, 2304, 4825
    see also: Cash crops
Cross-cultural analysis 167, 182, 980, 1584,
    1772, 2374, 2579, 2649, 2680, 2712,
    2791, 3193, 3791, 3942, 4419, 4521,
    4527, 4540, 4593, 4641
Cross-national analysis 1375, 2207, 2289,
    2568, 2706, 3028, 3112
Cross-sectional analysis 1541, 1578
Cult of the dead 2929
Cult of the saints 3240
Cult places 829
Cultivation practices 2260, 2269, 2272, 2295,
    2296, 2302, 2304, 2319, 2321, 4766, 4774
Cults 105, 521, 1040, 2321, 2345, 3175, 3217,
    3231, 3284, 3347, 3496, 3519-3521, 3528,
    3534, 3535, 3554, 3562, 3563, 3578,
    3579, 3591, 3601, 3611, 3715, 3822, 4386
    see also: Ancestor cults, Cargo cults
Cultural adaptation 1543, 2325, 3904, 4419,
    4603, 4619, 4761
Cultural alienation 2691
Cultural anthropology 45, 115, 120, 157, 163,
    166, 177, 182, 197, 205, 213, 245, 259,
    262, 414, 438, 572, 869, 1739, 1810,
    1878, 2428, 2472, 2518, 2563, 2699,
    2992, 3065, 3107, 3109, 3513, 3548,
    3649, 3698, 3948, 3954, 4049, 4093,
    4100, 4149, 4261, 4308, 4427, 4428,
    4439, 4491, 4500, 4513, 4517, 4593, 4625
Cultural areas 1849
Cultural assimilation 1551, 2685, 3097, 3193,
    3943, 4458, 4479, 4597
Cultural attitudes 399
Cultural authenticity 1774, 3698, 3699
Cultural behaviour 393
Cultural capital 130, 353, 2215, 4491
Cultural change 338, 597, 880, 980, 1745,
    2003, 2126, 2212, 2325, 2370, 2427,
    2473, 2482, 2527, 2630, 2643, 2990,
    3555, 3660, 3674, 3903, 4126, 4367,

4408, 4414, 4487, 4583, 4590, 4592,
    4593, 4595, 4601, 4610, 4620, 4685, 4812
Cultural contact 228, 326, 391, 447, 531, 532,
    553, 554, 583, 585, 593, 611, 625, 627,
    637, 641, 643, 665, 673, 677, 696, 714,
    720, 738, 742, 747, 770, 786, 798, 808,
    810, 916, 991, 1015, 1039, 1343, 1362,
    1733, 1757, 1809, 1871, 1985, 2016,
    2334, 2370, 2477, 2497, 2563, 2608,
    2990, 3042, 3044, 3079, 3097, 3137,
    3230, 3268, 3533, 3576, 3612, 3624,
    3625, 3743, 3829, 3918, 3925, 3926,
    3965, 4026, 4115, 4150, 4227, 4265, 4405,
    4408, 4430, 4441, 4516, 4590, 4597, 4620
Cultural continuity 487, 1298, 3690, 4414,
    4507
Cultural crises 867, 2691, 3543
Cultural development 556, 572, 881, 3380,
    4481
Cultural differences 147, 215, 269, 663, 787,
    1323, 1766, 1796, 1925, 2699, 2853,
    3055, 3112, 3397, 3613, 3653, 4395, 4484,
    4494, 4603, 4625, 4761
Cultural diffusion 3097, 4115, 4119, 4597
Cultural diversity 3108, 4129, 4336, 4408,
    4420, 4590, 4649
Cultural dualism 3065
Cultural dynamics 3733, 3994, 4633
Cultural ecology 867, 1584
Cultural exhibitions 347, 2933, 2940, 4110
Cultural factors 193, 1486, 1512, 1737, 2116,
    2118, 2139, 2150, 2345, 2363, 3029, 3050,
    3175, 3695, 3803, 4549
Cultural heritage 78, 155, 323, 326, 434, 487,
    524, 530, 683, 707, 962, 968, 969, 996,
    1028, 1033, 1035, 1039, 1043, 1053,
    1071, 1169, 1179, 1187, 1189, 1212, 1223,
    1226, 1232, 1255, 1386, 1438, 1774,
    2291, 2317, 2691, 3049, 3078, 3365,
    3558, 3624, 3671, 3698-3701, 3847, 3858,
    3861, 3866, 3926, 3949, 4000, 4080,
    4299, 4308, 4325, 4327, 4329, 4331,
    4346, 4360, 4401, 4468, 4604, 4775
    see also: Preservation of cultural heritage
Cultural history 12, 27, 48, 58, 81, 141, 200,
    231, 254, 273, 298, 326, 340, 371, 376,
    508, 543, 550, 555, 556, 578, 585, 596,
    606, 611, 631, 642, 647, 649, 651-653,
    659, 662, 664, 666, 694, 714, 747, 782,
    810, 946, 962, 999, 1032, 1035, 1060,
    1189, 1333, 1361, 1395, 1760, 2134, 2175,
    2324, 2482, 2691, 2740, 2857, 2936,
    2957, 2986, 2995, 3042, 3076, 3085,
    3132, 3333, 3353, 3357, 3431, 3458,
    3479, 3483, 3513, 3535, 3554, 3576,

3697, 3709, 3852, 3880, 3928, 3939,
3948, 3951, 3965, 3966, 3991, 4007,
4021, 4049, 4050, 4053, 4066, 4093,
4107, 4150, 4167, 4231, 4233, 4247,
4267, 4343, 4401, 4439, 4457, 4458, 4500
Cultural identity 130, 353, 599, 887, 2096,
2193, 2201, 2601, 2616, 2936, 2937,
3026, 3401, 3600, 3616, 3660, 3727,
3969, 4013, 4334, 4407, 4419, 4424,
4433, 4438, 4446, 4451, 4454
Cultural imperialism 611, 3042
Cultural influence 626, 798, 1443, 1874, 1932,
2744, 3049, 3078, 3122, 3848, 4044,
4160, 4383
Cultural materialism 204, 3292
Cultural nationalism 253
Cultural norms 2089, 2626, 2836
Cultural policy 972
Cultural practices 142, 1584, 2236, 2682,
2712, 2863, 3599
Cultural property 2937, 3701, 4438, 4617,
4619, 4651
Cultural relations 3037, 4311, 4479
  see also: International cultural relations
Cultural segregation 387
Cultural specificity 177, 245, 1723, 1728
Cultural studies 27, 117, 124, 149, 150, 177,
206, 244, 254, 284, 290, 316, 322, 330,
334, 341, 344, 360, 379, 382, 467, 474,
522, 527, 560, 576, 578, 579, 586, 603,
615, 620, 632, 640, 652, 653, 668, 708,
716, 729, 735, 751, 762, 769, 804, 811,
823, 878, 1012, 1015, 1032, 1055, 1067,
1076, 1086, 1096, 1316, 1331, 1333,
1336, 1339, 1395, 1423, 1433, 1527,
1774, 1783, 1805, 1819, 1862, 1865,
1871, 1945, 1950, 2047, 2078, 2090,
2092, 2100, 2113, 2117, 2176, 2234, 2241,
2260, 2330, 2384, 2395, 2436, 2440,
2451, 2467, 2476, 2484, 2492, 2496,
2501, 2526, 2556, 2580, 2592, 2600,
2622, 2632, 2641, 2658, 2685, 2695,
2716, 2733, 2759, 2760, 2762, 2805,
2817, 2848, 2857, 2861, 2866-2868, 2873,
2877, 2879, 2884, 2892, 2894, 2895,
2901, 2902, 2910, 2911, 2913, 2914, 2916,
2918, 2933, 2936, 2937, 2944, 2947,
2955, 2957, 2973, 2974, 2985, 3005,
3076, 3087, 3110, 3115, 3125, 3134, 3141,
3144, 3148, 3167, 3168, 3173, 3177,
3179, 3185, 3194-3198, 3203, 3206, 3209,
3214, 3225, 3254, 3268, 3271, 3273,
3284, 3293, 3296, 3312, 3315, 3317-3319,
3322, 3332, 3338, 3339, 3412, 3415,
3443, 3444, 3556, 3573, 3594, 3624,

3631, 3693, 3698-3700, 3702, 3707, 3717,
3796, 3810, 3831, 3839, 3852, 3869,
3874, 3885, 3890, 3891, 3906, 3909,
3943, 3954, 4007, 4025, 4028, 4061,
4064, 4076, 4086, 4093, 4115, 4154, 4155,
4167, 4170, 4177, 4178, 4194, 4203,
4207, 4227, 4228, 4231, 4233, 4238,
4246, 4247, 4261, 4267, 4280, 4303,
4333, 4364, 4365, 4380, 4427, 4434,
4438, 4446, 4452, 4457, 4468, 4470,
4483, 4491, 4499, 4500, 4548, 4561,
4563, 4570, 4612, 4631, 4637, 4641,
4729, 4758, 4771, 4878, 4891, 4898
Cultural survival 3083, 3989
Cultural systems 2449, 3158, 4908
Cultural tradition 153, 625, 666, 1024, 1033,
1782, 2202, 2482, 2588, 2598, 2691,
2707, 2734, 2777, 2834, 2911, 3431, 3458,
3548, 3551, 3627, 3664, 3669, 3684,
3696, 3701, 3732, 3840, 3866, 3891,
3902, 3928, 3981, 3984, 3992, 4097,
4351, 4355, 4363, 4365, 4396, 4406,
4507, 4512, 4586
Cultural unity 457, 2490
Cultural values 1475, 2166, 2691, 2694, 2762,
3036, 3059, 3660, 3693, 4570, 4625
Culture 31, 52, 88, 98, 115, 138, 159, 196,
210, 213, 217, 235, 240, 244, 262, 268,
274, 299, 373, 397, 433, 543, 572, 597,
712, 716, 729, 751, 851, 959, 1745, 1758,
1798, 1800, 1817, 1821, 1824, 1971,
2005, 2064, 2070, 2080, 2114, 2115, 2164,
2193, 2207, 2327, 2482, 2503, 2525,
2592, 2601, 2643, 2694, 2823, 2859,
2874, 2876, 2908, 2922, 2940, 2953,
2955, 2958, 2992, 3026, 3035, 3047,
3052, 3063, 3189, 3226, 3398, 3401,
3410, 3512, 3543, 3545, 3561, 3662,
3663, 3675, 3702, 3728, 3758, 3760,
3761, 3782, 3960, 4014, 4102, 4110, 4120,
4143, 4193, 4359, 4367, 4371, 4379,
4429, 4432, 4452, 4467, 4468, 4478,
4487, 4491, 4514, 4569, 4585, 4593,
4603, 4634, 4653, 4673, 4729, 4761,
4804, 4820, 4864
  see also: Access to culture, Ancient
  cultures, Corporate culture, Cultural
  differences, Cultural diversity, Cultural
  survival, Dominant culture, Economics of
  culture, Indigenous culture, Local culture,
  Material culture, Musical culture, National
  culture, Peasant cultures, Political culture,
  Popular culture, Sociology of culture,
  Subculture, Traditional culture, Youth
  culture

Currencies 551, 743, 2261, 2268, 2348, 2366, 2389
see also: Dollar
Current research 4582
Curriculum 3376, 4556
Customary law 268, 2416, 2417, 2425, 2972, 3015, 3017, 3018, 3020, 4418, 4659, 4722
Customary marriage 2736, 2739, 2750, 3010, 3012, 3019
Customers 1788, 2471, 4018
Customs 127, 147, 262, 651, 756, 760, 790, 809, 1323, 2149, 2291, 2374, 2472, 2474, 2579, 2613, 2647, 2649, 2684, 2720, 2738, 2785, 2789, 2838, 2942, 2992, 3065, 3109, 3512, 3536, 3678, 3694, 3807, 4358, 4369, 4373, 4376, 4403, 4496, 4579
see also: Birth customs, Marriage customs
Cybernetics 301, 4100
Cyprian [Saint] 473, 3411
Czechs 138
Dagari 2512, 4001
Dago, Ousmane Ndiaye 3714
Dalit 3082
Damage 1030
Dams 2079, 2164, 2271, 4594
Dance 166, 2291, 2838, 2943, 3513, 3585, 3649, 3867, 3868, 3871, 3879, 3886, 3890, 3892, 3906, 3933, 3939, 3949, 3960, 3967, 4059, 4428
see also: Anthropology of dance, Folk dances, Traditional dances
Dani 2629, 2714
Dante, Alighieri 3728
Dar'ī, Moses 3429
Darwich, Mahmoud 4062
Darwin, Charles 1517
Darwinism 1529, 1538
Dasan 3079, 3743
Data analysis 203, 282, 301, 313, 403, 423, 435, 436, 533, 1558, 1578, 1666, 4353, 4473, 4554, 4756, 4783, 4803, 4804
Data collection 78, 282, 286, 287, 290, 309, 403, 429, 436, 2119, 2124, 2146
Databases 313, 2057
Dating 274, 445, 509, 519, 826, 839, 849, 868, 906, 935, 1053, 1376, 1382, 3249, 3442
see also: Archaeological dating
Daughters 2131, 2722, 4006, 4835
Dayak 1067, 4320, 4598
Dead languages 1727, 3401
Deafness 40
Dealers 692
Deane, Seamus 3961

Death 147, 822, 970, 1088, 1294, 1296, 1297, 1308, 1323, 1358, 1965, 2128, 2615, 2636, 2643, 2762, 2766, 2778, 2780-2782, 2784, 2787-2791, 2800, 2924, 2929, 3036, 3059, 3207, 3225, 3515, 3722, 3803, 3828, 3949, 4003, 4047, 4083, 4189, 4231, 4263, 4276, 4512, 4518, 4539, 4541, 4546
Death rate 2636, 2778
Debī, Āśāpūrnā 2788, 4189
Debt 2336, 3344
Decadence 3909
Deceit 613, 3492, 3991, 3994, 3995, 4130
Decentralization 2210, 2219, 2288, 4612, 4616, 4671, 4710, 4874, 4882, 4907, 4932
Decision making 1539, 1639, 1693, 2174, 2185, 2322, 2713, 2721, 2772, 2948, 2965, 3015, 3395, 4307, 4660, 4742, 4790, 4928
Decolonization 611, 702, 753, 765, 784, 2989, 3042, 4171
Deconstruction 2092
Decorative art 316, 1016, 1396, 2234, 2243, 3839, 3840
Deforestation 2083, 2430, 4618, 4771, 4772, 4787, 4794, 4800, 4804
Deformations 1663
Deindustrialization 2355
Deities 105, 1040, 1072, 1941, 3150, 3177, 3231, 3270, 3273, 3281, 3284, 3298, 3302, 3535, 3717
Delinquency 2223
Demand 2141
Democracy 510, 2210, 2288, 2487, 2489, 2496, 2505, 2536, 2548, 2559, 2570, 2627, 2834, 3057, 4238, 4249, 4406, 4588, 4616, 4640, 4662, 4881, 4882, 4938
see also: Liberal democracy, Representative democracy
Democratic regimes 4649
Democratization 95, 234, 2518, 2548, 4588, 4672, 4679, 4682
Demographic change 1712, 2125, 2155, 2637, 4582
Demographic research 2626
Demography 246, 295, 646, 684, 757, 776, 838, 1488, 1522, 1558, 1625, 2105, 2120, 2126, 2127, 2130, 2133, 2135, 2144, 2147, 2155, 2380, 2406, 2540, 2634, 2637, 2655, 2662, 2710, 2742, 2743, 2749, 2752, 2768, 2770, 2876, 3615, 3704, 3739, 4431, 4479, 4736, 4840, 4859
see also: Historical demography, Paleodemography
Denominationalism 3158

Dentistry 1470
Dentition 898, 1461, 1464, 1467, 1468, 1471-1476, 1478, 1480-1485, 1590
Deontology 417, 425
Dependence relationships 2185, 2459, 4804
Deportation 323, 698, 707
Depression 4518, 4546
Deprivation 4075
Deregulation 1786, 4671, 4881
Dermatoglyphs 1454, 1455
Descent 2498, 2677, 2814
 see also: Matrilineal descent, Patrilineal descent
Desert 1211, 1335, 1366, 2102, 2473, 2609, 3658, 4046, 4798
Design 1009, 1021, 1032, 1034, 1045, 1054, 1357, 2227, 2245, 3511, 3736, 3838, 3842, 3843, 3846, 3847, 3851-3853, 3855, 4247, 4749
Desta, Makonnen 3046
Determinants 2077, 2140
Determinism 4513
 see also: Social determinism
Devaluation 2268
Developing countries 59, 621, 805, 1565, 2129, 2140, 2156, 2213, 2221, 2289, 2396, 2529, 2686, 2704, 2721, 2758, 2978, 3003, 3739, 3762, 4316, 4609, 4666, 4672, 4708, 4713, 4722, 4728, 4734, 4741, 4745, 4762, 4765, 4773, 4779, 4786, 4834, 4840, 4841, 4855, 4856, 4860, 4868, 4873, 4882, 4888, 4890, 4899, 4900, 4905, 4926, 4936
 see also: Less developed countries
Development 137, 267, 685, 770, 2111, 4300, 4329, 4340, 4596, 4682, 4692, 4712, 4727, 4729, 4732, 4768, 4799, 4829, 4839, 4855, 4856, 4859
 see also: Economic development, Rural development, Socioeconomic development, Sustainable development, Urban development
Development administration 4713, 4759
Development aid 4707, 4715, 4737, 4750, 4752, 4937
Development anthropology 3028, 4612, 4663, 4710, 4784
Development banks 4937
Development literature 4713
Development models 4784, 4802
Development planning 2219, 4711, 4713, 4714, 4726, 4735, 4738, 4763, 4779
Development plans 4717

Development policy 1573, 2222, 4340, 4612, 4720, 4739, 4763, 4788, 4838, 4845, 4847, 4874, 4915
Development programmes 2210, 4339, 4666, 4667, 4681, 4683, 4684, 4714, 4725, 4732, 4734, 4741, 4742, 4747, 4788, 4827, 4846, 4854, 4859, 4886, 4890, 4899, 4913, 4915, 4916, 4924, 4928, 4929, 4933, 4937
Development projects 2210, 2269, 2292, 2578, 3056, 3075, 4612, 4689, 4696, 4702, 4706, 4710, 4716, 4720, 4727, 4729, 4733, 4739, 4782, 4783, 4789, 4795, 4800, 4804, 4805, 4831, 4836, 4850, 4851, 4854, 4887, 4914, 4926, 4929, 4937
Development research 305, 306, 4675, 4676, 4910
Development strategies 2222, 4339, 4609, 4683, 4764, 4848, 4881, 4883, 4897
Development studies 2089, 2094, 2115, 2136, 2152, 2164, 2189, 2210, 2284, 2289, 2320, 2404, 2410, 2427, 2441, 2452, 2469, 2818, 2823, 2836, 2843, 2844, 2846, 2859, 3568, 4353, 4536, 4554, 4594, 4609, 4616, 4663, 4671-4673, 4682, 4705, 4707, 4711-4713, 4717, 4721, 4722, 4730, 4731, 4735, 4737, 4738, 4744, 4746, 4747, 4755, 4780, 4783, 4818, 4820, 4825, 4827, 4828, 4834, 4838, 4840, 4845, 4846, 4851, 4858, 4862, 4863, 4868, 4879, 4885, 4892, 4897, 4908, 4911, 4912, 4924, 4928
Development theory 4609, 4613, 4679, 4713, 4719, 4755, 4854
Developmental psychology 1513, 1561, 1790
Deviance 2912
Devils 2875, 3065, 3578
Devolution 4750
Diabetes 1560, 3836
Dialectics 79, 280, 985, 1451, 2198, 2334, 2428, 2450, 2591, 2790, 2858, 3178, 4068, 4517, 4519, 4685
Dialectology 1915, 1917, 1944, 1946, 1992
Dialects 1732, 1795, 1814, 1854, 1873, 1874, 1906, 1911, 1915, 1917, 1922-1924, 1954, 1973, 1981, 1989, 1991-1993, 1999, 2019, 2024, 2025, 2037, 2040, 2055-2057, 4032, 4446
Dialogue 66, 194, 420, 3000, 4058
Diana [Princess of Wales] 3693
Diary 97, 566, 584, 594, 637, 690, 731, 4108, 4263, 4277, 4572
Diaspora 184, 253, 538, 764, 830, 1773, 2125, 2157, 2161, 2170, 2172, 2173, 2182,

2408, 3061, 3077, 3081, 3083, 3401,
3616, 3708, 3960, 4410, 4417, 4421,
4427, 4455, 4468, 4622, 4650
Díaz del Castillo, Bernal 4245
Dictatorship 3891
Dictionaries 64, 65, 67, 68, 73, 75, 540, 570,
1769, 1770, 1778, 1779, 2055, 3545, 4176
Diet 155, 530, 744, 867, 909, 969, 1283, 1291,
1485, 1540, 1546, 1551, 1556, 1565,
1584, 1627, 1641, 1642, 1671, 1677,
1701, 2066, 2208, 3751, 3833, 4354,
4378, 4383, 4385, 4392, 4754, 4923
Dieterlen, Germaine 9, 108
Dieu, Michel 113, 1802
Difference 240, 247, 397, 2596, 3199, 4436,
4471, 4486
Digital technology 291, 436, 440, 983, 1003,
1105
Diglossia 1959
Dīn Khwārizmshāh, Jalāl al [Sultan] 446
Din Mozahheb, Nasir al 4223
Diocese 544, 700, 2209, 3219, 3654
Diplomacy 788, 2492, 4712
Diplomatic relations 658, 788, 2492
Diplomats 4712
Disability 1652, 2922, 2925, 2933, 2955
Disabled persons 40
Disaster relief 2148, 4816
Disasters 2119, 2148, 2549, 3563, 3976, 4719,
4816, 4824
see also: Natural disasters
Discourse 10, 169, 196, 230, 235, 248, 253,
266, 268, 613, 629, 1735, 1736, 1749,
1762, 1780, 1796, 1809, 1846, 1978,
2045, 2076, 2212, 2510, 2531, 2548,
2746, 2786, 2834, 2867, 2877, 2895,
2907, 3000, 3005, 3040, 3063, 3077,
3091, 3481, 3671, 3733, 3762, 3958,
3974, 4000, 4067, 4143, 4200, 4202,
4239, 4276, 4406, 4421, 4534, 4634
Discourse analysis 10, 196, 230, 235, 266,
1735, 1736, 1749, 1776, 1780, 1796,
1868, 2807, 2895, 2901, 3091, 3404,
4226, 4303, 4417, 4434, 4499, 4515,
4536, 4563
Discrimination 2714, 4581
see also: Racial discrimination, Sex
discrimination
Diseases 566, 1289, 1489, 1498, 1563, 1570,
1572, 1575, 1626, 1657, 1688, 1701,
2137, 2310, 2657, 2885, 3124, 3761-3763,
3771-3773, 3777, 3779, 3798, 3803, 3804,
3809, 3811, 3823, 3828, 3986, 4777, 4867,
4882
see also: AIDS, Epilepsy, Heart disease,

Leprosy, Malaria, Mental illness, Sexually
transmitted diseases, Smallpox
Displaced persons 2119, 2159, 2180, 2582,
4442, 4594, 4714
Displacement 2159, 2180
Dissent 3544
Distribution 861, 2338, 2390, 4382, 4394
Distribution costs 861
Districts 642, 876, 904, 950, 1048, 1512,
1579, 2419, 2510, 3281, 3854
Divākara, Siddhasena 3212
Divergence 4400
Diversification 2207
see also: Crop diversification, Production
diversification
Divination 3038, 3217, 3569, 3778
Divinities 3335, 3478
Division of labour 2081, 2431, 2651, 2692,
2828, 4853
Divorce 606, 776, 2736, 2739, 2743, 2756,
2986, 3010, 3012, 3457, 3704, 4539
DNA 1511, 1515, 1522, 1617, 1649, 1650,
1666
Doctor-patient relationship 1796
Doctors 99, 481, 2470, 2854, 3429, 3781,
3787, 4174, 4577
Documentary analysis 4183
Documentation 78, 438, 930, 1358, 3531,
4105, 4523
Documents 15, 76, 77, 80, 136, 320, 323, 355,
359, 369, 381, 581, 672, 707, 753, 801,
973, 2060, 2231, 3204, 3297, 3628, 4103,
4180, 4214
Dogma 3335
Dogon 2004, 3122, 3702
Dogs 2445
Dolgan 3101
Dollar 2533, 3073
Dolls 811, 1364
Domestic animals 920, 2340, 2445
Domestic architecture 2594
Domestic violence 2987, 3028, 3030, 4872
Domestic workers 2459, 2644, 2827, 3104
Dominant culture 3077, 4421
Domination 4037
Dominici, Gaston 3005
Doubrovsky, Serge 4562
Downward mobility 4661
Dowry 2738, 2744, 2745, 2785, 4780
Drama 3314, 3790, 3862-3866, 3872, 3874-
3876, 3878, 3882, 3885, 4226, 4349,
4425, 4465
Dramatic art 3878

Dravidian 250, 497, 1750, 1891, 1892, 1894, 1897-1900, 1902, 1907, 1908, 1956, 2638, 3968

Drawing 581, 832, 3868, 4098, 4528, 4591

Dreams 3208, 3280, 3454, 3641, 3671, 4000, 4004, 4282, 4514

Dress 991, 2928, 2936, 2946, 2948, 2951, 2957, 4116, 4164

Drinks 4379, 4390

Drought 2065, 2105, 2106, 2303, 2380, 2446, 4691, 4736, 4764, 4767, 4792

Drug abuse 3770

Drug addiction 3004

Drug trafficking 3946

Drug use 3765, 3929

Drugs 215, 507, 2109, 2874, 3766, 3782
    see also: Cocaine, Drug trafficking, Drug use, Heroin, Opiates

Drums 365, 3556, 3715, 3933, 3935, 3967, 4059

Dualism 412, 2474, 2727, 2926, 3527, 4297, 4507

Dumont, Fernand 2232

Dutch 640, 812, 1791, 1923, 3443, 3777

Dyad 1692

Dynamics 3756

Dynasty 477, 480, 481, 506, 902, 1341, 1401, 1437, 2528, 2566, 4095
    see also: Qing Dynasty, Tang dynasty

Early modern history 534, 561, 563, 606, 625, 738, 2986, 3532

Earnings 3344

Earth 2069, 3619, 3657, 3930

Earthquakes 3855, 4724

East-West relations 3079, 3137, 3743

Eastern civilization 3079

Eastern countries 2544

Ecological movements 3686

Ecologism 3619

Ecology 46, 646, 750, 1368, 1521, 1524, 1537, 1624, 1627, 1638, 1641, 1648, 1669, 1671, 1674, 1676, 1677, 1689, 1703, 1707, 1710, 1714, 1715, 1718, 1720, 2069, 2073, 2074, 2076, 2077, 2082, 2085, 2087, 2088, 2099, 2101, 2105, 2106, 2108, 2109, 2111, 2128, 2190, 2207, 2210, 2280, 2283, 2297, 2433, 2610, 2752, 2817, 3141, 3142, 3155, 3292, 3657, 3667, 4129, 4310, 4335, 4394, 4425, 4727, 4781, 4799, 4804, 4831, 4908
    see also: Animal ecology, Cultural ecology, Human ecology, Paleoecology, Social ecology

Econometrics 172

Economic activity 2244, 2347, 2385, 2394, 2819, 4809

Economic aid 4734, 4776, 4841, 4913, 4936

Economic anthropology 218, 2328, 2331, 2332, 2334, 2337, 2344, 2345, 2353, 2363, 2387, 2390, 2428, 2471, 2963, 3175, 4632, 4745

Economic behaviour 2364, 2371

Economic change 587, 633, 743, 2136, 2284, 2348, 2572, 2644, 3008, 4804, 4849, 4920

Economic conditions 288, 463, 551, 750, 809, 2082, 2150, 2196, 2210, 2343, 2345, 2383, 2424, 2430, 2637, 2833, 3175, 4266, 4367, 4447, 4645, 4667, 4713, 4739, 4829, 4831, 4832, 4842, 4854

Economic crisis 2221, 2284, 2318, 3884, 4608, 4836, 4875

Economic decline 4812

Economic development 59, 833, 1573, 2081, 2128, 2222, 2292, 2307, 2308, 2337, 2391, 2420, 2424, 2427, 2630, 2828, 2978, 2984, 3003, 4606, 4615, 4621, 4632, 4670, 4678, 4679, 4689, 4690, 4694, 4697, 4699, 4702, 4703, 4720, 4745, 4769, 4775, 4804, 4839, 4840, 4842, 4863, 4908, 4912, 4917

Economic differentiation 2426

Economic dynamics 4875

Economic geography 4609

Economic growth 4608, 4618, 4677, 4682, 4705, 4707, 4738, 4794, 4847, 4863, 4886, 4939
    see also: Endogenous growth

Economic hardship 2745

Economic history 463, 508, 551, 595, 671, 718, 726, 753, 757, 789, 835, 860, 2128, 2231, 2279, 2282, 2329, 2332, 2338, 2341, 2343, 2344, 2355, 2356, 2368, 2406, 2424, 2522, 2575, 2590, 2744, 2995, 3755, 4050, 4052, 4176, 4447, 4571
    see also: Recent economic history

Economic indicators 4817
    see also: Signalling

Economic inequality 2570

Economic integration 2359, 4614, 4682

Economic life 276, 2364

Economic organization 2364, 4790

Economic performance 2265, 2730, 4863

Economic planning 718, 4608

Economic policy 4338, 4662, 4669, 4671, 4677, 4678, 4680, 4704, 4793, 4842
    see also: Industrial policy

Economic reform 2315, 2380, 4671, 4736, 4806

Economic relations 2331, 2359, 2391, 4804
    see also: Bilateral economic relations
Economic research 43
Economic resources 2767, 3523
Economic sociology 2341, 2471
Economic systems 2345, 2448, 3175
Economic theory 218, 2141, 2331
Economics 679, 1571, 1768, 2136, 2202,
    2285, 2331, 2342, 2353, 2392, 2620,
    3063, 4339, 4634, 4668, 4683, 4804,
    4827, 4859
Economics of culture 2345, 3175
Economists 218
Ecosystems 1, 120, 2087, 2113, 2117, 2262,
    2290, 2300, 2358, 2429, 4693, 4780, 4820
Edo 1489, 3176, 3181, 3186, 3204, 3531,
    3532, 3972, 3987
Education 7, 235, 326, 352, 645, 1475, 1554,
    1749, 1816, 1969, 2085, 2463, 2675,
    2715, 2863, 2917, 2931, 3163, 3474,
    3615, 3661, 3761, 3772, 4310, 4336,
    4378, 4551, 4555-4558, 4603, 4647, 4663,
    4682, 4722, 4749, 4750, 4752, 4754,
    4755, 4757, 4758, 4760, 4761, 4858
    see also: Access to education, Agricultural
    education, Anthropology of education,
    Bilingual education, Health education,
    Higher education, History of education,
    Minority education, Pedagogy, Primary
    education, Religious education, Vocational
    education, Women's education
Education policy 1745, 1749, 1969, 3095,
    3471, 4553, 4663, 4753
Education reform 1513, 3675, 4556, 4559
Education systems 235, 3470, 4433, 4548,
    4551, 4552, 4555, 4559, 4663, 4753,
    4756, 4757
Educational development 4558, 4750, 4755
Educational institutions 26, 54, 93, 2783, 4550
Educational sociology 4551
Effects
    see: Environmental effects, Psychological
    effects
Egharevba, Jacob 4165
Ego 3508, 4540
Eisenstein, Sergei Mikhailovich 4068
Ejagham 2195
Elections 2505, 4058, 4415
    see also: Presidential elections
Electoral campaigning 1776
Electricity 4671
Electronic equipment 313
Elias, Norbert 2790

Elites 247, 253, 465, 494, 795, 1797, 2299,
    2370, 2495, 2521, 2535, 2596, 2600,
    2850, 2990, 3523, 4299, 4620, 4700
Elliott, J.H. 3227
Emancipation 681, 693, 694, 991, 4336, 4581,
    4596
Embassies 733
Embu 2094, 2843
Emigrants 99
Emigration 2460, 4479
Emotions 38, 170, 998, 1561, 1629, 1672,
    1855, 1864, 2346, 2931, 3174, 3275,
    3276, 3360, 3449, 3653, 3795, 3910,
    4060, 4283, 4484, 4509, 4512, 4518,
    4526, 4529, 4531, 4532, 4535, 4538,
    4541, 4562, 4846
    see also: Depression, Love
Empathy 2024
Empires 318, 366, 481, 501, 506, 541, 629,
    641, 678, 716, 724, 729, 735, 773, 775,
    814, 903, 933, 984, 1084, 1086, 1103,
    1934, 2168, 2479, 2488, 2493, 2497,
    2531, 2608, 2741, 2971, 3046, 3322,
    3520, 3746, 3829, 4155, 4188, 4191, 4483
    see also: British Empire, Byzantine
    Empire, Ottoman Empire
Empirical research 172, 1840, 3734, 4847
Empiricism 266, 275, 415, 2539, 3675
Employees 2468, 2955
Employers 753, 2459
Employers' organizations 753
Employment 1587, 2158, 2466, 4647, 4671,
    4672, 4827, 4828, 4858, 4914, 4929
    see also: Youth employment
Employment creation 4723
Employment opportunities 2163, 2825, 4722
Empowerment 562, 2222, 2470, 2818, 2835,
    2854, 2863, 4126, 4569, 4616, 4684,
    4722, 4723, 4746, 4820, 4828, 4833,
    4834, 4836, 4848, 4859, 4904, 4913
Enculturation 4586
Encyclopaedias 4219
Endangered species 1613, 1712, 1714
Endogenous growth 4609
Energy 429, 1556, 1600, 1628, 1676, 2324,
    3728, 4810
    see also: Wind energy
Engineering 863, 965, 3855, 4766
English language 63-65, 68, 70, 1723, 1728,
    1744, 1761, 1769, 1770, 1789, 1791,
    1797, 1801, 1803, 1808, 1810, 1814,
    1815, 1911, 1918, 1926, 1927, 1940, 1944,
    1947-1949, 1951, 1953, 1954, 1957, 1961,
    1963, 2005, 2018, 3874, 3989, 4160,
    4175, 4176, 4193, 4195

Engraving 1006, 1042, 1097, 4112
Enlightenment 3170, 3183, 3201, 3379
Enlightenment thought 16, 4466
Enterprises 986, 2468, 2471, 2644, 4820
    see also: Agricultural enterprises, Family
    firms, Multinational enterprises, Small and
    medium sized enterprises
Entertainment 371, 2584, 3731, 3972, 3987,
    4038, 4090, 4100, 4119, 4143, 4296, 4373
Entrepreneurs 2368, 4700, 4847
Entrepreneurship 2644, 2822, 4847
Environment 301, 455, 759, 838, 858, 867,
    882, 893, 913, 1190, 1524, 1533, 1562,
    1571, 1574, 1587, 1638, 1648, 1656,
    1658, 1674, 1710, 1711, 2061, 2065, 2077,
    2087, 2095, 2097, 2099, 2105, 2108, 2110,
    2111, 2190, 2210, 2213, 2218, 2224, 2225,
    2276, 2283, 2404, 2443, 2687, 3068,
    3155, 3712, 4294, 4300, 4335, 4545,
    4645, 4716, 4717, 4727, 4731, 4735,
    4763, 4768-4771, 4773, 4775, 4776, 4782,
    4787, 4790, 4797, 4799, 4806, 4807,
    4880, 4888, 4928
    see also: Environmentalism, Human
    environment, Physical environment, Rural
    environment, Social environment, Urban
    environment, Work environment
Environmental change 913
Environmental degradation 833, 1043, 2096,
    2099, 2102, 2111, 2113, 2434, 2448, 3155,
    4617, 4651, 4691, 4772, 4773, 4789,
    4793, 4799
Environmental economics 4666, 4787
Environmental effects 3759, 4776
Environmental law 4762
Environmental management 4618, 4778-4780,
    4786, 4792, 4794, 4939
Environmental movements 2311, 2587, 4796
Environmental planning 4779
Environmental policy 2445, 4666, 4791, 4842
Environmental protection 2076, 4773, 4796,
    4888
Environmental quality 2067, 4937
Environmental sociology 2587
Environmentalism 2069, 2074, 2076, 2190,
    2276, 2311, 3619, 3657, 3686, 3975, 4611,
    4612, 4799
Epic 1081, 1088, 2624, 3110, 3115, 3274,
    3290, 3293, 3295, 3302, 3305, 3863,
    3865, 3867, 3885, 3945, 3967, 4025,
    4027, 4215, 4253, 4349
Epic literature 3991, 4022
Epic poetry 3116, 3993, 4015, 4231
Epidemics 566, 3784, 4276
Epidemiology 1489, 2988, 3770, 3772

Epigraphs 916
Epigraphy 461, 1136, 1319, 1344, 1358, 3179,
    4268
Epilepsy 3777
Epistemology 199, 203, 213, 219, 238, 242,
    254, 260, 261, 275, 398, 407, 423, 542,
    2037, 2539, 2804, 2975, 3182, 3208,
    3381, 3388, 3669, 3670, 3675, 3677,
    3725, 3730, 4198, 4457, 4519, 4530, 4548
Equal opportunities 134, 4879
Equality 1529, 2626, 4238, 4510, 4829
    see also: Sex equality, Social equality
Equity 2093, 2111, 2757, 2856, 4666, 4677,
    4780, 4829, 4904
Ergonomics 296
Erosion control 4766
Eroticism 502, 2899, 3714, 3929
Error 1
Eschatology 3435, 3679
Esquivel, Laura 4242
Estates 726
Estimation 1468, 1477, 2433, 3792
Ethics 40, 153, 158, 236, 239, 277, 395, 396,
    415, 2074, 2099, 2381, 2469, 2705, 2728,
    2881, 2925, 2930, 2945, 2954, 2956,
    2970, 3000, 3002, 3138, 3155, 3174,
    3529, 3576, 3750, 3912, 4077, 4185,
    4245, 4444, 4556, 4804
    see also: Bioethics, Medical ethics,
    Professional ethics
Ethnic assimilation 2523, 2685
Ethnic communities 1822, 2074, 3956, 4012,
    4404
Ethnic development 1361, 3697
Ethnic groups 10, 215, 309, 399, 432, 574,
    648, 1426, 1491, 1492, 1503, 1579, 1583,
    1876, 2077, 2146, 2349, 2409, 2475,
    2523, 2552, 2559, 2564, 2566, 2568,
    2570, 2577, 2593, 2609, 2630, 2707,
    2712, 2802, 2834, 2876, 3060, 3069,
    3083, 3087, 3088, 3091, 3093, 3099,
    3101, 3102, 3410, 3489, 3522, 3607,
    3691, 3708, 3757, 3798, 3956, 4359,
    4398, 4400, 4406, 4409, 4410, 4413,
    4420, 4533, 4603, 4627, 4761
Ethnic minorities 41, 190, 1746, 2081, 2267,
    2432, 3083, 3760, 4433, 4474, 4627,
    4656, 4931
Ethnic pluralism 2523, 2564
Ethnic policy 4012
Ethnicity 10, 58, 146, 235, 253, 263, 376, 410,
    467, 515, 554, 582, 689, 694, 695, 708,
    812, 887, 1077, 1368, 1497, 1583, 1588,
    1749, 1773, 1822, 1925, 2066, 2109,
    2140, 2154, 2157, 2160, 2172, 2201,

2202, 2218, 2475, 2476, 2504, 2532,
2533, 2564, 2566, 2603, 2616, 2680,
2834, 2955, 3016, 3020, 3043, 3048,
3061, 3068, 3070, 3073, 3074, 3077,
3083, 3088, 3090, 3091, 3093, 3096,
3105, 3128, 3401, 3409, 3451, 3590,
3592, 3652, 4021, 4313, 4352, 4358,
4362, 4363, 4377, 4398, 4400-4421, 4424,
4426, 4431, 4433, 4434, 4447, 4450,
4453, 4463, 4468, 4475, 4479, 4485,
4488, 4492, 4498, 4504, 4528, 4587,
4590, 4591, 4603, 4639, 4653, 4657,
4720, 4761, 4798

Ethnoarchaeology 387, 555, 631, 720, 861,
  939, 992, 998, 1033, 1281, 1415, 1446,
  1760, 2236, 3845, 4377
Ethnobiology 1832, 2080, 2088, 3662, 3667,
  3747, 3753, 3785, 3786
Ethnobotany 1722, 2066, 2084, 2117, 3742,
  3747, 3757, 3785, 3833, 4636
Ethnocentrism 134, 143, 167, 227, 1766, 4395
Ethnogenesis 631, 1760
Ethnographers 92, 128, 135, 141, 142, 145,
  149, 172, 203, 237, 242, 264, 277, 293,
  392, 393, 398, 416, 419, 423, 427, 3599,
  4602
Ethnographic atlases 303
Ethnographic collections 13, 31, 130, 320,
  326, 328, 345, 353, 371
Ethnographic exhibitions 347
Ethnographic films 133, 151, 427, 439, 440,
  444
Ethnographic museums 331, 345
Ethnographic research 15, 28, 33, 47, 72, 91,
  107, 136, 141, 145, 153, 194, 211, 227,
  258, 287, 291, 293, 294, 302, 386, 388-
  390, 393, 394, 402, 405, 406, 411, 417,
  418, 420-422, 425, 426, 429, 430, 432,
  436, 783, 1505, 1825, 2214, 2321, 2377,
  2454, 2458, 2561, 2626, 2674, 2821,
  2831, 2910, 3064, 3262, 3550, 3790,
  3930, 4751, 4798
Ethnography 12, 13, 15, 31, 33, 39, 45, 47, 48,
  55, 72, 90-92, 101, 103, 105, 107, 121,
  123, 128, 130, 133, 136, 137, 141, 145,
  146, 148, 149, 158, 172, 173, 179, 191,
  193, 194, 200, 202, 203, 211, 212, 216,
  224, 225, 231, 236, 237, 239-243, 257,
  264, 267, 277, 283, 284, 293, 308, 309,
  319, 325, 326, 328, 334, 345, 351, 353,
  365, 372, 373, 376, 378, 380, 385-388,
  390-399, 403-411, 413, 417-421, 423, 425,
  426, 428, 430-433, 439-442, 487, 539,
  573, 574, 590, 597, 610, 628, 631, 783,
  804, 874, 888, 936, 1088, 1324, 1520,

1530, 1554, 1745, 1760, 1775, 1782,
1825, 1833, 1924, 1988, 2066, 2067,
2075, 2098, 2102, 2123, 2125, 2145,
2146, 2230, 2243, 2256, 2321, 2323,
2334, 2391, 2394, 2458, 2475-2477, 2479,
2481, 2524, 2538, 2540, 2604, 2652,
2656, 2672, 2675, 2676, 2696, 2751,
2812, 2821, 2823, 2831, 2837, 2938,
2964, 2979, 2988, 2999, 3004, 3021,
3062, 3083, 3092, 3096, 3101, 3142,
3152, 3231, 3245, 3288, 3345, 3347,
3349, 3356, 3361, 3446, 3519, 3536,
3550, 3555, 3565, 3575, 3581, 3585,
3589, 3594, 3625, 3628, 3656, 3661,
3664, 3700, 3715, 3737, 3767, 3858,
3870, 3878, 3926, 3936, 3945, 3948,
3988, 4026, 4032, 4125, 4133, 4178,
4255, 4265, 4331, 4366, 4386, 4410-4412,
4436, 4469, 4473, 4488, 4495, 4517,
4543, 4572, 4573, 4579, 4582, 4586, 4611,
4612, 4623, 4643, 4646, 4648, 4649,
4658, 4785, 4791
  see also: Historical ethnography
Ethnohistory 189, 214, 238, 555, 559, 607,
  631, 657, 1369, 1760, 2162, 2256, 2547,
  2627, 3057, 3515, 3585, 4183
Ethnolinguistics 631, 796, 1370, 1760, 1822,
  1845, 1972-1975, 1977, 1978, 1980, 1982-
  1986, 3126, 3672, 3745, 3752
Ethnological research 8, 17, 20, 32, 54, 78,
  101, 131, 143, 166, 281, 303, 346, 400,
  401, 410, 427, 438, 645, 1386, 2663,
  2915, 3649, 3825, 4008, 4428, 4454,
  4557, 4664
Ethnologists 8, 15, 32, 35, 100, 104, 136, 140,
  197, 199, 281, 740
Ethnology 8, 17, 20, 32, 54, 72, 78, 90, 91,
  101, 103, 121, 131, 140, 146, 152, 160,
  163, 166, 169, 173, 179, 197, 199, 204,
  205, 223, 243, 269, 281, 331, 346, 348,
  371, 372, 378, 380, 385, 386, 389, 394,
  400, 401, 406, 408, 410, 412, 424, 427,
  438, 645, 667, 722, 920, 950, 980, 1282,
  1386, 1520, 1733, 1832, 2074, 2085,
  2096, 2103, 2104, 2108, 2116, 2184, 2194,
  2195, 2203, 2260, 2346, 2374, 2382,
  2442, 2453, 2468, 2474, 2486, 2509,
  2512, 2523, 2579, 2613, 2649, 2666,
  2676, 2682, 2683, 2735, 2736, 2739,
  2750, 2751, 2847, 2915, 2947, 2975,
  3009, 3010, 3012, 3015, 3019, 3020,
  3055, 3093, 3114, 3163, 3241, 3357, 3360,
  3571, 3596, 3600, 3649, 3680, 3695,
  3702, 3713, 3737, 3807, 3812, 3815,
  3816, 3825, 3870, 3895, 3899, 3900,

3905, 3907, 3910, 3915, 3921, 3925,
3934, 3935, 3942, 3946, 3951, 3953,
3958, 3959, 3965, 4001, 4017, 4024,
4031, 4308-4310, 4319, 4325, 4326, 4334,
4335, 4344, 4345, 4361, 4382, 4384,
4400, 4413, 4416, 4418, 4424, 4428,
4430, 4454, 4465, 4485, 4493, 4498,
4557, 4586, 4600, 4664, 4732, 4809
see also: History of ethnology
Ethnology of religion 3241
Ethnomethodology 297, 435
Ethnomusicology 166, 323, 707, 3081, 3357,
3649, 3719, 3871, 3895, 3897, 3899,
3905, 3910, 3912, 3914, 3915, 3917,
3919, 3921, 3923, 3925, 3929, 3933,
3934, 3940-3942, 3946, 3947, 3951-3953,
3955-3960, 3965, 4059, 4428, 4455, 4465
Ethnonyms 554, 1876, 2475, 3691
Ethnonymy 554
Ethnopsychology 3512, 3729
Ethnosociology 2114, 3970
Ethnozoology 3744, 3786
Ethology 1493, 1494, 1496, 1560, 2872, 4396
Etiology 3124, 3770
Etymology 1729, 1738, 1813, 1836, 1837,
1926, 1927, 1942, 2056, 3381, 3587,
3726, 3757, 3913
Euba, Akin 3933, 4059
Euclid 3754
Eugenics 135, 416, 769, 1652, 2944, 4556
European integration 2486
European policy 2486
European Union 972, 2190, 2486, 4340, 4423,
4429, 4796, 4915
Europeanization 4454
Europeans 4348, 4405, 4423
Euthanasia 2791
Evaluation 44, 295, 296, 1576, 1580, 1844,
1890, 2130, 2878, 3788, 3820, 4876, 4877
see also: Aid evaluation, Programme
evaluation, Project evaluation
Evaluation techniques 4788
Evangelism 736, 774, 3222, 3228, 3241, 3612,
3620, 3887
Evangelization 701, 3220, 3617, 3618
Everyday life 32, 103, 161, 291, 323, 487,
656, 707, 911, 1430, 2200, 2210, 2213,
2217, 2259, 2294, 2459, 2462, 2946,
3034, 3523, 3538, 3580, 3581, 3601,
3870, 3974, 4038, 4105, 4116, 4356, 4378,
4495, 4523, 4570, 4572, 4754
Evidence 449, 903, 944, 1056, 1340, 1515,
1544, 1548, 1673, 2527, 2561, 3307,
3771, 3945, 4534, 4751

Evil 2532, 2635, 3025, 3578, 3590, 3738,
4035, 4087
Evolution 144, 456, 533, 1451, 1465, 1472,
1480, 1516, 1519, 1520, 1523, 1524,
1528, 1537, 1538, 1547, 1577, 1604,
1610, 1617, 1635, 1662, 1679, 1721,
3970, 3992, 4822
see also: Biological evolution, Darwinism,
Human development, Human evolution,
Natural selection
Evolutionary psychology 1539, 2645, 4019
Evolutionism 279, 1618
Ewe 3933, 4059
Examinations 63, 2521
Excavations 85, 463, 513, 520, 829, 840, 850,
871, 920, 922, 924, 926-928, 933, 934,
941, 945, 953, 961, 963, 966, 967, 970,
1001, 1014, 1021, 1022, 1028, 1046,
1051, 1068, 1070, 1074, 1075, 1079,
1087, 1092, 1098, 1111, 1113, 1114, 1120-
1122, 1124, 1135, 1144, 1145, 1153, 1161,
1164, 1165, 1167, 1169, 1172, 1173, 1175,
1177, 1179-1181, 1186, 1187, 1189, 1192,
1196, 1202, 1206, 1212, 1213, 1221-1223,
1225, 1231, 1232, 1234, 1237-1239, 1248,
1252, 1255, 1258, 1262-1264, 1268-1271,
1274-1276, 1278, 1292, 1297, 1300, 1302,
1305, 1309, 1310, 1313-1315, 1346, 1355,
1388, 1389, 1399, 1431, 1438, 1441,
2343, 4250
see also: Archaeological excavation
Exchange 247, 255, 463, 868, 1143, 1363,
1372, 1768, 2266, 2331, 2337, 2341-2343,
2367, 2369, 2373, 2382, 2393, 2596,
2615, 2781, 2983, 3468, 3730, 4389,
4426, 4782, 4804
see also: Marriage exchange, Social
exchange
Exchange theory 2328, 2963
Exhibitions 13, 332, 347, 362, 1332, 4102,
4487
see also: Cultural exhibitions,
Ethnographic exhibitions
Exile 92
Existentialism 4239
Exogamy 2690
Exorcism 3591, 3822
Exoticism 811, 3929, 3972, 4263
Expansionism 612, 810, 1333, 2484, 2493,
2501, 4191
Expectation 2285, 2545, 3006, 3730
Expeditions 33, 492, 940, 1141, 1259, 1261,
4103
see also: Archaeological expeditions

Experimental archaeology 995, 1011, 1526, 2304, 3941
Experimentation 3765, 3914
Experiments 1457, 1612, 1693, 1751, 3755, 3765
Experts 10, 3091, 4855, 4910
Explanation 3026, 4569
Exploitation 247, 2457, 2596, 2627, 2863, 4206, 4728
  see also: Overexploitation, Resource exploitation
Exploration 391, 584, 594, 625, 690, 691, 699, 713, 725, 728, 746, 756, 759, 762, 768, 779, 802, 942, 1690, 1820, 1833, 2060, 2507, 2563, 3121, 3617, 4103, 4208, 4347
Exports 2273, 2358, 4793
  see also: Agricultural exports
Fables 2546, 3688, 3997, 4002, 4212
Factories 2231, 2453
Faidherbe, Louis 582
Failure 1675
Fairy tales 141, 3686, 3990, 3998, 4016, 4017
Faith 119, 185, 2092, 3157, 3220, 3228, 3230, 3368, 3377, 3402, 3456, 3481, 3482, 3490, 3501, 3507, 3548, 3623, 4384, 4441, 4931
Falcone, Giovanni 2975
Family 198, 291, 557, 606, 1319, 1407, 1476, 1498, 1505, 1587, 1731, 1817, 2127, 2142, 2143, 2151, 2155, 2183, 2204, 2294, 2306, 2388, 2411, 2440, 2459, 2463, 2466, 2502, 2521, 2631, 2637, 2639, 2642-2644, 2650, 2651, 2655-2657, 2661, 2668, 2669, 2673, 2674, 2677, 2679, 2687, 2688, 2691, 2698, 2735, 2739, 2760, 2770, 2777, 2805, 2815, 2837, 2861, 2863, 2917, 2943, 2986, 2991, 3012, 3105, 3572, 3696, 3730, 4204, 4281, 4561, 4572, 4780, 4821
  see also: Nuclear family, One-parent families
Family farms 795, 2299
Family firms 2644
Family group 2022
Family history 557, 776, 2142, 2183, 2463, 2466, 2637, 2639, 2688, 2743, 2749, 3704, 4204, 4821
Family life 2394, 2655, 2770, 2878, 3157, 3788, 4877
Family planning 2136, 2640, 2710, 2714, 2717, 2721, 2725, 2726, 2893, 2894, 4668, 4885, 4891, 4899
Family relations 443, 649, 1685, 2158, 2160, 2166, 2171, 2174, 2183, 2410, 2643,

2644, 2662, 2688, 2691, 2740, 2745, 2764, 2772, 2793, 2815, 3730, 3966
Family size 4835
Family structure 557, 1587, 2141, 2637, 2639, 2642, 2651, 2655, 2770, 4584, 4780
Family studies 776, 2160, 2171, 2174, 2460, 2636, 2644, 2743, 2749, 2772, 3704
Famine 4437, 4719, 4812
Fanaticism 371
FAO 4802
Farag Hārūn, Abū 3329
Farid, Ibn Al- 4088
Farm management 4692
Farmers 795, 877, 1291, 2090, 2137, 2177, 2189, 2259, 2260, 2265, 2267, 2281, 2288, 2292, 2294, 2299, 2308-2310, 2312, 2313, 2319, 2376, 2382, 2417, 2452, 2730, 3018, 4604, 4686, 4691, 4696, 4697, 4699, 4700, 4703, 4769, 4783, 4804, 4820
  see also: Tenant farmers
Farming 830, 866, 2151, 2290, 2295, 2297, 2298, 2306, 2311, 2315, 2317, 2320, 2397, 2607, 2735, 4691, 4694, 4820, 4862, 4909
  see also: Fish farming
Farming methods 795, 2299, 4688, 4888
Farming systems 2255, 4661, 4687
Farms 2191, 2394
  see also: Family farms, Small farms
Fascism 3107
Fashion 174, 2928, 2936, 2946, 2948, 2957, 4116, 4121, 4122, 4164
Fasting 2718, 3814
Fatherhood 2711, 4844
Fathers 3267, 4022, 4521
Fatigue 3777
Fauna 460, 841, 842, 884, 889, 1137, 1190, 1818, 2063, 2098
Fauset, Jessie Redmon 2622
Fear 2102, 2533, 3073, 4003
Federal states 358
Federalism 2485, 2511, 4649, 4671
Federation 2210
Feeding 1599, 1601, 1639, 1641, 1642, 1651, 1691, 2713, 4816, 4824
  see also: Animal feeding
Feelings 1637, 4181, 4514
Females 514, 1450, 1455, 1508, 1511, 1539, 1603, 1606, 1631, 1640, 1643, 1658, 1665, 1667, 1668, 1692, 1704, 1706, 1708, 2139, 2431, 2706, 2733, 2796, 2834, 2852, 2883, 2890, 2909, 3991, 4406, 4661
Femininity 280, 769, 1777, 2858, 2934, 2944, 3781, 4175, 4560

Feminism 222, 245, 264, 280, 384, 419, 432,
    680, 694, 755, 978, 985, 2533, 2591,
    2760, 2771, 2807, 2810, 2817, 2820,
    2826, 2827, 2835, 2839, 2858, 2861,
    2873, 2932, 2962, 2966, 3073, 3104,
    3141, 3340, 3640, 4108, 4239, 4548,
    4577, 4612
Feminist theory 245, 264, 419, 432
Fernando, Lloyd 4177
Fertility 1486, 1488, 1720, 2118, 2122, 2139,
    2141, 2153, 2634, 2637, 2683, 2708,
    2737, 3270, 3399, 3719, 4892
    see also: Soil fertility
Fertility decline 2136
Fertility rate 295, 1486, 2118, 2121, 2130,
    2153
Fertilizers 2265, 2303, 2730
Festivals 58, 1818, 2063, 2211, 2256, 2340,
    2684, 2776, 2801, 2907, 3152, 3240,
    3410, 3536, 3549, 3689, 3708, 3863,
    3867, 4262, 4349-4353, 4355-4357, 4359-
    4361, 4363-4372, 4387, 4391, 4431, 4505,
    4522
    see also: Religious festivals
Fetishism 2387, 2921, 3526
Feudalism 624, 2550, 3092
Fichte, Johann Gottlieb 4489
Fiction 149, 409, 3005, 4146, 4149, 4154,
    4188, 4195, 4199, 4205, 4211, 4217, 4242,
    4265, 4272, 4287, 4288, 4562
    see also: Science fiction
Field archaeology 824, 997
Field work 7, 15, 33, 48, 49, 85, 91, 102, 123,
    136, 145, 158, 177, 194, 200, 202, 222,
    239, 241, 254, 277, 291, 292, 297, 302,
    304, 311-313, 371, 384, 386, 390, 391,
    393, 396, 400, 402, 403, 407, 413, 420,
    422, 424, 425, 429, 435, 436, 512, 827,
    829, 885, 907, 922-924, 927, 930, 945,
    967, 968, 1021, 1111, 1114, 1120, 1123,
    1124, 1130, 1134, 1154, 1155, 1158, 1159,
    1163, 1167, 1168, 1173, 1175, 1179, 1181,
    1186, 1196, 1197, 1222, 1223, 1225, 1238,
    1248, 1255, 1263, 1269-1271, 1274, 1276,
    1277, 1292, 1315, 1330, 1386, 1399, 1411,
    1436, 1799, 2438, 2663, 2821, 2897,
    3027, 3102, 3361, 3812, 3871, 4008,
    4410, 4424, 4457, 4533, 4740
Fighting techniques 3912
Figurative art 1071, 4118, 4132
Figurines 336, 1391, 1430, 2329, 4132
Filipinos 2161, 2534, 4478
Film makers 427, 440
Films 55, 133, 151, 409, 439, 442, 444, 2198,
    2482, 2933, 3731, 3873, 3977, 4099,

    4100, 4105, 4108, 4120, 4126, 4136,
    4190, 4296, 4366, 4470, 4523
    see also: Ethnographic films
Finance 2210, 2740, 3186, 4369, 4698, 4737,
    4739, 4908, 4911
    see also: Financial history, Public finance
Financial crisis 2258, 2268, 2305, 2314, 4663
Financial history 734
Financial institutions 4911
Financial liberalization 4662
Financial services 4671, 4730
Financing methods 4325
Fine arts 4103, 4142
Finkielkraut, Alain 4238
Finno-Ugrians 42
Fire 2060, 2272, 2797, 3126, 4774
Fish 2070, 2444, 4394
Fish farming 2452
Fisheries 2436, 2440, 3786, 4804, 4850
Fishermen 2070, 2451, 2467, 4729
Fishery co-operatives 2440
Fishery management 2404
Fishery resources 4804
Fishing 2344, 2428, 2429, 2436, 2451, 2467,
    3786, 4793, 4804
Fishing techniques 2436
Fishing villages 2194
Flexible specialization 4748
Floods 402, 2061, 2079, 3860
Flora 361, 362, 488, 756, 896, 1322, 1694,
    1701, 1722, 1818, 1832, 2063, 2066,
    2084, 2088, 2098, 2117, 2201, 2266, 2272,
    2296, 2304, 2377, 2435, 2444, 3570,
    3667, 3742, 3747, 3778, 3783, 3815,
    3816, 4774
Flour-mills 2203
Flute 3719
Focus groups 286, 290, 2124, 2734
Foetus 1555, 2706
Folk art 92, 3256, 4095, 4106, 4129, 4131
Folk beliefs 1768, 3535, 3678, 3686, 3694
Folk costumes 2951, 3678
Folk culture 2243, 2482, 2607, 3554, 3678,
    3684, 3918, 3970
Folk dances 3890, 3908
Folk literature 3679, 3991, 4022
Folk music 118, 3923, 3926, 3931, 3933,
    3948, 3967, 4059, 4367
Folk poetry 4038
Folk songs 3908, 3918, 3919, 3970
Folk tales 229, 289, 1788, 3116, 3979, 3983,
    3990, 3991, 3993, 3994, 3997, 3998,
    4002, 4006, 4010, 4015, 4016, 4018-4020,
    4022, 4026, 4032, 4033, 4243, 4372

Folk traditions 153, 166, 289, 2482, 3528, 3649, 3678, 3694, 3708, 3923, 3983, 4022, 4351, 4367, 4428
Folk wisdom 2088, 2364, 3667, 4070, 4233
Folklore 14, 92, 127, 149, 152, 160, 163, 166, 171, 181, 188, 229, 376, 564, 1782, 1788, 1858, 2080, 2187, 2204, 2291, 2364, 2437, 2438, 2678, 2828, 2830, 2943, 3065, 3116, 3124, 3242, 3528, 3535, 3582, 3649, 3661, 3662, 3664, 3670, 3679, 3682, 3686, 3694, 3698, 3721, 3763, 3785, 3863, 3903, 3918, 3930, 3945, 3949, 3970, 3976, 3979, 3982, 3987, 3991-3995, 3998, 4003, 4006, 4010, 4015, 4016, 4018, 4019, 4021, 4022, 4026, 4028, 4070, 4198, 4240, 4255, 4306, 4331, 4349, 4360, 4428
Folkloristics 143, 152, 153, 163, 166, 171, 181, 188, 229, 3649, 3979, 4022, 4255, 4360, 4428
Folklorists 127, 171
Fon 336, 2579
Fonseca, André Velho da 806
Food 20, 284, 744, 896, 1324, 1421, 1540, 1577, 1599, 1608, 1609, 1611, 1627, 1628, 1639, 1642, 1644, 1647, 1648, 1672, 1677, 1693, 1702-1704, 1720, 2191, 2210, 2275, 2316, 2444, 2824, 3310, 3678, 3747, 3751, 3779, 3786, 3992, 4308, 4371, 4377, 4380, 4381, 4383-4386, 4388, 4389, 4393, 4618, 4747, 4794, 4804, 4809, 4811-4813, 4815, 4822, 4823, 4825, 4923, 4940
    see also: Anthropology of food
Food aid 4814, 4817, 4820
Food beliefs 4378, 4386, 4754
Food consumption 1556, 2277, 3678, 4387, 4810
Food habits 1551, 1644, 4358, 4376, 4378, 4379, 4403, 4754
Food policy 4814
Food preparation
    see: Cooking
Food prices 2268
Food production 867, 892, 966, 1446, 2268, 2283, 2380, 4388, 4736
Food products 4380
Food resources 1645, 1694, 3751, 4385, 4923
Food security 1573, 1611, 1645, 1646, 2380, 4701, 4719, 4736, 4807, 4808, 4811, 4814, 4815, 4817-4820, 4834
Food sharing 1646, 1647, 2352, 4393, 4394
Food shortages 2129, 2704
Food supply 861, 1556, 4807, 4810, 4811, 4813-4815, 4817, 4819, 4826

Food taboos 4395
Football 40, 4309, 4336
Foragers 1584, 2302, 2382, 2431, 2834, 3992, 4406
Foraging 1408, 1600, 1609, 1671, 1711, 1715, 2433, 3084, 4394
Forced labour 807
Forced migration 531, 2159, 4714, 4725
Fordism
    see: Post-Fordism
Forecasts 388, 1583, 3038, 3569
Foreign aid 4707, 4724, 4725, 4737, 4781
Foreign direct investment 2113, 2318
Foreign languages 2047
Foreign occupation 642, 704, 705, 717, 768, 794, 2333, 3005, 4098
Foreign policy 677, 2357, 2455, 2533, 3041, 3073, 4663
Foreign relations 106, 658, 737, 741, 752, 2495, 2533, 3073, 4615, 4937
Foreign trade 1447, 2330, 2357
Foreigners 281, 4010
Forensic anthropology 970
Forensic science 970, 2780, 2924
Forest management 2081, 2090, 2115, 2404, 2413, 2818, 2828, 2829, 2844, 2859, 4779, 4780, 4792
Forest policy 2828, 4779
Forest resources 1686, 1691, 2081, 2090, 2413, 2808, 2828
Forestry 2264, 2292, 2307, 2309, 2311, 4399, 4690, 4694, 4696, 4697, 4699, 4702, 4799, 4804
Forestry development 2808, 2828
Forests 1359, 1609, 1651, 1663, 1669, 1674, 1686, 1687, 1709, 1717, 2087, 2091, 2095, 2115, 2191, 2207, 2264, 2284, 2431, 2808, 2828, 2859, 3056, 3075, 3084, 3547, 3819, 4399, 4666, 4695, 4780, 4787, 4791, 4799, 4805, 4923
    see also: Rain forest
Fortes, Meyer 9, 108
Fortifications 483, 620, 806, 1009, 1037, 1058, 1082, 1101, 1104, 1199, 1200, 1328, 1334, 1346, 1411, 1412, 3852, 3859
Fossil man 870, 1469, 1530
Fossil primates 1479, 1485
Fossils 460, 872, 873, 884, 899, 1137, 1363, 1379, 1458, 1472, 1473, 1523, 1528, 1532, 1534, 1536, 2086
Foucauld, Charles de 122, 600
Foucault, Michel 514, 2909
Francis, Newell S. 3588
Franciscans 3618
Frank, Waldo 4282

Fraser Russell, Alexander 792
Free trade 4611
Freedom 585, 2408, 2496, 2548, 3009, 3216,
    3846, 3862, 3869, 3889, 4650
    see also: Academic freedom
Freedom of association 4820
Freedom of religion 3563, 3634
Freedom of speech 134
French language 75, 1749, 1762, 1801, 1813,
    1919, 1981, 1986
Frequency 2634
Freud, Sigmund 176, 379, 4524
Friendship 2557, 2882, 4172
Frisian language 1964
Fruit 1609, 1627, 1642, 1648, 1671, 1715,
    1720, 2377
    see also: Bananas
Fuels 2083
Fugard, Athol 3874, 4200
Fulani 582, 1749
Fulbe 2073, 2510
Functionalism 138
    see also: Structural functionalism
Funeral art 1077
    see also: Ancient funeral art
Funeral monuments 1311, 1316, 1318, 2494
Funeral songs 3967
Funerals 58, 874, 1324, 2604, 2786, 2787,
    2791
Funerary masks 1077
Funerary rites 147, 360, 448, 838, 892, 1063,
    1288, 1301, 1319, 1323, 2784, 2786,
    2787, 2789, 2791, 3225, 3581
    see also: Ancient funeral rites, Burial
Furniture 2242
Gambling 4315, 4337
Games 730, 1783, 3549, 3930, 3976, 4306,
    4307, 4313-4315, 4333, 4492
Gandhi, Mohandas Karamchand 3079
Gardens 161, 1073, 2260, 4443
Gardner, Don 159, 217
Garifuna 1986
Gastronomy 4396
Gathering 371, 896, 2428, 2429
Gaudapāda 3291
Gawzī, Ibn al 3354
Geertz, Clifford 138, 244
Geiger, Abraham 3666, 4445
Gellner, Ernest 138
Gender 105, 214, 225, 248, 258, 528, 539,
    565, 643, 663, 676, 680, 694, 717, 1041,
    1360, 1466, 1549, 1563, 1628, 1639,
    1692, 1740, 1752, 1775, 1828, 1896,
    1943, 2133, 2142, 2169, 2174, 2176,
    2213, 2244, 2266, 2284, 2375, 2410,

2441, 2442, 2464, 2469, 2470, 2571,
    2603, 2605, 2611, 2622, 2629, 2644, 2660,
    2686, 2693, 2697, 2723, 2729, 2746,
    2757, 2759, 2761, 2765, 2769, 2771,
    2772, 2796, 2803-2805, 2809, 2810, 2812,
    2813, 2820-2824, 2826-2828, 2831, 2832,
    2834, 2835, 2838, 2840, 2841, 2845,
    2847-2849, 2852-2857, 2862, 2864, 2873,
    2888, 2895, 2905, 2918, 2928, 2932,
    2933, 2936, 2946, 2948, 2955, 2957,
    2959, 3028, 3030, 3056, 3075, 3076,
    3104, 3113, 3231, 3254, 3340, 3357, 3497,
    3525, 3615, 3640, 3751, 3871, 3873,
    3922, 3934, 3951, 3994, 3995, 4005,
    4009, 4041, 4052, 4073, 4108, 4116, 4158,
    4164, 4171, 4247, 4342, 4358, 4361,
    4385, 4403, 4406, 4440, 4450, 4468,
    4470, 4505, 4528, 4561, 4563, 4577,
    4591, 4611, 4645, 4780, 4790, 4821, 4829,
    4831, 4837-4841, 4845, 4851, 4856, 4879,
    4890, 4904, 4911
    see also: Gender studies
Gender differentiation 105, 1283, 1325, 1478,
    1506, 1508, 1509, 1568, 1588, 1643,
    1695, 1732, 1775, 1882, 2163, 2350,
    2453, 2594, 2667, 2765, 2768, 2812,
    2825, 2840, 2846, 2872, 2941, 3231,
    4612, 4840
Gender relations 606, 643, 1762, 1775, 2081,
    2442, 2498, 2645, 2683, 2724, 2758,
    2806-2808, 2812, 2814, 2828, 2829, 2834,
    2846, 2847, 2851, 2860, 2986, 3086,
    3216, 3781, 4406, 4828, 4858, 4873,
    4876, 4911
Gender roles 564, 694, 2089, 2094, 2163,
    2347, 2410, 2481, 2633, 2651, 2692,
    2810, 2819, 2821, 2825, 2830, 2835,
    2836, 2841, 2843, 2846, 2932, 2966,
    3934, 4839, 4845, 4853
    see also: Men's role, Women's role
Gender studies 2089, 2094, 2115, 2164, 2320,
    2452, 2818, 2823, 2827, 2836, 2843,
    2844, 2859, 3104, 3568, 4577, 4780,
    4834, 4862
Genealogy 649, 1615, 1828, 1830, 2132,
    2634, 2646, 2652, 2666, 2671, 3117, 3345,
    3353, 3420, 3421, 3669, 4460, 4493, 4717
Generalization 209, 1693, 2170, 3560
Generation conflicts 2675
Generation differences 3074
Generations 1511, 1817, 2155, 2375, 2605,
    2613, 2628, 2675, 2693, 4204
Genes 830, 1453, 1487, 1490, 1494-1500,
    1502, 1503, 1506, 1507, 1510, 1515,
    1538, 1615, 1650, 1666, 2657

Genetic engineering 236, 2310, 4825
Genetic psychology 1520
Genetics 1451, 1459, 1476, 1487, 1497, 1501,
    1503-1505, 1508-1511, 1520, 1522, 1587,
    1616, 1617, 1649, 1650, 1652, 1666,
    1679, 1688, 1714, 1781, 1822, 2132,
    2297, 2445, 2478, 2646, 2674, 3793,
    4697, 4825
    see also: Cloning, DNA, Human genetics
Genital mutilation 285, 459, 2705, 2733,
    2870, 2871, 2880, 2881, 2883, 2887,
    2890, 2982
Genocide 192, 618, 970, 2578, 3029, 3050
Gentileschi, Orazio 3728
Geoarchaeology 1183, 1185
Geographic distribution 2133
Geographic location 1495
Geographic mobility 2420
Geographical information systems 840, 1002,
    2138, 2287, 3800, 4735
Geography 214, 291, 474, 525, 541, 648, 806,
    872, 913, 983, 1002, 1737, 1820, 1833,
    2060, 2112, 2181, 2219, 2222, 2244, 2272,
    2274, 2287, 2313, 2362, 2402, 2418,
    2713, 2801, 3247, 3334, 3660, 3689,
    3868, 4103, 4124, 4171, 4186, 4226,
    4300, 4339, 4347, 4356, 4388, 4464,
    4478, 4618, 4626, 4654, 4660, 4678,
    4681, 4683, 4684, 4727, 4752, 4759,
    4768, 4774, 4794, 4797, 4798, 4800,
    4803, 4836, 4850, 4854, 4910, 4917, 4926
    see also: Economic geography, Historical
    geography, Human geography, Industrial
    geography, Political geography
Geology 390, 499, 500, 806, 839, 901, 913,
    1260, 1382, 2086, 2240, 3855
Geometry 832, 1044, 2324, 2329, 3754, 3857
Geophagy 1601, 1651
Geopolitics 2289, 4258, 4673, 4720
German language 69, 74, 83, 1751
German unification 3656
Germans 4292, 4347, 4603, 4761
Gerontocracy 2502, 2682, 2767, 3572
Gerontology 2650, 2655, 2763, 2770, 2777,
    3696
Gestures 1775, 2812
Ghazālī, Abu Hamid Mohammed al 2998,
    3366
Ghetto 4468
Gift 175, 2341, 2351, 2381, 2615, 2745, 2956,
    4381
Gikuyu 3548
Gilgamesh [King] 4253
Gimbutas, Marija 2175

Girls 2697, 2729, 2803, 2863, 2931, 2962,
    4835
Gjalski, Ksaver Sandor 3996
Glassware 1447
Gling pa, 'Jigs med 3205
Glissant, Edouard 4187
Global warming 2065
Globalization 178, 179, 189, 219, 254, 777,
    1826, 2182, 2207, 2210, 2216, 2257,
    2332, 2370, 2496, 2502, 2552, 2863,
    2990, 3041, 3056, 3075, 3232, 3534,
    3572, 3612, 3639, 3652, 3758, 3884,
    4030, 4218, 4301, 4315, 4316, 4338,
    4355, 4400, 4407, 4417, 4442, 4449,
    4450, 4452, 4454, 4457, 4587, 4604-4615,
    4617, 4618, 4620-4623, 4632, 4651, 4662,
    4663, 4680, 4700, 4722, 4793, 4794,
    4797, 4809, 4820, 4867, 4880, 4904,
    4909, 4917
Gluckman, Max 126, 3054
Gnosticism 476, 3527
Goddesses 105, 1040, 1078, 1334, 2324, 3231,
    3270, 3284, 3311, 3524
Gods 521, 1014, 1025, 1051, 1093, 1755,
    1837, 1863, 1941, 2439, 2532, 3111, 3115,
    3133, 3150, 3151, 3170, 3234, 3275,
    3276, 3283, 3290, 3294, 3295, 3302,
    3308, 3359, 3382, 3396, 3432, 3465,
    3466, 3499, 3513, 3519, 3528, 3535,
    3537, 3542, 3549, 3590, 3598, 3601,
    3837, 4095
Gold 506, 1438, 2439
Gold mines 791, 2373
Gond 2153
Gonne, Maud 4563
González, José Luis 4271
Gorillas 1481, 1607, 1656, 1667, 1671, 1704,
    1714
Goupil, Eugène 214
Governance 474, 2404, 2524, 2569, 3063,
    4615, 4634, 4720, 4721, 4764, 4843,
    4861, 4870, 4874, 4915
Government 818, 2210, 2288, 2403, 2487,
    2504, 2538, 2558, 2570, 2979, 2988,
    3036, 3059, 3349, 4185, 4301, 4481,
    4607, 4653, 4933
    see also: Colonial government, Local
    government, Regional government,
    Subnational government, Tribal
    government, Urban government
Government departments 1786, 4926, 4937
Government policy 153, 613, 2308, 2463,
    2576-2578, 2706, 2828, 3108, 4339, 4621,
    4655, 4683, 4703, 4738, 4756, 4770,
    4806, 4812, 4826, 4868, 4901, 4918, 4928

Government programmes 2090, 2412, 4742
Government relations 809, 2403, 4647
Government-business relations 2558
Governors 323, 707, 721, 2550, 2971
Goytisolo, Juan 4202
Grain 1704
Grammar 69, 71, 83, 109, 248, 1724, 1742,
    1752, 1753, 1789, 1807, 1812, 1836,
    1843, 1852, 1854, 1860, 1862, 1863,
    1866, 1867, 1875, 1892, 1896, 1918,
    1929, 1930, 1933, 1935, 1936, 1938,
    1948, 1960, 1963, 1982, 1987, 1995,
    1999, 2006, 2007, 2010, 2012, 2014,
    2017, 2023, 2029, 2031, 2032, 2035,
    2037, 2038, 2043, 2046, 2053, 3147,
    3165, 3273, 3359, 3754, 4262
    see also: Clause
Grandparents 2654, 2686, 2863
Graphic arts 1031
Graves 620, 855, 858, 859, 906, 970, 1010,
    1063, 1074, 1122, 1158, 1163, 1280, 1282,
    1288, 1290, 1292, 1296, 1298-1300, 1302,
    1303, 1305, 1306, 1309, 1310, 1313-1316,
    1319, 1325-1327, 1336, 1391, 1399, 2782
Great Depression 2300
Greek language 560, 1850, 1912, 1922, 1959,
    3412
Green Revolution 4693, 4698
Gregory, Augusta 2622
Grogan, Ewart Scott 773
Gross domestic product 4787
Gross national product 4733, 4797
Grosseteste, Robert 3728
Groundwater 525, 2112, 2376
Group analysis 220, 1607, 2125, 2585, 2606,
    2953
Group behaviour 220, 1598, 1599, 1605,
    1623, 1628, 1653, 1661, 1705, 1716,
    2126, 2585, 2606
Group cohesiveness 220, 2585
Group composition 1453, 1654
Group dynamics 1639, 1655, 1692, 1713,
    2606, 2882
Group functioning 2606
Group identity 220, 262, 2585, 2992, 3633,
    4126, 4309, 4423, 4435, 4459, 4604, 4741
Group interaction 1664
Group participation 2210, 4702
Group psychotherapy 220, 2585
Group size 1598, 1677
Group theory 2603
Growth rates 1470, 1553, 1557, 4705
Guaman Poma de Ayala, Felipe 4098
Guarani 1976, 2798
Guest, Barbara 4041

Guidar 2700
Guilt 4526
Gulf War 2860, 3086
Gundert, Hermann 1894
Gunwinggu 2670, 2747
Gurage 1845
Gusii 2635, 3025
Guthrie, Malcolm 1996
Gypsies 10, 14, 139, 399, 425, 3091, 3099,
    3124, 3710, 4006
Habitats 1525, 1598, 1624, 1627, 1630, 1638,
    1648, 1656, 1674, 1680, 1686, 1712,
    2077, 2098
Habits
    see: Food habits
Hadza 1281, 2352, 2651
Hagiography 514, 2909, 3414, 4255
Hahn, Reynaldo 4263
Haida 4134
Hair 1719, 2940, 4110
Hallucinogenic plants 3566, 3833
Hammarskjöld, Dag 4712
Hammurabi [King] 477
Han 41, 190, 649, 3713
Han, Yongun 3079
Handbooks 3206
Handicrafts 2239, 2244, 2644, 3678
Hanihara 246, 2135
Hanson, Pauline 3107
Harvesting 2377
Hasidism 253, 3976
Hau'ofa, Epeli 3650
Hausa 402, 1749
Head, Bessie 4160
Heads of state 537, 575, 583, 620, 639, 710,
    724, 792, 2330, 2519
Healers 17, 3591, 3812, 3822, 3825, 3830
Healing 17, 105, 2727, 3011, 3062, 3181,
    3231, 3259, 3535, 3541, 3565, 3586,
    3596, 3645, 3776, 3790, 3791, 3809,
    3813, 3825, 3830, 3833, 3835, 3991, 4511
Health 285, 290, 909, 1494, 1512, 1529, 1543,
    1569, 1572, 1589, 1657, 1688, 2140,
    2149, 2150, 2152, 2173, 2208, 2210,
    2213, 2277, 2311, 2695, 2696, 2701, 2702,
    2707-2711, 2720, 2721, 2733, 2758, 2759,
    2763, 2773, 2775, 2848, 2865-2868, 2870,
    2873, 2874, 2879, 2884, 2888-2890, 2892,
    2894-2896, 2898, 2902, 2910, 2913, 2914,
    2916, 2918, 2941, 2953, 3159, 3254,
    3510, 3764, 3774, 3775, 3780, 3782,
    3792, 3795-3798, 3806, 3810, 3813, 3821,
    3827, 3831, 3832, 3834, 3835, 4181, 4211,
    4328, 4396, 4397, 4526, 4531, 4647,
    4818, 4823, 4844, 4864, 4871, 4873,

4876, 4878, 4883, 4884, 4886, 4889, 4891, 4893, 4895, 4898-4901, 4903
see also: Child health, Health promotion, Men's health, Mental health, Public health, Reproductive health, Sexual health, Women's health
Health care 285, 1572, 2138, 2189, 2464, 2702, 2709, 2711, 2870, 2889, 3761, 3775, 3800, 3806, 4740, 4844, 4865, 4867, 4879, 4882, 4889, 4894, 4897, 4901
see also: Medical care, Primary health care
Health economics 4863
Health education 1559, 2711, 2878, 3761, 3788, 4844, 4877
Health planning 4876
Health policy 1470, 2128, 3761, 4823, 4863, 4864, 4875, 4876, 4882, 4890, 4892, 4894
Health promotion 3827
Health services 2702, 2863, 3775, 3794, 3821, 4328, 4866-4868, 4895, 4901
Hearing 4029
Heart disease 1585
Hebrew 1338, 1762, 1816, 1831, 1840, 1843, 1844, 1846, 1848, 1850, 1855, 1857, 1859, 1860, 1864, 1866, 1870, 3392, 3396, 3405, 3427, 3431, 3434, 3436, 3449, 3453, 3459, 3460, 3973, 4040, 4054, 4224, 4444, 4461, 4467, 4503
Hegemony 95, 234, 657, 2510, 2547, 3077, 3601, 3650, 3794, 4336, 4421, 4626, 4861
Height 1456, 1541, 1550, 4307
Heisenberg, Karl 60
Hemingway, Ernest 4199
Henricus Martellus Germanus 768
Hepworth, Barbara 4712
Herding 2105, 2442, 2610, 2847, 4604, 4784
Heredity 1476, 1835, 2132, 2195, 2646
Heresies 568, 3413
Hermeneutics 34, 257, 281, 772, 841, 987, 996, 1226, 1798, 3136, 3326, 3509
Hermits 905
Herod [King] 1328
Heroes 1539, 2911, 3271, 4019, 4289
Heroin 3004, 3765
Herskovits, Melville J. 4468
Hesiod 3115
Heterosexuality 1452, 2840, 2841, 2873, 2891
Heuristics 1385
Hidden economy 4621
Hierarchy 53, 504, 1631, 1775, 2530, 2627, 2735, 2812, 3523, 4254, 4299, 4365, 4387, 4549
Hieroglyphic script 4275
Hieroglyphics 102, 1345, 1799, 4275

Higher education 4548, 4572, 4748
Hindi 1896, 4173
Hinduism 22, 105, 732, 1081, 2099, 2485, 2515, 2615, 2788, 2926, 2991, 3079, 3155, 3214, 3231, 3269-3271, 3276-3280, 3283-3286, 3288-3291, 3295-3299, 3302-3304, 3306, 3309-3317, 3319, 3549, 3837, 3854, 3898, 3962, 4020, 4140, 4189, 4297, 4474, 4577
see also: Saivism
Hindus 2121, 2757, 2788, 2856, 3286, 3292, 4189, 4281, 4362, 4364
Hispanic-Americans 443, 2661, 2724, 2851, 4305
Hispanics 2533, 3073, 3769, 3946
Historians 36, 96, 116, 339, 471, 588, 615, 683, 701, 3220, 3985, 4326
Historic monuments 609, 1030, 1048, 1358, 1386, 1412, 3653, 3673, 3703, 3854, 4263, 4484
Historic sites 3848, 4299, 4317
Historical analysis 22, 30, 41, 109, 124, 190, 358, 541, 593, 599, 615, 656, 876, 904, 913, 1048, 1350, 1375, 1437, 1495, 1738, 1805, 1821, 1823, 1839, 1934, 1995, 2023, 2136, 2229, 2262, 2385, 2472, 2510, 2528, 2554, 2658, 2877, 2949, 3026, 3109, 3276, 3281, 3527, 3716, 3718, 3854, 4140, 4156, 4214, 4272, 4405, 4489, 4594
Historical anthropology 278, 869, 920, 2519, 2649, 3741, 4336
Historical archaeology 155, 251, 530, 624, 664, 969, 970, 973, 978, 979, 982, 988, 1009, 1058, 1245, 1361, 1392, 1407, 1429, 2338, 3697
Historical demography 246, 866, 2122, 2131, 2135, 2147, 2150
Historical ethnography 2052, 3595
Historical geography 768, 806, 1820, 2173, 2296, 3961
Historical museums 366
Historicism 650, 3888, 3974
Historiography 12, 25, 48, 97, 116, 125, 155, 200, 214, 228, 231, 278, 333, 335, 351, 367, 530, 532, 537, 542, 547, 549, 552, 569, 573, 575, 582, 588, 589, 595, 602, 607, 610, 612, 614-616, 622, 635, 641, 655, 665, 670, 671, 701, 713, 733, 758, 969, 971, 1004, 1353, 2167, 2392, 2465, 2493, 2532, 2533, 2608, 2625, 2697, 2803, 3073, 3085, 3146, 3167, 3174, 3331, 3445, 3477, 3590, 3635, 3656, 3705, 3902, 4023, 4185, 4245, 4260, 4306, 4472, 4544, 4580

History 7, 11, 12, 16, 18, 31, 40, 62, 73, 88,
    97, 99, 101, 106, 109, 116, 117, 122, 132,
    149, 150, 155, 159, 162, 217, 225, 231,
    246, 279, 317, 319, 326, 333, 335, 344,
    345, 351, 357, 364, 367, 375, 376, 382,
    412, 434, 437, 441, 446, 465, 467, 473,
    486, 491, 495, 509, 514, 519, 522, 527,
    528, 530-532, 535, 537-539, 541, 545-
    550, 552, 553, 564, 567, 569, 571-575,
    578, 579, 582, 586-589, 592, 597, 600,
    601, 607, 609, 610, 612, 614-616, 619,
    620, 622, 626, 635, 637, 639, 643-645,
    647, 648, 650, 652, 653, 655, 657, 660,
    661, 665, 668, 674, 677, 678, 686, 687,
    695, 696, 702, 703, 708, 709, 714-716,
    724, 728, 744, 752, 755, 760, 762, 771,
    773, 776, 778, 785, 786, 797, 801, 807,
    814, 817, 823, 878, 893, 895, 926, 928,
    934, 936, 937, 969, 971, 979, 984, 992,
    1004, 1012, 1015, 1019, 1032, 1054,
    1055, 1084, 1086, 1094, 1096, 1097, 1101,
    1123, 1154, 1159, 1172, 1180, 1213, 1223,
    1249, 1264, 1276, 1305, 1330, 1333,
    1336, 1338, 1339, 1346, 1355, 1357,
    1369, 1389, 1395, 1420, 1421, 1423,
    1433, 1463, 1520, 1524, 1740, 1743,
    1786, 1827, 1828, 1830, 1831, 1840,
    1841, 1856, 1862, 1865, 1871, 1901,
    1904, 1905, 1910, 1914, 1940, 1988-1990,
    1992-1995, 2003, 2009, 2036, 2078, 2092,
    2095, 2100, 2110, 2111, 2135, 2142, 2147,
    2151, 2168, 2173, 2175, 2197, 2205,
    2230, 2233, 2243, 2250, 2253, 2254,
    2259, 2267, 2276, 2286, 2294, 2306,
    2335, 2365, 2367, 2371, 2383, 2386,
    2392, 2395, 2397, 2398, 2422, 2423,
    2429, 2447, 2451, 2460, 2464, 2479,
    2484, 2493, 2496, 2500, 2501, 2519,
    2526, 2541, 2545, 2547, 2548, 2556,
    2563, 2566, 2572, 2573, 2577, 2599,
    2610, 2623, 2636, 2644, 2648, 2652,
    2658, 2671, 2689, 2743, 2749, 2754,
    2789, 2792, 2828, 2830, 2832-2834, 2860,
    2909, 2912, 2942, 2949, 2964, 2965,
    2974, 2981, 2998, 2999, 3007, 3023,
    3041, 3051, 3058, 3071, 3086, 3108, 3114,
    3117, 3146, 3161, 3172, 3180, 3185, 3189,
    3236, 3266, 3268, 3322, 3327, 3332,
    3334, 3338, 3339, 3343, 3345, 3346,
    3350, 3358, 3366, 3394, 3395, 3398,
    3400, 3411, 3416, 3509, 3571, 3628, 3629,
    3643, 3648, 3655, 3656, 3666, 3668,
    3673, 3683, 3687, 3704, 3705, 3707,
    3720, 3739, 3749, 3766, 3768, 3776,
    3779, 3785, 3787, 3797, 3802, 3813,
    3826, 3828, 3836, 3852, 3868, 3882,
    3923, 3944, 3974, 3986, 4009, 4012,
    4023, 4040, 4054, 4056, 4060, 4089, 4115,
    4124, 4144, 4155, 4156, 4161, 4165,
    4167, 4174, 4186, 4190, 4201, 4205,
    4219, 4221, 4227, 4232, 4240, 4242,
    4247, 4260, 4267, 4269, 4280, 4302,
    4308, 4333, 4336, 4344, 4347, 4348,
    4350, 4379, 4384, 4406, 4416, 4444,
    4445, 4448, 4460, 4467, 4468, 4504,
    4505, 4508, 4557, 4558, 4568, 4573,
    4592, 4625, 4638-4640, 4642, 4657, 4711,
    4739, 4799, 4804, 4821, 4861, 4908, 4912
    see also: Agricultural history, Ancien
    Régime, Ancient history, Business history,
    Church history, Colonial history,
    Constitutional history, Cultural history,
    Early modern history, Economic history,
    Family history, Industrial history, Labour
    history, Language history, Life history,
    Local history, Maritime history, Medieval
    history, Military history, Modern history,
    National history, Oral history, Political
    history, Post-war history, Pre-Columbian
    history, Religious history, Rural history,
    Social history, Urban history
History of anthropology 1-3, 7, 9, 11, 12, 18,
    43, 45, 99, 108, 110, 121, 126, 160, 198,
    232, 249, 254, 399, 408, 621, 636, 1531,
    2612, 2658, 2679, 3054, 3107, 3533,
    3596, 3692, 3799, 4457
History of archaeology 87, 971, 974, 975, 980,
    995
History of art 338, 371, 1005, 3249, 4093-
    4095, 4097, 4114, 4128, 4130, 4235
History of civilization 377
History of education 645, 4552, 4557
History of ethnology 8
History of ideas 164, 214, 259, 414, 514, 737,
    2909, 3178, 3208, 4476
History of law 508, 516, 638, 771, 2981, 2991,
    2995, 2996, 4247
History of medicine 62, 110, 605, 1489, 1953,
    2912, 3358, 3595, 3749, 3766-3768, 3778,
    3779, 3784, 3785, 3787, 3794, 3797,
    3799, 3802, 3808, 3828, 3836, 4174, 4525
History of music 647, 3914, 3926, 3929, 3933,
    3943, 3952, 4059
History of philosophy 79, 588, 758, 1738,
    3129, 3208
History of political ideas 138
History of religion 154, 168, 210, 585, 591,
    634, 640, 1025, 1100, 3139, 3152, 3161,
    3167, 3169, 3171, 3174, 3183, 3190,
    3197, 3200, 3253, 3263, 3264, 3330,

3331, 3334, 3342, 3370, 3379, 3385-3387,
  3415, 3417, 3428, 3441, 3443, 3461,
  3473, 3476, 3484, 3490, 3493, 3502,
  3521, 3528, 3561, 3562, 3615, 3642, 3647
History of science 16, 132, 371, 437, 459, 464,
  2871, 3746, 3749, 3754, 3755, 3768
History of slavery 807
History of technology 455, 789, 1202, 1388,
  1397, 1421, 2225, 2229
History of the social sciences 5, 6, 11, 94, 138,
  226
History of trade 150, 382, 449, 503, 633, 709,
  764, 793, 806, 908, 1392, 2330, 2335,
  2339, 2344, 2357, 2358, 2360, 2362,
  2372, 2383, 2533, 3008, 3073, 3797, 4272
History of travels 3263, 4179, 4225, 4236,
  4237, 4290, 4292, 4321-4323, 4332
Hitler, Adolf 576, 3573
Hittites 478, 479, 1394
HIV 44, 52, 264, 419, 1580, 2156, 2695, 2865,
  2866, 2869, 2874, 2884, 2885, 2889,
  2892, 2896, 2902, 2903, 2908, 2913,
  2916, 3761, 3762, 3770, 3771, 3773,
  3780, 3782, 3796, 3810, 3820, 3831,
  3834, 4863, 4869, 4873, 4889, 4893,
  4897, 4898
Hmong 2028, 2323
Hobsbawm, Eric 3929
Holidays 2482, 2778, 4350
Holism 3558, 4294, 4842
Holocaust 357, 434, 695, 4049, 4439
Holocene 543, 837, 847, 857, 913, 1183, 1304
Holy persons 3134
Holy places 257, 829, 1361, 1381, 3230, 3452,
  3697, 4441
Holy war 611, 3042, 3049
Holý, Ladislav 138
Home 291, 694, 2100, 2154, 2461, 2766,
  2900, 2907, 3707, 3843, 4111, 4184, 4330,
  4384
Home ownership 2210
Home rule 2540
Homelessness 2210, 4543, 4571, 4722
Homer 3680
Homicide 977, 3024
  see also: Murder
Hominids 822, 841, 842, 898, 899, 914, 1137,
  1368, 1458, 1467, 1472, 1479, 1481,
  1518, 1521, 1523, 1525, 1526, 1528,
  1530, 1532, 1534, 1604
Homosexuality 514, 562, 1507, 2841, 2866,
  2877, 2882, 2885, 2900-2902, 2907, 2909,
  2912, 2933, 4330, 4470, 4499, 4898
Honorius, Iulius 4167

Honour and shame 1872, 2586, 3258, 3267,
  3644, 3912
Hopi 3742
Horace 4172
Hormones 1460, 1553, 1613, 1622, 1658,
  1668, 1670, 1697, 1699
Horse-riding 1383
Horse-riding equipment 1383
Horses 502, 1406, 2438, 2445, 2899, 3213,
  3240, 4331
Horticulture 2469
Hospitality 916
Hospitals 401, 1200, 2632, 2709
  see also: Mental hospitals
House 911, 1035, 1365, 2187, 2394, 2459,
  2594, 2602, 2642, 2665, 2777, 3660,
  3696, 3713, 4319
Household economics 2142, 2644, 4808, 4821
Household expenditure 4353
Household income 2141, 2210
Households 848, 911, 2137, 2151, 2181, 2185,
  2221, 2306, 2375, 2455, 2605, 2636,
  2654, 2690, 2823, 4661, 4719
Housewives 4584
Housework 2692, 4853
Housing 1054, 1196, 2141, 2171, 2210, 3660,
  3842, 3843, 4364, 4647, 4681, 4838,
  4930, 4934, 4935, 4941
  see also: Rural dwellings, Social housing,
  Urban housing
Housing policy 4838, 4934
Housing prices 4681
Howard, Albert 2311
Hrozný, Bedřich 87, 975, 976
HsShelishi, Shemu'el 4054
Huichol 2602, 2665, 3598
Human behaviour 38, 138, 210, 822, 1452,
  1487, 1488, 1496, 1499, 1507, 1754,
  2872, 2891, 3360, 3561, 3761, 3992,
  4019, 4393, 4394, 4529, 4532, 4539
Human biology 193, 1451, 1487, 1492, 1499,
  1521, 1543, 1575, 1584, 2080, 2699,
  3662, 3750, 3771
Human body 174, 310, 433, 760, 769, 1448-
  1450, 1455, 1457, 1514, 1531, 1541,
  1542, 1547, 1549, 1555, 1556, 1560,
  1563, 1564, 1569, 1581, 1588, 1777,
  2374, 2381, 2676, 2719, 2727, 2780,
  2791, 2810, 2827, 2920-2926, 2929, 2930,
  2932-2935, 2939-2942, 2944, 2947, 2949,
  2952, 2954-2959, 2961, 2962, 3104, 3225,
  3653, 3714, 3760, 3777, 3779, 3817,
  3929, 4110, 4239, 4297, 4312, 4348, 4484,
  4510, 4560, 4872

see also: Anthropology of the body, Organs

Human capital 2315, 4711, 4865

Human development 186, 894, 914, 1470, 1496, 1518, 1545-1547, 1550, 1552, 1553, 1555, 1557, 1562, 1564, 1571, 1573, 1574, 1578, 1579, 1590, 1592, 2715, 2860, 3086, 3149, 4575, 4621, 4672, 4711, 4721, 4738, 4747, 4756, 4789

Human ecology 646, 685, 1303, 2061, 2072, 2098, 2109, 2190, 2217, 2224, 2283, 2296, 2435, 2594, 2752, 2834, 4406, 4666, 4782, 4797, 4923

Human environment 1, 2095, 2133, 2834, 4406

Human evolution 156, 198, 272, 429, 845, 846, 849, 870, 898, 899, 1379, 1413, 1450, 1458, 1459, 1467, 1472, 1477, 1484, 1514, 1515, 1517, 1521-1526, 1529-1534, 1536, 1537, 1543, 1567, 1584, 1703, 1715, 2126, 2589, 2645, 2679, 2872, 3131, 3771

Human genetics 1453, 1486-1488, 1491-1496, 1498, 1499, 1502, 1506, 1507, 1511-1515, 1517, 1558, 1561, 1582, 1741, 2118, 2657, 2722

Human geography 254, 291, 409, 611, 684, 757, 1043, 1066, 1303, 2120, 2170, 2207, 2386, 2406, 2594, 3042, 3615, 3961, 4347, 4431, 4457, 4487, 4624

Human nature 1451, 2080, 3009, 3662

Human origins 914, 1515, 1518, 1522, 1525, 4463

Human race 1492, 2229, 4199

Human relations 134, 4854

Human resources 29, 4701, 4755

Human rights 134, 395, 562, 765, 1652, 2414, 2570, 2577, 2582, 2728, 2863, 2954, 3009, 3020, 3028, 3036, 3059, 3063, 3551, 3798, 4012, 4418, 4613, 4616, 4625, 4634, 4640, 4641, 4644, 4653, 4733, 4829, 4904

Human settlements 455, 483, 835, 843, 854, 869, 870, 907, 920, 936, 965, 994, 1130, 1155, 1183, 1205, 1240, 1319, 2095, 2103, 2104, 2164, 2168, 2178, 2184, 2195, 2225, 2276, 2474, 2512, 2590, 4001, 4024, 4031, 4666, 4759

Humanism 35, 104, 110, 115, 758, 2099, 2232, 3155, 3354, 3799, 3862, 4191, 4264

Humanitarian intervention 4708, 4725, 4834, 4839

Humanities 106, 132, 437, 451, 485, 501, 542, 546, 596, 683, 701, 713, 725, 733, 745, 752, 758, 783, 802, 946, 1005, 1024, 1136, 1294, 1319, 1344, 1347, 1758, 1770, 1787, 1810, 1812, 1868, 1925, 1926, 1970, 1979, 2139, 2361, 2813, 3032, 3113, 3119, 3133, 3216, 3255, 3258, 3365, 3617, 3618, 3626, 3632, 3637, 3642, 3644, 3738, 3741, 3778, 3891, 3902, 3911, 3928, 3933, 3981, 3984, 4014, 4030, 4036, 4045, 4047, 4053, 4059, 4065, 4066, 4075, 4077, 4080, 4083, 4084, 4087, 4088, 4097, 4101, 4121, 4122, 4147, 4196, 4201, 4220, 4222, 4234, 4235, 4242, 4245, 4260, 4270, 4271, 4275, 4306

Humanity 1525, 3035, 3475, 4238

Humour 1767, 1864, 3354, 3449, 4033, 4194, 4243, 4254

see also: Jokes

Humsi, Deek al-Jin al- 4083

Hunger 4817, 4820, 4872

Hunter-gatherers 371, 833, 887, 1041, 1281, 1304, 1408, 1550, 2266, 2352, 2432, 2433, 2449, 2651, 2834, 3084, 3992, 4393, 4406

see also: Gathering

Hunters 3991, 3998

Hunting 222, 384, 564, 746, 841, 1072, 1281, 1406, 1600, 1663, 2075, 2429, 2431, 2433, 2830, 2834, 3674, 3991, 3998, 4208, 4406, 4595

Huron 4321

Hurrian 479

Husbandry 2441

see also: Animal husbandry

Husbands 2645, 2758

Hutterites 2122

Hutu 192, 618

Hydrology 2091, 4766

Hygiene 1474, 1475, 1569, 3798, 4396, 4903

Hymns 3211, 3282, 3289, 3307, 3484, 3920

Hypothesis 298, 428, 1449, 1604, 1608, 1662, 1931, 2134, 2235, 2352, 2790, 2935, 3516, 4705

Iatmul 3550

Iban 2181

Ibn Khaldun 1830

Iconography 433, 461, 567, 581, 828, 1005, 1013, 1044, 1055, 1060, 1385, 3051, 3118, 3515, 3520, 3585, 3735, 3999, 4095, 4140

Icons 166, 1024, 1077, 3118, 3249, 3649, 3733, 3830, 3947, 3999, 4428

Idealism 4045, 4191, 4489

Identification 1764, 1820, 4489, 4494

Identity 155, 158, 166, 228, 252-254, 263, 291, 383, 415, 530, 579, 582, 599, 611, 625, 627, 659, 669, 689, 694, 708, 716, 729, 735, 748, 751, 798, 852, 886, 936,

969, 972, 991, 991, 1004, 1083, 1361,
1426, 1554, 1733, 1749, 1758, 1787,
1798, 1816, 1816, 1817, 1824, 1925,
1965, 2005, 2013, 2092, 2104, 2192,
2193, 2195, 2207, 2257, 2323, 2324,
2327, 2476, 2478, 2496, 2510, 2533,
2600, 2601, 2603, 2603, 2623, 2628,
2648, 2652, 2668, 2692, 2762, 2779,
2831, 2834, 2842, 2900, 2919, 2921,
2955, 2976, 3005, 3016, 3039, 3042,
3043, 3071, 3073, 3081, 3094, 3096,
3102, 3105, 3106, 3132, 3199, 3230,
3250, 3345, 3348, 3409, 3410, 3414,
3422, 3487, 3489, 3494, 3516, 3570,
3591, 3621, 3625, 3633, 3639, 3649,
3665, 3666, 3683, 3697, 3700, 3701,
3712, 3722, 3723, 3739, 3777, 3783,
3822, 3871, 3873, 3891, 3917, 3938,
3939, 3946, 3958, 3960, 3961, 3969,
3994, 4014, 4041, 4049, 4056, 4073,
4074, 4093, 4108, 4111, 4126, 4184, 4191,
4205, 4238, 4239, 4265, 4313, 4316,
4330, 4337, 4352, 4355, 4356, 4359,
4361, 4377-4379, 4395, 4398, 4401, 4402,
4405, 4406, 4408-4412, 4414, 4415, 4419,
4422, 4425-4432, 4434, 4436, 4437, 4439,
4440, 4440, 4441, 4443-4453, 4455-4459,
4461, 4462, 4464, 4466-4468, 4470, 4471,
4473-4477, 4479, 4481, 4483, 4485, 4488,
4489, 4492, 4494, 4504, 4516, 4528,
4540, 4582, 4590, 4591, 4605, 4652,
4708, 4754, 4758, 4839, 4845, 4853, 4861
see also: Cultural identity, Group identity,
National identity, Regional identity, Social
identity
Identity formation 15, 136, 278, 504, 2475,
2530, 2671, 2834, 3026, 3230, 3708,
3777, 4405, 4406, 4414, 4441, 4443,
4447, 4458, 4460, 4468, 4486, 4496
Identity politics 2157, 3061, 3404, 3969,
4407, 4515
Ideology 35, 104, 204, 215, 228, 271, 329,
656, 769, 800, 1735, 1736, 1785, 1792,
2096, 2100, 2535, 2538, 2544, 2549,
2600, 2619, 2630, 2666, 2791, 2822,
2826, 2850, 2927, 2944, 3030, 3066,
3142, 3233, 3288, 3340, 3367, 3518,
3523, 3538, 3707, 3838, 3846, 3887,
3933, 4023, 4059, 4102, 4415, 4452,
4482, 4490, 4493, 4502
see also: Political ideology
Igbo 2005, 2513, 2659, 2682, 2683, 2733,
4193
Igbo-Ukwu 532
Igorot 4852

Ikwerre 1998
Ila 3245
Illegal immigrants 2169, 2660
Illiteracy 3710, 4247, 4721, 4733
Illness 566, 1560, 1570, 1651, 1657, 2128,
2701, 3761, 3763, 3774, 3777, 3805, 3811,
3813, 3815, 3819, 3835, 3836, 4211, 4276,
4526, 4871, 4882, 4896
Images 110, 133, 231, 257, 322, 360, 380,
389, 409, 439, 441, 582, 759, 813, 997,
1006, 1044, 1051, 1088, 1364, 1394,
1442, 1460, 1777, 2774, 2934, 2950, 3119,
3189, 3217, 3242, 3396, 3511, 3516, 3660,
3718, 3721, 3799, 3873, 4098, 4104,
4105, 4126, 4139, 4140, 4160, 4195,
4199, 4316, 4382, 4523
Imagination 2085, 2324, 3330, 3933, 4029,
4059, 4263, 4310, 4514, 4599
Imbuga, Francis 2499
IMF 4338, 4667, 4680
Immigrant adaptation 2178, 2616, 4603, 4761
Immigrant assimilation 1798
Immigrants 253, 489, 732, 763, 787, 2154,
2186, 2259, 2453, 2599, 2883, 2887,
2982, 3070, 3629, 4397, 4603, 4761
see also: Illegal immigrants
Immigration 246, 1551, 1659, 2135, 3056,
3075, 3077, 4191, 4421
Immigration policy 4632
Immunization 2140, 4880, 4884, 4885
Imperialism 529, 611, 650, 694, 702, 703,
715, 718, 742, 805, 817, 903, 984, 2092,
2741, 2745, 3042, 4150, 4171, 4182,
4284, 4298
see also: Cultural imperialism
Implements 1393
see also: Agricultural implements
Imports 2305
Inca 766, 1784, 2597, 3538, 4098
Incest 3966
Income 485, 2210, 2290, 2293, 2309, 2350,
2361, 2430, 2434, 2466, 2620, 2631,
2726, 2763, 4787, 4820, 4827
see also: Household income, Low income,
National income, Per capita income
Income inequality 2264, 2620, 4399, 4682
Income redistribution 4609, 4929
Incompatibility 1486, 1491, 2118
Independence 37, 114, 529, 541, 609, 675,
792, 793, 2506, 2559, 2653, 2977, 3673,
3869, 3949, 4102, 4589, 4629
Indians 225, 539, 732, 761, 1945, 2098, 2356,
2621, 2886, 3053, 3107, 3214, 3271,
3272, 3296, 3317, 3570, 3605, 3754,
3783, 4363

Indicators 1568, 1629, 2149, 2720, 3674, 4595
  see also: Economic indicators
Indigenism 3911, 4655
Indigenous culture 1787, 1970, 3071, 3107,
  3891, 3911, 3981, 4196, 4201, 4293, 4295,
  4463, 4617, 4651
Indigenous knowledge 1513, 2094, 2098,
  2370, 2432, 2447, 2733, 2806, 2828,
  2843, 2990, 3015, 3566, 3655, 3757,
  3786, 3815, 4129, 4620, 4637, 4658,
  4693, 4780, 4820, 4910
Indigenous populations 1, 90, 95, 100, 103,
  135, 139, 214, 225, 234, 254, 258, 269,
  385, 404, 416, 531, 539, 542, 566, 648,
  682, 699, 720, 721, 725, 733, 739, 740,
  745, 758, 763, 783, 784, 790, 803, 806,
  810, 942, 991, 1289, 1294, 1322, 1456,
  1749, 1787, 1797, 1824, 1970, 2062,
  2067, 2075, 2078, 2084, 2102, 2164,
  2167, 2197, 2207, 2262, 2391, 2398,
  2403, 2414, 2426, 2472, 2477, 2524,
  2540, 2541, 2570, 2576-2578, 2582, 2592,
  2691, 2750, 2827, 2834, 2849, 2857,
  2904, 2989, 3011, 3016, 3019, 3026, 3032,
  3036, 3039, 3045, 3055, 3056, 3059,
  3063, 3071, 3074-3076, 3092, 3104, 3107-
  3109, 3130, 3348, 3548, 3559, 3588,
  3635, 3659, 3669, 3671, 3735, 3742,
  3757, 3761, 3870, 3902, 3911, 3915, 4000,
  4044, 4129, 4136, 4196, 4201, 4278,
  4293, 4295, 4320, 4377, 4406, 4408,
  4412, 4420, 4422, 4425, 4457, 4465,
  4535, 4569, 4584, 4590, 4598, 4612,
  4623, 4624, 4633-4638, 4642-4649, 4652-
  4658, 4660, 4785, 4791, 4798, 4799,
  4801, 4802, 4852
Indigenous rights 24, 2062, 2398, 2425, 2524,
  3026, 3056, 3075, 3107, 4633, 4635,
  4638, 4644-4647, 4658-4660, 4799
Individual and society 2595
Individual behaviour 1608, 1629, 1697, 1704,
  2097, 2588, 3761, 3795, 3827, 3834
Individual rights 4625
Individualism 371, 2618, 3112, 3166
Individuality 2367
Individuals 159, 217, 2324, 2490, 2643, 2790,
  2921, 3812, 4126, 4469, 4540, 4890
Indo-European languages 1729, 1912, 1916,
  1920, 1928, 1930, 1931, 1935, 1942,
  1943, 1956, 1966, 2059
  see also: Sanskrit
Indo-Europeans 559, 1729, 2162, 2175, 2612,
  3110, 3115, 3125, 3692
Indonesians 4071
Industrial development 1829

Industrial geography 4663
Industrial history 811, 2619, 3066
Industrial policy 2355
Industrial pollution 2210
Industrial revolution 2229
Industrial sector 4678
Industrial workers 2453
Industrialization 580, 909, 2208, 2279
Industrialized countries 1033
Industry 463, 580, 850, 864, 1395, 2236,
  2279, 2343, 2644
  see also: Agricultural industry, Agrofood
  industry, Automobile industry, Clothing
  industry, Coal industry, Construction
  industry, Location of industry,
  Manufacturing, Milling industry, Nuclear
  industry, Prehistoric industry, Processing
  industry, Record industry, Rubber industry,
  Shipbuilding, Small-scale industry, Sugar
  industry, Telecommunications industry,
  Textile industry
Inequality 183, 247, 978, 1456, 2101, 2387,
  2410, 2513, 2596, 2618, 2626, 2659,
  2795, 2846, 3597, 3801, 4609, 4611, 4618,
  4682, 4794, 4875, 4895
  see also: Economic inequality, Social
  inequality
Infant mortality 1548, 1583, 1675, 2140
Infanticide 1605, 1683, 2722, 2738, 2785,
  4835
Infants 1548, 1574, 1584, 1602, 1603, 1607,
  1612, 1672, 1675, 1676, 1693, 1708,
  2699, 2712, 2713, 3515, 4816, 4824
Infertility 1450, 1491
Infibulation 2880, 2883
Inflation 485, 2361
Informal sector 2169, 2347, 2660, 2819, 4426,
  4663, 4911
Information 25, 61, 78, 291, 301, 635, 2057,
  2241, 2589
  see also: Access to information
Information dissemination 4548
Information exchange 3992
Information processing 320, 3159
Information sources 61, 471, 2497, 4180, 4327
Information systems 4819
Information technology 1773, 1778, 1779,
  2229
Ingalls, Daniel Henry Holmes 1945
Inheritance 1498, 2350, 2410, 2416, 2645,
  2657, 2740, 2753, 2863, 2906, 2973,
  2991, 3017, 3173, 4780
Initiation 166, 2731, 3511, 3591, 3649, 3822,
  4199, 4428
Initiation rites 2729, 3512, 3550, 3626

Injuries 1663

Innovation 188, 879, 1397, 1684, 2085, 2253, 2436, 3730, 3892, 4310, 4743
see also: Agricultural innovations

Innovation diffusion 2588

Insects 4, 165, 507, 2109, 3746

Institutional change 337, 2264, 2376, 2404, 4399, 4682, 4699, 4769, 4894, 4937

Institutional reform 2289

Institutionalism 4787

Institutionalization 4816

Institutions 337, 380, 722, 2067, 2289, 2376, 2404, 2416, 2514, 2999, 3017, 3030, 4710, 4726, 4789, 4907
see also: Aid institutions, Educational institutions, Financial institutions, Religious institutions

Insurrection 816

Integrated development 4788, 4915

Intellectual property 4566, 4636

Intellectual work 175, 254, 4457

Intellectuals 123, 176, 587, 634, 2495, 2572, 3079, 3100, 3441, 3616, 3675, 4187, 4210, 4524

Intelligence 1492, 1513, 1711, 1715, 4527

Intelligence services 552
see also: KGB

Intelligence tests 1463

Intercultural communication 1796, 3037, 3062, 3079, 3565

Intercultural influences 81, 323, 707, 3933, 4059

Interdependence 254, 2185, 3388, 4457, 4615, 4804

Interdisciplinary relations 154, 172, 178, 189, 197, 211, 215, 430, 2915

Interdisciplinary research 154, 156, 163, 170, 172, 187, 189, 194, 420, 974, 2172, 2915, 3015, 4017

Interethnic conflict 395, 447, 712, 2511, 2610, 2827, 3047, 3048, 3088, 3104, 4082, 4603, 4741, 4761

Interethnic relations 10, 447, 509, 553, 554, 582, 593, 760, 782, 2497, 2564, 2578, 2621, 2742, 2886, 2942, 3045, 3062, 3064, 3067, 3069, 3070, 3072, 3074, 3077, 3080, 3082, 3083, 3087, 3090, 3091, 3093, 3094, 3099, 3101, 3102, 3519, 3565, 3592, 3596, 3671, 4000, 4413, 4421

Intergenerational relations 197, 2350, 2662, 2767

Intergroup relations 853, 4468, 4741

Intermarriage 2754, 3058, 3101, 4416

Internal migration 597, 1453, 2167, 2460

Internal trade 2358

International banks 2210

International community 4613, 4621

International conferences 19-21, 23, 27, 41, 42, 184, 190, 211, 430, 590, 658, 679, 1594-1596, 3470, 4646, 4899

International conflicts 793

International cooperation 29, 153, 2289, 4666, 4874, 4933

International cultural relations 3193

International economics 4614

International law 771, 2981, 4203, 4629

International market 2280

International migration 253, 2185

International political economy 183, 3801

International politics 1517

International relations 553, 677, 771, 2189, 2210, 2391, 2549, 2576, 2981, 3036, 3041, 3059, 4483, 4516, 4536, 4673, 4705, 4706, 4712, 4737, 4744, 4746, 4804, 4825
see also: East-West relations, North-South relations

International security 1517

International system 1517

International trade 692, 2391
see also: Exports, Imports

International travels 594, 674, 756, 1820, 3600, 3749, 3797, 3821, 3952, 4263, 4320, 4328, 4334, 4565, 4598, 4618, 4794

Internationalization 29, 2385

Internet 1773, 1782, 2324, 3664

Interpersonal attraction 1449, 1452, 1493, 1494, 2891, 2935

Interpersonal communication 1772

Interpersonal relations 247, 874, 1539, 1775, 1811, 2449, 2596, 2604, 2621, 2691, 2732, 2755, 2758, 2812, 2868, 2882, 2886, 2888, 2914, 3553, 3940, 4172, 4193, 4447

Interracial marriages 2742

Interviews 215, 235, 306, 313, 357, 407, 422, 424, 979, 1586, 2890, 3040, 3747, 3751, 3781, 3792, 3805, 3824, 4170, 4303, 4385, 4473, 4533, 4676

Interwar years 345, 2669, 2827, 3104

Intifada 3026, 4495

Intimacy 2868

Inuit 2066, 2075, 2524, 3514, 3660, 4645, 4785, 4811

Invasions 535, 612, 3023

Inventions 613, 879, 1704, 2230

Inventories 1386

Investment 1571, 2158, 2251, 2399, 4647, 4866, 4900, 4932
see also: Foreign direct investment

Investment returns
   see: Rent
Iranian Revolution 3957
Iranians 559, 626, 2162, 4358, 4403
Iraqw 2487
Iron 709, 2335
Iron Age 363, 387, 448, 449, 512, 523, 669,
   823, 826, 828, 838, 859, 878, 881, 885,
   895, 916, 920, 921, 924, 927, 928, 950,
   965, 981, 1013, 1036, 1053, 1057, 1263,
   1324, 1398, 1399, 1402, 1439, 1443,
   2360, 3111
Iroquois 102, 1799
Irrigation 789, 2062, 2070, 2093, 2271, 2287,
   2289, 2293, 2295, 2376, 3536, 4635,
   4688, 4769, 4771, 4783, 4926
Ishi 887
Islam 154, 191, 202, 228, 245, 260, 292, 356,
   413, 484, 527, 579, 596, 606, 611, 617,
   782, 1015, 1032, 1082, 1100, 1333, 1373,
   1749, 1852, 1863, 2073, 2099, 2182,
   2227, 2395, 2484, 2501, 2652, 2682,
   2748, 2826, 2910, 2967, 2979, 2986,
   2998, 3014, 3027, 3042, 3155, 3230,
   3236, 3320, 3321, 3323-3336, 3336, 3338,
   3338-3342, 3344, 3345, 3347-3350, 3353-
   3357, 3359-3361, 3364-3366, 3580, 3616,
   3621, 3625, 3634, 3646, 3767, 3802,
   3840, 3853, 3951, 4052, 4058, 4080, 4115,
   4185, 4215, 4218, 4232, 4441, 4447,
   4558, 4585, 4615, 4622, 4629, 4685
   see also: Koran, Shiism, Sufism
Islam and politics 2484, 2501, 2541, 3353,
   4585, 4615
Islamic art 1015, 3840, 4115
Islamic countries 1874, 4551, 4615
Islamic law 606, 748, 1852, 2417, 2417, 2664,
   2976, 2979, 2986, 2993, 3014, 3018,
   3018, 3324, 3330, 3341, 3349, 3352,
   3364, 3646
Islamization 245, 2495, 2652, 3345, 4185
Islands 323, 365, 511, 556, 566, 630, 691,
   707, 721, 1088, 1462, 1820, 1827, 2085,
   2344, 2384, 2498, 2559, 2647, 2814,
   3546, 3650, 3847, 3847, 4228, 4237,
   4300, 4310, 4311, 4323, 4443, 4601, 4647,
   4768
Ismail, Husin bin 4215
Isolate 1731
Isolationism 2478
Isonymy 1822
Italian language 1932
Italians 2476, 4397
Ivory 1366
Jackson, Andrew 2330

Jacob, Ephraim ben 3089
Jaddus 3454
Jainism 185, 2099, 3155, 3164, 3183, 3235,
   3368-3380, 3382-3391, 4117
Jains 185, 3183, 3235, 3369-3379, 3381,
   3384-3386, 3388-3391, 4117
Jamālzāde, Mohammad Ali 4169
Jansen, Jan 2488
Japanese 787, 3078, 3956, 4419, 4583
Japanese language 1737, 1769, 1770, 1872,
   1875
Japanese studies 330, 331, 337, 338, 347, 361,
   362, 364, 374, 377
Jaspers, Karl 260
Jazz 118, 2857, 3076, 3900, 3929, 3931, 3933,
   3935, 3943, 4059
Jealousy 2682
Jesuits 721, 806, 3220, 3632
Jewellery 1373, 1382, 1396
   see also: Beads
Jews 253, 468, 472, 476, 515, 519, 560, 592,
   593, 1773, 1816, 2160, 2422, 2573, 2778,
   2799, 3089, 3098, 3100, 3327, 3392,
   3394, 3397, 3401, 3404, 3406, 3408-3410,
   3412, 3414, 3422, 3428, 3446, 3447,
   3451, 3452, 3613, 3665, 3666, 3899,
   4002, 4049, 4093, 4141, 4359, 4384,
   4402, 4424, 4427, 4439, 4445, 4451,
   4461, 4468, 4479, 4503, 4515, 4581, 4628
Job performance 2468
Job search 2458
Job security 1573
John [Saint] 3261
Johnson, Samuel 4176
Johnson, William 2857, 3076
Joint consultation 2113
Jokes 1754, 1767, 4243, 4450
Jomon 1461, 1464, 2235
Josephus, Flavius 3420, 3421, 3428, 3454,
   4258
Joshee, Anandibai 4577
Journalism 805, 1781, 3037, 3793, 4280
Journalists 106, 752
Joyce, James 4182
Jubair, Ibn 596
Judaism 208, 253, 447, 468, 472, 473, 476,
   514, 515, 560, 568, 591-593, 604, 606,
   634, 640, 666, 897, 1103, 1308, 1864,
   1965, 2099, 2573, 2748, 2756, 2799,
   2909, 2965, 2986, 3155, 3327, 3392-3395,
   3397, 3398, 3400-3403, 3405-3409, 3411-
   3413, 3415-3419, 3422-3426, 3428-3430,
   3432-3435, 3437-3444, 3447-3458, 3460,
   3613, 3666, 3748, 3997, 4141, 4258,

4384, 4402, 4427, 4445, 4581
see also: Hasidism, Hebrew
Judgement 4466
Judges 485, 792, 2361, 2987
Judiciary 59, 2975, 2994, 3003, 3705
Judiciary power 606, 2986
Jurisdiction
see: Criminal jurisdiction
Jurisprudence 516, 784, 2989, 2996, 3014, 3341
Justice 214, 485, 510, 2218, 2361, 2536, 2933, 2971, 3013, 3032, 3063, 3068, 4012, 4449, 4634
see also: Criminal justice, Social justice
Kaberry, Phyllis 105, 3231
Kabyle 1854
Kafka, Franz 4093
Kālidāsa 3305, 3885
Kalmyk 3945, 4410
Kamuleta, Kadima 1994, 2009
Kanak 2096
Karen 4791
Karo Batak 334, 4178
Kasena 2103, 4024
Kaur, Satwant 3492, 3493
Keats, John 3728
Kenyah 4320, 4598
Kety 1768
KGB 319, 2964
Khaldun, Ibn 575
Khaled bn 'Abd el-Malik bn al-Harth bn Al-Hakam, Mohammed bn [Prince] 1319
Khanty 2057
Khatri 2541
Khmer 1076, 4547
Khoi 4151
Khoikhoi 682
Khoisan 1726, 2377
Kikuyu 1997
Kinberg, Naphtali 129, 1853
Kingdoms 358, 495, 541, 583, 626, 639, 648, 721, 724, 739, 806, 895, 1088, 1437, 2073, 2417, 2501, 2546, 2574, 2581, 3018, 3688, 4007, 4153, 4253
Kingship 587, 1838, 2282, 2392, 2572, 2575, 2584, 4090, 4165
Kinguri 2168
Kinship 138, 198, 666, 1498, 1505, 1685, 1882, 1900, 2020, 2143, 2161, 2169, 2171, 2188, 2266, 2285, 2351, 2474, 2509, 2513, 2554, 2557, 2586, 2602, 2628-2631, 2634, 2638, 2641, 2647, 2650, 2654-2660, 2662-2665, 2667, 2670, 2672-2674, 2676, 2677, 2679-2681, 2683, 2684, 2687, 2689, 2690, 2740, 2747, 2748,

2751, 2770, 2837, 2933, 2952, 3030, 3105, 3352, 3353, 3458, 4008, 4790
Kinship systems 2597, 2658
see also: Exogamy
Kinship terminology 2020, 2022
Kintō, Fujiwara 4051
Kipling, Rudyard 4284
Kipsigis 2611, 2611
Kirghiz 145, 1834
Klong-rdol bla ma 3184
Knots 1784
Knotting 1784
Knowledge 53, 99, 156, 160, 173, 182, 239, 243, 261, 275, 305, 329, 396, 407, 476, 691, 996, 1226, 1609, 1743, 2201, 2232, 2297, 2308, 2309, 2370, 2539, 2598, 2633, 2686, 2726, 2804, 2937, 2949, 2990, 3170, 3172, 3252, 3346, 3621, 3627, 3659, 3668, 3669, 3675-3677, 3728, 3730, 3739, 3753, 4275, 4438, 4548, 4549, 4612, 4620, 4675, 4696, 4703
see also: Anthropology of knowledge, Indigenous knowledge, Sociology of knowledge
Koentjaraningrat, R.M. 37, 114
Kohnen, Bernardo 88
Komi 2050, 2053, 2054, 2056
Koran 3120, 3330, 3333, 3338, 3344, 3346, 3351, 3355, 3358, 3362, 3365, 3802, 4080
Korean language 1962
Koresh, David 3563
Kota 3910, 3967
Krčelić, Baltazar Adam 3974
Kuhn, Thomas S. 259, 414
Kumaraswamy Iyer, K.R. 3932
Kuna 3550
Kunama 2010
Kuru 3803
Kurzman, Steven L. 2955
Kusu 1996
Kwahu 2773, 2898
Kwakiutl 98, 2503
Kwara'ae 3669, 4519
Kyong'ae, Kang 2933
Kyrillos VI [Saint] 3253
Labdron, Machig 3192
Labelling 4388
Laboratory 1509
Labour 693, 2200, 2222, 2229, 2293, 2342, 2411, 2418, 2457, 2460, 2461, 2471, 3889, 4311, 4331
see also: Agricultural labour, Child labour, Division of labour, Forced labour
Labour costs 2279
Labour force 687, 2254

Labour history 2460, 2467
Labour market 2359, 2460, 2466, 2768, 4606, 4916
Labour migration 2161, 2166, 2207, 2439, 4632
Labour mobility 2279
Labour relations 2089, 2467, 2836
Labour supply 807, 4916
Labour value 2342
Lactation 1670
Lakes 2086
Lamaism 3202
Laments 4011
Land 155, 530, 541, 721, 797, 803, 810, 969, 2127, 2316, 2321, 2337, 2350, 2399, 2401-2403, 2405, 2408, 2409, 2414, 2418, 2421, 2422, 2424, 2425, 2517, 2609, 2997, 3056, 3075, 4442, 4650, 4659, 4796, 4917, 4939, 4940
Land claims 4645, 4654
Land economics 2427, 4805
Land policy 2265, 2397, 2407, 2411, 2412, 2419, 2730, 2980, 4934
Land reform 184, 726, 2396, 2402, 2412, 2419, 2420, 2600, 4669, 4682, 4820, 4905, 4917
Land settlement 797, 803, 994, 2103, 2184, 2422, 2512, 2599, 3629, 4001, 4024, 4031
Land tenure 795, 806, 2299, 2314, 2396-2401, 2403, 2404, 2409, 2414-2418, 2420, 2422, 2425, 2426, 2609, 2669, 2968, 3017, 3018, 3106, 3659, 4618, 4630, 4638, 4659, 4682, 4794, 4820, 4887, 4905
Land use 249, 488, 831, 882, 913, 926, 1153, 1310, 1834, 2079, 2084, 2137, 2287, 2292, 2313, 2319, 2371, 2411, 2413, 2420, 3107, 4301, 4607, 4669, 4766, 4804, 4819
Landowners 757, 2281, 2397, 2405, 2406, 2600, 2681, 4619, 4799
Landscape 291, 458, 806, 852, 885, 888, 892, 893, 915, 923, 932, 962, 1000, 1011, 1041, 1053, 1084, 1123, 1148, 1150, 1153, 1155, 1163, 1188, 1196, 1197, 1222, 1263, 1310, 1824, 2060, 2084, 2087, 2095, 2096, 2110, 2170, 2207, 2317, 2509, 3653, 3727, 3845, 3847, 4127, 4128, 4425, 4484, 4487, 4626, 4789, 4792
Language 99, 110, 129, 230, 248, 266, 271, 291, 308, 320, 344, 540, 542, 550, 586, 597, 651, 735, 745, 830, 1005, 1036, 1042, 1338, 1339, 1723, 1726-1736, 1739, 1741, 1742, 1745-1749, 1756, 1759, 1763, 1765, 1773, 1775, 1778-1780, 1784, 1785, 1787, 1789-1791, 1794, 1795, 1797, 1798, 1800, 1801, 1803, 1804, 1807-1810, 1812-
1814, 1816, 1824, 1826, 1831, 1834, 1839-1841, 1845-1849, 1853, 1854, 1856, 1858, 1865-1867, 1870-1872, 1877, 1880, 1892, 1894, 1895, 1897-1901, 1904-1906, 1908-1911, 1913, 1915-1918, 1920, 1924, 1925, 1927-1931, 1933-1941, 1943, 1944, 1946-1949, 1951-1958, 1961, 1962, 1964, 1965, 1968-1971, 1974, 1976-1983, 1986-1988, 1990, 1991, 1994, 1997, 1998, 2002-2007, 2009, 2011, 2012, 2017, 2020-2046, 2048-2051, 2053-2055, 2057, 2059, 2145, 2324, 2529, 2638, 2641, 2689, 2812, 3014, 3080, 3150, 3226, 3229, 3233, 3258, 3268, 3282, 3312, 3333, 3341, 3362, 3433, 3459, 3511, 3537, 3588, 3644, 3652, 3653, 3799, 3874, 3887, 3915, 3927, 3973, 3996, 4017, 4035, 4039, 4061, 4065, 4067, 4170, 4224, 4250, 4252, 4256, 4263, 4286, 4409, 4419, 4426, 4430, 4434, 4437, 4446, 4474, 4478, 4484, 4488, 4490, 4506, 4562, 4587, 4640
  see also: Albanian language, Arabic language, Dead languages, Foreign languages, Hindi, Indo-European languages, Korean language, National language, Official languages, Philology, Polish language, Portuguese language, Sentences, Sign language, Unwritten languages, Urdu, Vernacular languages, Written language
Language acquisition 1790, 1936, 4506
Language change 1724, 1725, 1727, 1730, 1734, 1744, 1745, 1749, 1757, 1789, 1806, 1807, 1810, 1813-1815, 1851, 1870, 1874, 1879, 1911, 1915, 1927, 1929, 1930, 1935, 1938, 1942, 1947, 1951, 1954, 1955, 1958, 1964, 1979, 1981, 1985, 1988, 1990, 2003, 2011, 2012, 2016, 2018, 2051, 2052, 2058, 4268
Language disorder 110, 3799
Language history 117, 1729, 1732, 1785, 1794, 1797, 1808, 1810, 1841, 1857, 1869, 1873, 1877-1879, 1881, 1886-1888, 1892, 1901, 1902, 1905, 1910-1913, 1915, 1916, 1918, 1920, 1927, 1929, 1930, 1934, 1935, 1937, 1938, 1942-1944, 1946, 1948, 1949, 1951-1956, 1961, 1964, 1965, 1988, 1990, 2003, 2021, 2023, 2037, 2039, 2042, 2044, 2051, 2052, 2058, 2059, 2302, 4268
Language planning 1983, 2529
Language policy 1759, 1797, 1916
Language teaching 1975, 3095, 4553
Lapita 556, 598, 623, 931, 1404

Lapp 4624
Latin 461, 490, 774, 1358, 1912, 1941, 1942, 3150
Latin American studies 214, 750, 763, 2082
Laughter 1864, 3449
Law 59, 158, 214, 342, 508, 568, 624, 1852, 2400, 2407, 2408, 2418, 2738, 2785, 2887, 2954, 2965, 2968, 2969, 2972-2974, 2978, 2980, 2982-2985, 2994, 2995, 3001, 3003, 3013, 3014, 3016, 3030, 3056, 3075, 3173, 3303, 3341, 3346, 3395, 3413, 3418, 3428, 3468, 3701, 4152, 4247, 4613, 4617, 4619, 4644, 4650, 4651, 4654, 4670, 4762, 4820, 4935
  see also: Anthropology of law, Commercial law, Common law, Criminal law, Customary law, Environmental law, History of law, International law, Islamic law, Litigation, Natural law, Sociology of law, Traditional law
Lawrence, David 4303
Lawyers 2618, 3638
Leaders 537, 649, 2199, 2563, 2566, 3488
  see also: Charismatic leaders, Political leaders
Leadership 724, 739, 2560, 2561, 2566, 2569, 2571, 2681, 3015, 4374, 4751, 4752, 4843
  see also: Political leadership
Learned societies 19, 21, 23, 27, 427, 1594-1596
Learning 66, 69, 84, 291, 352, 407, 1405, 1427, 1637, 2236, 2588, 2589, 3474, 4549, 4554, 4559, 4690, 4749, 4860
Least squares method 4886
Leer, Willem van 4581
Left 270, 2537
Legal aspects 2998, 3366
Legal culture 2400, 2968, 3016
Legal protection 667
Legal reform 59, 2407, 2980, 2994, 3003
Legal status 694, 748, 2976, 2983, 4606, 4644
Legal systems 516, 606, 748, 771, 2750, 2969, 2972, 2975, 2976, 2981, 2984-2986, 2996, 3019, 3112, 4670
  see also: Legal culture
Legal theory 59, 235, 268, 3003
Legends 505, 639, 659, 662, 713, 3116, 3118, 3120, 3132, 3351, 3353, 3354, 3493, 3514, 3528, 3679, 3709, 3974, 3993, 3997, 3999, 4003, 4005, 4013, 4015, 4026, 4154, 4214, 4221, 4253
Leger, Alexis 4712
Legislation 719, 2259, 2582, 2736, 2739, 2750, 2863, 2883, 2954, 3010, 3012,

3019, 3096, 4617, 4642, 4644, 4651, 4791, 4804, 4861
Legitimacy 1159, 2937, 3739, 3861, 4438
Legitimation 4257
Leisure 371, 2085, 2234, 2946, 3972, 4116, 4295, 4310, 4314, 4318, 4324
Leisure time 4350
Leitão, Manoel Correia 690
Lele 3685
Lenca 2084
Leopardi, Giacomo 3728
Leprosy 739
Lesbianism 514, 2900, 2909, 4330
Less developed countries 1552, 4734
Level of education 2153, 2410, 3769
Levi, Maklouf 615
Lévi-Povençal, Evariste 615
Lévi-Strauss, Claude 2602, 2665
Levirate 2753, 2906
Lexicography 745, 1728, 1769, 1770, 1779, 2055
Lexicology 1730, 1751, 1877, 1879, 1889, 1932, 1987, 2007, 2014, 2015, 2021, 4262
Li 2678, 3682
Li Po 4056
Liberal democracy 4778
Liberal parties 754
Liberalism 815, 3846, 4682
  see also: Neoliberalism
Liberalization 4661, 4671, 4672
  see also: Financial liberalization
Liberation 215, 3188, 3299, 3376, 3679
Libertarians 3846
Librarians 2465
Libraries 25, 82, 291, 323, 324, 354, 370, 375, 707, 2465, 4215, 4223
Life cycles 565, 676, 1407, 2697, 2761, 2768, 2769, 2771, 2776, 2803, 2845, 2862, 2864, 3269, 3678, 3684
Life expectancy 2152, 2768, 4859
Life history 103, 297, 357, 1481, 1546, 1718, 2938, 3870, 4574, 4575, 4577
Life stories 88, 101, 128, 375, 570, 4012, 4249, 4564, 4567-4570, 4572
Life styles 905, 1456, 2326, 2502, 3378, 3572, 3795
Limb 2955
Limbu 2032, 2035
Liminality 201, 222, 237, 239, 384, 392, 396, 2190, 2615, 3777
Lindfors, Bernth 89
Lineage 1577, 2188, 2421, 2617, 2653, 2662, 2677, 2977, 3185, 3519, 4822
Linear models 4554

Linguistic anthropology 102, 113, 119, 129, 196, 230, 235, 248, 266, 1732, 1736, 1772, 1780, 1799, 1802, 1849, 1853, 1878, 1881-1884, 1886, 1968, 2667, 3233
Linguistic areas 1849
Linguistic atlases 113, 1802
Linguistic conflict 1759
Linguistic contact 1757, 1759, 1789, 1791, 1792, 1794, 1795, 1804, 1806, 1808, 1810, 1815, 1849, 1851, 1877, 1915, 1932, 1985, 1999, 2021, 2056
Linguistic groups 1845, 1881, 1886, 1888
Linguistic minorities 1746, 1768, 1916
Linguistic pluralism 4649
Linguistic research 42, 57, 109, 117, 124, 139, 1792, 1805, 1881-1888, 1914, 1989, 1994, 1995, 1999, 2009, 2052, 2667
Linguistic theory 1766, 1860, 1869, 1882-1888, 1890, 1933, 2667, 3330
Linguistics 30, 42, 57, 109, 113, 117, 124, 139, 150, 163, 250, 252, 271, 382, 522, 540, 609, 631, 745, 762, 1025, 1331, 1435, 1723-1726, 1728-1730, 1732, 1734, 1740-1742, 1744, 1747, 1749-1753, 1756, 1757, 1760, 1765, 1766, 1776, 1778, 1779, 1783, 1785, 1789, 1791-1797, 1801, 1802, 1805-1808, 1810-1814, 1819, 1821, 1826, 1831, 1832, 1837-1840, 1842-1850, 1854, 1855, 1858, 1860, 1866-1870, 1872, 1875, 1877-1892, 1894-1911, 1913-1915, 1917, 1918, 1920-1922, 1924, 1927-1930, 1932-1938, 1940, 1943, 1944, 1946-1949, 1951-1964, 1967, 1968, 1971, 1976, 1977, 1979-1981, 1984, 1986, 1987, 1989, 1991-1999, 2001, 2002, 2005-2016, 2020-2022, 2024, 2025, 2027-2046, 2048-2052, 2054, 2055, 2058, 2100, 2301, 2526, 2544, 2550, 2638, 2667, 2832, 2973, 3134, 3146, 3147, 3165, 3173, 3179, 3185, 3195, 3203, 3233, 3267, 3273, 3293, 3301, 3319, 3322, 3539, 3576, 3588, 3673, 3707, 3728, 3885, 3944, 3950, 3973, 3989, 4025, 4040, 4064, 4082, 4147, 4151, 4155, 4188, 4203, 4206, 4224, 4244, 4249, 4273, 4285, 4286, 4409, 4422, 4444, 4461, 4467, 4503, 4548 *see also:* Accent, Comparative linguistics, Diglossia, Sociolinguistics
Linguists 119, 139, 1878, 1994, 2009
Lips, Julius E. 3045
Lisnianskaia, Inna 4073
Lisu 2022
Literacy 248, 1568, 1743, 1744, 1790, 2121, 2561, 2598, 2760, 2861, 3627, 3668, 4229, 4247, 4751, 4756, 4902

Literary criticism 89, 236, 650, 2533, 2955, 3073, 3405, 3911, 3996, 4036, 4053, 4083, 4086, 4147, 4149, 4157, 4175, 4182, 4191, 4196, 4200, 4201, 4217, 4220, 4222, 4287, 4563
Literary genres 3995, 3996, 4052, 4060, 4156, 4204
Literary history 89, 107, 405, 1911, 2533, 2839, 2857, 3005, 3073, 3076, 3079, 3211, 3263, 3305, 3437, 3665, 3911, 3974, 3987, 3990, 3991, 3996, 4042, 4044, 4047, 4048, 4053, 4057, 4069, 4071, 4079, 4085, 4112, 4139, 4157, 4160, 4168, 4179, 4191, 4192, 4210, 4211, 4220, 4225, 4231, 4233-4237, 4240, 4247, 4248, 4254, 4255, 4257, 4260, 4264, 4271, 4274, 4277, 4279, 4282, 4287, 4290, 4292, 4322, 4323, 4578, 4581
Literary movements 4053
Literary works 628
Literature 62, 89, 107, 129, 141, 163, 201, 326, 376, 405, 409, 452, 471, 514, 528, 651, 663, 799, 805, 1739, 1827, 1853, 1865, 1950, 1974, 2005, 2025, 2533, 2622, 2641, 2813, 2834, 2839, 2853, 2857, 2909, 2928, 2933, 3005, 3073, 3076, 3079, 3080, 3113, 3118, 3172, 3179, 3180, 3211, 3255, 3272, 3274, 3296, 3305, 3330, 3354, 3369, 3390, 3437, 3535, 3655, 3665, 3698, 3718, 3728, 3740, 3823, 3911, 3961, 3980, 3981, 3984, 3996, 3999, 4011, 4027, 4030, 4039, 4040, 4043, 4046, 4048, 4049, 4051, 4053-4055, 4058, 4064, 4079, 4081, 4082, 4084, 4085, 4088, 4112, 4146, 4147, 4149-4151, 4153, 4156-4159, 4162-4164, 4166-4170, 4173, 4174, 4177, 4179, 4182, 4184, 4187, 4188, 4190-4192, 4195-4197, 4199-4202, 4204, 4206, 4209-4214, 4216-4222, 4226, 4228, 4230, 4235, 4242, 4244-4249, 4251, 4252, 4260-4265, 4269, 4271-4273, 4275, 4279, 4282, 4283, 4287-4289, 4296, 4341, 4354, 4375, 4406, 4439, 4503, 4569, 4581 *see also:* Classical literature, Development literature, Epic literature, Folk literature, Literary history, Novels, Oral literature, Poems, Poetry, Popular literature, Prose, Traditional literature
Lithics 820, 836, 842, 850, 864, 875, 881, 890, 991, 1378, 1403, 1408, 1409, 2107, 3941
Lithographies 4128, 4240
Litigation 342, 2987, 2994, 3638, 4762
Liturgies 468, 472, 3336, 3406-3408, 3423, 3748, 4054
Liver 1570

Livestock 730, 2083, 2367, 2447, 3678, 4536, 4780
Livestock production 2448
Living conditions 1543, 2171, 4531, 4748, 4907, 4922
Loans 1801, 2210, 4671
Lobi 2945, 3529
Local communities 2083, 2085, 2090, 2091, 2103, 2104, 2192, 2195, 2601, 3064, 4024, 4294, 4310, 4311, 4454, 4648, 4718, 4723, 4779, 4793, 4795, 4852
Local culture 303, 2291, 2601, 2713, 3181, 3186, 3531, 3532, 3727, 3886, 4311, 4454, 4664
Local economy 4917
Local government 1786, 2210, 2222, 3230, 3703, 4441, 4717, 4740, 4786
Local history 251, 335, 688, 2003, 2104
Local politics 2101, 2207, 2735, 3064, 4882
Local power 2829
Localization 189, 3723, 4355, 4456
Location of industry 4663
Logic 261, 275, 428, 2539, 3153, 3162, 3178, 3381, 3677, 3947
Lohana 3284
Lolo 2022
Lom D'Arce, Louis-Armand de 100, 740
Loneliness 2868
Longowal, Sant 2515
López Dàvalos, Ruy 3852
López-Baralt, Mercedes 4098
Loss 4538, 4539
Loti, Pierre 4179, 4236, 4263, 4322
Lounsbury, Floyd Glenn 102, 1799
Love 514, 2453, 2683, 2909, 3244, 3276, 3305, 3508, 4034, 4057, 4060, 4062, 4088, 4139, 4218, 4259, 4263, 4571
Love stories 4046
Low income 2210, 2941, 4902
Lower chamber
  see: Members of the lower chamber
Loyalty 2104, 2557, 2631, 2635, 3025
Lua 2806, 2828
Luba 2168
Lucas, Claude 3005
Lugbara 3542
Lunda 2168
Lutheranism 3230, 4441
Lyre 3896
Ma'ari, Abul Ala'a al- 4047
Macushi 2297, 3067
Madness 775, 3873, 4263
Madumo 3579
Maeterlinck, Maurice 3728
Mafia 2663, 2975, 4008

Magic 233, 256, 371, 502, 514, 576, 1006, 1317, 1489, 1738, 2802, 2899, 2909, 2923, 3060, 3555, 3557, 3567, 3570, 3573-3576, 3580, 3581, 3583, 3591, 3602, 3604, 3605, 3607, 3626, 3778, 3783, 3809, 3822, 3830, 4017, 4287, 4354
Magyars 3094, 3095, 3102, 3703, 4553
Mahafaly 2507
Mahākassapa 3190
Mahāvīra, Bhagavān 3368, 3375, 3385, 3386, 4117
Mahavira, Vardhamāna 3370, 3384
Mahmoud, Haidar 3365, 4080
Maimonides, Moses 3403
Maize 323, 707, 2275, 2302, 2312, 2319, 4609
Makonde 4145
Makoni [Chief] 711
Makuzu, Tadano 4266
Malanggan 2241
Malaria 2128, 4870, 4880, 4888
Malays 4215
Male-female relationships 1653, 2461, 2498, 2692, 2724, 2814, 2851, 3940, 4062, 4266, 4853
  see also: Partners
Males 1508, 1539, 1602, 1605, 1623, 1628, 1635, 1643, 1661, 2875, 2890
Malet, Léo 3005
Malnutrition 1540, 1551, 1557, 1565, 1568, 4823, 4895
Management 255, 2369, 4548, 4744, 4757, 4801, 4804, 4820
  see also: Agricultural management, Crisis management, Environmental management, Farm management, Fishery management, Forest management, Personnel management, Public management, Resource management, Risk management, Soil management, Urban management, Waste management, Water management
Managers 2368
Manasseh [King] 3424
Mande 625, 629, 641, 643, 2488, 2531, 2608, 4447
Manggarai 3939
Mangyan 4772
Mani 3527
Mankind 2296
Manobo 2409
Mansi 2055, 2057
Manual workers 682
Manuel I [King] 323, 707
Manufacturing 2231, 2251, 2338, 4678
Manufacturing techniques 1388, 1425

Maori 811, 2408, 2525, 2712, 2937, 3655, 4293, 4432, 4438, 4650
Mapping 132, 294, 393, 437, 494, 768, 802, 1084, 1197, 1737
Maps 132, 323, 393, 437, 707, 721, 768, 802, 1727, 1737, 3111, 3121
Mapuche 1586, 3824, 4315
Marathi 124, 1805, 4197
Marcellini, Margarita 3828
Marcos, Ferdinand 4679
Marginality 994, 4200
Marginalized people 239, 254, 396, 2933, 3082, 4457, 4630, 4646, 4722
Mari 3087, 3708
Marine resources 1291, 4850
Marital conflict 2757, 2856
Marital status 3769
Maritime anthropology 2117
Maritime borders 2070
Maritime history 820
Market 529, 1357, 2196, 2322, 2331, 2332, 2334, 2338, 2341, 2359, 2450, 4426, 4661, 4820, 4827
  see also: Agricultural and food market, Art market, Capital market, Credit market, International market, Labour market, Regional markets, World market
Market economy 2318, 2364, 2447, 2782
Market failure 4894
Market forces 4281
Market research 2326
Market structure 2277
Marketing 2353, 2363
  see also: Advertising
Marold, Luděk 4112
Marquez-Benitez, Paz 4195
Marriage 127, 502, 606, 646, 666, 676, 776, 1453, 1900, 2163, 2252, 2351, 2474, 2554, 2586, 2628, 2629, 2638, 2651, 2658, 2666, 2670, 2683, 2687, 2735, 2737, 2738, 2740-2747, 2749-2753, 2755-2758, 2781, 2785, 2825, 2833, 2856, 2862-2864, 2899, 2906, 2986, 3019, 3267, 3319, 3399, 3457, 3458, 3704, 4373, 4493, 4541
  see also: Age at marriage, Consanguineous marriage, Customary marriage, Intermarriage, Interracial marriages
Marriage customs 2734, 4011
Marriage exchange 2742
Martí, José 4234
Martial arts 2625, 3867
Martin, Jean 3105
Martino, Ernesto de 121, 408

Martyr, Justin [Saint] 3437
Marxism 204, 218, 3616
Masai 673, 3806
Masculinity 215, 280, 433, 2807, 2810, 2820, 2840, 2841, 2848, 2855, 2858, 2865, 2911, 2932, 3254, 4305, 4309, 4336, 4342, 4520, 4560
Maseet, Ki 3363, 3498
Mask
  see: Funerary masks
Masks 1067, 2571, 2731, 2945, 3122, 3529, 3559, 3614, 3722, 4133, 4296
Masochism 3877
Mass consumption 2324, 4602
Mass production 2324
Mate selection 1493, 1494, 1697, 2872, 3307
Material culture 85, 175, 178, 284, 314, 321, 343, 346, 350, 351, 379, 387, 505, 610, 714, 720, 809, 844, 853, 855, 871, 874, 885, 909, 926, 967, 1039, 1040, 1071, 1098, 1248, 1300, 1322, 1336, 1361, 1362, 1374, 1377, 1383, 1385, 1410, 1413, 1418, 1421, 1424, 1426, 1427, 1431, 1432, 1434-1436, 1438, 1439, 1445, 1526, 1608, 2208, 2236, 2237, 2252, 2323, 2325, 2387, 2604, 2632, 2692, 2766, 2923, 2948, 3034, 3256, 3440, 3697, 3712, 3773, 3843, 3905, 4091, 4109, 4118, 4125, 4131, 4133, 4138, 4241, 4250, 4256, 4853
Materialism 164, 218, 3373
  see also: Cultural materialism
Mathematical methods 310
Mathematical models 1537, 1545
Mathematics 832, 1612, 3743, 3857
Matriarchy 2546, 2690, 2835, 3688
Matrilineal descent 2676, 2678, 2690, 2744, 3682
Matsigenka 2098
Mauss, Marcel 223
Maxims 3661
Maya 453, 494, 499, 525, 657, 851, 929, 1016, 1345, 1370, 1372, 1970, 1979, 2112, 2165, 2240, 2444, 2547, 2562, 2794, 2811, 2955, 3517, 3523, 3672, 3735, 3745, 3752, 3757, 4183, 4387, 4414, 4450
Mayan language 102, 1799
Mazahua 1812
Meals 4381, 4387
Measurement 235, 268, 296, 310, 870, 1454, 1462, 1466, 1493, 1543, 1563, 1576, 1578, 1579, 1583, 1619, 1665, 1667, 1668, 1670, 1719, 3269, 3792, 3959, 4527, 4823, 4911

Meat 2352, 4380, 4389, 4391
    see also: Butchering
Meddeb, Abdelwahab 2641
Media 106, 389, 432, 434, 661, 752, 785,
    1781, 2317, 2462, 2495, 2780, 2800,
    2866, 2924, 2927, 2967, 3037, 3207,
    3328, 3761, 3793, 3823, 3893, 3895,
    3921, 3976, 4043, 4094, 4096, 4119, 4136,
    4143, 4280, 4316, 4368, 4415, 4446,
    4482, 4516, 4544, 4548
    see also: Multimedia, Press
Mediation 3176
Medical anthropology 183, 605, 1474-1476,
    1508, 1512, 1545, 1555, 1564, 1569,
    1570, 1572, 1575, 1585, 1589, 1591,
    1593, 2703, 2719, 2887, 2930, 2952,
    2982, 3586, 3760, 3767, 3770, 3772,
    3777, 3789, 3791, 3801, 3804, 3806-3809,
    3813, 3815, 3817, 4871
Medical beliefs 313, 3811, 4397
Medical care 1470
Medical ethics 2887, 2925, 2929, 2982, 3802
Medical personnel 1809, 2119, 2470, 2718,
    2854, 3789, 3790, 3814
Medical research 1542, 4525
Medical sociology 1529, 1809
Medical treatment 1460, 2884, 3796, 4546,
    4547
Medicinal plants 3566, 3766
Medicine 17, 62, 459, 605, 729, 909, 1470,
    1505, 1542, 1555, 1575, 1585, 1953,
    2149, 2150, 2208, 2661, 2674, 2701,
    2712, 2720, 2728, 2773, 2775, 2871,
    2890, 2898, 2912, 2952, 2959, 3159,
    3358, 3510, 3580, 3739, 3749, 3750,
    3764, 3766, 3768, 3770, 3774, 3778-3780,
    3784-3787, 3795, 3797, 3798, 3802, 3803,
    3805, 3807-3809, 3818, 3821, 3825-3829,
    3832, 3834, 3836, 4174, 4186, 4328,
    4525, 4531, 4637
    see also: Alternative medicine,
    Biomedicine, History of medicine,
    Surgery, Traditional medicine, Veterinary
    medicine
Medieval art 3249
Medieval civilization 30, 634, 638, 671, 779,
    1146, 1325, 1444, 1833, 1857, 1937, 1953,
    2378, 3089, 3167, 3441, 3859, 3863,
    4034, 4349, 4381
Medieval history 606, 629, 666, 671, 676,
    715, 779, 951, 953, 1280, 1288, 1381,
    1833, 1937, 1953, 2531, 2864, 2965,
    2986, 3089, 3249, 3338, 3382, 3395,
    3458, 3679, 4002, 4097, 4221, 4247, 4580

Meditation 1876, 2800, 3205, 3207, 3278,
    3299, 3463, 3486, 3691
Megacities 4938
Megalithism 1056, 1063, 4601
Megaliths 852, 863, 888, 1011, 1067, 1095,
    1205, 3123, 4601
Meiji period 501, 4266
Meinecke, Michael 989
Meitei 1579
Meithei 2029
Melo, Fontes Pereira de 323, 707
Melville, Herman 4162
Member States 3169, 4623
Members of the lower chamber 323, 707
Memoirs 76, 355, 637, 731, 3214, 3317, 3628,
    4217, 4271
Memorials 364, 4508
Memory 171, 319, 434, 544, 621, 637, 1432,
    1637, 1784, 1828, 2092, 2211, 2766, 2964,
    3005, 3243, 3438, 3634, 3654, 3665,
    3666, 3693, 3702, 3900, 3947, 4012,
    4049, 4126, 4181, 4201, 4416, 4423,
    4439, 4445, 4508, 4511, 4533, 4570, 4573
    see also: Collective memory, National
    memory
Men 514, 1452, 2820, 2840, 2841, 2848,
    2865, 2874, 2891, 2894, 2909, 2955,
    3106, 3254, 3782, 4520, 4891
Men's health 2889, 4889
Men's role 2848, 3254, 4833
Menchú, Rigoberta 95, 234, 4569
Mende 3034
Mendi 3586
Menges, Karl Heinrich 117
Mennonites 4184
Menopause 1593
Menstruation 1544, 1558, 1581, 1613, 1640,
    1665, 1667, 1668, 1670, 2811, 3517
Mental health 775, 1513, 2762, 3404, 3791,
    4513, 4515, 4543, 4547, 4722
Mental hospitals 4545
Mental illness 1781, 3404, 3777, 3793, 4515,
    4543, 4545
Mental stress 1629, 2758, 4539, 4846
Mentality 3258, 3644
Mentally disabled 2933
Mercantilism 633, 3008
Mercenaries 448
Merchant navy 4724
Merchants 764, 2196, 2356, 2386, 4497
MERCOSUR 4663
Mergers 282
Meru 2613
Mesolithic Age 834, 883, 1000, 1291, 1304,
    1413

Mesopotamian civilization 482, 508, 2261, 2354, 2358, 2995, 3289, 3868, 4279
Messiah 3427
Messianism 3427, 3632
Mestizos 214, 2197, 3070
Metallurgy 1376, 1434
Metals 363, 474, 908, 912, 1326, 1387, 1397, 1414, 1444
Metalwork 363, 1017, 1383, 1402
  see also: Art metalwork
Metaphor 151, 169, 209, 233, 444, 502, 888, 1855, 2899, 2955, 3326, 3560, 3567, 3587, 3726, 3728, 3731, 4065, 4286, 4296, 4429
Metaphysics 121, 227, 408, 2800, 3123, 3143, 3207, 3466, 3595, 3728
Meteorology 3680, 3759
Methodist churches 3239, 3266, 3648
Methodology 33, 72, 107, 146, 187, 196, 219, 266, 279, 283, 286, 287, 294, 302, 303, 306, 308, 309, 389, 394, 405, 406, 410, 429, 589, 616, 772, 875, 930, 1001, 1123, 1562, 1571, 1618, 1723, 2123, 2124, 2145, 2146, 2233, 2569, 2618, 2860, 3086, 3754, 4009, 4326, 4473, 4676, 4702, 4746, 4756, 4804, 4843, 4924
  see also: Anthropological methodology, Archaeological methodology, Sociological methodology
Metropolitan areas 2222, 4937
Mexica 1024, 3119, 3133, 3711
Mexicans 432, 2661, 3065
Miao 2149, 2720, 4605
Michel, Natacha 2453
Microeconomics 2418
Microfinance 288, 4730, 4846, 4848, 4851, 4885, 4911
Middendorf, Ernst W. 99
Middle Ages 529, 624, 715, 943, 951, 1283, 1326, 1422, 1424, 1444, 2965, 3322, 3395, 4002, 4035, 4247, 4580
Middle class 4336
Migrant workers 877, 2177, 2179
Migrants 154, 2158, 2176, 2183, 2184, 2356, 2631, 2688, 2802, 3060, 3105, 3250, 3607, 3700, 3960, 4031, 4462, 4611
Migration 193, 228, 246, 254, 559, 585, 669, 684, 877, 880, 1280, 1495, 1497, 1502, 1521, 1635, 1669, 1773, 1809, 1841, 2092, 2104, 2106, 2120, 2135, 2151, 2156, 2158, 2160, 2162, 2163, 2166-2169, 2171-2177, 2179, 2181, 2183, 2185, 2243, 2306, 2356, 2421, 2621, 2655, 2660, 2688, 2770, 2772, 2825, 2886, 3070, 3090, 3103, 3228, 3519, 3791, 4013, 4411,

4417, 4457, 4479, 4606, 4804, 4882
  see also: Forced migration, Internal migration, International migration, Labour migration, Return migration, Rural-urban migration, Urban-rural migration
Miklukho-Maklai, Nikolai 365
Miles, Josephine 2933
Milhaud, Darius 3929
Militancy 2504, 2520
Militants 2453, 2520
Militarization 2577, 2578, 2582, 4653
Military 433, 498, 512, 546, 558, 917, 1076, 2494, 2508, 2521, 3022, 3036, 3059, 4706
Military alliances
  see: NATO
Military bases 498
Military history 323, 498, 534, 546, 563, 577, 581, 705, 707, 761, 1009, 1029, 2521
Military intervention 395
Military personnel
  see: Soldiers
Military relations 3022
Millar, Fergus 593
Millenarianism 3643, 4097
Milling industry 2203
Mills 2203
Minang Kabu 2849
Mind 634, 1520, 1547, 1751, 2800, 3207, 3299, 3431, 3441, 3480, 4469, 4525, 4530
Mineral resources 2107
Minerals 1651
Miners 1414, 1829, 2453
Mines 791, 1403
  see also: Copper mines, Gold mines, Silver mines
Mining 936, 2226, 2439, 4619
  see also: Coal mining
Ministers 632, 2580
Minorities 3077, 3097, 3098, 3103, 3160, 4421, 4597, 4624, 4628
  see also: Ethnic minorities, Linguistic minorities, National minorities
Minority education 3097, 4597
Minority groups 41, 119, 190, 2432, 2554, 3056, 3070, 3075, 3084, 3798, 4433, 4605
Minority rights 4627, 4656
Miskito 2731
Missiles 2576
Missionaries 25, 88, 122, 155, 530, 540, 600, 608, 644, 700, 722, 732, 736, 750, 766, 781, 794, 808, 813, 969, 1744, 2082, 2682, 2746, 2754, 2755, 2774, 3058, 3219, 3224, 3230, 3234, 3245, 3266, 3533, 3608, 3614, 3635, 3640, 3648, 4441
Mixtec 214, 1812, 3735

Moabite 934
Modelling 298, 388, 455, 866, 1488, 2134, 2225, 4847
Models 198, 209, 210, 305, 1558, 1631, 1670, 2364, 2430, 2679, 2791, 3125, 3534, 3560, 3561, 3761, 3765, 3942, 4675
see also: Development models, Linear models, Mathematical models, Stochastic models
Modern civilization 4592
Modern history 3082, 3204
Modern society 34, 987, 1451, 2324, 2790, 3262, 3385, 3386, 4177, 4449, 4596
Modernism 158, 3168, 3725, 4061, 4071, 4072, 4234, 4277, 4407, 4596
Modernity 3, 178, 216, 261, 276, 777, 2232, 2241, 2322, 2417, 2502, 2516, 2532, 2641, 2801, 2831, 2928, 2999, 3018, 3033, 3156, 3166, 3233, 3246, 3534, 3572, 3590, 3595, 3603, 3636, 3677, 3681, 3689, 3700, 3933, 4059, 4164, 4287, 4378, 4407, 4500, 4502, 4544, 4596, 4602, 4754
Modernization 580, 2179, 2204, 2257, 2300, 2477, 2552, 2644, 2650, 3013, 3070, 3078, 3108, 3169, 3660, 3784, 3884, 4101, 4106, 4126, 4294, 4592, 4605, 4679, 4682, 4882
Mokeddem, Malika 2092
Molina, Luís de 774
Monarchy 323, 358, 453, 477, 511, 537, 571, 620, 627, 705, 707, 724, 739, 747, 800, 814, 815, 1284, 1319, 1329, 1331, 1341, 1437, 1818, 2063, 2282, 2339, 2519, 2562, 2574, 2575, 2579, 2581, 2838, 3305, 3343, 3473, 3928, 4248, 4253
Monasteries 1065, 2389, 3495, 3642, 4381
Monasticism 514, 2875, 2909
Monetary circulation 4663
Monetary systems 2329, 2336
Monetary unions 551
Money 321, 356, 363, 491, 617, 1143, 2336, 2365, 2366, 2378, 2384, 2392, 2533, 3073, 3716, 3730, 4218, 4730
Mongo 1992
Mongol Empire 607, 4185
Monk, Thelonious 3929
Monks 452, 1026, 2389, 3187, 3191, 3312, 3376, 3642, 4375
Monogamy 2737, 3399
Monolingualism 1895
Monotheism 3264, 3527, 3647
Mood 1961
Moodie, Donald 96, 3985
Moon 3120, 3269, 3351

Moor 705
Moral philosophy 2970, 3002, 3138, 4226, 4233
Morales Bermúdez, Jesús 4201
Morality 239, 395, 396, 2119, 2381, 2595, 2643, 2705, 2715, 2724, 2851, 2881, 2930, 2956, 2961, 2966, 2970, 3002, 3138, 3621, 3712, 3761, 3776, 4549
Morals 1044, 2093, 2371, 2896, 3293, 3507, 3521, 3661, 4233, 4469, 4893
Morbidity 1566, 3821, 3828, 4328, 4899
Mores 3863, 4349
Morgan, L.H. 2658
Morio, Kita 4204
Morphology 144, 310, 870, 890, 898, 1379, 1455, 1459, 1464, 1465, 1467, 1471, 1479, 1483, 1484, 1509, 1524, 1528, 1534, 1535, 1560, 1590, 1617, 1620, 1641, 1649, 1719, 1725, 1726, 1734, 1751, 1765, 1807, 1847, 1872, 1879, 1899, 1935, 1937, 1938, 1960, 1984, 2015, 2022, 2032, 2034, 2088, 3667, 3736
Morphometrics 1280, 1480
Morris, Jan 4171
Morrison, Toni 2857, 3076
Mortality 1706, 2128, 2133, 2138, 2142, 2144, 2150, 2152, 2173, 2701, 2709, 2778, 3774, 3800, 3986, 4821, 4884, 4899
see also: Child mortality, Infant mortality
Morteira, Hakham Saul Levi 3444
Mortuary customs 383, 1289, 1304, 2779, 2781, 2794, 2929
see also: Ancient mortuary customs, Funerary rites
Mosaics 1026, 1044, 1357
Moses 3420, 3421
Moso 2741
Mosques 316, 402, 1032, 1099, 1100, 2227, 3839, 3848, 3849
Mossi 727, 2270
Mother tongue 309, 2146, 3095, 4553
Motherhood 557, 1658, 1676, 2632, 2639, 2693, 2702, 2707, 2709, 2721, 2863, 2966, 3693, 3775
Mothers 1544, 1560, 1584, 1587, 1607, 1614, 1672, 1675, 2654, 2685, 2694, 2696, 2701, 2703, 3774, 3806, 4897
Motivation 1675, 2326, 2468
Motivational analysis 422, 3687
Motu 4602
Mountains 1026, 1027, 1058, 1129, 1131, 1249, 1328, 1371, 1514, 1608, 2075, 2187, 2274, 2319, 2417, 2425, 2438, 2653, 2855, 2977, 3018, 3121, 3130, 3536, 3593, 3818, 4186, 4342, 4502, 4659

Mourning 1294, 2787, 2793, 3967
Mouseli, Ibn Danial Al- 4075
Mughal Empire 2528, 3414, 3461, 3484, 3502
Muhammad V [King] 620
Mukasa, Ham 674
Mulattoes 2197
Multiculturalism 228, 269, 399, 572, 782,
    1280, 1815, 3020, 3053, 3055, 3064,
    3088, 3093, 3096, 3098, 3410, 3612,
    3700, 3727, 3918, 4313, 4359, 4365,
    4407, 4413, 4418, 4419, 4433, 4492, 4628
Multiethnic countries 2077, 2587, 3072, 3098,
    4468, 4628
Multilingualism 113, 1798, 1802, 1803, 1815,
    1849, 1969, 4419
Multimedia 4242
Multinational enterprises 4762
Multivariate analysis 1462, 2150, 2235
Mummies 490, 1077
Murder 970, 2705, 2881, 3026, 3033, 3036,
    3059, 3089, 3603, 4280
    see also: Ritual murders
Murid 2182, 2375, 2605, 3591, 3822, 4622
Murik 2694
Murray, Margaret 143
Museology 376
Museum collections 13, 314, 316, 321, 322,
    324, 326, 328, 331, 332, 334, 336, 340,
    341, 346, 348-351, 358, 360-362, 364-
    368, 371, 372, 374, 377, 378, 610, 714,
    1332, 1410, 1527, 1673, 3737, 3839,
    4091, 4118, 4178, 4215, 4231
Museum policy 352
Museums 13, 25, 31, 32, 144, 145, 214, 314,
    315, 321, 325, 326, 328, 331, 340-342,
    348, 351, 352, 357, 364, 367, 368, 371,
    373, 376, 377, 434, 518, 610, 714, 1432,
    1527, 2202, 3653, 4091, 4092, 4484, 4508
    see also: Art museums, Ethnographic
    museums, Historical museums, National
    museums
Music 166, 371, 647, 1749, 2324, 2481, 2842,
    2857, 3076, 3081, 3309, 3357, 3649,
    3652, 3724, 3871, 3879, 3894, 3897-3899,
    3904, 3906, 3909-3914, 3916, 3917, 3919,
    3921, 3922, 3925, 3927, 3932-3935, 3937-
    3941, 3943-3946, 3951, 3953, 3954, 3957,
    3958, 3961-3965, 3967, 4051, 4059, 4119,
    4145, 4362, 4428, 4455, 4505, 4587
    see also: Classical music, Contemporary
    music, Ethnomusicology, Folk music,
    History of music, Pop music, Religious
    music, Ritual music, Rock music,
    Traditional music
Music research 118, 3931

Musical culture 3926
Musical instruments 2247, 3587, 3719, 3724,
    3726, 3911, 3923, 3926, 3929, 3935-3937,
    3945, 3948, 3954, 3967, 4505
    see also: Wind instruments
Musical styles 3894, 3899, 3901, 3929, 3933,
    3953, 3964, 4059
Musical traditions 3653, 3932, 4484
Musicians 118, 3518, 3903, 3914, 3922, 3923,
    3925, 3929, 3931-3934, 4059
Musicology 118, 3719, 3922, 3929, 3931,
    3936, 3954, 3960
Muslims 748, 2121, 2347, 2386, 2535, 2541,
    2652, 2757, 2819, 2850, 2856, 2910,
    2967, 2976, 2993, 2998, 3026, 3230,
    3324, 3328, 3339, 3344, 3345, 3348,
    3355, 3363, 3364, 3366, 3367, 3498,
    3615, 3646, 3660, 3767, 3802, 4052,
    4362, 4441, 4551, 4558, 4685
Mutesa I 583
Muti 2792, 3007
Mysticism 186, 568, 3123, 3149, 3153, 3183,
    3192, 3330, 3342, 3379, 3413, 3414,
    3430, 4412
Myth 192, 535, 542, 564, 618, 639, 656, 659,
    669, 725, 1762, 2198, 2813, 2828, 2830,
    2835, 2838, 3023, 3110, 3113, 3115-3123,
    3125-3127, 3129, 3131-3133, 3246, 3270,
    3271, 3351, 3400, 3424, 3513, 3537,
    3744, 3861, 3974, 3991, 3993, 3995,
    3999, 4004, 4010, 4048, 4151, 4263,
    4296, 4463, 4486, 4502
    see also: Creation myths
Mythical animals 3116, 3127, 3993
Mythology 257, 461, 505, 1047, 1364, 1707,
    2512, 3110, 3115, 3117, 3119, 3121, 3124,
    3125, 3127-3129, 3177, 3269, 3270, 3283,
    3290, 3294, 3431, 3448, 3495, 3514,
    3535, 3674, 3717, 3885, 4001, 4020,
    4140, 4148, 4470, 4595
NAFTA 4700
Nahuatl 1979, 3537, 3735, 3741, 3757, 4065,
    4066, 4196, 4222, 4270
Nakibinge [King] 639
Namaganda, Irene Drusilla 627
Names 477, 1334, 1347, 1722, 1749, 1817-
    1821, 1824-1827, 1831-1837, 1905, 1912,
    1924, 1941, 1979, 2063, 2666, 3150,
    3301, 3582, 3887, 3896, 4493
Naming 1749, 1818, 1822, 1826, 1828, 1831,
    1834-1836, 2063, 2700, 3582, 3887
Nanaï 3589
Nanak 3496
Narcotics 3946

Narratives 3, 96, 216, 229, 230, 236, 257, 273,
    278, 289, 319, 508, 660, 662, 999, 1498,
    1740, 1754, 1758, 1762, 1793, 1828,
    1846, 1978, 2037, 2094, 2103, 2184,
    2512, 2533, 2635, 2657, 2762, 2832,
    2834, 2843, 2964, 2995, 3005, 3025,
    3026, 3073, 3077, 3131, 3174, 3255,
    3274, 3293, 3296, 3404, 3424, 3438,
    3516, 3643, 3659, 3687, 3709, 3790,
    3805, 3955, 3976-3979, 3982, 3983, 3985,
    3988, 3991, 3992, 3994, 3997, 4001,
    4002, 4014, 4016, 4022, 4024, 4025,
    4031, 4032, 4046, 4069, 4108, 4147,
    4149, 4161, 4181, 4243, 4245, 4251,
    4254, 4255, 4313, 4362, 4372, 4405,
    4406, 4421, 4437, 4492, 4515, 4534,
    4562, 4568, 4575, 4578, 4580
Nation 173, 243, 410, 801, 2161, 2324, 2522,
    2533, 2955, 3005, 3073, 3088, 3687,
    3886, 4420, 4468, 4504, 4505, 4600, 4758
Nation building 2523, 3020, 3723, 4352,
    4418, 4456, 4481, 4494, 4600
Nation state 178, 777, 1426, 1562, 2523,
    3730, 4417, 4544, 4624, 4655
National archives 76, 355, 427
National character 3653, 4221, 4484, 4486
National commemoration 609, 3673, 4544
National consciousness 3480, 3653, 4484
National culture 433, 2249, 3701, 3708, 3886,
    4343, 4481
National history 590, 683
National identity 15, 136, 166, 647, 1746,
    1774, 1777, 2018, 2198, 2487, 2666,
    2855, 2901, 2927, 2934, 3071, 3088,
    3096, 3649, 3653, 3693, 3699, 3703,
    3886, 3891, 3958, 4120, 4221, 4336,
    4342, 4369, 4411, 4423, 4428, 4448, 4470,
    4482, 4484, 4486, 4487, 4490, 4493,
    4496, 4498, 4499, 4502-4505, 4626, 4758
National income 4787
National language 1749
National memory 2211
National minorities 3094, 3095, 3102, 3160,
    4479, 4553
National museums 118, 371, 3931
National parks 1605, 2107
National product
    see: Gross national product
Nationalism 3, 41, 138, 190, 192, 253, 618,
    647, 683, 735, 769, 801, 1361, 1426,
    1532, 1749, 2172, 2482, 2486, 2514,
    2533, 2564, 2666, 2855, 2857, 2901,
    2927, 2944, 3073, 3076, 3088, 3093,
    3480, 3697, 3723, 3958, 4053, 4102,
    4313, 4342, 4352, 4413, 4425, 4447,

    4448, 4456, 4472, 4481, 4482, 4485,
    4486, 4490, 4492-4495, 4497, 4499, 4501,
    4502, 4504, 4618, 4632, 4794
    see also: Cultural nationalism
Nationalists 1773, 3312
Nationality 41, 190, 309, 689, 694, 784, 2146,
    2989, 4480, 4488, 4497
Nationalization 726
Native art 130, 353
Native reservations 803, 2614, 3727
Nativism 254, 4266, 4457
NATO 4706
Natural disasters 2394, 2432, 2780, 2924,
    4764, 4792
Natural history 4, 165, 326, 361, 362, 368,
    756, 1715
Natural law 3418
Natural resources 960, 1571, 2061, 2067,
    2073, 2075, 2089, 2116, 2164, 2207, 2288,
    2309, 2404, 2413, 2415, 2434, 2439,
    2449, 2836, 3695, 3751, 4385, 4612,
    4690, 4693, 4767, 4770, 4779, 4780,
    4799, 4801, 4803, 4805, 4806, 4819, 4820
Natural sciences 501, 974, 1770, 1926
Natural selection 1649, 2275, 2297
Naturalism 3373, 4216
Naturalization 784, 2563, 2989
Nature 361, 362, 596, 685, 1499, 1818, 2061,
    2063, 2064, 2068, 2069, 2072, 2085,
    2088, 2096, 2105, 2111, 2114, 2198, 3144,
    3619, 3657, 3667, 3728, 3862, 4063,
    4127, 4199, 4310, 4712
Nature conservation 1714, 2067, 2083, 2222,
    3056, 3075, 4781, 4784, 4791, 4800
Nature reserves 667, 1686, 2191, 2203, 2272,
    4319, 4773, 4774
Naumann, Nelly 181
Navaho 2435, 3510, 3742, 3764
Navigation 503, 594, 691, 1375, 2372, 3680
Nazism 98, 2503, 2693, 3099, 4508
Neanderthals 845, 914, 1406, 1468, 1469,
    1516, 1518, 1530, 1533, 1536
Neighbourhoods 909, 2208, 2607, 2664, 3064,
    3352
Nelson, Diane M. 2955
Nenet 1771, 3606
Neoclassical economics 2342
Neoliberalism 235, 2411, 3584, 4611, 4623,
    4662, 4674, 4731, 4775
Neolithic Age 830, 844, 852, 853, 858, 866,
    867, 874, 877, 883, 886, 891, 935, 995,
    1000, 1007, 1013, 1029, 1066, 1114, 1139,
    1140, 1299, 1303, 1309, 1375, 1403, 1430,
    2177, 2206, 2304, 2340, 2604
Neruda, Pablo 4192

Nerval, Gérard de 4179, 4225
Nervo, Amado 4234
Network analysis 131
Networks 286, 679, 764, 2124, 2196, 2356,
    2447, 2634, 2663, 4008, 4746
Neurology 110, 170, 1513, 1561, 3789, 3799
Nevsky, Nikolai 3546
New technology 436, 687, 2254, 2588, 2632,
    4743
New World monkeys 1501, 1509, 1598, 1602,
    1606, 1609, 1610, 1612, 1616, 1627,
    1635, 1640, 1646, 1647, 1661, 1669,
    1675, 1677-1679, 1691, 1698, 1702, 1705,
    1706, 1708, 1710, 1711, 1715, 1717, 1718
Newar 3663
Newly industrializing countries 4679
News 1781, 3793, 4250
Ngaitahu 3655
Ngata, Apirana 4722
Nias 4601
Nicknames 1829
Nietzsche, Friedrich 280, 2858, 3129
Niger-Congo languages 1988, 1990, 1994,
    1998, 2004, 2009
Nihilism 4277
Nilo Saharan 1994, 2009
Nilote 1987, 2007
Nizan, Paul 2453
Nkrumah, Kwame 4102
Nobility 815, 3230, 4441
Noboru, Miyata 127
Nodilo, Natko 147, 1323
Nomadism 2623, 3683
    see also: Pastoral nomadism
Nomads 145, 283, 487, 555, 882, 2092, 2123,
    2473, 2491, 2610, 2690
Nomenclature 1673, 1818, 1820, 2063
Non-alignment 1765
Non-governmental organizations 158, 2210,
    3761, 4594, 4708, 4714, 4722, 4725,
    4727, 4728, 4731, 4740, 4742, 4752,
    4778, 4781, 4800, 4824, 4836, 4868,
    4870, 4887, 4888, 4904
Non-verbal communication 2955, 4560
Non-violence 3213, 3368, 3380, 3383, 3391,
    3889
Normal 2953
North Amerindians 100, 215, 225, 531, 539,
    699, 740, 786, 887, 2072, 2330, 3514,
    3547, 3674, 4576, 4595, 4644
North-South relations 2269
Nortje, Arthur Kenneth 4079
Norwegian language 1921
Nostalgia 327, 1762, 3730, 3903, 4416
Nouns 1347, 2022

Novais, Paulo Dias de 721
Novelists 4157, 4191, 4192
Novels 663, 1739, 2453, 2534, 2788, 2834,
    2853, 2928, 3005, 3118, 3885, 3999, 4112,
    4149, 4151, 4152, 4157-4160, 4162-4164,
    4175, 4188-4193, 4200, 4204, 4216, 4218,
    4230, 4242, 4247, 4249, 4254, 4257,
    4262, 4263, 4272, 4273, 4284, 4285, 4406
Noves, Laure de 4179, 4264
Ntomba 1993
Nuclear family 557, 2639
Nuclear industry 2454
Nuclear power plants 3976
Nuclear testing 2576, 4617, 4651
Nuclear weapons 3758
Numbers 3745, 3971
Numismatics 321, 363
Núñez de Miranda, Antonio 3216
Nuns 565, 2617, 2769, 3216, 3258, 3637,
    3644
Nurses 603, 2716, 3781
Nutrition 1541, 1543, 1550, 1552, 1563, 1569,
    1577-1579, 1588, 1589, 1611, 1671, 1677,
    2651, 2654, 2686, 3804, 4671, 4809-4811,
    4814, 4815, 4818, 4820, 4822, 4823,
    4827, 4867, 4886, 4897, 4902, 4923
Nutritional anthropology 1541
Nzema 4475
Oases 3658, 4798
Obesity 1551, 1556, 1588, 1589
Object 1763
Objectivity 143, 276, 2949, 4077
Obligation 534, 2676, 2983
Obrębski, Józef 15, 136
Obregón, Alejandro 4235
Observation 291, 428, 654, 691, 806, 1644,
    1667, 2786
Ocampo, Silvina 4147
Occultism 199, 576, 3573, 3578
Occupational health 3789
Occupational safety 3986
Occupational status 3781
Occupations 1535, 2220, 2464, 2465, 2845,
    3903
    see also: Academic profession
Official languages 1797
Oil 488
Okojie, C.G. 4161
Old age 813, 2655, 2770, 2773, 2774, 2898
Old World monkeys 1510, 1511, 1599, 1601,
    1603, 1611-1614, 1619, 1622, 1623, 1625,
    1626, 1628, 1630, 1631, 1633, 1641,
    1642, 1644, 1649, 1651, 1654, 1655,
    1657-1660, 1662, 1664-1666, 1668, 1670,

1672, 1681, 1682, 1690, 1692-1694, 1700,
  1707, 1712, 1713
Olmec 1970
Olympic games 4336, 4574
One-parent families 2696, 4521
Onitsura, Uejima 4063
Onomastics 30, 1831, 1836, 4258
Ontogeny 1465, 1466, 1567
Ontology 213, 2232, 3381, 3527, 3675, 3690,
  3733, 3878, 4466
  see also: Paleontology
Open economies 2280
Opera 3866, 3880, 3888, 3906, 4263
Opiates 896, 2296, 4720
Opinion 2453, 2791
  see also: Political opinions, Public opinion
Opportunity cost 2433
Oppression 3089, 4082
Oracles 3812
Oral communication 1758, 1898, 3973, 3989,
  4014
Oral history 40, 96, 291, 357, 375, 544, 562,
  575, 607, 613, 614, 619, 665, 1787, 2087,
  2548, 2648, 2663, 3118, 3510, 3654, 3764,
  3981, 3984-3986, 3999, 4008, 4012, 4023,
  4232, 4568, 4804
Oral literature 1758, 3990, 3995, 3996, 4014,
  4021, 4027, 4029, 4030
Oral tradition 153, 169, 544, 619, 665, 799,
  1316, 1743, 1754, 1767, 1787, 1829,
  2103, 2104, 2184, 2481, 2489, 2512,
  3124, 3514, 3654, 3668, 3968, 3972,
  3974, 3977, 3980-3982, 3984, 3989, 3990,
  4001, 4004, 4005, 4007, 4009-4011, 4013,
  4016, 4021, 4023, 4024, 4027, 4031,
  4201, 4232, 4463, 4490
Orang-utans 1480, 1629, 1674
Oraon 1453, 1454
Orchestras 3935
Organic produce 2311, 4820
Organization 255, 308, 371, 2145, 2244, 2269,
  2369, 3021, 3022, 3144, 4730
  see also: Administrative organization,
  Community organization, Economic
  organization, Social organization
Organization of space 3845
Organization theory 249, 306, 2202, 2456,
  2606, 2822, 2887, 2982, 4129, 4320,
  4598, 4676, 4700, 4848, 4852, 4871
Organizational behaviour 2606
Organizational change 4804
Organizational culture 255, 2369, 2468, 4400
Organizational effectiveness 2468
Organizational structure 4742

Organizations 986, 2307, 2514, 3957
  see also: Employers' organizations, Non-
  governmental organizations
Organs 1575, 2930
Oriental studies 6, 94, 934, 3002
Orientalism 14, 260, 329, 4217
Ornithology 3744, 3753
Orok 2477
Orosius, Paulus 519
Orphans 4897
Orthodox Church 3230, 3628, 3634, 4441
Orthography 334, 1911, 1919, 4178
Osteology 1283, 1287
Otomanguean 1812, 1967
Ottoman Empire 1301, 2479, 2494, 3120,
  3236, 3327, 3350, 3351, 4070
Overexploitation 867
Ownership 1448, 2328, 2373, 2377, 2398,
  2402, 2417, 2427, 2920, 2963, 2991,
  2997, 3018, 3106, 4638, 4882
Oxen 2291
Oyo 4009
Pacifism 3489
Paganism 1381, 3521, 3554, 3619, 3686
Pagis, Dan 4049, 4439
Pai 3585
Painters 3841, 4089, 4095, 4112
Painting 337, 937, 1007, 1023, 1060, 1072,
  1074, 1077, 1081, 1084, 1095, 1105, 3728,
  3736, 3841, 4041, 4089, 4095, 4097,
  4101, 4106, 4109, 4113, 4114, 4128, 4130,
  4144, 4235
Paiute 3585
Palawan 3813
Paleoanthropology 1479, 1532
Paleodemography 246, 298, 1379, 1516, 2134,
  2135, 2144
Paleoecology 155, 530, 744, 858, 882, 947,
  969, 994, 1000, 1368, 1533
Paleography 1340, 1535, 3179, 3203
Paleolithic Age 819, 834, 836, 845, 849, 850,
  856, 862, 873, 894, 914, 932, 959, 1023,
  1153, 1245, 1273, 1298, 1362, 1378, 1406,
  1518
Paleontology 824, 837, 842, 846, 872, 889,
  898, 899, 1137, 1458, 1467, 1528, 1534
Paleopathology 538
Paleozoology 144
Palestinians 2456, 3040, 4062
Pali, Avtar Singh 3855
Pampas 837
Panassié, Hugues 3929
Pandit 4176
Panic 2896, 4547, 4893
Pānini 1960, 3754

Pano 1506, 3128
Papon, Maurice 3005
Paradigms 194, 204, 259, 268, 414, 420, 2035,
    2958, 3079, 3170, 3670, 3730, 3743,
    4198, 4586, 4627, 4757
Parent-child relations 557, 1584, 1602, 1603,
    1614, 1672, 2635, 2639, 2694, 2933,
    3025, 4022
Parenthood 1577, 1587, 2636, 2694, 2696,
    2713, 2717, 2863, 2893, 4822
Parenting 603, 2716
Parents 1574, 1615, 1675, 2350, 2636, 2713,
    4244, 4433, 4506
Parishes 2599, 3629, 3636
Parliament 815, 2402, 2483
Parliamentary bills 4861
Parlo, Giancarlo De 3846
Parsi 3331, 3880, 3882
Participant observation 291, 424
Partition 3730
Partners 2868
Paschoal, Hermeto 3914
Passamaquoddy 3588
Past 278, 434, 573, 613, 1828, 1835, 2017,
    3710, 4161, 4260
Pastoral nomadism 283, 2123, 3806, 4725
Pastoralism 682, 882, 913, 1584, 2073, 2126,
    2367, 2425, 2429, 2434, 2435, 2446,
    2446, 2447, 2610, 2626, 2767, 3678,
    4659, 4764, 4784, 4797, 4820
Patents 2241, 4880
Paternalism 723, 2273
Pathology 110, 1591, 2703, 3799
    see also: Paleopathology
Patients 3159, 3790, 3805, 4545
Paton, Alan 4249
Patriarchy 198, 470, 2535, 2567, 2679, 2767,
    2811, 2846, 2850, 2873, 3258, 3517, 3525,
    3644, 4830
Patrilineal descent 2658, 2676
Patriotism 2281, 3312, 3653, 4484, 4487,
    4489
Patronage 2382, 2513, 2617, 2659, 2795,
    3597, 3884
Paulmier de Gonneville, Jean 783
Paz, Octavio 3728, 4220
Peace 364, 2533, 3073, 3170, 3275, 3354,
    3489
Peace agreement 4733
Peace keeping 395, 4712, 4820
Peace negotiations 2577
Peace studies 4706
Peaceful co-existence 3040
Peacock, Kenneth Howard 118, 3931
Peanuts 749

Peasant cultures 17, 2371, 3825
Peasant societies 2371, 2400, 2968, 4912
Peasantry 2200, 2205, 2280, 2282, 2423,
    2480, 2575, 3223, 4381
Peasants 624, 1823, 2183, 2194, 2197, 2200,
    2255, 2258, 2261, 2269, 2336, 2371,
    2397, 2399, 2412, 2478, 2688, 3176,
    3223, 3538, 4502, 4569, 4573, 4687
Pedagogy 3661, 4433, 4559
Pedi 2750, 3019
Peer groups 2882
Peformance
    see: Job performance
Peirce, C.S. 3728
Penashue, Elizabeth 2075
Pentecostalism 3221, 3232, 3237, 3250, 3252,
    3257, 3259, 3636, 3645, 4462
Per capita income 1568
Perception 307, 661, 1492, 1506, 1703, 1737,
    1958, 2047, 2080, 2091, 2095, 2096, 2116,
    2284, 2441, 2718, 2739, 2753, 2906,
    2933, 3012, 3212, 3658, 3662, 3695,
    3728, 3814, 3816, 3897, 4029, 4107,
    4190, 4498, 4528, 4536, 4591, 4783
    see also: Social perception, Visual
    perception
Perception of others 1793, 2802, 2914, 3060,
    3397, 3607, 3613
Perec, Georges 107, 405
Performance 1629, 1793, 2907, 2945, 3006,
    3290, 3410, 3529, 3596, 3625, 3830,
    3871, 3873, 3875-3877, 3881, 3883, 3907,
    3933, 3955, 3965, 3982, 4043, 4059,
    4102, 4113, 4121, 4122, 4263, 4316, 4355,
    4356, 4359, 4362, 4366, 4367, 4505, 4519
Performers 2842, 3884, 3903, 3938
Performing arts 364, 3881, 3903, 4605
Periodicals 50, 51, 3100, 4243, 4525, 4548
Personal power 1828
Personality 111, 176, 486, 627, 649, 815,
    3553, 3712, 4074, 4524
Personality cult 3262
Personality tests 1463
Personnel management 2468
Persuasion 2887, 2982
Pessimism 3869
Pestana, Catalino 2260
Pesticides 4888
Pétrarque, François 4179, 4264
Petroglyphs 1062
Petrol 2242
Peul 2718, 3814
Pharmaceuticals 4636
Phenomenology 5, 45, 226, 227, 1753, 1798,
    2170, 2958, 3217, 3533, 3777

Philip, M. Nourbese 4039

Philology 1792, 1801, 1814, 1819, 1859, 1928, 2071, 3196, 3229, 3251, 3436, 3826, 3966

Philosophers 79, 588, 2232, 3129, 3291, 3403, 3437, 4172, 4174

Philosophical anthropology 395, 4530

Philosophical thought 100, 121, 408, 588, 660, 740, 758, 2114, 2457, 2970, 3002, 3079, 3138, 3143, 3162, 3164, 3170, 3178, 3182, 3208, 3210, 3280, 3291, 3311, 3335, 3381, 3728, 4063, 4067, 4073, 4172, 4191, 4489, 4510

Philosophy 11, 79, 151, 167, 216, 221, 223, 224, 244, 259, 280, 414, 444, 464, 588, 589, 758, 807, 998, 1538, 1863, 1945, 1960, 1965, 2072, 2092, 2111, 2114, 2232, 2435, 2705, 2858, 2881, 2970, 2991, 3000, 3002, 3079, 3129, 3138, 3143, 3148, 3153, 3162, 3164, 3165, 3170, 3178, 3182, 3201, 3208, 3210, 3212, 3214, 3251, 3271, 3272, 3290, 3296, 3315, 3317, 3318, 3320, 3335, 3339, 3359, 3376, 3380-3382, 3389, 3403, 3438, 3462, 3477, 3620, 3659, 3669, 3675, 3725, 3728, 3743, 3754, 3756, 3857, 3862, 3971, 4023, 4063, 4067, 4077, 4179, 4191, 4207, 4220, 4238, 4261, 4510
see also: Dualism, History of philosophy, Moral philosophy, Political philosophy, Public philosophy, Social philosophy

Philosophy of art 3728

Philosophy of language 3165

Philosophy of religion 208, 275, 2539, 3182, 3202, 3303, 3389, 3455

Philosophy of science 5, 16, 226, 998, 3753

Phoenicians 1722

Phonetics 122, 600, 1764, 1813, 1858, 1866, 1873, 1891, 1899, 1907, 1922, 1923, 1937, 1958, 1959, 1968, 1976, 1979, 2001, 2008, 2010, 2041, 2051, 2058

Phonology 113, 1802, 1813, 1847, 1858, 1870, 1890, 1927, 1976, 1981, 1984, 1992, 2001, 2039, 2041, 2048, 3874

Photograph collections 367

Photography 92, 101, 231, 273, 326, 367, 417, 438, 441, 443, 769, 923, 932, 983, 999, 1003, 1105, 2210, 2287, 2933, 2944, 3929, 4094, 4104, 4107, 4121, 4126, 4127, 4138

Phraseology 1761

Phrenology 110, 3799

Phylogeny 279, 898, 899, 1458, 1467, 1534, 1618, 1666, 1679, 2687

Physical activity 1457, 1559, 1585, 1588, 1589, 3804, 4348

Physical anthropology 46, 110, 144, 538, 845, 1453, 1459, 1466, 1474, 1476, 1483, 1500, 1504, 1510, 1531, 1536, 1546, 1547, 1549, 1559, 1563, 1569, 1574, 1588, 1589, 1600, 1620, 1623, 1624, 1645, 1646, 1685, 1689, 1694, 1716, 3799

Physical appearance 1449, 1493, 1494, 2935

Physical constitution 1545, 1610

Physical environment 2428

Physics 60, 371, 464, 1549, 3728, 3758

Physiology 1485, 1491, 1499, 1555, 1558, 1591, 1632-1634, 1663, 1695, 1859, 2917, 3436, 3759, 3789

Pialoux, Michel 2453

Picón Salas, Mariano 4192

Pictography 214

Pidgin languages 252, 1749, 1757, 1789, 2011-2018

Pietism 3430

Pigs 2442, 2445, 2450, 2847

Pike, Kenneth Lee 119

Pilgrimages 166, 2900, 3133, 3181, 3230, 3256, 3263, 3287, 3532, 3649, 4131, 4179, 4225, 4236, 4264, 4321, 4322, 4330, 4428, 4441

Piłsudski, Bronisław 92

Piro 2472, 3109

Planning methods 1763, 2210, 2221, 2894, 4702, 4717, 4731, 4735, 4891, 4928

Planning systems 2782

Plant domestication 2266, 2304, 2435

Plantations 2167, 2273, 2619, 2822, 3066

Plastic arts 4610

Plato 1738

Play 1783, 4519

Pleistocene 460, 824, 831, 837, 839, 841, 842, 846, 870, 872, 875, 884, 889, 890, 899, 1137, 1190, 1368, 1379, 1458, 1469, 1521, 1525, 1533-1535

Plots 3878

Pluralism 268, 798, 974, 1726, 3092, 3096, 4411, 4510
see also: Ethnic pluralism, Linguistic pluralism, Religious pluralism

Poe, Edgar Allen 2857, 3076

Poems 4036, 4046, 4063, 4070, 4074, 4083

Poetry 96, 141, 151, 206, 444, 660, 1844, 1859, 1945, 1965, 1970, 2099, 2324, 2805, 2933, 3155, 3195, 3272, 3278, 3294, 3321, 3330, 3365, 3423, 3429, 3436, 3500, 3738, 3865, 3885, 3928, 3933, 3968, 3985, 4004, 4029, 4035-4045, 4047, 4049-4063, 4065-4089, 4147, 4179, 4192, 4214, 4231, 4242, 4264, 4266,

4439, 4561, 4563, 4578
see also: Epic poetry, Folk poetry
Poison 2615, 3570, 3783, 4003
Poles 4488
Police 3006, 3013, 3107
Policing 2969
Policy analysis 4788, 4828, 4865, 4928
Policy implementation 152, 2828, 2829
Policy making 2221, 2469, 3761, 4672, 4702,
  4705, 4744, 4756, 4864
Policy studies 2662
Polish language 1958
Political action 253
Political actors 2502, 2517, 2533, 3073, 3572
Political anthropology 270, 629, 985, 2486,
  2488, 2531, 2532, 2537, 2538, 2568,
  2591, 2595, 2597, 3064, 3590, 4351, 4632
Political authority 2212, 2487, 4643
Political behaviour 2505
Political change 993, 2210, 2518, 2548, 3090,
  3222, 3944, 4084, 4487, 4728, 4778,
  4804, 4820
Political communication 1776, 4243
Political conditions 986, 2210, 2491, 2500,
  2518, 3039, 3869, 4152, 4266, 4447,
  4571, 4652
Political conflicts 373, 535, 816, 2491, 3023,
  3093, 4413
Political consciousness 2795, 3597
Political control 484
Political correctness 2525
Political corruption 2558
Political crises 4152, 4618, 4794
Political culture 668, 2392, 2496, 2529, 2556,
  3969, 4435, 4938
Political development 633, 993, 2486, 2984,
  3008, 4615, 4670, 4769
Political economy 52, 215, 225, 539, 2202,
  2513, 2659, 2908, 4673, 4708
  see also: International political economy
Political geography 2418
Political groups 765
Political history 501, 510, 535, 546, 577, 607,
  619, 654, 688, 703, 705, 773, 787, 816,
  818, 2155, 2330, 2475, 2478, 2491, 2493,
  2500, 2533, 2536, 2545, 2558, 2566,
  3023, 3029, 3050, 3073, 3080, 3100,
  3145, 4105, 4369, 4447, 4523, 4571, 4921
Political ideas
  see: History of political ideas
Political ideology 1084, 2399, 3107, 3357,
  3951
Political instability 787, 2102
Political leaders 501, 576, 2564, 3322, 3573,
  4533

Political leadership 470, 2567, 2979, 3349
Political life 110, 2551, 2554, 3799
Political mobilization 4472
Political movements 215, 681, 765, 2541,
  2829, 3889
Political opinions 2534
Political opposition 3703
Political order 2509, 2682
Political participation 675, 700, 2515, 3219,
  4230, 4611, 4648, 4882
  see also: Activism
Political parties 2483, 3944
  see also: Communist parties, Liberal
  parties
Political philosophy 79, 3850
Political power 383, 453, 474, 558, 632, 2494,
  2498, 2508, 2509, 2512, 2553, 2562,
  2568, 2580, 2779, 2814, 3145, 3353,
  3538, 4001, 4548
Political prisoners 395, 698, 4477
Political protest 2483, 3969
Political reform 383, 2779
Political regimes 192, 609, 618, 721, 3090,
  3584, 3673, 4674, 4778
Political representation 253, 2524, 2540, 3880
Political roles 2584, 4090
Political science 2502, 2532, 3572, 3590,
  4205, 4251, 4718
Political sociology 3001, 4845
Political stability 2504, 2595
Political structure 657, 2517, 2547, 2553
Political support 3029, 3050, 4594
Political systems 2538, 2565
Political theory 2954, 4485, 4637
Political thought 3107, 4485
Political violence 395, 2515, 2558, 2714,
  3029, 3050
Politicians 92, 815
Politicization 4389, 4400
Politics 253, 418, 474, 657, 991, 2076, 2210,
  2499, 2505, 2525, 2529, 2532, 2534,
  2543, 2547, 2570, 2582, 2911, 2955, 3034,
  3063, 3108, 3246, 3570, 3590, 3761,
  3777, 3783, 3784, 3908, 3975, 4058,
  4084, 4129, 4230, 4447, 4469, 4496,
  4502, 4599, 4634, 4637, 4642, 4643,
  4700, 4820, 4841, 4907
Polls
  see: Public opinion polls
Pollution 2311, 4765, 4770, 4941
  see also: Air pollution, Industrial pollution
Pollution control 2210
Polo, Marco 779
Polygamy 2755
Polygyny 295, 2130, 2736, 3010

Poor 2189, 2408, 2452, 3566, 4075, 4536, 4611, 4616, 4650, 4662, 4743, 4744, 4823, 4842, 4872
Pop music 3903
Pope 3230, 3253, 4441
Popular culture 171, 188, 576, 668, 1774, 1777, 2072, 2556, 2934, 3573, 3631, 3699, 3725, 3880, 3908, 3909, 3918, 3943, 3961, 3990, 4038, 4119, 4121, 4122, 4143, 4146, 4240, 4303, 4373, 4378, 4380, 4392, 4464, 4754
Popular literature 3991, 3995, 4240
Popular music 1748, 3940, 3961, 3969
Popular religion 86, 3215, 3531, 3554, 3639
Popular theatre 103, 3870
Popularity 4217
Population 286, 298, 309, 646, 684, 757, 866, 1502, 1538, 1550, 1615, 1669, 1677, 1705, 1712, 2120, 2124, 2125, 2134, 2144, 2146-2148, 2151, 2155, 2306, 2406, 2551, 2752, 3739, 3762, 4840, 4892, 4899 *see also:* Indigenous populations, Rural population, Urban population
Population censuses 308, 309, 2145, 2146
Population decline 1686, 2151, 2306, 3797
Population density 1687, 1705, 2148, 2271
Population distribution 1597, 1630, 1712
Population dynamics 1597, 1822, 2132, 2646
Population economics 2143, 2673
Population growth 2127, 4941
Population increase 2079
Population movements 559, 2162, 2163, 2175, 2178, 2180, 2184, 2825, 4031, 4725
Population pressure 2416, 3017
Population theory 1563
Populism 4336
Porcelain 1429
Pornography 2950
Ports 806, 1049, 1061, 1233, 1235, 2092, 2360
Portuguese language 66, 68, 71
Positivism 998
Post-apartheid society 1432, 2166, 2388, 2453, 2675, 3579, 4548, 4588, 4717
Post-communist societies 179, 319, 781, 2100, 2391, 2548, 2964, 3081, 3593, 3634, 3703, 3707, 4411, 4440, 4448, 4455, 4479, 4582
Post-Fordism 2502, 3572
Post-materialism 2326
Post-Soviet studies 319, 2964, 3409, 4402, 4440, 4468
Post-structuralism 180, 650
Post-war history 3956, 4105, 4479, 4523

Postcolonial societies 228, 335, 689, 702, 712, 723, 742, 799, 2397, 2401, 2506, 2522, 2529, 2551, 2553, 2560, 2641, 3039, 3046, 3047, 3071, 3222, 3287, 3438, 3625, 3671, 3687, 3698, 3844, 3949, 3969, 4000, 4039, 4134, 4150, 4182, 4244, 4265, 4278, 4288, 4293, 4295, 4298, 4299, 4312, 4343, 4352, 4374, 4378, 4432, 4453, 4475, 4500, 4516, 4548, 4574, 4589, 4652, 4655, 4685, 4754
Postcolonialism 254, 702, 735, 2172, 2182, 2499, 2502, 2877, 3572, 3586, 3933, 4059, 4071, 4120, 4151, 4171, 4177, 4425, 4452, 4457, 4483, 4622, 4639, 4731
Postmodernism 115, 180, 250, 253, 260, 300, 304, 364, 998, 1750, 2326, 2552, 2897, 2948, 3130, 3401, 3639, 3650, 3725, 3838, 3877, 4068, 4138, 4151
Potatoes 2269, 2275
Potters 2238
Pottery 378, 387, 853, 871, 883, 919, 943, 1034, 1056, 1058, 1288, 1309, 1374, 1376, 1380, 1385, 1388, 1389, 1403-1405, 1415-1417, 1424, 1425, 1427, 1431, 1439, 1442, 1444, 1445, 2206, 2233, 2235, 2237-2239, 2249, 2250, 3737 *see also:* Ceramics
Pound, Ezra 4068
Poverty 59, 548, 1573, 2152, 2210, 2289, 2340, 2362, 2400, 2407, 2582, 2627, 2961, 2968, 2969, 2972, 2978, 2980, 2984, 2994, 3001, 3003, 3004, 3819, 4536, 4543, 4611, 4613, 4621, 4661, 4668, 4670, 4672, 4677, 4682, 4690, 4699, 4707, 4719, 4721, 4728, 4730, 4732, 4733, 4739, 4744-4747, 4755, 4762, 4793, 4817, 4820, 4823, 4825, 4863-4865, 4867, 4870, 4872, 4874-4876, 4880, 4881, 4883, 4894, 4896, 4897, 4900, 4904, 4918, 4939 *see also:* Rural poverty, Urban poverty
Poverty alleviation 2210, 2222, 2396, 4666, 4671, 4707, 4723, 4732, 4744, 4817, 4825, 4832, 4841, 4847, 4848, 4865, 4896, 4905, 4911, 4913, 4914, 4918, 4919, 4936, 4937
Power 52, 98, 105, 191, 196, 247, 255, 612, 620, 627, 649, 716, 722, 729, 751, 1102, 1716, 1777, 2214, 2369, 2487, 2489, 2490, 2493, 2499, 2503, 2513, 2532, 2533, 2552, 2554, 2555, 2560, 2571, 2596, 2618, 2659, 2669, 2719, 2908, 2934, 3000, 3073, 3077, 3216, 3231, 3353, 3356, 3586, 3590, 3592, 3602, 3730, 3776, 3816, 3817, 3850, 3925, 3947, 4200, 4374, 4421, 4468, 4619,

4630, 4700
see also: Political power
Power relations 269, 514, 1066, 1647, 2101, 2489, 2490, 2555, 2834, 2909, 2959, 3055, 3367, 3592, 3829, 4406, 4648, 4780
Practice 3912
Pragmatics 266, 1753, 1766, 1811, 1921, 1951, 1961
Prairies 2187
Prayer 472, 1871, 3170, 3233, 3268, 3299, 3336, 3360, 3407, 3408, 3439, 3440, 3452, 3465, 3748, 3899
Pre-Columbian history 504, 903, 1294, 1375, 2530, 2764, 3745, 4066, 4220
Pre-industrial society 1584, 2143, 2673, 2749
Preaching 640, 2967, 3328, 3443, 3508
Precipitation 2065, 2079, 2417, 2517, 3018, 3114, 3571, 4691, 4727, 4777
Precolonial history 73, 214, 228, 335, 533, 542, 573, 633, 670, 821, 1385, 1405, 2653, 2977, 3008, 3353, 3902
Preferences 1452, 1656, 2342, 2670, 2747, 2891, 3200, 3751, 4385, 4835
Pregnancy 1491, 1542, 1613, 1708, 2711, 2717-2719, 2727, 2811, 2869, 2893, 3517, 3539, 3814, 3817, 3950, 4844, 4869
Prehistoric agriculture 851, 854, 1413
Prehistoric art 1384
Prehistoric caves 836, 894, 898, 1007, 1013, 1023, 1467
Prehistoric industry 1359
Prehistoric man 822, 841, 875, 890
Prehistoric religions 1052
Prehistoric technology 1010, 1359, 1415, 1526
Prehistoric tools 890
Prehistory 34, 374, 460, 598, 623, 720, 821-823, 825, 827, 829, 832, 833, 835, 836, 844-846, 848-852, 856, 857, 859-861, 863, 864, 866, 868, 870, 873, 876-879, 882, 883, 886, 892-894, 896, 906, 916, 921, 924, 926, 932, 947, 966, 977, 981, 987, 1000, 1004, 1011, 1013, 1017, 1020, 1050, 1052, 1066, 1067, 1095, 1097, 1153, 1160, 1172, 1173, 1184, 1223, 1225, 1245, 1248, 1249, 1264, 1271, 1281, 1292, 1296, 1298-1300, 1303, 1305, 1314, 1315, 1324, 1362, 1363, 1366, 1368, 1374, 1376, 1379, 1390, 1397, 1406, 1408, 1409, 1413, 1415, 1439, 1459, 1461, 1484, 1514, 1516, 1522, 1526, 1533, 1536, 1563, 1934, 2110, 2177, 2229, 2340, 2590, 3024, 3941, 4268, 4501
Preservation of cultural heritage 78, 152, 316, 524, 667, 962, 1028, 1169, 1203, 1240, 1386, 2203, 2691, 2838, 3196, 3818,

3839, 4317, 4319, 4325-4327, 4329, 4344-4346, 4429, 4573
Presidential elections 4618, 4794
Press 661, 785, 1785, 1915, 2821, 2866, 3335, 4081, 4415, 4496, 4497
Prestige 2328, 2589, 2963
Prevention 44, 1580, 2885, 3761, 3820, 3834
Prices 150, 382, 2342
see also: Agricultural prices, Commodity prices, Food prices, Housing prices
Priests 3187, 3220, 3230, 3277, 3454, 3461, 3524, 3637, 3672, 3752, 4234, 4441
Primary education 4554
Primary health care 3819, 4896
Primates 19, 21, 23, 46, 1472, 1480, 1481, 1485, 1500, 1501, 1509-1511, 1567, 1594-1616, 1618-1628, 1630-1647, 1650, 1652, 1654-1662, 1664, 1665, 1667-1671, 1674, 1676-1680, 1682-1692, 1694, 1696-1703, 1705-1714, 1717, 1718, 1720, 1721
Primatology 19, 21, 23, 46, 1465, 1479-1481, 1500, 1501, 1509-1511, 1594-1611, 1613-1616, 1618-1651, 1653-1664, 1666-1674, 1676, 1678-1681-1692, 1694-1702, 1704-1714, 1716-1721
Primitive art 1033, 1088, 2346
Primitivism 233, 628, 3567, 4061
Pringle, Thomas 4082
Printing 1743, 2253, 3354, 3668, 4144, 4240
Prisoners 698, 2959, 3005, 3009
see also: Political prisoners
Prisoners of war 4477
Prisons 698, 2938, 2999, 3009, 3803
Privacy 2459
Private collections 13, 365, 371, 379
Private property 2420
Private sector 2210, 4932, 4937
Private sphere 2450, 2502, 3572
Privatization 2210, 4609, 4718, 4874, 4882
Processing industry 4678
Production 175, 718, 749, 864, 1405, 1413, 1415, 1428, 1439, 2226, 2233, 2236, 2237, 2257, 2338, 2390, 2399, 2442, 2450, 2462, 2847, 4696
see also: Agricultural production, Cattle production, Cotton production, Mass production
Production costs 2305
Production diversification 4688
Production factors 2143, 2673
Production functions 2277
Production systems 833, 1041, 1406, 2349, 2437, 2443, 2448, 2593, 4689, 4698
Productivity 2091
see also: Agricultural productivity

Productivity growth 4698
Professional ethics 24, 135, 148, 258, 416
Professional workers 1505, 2674
Professionalism 963
Professionalization 909, 2208, 3884
Professors 37, 102, 114, 1799
Programme evaluation 4345, 4740, 4741, 4841
Project evaluation 4325, 4851
Pronoun 1929, 1930, 1949
Pronunciation 1957
Propaganda 2693, 3048, 4105, 4523
Property 757, 2062, 2337, 2349, 2373, 2374, 2377, 2404, 2406, 2408, 2421, 2442, 2593, 2736, 2847, 2954, 2997, 3010, 4635, 4650
    see also: Cultural property, Intellectual property, Private property
Property rights 1448, 2284, 2289, 2376, 2404, 2408, 2416, 2920, 2954, 3017, 4617, 4636, 4650, 4651, 4780
Prophecy 3424, 3591, 3822
Prophets 2534, 2748, 3368, 3420, 3421, 3591, 3822
Prose 1844, 3195, 3321, 3331, 4032, 4169, 4234, 4252
Proselytism 732
Prosimians 1600, 1615, 1617, 1619, 1624, 1632-1634, 1639, 1643, 1645, 1650, 1680, 1695-1697, 1699, 1719
Prosody 1890
Prostitution 2220, 2821, 2896, 2988, 3004, 3119, 4826, 4893
Protest movements 2614, 3686
Protestant churches 3224
Protestantism 2085, 3230, 3252, 3610, 3653, 4310, 4441, 4474, 4484
Protestants 3243, 3252, 3610
Proto-Dravidian languages 1903, 2301
Protohistory 569
Proverbs 1788, 2200, 2364, 3321, 3354, 3997, 4018, 4070, 4600, 4640
Provinces 296, 366, 1442, 1576, 2159, 2209, 2267, 2437, 2550, 3581, 3586, 3916, 4186, 4480, 4629, 4669, 4772
Psychiatry 775, 3595, 3638, 4525, 4547
    see also: Social psychiatry
Psychoanalysis 176, 186, 195, 221, 379, 3149, 3791, 4022, 4524, 4537, 4562, 4745
Psychological anthropology 2635, 2694, 3025, 3790, 4511, 4520, 4530, 4542
Psychological effects 2890, 3044, 4538
Psychology 38, 176, 186, 193, 195, 221, 236, 1556, 1561, 1637, 2030, 2037, 2480, 2555, 2611, 2633, 2684, 2719, 2872, 2931,

2962, 3044, 3149, 3365, 3404, 3595, 3712, 3759, 3817, 4080, 4434, 4509, 4512-4516, 4518-4521, 4524, 4525, 4527, 4529, 4532, 4534, 4537-4543, 4547, 4549
    see also: Clinical psychology, Developmental psychology, Evolutionary psychology, Genetic psychology, Social psychology
Psychopathology 121, 408, 4513, 4543
Psychopharmacology 1591
Psychosociology 1664, 3575
Psychotherapy
    see: Group psychotherapy
Puberty 676, 1466, 1553, 1557, 1592, 2864
Puberty rites 2729
Public administration 2407, 2569, 2980, 3325, 3334, 3344, 4716, 4843, 4861
Public finance 4671
Public goods 2595, 4718, 4880
Public health 44, 1565, 1566, 1580, 2140, 2696, 2707, 2709, 2711, 2865, 2869, 2878, 2888, 2889, 3739, 3788, 3804, 3811, 3820, 3821, 4328, 4709, 4808, 4814, 4823, 4844, 4865, 4867, 4869, 4870, 4872, 4874-4877, 4880, 4881, 4883, 4884, 4887-4889, 4892, 4894, 4896, 4900, 4903, 4904
Public infrastructure 4688, 4907, 4932, 4939, 4941
Public interest 4718
Public management 4665, 4717
Public opinion 737, 759, 2072, 2092, 2113, 2495, 2518, 2524, 3074, 3804, 3823, 4496, 4773
Public opinion polls 2518
Public philosophy 2967, 3328
Public policy 2887, 2982, 3819, 4665
Public sector 4671, 4935
Public servants 2584, 4090
Public spaces 373, 2502, 3572, 3850, 4715, 4930
Public sphere 662, 2668, 3709, 4356, 4368, 4390, 4832
Publishing 4032, 4567
Pudumaippittan 4213
Punishment
    see: Capital punishment
Punjabi 3470
Puppets 4138
Purves, Andrew 4579
Pygmies 4555
Qing Dynasty 2460, 2928, 4164
Qualitative analysis 28, 215, 282, 306, 435, 443, 2712, 2880, 3159, 3781, 4676
Quality of life 1283, 3064, 4759, 4883

Quantitative analysis 282, 306, 443, 1885, 2880, 4676
Quarrying 500, 1143, 2107
Quechua 1823, 1974, 1983
Questionnaires 313, 2083, 3101, 3157, 4531
Qutb, Sayyid 3320
Rabban al-Tabari, Ali ibn 4232
Race 144, 155, 263, 530, 562, 628, 659, 673, 680, 695, 696, 719, 760, 812, 969, 1483, 1492, 1502-1504, 1531, 1582, 1583, 1729, 1777, 1934, 2157, 2172, 2327, 2496, 2551, 2622, 2671, 2746, 2827, 2857, 2875, 2877, 2934, 2939, 2942, 3026, 3043, 3046, 3061, 3076, 3082, 3104, 3107, 3132, 3693, 3893, 4086, 4170, 4183, 4249, 4298, 4361, 4401, 4431, 4460, 4468, 4478, 4639, 4684
Race relations 673, 786, 809, 2533, 2587, 2619, 2820, 2827, 2857, 3026, 3066, 3073, 3076, 3085, 3099, 3104, 3106, 3107, 3671, 4000, 4012, 4183
Racial attitudes 696, 3106
Racial differentiation 1531
Racial discrimination 2157, 2533, 3056, 3061, 3073, 3075, 4012
Racial segregation 126, 269, 3054, 3055
Racism 134, 135, 254, 416, 2570, 3036, 3048, 3056, 3059, 3075, 3099, 4395, 4457, 4559, 4646, 4881
Radama I [King] 800
Radicalism 778, 4249
Radicals 765
Radio 375, 1786, 1788, 4018, 4263
Railway networks 4608
Railways 749, 4608, 4766
Rain forest 857, 1598, 1649, 1691, 2098, 2104, 2108, 2195, 4335
Rajagopalan, L.S. 3304
Rameses II [King] 507
Ranganātha 3305
Rape 2533, 3073
Rapport, Nigel 159, 217
Rationalism 138
Rationality 255, 275, 630, 2062, 2346, 2369, 2539, 4635
Ratnākara 4067
Raw materials 2107, 2235
Ray, Bharatcandra 4257
Read, James 644
Reading 257, 1740, 2561, 2832, 4217, 4247, 4751
Realism 438, 1517, 1781, 3793, 4045, 4287, 4556
Reason 998, 2933, 3153, 3552, 3564, 4449

Rebellions 522, 548, 711, 763, 1012, 2197, 3063, 3525, 4634
Recent economic history 2345, 3175
Recession 2258, 2268, 4291, 4906
Reciprocity 404, 1647, 1692, 2351, 2379, 2382, 4390, 4393
Record industry 3922
Recreation 2085, 2697, 2803, 4310
Recruitment 4927
Recycling 908, 2114
Refiki 4070
Reflexivity 133, 158, 196, 216, 219, 222, 228, 235, 237, 241, 242, 261, 275, 326, 351, 383, 384, 392, 398, 403, 422, 439, 610, 613, 635, 670, 2477, 2539, 2779, 3677, 3905, 4641
Reform 3, 2404, 4778
    see also: Agrarian reform, Constitutional reform, Economic reform, Education reform, Land reform, Legal reform, Political reform, Religious reform, Social reform
Reformation 3230, 4441
Refugees 489, 1282, 2119, 2148, 2159, 2165, 2176, 2178, 3105, 3519, 3730, 4547, 4820, 4826, 4899
    see also: Displaced persons
Regime transition 4682
Regional analysis 663, 2150, 2210, 2749, 2853, 4452, 4707
Regional conflicts 254, 4457
Regional cooperation 3169, 4721
Regional development 4614, 4664, 4734, 4753, 4755
Regional disparities 4021, 4338, 4609, 4680
Regional economics 4614
Regional government 2222
Regional identity 402, 2614, 3094, 3102, 3917, 4382
Regional integration 551, 2318, 2385, 4682, 4688
Regional markets 2255, 4687
Regional planning 4326, 4831
Regional politics 4664
Regional studies 27, 35, 53, 54, 61, 87, 104, 109, 124, 126, 129, 307, 321, 324, 332, 336, 350, 366, 447-449, 474, 477-479, 481, 482, 493, 495, 506, 518, 558, 566, 567, 595, 609, 630, 642, 661, 666, 678, 694, 712, 719, 741, 761, 780, 795, 801, 843, 847, 895, 897, 902, 906, 907, 925, 934, 962, 975, 976, 1006, 1019, 1049, 1056, 1063, 1072, 1076, 1081, 1083, 1084, 1089, 1097, 1102, 1104, 1249, 1284, 1301, 1308, 1316, 1328, 1332, 1334,

1335, 1394, 1410, 1411, 1428, 1731, 1746,
1748, 1800, 1805, 1821, 1835, 1851,
1853, 1857, 1893, 1913, 1914, 1917,
1931, 1932, 1938, 1939, 1950, 1966,
1989, 1993, 1995, 1996, 1999, 2019,
2023, 2059, 2061, 2064, 2086, 2097,
2125, 2151, 2155, 2159, 2161, 2178,
2180, 2197, 2238, 2246, 2248, 2252,
2261, 2263, 2271, 2278, 2283, 2289,
2290, 2295, 2299, 2306, 2339, 2351,
2354, 2356, 2357, 2366, 2367, 2389,
2405, 2409, 2429, 2439, 2447, 2464,
2490, 2497, 2499, 2504, 2506, 2508,
2521, 2534, 2546, 2558, 2559, 2561,
2574, 2581, 2610, 2614, 2616, 2624,
2629, 2640, 2670, 2698, 2714, 2718,
2725, 2734, 2745, 2747, 2756, 2786,
2788, 2797, 2809, 2815, 2839, 2857,
2877, 2904, 2911, 2960, 2965, 2971, 3029,
3031, 3039, 3047, 3048, 3050, 3051,
3054, 3057, 3076, 3078, 3079, 3084,
3087, 3114, 3120, 3137, 3157, 3167-3169,
3171, 3177, 3184, 3192-3194, 3196-3198,
3205, 3206, 3209, 3213, 3218, 3220,
3251, 3261, 3274, 3275, 3277, 3279,
3282-3285, 3289, 3295, 3299, 3303, 3304,
3306-3308, 3310, 3321, 3323, 3329, 3351,
3354, 3362, 3364, 3371, 3392, 3395,
3400, 3402, 3416, 3418, 3424, 3425,
3433, 3439, 3440, 3450, 3456-3459, 3513,
3524, 3528, 3539, 3556, 3557, 3571,
3635, 3646, 3663, 3673, 3676, 3688,
3701, 3717, 3732, 3740, 3743, 3761,
3784, 3794, 3814, 3818, 3833, 3837,
3851, 3853, 3860, 3862, 3866, 3868,
3872, 3886, 3888, 3893, 3896, 3918,
3920, 3924, 3927, 3933, 3939, 3944,
3950, 3955, 4005, 4012, 4020, 4029,
4033, 4042-4044, 4048, 4051, 4054-4056,
4059, 4062, 4068, 4069, 4072, 4073,
4095, 4112, 4137, 4141, 4144, 4148, 4153,
4157, 4162, 4166, 4169, 4173, 4185,
4189, 4192, 4195, 4197, 4199, 4204-4206,
4209-4211, 4213, 4217, 4223, 4246, 4248,
4251, 4252, 4254, 4256, 4257, 4263,
4274, 4279, 4281-4284, 4287, 4314, 4347,
4357, 4360, 4368, 4369, 4383, 4392,
4398, 4443, 4458, 4463, 4481, 4494,
4497, 4522, 4556, 4578, 4588, 4589,
4596, 4605, 4609, 4640, 4642, 4652,
4663, 4671, 4679, 4682, 4688, 4723,
4725, 4740, 4751, 4757, 4758, 4772,
4777, 4792, 4799, 4804, 4830, 4833,
4929, 4931
Regional trade 150, 382, 2357, 2362

Regionalism 801, 3917, 4671
Regions 39, 80, 150, 171, 184, 303, 369, 382,
919, 957, 1061, 1127, 2054, 2060, 2078,
2419, 2528, 2614, 2951, 3098, 3099,
3935, 4186, 4336, 4371, 4628, 4664, 4734
see also: Regional politics, Regional
studies
Regression analysis 910, 1675, 2137, 2430,
4886
Regulation 4301, 4326, 4607, 4621, 4935
Reincarnation 2791, 3153, 3192
Reinel, Pedro 768
Reis, Piris 768
Relativism 138, 1723, 1728, 4216, 4513, 4641
Religion 86, 105, 166, 185, 186, 191, 195,
202, 208, 209, 214, 256, 300, 413, 447,
468, 473, 476, 509, 531, 568, 577, 585,
596, 604, 626, 639, 644, 700, 725, 735,
736, 766, 782, 808, 829, 897, 1025, 1050-
1052, 1070, 1121, 1165, 1320, 1348, 1519,
1749, 1755, 1837, 1863, 2018, 2069,
2099, 2115, 2160, 2186, 2217, 2375, 2388,
2392, 2482, 2483, 2532, 2542-2544, 2574,
2579, 2598, 2605, 2675, 2684, 2729,
2746, 2755, 2756, 2764, 2776, 2808,
2817, 2826, 2828, 2834, 2859, 2952,
2965, 2967, 2998, 3014, 3079, 3103, 3112,
3131, 3135, 3141, 3142, 3149, 3151-3158,
3161, 3170, 3172, 3174, 3180, 3186,
3188, 3189, 3191, 3215, 3217, 3219-3222,
3225, 3227, 3228, 3230-3232, 3234, 3236,
3237, 3241, 3246, 3247, 3250, 3257,
3259, 3265, 3286, 3287, 3292, 3294,
3300, 3320, 3324, 3325, 3328, 3334,
3335, 3337, 3338, 3340, 3341, 3344,
3346-3348, 3350, 3356, 3359-3361, 3363,
3365-3367, 3370, 3371, 3377, 3380, 3382,
3394, 3395, 3402, 3406, 3410, 3411, 3413,
3416, 3419, 3422, 3425, 3426, 3432,
3433, 3439, 3448, 3455-3457, 3462 3465,
3467-3471, 3473-3483, 3485, 3487-3495,
3497, 3498, 3501, 3505, 3507-3509, 3513,
3514, 3526, 3528, 3533, 3535, 3540-3545,
3547, 3549, 3557, 3560, 3562, 3574,
3578, 3583, 3584, 3589-3591, 3593, 3602,
3609, 3612, 3616, 3619, 3620, 3622,
3625, 3627, 3631-3633, 3636, 3637, 3639,
3640, 3642, 3645, 3649, 3652, 3653,
3657, 3666, 3681, 3706, 3711, 3728, 3734,
3741, 3761, 3822, 3826, 4034, 4043,
4080, 4095, 4105, 4184, 4247, 4259,
4264, 4269, 4304, 4359, 4383, 4406,
4412, 4428, 4441, 4445, 4459, 4461,
4462, 4468, 4474, 4484, 4503, 4523,
4537, 4585, 4585, 4587, 4599, 4674, 4724

see also: Ancient religions, Anthropology of religion, Comparative religion, Ethnology of religion, History of religion, Monotheism, Philosophy of religion, Popular religion, Prehistoric religions, Religious texts, Sociology of religion, Traditional religion, Tribal religion, World religions

Religion and politics 1361, 2515, 2979, 3324, 3349, 3353, 3438, 3448, 3470, 3625, 3697, 4415

see also: Islam and politics

Religiosity 257, 2515, 2816, 3140, 3154, 3157, 3259, 3262, 3378, 3512, 3574, 3593, 3639, 3645, 4179

Religious art 1081, 3230, 3249, 3256, 3452, 3624, 4095, 4106, 4114, 4117, 4131, 4137, 4140, 4441

Religious authorities 275, 2539

Religious behaviour 3157, 3230, 3332, 3360, 3446, 3621, 4371, 4441

Religious beliefs 22, 142, 143, 168, 1489, 2791, 2816, 2945, 3131, 3134, 3139, 3140, 3160, 3194, 3230, 3269, 3316, 3325, 3330, 3338, 3342, 3446, 3464, 3466, 3467, 3472, 3478, 3488, 3490, 3492-3494, 3501, 3515, 3529, 3542, 3555, 3563, 3599, 3621, 3623, 3631, 3713, 3734, 4441

Religious broadcasting 3621

Religious change 86, 701, 1025, 3215, 3234, 3257, 3264, 3557, 3593, 3609, 3610, 3612, 3617, 3618, 3623, 3631-3636, 3639-3641, 3647, 3887, 4459, 4804

Religious communities 2652, 2764, 3186, 3194, 3222, 3226, 3241, 3345, 3376, 3394, 3422, 3544, 3555, 4451, 4581, 4931

Religious conflicts 383, 593, 611, 1361, 2779, 3040, 3042, 3230, 3697, 4441, 4476

Religious conversion 3230, 3264, 3484, 3647, 3887, 4441

Religious doctrines 515, 568, 2931, 3330, 3413, 3440, 3442, 3451, 3485, 3515

Religious education 86, 3215, 3471

Religious experiences 105, 3231, 3338

Religious festivals 2778, 3269, 3741, 4362, 4370

Religious fundamentalism 3326, 3367, 3548, 3643

Religious groups 592, 1454, 2573, 3342, 3534, 4424

Religious history 451, 592, 606, 782, 1344, 1353, 2573, 2986, 3216, 3224, 3230, 3247, 3260, 3266, 3405, 3419, 3445,

3460, 3531, 3535, 3632, 3637, 3648, 3856, 3974, 4114, 4441

Religious ideas 3427, 3439

Religious influences 2267, 3193, 3234, 3416, 3641

Religious institutions 2485, 2997, 3194, 3197, 3204

Religious leaders 470, 700, 1336, 2567, 3014, 3185, 3219, 3312, 3330, 3341, 3368, 3387, 3394, 3427, 3461, 3473, 3475, 3476, 3484, 3485, 3490, 3496, 3500, 3506, 3508, 3532, 3623, 4078

Religious life 210, 766, 2617, 2811, 2979, 3204, 3349, 3512, 3517, 3526, 3531, 3561, 3562, 3574, 3579

Religious missions 318, 608, 721, 722, 750, 813, 2082, 2754, 2774, 3058, 3608, 3614, 3615, 3617, 3618, 3628, 3630, 3635, 3640, 3727, 4472, 4474

Religious movements 2069, 2485, 3262, 3265, 3276, 3423, 3429, 3548, 3595, 3611, 3631, 3657

Religious music 3309, 3463, 3901, 3915, 3927, 3962

Religious orders 323, 565, 707, 2769, 3198

Religious persecution 3089, 3100, 3230, 3484, 3502, 4441

Religious pluralism 3394

Religious practice 142, 568, 3152, 3163, 3171, 3188, 3198, 3230, 3235, 3281, 3310, 3332, 3374, 3383, 3413, 3447, 3461, 3486, 3499, 3503, 3546, 3599, 3621, 3625, 3639, 4441, 4451

Religious reform 3286, 3333

Religious representation 3396

Religious revival 245, 3198, 3364, 3646

Religious separatism 3248

Religious studies 5, 154, 167, 185, 195, 208-210, 226, 227, 300, 591, 782, 1103, 1489, 1738, 1755, 2375, 2388, 2605, 2675, 2973, 3111, 3129, 3136, 3142, 3151, 3161, 3173, 3179, 3181, 3183, 3187, 3188, 3195, 3199, 3203, 3222, 3227, 3229, 3235, 3238, 3239, 3243, 3244, 3247, 3264, 3273, 3293, 3303, 3315, 3318, 3368-3375, 3377, 3379, 3383, 3385-3388, 3391, 3396, 3414, 3417, 3430, 3435, 3455, 3463, 3520, 3521, 3527, 3531, 3533, 3545, 3546, 3560, 3561, 3584, 3591, 3611, 3619, 3620, 3638, 3647, 3706, 3822, 3885, 4034, 4117, 4471, 4537, 4674

Religious symbolism 3703, 3711

Religious syncretism 3335

Religious systems 3522

Religious teachings 560, 568, 640, 1349, 2000, 3136, 3168-3170, 3200, 3205, 3209, 3210, 3285, 3297, 3308, 3313, 3315, 3321, 3323, 3354, 3370, 3373, 3375, 3385, 3386, 3391, 3393, 3412, 3413, 3415, 3428, 3430, 3442-3444, 3447, 3453, 3471, 3476, 3481, 3494, 3496, 3504, 3506, 4284

Religious texts 22, 208, 472, 476, 515, 604, 796, 1103, 1129, 1344, 1349, 1353, 1843, 1861, 1864, 1893, 2000, 2973, 3120, 3136, 3146, 3148, 3164, 3169, 3173, 3174, 3179, 3184, 3190, 3195-3197, 3200, 3203, 3205, 3206, 3209, 3212, 3218, 3227, 3229, 3237, 3238, 3244, 3248, 3253, 3255, 3272, 3273, 3277, 3278, 3281, 3282, 3291, 3293, 3294, 3297, 3298, 3300, 3302, 3307, 3308, 3310, 3313, 3320, 3330-3333, 3336-3338, 3344, 3351, 3355, 3358, 3362, 3369, 3390, 3392, 3393, 3396, 3398, 3400, 3405, 3407, 3408, 3420, 3421, 3424-3427, 3430, 3432-3435, 3437, 3439, 3440, 3442, 3445, 3449-3451, 3453, 3455, 3456, 3460, 3465, 3479, 3485, 3495, 3504, 3521, 3632, 3748, 4224, 4231, 4283, 4286

Religious thought 185, 634, 3143, 3162, 3164, 3165, 3170, 3178, 3182, 3183, 3200, 3201, 3208, 3210, 3252, 3270, 3280, 3283, 3291, 3297, 3303, 3311, 3320, 3368, 3369, 3372, 3373, 3375, 3377, 3379, 3381, 3383, 3385, 3386, 3388, 3389, 3391, 3441, 3477, 3481, 3496, 4026, 4284

Religious traditions 147, 186, 208, 490, 1006, 1323, 2099, 2737, 3149, 3155, 3163, 3166, 3168, 3180, 3192, 3194, 3197, 3200, 3201, 3286, 3300, 3304, 3338, 3364, 3376, 3399, 3434, 3455, 3463, 3481, 3646, 3706, 4284

Remittances 2631, 4804

Renaissance 1031, 3787

Rendille 2126, 2434, 2626, 2767, 2879, 4878

Rent 2293

Representations of the body 766, 769, 1361, 2727, 2944, 2947, 2953, 3697, 3994

Representative democracy 4929

Repression 2496

Reproductive health 1586, 3824

Reproductive technology 2722

Rescue archaeology 1135, 1144, 1145, 1158, 1206, 1221, 1238, 1239, 1275, 1295, 1313-1315, 1391, 1436

Research 22, 25, 29, 36, 48, 50, 51, 184, 200, 225, 297, 317, 324, 333, 339, 352, 354, 381, 389, 394, 413, 533, 536, 539, 547, 552, 589, 613, 622, 635, 655, 672, 907, 910, 927, 930, 953, 1101, 1111, 1120, 1123, 1124, 1154, 1158, 1168, 1172, 1192, 1206, 1231, 1237, 1252, 1258, 1274, 1276, 1310, 1840, 2148, 2308, 2838, 2880, 2953, 3761, 4306, 4696, 4697, 4703, 4705, 4746, 4931
see also: Agricultural research, Anthropological research, Archaeological research, Current research, Demographic research, Development research, Economic research, Empirical research, Ethnographic research, Ethnological research, Interdisciplinary research, Linguistic research, Market research, Medical research, Music research, Scientific research, Social research, Social science research, Sociological research

Research and development 2307, 4699, 4743

Research centres 29, 160, 1205, 3600, 4334

Research equipment 963, 1001

Research methodology 282, 407, 443, 3765

Research methods 28, 33, 36, 72, 170, 187, 225, 277, 287, 290, 291, 294, 300, 302, 306, 307, 339, 394, 404, 406, 410, 411, 422, 426, 429, 536, 539, 616, 635, 655, 930, 970, 1003, 1468, 1815, 2880, 4009, 4676, 4709, 4818, 4910
see also: Field work

Research programmes 29

Research projects 30, 32, 290, 313, 1038, 1109, 1254, 1273, 3566

Research trends 1914, 2052

Research workers 291, 304, 443, 608, 2324, 2897

Residence 2654

Residential areas 1083, 3660

Residential segregation 2222

Resistance 531, 601, 1616, 1762, 2190, 2382, 2933, 3032, 4037, 4112, 4495, 4637

Resistance movements 767, 3577

Resistance to change 3286, 4442

Resource allocation 2449, 4801, 4810

Resource exploitation 2417, 2446, 2448, 3018, 4850

Resource management 968, 2067, 2073, 2083, 2116, 2210, 2264, 2272, 2288, 2289, 2404, 2413, 2427, 3695, 4399, 4660, 4691, 4769, 4770, 4773, 4774, 4780, 4799, 4801, 4805

Resource scarcity 2303

Resource utilization 3742, 4779, 4802, 4806

Responsibility 395, 1578, 2544, 2656, 2668, 2837, 3508, 4666, 4882

Return migration 2165

Revenge 510, 790, 2536, 2653, 2977
Revisionism 348
Revolt 323, 707
Revolution 754, 778, 982, 1823, 2281, 2534,
    4352, 4921
    see also: Industrial revolution, Iranian
    Revolution, Russian Revolution
Revolutionaries 2557, 4277
Reyes, Alfonso 3862, 4192, 4282
Reyes, Bernardo 546
Rhetoric 560, 805, 1776, 3000, 3258, 3354,
    3412, 3444, 3644, 4035, 4113
Rhodes, Cecil 710
Ricci, Matteo 3079, 3743
Rice 726, 2142, 2255, 2271, 2304, 2305,
    2314, 2735, 4687, 4693, 4821, 4827
Riddles 1788, 4018
Riehl, Wilhelm Heinrich 149
Right 270, 2537
Rights 59, 2083, 2289, 2400, 2407, 2415,
    2420, 2427, 2457, 2728, 2933, 2968,
    2969, 2972, 2978, 2980, 2984, 2994,
    2997, 3001, 3003, 3791, 4613, 4630,
    4640, 4642, 4654, 4670, 4762
    see also: Children's rights, Civil rights,
    Human rights, Indigenous rights,
    Individual rights, Minority rights, Property
    rights, Women's rights
Riots 609, 2318, 3673
Risk 422, 879, 1539, 1544, 1548, 1713, 2106,
    2149, 2371, 2454, 2695, 2720, 2867,
    2885, 2889, 2896, 2916, 3575, 3680,
    3769, 3780, 3795, 3831, 4497, 4889, 4893
Risk management 4865
Rites of passage 2731, 2776, 3609, 4017
Ritual 105, 166, 214, 222, 233, 271, 374, 384,
    459, 468, 656, 804, 880, 911, 929, 1000,
    1024, 1052, 1063, 1300, 1302, 1304,
    1430, 1446, 1733, 1771, 1965, 2109,
    2252, 2256, 2291, 2337, 2388, 2514,
    2571, 2579, 2682, 2684, 2700, 2727,
    2731, 2753, 2766, 2781, 2784, 2787,
    2791, 2794, 2795, 2811, 2835, 2838, 2871,
    2876, 2906, 3014, 3119, 3156, 3163, 3171,
    3198, 3221, 3228, 3231, 3232, 3234,
    3237, 3250, 3257, 3259, 3265, 3296,
    3301, 3306, 3310, 3316, 3338, 3341,
    3348, 3353, 3357, 3360, 3367, 3382,
    3406, 3409, 3439, 3509, 3511, 3514, 3517,
    3518, 3521, 3523-3525, 3530, 3537-3539,
    3549, 3550, 3552, 3556, 3558, 3559,
    3564, 3567, 3581, 3586, 3594, 3596,
    3597, 3600-3602, 3606, 3609, 3622, 3625,
    3645, 3649, 3678, 3681, 3694, 3713,
    3715, 3736, 3776, 3812, 3910, 3939,

3950, 3951, 3982, 4011, 4013, 4017, 4126,
    4138, 4231, 4315, 4334, 4354, 4361,
    4362, 4364, 4367, 4373, 4387, 4390,
    4402, 4423, 4428, 4430, 4462, 4496, 4758
    see also: Initiation rites, Puberty rites
Ritual murders 2792, 2795, 3007, 3089, 3597
Ritual music 3539, 3950
Ritual songs 3539, 3950
Rivalry 1606, 2188, 2682
Rivers 721, 806, 893, 942, 957, 1597, 2070,
    2079, 2086, 2101, 2110, 2274, 2289, 2678,
    3536, 3682, 4775
Rivière, Peter 90, 385
Rizal, José 2534
Roads 466, 496, 524, 1138, 2228, 4346
Robert, Shaaban 4163
Robots 4100
Roche, Yves 4263
Rock art 894, 968, 1007, 1013, 1023, 1041,
    1087, 1095, 1105, 1335, 3585
Rock music 3518
Rodó, José Enrique 4157, 4191
Rohe, Ludwig Mies van der 3660
Role 3869
Role prescriptions 365
Rom 14, 399, 1924, 3798, 4006
Roman Empire 454, 465, 468, 471, 498, 500,
    513, 519, 524, 529, 593, 1029, 1090,
    1234, 1236, 1302, 1358, 1367, 1418,
    1419, 3406, 4346
Romanticism 149, 630, 3129, 3940, 4263
Romany languages 1924
Römer, Ludewig Ferdinand 4007
Rougier, Berthe 566
Rousseau, Jean Jacques 3929
Roussel, Raymond 4263
Rsabhadeva 3387
Rubber industry 893, 2110
Rübner, Tuvia 4049, 4439
Rule of law 2972, 2978, 2984, 2994, 4616,
    4670
Rumours 3114, 3571, 3974
Rungu 2808, 2828
Rūparām 2624
Ruqayyat, Ibn Qais Al- 4077
Rural anthropology 41, 190, 2204, 2206, 4369
Rural areas 2133, 2137, 2138, 2180, 2185,
    2202, 2286, 2336, 2396, 2413, 2441,
    2599, 2620, 2718, 2793, 2818, 3629,
    3678, 3800, 3814, 3819, 3858, 4291,
    4353, 4669, 4699, 4757, 4766, 4796,
    4858, 4866, 4902, 4905, 4906, 4908,
    4909, 4918-4920, 4922, 4925
Rural communities 15, 136, 646, 668, 2192,
    2194, 2195, 2207, 2294, 2413, 2426,

2556, 2561, 2735, 2752, 2786, 3819,
3827, 3858, 4309, 4742, 4751, 4795,
4818, 4910
Rural credit 288, 4671, 4855
Rural development 288, 2062, 2318, 2396,
2422, 4635, 4696, 4701, 4781, 4796,
4820, 4833, 4855, 4905, 4907, 4910,
4912-4926
Rural dwellings 2394
Rural economics 288, 2196, 2316, 2371, 2416,
3017, 4291, 4906, 4916-4918, 4921, 4922,
4925, 4940
Rural environment 3861
Rural history 757, 2205, 2406, 2423, 2463,
2607, 4325
Rural life 667, 917, 1759, 2197, 2200, 2203,
2205, 2206, 2256, 2388, 2423, 2463,
2655, 2702, 2770, 2949, 3005, 3669,
3775, 4135, 4369, 4448, 4764, 4799,
4884, 4909, 4922
Rural policy 4915
Rural population 17, 1543, 1578, 1586, 2553,
2726, 2773, 2898, 3824, 3825, 4789
Rural poverty 2196, 2288, 2396, 2434, 2620,
4291, 4846, 4885, 4905, 4906, 4911, 4913,
4914, 4919
Rural society 1759, 2204, 2207, 2600, 2675,
4291, 4906
Rural sociology 2655, 2757, 2770, 2856, 2913
Rural studies 730, 2188, 2257, 2275, 2317,
2336, 2417, 2586, 2628, 3018, 3735,
4391, 4604, 4796
Rural women 2094, 2320, 2702, 2793, 2843,
3775, 4760, 4862
Rural-urban migration 2167, 2181
Rural-urban relations 684, 2120, 2179, 3772
Russian Empire 2644
Russian language 1909, 1936, 3100
Russian Orthodox Church 2599, 3555, 3629,
4476
Russian Revolution 658, 2545
Russians 2480, 2599, 3100, 3101, 3446, 3628,
3629, 3918
Sa'd, Abdullah ibn 4232
Saadia Gaon, R. 3251
Sacred 105, 656, 1006, 1049, 1322, 1859,
2099, 2782, 3142, 3155, 3196, 3231,
3367, 3436, 3659, 4257
Sacred cows 3292
Sacrifice 829, 929, 1818, 2063, 3213, 3447,
3537, 3556, 4231
Safety 2721, 3986
   see also: Occupational safety
Sahib, Granth 2997
Sahib, Hargobind 3476

Saikaku, Ihara 4254
Saints 142, 166, 473, 514, 1065, 2909, 3152,
3220, 3240, 3242, 3253, 3261, 3347, 3411,
3414, 3472, 3516, 3554, 3599, 3649,
3721, 4391, 4428
Saivism 3854
Sakalava 2392
Sakhawat Hossain, Rokeya 2839
Salih, Ali M.A. 111
Salish 1322, 1837
Salt 2355, 2806, 2828, 3318
Samburu 2447, 2824
Sami 3535, 4624
Samples 296, 1510
Sampling 282, 296, 388, 1456, 2148, 4527
San 2398, 4638
Sanballat 2550
Sango 2017
Sanitation 4811
Sanitation services 4887, 4937
Sankara 3200
Sanskrit 14, 1907, 1939, 1945, 1950, 1960,
3148, 3162, 3179, 3184, 3195, 3203,
3212, 3214, 3272, 3282, 3290, 3296,
3301, 3302, 3314, 3317, 3390, 3865,
3875, 3876, 4057, 4067, 4168, 4207,
4246, 4261, 4596
Santal 2359
Sarah 2748
Sargon II [King] 1341
Sarmad, Sa'id 3414
Sarmiento, Domingo Faustino 4048, 4210
Sarrazin, Albertine 3005
Satanism 3578
Satellites 1615, 2287
Sati 2738, 2785
Satire 4058, 4194, 4243
Satisfaction 2768
Sauer, James A. 112
Savanna 900, 1359, 2104, 2448, 4784
Savings 2210, 4911
Scandals 148, 644, 2966
Scarcity 2289
   see also: Resource scarcity
Schaden, Egon 2798
Schaeffner, André 3929
Schenda, Rudolf 141
Schmitz, C.A. 26, 93
School leavers 2223
Schooling 1559, 2350, 4542, 4555, 4682
Schools 1387, 1554, 2783, 2869, 4550, 4560,
4603, 4757, 4761, 4869
Schwarz-Bart, Simone 3980
Schweizer, Thomas 131

Science 4, 5, 24, 60, 99, 132, 144, 156, 165,
170, 188, 226, 274, 437, 464, 908, 947,
971, 974, 1002, 1163, 1451, 1504, 1519,
1781, 2099, 2300, 3005, 3014, 3131,
3153, 3155, 3341, 3491, 3685, 3728,
3739, 3746, 3750, 3753, 3755, 3793,
3975, 4142, 4763
see also: Anthropology of science,
Behavioural sciences, Forensic science,
History of science, Natural sciences,
Philosophy of science
Science and technology 1577, 1683, 2094,
2129, 2131, 2320, 2452, 2704, 2818,
2823, 2843, 2844, 3568, 4822, 4862
Science fiction 4197
Scientific communities 197
Scientific discoveries 2310
Scientific progress 16
Scientific research 33, 988, 1517, 1616, 1683,
3209, 4473, 4664, 4785
Scientific thought 16
Scientists 4, 110, 156, 165, 3755, 3799
see also: Social scientists
Scripts 4268, 4269
see: Ancient scripts, Hieroglyphic script
Sculpture and carving 322, 336, 360, 461,
1006, 1014, 1024, 1030, 1043, 1051,
1062, 1067, 1068, 1071, 1078, 1086,
1087, 1093, 1096-1098, 1341, 1350, 1364,
1387, 1432, 1531, 2241, 3714, 4095, 4117,
4124, 4134, 4145, 4712
Sea 39, 948, 1151, 2065, 2070, 2085, 2092,
2428, 3242, 3650, 3721, 3847, 4310
Sea transport 503, 2372
Seafarers 323, 707
Seafaring 455, 820, 2225
Seasonality 646, 1695, 1699, 1700, 1718,
2060, 2752
Seasons 1034, 1107, 1112, 1115, 1119, 1128,
1131, 1139, 1147, 1174, 1176, 1178, 1182,
1204, 1218, 1219, 1227, 1241, 1243,
1246, 1253, 1257, 1261, 1266, 1609,
1638, 1718, 2085, 2187, 2610, 3242,
3721, 3740, 4310
Secrecy 201, 3643
Secret societies 3519
Sectarianism 3167, 3257, 3327
Sects 571, 3198, 3248, 3342, 3343, 3429,
3496, 3631
Secularism 275, 606, 2099, 2539, 2986, 3155,
3544
Secularization 3734
Sedakova, Olga 4073
Sedentarization 1301, 2434

Segregation 263, 3043
see also: Cultural segregation, Racial
segregation, Residential segregation
Self 215, 1066, 1448, 1793, 2322, 2533, 2766,
2920, 2923, 2926, 2933, 2948, 2961,
3073, 3144, 3499, 3516, 3760, 4069,
4073, 4083, 4297, 4437, 4443, 4510,
4514, 4517, 4534, 4535, 4540, 4578
Self-concept 4530
Self-consciousness 3103, 3653, 4484, 4580
Self-determination 2538, 2954, 3026, 4627,
4629, 4646, 4649, 4656, 4785
Self-esteem 2962
Self-expression 3760, 3929, 4011, 4562
Self-government 2540, 4656
Self-help 4511
Self-management 2210
Self-perception 3112, 3760, 4468, 4486
Self-sufficiency 2210, 2262
Selkup 3587, 3726
Selous, Frederick Courteney 746, 4208
Semai 2698
Semantics 1723, 1728, 1737, 1738, 1749,
1752, 1811, 1866, 1880, 1881, 1889, 1921,
1960, 1963, 1977, 1980, 1982, 1987,
2007, 2015, 2016, 2037, 3165, 3210,
3273, 3753, 3874, 4206, 4600
Seminars 2485
Semiology 3670, 3715, 3756, 4098, 4198
Semiotics 1763, 2387, 2685, 2958, 3021,
3728, 3731, 4136
Senapati, Fakir Mohan 4272
Senn, Nicholas 3749
Senses 1703, 2324, 2800, 2949, 3188, 3207
see also: Hearing, Sight, Smell, Taste
Sensory organs 1556
Sentences 1769, 1848, 1868, 1895, 1921, 3011
Sentongo, Z.K. 677
Separatism
see: Religious separatism
Setswana 1783
Settlement archaeology 445, 448, 475, 483,
512, 556, 598, 623, 825, 831, 840, 843,
854-856, 859, 860, 885, 886, 892, 905,
907, 909, 917, 922, 924, 927, 931, 938,
944, 957, 965, 966, 968, 982, 1035, 1036,
1114, 1130, 1148, 1152, 1155, 1173, 1185,
1196, 1238, 1240, 1245, 1263, 1264, 1285,
1301, 1303, 1306, 1309, 1355, 1392,
1433, 1444, 2208, 2340
Sex 44, 1507, 1580, 1621, 1654, 1660, 1684,
1752, 2621, 2706, 2723, 2725, 2759,
2773, 2827, 2869, 2886, 2894, 2898,
2903-2905, 2911, 2913, 2918, 2919, 3104,
3130, 3820, 3929, 4461, 4542, 4869, 4891

Sex differentiation 1684, 2831
Sex discrimination 4645, 4835
Sex distribution 2722
Sex education 2710, 2869, 2878, 2879, 3788,
   4869, 4877, 4878
Sex equality 2863
Sex roles 2810, 2831, 2932, 3034, 3525
Sex workers 2220, 2710, 2884, 2902, 2988,
   3796, 4218, 4898
Sexology 1945
Sexual abuse 2533, 3073
Sexual behaviour 44, 1507, 1580, 2153, 2156,
   2710, 2717, 2759, 2840, 2848, 2867,
   2868, 2876, 2878, 2879, 2884, 2885,
   2893, 2895, 2902-2904, 2910, 2912, 2914,
   2916-2919, 2966, 3254, 3780, 3788, 3796,
   3820, 3831, 3966, 4877, 4878, 4898
Sexual health 285, 2696, 2707, 2723, 2865,
   2866, 2869, 2870, 2878, 2888, 2892,
   2894, 2905, 2913, 2914, 3788, 3810, 3811,
   4722, 4869, 4877, 4891, 4892, 4901
Sexual intercourse 2621, 2886, 2903
Sexual reproduction 1283, 1488, 1491, 1500,
   1586, 1605, 1613, 1619, 1658, 1662,
   1667-1669, 1676, 1695, 1697-1699, 1705,
   1706, 1708, 2131, 2381, 2723, 2724,
   2851, 2863, 2876, 2905, 2941, 2956,
   3358, 3824, 4890, 4892
Sexual symbolism 280, 2858
Sexuality 44, 52, 290, 304, 502, 514, 562,
   1507, 1580, 1697, 1777, 2695, 2717,
   2723, 2746, 2753, 2759, 2820, 2821,
   2848, 2865-2869, 2872-2875, 2877-2879,
   2882, 2884, 2885, 2888, 2892-2895, 2897,
   2899, 2902, 2903, 2905, 2906, 2908-2914,
   2916-2919, 2934, 2941, 2953, 3254, 3719,
   3782, 3788, 3796, 3810, 3820, 3831,
   4468, 4548, 4869, 4877, 4878, 4891, 4898
   see also: Bisexuality, Heterosexuality,
   Homosexuality, Lesbianism,
   Transsexuality
Sexually transmitted diseases 44, 1580, 2723,
   2879, 2884, 2885, 2892, 2905, 3761,
   3796, 3810, 3820, 4878
Shakespeare, William 3878
Shamanism 105, 828, 1041, 1771, 3062, 3128,
   3231, 3535, 3550, 3565, 3566, 3580,
   3587, 3589, 3592, 3593, 3600-3602, 3605,
   3606, 3726, 3833, 4334, 4360, 4480
Shamans 1771, 1834, 3062, 3565, 3566, 3582,
   3585, 3587-3589, 3592, 3598, 3600, 3605,
   3606, 3626, 3726, 4334, 4360
Shambhu Hedge, Keremane 3892
Shanty towns 2180
Sharecropping 2285

Sheep 2310, 2437, 2445
Shells 1097, 1362, 1382, 1420
Shepherds 4579
Shia 3337
Shifting cultivation 2181
Shiism 470, 571, 2567, 3337, 3343
Shilluk 88
Shintoism 3177, 3187, 3532, 3706, 3717
Shipbuilding 1395
Shipibo 1969
Ships 4724
Shivarama Karanth, Kota 3892
Shona 711, 767, 2001, 3577
Shopping 2322
Shortage
   see: Food shortages
Shotridge, Louis 130, 353
Shrines 105, 2682, 3204, 3231, 3239, 3495,
   3548, 3703
Shvarts, Elena 4073
Sibawayh 3362
Siblings 1614
Siddhi Nara Simha [King] 2519
Sight 1688, 3728
Sigillography 2497
Sign language 40
Signalling 1617
Signs 545, 1778, 2246, 3158, 3670, 3828,
   4198
Sigüenza y Góngora, Carlos de 132, 437
Sikhism 577, 2186, 2483, 2485, 2495, 2511,
   2515, 2520, 2542, 2543, 2997, 3331,
   3363, 3461-3484, 3486-3508, 3705, 3716,
   3855, 4078, 4269, 4304, 4370, 4724
Sikhs 2186, 2483, 2515, 2520, 2542, 3363,
   3462, 3464, 3466, 3469-3473, 3475, 3476,
   3478, 3480, 3487, 3490-3493, 3498, 3501-
   3503, 3505, 3716, 3855, 4304, 4370
Silk 2231
Silva, Francisco Correia da 323, 707
Silver 506, 1428, 1444
Silver mines 4608
Simonović, Radivoj 101
Simulation 295, 455, 2130, 2225, 2634, 3765
Singers 2584, 2842, 3933, 3938, 4059, 4090
Singh, Gobind 3500, 4078
Singh, Harbhajan 4304
Singh, Ranjit 3473
Singh, Sardar Khushwant 2483
Singh, Sukhvinder 4724
Singhalese 2489, 3194
Sisala 2512, 4001
Sisterhoods 4193
Śivānī 4281
Size of enterprise 4671

Skills 970, 1427, 2464, 4760, 4836, 4866
Skin 2248
Skis 2230
Slave trade 554, 692, 695, 734, 778, 806, 807,
    961, 2383, 2671, 2857, 3076, 3230, 4007,
    4441, 4460, 4548
Slavery 228, 323, 538, 554, 601, 680, 681,
    687, 693, 707, 724, 774, 807, 2167, 2254,
    2383, 2616, 2857, 3076, 3484, 3609, 4461
    see also: History of slavery
Slaves 528, 681, 692, 961, 2616, 2857, 3076
Slavic languages 117, 1933, 1958, 3103
Slavic studies 1933, 3918, 4069, 4578
Slavs 147, 1320, 1323, 1381, 3103, 3135,
    4306, 4476
Sleep 1713
Slums 909, 2208, 2214, 2222, 4937
Small and medium sized enterprises 2244,
    2644
Small farms 4926
Small-scale industry 4671
Smallpox 1489
Smell 2939, 3653, 3766, 4484
Smith, Morton 3428
Smith, Pauline 4244
Smoking 1591, 2917, 4722
Social action 428, 638, 4665, 4723
Social anthropology 28, 45, 47, 91, 115, 120,
    126, 142, 154, 157, 159, 205, 217, 262,
    265, 288, 386, 415, 421, 985, 1878, 2373,
    2472, 2551, 2587, 2591, 2595, 2699,
    2807, 2907, 2992, 3001, 3040, 3054,
    3109, 3518, 3599, 3929, 4351, 4361,
    4394, 4449, 4602, 4612, 4745
Social behaviour 138, 428, 1606, 1635, 1645,
    1661, 1664, 1681, 1682, 1684, 2937,
    4016, 4378, 4438, 4754
Social biology 2699
Social capital 2210, 2289, 4726, 4808
Social change 137, 179, 267, 338, 504, 587,
    619, 621, 743, 1361, 1432, 1823, 2136,
    2164, 2196, 2284, 2348, 2506, 2530,
    2548, 2560, 2572, 2643, 2650, 2689,
    2806, 3030, 3033, 3041, 3090, 3101,
    3582, 3603, 3697, 3718, 3905, 3934,
    3988, 4012, 4021, 4191, 4302, 4374,
    4417, 4440, 4447, 4528, 4582, 4584,
    4589, 4591-4593, 4599, 4708, 4849, 4902,
    4909
Social cognition 170
Social cohesion 2776, 4610
Social conditions 373, 548, 717, 723, 778,
    786, 814, 2205, 2268, 2398, 2403, 2411,
    2423, 2472, 2480, 2481, 2729, 2780,
    2793, 2821, 2833, 2924, 2962, 3011, 3033,

3039, 3109, 3603, 4152, 4302, 4358,
    4367, 4403, 4435, 4579, 4585, 4638,
    4639, 4645, 4652, 4662, 4739, 4747,
    4765, 4829, 4831, 4835, 4840, 4856,
    4857, 4860, 4864
Social conflicts 2191, 3001, 3176
Social consciousness 2583, 3784
Social construction 168, 1505, 2326, 2470,
    2490, 2609, 2674, 2796, 2852, 2854,
    3139, 4483
Social control 201, 722, 2176, 2370, 2401,
    2969, 2990, 4620
Social costs 4594, 4662
Social determinism 159, 217
Social development 1565, 2475, 2589, 2630,
    3035, 3664, 4795, 4840, 4857, 4894
Social differentiation 2397, 2407, 2426, 2980
Social doctrines 4102
Social dynamics 247, 2105, 2132, 2595, 2596,
    2646
Social ecology 1653, 1685, 1694, 1698, 1707
Social environment 3845
Social equality 835, 2590
Social exchange 2210, 2352, 2589
Social exclusion 247, 812, 2459, 2596, 2938,
    2988, 3056, 3075, 3404, 3520, 3986,
    4361, 4515, 4559, 4626, 4672, 4722,
    4860, 4882, 4931
Social factors 1486, 1512, 1656, 1919, 2118,
    2139, 2153, 2196, 2374, 2912, 4575,
    4662, 4854, 4866, 4895
Social facts 223, 3038, 3569
Social history 12, 18, 48, 172, 200, 337, 340,
    347, 361, 362, 377, 508, 527, 548, 557,
    576, 579, 595, 603, 613, 631, 646, 647,
    651, 663, 664, 671, 674, 675, 682, 691,
    719, 738, 744, 775, 776, 1336, 1760,
    1829, 1916, 2085, 2128, 2183, 2204, 2211,
    2215, 2217, 2282, 2324, 2341, 2355,
    2368, 2395, 2466, 2475, 2489, 2522,
    2533, 2575, 2607, 2617, 2621, 2636,
    2639, 2688, 2697, 2716, 2741, 2743,
    2752, 2761, 2771, 2789, 2803, 2822,
    2845, 2853, 2857, 2862, 2886, 2995,
    3073, 3076, 3082, 3085, 3098, 3099,
    3402, 3562, 3573, 3665, 3704, 3739,
    3755, 3829, 3909, 3929, 4015, 4016,
    4050, 4052, 4105, 4176, 4211, 4227, 4254,
    4302, 4310, 4390, 4437, 4472, 4501,
    4523, 4568, 4571, 4628
Social housing 4934
Social identity 252, 263, 504, 708, 804, 2013,
    2327, 2530, 2672, 2928, 3043, 3367,
    3594, 3616, 3777, 3842, 4164, 4435
Social inequality 235, 760, 2942, 4665, 4895

Social infrastructure 4723
Social inheritance 1835
Social integration 1661, 1816, 2655, 2770, 3067, 4682
Social interaction 916, 957, 1404, 1430, 1636, 1653, 1735, 1752, 1803, 2457, 3000, 3398, 3843, 4390, 4511, 4882
Social justice 95, 234, 516, 2090, 2485, 2496, 2544, 2969, 2984, 2996, 3074, 4012, 4611, 4613, 4670, 4671, 4752, 4762
Social life 137, 267, 271, 277, 299, 373, 393, 422, 531, 651, 756, 760, 1502, 2217, 2291, 2374, 2386, 2472, 2474, 2583, 2611, 2613, 2647, 2649, 2684, 2738, 2785, 2790, 2919, 2942, 3034, 3052, 3065, 3109, 3575, 3807, 4358, 4376, 4403, 4540, 4579
Social mobility 880, 2609, 2746
Social mobilization 4730
Social movements 548, 681, 1652, 2197, 2210, 2216, 2218, 2222, 2505, 2587, 2955, 3068, 4612, 4633, 4775
Social networks 252, 2013, 2169, 2373, 2610, 2611, 2631, 2660, 2672, 3105, 4726, 4808
Social norms 201, 723, 1752, 1766, 1803, 2586, 2763, 3038, 3543, 3569, 4409
Social order 131, 1066, 2349, 2442, 2593, 2595, 2607, 2767, 2847, 2896, 3005, 4893
Social organization 670, 835, 838, 848, 921, 942, 1374, 1607, 1645-1647, 1680-1682, 1685, 1690, 1698, 1706, 1707, 1716, 2143, 2166, 2245, 2358, 2538, 2552, 2587, 2590, 2597, 2602, 2612, 2616, 2630, 2658, 2665, 2673, 3092, 3353, 3692, 3733
Social origin 659, 3132, 3134, 3710
Social participation 2469, 4353, 4435, 4716, 4818, 4820, 4871
Social perception 3861
Social philosophy 572, 4261
Social policy 2152, 2627, 2655, 2770, 4662, 4900
Social problems 215, 2220, 2221, 2432, 2581, 3543, 3762, 4390, 4520, 4521, 4571
Social psychiatry 3760
Social psychology 399, 1449, 1554, 1796, 2165, 2589, 2606, 2758, 2888, 2917, 2935, 3665, 4181, 4757
Social reform 3286, 3530
Social rehabilitation 4545
Social relations 34, 203, 326, 423, 793, 874, 886, 916, 987, 1606, 1621, 1631, 1647, 1685, 1713, 1753, 1775, 2115, 2179, 2191, 2213, 2237, 2324, 2377, 2386, 2513, 2583, 2603, 2604, 2611, 2615, 2621, 2629, 2659, 2664, 2715, 2719, 2763, 2777, 2781, 2795, 2812, 2859, 2886, 3009, 3093, 3352, 3398, 3534, 3596, 3597, 3696, 3817, 3907, 3966, 4193, 4377, 4378, 4413, 4416, 4498, 4511, 4754, 4804, 4852, 4873, 4882
Social representations 261, 3677, 4305, 4633
Social reproduction 880, 1405, 1427, 1733, 2237, 2346, 2381, 2506, 2633, 2956, 3690, 3710, 3845, 4430, 4465, 4507, 4589
Social research 43, 215, 287, 302, 974, 2478, 2807, 4509, 4532, 4642, 4871
Social roles 490, 2686, 2764, 3006, 4337
Social science research 28, 53, 435, 2903, 3665, 3833
Social sciences 28, 30, 90, 120, 173, 176, 182, 224, 227, 243, 259, 385, 414, 451, 485, 596, 638, 1136, 1319, 1342, 1344, 1347, 1517, 1562, 1804, 1842, 1852, 1856, 1867, 1868, 2139, 2140, 2149, 2200, 2278, 2359, 2361, 2397, 2629, 2661, 2698, 2701, 2720, 2773, 2775, 2809, 2890, 2898, 2958, 2993, 3037, 3159, 3252, 3288, 3320, 3330, 3336, 3337, 3342, 3355, 3365, 3540, 3738, 3774, 3780, 3792, 3795, 3821, 3827, 3832, 3834, 3978, 4036, 4044, 4045, 4047, 4075, 4077, 4080, 4083, 4084, 4087, 4088, 4101, 4105, 4232, 4247, 4276, 4328, 4474, 4485, 4523, 4524, 4531, 4830, 4907
Social scientists 149, 176, 300, 4524
Social services 305, 2152, 4675, 4900
Social space 886, 2176, 2459, 2642, 3845
Social stability 2504, 4806
Social status 247, 641, 880, 1552, 1606, 1684, 1759, 2488, 2560, 2584, 2589, 2596, 2608, 2625, 2682, 2742, 2764, 2860, 3021, 3086, 3566, 3642, 3751, 3922, 4090, 4353, 4374, 4378, 4385, 4754, 4782, 4902
Social stratification 247, 629, 694, 818, 835, 920, 1915, 1955, 2245, 2349, 2488, 2521, 2531, 2590, 2593, 2596, 2603, 2622, 2627, 2925, 2938, 3022, 3092, 4075, 4299, 4732
Social structure 131, 138, 155, 530, 697, 848, 969, 1705, 2132, 2199, 2324, 2478, 2553, 2597, 2646, 2650, 2682, 3001, 3049, 3518, 3530, 3610, 3626, 4521
Social support 1591, 2169, 2174, 2650, 2655, 2660, 2661, 2770, 2772, 2882
Social surveys 3157

Social systems 727, 2270, 2349, 2449, 2593, 2607, 2672, 3522, 3534, 3653, 4409, 4484, 4730, 4908
Social theory 90, 137, 164, 203, 223, 236, 237, 260, 267, 274, 276, 385, 392, 423, 589, 613, 947, 971, 985, 1743, 2092, 2589, 2591, 2840, 3652, 3668, 4466, 4587
Social values 1766, 2156
Social welfare 4738, 4808
Social work 305, 401, 2623, 3683, 4675
Socialism 218, 693, 2167, 2480, 2545, 3530, 3975, 3988, 4351
Socialist economies 2318
Socialist states 4477
Socialists 765
Socialization 606, 736, 1749, 2470, 2698, 2715, 2854, 2917, 2986, 3106, 3739, 4378, 4433, 4507, 4534, 4586, 4754
Society 107, 212, 400, 405, 431, 533, 550, 587, 664, 713, 1736, 1748, 2064, 2183, 2249, 2340, 2516, 2572, 2582, 2586, 2592, 2602, 2613, 2665, 2668, 2688, 2775, 3543, 3651, 3832, 4061, 4152, 4210, 4444, 4469, 4483, 4592, 4673, 4729, 4758
see also: Agrarian society, Capitalist society, Civil society, Complex societies, Consumer society, Individual and society, Learned societies, Modern society, Peasant societies, Post-communist societies, Pre-industrial society, Rural society, Secret societies, Traditional society, Tribal society
Sociobiology 227, 1493, 1494, 1496, 1507, 1529, 1552, 1560, 1581, 1592, 2352, 2589, 2872, 3750, 4396
Socioeconomic development 2287, 2620, 2846, 2972, 2978, 3028, 4294, 4668, 4707, 4722, 4726, 4755, 4789, 4797, 4831, 4840, 4852, 4857, 4863, 4886, 4903
Socioeconomic status 909, 1475, 1493, 1540, 1558, 1566, 1568, 1579, 1733, 2141, 2171, 2208, 2426, 2477, 2488, 2742, 2763, 2775, 2834, 2914, 2917, 3028, 3832, 4406, 4430
Sociolinguistics 196, 235, 250, 631, 1732, 1735, 1746, 1749, 1750, 1760, 1767, 1785, 1792-1795, 1798, 1814, 1815, 1842, 1867, 1870, 1882, 1892, 1904, 1915, 1919, 1936, 1946, 1952, 1955, 1968, 1969, 1972, 1973, 1977, 1980, 1984, 1986, 1987, 2007, 2667, 3000, 3805, 4039, 4061, 4409
Sociological anthropology 4584
Sociological methodology 388

Sociological research 28, 157, 221, 232, 238, 265, 290, 411, 510, 1745, 2536, 2662, 2946, 3227, 3262, 3734, 4116, 4446, 4715
Sociological theory 138, 224, 249, 265, 388, 510, 2404, 2536, 2790, 4485
Sociologists 2453, 3105
Sociology 14, 41, 175, 189, 190, 205, 261, 692, 754, 815, 1544, 1548, 1582, 1773, 1915, 2122, 2129, 2131, 2136, 2262, 2281, 2341, 2363, 2489, 2704, 2757, 2778, 2790, 2856, 2999, 3128, 3166, 3610, 3643, 3677, 3730, 4105, 4264, 4291, 4363, 4364, 4523, 4665, 4906
see also: Economic sociology, Educational sociology, Medical sociology, Political sociology, Rural sociology, Urban sociology
Sociology of culture 3065
Sociology of knowledge 259, 414, 4096
Sociology of law 59, 2984, 2994, 3003, 4670
Sociology of religion 168, 3139, 3166, 3227, 3541, 3543, 3636, 3643, 3734
Sociology of work 2453, 2457, 2471
Sociometry 252, 2013
Soil conservation 2276, 2319, 4792
Soil degradation 2319, 4804
Soil erosion 687, 2079, 2106, 2254, 2265, 2412, 2730, 4766, 4803
Soil fertility 2303, 2307, 2313
Soil management 2313
Soils 938, 1651, 1691, 2272, 2313, 4774
Soldiers 546, 1077, 1302, 1326, 2494, 2502, 3021, 3572
Solidarity 2210, 2453
Soltān, Ebrāhim 4223
Soltāni, Nasr al 4223
Songs 166, 1788, 1859, 2481, 2700, 2842, 3436, 3539, 3649, 3653, 3892, 3894, 3897, 3902, 3907, 3908, 3912, 3915, 3919, 3924, 3927, 3928, 3930, 3933, 3938, 3940, 3944, 3949, 3950, 3955, 3956, 3964, 3966, 3968, 3984, 4018, 4051, 4059, 4065, 4263, 4428, 4484
see also: Folk songs, Funeral songs, Ritual songs
Sons 2722, 3244, 3267, 4022
Sorb 1933
Sotho 1832, 3816
Soul 2791, 3148, 3202, 3311, 3338, 3368, 3372, 3499, 3504, 3516, 3553, 3685
Sound 1909, 1958, 1968, 2041, 3959
South Amerindians 90, 385, 756, 4644
Sovereignty 254, 688, 2408, 3716, 4417, 4457, 4629, 4643, 4650

Soviet studies 345, 2154, 4073
    see also: Post-Soviet studies
Soyinka, Wole 3869, 4152, 4200
Space 260, 291, 383, 599, 621, 691, 886, 886,
    1066, 1598, 1621, 1691, 1773, 1880,
    1973, 2092, 2187, 2211, 2459, 2509, 2594,
    2779, 2801, 2855, 2907, 2947, 3156,
    3625, 3650, 3659, 3660, 3681, 3689,
    3713, 3756, 3838, 3842, 3845, 3942,
    3961, 4086, 4113, 4262, 4342, 4356, 4364,
    4498, 4548, 4580, 4611, 4749
    see also: Spatial analysis
Spaniards 743, 763, 2348, 4305
Spanish Civil War 323, 707, 4105, 4523
Spanish Empire 730
Spanish language 65, 67, 84, 1785, 1794,
    1795, 1806, 1810, 1862, 1915, 1925,
    1946, 1952, 1985, 3930, 4167, 4267, 4270
Spatial analysis 950, 1659, 1973, 2138, 2412,
    3800, 4339, 4683, 4831
Spatial distribution 2077
Spears 1402
Species 1528, 1530, 1567, 1609, 1643, 1649,
    1650, 1652, 1660, 1666, 1673, 1678,
    1686, 1719, 1721, 1818, 2063, 2066,
    2088, 2117, 2272, 3667, 3816, 4774
    see also: Endangered species
Speech 66, 70, 407, 560, 1735, 1739, 1764,
    1767, 1771, 1806, 1824, 1846, 1957-1959,
    1967, 1976, 1997, 2001, 2008, 2027,
    2037, 2040, 2807, 3165, 3412, 3606,
    3702, 3744, 3874, 4035, 4392, 4409,
    4569, 4602
    see also: Pronunciation
Spelling 1919
Spinning 2243, 2251, 3116, 3993
Spirit possession 767, 3275, 3577, 3579, 3582,
    3584, 3591, 3612, 3822, 4674
Spirits 142, 767, 790, 1771, 2802, 3060, 3130,
    3577, 3582, 3584, 3587, 3589, 3591,
    3599, 3606, 3607, 3626, 3722, 3726,
    3791, 3822, 4674
Spiritualism 2802, 2945, 3060, 3262, 3529,
    3579, 3595, 3607
Spirituality 186, 188, 323, 476, 585, 707,
    2069, 2816, 3136, 3140, 3149, 3159,
    3235, 3259, 3292, 3309, 3330, 3338,
    3372, 3374, 3387, 3425, 3468, 3486,
    3497, 3499, 3503, 3504, 3506, 3540,
    3541, 3589, 3598, 3619, 3620, 3626,
    3641, 3645, 3657, 3686, 3812, 3854,
    3962, 4332, 4454, 4666
Sport 4336
    see also: Anthropology of sport

Sports 40, 730, 1559, 2855, 2926, 2961, 3071,
    4182, 4293, 4295, 4297, 4298, 4303,
    4304, 4307, 4312-4314, 4331, 4337, 4342,
    4343, 4348, 4492, 4574
    see also: Baseball, Football
Squatters 2213, 2419
St. John, Spenser 4150
Stabilization policy 4662
Staff 2462
Stages 3888
Stakeholder 2469, 4786
Stalinism 3107
Standard of living 1456, 1565, 1566, 2191,
    2277, 4883
Standardization 1785, 1913, 1915, 1952, 2004,
    4527
Stars 3672, 3752
State 456, 482, 517, 521, 921, 985, 993, 1372,
    2273, 2274, 2354, 2417, 2422, 2450,
    2456, 2487, 2491, 2516, 2527, 2543,
    2553, 2559, 2565, 2568, 2583, 2591,
    2806, 2828, 2926, 3005, 3018, 3057,
    3085, 3523, 3530, 3568, 3755, 3850,
    4297, 4300, 4624, 4642, 4673, 4679,
    4768, 4778, 4806, 4929
    see also: Church and state, Heads of state,
    Nation state, Socialist states
State formation 228, 470, 611, 685, 921, 993,
    2282, 2527, 2567, 2575, 3042, 4352
State structure 456, 2565, 4494
State-society relations 684, 809, 2120, 4616,
    4714, 4779
Statistical analysis 1453, 1462, 1486, 1490,
    1603, 2118, 2778, 4719
Statistical methods 301, 4340
Statistics 310, 2293, 2312, 3770, 4847
Statues 518, 1040, 1093, 1422, 3837
Stereotypes 2321, 2364, 3009, 3084, 3293,
    3893, 4395, 4516
Sterilization 2726, 4901
Stimuli 1693
Stochastic models 295, 2130
Stochastic processes 456
Stoll, David 95, 234, 4569
Stone Age 864, 1042, 1359
Stories 169, 222, 229, 289, 384, 1782, 1978,
    2103, 2582, 3118, 3121, 3172, 3424, 3437,
    3448, 3664, 3679, 3805, 3968, 3972,
    3974, 3979, 3983, 3989, 3997, 3999,
    4004, 4006, 4013, 4015, 4016, 4019,
    4024-4026, 4042, 4046, 4169, 4175, 4195,
    4199, 4206, 4213, 4234, 4244, 4281,
    4517, 4570
    see also: Life stories, Love stories
Story tellers 3995, 4016

Story telling 204, 225, 229, 539, 1762, 1767,
    1864, 3449, 3714, 3979, 3982, 3987,
    4012, 4016, 4030, 4161, 4212, 4372, 4534
Strategic planning 2289, 4711, 4744, 4924
Strikes 723, 2453
Structural adaptation 1806
Structural adjustment 3584, 4338, 4661, 4662,
    4665, 4667-4669, 4671, 4674, 4677, 4678,
    4680, 4681, 4704, 4828, 4930, 4932
Structural analysis 1918, 1948, 4372
Structural change 2315, 4682, 4866
Structural functionalism 2612, 3692
Structuralism 260, 3252, 3422
Stuart, James 125, 602
Students 145, 1449, 2097, 2734, 2809, 2916,
    2935, 3214, 3317, 3831, 4560, 4572, 4748
Suaznábar, Marcelo 4097
Subaltern 95, 234, 605, 717, 729, 751, 3039,
    3808, 4652
Subculture 2220
Subjectivity 130, 180, 237, 275, 276, 304,
    353, 392, 991, 2324, 2342, 2539, 2791,
    2897, 3005, 3792, 4077, 4356
Subnational government 4301, 4607
Subsidies 2210, 4827
Subsistence economy 164, 371, 2181, 2297,
    2409, 2444, 2447, 2834, 4393, 4406
Substance abuse 4722
Substance use 738
Suburban areas 417, 2215
Suburbanization 2222
Subversion 4230
Suetonius 519
Sufism 3049, 3322, 3342, 3364, 3414, 3646,
    4088
Sugali 1490
Sugar 812
Sugar industry 2300, 2619, 3066
Suicide 2797, 2798, 4231
Sumba 3744
Sumerians 4253
Summit conferences 4623, 4648, 4658
Sun 1381, 3111, 3133, 3177, 3711, 3717,
    3740, 4220
Sung 632, 2580
Supermarkets 161
Supernatural 2532, 3579, 3590, 3626, 3972,
    3987, 3998, 4010
Superstition 2439, 2682, 3153, 3230, 3480,
    3972, 4441
Supervisors 2955
Supply
    see: Food supply, Labour supply, Water
    supply
Supply and demand 4701

Supranationality 1946
Supreme Court 2511, 2997, 4643
Surgery 110, 1583, 3749, 3799
Suri, Haribhadra 3372, 3373
Surname 1823, 1834, 2677
Surveys 41, 190, 286, 458, 492, 885, 923, 936,
    939, 940, 953-956, 1069, 1079, 1109,
    1113, 1116, 1127, 1134, 1144, 1145, 1147-
    1151, 1153, 1159, 1163, 1175, 1196, 1197,
    1202, 1214, 1215, 1222, 1247, 1249,
    1260, 1264, 1269, 1277, 1278, 1313,
    1316, 1436, 2124, 2129, 2141, 2285,
    2430, 2518, 2620, 2654, 2704, 2726,
    2791, 2799, 3112, 4420
    see also: Social surveys
Survival strategy 299, 3052, 3761, 4661, 4820
Sustainability 1571, 2090, 2116, 2419, 3695,
    4626, 4662, 4666, 4689, 4695, 4698,
    4732, 4740, 4785, 4797, 4803, 4804,
    4820, 4911, 4922, 4933, 4937, 4938
Sustainable development 2255, 2290, 4618,
    4623, 4648, 4658, 4666, 4672, 4682,
    4687, 4694, 4697, 4780, 4781, 4785,
    4788, 4789, 4794, 4795, 4799-4802, 4804,
    4833, 4842, 4883, 4922, 4930, 4933, 4939
Svobida, Lawrence 2259
Swahili 550, 2386, 3944, 4163, 4564
Swedish language 1963
Swords 338, 3125
Symbolism 209, 233, 240, 397, 426, 828, 832,
    929, 1020, 1042, 1051, 1114, 1363, 1385,
    2068, 2188, 2215, 2232, 2346, 2363,
    2632, 2675, 2791, 2900, 2923, 3006,
    3177, 3292, 3513, 3537, 3556, 3560,
    3567, 3587, 3686, 3711, 3713-3715, 3717,
    3719, 3720, 3722, 3723, 3725, 3726,
    3728-3736, 3740, 3744, 3830, 3877, 4035,
    4041, 4061, 4062, 4065, 4141, 4191,
    4220, 4222, 4275, 4286, 4330, 4343,
    4383, 4384, 4387, 4456, 4758
    see also: Body symbolism, Religious
    symbolism, Sexual symbolism
Symbols 156, 504, 656, 1056, 1334, 1369,
    2070, 2071, 2514, 2530, 2560, 2777,
    2782, 3129, 3158, 3242, 3396, 3670,
    3696, 3711, 3716, 3718, 3720, 3721, 3723,
    3727-3729, 3733, 3734, 3738, 3838, 3863,
    4087, 4088, 4198, 4349, 4374, 4456
Sympathy 3693
Synagogues 1050, 3409, 3452, 4402
Syncretism 461, 3335, 3625, 3904
    see also: Religious syncretism
Syntax 1726, 1734, 1742, 1756, 1765, 1770,
    1807, 1811, 1838, 1843, 1844, 1847, 1860,

1868, 1937, 1947, 1949, 1951, 1960, 1961, 1963, 2014, 2034, 2037, 2054, 3576
Systems analysis 1908
Ta'ālibī, Abū Mansūr al- 3330
Taboo 201, 2507, 2811, 3510, 3517, 3539, 3764, 3773, 3950, 4017, 4389
  see also: Food taboos
Tagore, Rabindranath 3500, 3924, 4078, 4274
Taita 3584, 4674
Tales 3588, 3738, 3972, 3984, 3987, 3988, 4005, 4028, 4032, 4034, 4087, 4147, 4153, 4215, 4234
  see also: Fairy tales, Folk tales
Talismans 1006, 3580
Tallensi 2594
Tamils 1892, 1895, 3085, 3180, 3375, 4020, 4213
Tang dynasty 522, 4130
Taoism 79, 2099, 2817, 3141, 3144, 3155
Tapestry 4114
Taste 1506, 1703, 4618, 4794
Tatar 2125
Tattooing 2921, 2937, 2938, 4438
Tax evasion 489
Taxation 482, 2354, 4663
Taxes 506, 527, 2336, 2395
Taxonomy 5, 226, 263, 327, 1455, 1530, 1617, 1673, 1714, 1719, 1721, 1832, 1837, 2080, 2088, 2109, 3043, 3662, 3667, 3744, 3757, 3786
Tea 374, 738
Teachers 235, 3214, 3317, 3635, 4560
Teaching 37, 57, 83, 110, 114, 116, 291, 3799, 3932, 4029, 4132, 4559, 4610
  see also: Language teaching, Religious teachings
Technical cooperation 4734, 4737
Technological change 845, 879, 1383, 1521, 2265, 2730, 4743, 4804
Technology 236, 363, 427, 534, 543, 563, 845, 849, 863, 864, 875, 887, 890, 892, 960, 963, 1001, 1007, 1010, 1017, 1374, 1388, 1395, 1396, 1408, 1413, 1419, 1425, 1439, 1445, 1710, 1739, 2230, 2233, 2241, 2249, 2253, 2283, 2292, 2303, 2307, 2312, 2387, 2462, 2692, 3742, 3975, 4096, 4120, 4126, 4142, 4690, 4696, 4711, 4804, 4853, 4885
  see also: Agricultural technology, Appropriate technology, Biotechnology, Communications technology, Digital technology, History of technology, Information technology, New technology, Prehistoric technology, Reproductive technology

Teeth 460, 1280, 1461, 1468, 1469, 1471-1473, 1475-1482, 1485, 1590
Tehuelche 1586, 3126, 3824
Telecommunications 435
Telecommunications industry 2471
Telefol 3117
Television 55, 432, 442, 1774, 2379, 3623, 3699, 4043, 4120, 4143, 4446
Tello, Antonio 701
Telugu 1909, 3968
Temperate zones 2275
Temples 105, 852, 911, 918, 934, 1019, 1025, 1048, 1049, 1064, 1072, 1078, 1103, 1113, 1116, 1118, 1121, 1156, 1157, 1161, 1165, 1343, 1348, 1350, 1354, 1401, 1417, 1838, 3152, 3176, 3186, 3204, 3231, 3454, 3857, 3860
Temur, Amîr 3322
Tenant farmers 2426
Tenetehara 3067
Terminology 56, 173, 207, 243, 1882, 1903, 2095, 2301, 2658, 2667, 2670, 2689, 2747, 3088, 3208, 3358
Territoriality 612, 641, 993, 1426, 1599, 1661, 1690, 1716, 2608, 2927, 4309, 4475, 4482, 4624
Territory 146, 283, 446, 721, 763, 806, 841, 955, 1690, 1716, 1825, 2123, 2497, 2517, 2550, 2664, 2993, 3352, 4309, 4405, 4609, 4629, 4631, 4660
Terrorism 292, 395, 2549, 2927, 3027, 3199, 3638, 4471, 4482
Teulé, Jean 3005
Textbooks 66, 70, 71, 570, 2519, 3705
Textile industry 727, 2270, 2863
Textiles 174, 284, 909, 1360, 1411, 2208, 2245, 2251-2253, 2644
Texts 14, 25, 36, 62, 82, 109, 124, 125, 228, 239, 242, 324, 326, 332, 339, 344, 370, 372, 396, 398, 435, 472, 486, 516, 519, 536, 552, 569, 570, 578, 582, 584, 586, 602, 604, 622, 625, 653, 655, 696, 701, 741, 774, 796, 799, 806, 832, 897, 905, 1329-1332, 1334, 1338-1341, 1346, 1349, 1351, 1355, 1377, 1435, 1742, 1805, 1808, 1844, 1850, 1862, 1875, 1945, 1966, 1972, 1995, 2000, 2011, 2114, 2282, 2499, 2575, 2748, 2967, 2974, 2991, 2996, 3038, 3120, 3146, 3147, 3164, 3180, 3214, 3242, 3294, 3300, 3316, 3317, 3319, 3320, 3328, 3329, 3333, 3336, 3351, 3407, 3408, 3418, 3419, 3425, 3426, 3432, 3485, 3495, 3500, 3569, 3632, 3670, 3721, 3748, 3787, 3874, 3876, 3933, 3995-3997, 4002, 4059,

4064, 4074, 4078, 4167, 4180, 4183-4185,
    4198, 4203, 4206, 4207, 4215, 4216,
    4222, 4227, 4229, 4230, 4232, 4233,
    4238, 4241, 4245, 4247, 4250, 4252,
    4256, 4258, 4267, 4270, 4276, 4280,
    4283, 4490, 4564, 4566, 4567
Thai 1747
Thanatology 2787
Thao 1889
Thapa, Bhimsen 2519
Theatre 103, 660, 1008, 1031, 1090, 2482,
    3305, 3314, 3728, 3862, 3864-3866, 3870,
    3872, 3873, 3875, 3876, 3880, 3882,
    3883, 3887-3889, 3891-3893, 3909, 4138,
    4263, 4722
    see also: Popular theatre
Theft 342, 2382, 2384
Theology 208, 451, 461, 509, 604, 1863,
    3147, 3160, 3222, 3229, 3244, 3294,
    3320, 3326, 3332, 3338, 3339, 3359,
    3380, 3407, 3418, 3426, 3431, 3432,
    3435, 3437, 3439, 3448, 3450, 3455,
    3462, 3466, 3477, 3479, 3527, 3620,
    3728, 3748, 4255
    see also: Eschatology
Therapy 1591, 3790
Thieves 4015
Thiongo, Ngugi wa 2499
Third-party intervention 4728
Thompson, Laura Maud 120
Threat 2210, 2549
Tibbon, Samuel Ibn 3403
Tiele, C.P. 5, 226
Tierney, Patrick 135, 148, 416
Timber 2207, 4772
Time 56, 127, 138, 207, 278, 621, 662, 1633,
    1724, 2211, 2256, 2522, 2801, 3144, 3156,
    3643, 3651, 3658, 3681, 3689, 3709,
    3756, 3850, 3942, 4049, 4055, 4097,
    4308, 4439
Tin 908
Tingatinga, Eduardo S. 4145
Titian 3728
Tlingit 130, 249, 353, 1968, 2834, 4406
Tobacco 215, 507, 687, 2254, 4128, 4609,
    4722, 4867
Tobia 2550
Tolai 158
Tolerance 2998, 3072, 3154, 3366, 4548, 4625
Toltec 1970
Tomatoes 2275
Tonga (Polynesia) 1890
Tools 460, 499, 543, 836, 845, 849, 850, 860,
    864, 875, 881, 883, 887, 890, 892, 1359,
    1363, 1393, 1398, 1403, 1409, 1414,

1441, 1672, 1702, 1710, 1711, 1715, 2107,
    2240, 2248, 2251, 4686
    see also: Prehistoric tools
Toponyms 2475
Toraja 2325
Torture 2959, 4477
Totem 2403
Totemism 255, 2369, 3690, 3869
Tourism 2068, 2081, 2085, 2092, 2102, 2108,
    2244, 2325, 2828, 2900, 3121, 3600,
    3884, 4038, 4136, 4179, 4291, 4292,
    4294, 4299-4302, 4308, 4310, 4311, 4316,
    4320, 4329, 4330, 4334, 4335, 4338-4341,
    4355, 4363, 4365, 4598, 4607, 4680,
    4683, 4684, 4714, 4768, 4906
Tourist policy 4301, 4607
Tourist trade 2108, 4300, 4335, 4338, 4340,
    4680, 4768
Towns 529, 895, 1265, 1386, 1447, 2159,
    2180, 3660, 4317
    see also: Shanty towns
Toys 811, 2632
Trade 356, 463, 503, 617, 749, 895, 908,
    1362, 1392, 2182, 2329, 2343, 2344,
    2356, 2360, 2362, 2372, 2383, 2390,
    2393, 2447, 2469, 2806, 2828, 4272, 4622
    see also: Agricultural trade, Foreign trade,
    Free trade, History of trade, Internal trade,
    International trade, Regional trade, Slave
    trade, Tourist trade
Trade relations 2391
Trade unionism 4671
Trade unions 2222, 2618
Trade-off 1452, 2390, 2891, 4677
Trademarks 1447
Tradition 127, 175, 178, 188, 216, 409, 527,
    544, 550, 564, 597, 601, 613, 776, 1015,
    1094, 1360, 1733, 1817, 1836, 2085,
    2100, 2126, 2156, 2166, 2179, 2217,
    2234, 2245, 2291, 2341, 2395, 2478,
    2484, 2489, 2532, 2641, 2733, 2743,
    2745, 2782, 2801, 2828, 2830, 2904,
    2943, 3014, 3166, 3226, 3240, 3300,
    3341, 3448, 3483, 3536, 3590, 3654,
    3663, 3666, 3674, 3678, 3684, 3689,
    3702, 3704, 3706, 3707, 3732, 3826,
    3858, 3892, 3895, 3902, 3984, 4005,
    4052, 4106, 4161, 4201, 4242, 4281,
    4310, 4382, 4388, 4391, 4392, 4427,
    4430, 4445, 4496, 4548, 4595, 4818, 4873
    see also: Cultural tradition, Folk
    traditions, Musical traditions, Oral
    tradition, Religious traditions, Written
    tradition
Traditional architecture 3840

Traditional art 2325, 3908, 4096, 4130, 4145
Traditional culture 152, 487, 2198, 2364,
    2371, 2473, 2481, 2834, 3551, 3555,
    3736, 3742, 3751, 3818, 3976, 4011, 4046,
    4113, 4385, 4406, 4432, 4535, 4573, 4583
Traditional dances 3867, 3890
Traditional law 158, 606, 2416, 2739, 2945,
    2986, 3012, 3013, 3017, 3529, 4006
Traditional literature 206, 4076, 4215
Traditional medicine 62, 1446, 2066, 2138,
    2260, 2764, 3678, 3739, 3766-3768, 3779,
    3784, 3785, 3797, 3800, 3807, 3815,
    3816, 3818, 3819, 3835, 4188
Traditional music 2247, 3897, 3933, 3948,
    3949, 3952, 3967, 3971, 4059
Traditional religion 1454, 2435, 3264, 3602,
    3647
Traditional science 156
Traditional society 2473, 2767, 2808, 2828,
    2834, 3558, 4406, 4600
Traditionalism 2417, 3018, 3167, 4631
Traffic 697, 3759
    see also: Urban traffic
Tragedy 2092, 4083
Training 1664, 2955, 4688, 4760, 4914
Trances 1095, 3486, 3812
Transaction costs 2376
Transition economies 2315, 2380, 4736
Translation 40, 334, 595, 650, 1755, 1800,
    1803, 1838, 1848, 1850, 1855, 1861,
    1868, 1880, 1893, 1945, 1972, 1996,
    3151, 3197, 3203, 3206, 3209, 3211, 3218,
    3248, 3253, 3333, 3393, 3453, 3459,
    3545, 4048, 4056, 4165, 4178, 4203,
    4207, 4231, 4250, 4270
Transnationalism 36, 253, 339, 2171, 3700,
    4106, 4401, 4417, 4606, 4611, 4728
Transplants 2930, 2952
Transport 454, 466, 749, 861, 1076, 1367,
    1383, 2933, 4933
    see also: Sea transport, Urban transport
Transsexuality 2809, 2915
Transvestism 2915
Trauma 2165, 2582, 4181, 4509, 4538, 4539
Travel 88, 99, 584, 596, 690, 742, 779, 1419,
    1611, 2092, 3111, 4171, 4208, 4302,
    4316, 4318, 4324, 4332, 4340, 4341,
    4347, 4565
    see also: History of travels, International
    travels
Travel records 4179, 4225, 4236, 4237, 4290,
    4292, 4321-4323, 4341
Trees 1711, 2084, 2087, 2091, 2427, 4697
Triad 2612, 3692
Tribal art 327

Tribal economy 2359
Tribal government 2565
Tribal religion 2435, 3625
Tribal society 2691, 4337, 4633
Tribalism 2552, 2564, 3353, 4407, 4653
Tribes 88, 96, 659, 895, 946, 1301, 1347,
    1456, 1490, 1495, 1508, 1512, 1830,
    1876, 1897, 2417, 2425, 2553, 2554,
    2568, 2610, 2623, 2664, 2691, 2703,
    2741, 3016, 3018, 3049, 3056, 3067,
    3069, 3075, 3132, 3352, 3353, 3568,
    3683, 3691, 3772, 3815, 3910, 3967,
    3985, 4037, 4084, 4474, 4576, 4659, 4689
Tropical zones 900, 1717, 2091, 2443, 3746,
    3809
Trucks 3780
Trujillo Molina, Rafael Leónidas 787
Trust 2867, 3492, 3575, 4447, 4726
Truth 95, 159, 217, 234, 291, 428, 1538, 3170,
    3383, 3388, 3499, 3877, 4006, 4063, 4508
Tsimshian 1835
Tswana 278, 2672
Tu Fu 4056
Tuareg 122, 600, 2102, 2776, 3057, 3807
Tubu 2491, 2586
Tucker, Alfred 700, 3219
Tupi-Guarani 783
Tupinamba 756
Turkana 558, 2367, 2508
Turks 522, 2479, 4603, 4761
Tuva 1746, 1876, 2690, 3691
Twins 1488, 2682, 3273
Typology 865, 1101, 1369, 1724, 1756, 1765,
    1928, 1947, 1954, 1956, 1971, 2022,
    2026, 2054, 2569, 3582, 3747, 4843
Tzeltal 3516
Ubangi 1994, 2009
Uddālaka 3315
Udmurt 2056
Uigur 522, 4605
UN Conventions 4636, 4658, 4722
UN General Assembly 4666
Uncertainty 1573, 1602, 2404, 3326, 4763
Unemployment 2223, 2388, 2458, 4663, 4682
UNESCO 152, 962
UNHCR 4824
Uniate churches 4476
UNICEF 4816, 4824
United Nations 4646, 4712, 4802
    see also: UN Conventions
Universalism 138, 167, 182, 209, 210, 220,
    300, 2585, 3367, 3504, 3560, 3561, 3676,
    4019
Universities 7, 29, 36, 57, 62, 77, 188, 197,
    339, 341, 359, 438, 613, 1156, 1157, 1176,

1199-1201, 1211, 1215, 1242, 1417, 1527,
  2916, 3831, 4548, 4759
Unwritten languages 139, 1784
Upreti, Mohan 3919
Urban agglomeration 4927
Urban anthropology 265, 2154, 2215, 2217,
  2224, 2766, 3096, 3575, 3900, 4611, 4882
Urban archaeology 466, 901, 909, 917, 948,
  1146, 1233, 1235, 1251, 1272, 1422, 2208
Urban areas 1576, 2133, 2180, 2181, 2209,
  2218, 2220, 2222, 2502, 3068, 3505,
  3572, 3660, 4533, 4765, 4927
Urban communities 4119, 4927
Urban development 494, 1089, 2210, 2212,
  2219, 2222, 4759, 4786, 4806, 4838,
  4927, 4928, 4932-4935, 4938, 4939, 4941
Urban economics 917, 1235
Urban environment 2101
Urban government 2222
Urban growth 2216, 2219, 2222, 4941
Urban history 2223
Urban housing 4937
Urban life 917, 1272, 2206, 3900, 3907, 4075
Urban management 2401, 4786
Urban movements 2216, 2222
Urban planning 1021, 2212, 2219, 2421, 3846,
  4326, 4786, 4930, 4934, 4935
Urban policy 2216, 2219, 4317, 4930
Urban population 2216, 3090, 4813, 4941
Urban poverty 2210, 2214-2216, 2221, 2222,
  4666, 4851, 4930, 4934-4938
Urban renewal 2101, 2222, 4931
Urban sociology 4435
Urban space 466, 4749, 4927, 4930, 4938
Urban studies 2210, 2224, 4611
Urban traffic 3759
Urban transport 4937
Urban-rural migration 4135
Urbanism 906, 1355, 1372, 2212, 3838, 4749
Urbanization 906, 909, 1263, 2159, 2179,
  2208, 2210, 2222, 2223, 2316, 2380,
  2421, 2501, 3505, 3610, 4618, 4736,
  4794, 4882, 4940
Urdu 3768, 4043, 4052
Urhobo 3933, 4059
Utopianism 100, 740, 2926, 3544, 4163, 4297
Utopias 100, 713, 740, 3617, 3618
Vailland, Roger 2453
Validity 306, 2750, 3019, 3182, 4676
Valikhanov, Chokan 150, 382
Valleys 303, 721, 1241, 2437, 2438, 4263
Valuation 4925
Value 327, 2328, 2329, 2349, 2375, 2381,
  2593, 2605, 2956, 2963, 3196
  see also: Labour value

Value systems 2950, 3158
Value theory 2392
Values 2097, 2160, 2388, 2478, 2668, 3020,
  3083, 3137, 3348, 3551, 3661, 4418,
  4510, 4536, 4548, 4556, 4660
  see also: Cultural values
Variance 70, 1457, 1462, 1488, 1528, 1567,
  1709, 1721, 1764, 3970
Veblen, Thorstein Bunde 2946, 4116
Vedas 3301, 3316, 3319
Vedism 22, 457, 2623, 2973, 3173, 3213,
  3277, 3280, 3282, 3295, 3297, 3298,
  3301, 3303, 3306-3308, 3310, 3313, 3316,
  3318, 3319, 3466, 3683, 3857
Vegetables 4396
Vegetarianism 3288
Veils 3240, 3384
Vendors 2210
Verbal behaviour 1754, 4477
Verbal communication 1754
Verbs 1724, 1751, 1769, 1812, 1854, 1860,
  1872, 1879, 1889, 1910, 1939, 1940,
  1947-1949, 1962, 1986, 1989, 2002, 2006,
  2014, 2024, 2025, 2031, 2040, 2042,
  2046, 2053, 3147, 3290
Verification 1764
Vernacular languages 1795, 1915
Veterans 2467
Veterinary medicine 2189
Vezo 4507
Viaud, Gustave 4263
Viaud, Julien 4263
Vichy Regime 3005
Victims 2137, 4508, 4538
Victorian Age 4298
Vidal, Peire 4035
Videos 357, 440, 4119
Vikings 2360
Vila, Vargas 4277
Villages 37, 41, 114, 190, 402, 942, 951, 1037,
  1061, 1117, 1176, 1265, 1454, 1477, 1577,
  1993, 2085, 2127, 2187, 2188, 2192,
  2194, 2195, 2200, 2404, 2417, 2557,
  2663, 2669, 2676, 2943, 3018, 3094,
  3176, 3530, 3811, 3889, 3930, 3988, 4008,
  4310, 4320, 4345, 4369, 4448, 4598,
  4684, 4689, 4718, 4777, 4799, 4822,
  4849, 4852
  see also: Fishing villages
Villegaignon, Nicolas Durand de 756
Violence 192, 291, 292, 299, 395, 618, 717,
  780, 790, 977, 2076, 2222, 2439, 2456,
  2502, 2533, 2558, 2583, 2609, 2635,
  2714, 2961, 3013, 3021, 3022, 3024-3027,
  3029, 3031-3035, 3048, 3050, 3052, 3073,

3107, 3199, 3572, 3603, 3608, 3730,
3900, 4100, 4450, 4471, 4477, 4520,
4538, 4543, 4741, 4828, 4872
see also: Domestic violence, Political
violence
Violent crime 4280
Violin 3967
Visual anthropology 55, 293, 389, 440, 442,
3977, 4126, 4366
Visual arts 3354, 3718, 4098, 4123, 4126,
4127, 4366
Visual communication 4126
Visual perception 231, 4123, 4127, 4134, 4453
Viticulture 1106, 1236, 4382, 4397
Vivekananda 3312
Vocabulary 68, 745, 1723, 1728, 1730, 1737,
1768, 1791, 1806, 1873, 1889, 1926,
1932, 1992, 1993, 2039, 2048, 2055, 2056
Vocational education 4760
Volcanoes 2432
Voluntary work 4709
Voulet, Paul 3608
Vowel 1722, 1801, 1858, 1870, 1912, 1957,
1997, 2051
Wa 3715
Wage differentials 4609
Wages 485, 2251, 2350, 2361, 2453, 2466
Walcott, Derek 4200
Wallach, Yona 4040
Walsperger, Andreas 768
Wancho 2048
Wang, Fuzhi 588
Wapishana 3069
War 299, 534, 551, 567, 599, 654, 695, 721,
761, 786, 1370, 1569, 2197, 2549, 2578,
2610, 2653, 2693, 2860, 2977, 3035,
3036, 3051, 3052, 3059, 3086, 3196,
3428, 3570, 3687, 3711, 3758, 3783, 4216,
4258, 4477, 4864
see also: Civil war, Cold War, Holy war
War crimes 970
Ward, Henry George 1428
Warfare 395, 624, 688
Warhol, Andy 4093
Warriors 1326, 2625, 3502
Washburn, Sherwood Larned 144
Waste 2114
Waste management 4887, 4933, 4941
Water 960, 2061, 2062, 2070, 2071, 2091,
2093, 2113, 2210, 2271, 2274, 2295, 3236,
3318, 3350, 3447, 3835, 4635
see also: Groundwater
Water management 960, 1202, 2061, 2289,
4710, 4718, 4777, 4780, 4887, 4937
Water policy 2289

Water quality 525, 2112, 3827, 4777
Water resources 525, 957, 960, 1202, 2062,
2070, 2086, 2112, 2289, 2417, 3018, 4635,
4710, 4718, 4771, 4777, 4798
Water supply 957, 2070, 2113, 2289, 4771,
4910
Water utilization 525, 2093, 2112, 4710, 4777
Waterways 2070
Way of life 204, 2199, 2478, 3378, 3506, 4653
Wayana 3570, 3783
Wealth 307, 2340, 2375, 2390, 2430, 2535,
2605, 2744, 2850, 3260, 3642, 3856
Weapons 338, 534, 558, 563, 581, 1443, 1526,
2508, 2576
see also: Nuclear weapons
Weather 127, 1008, 1030, 2313, 3114, 3571
see also: Precipitation
Weaving 349, 2231, 2251
Weddings 3581, 3684, 3706
Weights and measures 349, 2329
Welby, Victoria 3728
Welfare 43, 977, 2644, 3024, 4836
see also: Social welfare
Well-being 3159, 3795, 4181, 4689, 4738,
4846, 4890
Wells, H.G. 3746
Wesley, John 3239
Westermarck, Edvard 142, 3599
Western civilization 135, 199, 416, 605, 2465,
3079, 3803, 3808, 3809, 4101, 4263,
4449, 4489
Western countries 41, 190, 3166, 4154
Westernization 2736, 3010, 4600
Wheat 896, 1704
Whitehead, Alfred North 3170
Whites 567, 1503, 1582, 1773, 3026, 3045,
3051, 3053, 3266, 3648, 4012, 4425
Widowhood 2793
Widows 2753, 2793, 2906, 4231
Wiener, Jean 3929
Wierzbicka, Anna 1723
Wijeyewardene, Gehan 35, 104
Wilber, Ken 186, 3149
Wildlife 1, 1818, 2063, 4318, 4782, 4805
Wildlife protection 2412, 4784
Williams, Tennessee 2857, 3076
Willumsen, J.F. 371
Wind energy 4795
Wind instruments 3935, 3936
Wine 1106, 1236, 4382, 4397
Wiru 809
Witchcraft 143, 2502, 2532, 2635, 2795, 3013,
3025, 3033, 3114, 3540, 3568, 3571, 3572,
3579, 3586, 3588, 3590, 3591, 3597,
3602, 3603, 3605, 3815, 3822

Witches 3033, 3230, 3603, 4005, 4441
Wittgenstein, Ludwig 3728
Wives 2629, 2645, 2737, 2744, 2758, 2824, 3399
Wo'daa'be 2064
Wojciech [Saint] 3554
Wolf, Eric R. 98, 2503
Wolves 3738, 4087
Women 105, 264, 280, 285, 378, 419, 495, 502, 514, 515, 528, 564, 565, 606, 676, 742, 755, 767, 1055, 1449, 1452, 1542, 1573, 1581, 1593, 1732, 1740, 1828, 2081, 2089, 2115, 2153, 2169, 2174, 2213, 2220, 2251, 2427, 2434, 2452, 2455, 2481, 2535, 2546, 2569, 2644, 2656, 2660, 2661, 2686, 2690, 2693, 2695, 2717, 2721, 2728, 2737, 2738, 2760, 2761, 2765, 2769, 2771, 2772, 2785, 2804, 2805, 2813, 2815, 2816, 2818, 2821, 2822, 2826, 2828-2830, 2832, 2833, 2835-2837, 2842, 2844-2846, 2850, 2855, 2858-2862, 2864, 2870, 2873, 2891, 2893, 2899, 2909, 2935, 2941, 2943, 2946, 2948, 2953, 2959, 2962, 2986, 2987, 3056, 3075, 3086, 3113, 3140, 3191, 3192, 3216, 3231, 3258, 3319, 3340, 3399, 3451, 3497, 3520, 3577, 3640, 3644, 3688, 3730, 3737, 3863, 3922, 3923, 3934, 3938, 3955, 4005, 4011, 4041, 4045, 4069, 4072, 4073, 4088, 4108, 4116, 4132, 4158, 4193, 4205, 4211, 4231, 4239, 4247, 4251, 4336, 4342, 4349, 4358, 4403, 4426, 4447, 4453, 4531, 4538, 4542, 4552, 4561, 4565, 4576-4578, 4645, 4685, 4686, 4690, 4692, 4728, 4742, 4760, 4780, 4820, 4826, 4828, 4829, 4832-4834, 4837-4843, 4845, 4846, 4848, 4849, 4851, 4852, 4855-4861, 4873, 4876, 4882, 4890, 4903
   see also: Rural women
Women and politics 4841
Women workers 2453, 2455, 2470, 2822, 2854, 3781, 4780, 4850
Women's education 4552, 4753
Women's health 285, 1560, 2702, 2707, 2709, 2728, 2870, 3769, 3775, 3811, 4780, 4866, 4885, 4901-4904
Women's participation 4832, 4836, 4854
Women's rights 606, 680, 2656, 2728, 2765, 2837, 2863, 2986, 3551, 4780, 4850, 4856, 4860
Women's role 215, 516, 2163, 2470, 2806, 2813, 2825, 2828, 2844, 2849, 2854, 2996, 3922, 4072, 4105, 4175, 4523, 4584, 4780

Women's status 2656, 2738, 2759, 2785, 2811, 2815, 2837, 2849, 2918, 3517, 4835, 4858, 4859
Women's studies 2835, 4041
Women's work 2347, 2819
Wood products 2099, 3155
Word order 1756, 1940, 1947, 1949, 2054
Words 320, 1334, 1347, 1355, 1723, 1728, 1731, 1751, 1767, 1851, 1869, 1874, 1903, 1905, 1907, 1942, 2039, 2048, 2054, 2055, 2057, 2301, 3511, 4040, 4139, 4224, 4506
Work at home 2347, 2461, 2819
Work environment 3789
Work place 2454, 2459, 2461, 2468, 3986
Workers 723, 2461, 2462, 2471, 2607, 2949
   see also: Agricultural workers, Domestic workers, Industrial workers, Manual workers, Migrant workers, Professional workers, Research workers, Women workers
Working class 909, 2208, 2644, 3900, 4519
Working conditions 807, 2231, 2454, 2469
Working parents 2694
Works of art 337, 371, 4130
Workshops 418, 1387, 2037, 4623
World Bank 4338, 4612, 4667, 4678, 4680, 4737, 4781, 4800, 4937
World economy 183, 2158, 2245, 2385, 3650, 3801, 4614, 4633
World Health Organization 4816
World market 2305, 4809
World religions 2099, 3155
   see also: Christianity, Hinduism, Islam, Judaism
World view 151, 164, 444, 813, 1320, 2114, 2116, 2260, 2612, 2774, 3002, 3041, 3135, 3318, 3620, 3625, 3652, 3655, 3692, 3695, 3833, 4587, 4661, 4790
World War Two 357, 658, 769, 2944, 3005
Worship 105, 166, 560, 640, 3211, 3231, 3270, 3299, 3338, 3387, 3412, 3443, 3444, 3480, 3504, 3548, 3649, 4362, 4428
Wright, Melissa W. 2955
Writers 471, 578, 2092, 2533, 2813, 2987, 3073, 3113, 3184, 3205, 3255, 3291, 3429, 3500, 3980, 4042, 4057, 4062, 4071, 4078, 4079, 4081, 4151, 4158-4160, 4163, 4165, 4169, 4179, 4184, 4187, 4188, 4200, 4204, 4210, 4213, 4215, 4216, 4225, 4227, 4230, 4236, 4238, 4263, 4273, 4274, 4281, 4282, 4285, 4288, 4289, 4322, 4581
   see also: Novelists

Writing 37, 55, 107, 114, 122, 312, 334, 405,
    433, 442, 453, 545, 600, 607, 628, 671,
    742, 805, 1330, 1338, 1340, 1342, 1347,
    1348, 1354, 1356, 1419, 1722, 1740,
    1787, 1841, 1950, 1972, 1974, 2005,
    2019, 2092, 2562, 2598, 2624, 2641,
    2821, 2832, 2849, 3005, 3049, 3170,
    3206, 3212, 3255, 3305, 3627, 3745,
    3802, 3952, 3973, 3980, 4004, 4009,
    4030, 4054, 4055, 4060, 4077, 4089,
    4147, 4158, 4159, 4165, 4166, 4171,
    4174, 4177, 4178, 4180, 4181, 4190,
    4194, 4197, 4202, 4205, 4208, 4213,
    4215, 4219, 4228, 4229, 4231, 4241,
    4245, 4246, 4248, 4250, 4255, 4257,
    4259, 4268, 4269, 4275, 4278, 4284,
    4288, 4548, 4562, 4564, 4566, 4567
Writing systems 214, 545, 1334, 1966, 2019
Written language 545, 1744, 1875, 2017
Written tradition 125, 344, 471, 540, 570, 574,
    578, 584, 586, 602, 625, 653, 675, 690,
    772, 799, 1333, 1336, 1337, 1339, 1435,
    1742, 1862, 1865, 1972, 2974, 3146,
    4016, 4184, 4227, 4229, 4232, 4256,
    4267, 4278, 4288, 4289, 4564, 4566, 4567
Wu-chu, Hsia 481
Xenophobia 2802, 3060, 3607, 4395
Xhosa 813, 2774, 3829, 4082
Xie, Wanying 4042
Xingu 3605
Yagnik, Indulal 4571
Yahi 887
Yang, Shang 2985
Yanomami 24, 135, 148, 416, 1577, 3750,
    4822
Yao (Thailand) 4689
Yap 2384
Yāska, Acharya 1738
Yazīd Makhlad, Abū 470, 2567
Yeats, William Butler 3698, 4563
Yehudah, Yeshu'ah ben 3393
Yerukala 1490
Yoga 3299, 3304, 3372, 3496, 4207
Yolngu 2670, 2747, 3955
Yombe 3557
Yoruba 2252, 2320, 2584, 2682, 3533, 3732,
    3835, 4090, 4289, 4862
Youth 1589, 1748, 2085, 2502, 2734, 2882,
    2914, 2917, 3040, 3154, 3474, 3508,
    3572, 4310, 4447, 4722, 4733, 4937
Youth and politics 2502, 3572
Youth culture 2326
Youth employment 4722
Yuan 4089
Yucatec 1970, 3753

Yukagir 1825
Yupik 3514
Yuson, Alfred A. 4199
Zapotec 733, 993, 1812, 1967
Zarma 1749
Zedong, Mao 2936
Zen 3168
Zhang, Tianyi 4194
Zheng, Liu 2933
Zigmund-Cerbu, Anton 6, 94
Zigmund-Cerbu, Liza 6, 94
Zionism 3438, 4427
Zola, Émile 3005
Zoology 371, 974, 1673, 1819, 3785
    see also: Archaeozoology, Paleozoology
Zoomorphic arts 1391, 1430
Zulu 817, 2006, 2739, 3012, 4363
Zuni 4103

SUBJECT INDEX IN FRENCH

INDEX DES MATIÈRES

Abdulkadir Munsyi, Abdullah bin 4215
Abelam 158, 3511
Abolitionnism 680, 681, 692, 2857, 3076
Aborigènes 298, 662, 706, 2060, 2074, 2078,
    2134, 2403, 2408, 2685, 2827, 3056,
    3074, 3075, 3104, 3106, 3107, 3625,
    3641, 3659, 3671, 3709, 3989, 4000,
    4096, 4278, 4626, 4647, 4650, 4656, 4657
Abraham 2748
Abramzon, S.M. 145
Abus de drogues 3770
Abus de substances toxiques 4722
Abus sexuel 2533, 3073
Accent 1844, 1957
Accès à la culture 4329
Accès à l'éducation 4748
Accès à l'information 4820
Accès aux soins médicaux généraux 1529,
    2138, 2863, 3800, 4609
Accord de paix 4733
Accroissement de la productivité 4698
Accroissement de population 2079
Acculturation 259, 414, 637, 708, 887, 2409,
    2616, 2661, 2798, 3098, 4479, 4600, 4628
Aché 4393
Acquisition de connaissances 66, 69, 84, 291,
    352, 407, 1405, 1427, 1637, 2236, 2588,
    2589, 3474, 4549, 4554, 4559, 4690,
    4749, 4860
Acquisition du langage 1790, 1936, 4506
Acteurs 3040, 3878, 4206
Acteurs politiques 2502, 2517, 2533, 3073,
    3572
Actif 3344
Action collective 2264, 4399
Action politique 253
Action sociale 428, 638, 4665, 4723
Activisme 2108, 2827, 3104, 3758, 4335,
    4495, 4775
Activistes 2218, 3068
Activité bancaire 380, 734, 4671
Activité de construction 1012, 1104, 1375,
    1838, 2394, 3855, 4594
Activité économique 2244, 2347, 2385, 2394,
    2819, 4809

Activité militante 2504, 2520
Activité physique 1457, 1559, 1585, 1588,
    1589, 3804, 4348
Adaptation au changement 1601, 4010
Adaptation culturelle 1543, 2325, 3904, 4419,
    4603, 4619, 4761
Adaptation des immigrants 2178, 2616, 4603,
    4761
Administration 125, 482, 602, 2354, 2484,
    2504
Administration coloniale 125, 323, 592, 602,
    636, 681, 682, 684-686, 688, 703, 705,
    707, 715, 721, 727, 731, 748, 770, 771,
    773, 780, 785, 788, 805, 816-818, 2120,
    2270, 2362, 2573, 2828, 2829, 2976,
    2981, 3031, 3057, 4215
Administration du développement 4713, 4759
Administration locale 1786, 2210, 2222, 3230,
    3703, 4441, 4717, 4740, 4786
Administration publique 2407, 2569, 2980,
    3325, 3334, 3344, 4716, 4843, 4861
Administration régionale 2222
Administration territoriale 4301, 4607
ADN 1511, 1515, 1522, 1617, 1649, 1650,
    1666
Adolescence 1553, 1557, 1592, 2731, 2732,
    2962
Adolescents 1466, 1477, 1578, 2223, 2696,
    2732, 2733, 2879, 2883, 2895, 2913,
    2931, 2962, 4878
Adoption d'enfant 2648, 2685, 4416
Adorno, Theodor W. 3698
Adultes 1602, 1654, 1693, 2662, 2732
Adverbe 1756, 1769, 2017, 2050
Aéroports 4311
Aeta 2432
Affaires 74, 1926, 2257, 2644, 2740
Affectation des ressources 2449, 4801, 4810
Affiliation 1653, 2791
Africains 253, 279, 567, 692, 774, 806, 1536,
    2070, 2173, 2535, 2755, 2820, 2850,
    2883, 3051, 3616, 3929, 4107, 4398
Afro-américains 215, 538, 680, 978, 1582,
    2327, 2466, 2533, 2622, 2857, 3073,
    3076, 3900, 3929, 4363

Afro-brésilien 4158
Âge 565, 676, 1466, 1468, 1469, 1474, 1477,
 1515, 1544, 1558, 1574, 1633, 1684,
 1752, 2142, 2156, 2535, 2560, 2603,
 2613, 2645, 2655, 2669, 2697, 2731,
 2761, 2765, 2768-2771, 2803, 2804, 2845,
 2850, 2862, 2864, 2950, 3751, 3772,
 3792, 4374, 4385, 4542, 4748, 4821
 voir aussi: Vieillesse
Âgé 2133, 2650, 2763, 2764, 2768, 2773,
 2777, 2786, 2824, 2898, 3540, 3545,
 3696, 3777, 3791, 3792, 3827, 4573
 voir aussi: Aide aux personnes âgées
Âge adulte 676, 2731, 2775, 2864, 3832
Âge au mariage 2139, 2153, 2726, 2749
Âge chalcolithique 825, 1158, 1243, 1440
Âge de la pierre 864, 1042, 1359
Âge des lumières 3170, 3183, 3201, 3379
 voir aussi: Pensée des lumières
Âge du bronze 445, 449, 516, 820, 835, 838,
 840, 868, 881, 882, 885, 906, 908, 912,
 924, 965, 991, 995, 1000, 1017, 1052,
 1053, 1158, 1184, 1205, 1263, 1285, 1292,
 1305, 1307, 1309, 1314, 1315, 1324,
 1366, 1391, 1397, 1409, 2226, 2590, 2996
Âge du cuivre 820, 1376, 1397
Âge du fer 363, 387, 448, 449, 512, 523, 669,
 823, 826, 828, 838, 859, 878, 881, 885,
 895, 916, 920, 921, 924, 927, 928, 950,
 965, 981, 1013, 1036, 1053, 1057, 1263,
 1324, 1398, 1399, 1402, 1439, 1443,
 2360, 3111
Âge mésolithique 834, 883, 1000, 1291, 1304,
 1413
Âge néolithique 830, 844, 852, 853, 858, 866,
 867, 874, 877, 883, 886, 891, 935, 995,
 1000, 1007, 1013, 1029, 1066, 1114, 1139,
 1140, 1299, 1303, 1309, 1375, 1403, 1430,
 2177, 2206, 2304, 2340, 2604
Âge paléolithique 819, 834, 836, 845, 849,
 850, 856, 862, 873, 894, 914, 932, 959,
 1023, 1153, 1245, 1273, 1298, 1362, 1378,
 1406, 1518
Agence 95, 234, 248, 276, 686, 991, 1777,
 2241, 2502, 2934, 3030, 3170, 3510,
 3541, 3572, 3625, 3764, 3843, 3878,
 4506, 4726
Agglomération urbaine 4927
Agressivité 1614, 1631, 1653, 3062, 3565
Agriculteurs 795, 877, 1291, 2090, 2137,
 2177, 2189, 2259, 2260, 2265, 2267,
 2281, 2288, 2292, 2294, 2299, 2308-2310,
 2312, 2313, 2319, 2376, 2382, 2417,
 2452, 2730, 3018, 4604, 4686, 4691,
 4696, 4697, 4699, 4700, 4703, 4769,

 4783, 4804, 4820
 voir aussi: Fermiers
Agriculture 24, 488, 525, 596, 687, 709, 726,
 757, 851, 857, 867, 1236, 1446, 1550,
 1903, 2070, 2105, 2106, 2112, 2199, 2205,
 2206, 2254-2259, 2263, 2266-2268, 2271,
 2273, 2276, 2278-2281, 2283, 2285, 2286,
 2288, 2290, 2292, 2294, 2297, 2298,
 2301, 2303-2305, 2307-2309, 2314, 2316-
 2319, 2335, 2397, 2400, 2405, 2406,
 2423, 2430, 2441, 2463, 2619, 2968,
 3066, 3538, 3674, 3678, 4291, 4595,
 4609, 4686, 4687, 4689, 4690, 4692-4695,
 4697-4700, 4702-4704, 4720, 4764, 4765,
 4767, 4780, 4803, 4804, 4812, 4837,
 4906, 4909, 4911, 4924, 4940
 voir aussi: Métayage, Systèmes agricoles
Agriculture itinérante 2181
Agriculture préhistorique 851, 854, 1413
Agriexploitation 830, 866, 2151, 2290, 2295,
 2297, 2298, 2306, 2311, 2315, 2317, 2320,
 2397, 2607, 2735, 4691, 4694, 4820,
 4862, 4909
 voir aussi: Pisciculture
Agroindustrie 2279
Agronomie 4807
Aide 4705, 4708, 4737, 4744, 4747, 4812,
 4834, 4839, 4937
Aide à l'étranger 4707, 4724, 4725, 4737,
 4781
Aide alimentaire 4814, 4817, 4820
Aide au développement 4707, 4715, 4737,
 4750, 4752, 4937
Aide aux enfants 603, 2648, 2654, 2668, 2701,
 2712, 2716, 2863, 3774
Aide aux personnes âgées 2655, 2770
Aide économique 4734, 4776, 4841, 4913,
 4936
Ainley, John 2298
Ainu 92
Air 1514, 4765
Aires culturelles 1849
Aires linguistiques 1849
Aires métropolitaines 2222, 4937
Aït Youssi 3049
Ajustement structurel 1806, 3584, 4338, 4661,
 4662, 4665, 4667-4669, 4671, 4674, 4677,
 4678, 4680, 4681, 4704, 4828, 4930, 4932
Aka 2431
Akan 2329, 2777, 2786, 3696, 4188
Akhtal Al- 4036
Aklan 2592
'Alawi 571, 3343
Albanais 1913, 1932, 1938
Alberdi, Juan Bautista 4210

Alchimie 643, 3787
Alcool 215, 719, 2824, 3547
Alcoolisme 215, 1570, 4511
ALÉNA 4700
Aliénation 1448, 2920, 4038
Aliénation culturelle 2691
Alimentation 1599, 1601, 1639, 1641, 1642,
    1651, 1691, 2713, 4816, 4824
Alimentation animale 1700
Aliments 20, 284, 744, 896, 1324, 1421, 1540,
    1577, 1599, 1608, 1609, 1611, 1627, 1628,
    1639, 1642, 1644, 1647, 1648, 1672,
    1677, 1693, 1702-1704, 1720, 2191, 2210,
    2275, 2316, 2444, 2824, 3310, 3678,
    3747, 3751, 3779, 3786, 3992, 4308,
    4371, 4377, 4380, 4381, 4383-4386, 4388,
    4389, 4393, 4618, 4747, 4794, 4804,
    4809, 4811-4813, 4815, 4822, 4823, 4825,
    4923, 4940
    voir aussi: Anthropologie de la nourriture
Allaitement 1670
Allaitement naturel 1540, 1548, 1551, 1584,
    2129, 2699, 2704, 2713, 2863, 4816, 4824
Allemands 4292, 4347, 4603, 4761
Alliances 470, 688, 1646, 1900, 2210, 2474,
    2567, 2638, 2658, 2983, 3355, 3502
Alliances militaires
    voir: OTAN
Alphabet 545, 1913, 1996, 2019, 4229
Alphabétisation 248, 1568, 1743, 1744, 1790,
    2121, 2561, 2598, 2760, 2861, 3627,
    3668, 4229, 4247, 4751, 4756, 4902
Alternance 1962
Altruisme 220, 1539, 2585, 3468
Ambassades 733
Âme 2791, 3148, 3202, 3311, 3338, 3368,
    3372, 3499, 3504, 3516, 3553, 3685
Aménagement de l'espace 3845
Aménagement hydraulique 960, 1202, 2061,
    2289, 4710, 4718, 4777, 4780, 4887, 4937
Aménagement urbain 1021, 2212, 2219, 2421,
    3846, 4326, 4786, 4930, 4934, 4935
Américain d'origine asiatique 2161, 2533,
    3073, 3700
Américains 743, 2348, 2533, 3073
Amérindiens 102, 119, 404, 774, 783, 1799,
    2099, 2691, 2834, 3155, 3550, 3617,
    3915, 4406
Amérindiens du Nord 100, 215, 225, 531, 539,
    699, 740, 786, 887, 2072, 2330, 3514,
    3547, 3674, 4576, 4595, 4644
Amérindiens du Sud 90, 385, 756, 4644
Amiante 3986
Amichai, Yehuda 4049, 4439
Amitié 2557, 2882, 4172

Amour 514, 2453, 2683, 2909, 3244, 3276,
    3305, 3508, 4034, 4057, 4060, 4062,
    4088, 4139, 4218, 4259, 4263, 4571
Amuzgo 1967
An, Lu-shan 522
Analphabétisme 3710, 4247, 4721, 4733
Analyse anthropologique 177, 212, 213, 431
Analyse comparative 286, 330, 415, 663, 733,
    984, 1283, 1424, 1445, 1455, 1471, 1479,
    1618, 1743, 1909, 1932, 2002, 2124,
    2413, 2425, 2499, 2527, 2687, 2689,
    2853, 3092, 3110, 3112, 3115, 3125, 3313,
    3383, 3661, 3668, 3713, 3743, 3848,
    3906, 4048, 4167, 4219, 4270, 4282,
    4513, 4656, 4659, 4710
Analyse contextuelle 212, 230, 415, 431,
    1753, 1780
Analyse coût-avantage 2588
Analyse de contenu 331, 1921
Analyse de discours 10, 196, 230, 235, 266,
    1735, 1736, 1749, 1776, 1780, 1796,
    1868, 2807, 2895, 2901, 3091, 3404,
    4226, 4303, 4417, 4434, 4499, 4515,
    4536, 4563
Analyse de données croisées 1541, 1578
Analyse de groupe 220, 1607, 2125, 2585,
    2606, 2953
Analyse de motivation 422, 3687
Analyse de régression 910, 1675, 2137, 2430,
    4886
Analyse de réseau 131
Analyse de systèmes 1908
Analyse des données 203, 282, 301, 313, 403,
    423, 435, 436, 533, 1558, 1578, 1666,
    4353, 4473, 4554, 4756, 4783, 4803, 4804
Analyse des politiques gouvernementales
    4788, 4828, 4865, 4928
Analyse documentaire 4183
Analyse historique 22, 30, 41, 109, 124, 190,
    358, 541, 593, 599, 615, 656, 876, 904,
    913, 1048, 1350, 1375, 1437, 1495, 1738,
    1805, 1821, 1823, 1839, 1934, 1995,
    2023, 2136, 2229, 2262, 2385, 2472,
    2510, 2528, 2554, 2658, 2877, 2949,
    3026, 3109, 3276, 3281, 3527, 3716,
    3718, 3854, 4140, 4156, 4214, 4272,
    4405, 4489, 4594
Analyse multivariée 1462, 2150, 2235
Analyse par cohorte 2121, 2131, 3074, 4575
Analyse par grappe 943
Analyse qualitative 28, 215, 282, 306, 435,
    443, 2712, 2880, 3159, 3781, 4676
Analyse quantitative 282, 306, 443, 1885,
    2880, 4676

Analyse régionale 663, 2150, 2210, 2749, 2853, 4452, 4707
Analyse spatiale 950, 1659, 1973, 2138, 2412, 3800, 4339, 4683, 4831
Analyse statistique 1453, 1462, 1486, 1490, 1603, 2118, 2778, 4719
Analyse structurale 1918, 1948, 4372
Analyse transculturale 167, 182, 980, 1584, 1772, 2374, 2579, 2649, 2680, 2712, 2791, 3193, 3791, 3942, 4419, 4521, 4527, 4540, 4593, 4641
Analyse transnationale 1375, 2207, 2289, 2568, 2706, 3028, 3112
Anatomie 110, 1464, 1465, 1469, 1523, 1531, 1590, 1593, 1610, 1620, 1678, 3779, 3799
Ancien Régime 2205, 2423
Anciens combattants 2467
Androgynie 2838
Angoisse 4504
Anikulapo-Kuti, Fela 3933, 4059
Animaux 46, 462, 638, 730, 749, 824, 872, 884, 889, 929, 947, 1020, 1366, 1501, 1620, 1624, 1657, 1678, 1679, 1689, 1696, 1700, 2068, 2189, 2291, 2445, 3998, 4212, 4391, 4496
   voir aussi: Boeufs, Droits des animaux, Moutons
Animaux domestiques 920, 2340, 2445
Animaux mythiques 3116, 3127, 3993
Animaux sauvages 1, 1818, 2063, 4318, 4782, 4805
Animisme 3609, 3690, 3702, 3939
Ankutshu 1996
Anomie 4152
Antécédents financiers 734
Anthologie 4074
Anthropocentrisme 167
Anthropologie 2, 3, 6-9, 11, 13, 16, 18, 26, 29, 31, 35, 37, 41, 43, 48-52, 56, 76, 77, 80-82, 90, 93-98, 100, 104, 108, 110, 114, 115, 119-121, 127, 131, 133, 134, 137, 151, 155-157, 159-164, 169, 171, 175, 176, 180, 182-184, 187, 189, 190, 192, 193, 195, 198-200, 202, 207, 212-214, 216, 217, 219, 221, 223, 224, 232-234, 237, 238, 241, 244, 246-248, 256, 262, 267, 269-272, 275, 276, 279-281, 291, 293, 295-297, 299, 301, 303, 304, 310-312, 317, 318, 328, 341, 348, 354, 355, 359, 365, 369-371, 385, 391, 392, 402, 408, 410-413, 418, 424, 428, 431, 439, 444, 456, 482, 504, 521, 530, 532, 533, 538, 545, 549, 552, 561, 572-574, 587, 590, 597, 605, 614, 618, 621, 626, 636, 638, 648, 655, 657, 660, 665, 674, 677,
679, 688, 689, 697, 736, 740, 742, 743, 745, 767, 774, 790, 793, 796, 800, 821, 830, 832, 836, 849, 850, 866, 870, 876, 879, 903, 937, 969, 974, 977, 980, 985, 992, 993, 1007, 1095, 1101, 1280, 1291, 1345, 1357, 1360, 1369, 1370, 1372, 1374, 1387, 1389, 1420, 1450, 1451, 1457, 1459-1465, 1468, 1469, 1471, 1473, 1477, 1478, 1482-1484, 1492, 1495, 1497, 1502-1504, 1512-1515, 1520, 1521, 1523-1528, 1538, 1542, 1545, 1550, 1552, 1561, 1566, 1567, 1572, 1576, 1584, 1586, 1590, 1592, 1593, 1622, 1662, 1703, 1721, 1752, 1753, 1761, 1772, 1773, 1792, 1800, 1809, 1815, 1823, 1827, 1830, 1837, 1841, 1845, 1880, 1912, 1962, 1967, 1968, 1971-1975, 1977, 1978, 1980, 1982-1986, 2018, 2022, 2036, 2052, 2068, 2070, 2071, 2076, 2077, 2093, 2101, 2116, 2126, 2127, 2130, 2135, 2157, 2168, 2170, 2172, 2185, 2190, 2194, 2198, 2216, 2218, 2220, 2224, 2233, 2235, 2247, 2250, 2253, 2302, 2328, 2334, 2348, 2354, 2367, 2373, 2379, 2387, 2428, 2429, 2431, 2433, 2447, 2450, 2475, 2485, 2498, 2503, 2505, 2507, 2510, 2516, 2517, 2519, 2525, 2527, 2530, 2537, 2539, 2547, 2549, 2551, 2557, 2561, 2563, 2571, 2572, 2583, 2588, 2591, 2596, 2609-2611, 2623, 2633, 2647, 2670, 2679, 2687, 2689, 2700, 2703, 2706, 2714, 2731, 2732, 2737, 2740, 2747, 2751, 2776, 2784, 2796, 2798, 2814, 2824, 2842, 2852, 2858, 2883, 2896, 2897, 2908, 2915, 2919, 2926, 2927, 2929, 2939, 2955, 2958, 2963, 2987, 2992, 2998, 2999, 3004, 3021, 3024, 3038, 3044-3046, 3052, 3055, 3061, 3067-3069, 3071, 3072, 3084, 3108, 3117, 3122, 3123, 3126-3128, 3130, 3172, 3189-3191, 3202, 3233, 3235, 3236, 3245, 3246, 3252, 3264, 3288, 3292, 3301, 3302, 3309, 3314, 3326, 3346, 3347, 3350, 3361, 3366, 3374, 3384, 3399, 3409, 3509, 3511, 3518, 3522, 3540, 3542, 3544, 3547, 3552, 3553, 3558, 3559, 3564, 3567, 3569, 3570, 3577, 3583, 3588, 3592, 3598, 3605, 3614, 3622, 3623, 3630, 3633, 3641, 3647, 3651, 3653, 3658, 3672, 3674, 3683, 3685, 3686, 3695, 3710, 3715, 3719, 3720, 3722, 3724, 3729, 3739, 3741, 3745, 3747, 3752, 3763, 3769, 3771, 3776, 3777, 3783, 3799, 3801, 3803, 3806, 3808, 3809, 3824, 3826,

3851, 3867, 3868, 3875-3877, 3879-3883,
3889, 3892, 3894, 3898, 3901, 3904,
3905, 3913, 3916, 3919, 3929, 3932,
3937, 3938, 3955, 3962-3964, 3967, 3968,
3975, 3981, 3985, 4003, 4004, 4009,
4013, 4039, 4056, 4060, 4071, 4081,
4089, 4105, 4109, 4111, 4124, 4125, 4134,
4143-4145, 4150, 4156, 4165, 4172, 4180,
4182, 4190, 4208, 4209, 4219, 4259,
4265, 4269, 4278, 4288, 4293-4295, 4297,
4298, 4312, 4315, 4337, 4343, 4381,
4387, 4388, 4402, 4415, 4424, 4426,
4429, 4432, 4436, 4437, 4443, 4447,
4449, 4452, 4453, 4459, 4466, 4468,
4469, 4481, 4482, 4484, 4489, 4490,
4513, 4514, 4517, 4519-4521, 4523, 4524,
4526, 4527, 4533, 4534, 4537, 4540,
4542, 4544, 4545, 4549, 4555, 4559,
4566-4568, 4574, 4582, 4595, 4599, 4601,
4602, 4611, 4630, 4633, 4636, 4641, 4685,
4751, 4775, 4790, 4799, 4802, 4804, 4893
voir aussi: Histoire de l'anthropologie,
Paléoanthropologie
Anthropologie appliquée 41, 45, 190, 249,
401, 2587, 4632, 4808
Anthropologie biologique 1465, 1472, 1502,
1522, 1523, 1545, 1564, 1581, 1593,
1610, 1635, 2699
Anthropologie criminelle 633, 3008
Anthropologie culturelle 45, 115, 120, 157,
163, 166, 177, 182, 197, 205, 213, 245,
259, 262, 414, 438, 572, 869, 1739, 1810,
1878, 2428, 2472, 2518, 2563, 2699,
2992, 3065, 3107, 3109, 3513, 3548,
3649, 3698, 3948, 3954, 4049, 4093,
4100, 4149, 4261, 4308, 4427, 4428,
4439, 4491, 4500, 4513, 4517, 4593, 4625
Anthropologie de la connaissance 199, 3655
Anthropologie de la danse 3890
Anthropologie de la nourriture 4354, 4376-
4379, 4386, 4395, 4754, 4809
Anthropologie de la science 3739, 3750, 3758,
3759
Anthropologie de l'alimentation 1541
Anthropologie de l'art 4149
Anthropologie de l'éducation 47, 421
Anthropologie du corps 1448, 1459, 1483,
2715, 2780, 2920, 2921, 2923, 2924,
2927, 2929, 2930, 2938, 2947, 2950,
2952, 2958, 2961, 3338, 4482
Anthropologie du développement 3028, 4612,
4663, 4710, 4784
Anthropologie du droit 59, 262, 2400, 2407,
2968, 2972, 2978, 2980, 2984, 2991,
2992, 3003, 3016, 4670

Anthropologie du sport 1559
Anthropologie du travail 2453, 2468, 2471
Anthropologie économique 218, 2328, 2331,
2332, 2334, 2337, 2344, 2345, 2353,
2363, 2387, 2390, 2428, 2471, 2963,
3175, 4632, 4745
Anthropologie historique 278, 869, 920, 2519,
2649, 3741, 4336
Anthropologie légale 970
Anthropologie linguistique 102, 113, 119, 129,
196, 230, 235, 248, 266, 1732, 1736,
1772, 1780, 1799, 1802, 1849, 1853,
1878, 1881-1884, 1886, 1968, 2667, 3233
Anthropologie maritime 2117
Anthropologie médicale 183, 605, 1474-1476,
1508, 1512, 1545, 1555, 1564, 1569,
1570, 1572, 1575, 1585, 1589, 1591,
1593, 2703, 2719, 2887, 2930, 2952,
2982, 3586, 3760, 3767, 3770, 3772,
3777, 3789, 3791, 3801, 3804, 3806-3809,
3813, 3815, 3817, 4871
Anthropologie philosophique 395, 4530
Anthropologie physique 46, 110, 144, 538,
845, 1453, 1459, 1466, 1474, 1476, 1483,
1500, 1504, 1510, 1531, 1536, 1546,
1547, 1549, 1559, 1563, 1569, 1574,
1588, 1589, 1600, 1620, 1623, 1624,
1645, 1646, 1685, 1689, 1694, 1716, 3799
Anthropologie politique 270, 629, 985, 2486,
2488, 2531, 2532, 2537, 2538, 2568,
2591, 2595, 2597, 3064, 3590, 4351, 4632
Anthropologie psychologique 2635, 2694,
3025, 3790, 4511, 4520, 4530, 4542
Anthropologie religieuse 86, 105, 191, 202,
208, 256, 275, 413, 869, 1353, 2539,
3145, 3215, 3221, 3227, 3228, 3231,
3232, 3234, 3237, 3250, 3257, 3259,
3265, 3326, 3347, 3356, 3361, 3405,
3422, 3427, 3431, 3445, 3455, 3460,
3583, 3645, 4462
Anthropologie rurale 41, 190, 2204, 2206,
4369
Anthropologie sociale 28, 45, 47, 91, 115,
120, 126, 142, 154, 157, 159, 205, 217,
262, 265, 288, 386, 415, 421, 985, 1878,
2373, 2472, 2551, 2587, 2591, 2595,
2699, 2807, 2907, 2992, 3001, 3040,
3054, 3109, 3518, 3599, 3929, 4351,
4361, 4394, 4449, 4602, 4612, 4745
Anthropologie sociologique 4584
Anthropologie urbaine 265, 2154, 2215, 2217,
2224, 2766, 3096, 3575, 3900, 4611, 4882
Anthropologie visuelle 55, 293, 389, 440, 442,
3977, 4126, 4366

Anthropologues 1, 6, 9, 18, 24, 26, 35, 37, 41,
    91, 93, 94, 102-105, 108, 110, 113-115,
    120, 123, 128, 134, 138, 143, 144, 148,
    157, 169, 180, 190, 193, 214, 223, 244,
    304, 386, 404, 1799, 1802, 2170, 2658,
    2798, 2834, 2897, 3231, 3799, 3870,
    4406, 4408, 4590, 4625, 4804
Anthropométrie 296, 310, 628, 898, 1455,
    1456, 1467, 1531, 1541, 1542, 1549,
    1557, 1566, 1576, 1587, 1589, 3772,
    3804, 4307, 4810
Anthropomorphisme 828, 1067, 1430, 3601,
    4386
Anthropophagie 751, 822, 977, 2796, 2852,
    3024, 3588
Anticléricalisme 4277
Anticolonialisme 4544
Antiquité 342, 379, 445, 453, 454, 462, 463,
    467, 475, 514, 526, 591, 669, 826, 863,
    900, 961, 1003, 1042, 1044, 1086, 1096,
    1097, 1285, 1358, 1367, 1390, 1408,
    1423, 1433, 1441, 1516, 2093, 2343,
    2562, 2875, 2909, 3417, 3454, 3680, 3701
Antiquité egypte 387, 452, 459, 490, 507, 517,
    902, 1335, 1818, 1928, 2063, 2871, 4375
Antiquité grecque 448, 449, 490, 491, 496,
    510, 521, 1044, 1738, 2228, 2324, 2365,
    2536, 2612, 3692, 3754, 3756, 4066,
    4148, 4290
Antiquité romaine 454, 490, 512, 528, 1031,
    1200, 1364, 1367
Antisémitisme 4479
Apache 1824
Apartheid 126, 269, 613, 2219, 2969, 3054,
    3055, 4012, 4293, 4548, 4663, 4881
    voir aussi: Société post-apartheid
Apiculture 4800
Apin, Rivai 4071
Apostasie 2998, 3366
Apparence physique 1449, 1493, 1494, 2935
Apprentis 2227
Apprentissage 424, 2237
Approvisionnement en eau 957, 2070, 2113,
    2289, 4771, 4910
Après-guerre 3956, 4105, 4479, 4523
Aquaculture 2117, 2452
Arabes 253, 484, 555, 579, 1830, 1856, 2422,
    2628, 3848, 3954, 4084, 4583, 4585
Arachides 749
Aragão, Baltasar Rebelo de 806
Araucana 3126
Araucanian 3126
Arawak 1982
Arbres 1711, 2084, 2087, 2091, 2427, 4697

Archébotanique 452, 858, 896, 900, 2296,
    2304, 4375
Archéologie 34, 60, 85, 111, 112, 117, 150,
    155, 162, 164, 178, 211, 246, 251, 258,
    260, 273, 274, 298, 325, 326, 332, 342,
    343, 363, 382, 409, 430, 445, 448, 452-
    454, 456, 458, 459, 462-464, 466, 469,
    471, 475, 483, 484, 488, 492, 494, 496-
    500, 503-505, 507, 511-513, 518, 520,
    522-524, 526, 530, 533, 538, 543, 545,
    550, 555, 556, 595, 598, 619, 623, 631,
    646, 656, 657, 664, 669, 744, 762, 789,
    819, 820, 823, 825-827, 829, 831, 832,
    834-838, 840, 843, 844, 846-848, 850,
    851, 853-863, 865, 866, 868, 869, 871,
    873, 874, 877, 879-883, 885, 888, 891,
    894, 896, 898, 900-910, 912, 914-924,
    926-933, 935, 937-941, 943-960, 962-974,
    977-985, 985-992, 994-1003, 1008-1014,
    1017, 1018, 1020-1023, 1026-1030, 1034-
    1043, 1045-1047, 1050-1054, 1057-1065,
    1068-1071, 1073-1075, 1078-1080, 1082,
    1085, 1087, 1089-1094, 1098-1101, 1105-
    1198, 1201-1204, 1206-1282, 1284-1293,
    1295, 1297-1300, 1302, 1304-1307, 1309-
    1315, 1317, 1318, 1320-1322, 1325-1328,
    1330-1332, 1337, 1338, 1340, 1343, 1344,
    1346, 1348, 1351, 1352, 1354-1356, 1360,
    1362, 1363, 1365-1369, 1371, 1376-1378,
    1380-1384, 1388-1393, 1396-1402, 1404,
    1406-1409, 1411, 1412, 1414-1419, 1421,
    1424-1427, 1429, 1431-1436, 1438, 1440-
    1447, 1461, 1464, 1467, 1471, 1479,
    1516, 1518, 1532, 1533, 1546, 1760,
    2087, 2100, 2107, 2134, 2135, 2144,
    2170, 2175, 2177, 2206, 2208, 2226,
    2228, 2230, 2240, 2266, 2304, 2321,
    2338, 2340, 2343, 2360, 2372, 2393,
    2444, 2526, 2530, 2547, 2562, 2590,
    2591, 2604, 2642, 2752, 2794, 2871,
    3024, 3135, 3185, 3322, 3604, 3707,
    3849, 3859, 3973, 4155, 4241, 4250,
    4256, 4327, 4329, 4346, 4375, 4501
    voir aussi: Histoire de l'archéologie
Archéologie aérienne 932, 983
Archéologie biblique 87, 506, 897, 975, 976,
    1027, 1129, 1131, 1371, 3145, 3973
Archéologie classique 464, 505, 513, 520,
    569, 915, 1069, 1161, 1234, 1297, 1348
Archéologie de colonisation 445, 448, 475,
    483, 512, 556, 598, 623, 825, 831, 840,
    843, 854-856, 859, 860, 885, 886, 892,
    905, 907, 909, 917, 922, 924, 927, 931,
    938, 944, 957, 965, 966, 968, 982, 1035,
    1036, 1114, 1130, 1148, 1152, 1155, 1173,

1185, 1196, 1238, 1240, 1245, 1263, 1264, 1285, 1301, 1303, 1306, 1309, 1355, 1392, 1433, 1444, 2208, 2340

Archéologie expérimentale 995, 1011, 1526, 2304, 3941

Archéologie historique 155, 251, 530, 624, 664, 969, 970, 973, 978, 979, 982, 988, 1009, 1058, 1245, 1361, 1392, 1407, 1429, 2338, 3697

Archéologie sauvetage 1135, 1144, 1145, 1158, 1206, 1221, 1238, 1239, 1275, 1295, 1313-1315, 1391, 1436

Archéologie sur le terrain 824, 997

Archéologie urbaine 466, 901, 909, 917, 948, 1146, 1233, 1235, 1251, 1272, 1422, 2208

Archéologue 60, 85, 87, 111, 112, 851, 967, 972, 975, 976, 979, 989, 990, 4326

Archéozoologie 824, 841, 842, 872, 884, 889, 929, 947, 974

Architecte 1009, 1763, 3660, 3846, 3853

Architecture 316, 323, 343, 512, 620, 707, 798, 825, 880, 906, 918, 995, 1009-1012, 1015, 1019, 1021, 1022, 1025, 1032, 1035, 1043, 1045, 1047, 1048, 1050, 1052, 1054, 1057, 1063, 1069, 1070, 1075, 1079, 1082, 1089, 1091, 1092, 1100, 1110, 1113, 1121, 1165-1167, 1181, 1188, 1217, 1246, 1296, 1333, 1337, 1343, 1346, 1357, 1364, 1420, 1763, 2092, 2227, 2459, 3260, 3354, 3452, 3660, 3678, 3838, 3839, 3842-3844, 3846-3848, 3851-3853, 3856-3861, 3898, 4124, 4345, 4749

Architecture antique 469, 989, 1008, 1010, 1016, 1018, 1021, 1022, 1025, 1027, 1028, 1031, 1032, 1038, 1045, 1049, 1059, 1065, 1073, 1076, 1083, 1085, 1090, 1099, 1102-1104, 1106, 1113, 1116, 1118, 1121, 1156, 1157, 1199, 1200, 1217, 1229, 1311, 1318, 1321, 1351, 1371, 1416

Architecture domestique 2594

Architecture traditionnelle 3840

Archives 25, 36, 61, 76, 77, 80, 81, 89, 150, 283, 291, 317, 318, 320, 323, 329, 333, 335, 339, 340, 354, 355, 359, 369, 372, 375, 381, 382, 547, 672, 707, 753, 781, 902, 1745, 1825, 2123, 2642, 3546, 3929

Archives nationales 76, 355, 427

Argent 321, 356, 363, 491, 617, 1143, 2336, 2365, 2366, 2378, 2384, 2392, 2533, 3073, 3716, 3730, 4218, 4730

Argent (métal) 506, 1428, 1444

Argile 349, 2206

Aristocratie 557, 624, 2639, 4094

Armah, Ayi Kwei 4188

Armée 433, 498, 512, 546, 558, 917, 1076, 2494, 2508, 2521, 3022, 3036, 3059, 4706

Armée de l'air 3463

Armée de terre 283, 299, 498, 624, 1029, 1076, 2123, 2483, 2526, 2542, 2577, 2960, 3021, 3022, 3052, 3502, 3716

Armement 534, 581

Arméniens 253

Armes 338, 534, 558, 563, 581, 1443, 1526, 2508, 2576

Armes nucléaires 3758
  voir aussi: Essai nucléaire

Armstrong, Hamilton F. 2533, 3073

Arrestation 2570

Art 133, 151, 174, 201, 273, 314, 327, 330, 337, 338, 343, 368, 439, 444, 759, 828, 894, 937, 999, 1005, 1007, 1012-1014, 1016, 1017, 1020, 1039, 1048, 1051, 1068, 1071, 1074, 1084, 1087, 1094, 1097, 1098, 1102, 1110, 1114, 1337, 1343, 1352, 1384, 1387, 1391, 1420, 2234, 2245, 2250, 2253, 2324, 2353, 2453, 2921, 2933, 2945, 2950, 3354, 3529, 3598, 3624, 3714, 3731, 3736, 3773, 3838, 3841, 3850, 3852, 3866, 3906, 4041, 4091, 4093-4095, 4097, 4101-4103, 4106, 4109, 4111-4113, 4115, 4121-4123, 4125, 4127, 4128, 4130, 4133-4135, 4137, 4139, 4141, 4144, 4145, 4223, 4235, 4247, 4453
  voir aussi: Anthropologie de l'art, Beaux-arts, Histoire de l'art, Œuvres d'art, Philosophie de l'art

Art antique 1040, 1055, 1056, 1072, 1081, 1096, 1102

Art bouddhique 3211

Art contemporain 3881, 4107

Art culinaire 1398, 4376, 4379, 4396

Art de la guerre 395, 624, 688

Art décoratif 316, 1016, 1396, 2234, 2243, 3839, 3840

Art dramatique 3878

Art du fer-forgé 1017

Art figuratif 1071, 4118, 4132

Art funéraire 1077

Art funéraire antique 1311, 1317, 1318, 1321, 1385, 3604

Art indigène 130, 353

Art islamique 1015, 3840, 4115

Art médiéval 3249

Art populaire 92, 3256, 4095, 4106, 4129, 4131

Art préhistorique 1384

Art primitif 1033, 1088, 2346

Art religieux 1081, 3230, 3249, 3256, 3452,
3624, 4095, 4106, 4114, 4117, 4131, 4137,
4140, 4441
Art rupestre 894, 968, 1007, 1013, 1023,
1041, 1087, 1095, 1105, 1335, 3585
Art traditionnel 2325, 3908, 4096, 4130, 4145
Art tribal 327
Artefact archéologique 325, 342, 356, 460,
499, 507, 617, 837, 839, 846, 860, 890,
912, 943, 951, 968, 973, 1016, 1042,
1236, 1306, 1363, 1366, 1368, 1373,
1378, 1379, 1382, 1384, 1390, 1392,
1402-1404, 1407, 1412, 1422, 1429, 1440,
1441, 1443, 1447, 1536, 2240, 2360, 4268
Artisanat 2239, 2244, 2644, 3678
Artisans 1425, 2644
Artistes 1094, 3841, 3869, 4093, 4103, 4109,
4111, 4123, 4128, 4132, 4135, 4223, 4235
Artistes du spectacle 2842, 3884, 3903, 3938
Artistes peintres 3841, 4089, 4095, 4112
Arts 314, 315, 368, 1033, 1047, 1081, 1093,
1094, 1331, 1357, 1819, 2325, 2571,
2842, 2940, 3134, 3319, 3624, 3724,
3749, 3768, 3773, 3823, 3841, 3844,
3882, 3884, 3890, 3904, 3916, 3937,
3938, 3963, 3967, 4025, 4064, 4091,
4092, 4104, 4108-4111, 4118, 4123, 4125,
4127, 4132, 4133, 4138, 4203, 4610, 4712
Arts du spectacle 364, 3881, 3903, 4605
Arts graphiques 1031
Arts martiaux 2625, 3867
Arts plastiques 4610
Arts visuels 3354, 3718, 4098, 4123, 4126,
4127, 4366
Arts zoomorphes 1391, 1430
Ascendance 649, 804, 813, 2337, 2421, 2551,
2643, 2649, 2774, 2801, 2997, 3078,
3243, 3558, 3562, 3594, 3689, 3690,
4013, 4029, 4248, 4572, 4630
Ascétisme 2085, 3136, 4310
A'sha Al- 4084
Ashanti 2833
Ashkenaze 2965, 3394, 3395, 3997
Ashurnasirpal, II [King] 3920
Asiatiques 253, 4398, 4478
Asile 2186
Asma'u, Nana 4081
Aspects juridiques 2998, 3366
Assainissement 4811
    voir aussi: Services de voirie
Assemblée générale des Nations Unies 4666
Asseng, Protais 4206
Assimilation culturelle 1551, 2685, 3097,
3193, 3943, 4458, 4479, 4597
Assimilation des immigrants 1798

Assimilation ethnique 2523, 2685
Assistance 1571
Assistance socio-psychologique 2717, 2893,
3834
Association commerciale 2269, 4648, 4671,
4759, 4786
Associations 693, 4927
Assolement 2276
Assyriennes 450, 489, 1102, 1284, 1330,
1341, 1839, 3920
Astrologie 591, 3417
Astronomie 652, 653, 3269, 3672, 3740, 3752,
4095
Asturias, Miguel Ángel 4222
Ateliers 418, 1387, 2037, 4623
Athéisme 3131
Athlètes 4307, 4312, 4336, 4574
Ati 2592
Atlas 1727, 3247
Atlas ethnographiques 303
Atlas linguistiques 113, 1802
Attitudes 45, 53, 399, 625, 1748, 2047, 2097,
2443, 2502, 2791, 2802, 2809, 2892,
2910, 2931, 2933, 2988, 3060, 3078,
3092, 3442, 3572, 3607, 3810, 3811, 3813,
3893, 4668, 4722, 4805
Attitudes collectives 3074
Attitudes culturelles 399
Attitudes raciales 696, 3106
Attraction interpersonnelle 1449, 1452, 1493,
1494, 2891, 2935
Attribution du nom 1749, 1818, 1822, 1826,
1828, 1831, 1834-1836, 2063, 2700, 3582,
3887
Audition 4029
Austerlitz, Robert 139
Australien 1723, 1728
Autarcie 2507
Auteur 799, 1833, 2998, 3190, 3212, 3331,
3366, 3876, 3895, 4162, 4170, 4194,
4202, 4239, 4258, 4263, 4266, 4272,
4277, 4278, 4566
Authenticité culturelle 1774, 3698, 3699
Autoassistance 4511
Autobiographies 1740, 2832, 3988, 4062,
4069, 4171, 4215, 4251, 4511, 4517, 4562,
4566-4568, 4570, 4571, 4575, 4578-4580
Autodétermination 2538, 2954, 3026, 4627,
4629, 4646, 4649, 4656, 4785
Autogestion 2210
Automobiles 161, 697, 3712
Autonomie 739, 2417, 2524, 2540, 2614,
2672, 2834, 2933, 3018, 3063, 3967,
4406, 4480, 4634, 4656, 4858, 4902
Autoritarisme 4778

Autorité 563, 2176, 2324, 2480, 2528, 2560, 2583, 2598, 2669, 3627, 3803, 4374, 4560
Autorité politique 2212, 2487, 4643
Autorités religieuses 275, 2539
Autosuffisance 2210, 2262
Avantage comparé 2226
Ávila, António José de 815
Avortement 2705, 2706, 2722, 2724, 2725, 2851, 2881, 2966, 4531
Aztec 98, 214, 802, 1005, 1024, 2302, 2503, 3515, 4242
Bablot, Alfredo J. 106, 752
Baga 574
Bagley, Ray 4038
Baidawī, Qāḍī 4185
Baisse de la fécondité 2136
Baker, Reginald 4574
Bakgatla 215
Balādurī, Ahmad Ibn Yahya al 3323
Baldeep Singh, Bhai 3463
Balkar 2321, 2979, 3349
Bambara 1818, 2063
Bananes 723
Banditisme 633, 3008, 3991, 4015, 4500
Bankimchandra, Rishi 3312
Banque mondiale 4338, 4612, 4667, 4678, 4680, 4737, 4781, 4800, 4937
Banques 734, 4911
Banques de développement 4937
Banques internationales 2210
Bantou 1987, 1988, 1990, 1996, 1997, 1999, 2003, 2007
Baptisme 4183
Baraka, Sayyid 3322
Barrages 2079, 2164, 2271, 4594
Base militaire 498
Base-ball 4336
Bases de données 313, 2057
Basotho 1821
Basques 1522, 2187, 2666, 4493
Bateau 868, 1395, 2248, 3680
Bâtiment 667, 906, 965, 1015, 1016, 1021, 1022, 1046, 1053, 1069, 1091, 1102, 1166, 1167, 1181, 1207, 1420, 2227, 3354, 3840, 3842-3844, 3855, 3861, 4148, 4319, 4345, 4749
Baudelaire, Charles 3728
Baudot, Georges 106, 752
Baudrillard, Jean 3698
Bazié, Jean-Hubert 1749
Beaud, Stéphane 2453
Beaux-arts 4103, 4142
Bédouin 555, 939, 1301, 2287, 2417, 2473, 3018, 4604
Behn, Aphra 4285

Bemba 2729
Bengali 1893, 1906, 2282, 2575, 3218, 4072
Benjamin, Sathima Bea 3933, 4059
Benjamin, Walter 4068
Berbère 122, 470, 600, 1830, 1854, 1858, 2274, 2417, 2567, 2653, 2977, 3018, 4037
Berberova, Nina 4069, 4578
Berenicianus, Alexander 486
Bergers 4579
Besoins fondamentaux 2640, 2863, 4665
Bétail 2430, 2437, 2438, 2445, 3917
Bhagat Nam Devji [Saint] 3472
Bhangi 1455
Bhāsa 3314, 3865, 3875, 3876
Bialik, H.N. 4444
Bible 87, 506, 604, 975, 1353, 1831, 1838, 1843, 1846, 1848, 1850, 1855, 1859, 1861, 1864, 1893, 2310, 2598, 2737, 2748, 3146, 3147, 3218, 3227, 3229, 3237, 3238, 3244, 3251, 3255, 3267, 3337, 3392, 3393, 3396, 3399, 3400, 3405, 3420, 3421, 3426, 3427, 3431, 3434-3436, 3445, 3447, 3449, 3453, 3459, 3460, 3627, 3899, 3973, 4026, 4114, 4224, 4283
Bibliographes 3206
Bibliographies 79, 109, 340, 1995, 4079, 4404
Bibliothécaires 2465
Bibliothèques 25, 82, 291, 323, 324, 354, 370, 375, 707, 2465, 4215, 4223
Biculturalisme 2525
Bidayuh 4584
Bidonville 2180
Bidonvilles 909, 2208, 2214, 2222, 4937
Bien-être 43, 977, 2644, 3024, 4836
Bien-être des enfants 2648
Bien-être (personnel) 3159, 3795, 4181, 4689, 4738, 4846, 4890
Bien-être social 4738, 4808
Biens culturels 2937, 3701, 4438, 4617, 4619, 4651
Biens publics 2595, 4718, 4880
Bière 2277, 2824
Big Man 2199
Biggs, Bruce 1878
Bilinguisme 1770, 1790, 1793, 1798, 1803, 1895, 1969, 1985, 2005, 3989, 4548
Bini 4007
Biodiversité 2105, 2272, 2445, 4636, 4658, 4767, 4774, 4781, 4820
Bioéthique 2728
Biographies 88, 92, 99, 106, 111, 123, 128, 181, 371, 433, 570, 615, 627, 675, 752, 773, 817, 979, 990, 1878, 2281, 2298,

2465, 3841, 4192, 4271, 4477, 4563-4568, 4574-4577, 4579, 4712
Biologie 46, 263, 279, 910, 1465, 1500, 1501, 1504, 1508, 1519, 1520, 1537, 1538, 1593, 1616, 1618, 1632, 1634, 1640, 1689, 1695, 3043, 4507, 4770
Biologie humaine 193, 1451, 1487, 1492, 1499, 1521, 1543, 1575, 1584, 2080, 2699, 3662, 3750, 3771
Biologie sociale 2699
Bioméchanique 1549, 1610
Biomédecine 1498, 2657, 2719, 2959, 3817
Biométrie 1553, 1564, 1566, 1572, 1581, 1592
Biopolitique 1448, 2920
Biotechnologie 2930
Bisa 2509
Bisexualité 1454, 2874, 2919, 3782
Bislama 1724, 2018
Blancs 567, 1503, 1582, 1773, 3026, 3045, 3051, 3053, 3266, 3648, 4012, 4425
Blé 896, 1704
Bloch, Jules 124, 1805
Boas, Franz 134
Bochiman 2398, 4436, 4638
Bodi 2610
Boeck, Egide De 109, 1995
Boeufs 2291
Bohémiens 10, 14, 139, 399, 425, 3091, 3099, 3124, 3710, 4006
Bois de construction 2207, 4772
Boisement 2448
Boissons 4379, 4390
Boissons alcoolisées 215, 490, 4390
    voir aussi: Bière, Vin
Bombal, María Luisa 4239
Bon sens populaire 2088, 2364, 3667, 4070, 4233
Bonaventure [Saint] 3728
Boruca 1984
Bosatsu, Gyōki 3187
Bosch, Hieronymous 4097
Botanique 900, 1722, 2066, 2201, 2297
    voir aussi: Archébotanique
Boucherie 1281
Bouddhisme 105, 2099, 2345, 2800, 2973, 3079, 3155, 3162-3164, 3166-3177, 3180-3195, 3197-3208, 3210-3214, 3231, 3261, 3291, 3297, 3313, 3317, 3379, 3496, 3531, 3532, 3549, 3593, 3717, 3826, 3860, 4095, 4284, 4471
Bourdieu, Pierre 2609
Brahmanes 3277
Branco, García Mendes Castelo 806
Brevets 2241, 4880
Brink, André 4151

Broca, Paul 110, 3799
Brong 992
Bronze 322, 912, 1017, 1067, 1199, 3556
Buck, Pearl S. 3079
Budha, Baba 3461
Bunting, Edward 647
Bureaucratie 818, 2625, 3107, 4365
Burgh, James 713
Burton, Richard F. 291
Butler, William 97
Bwa 2945, 3529
Cabanis, Pierre-Jean-Georges 3728
Cabrera, Lydia 3981
Cacao 2258, 2275, 2400, 2968
Cadornega, António de Oliveira de 806
Café 738
Calderón de la Barca, Pedro 3862
Caldwell, Robert 1894
Calendriers 166, 1979, 2256, 3407, 3649, 3740, 3741, 3745, 3748, 4095, 4428
Calligraphie 3330, 4223
Calungsod, Pedro 3220
Camions 3780
Camp 498, 698, 1282, 2119, 2148, 2697, 2803
Campagne 2198, 2578, 4332, 4796
Campagne électorale 1776
Camping 2085, 4310
Camps de concentration 654, 4508
Camus, Albert 3728
Canadien 1796, 2122
Cancer 3769, 3805
Canoes 360, 1375, 4343
Canto, José do 2281
Capacité 1463, 4593
Capital 2068, 2293, 2456, 4932
Capital culturel 130, 353, 2215, 4491
Capital humain 2315, 4711, 4865
Capital social 2210, 2289, 4726, 4808
Capitalisme 777, 778, 2229, 2290, 2323, 2325, 2332, 2345, 2363, 2385, 2399, 2459, 2955, 3175, 3409, 3895, 4218, 4351, 4402, 4483
Caractère 3110, 3467, 3878, 3991, 3995, 4162
Caractère national 3653, 4221, 4484, 4486
Cardew, Michael 2238
Carlos de Chelmichi, José Conrado 323, 707
Carnavals 2334, 3877, 4363, 4366
Carpo, Arsénio Pompílio Pompeu de 692
Cartes géographiques 132, 323, 393, 437, 707, 721, 768, 802, 1727, 1737, 3111, 3121
Cartographie 132, 294, 393, 437, 494, 768, 802, 1084, 1197, 1737
Casas, Bartolomé de las 4234
Casement, Roger 4182

Castes 1506, 1508, 2197, 2569, 2614, 2615,
    2617, 2620, 2623, 2624, 2627, 3056,
    3075, 3082, 3284, 3288, 3683, 4106,
    4596, 4843
Catastrophes naturelles 2394, 2432, 2780,
    2924, 4764, 4792
Catholicisme 105, 565, 732, 736, 2617, 2729,
    2769, 2966, 3217, 3225, 3230, 3231,
    3256, 3263, 3637, 4131, 4441
Catholiques 754, 3230, 4441
Causalité 1567, 1872, 2137, 2490, 2532, 3590
Cause 4812
Cécité des couleurs 1506
Célibat 2127, 2904
Cellules 1699, 3728
Celtes 916, 1361, 1928, 3240, 3697
Censure 3714
Centrales nucléaires 3976
Centres de recherche 29, 160, 1205, 3600,
    4334
Céramique 316, 378, 838, 909, 951, 1324,
    1369, 1370, 1374, 1376, 1388, 1404,
    1415, 1424, 1425, 1427, 1431, 1439,
    1440, 1445, 2208, 2249, 2250, 3737, 3839
Céréales 900, 2261, 4671
Cérémonie de mariage 3581, 3684, 3706
Cérémonies 285, 374, 911, 2252, 2563, 2579,
    2602, 2665, 2700, 2870, 2943, 3307,
    3514, 3525, 3556, 3778, 4011, 4373, 4602
Cerveau 110, 170, 1481, 1496, 1547, 1561,
    1567, 1612, 1730, 3799
Césaire, Aimée 4159
Cœuroy, André 3929
Chalukya Bhima [II] 1437
Cham 4153
Chamanisme 105, 828, 1041, 1771, 3062,
    3128, 3231, 3535, 3550, 3565, 3566,
    3580, 3587, 3589, 3592, 3593, 3600-3602,
    3605, 3606, 3726, 3833, 4334, 4360, 4480
Chamans 1771, 1834, 3062, 3565, 3566, 3582,
    3585, 3587-3589, 3592, 3598, 3600, 3605,
    3606, 3626, 3726, 4334, 4360
Chambri 2370, 2990, 4620
Chameaux 454, 462, 1367, 2429
Chamoiseau, Patrick 3980
Chamorro 120, 2637, 4028
Chances d'obtenir un emploi 2163, 2825, 4722
Chane 3559
Changement culturel 338, 597, 880, 980,
    1745, 2003, 2126, 2212, 2325, 2370,
    2427, 2473, 2482, 2527, 2630, 2643,
    2990, 3555, 3660, 3674, 3903, 4126,
    4367, 4408, 4414, 4487, 4583, 4590,
    4592, 4593, 4595, 4601, 4610, 4620,
    4685, 4812

Changement d'attitude 3074, 3813
Changement de climat 833, 847, 857, 1190,
    4666, 4763, 4785
Changement démographique 1712, 2125,
    2155, 2637, 4582
Changement d'organisation 4804
Changement économique 587, 633, 743, 2136,
    2284, 2348, 2572, 2644, 3008, 4804,
    4849, 4920
Changement linguistique 1724, 1725, 1727,
    1730, 1734, 1744, 1745, 1749, 1757,
    1789, 1806, 1807, 1810, 1813-1815, 1851,
    1870, 1874, 1879, 1911, 1915, 1927, 1929,
    1930, 1935, 1938, 1942, 1947, 1951,
    1954, 1955, 1958, 1964, 1979, 1981,
    1985, 1988, 1990, 2003, 2011, 2012, 2016,
    2018, 2051, 2052, 2058, 4268
Changement politique 993, 2210, 2518, 2548,
    3090, 3222, 3944, 4084, 4487, 4728,
    4778, 4804, 4820
Changement religieux 86, 701, 1025, 3215,
    3234, 3257, 3264, 3557, 3593, 3609,
    3610, 3612, 3617, 3618, 3623, 3631-3636,
    3639-3641, 3647, 3887, 4459, 4804
Changement social 137, 179, 267, 338, 504,
    587, 619, 621, 743, 1361, 1432, 1823,
    2136, 2164, 2196, 2284, 2348, 2506,
    2530, 2548, 2560, 2572, 2643, 2650,
    2689, 2806, 3030, 3033, 3041, 3090,
    3101, 3582, 3603, 3697, 3718, 3905,
    3934, 3988, 4012, 4021, 4191, 4302,
    4374, 4417, 4440, 4447, 4528, 4582,
    4584, 4589, 4591-4593, 4599, 4708, 4849,
    4902, 4909
Changement structurel 2315, 4682, 4866
Changement technologique 845, 879, 1383,
    1521, 2265, 2730, 4743, 4804
Chanoine, Julien 3608
Chansons populaires 3908, 3918, 3919, 3970
Chantepie de la Saussaye, P.D. 5, 226
Chanteurs 2584, 2842, 3933, 3938, 4059,
    4090
Chants 166, 1788, 1859, 2481, 2700, 2842,
    3436, 3539, 3649, 3653, 3892, 3894,
    3897, 3902, 3907, 3908, 3912, 3915,
    3919, 3924, 3927, 3928, 3930, 3933,
    3938, 3940, 3944, 3949, 3950, 3955,
    3956, 3964, 3966, 3968, 3984, 4018,
    4051, 4059, 4065, 4263, 4428, 4484
Chants funèbres 3967
Chants rituels 3539, 3950
Charbon 1829
Charbonnages 1829
Charisme 3221, 3265
Charité 3163, 3187, 3468, 3693, 4381, 4708

Charwe 767, 3577
Chasse 222, 384, 564, 746, 841, 1072, 1281,
    1406, 1600, 1663, 2075, 2429, 2431,
    2433, 2830, 2834, 3674, 3991, 3998,
    4208, 4406, 4595
Chasseurs 3991, 3998
Chasseurs-cueilleurs 371, 833, 887, 1041,
    1281, 1304, 1408, 1550, 2266, 2352,
    2432, 2433, 2449, 2651, 2834, 3084,
    3992, 4393, 4406
    voir aussi: Cueillette
Châtiment
    voir: Peine de mort
Chavin 3601
Chefferie 2568
Chefs 711, 733, 2195, 2564, 2792, 3007
Chefs d'entreprise 2368, 4700, 4847
Chefs d'État 537, 575, 583, 620, 639, 710,
    724, 792, 2330, 2519
Chemins de fer 749, 4608, 4766
Cheptel 730, 2083, 2367, 2447, 3678, 4536,
    4780
Chercheurs 291, 304, 443, 608, 2324, 2897
Cherokee 2330
Chevaux 502, 1406, 2438, 2445, 2899, 3213,
    3240, 4331
Ch'ien-lung [Emperor] 4155
Chiens 2445
Chiisme 470, 571, 2567, 3337, 3343
Chimalpahin, Domingo 214
Chimie 60
Chimpanzés 1604, 1605, 1608, 1636, 1638,
    1648, 1653, 1663, 1673, 1701, 1709,
    1716, 1720, 3771
Chin 2044, 2045
Chinois 642, 1796, 1803, 1877, 2021, 2036,
    2722, 3156, 3397, 3613, 3681, 3700,
    4203, 4451
Chirurgie 110, 1583, 3749, 3799
Choix du conjoint 1493, 1494, 1697, 2872,
    3307
Chokwe 3614
Chokye Gyaltsen, Jampal Namdol 3185
Chômage 2223, 2388, 2458, 4663, 4682
Chongjo [King] 2339, 2574, 2581
Chorégraphie 3867
Chrétiens 451, 473, 1454, 2121, 2993, 3026,
    3089, 3223, 3235, 3239, 3327, 3374, 3411,
    3615, 3630
Christianisation 3233, 3622
Christianisme 86, 119, 329, 451, 473, 514,
    591, 611, 644, 722, 732, 777, 796, 808,
    1046, 1070, 1092, 1871, 2099, 2232,
    2598, 2682, 2755, 2875, 2909, 3042,
    3155, 3160, 3215, 3217, 3221-3223, 3227,

3228, 3232, 3236-3238, 3242, 3245, 3248-
    3250, 3253, 3259-3261, 3264-3266, 3268,
    3350, 3400, 3411, 3417, 3435, 3437, 3460,
    3521, 3535, 3554, 3580, 3591, 3593,
    3622, 3625, 3627, 3635, 3636, 3640,
    3641, 3645, 3647, 3648, 3721, 3822,
    3856, 3915, 4114, 4183, 4264, 4462, 4472
    voir aussi: Catholicisme, Pentecôtisme
Chromosomes 1500, 1501, 1721
Chronologie 387, 445, 460, 475, 523, 537,
    575, 824, 826, 839, 842, 884, 889, 902,
    912, 926, 943, 951, 1016, 1248, 1290,
    1324, 1340, 1341, 1352, 1373, 1376,
    1403, 1430, 1443, 1468, 1516, 1535,
    2302, 3369, 4161
Chung, Kuan 2985
Cinéastes 427, 440
Cinéma 55, 442, 3731, 3977, 4099, 4105,
    4136, 4139, 4523, 4574
Circoncision 2888, 2889, 3267, 4889
Circonscriptions administratives 642, 876,
    904, 950, 1048, 1512, 1579, 2419, 2510,
    3281, 3854
Circulation 697, 3759
Circulation monétaire 4663
Circulation urbaine 3759
Cirque 3877
Citoyenneté 784, 2457, 2516, 2933, 2936,
    2989, 4606
Citoyens 748, 2457, 2967, 2976, 3006, 3328
Civilisation 148, 371, 467, 596, 638, 702, 737,
    799, 2476, 2480, 2647, 3035, 3079, 3137,
    3199, 3656, 3743, 4221, 4471, 4501, 4592
    voir aussi: Histoire des civilisations
Civilisation ancienne 73, 214, 343, 349, 356,
    366, 446, 447, 449-453, 455-457, 462,
    465, 467, 474, 477-481, 483, 486, 487,
    489, 491, 493, 494, 496, 497, 499, 500,
    503, 510, 515, 517, 521, 523, 524, 526,
    535, 541, 617, 632, 669, 802, 881, 903,
    925, 942, 984, 1005, 1024, 1036, 1049,
    1083, 1106, 1224, 1294, 1317, 1329,
    1341-1343, 1352, 1370, 1373, 1377, 1495,
    1738, 2092, 2225, 2228, 2240, 2261,
    2358, 2365, 2366, 2372, 2378, 2444,
    2536, 2544, 2546, 2550, 2562, 2580,
    2642, 2797, 3023, 3119, 3301, 3387, 3398,
    3451, 3604, 3680, 3688, 3896, 3920,
    3928, 3973, 4066, 4253, 4279, 4314,
    4346, 4375, 4548
Civilisation byzantine 484, 1021, 1022, 1122,
    1205, 1287, 1293, 1365, 1434, 1438,
    1722, 4247
Civilisation classique 451, 459, 463, 464, 471,
    505, 513, 520, 528, 569, 905, 915, 1014,

1047, 1069, 1093, 1098, 1110, 1113, 1134,
1161, 1165, 1173, 1225, 1234, 1252, 1255,
1297, 1348, 1361, 2343, 2871, 3697, 4592
Civilisation contemporaine 4592
Civilisation médiévale 30, 634, 638, 671, 779,
1146, 1325, 1444, 1833, 1857, 1937, 1953,
2378, 3089, 3167, 3441, 3859, 3863,
4034, 4349, 4381
Civilisation mésopotamienne 482, 508, 2261,
2354, 2358, 2995, 3289, 3868, 4279
Civilisation occidentale 135, 199, 416, 605,
2465, 3079, 3803, 3808, 3809, 4101,
4263, 4449, 4489
Civilisation orientale 3079
Clans 41, 190, 470, 1834, 2509, 2567, 2597,
2681
Clapperton, Hugh 584
Clark-Bekederemo, J.P. 3933, 4059
Classe 247, 563, 629, 760, 909, 1529, 1540,
1735, 1817, 1989, 2196, 2208, 2496,
2531, 2596, 2618, 2619, 2622, 2625,
2626, 2746, 2942, 2955, 3066, 3105,
3843, 4266, 4298, 4378, 4414, 4435,
4468, 4754, 4831, 4858, 4895
voir aussi: Aristocratie
Classe moyenne 4336
Classe ouvrière 909, 2208, 2644, 3900, 4519
Classification 223, 270, 284, 310, 910, 1062,
1373, 1385, 1719, 1729, 1741, 1752,
1996, 1999, 2022, 2098, 2537, 2950,
2999, 3753, 3757, 3905, 3953
Clergé 3618, 3637, 3642
Client 1788, 2471, 4018
Clientélisme 2558
Clignotement des indicateurs économiques
1617
Climat 455, 857, 1382, 1533, 2065, 2225,
2271, 2283, 4772
voir aussi: Changement de climat,
Météorologie, Temps
Clinton, Bill 4548
Clonage 1616
Clubs 2085, 2586, 3909, 4309, 4310
Coalition 2218, 2587, 3068
Coast Salish 1322
Cocaïne 3004
Code déontologique médical 2887, 2925,
2929, 2982, 3802
Coexistence pacifique 3040
Cognition 38, 170, 224, 302, 438, 542, 1004,
1405, 1520, 1547, 1612, 1636, 1693,
1730, 1790, 1832, 1921, 1973, 2080,
2201, 2895, 3512, 3574, 3662, 3789,
3842, 3941, 4507, 4529
Cognition sociale 170

Cohabitation 2160
Cohésion du groupe 220, 2585
Cohésion sociale 2776, 4610
Colenso, Harriette 817
Collaboration 53, 291, 404, 3005, 4548
Collection archéologique 325, 330, 342, 959
Collection d'art 315, 327, 330, 337, 347, 379,
380, 2346, 2353, 4092, 4118, 4125
Collections de musées 13, 314, 316, 321, 322,
324, 326, 328, 331, 332, 334, 336, 340,
341, 346, 348-351, 358, 360-362, 364-
368, 371, 372, 374, 377, 378, 610, 714,
1332, 1410, 1527, 1673, 3737, 3839,
4091, 4118, 4178, 4215, 4231
Collections ethnographiques 13, 31, 130, 320,
326, 328, 345, 353, 371
Collections photographiques 367
Collections privées 13, 365, 371, 379
Collectivisation 2278
Collectivisme 2376
Collectivité 3, 253, 307, 425, 717, 937, 1361,
1426, 1623, 1716, 1773, 1786, 2067,
2075, 2078, 2089, 2103, 2104, 2154,
2158, 2164, 2165, 2184, 2201, 2202,
2204, 2210, 2264, 2284, 2294, 2307,
2324, 2331, 2332, 2359, 2487, 2509,
2557, 2592, 2599, 2602, 2647, 2664,
2665, 2668, 2672, 2686, 2818, 2828,
2829, 2836, 2844, 2907, 3011, 3026, 3105,
3352, 3450, 3483, 3530, 3558, 3629,
3697, 3710, 3720, 3723, 3739, 3847,
3886, 4024, 4031, 4075, 4134, 4184,
4262, 4337, 4353, 4355, 4399, 4431,
4451, 4456, 4475, 4478, 4479, 4498,
4536, 4545, 4573, 4611, 4654, 4752, 4780,
4799, 4804, 4820, 4871, 4882, 4938
voir aussi: Communauté internationale,
Communauté scientifique, Communautés
ethniques, Communautés religieuses
Collectivités locales 2083, 2085, 2090, 2091,
2103, 2104, 2192, 2195, 2601, 3064,
4024, 4294, 4310, 4311, 4454, 4648, 4718,
4723, 4779, 4793, 4795, 4852
Collectivités rurales 15, 136, 646, 668, 2192,
2194, 2195, 2207, 2294, 2413, 2426,
2556, 2561, 2735, 2752, 2786, 3819,
3827, 3858, 4309, 4742, 4751, 4795,
4818, 4910
Collectivités urbaines 4119, 4927
Colonialisme 2, 14, 43, 97, 125, 155, 326,
328, 329, 530, 532, 540, 553, 580, 583,
602, 611, 622, 637, 641, 643, 647, 650,
651, 662, 665, 670, 673, 675, 683, 689,
690, 693, 694, 698, 700, 708-710, 715,
716, 718, 720, 722, 726, 729, 731, 732,

735, 736, 738, 746, 747, 750, 751, 753, 754, 759, 764, 765, 770, 772, 775, 777, 780, 787, 793, 794, 797-799, 801, 803, 804, 808, 810, 812, 818, 969, 1432, 2082, 2179, 2199, 2223, 2335, 2359, 2397, 2507, 2534, 2608, 2671, 2682, 2808, 2828, 3031, 3042, 3219, 3245, 3353, 3594, 3596, 3624, 3709, 3829, 3844, 4037, 4086, 4160, 4166, 4173, 4187, 4213, 4226, 4293, 4299, 4312, 4336, 4460, 4639, 4657, 4679, 4772

Colonies 348, 360, 493, 592, 681, 686, 697-699, 706, 710, 714, 721, 727, 728, 739, 743, 746, 764, 780, 784, 787, 788, 794, 795, 809, 811, 812, 814, 816, 817, 1617, 1625, 1955, 2078, 2222, 2270, 2298, 2299, 2348, 2408, 2424, 2559, 2573, 2989, 3031, 3415, 3608, 3746, 4135, 4166, 4173, 4458, 4472, 4650

Colonisation 295, 329, 391, 449, 567, 583, 584, 598, 608, 623, 690, 691, 696, 713, 715, 725, 728, 759, 761, 781, 787, 797, 803, 806, 809, 814, 1130, 1137, 1289, 1290, 1413, 1497, 2130, 2161, 2385, 2448, 2507, 3032, 3051, 3078, 3608, 3746, 4195, 4215, 4630, 4639, 4643, 4655

Colonisation rurale 797, 803, 994, 2103, 2184, 2422, 2512, 2599, 3629, 4001, 4024, 4031

Columbus, Christopher 2551

Combustibles 2083

Comédie 1754, 3279, 4254

Commerce 356, 463, 503, 529, 617, 709, 734, 749, 764, 895, 908, 1362, 1392, 2182, 2256, 2329, 2335, 2343, 2344, 2356, 2360, 2362, 2372, 2383, 2386, 2390, 2393, 2447, 2469, 2806, 2828, 3575, 4272, 4622
    voir aussi: Histoire du commerce, Libre échange, Tourisme international

Commerce agricole 749

Commerce des esclaves 554, 692, 695, 734, 778, 806, 807, 961, 2383, 2671, 2857, 3076, 3230, 4007, 4441, 4460, 4548

Commerce extérieur 1447, 2330, 2357

Commerce intérieur 2358

Commerce international 692, 2391
    voir aussi: Exportations, Importations

Commerce régional 150, 382, 2357, 2362

Commercialisation 3706

Commodification 738, 1448, 2325, 2363, 2381, 2780, 2920, 2923, 2924, 2929, 2952, 2956, 2961, 3895, 3921

Commonwealth 43, 616

Communalisme 2408, 4650

Communauté internationale 4613, 4621

Communauté scientifique 197

Communautés ethniques 1822, 2074, 3956, 4012, 4404

Communautés religieuses 2652, 2764, 3186, 3194, 3222, 3226, 3241, 3345, 3376, 3394, 3422, 3544, 3555, 4451, 4581, 4931

Communes 3544, 4105, 4523

Communication 148, 182, 271, 526, 544, 991, 1362, 1525, 1743, 1754, 1762, 1771-1773, 1798, 1803, 1809, 1811, 1921, 1925, 2453, 2955, 3015, 3537, 3598, 3606, 3654, 3668, 4030, 4094, 4096, 4099, 4119, 4143, 4202, 4434

Communication interculturelle 1796, 3037, 3062, 3079, 3565

Communication interpersonnelle 1772

Communication non-verbale 2955, 4560

Communication orale 1758, 1898, 3973, 3989, 4014

Communication politique 1776, 4243

Communication verbale 1754

Communication visuelle 4126

Communisme 218, 319, 2480, 2500, 2964, 3968, 3988

Communistes 2557

Compensation 2373

Compétences 970, 1427, 2464, 4760, 4836, 4866

Compétitivité 718, 4671

Complots 3878

Comportement collectif 3048, 3633, 4459

Comportement culturel 393

Comportement de l'organisation 2606

Comportement du consommateur 1409

Comportement du groupe 220, 1598, 1599, 1605, 1623, 1628, 1653, 1661, 1705, 1716, 2126, 2585, 2606

Comportement économique 2364, 2371

Comportement humain 38, 138, 210, 822, 1452, 1487, 1488, 1496, 1499, 1507, 1754, 2872, 2891, 3360, 3561, 3761, 3992, 4019, 4393, 4394, 4529, 4532, 4539

Comportement individuel 1608, 1629, 1697, 1704, 2097, 2588, 3761, 3795, 3827, 3834

Comportement politique 2505

Comportement religieux 3157, 3230, 3332, 3360, 3446, 3621, 4371, 4441

Comportement sexuel 44, 1507, 1580, 2153, 2156, 2710, 2717, 2759, 2840, 2848, 2867, 2868, 2876, 2878, 2879, 2884, 2885, 2893, 2895, 2902-2904, 2910, 2912, 2914, 2916-2919, 2966, 3254, 3780, 3788, 3796, 3820, 3831, 3966, 4877, 4878, 4898

Comportement social 138, 428, 1606, 1635, 1645, 1661, 1664, 1681, 1682, 1684, 2937, 4016, 4378, 4438, 4754
Comportement verbal 1754, 4477
Compositeur 118, 3904, 3919, 3924, 3931, 3933, 4059, 4263
Composition du groupe 1453, 1654
Conception 1009, 1021, 1032, 1034, 1045, 1054, 1357, 2227, 2245, 3511, 3736, 3838, 3842, 3843, 3846, 3847, 3851-3853, 3855, 4247, 4749
Conception de soi 4530
Conceptualisation 56, 98, 154, 167, 195, 207, 213, 233, 262, 272, 320, 388, 435, 436, 634, 1751, 1855, 2490, 2503, 2992, 3062, 3111, 3162, 3199, 3280, 3298, 3431, 3441, 3466, 3565, 3567, 3685, 3728, 3816, 3942, 4107, 4463, 4471, 4537, 4549
Concurrence 1621, 2334, 2436, 3907, 3956, 4320, 4368, 4447, 4598, 4750
Condé, Maryse 4170
Conditions de travail 807, 2231, 2454, 2469
Conditions de vie 1543, 2171, 4531, 4748, 4907, 4922
Conditions économiques 288, 463, 551, 750, 809, 2082, 2150, 2196, 2210, 2343, 2345, 2383, 2424, 2430, 2637, 2833, 3175, 4266, 4367, 4447, 4645, 4667, 4713, 4739, 4829, 4831, 4832, 4842, 4854
Conditions politiques 986, 2210, 2491, 2500, 2518, 3039, 3869, 4152, 4266, 4447, 4571, 4652
Conditions sociales 373, 548, 717, 723, 778, 786, 814, 2205, 2268, 2398, 2403, 2411, 2423, 2472, 2480, 2481, 2729, 2780, 2793, 2821, 2833, 2924, 2962, 3011, 3033, 3039, 3109, 3603, 4152, 4302, 4358, 4367, 4403, 4435, 4579, 4585, 4638, 4639, 4645, 4652, 4662, 4739, 4747, 4765, 4829, 4831, 4835, 4840, 4856, 4857, 4860, 4864
Conférences au sommet 4623, 4648, 4658
Conférences internationales 19-21, 23, 27, 41, 42, 184, 190, 211, 430, 590, 658, 679, 1594-1596, 3470, 4646, 4899
Confessionellisme 3158
Confiance 2867, 3492, 3575, 4447, 4726
Conflit 329, 395, 641, 654, 705, 712, 719, 993, 1496, 1643, 1681, 1682, 2076, 2127, 2188, 2202, 2221, 2278, 2289, 2409, 2436, 2456, 2529, 2532, 2550, 2583, 2608, 2653, 2724, 2782, 2851, 2977, 2987, 3035, 3038, 3040, 3047, 3048, 3057, 3115, 3267, 3470, 3492, 3569, 3570,

3590, 3783, 3907, 4032, 4034, 4475, 4630, 4706, 4799, 4820
Conflit conjugal 2757, 2856
Conflit israélo-arabe 4495
Conflits de générations 2675
Conflits frontaliers 611, 3042
Conflits interethniques 395, 447, 712, 2511, 2610, 2827, 3047, 3048, 3088, 3104, 4082, 4603, 4741, 4761
Conflits internationaux 793
Conflits linguistiques 1759
Conflits politiques 373, 535, 816, 2491, 3023, 3093, 4413
Conflits régionaux 254, 4457
Conflits religieux 383, 593, 611, 1361, 2779, 3040, 3042, 3230, 3697, 4441, 4476
Conflits sociaux 2191, 3001, 3176
Confréries 2182, 2485, 2628, 4622
Confucianisme 79, 2099, 2574, 2970, 3136-3138, 3155, 3518
Congrégations 640, 3230, 3443, 3461, 3464, 3623, 4441
Congrès National Africain 77, 359, 2523
Conjoncture démographique 559, 2162, 2163, 2175, 2178, 2180, 2184, 2825, 4031, 4725
Connaissance 53, 99, 156, 160, 173, 182, 239, 243, 261, 275, 305, 329, 396, 407, 476, 691, 996, 1226, 1609, 1743, 2201, 2232, 2297, 2308, 2309, 2370, 2539, 2598, 2633, 2686, 2726, 2804, 2937, 2949, 2990, 3170, 3172, 3252, 3346, 3621, 3627, 3659, 3668, 3669, 3675-3677, 3728, 3730, 3739, 3753, 4275, 4438, 4548, 4549, 4612, 4620, 4675, 4696, 4703
voir aussi: Anthropologie de la connaissance, Sociologie de la connaissance
Connaissance indigène 1513, 2094, 2098, 2370, 2432, 2447, 2733, 2806, 2828, 2843, 2990, 3015, 3566, 3655, 3757, 3786, 3815, 4129, 4620, 4637, 4658, 4693, 4780, 4820, 4910
Connaissance sociale 2583, 3784
Consanguinité 2748
Conscience 173, 186, 243, 303, 660, 1739, 1876, 2840, 3079, 3143, 3149, 3291, 3481, 3494, 3499, 3691, 3728, 3761, 3821, 3833, 4328, 4450, 4668
Conscience collective 3074
Conscience de soi 3103, 3653, 4484, 4580
Conscience nationale 3480, 3653, 4484
Conscience politique 2795, 3597
Conseil de l'Europe 972
Consensus 2724, 2851, 3544, 4824
Conservateurs 754

Conservation de la faune 2412, 4784
Conservation de la nature 1714, 2067, 2083,
    2222, 3056, 3075, 4781, 4784, 4791, 4800
Conservation des sols 2276, 2319, 4792
Conservatisme 754
Consommateurs 2189, 2390, 4388, 4610,
    4618, 4794
Consommation 175, 1407, 2323, 2324, 2327,
    2328, 2390, 2401, 2450, 2462, 2923,
    2946, 2948, 2963, 3256, 3725, 4116, 4131,
    4382, 4389, 4391, 4394, 4397, 4440, 4809
Consommation alimentaire 1556, 2277, 3678,
    4387, 4810
Consommation de masse 2324, 4602
Consonnes 1858, 1922, 1989, 1991, 2058
Constitution 2511, 2523, 2540, 3036, 3059,
    4253, 4629, 4643
Constitution physique 1545, 1610
Constitutionalisme 815, 4631
Construction de l'État 228, 470, 611, 685, 921,
    993, 2282, 2527, 2567, 2575, 3042, 4352
Construction nationale 2523, 3020, 3723,
    4352, 4418, 4456, 4481, 4494, 4600
Construction navale 1395
Construction sociale 168, 1505, 2326, 2470,
    2490, 2609, 2674, 2796, 2852, 2854,
    3139, 4483
Constructivisme 56, 168, 207, 244, 3139,
    3708, 3739, 4289, 4412
Consulats 658, 721
Consultation mixte 2113
Consumer culture 2322, 2326, 2462
Contact entre les cultures 228, 326, 391, 447,
    531, 532, 553, 554, 583, 585, 593, 611,
    625, 627, 637, 641, 643, 665, 673, 677,
    696, 714, 720, 738, 742, 747, 770, 786,
    798, 808, 810, 916, 991, 1015, 1039,
    1343, 1362, 1733, 1757, 1809, 1871,
    1985, 2016, 2334, 2370, 2477, 2497,
    2563, 2608, 2990, 3042, 3044, 3079,
    3097, 3137, 3230, 3268, 3533, 3576,
    3612, 3624, 3625, 3743, 3829, 3918,
    3925, 3926, 3965, 4026, 4115, 4150, 4227,
    4265, 4405, 4408, 4430, 4441, 4516,
    4590, 4597, 4620
Contact linguistique 1757, 1759, 1789, 1791,
    1792, 1794, 1795, 1804, 1806, 1808,
    1810, 1815, 1849, 1851, 1877, 1915,
    1932, 1985, 1999, 2021, 2056
Contes 3588, 3738, 3972, 3984, 3987, 3988,
    4005, 4028, 4032, 4034, 4087, 4147,
    4153, 4215, 4234
Contes de fées 141, 3686, 3990, 3998, 4016,
    4017

Contes populaires 229, 289, 1788, 3116, 3979,
    3983, 3990, 3991, 3993, 3994, 3997,
    3998, 4002, 4006, 4010, 4015, 4016,
    4018-4020, 4022, 4026, 4032, 4033, 4243,
    4372
Contestation politique 2483, 3969
Conteurs 3995, 4016
Continuité culturelle 487, 1298, 3690, 4414,
    4507
Contraception 2640, 2695, 2710, 2717, 2723,
    2857, 2869, 2889, 2892, 2893, 2903,
    2905, 3076, 3810, 4869, 4889, 4901
Contrats 2983
Contre-culture 3619
Contremaîtres 2955
Contrôle de pollution 2210
Contrôle politique 484
Conventions des Nations Unies 4636, 4658,
    4722
Convergence 1791, 4400
Conversion religieuse 3230, 3264, 3484, 3647,
    3887, 4441
Coopération 172, 2093, 2285, 2352, 4393,
    4660
Coopération internationale 29, 153, 2289,
    4666, 4874, 4933
Coopération régionale 3169, 4721
Coopération technique 4734, 4737
Coopératives 2440, 4609
Coopératives de pêche 2440
Coquillages 1097, 1362, 1382, 1420
Coran 3120, 3330, 3333, 3338, 3344, 3346,
    3351, 3355, 3358, 3362, 3365, 3802, 4080
Coréen 1962
Corps humain 174, 310, 433, 760, 769, 1448-
    1450, 1455, 1457, 1514, 1531, 1541,
    1542, 1547, 1549, 1555, 1556, 1560,
    1563, 1564, 1569, 1581, 1588, 1777,
    2374, 2381, 2676, 2719, 2727, 2780,
    2791, 2810, 2827, 2920-2926, 2929, 2930,
    2932, 2932-2935, 2939-2942, 2944, 2947,
    2949, 2952, 2954-2959, 2961, 2962, 3104,
    3225, 3653, 3714, 3760, 3777, 3779,
    3817, 3929, 4110, 4239, 4297, 4312, 4348,
    4484, 4510, 4560, 4872
    voir aussi: Anthropologie du corps,
    Organes
Correction politique 2525
Corrélation 283, 1449, 1457, 1481, 1542,
    2123, 2634, 2687, 2935, 3028, 3142, 3780
Correll family 2265, 2730
Correspondance 110, 122, 334, 600, 721,
    1926, 2259, 2987, 3304, 3403, 3799,
    3945, 4178, 4372

Corruption 2258, 2278, 2513, 2555, 2659, 2971
Corruption politique 2558
Cortés, Hernán 802
Cosmogonie 3124, 3236, 3350, 3711
Cosmologie 105, 214, 299, 588, 652, 828, 852, 1036, 1320, 1837, 2069, 2099, 2544, 2551, 2602, 2665, 3052, 3111, 3128, 3131, 3135, 3155, 3168, 3231, 3400, 3510, 3605, 3650, 3653, 3657, 3659, 3672, 3680, 3730, 3752, 3764, 4035, 4098, 4397, 4484
Cosmopolitisme 777, 2182, 4622
Costume 991, 2928, 2936, 2946, 2948, 2951, 2957, 4116, 4164
Costumes traditionnels 2951, 3678
Côtes 251, 2429
  voir aussi: Littoraux
Coton 727, 2270, 4912
Couceiro, Henrique Mitchel Paiva 754
Couleur 1912, 3598, 3728, 3840
Coup d'État 4533
Cour 2683
Cour Suprême 2511, 2997, 4643
Cours d'eau 721, 806, 893, 942, 957, 1597, 2070, 2079, 2086, 2101, 2110, 2274, 2289, 2678, 3536, 3682, 4775
Courses 2322
Coût 2226, 3011, 4804
Coût de la distribution 861
Coût d'opportunité 2433
Coûts de la vie 2455
Coûts de main d'œuvre 2279
Coûts de production 2305
Coûts de transaction 2376
Coûts sociaux 4594, 4662
Coutume mortuaire 383, 1289, 1304, 2779, 2781, 2794, 2929
  voir aussi: Pratique mortuaire antique, Rites funéraires
Coutumes 127, 147, 262, 651, 756, 760, 790, 809, 1323, 2149, 2291, 2374, 2472, 2474, 2579, 2613, 2647, 2649, 2684, 2720, 2738, 2785, 2789, 2838, 2942, 2992, 3065, 3109, 3512, 3536, 3678, 3694, 3807, 4358, 4369, 4373, 4376, 4403, 4496, 4579
  voir aussi: Coutumes liées à la naissance, Coutumes matrimoniales
Coutumes liées à la naissance 2700
Coutumes matrimoniales 2734, 4011
Craniologie 899, 1458, 1460-1462, 1464-1466, 1509, 1524
Craniométrie 628, 1460, 1462, 1463
Création artistique 1033

Création d'emplois 4723
Créativité 1033, 3170, 3255, 3354, 3731, 3841, 3886, 3929, 3958, 3965, 4039, 4099, 4111, 4123, 4126, 4133, 4184, 4265, 4465, 4593, 4610
Crédit 4851, 4897, 4911
  voir aussi: Microfinancement
Crédit rural 288, 4671, 4855
Cree 1981, 3545
Crémation 147, 1323, 3225
Créole 252, 821, 1791, 2013, 2621, 2886, 3980, 4452
Créolisation 2157, 2312, 3061, 3981
Crime 599, 970, 2738, 2785, 3005, 3006, 4280
Crime violent 4280
Crimes de guerre 970
Criminalité 3005
Criminologie 3005
Crise économique 2221, 2284, 2318, 3884, 4608, 4836, 4875
Crise financière 2258, 2268, 2305, 2314, 4663
Crise politique 4152, 4618, 4794
Crises culturelles 867, 2691, 3543
Crispina, Julia 486
Critique 180, 230, 266, 514, 1723, 1735, 1736, 1780, 2570, 2909, 2955, 3229, 3238, 3444
Critique littéraire 89, 236, 650, 2533, 2955, 3073, 3405, 3911, 3996, 4036, 4053, 4083, 4086, 4147, 4149, 4157, 4175, 4182, 4191, 4196, 4200, 4201, 4217, 4220, 4222, 4287, 4563
Croissance démographique 2127, 4941
Croissance économique 4608, 4618, 4677, 4682, 4705, 4707, 4738, 4794, 4847, 4863, 4886, 4939
Croissance endogène 4609
Croissance urbaine 2216, 2219, 2222, 4941
Croyance 143, 191, 199, 468, 487, 544, 790, 804, 828, 1308, 1320, 1586, 1863, 2727, 2791, 2808, 2823, 2828, 3006, 3015, 3016, 3135, 3148, 3153, 3156, 3225, 3300, 3318, 3325, 3334, 3356, 3359, 3382, 3406, 3440, 3465, 3479, 3483, 3485, 3509, 3536, 3553, 3557, 3589, 3591, 3594, 3602, 3616, 3620, 3622, 3654, 3681, 3690, 3736, 3739, 3769, 3787, 3822, 3824, 3830, 4535
Croyances liées à l'alimentation 4378, 4386, 4754
Croyances médicales 313, 3811, 4397
Croyances populaires 1768, 3535, 3678, 3686, 3694
Croyances religieuses 22, 142, 143, 168, 1489, 2791, 2816, 2945, 3131, 3134, 3139, 3140, 3160, 3194, 3230, 3269, 3316,

3325, 3330, 3338, 3342, 3446, 3464,
3466, 3467, 3472, 3478, 3488, 3490,
3492-3494, 3501, 3515, 3529, 3542, 3555,
3563, 3599, 3621, 3623, 3631, 3713,
3734, 4441
Cueillette 371, 896, 2428, 2429
Cuivre 358, 908, 912, 1397, 2226
Culpabilité 4526
Culte 105, 166, 560, 640, 3211, 3231, 3270,
3299, 3338, 3387, 3412, 3443, 3444,
3480, 3504, 3548, 3649, 4362, 4428
Culte de personalité 3262
Culte des ancêtres 804, 3594
Culte des morts 2929
Culte des saints 3240
Culte du cargo 3512
Cultes 105, 521, 1040, 2321, 2345, 3175,
3217, 3231, 3284, 3347, 3496, 3519-3521,
3528, 3534, 3535, 3554, 3562, 3563,
3578, 3579, 3591, 3601, 3611, 3715, 3822,
4386
Culture 31, 52, 88, 98, 115, 138, 159, 196,
210, 213, 217, 235, 240, 244, 262, 268,
274, 299, 373, 397, 433, 543, 572, 597,
712, 716, 729, 751, 851, 959, 1745, 1758,
1798, 1800, 1817, 1821, 1824, 1971,
2005, 2064, 2070, 2080, 2114, 2115, 2164,
2193, 2207, 2327, 2482, 2503, 2525,
2592, 2601, 2643, 2694, 2823, 2859,
2874, 2876, 2908, 2922, 2940, 2953,
2955, 2958, 2992, 3026, 3035, 3047,
3052, 3063, 3189, 3226, 3398, 3401,
3410, 3512, 3543, 3545, 3561, 3662,
3663, 3675, 3702, 3728, 3758, 3760,
3761, 3782, 3960, 4014, 4102, 4110, 4120,
4143, 4193, 4359, 4367, 4371, 4379,
4429, 4432, 4452, 4467, 4468, 4478,
4487, 4491, 4514, 4569, 4585, 4593,
4603, 4634, 4653, 4673, 4729, 4761,
4804, 4820, 4864
voir aussi: Accès à la culture, Différence
culturelle, Diversité des cultures,
Économie de la culture, Sociologie de la
culture, Subculture, Survivance culturelle
Culture ancienne 356, 617, 1373, 1437, 3991
Culture commerciale 2207, 4689
Culture de jeunes 2326
Culture d'entreprise 380
Culture dominante 3077, 4421
Culture folklorique 2243, 2482, 2607, 3554,
3678, 3684, 3918, 3970
Culture indigène 1787, 1970, 3071, 3107,
3891, 3911, 3981, 4196, 4201, 4293, 4295,
4463, 4617, 4651
Culture juridique 2400, 2968, 3016

Culture locale 303, 2291, 2601, 2713, 3181,
3186, 3531, 3532, 3727, 3886, 4311, 4454,
4664
Culture matérielle 85, 175, 178, 284, 314, 321,
343, 346, 350, 351, 379, 387, 505, 610,
714, 720, 809, 844, 853, 855, 871, 874,
885, 909, 926, 967, 1039, 1040, 1071,
1098, 1248, 1300, 1322, 1336, 1361,
1362, 1374, 1377, 1383, 1385, 1410,
1413, 1418, 1421, 1424, 1426, 1427,
1431, 1432, 1434-1436, 1438, 1439, 1445,
1526, 1608, 2208, 2236, 2237, 2252,
2323, 2325, 2387, 2604, 2632, 2692,
2766, 2923, 2948, 3034, 3256, 3440,
3697, 3712, 3773, 3843, 3905, 4091,
4109, 4118, 4125, 4131, 4133, 4138, 4241,
4250, 4256, 4853
Culture musicale 3926
Culture nationale 433, 2249, 3701, 3708,
3886, 4343, 4481
Culture organisationnelle 255, 2369, 2468,
4400
Culture paysanne 17, 2371, 3825
Culture politique 668, 2392, 2496, 2529,
2556, 3969, 4435, 4938
Culture populaire 171, 188, 576, 668, 1774,
1777, 2072, 2556, 2934, 3573, 3631,
3699, 3725, 3880, 3908, 3909, 3918,
3943, 3961, 3990, 4038, 4119, 4121, 4122,
4143, 4146, 4240, 4303, 4373, 4378,
4380, 4392, 4464, 4754
Culture traditionnelle 152, 487, 2198, 2364,
2371, 2473, 2481, 2834, 3551, 3555,
3736, 3742, 3751, 3818, 3976, 4011, 4046,
4113, 4385, 4406, 4432, 4535, 4573, 4583
Cultures agricoles 2261, 2304, 4825
Curriculum 3376, 4556
Cybernétique 301, 4100
Cycle de vie 565, 676, 1407, 2697, 2761,
2768, 2769, 2771, 2776, 2803, 2845,
2862, 2864, 3269, 3678, 3684
Cyprian [Saint] 473, 3411
Dagari 2512, 4001
Dago, Ousmane Ndiaye 3714
Dalit 3082
Dani 2629, 2714
Danse 166, 2291, 2838, 2943, 3513, 3585,
3649, 3867, 3868, 3871, 3879, 3886,
3890, 3892, 3906, 3933, 3939, 3949,
3960, 3967, 4059, 4428
voir aussi: Anthropologie de la danse
Danses folkloriques 3890, 3908
Danses traditionnelles 3867, 3890
Dante, Alighieri 3728
Dar'ī, Moses 3429

Darwich, Mahmoud 4062
Darwin, Charles 1517
Darwinisme 1529, 1538
Dasan 3079, 3743
Datation 274, 445, 509, 519, 826, 839, 849,
  868, 906, 935, 1053, 1376, 1382, 3249,
  3442
Datation archéologique 34, 523, 819, 839,
  869, 902, 948, 951, 987, 1130, 1290, 1291,
  1316, 1378, 1422
Dayak 1067, 4320, 4598
Deane, Seamus 3961
Debī, Āśāpūrnā 2788, 4189
Déboisement 2083, 2430, 4618, 4771, 4772,
  4787, 4794, 4800, 4804
Début de l'époque moderne 534, 561, 563,
  606, 625, 738, 2986, 3532
Décadence 3909
Décentralisation 2210, 2219, 2288, 4612,
  4616, 4671, 4710, 4874, 4882, 4907, 4932
Déchets 2114
Déclin économique 4812
Décolonisation 611, 702, 753, 765, 784, 2989,
  3042, 4171
Déconstruction 2092
Découvert archéologique 322, 332, 448, 469,
  872, 904, 925, 944, 952, 959, 961, 1014,
  1016, 1034, 1080, 1107, 1115, 1117, 1119,
  1126, 1133, 1138, 1146, 1161, 1162, 1171,
  1178, 1182, 1195, 1199-1201, 1204, 1205,
  1207, 1208, 1210, 1216, 1218, 1220,
  1250, 1253, 1259, 1260, 1272, 1279,
  1306, 1307, 1312, 1316, 1317, 1332,
  1365, 1372, 1380, 1393, 1401, 1412,
  1414, 1417, 1422, 1443, 1530, 2378, 3604
Découvertes scientifiques 2310
Déesse 105, 1040, 1078, 1334, 2324, 3231,
  3270, 3284, 3311, 3524
Defaut du marché 4894
Déformation 1663
Déformations congénitales 1663
Dégâts 1030
Dégradation de l'environnement 833, 1043,
  2096, 2099, 2102, 2111, 2113, 2434, 2448,
  3155, 4617, 4651, 4691, 4772, 4773,
  4789, 4793, 4799
Dégradation du sol 2319, 4804
Déités 105, 1040, 1072, 1941, 3150, 3177,
  3231, 3270, 3273, 3281, 3284, 3298,
  3302, 3535, 3717
Délinquance 2223
Demande 2141
Démocratie 510, 2210, 2288, 2487, 2489,
  2496, 2505, 2536, 2548, 2559, 2570,

  2627, 2834, 3057, 4238, 4249, 4406,
  4588, 4616, 4640, 4662, 4881, 4882, 4938
Démocratie libérale 4778
Démocratie représentative 4929
Démocratisation 95, 234, 2518, 2548, 4588,
  4672, 4679, 4682
Démographie 246, 295, 646, 684, 757, 776,
  838, 1488, 1522, 1558, 1625, 2105, 2120,
  2126, 2127, 2130, 2133, 2135, 2144,
  2147, 2155, 2380, 2406, 2540, 2634,
  2637, 2655, 2662, 2710, 2742, 2743,
  2749, 2752, 2768, 2770, 2876, 3615,
  3704, 3739, 4431, 4479, 4736, 4840, 4859
  voir aussi: Paléodémographie
Démographie historique 246, 866, 2122, 2131,
  2135, 2147, 2150
Densité de population 1687, 1705, 2148, 2271
Dentisterie 1470
Dentition 898, 1461, 1464, 1467, 1468, 1471-
  1476, 1478, 1480-1485, 1590
Dents 460, 1280, 1461, 1468, 1469, 1471-
  1473, 1475-1482, 1485, 1590
Déontologie 24, 135, 148, 258, 416, 417, 425
Dépendance 1591, 2322
  voir aussi: Toxicomanie
Dépenses de ménage 4353
Dépeuplement 1686, 2151, 2306, 3797
Déplacement 2159, 2180
Dépositaire d'enjeux 2469, 4786
Depression 4518, 4546
Déréglementation 1786, 4671, 4881
Dermatoglyphes 1454, 1455
Désastres 2119, 2148, 2549, 3563, 3976,
  4719, 4816, 4824
  voir aussi: Catastrophes naturelles
Désert 1211, 1335, 1366, 2102, 2473, 2609,
  3658, 4046, 4798
Désindustrialisation 2355
Dessin 581, 832, 3868, 4098, 4528, 4591
Dessins humoristiques 4100
Desta, Makonnen 3046
Déterminants 2077, 2140
Déterminisme 4513
Déterminisme social 159, 217
Dette 2336, 3344
Deuil 1294, 2787, 2793, 3967
Deuxième guerre mondiale 357, 658, 769,
  2944, 3005
Dévaluation 2268
Développement 137, 267, 685, 770, 2111,
  4300, 4329, 4340, 4596, 4682, 4692,
  4712, 4727, 4729, 4732, 4768, 4799,
  4829, 4839, 4855, 4856, 4859
Développement agricole 830, 2267, 2274,
  2280, 2300, 2315, 4618, 4692, 4694,

4700, 4701, 4743, 4794, 4798, 4802, 4919
voir aussi: Révolution verte
Développement capitaliste 2337
Développement cognitif 1547, 4506, 4507
Développement culturel 556, 572, 881, 3380, 4481
Développement de l'éducation 4558, 4750, 4755
Développement de l'enfant 1405, 1460, 1469, 1470, 1540, 1550-1554, 1557, 1559, 1569, 1576, 1790, 1936, 2698, 2715, 2775, 3832, 4378, 4506, 4542, 4754
Développement des collectivités 32, 2210, 4709, 4723, 4726, 4733, 4741, 4795, 4832, 4833, 4866, 4868, 4873, 4915, 4929, 4931
Développement durable 2255, 2290, 4618, 4623, 4648, 4658, 4666, 4672, 4682, 4687, 4694, 4697, 4780, 4781, 4785, 4788, 4789, 4794, 4795, 4799-4802, 4804, 4833, 4842, 4883, 4922, 4930, 4933, 4939
Développement économique 59, 833, 1573, 2081, 2128, 2222, 2292, 2307, 2308, 2337, 2391, 2420, 2424, 2427, 2630, 2828, 2978, 2984, 3003, 4606, 4615, 4621, 4632, 4670, 4678, 4679, 4689, 4690, 4694, 4697, 4699, 4702, 4703, 4720, 4745, 4769, 4775, 4804, 4839, 4840, 4842, 4863, 4908, 4912, 4917
Développement ethnique 1361, 3697
Développement forestier 2808, 2828
Développement humain 186, 894, 914, 1470, 1496, 1518, 1545-1547, 1550, 1552, 1553, 1555, 1557, 1562, 1564, 1571, 1573, 1574, 1578, 1579, 1590, 1592, 2715, 2860, 3086, 3149, 4575, 4621, 4672, 4711, 4721, 4738, 4747, 4756, 4789
Développement industriel 1829
Développement intégré 4788, 4915
Développement politique 633, 993, 2486, 2984, 3008, 4615, 4670, 4769
Développement régional 4614, 4664, 4734, 4753, 4755
Développement rural 288, 2062, 2318, 2396, 2422, 4635, 4696, 4701, 4781, 4796, 4820, 4833, 4855, 4905, 4907, 4910, 4912-4926
Développement social 1565, 2475, 2589, 2630, 3035, 4664, 4795, 4840, 4857, 4894
Développement socioéconomique 2287, 2620, 2846, 2972, 2978, 3028, 4294, 4668, 4707, 4722, 4726, 4755, 4789, 4797, 4831, 4840, 4852, 4857, 4863, 4886, 4903

Développement urbain 494, 1089, 2210, 2212, 2219, 2222, 4759, 4786, 4806, 4838, 4927, 4928, 4932-4935, 4938, 4939, 4941
Déviance 2912
Devinettes 1788, 4018
Dévolution 4750
Diabète 1560, 3836
Diable 2875, 3065, 3578
Dialectes 1732, 1795, 1814, 1854, 1873, 1874, 1906, 1911, 1915, 1917, 1922-1924, 1954, 1973, 1981, 1989, 1991-1993, 1999, 2019, 2024, 2025, 2037, 2040, 2055-2057, 4032, 4446
Dialectes créoles 252, 1724, 1749, 1757, 1789, 1791, 2011-2017, 4170
Dialectes pidgin 252, 1749, 1757, 1789, 2011-2018
Dialectique 79, 280, 985, 1451, 2198, 2334, 2428, 2450, 2591, 2790, 2858, 3178, 4068, 4517, 4519, 4685
Dialectologie 1915, 1917, 1944, 1946, 1992
Dialogue 66, 194, 420, 3000, 4058
Diana [Princess of Wales] 3693
Diaspora 184, 253, 538, 764, 830, 1773, 2125, 2157, 2161, 2170, 2172, 2173, 2182, 2408, 3061, 3077, 3081, 3083, 3401, 3616, 3708, 3960, 4410, 4417, 4421, 4427, 4455, 4468, 4622, 4650
Díaz del Castillo, Bernal 4245
Dictature 3891
Dictionnaires 64, 65, 67, 68, 73, 75, 540, 570, 1769, 1770, 1778, 1779, 2055, 3545, 4176
Dieterlen, Germaine 9, 108
Dieu, Michel 113, 1802
Dieux 521, 1014, 1025, 1051, 1093, 1755, 1837, 1863, 1941, 2439, 2532, 3111, 3115, 3133, 3150, 3151, 3170, 3234, 3275, 3276, 3283, 3290, 3294, 3295, 3302, 3308, 3359, 3382, 3396, 3432, 3465, 3466, 3499, 3513, 3519, 3528, 3535, 3537, 3542, 3549, 3590, 3598, 3601, 3837, 4095
Différence 240, 247, 397, 2596, 3199, 4436, 4471, 4486
Différence culturelle 147, 215, 269, 663, 787, 1323, 1766, 1796, 1925, 2699, 2853, 3055, 3112, 3397, 3613, 3653, 4395, 4484, 4494, 4603, 4625, 4761
Différence d'âge 1283, 2594, 4748
Différences de generations 3074
Différenciation de classes 4748
Différenciation économique 2426
Différenciation raciale 1531
Différenciation sexuelle 1684, 2831

Différenciation sexuelle (culturelle) 105, 1283, 1325, 1478, 1506, 1508, 1509, 1568, 1588, 1643, 1695, 1732, 1775, 1882, 2163, 2350, 2453, 2594, 2667, 2765, 2768, 2812, 2825, 2840, 2846, 2872, 2941, 3231, 4612, 4840
Différenciation sociale 2397, 2407, 2426, 2980
Difficulté de langue 110, 3799
Difficultés économiques 2745
Diffusion de la culture 3097, 4115, 4119, 4597
Diffusion de l'information 4548
Diffusion des innovations 2588
Diffusion religieuse 3621
Diglossie 1959
Dimension de la famille 4835
Dimension de l'entreprise 4671
Dimension du groupe 1598, 1677
Dīn Khwārizmshāh, Jalāl al [Sultan] 446
Din Mozahheb, Nasir al 4223
Diocèse 544, 700, 2209, 3219, 3654
Diplomates 4712
Diplomatie 788, 2492, 4712
Directeurs 2368
Direction 724, 739, 2560, 2561, 2566, 2569, 2571, 2681, 3015, 4374, 4751, 4752, 4843
Direction de crise 2549
Direction de l'entreprise 2644, 2822, 4847
Direction politique 470, 2567, 2979, 3349
Dirigeant religieux 470, 700, 1336, 2567, 3014, 3185, 3219, 3312, 3330, 3341, 3368, 3387, 3394, 3427, 3461, 3473, 3475, 3476, 3484, 3485, 3490, 3496, 3500, 3506, 3508, 3532, 3623, 4078
Discipline intellectuelle 3, 4, 11, 24, 32, 41, 53, 115, 146, 152, 160, 165, 178, 180, 189, 190, 193, 198, 213, 215, 399, 996, 1004, 1226, 1914, 2679, 3142, 3288, 4745
Discours 10, 169, 196, 230, 235, 248, 253, 266, 268, 613, 629, 1735, 1736, 1749, 1762, 1780, 1796, 1809, 1846, 1978, 2045, 2076, 2212, 2510, 2531, 2548, 2746, 2786, 2834, 2867, 2877, 2895, 2907, 3000, 3005, 3040, 3063, 3077, 3091, 3481, 3671, 3733, 3762, 3958, 3974, 4000, 4067, 4143, 4200, 4202, 4239, 4276, 4406, 4421, 4534, 4634
Discrimination 2714, 4581
Discrimination raciale 2157, 2533, 3056, 3061, 3073, 3075, 4012
Discrimination sexuelle 4645, 4835
Disparités régionales 4021, 4338, 4609, 4680
Disponibilités alimentaires 861, 1556, 4807, 4810, 4811, 4813-4815, 4817, 4819, 4826
Dissensus 3544

Distribution 861, 2338, 2390, 4382, 4394
Divākara, Siddhasena 3212
Divergence 4400
Diversification 2207
Diversification de la production 4688
Diversification des cultures 2258, 2277, 2314
Diversité des cultures 3108, 4129, 4336, 4408, 4420, 4590, 4649
Divertissement 371, 2584, 3731, 3972, 3987, 4038, 4090, 4100, 4119, 4143, 4296, 4373
Divination 3038, 3217, 3569, 3778
Divinités 3335, 3478
Division du travail 2081, 2431, 2651, 2692, 2828, 4853
Divorce 606, 776, 2736, 2739, 2743, 2756, 2986, 3010, 3012, 3457, 3704, 4539
Doctrines religieuses 515, 568, 2931, 3330, 3413, 3440, 3442, 3451, 3485, 3515
Doctrines sociales 4102
Documentation 78, 438, 930, 1358, 3531, 4105, 4523
Documents 15, 76, 77, 80, 136, 320, 323, 355, 359, 369, 381, 581, 672, 707, 753, 801, 973, 2060, 2231, 3204, 3297, 3628, 4103, 4180, 4214
Dogme 3335
Dogon 2004, 3122, 3702
Dolgan 3101
Dollar 2533, 3073
Domestication animale 966, 2310
Domestication végétale 2266, 2304, 2435
Domination 4037
Dominici, Gaston 3005
Don 175, 2341, 2351, 2381, 2615, 2745, 2956, 4381
Dot 2738, 2744, 2745, 2785, 4780
Doubrovsky, Serge 4562
Dravidian 250, 497, 1750, 1891, 1892, 1894, 1897-1900, 1902, 1907, 1908, 1956, 2638, 3968
Droit 59, 158, 214, 342, 508, 568, 624, 1852, 2400, 2407, 2408, 2418, 2738, 2785, 2887, 2954, 2965, 2968, 2969, 2972-2974, 2978, 2980, 2982-2985, 2994, 2995, 3001, 3003, 3013, 3014, 3016, 3030, 3056, 3075, 3173, 3303, 3341, 3346, 3395, 3413, 3418, 3428, 3468, 3701, 4152, 4247, 4613, 4617, 4619, 4644, 4650, 4651, 4654, 4670, 4762, 4820, 4935
    voir aussi: Anthropologie du droit, Histoire du droit, Litige, Loi environnementale, Loi islamique, Sociologie du droit
Droit commercial 734
Droit commun 2656, 2837, 2972

Droit coutumier 268, 2416, 2417, 2425, 2972, 3015, 3017, 3018, 3020, 4418, 4659, 4722
Droit criminel 2988
Droit d'auteur 3895, 3921
Droit international 771, 2981, 4203, 4629
Droit naturel 3418
Droit traditionnel 158, 606, 2416, 2739, 2945, 2986, 3012, 3013, 3017, 3529, 4006
Droite 270, 2537
Droits 59, 2083, 2289, 2400, 2407, 2415, 2420, 2427, 2457, 2728, 2933, 2968, 2969, 2972, 2978, 2980, 2984, 2994, 2997, 3001, 3003, 3791, 4613, 4630, 4640, 4642, 4654, 4670, 4762
Droits de la femme 606, 680, 2656, 2728, 2765, 2837, 2863, 2986, 3551, 4780, 4850, 4856, 4860
Droits de l'enfant 2863, 4722
Droits de l'homme 134, 459, 562, 765, 1652, 2414, 2570, 2577, 2582, 2728, 2863, 2954, 3009, 3020, 3028, 3036, 3059, 3063, 3551, 3798, 4012, 4418, 4613, 4616, 4625, 4634, 4640, 4641, 4644, 4653, 4733, 4829, 4904
Droits de propriété 1448, 2284, 2289, 2376, 2404, 2408, 2416, 2920, 2954, 3017, 4617, 4636, 4650, 4651, 4780
Droits des animaux 1652
Droits des minorités 4627, 4656
Droits du citoyen 680, 4465, 4627, 4791
Droits indigènes 24, 2062, 2398, 2425, 2524, 3026, 3056, 3075, 3107, 4633, 4635, 4638, 4644-4647, 4658-4660, 4799
Droits individuels 4625
Dualisme 412, 2474, 2727, 2926, 3527, 4297, 4507
Dualisme culturel 3065
Dumont, Fernand 2232
Durabilité 1571, 2090, 2116, 2419, 3695, 4626, 4662, 4666, 4689, 4695, 4698, 4732, 4740, 4785, 4797, 4803, 4804, 4820, 4911, 4922, 4933, 4937, 4938
Dyade 1692
Dynamique 3756
Dynamique culturelle 3733, 3994, 4633
Dynamique de groupe 1639, 1655, 1692, 1713, 2606, 2882
Dynamique de la population 1597, 1822, 2132, 2646
Dynamique économique 4875
Dynamique sociale 247, 2105, 2132, 2595, 2596, 2646
Dynastie 477, 480, 481, 506, 902, 1341, 1401, 1437, 2528, 2566, 4095
Dynastie des Qing 2460, 2928, 4164

Dynastie des Tang 522, 4130
Eau 960, 2061, 2062, 2070, 2071, 2091, 2093, 2113, 2210, 2271, 2274, 2295, 3236, 3318, 3350, 3447, 3835, 4635
Eaux souterraines 525, 2112, 2376
Écart des salaires 4609
Échange 247, 255, 463, 868, 1143, 1363, 1372, 1768, 2266, 2331, 2337, 2341-2343, 2367, 2369, 2373, 2382, 2393, 2596, 2615, 2781, 2983, 3468, 3730, 4389, 4426, 4782, 4804
Échange d'information 3992
Échange matrimonial 2742
Échange social 2210, 2352, 2589
Échantillon 296, 1510
Échantillonnage 282, 296, 388, 1456, 2148, 4527
Échec 1675
Écoles 1387, 1554, 2783, 2869, 4550, 4560, 4603, 4757, 4761, 4869
Écologie 46, 646, 750, 1368, 1521, 1524, 1537, 1624, 1627, 1638, 1641, 1648, 1669, 1671, 1674, 1676, 1677, 1689, 1703, 1707, 1710, 1714, 1715, 1718, 1720, 2069, 2073, 2074, 2076, 2077, 2082, 2085, 2087, 2088, 2099, 2101, 2105, 2106, 2108, 2109, 2111, 2128, 2190, 2207, 2210, 2280, 2283, 2297, 2433, 2610, 2752, 2817, 3141, 3142, 3155, 3292, 3657, 3667, 4129, 4310, 4335, 4394, 4425, 4727, 4781, 4799, 4804, 4831, 4908
voir aussi: Paléoécologie
Écologie animale 46, 1510, 1597, 1599, 1600, 1611, 1623, 1624, 1627, 1638, 1641, 1642, 1646, 1648, 1657, 1658, 1661, 1664, 1671, 1674, 1676, 1677, 1682, 1683, 1689, 1690, 1698, 1700, 1710, 1720, 2109
Écologie culturelle 867, 1584
Écologie humaine 646, 685, 1303, 2061, 2072, 2098, 2109, 2190, 2217, 2224, 2283, 2296, 2435, 2594, 2752, 2834, 4406, 4666, 4782, 4797, 4923
Écologie sociale 1653, 1685, 1694, 1698, 1707
Écologisme 3619
Économétrie 172
Économie 679, 1571, 1768, 2136, 2202, 2285, 2331, 2342, 2353, 2392, 2620, 3063, 4339, 4634, 4668, 4683, 4804, 4827, 4859
Économie agricole 2285, 2316, 2424, 4704, 4807, 4888, 4940
Économie antique 356, 482, 488, 503, 517, 527, 617, 897, 2354, 2372, 2395
Économie capitaliste 2290

Économie de la culture 2345, 3175
Économie de la population 2143, 2673
Économie de la santé 4863
Économie de l'environnement 4666, 4787
Économie de marché 2318, 2364, 2447, 2782
Économie de subsistance 164, 371, 2181,
    2297, 2409, 2444, 2447, 2834, 3972, 3987
Économie du ménage 2142, 2644, 4808, 4821
Économie foncière 2427, 4805
Économie internationale 4614
Économie locale 4917
Économie mondiale 183, 2158, 2245, 2385,
    3650, 3801, 4614, 4633
Économie néoclassique 2342
Économie occulte 4621
Économie ouverte 2280
Économie politique 52, 215, 225, 539, 2202,
    2513, 2659, 2908, 4673, 4708
Économie politique internationale 183, 3801
Économie régionale 4614
Économie rurale 288, 2196, 2316, 2371, 2416,
    3017, 4291, 4906, 4916-4918, 4921, 4922,
    4925, 4940
Économie socialiste 2318
Économie tribale 2359
Économie urbaine 917, 1235
Économies de transition 2315, 2380, 4736
Économistes 218
Écosystèmes 1, 120, 2087, 2113, 2117, 2262,
    2290, 2300, 2358, 2429, 4693, 4780, 4820
Écriture 37, 55, 107, 114, 122, 312, 334, 405,
    433, 442, 453, 545, 600, 607, 628, 671,
    742, 805, 1330, 1338, 1340, 1342, 1347,
    1348, 1354, 1356, 1419, 1722, 1740,
    1787, 1841, 1950, 1972, 1974, 2005,
    2019, 2092, 2562, 2598, 2624, 2641,
    2821, 2832, 2849, 3005, 3049, 3170,
    3206, 3212, 3255, 3305, 3627, 3745,
    3802, 3952, 3973, 3980, 4004, 4009,
    4030, 4054, 4055, 4060, 4077, 4089,
    4147, 4158, 4159, 4165, 4166, 4171,
    4174, 4177, 4178, 4180, 4181, 4190,
    4194, 4197, 4202, 4205, 4208, 4213,
    4215, 4219, 4228, 4229, 4231, 4241,
    4245, 4246, 4248, 4250, 4255, 4257,
    4259, 4268, 4269, 4275, 4278, 4284,
    4288, 4548, 4562, 4564, 4566, 4567
Écriture ancienne 1331, 1349, 2000
Écriture hiéroglyphique 4275
Écrivains 471, 578, 2092, 2533, 2813, 2987,
    3073, 3113, 3184, 3205, 3255, 3291, 3429,
    3500, 3980, 4042, 4057, 4062, 4071,
    4078, 4079, 4081, 4151, 4158-4160, 4163,
    4165, 4169, 4179, 4184, 4187, 4188,
    4200, 4204, 4210, 4213, 4215, 4216,
    4225, 4227, 4230, 4236, 4238, 4263,
    4273, 4274, 4281, 4282, 4285, 4288,
    4289, 4322, 4581
    voir aussi: Romancier
Édition 4032, 4567
Edo 1489, 3176, 3181, 3186, 3204, 3531,
    3532, 3972, 3987
Éducation 7, 235, 326, 352, 645, 1475, 1554,
    1749, 1816, 1969, 2085, 2463, 2675,
    2715, 2863, 2917, 2931, 3163, 3474,
    3615, 3661, 3761, 3772, 4310, 4336,
    4378, 4551, 4555-4558, 4603, 4647, 4663,
    4682, 4722, 4749, 4750, 4752, 4754,
    4755, 4757, 4758, 4760, 4761, 4858
    voir aussi: Accès à l'éducation,
    Anthropologie de l'éducation,
    Enseignement agricole, Enseignement
    bilingue, Enseignement primaire,
    Enseignement professionnel,
    Enseignement supérieur, Histoire de
    l'éducation, Hygiène publique, Pédagogie
Éducation des femmes 4552, 4753
Éducation des minorités 3097, 4597
Éducation religieuse 86, 3215, 3471
Éducation sexuelle 2710, 2869, 2878, 2879,
    3788, 4869, 4877, 4878
Effets psychologiques 2890, 3044, 4538
Effets sur l'environnement 3759, 4776
Efficacité organisationnelle 2468
Efficacité-coût 3011, 4870
Égalité 1529, 2626, 4238, 4510, 4829
Égalité de chances 134, 4879
Égalité des sexes 2863
Égalité sociale 835, 2590
Egharevba, Jacob 4165
Église catholique 110, 122, 567, 600, 766,
    2760, 2861, 3051, 3246, 3634, 3799,
    4371, 4476
Eglise copte 502, 1861, 2899
Église et État 3186, 3287, 3610
Église méthodiste 3239, 3266, 3648
Église orthodox russe 2599, 3555, 3629, 4476
Église orthodoxe 3230, 3628, 3634, 4441
Église unaite 4476
Églises 81, 323, 700, 707, 1012, 1018, 1022,
    1026, 1038, 1046, 1070, 1075, 1080,
    1085, 1092, 1167, 1351, 1381, 2018, 2755,
    3152, 3219, 3241, 3256, 3260, 3591,
    3610, 3623, 3631, 3636, 3642, 3727,
    3822, 3856, 3915, 4131
Églises chrétiennes 3226, 3241, 4371
    voir aussi: Confessionellisme, Hutterite,
    Luthéranisme, Mennonites, Piétisme
Églises protestantes 3224
Ego 3508, 4540

Eisenstein, Sergei Mikhailovich 4068
Ejagham 2195
Élaboration d'une politique 2221, 2469, 3761, 4672, 4702, 4705, 4744, 4756, 4864
Élections 2505, 4058, 4415
Élections présidentielles 4618, 4794
Électricité 4671
Élevage 757, 2406, 2433, 2441, 2443, 2445, 2450
Élevage du bétail 101, 2437, 2438, 2690
Élevage du cheptel 2105, 2442, 2610, 2847, 4604, 4784
Élèves sortants 2223
Éleveurs de bestiaux 4038
Elias, Norbert 2790
Élite 247, 253, 465, 494, 795, 1797, 2299, 2370, 2495, 2521, 2535, 2596, 2600, 2850, 2990, 3523, 4299, 4620, 4700
Elliott, J.H. 3227
Émancipation 681, 693, 694, 991, 4336, 4581, 4596
Embu 2094, 2843
Émeutes 609, 2318, 3673
Émigrants 99
Émigration 2460, 4479
Émotion 38, 170, 998, 1561, 1629, 1672, 1855, 1864, 2346, 2931, 3174, 3275, 3276, 3360, 3449, 3653, 3795, 3910, 4060, 4283, 4484, 4509, 4512, 4518, 4526, 4529, 4531, 4532, 4535, 4538, 4541, 4562, 4846
    voir aussi: Amour, Depression
Empathie 2024
Empire 318, 366, 481, 501, 506, 541, 629, 641, 678, 716, 724, 729, 735, 773, 775, 814, 903, 933, 984, 1084, 1086, 1103, 1934, 2168, 2479, 2488, 2493, 2497, 2531, 2608, 2741, 2971, 3046, 3322, 3520, 3746, 3829, 4155, 4188, 4191, 4483
Empire britannique 694, 696, 702, 703, 710, 717, 762, 791, 792, 3755, 4215, 4336
Empire byzantin 529
Empire espagnol 730
Empire moghal 2528, 3414, 3461, 3484, 3502
Empire mongol 607, 4185
Empire ottoman 1301, 2479, 2494, 3120, 3236, 3327, 3350, 3351, 4070
Empire romain 454, 465, 468, 471, 498, 500, 513, 519, 524, 529, 593, 1029, 1090, 1234, 1236, 1302, 1358, 1367, 1418, 1419, 3406, 4346
Empire russe 2644
Empirisme 266, 275, 415, 2539, 3675

Emploi 1587, 2158, 2466, 4647, 4671, 4672, 4827, 4828, 4858, 4914, 4929
    voir aussi: Emploi des jeunes
Emploi des jeunes 4722
Employés 2468, 2955
Employés des services publics 2584, 4090
Employeurs 753, 2459
Emprunts 4911
Enchères 2346
Enculturation 4586
Encyclopédies 4219
Énergie 429, 1556, 1600, 1628, 1676, 2324, 3728, 4810
Énergie éolienne 4795
Enfance 1541, 2697, 2803, 2805, 4271, 4561
Enfants 557, 1327, 1427, 1460, 1466, 1475, 1540, 1541, 1554, 1561, 1565, 1568, 1572, 1576, 1588, 1592, 1783, 1790, 1936, 2085, 2119, 2138, 2463, 2502, 2633, 2639, 2645, 2648, 2698, 2703, 2708, 3278, 3572, 3574, 3800, 3930, 3982, 3990, 4004, 4244, 4306, 4310, 4433, 4519, 4521, 4586, 4826, 4879, 4884
    voir aussi: Petits enfants
Engrais 2265, 2303, 2730
Enquêtes 41, 190, 286, 458, 492, 885, 923, 936, 939, 940, 953-956, 1069, 1079, 1109, 1113, 1116, 1127, 1134, 1144, 1145, 1147-1151, 1153, 1159, 1163, 1175, 1196, 1197, 1202, 1214, 1215, 1222, 1247, 1249, 1260, 1264, 1269, 1277, 1278, 1313, 1316, 1436, 2124, 2129, 2141, 2285, 2430, 2518, 2620, 2654, 2704, 2726, 2791, 2799, 3112, 4420
Enquêtes sociales 3157
Enseignants 235, 3214, 3317, 3635, 4560
Enseignement 37, 57, 83, 110, 114, 116, 291, 3799, 3932, 4029, 4132, 4559, 4610
Enseignement agricole 4, 165, 4701, 4833
Enseignement bilingue 1969
Enseignement des langues 1975, 3095, 4553
Enseignement primaire 4554
Enseignement professionnel 4760
Enseignement religieux 560, 568, 640, 1349, 2000, 3136, 3168-3170, 3200, 3205, 3209, 3210, 3285, 3297, 3308, 3313, 3315, 3321, 3323, 3354, 3370, 3373, 3375, 3385, 3386, 3391, 3393, 3412, 3413, 3415, 3428, 3430, 3442-3444, 3447, 3453, 3471, 3476, 3481, 3494, 3496, 3504, 3506, 4284
Enseignement supérieur 4548, 4572, 4748
Enterrement 147, 258, 365, 475, 838, 869, 873, 874, 878, 970, 991, 1129, 1205, 1220, 1240, 1267, 1279, 1282, 1284-1287, 1291,

1293, 1296, 1298, 1300, 1301, 1304, 1307, 1308, 1311, 1312, 1317, 1318, 1320, 1321, 1323, 1325, 1327, 1328, 1464, 2494, 2604, 2783, 2794, 2799, 2801, 3135, 3604, 3689
Entre deux guerres 345, 2669, 2827, 3104
Entreprises 986, 2468, 2471, 2644, 4820
    voir aussi: Petites et moyennes entreprises
Entreprises agricoles 2277
Entreprises familiales 2644
Entreprises multinationales 4762
Entretiens 215, 235, 306, 313, 357, 407, 422, 424, 979, 1586, 2890, 3040, 3747, 3751, 3781, 3792, 3805, 3824, 4170, 4303, 4385, 4473, 4533, 4676
Environnement 301, 455, 759, 838, 858, 867, 882, 893, 913, 1190, 1524, 1533, 1562, 1571, 1574, 1587, 1638, 1648, 1656, 1658, 1674, 1710, 1711, 2061, 2065, 2077, 2087, 2095, 2097, 2099, 2105, 2108, 2110, 2111, 2190, 2210, 2213, 2218, 2224, 2225, 2276, 2283, 2404, 2443, 2687, 3068, 3155, 3712, 4294, 4300, 4335, 4545, 4645, 4716, 4717, 4727, 4731, 4735, 4763, 4768-4771, 4773, 4775, 4776, 4782, 4787, 4790, 4797, 4799, 4806, 4807, 4880, 4888, 4928
    voir aussi: Milieu de travail, Milieu rural, Milieu social, Milieu urbain, Transformation de l'environnement
Environnement humain 1, 2095, 2133, 2834, 4406
Environnement physique 2428
Environnementalisme 2069, 2074, 2076, 2190, 2276, 2311, 3619, 3657, 3686, 3975, 4611, 4612, 4799
Envois de fonds 2631, 4804
Épargne 2210, 4911
Épées 338, 3125
Épidémie 566, 3784, 4276
Épidémiologie 1489, 2988, 3770, 3772
Epigraphes 916
Epigraphie 461, 1136, 1319, 1344, 1358, 3179, 4268
Epilepsie 3777
Épistémologie 199, 203, 213, 219, 238, 242, 254, 260, 261, 275, 398, 407, 423, 542, 2037, 2539, 2804, 2975, 3182, 3208, 3381, 3388, 3669, 3670, 3675, 3677, 3725, 3730, 4198, 4457, 4519, 4530, 4548
Épopée 1081, 1088, 2624, 3110, 3115, 3274, 3290, 3293, 3295, 3302, 3305, 3863, 3865, 3867, 3885, 3945, 3967, 4025, 4027, 4215, 4253, 4349
Époque victorienne 4298

Épouses 2629, 2645, 2737, 2744, 2758, 2824, 3399
Époux 2868
Équilibre des forces 228, 612, 2488, 3925
Équipement agricole
    voir: Engrais
Équipement de recherche 963, 1001
Équipement électronique 313
Équitation 1383
Équité 2093, 2111, 2757, 2856, 4666, 4677, 4780, 4829, 4904
Ère des Meiji 501, 4266
Ergonomie 296
Ermites 905
Érosion du sol 687, 2079, 2106, 2254, 2265, 2412, 2730, 4766, 4803
Erotisme 502, 2899, 3714, 3929
Erreur 1
Eschatologie 3435, 3679
Esclavage 228, 323, 538, 554, 601, 680, 681, 687, 693, 707, 724, 774, 807, 2167, 2254, 2383, 2616, 2857, 3076, 3484, 3609, 4461
    voir aussi: Histoire de l'esclavage
Esclaves 528, 681, 692, 961, 2616, 2857, 3076
Espace 260, 291, 383, 599, 621, 691, 886, 886, 1066, 1598, 1621, 1691, 1773, 1880, 1973, 2092, 2187, 2211, 2459, 2509, 2594, 2779, 2801, 2855, 2907, 2947, 3156, 3625, 3650, 3659, 3660, 3681, 3689, 3713, 3756, 3838, 3842, 3845, 3942, 3961, 4086, 4113, 4262, 4342, 4356, 4364, 4498, 4548, 4580, 4611, 4749
    voir aussi: Analyse spatiale
Espace publique 373, 2502, 3572, 3850, 4715, 4930
Espace social 886, 2176, 2459, 2642, 3845
Espace urbain 466, 4749, 4927, 4930, 4938
Espacement des naissances 2129, 2704
Espagnols 743, 763, 2348, 4305
Espèce 1528, 1530, 1567, 1609, 1643, 1649, 1650, 1652, 1660, 1666, 1673, 1678, 1686, 1719, 1721, 1818, 2063, 2066, 2088, 2117, 2272, 3667, 3816, 4774
Espèce menacée 1613, 1712, 1714
Espérance de vie 2152, 2768, 4859
Esprit 634, 1520, 1547, 1751, 2800, 3207, 3299, 3431, 3441, 3480, 4469, 4525, 4530
Esprits 142, 767, 790, 1771, 2802, 3060, 3130, 3577, 3582, 3584, 3587, 3589, 3591, 3599, 3606, 3607, 3626, 3722, 3726, 3791, 3822, 4674
Esquivel, Laura 4242
Essai nucléaire 2576, 4617, 4651
Essence 2242

Esthétique 171, 253, 314, 368, 2571, 3136, 3256, 3660, 3773, 3844, 3850, 4071, 4091, 4109, 4111, 4118, 4125, 4131, 4133, 4261, 4469
Estimation 1468, 1477, 2433, 3792
Estime de soi 2962
Établissement du budget 4937
Établissements d'enseignement 26, 54, 93, 2783, 4550
Établissements humains 455, 483, 835, 843, 854, 869, 870, 907, 920, 936, 965, 994, 1130, 1155, 1183, 1205, 1240, 1319, 2095, 2103, 2104, 2164, 2168, 2178, 2184, 2195, 2225, 2276, 2474, 2512, 2590, 4001, 4024, 4031, 4666, 4759
Étain 908
Étapes 3888
État 456, 482, 517, 521, 921, 985, 993, 1372, 2273, 2274, 2354, 2417, 2422, 2450, 2456, 2487, 2491, 2516, 2527, 2543, 2553, 2559, 2565, 2568, 2583, 2591, 2806, 2828, 2926, 3005, 3018, 3057, 3085, 3523, 3530, 3568, 3755, 3850, 4297, 4300, 4624, 4642, 4673, 4679, 4768, 4778, 4806, 4929
  voir aussi: Chefs d'État, Église et État, Relations État-société
État fédéral 358
État socialiste 4477
État-nation 178, 777, 1426, 1562, 2523, 3730, 4417, 4544, 4624, 4655
États membres 3169, 4623
Éthique 40, 153, 158, 236, 239, 277, 395, 396, 415, 2074, 2099, 2381, 2469, 2705, 2728, 2881, 2925, 2930, 2945, 2954, 2956, 2970, 3000, 3002, 3138, 3155, 3174, 3529, 3576, 3750, 3912, 4077, 4185, 4245, 4444, 4556, 4804
  voir aussi: Bioéthique, Code déontologique médical, Déontologie
Ethnicité 10, 58, 146, 235, 253, 263, 376, 410, 467, 515, 554, 582, 689, 694, 695, 708, 812, 887, 1077, 1368, 1497, 1583, 1588, 1749, 1773, 1822, 1925, 2066, 2109, 2140, 2154, 2157, 2160, 2172, 2201, 2202, 2218, 2475, 2476, 2504, 2532, 2533, 2564, 2566, 2603, 2616, 2680, 2834, 2955, 3016, 3020, 3043, 3048, 3061, 3068, 3070, 3073, 3074, 3077, 3083, 3088, 3090, 3091, 3093, 3096, 3105, 3128, 3401, 3409, 3451, 3590, 3592, 3652, 4021, 4313, 4352, 4358, 4362, 4363, 4377, 4398, 4400-4421, 4424, 4426, 4431, 4433, 4434, 4447, 4450, 4453, 4463, 4468, 4475, 4479, 4485, 4488, 4492, 4498, 4504, 4528, 4587, 4590, 4591, 4603, 4639, 4653, 4657, 4720, 4761, 4798
Ethnoarchéologie 387, 555, 631, 720, 861, 939, 992, 998, 1033, 1281, 1415, 1446, 1760, 2236, 3845, 4377
Ethnobiologie 1832, 2080, 2088, 3662, 3667, 3747, 3753, 3785, 3786
Ethnobotanique 1722, 2066, 2084, 2117, 3742, 3747, 3757, 3785, 3833, 4636
Ethnocentrisme 134, 143, 167, 227, 1766, 4395
Ethnogenèse 631, 1760
Ethnographes 92, 128, 135, 141, 142, 145, 149, 172, 203, 237, 242, 264, 277, 293, 392, 393, 398, 416, 419, 423, 427, 3599, 4602
Ethnographie 12, 13, 15, 31, 33, 39, 45, 47, 48, 55, 72, 90-92, 101, 103, 105, 107, 121, 123, 128, 130, 133, 136, 137, 141, 145, 146, 148, 149, 158, 172, 173, 179, 191, 193, 194, 200, 202, 203, 211, 212, 216, 224, 225, 231, 236, 237, 239-243, 257, 264, 267, 277, 283, 284, 293, 308, 309, 319, 325, 326, 328, 334, 345, 351, 353, 365, 372, 373, 376, 378, 380, 385-388, 390-399, 403-411, 413, 417-421, 423, 425, 426, 428, 430-433, 439-442, 487, 539, 573, 574, 590, 597, 610, 628, 631, 783, 804, 874, 888, 936, 1088, 1324, 1520, 1530, 1554, 1745, 1760, 1775, 1782, 1825, 1833, 1924, 1988, 2066, 2067, 2075, 2098, 2102, 2123, 2125, 2145, 2146, 2230, 2243, 2256, 2321, 2323, 2334, 2391, 2394, 2458, 2475-2477, 2479, 2481, 2524, 2538, 2540, 2604, 2652, 2656, 2672, 2675, 2676, 2696, 2751, 2812, 2821, 2823, 2831, 2837, 2938, 2964, 2979, 2988, 2999, 3004, 3021, 3062, 3083, 3092, 3096, 3101, 3142, 3152, 3231, 3245, 3288, 3345, 3347, 3349, 3356, 3361, 3446, 3519, 3536, 3550, 3555, 3565, 3575, 3581, 3585, 3589, 3594, 3625, 3628, 3656, 3661, 3664, 3700, 3715, 3737, 3767, 3858, 3870, 3878, 3926, 3936, 3945, 3948, 3988, 4026, 4032, 4125, 4133, 4178, 4255, 4265, 4331, 4366, 4386, 4410-4412, 4436, 4469, 4473, 4488, 4495, 4517, 4543, 4572, 4573, 4579, 4582, 4586, 4611, 4612, 4623, 4643, 4646, 4648, 4649, 4658, 4785, 4791
Ethnographie historique 2052, 3595

Ethnohistoire 189, 214, 238, 555, 559, 607, 631, 657, 1369, 1760, 2162, 2256, 2547, 2627, 3057, 3515, 3585, 4183

Ethnolinguistique 631, 796, 1370, 1760, 1822, 1845, 1972-1975, 1977, 1978, 1980, 1982-1986, 3126, 3672, 3745, 3752

Ethnologie 8, 17, 20, 32, 54, 72, 78, 90, 91, 101, 103, 121, 131, 140, 146, 152, 160, 163, 166, 169, 173, 179, 197, 199, 204, 205, 223, 243, 269, 281, 331, 346, 348, 371, 372, 378, 380, 385, 386, 389, 394, 400, 401, 406, 408, 410, 412, 424, 427, 438, 645, 667, 722, 920, 950, 980, 1282, 1386, 1520, 1733, 1832, 2074, 2085, 2096, 2103, 2104, 2108, 2116, 2184, 2194, 2195, 2203, 2260, 2346, 2374, 2382, 2442, 2453, 2468, 2474, 2486, 2509, 2512, 2523, 2579, 2613, 2649, 2666, 2676, 2682, 2683, 2735, 2736, 2739, 2750, 2751, 2847, 2915, 2947, 2975, 3009, 3010, 3012, 3015, 3019, 3020, 3055, 3093, 3114, 3163, 3241, 3357, 3360, 3571, 3596, 3600, 3649, 3680, 3695, 3702, 3713, 3737, 3807, 3812, 3815, 3816, 3825, 3870, 3895, 3899, 3900, 3905, 3907, 3910, 3915, 3921, 3925, 3934, 3935, 3942, 3946, 3951, 3953, 3958, 3959, 3965, 4001, 4017, 4024, 4031, 4308-4310, 4319, 4325, 4326, 4334, 4335, 4344, 4345, 4361, 4382, 4384, 4400, 4413, 4416, 4418, 4424, 4428, 4430, 4454, 4465, 4485, 4493, 4498, 4557, 4586, 4600, 4664, 4732, 4809 *voir aussi:* Histoire de l'ethnologie

Ethnologie religieuse 3241

Ethnologues 8, 15, 32, 35, 100, 104, 136, 140, 197, 199, 281, 740

Ethnométhodologie 297, 435

Ethnomusicologie 166, 323, 707, 3081, 3357, 3649, 3719, 3871, 3895, 3897, 3899, 3905, 3910, 3912, 3914, 3915, 3917, 3919, 3921, 3923, 3925, 3929, 3933, 3934, 3940-3942, 3946, 3947, 3951-3953, 3955-3960, 3965, 4059, 4428, 4455, 4465

Ethnonymes 554, 1876, 2475, 3691

Ethnonymie 554

Ethnopsychologie 3512, 3729

Ethnosociologie 2114, 3970

Ethnozoologie 3744, 3786

Ethologie 1493, 1494, 1496, 1560, 2872, 4396

Étiologie 3124, 3770

Étiquetage 4388

Étoiles 3672, 3752

Étrangers 281, 4010

Études africaines 53, 116, 187, 558, 619, 695, 1748, 1821, 1988, 1990, 2003, 2064, 2347, 2494, 2499, 2508, 2584, 2819, 3226, 3835, 3908, 4012, 4090, 4126, 4160, 4175, 4193, 4548, 4640

Études asiatiques 27, 1746, 3364, 3646, 4458

Études culturelles 27, 117, 124, 149, 150, 177, 206, 244, 254, 284, 290, 316, 322, 330, 334, 341, 344, 360, 379, 382, 467, 474, 522, 527, 560, 576, 578, 579, 586, 603, 615, 620, 632, 640, 652, 653, 668, 708, 716, 729, 735, 751, 762, 769, 804, 811, 823, 878, 1012, 1015, 1032, 1055, 1067, 1076, 1086, 1096, 1316, 1331, 1333, 1336, 1339, 1395, 1423, 1433, 1527, 1774, 1783, 1805, 1819, 1862, 1865, 1871, 1945, 1950, 2047, 2078, 2090, 2092, 2100, 2113, 2117, 2176, 2234, 2241, 2260, 2330, 2384, 2395, 2436, 2440, 2451, 2467, 2476, 2484, 2492, 2496, 2501, 2526, 2556, 2580, 2592, 2600, 2622, 2632, 2641, 2658, 2685, 2695, 2716, 2733, 2759, 2760, 2762, 2805, 2817, 2848, 2857, 2861, 2866-2868, 2873, 2877, 2879, 2884, 2892, 2894, 2895, 2901, 2902, 2910, 2911, 2913, 2914, 2916, 2918, 2933, 2936, 2937, 2944, 2947, 2955, 2957, 2973, 2974, 2985, 3005, 3076, 3087, 3110, 3115, 3125, 3134, 3141, 3144, 3148, 3167, 3168, 3173, 3177, 3179, 3185, 3194-3198, 3203, 3206, 3209, 3214, 3225, 3254, 3268, 3271, 3273, 3284, 3293, 3296, 3312, 3315, 3317-3319, 3322, 3332, 3338, 3339, 3412, 3415, 3443, 3444, 3556, 3573, 3594, 3624, 3631, 3693, 3698-3700, 3702, 3707, 3717, 3796, 3810, 3831, 3839, 3852, 3869, 3874, 3885, 3890, 3891, 3906, 3909, 3943, 3954, 4007, 4025, 4028, 4061, 4064, 4076, 4086, 4093, 4115, 4154, 4155, 4167, 4170, 4177, 4178, 4194, 4203, 4207, 4227, 4228, 4231, 4233, 4238, 4246, 4247, 4261, 4267, 4280, 4303, 4333, 4364, 4365, 4380, 4427, 4434, 4438, 4446, 4452, 4457, 4468, 4470, 4483, 4491, 4499, 4500, 4548, 4561, 4563, 4570, 4612, 4631, 4637, 4641, 4729, 4758, 4771, 4878, 4891, 4898

Études d'aire 27, 39, 82, 184, 370, 559, 1342, 1941, 1942, 2099, 2162, 2612, 2677, 3087, 3150, 3155, 3692, 4268, 4506

Études de cas 98, 159, 217, 282, 352, 508, 910, 1568, 1786, 1897, 1904, 1909, 2115, 2164, 2189, 2213, 2244, 2292, 2308, 2309, 2312, 2402, 2441, 2446, 2455,

2503, 2504, 2527, 2859, 2874, 2876,
2995, 3163, 3579, 3782, 4339, 4353,
4472, 4497, 4545, 4588, 4645, 4683,
4692, 4698, 4703, 4706, 4716, 4719,
4730, 4731, 4740, 4743, 4752, 4756,
4769, 4783, 4788, 4849, 4871, 4879,
4912, 4916, 4924, 4926, 4928, 4937
Études de genre 2089, 2094, 2115, 2164,
2320, 2452, 2818, 2823, 2827, 2836,
2843, 2844, 2859, 3104, 3568, 4577,
4780, 4834, 4862
Études de la famille 2160, 2171, 2174, 2460,
2636, 2644, 2743, 2749, 2772, 3704
Études de marché 2326
Études de politique 2662
Études des femmes 2835, 4041
Études japonaises 330, 331, 337, 338, 347,
361, 362, 364, 374, 377
Études latino-américaines 214, 750, 763, 2082
Études orientales 6, 94, 934, 3002
Études post-soviétiques 319, 2964, 3409,
4402, 4440, 4468
Études régionales 27, 35, 53, 54, 61, 87, 104,
109, 124, 126, 129, 307, 321, 324, 332,
336, 350, 366, 447-449, 474, 477-479,
481, 482, 493, 495, 506, 518, 558, 566,
567, 595, 609, 630, 642, 661, 666, 678,
694, 712, 719, 741, 761, 780, 795, 801,
843, 847, 895, 897, 902, 906, 907, 925,
934, 962, 975, 976, 1006, 1019, 1049,
1056, 1063, 1072, 1076, 1081, 1083,
1084, 1089, 1097, 1102, 1104, 1249, 1284,
1301, 1308, 1316, 1328, 1332, 1334,
1335, 1394, 1410, 1411, 1428, 1731, 1746,
1748, 1800, 1805, 1821, 1835, 1851,
1853, 1857, 1893, 1913, 1914, 1917,
1931, 1932, 1938, 1939, 1950, 1966,
1989, 1993, 1995, 1996, 1999, 2019,
2023, 2059, 2061, 2064, 2086, 2097,
2125, 2151, 2155, 2159, 2161, 2178,
2180, 2197, 2238, 2246, 2248, 2252,
2261, 2263, 2271, 2278, 2283, 2289,
2290, 2295, 2299, 2306, 2339, 2351,
2354, 2356, 2357, 2366, 2367, 2389,
2405, 2409, 2429, 2439, 2447, 2464,
2490, 2497, 2499, 2504, 2506, 2508,
2521, 2534, 2546, 2558, 2559, 2561,
2574, 2581, 2610, 2614, 2616, 2624,
2629, 2640, 2670, 2698, 2714, 2718,
2725, 2734, 2745, 2747, 2756, 2786,
2788, 2797, 2809, 2815, 2839, 2857,
2877, 2904, 2911, 2960, 2965, 2971, 3029,
3031, 3039, 3047, 3048, 3050, 3051,
3054, 3057, 3076, 3078, 3079, 3084,
3087, 3114, 3120, 3137, 3157, 3167-3169,
3171, 3177, 3184, 3192-3194, 3196-3198,
3205, 3206, 3209, 3213, 3218, 3220,
3251, 3261, 3274, 3275, 3277, 3279,
3282-3285, 3289, 3295, 3299, 3303, 3304,
3306-3308, 3310, 3321, 3323, 3329, 3351,
3354, 3362, 3364, 3371, 3392, 3395,
3400, 3402, 3416, 3418, 3424, 3425,
3433, 3439, 3440, 3450, 3456-3459, 3513,
3524, 3528, 3539, 3556, 3557, 3571,
3635, 3646, 3663, 3673, 3676, 3688,
3701, 3717, 3732, 3740, 3743, 3761,
3784, 3794, 3814, 3818, 3833, 3837,
3851, 3853, 3860, 3862, 3866, 3868,
3872, 3886, 3888, 3893, 3896, 3918,
3920, 3924, 3927, 3933, 3939, 3944,
3950, 3955, 4005, 4012, 4020, 4029,
4033, 4042-4044, 4048, 4051, 4054-4056,
4059, 4062, 4068, 4069, 4072, 4073,
4095, 4112, 4137, 4141, 4144, 4148, 4153,
4157, 4162, 4166, 4169, 4173, 4185,
4189, 4192, 4195, 4197, 4199, 4204-4206,
4209-4211, 4213, 4217, 4223, 4246, 4248,
4251, 4252, 4254, 4256, 4257, 4263,
4274, 4279, 4281-4284, 4287, 4314, 4347,
4357, 4360, 4368, 4369, 4383, 4392,
4398, 4443, 4458, 4463, 4481, 4494,
4497, 4522, 4556, 4578, 4588, 4589,
4596, 4605, 4609, 4640, 4642, 4652,
4663, 4671, 4679, 4682, 4688, 4723,
4725, 4740, 4751, 4757, 4758, 4772,
4777, 4792, 4799, 4804, 4830, 4833,
4929, 4931
Études religieuses 5, 154, 167, 185, 195, 208-
210, 226, 227, 300, 591, 782, 1103, 1489,
1738, 1755, 2375, 2388, 2605, 2675,
2973, 3111, 3129, 3136, 3142, 3151, 3161,
3173, 3179, 3181, 3183, 3187, 3188,
3195, 3199, 3203, 3222, 3227, 3229,
3235, 3238, 3239, 3243, 3244, 3247,
3264, 3273, 3293, 3303, 3315, 3318,
3368-3375, 3377, 3379, 3383, 3385-3388,
3391, 3396, 3414, 3417, 3430, 3435,
3455, 3463, 3520, 3521, 3527, 3531,
3533, 3545, 3546, 3560, 3561, 3584,
3591, 3611, 3619, 3620, 3638, 3647, 3706,
3822, 3885, 4034, 4117, 4471, 4537, 4674
Études rurales 730, 2188, 2257, 2275, 2317,
2336, 2417, 2586, 2628, 3018, 3735,
4391, 4604, 4796
Études slaves 1933, 3918, 4069, 4578
Études soviétiques 345, 2154, 4073
Études sur le développement 2089, 2094,
2115, 2136, 2152, 2164, 2189, 2210, 2284,
2289, 2320, 2404, 2410, 2427, 2441,
2452, 2469, 2818, 2823, 2836, 2843,

2844, 2846, 2859, 3568, 4353, 4536, 4554, 4594, 4609, 4616, 4663, 4671-4673, 4682, 4705, 4707, 4711-4713, 4717, 4721, 4722, 4730, 4731, 4735, 4737, 4738, 4744, 4746, 4747, 4755, 4780, 4783, 4818, 4820, 4825, 4827, 4828, 4834, 4838, 4840, 4845, 4846, 4851, 4858, 4862, 4863, 4868, 4879, 4885, 4892, 4897, 4908, 4911, 4912, 4924, 4928

Études sur le paix 4706

Études urbaines 2210, 2224, 4611

Étudiants 145, 1449, 2097, 2734, 2809, 2916, 2935, 3214, 3317, 3831, 4560, 4572, 4748

Étymologie 1729, 1738, 1813, 1836, 1837, 1926, 1927, 1942, 2056, 3381, 3587, 3726, 3757, 3913

Euba, Akin 3933, 4059

Euclid 3754

Eugénisme 135, 416, 769, 1652, 2944, 4556

Européanisation 4454

Européens 4348, 4405, 4423

Euthanasie 2791

Évaluation 44, 295, 296, 1576, 1580, 1844, 1890, 2130, 2878, 3788, 3820, 4876, 4877

Évaluation de l'aide 4744

Évaluation de programme 4345, 4740, 4741, 4841

Évaluation de projet 4325, 4851

Évangélisation 701, 3220, 3617, 3618

Évangélisme 736, 774, 3222, 3228, 3241, 3612, 3620, 3887

Évolution 144, 456, 533, 1451, 1465, 1472, 1480, 1516, 1519, 1520, 1523, 1524, 1528, 1537, 1538, 1547, 1577, 1604, 1610, 1617, 1635, 1662, 1679, 1721, 3970, 3992, 4822

voir aussi: Darwinisme, Développement humain, Sélection naturelle

Évolution biologique 1485

Évolution humaine 156, 198, 272, 429, 845, 846, 849, 870, 898, 899, 1379, 1413, 1450, 1458, 1459, 1467, 1472, 1477, 1484, 1514, 1515, 1517, 1521-1526, 1529-1534, 1536, 1537, 1543, 1567, 1584, 1703, 1715, 2126, 2589, 2645, 2679, 2872, 3131, 3771

Évolutionnisme 279, 1618

Ewe 3933, 4059

Examens 63, 2521

Exclusion sociale 247, 812, 2459, 2596, 2938, 2988, 3056, 3075, 3404, 3520, 3986, 4361, 4515, 4559, 4626, 4672, 4722, 4860, 4882, 4931

Exilé 92

Existentialisme 4239

Exode des compétences 4875

Exogamie 2690

Exorcisme 3591, 3822

Exotisme 811, 3929, 3972, 4263

Expansionnisme 612, 810, 1333, 2484, 2493, 2501, 4191

Expectation 2285, 2545, 3006, 3730

Expédition 33, 492, 940, 1141, 1259, 1261, 4103

Expédition archéologique 1199, 1257

Expérience religieuse 105, 3231, 3338

Expériences 1457, 1612, 1693, 1751, 3755, 3765

Expérimentation 3765, 3914

Expertise 4925

Experts 10, 3091, 4855, 4910

Explication 3026, 4569

Exploitation 247, 2457, 2596, 2627, 2863, 4206, 4728

voir aussi: Surexploitation

Exploitation de carrières 500, 1143, 2107

Exploitation des ressources 2417, 2446, 2448, 3018, 4850

Exploration 391, 584, 594, 625, 690, 691, 699, 713, 725, 728, 746, 756, 759, 762, 768, 779, 802, 942, 1690, 1820, 1833, 2060, 2507, 2563, 3121, 3617, 4103, 4208, 4347

Exportations 2273, 2358, 4793

Exportations agricoles 727, 743, 2270, 2273, 2300, 2348

Expositions 13, 332, 347, 362, 1332, 4102, 4487

Expositions culturelles 347, 2933, 2940, 4110

Expositions ethnographiques 347

Expression de soi 3760, 3929, 4011, 4562

Expulsion 323, 698, 707

Fables 2546, 3688, 3997, 4002, 4212

Fabrication de noeuds 1784

Fabrication industrielle 2231, 2251, 2338, 4678

Facteurs culturels 193, 1486, 1512, 1737, 2116, 2118, 2139, 2150, 2345, 2363, 3029, 3050, 3175, 3695, 3803, 4549

Facteurs de production 2143, 2673

Facteurs sociaux 1486, 1512, 1656, 1919, 2118, 2139, 2153, 2196, 2374, 2912, 4575, 4662, 4854, 4866, 4895

Facture

voir: Proposition de loi

Faible revenu 2210, 2941, 4902

Faidherbe, Louis 582

Faim 4817, 4820, 4872

Faire un compromis 1452, 2390, 2891, 4677

Faits sociaux 223, 3038, 3569

Falcone, Giovanni 2975

Famille 198, 291, 557, 606, 1319, 1407, 1476, 1498, 1505, 1587, 1731, 1817, 2127, 2142, 2143, 2151, 2155, 2183, 2204, 2294, 2306, 2388, 2411, 2440, 2459, 2463, 2466, 2502, 2521, 2631, 2637, 2639, 2642-2644, 2650, 2651, 2655-2657, 2661, 2668, 2669, 2673, 2674, 2677, 2679, 2687, 2688, 2691, 2698, 2735, 2739, 2760, 2770, 2777, 2805, 2815, 2837, 2861, 2863, 2917, 2943, 2986, 2991, 3012, 3105, 3572, 3696, 3730, 4204, 4281, 4561, 4572, 4780, 4821

Famille conjugale 557, 2639
Famille monoparentale 2696, 4521
Famine 4437, 4719, 4812
Fanatisme 371
FAO 4802
Farag Hārūn, Abū 3329
Farid, Ibn Al- 4088
Fascisme 3107
Fatigue 3777
Faune 460, 841, 842, 884, 889, 1137, 1190, 1818, 2063, 2098
Fauset, Jessie Redmon 2622
Fécondité 1486, 1488, 1720, 2118, 2122, 2139, 2141, 2153, 2634, 2637, 2683, 2708, 2737, 3270, 3399, 3719, 4892
    voir aussi: Fertilité du sol
Fédéralisme 2485, 2511, 4649, 4671
Fédération 2210
Femelle 514, 1450, 1455, 1508, 1511, 1539, 1603, 1606, 1631, 1640, 1643, 1658, 1665, 1667, 1668, 1692, 1704, 1706, 1708, 2139, 2431, 2706, 2733, 2796, 2834, 2852, 2883, 2890, 2909, 3991, 4406, 4661
Fémininité 280, 769, 1777, 2858, 2934, 2944, 3781, 4175, 4560
Féminisme 222, 245, 264, 280, 384, 419, 432, 680, 694, 755, 978, 985, 2533, 2591, 2760, 2771, 2807, 2810, 2817, 2820, 2826, 2827, 2835, 2839, 2858, 2861, 2873, 2932, 2962, 2966, 3073, 3104, 3141, 3340, 3640, 4108, 4239, 4548, 4577, 4612
Femmes 105, 264, 280, 285, 378, 419, 495, 502, 514, 515, 528, 564, 565, 606, 676, 742, 755, 767, 1055, 1449, 1452, 1542, 1573, 1581, 1593, 1732, 1740, 1828, 2081, 2089, 2115, 2153, 2169, 2174, 2213, 2220, 2251, 2427, 2434, 2452, 2455, 2481, 2535, 2546, 2569, 2644, 2656, 2660, 2661, 2686, 2690, 2693, 2695, 2717, 2721, 2728, 2737, 2738, 2760, 2761, 2765, 2769, 2771, 2772, 2785, 2804, 2805, 2813, 2815, 2816, 2818, 2821, 2822, 2826, 2828-2830, 2832, 2833, 2835-2837, 2842, 2844-2846, 2850, 2855, 2858-2862, 2864, 2870, 2873, 2891, 2893, 2899, 2909, 2935, 2941, 2943, 2946, 2948, 2953, 2959, 2962, 2986, 2987, 3056, 3075, 3086, 3113, 3140, 3191, 3192, 3216, 3231, 3258, 3319, 3340, 3399, 3451, 3497, 3520, 3577, 3640, 3644, 3688, 3730, 3737, 3863, 3922, 3923, 3934, 3938, 3955, 4005, 4011, 4041, 4045, 4069, 4072, 4073, 4088, 4108, 4116, 4132, 4158, 4193, 4205, 4211, 4231, 4239, 4247, 4251, 4336, 4342, 4349, 4358, 4403, 4426, 4447, 4453, 4531, 4538, 4542, 4552, 4561, 4565, 4576-4578, 4645, 4685, 4686, 4690, 4692, 4728, 4742, 4760, 4780, 4820, 4826, 4828, 4829, 4832-4834, 4837-4843, 4845, 4846, 4848, 4849, 4851, 4852, 4855-4861, 4873, 4876, 4882, 4890, 4903
Femmes au foyer 4584
Femmes et politique 4841
Femmes rurales 2094, 2320, 2702, 2793, 2843, 3775, 4760, 4862
Féodalisme 624, 2550, 3092
Fer 709, 2335
Ferme 2191, 2394
    voir aussi: Petites entreprises agricoles
Fermes familiales 795, 2299
Fermiers 2426
Fernando, Lloyd 4177
Fertilité du sol 2303, 2307, 2313
Fête nationale 609, 3673, 4544
Fêtes 58, 1818, 2063, 2211, 2256, 2340, 2684, 2776, 2801, 2907, 3152, 3240, 3410, 3536, 3549, 3689, 3708, 3863, 3867, 4262, 4349-4353, 4355-4357, 4359-4361, 4363-4372, 4387, 4391, 4431, 4505, 4522
Fêtes religieuse 2778, 3269, 3741, 4362, 4370
Fétichisme 2387, 2921, 3526
Fœtus 1555, 2706
Feu 2060, 2272, 2797, 3126, 4774
Fiancée 2744
Fichte, Johann Gottlieb 4489
Figurines 336, 1391, 1430, 2329, 4132
Filage au rouet 2243, 2251, 3116, 3993
Filiation 2498, 2677, 2814
Filiation matrilinéaire 2676, 2678, 2690, 2744, 3682
Filiation patrilinéaire 2658, 2676
Fille 2131, 2722, 4006, 4835
Films 55, 133, 151, 409, 439, 442, 444, 2198, 2482, 2933, 3731, 3873, 3977, 4099,

4100, 4105, 4108, 4120, 4126, 4136, 4190, 4296, 4366, 4470, 4523
Films ethnographiques 133, 151, 427, 439, 440, 444
Fils 2722, 3244, 3267, 4022
Finance 2210, 2740, 3186, 4369, 4698, 4737, 4739, 4908, 4911
    voir aussi: Antécédents financiers
Finances publiques 4671
Finkielkraut, Alain 4238
Finno-Ougriens 42
Fiscalité 482, 2354, 4663
Flore 361, 362, 488, 756, 896, 1322, 1694, 1701, 1722, 1818, 1832, 2063, 2066, 2084, 2088, 2098, 2117, 2201, 2266, 2272, 2296, 2304, 2377, 2435, 2444, 3570, 3667, 3742, 3747, 3778, 3783, 3815, 3816, 4774
Flûte 3719
FMI 4338, 4667, 4680
Foi 119, 185, 2092, 3157, 3220, 3228, 3230, 3368, 3377, 3402, 3456, 3481, 3482, 3490, 3501, 3507, 3548, 3623, 4384, 4441, 4931
Foie 1570
Folie 775, 3873, 4263
Folklore 14, 92, 127, 149, 152, 160, 163, 166, 171, 181, 188, 229, 376, 564, 1782, 1788, 1858, 2080, 2187, 2204, 2291, 2364, 2437, 2438, 2678, 2828, 2830, 2943, 3065, 3116, 3124, 3242, 3528, 3535, 3582, 3649, 3661, 3662, 3664, 3670, 3679, 3682, 3686, 3694, 3698, 3721, 3763, 3785, 3863, 3903, 3918, 3930, 3945, 3949, 3970, 3976, 3979, 3982, 3987, 3991-3995, 3998, 4003, 4006, 4010, 4015, 4016, 4018, 4019, 4021, 4022, 4026, 4028, 4070, 4198, 4240, 4255, 4306, 4331, 4349, 4360, 4428
Folkloristes 127, 171
Fon 336, 2579
Fonctionnalisme 138
Fonctionnalisme structurel 2612, 3692
Fonctionnement du groupe 2606
Fonctions de production 2277
Fondamentalisme religieux 3326, 3367, 3548, 3643
Fonseca, André Velho da 806
Football 40, 4309, 4336
Force du marché 4281
Forces armées 2577, 2578, 4653
Fordisme
    voir: Post-fordisme

Foresterie 2264, 2292, 2307, 2309, 2311, 4399, 4690, 4694, 4696, 4697, 4699, 4702, 4799, 4804
Forêt tropicale 857, 1598, 1649, 1691, 2098, 2104, 2108, 2195, 4335
Forêts 1359, 1609, 1651, 1663, 1669, 1674, 1686, 1687, 1709, 1717, 2087, 2091, 2095, 2115, 2191, 2207, 2264, 2284, 2431, 2808, 2828, 2859, 3056, 3075, 3084, 3547, 3819, 4399, 4666, 4695, 4780, 4787, 4791, 4799, 4805, 4923
Formation 1664, 2955, 4688, 4760, 4914
Formation d'identité 15, 136, 278, 504, 2475, 2530, 2671, 2834, 3026, 3230, 3708, 3777, 4405, 4406, 4414, 4441, 4443, 4447, 4458, 4460, 4468, 4486, 4496
Fortes, Meyer 9, 108
Fortifications 483, 620, 806, 1009, 1037, 1058, 1082, 1101, 1104, 1199, 1200, 1328, 1334, 1346, 1411, 1412, 3852, 3859
Fossile 460, 872, 873, 884, 899, 1137, 1363, 1379, 1458, 1472, 1473, 1523, 1528, 1532, 1534, 1536, 2086
Foucauld, Charles de 122, 600
Foucault, Michel 514, 2909
Fouille archéologique 85, 356, 445, 452, 454, 460, 469, 494, 498, 499, 507, 512, 513, 556, 598, 617, 623, 744, 819, 820, 822-826, 831, 837, 839, 840, 842, 856, 859, 860, 865, 868, 872, 873, 883, 884, 888, 889, 891, 899, 900, 906, 911, 915, 917, 918, 922, 925, 927-929, 931, 935, 938, 941, 943, 944, 948, 950, 954, 956, 958, 959, 961, 964, 967, 968, 970, 973, 976, 979, 981, 982, 1009, 1010, 1014, 1018, 1020, 1023, 1026-1028, 1034-1036, 1038, 1042, 1050, 1057, 1068, 1070, 1072, 1073, 1075, 1078-1080, 1082, 1085, 1087, 1092, 1100, 1107-1112, 1114-1122, 1124-1129, 1131-1136, 1138-1145, 1147, 1150-1154, 1156-1162, 1164-1171, 1174-1176, 1178-1182, 1185-1187, 1189-1195, 1198, 1200-1213, 1215-1222, 1224, 1227-1232, 1234, 1236, 1237, 1239, 1241-1247, 1250-1254, 1256-1262, 1265-1270, 1272-1275, 1277-1279, 1285, 1293, 1295-1297, 1307, 1312-1314, 1318, 1326-1328, 1330, 1337, 1344, 1363-1367, 1371, 1378, 1379, 1381, 1382, 1384, 1390, 1398, 1400, 1402-1404, 1407-1409, 1416, 1417, 1419, 1429, 1433, 1440-1442, 1458, 1461, 1464, 1471, 1535, 2240, 2304, 2360, 2393, 2444, 3853, 4007, 4375
Fouilles 85, 463, 513, 520, 829, 840, 850, 871, 920, 922, 924, 926-928, 933, 934, 941,

945, 953, 961, 963, 966, 967, 970, 1001,
1014, 1021, 1022, 1028, 1046, 1051,
1068, 1070, 1074, 1075, 1079, 1087,
1092, 1098, 1111, 1113, 1114, 1120-1122,
1124, 1135, 1144, 1145, 1153, 1161, 1164,
1165, 1167, 1169, 1172, 1173, 1175, 1177,
1179-1181, 1186, 1187, 1189, 1192, 1196,
1202, 1206, 1212, 1213, 1221-1223, 1225,
1231, 1232, 1234, 1237-1239, 1248, 1252,
1255, 1258, 1262-1264, 1268-1271, 1274-
1276, 1278, 1292, 1297, 1300, 1302,
1305, 1309, 1310, 1313-1315, 1346, 1355,
1388, 1389, 1399, 1431, 1438, 1441,
2343, 4250
Foulbe 2073, 2510
Fourrager 1408, 1600, 1609, 1671, 1711,
1715, 2433, 3084, 4394
Fourrageurs 1584, 2302, 2382, 2431, 2834,
3992, 4406
Foyer 291, 694, 2100, 2154, 2461, 2766,
2900, 2907, 3707, 3843, 4111, 4184, 4330,
4384
Francis, Newell S. 3588
Franciscaines 3618
Frank, Waldo 4282
Fraser Russell, Alexander 792
Fratrie 1614
Fraude fiscale 489
Fréquence 2634
Frère 3125
Freud, Sigmund 176, 379, 4524
Frontières 383, 599, 641, 670, 750, 763, 777,
2082, 2092, 2125, 2456, 2608, 2779,
2827, 3085, 3098, 3104, 4619, 4624,
4626, 4628, 4632
voir aussi: Régions frontalières
Frontières maritimes 2070
Fruits 1609, 1627, 1642, 1648, 1671, 1715,
1720, 2377
voir aussi: Bananes
Fugard, Athol 3874, 4200
Fulani 582, 1749
Funèbres 58, 874, 1324, 2604, 2786, 2787,
2791
Fusions d'entreprises 282
Gains 3344
Gandhi, Mohandas Karamchand 3079
Garçons 1579
Garde des enfants 2736, 3010
Gardner, Don 159, 217
Garifuna 1986
Gastronomie 4396
Gauche 270, 2537
Gaudapāda 3291
Gawzī, Ibn al 3354

Geertz, Clifford 138, 244
Geiger, Abraham 3666, 4445
Gellner, Ernest 138
Généalogie 649, 1615, 1828, 1830, 2132,
2634, 2646, 2652, 2666, 2671, 3117, 3345,
3353, 3420, 3421, 3669, 4460, 4493, 4717
Généralisation 209, 1693, 2170, 3560
Génération 1511, 1817, 2155, 2375, 2605,
2613, 2628, 2675, 2693, 4204
Gènes 830, 1453, 1487, 1490, 1494-1500,
1502, 1503, 1506, 1507, 1510, 1515,
1538, 1615, 1650, 1666, 2657
Génétique 1451, 1459, 1476, 1487, 1497,
1501, 1503-1505, 1508-1511, 1520, 1522,
1587, 1616, 1617, 1649, 1650, 1652,
1666, 1679, 1688, 1714, 1781, 1822,
2132, 2297, 2445, 2478, 2646, 2674,
3793, 4697, 4825
voir aussi: ADN, Clonage
Génétique humaine 1453, 1486-1488, 1491-
1496, 1498, 1499, 1502, 1506, 1507,
1511-1515, 1517, 1558, 1561, 1582, 1741,
2118, 2657, 2722
Génie génétique 236, 2310, 4825
Génocide 192, 618, 970, 2578, 3029, 3050
Genre 105, 214, 225, 248, 258, 528, 539, 565,
643, 663, 676, 680, 694, 717, 1041, 1360,
1466, 1549, 1563, 1628, 1639, 1692,
1740, 1752, 1775, 1828, 1896, 1943,
2133, 2142, 2169, 2174, 2176, 2213,
2244, 2266, 2284, 2375, 2410, 2441,
2442, 2464, 2469, 2470, 2571, 2603,
2605, 2611, 2622, 2629, 2644, 2660, 2686,
2693, 2697, 2723, 2729, 2746, 2757,
2759, 2761, 2765, 2769, 2771, 2772,
2796, 2803-2805, 2809, 2810, 2812, 2813,
2820-2824, 2826-2828, 2831, 2832, 2834,
2835, 2838, 2840, 2841, 2845, 2847-2849,
2852-2857, 2862, 2864, 2873, 2888, 2895,
2905, 2918, 2928, 2932, 2933, 2936,
2946, 2948, 2955, 2957, 2959, 3028,
3030, 3056, 3075, 3076, 3104, 3113, 3231,
3254, 3340, 3357, 3497, 3525, 3615,
3640, 3751, 3871, 3873, 3922, 3934,
3951, 3994, 3995, 4005, 4009, 4041,
4052, 4073, 4108, 4116, 4158, 4164, 4171,
4247, 4342, 4358, 4361, 4385, 4403,
4406, 4440, 4450, 4468, 4470, 4505,
4528, 4561, 4563, 4577, 4591, 4611, 4645,
4780, 4790, 4821, 4829, 4831, 4837-4841,
4845, 4851, 4856, 4879, 4890, 4904, 4911
voir aussi: Études de genre
Genre de vie 204, 2199, 2478, 3378, 3506,
4653
Genre humain 2296

Genres littéraires 3995, 3996, 4052, 4060,
    4156, 4204
Gens de maison 2459, 2644, 2827, 3104
Gentileschi, Orazio 3728
Géoarchéologie 1183, 1185
Géographie 214, 291, 474, 525, 541, 648, 806,
    872, 913, 983, 1002, 1737, 1820, 1833,
    2060, 2112, 2181, 2219, 2222, 2244, 2272,
    2274, 2287, 2313, 2362, 2402, 2418,
    2713, 2801, 3247, 3334, 3660, 3689,
    3868, 4103, 4124, 4171, 4186, 4226,
    4300, 4339, 4347, 4356, 4388, 4464,
    4478, 4618, 4626, 4654, 4660, 4678,
    4681, 4683, 4684, 4727, 4752, 4759,
    4768, 4774, 4794, 4797, 4798, 4800,
    4803, 4836, 4850, 4854, 4910, 4917, 4926
Géographie économique 4609
Géographie historique 768, 806, 1820, 2173,
    2296, 3961
Géographie humaine 254, 291, 409, 611, 684,
    757, 1043, 1066, 1303, 2120, 2170, 2207,
    2386, 2406, 2594, 3042, 3615, 3961,
    4347, 4431, 4457, 4487, 4624
Géographie industrielle 4663
Géographie politique 2418
Géologie 390, 499, 500, 806, 839, 901, 913,
    1260, 1382, 2086, 2240, 3855
Géométrie 832, 1044, 2324, 2329, 3754, 3857
Géophagie 1601, 1651
Géopolitique 2289, 4258, 4673, 4720
Gérontocratie 2502, 2682, 2767, 3572
Gérontologie 2650, 2655, 2763, 2770, 2777,
    3696
Gestes 1775, 2812
Gestion 255, 2369, 4548, 4744, 4757, 4801,
    4804, 4820
    voir aussi: Aménagement hydraulique,
    Direction de crise, Mise en valeur du sol
Gestion administrative 4665, 4717
Gestion agricole 4692, 4767, 4780
Gestion de l'environnement 4618, 4778-4780,
    4786, 4792, 4794, 4939
Gestion de risque 4865
Gestion d'entreprise agricole 4692
Gestion des déchets 4887, 4933, 4941
Gestion des pêches 2404
Gestion des ressources 968, 2067, 2073, 2083,
    2116, 2210, 2264, 2272, 2288, 2289, 2404,
    2413, 2427, 3695, 4399, 4660, 4691,
    4769, 4770, 4773, 4774, 4780, 4799,
    4801, 4805
Gestion du personnel 2468
Gestion forestière 2081, 2090, 2115, 2404,
    2413, 2818, 2828, 2829, 2844, 2859,
    4779, 4780, 4792

Gestion urbaine 2401, 4786
Ghazālī, Abu Hamid Mohammed al 2998,
    3366
Ghetto 4468
Gikuyu 3548
Gilgamesh [King] 4253
Gimbutas, Marija 2175
Gjalski, Ksaver Sandor 3996
Gling pa, 'Jigs med 3205
Glissant, Edouard 4187
Gluckman, Max 126, 3054
Gnosticisme 476, 3527
Gond 2153
Gonne, Maud 4563
González, José Luis 4271
Gorilles 1481, 1607, 1656, 1667, 1671, 1704,
    1714
Goupil, Eugène 214
Goût 1506, 1703, 4618, 4794
Gouvernance 474, 2404, 2524, 2569, 3063,
    4615, 4634, 4720, 4721, 4764, 4843,
    4861, 4870, 4874, 4915
Gouvernement 818, 2210, 2288, 2403, 2487,
    2504, 2538, 2558, 2570, 2979, 2988,
    3036, 3059, 3349, 4185, 4301, 4481,
    4607, 4653, 4933
    voir aussi: Administration coloniale,
    Administration locale, Administration
    régionale, Administration territoriale
Gouvernement tribal 2565
Gouvernement urbain 2222
Gouverneurs 323, 707, 721, 2550, 2971
Goytisolo, Juan 4202
Grain 1704
Grammaire 69, 71, 83, 109, 248, 1724, 1742,
    1752, 1753, 1789, 1807, 1812, 1836,
    1843, 1852, 1854, 1860, 1862, 1863,
    1866, 1867, 1875, 1892, 1896, 1918,
    1929, 1930, 1933, 1935, 1936, 1938,
    1948, 1960, 1963, 1982, 1987, 1995,
    1999, 2006, 2007, 2010, 2012, 2014,
    2017, 2023, 2029, 2031, 2032, 2035,
    2037, 2038, 2043, 2046, 2053, 3147,
    3165, 3273, 3359, 3754, 4262
    voir aussi: Proposition
Grande depression 2300
Grandes villes 450, 496, 563, 906, 989, 1083,
    1090, 1099, 1102, 1106, 1115, 1116, 1149,
    1203, 1204, 1229, 1250, 1942, 2092,
    2209, 2211, 2212, 2217, 2224, 2228, 2789,
    3145, 3650, 3656, 3853, 3918, 4124,
    4168, 4186, 4317, 4580, 4604, 4759,
    4806, 4813, 4934, 4937, 4939
    voir aussi: Mégacité, Villes capitales
Grands-parents 2654, 2686, 2863

Gravure 1006, 1042, 1097, 4112
Greffe 2930, 2952
Gregory, Augusta 2622
Grèves 723, 2453
Grogan, Ewart Scott 773
Grossesse 1491, 1542, 1613, 1708, 2711,
    2717-2719, 2727, 2811, 2869, 2893, 3517,
    3539, 3814, 3817, 3950, 4844, 4869
Grosseteste, Robert 3728
Grottes préhistoriques 836, 894, 898, 1007,
    1013, 1023, 1467
Groupe cible 286, 290, 2124, 2734
Groupe familial 2022
Groupes d'égaux 2882
Groupes ethniques 10, 215, 309, 399, 432,
    574, 648, 1426, 1491, 1492, 1503, 1579,
    1583, 1876, 2077, 2146, 2349, 2409,
    2475, 2523, 2552, 2559, 2564, 2566,
    2568, 2570, 2577, 2593, 2609, 2630,
    2707, 2712, 2802, 2834, 2876, 3060,
    3069, 3083, 3087, 3088, 3091, 3093,
    3099, 3101, 3102, 3410, 3489, 3522,
    3607, 3691, 3708, 3757, 3798, 3956,
    4359, 4398, 4400, 4406, 4409, 4410,
    4413, 4420, 4533, 4603, 4627, 4761
Groupes linguistiques 1845, 1881, 1886, 1888
Groupes minoritaires 41, 119, 190, 2432,
    2554, 3056, 3070, 3075, 3084, 3798,
    4433, 4605
Groupes politiques 765
Groupes religieux 592, 1454, 2573, 3342,
    3534, 4424
Groupes sanguins 1486, 1490, 1491, 2118
Guaman Poma de Ayala, Felipe 4098
Guarani 1976, 2798
Guérison 17, 105, 2727, 3011, 3062, 3181,
    3231, 3259, 3535, 3541, 3565, 3586,
    3596, 3645, 3776, 3790, 3791, 3809,
    3813, 3825, 3830, 3833, 3835, 3991, 4511
Guérisseurs 17, 3591, 3812, 3822, 3825, 3830
Guerre 299, 534, 551, 567, 599, 654, 695, 721,
    761, 786, 1370, 1569, 2197, 2549, 2578,
    2610, 2653, 2693, 2860, 2977, 3035,
    3036, 3051, 3052, 3059, 3086, 3196,
    3428, 3570, 3687, 3711, 3758, 3783, 4216,
    4258, 4477, 4864
    voir aussi: Art de la guerre
Guerre civile 2532, 3590, 4792
Guerre civile américaine 982
Guerre civile espagnole 323, 707, 4105, 4523
Guerre de boer 654, 1282, 4182
Guerre du Golfe 2860, 3086
Guerre froide 658, 2857, 3076, 3975
Guerre sainte 611, 3042, 3049
Guerriers 1326, 2625, 3502

Guest, Barbara 4041
Guidar 2700
Gundert, Hermann 1894
Gunwinggu 2670, 2747
Gurage 1845
Gusii 2635, 3025
Guthrie, Malcolm 1996
Habitat 1525, 1598, 1624, 1627, 1630, 1638,
    1648, 1656, 1674, 1680, 1686, 1712,
    2077, 2098
Habitations rurales 2394
Habitudes alimentaires 1551, 1644, 4358,
    4376, 4378, 4379, 4403, 4754
Hadza 1281, 2352, 2651
Hagiographie 514, 2909, 3414, 4255
Hahn, Reynaldo 4263
Haida 4134
Hammarskjöld, Dag 4712
Hammurabi [King] 477
Han 41, 190, 649, 3713
Han, Yongun 3079
Handicapés 40
Handicapés mentaux 2933
Hanihara 246, 2135
Hanson, Pauline 3107
Hassidisme 253, 3976
Hau'ofa, Epeli 3650
Hausa 402, 1749
Head, Bessie 4160
Hébreu 1338, 1762, 1816, 1831, 1840, 1843,
    1844, 1846, 1848, 1850, 1855, 1857,
    1859, 1860, 1864, 1866, 1870, 3392,
    3396, 3405, 3427, 3431, 3434, 3436,
    3449, 3453, 3459, 3460, 3973, 4040,
    4054, 4224, 4444, 4461, 4467, 4503
Hégémonie 95, 234, 657, 2510, 2547, 3077,
    3601, 3650, 3794, 4336, 4421, 4626, 4861
Heisenberg, Karl 60
Hemingway, Ernest 4199
Henricus Martellus Germanus 768
Hepworth, Barbara 4712
Hérédité 1476, 1835, 2132, 2195, 2646
Hérésies 568, 3413
Héritage 1498, 2350, 2410, 2416, 2645, 2657,
    2740, 2753, 2863, 2906, 2973, 2991,
    3017, 3173, 4780
Héritage social 1835
Herméneutique 34, 257, 281, 772, 844, 987,
    996, 1226, 1798, 3136, 3326, 3509
Herod [King] 1328
Héroïne 3004, 3765
Héros 1539, 2911, 3271, 4019, 4289
Herskovits, Melville J. 4468
Hesiod 3115
Hétérosexualité 1452, 2840, 2841, 2873, 2891

Heuristique 1385
Hiérarchie 53, 504, 1631, 1775, 2530, 2627, 2735, 2812, 3523, 4254, 4299, 4365, 4387, 4549
Hieroglyphes 102, 1345, 1799, 4275
Hindi 1896, 4173
Hindouisme 22, 105, 732, 1081, 2099, 2485, 2515, 2615, 2788, 2926, 2991, 3079, 3155, 3214, 3231, 3269-3271, 3276-3280, 3283-3286, 3288-3291, 3295-3299, 3302-3304, 3306, 3309-3317, 3319, 3549, 3837, 3854, 3898, 3962, 4020, 4140, 4189, 4297, 4474, 4577
voir aussi: Saivisme
Hindous 2121, 2757, 2788, 2856, 3286, 3292, 4189, 4281, 4362, 4364
Hispaniques 2533, 3073, 3769, 3946
Hispano-américains 443, 2661, 2724, 2851, 4305
Histoire 7, 11, 12, 16, 18, 31, 40, 62, 73, 88, 97, 99, 101, 106, 109, 116, 117, 122, 132, 149, 150, 155, 159, 162, 217, 225, 231, 246, 279, 317, 319, 326, 333, 335, 344, 345, 351, 357, 364, 367, 375, 376, 382, 412, 434, 437, 441, 446, 465, 467, 473, 486, 491, 495, 509, 514, 519, 522, 527, 528, 530-532, 535, 537-539, 541, 545-550, 552, 553, 564, 567, 569, 571-575, 578, 579, 582, 586-589, 592, 597, 600, 601, 607, 609, 610, 612-616, 619, 620, 622, 626, 635, 637, 639, 643-645, 647, 648, 650, 652, 653, 655, 657, 660, 661, 665, 668, 674, 677, 678, 686, 687, 695, 696, 702, 703, 708, 709, 714-716, 724, 728, 744, 752, 755, 760, 762, 771, 773, 776, 778, 785, 786, 797, 801, 807, 814, 817, 823, 878, 893, 895, 926, 928, 934, 936, 937, 969, 971, 979, 984, 992, 1004, 1012, 1015, 1019, 1032, 1054, 1055, 1084, 1086, 1094, 1096, 1097, 1101, 1123, 1154, 1159, 1172, 1180, 1213, 1223, 1249, 1264, 1276, 1305, 1330, 1333, 1336, 1338, 1339, 1346, 1355, 1357, 1369, 1389, 1395, 1420, 1421, 1423, 1433, 1463, 1520, 1524, 1740, 1743, 1786, 1827, 1828, 1830, 1831, 1840, 1841, 1856, 1862, 1865, 1871, 1901, 1904, 1905, 1910, 1914, 1940, 1988-1990, 1992-1995, 2003, 2009, 2036, 2078, 2092, 2095, 2100, 2110, 2111, 2135, 2142, 2147, 2151, 2168, 2173, 2175, 2197, 2205, 2230, 2233, 2243, 2250, 2253, 2254, 2259, 2267, 2276, 2286, 2294, 2306, 2335, 2365, 2367, 2371, 2383, 2386, 2392, 2395, 2397, 2398, 2422, 2423,

2429, 2447, 2451, 2460, 2464, 2479, 2484, 2493, 2496, 2500, 2501, 2519, 2526, 2541, 2545, 2547, 2548, 2556, 2563, 2566, 2572, 2573, 2577, 2599, 2610, 2623, 2636, 2644, 2648, 2652, 2658, 2671, 2689, 2743, 2749, 2754, 2789, 2792, 2828, 2830, 2832-2834, 2860, 2909, 2912, 2942, 2949, 2964, 2965, 2974, 2981, 2998, 2999, 3007, 3023, 3041, 3051, 3058, 3071, 3086, 3108, 3114, 3117, 3146, 3161, 3172, 3180, 3185, 3189, 3236, 3266, 3268, 3322, 3327, 3332, 3334, 3338, 3339, 3343, 3345, 3346, 3350, 3358, 3366, 3394, 3395, 3398, 3400, 3411, 3416, 3509, 3571, 3628, 3629, 3643, 3648, 3655, 3656, 3666, 3668, 3673, 3683, 3687, 3704, 3705, 3707, 3720, 3739, 3749, 3766, 3768, 3776, 3779, 3785, 3787, 3797, 3802, 3813, 3826, 3828, 3836, 3852, 3868, 3882, 3923, 3944, 3974, 3986, 4009, 4012, 4023, 4040, 4054, 4056, 4060, 4089, 4115, 4124, 4144, 4155, 4156, 4161, 4165, 4167, 4174, 4186, 4190, 4201, 4205, 4219, 4221, 4227, 4232, 4240, 4242, 4247, 4260, 4267, 4269, 4280, 4302, 4308, 4333, 4336, 4344, 4347, 4348, 4350, 4379, 4384, 4406, 4416, 4444, 4445, 4448, 4460, 4467, 4468, 4504, 4505, 4508, 4557, 4558, 4568, 4573, 4592, 4625, 4638-4640, 4642, 4657, 4711, 4739, 4799, 4804, 4821, 4861, 4908, 4912
voir aussi: Ancien Régime, Après-guerre, Début de l'époque moderne, Vie
Histoire agricole 4, 165, 323, 682, 707, 727, 857, 2259, 2261, 2265, 2267, 2270, 2276, 2281, 2282, 2286, 2294, 2300, 2304, 2405, 2418, 2424, 2575, 2619, 2730, 3066
Histoire ancienne 73, 214, 446, 447, 457-459, 462, 465, 468, 473, 478, 480-482, 486, 491, 493-495, 499, 508-510, 520, 523, 525, 528, 535, 559, 632, 918, 925, 933, 1004, 1005, 1024, 1036, 1047, 1055, 1060, 1093, 1103, 1308, 1329, 1338, 1343, 1353, 2112, 2162, 2240, 2354, 2365, 2444, 2536, 2580, 2871, 2995, 3023, 3119, 3145, 3398, 3406, 3411, 3419, 3440, 3445, 3459, 3753, 3928, 4066, 4209, 4241, 4258, 4268
Histoire coloniale 43, 97, 100, 106, 125, 132, 155, 184, 228, 254, 317, 318, 323, 326, 335, 348, 391, 437, 530, 532, 540, 548, 551, 553, 558, 575, 580, 583, 584, 592, 601, 602, 613, 614, 616, 619, 622, 627, 636, 637, 641, 643, 644, 650, 651, 658, 664, 673, 675, 678, 681-686, 688-690,

692-694, 696, 697, 699, 701-703, 705-707, 710-715, 717-721, 725, 726, 728, 730, 731, 733, 734, 736, 737, 739-742, 745-748, 750, 752, 754, 760-763, 766, 768, 770-773, 775, 780-783, 786, 789-791, 793-798, 800-803, 806, 808, 810-814, 816-818, 893, 969, 991, 1289, 1392, 1428, 1429, 1761, 1792, 1794, 1915, 2078, 2082, 2110, 2120, 2128, 2223, 2262, 2274, 2298, 2299, 2336, 2355, 2362, 2368, 2383, 2385, 2401, 2424, 2443, 2500, 2507, 2508, 2510, 2522, 2553, 2559, 2573, 2608, 2617, 2630, 2744, 2754, 2774, 2827, 2833, 2933, 2942, 2976, 2981, 2993, 3031, 3032, 3047, 3057, 3058, 3104, 3216, 3224, 3286, 3287, 3353, 3402, 3415, 3533, 3608, 3614, 3617, 3618, 3630, 3637, 3701, 3735, 3755, 3778, 3829, 3844, 3880, 4005, 4007, 4098, 4128, 4134, 4150, 4166, 4173, 4176, 4182, 4183, 4187, 4191, 4215, 4234, 4245, 4260, 4270, 4275, 4285, 4298, 4302, 4312, 4431, 4437, 4457, 4458, 4501, 4608, 4657

Histoire constitutionnelle 2511
Histoire culturelle 12, 27, 48, 58, 81, 141, 200, 231, 254, 273, 298, 326, 340, 371, 376, 508, 543, 550, 555, 556, 578, 585, 596, 606, 611, 631, 642, 647, 649, 651-653, 659, 662, 664, 666, 694, 714, 747, 782, 810, 946, 962, 999, 1032, 1035, 1060, 1189, 1333, 1361, 1395, 1760, 2134, 2175, 2324, 2482, 2691, 2740, 2857, 2936, 2957, 2986, 2995, 3042, 3076, 3085, 3132, 3333, 3353, 3357, 3431, 3458, 3479, 3483, 3513, 3535, 3554, 3576, 3697, 3709, 3852, 3880, 3928, 3939, 3948, 3951, 3965, 3966, 3991, 4007, 4021, 4049, 4050, 4053, 4066, 4093, 4107, 4150, 4167, 4231, 4233, 4247, 4267, 4343, 4401, 4439, 4457, 4458, 4500
Histoire de la famille 557, 776, 2142, 2183, 2463, 2466, 2637, 2639, 2688, 2743, 2749, 3704, 4204, 4821
Histoire de la marine 820
Histoire de la médecine 62, 110, 605, 1489, 1953, 2912, 3358, 3595, 3749, 3766-3768, 3778, 3779, 3784, 3785, 3787, 3794, 3797, 3799, 3802, 3808, 3828, 3836, 4174, 4525
Histoire de la musique 647, 3914, 3926, 3929, 3933, 3943, 3952, 4059
Histoire de la philosophie 79, 588, 758, 1738, 3129, 3208

Histoire de la religion 154, 168, 210, 585, 591, 634, 640, 1025, 1100, 3139, 3152, 3161, 3167, 3169, 3171, 3174, 3183, 3190, 3197, 3200, 3253, 3263, 3264, 3330, 3331, 3334, 3342, 3370, 3379, 3385-3387, 3415, 3417, 3428, 3441, 3443, 3461, 3473, 3476, 3484, 3490, 3493, 3502, 3521, 3528, 3561, 3562, 3615, 3642, 3647
Histoire de la technologie 455, 789, 1202, 1388, 1397, 1421, 2225, 2229
Histoire de l'anthropologie 1-3, 7, 9, 11, 12, 18, 43, 45, 99, 108, 110, 121, 126, 160, 198, 232, 249, 254, 399, 408, 621, 636, 1531, 2612, 2658, 2679, 3054, 3107, 3533, 3596, 3692, 3799, 4457
Histoire de l'archéologie 87, 971, 974, 975, 980, 995
Histoire de l'art 338, 371, 1005, 3249, 4093-4095, 4097, 4114, 4128, 4130, 4235
Histoire de l'éducation 645, 4552, 4557
Histoire de l'Église 86, 3215, 3224, 3247, 3266, 3648
Histoire de l'entreprise 2368
Histoire de l'esclavage 807
Histoire de l'ethnologie 8
Histoire des civilisations 377
Histoire des idées 164, 214, 259, 414, 514, 737, 2909, 3178, 3208, 4476
Histoire des idées politiques 138
Histoire des langues 117, 1729, 1732, 1785, 1794, 1797, 1808, 1810, 1841, 1857, 1869, 1873, 1877-1879, 1881, 1886-1888, 1892, 1901, 1902, 1905, 1910-1913, 1915, 1916, 1918, 1920, 1927, 1929, 1930, 1934, 1935, 1937, 1938, 1942-1944, 1946, 1948, 1949, 1951-1956, 1961, 1964, 1965, 1988, 1990, 2003, 2021, 2023, 2037, 2039, 2042, 2044, 2051, 2052, 2058, 2059, 2302, 4268
Histoire des science sociales 5, 6, 11, 94, 138, 226
Histoire des sciences 16, 132, 371, 437, 459, 464, 2871, 3746, 3749, 3754, 3755, 3768
Histoire des voyages 3263, 4179, 4225, 4236, 4237, 4290, 4292, 4321-4323, 4332
Histoire du commerce 150, 382, 449, 503, 633, 709, 764, 793, 806, 908, 1392, 2330, 2335, 2339, 2344, 2357, 2358, 2360, 2362, 2372, 2383, 2533, 3008, 3073, 3797, 4272
Histoire du droit 508, 516, 638, 771, 2981, 2991, 2995, 2996, 4247
Histoire du travail 2460, 2467
Histoire économique 463, 508, 551, 595, 671, 718, 726, 753, 757, 789, 835, 860, 2128,

2231, 2279, 2282, 2329, 2332, 2338, 2341, 2343, 2344, 2355, 2356, 2368, 2406, 2424, 2522, 2575, 2590, 2744, 2995, 3755, 4050, 4052, 4176, 4447, 4571

Histoire économique récente 2345, 3175

Histoire industrielle 811, 2619, 3066

Histoire littéraire 89, 107, 405, 1911, 2533, 2839, 2857, 3005, 3073, 3076, 3079, 3211, 3263, 3305, 3437, 3665, 3911, 3974, 3987, 3990, 3991, 3996, 4042, 4044, 4047, 4048, 4053, 4057, 4069, 4071, 4079, 4085, 4112, 4139, 4157, 4160, 4168, 4179, 4191, 4192, 4210, 4211, 4220, 4225, 4231, 4233-4237, 4240, 4247, 4248, 4254, 4255, 4257, 4260, 4264, 4271, 4274, 4277, 4279, 4282, 4287, 4290, 4292, 4322, 4323, 4578, 4581

Histoire locale 251, 335, 688, 2003, 2104

Histoire médiévale 606, 629, 666, 671, 676, 715, 779, 951, 953, 1280, 1288, 1381, 1833, 1937, 1953, 2531, 2864, 2965, 2986, 3089, 3249, 3338, 3382, 3395, 3458, 3679, 4002, 4097, 4221, 4247, 4580

Histoire militaire 323, 498, 534, 546, 563, 577, 581, 705, 707, 761, 1009, 1029, 2521

Histoire moderne 3082, 3204

Histoire nationale 590, 683

Histoire naturelle 4, 165, 326, 361, 362, 368, 756, 1715

Histoire orale 40, 96, 291, 357, 375, 544, 562, 575, 607, 613, 614, 619, 665, 1787, 2087, 2548, 2648, 2663, 3118, 3510, 3654, 3764, 3981, 3984-3986, 3999, 4008, 4012, 4023, 4232, 4568, 4804

Histoire politique 501, 510, 535, 546, 577, 607, 619, 654, 688, 703, 705, 773, 787, 816, 818, 2155, 2330, 2475, 2478, 2491, 2493, 2500, 2533, 2536, 2545, 2558, 2566, 3023, 3029, 3050, 3073, 3080, 3100, 3145, 4105, 4369, 4447, 4523, 4571, 4921

Histoire précolombien 504, 903, 1294, 1375, 2530, 2764, 3745, 4066, 4220

Histoire précoloniale 73, 214, 228, 335, 533, 542, 573, 633, 670, 821, 1385, 1405, 2653, 2977, 3008, 3353, 3902

Histoire religieuse 451, 592, 606, 782, 1344, 1353, 2573, 2986, 3216, 3224, 3230, 3247, 3260, 3266, 3405, 3419, 3445, 3460, 3531, 3535, 3632, 3637, 3648, 3856, 3974, 4114, 4441

Histoire rurale 757, 2205, 2406, 2423, 2463, 2607, 4325

Histoire sociale 12, 18, 48, 172, 200, 337, 340, 347, 361, 362, 377, 508, 527, 548, 557,

576, 579, 595, 603, 613, 631, 646, 647, 651, 663, 664, 671, 674, 675, 682, 691, 719, 738, 744, 775, 776, 1336, 1760, 1829, 1916, 2085, 2128, 2183, 2204, 2211, 2215, 2217, 2282, 2324, 2341, 2355, 2368, 2395, 2466, 2475, 2489, 2522, 2533, 2575, 2607, 2617, 2621, 2636, 2639, 2688, 2697, 2716, 2741, 2743, 2752, 2761, 2771, 2789, 2803, 2822, 2845, 2853, 2857, 2862, 2886, 2995, 3073, 3076, 3082, 3085, 3098, 3099, 3402, 3562, 3573, 3665, 3704, 3739, 3755, 3829, 3909, 3929, 4015, 4016, 4050, 4052, 4105, 4176, 4211, 4227, 4254, 4302, 4310, 4390, 4437, 4472, 4501, 4523, 4568, 4571, 4628

Histoire urbaine 2223

Histoires 169, 222, 229, 289, 384, 1782, 1978, 2103, 2582, 3118, 3121, 3172, 3424, 3437, 3448, 3664, 3679, 3805, 3968, 3972, 3974, 3979, 3983, 3989, 3997, 3999, 4004, 4006, 4013, 4015, 4016, 4019, 4024-4026, 4042, 4046, 4169, 4175, 4195, 4199, 4206, 4213, 4234, 4244, 4281, 4517, 4570

Histoires d'amour 4046

Histoires de vies 88, 101, 128, 375, 570, 4012, 4249, 4564, 4567-4570, 4572

Historicisme 650, 3888, 3974

Historiens 36, 96, 116, 339, 471, 588, 615, 683, 701, 3220, 3985, 4326

Historiographie 12, 25, 48, 97, 116, 125, 155, 200, 214, 228, 231, 278, 333, 335, 351, 367, 530, 532, 537, 542, 547, 549, 552, 569, 573, 575, 582, 588, 589, 595, 602, 607, 610, 612, 614-616, 622, 635, 641, 655, 665, 670, 671, 701, 713, 733, 758, 969, 971, 1004, 1353, 2167, 2392, 2465, 2493, 2532, 2533, 2608, 2625, 2697, 2803, 3073, 3085, 3146, 3167, 3174, 3331, 3445, 3477, 3590, 3635, 3656, 3705, 3902, 4023, 4185, 4245, 4260, 4306, 4472, 4544, 4580

Hitler, Adolf 576, 3573

Hittites 478, 479, 1394

Hmong 2028, 2323

Hobsbawm, Eric 3929

Holisme 3558, 4294, 4842

Holocauste 357, 434, 695, 4049, 4439

Holocène 543, 837, 847, 857, 913, 1183, 1304

Holý, Ladislav 138

Homer 3680

Homicide 977, 3024

voir aussi: Meurtre

Hominidés 822, 841, 842, 898, 899, 914,
    1137, 1368, 1458, 1467, 1472, 1479, 1481,
    1518, 1521, 1523, 1525, 1526, 1528,
    1530, 1532, 1534, 1604
Homme fossile 870, 1469, 1530
Homme préhistorique 822, 841, 875, 890
Hommes 514, 1452, 2820, 2840, 2841, 2848,
    2865, 2874, 2891, 2894, 2909, 2955,
    3106, 3254, 3782, 4520, 4891
Hommes de loi 2618, 3638
Hommes de métier 1441, 2246, 4848
Homosexualité 514, 562, 1507, 2841, 2866,
    2877, 2882, 2885, 2900-2902, 2907, 2909,
    2912, 2933, 4330, 4470, 4499, 4898
Honneur et honte 1872, 2586, 3258, 3267,
    3644, 3912
Honorius, Iulius 4167
Hopi 3742
Hôpitaux 401, 1200, 2632, 2709
Hôpitaux psychiatriques 4545
Horace 4172
Hormones 1460, 1553, 1613, 1622, 1658,
    1668, 1670, 1697, 1699
Horticulture 2469
Hospitalité 916
Howard, Albert 2311
Hrozný, Bedřich 87, 975, 976
HsShelishi, Shemu'el 4054
Huichol 2602, 2665, 3598
Huile 488
Humanisme 35, 104, 110, 115, 758, 2099,
    2232, 3155, 3354, 3799, 3862, 4191, 4264
Humanité 1525, 3035, 3475, 4238
Humanités 106, 132, 437, 451, 485, 501, 542,
    546, 596, 683, 701, 713, 725, 733, 745,
    752, 758, 783, 802, 946, 1005, 1024, 1136,
    1294, 1319, 1344, 1347, 1758, 1770,
    1787, 1810, 1812, 1868, 1925, 1926,
    1970, 1979, 2139, 2361, 2813, 3032, 3113,
    3119, 3133, 3216, 3255, 3258, 3365, 3617,
    3618, 3626, 3632, 3637, 3642, 3644,
    3738, 3741, 3778, 3891, 3902, 3911, 3928,
    3933, 3981, 3984, 4014, 4030, 4036,
    4045, 4047, 4053, 4059, 4065, 4066,
    4075, 4077, 4080, 4083, 4084, 4087,
    4088, 4097, 4101, 4121, 4122, 4147,
    4196, 4201, 4220, 4222, 4234, 4235,
    4242, 4245, 4260, 4270, 4271, 4275, 4306
Humeur 1961
Humour 1767, 1864, 3354, 3449, 4033, 4194,
    4243, 4254
    voir aussi: Plaisanteries
Humsi, Deek al-Jin al- 4083
Huron 4321
Hurrian 479

Hutte 2441
    voir aussi: Élevage
Hutterite 2122
Hutu 192, 618
Hydrologie 2091, 4766
Hygiène publique 1559, 2711, 2878, 3761,
    3788, 4844, 4877
Hymnes 3211, 3282, 3289, 3307, 3484, 3920
Hypothèse 298, 428, 1449, 1604, 1608, 1662,
    1931, 2134, 2235, 2352, 2790, 2935,
    3516, 4705
Iatmul 3550
Iban 2181
Ibn Khaldun 1830
Icônes 166, 1024, 1077, 3118, 3249, 3649,
    3733, 3830, 3947, 3999, 4428
Iconographie 433, 461, 567, 581, 828, 1005,
    1013, 1044, 1055, 1060, 1385, 3051, 3118,
    3515, 3520, 3585, 3735, 3999, 4095, 4140
Idéalisme 4045, 4191, 4489
Idées politiques
    voir: Histoire des idées politiques
Idées religieuses 3427, 3439
Identification 1764, 1820, 4489, 4494
Identité 155, 158, 166, 228, 252-254, 263,
    291, 383, 415, 530, 579, 582, 599, 611,
    625, 627, 659, 669, 689, 694, 708, 716,
    729, 735, 748, 751, 798, 852, 886, 936,
    969, 972, 991, 991, 1004, 1083, 1361,
    1426, 1554, 1733, 1749, 1758, 1787,
    1798, 1816, 1816, 1817, 1824, 1925,
    1965, 2005, 2013, 2092, 2104, 2192,
    2193, 2195, 2207, 2257, 2323, 2324,
    2327, 2476, 2478, 2496, 2510, 2533,
    2600, 2601, 2603, 2603, 2623, 2628,
    2648, 2652, 2668, 2692, 2762, 2779,
    2831, 2834, 2842, 2900, 2919, 2921,
    2955, 2976, 3005, 3016, 3039, 3042,
    3043, 3071, 3073, 3081, 3094, 3096,
    3102, 3105, 3106, 3132, 3199, 3230,
    3250, 3345, 3348, 3409, 3410, 3414,
    3422, 3487, 3489, 3494, 3516, 3570,
    3591, 3621, 3625, 3633, 3639, 3649,
    3665, 3666, 3683, 3697, 3700, 3701,
    3712, 3722, 3723, 3739, 3777, 3783,
    3822, 3871, 3873, 3891, 3917, 3938,
    3939, 3946, 3958, 3960, 3961, 3969,
    3994, 4014, 4041, 4049, 4056, 4073,
    4074, 4093, 4108, 4111, 4126, 4184, 4191,
    4205, 4238, 4239, 4265, 4313, 4316,
    4330, 4337, 4352, 4355, 4356, 4359,
    4361, 4377-4379, 4395, 4398, 4401, 4402,
    4405, 4406, 4408-4412, 4414, 4415, 4419,
    4422, 4425-4432, 4434, 4436, 4437, 4439,
    4440, 4440, 4441, 4443-4453, 4455-4459,

4461, 4462, 4464, 4466-4468, 4470, 4471, 4473-4477, 4479, 4481, 4483, 4485, 4488, 4489, 4492, 4494, 4504, 4516, 4528, 4540, 4582, 4590, 4591, 4605, 4652, 4708, 4754, 4758, 4839, 4845, 4853, 4861
voir aussi: Formation d'identité, Politique d'identité
Identité culturelle 130, 353, 599, 887, 2096, 2193, 2201, 2601, 2616, 2936, 2937, 3026, 3401, 3600, 3616, 3660, 3727, 3969, 4013, 4334, 4407, 4419, 4424, 4433, 4438, 4446, 4451, 4454
Identité de groupe 220, 262, 2585, 2992, 3633, 4126, 4309, 4423, 4435, 4459, 4604, 4741
Identité nationale 15, 136, 166, 647, 1746, 1774, 1777, 2018, 2198, 2487, 2666, 2855, 2901, 2927, 2934, 3071, 3088, 3096, 3649, 3653, 3693, 3699, 3703, 3886, 3891, 3958, 4120, 4221, 4336, 4342, 4369, 4411, 4423, 4428, 4448, 4470, 4482, 4484, 4486, 4487, 4490, 4493, 4496, 4498, 4499, 4502-4505, 4626, 4758
Identité régionale 402, 2614, 3094, 3102, 3917, 4382
Identité sociale 252, 263, 504, 708, 804, 2013, 2327, 2530, 2672, 2928, 3043, 3367, 3594, 3616, 3777, 3842, 4164, 4435
Idéologie 35, 104, 204, 215, 228, 271, 329, 656, 769, 800, 1735, 1736, 1785, 1792, 2096, 2100, 2535, 2538, 2544, 2549, 2600, 2619, 2630, 2666, 2791, 2822, 2826, 2850, 2927, 2944, 3030, 3066, 3142, 3233, 3288, 3340, 3367, 3518, 3523, 3538, 3707, 3838, 3846, 3887, 3933, 4023, 4059, 4102, 4415, 4452, 4482, 4490, 4493, 4502
Idéologies politiques 1084, 2399, 3107, 3357, 3951
Igbo 2005, 2513, 2659, 2682, 2683, 2733, 4193
Igbo-Ukwu 532
Igorot 4852
Ikwerre 1998
Ila 3245
Îles 323, 365, 511, 556, 566, 630, 691, 707, 721, 1088, 1462, 1820, 1827, 2085, 2344, 2384, 2498, 2559, 2647, 2814, 3546, 3650, 3847, 3847, 4228, 4237, 4300, 4310, 4311, 4323, 4443, 4601, 4647, 4768
Images 110, 133, 231, 257, 322, 360, 380, 389, 409, 439, 441, 582, 759, 813, 997, 1006, 1044, 1051, 1088, 1364, 1394, 1442, 1460, 1777, 2774, 2934, 2950, 3119, 3189, 3217, 3242, 3396, 3511, 3516, 3660, 3718, 3721, 3799, 3873, 4098, 4104,

4105, 4126, 4139, 4140, 4160, 4195, 4199, 4316, 4382, 4523
Imagination 2085, 2324, 3330, 3933, 4029, 4059, 4263, 4310, 4514, 4599
Imbuga, Francis 2499
Immigrants 253, 489, 732, 763, 787, 2154, 2186, 2259, 2453, 2599, 2883, 2887, 2982, 3070, 3629, 4397, 4603, 4761
Immigrants clandestins 2169, 2660
Immigration 246, 1551, 1659, 2135, 3056, 3075, 3077, 4191, 4421
Immunisation 2140, 4880, 4884, 4885
Impérialisme 529, 611, 650, 694, 702, 703, 715, 718, 742, 805, 817, 903, 984, 2092, 2741, 2745, 3042, 4150, 4171, 4182, 4284, 4298
Impérialisme culturel 611, 3042
Importations 2305
Impôts 506, 527, 2336, 2395
Impression 1743, 2253, 3354, 3668, 4144, 4240
Inca 766, 1784, 2597, 3538, 4098
Incertitude 1573, 1602, 2404, 3326, 4763
Inceste 3966
Incompatibilités 1486, 1491, 2118
Indépendance 37, 114, 529, 541, 609, 675, 792, 793, 2506, 2559, 2653, 2977, 3673, 3869, 3949, 4102, 4589, 4629
Indicateurs 1568, 1629, 2149, 2720, 3674, 4595
Indicateurs économiques 4817
voir aussi: Clignotement des indicateurs économiques
Indiens 225, 539, 732, 761, 1945, 2098, 2356, 2621, 2886, 3053, 3107, 3214, 3271, 3272, 3296, 3317, 3570, 3605, 3754, 3783, 4363
Indigénisme 3911, 4655
Individu et société 2595
Individualisme 371, 2618, 3112, 3166
Individualité 2367
Individus 159, 217, 2324, 2490, 2643, 2790, 2921, 3812, 4126, 4469, 4540, 4890
Indo-europénnes 559, 1729, 2162, 2175, 2612, 3110, 3115, 3125, 3692
Indonésiens 4071
Industrialisation 580, 909, 2208, 2279
Industrie 463, 580, 850, 864, 1395, 2236, 2279, 2343, 2644
voir aussi: Agroindustrie, Construction navale, Fabrication industrielle, Localisation industrielle, Minoterie, Petite industrie
Industrie agro-alimentaire 4784
Industrie automobile 4671

Industrie de la construction 2456
Industrie de transformation 4678
Industrie des télécommunications 2471
Industrie du caoutchouc 893, 2110
Industrie du charbon 1829
Industrie du disque 3922
Industrie du sucre 2300, 2619, 3066
Industrie du vêtement 2456
Industrie minière 936, 2226, 2439, 4619
    voir aussi: Charbonnages
Industrie nucléaire 2454
Industrie textile 727, 2270, 2863
Industries préhistoriques 1359
Inégalité 183, 247, 978, 1456, 2101, 2387,
    2410, 2513, 2596, 2618, 2626, 2659,
    2795, 2846, 3597, 3801, 4609, 4611, 4618,
    4682, 4794, 4875, 4895
Inégalité de revenu 2264, 2620, 4399, 4682
Inégalité économique 2570
Inégalité sociale 235, 760, 2942, 4665, 4895
Infanticide 1605, 1683, 2722, 2738, 2785,
    4835
Inférence causale 224
Infibulation 2880, 2883
Infirmières 603, 2716, 3781
Inflation 485, 2361
Influence culturelle 626, 798, 1443, 1874,
    1932, 2744, 3049, 3078, 3122, 3848,
    4044, 4160, 4383
Influence interculturelle 81, 323, 707, 3933,
    4059
Influences religieuses 2267, 3193, 3234, 3416,
    3641
Information 25, 61, 78, 291, 301, 635, 2057,
    2241, 2589
    voir aussi: Accès à l'information
Infrastructure publique 4688, 4907, 4932,
    4939, 4941
Infrastructure sociale 4723
Ingalls, Daniel Henry Holmes 1945
Ingénierie 863, 965, 3855, 4766
Initiation 166, 2731, 3511, 3591, 3649, 3822,
    4199, 4428
Injures 1663
Innovation 188, 879, 1397, 1684, 2085, 2253,
    2436, 3730, 3892, 4310, 4743
Innovation agricole 2255, 2273, 2280, 2308,
    4687, 4694, 4703
Inondations 402, 2061, 2079, 3860
Insectes 4, 165, 507, 2109, 3746
Instabilité politique 787, 2102
Institutionnalisation 4816
Institutionnalisme 4787
Institutions 337, 380, 722, 2067, 2289, 2376,
    2404, 2416, 2514, 2999, 3017, 3030,

4710, 4726, 4789, 4907
    voir aussi: Établissements d'enseignement,
    Modification institutionnelle, Organismes
    d'aide, Réforme institutionnelle
Institutions financières 4911
Institutions religieuses 2485, 2997, 3194,
    3197, 3204
Instrument 1393
    voir aussi: Outil agricole
Instruments à vent 3935, 3936
Instruments de musique 2247, 3587, 3719,
    3724, 3726, 3911, 3923, 3926, 3929,
    3935-3937, 3945, 3948, 3954, 3967, 4505
Insurrection 816
Intégration économique 2359, 4614, 4682
Intégration européenne 2486
Intégration régionale 551, 2318, 2385, 4682,
    4688
Intégration sociale 1661, 1816, 2655, 2770,
    3067, 4682
Intellectuels 123, 176, 587, 634, 2495, 2572,
    3079, 3100, 3441, 3616, 3675, 4187,
    4210, 4524
Intelligence 1492, 1513, 1711, 1715, 4527
Intensification agricole 2314
Interaction en groupe 1664
Interaction sociale 916, 957, 1404, 1430,
    1636, 1653, 1735, 1752, 1803, 2457,
    3000, 3398, 3843, 4390, 4511, 4882
Interdépendance 254, 2185, 3388, 4457, 4615,
    4804
Interdit alimentaire 4395
Intérêt public 4718
Intermariage 2754, 3058, 3101, 4416
Internationalisation 29, 2385
Internet 1773, 1782, 2324, 3664
Intervalles génésiques 2131, 2708
Intervention d'une troisième partie 4728
Intervention humanitaire 4708, 4725, 4834,
    4839
Intervention militaire 395
Intifada 3026, 4495
Intimité 2868
Inuit 2066, 2075, 2524, 3514, 3660, 4645,
    4785, 4811
Invalidité 1652, 2922, 2925, 2933, 2955
Invasions 535, 612, 3023
Inventions 613, 879, 1704, 2230
Inventaire 1386
Investissements 1571, 2158, 2251, 2399,
    4647, 4866, 4900, 4932
Investissements directs étrangers 2113, 2318
Iraniens 559, 626, 2162, 4358, 4403
Iraqw 2487
Iroquois 102, 1799

Irrigation 789, 2062, 2070, 2093, 2271, 2287, 2289, 2293, 2295, 2376, 3536, 4635, 4688, 4769, 4771, 4783, 4926
Ishi 887
Islam 154, 191, 202, 228, 245, 260, 292, 356, 413, 484, 527, 579, 596, 606, 611, 617, 782, 1015, 1032, 1082, 1100, 1333, 1373, 1749, 1852, 1863, 2073, 2099, 2182, 2227, 2395, 2484, 2501, 2652, 2682, 2748, 2826, 2910, 2967, 2979, 2986, 2998, 3014, 3027, 3042, 3155, 3230, 3236, 3320, 3321, 3323-3336, 3338, 3338-3342, 3344, 3345, 3347-3350, 3353-3357, 3359-3361, 3364-3366, 3580, 3616, 3621, 3625, 3634, 3646, 3767, 3802, 3840, 3853, 3951, 4052, 4058, 4080, 4115, 4185, 4215, 4218, 4232, 4441, 4447, 4558, 4585, 4615, 4622, 4629, 4685
    voir aussi: Chiisme, Coran, Soufisme
Islam et politique 2484, 2501, 2541, 3353, 4585, 4615
Islamisation 245, 2495, 2652, 3345, 4185
Ismail, Husin bin 4215
Isolat 1731
Isolationnisme 2478
Isonymie 1822
Italiens 2476, 4397
Ivoires 1366
Jackson, Andrew 2330
Jacob, Ephraim ben 3089
Jaddus 3454
Jaïn 185, 3183, 3235, 3369-3379, 3381, 3384-3386, 3388-3391, 4117
Jaïnisme 185, 2099, 3155, 3164, 3183, 3235, 3368-3380, 3382-3391, 4117
Jalousie 2682
Jamālzāde, Mohammad Ali 4169
Jansen, Jan 2488
Japonais 787, 3078, 3956, 4419, 4583
Jardins 161, 1073, 2260, 4443
Jaspers, Karl 260
Jazz 118, 2857, 3076, 3900, 3929, 3931, 3933, 3935, 3943, 4059
Jésuite 721, 806, 3220, 3632
Jeu 1783, 4519
Jeu d'échecs 4333
Jeûne 2718, 3814
Jeunes et politique 2502, 3572
Jeunes filles 2697, 2729, 2803, 2863, 2931, 2962, 4835
Jeunesse 1589, 1748, 2085, 2502, 2734, 2882, 2914, 2917, 3040, 3154, 3474, 3508, 3572, 4310, 4447, 4722, 4733, 4937
Jeux 730, 1783, 3549, 3930, 3976, 4306, 4307, 4313-4315, 4333, 4492

Jeux d'argent 4315, 4337
Jeux de balle 4304, 4336, 4337
Jeux olympiques 4336, 4574
Joaillerie 1373, 1382, 1396
    voir aussi: Perles
John [Saint] 3261
Johnson, Samuel 4176
Johnson, William 2857, 3076
Jomon 1461, 1464, 2235
Josephus, Flavius 3420, 3421, 3428, 3454, 4258
Joshee, Anandibai 4577
Jouets 811, 2632
Journal 97, 566, 584, 594, 637, 690, 731, 4108, 4263, 4277, 4572
Journalisme 805, 1781, 3037, 3793, 4280
Journalistes 106, 752
Joyce, James 4182
Jubair, Ibn 596
Judaïsme 208, 253, 447, 468, 472, 473, 476, 514, 515, 560, 568, 591-593, 604, 606, 634, 640, 666, 897, 1103, 1308, 1864, 1965, 2099, 2573, 2748, 2756, 2799, 2909, 2965, 2986, 3155, 3327, 3392-3395, 3397, 3398, 3400-3403, 3405-3409, 3411-3413, 3415-3419, 3422-3426, 3428-3430, 3432-3435, 3437-3444, 3447-3458, 3460, 3613, 3666, 3748, 3997, 4141, 4258, 4384, 4402, 4427, 4445, 4581
    voir aussi: Hassidisme, Hébreu
Judiciaire 59, 2975, 2994, 3003, 3705
Jugement 4466
Juges 485, 792, 2361, 2987
Juifs 253, 468, 472, 476, 515, 519, 560, 592, 593, 1773, 1816, 2160, 2422, 2573, 2778, 2799, 3089, 3098, 3100, 3327, 3392, 3394, 3397, 3401, 3404, 3406, 3408-3410, 3412, 3414, 3422, 3428, 3446, 3447, 3451, 3452, 3613, 3665, 3666, 3899, 4002, 4049, 4093, 4141, 4359, 4384, 4402, 4424, 4427, 4439, 4445, 4451, 4461, 4468, 4479, 4503, 4515, 4581, 4628
Jumeaux 1488, 2682, 3273
Juridiction criminelle 3011
Jurisprudence 516, 784, 2989, 2996, 3014, 3341
Justice 214, 485, 510, 2218, 2361, 2536, 2933, 2971, 3013, 3032, 3063, 3068, 4012, 4449, 4634
Justice pénale 3004, 3011
Justice sociale 95, 234, 516, 2090, 2485, 2496, 2544, 2969, 2984, 2996, 3074, 4012, 4611, 4613, 4670, 4671, 4752, 4762
Kaberry, Phyllis 105, 3231
Kabyle 1854

Kafka, Franz 4093
Kālidāsa 3305, 3885
Kalmyk 3945, 4410
Kamuleta, Kadima 1994, 2009
Kanak 2096
Karen 4791
Karo Batak 334, 4178
Kasena 2103, 4024
Kaur, Satwant 3492, 3493
Keats, John 3728
Kenyah 4320, 4598
Kety 1768
KGB 319, 2964
Khaldun, Ibn 575
Khaled bn 'Abd el-Malik bn al-Harth bn Al-
    Hakam, Mohammed bn [Prince] 1319
Khanty 2057
Khatri 2541
Khmer 1076, 4547
Khoi 4151
Khoikhoi 682
Khoisan 1726, 2377
Kikuyu 1997
Kinberg, Naphtali 129, 1853
Kinguri 2168
Kintō, Fujiwara 4051
Kipling, Rudyard 4284
Kipsigis 2611, 2611
Kirghiz 145, 1834
Klong-rdol bla ma 3184
Koentjaraningrat, R.M. 37, 114
Kohnen, Bernardo 88
Komi 2050, 2053, 2054, 2056
Koresh, David 3563
Kota 3910, 3967
Krčelić, Baltazar Adam 3974
Kuhn, Thomas S. 259, 414
Kumaraswamy Iyer, K.R. 3932
Kuna 3550
Kunama 2010
Kuru 3803
Kurzman, Steven L. 2955
Kusu 1996
Kwahu 2773, 2898
Kwakiutl 98, 2503
Kwara'ae 3669, 4519
Kyong'ae, Kang 2933
Kyrillos VI [Saint] 3253
Labdron, Machig 3192
Laboratoire 1509
Lac 2086
Laïcisme 275, 606, 2099, 2539, 2986, 3155,
    3544
Lamaïsme 3202
Lamentations 4011

Lances 1402
Langage 99, 110, 129, 230, 248, 266, 271,
    291, 308, 320, 344, 540, 542, 550, 586,
    597, 651, 735, 745, 830, 1005, 1036,
    1042, 1338, 1339, 1723, 1726-1736, 1739,
    1741, 1742, 1745-1749, 1756, 1759, 1763,
    1765, 1773, 1775, 1778-1780, 1784, 1785,
    1787, 1789-1791, 1794, 1795, 1797, 1798,
    1800, 1801, 1803, 1804, 1807-1810, 1812-
    1814, 1816, 1824, 1826, 1831, 1834,
    1839-1841, 1845-1849, 1853, 1854, 1856,
    1858, 1865-1867, 1870-1872, 1877, 1880,
    1892, 1894, 1895, 1897-1901, 1904-1906,
    1908-1911, 1913, 1915-1918, 1920, 1924,
    1925, 1927-1931, 1933-1941, 1943, 1944,
    1946-1949, 1951-1958, 1961, 1962, 1964,
    1965, 1968-1971, 1974, 1976-1983, 1986-
    1988, 1990, 1991, 1994, 1997, 1998,
    2002-2007, 2009, 2011, 2012, 2017, 2020-
    2046, 2048-2051, 2053-2055, 2057, 2059,
    2145, 2324, 2529, 2638, 2641, 2689,
    2812, 3014, 3080, 3150, 3226, 3229,
    3233, 3258, 3268, 3282, 3312, 3333,
    3341, 3362, 3433, 3459, 3511, 3537, 3588,
    3644, 3652, 3653, 3799, 3874, 3887,
    3915, 3927, 3973, 3996, 4017, 4035,
    4039, 4061, 4065, 4067, 4170, 4224,
    4250, 4252, 4256, 4263, 4286, 4409,
    4419, 4426, 4430, 4434, 4437, 4446,
    4474, 4478, 4484, 4488, 4490, 4506,
    4562, 4587, 4640
    voir aussi: Albanais, Coréen, Hindi,
    Philologie, Phrases, Portugais, Urdu
Langage par signes 40
Langue allemande 69, 74, 83, 1751
Langue anglaise 63-65, 68, 70, 1723, 1728,
    1744, 1761, 1769, 1770, 1789, 1791,
    1797, 1801, 1803, 1808, 1810, 1814,
    1815, 1911, 1918, 1926, 1927, 1940, 1944,
    1947-1949, 1951, 1953, 1954, 1957, 1961,
    1963, 2005, 2018, 3874, 3989, 4160,
    4175, 4176, 4193, 4195
Langue arabe 129, 324, 344, 586, 1136, 1339,
    1347, 1356, 1762, 1804, 1819, 1840-1842,
    1847, 1851-1853, 1860, 1862, 1863, 1865,
    1867-1869, 1871, 1874, 3268, 3354, 3359,
    3393, 3738, 4087, 4155, 4167, 4267
Langue bulgare 1917
Langue espagnole 65, 67, 84, 1785, 1794,
    1795, 1806, 1810, 1862, 1915, 1925,
    1946, 1952, 1985, 3930, 4167, 4267, 4270
Langue française 75, 1749, 1762, 1801, 1813,
    1919, 1981, 1986
Langue frisonne 1964

Langue grecque 560, 1850, 1912, 1922, 1959, 3412

Langue italienne 1932

Langue japonaise 1737, 1769, 1770, 1872, 1875

Langue maternelle 309, 2146, 3095, 4553

Langue maya 102, 1799

Langue nationale 1749

Langue polonaise 1958

Langue proto-dravidian 1903, 2301

Langue roumaine 1924

Langue russe 1909, 1936, 3100

Langue suédois 1963

Langues asiatiques et du pacifique 1725, 1744, 1883

Langues chinoises 54, 2019, 2026, 2047

Langues écrites 545, 1744, 1875, 2017

Langues étrangères 2047

Langues indo-européennes 1729, 1912, 1916, 1920, 1928, 1930, 1931, 1935, 1942, 1943, 1956, 1966, 2059
    voir aussi: Sanscrit

Langues mortes 1727, 3401

Langues nigéro-congolaises 1988, 1990, 1994, 1998, 2004, 2009

Langues non-écrites 139, 1784

Langues officielles 1797

Langues slavs 117, 1933, 1958, 3103

Langues vernaculaires 1795, 1915

Lapita 556, 598, 623, 931, 1404

Lapon 4624

Latin 461, 490, 774, 1358, 1912, 1941, 1942, 3150

Lawrence, David 4303

Leaders 537, 649, 2199, 2563, 2566, 3488

Leaders charismatiques 3262

Leaders politiques 501, 576, 2564, 3322, 3573, 4533

Lecture 257, 1740, 2561, 2832, 4217, 4247, 4751

Leer, Willem van 4581

Légendes 505, 639, 659, 662, 713, 3116, 3118, 3120, 3132, 3351, 3353, 3354, 3493, 3514, 3528, 3679, 3709, 3974, 3993, 3997, 3999, 4003, 4005, 4013, 4015, 4026, 4154, 4214, 4221, 4253

Leger, Alexis 4712

Législation 719, 2259, 2582, 2736, 2739, 2750, 2863, 2883, 2954, 3010, 3012, 3019, 3096, 4617, 4642, 4644, 4651, 4791, 4804, 4861

Légitimation 4257

Légitimité 1159, 2937, 3739, 3861, 4438

Légumes 4396

Leitão, Manoel Correia 690

Lele 3685

Lenca 2084

Leopardi, Giacomo 3728

Lèpre 739

Lesbianisme 514, 2900, 2909, 4330

Levi, Maklouf 615

Lévi-Povençal, Evariste 615

Lévirat 2753, 2906

Lévi-Strauss, Claude 2602, 2665

Lexicographie 745, 1728, 1769, 1770, 1779, 2055

Lexicologie 1730, 1751, 1877, 1879, 1889, 1932, 1987, 2007, 2014, 2015, 2021, 4262

Li 2678, 3682

Li Po 4056

Libéralisation 4661, 4671, 4672

Libéralisation financière 4662

Libéralisme 815, 3846, 4682
    voir aussi: Néolibéralisme

Libération 215, 3188, 3299, 3376, 3679

Libertariens 3846

Liberté 585, 2408, 2496, 2548, 3009, 3216, 3846, 3862, 3869, 3889, 4650

Liberté d'association 4820

Liberté de l'enseignement 4748

Liberté d'expression 134

Liberté religieuse 3563, 3634

Libre échange 4611

Lieu de travail 2454, 2459, 2461, 2468, 3986

Lieux de culte 829

Lieux sacrés 105, 2682, 3204, 3231, 3239, 3495, 3548, 3703

Lieux saints 257, 829, 1361, 1381, 3230, 3452, 3697, 4441

Lignage 1577, 2188, 2421, 2617, 2653, 2662, 2677, 2977, 3185, 3519, 4822

Limbu 2032, 2035

Liminalité 201, 222, 237, 239, 384, 392, 396, 2190, 2615, 3777

Lindfors, Bernth 89

Linguistes 119, 139, 1878, 1994, 2009

Linguistique 30, 42, 57, 109, 113, 117, 124, 139, 150, 163, 250, 252, 271, 382, 522, 540, 609, 631, 745, 762, 1025, 1331, 1435, 1723-1726, 1728-1730, 1732, 1734, 1740-1742, 1744, 1747, 1749-1753, 1756, 1757, 1760, 1765, 1766, 1776, 1778, 1779, 1783, 1785, 1789, 1791-1797, 1801, 1802, 1805-1808, 1810-1814, 1819, 1821, 1826, 1831, 1832, 1837-1840, 1842-1850, 1854, 1855, 1858, 1860, 1866-1870, 1872, 1875, 1877-1892, 1894-1911, 1913-1915, 1917, 1918, 1920-1922, 1924, 1927-1930, 1932-1938, 1940, 1943, 1944, 1946-1949, 1951-1964, 1967, 1968, 1971, 1976, 1977,

1979-1981, 1984, 1986, 1987, 1989, 1991-1999, 2001, 2002, 2005-2016, 2020-2022, 2024, 2025, 2027-2046, 2048-2052, 2054, 2055, 2058, 2100, 2301, 2526, 2544, 2550, 2638, 2667, 2832, 2973, 3134, 3146, 3147, 3165, 3173, 3179, 3185, 3195, 3203, 3233, 3267, 3273, 3293, 3301, 3319, 3322, 3539, 3576, 3588, 3673, 3707, 3728, 3885, 3944, 3950, 3973, 3989, 4025, 4040, 4064, 4082, 4147, 4151, 4155, 4188, 4203, 4206, 4224, 4244, 4249, 4273, 4285, 4286, 4409, 4422, 4444, 4461, 4467, 4503, 4548
voir aussi: Accent, Diglossie, Sociolinguistique
Linguistique comparée 1847, 1885, 1896, 1920, 2002
Lips, Julius E. 3045
Lisnianskaia, Inna 4073
Lisu 2022
Lithographies 4128, 4240
Litige 342, 2987, 2994, 3638, 4762
Littérature 62, 89, 107, 129, 141, 163, 201, 326, 376, 405, 409, 452, 471, 514, 528, 651, 663, 799, 805, 1739, 1827, 1853, 1865, 1950, 1974, 2005, 2025, 2533, 2622, 2641, 2813, 2834, 2839, 2853, 2857, 2909, 2928, 2933, 3005, 3073, 3076, 3079, 3080, 3113, 3118, 3172, 3179, 3180, 3211, 3255, 3272, 3274, 3296, 3305, 3330, 3354, 3369, 3390, 3437, 3535, 3655, 3665, 3698, 3718, 3728, 3740, 3823, 3911, 3961, 3980, 3981, 3984, 3996, 3999, 4011, 4027, 4030, 4039, 4040, 4043, 4046, 4048, 4049, 4051, 4053-4055, 4058, 4064, 4079, 4081, 4082, 4084, 4085, 4088, 4112, 4146, 4147, 4149-4151, 4153, 4156-4159, 4162-4164, 4166-4170, 4173, 4174, 4177, 4179, 4182, 4184, 4187, 4188, 4190-4192, 4195-4197, 4199-4202, 4204, 4206, 4209-4214, 4216-4222, 4226, 4228, 4230, 4235, 4242, 4244-4249, 4251, 4252, 4260-4265, 4269, 4271-4273, 4275, 4279, 4282, 4283, 4287-4289, 4296, 4341, 4354, 4375, 4406, 4439, 4503, 4569, 4581
voir aussi: Histoire littéraire, Poèmes, Poésie, Prose, Romans
Littérature classique 1819, 4215, 4231
Littérature épique 3991, 4022
Littérature folklorique 3679, 3991, 4022
Littérature orale 1758, 3990, 3995, 3996, 4014, 4021, 4027, 4029, 4030
Littérature populaire 3991, 3995, 4240
Littérature sur le développement 4713
Littérature traditionnelle 206, 4076, 4215

Littoraux 298, 806, 1151, 1246, 1825, 2079, 2117, 2134, 2260, 2313, 2362, 3084, 4618, 4794
Liturgie 468, 472, 3336, 3406-3408, 3423, 3748, 4054
Livres 124, 593, 796, 1044, 1761, 1805, 1865, 3164, 3209, 3323, 3485, 3766, 3768, 4154, 4165, 4186, 4200, 4223, 4244, 4247, 4249
Lobi 2945, 3529
Localisation 189, 3723, 4355, 4456
Localisation géographique 1495
Localisation industrielle 4663
Logement 1054, 1196, 2141, 2171, 2210, 3660, 3842, 3843, 4364, 4647, 4681, 4838, 4930, 4934, 4935, 4941
voir aussi: Habitations rurales
Logement urbain 4937
Logements sociaux 4934
Logique 261, 275, 428, 2539, 3153, 3162, 3178, 3381, 3677, 3947
Lohana 3284
Loi environnementale 4762
Loi islamique 606, 748, 1852, 2417, 2417, 2664, 2976, 2979, 2986, 2993, 3014, 3018, 3018, 3324, 3330, 3341, 3349, 3352, 3364, 3646
Loisir 371, 2085, 2234, 2946, 3972, 4116, 4295, 4310, 4314, 4318, 4324
Lolo 2022
Lom D'Arce, Louis-Armand de 100, 740
Longowal, Sant 2515
López Dàvalos, Ruy 3852
López-Baralt, Mercedes 4098
Loti, Pierre 4179, 4236, 4263, 4322
Lounsbury, Floyd Glenn 102, 1799
Loups 3738, 4087
Loyauté 2104, 2557, 2631, 2635, 3025
Loyer 2293
Lua 2806, 2828
Luba 2168
Lucas, Claude 3005
Lugbara 3542
Lunda 2168
Lune 3120, 3269, 3351
Luthéranisme 3230, 4441
Lutte anti-érosion 4766
Lyre 3896
Ma'ari, Abul Ala'a al- 4047
Macushi 2297, 3067
Madumo 3579
Maeterlinck, Maurice 3728
Mafia 2663, 2975, 4008
Magie 233, 256, 371, 502, 514, 576, 1006, 1317, 1489, 1738, 2802, 2899, 2909,

2923, 3060, 3555, 3557, 3567, 3570,
3573-3576, 3580, 3581, 3583, 3591, 3602,
3604, 3605, 3607, 3626, 3778, 3783,
3809, 3822, 3830, 4017, 4287, 4354
Magyar 3094, 3095, 3102, 3703, 4553
Mahafaly 2507
Mahākassapa 3190
Mahāvīra, Bhagavān 3368, 3375, 3385, 3386,
4117
Mahavira, Vardhamāna 3370, 3384
Mahmoud, Haidar 3365, 4080
Maimonides, Moses 3403
Main d'œuvre 687, 2254
Maintien de l'ordre 2969
Maïs 323, 707, 2275, 2302, 2312, 2319, 4609
Maison 911, 1035, 1365, 2187, 2394, 2459,
2594, 2602, 2642, 2665, 2777, 3660,
3696, 3713, 4319
Makonde 4145
Makoni [Chief] 711
Makuzu, Tadano 4266
Mal 2532, 2635, 3025, 3578, 3590, 3738,
4035, 4087
Malades 3159, 3790, 3805, 4545
Maladie 566, 1560, 1570, 1651, 1657, 2128,
2701, 3761, 3763, 3774, 3777, 3805, 3811,
3813, 3815, 3819, 3835, 3836, 4211, 4276,
4526, 4871, 4882, 4896
Maladie mentale 1781, 3404, 3777, 3793,
4515, 4543, 4545
Maladie sexuellement transmissible 44, 1580,
2723, 2879, 2884, 2885, 2892, 2905,
3761, 3796, 3810, 3820, 4878
Maladies 566, 1289, 1489, 1498, 1563, 1570,
1572, 1575, 1626, 1657, 1688, 1701,
2137, 2310, 2657, 2885, 3124, 3761-3763,
3771-3773, 3777, 3779, 3798, 3803, 3804,
3809, 3811, 3823, 3828, 3986, 4777, 4867,
4882
voir aussi: Epilepsie, Lèpre, SIDA,
Variole
Maladies de coeur 1585
Malais 4215
Malanggan 2241
Malaria 2128, 4870, 4880, 4888
Mâle 1508, 1539, 1602, 1605, 1623, 1628,
1635, 1643, 1661, 2875, 2890
Malet, Léo 3005
Manasseh [King] 3424
Mande 625, 629, 641, 643, 2488, 2531, 2608,
4447
Manggarai 3939
Mangyan 4772
Mani 3527
Manioc 2297

Manobo 2409
Mansi 2055, 2057
Manuel I [King] 323, 707
Manuels 3206
Manuels scolaires 66, 70, 71, 570, 2519, 3705
Maori 811, 2408, 2525, 2712, 2937, 3655,
4293, 4432, 4438, 4650
Mapuche 1586, 3824, 4315
Marathi 124, 1805, 4197
Marcellini, Margarita 3828
Marchands 764, 2196, 2356, 2386, 4497
Marché 529, 1357, 2196, 2322, 2331, 2332,
2334, 2338, 2341, 2359, 2450, 4426,
4661, 4820, 4827
Marché agricole et alimentaire 709, 2335,
4693
Marché de l'art 2353
Marché du crédit 4911
Marché du travail 2359, 2460, 2466, 2768,
4606, 4916
Marché financier 4671
Marché international 2280
Marché mondial 2305, 4809
Marché régional 2255, 4687
Marcos, Ferdinand 4679
Marginalité 994, 4200
Marginaux 239, 254, 396, 2933, 3082, 4457,
4630, 4646, 4722
Mari (ethnie) 3087, 3708
Mariage 127, 502, 606, 646, 666, 676, 776,
1453, 1900, 2163, 2252, 2351, 2474,
2554, 2586, 2628, 2629, 2638, 2651,
2658, 2666, 2670, 2683, 2687, 2735,
2737, 2738, 2740-2747, 2749-2753, 2755-
2758, 2781, 2785, 2825, 2833, 2856,
2862-2864, 2899, 2906, 2986, 3019, 3267,
3319, 3399, 3457, 3458, 3704, 4373,
4493, 4541
voir aussi: Âge au mariage, Intermariage
Mariage consanguin 2748
Mariage coutumier 2736, 2739, 2750, 3010,
3012, 3019
Mariages interraciaux 2742
Marine marchande 4724
Marins 323, 707
Marionnettes 4138
Maris 2645, 2758
Marketing 2353, 2363
voir aussi: Publicité
Marold, Luděk 4112
Marque 2363, 3893
Marques commerciales 1447
Marquez-Benitez, Paz 4195
Martí, José 4234
Martin, Jean 3105

Martino, Ernesto de 121, 408
Martyr, Justin [Saint] 3437
Marxisme 204, 218, 3616
Masai 673, 3806
Masculinité 215, 280, 433, 2807, 2810, 2820,
    2840, 2841, 2848, 2855, 2858, 2865, 2911,
    2932, 3254, 4305, 4309, 4336, 4342,
    4520, 4560
Maseet, Ki 3363, 3498
Masochisme 3877
Masques 1067, 2571, 2731, 2945, 3122, 3529,
    3559, 3614, 3722, 4133, 4296
Masques funéraires 1077
Matérialisme 164, 218, 3373
Matérialisme culturel 204, 3292
Matériel d'équitation 1383
Maternité 557, 1658, 1676, 2632, 2639, 2693,
    2702, 2707, 2709, 2721, 2863, 2966,
    3693, 3775
Mathématiques 832, 1612, 3743, 3857
Matières premières 2107, 2235
Matriarcat 2546, 2690, 2835, 3688
Matsigenka 2098
Maure 705
Mauss, Marcel 223
Mauvais traitements infligés à un enfant 4722
Maximes 3661
Maya 453, 494, 499, 525, 657, 851, 929, 1016,
    1345, 1370, 1372, 1970, 1979, 2112, 2165,
    2240, 2444, 2547, 2562, 2794, 2811, 2955,
    3517, 3523, 3672, 3735, 3745, 3752,
    3757, 4183, 4387, 4414, 4450
Mazahua 1812
Meddeb, Abdelwahab 2641
Médecine 17, 62, 459, 605, 729, 909, 1470,
    1505, 1542, 1555, 1575, 1585, 1953,
    2149, 2150, 2208, 2661, 2674, 2701,
    2712, 2720, 2728, 2773, 2775, 2871,
    2890, 2898, 2912, 2952, 2959, 3159,
    3358, 3510, 3580, 3739, 3749, 3750,
    3764, 3766, 3768, 3770, 3774, 3778-3780,
    3784-3787, 3795, 3797, 3798, 3802, 3803,
    3805, 3807-3809, 3818, 3821, 3825-3829,
    3832, 3834, 3836, 4174, 4186, 4328,
    4525, 4531, 4637
    voir aussi: Biomédecine, Chirurgie,
    Histoire de la médecine
Médecine alternative 17, 3825
Médecine du travail 3789
Médecine légal 970, 2780, 2924
Médecine traditionnelle 62, 1446, 2066, 2138,
    2260, 2764, 3678, 3739, 3766-3768, 3779,
    3784, 3785, 3797, 3800, 3807, 3815,
    3816, 3818, 3819, 3835, 4188
Médecine vétérinaire 2189

Médecins 99, 481, 2470, 2854, 3429, 3781,
    3787, 4174, 4577
Médias 106, 389, 432, 434, 661, 752, 785,
    1781, 2317, 2462, 2495, 2780, 2800,
    2866, 2924, 2927, 2967, 3037, 3207,
    3328, 3761, 3793, 3823, 3893, 3895,
    3921, 3976, 4043, 4094, 4096, 4119, 4136,
    4143, 4280, 4316, 4368, 4415, 4446,
    4482, 4516, 4544, 4548
    voir aussi: Multimédia, Presse
Médiation 3176
Médicaments 215, 507, 2109, 2874, 3766,
    3782
    voir aussi: Cocaïne, Héroïne, Opiat, Trafic
    de la drogue, Usage de stupéfiants
Méditation 1876, 2800, 3205, 3207, 3278,
    3299, 3463, 3486, 3691
Mégacité 4938
Mégalithes 852, 863, 888, 1011, 1067, 1095,
    1205, 3123, 4601
Mégalithisme 1056, 1063, 4601
Meinecke, Michael 989
Meitei 1579
Meithei 2029
Melo, Fontes Pereira de 323, 707
Melville, Herman 4162
Membre 2955
Membres de la Première Chambre 323, 707
Mémoire 171, 319, 434, 544, 621, 637, 1432,
    1637, 1784, 1828, 2092, 2211, 2766, 2964,
    3005, 3243, 3438, 3634, 3654, 3665,
    3666, 3693, 3702, 3900, 3947, 4012,
    4049, 4126, 4181, 4201, 4416, 4423,
    4439, 4445, 4508, 4511, 4533, 4570, 4573
Mémoire collective 155, 373, 530, 544, 969,
    1782, 1828, 2165, 3654, 3656, 3664-3666,
    3687, 3735, 3912, 4012, 4105, 4357,
    4445, 4477, 4498, 4522, 4523, 4544
Mémoire nationale 2211
Mémoires 76, 355, 637, 731, 3214, 3317,
    3628, 4217, 4271
Mémorials 364, 4508
Menace 2210, 2549
Ménages 848, 911, 2137, 2151, 2181, 2185,
    2221, 2306, 2375, 2455, 2605, 2636,
    2654, 2690, 2823, 4661, 4719
Menchú, Rigoberta 95, 234, 4569
Mende 3034
Mendi 3586
Menges, Karl Heinrich 117
Mennonites 4184
Ménopause 1593
Menstruation 1544, 1558, 1581, 1613, 1640,
    1665, 1667, 1668, 1670, 2811, 3517
Mentalité 3258, 3644

Mer 39, 948, 1151, 2065, 2070, 2085, 2092, 2428, 3242, 3650, 3721, 3847, 4310
Mercantilisme 633, 3008
Mercenaires 448
Mercosur 4663
Mère 1544, 1560, 1584, 1587, 1607, 1614, 1672, 1675, 2654, 2685, 2694, 2696, 2701, 2703, 3774, 3806, 4897
Meru 2613
Messianisme 3427, 3632
Messies 3427
Mesure 235, 268, 296, 310, 870, 1454, 1462, 1466, 1493, 1543, 1563, 1576, 1578, 1579, 1583, 1619, 1665, 1667, 1668, 1670, 1719, 3269, 3792, 3959, 4527, 4823, 4911
Métallurgie 1376, 1434
Métaphore 151, 169, 209, 233, 444, 502, 888, 1855, 2899, 2955, 3326, 3560, 3567, 3587, 3726, 3728, 3731, 4065, 4286, 4296, 4429
Métaphysique 121, 227, 408, 2800, 3123, 3143, 3207, 3466, 3595, 3728
Métaux 363, 474, 908, 912, 1326, 1387, 1397, 1414, 1444
Métayage 2285
Météorologie 3680, 3759
Méthode de moindres carrés 4886
Méthodes contraceptives 2695, 2723, 2726, 2892, 2903, 2905, 3810
Méthodes de financement 4325
Méthodes de planification 1763, 2210, 2221, 2894, 4702, 4717, 4731, 4735, 4891, 4928
Méthodes de recherche 28, 33, 36, 72, 170, 187, 225, 277, 282, 287, 290, 291, 294, 300, 302, 306, 307, 339, 394, 404, 406, 407, 410, 411, 422, 426, 429, 443, 536, 539, 616, 635, 655, 930, 970, 1003, 1468, 1815, 2880, 3765, 4009, 4676, 4709, 4818, 4910
    voir aussi: Travail sur le terrain
Méthodes d'exploitation agricole 795, 2299, 4688, 4888
Méthodes mathématiques 310
Méthodes statistiques 301, 4340
Méthodologie 33, 72, 107, 146, 187, 196, 219, 266, 279, 283, 286, 287, 294, 302, 303, 306, 308, 309, 389, 394, 405, 406, 410, 429, 589, 616, 772, 875, 930, 1001, 1123, 1562, 1571, 1618, 1723, 2123, 2124, 2145, 2146, 2233, 2569, 2618, 2860, 3086, 3754, 4009, 4326, 4473, 4676, 4702, 4746, 4756, 4804, 4843, 4924
Méthodologie anthropologique 126, 158, 174, 177, 179, 197, 212, 232, 240-242, 259, 275, 277, 346, 397, 398, 403, 414, 424, 431, 440, 1564, 2539, 3054
    voir aussi: Observation participante
Méthodologie archéologique 60, 258, 458, 923, 938, 941, 945, 953, 970, 980, 983, 988, 996, 997, 1002, 1010, 1046, 1054, 1064, 1074, 1075, 1079, 1082, 1110, 1111, 1113, 1120, 1123, 1124, 1134, 1144, 1145, 1148, 1150, 1154, 1163, 1164, 1169, 1172, 1179, 1180, 1186, 1187, 1189, 1192, 1197, 1206, 1212, 1213, 1221, 1225, 1226, 1231, 1232, 1237, 1239, 1252, 1255, 1258, 1262, 1268, 1269, 1271, 1274-1276, 1278, 1305, 1310, 1360, 1407, 1418, 1419, 1436, 2144
Méthodologie sociologique 388
Métier 322, 1365, 1400, 1405, 1423, 1439, 2233, 2234, 2236-2239, 2242, 2243, 2246, 2247, 2249, 2250, 2253, 2644, 4129, 4453, 4848
Métis 214, 2197, 3070
Meubles 2242
Mœurs 3863, 4349
Meurtre 970, 2705, 2881, 3026, 3033, 3036, 3059, 3089, 3603, 4280
Meurtres rituels 2792, 2795, 3007, 3089, 3597
Mexica 1024, 3119, 3133, 3711
Mexicains 432, 2661, 3065
Miao 2149, 2720, 4605
Michel, Natacha 2453
Microéconomie 2418
Microfinancement 288, 4730, 4846, 4848, 4851, 4885, 4911
Middendorf, Ernst W. 99
Migrateurs 154, 2158, 2176, 2183, 2184, 2356, 2631, 2688, 2802, 3060, 3105, 3250, 3607, 3700, 3960, 4031, 4462, 4611
Migration 193, 228, 246, 254, 559, 585, 669, 684, 877, 880, 1280, 1495, 1497, 1502, 1521, 1635, 1669, 1773, 1809, 1841, 2092, 2104, 2106, 2120, 2135, 2151, 2156, 2158, 2160, 2162, 2163, 2166-2169, 2171-2177, 2179, 2181, 2183, 2185, 2243, 2306, 2356, 2421, 2621, 2655, 2660, 2688, 2770, 2772, 2825, 2886, 3070, 3090, 3103, 3228, 3519, 3791, 4013, 4411, 4417, 4457, 4479, 4606, 4804, 4882
Migration de retour 2165
Migration de travail 2161, 2166, 2207, 2439, 4632
Migration forcée 531, 2159, 4714, 4725
Migration internationale 253, 2185
Migration interne 597, 1453, 2167, 2460
Migration rurale-urbaine 2167, 2181
Migration urbaine-rurale 4135

Miklukho-Maklai, Nikolai 365
Miles, Josephine 2933
Milhaud, Darius 3929
Milieu de travail 3789
Milieu rural 3861
Milieu social 3845
Milieu urbain 2101
Militaires
    voir: Soldat
Militants 2453, 2520
Militarisation 2577, 2578, 2582, 4653
Millar, Fergus 593
Millénarisme 3643, 4097
Minang Kabu 2849
Mine d'argent 4608
Minéraux 1651
Mines 791, 1403
Mines de cuivre 580
Mines d'or 791, 2373
Mineurs 1414, 1829, 2453
Ministères 1786, 4926, 4937
Ministres 632, 2580
Minorités 3077, 3097, 3098, 3103, 3160,
    4421, 4597, 4624, 4628
Minorités ethniques 41, 190, 1746, 2081,
    2267, 2432, 3083, 3760, 4433, 4474,
    4627, 4656, 4931
Minorités linguistiques 1746, 1768, 1916
Minorités nationales 3094, 3095, 3102, 3160,
    4479, 4553
Minoterie 2203
Mise en œuvre d'une politique 152, 2828,
    2829
Mise en valeur du sol 2313
Miskito 2731
Missiles 2576
Missionnaires 25, 88, 122, 155, 530, 540, 600,
    608, 644, 700, 722, 732, 736, 750, 766,
    781, 794, 808, 813, 969, 1744, 2082,
    2682, 2746, 2754, 2755, 2774, 3058,
    3219, 3224, 3230, 3234, 3245, 3266,
    3533, 3608, 3614, 3635, 3640, 3648, 4441
Missions religieuses 318, 608, 721, 722, 750,
    813, 2082, 2754, 2774, 3058, 3608, 3614,
    3615, 3617, 3618, 3628, 3630, 3635,
    3640, 3727, 4472, 4474
Mixtèque 214, 1812, 3735
Moabite 934
Mobilisation politique 4472
Mobilisation sociale 4730
Mobilité de la main d'œuvre 2279
Mobilité descendante 4661
Mobilité géographique 2420
Mobilité sociale 880, 2609, 2746

Mode 174, 2928, 2936, 2946, 2948, 2957,
    4116, 4121, 4122, 4164
Modèles 198, 209, 210, 305, 1558, 1631,
    1670, 2364, 2430, 2679, 2791, 3125,
    3534, 3560, 3561, 3761, 3765, 3942, 4675
Modèles de développement 4784, 4802
Modèles linéaires 4554
Modèles mathématiques 1537, 1545
Modèles stochastiques 295, 2130
Modélisation 298, 388, 455, 866, 1488, 2134,
    2225, 4847
Modernisation 580, 2179, 2204, 2257, 2300,
    2477, 2552, 2644, 2650, 3013, 3070,
    3078, 3108, 3169, 3660, 3784, 3884,
    4101, 4106, 4126, 4294, 4592, 4605,
    4679, 4682, 4882
Modernisme 158, 3168, 3725, 4061, 4071,
    4072, 4234, 4277, 4407, 4596
Modernité 3, 178, 216, 261, 276, 777, 2232,
    2241, 2322, 2417, 2502, 2516, 2532,
    2641, 2801, 2831, 2928, 2999, 3018,
    3033, 3156, 3166, 3233, 3246, 3534,
    3572, 3590, 3595, 3603, 3636, 3677,
    3681, 3689, 3700, 3933, 4059, 4164,
    4287, 4378, 4407, 4500, 4502, 4544,
    4596, 4602, 4754
Modes de vie 905, 1456, 2326, 2502, 3378,
    3572, 3795
Modification institutionnelle 337, 2264, 2376,
    2404, 4399, 4682, 4699, 4769, 4894, 4937
Moines 452, 1026, 2389, 3187, 3191, 3312,
    3376, 3642, 4375
Mokeddem, Malika 2092
Molina, Luís de 774
Momies 490, 1077
Monachisme 514, 2875, 2909
Monarchie 323, 358, 453, 477, 511, 537, 571,
    620, 627, 705, 707, 724, 739, 747, 800,
    814, 815, 1284, 1319, 1329, 1331, 1341,
    1437, 1818, 2063, 2282, 2339, 2519,
    2562, 2574, 2575, 2579, 2581, 2838,
    3305, 3343, 3473, 3928, 4248, 4253
Monastères 1065, 2389, 3495, 3642, 4381
Mondialisation 178, 179, 189, 219, 254, 777,
    1826, 2182, 2207, 2210, 2216, 2257,
    2332, 2370, 2496, 2502, 2552, 2863,
    2990, 3041, 3056, 3075, 3232, 3534,
    3572, 3612, 3639, 3652, 3758, 3884,
    4030, 4218, 4301, 4315, 4316, 4338,
    4355, 4400, 4407, 4417, 4442, 4449,
    4450, 4452, 4454, 4457, 4587, 4604-4615,
    4617, 4618, 4620-4623, 4632, 4651, 4662,
    4663, 4680, 4700, 4722, 4793, 4794,
    4797, 4809, 4820, 4867, 4880, 4904,
    4909, 4917

Mongo 1992
Monk, Thelonious 3929
Monnaies 551, 743, 2261, 2268, 2348, 2366, 2389
  voir aussi: Dollar
Monogamie 2737, 3399
Monolinguisme 1895
Monothéisme 3264, 3527, 3647
Montagnes 1026, 1027, 1058, 1129, 1131, 1249, 1328, 1371, 1514, 1608, 2075, 2187, 2274, 2319, 2417, 2425, 2438, 2653, 2855, 2977, 3018, 3121, 3130, 3536, 3593, 3818, 4186, 4342, 4502, 4659
Monuments funéraires 1311, 1316, 1318, 2494
Monuments historiques 609, 1030, 1048, 1358, 1386, 1412, 3653, 3673, 3703, 3854, 4263, 4484
Moodie, Donald 96, 3985
Morale 2970, 3002, 3138, 4226, 4233
Morales 1044, 2093, 2371, 2896, 3293, 3507, 3521, 3661, 4233, 4469, 4893
Morales Bermúdez, Jesús 4201
Moralité 239, 395, 396, 2119, 2381, 2595, 2643, 2705, 2715, 2724, 2851, 2881, 2930, 2956, 2961, 2966, 2970, 3002, 3138, 3621, 3712, 3761, 3776, 4549
Morbidité 1566, 3821, 3828, 4328, 4899
Morgan, L.H. 2658
Morio, Kita 4204
Morphologie 144, 310, 870, 890, 898, 1379, 1455, 1459, 1464, 1465, 1467, 1471, 1479, 1483, 1484, 1509, 1524, 1528, 1534, 1535, 1560, 1590, 1617, 1620, 1641, 1649, 1719, 1725, 1726, 1734, 1751, 1765, 1807, 1847, 1872, 1879, 1899, 1935, 1937, 1938, 1960, 1984, 2015, 2022, 2032, 2034, 2088, 3667, 3736
Morphométrie 1280, 1480
Morris, Jan 4171
Morrison, Toni 2857, 3076
Mort 147, 822, 970, 1088, 1294, 1296, 1297, 1308, 1323, 1358, 1965, 2128, 2615, 2636, 2643, 2762, 2766, 2778, 2780-2782, 2784, 2787-2791, 2800, 2924, 2929, 3036, 3059, 3207, 3225, 3515, 3722, 3803, 3828, 3949, 4003, 4047, 4083, 4189, 4231, 4263, 4276, 4512, 4518, 4539, 4541, 4546
Mortalité 1706, 2128, 2133, 2138, 2142, 2144, 2150, 2152, 2173, 2701, 2709, 2778, 3774, 3800, 3986, 4821, 4884, 4899
Mortalité des enfants 2129, 2149, 2701, 2704, 2720, 3774
Mortalité infantile 1548, 1583, 1675, 2140
Morteira, Hakham Saul Levi 3444

Mosaïque 1026, 1044, 1357
Moses 3420, 3421
Moso 2741
Mosquées 316, 402, 1032, 1099, 1100, 2227, 3839, 3848, 3849
Mossi 727, 2270
Motivation 1675, 2326, 2468
Motivation d'accomplissement
  voir: Réussite intellectuelle
Mots 320, 1334, 1347, 1355, 1723, 1728, 1731, 1751, 1767, 1851, 1869, 1874, 1903, 1905, 1907, 1942, 2039, 2048, 2054, 2055, 2057, 2301, 3511, 4040, 4139, 4224, 4506
  voir aussi: Ordre des mots
Motu 4602
Moulins 2203
Moulins à blé 2203
Mouseli, Ibn Danial Al- 4075
Moutons 2310, 2437, 2445
Mouvements contestataires 2614, 3686
Mouvements de résistance 767, 3577
Mouvements écologiques 2311, 2587, 3686, 4796
Mouvements littéraires 4053
Mouvements politiques 215, 681, 765, 2541, 2829, 3889
Mouvements religieux 2069, 2485, 3262, 3265, 3276, 3423, 3429, 3548, 3595, 3611, 3631, 3657
Mouvements sociaux 548, 681, 1652, 2197, 2210, 2216, 2218, 2222, 2505, 2587, 2955, 3068, 4612, 4633, 4775
Mouvements urbains 2216, 2222
Moyen âge 529, 624, 715, 943, 951, 1283, 1326, 1422, 1424, 1444, 2965, 3322, 3395, 4002, 4035, 4247, 4580
Muhammad V [King] 620
Mukasa, Ham 674
Mulâtres 2197
Multiculturalisme 228, 269, 399, 572, 782, 1280, 1815, 3020, 3053, 3055, 3064, 3088, 3093, 3096, 3098, 3410, 3612, 3700, 3727, 3918, 4313, 4359, 4365, 4407, 4413, 4418, 4419, 4433, 4492, 4628
Multimédia 4242
Murid 2182, 2375, 2605, 3591, 3822, 4622
Murik 2694
Murray, Margaret 143
Musée d'art 314, 366, 374, 4091
Musées 13, 25, 31, 32, 144, 145, 214, 314, 315, 321, 325, 326, 328, 331, 340-342, 348, 351, 352, 357, 364, 367, 368, 371, 373, 376, 377, 434, 518, 610, 714, 1432, 1527, 2202, 3653, 4091, 4092, 4484, 4508

Musées ethnographiques 331, 345
Musées historiques 366
Musées nationaux 118, 371, 3931
Muséologie 376
Musiciens 118, 3518, 3903, 3914, 3922, 3923, 3925, 3929, 3931-3934, 4059
Musicologie 118, 3719, 3922, 3929, 3931, 3936, 3954, 3960
Musique 166, 371, 647, 1749, 2324, 2481, 2842, 2857, 3076, 3081, 3309, 3357, 3649, 3652, 3724, 3871, 3879, 3894, 3897-3899, 3904, 3906, 3909-3914, 3916, 3917, 3919, 3921, 3922, 3925, 3927, 3932-3935, 3937-3941, 3943-3947, 3951, 3953, 3954, 3957, 3958, 3961-3965, 3967, 4051, 4059, 4119, 4145, 4362, 4428, 4455, 4505, 4587
  voir aussi: Ethnomusicologie, Histoire de la musique
Musique classique 118, 3894, 3931, 3964
Musique contemporaine 3969
Musique folklorique 118, 3923, 3926, 3931, 3933, 3948, 3967, 4059, 4367
Musique pop 3903
Musique populaire 1748, 3940, 3961, 3969
Musique religieuse 3309, 3463, 3901, 3915, 3927, 3962
Musique rituelle 3539, 3950
Musique rock 3518
Musique traditionnelle 2247, 3897, 3933, 3948, 3949, 3952, 3967, 3971, 4059
Musulmans 748, 2121, 2347, 2386, 2535, 2541, 2652, 2757, 2819, 2850, 2856, 2910, 2967, 2976, 2993, 2998, 3026, 3230, 3324, 3328, 3339, 3344, 3345, 3348, 3355, 3363, 3364, 3366, 3367, 3498, 3615, 3646, 3660, 3767, 3802, 4052, 4362, 4441, 4551, 4558, 4685
Mutesa I 583
Muti 2792, 3007
Mutilation génitale 285, 459, 2705, 2733, 2870, 2871, 2880, 2881, 2883, 2887, 2890, 2982
Mutilations corporelles 2921
Mysticisme 186, 568, 3123, 3149, 3153, 3183, 3192, 3330, 3342, 3379, 3413, 3414, 3430, 4412
Mythes 192, 535, 542, 564, 618, 639, 656, 659, 669, 725, 1762, 2198, 2813, 2828, 2830, 2835, 2838, 3023, 3110, 3113, 3115-3123, 3125-3127, 3129, 3131-3133, 3246, 3270, 3271, 3351, 3400, 3424, 3513, 3537, 3744, 3861, 3974, 3991, 3993, 3995, 3999, 4004, 4010, 4048, 4151, 4263, 4296, 4463, 4486, 4502

Mythes de création 3124, 3131, 3133, 3625
Mythologie 257, 461, 505, 1047, 1364, 1707, 2512, 3110, 3115, 3117, 3119, 3121, 3124, 3125, 3127-3129, 3177, 3269, 3270, 3283, 3290, 3294, 3431, 3448, 3495, 3514, 3535, 3674, 3717, 3885, 4001, 4020, 4140, 4148, 4470, 4595
Nahuatl 1979, 3537, 3735, 3741, 3757, 4065, 4066, 4196, 4222, 4270
Naissance 378, 1500, 1544, 1566, 1582, 1583, 1614, 1708, 1718, 2121, 2122, 2632, 2702, 2707, 2709, 2711, 2718, 2727, 3192, 3581, 3737, 3775, 3814, 4844
Nakibinge [King] 639
Namaganda, Irene Drusilla 627
Nanaï 3589
Nanak 3496
Narration d'histoires 204, 225, 229, 539, 1762, 1767, 1864, 3449, 3714, 3979, 3982, 3987, 4012, 4016, 4030, 4161, 4212, 4372, 4534
Nation 173, 243, 410, 801, 2161, 2324, 2522, 2533, 2955, 3005, 3073, 3088, 3687, 3886, 4420, 4468, 4504, 4505, 4600, 4758
Nationalisation 726
Nationalisme 3, 41, 138, 190, 192, 253, 618, 647, 683, 735, 769, 801, 1361, 1426, 1532, 1749, 2172, 2482, 2486, 2514, 2533, 2564, 2666, 2855, 2857, 2901, 2927, 2944, 3073, 3076, 3088, 3093, 3480, 3697, 3723, 3958, 4053, 4102, 4313, 4342, 4352, 4413, 4425, 4447, 4448, 4456, 4472, 4481, 4482, 4485, 4486, 4490, 4492-4495, 4497, 4499, 4501, 4502, 4504, 4618, 4632, 4794
Nationalisme culturel 253
Nationalistes 1773, 3312
Nationalité 41, 190, 309, 689, 694, 784, 2146, 2989, 4480, 4488, 4497
Nations Unies 4646, 4712, 4802
  voir aussi: Conventions des Nations Unies
Nativisme 254, 4266, 4457
Naturalisation 784, 2563, 2989
Naturalisme 3373, 4216
Nature 361, 362, 596, 685, 1499, 1818, 2061, 2063, 2064, 2068, 2069, 2072, 2085, 2088, 2096, 2105, 2111, 2114, 2198, 3144, 3619, 3657, 3667, 3728, 3862, 4063, 4127, 4199, 4310, 4712
Nature humaine 1451, 2080, 3009, 3662
Naumann, Nelly 181
Navaho 2435, 3510, 3742, 3764
Navigation 503, 594, 691, 1375, 2372, 3680
Navires 4724
Nazisme 98, 2503, 2693, 3099, 4508

Néanderthaliens 845, 914, 1406, 1468, 1469, 1516, 1518, 1530, 1533, 1536
Néerlandais 640, 812, 1791, 1923, 3443, 3777
Négociation 2446, 2681, 2759, 2918, 3354
Négociations de paix 2577
Nelson, Diane M. 2955
Nenet 1771, 3606
Néolibéralisme 235, 2411, 3584, 4611, 4623, 4662, 4674, 4731, 4775
Neruda, Pablo 4192
Nerval, Gérard de 4179, 4225
Nervo, Amado 4234
Neurologie 110, 170, 1513, 1561, 3789, 3799
Nevsky, Nikolai 3546
Néwar 3663
Ngaitahu 3655
Ngata, Apirana 4722
Nias 4601
Nietzsche, Friedrich 280, 2858, 3129
Nihilisme 4277
Nilo-Saharienne 1994, 2009
Nilote 1987, 2007
Niveau de vie 1456, 1565, 1566, 2191, 2277, 4883
Niveaux d'enseignement 2153, 2410, 3769
Nizan, Paul 2453
Nkrumah, Kwame 4102
Noblesse 815, 3230, 4441
Noboru, Miyata 127
Nodilo, Natko 147, 1323
Noël 4372
Nœuds 1784
Noirs 562, 695, 774, 978, 1503, 1582, 2173, 2327, 2505, 2671, 2875, 3266, 3609, 3648, 4012, 4030, 4401, 4460, 4468
Nom de famille 1823, 1834, 2677
Nomades 145, 283, 487, 555, 882, 2092, 2123, 2473, 2491, 2610, 2690
Nomadisme 2623, 3683
Nomadisme pastoral 283, 2123, 3806, 4725
Nombre 3745, 3971
Nomenclature 1673, 1818, 1820, 2063
Noms 477, 1334, 1347, 1722, 1749, 1817-1821, 1824-1827, 1831-1837, 1905, 1912, 1924, 1941, 1979, 2063, 2666, 3150, 3301, 3582, 3887, 3896, 4493
Non-alignement 1765
Non-violence 3213, 3368, 3380, 3383, 3391, 3889
Normal 2953
Normalisation 1785, 1913, 1915, 1952, 2004, 4527
Normes culturelles 2089, 2626, 2836
Normes sociales 201, 723, 1752, 1766, 1803, 2586, 2763, 3038, 3543, 3569, 4409

Nortje, Arthur Kenneth 4079
Norvégien 1921
Nostalgie 327, 1762, 3730, 3903, 4416
Nourriture 155, 530, 744, 867, 909, 969, 1283, 1291, 1485, 1540, 1546, 1551, 1556, 1565, 1584, 1627, 1641, 1642, 1671, 1677, 1701, 2066, 2208, 3751, 3833, 4354, 4378, 4383, 4385, 4392, 4754, 4923
Nouvelles 1781, 3793, 4250
Novais, Paulo Dias de 721
Noves, Laure de 4179, 4264
Ntomba 1993
Numismatique 321, 363
Núñez de Miranda, Antonio 3216
Nutrition 1541, 1543, 1550, 1552, 1563, 1569, 1577-1579, 1588, 1589, 1611, 1671, 1677, 2651, 2654, 2686, 3804, 4671, 4809-4811, 4814, 4815, 4818, 4820, 4822, 4823, 4827, 4867, 4886, 4897, 4902, 4923
Nzema 4475
Oasis 3658, 4798
Obesité 1551, 1556, 1588, 1589
Objectivité 143, 276, 2949, 4077
Objet 1763
Obligation 534, 2676, 2983
Obligations 2983
Obrębski, Józef 15, 136
Obregón, Alejandro 4235
Observation 291, 428, 654, 691, 806, 1644, 1667, 2786
Observation participante 291, 424
Ocampo, Silvina 4147
Occidentalisation 2736, 3010, 4600
Occultisme 199, 576, 3573, 3578
Occupation étrangère 642, 704, 705, 717, 768, 794, 2333, 3005, 4098
Odorat 2939, 3653, 3766, 4484
Œuvre dramatique 3314, 3790, 3862-3866, 3872, 3874-3876, 3878, 3882, 3885, 4226, 4349, 4425, 4465
Œuvres d'art 337, 3771, 4130
Œuvres littéraires 628
Offre
    voir: Approvisionnement en eau, Disponibilités alimentaires
Offre de main d'œuvre 807, 4916
Offre et demande 4701
Oiseaux 360, 371, 1818, 1819, 2063, 2064, 2108, 2445, 3744, 3753, 4335
Okojie, C.G. 4161
Olmèque 1970
Onitsura, Uejima 4063
Onomastique 30, 1831, 1836, 4258
Ontogénie 1465, 1466, 1567

Ontologie 213, 2232, 3381, 3527, 3675, 3690, 3733, 3878, 4466
  voir aussi: Paléontologie
Opéra 3866, 3880, 3888, 3906, 4263
Opiat 896, 2296, 4720
Opinion 2453, 2791
Opinion politique 2534
Opinion publique 737, 759, 2072, 2092, 2113, 2495, 2518, 2524, 3074, 3804, 3823, 4496, 4773
Opposition politique 3703
Oppression 3089, 4082
Or 506, 1438, 2439
Oracles 3812
Orang-outans 1480, 1629, 1674
Oraon 1453, 1454
Orchestres 3935
Ordinateurs 30, 436, 1629, 1773, 1778, 1779, 1782, 2019, 3664, 3964
Ordre des mots 1756, 1940, 1947, 1949, 2054
Ordre politique 2509, 2682
Ordre social 131, 1066, 2349, 2442, 2593, 2595, 2607, 2767, 2847, 2896, 3005, 4893
Ordres 726
Ordres chrétiens
  voir: Franciscaines, Jésuite
Ordres religieux 323, 565, 707, 2769, 3198
Organes 1575, 2930
Organes sensoriels 1556
Organisation 255, 308, 371, 2145, 2244, 2269, 2369, 3021, 3022, 3144, 4730
Organisation administrative 2528
Organisation communautaire 2210, 4442, 4924
Organisation économique 2364, 4790
Organisation mondiale de la santé 4816
Organisations 986, 2307, 2514, 3957
  voir aussi: Culture organisationnelle
Organisations non-gouvernementales 158, 2210, 3761, 4594, 4708, 4714, 4722, 4725, 4727, 4728, 4731, 4740, 4742, 4752, 4778, 4781, 4800, 4824, 4836, 4868, 4870, 4887, 4888, 4904
Organisations patronales 753
Organisme social 670, 835, 838, 848, 921, 942, 1374, 1607, 1645-1647, 1680-1682, 1685, 1690, 1698, 1706, 1707, 1716, 2143, 2166, 2245, 2358, 2538, 2552, 2587, 2590, 2597, 2602, 2612, 2616, 2630, 2658, 2665, 2673, 3092, 3353, 3692, 3733
Organismes d'aide 4750
Orientalisme 14, 260, 329, 4217
Origine humaine 914, 1515, 1518, 1522, 1525, 4463

Origine sociale 659, 3132, 3134, 3710
Ornithologie 3744, 3753
Orok 2477
Orosius, Paulus 519
Orphelins 4897
Orthographe 1919
Orthographie 334, 1911, 1919, 4178
Ostéologie 1283, 1287
OTAN 4706
Otomanguean 1812, 1967
Oudmourte 2056
Ours 1368
Outil agricole 4686
Outils 460, 499, 543, 836, 845, 849, 850, 860, 864, 875, 881, 883, 887, 890, 892, 1359, 1363, 1393, 1398, 1403, 1409, 1414, 1441, 1672, 1702, 1710, 1711, 1715, 2107, 2240, 2248, 2251, 4686
Outils en pierre 820, 836, 842, 850, 864, 875, 881, 890, 991, 1378, 1403, 1408, 1409, 2107, 3941
Outils préhistoriques 890
Ouvriers industriels 2453
Ouvriers sexuels 2220, 2710, 2884, 2902, 2988, 3796, 4218, 4898
Oyo 4009
Pacification 395, 4712, 4820
Pacifisme 3489
Paganisme 1381, 3521, 3554, 3619, 3686
Pagis, Dan 4049, 4439
Pai 3585
Pain 1398, 4354
Paiute 3585
Paix 364, 2533, 3073, 3170, 3275, 3354, 3489
  voir aussi: Accord de paix
Palawan 3813
Paléoanthropologie 1479, 1532
Paléodémographie 246, 298, 1379, 1516, 2134, 2135, 2144
Paléoécologie 155, 530, 744, 858, 882, 947, 969, 994, 1000, 1368, 1533
Paléographie 1340, 1535, 3179, 3203
Paléontologie 824, 837, 842, 846, 872, 889, 898, 899, 1137, 1458, 1467, 1528, 1534
Paléopathologie 538
Paléozoologie 144
Palestiniens 2456, 3040, 4062
Pali, Avtar Singh 3855
Pampa 837
Panassié, Hugues 3929
Pandit 4176
Pāṇini 1960, 3754
Panique 2896, 4547, 4893
Pano 1506, 3128
Pape 3230, 3253, 4441

Papon, Maurice 3005
Paradigmes 194, 204, 259, 268, 414, 420, 2035, 2958, 3079, 3170, 3670, 3730, 3743, 4198, 4586, 4627, 4757
Parcs nationaux 1605, 2107
Parentalité 603, 2716
Parenté 138, 198, 666, 1498, 1505, 1685, 1882, 1900, 2020, 2143, 2161, 2169, 2171, 2188, 2266, 2285, 2351, 2474, 2509, 2513, 2554, 2557, 2586, 2602, 2628-2631, 2634, 2638, 2641, 2647, 2650, 2654-2660, 2662-2665, 2667, 2670, 2672-2674, 2676, 2677, 2679-2681, 2683, 2684, 2687, 2689, 2690, 2740, 2747, 2748, 2751, 2770, 2837, 2933, 2952, 3030, 3105, 3352, 3353, 3458, 4008, 4790
Parents 1574, 1615, 1675, 2350, 2636, 2713, 4244, 4433, 4506
Parents actifs 2694
Parlement 815, 2402, 2483
Parlo, Giancarlo De 3846
Paroisse 2599, 3629, 3636
Parole 66, 70, 407, 560, 1735, 1739, 1764, 1767, 1771, 1806, 1824, 1846, 1957-1959, 1967, 1976, 1997, 2001, 2008, 2027, 2037, 2040, 2807, 3165, 3412, 3606, 3702, 3744, 3874, 4035, 4392, 4409, 4569, 4602
  voir aussi: Prononciation
Parsi 3331, 3880, 3882
Partage de nourriture 1646, 1647, 2352, 4393, 4394
Parti pris 228, 241, 258, 635, 1548, 2588, 4415, 4879
Participation au groupe 2210, 4702
Participation de la citoyenneté 2826, 2834, 3340, 4406, 4742
Participation de la collectivité 2309, 2402, 4714, 4732, 4795, 4832, 4927, 4937
Participation des femmes 4832, 4836, 4854
Participation politique 675, 700, 2515, 3219, 4230, 4611, 4648, 4882
  voir aussi: Activisme
Participation sociale 2469, 4353, 4435, 4716, 4818, 4820, 4871
Partis communistes 2500
Partis libéraux 754
Partis politiques 2483, 3944
Partition 3730
Parure 1373, 1777, 2934
Paschoal, Hermeto 3914
Passamaquoddy 3588
Passé 278, 434, 573, 613, 1828, 1835, 2017, 3710, 4161, 4260

Pastoralisme 682, 882, 913, 1584, 2073, 2126, 2367, 2425, 2429, 2434, 2435, 2446, 2446, 2447, 2610, 2626, 2767, 3678, 4659, 4764, 4784, 4797, 4820
Paternalisme 723, 2273
Paternité 2711, 4844
Paternité-maternité 1577, 1587, 2636, 2694, 2696, 2713, 2717, 2863, 2893, 4822
Pathologie 110, 1591, 2703, 3799
  voir aussi: Paléopathologie
Paton, Alan 4249
Patriarcat 198, 470, 2535, 2567, 2679, 2767, 2811, 2846, 2850, 2873, 3258, 3517, 3525, 3644, 4830
Patrimoine culturel 78, 155, 323, 326, 434, 487, 524, 530, 683, 707, 962, 968, 969, 996, 1028, 1033, 1035, 1039, 1043, 1053, 1071, 1169, 1179, 1187, 1189, 1212, 1223, 1226, 1232, 1255, 1386, 1438, 1774, 2291, 2317, 2691, 3049, 3078, 3365, 3558, 3624, 3671, 3698-3701, 3847, 3858, 3861, 3866, 3926, 3949, 4000, 4080, 4299, 4308, 4325, 4327, 4329, 4331, 4346, 4360, 4401, 4468, 4604, 4775
  voir aussi: Préservation du patrimoine culturel
Patriotisme 2281, 3312, 3653, 4484, 4487, 4489
Patronage 2382, 2513, 2617, 2659, 2795, 3597, 3884
Paulmier de Gonneville, Jean 783
Pauvres 2189, 2408, 2452, 3566, 4075, 4536, 4611, 4616, 4650, 4662, 4743, 4744, 4823, 4842, 4872
Pauvreté 59, 548, 1573, 2152, 2210, 2289, 2340, 2362, 2400, 2407, 2582, 2627, 2961, 2968, 2969, 2972, 2978, 2980, 2984, 2994, 3001, 3003, 3004, 3819, 4536, 4543, 4611, 4613, 4621, 4661, 4668, 4670, 4672, 4677, 4682, 4690, 4699, 4707, 4719, 4721, 4728, 4730, 4732, 4733, 4739, 4744-4747, 4755, 4762, 4793, 4817, 4820, 4823, 4825, 4863-4865, 4867, 4870, 4872, 4874-4876, 4880, 4881, 4883, 4894, 4896, 4897, 4900, 4904, 4918, 4939
  voir aussi: Réduction de pauvreté
Pauvreté rurale 2196, 2288, 2396, 2434, 2620, 4291, 4846, 4885, 4905, 4906, 4911, 4913, 4914, 4919
Pauvreté urbaine 2210, 2214-2216, 2221, 2222, 4666, 4851, 4930, 4934-4938
Pays arabes 1342, 2417, 2554, 3018, 3327, 3339, 4101
Pays de l'Est 2544

Pays en développement 59, 621, 805, 1565,
2129, 2140, 2156, 2213, 2221, 2289,
2396, 2529, 2686, 2704, 2721, 2758,
2978, 3003, 3739, 3762, 4316, 4609,
4666, 4672, 4708, 4713, 4722, 4728,
4734, 4741, 4745, 4762, 4765, 4773,
4779, 4786, 4834, 4840, 4841, 4855,
4856, 4860, 4868, 4873, 4882, 4888,
4890, 4899, 4900, 4905, 4926, 4936
Pays industrialisés 1033
Pays islamiques 1874, 4551, 4615
Pays moins développés 1552, 4734
Pays multiethniques 2077, 2587, 3072, 3098,
4468, 4628
Pays nouvellement industrialisés 4679
Pays occidentaux 41, 190, 3166, 4154
Paysage 291, 458, 806, 852, 885, 888, 892,
893, 915, 923, 932, 962, 1000, 1011, 1041,
1053, 1084, 1123, 1148, 1150, 1153, 1155,
1163, 1188, 1196, 1197, 1222, 1263, 1310,
1824, 2060, 2084, 2087, 2095, 2096, 2110,
2170, 2207, 2317, 2509, 3653, 3727,
3845, 3847, 4127, 4128, 4425, 4484,
4487, 4626, 4789, 4792
Paysannerie 2200, 2205, 2280, 2282, 2423,
2480, 2575, 3223, 4381
Paysans 624, 1823, 2183, 2194, 2197, 2200,
2255, 2258, 2261, 2269, 2336, 2371,
2397, 2399, 2412, 2478, 2688, 3176,
3223, 3538, 4502, 4569, 4573, 4687
Paz, Octavio 3728, 4220
Peacock, Kenneth Howard 118, 3931
Peau 2248
Pêcheries 2436, 2440, 3786, 4804, 4850
Pêcheurs 2070, 2451, 2467, 4729
Pédagogie 3661, 4433, 4559
Pedi 2750, 3019
Peformance
    voir: Rendement du travail
Peignes 3663
Peine de mort 3013
Peinture 337, 937, 1007, 1023, 1060, 1072,
1074, 1077, 1081, 1084, 1095, 1105, 3728,
3736, 3841, 4041, 4089, 4095, 4097,
4101, 4106, 4109, 4113, 4114, 4128, 4130,
4144, 4235
Peirce, C.S. 3728
Pèlerinages 166, 2900, 3133, 3181, 3230,
3256, 3263, 3287, 3532, 3649, 4131,
4179, 4225, 4236, 4264, 4321, 4322,
4330, 4428, 4441
Penashue, Elizabeth 2075
Pensée des lumières 16, 4466
Pensée philosophique 100, 121, 408, 588, 660,
740, 758, 2114, 2457, 2970, 3002, 3079,

3138, 3143, 3162, 3164, 3170, 3178,
3182, 3208, 3210, 3280, 3291, 3311, 3335,
3381, 3728, 4063, 4067, 4073, 4172,
4191, 4489, 4510
Pensée politique 3107, 4485
Pensée religieuse 185, 634, 3143, 3162, 3164,
3165, 3170, 3178, 3182, 3183, 3200,
3201, 3208, 3210, 3252, 3270, 3280,
3283, 3291, 3297, 3303, 3311, 3320, 3368,
3369, 3372, 3373, 3375, 3377, 3379,
3381, 3383, 3385, 3386, 3388, 3389,
3391, 3441, 3477, 3481, 3496, 4026, 4284
Pensée scientifique 16
Pentecôtisme 3221, 3232, 3237, 3250, 3252,
3257, 3259, 3636, 3645, 4462
Pénurie alimentaire 2129, 2704
Pénurie de ressources 2303
Perception 307, 661, 1492, 1506, 1703, 1737,
1958, 2047, 2080, 2091, 2095, 2096, 2116,
2284, 2441, 2718, 2739, 2753, 2906,
2933, 3012, 3212, 3658, 3662, 3695,
3728, 3814, 3816, 3897, 4029, 4107,
4190, 4498, 4528, 4536, 4591, 4783
Perception d'autrui 1793, 2802, 2914, 3060,
3397, 3607, 3613
Perception de soi 3112, 3760, 4468, 4486
Perception sociale 3861
Perception visuelle 231, 4123, 4127, 4134,
4453
Père 3267, 4022, 4521
Perec, Georges 107, 405
Périodiques 50, 51, 3100, 4243, 4525, 4548
Périurbanisation 2222
Perles 1392
Persécution religieuse 3089, 3100, 3230,
3484, 3502, 4441
Personnalité 111, 176, 486, 627, 649, 815,
3553, 3712, 4074, 4524
Personnel 2462
Personnel médical 1809, 2119, 2470, 2718,
2854, 3789, 3790, 3814
Personnes deplacées 2119, 2159, 2180, 2582,
4442, 4594, 4714
Personnes sacrées 3134
Perspective mondiale 151, 164, 444, 813,
1320, 2114, 2116, 2260, 2612, 2774, 3002,
3041, 3135, 3318, 3620, 3625, 3652,
3655, 3692, 3695, 3833, 4587, 4661, 4790
Persuasion 2887, 2982
Perte 38, 2787, 4509, 4512, 4518, 4529, 4532,
4538, 4539, 4541, 4546
Pessimisme 3869
Pestana, Catalino 2260
Pesticides 4888
Petite industrie 4671

Petites entreprises agricoles 4926
Petites et moyennes entreprises 2244, 2644
Petits enfants 1548, 1574, 1584, 1602, 1603,
   1607, 1612, 1672, 1675, 1676, 1693,
   1708, 2699, 2712, 2713, 3515, 4816, 4824
Pétrarque, François 4179, 4264
Pétroglyphes 1062
Peul 2718, 3814
Peur 2102, 2533, 3073, 4003
Phéniciens 1722
Phénoménologie 5, 45, 226, 227, 1753, 1798,
   2170, 2958, 3217, 3533, 3777
Philip, M. Nourbese 4039
Philippins 2161, 2534, 4478
Philologie 1792, 1801, 1814, 1819, 1859,
   1928, 2071, 3196, 3229, 3251, 3436,
   3826, 3966
Philosophes 79, 588, 2232, 3129, 3291, 3403,
   3437, 4172, 4174
Philosophie 11, 79, 151, 167, 216, 221, 223,
   224, 244, 259, 280, 414, 444, 464, 588,
   589, 758, 807, 998, 1538, 1863, 1945,
   1960, 1965, 2072, 2092, 2111, 2114, 2232,
   2435, 2705, 2858, 2881, 2970, 2991,
   3000, 3002, 3079, 3129, 3138, 3143,
   3148, 3153, 3162, 3164, 3165, 3170,
   3178, 3182, 3201, 3208, 3210, 3212,
   3214, 3251, 3271, 3272, 3290, 3296,
   3315, 3317, 3318, 3320, 3335, 3339,
   3359, 3376, 3380-3382, 3389, 3403, 3438,
   3462, 3477, 3620, 3659, 3669, 3675,
   3725, 3728, 3743, 3754, 3756, 3857,
   3862, 3971, 4023, 4063, 4067, 4077,
   4179, 4191, 4207, 4220, 4238, 4261, 4510
   voir aussi: Dualisme, Histoire de la
   philosophie, Morale
Philosophie de la religion 208, 275, 2539,
   3182, 3202, 3303, 3389, 3455
Philosophie de la science 5, 16, 226, 998,
   3753
Philosophie de langue 3165
Philosophie de l'art 3728
Philosophie politique 79, 3850
Philosophie publique 2967, 3328
Philosophie sociale 572, 4261
Phonétique 122, 600, 1764, 1813, 1858, 1866,
   1873, 1891, 1899, 1907, 1922, 1923,
   1937, 1958, 1959, 1968, 1976, 1979,
   2001, 2008, 2010, 2041, 2051, 2058
Phonologie 113, 1802, 1813, 1847, 1858,
   1870, 1890, 1927, 1976, 1981, 1984,
   1992, 2001, 2039, 2041, 2048, 3874
Photographie 92, 101, 231, 273, 326, 367,
   417, 438, 441, 443, 769, 923, 932, 983,
   999, 1003, 1105, 2210, 2287, 2933, 2944,

3929, 4094, 4104, 4107, 4121, 4126,
   4127, 4138
Phraséologie 1761
Phrases 1769, 1848, 1868, 1895, 1921, 3011
Phrénologie 110, 3799
Phylogénie 279, 898, 899, 1458, 1467, 1534,
   1618, 1666, 1679, 2687
Physiologie 1485, 1491, 1499, 1555, 1558,
   1591, 1632-1634, 1663, 1695, 1859, 2917,
   3436, 3759, 3789
Physique 60, 371, 464, 1549, 3728, 3758
Pialoux, Michel 2453
Picón Salas, Mariano 4192
Pictographie 214
Piétisme 3430
Pike, Kenneth Lee 119
Piłsudski, Bronisław 92
Piro 2472, 3109
Pisciculture 2452
Placement familial 2648, 2685
Plaisanteries 1754, 1767, 4243, 4450
Planification agricole 4692
Planification de la famille 2136, 2640, 2710,
   2714, 2717, 2721, 2725, 2726, 2893,
   2894, 4668, 4885, 4891, 4899
Planification de la santé 4876
Planification de l'environnement 4779
Planification du développement 2219, 4711,
   4713, 4714, 4726, 4735, 4738, 4763, 4779
Planification économique 718, 4608
Planification linguistique 1983, 2529
Planification régionale 4326, 4831
Planification stratégique 2289, 4711, 4744,
   4924
Plans de développement 4717
Plantations 2167, 2273, 2619, 2822, 3066
Plantes hallucinogènes 3566, 3833
Plantes médicinales 3566, 3766
Plato 1738
Pléistocène 460, 824, 831, 837, 839, 841, 842,
   846, 870, 872, 875, 884, 889, 890, 899,
   1137, 1190, 1368, 1379, 1458, 1469, 1521,
   1525, 1533-1535
Pluralisme 268, 798, 974, 1726, 3092, 3096,
   4411, 4510
Pluralisme ethnique 2523, 2564
Pluralisme linguistique 4649
Pluralisme religieux 3394
Plurilinguisme 113, 1798, 1802, 1803, 1815,
   1849, 1969, 4419
Poe, Edgar Allen 2857, 3076
Poèmes 4036, 4046, 4063, 4070, 4074, 4083
Poésie 96, 141, 151, 206, 444, 660, 1844,
   1859, 1945, 1965, 1970, 2099, 2324,
   2805, 2933, 3155, 3195, 3272, 3278,

3294, 3321, 3330, 3365, 3423, 3429,
3436, 3500, 3738, 3865, 3885, 3928,
3933, 3968, 3985, 4004, 4029, 4035-4045,
4047, 4049-4063, 4065-4089, 4147, 4179,
4192, 4214, 4231, 4242, 4264, 4266,
4439, 4561, 4563, 4578
Poésie épique 3116, 3993, 4015, 4231
Poésie folklorique 4038
Poids et mesures 349, 2329
Poison 2615, 3570, 3783, 4003
Poisson 2070, 2444, 4394
Police 3006, 3013, 3107
Politiciens 92, 815
Politique 253, 418, 474, 657, 991, 2076, 2210,
2499, 2505, 2525, 2529, 2532, 2534,
2543, 2547, 2570, 2582, 2911, 2955, 3034,
3063, 3108, 3246, 3570, 3590, 3761,
3777, 3783, 3784, 3908, 3975, 4058,
4084, 4129, 4230, 4447, 4469, 4496,
4502, 4599, 4634, 4637, 4642, 4643,
4700, 4820, 4841, 4907
Politique agricole 249, 2273, 2305, 2310,
2315, 4671, 4767
Politique alimentaire 4814
Politique coloniale 636, 684, 784, 2120, 2989,
3746, 4195
Politique commerciale 2339
Politique culturelle 972
Politique de développement 1573, 2222, 4340,
4612, 4720, 4739, 4763, 4788, 4838,
4845, 4847, 4874, 4915
Politique de l'eau 2289
Politique de l'éducation 1745, 1749, 1969,
3095, 3471, 4553, 4663, 4753
Politique de l'environnement 2445, 4666,
4791, 4842
Politique de l'Union européenne 2486
Politique de stabilisation 4662
Politique des musées 352
Politique d'identité 2157, 3061, 3404, 3969,
4407, 4515
Politique d'immigration 4632
Politique du crédit 4847
Politique du logement 4838, 4934
Politique économique 4338, 4662, 4669, 4671,
4677, 4678, 4680, 4704, 4793, 4842
Politique ethnique 4012
Politique étrangère 677, 2357, 2455, 2533,
3041, 3073, 4663
Politique foncière 2265, 2397, 2407, 2411,
2412, 2419, 2730, 2980, 4934
Politique forestière 2828, 4779
Politique gouvernementale 153, 613, 2308,
2463, 2576-2578, 2706, 2828, 3108, 4339,
4621, 4655, 4683, 4703, 4738, 4756,

4770, 4806, 4812, 4826, 4868, 4901,
4918, 4928
Politique industrielle 2355
Politique internationale 1517
Politique linguistique 1759, 1797, 1916
Politique locale 2101, 2207, 2735, 3064, 4882
Politique Noire 3929
Politique publique 2887, 2982, 3819, 4665
Politique rurale 4915
Politique sanitaire 1470, 2128, 3761, 4823,
4863, 4864, 4875, 4876, 4882, 4890,
4892, 4894
Politique sociale 2152, 2627, 2655, 2770,
4662, 4900
Politique touristique 4301, 4607
Politique urbaine 2216, 2219, 4317, 4930
Politiques régionales 4664
Politisation 4389, 4400
Pollution 2311, 4765, 4770, 4941
Pollution de l'air 2210, 4765
Pollution industrielle 2210
Polo, Marco 779
Polonais 4488
Polygamie 2755
Polygynie 295, 2130, 2736, 3010
Pommes de terre 2269, 2275
Ponts 1076
Popularité 4217
Population 286, 298, 309, 646, 684, 757, 866,
1502, 1538, 1550, 1615, 1669, 1677,
1705, 1712, 2120, 2124, 2125, 2134,
2144, 2146-2148, 2151, 2155, 2306, 2406,
2551, 2752, 3739, 3762, 4840, 4892, 4899
Population indigène 1, 90, 95, 100, 103, 135,
139, 214, 225, 234, 254, 258, 269, 385,
404, 416, 531, 539, 542, 566, 648, 682,
699, 720, 721, 725, 733, 739, 740, 745,
758, 763, 783, 784, 790, 803, 806, 810,
942, 991, 1289, 1294, 1322, 1456, 1749,
1787, 1797, 1824, 1970, 2062, 2067,
2075, 2078, 2084, 2102, 2164, 2167,
2197, 2207, 2262, 2391, 2398, 2403,
2414, 2426, 2472, 2477, 2524, 2540,
2541, 2570, 2576-2578, 2582, 2592, 2691,
2750, 2827, 2834, 2849, 2857, 2904,
2989, 3011, 3016, 3019, 3026, 3032, 3036,
3039, 3045, 3055, 3056, 3059, 3063,
3071, 3074-3076, 3092, 3104, 3107-3109,
3130, 3348, 3548, 3559, 3588, 3635,
3659, 3669, 3671, 3735, 3742, 3757,
3761, 3870, 3902, 3911, 3915, 4000, 4044,
4129, 4136, 4196, 4201, 4278, 4293,
4295, 4320, 4377, 4406, 4408, 4412,
4420, 4422, 4425, 4457, 4465, 4535,
4569, 4584, 4590, 4598, 4612, 4623,

4624, 4633-4638, 4642-4649, 4652-4658, 4660, 4785, 4791, 4798, 4799, 4801, 4802, 4852

Population rurale 17, 1543, 1578, 1586, 2553, 2726, 2773, 2898, 3824, 3825, 4789

Population urbaine 2216, 3090, 4813, 4941

Populisme 4336

Porcelaine 1429

Porcs 2442, 2445, 2450, 2847

Pornographie 2950

Ports 806, 1049, 1061, 1233, 1235, 2092, 2360

Portugais 66, 68, 71

Position socioéconomique 909, 1475, 1493, 1540, 1558, 1566, 1568, 1579, 1733, 2141, 2171, 2208, 2426, 2477, 2488, 2742, 2763, 2775, 2834, 2914, 2917, 3028, 3832, 4406, 4430

Positivisme 998

Possession 767, 1448, 2328, 2373, 2377, 2398, 2402, 2417, 2427, 2920, 2963, 2991, 2997, 3018, 3106, 3275, 3577, 3579, 3582, 3584, 3591, 3612, 3822, 4638, 4674, 4882

Postcolonialisme 254, 702, 735, 2172, 2182, 2499, 2502, 2877, 3572, 3586, 3933, 4059, 4071, 4120, 4151, 4171, 4177, 4425, 4452, 4457, 4483, 4622, 4639, 4731

Post-fordisme 2502, 3572

Post-matérialisme 2326

Postmodernisme 115, 180, 250, 253, 260, 300, 304, 364, 998, 1750, 2326, 2552, 2897, 2948, 3130, 3401, 3639, 3650, 3725, 3838, 3877, 4068, 4138, 4151

Post-structuralisme 180, 650

Poterie 378, 387, 853, 871, 883, 919, 943, 1034, 1056, 1058, 1288, 1309, 1374, 1376, 1380, 1385, 1388, 1389, 1403-1405, 1415-1417, 1424, 1425, 1427, 1431, 1439, 1442, 1444, 1445, 2206, 2233, 2235, 2237-2239, 2249, 2250, 3737
   voir aussi: Céramique

Potiers 2238

Pound, Ezra 4068

Poupées 811, 1364

Pouvoir 52, 98, 105, 191, 196, 247, 255, 612, 620, 627, 649, 716, 722, 729, 751, 1102, 1716, 1777, 2214, 2369, 2487, 2489, 2490, 2493, 2499, 2503, 2513, 2532, 2533, 2552, 2554, 2555, 2560, 2571, 2596, 2618, 2659, 2669, 2719, 2908, 2934, 3000, 3073, 3077, 3216, 3231, 3353, 3356, 3586, 3590, 3592, 3602, 3730, 3776, 3816, 3817, 3850, 3925, 3947, 4200, 4374, 4421, 4468, 4619,

4630, 4700
   voir aussi: Rapports de pouvoirs

Pouvoir de la collectivité 4301, 4607

Pouvoir de négociation 2983

Pouvoir judiciaire 606, 2986

Pouvoir local 2829

Pouvoir personnel 1828

Pouvoir politique 383, 453, 474, 558, 632, 2494, 2498, 2508, 2509, 2512, 2553, 2562, 2568, 2580, 2779, 2814, 3145, 3353, 3538, 4001, 4548

Pragmatique 266, 1753, 1766, 1811, 1921, 1951, 1961

Prairies 2187

Pratique 3912

Pratique de la pêche 2344, 2428, 2429, 2436, 2451, 2467, 3786, 4793, 4804

Pratique mortuaire antique 343, 859, 906, 991, 1074, 1280, 1292, 1294, 1298, 1302-1304, 1308, 1322, 1327

Pratique religieuse 142, 568, 3152, 3163, 3171, 3188, 3198, 3230, 3235, 3281, 3310, 3332, 3374, 3383, 3413, 3447, 3461, 3486, 3499, 3503, 3546, 3599, 3621, 3625, 3639, 4441, 4451

Pratiques culturales 2260, 2269, 2272, 2295, 2296, 2302, 2304, 2319, 2321, 4766, 4774

Pratiques culturelles 142, 1584, 2236, 2682, 2712, 2863, 3599

Précipitation 2065, 2079, 2417, 2517, 3018, 3114, 3571, 4691, 4727, 4777

Prédication 640, 2967, 3328, 3443, 3508

Préférences 1452, 1656, 2342, 2670, 2747, 2891, 3200, 3751, 4385, 4835

Préhistoire 34, 374, 460, 598, 623, 720, 821-823, 825, 827, 829, 832, 833, 835, 836, 844-846, 848-852, 856, 857, 859-861, 863, 864, 866, 868, 870, 873, 876-879, 882, 883, 886, 892-894, 896, 906, 916, 921, 924, 926, 932, 947, 966, 977, 981, 987, 1000, 1004, 1011, 1013, 1017, 1020, 1050, 1052, 1066, 1067, 1095, 1097, 1153, 1160, 1172, 1173, 1184, 1223, 1225, 1245, 1248, 1249, 1264, 1271, 1281, 1292, 1296, 1298-1300, 1303, 1305, 1314, 1315, 1324, 1362, 1363, 1366, 1368, 1374, 1376, 1379, 1390, 1397, 1406, 1408, 1409, 1413, 1415, 1439, 1459, 1461, 1484, 1514, 1516, 1522, 1526, 1533, 1536, 1563, 1934, 2110, 2177, 2229, 2340, 2590, 3024, 3941, 4268, 4501

Première Chambre
   voir: Membres de la Première Chambre

Préparation des aliments
   voir: Art culinaire

Prescription de rôle 365
Préservation 158, 564, 667, 909, 1028, 1064,
    1510, 1626, 1669, 2084, 2203, 2208, 2311,
    2402, 2830, 2844, 3849, 4294, 4319,
    4344, 4345, 4671, 4694, 4773, 4782,
    4799, 4805, 4850
    voir aussi: Conservation de la nature,
    Conservation des sols
Préservation du patrimoine culturel 78, 152,
    316, 524, 667, 962, 1028, 1169, 1203,
    1240, 1386, 2203, 2691, 2838, 3196,
    3818, 3839, 4317, 4319, 4325-4327, 4329,
    4344-4346, 4429, 4573
Presse 661, 785, 1785, 1915, 2821, 2866,
    3335, 4081, 4415, 4496, 4497
Pression démographique 2416, 3017
Prestige 2328, 2589, 2963
Prêtres 3187, 3220, 3230, 3277, 3454, 3461,
    3524, 3637, 3672, 3752, 4234, 4441
Prêts 1801, 2210, 4671
Prévention 44, 1580, 2885, 3761, 3820, 3834
Prévisions 388, 1583, 3038, 3569
Prière 472, 1871, 3170, 3233, 3268, 3299,
    3336, 3360, 3407, 3408, 3439, 3440,
    3452, 3465, 3748, 3899
Primates 19, 21, 23, 46, 1472, 1480, 1481,
    1485, 1500, 1501, 1509-1511, 1567, 1594-
    1616, 1618-1628, 1630-1647, 1650, 1652,
    1654-1662, 1664, 1665, 1667-1671, 1674,
    1676-1680, 1682-1692, 1694, 1696-1703,
    1705-1714, 1717, 1718, 1720, 1721
Primates fossiles 1479, 1485
Primatologie 19, 21, 23, 46, 1465, 1479-1481,
    1500, 1501, 1509-1511, 1594-1611, 1613-
    1616, 1618-1651, 1653-1664, 1666-1674,
    1676, 1678-1692, 1694-1702, 1704-1714,
    1716-1721
Primitivisme 233, 628, 3567, 4061
Principauté 2073, 2488, 2565
Pringle, Thomas 4082
Prise de décision 1539, 1639, 1693, 2174,
    2185, 2322, 2713, 2721, 2772, 2948,
    2965, 3015, 3395, 4307, 4660, 4742,
    4790, 4928
Prise en charge 562, 2222, 2470, 2818, 2835,
    2854, 2863, 4126, 4569, 4616, 4684,
    4722, 4723, 4746, 4820, 4828, 4833,
    4834, 4836, 4848, 4859, 4904, 4913
Prison 698, 2938, 2999, 3009, 3803
Prisonniers 698, 2959, 3005, 3009
Prisonniers de guerre 4477
Prisonniers politiques 395, 698, 4477
Privation 4075
Privatisation 2210, 4609, 4718, 4874, 4882
Prix 150, 382, 2342

Prix agricole 2142, 4821
Prix alimentaires 2268
Prix de la fiancée 2734
Prix des produits de base 4663
Prix du logement 4681
Problèmes sociaux 215, 2220, 2221, 2432,
    2581, 3543, 3762, 4390, 4520, 4521, 4571
Processus stochastiques 456
Production 175, 718, 749, 864, 1405, 1413,
    1415, 1428, 1439, 2226, 2233, 2236,
    2237, 2257, 2338, 2390, 2399, 2442,
    2450, 2462, 2847, 4696
Production agricole 709, 1454, 2255, 2258,
    2262, 2263, 2278, 2280, 2293, 2305,
    2312, 2314, 2335, 2419, 3678, 4687,
    4688, 4693, 4727, 4793
Production alimentaire 867, 892, 966, 1446,
    2268, 2283, 2380, 4388, 4736
Production de bétail 2437, 2438
Production de cheptel 2448
Production de coton 2415
Production de masse 2324
Productivité 2091
    voir aussi: Accroissement de la
    productivité
Productivité agricole 2303, 2358, 4663
Produit agricole 4443
Produit intérieur brut 4787
Produit national
Produit national brut 4733, 4797
Produits alimentaires 4380
Produits biologiques 2311, 4820
Produits chimiques 912, 2235, 3789
Produits de base 2323
Produits de bois 2099, 3155
Produits ouvrés 130, 330, 331, 353, 379, 380,
    505, 869, 981, 1039, 1040, 1071, 1098,
    1299, 1322, 1372, 1396, 1418, 1421,
    1424, 1431, 1434, 1436, 1438, 3580, 4241
Produits pharmaceutiques 4636
Professeurs 37, 102, 114, 1799
Professionnalisation 909, 2208, 3884
Professionnalisme 963
Professions 1535, 2220, 2464, 2465, 2845,
    3903
Professorat 2845
Programme de gouvernement 2090, 2412,
    4742
Programmes de développement 2210, 4339,
    4666, 4667, 4681, 4683, 4684, 4714,
    4725, 4732, 4734, 4741, 4742, 4747,
    4788, 4827, 4846, 4854, 4859, 4886,
    4890, 4899, 4913, 4915, 4916, 4924,
    4928, 4929, 4933, 4937
Programmes de recherche 29

Progrès scientifique 16
Projets de développement 2210, 2269, 2292,
     2578, 3056, 3075, 4612, 4689, 4696,
     4702, 4706, 4710, 4716, 4720, 4727,
     4729, 4733, 4739, 4782, 4783, 4789,
     4795, 4800, 4804, 4805, 4831, 4836,
     4850, 4851, 4854, 4887, 4914, 4926,
     4929, 4937
Projets de recherche 30, 32, 290, 313, 1038,
     1109, 1254, 1273, 3566
Promotion de la santé 3827
Pronom 1929, 1930, 1949
Prononciation 1957
Propagande 2693, 3048, 4105, 4523
Prophètes 2534, 2748, 3368, 3420, 3421,
     3591, 3822
Prophétie 3424, 3591, 3822
Proposition 1756, 1848, 1992
Proposition de loi 4861
Propreté 1474, 1475, 1569, 3798, 4396, 4903
Propriétaires fonciers 757, 2281, 2397, 2405,
     2406, 2600, 2681, 4619, 4799
Propriété 757, 2062, 2337, 2349, 2373, 2374,
     2377, 2404, 2406, 2408, 2421, 2442,
     2593, 2736, 2847, 2954, 2997, 3010,
     4635, 4650
     voir aussi: Biens culturels
Propriété du domicile 2210
Propriété intellectuelle 4566, 4636
Propriété privée 2420
Prose 1844, 3195, 3321, 3331, 4032, 4169,
     4234, 4252
Prosélytisme 732
Prosimiens 1600, 1615, 1617, 1619, 1624,
     1632-1634, 1639, 1643, 1645, 1650, 1680,
     1695-1697, 1699, 1719
Prosodie 1890
Prostitution 2220, 2821, 2896, 2988, 3004,
     3119, 4826, 4893
Protection de l'enfance 4722
Protection de l'environnement 2076, 4773,
     4796, 4888
Protection des monuments 1358
Protection légale 667
Protestantisme 2085, 3230, 3252, 3610, 3653,
     4310, 4441, 4474, 4484
Protestants 3243, 3252, 3610
Protohistoire 569
Proverbes 1788, 2200, 2364, 3321, 3354,
     3997, 4018, 4070, 4600, 4640
Provinces 296, 366, 1442, 1576, 2159, 2209,
     2267, 2437, 2550, 3581, 3586, 3916,
     4186, 4480, 4629, 4669, 4772
Psychanalyse 176, 186, 195, 221, 379, 3149,
     3791, 4022, 4524, 4537, 4562, 4745

Psychiatre 775, 3595, 3638, 4525, 4547
Psychiatrie sociale 3760
Psychologie 38, 176, 186, 193, 195, 221, 236,
     1556, 1561, 1637, 2030, 2037, 2480,
     2555, 2611, 2633, 2684, 2719, 2872, 2931,
     2962, 3044, 3149, 3365, 3404, 3595,
     3712, 3759, 3817, 4080, 4434, 4509,
     4512-4516, 4518-4521, 4524, 4525, 4527,
     4529, 4532, 4534, 4537-4543, 4547, 4549
Psychologie clinique 221, 4525, 4543, 4546,
     4547
Psychologie du développement 1513, 1561,
     1790
Psychologie évolutionniste 1539, 2645, 4019
Psychologie génétique 1520
Psychologie sociale 399, 1449, 1554, 1796,
     2165, 2589, 2606, 2758, 2888, 2917,
     2935, 3665, 4181, 4757
Psychopathologie 121, 408, 4513, 4543
Psychopharmacologie 1591
Psychosociologie 1664, 3575
Psychothérapie de groupe 220, 2585
Puberté 676, 1466, 1553, 1557, 1592, 2864
Public 660
Publicité 1774, 1788, 2317, 2326, 2327, 2950,
     3698, 3699, 3903, 4018, 4388
Pudumaippittan 4213
Puériculture 603, 1584, 1603, 1706, 2633,
     2698, 2716, 4528, 4591
Punjabi 3470
Purves, Andrew 4579
Pygmées 4555
Qualité de la vie 1283, 3064, 4759, 4883
Qualité de l'eau 525, 2112, 3827, 4777
Qualité de l'environnement 2067, 4937
Quartier 909, 2208, 2607, 2664, 3064, 3352
Quechua 1823, 1974, 1983
Questionnaires 313, 2083, 3101, 3157, 4531
Qutb, Sayyid 3320
Rabban al-Tabari, Ali ibn 4232
Race 144, 155, 263, 530, 562, 628, 659, 673,
     680, 695, 696, 719, 760, 812, 969, 1483,
     1492, 1502-1504, 1531, 1582, 1583, 1729,
     1777, 1934, 2157, 2172, 2327, 2496,
     2551, 2622, 2671, 2746, 2827, 2857,
     2875, 2877, 2934, 2939, 2942, 3026,
     3043, 3046, 3061, 3076, 3082, 3104,
     3107, 3132, 3693, 3893, 4086, 4170,
     4183, 4249, 4298, 4361, 4401, 4431,
     4460, 4468, 4478, 4639, 4684
Races humaines 1492, 2229, 4199
Racisme 134, 135, 254, 416, 2570, 3036,
     3048, 3056, 3059, 3075, 3099, 4395,
     4457, 4559, 4646, 4881
Radama I [King] 800

Radicalisme 778, 4249
Radicaux 765
Radio 375, 1786, 1788, 4018, 4263
Radiodiffusion 375, 1786
   voir aussi: Diffusion religieuse
Raison 998, 2933, 3153, 3552, 3564, 4449
Rajagopalan, L.S. 3304
Rameses II [King] 507
Ranganātha 3305
Rapport, Nigel 159, 217
Rapports de pouvoirs 269, 514, 1066, 1647,
   2101, 2489, 2490, 2555, 2834, 2909,
   2959, 3055, 3367, 3592, 3829, 4406,
   4648, 4780
Rareté 2289
   voir aussi: Pénurie de ressources
Rassemblement des données 78, 282, 286,
   287, 290, 309, 403, 429, 436, 2119, 2124,
   2146
Rationalisme 138
Rationalité 255, 275, 630, 2062, 2346, 2369,
   2539, 4635
Ratnākara 4067
Ray, Bharatcandra 4257
Read, James 644
Réadaptation sociale 4545
Réalisme 438, 1517, 1781, 3793, 4045, 4287,
   4556
Rébellion 522, 548, 711, 763, 1012, 2197,
   3063, 3525, 4634
Recensements 308, 2143, 2145, 2673
Recensements de population 308, 309, 2145,
   2146
Récession 2258, 2268, 4291, 4906
Réchauffement de l'atmosphère 2065
Recherche 22, 25, 29, 36, 48, 50, 51, 184, 200,
   225, 297, 317, 324, 333, 339, 352, 354,
   381, 389, 394, 413, 533, 536, 539, 547,
   552, 589, 613, 622, 635, 655, 672, 907,
   910, 927, 930, 953, 1101, 1111, 1120,
   1123, 1124, 1154, 1158, 1168, 1172, 1192,
   1206, 1231, 1237, 1252, 1258, 1274,
   1276, 1310, 1840, 2148, 2308, 2838,
   2880, 2953, 3761, 4306, 4696, 4697,
   4703, 4705, 4746, 4931
   voir aussi: Études de marché
Recherche agricole 4, 165, 4825
Recherche anthropologique 1, 2, 6, 7, 9, 24,
   26, 28, 35, 37, 41, 45-47, 49-52, 55, 56,
   58, 93, 94, 104, 105, 108, 114, 135, 142,
   147, 148, 157, 158, 160, 169, 174, 177,
   183, 189, 190, 207, 212, 215, 219, 232,
   238, 240, 242, 253, 265, 288, 292, 297,
   301, 302, 304, 311, 312, 317, 333, 341,
   354, 367, 381, 390, 397, 398, 400, 404,

   411, 413, 416, 421, 424, 431, 440, 442,
   547, 552, 562, 574, 595, 655, 672, 793,
   961, 1323, 1359, 1514, 1527, 1689, 1823,
   2157, 2214, 2344, 2458, 2568, 2597,
   2680, 2751, 2777, 2798, 2897, 2908,
   2910, 2941, 3022, 3027, 3061, 3231,
   3245, 3540, 3558, 3599, 3656, 3696,
   3729, 3765, 3801, 3804, 4105, 4182,
   4295, 4312, 4364, 4378, 4408, 4410,
   4420, 4473, 4495, 4523, 4584, 4590,
   4641, 4655, 4715, 4754, 4793, 4799
Recherche archéologique 34, 60, 87, 155, 162,
   211, 251, 273, 274, 430, 445, 450, 454,
   469, 475, 492, 513, 520, 526, 530, 550,
   556, 598, 623, 664, 669, 789, 819, 820,
   825-827, 831, 834, 837, 846, 858-860,
   862, 863, 865, 883, 891, 893, 897, 900,
   901, 903, 904, 906, 908, 910, 918, 922,
   923, 925, 928, 930, 931, 935, 939-942,
   944, 948-950, 952, 954-956, 958, 960,
   961, 964, 968-970, 972, 975-979, 981,
   983, 984, 986, 987, 989, 995-997, 999,
   1002, 1003, 1018, 1020, 1031, 1038,
   1041, 1042, 1050, 1057, 1059, 1068,
   1069, 1073-1075, 1077, 1079, 1080, 1092,
   1107-1112, 1114, 1116, 1117, 1119, 1121-
   1129, 1131-1135, 1137-1152, 1154-1157,
   1160-1162, 1164, 1168, 1170, 1171, 1174-
   1176, 1179, 1180, 1182-1189, 1191, 1193-
   1195, 1198-1204, 1206, 1208-1216, 1218,
   1219, 1222, 1224, 1226-1228, 1230, 1232-
   1235, 1237, 1239, 1241-1247, 1250, 1251,
   1253, 1254, 1256, 1257, 1259, 1261,
   1262, 1265-1268, 1270, 1273-1275, 1277-
   1279, 1282, 1285-1287, 1289, 1294, 1296,
   1297, 1307, 1329, 1343, 1351, 1352,
   1360, 1367, 1375, 1377, 1380, 1390,
   1393, 1398-1400, 1404, 1407, 1408, 1414,
   1416, 1418, 1421, 1434, 1436, 1441,
   1442, 1516, 1546, 2110, 2144, 2296, 2393,
   2794, 3024, 3520, 3859, 3941, 4215,
   4241, 4256
Recherche démographique 2626
Recherche d'emploi 2458
Recherche économique 43
Recherche empirique 172, 1840, 3734, 4847
Recherche en cours 4582
Recherche en sciences sociales 28, 53, 435,
   2903, 3665, 3833
Recherche et développement 2307, 4699,
   4743
Recherche ethnographique 15, 28, 33, 47, 72,
   91, 107, 136, 141, 145, 153, 194, 211, 227,
   258, 287, 291, 293, 294, 302, 386, 388-
   390, 393, 394, 402, 405, 406, 411, 417,

418, 420-422, 425, 426, 429, 430, 432, 436, 783, 1505, 1825, 2214, 2321, 2377, 2454, 2458, 2561, 2626, 2674, 2821, 2831, 2910, 3064, 3262, 3550, 3790, 3930, 4751, 4798

Recherche ethnologique 8, 17, 20, 32, 54, 78, 101, 131, 143, 166, 281, 303, 346, 400, 401, 410, 427, 438, 645, 1386, 2663, 2915, 3649, 3825, 4008, 4428, 4454, 4557, 4664

Recherche interdisciplinaire 154, 156, 163, 170, 172, 187, 189, 194, 420, 974, 2172, 2915, 3015, 4017

Recherche linguistique 42, 57, 109, 117, 124, 139, 1792, 1805, 1881-1888, 1914, 1989, 1994, 1995, 1999, 2009, 2052, 2667

Recherche médicale 1542, 4525

Recherche musicale 118, 3931

Recherche scientifique 33, 988, 1517, 1616, 1683, 3209, 4473, 4664, 4785

Recherche sociale 43, 215, 287, 302, 974, 2478, 2807, 4509, 4532, 4642, 4871

Recherche sociologique 28, 157, 221, 232, 238, 265, 290, 411, 510, 1745, 2536, 2662, 2946, 3227, 3262, 3734, 4116, 4446, 4715

Recherche sur le développement 305, 306, 4675, 4676, 4910

Réciprocité 404, 1647, 1692, 2351, 2379, 2382, 4390, 4393

Récits 3, 96, 216, 229, 230, 236, 257, 273, 278, 289, 319, 508, 660, 662, 999, 1498, 1740, 1754, 1758, 1762, 1793, 1828, 1846, 1978, 2037, 2094, 2103, 2184, 2512, 2533, 2635, 2657, 2762, 2832, 2834, 2843, 2964, 2995, 3005, 3025, 3026, 3073, 3077, 3131, 3174, 3255, 3274, 3293, 3296, 3404, 3424, 3438, 3516, 3643, 3659, 3687, 3709, 3790, 3805, 3955, 3976-3979, 3982, 3983, 3985, 3988, 3991, 3992, 3994, 3997, 4001, 4002, 4014, 4016, 4022, 4024, 4025, 4031, 4032, 4046, 4069, 4108, 4147, 4149, 4161, 4181, 4243, 4245, 4251, 4254, 4255, 4313, 4362, 4372, 4405, 4406, 4421, 4437, 4492, 4515, 4534, 4562, 4568, 4575, 4578, 4580

Récits de voyage 4179, 4225, 4236, 4237, 4290, 4292, 4321-4323, 4341

Récolte 2377

Récréation 2085, 2697, 2803, 4310

Recrutement 4927

Recyclage 908, 2114

Redistribution du revenu 4609, 4929

Réduction de pauvreté 2210, 2222, 2396, 4666, 4671, 4707, 4723, 4732, 4744,

4817, 4825, 4832, 4841, 4847, 4848, 4865, 4896, 4905, 4911, 4913, 4914, 4918, 4919, 4936, 4937

Refiki 4070

Réflexivité 133, 158, 196, 216, 219, 222, 228, 235, 237, 241, 242, 261, 275, 326, 351, 383, 384, 392, 398, 403, 422, 439, 610, 613, 635, 670, 2477, 2539, 2779, 3677, 3905, 4641

Réforme 3, 2404, 3230, 4441, 4778

Réforme agraire 2405, 4682

Réforme constitutionnelle 2511, 3020, 4418

Réforme de l'enseignement 1513, 3675, 4556, 4559

Réforme économique 2315, 2380, 4671, 4736, 4806

Réforme foncière 184, 726, 2396, 2402, 2412, 2419, 2420, 2600, 4669, 4682, 4820, 4905, 4917

Réforme institutionnelle 2289

Réforme légale 59, 2407, 2980, 2994, 3003

Réforme politique 383, 2779

Réforme religieuse 3286, 3333

Réforme sociale 3286, 3530

Réfugiés 489, 1282, 2119, 2148, 2159, 2165, 2176, 2178, 3105, 3519, 3730, 4547, 4820, 4826, 4899

voir aussi: Personnes deplacées

Régime de Vichy 3005

Régimes démocratiques 4649

Régimes fonciers 795, 806, 2299, 2314, 2396-2401, 2403, 2404, 2409-2418, 2420, 2422, 2425, 2426, 2609, 2669, 2968, 3017, 3018, 3106, 3659, 4618, 4630, 4638, 4659, 4682, 4794, 4820, 4887, 4905

Régimes politiques 192, 609, 618, 721, 3090, 3584, 3673, 4674, 4778

Régionalisme 801, 3917, 4671

Régions 39, 80, 150, 171, 184, 303, 369, 382, 919, 957, 1061, 1127, 2054, 2060, 2078, 2419, 2528, 2614, 2951, 3098, 3099, 3935, 4186, 4336, 4371, 4628, 4664, 4734

voir aussi: Études régionales, Politiques régionales

Régions frontalières 291, 599, 2192, 2495, 3098, 3121, 3694, 4488, 4628, 4632, 4695

Réglementation 4301, 4326, 4607, 4621, 4935

Régulation des naissances 2122, 2131, 2714

Régulation sociale 201, 722, 2176, 2370, 2401, 2969, 2990, 4620

Réincarnation 2791, 3153, 3192

Reinel, Pedro 768

Reis, Piris 768

Relations bilatérales 4632

Relations centre-périphérie 2511

Relations commerciales 2391
Relations culturelles 3037, 4311, 4479
Relations culturelles internationales 3193
Relations de classes 563
Relations de dépendance 2185, 2459, 4804
Relations des sexes 606, 643, 1762, 1775,
    2081, 2442, 2498, 2645, 2683, 2724,
    2758, 2806-2808, 2812, 2814, 2828, 2829,
    2834, 2846, 2847, 2851, 2860, 2986,
    3086, 3216, 3781, 4406, 4828, 4858,
    4873, 4876, 4911
Relations diplomatiques 658, 788, 2492
Relations du travail 2089, 2467, 2836
Relations économiques 2331, 2359, 2391,
    4804
Relations économiques bilatérales 4632
Relations entre générations 197, 2350, 2662,
    2767
Relations Est-Ouest 3079, 3137, 3743
Relations État-entreprises 2558
Relations État-société 684, 809, 2120, 4616,
    4714, 4779
Relations extérieures 106, 658, 737, 741, 752,
    2495, 2533, 3073, 4615, 4937
Relations familiales 443, 649, 1685, 2158,
    2160, 2166, 2171, 2174, 2183, 2410,
    2643, 2644, 2662, 2688, 2691, 2740,
    2745, 2764, 2772, 2793, 2815, 3730, 3966
Relations gouvernementales 809, 2403, 4647
Relations hommes-femmes 1653, 2461, 2498,
    2692, 2724, 2814, 2851, 3940, 4062,
    4266, 4853
    voir aussi: Époux
Relations humaines 134, 4854
Relations interdisciplinaires 154, 172, 178,
    189, 197, 211, 215, 430, 2915
Relations interethniques 10, 447, 509, 553,
    554, 582, 593, 760, 782, 2497, 2564,
    2578, 2621, 2742, 2886, 2942, 3045,
    3062, 3064, 3067, 3069, 3070, 3072,
    3074, 3077, 3080, 3082, 3083, 3087,
    3090, 3091, 3093, 3094, 3099, 3101,
    3102, 3519, 3565, 3592, 3596, 3671,
    4000, 4413, 4421
Relations intergroupes 853, 4468, 4741
Relations internationales 553, 677, 771, 2189,
    2210, 2391, 2549, 2576, 2981, 3036,
    3041, 3059, 4483, 4516, 4536, 4673,
    4705, 4706, 4712, 4737, 4744, 4746,
    4804, 4825
Relations interpersonnelles 247, 874, 1539,
    1775, 1811, 2449, 2596, 2604, 2621, 2691,
    2732, 2755, 2758, 2812, 2868, 2882,
    2886, 2888, 2914, 3553, 3940, 4172,
    4193, 4447

Relations médecin-malade 1796
Relations militaires 3022
Relations Nord-Sud 2269
Relations parents-enfants 557, 1584, 1602,
    1603, 1614, 1672, 2635, 2639, 2694,
    2933, 3025, 4022
Relations raciales 673, 786, 809, 2533, 2587,
    2619, 2820, 2827, 2857, 3026, 3066,
    3073, 3076, 3085, 3099, 3104, 3106,
    3107, 3671, 4000, 4012, 4183
Relations rurale-urbaine 684, 2120, 2179,
    3772
Relations sexuelles 2621, 2886, 2903
Relations sociales 34, 203, 326, 423, 793, 874,
    886, 916, 987, 1606, 1621, 1631, 1647,
    1685, 1713, 1753, 1775, 2115, 2179, 2191,
    2213, 2237, 2324, 2377, 2386, 2513,
    2583, 2603, 2604, 2611, 2615, 2621, 2629,
    2659, 2664, 2715, 2719, 2763, 2777,
    2781, 2795, 2812, 2859, 2886, 3009,
    3093, 3352, 3398, 3534, 3596, 3597,
    3696, 3817, 3907, 3966, 4193, 4377,
    4378, 4413, 4416, 4498, 4511, 4754, 4804,
    4852, 4873, 4882
Relativisme 138, 1723, 1728, 4216, 4513,
    4641
Religieuses 565, 2617, 2769, 3216, 3258,
    3637, 3644
Religion 86, 105, 166, 185, 186, 191, 195,
    202, 208, 209, 214, 256, 300, 413, 447,
    468, 473, 476, 509, 531, 568, 577, 585,
    596, 604, 626, 639, 644, 700, 725, 735,
    736, 766, 782, 808, 829, 897, 1025, 1050-
    1052, 1070, 1121, 1165, 1320, 1348, 1519,
    1749, 1755, 1837, 1863, 2018, 2069,
    2099, 2115, 2160, 2186, 2217, 2375, 2388,
    2392, 2482, 2483, 2532, 2542-2544, 2574,
    2579, 2598, 2605, 2675, 2684, 2729,
    2746, 2755, 2756, 2764, 2776, 2808,
    2817, 2826, 2828, 2834, 2859, 2952,
    2965, 2967, 2998, 3014, 3079, 3103, 3112,
    3131, 3135, 3141, 3142, 3149, 3151-3158,
    3161, 3170, 3172, 3174, 3180, 3186,
    3188, 3189, 3191, 3215, 3217, 3219-3222,
    3225, 3227, 3228, 3230-3232, 3234, 3236,
    3237, 3241, 3246, 3247, 3250, 3257,
    3259, 3265, 3286, 3287, 3292, 3294,
    3300, 3320, 3324, 3325, 3328, 3334,
    3335, 3337, 3338, 3340, 3341, 3344,
    3346-3348, 3350, 3356, 3359-3361, 3363,
    3365-3367, 3370, 3371, 3377, 3380, 3382,
    3394, 3395, 3402, 3406, 3410, 3411, 3413,
    3416, 3419, 3422, 3425, 3426, 3432,
    3433, 3439, 3448, 3455-3457, 3462-3465,
    3467-3471, 3473-3483, 3485, 3487-3495,

3497, 3498, 3501, 3505, 3507-3509, 3513, 3514, 3526, 3528, 3533, 3535, 3540-3545, 3547, 3549, 3557, 3560, 3562, 3574, 3578, 3583, 3584, 3589-3591, 3593, 3602, 3609, 3612, 3616, 3619, 3620, 3622, 3625, 3627, 3631-3633, 3636, 3637, 3639, 3640, 3642, 3645, 3649, 3652, 3653, 3657, 3666, 3681, 3706, 3711, 3728, 3734, 3741, 3761, 3822, 3826, 4034, 4043, 4080, 4095, 4105, 4184, 4247, 4259, 4264, 4269, 4304, 4359, 4383, 4406, 4412, 4428, 4441, 4445, 4459, 4461, 4462, 4468, 4474, 4484, 4503, 4523, 4537, 4585, 4585, 4587, 4599, 4674, 4724 *voir aussi:* Anthropologie religieuse, Ethnologie religieuse, Histoire de la religion, Monothéisme, Philosophie de la religion, Sociologie de la religion, Textes religieux

Religion comparée 5, 105, 167, 209, 210, 226, 227, 300, 3231, 3235, 3294, 3374, 3527, 3560, 3561

Religion de l'Antiquité 1025, 3515

Religion et politique 1361, 2515, 2979, 3324, 3349, 3353, 3438, 3448, 3470, 3625, 3697, 4415 *voir aussi:* Islam et politique

Religion mondiale 2099, 3155 *voir aussi:* Christianisme, Hindouisme, Islam, Judaïsme

Religion populaire 86, 3215, 3531, 3554, 3639

Religion traditionnelle 1454, 2435, 3264, 3602, 3647

Religion tribale 2435, 3625

Religions préhistoriques 1052

Religiosité 257, 2515, 2816, 3140, 3154, 3157, 3259, 3262, 3378, 3512, 3574, 3593, 3639, 3645, 4179

Renaissance 1031, 3787

Rendement du travail 2468

Rendille 2126, 2434, 2626, 2767, 2879, 4878

Rénovation urbaine 2101, 2222, 4931

Répartition de la population 1597, 1630, 1712

Répartition géographique 2133

Répartition par âge 4750

Répartition par sexe 2722

Répartition spatiale 2077

Repas 4381, 4387

Représentation 1629, 1793, 2907, 2945, 3006, 3290, 3410, 3529, 3596, 3625, 3830, 3871, 3873, 3875-3877, 3881, 3883, 3907, 3933, 3955, 3965, 3982, 4043, 4059, 4102, 4113, 4121, 4122, 4263, 4316, 4355, 4356, 4359, 4362, 4366, 4367, 4505, 4519

Représentation du corps 766, 769, 1361, 2727, 2944, 2947, 2953, 3697, 3994

Représentation politique 253, 2524, 2540, 3880

Représentations religieuses 3396

Représentations sociales 261, 3677, 4305, 4633

Répression 2496

Reproduction sexuelle 1283, 1488, 1491, 1500, 1586, 1605, 1613, 1619, 1658, 1662, 1667-1669, 1676, 1695, 1697-1699, 1705, 1706, 1708, 2131, 2381, 2723, 2724, 2851, 2863, 2876, 2905, 2941, 2956, 3358, 3824, 4890, 4892

Reproduction sociale 880, 1405, 1427, 1733, 2237, 2346, 2381, 2506, 2633, 2956, 3690, 3710, 3845, 4430, 4465, 4507, 4589

Réseaux 286, 679, 764, 2124, 2196, 2356, 2447, 2634, 2663, 4008, 4746

Réseaux ferroviaires 4608

Réseaux sociaux 252, 2013, 2169, 2373, 2610, 2611, 2631, 2660, 2672, 3105, 4726, 4808

Réserves indigènes 803, 2614, 3727

Réserves naturelles 667, 1686, 2191, 2203, 2272, 4319, 4773, 4774

Résidence 2654

Résistance 531, 601, 1616, 1762, 2190, 2382, 2933, 3032, 4037, 4442, 4495, 4637 *voir aussi:* Mouvements de résistance

Résistance au changement 3286, 4442

Résolution des conflits 395, 1681, 1682, 2446, 2529, 3001, 3038, 3176, 3569 *voir aussi:* Intervention d'une troisième partie

Responsabilité 395, 1578, 2544, 2656, 2668, 2837, 3508, 4666, 4882

Responsabilité financière 158

Ressources alimentaires 1645, 1694, 3751, 4385, 4923

Ressources de la mer 1291, 4850

Ressources de pêche 4804

Ressources économiques 2767, 3523

Ressources en eau 525, 957, 960, 1202, 2062, 2070, 2086, 2112, 2289, 2417, 3018, 4635, 4710, 4718, 4771, 4777, 4798

Ressources forestières 1686, 1691, 2081, 2090, 2413, 2808, 2828

Ressources humaines 29, 4701, 4755

Ressources minérales 2107

Ressources naturelles 960, 1571, 2061, 2067, 2073, 2075, 2089, 2116, 2164, 2207, 2288, 2309, 2404, 2413, 2415, 2434, 2439, 2449, 2836, 3695, 3751, 4385, 4612, 4690, 4693, 4767, 4770, 4779, 4780, 4799, 4801, 4803, 4805, 4806, 4819, 4820

Résultats économique 2265, 2730, 4863
Réussite intellectuelle 4554
Réveil religieux 245, 3198, 3364, 3646
Revendications foncières 4645, 4654
Revenu 485, 2210, 2290, 2293, 2309, 2350,
    2361, 2430, 2434, 2466, 2620, 2631,
    2726, 2763, 4787, 4820, 4827
    voir aussi: Faible revenu
Revenu des ménages 2141, 2210
Revenu national 4787
Revenu par tête 1568
Revenus d'investissement
    voir: Loyer
Rêves 3208, 3280, 3454, 3641, 3671, 4000,
    4004, 4282, 4514
Révisionnisme 348
Révolte 323, 707
Révolution 754, 778, 982, 1823, 2281, 2534,
    4352, 4921
Révolution industrielle 2229
Révolution iranienne 3957
Révolution russe 658, 2545
Révolution verte 4693, 4698
Révolutionnaires 2557, 4277
Reyes, Alfonso 3862, 4192, 4282
Reyes, Bernardo 546
Rhétorique 560, 805, 1776, 3000, 3258, 3354,
    3412, 3444, 3644, 4035, 4113
Rhodes, Cecil 710
Ricci, Matteo 3079, 3743
Richesse 307, 2340, 2375, 2390, 2430, 2535,
    2605, 2744, 2850, 3260, 3642, 3856
Riehl, Wilhelm Heinrich 149
Rire 1864, 3449
Risque 422, 879, 1539, 1544, 1548, 1713,
    2106, 2149, 2371, 2454, 2695, 2720,
    2867, 2885, 2889, 2896, 2916, 3575,
    3680, 3769, 3780, 3795, 3831, 4497,
    4889, 4893
Rites de la puberté 2729
Rites de passage 2731, 2776, 3609, 4017
Rites d'initiation 2729, 3512, 3550, 3626
Rites funéraires 147, 360, 448, 838, 892,
    1063, 1288, 1301, 1319, 1323, 2784,
    2786, 2787, 2789, 2791, 3225, 3581
    voir aussi: Enterrement, Funèbres
Rites funéraires antique 874, 2604
Rituelle 105, 166, 214, 222, 233, 271, 374,
    384, 459, 468, 656, 804, 880, 911, 929,
    1000, 1024, 1052, 1063, 1300, 1302,
    1304, 1430, 1446, 1733, 1771, 1965,
    2109, 2252, 2256, 2291, 2337, 2388,
    2514, 2571, 2579, 2682, 2684, 2700,
    2727, 2731, 2753, 2766, 2781, 2784,
    2787, 2791, 2794, 2795, 2811, 2835, 2838,

    2871, 2876, 2906, 3014, 3119, 3156, 3163,
    3171, 3198, 3221, 3228, 3231, 3232,
    3234, 3237, 3250, 3257, 3259, 3265,
    3296, 3301, 3306, 3310, 3316, 3338,
    3341, 3348, 3353, 3357, 3360, 3367,
    3382, 3406, 3409, 3439, 3509, 3511, 3514,
    3517, 3518, 3521, 3523-3525, 3530, 3537-
    3539, 3549, 3550, 3552, 3556, 3558,
    3559, 3564, 3567, 3581, 3586, 3594,
    3596, 3597, 3600-3602, 3606, 3609, 3622,
    3625, 3645, 3649, 3678, 3681, 3694,
    3713, 3715, 3736, 3776, 3812, 3910,
    3939, 3950, 3951, 3982, 4011, 4013, 4017,
    4126, 4138, 4231, 4315, 4334, 4354,
    4361, 4362, 4364, 4367, 4373, 4387,
    4390, 4402, 4423, 4428, 4430, 4462,
    4496, 4758
Rivalité 1606, 2188, 2682
Rivière, Peter 90, 385
Riz 726, 2142, 2255, 2271, 2304, 2305, 2314,
    2735, 4687, 4693, 4821, 4827
Rizal, José 2534
Robert, Shaaban 4163
Robots 4100
Roche, Yves 4263
Rodó, José Enrique 4157, 4191
Rohe, Ludwig Mies van der 3660
Rôle 3869
Rôle de sexes 564, 694, 2089, 2094, 2163,
    2347, 2410, 2481, 2633, 2651, 2692,
    2810, 2819, 2821, 2825, 2830, 2835,
    2836, 2841, 2843, 2846, 2932, 2966,
    3934, 4839, 4845, 4853
Rôle des femmes 215, 516, 2163, 2470, 2806,
    2815, 2825, 2828, 2844, 2849, 2854,
    2996, 3922, 4072, 4105, 4175, 4523,
    4584, 4780
Rôle des hommes 2848, 3254, 4833
Rôles politiques 2584, 4090
Rôles sexuels 2810, 2831, 2932, 3034, 3525
Rôles sociaux 490, 2686, 2764, 3006, 4337
Rom 14, 399, 1924, 3798, 4006
Roman 149, 409, 3005, 4146, 4149, 4154,
    4188, 4195, 4199, 4205, 4211, 4217, 4242,
    4265, 4272, 4287, 4288, 4562
    voir aussi: Science-fiction
Romancier 4157, 4191, 4192
Romans 663, 1739, 2453, 2534, 2788, 2834,
    2853, 2928, 3005, 3118, 3885, 3999, 4112,
    4149, 4151, 4152, 4157-4160, 4162-4164,
    4175, 4188-4193, 4200, 4204, 4216, 4218,
    4230, 4242, 4247, 4249, 4254, 4257,
    4262, 4263, 4272, 4273, 4284, 4285, 4406
Romantisme 149, 630, 3129, 3940, 4263
Römer, Ludewig Ferdinand 4007

Rougier, Berthe 566
Rousseau, Jean Jacques 3929
Roussel, Raymond 4263
Routes 466, 496, 524, 1138, 2228, 4346
Royaumes 358, 495, 541, 583, 626, 639, 648,
    721, 724, 739, 806, 895, 1088, 1437,
    2073, 2417, 2501, 2546, 2574, 2581,
    3018, 3688, 4007, 4153, 4253
Royauté 587, 1838, 2282, 2392, 2572, 2575,
    2584, 4090, 4165
Rsabhadeva 3387
Rübner, Tuvia 4049, 4439
Rumeurs 3114, 3571, 3974
Rungu 2808, 2828
Rūparām 2624
Ruqayyat, Ibn Qais Al- 4077
Russes 2480, 2599, 3100, 3101, 3446, 3628,
    3629, 3918
Saadia Gaon, R. 3251
Sacré 105, 656, 1006, 1049, 1322, 1859, 2099,
    2782, 3142, 3155, 3196, 3231, 3367,
    3436, 3659, 4257
Sacrifice 829, 929, 1818, 2063, 3213, 3447,
    3537, 3556, 4231
Sa'd, Abdullah ibn 4232
Sahib, Granth 2997
Sahib, Hargobind 3476
Saikaku, Ihara 4254
Saints 142, 166, 473, 514, 1065, 2909, 3152,
    3220, 3240, 3242, 3253, 3261, 3347, 3411,
    3414, 3472, 3516, 3554, 3599, 3649,
    3721, 4391, 4428
Saisonalité 646, 1695, 1699, 1700, 1718,
    2060, 2752
Saisons 1034, 1107, 1112, 1115, 1119, 1128,
    1131, 1139, 1147, 1174, 1176, 1178, 1182,
    1204, 1218, 1219, 1227, 1241, 1243,
    1246, 1253, 1257, 1261, 1266, 1609,
    1638, 1718, 2085, 2187, 2610, 3242,
    3721, 3740, 4310
Saivisme 3854
Sakalava 2392
Sakhawat Hossain, Rokeya 2839
Salaires 485, 2251, 2350, 2361, 2453, 2466
Salih, Ali M.A. 111
Salish 1322, 1837
Samburu 2447, 2824
Sami 3535, 4624
San 2398, 4638
Sanballat 2550
Sang 769, 1490, 1510, 1626, 1699, 2931,
    2944, 3510, 3764
Sango 2017
Sankara 3200
Sans foyer 2210, 4543, 4571, 4722

Sanscrit 14, 1907, 1939, 1945, 1950, 1960,
    3148, 3162, 3179, 3184, 3195, 3203,
    3212, 3214, 3272, 3282, 3290, 3296,
    3301, 3302, 3314, 3317, 3390, 3865,
    3875, 3876, 4057, 4067, 4168, 4207,
    4246, 4261, 4596
Santal 2359
Santé 285, 290, 909, 1494, 1512, 1529, 1543,
    1569, 1572, 1589, 1657, 1688, 2140,
    2149, 2150, 2152, 2173, 2208, 2210,
    2213, 2277, 2311, 2695, 2696, 2701, 2702,
    2707-2711, 2720, 2721, 2733, 2758, 2759,
    2763, 2773, 2775, 2848, 2865-2868, 2870,
    2873, 2874, 2879, 2884, 2888-2890, 2892,
    2894-2896, 2898, 2902, 2910, 2913, 2914,
    2916, 2918, 2941, 2953, 3159, 3254,
    3510, 3764, 3774, 3775, 3780, 3782,
    3792, 3795-3798, 3806, 3810, 3813, 3821,
    3827, 3831, 3832, 3834, 3835, 4181, 4211,
    4328, 4396, 4397, 4526, 4531, 4647,
    4818, 4823, 4844, 4864, 4871, 4873,
    4876, 4878, 4883, 4884, 4886, 4889,
    4891, 4893, 4895, 4898-4901, 4903
    voir aussi: Promotion de la santé
Santé de femmes 285, 1560, 2702, 2707,
    2709, 2728, 2870, 3769, 3775, 3811, 4780,
    4866, 4885, 4901-4904
Santé de la reproduction 1586, 3824
Santé d'enfants 443, 1544, 1548, 1572, 1577,
    1582, 1584, 2686, 2703, 2708, 2711, 4822,
    4844, 4885
Santé d'hommes 2889, 4889
Santé mentale 775, 1513, 2762, 3404, 3791,
    4513, 4515, 4543, 4547, 4722
Santé publique 44, 1565, 1566, 1580, 2140,
    2696, 2707, 2709, 2711, 2865, 2869, 2878,
    2888, 2889, 3739, 3788, 3804, 3811, 3820,
    3821, 4328, 4709, 4808, 4814, 4823,
    4844, 4865, 4867, 4869, 4870, 4872,
    4874-4877, 4880, 4881, 4883, 4884, 4887-
    4889, 4892, 4894, 4896, 4900, 4903, 4904
Santé sexuelle 285, 2696, 2707, 2723, 2865,
    2866, 2869, 2870, 2878, 2888, 2892,
    2894, 2905, 2913, 2914, 3788, 3810, 3811,
    4722, 4869, 4877, 4891, 4892, 4901
Sarah 2748
Sargon II [King] 1341
Sarmad, Sa'id 3414
Sarmiento, Domingo Faustino 4048, 4210
Sarrazin, Albertine 3005
Satanisme 3578
Satellites 1615, 2287
Sati 2738, 2785
Satire 4058, 4194, 4243
Satisfaction 2768

Sauer, James A. 112
Savane 900, 1359, 2104, 2448, 4784
Scandales 148, 644, 2966
Schaden, Egon 2798
Schaeffner, André 3929
Schenda, Rudolf 141
Schmitz, C.A. 26, 93
Schwarz-Bart, Simone 3980
Schweizer, Thomas 131
Science 4, 5, 24, 60, 99, 132, 144, 156, 165,
    170, 188, 226, 274, 437, 464, 908, 947,
    971, 974, 1002, 1163, 1451, 1504, 1519,
    1781, 2099, 2300, 3005, 3014, 3131,
    3153, 3155, 3341, 3491, 3685, 3728,
    3739, 3746, 3750, 3753, 3755, 3793,
    3975, 4142, 4763
    voir aussi: Anthropologie de la science,
    Histoire des sciences, Médecine légal,
    Philosophie de la science
Science du folklore 143, 152, 153, 163, 166,
    171, 181, 188, 229, 3649, 3979, 4022,
    4255, 4360, 4428
Science et technologie 1577, 1683, 2094,
    2129, 2131, 2320, 2452, 2704, 2818,
    2823, 2843, 2844, 3568, 4822, 4862
Science politique 2502, 2532, 3572, 3590,
    4205, 4251, 4718
Science traditionnelle 156
Science-fiction 4197
Sciences du comportement 1487, 1606, 1623,
    1662, 1683, 1694, 1698, 2691
Sciences naturelles 501, 974, 1770, 1926
Sciences sociales 28, 30, 90, 120, 173, 176,
    182, 224, 227, 243, 259, 385, 414, 451,
    485, 596, 638, 1136, 1319, 1342, 1344,
    1347, 1517, 1562, 1804, 1842, 1852,
    1856, 1867, 1868, 2139, 2140, 2149,
    2200, 2278, 2359, 2361, 2397, 2629,
    2661, 2698, 2701, 2720, 2773, 2775,
    2809, 2890, 2898, 2958, 2993, 3037,
    3159, 3252, 3288, 3320, 3330, 3336,
    3337, 3342, 3355, 3365, 3540, 3738,
    3774, 3780, 3792, 3795, 3821, 3827,
    3832, 3834, 3978, 4036, 4044, 4045,
    4047, 4075, 4077, 4080, 4083, 4084,
    4087, 4088, 4101, 4105, 4232, 4247,
    4276, 4328, 4474, 4485, 4523, 4524,
    4531, 4830, 4907
Scientifiques 4, 110, 156, 165, 3755, 3799
    voir aussi: Spécialistes en sciences
    sociales
Scolarité 1559, 2350, 4542, 4555, 4682
Script 4268, 4269
    voir aussi: Écriture ancienne, Écriture
    hiéroglyphique

Scrutin
    voir: Sondages d'opinion publique
Sculpture 322, 336, 360, 461, 1006, 1014,
    1024, 1030, 1043, 1051, 1062, 1067,
    1068, 1071, 1078, 1086, 1087, 1093,
    1096-1098, 1341, 1350, 1364, 1387, 1432,
    1531, 2241, 3714, 4095, 4117, 4124, 4134,
    4145, 4712
Sécheresse 2065, 2105, 2106, 2303, 2380,
    2446, 4691, 4736, 4764, 4767, 4792
Secours aux sinistrés 2148, 4816
Secret 201, 3643
Sectarisme 3167, 3257, 3327
Sectes 571, 3198, 3248, 3342, 3343, 3429,
    3496, 3631
Secteur agricole 2279, 4704
Secteur industriel 4678
Secteur informel 2169, 2347, 2660, 2819,
    4426, 4663, 4911
Secteur privé 2210, 4932, 4937
Secteur public 4671, 4935
Sécularisation 3734
Sécurité 2721, 3986
    voir aussi: Sécurité du travail
Sécurité alimentaire 1573, 1611, 1645, 1646,
    2380, 4701, 4719, 4736, 4807, 4808, 4811,
    4814, 4815, 4817-4820, 4834
Sécurité collective 4746
Sécurité de l'emploi 1573
Sécurité du travail 3986
Sécurité internationale 1517
Sedakova, Olga 4073
Sédentarisation 1301, 2434
Ségrégation 263, 3043
Ségrégation culturelle 387
Ségrégation raciale 126, 269, 3054, 3055
Ségrégation résidentielle 2222
Sel 2355, 2806, 2828, 3318
Sélection naturelle 1649, 2275, 2297
Selkoupe 3587, 3726
Selous, Frederick Courteney 746, 4208
Semai 2698
Sémantique 1723, 1728, 1737, 1738, 1749,
    1752, 1811, 1866, 1880, 1881, 1889, 1921,
    1960, 1963, 1977, 1980, 1982, 1987,
    2007, 2015, 2016, 2037, 3165, 3210,
    3273, 3753, 3874, 4206, 4600
Séminaires 2485
Sémiologie 3670, 3715, 3756, 4098, 4198
Sémiotique 1763, 2387, 2685, 2958, 3021,
    3728, 3731, 4136
Senapati, Fakir Mohan 4272
Senn, Nicholas 3749

Sens 1703, 2324, 2800, 2949, 3188, 3207
   voir aussi: Audition, Goût, Odorat, Son,
   Vue
Sentiments 1637, 4181, 4514
Sentongo, Z.K. 677
Séparatisme
Séparatisme religieux 3248
Services de santé 2702, 2863, 3775, 3794,
   3821, 4328, 4866-4868, 4895, 4901
Services de voirie 4887, 4937
Services d'espionnage 552
   voir aussi: KGB
Services financières 4671, 4730
Services sociaux 305, 2152, 4675, 4900
Setswana 1783
Sexe 44, 1507, 1580, 1621, 1654, 1660, 1684,
   1752, 2621, 2706, 2723, 2725, 2759,
   2773, 2827, 2869, 2886, 2894, 2898,
   2903-2905, 2911, 2913, 2918, 2919, 3104,
   3130, 3820, 3929, 4461, 4542, 4869, 4891
Sexologie 1945
Sexualité 44, 52, 290, 304, 502, 514, 562,
   1507, 1580, 1697, 1777, 2695, 2717,
   2723, 2746, 2753, 2759, 2820, 2821,
   2848, 2865-2869, 2872-2875, 2877-2879,
   2882, 2884, 2885, 2888, 2892-2895, 2897,
   2899, 2902, 2903, 2905, 2906, 2908-2914,
   2916-2919, 2934, 2941, 2953, 3254, 3719,
   3782, 3788, 3796, 3810, 3820, 3831,
   4468, 4548, 4869, 4877, 4878, 4891, 4898
   voir aussi: Bisexualité, Hétérosexualité,
   Homosexualité, Lesbianisme,
   Transsexualisme
Shakespeare, William 3878
Shambhu Hedge, Keremane 3892
Shia 3337
Shilluk 88
Shintoïsme 3177, 3187, 3532, 3706, 3717
Shipibo 1969
Shivarama Karanth, Kota 3892
Shona 711, 767, 2001, 3577
Shotridge, Louis 130, 353
Shvarts, Elena 4073
Sibawayh 3362
SIDA 52, 183, 264, 419, 2156, 2721, 2753,
   2865, 2867, 2879, 2884, 2896, 2902,
   2906, 2908, 2916, 2988, 3004, 3739,
   3761-3763, 3770, 3771, 3773, 3796, 3801,
   3823, 3831, 3834, 4666, 4808, 4863,
   4864, 4870, 4878, 4880, 4893, 4897, 4898
Siddhi Nara Simha [King] 2519
Sigillographie 2497
Signes 545, 1778, 2246, 3158, 3670, 3828,
   4198
Sigüenza y Góngora, Carlos de 132, 437

Sikhisme 577, 2186, 2483, 2485, 2495, 2511,
   2515, 2520, 2542, 2543, 2997, 3331,
   3363, 3461-3484, 3486-3508, 3705, 3716,
   3855, 4078, 4269, 4304, 4370, 4724
Sikhs 2186, 2483, 2515, 2520, 2542, 3363,
   3462, 3464, 3466, 3469-3473, 3475, 3476,
   3478, 3480, 3487, 3490-3493, 3498, 3501-
   3503, 3505, 3716, 3855, 4304, 4370
Silva, Francisco Correia da 323, 707
Simonović, Radivoj 101
Simulation 295, 455, 2130, 2225, 2634, 3765
Singes du Nouveau Monde 1501, 1509, 1598,
   1602, 1606, 1609, 1610, 1612, 1616,
   1627, 1635, 1640, 1646, 1647, 1661,
   1669, 1675, 1677-1679, 1691, 1698, 1702,
   1705, 1706, 1708, 1710, 1711, 1715, 1717,
   1718
Singes du Vieux Monde 1510, 1511, 1599,
   1601, 1603, 1611-1614, 1619, 1622, 1623,
   1625, 1626, 1628, 1630, 1631, 1633,
   1641, 1642, 1644, 1649, 1651, 1654,
   1655, 1657-1660, 1662, 1664-1666, 1668,
   1670, 1672, 1681, 1682, 1690, 1692-1694,
   1700, 1707, 1712, 1713
Singh, Gobind 3500, 4078
Singh, Harbhajan 4304
Singh, Ranjit 3473
Singh, Sardar Khushwant 2483
Singh, Sukhvinder 4724
Singhalese 2489, 3194
Sisala 2512, 4001
Sites archéologiques 85, 251, 458, 469, 475,
   488, 497, 518, 543, 822, 824, 827, 842,
   843, 847, 856, 862, 873, 888, 891, 900,
   907, 913, 915, 919, 922, 931, 933, 936,
   938, 942, 944, 950, 951, 954, 958, 964,
   967, 968, 973, 981-983, 989, 997, 1011,
   1018, 1021, 1026, 1034, 1037, 1038,
   1053, 1059, 1063, 1073, 1080, 1085,
   1089, 1091, 1106 1110, 1112, 1115-1119,
   1123, 1125, 1127, 1128, 1130-1133, 1139-
   1143, 1146, 1147, 1149, 1151-1153, 1155,
   1156, 1160, 1162, 1170, 1171, 1174, 1177,
   1182, 1185, 1191, 1193-1195, 1198, 1203,
   1204, 1208-1211, 1214-1216, 1218, 1219,
   1224, 1229, 1230, 1233, 1241, 1243-1247,
   1249-1251, 1254, 1256, 1259, 1261, 1265-
   1267, 1273, 1279, 1281, 1284-1286, 1295,
   1304, 1306, 1307, 1318, 1348, 1359,
   1365, 1378, 1380, 1381, 1384, 1393,
   1398, 1400, 1401, 1409, 1411, 1412, 1414,
   1416, 1417, 1429, 1442, 1536, 2235,
   2378, 2393, 3859
Sites historiques 3848, 4299, 4317
Situation de famille 3769

Śivānī 4281
Skis 2230
Slaves 147, 1320, 1323, 1381, 3103, 3135, 4306, 4476
Smith, Morton 3428
Smith, Pauline 4244
Socialisation 606, 736, 1749, 2470, 2698, 2715, 2854, 2917, 2986, 3106, 3739, 4378, 4433, 4507, 4534, 4586, 4754
Socialisme 218, 693, 2167, 2480, 2545, 3530, 3975, 3988, 4351
Socialistes 765
Société 107, 212, 400, 405, 431, 533, 550, 587, 664, 713, 1736, 1748, 2064, 2183, 2249, 2340, 2516, 2572, 2582, 2586, 2592, 2602, 2613, 2665, 2668, 2688, 2775, 3543, 3651, 3832, 4061, 4152, 4210, 4444, 4469, 4483, 4592, 4673, 4729, 4758
    voir aussi: Individu et société
Société agraire 633, 830, 2143, 2198, 2399, 2673, 3008, 4909
Société capitaliste 3534
Société civile 694, 2210, 2491, 2775, 3832, 3975, 4665, 4721, 4820, 4830
Société contemporaine 34, 987, 1451, 2324, 2790, 3262, 3385, 3386, 4177, 4449, 4596
Société de consommation 664, 2322
Société paysanne 2371, 2400, 2968, 4912
Société post-apartheid 1432, 2166, 2388, 2453, 2675, 3579, 4548, 4588, 4717
Société pré-industrielle 1584, 2143, 2673, 2749
Société rurale 1759, 2204, 2207, 2600, 2675, 4291, 4906
Société traditionnelle 2473, 2767, 2808, 2828, 2834, 3558, 4406, 4600
Société tribale 2691, 4337, 4633
Sociétés complexes 456, 1372, 2358, 4649
Sociétés postcoloniales 228, 335, 689, 702, 712, 723, 742, 799, 2397, 2401, 2506, 2522, 2529, 2551, 2553, 2560, 2641, 3039, 3046, 3047, 3071, 3222, 3287, 3438, 3625, 3671, 3687, 3698, 3844, 3949, 3969, 4000, 4039, 4134, 4150, 4182, 4244, 4265, 4278, 4288, 4293, 4295, 4298, 4299, 4312, 4343, 4352, 4374, 4378, 4432, 4453, 4475, 4500, 4516, 4548, 4574, 4589, 4652, 4655, 4685, 4754
Sociétés post-communistes 179, 319, 781, 2100, 2391, 2548, 2964, 3081, 3593, 3634, 3703, 3707, 4411, 4440, 4448, 4455, 4479, 4582

Sociétés savantes 19, 21, 23, 27, 427, 1594-1596
Sociétés secrètes 3519
Sociobiologie 227, 1493, 1494, 1496, 1507, 1529, 1552, 1560, 1581, 1592, 2352, 2589, 2872, 3750, 4396
Sociolinguistique 196, 235, 250, 631, 1732, 1735, 1746, 1749, 1750, 1760, 1767, 1785, 1792-1795, 1798, 1814, 1815, 1842, 1867, 1870, 1882, 1892, 1904, 1915, 1919, 1936, 1946, 1952, 1955, 1968, 1969, 1972, 1973, 1977, 1980, 1984, 1986, 1987, 2007, 2667, 3000, 3805, 4039, 4061, 4409
Sociologie 14, 41, 175, 189, 190, 205, 261, 692, 754, 815, 1544, 1548, 1582, 1773, 1915, 2122, 2129, 2131, 2136, 2262, 2281, 2341, 2363, 2489, 2704, 2757, 2778, 2790, 2856, 2999, 3128, 3166, 3610, 3643, 3677, 3730, 4105, 4264, 4291, 4363, 4364, 4523, 4665, 4906
Sociologie de la connaissance 259, 414, 4096
Sociologie de la culture 3065
Sociologie de la religion 168, 3139, 3166, 3227, 3541, 3543, 3636, 3643, 3734
Sociologie de l'éducation 4551
Sociologie du droit 59, 2984, 2994, 3003, 4670
Sociologie du milieu 2587
Sociologie du travail 2453, 2457, 2471
Sociologie économique 2341, 2471
Sociologie médicale 1529, 1809
Sociologie politique 3001, 4845
Sociologie rurale 2655, 2757, 2770, 2856, 2913
Sociologie urbaine 4435
Sociologues 2453, 3105
Sociométrie 252, 2013
Soi 215, 1066, 1448, 1793, 2322, 2533, 2766, 2920, 2923, 2926, 2933, 2948, 2961, 3073, 3144, 3499, 3516, 3760, 4069, 4073, 4083, 4297, 4437, 4443, 4510, 4514, 4517, 4534, 4535, 4540, 4578
Soie 2231
Soins 2762
Soins en dehors du milieu hospitalier 285, 2870
Soins médicaux 1470
Soins médicaux généraux 285, 1572, 2138, 2189, 2464, 2702, 2709, 2711, 2870, 2889, 3761, 3775, 3800, 3806, 4740, 4844, 4865, 4867, 4879, 4882, 4889, 4894, 4897, 4901
Soins médicaux primaires 3819, 4896

Soldat 546, 1077, 1302, 1326, 2494, 2502, 3021, 3572

Soleil 1381, 3111, 3133, 3177, 3711, 3717, 3740, 4220

Solidarité 2210, 2453

Solidarité féminine 4193

Solitude 2868

Sols 938, 1651, 1691, 2272, 2313, 4774

Soltān, Ebrāhim 4223

Soltāni, Nasr al 4223

Sommeil 1713

Son 1909, 1958, 1968, 2041, 3959

Sondages d'opinion publique 2518

Sorbe 1933

Sorcellerie 143, 2502, 2532, 2635, 2795, 3013, 3025, 3033, 3114, 3540, 3568, 3571, 3572, 3579, 3586, 3588, 3590, 3591, 3597, 3602, 3603, 3605, 3815, 3822

Sorciers 3033, 3230, 3603, 4005, 4441

Sotho 1832, 3816

Soufisme 3049, 3322, 3342, 3364, 3414, 3646, 4088

Sources d'information 61, 471, 2497, 4180, 4327

Sous-alimentation 1540, 1551, 1557, 1565, 1568, 4823, 4895

Soutien politique 3029, 3050, 4594

Soutien social 1591, 2169, 2174, 2650, 2655, 2660, 2661, 2770, 2772, 2882

Souveraineté 254, 688, 2408, 3716, 4417, 4457, 4629, 4643, 4650

Souveraineté interne 2540

Soyinka, Wole 3869, 4152, 4200

Spécialisation flexible 4748

Spécialistes en sciences sociales 149, 176, 300, 4524

Spécificité culturelle 177, 245, 1723, 1728

Sphère privée 2450, 2502, 3572

Sphère publique 662, 2668, 3709, 4356, 4368, 4390, 4832

Spiritisme 2802, 2945, 3060, 3262, 3529, 3579, 3595, 3607

Spiritualité 186, 188, 323, 476, 585, 707, 2069, 2816, 3136, 3140, 3149, 3159, 3235, 3259, 3292, 3309, 3330, 3338, 3372, 3374, 3387, 3425, 3468, 3486, 3497, 3499, 3503, 3504, 3506, 3540, 3541, 3589, 3598, 3619, 3620, 3626, 3641, 3645, 3657, 3686, 3812, 3854, 3962, 4332, 4454, 4666

Sport 40, 730, 1559, 2855, 2926, 2961, 3071, 4182, 4293, 4295, 4297, 4298, 4303, 4304, 4307, 4312-4314, 4331, 4336, 4337, 4342, 4343, 4348, 4492, 4574

voir aussi: Anthropologie du sport, Baseball, Football

Squatters 2213, 2419

St. John, Spenser 4150

Stabilité politique 2504, 2595

Stabilité sociale 2504, 4806

Stalinisme 3107

Statistique 310, 2293, 2312, 3770, 4847

Statues 518, 1040, 1093, 1422, 3837

Statut de la femme 2656, 2738, 2759, 2785, 2811, 2815, 2837, 2849, 2918, 3517, 4835, 4858, 4859

Statut juridique 694, 748, 2976, 2983, 4606, 4644

Statut professionnel 3781

Statut social 247, 641, 880, 1552, 1606, 1684, 1759, 2488, 2560, 2584, 2589, 2596, 2608, 2625, 2682, 2742, 2764, 2860, 3021, 3086, 3566, 3642, 3751, 3922, 4090, 4353, 4374, 4378, 4385, 4754, 4782, 4902

Stéréotypes 2321, 2364, 3009, 3084, 3293, 3893, 4395, 4516

Stérilisation 2726, 4901

Stérilité 1450, 1491

Stimulus 1693

Stoll, David 95, 234, 4569

Stratégie de développement 2222, 4339, 4609, 4683, 4764, 4848, 4881, 4883, 4897

Stratégie de survie 299, 3052, 3761, 4661, 4820

Stratification sociale 247, 629, 694, 818, 835, 920, 1915, 1955, 2245, 2349, 2488, 2521, 2531, 2590, 2593, 2596, 2603, 2622, 2627, 2925, 2938, 3022, 3092, 4075, 4299, 4732

Structuralisme 260, 3252, 3422

Structure de la famille 557, 1587, 2141, 2637, 2639, 2642, 2651, 2655, 2770, 4584, 4780

Structure de l'État 456, 2565, 4494

Structure de l'organisation 4742

Structure du marché 2277

Structure politique 657, 2517, 2547, 2553

Structure sociale 131, 138, 155, 530, 697, 848, 969, 1705, 2132, 2199, 2324, 2478, 2553, 2597, 2646, 2650, 2682, 3001, 3049, 3518, 3530, 3610, 3626, 4521

Stuart, James 125, 602

Stupéfiants 3946

Style artistique 1048, 3212, 3848, 4016, 4101, 4130, 4137, 4145

Styles musicaux 3894, 3899, 3901, 3929, 3933, 3953, 3964, 4059

Suaznábar, Marcelo 4097

Subalterne 95, 234, 605, 717, 729, 751, 3039, 3808, 4652
Subculture 2220
Subjectivité 130, 180, 237, 275, 276, 304, 353, 392, 991, 2324, 2342, 2539, 2791, 2897, 3005, 3792, 4077, 4356
Substantif 1347, 2022
Subventions 2210, 4827
Subversion 4230
Sucre 812
Suetonius 519
Sugali 1490
Suicide 2797, 2798, 4231
Sumba 3744
Sumérians 4253
Sung 632, 2580
Supermarchés 161
Superstition 2439, 2682, 3153, 3230, 3480, 3972, 4441
Supranationalité 1946
Suprématie du droit 2972, 2978, 2984, 2994, 4616, 4670
Surdité 40
Surexploitation 867
Suri, Haribhadra 3372, 3373
Surnaturel 2532, 3579, 3590, 3626, 3972, 3987, 3998, 4010
Surnoms 1829
Survivance culturelle 3083, 3989
Svobida, Lawrence 2259
Swahili 550, 2386, 3944, 4163, 4564
Symboles 156, 504, 656, 1056, 1334, 1369, 2070, 2071, 2514, 2530, 2560, 2777, 2782, 3129, 3158, 3242, 3396, 3670, 3696, 3711, 3716, 3718, 3720, 3721, 3723, 3727-3729, 3733, 3734, 3738, 3838, 3863, 4087, 4088, 4198, 4349, 4374, 4456
Symbolisme 209, 233, 240, 397, 426, 828, 832, 929, 1020, 1042, 1051, 1114, 1363, 1385, 2068, 2188, 2215, 2232, 2346, 2363, 2632, 2675, 2791, 2900, 2923, 3006, 3177, 3292, 3513, 3537, 3556, 3560, 3567, 3587, 3686, 3711, 3713-3715, 3717, 3719, 3720, 3722, 3723, 3725, 3726, 3728-3736, 3740, 3744, 3830, 3877, 4035, 4041, 4061, 4062, 4065, 4141, 4191, 4220, 4222, 4275, 4286, 4330, 4343, 4383, 4384, 4387, 4456, 4758
Symbolisme du corps 2938, 2947
Symbolisme religieux 3703, 3711
Symbolisme sexuel 280, 2858
Sympathie 3693
Synagogues 1050, 3409, 3452, 4402
Syncrétisme 461, 3335, 3625, 3904
Syncrétisme religieux 3335

Syndicalisme 4671
Syndicats 2222, 2618
Syntaxe 1726, 1734, 1742, 1756, 1765, 1770, 1807, 1811, 1838, 1843, 1844, 1847, 1860, 1868, 1937, 1947, 1949, 1951, 1960, 1961, 1963, 2014, 2034, 2037, 2054, 3576
Système international 1517
Système pileux 1719, 2940, 4110
Systèmes agricoles 2262, 2263, 2278, 2314, 2404, 2419, 2426, 4609, 4691, 4692, 4692
Systèmes culturels 2449, 3158, 4908
Systèmes de parenté 2597, 2658
    voir aussi: Exogamie
Systèmes de planification 2782
Systèmes de production 833, 1041, 1406, 2349, 2437, 2443, 2448, 2593, 4689, 4698
Systèmes de valeur 2950, 3158
Systèmes d'écriture 214, 545, 1334, 1966, 2019
Systèmes d'enseignement 235, 3470, 4433, 4548, 4551, 4552, 4555, 4559, 4663, 4753, 4756, 4757
Systèmes d'exploitation 2255, 4661, 4687
Systèmes d'information 4819
Systèmes d'information géographique 840, 1002, 2138, 2287, 3800, 4735
Systèmes économiques 2345, 2448, 3175
Systèmes juridiques 516, 606, 748, 771, 2750, 2969, 2972, 2975, 2976, 2981, 2984-2986, 2996, 3019, 3112, 4670
    voir aussi: Culture juridique
Systèmes monétaires 2329, 2336
Systèmes politiques 2538, 2565
Systèmes religieux 3522
Systèmes sociales 727, 2270, 2349, 2449, 2593, 2607, 2672, 3522, 3534, 3653, 4409, 4484, 4730, 4908
Ta'ālibī, Abū Mansūr al- 3330
Tabac 215, 507, 687, 2254, 4128, 4609, 4722, 4867
Tabou 201, 2507, 2811, 3510, 3517, 3539, 3764, 3773, 3950, 4017, 4389
    voir aussi: Interdit alimentaire
Tagore, Rabindranath 3500, 3924, 4078, 4274
Taille 1456, 1541, 1550, 4307
Taita 3584, 4674
Talismans 1006, 3580
Tallensi 2594
Tambour 365, 3556, 3715, 3933, 3935, 3967, 4059
Tamouls 1892, 1895, 3085, 3180, 3375, 4020, 4213
Taoïsme 79, 2099, 2817, 3141, 3144, 3155
Tapisserie 4114
Tatar 2125

Tatouage 2921, 2937, 2938, 4438
Tauromachie 4305
Taux de croissance 1470, 1553, 1557, 4705
Taux de fécondité 295, 1486, 2118, 2121, 2130, 2153
Taux de mortalité 2636, 2778
Taux de natalité 3739
Taxonomie 5, 226, 263, 327, 1455, 1530, 1617, 1673, 1714, 1719, 1721, 1832, 1837, 2080, 2088, 2109, 3043, 3662, 3667, 3744, 3757, 3786
Tchèques 138
Tchouktche 1732, 1825
Technique agricole 687, 2254
Technique archéologique 60, 819, 865, 868, 932, 935, 938, 963, 988, 997, 1001, 1059, 1105, 1162, 1290, 1295, 2304
Techniques de combat 3912
Techniques de fabrication 1388, 1425
Techniques de pêche 2436
Techniques d'évaluation 4788
Technologie 236, 363, 427, 534, 543, 563, 845, 849, 863, 864, 875, 887, 890, 892, 960, 963, 1001, 1007, 1010, 1017, 1374, 1388, 1395, 1396, 1408, 1413, 1419, 1425, 1439, 1445, 1710, 1739, 2230, 2233, 2241, 2249, 2253, 2283, 2292, 2303, 2307, 2312, 2387, 2462, 2692, 3742, 3975, 4096, 4120, 4126, 4142, 4690, 4696, 4711, 4804, 4853, 4885
  voir aussi: Biotechnologie, Histoire de la technologie, Science et technologie
Technologie agricole 2265, 2730, 4820
Technologie appropriée 1001
Technologie de l'information 1773, 1778, 1779, 2229
Technologie des communications 1782, 2800, 3207, 3664
Technologie numérique 291, 436, 440, 983, 1003, 1105
Technologie préhistorique 1010, 1359, 1415, 1526
Technologie reproductive 2722
Technologies nouvelles 436, 687, 2254, 2588, 2632, 4743
Tehuelche 1586, 3126, 3824
Télécommunications 435
Telefol 3117
Télévision 55, 432, 442, 1774, 2379, 3623, 3699, 4043, 4120, 4143, 4446
Tello, Antonio 701
Telugu 1909, 3968
Témoinage 449, 903, 944, 1056, 1340, 1515, 1544, 1548, 1673, 2527, 2561, 3307, 3771, 3945, 4534, 4751

Temples 105, 852, 911, 918, 934, 1019, 1025, 1048, 1049, 1064, 1072, 1078, 1103, 1113, 1116, 1118, 1121, 1156, 1157, 1161, 1165, 1343, 1348, 1350, 1354, 1401, 1417, 1838, 3152, 3176, 3186, 3204, 3231, 3454, 3857, 3860
Temps 56, 127, 138, 207, 278, 621, 662, 1633, 1724, 2211, 2256, 2522, 2801, 3144, 3156, 3643, 3651, 3658, 3681, 3689, 3709, 3756, 3850, 3942, 4049, 4055, 4097, 4308, 4439
Temps 127, 1008, 1030, 2313, 3114, 3571
  voir aussi: Précipitation
Temps de loisir 4350
Temur, Amîr 3322
Tendances de recherche 1914, 2052
Tenetehara 3067
Tension mentale 1629, 2758, 4539, 4846
Terminologie 56, 173, 207, 243, 1882, 1903, 2095, 2301, 2658, 2667, 2670, 2689, 2747, 3088, 3208, 3358
Terminologie de parenté 2020, 2022
Terrain 155, 530, 541, 721, 797, 803, 810, 969, 2127, 2316, 2321, 2337, 2350, 2399, 2401-2403, 2405, 2408, 2409, 2414, 2418, 2421, 2422, 2424, 2425, 2517, 2609, 2997, 3056, 3075, 4442, 4650, 4659, 4796, 4917, 4939, 4940
Terre 2069, 3619, 3657, 3930
Territoire 146, 283, 446, 721, 763, 806, 841, 955, 1690, 1716, 1825, 2123, 2497, 2517, 2550, 2664, 2993, 3352, 4309, 4405, 4609, 4629, 4631, 4660
Territorialité 612, 641, 993, 1426, 1599, 1661, 1690, 1716, 2608, 2927, 4309, 4475, 4482, 4624
Terrorisme 292, 395, 2549, 2927, 3027, 3199, 3638, 4471, 4482
Tests d'aptitude 1463
Tests de personnalité 1463
Teulé, Jean 3005
Textes 14, 25, 36, 62, 82, 109, 124, 125, 228, 239, 242, 324, 326, 332, 339, 344, 370, 372, 396, 398, 435, 472, 486, 516, 519, 536, 552, 569, 570, 578, 582, 584, 586, 602, 604, 622, 625, 653, 655, 696, 701, 741, 774, 796, 799, 806, 832, 897, 905, 1329-1332, 1334, 1338-1341, 1346, 1349, 1351, 1355, 1377, 1435, 1742, 1805, 1808, 1844, 1850, 1862, 1875, 1945, 1966, 1972, 1995, 2000, 2011, 2114, 2282, 2499, 2575, 2748, 2967, 2974, 2991, 2996, 3038, 3120, 3146, 3147, 3164, 3180, 3214, 3242, 3294, 3300, 3316, 3317, 3319, 3320, 3328, 3329, 3333,

3336, 3351, 3407, 3408, 3418, 3419,
3425, 3426, 3432, 3485, 3495, 3500,
3569, 3632, 3670, 3721, 3748, 3787,
3874, 3876, 3933, 3995-3997, 4002, 4059,
4064, 4074, 4078, 4167, 4180, 4183-4185,
4198, 4203, 4206, 4207, 4215, 4216,
4222, 4227, 4229, 4230, 4232, 4233,
4238, 4241, 4245, 4247, 4250, 4252,
4256, 4258, 4267, 4270, 4276, 4280,
4283, 4490, 4564, 4566, 4567

Textes religieux 22, 208, 472, 476, 515, 604,
796, 1103, 1129, 1344, 1349, 1353, 1843,
1861, 1864, 1893, 2000, 2973, 3120,
3136, 3146, 3148, 3164, 3169, 3173,
3174, 3179, 3184, 3190, 3195-3197, 3200,
3203, 3205, 3206, 3209, 3212, 3218,
3227, 3229, 3237, 3238, 3244, 3248,
3253, 3255, 3272, 3273, 3277, 3278,
3281, 3282, 3291, 3293, 3294, 3297,
3298, 3300, 3302, 3307, 3308, 3310,
3313, 3320, 3330-3333, 3336-3338, 3344,
3351, 3355, 3358, 3362, 3369, 3390,
3392, 3393, 3396, 3398, 3400, 3405,
3407, 3408, 3420, 3421, 3424-3427, 3430,
3432-3435, 3437, 3439, 3440, 3442, 3445,
3449-3451, 3453, 3455, 3456, 3460, 3465,
3479, 3485, 3495, 3504, 3521, 3632,
3748, 4224, 4231, 4283, 4286

Textiles 174, 284, 909, 1360, 1411, 2208,
2245, 2251-2253, 2644

Thai 1747

Thanatologie 2787

Thao 1889

Thapa, Bhimsen 2519

Thé 374, 738

Théâtre 103, 660, 1008, 1031, 1090, 2482,
3305, 3314, 3728, 3862, 3864-3866, 3870,
3872, 3873, 3875, 3876, 3880, 3882,
3883, 3887-3889, 3891-3893, 3909, 4138,
4263, 4722

Théâtre populaire 103, 3870

Théologie 208, 451, 461, 509, 604, 1863,
3147, 3160, 3222, 3229, 3244, 3294,
3320, 3326, 3332, 3338, 3339, 3359,
3380, 3407, 3418, 3426, 3431, 3432,
3435, 3437, 3439, 3448, 3450, 3455,
3462, 3466, 3477, 3479, 3527, 3620,
3728, 3748, 4255
voir aussi: Eschatologie

Théorie anthropologique 9, 12, 58, 108, 121,
123, 126, 127, 133, 137, 138, 146, 157,
158, 161, 164, 174, 179, 180, 203, 204,
212, 215, 216, 218, 219, 221-223, 228,
232, 233, 235, 238, 240-242, 244, 247,
249, 254-256, 263, 265, 267, 268, 270-

272, 275, 277-279, 284, 384, 395, 397,
398, 403, 408, 411, 415, 423, 426, 431,
439, 638, 911, 1584, 1772, 2369, 2387,
2527, 2537, 2539, 2552, 2596, 2612,
2658, 2680, 2751, 3022, 3043, 3054,
3567, 3583, 3622, 3653, 3692, 4378,
4414, 4457, 4484, 4485, 4490, 4715, 4754

Théorie archéologique 34, 85, 155, 164, 251,
274, 520, 530, 844, 865, 933, 965, 967,
969, 971, 978, 980-982, 987, 988, 991,
995, 996, 1002, 1135, 1221, 1226, 1239,
1361, 3697

Théorie critique 183, 1777, 2934, 3801, 4494

Théorie de chaos 3144

Théorie de la population 1563

Théorie de la valeur 2392

Théorie de l'organisation 249, 306, 2202,
2456, 2606, 2822, 2887, 2982, 4129,
4320, 4598, 4676, 4700, 4848, 4852, 4871

Théorie du change 2328, 2963

Théorie du développement 4609, 4613, 4679,
4713, 4719, 4755, 4854

Théorie du groupe 2603

Théorie économique 218, 2141, 2331

Théorie feministe 245, 264, 419, 432

Théorie juridique 59, 235, 268, 3003

Théorie linguistique 1766, 1860, 1869, 1882-
1888, 1890, 1933, 2667, 3330

Théorie politique 2954, 4485, 4637

Théorie sociale 90, 137, 164, 203, 223, 236,
237, 260, 267, 274, 276, 385, 392, 423,
589, 613, 947, 971, 985, 1743, 2092,
2589, 2591, 2840, 3652, 3668, 4466, 4587

Théorie sociologique 138, 224, 249, 265, 388,
510, 2404, 2536, 2790, 4485

Thérapie 1591, 3790

Thiongo, Ngugi wa 2499

Thompson, Laura Maud 120

Tibbon, Samuel Ibn 3403

Tiele, C.P. 5, 226

Tierney, Patrick 135, 148, 416

Tingatinga, Eduardo S. 4145

Tissage 349, 2231, 2251

Titian 3728

Tlingit 130, 249, 353, 1968, 2834, 4406

Tobia 2550

Tolai 158

Tolérance 2998, 3072, 3154, 3366, 4548, 4625

Toltèque 1970

Tomates 2275

Tombeaux 620, 855, 858, 859, 906, 970, 1010,
1063, 1074, 1122, 1158, 1163, 1280, 1282,
1288, 1290, 1292, 1296, 1298-1300, 1302,
1303, 1305, 1306, 1309, 1310, 1313-1316,
1319, 1325-1327, 1336, 1391, 1399, 2782

Tonga (Polynesia) 1890
Tonneliers 1401
Toponymes 2475
Toradja 2325
Torture 2959, 4477
Totem 2403
Totémisme 255, 2369, 3690, 3869
Touareg 122, 600, 2102, 2776, 3057, 3807
Tourisme 2068, 2081, 2085, 2092, 2102, 2108,
    2244, 2325, 2828, 2900, 3121, 3600,
    3884, 4038, 4136, 4179, 4291, 4292,
    4294, 4299-4302, 4308, 4310, 4311, 4316,
    4320, 4329, 4330, 4334, 4335, 4338-4341,
    4355, 4363, 4365, 4598, 4607, 4680,
    4683, 4684, 4714, 4768, 4906
Tourisme international 2108, 4300, 4335,
    4338, 4340, 4680, 4768
Toxicomanie 3004
Tradition 127, 175, 178, 188, 216, 409, 527,
    544, 550, 564, 597, 601, 613, 776, 1015,
    1094, 1360, 1733, 1817, 1836, 2085,
    2100, 2126, 2156, 2166, 2179, 2217,
    2234, 2245, 2291, 2341, 2395, 2478,
    2484, 2489, 2532, 2641, 2733, 2743,
    2745, 2782, 2801, 2828, 2830, 2904,
    2943, 3014, 3166, 3226, 3240, 3300,
    3341, 3448, 3483, 3536, 3590, 3654,
    3663, 3666, 3674, 3678, 3684, 3689,
    3702, 3704, 3706, 3707, 3732, 3826,
    3858, 3892, 3895, 3902, 3984, 4005,
    4052, 4106, 4161, 4201, 4242, 4281,
    4310, 4382, 4388, 4391, 4392, 4427,
    4430, 4445, 4496, 4548, 4595, 4818, 4873
Tradition culturelle 153, 625, 666, 1024, 1033,
    1782, 2202, 2482, 2588, 2598, 2691,
    2707, 2734, 2777, 2834, 2911, 3431, 3458,
    3548, 3551, 3627, 3664, 3669, 3684,
    3696, 3701, 3732, 3840, 3866, 3891,
    3902, 3928, 3981, 3984, 3992, 4097,
    4351, 4355, 4363, 4365, 4396, 4406,
    4507, 4512, 4586
Tradition écrite 125, 344, 471, 540, 570, 574,
    578, 584, 586, 602, 625, 653, 675, 690,
    772, 799, 1333, 1336, 1337, 1339, 1435,
    1742, 1862, 1865, 1972, 2974, 3146,
    4016, 4184, 4227, 4229, 4232, 4256,
    4267, 4278, 4288, 4289, 4564, 4566, 4567
Tradition orale 153, 169, 544, 619, 665, 799,
    1316, 1743, 1754, 1767, 1787, 1829,
    2103, 2104, 2184, 2481, 2489, 2512,
    3124, 3514, 3654, 3668, 3968, 3972,
    3974, 3977, 3980-3982, 3984, 3989, 3990,
    4001, 4004, 4005, 4007, 4009-4011, 4013,
    4016, 4021, 4023, 4024, 4027, 4031,
    4201, 4232, 4463, 4490

Traditionalisme 2417, 3018, 3167, 4631
Traditions artistiques 1031, 3714
Traditions musicales 3653, 3932, 4484
Traditions populaires 153, 166, 289, 2482,
    3528, 3649, 3678, 3694, 3708, 3923,
    3983, 4022, 4351, 4367, 4428
Traditions religieuses 147, 186, 208, 490,
    1006, 1323, 2099, 2737, 3149, 3155,
    3163, 3166, 3168, 3180, 3192, 3194,
    3197, 3200, 3201, 3286, 3300, 3304,
    3338, 3364, 3376, 3399, 3434, 3455,
    3463, 3481, 3646, 3706, 4284
Traduction 40, 334, 595, 650, 1755, 1800,
    1803, 1838, 1848, 1850, 1855, 1861,
    1868, 1880, 1893, 1945, 1972, 1996,
    3151, 3197, 3203, 3206, 3209, 3211, 3218,
    3248, 3253, 3333, 3393, 3453, 3459,
    3545, 4048, 4056, 4165, 4178, 4203,
    4207, 4231, 4250, 4270
Trafic de la drogue 3946
Trafiquants de drogue 692
Tragédie 2092, 4083
Traitement de l'information 320, 3159
Traitement médical 1460, 2884, 3796, 4546,
    4547
Tranche d'âge 1327, 1477, 2121, 2122, 2139
Transe 1095, 3486, 3812
Transformation de l'environnement 913
Transition de régime 4682
Transnationalisme 36, 253, 339, 2171, 3700,
    4106, 4401, 4417, 4606, 4611, 4728
Transport 454, 466, 749, 861, 1076, 1367,
    1383, 2933, 4933
Transport maritime 503, 2372
Transport urbain 4937
Transsexualisme 2809, 2915
Traumatisme 2165, 2582, 4181, 4509, 4538,
    4539
Travail 693, 2200, 2222, 2229, 2293, 2342,
    2411, 2418, 2457, 2460, 2461, 2471, 3889,
    4311, 4331
    voir aussi: Division du travail
Travail à domicile 2347, 2461, 2819
Travail agricole 2286, 4686, 4692, 4701, 4837
Travail bénévole 4709
Travail des enfants 2463, 2863, 4668
Travail des femmes 2347, 2819
Travail du métal 363, 1017, 1383, 1402
    voir aussi: Art du fer-forgé
Travail forcé 807
Travail intellectuel 175, 254, 4457
Travail ménager 2692, 4853
Travail social 305, 401, 2623, 3683, 4675
Travail sur le terrain 7, 15, 33, 48, 49, 85, 91,
    102, 123, 136, 145, 158, 177, 194, 200,

202, 222, 239, 241, 254, 277, 291, 292,
297, 302, 304, 311-313, 371, 384, 386,
390, 391, 393, 396, 400, 402, 403, 407,
413, 420, 422, 424, 425, 429, 435, 436,
512, 827, 829, 885, 907, 922-924, 927,
930, 945, 967, 968, 1021, 1111, 1114,
1120, 1123, 1124, 1130, 1134, 1154, 1155,
1158, 1159, 1163, 1167, 1168, 1173, 1175,
1179, 1181, 1186, 1196, 1197, 1222, 1223,
1225, 1238, 1248, 1255, 1263, 1269-1271,
1274, 1276, 1277, 1292, 1315, 1330,
1386, 1399, 1411, 1436, 1799, 2438, 2663,
2821, 2897, 3027, 3102, 3361, 3812,
3871, 4008, 4410, 4424, 4457, 4533, 4740
Travailleurs 723, 2461, 2462, 2471, 2607,
2949
    voir aussi: Chercheurs, Gens de maison,
    Ouvriers industriels
Travailleurs agricoles 1490, 2269, 4701, 4765,
4837
Travailleurs manuels 682
Travailleurs migrants 877, 2177, 2179
Travailleurs professionnels 1505, 2674
Travailleuses 2453, 2455, 2470, 2822, 2854,
3781, 4780, 4850
Travestisme 2915
Tremblements de terre 3855, 4724
Triade 2612, 3692
Tribalisme 2552, 2564, 3353, 4407, 4653
Tribunaux 516, 2996, 3330, 3724, 3916, 3937,
3963
    voir aussi: Cour Suprême
Tribus 88, 96, 659, 895, 946, 1301, 1347,
    1456, 1490, 1495, 1508, 1512, 1830,
    1876, 1897, 2417, 2425, 2553, 2554,
    2568, 2610, 2623, 2664, 2691, 2703,
    2741, 3016, 3018, 3049, 3056, 3067,
    3069, 3075, 3132, 3352, 3353, 3568,
    3683, 3691, 3772, 3815, 3910, 3967,
    3985, 4037, 4084, 4474, 4576, 4659, 4689
Tromperie 613, 3492, 3991, 3994, 3995, 4130
Trujillo Molina, Rafael Leónidas 787
Tsimshian 1835
Tswana 278, 2672
Tu Fu 4056
Tubu 2491, 2586
Tucker, Alfred 700, 3219
Tupi-Guarani 783
Tupinamba 756
Turcs 522, 2479, 4603, 4761
Turkana 558, 2367, 2508
Tuva 1746, 1876, 2690, 3691
Typologie 865, 1101, 1369, 1724, 1756, 1765,
    1928, 1947, 1954, 1956, 1971, 2022,
    2026, 2054, 2569, 3582, 3747, 4843

Tzeltal 3516
Ubangi 1994, 2009
Uddālaka 3315
Uigur 522, 4605
UNESCO 152, 962
UNHCR 4824
UNICEF 4816, 4824
Unification d'Allemagne 3656
Union européenne 972, 2190, 2486, 4340,
    4423, 4429, 4796, 4915
Unions monétaires 551
Unité culturelle 457, 2490
Universalisme 138, 167, 182, 209, 210, 220,
    300, 2585, 3367, 3504, 3560, 3561, 3676,
    4019
Universités 7, 29, 36, 57, 62, 77, 188, 197,
    339, 341, 359, 438, 613, 1156, 1157, 1176,
    1199-1201, 1211, 1215, 1242, 1417, 1527,
    2916, 3831, 4548, 4759
Upreti, Mohan 3919
Urbanisation 906, 909, 1263, 2159, 2179,
    2208, 2210, 2222, 2223, 2316, 2380,
    2421, 2501, 3505, 3610, 4618, 4736,
    4794, 4882, 4940
Urbanisme 906, 1355, 1372, 2212, 3838, 4749
Urdu 3768, 4043, 4052
Urhobo 3933, 4059
Usage de stupéfiants 3765, 3929
Usage de substances toxiques 738
Usage du tabac 1591, 2917, 4722
Usines 2231, 2453
Utilisation de l'eau 525, 2093, 2112, 4710,
    4777
Utilisation des ressources 3742, 4779, 4802,
    4806
Utilisation des terres 249, 488, 831, 882, 913,
    926, 1153, 1310, 1834, 2079, 2084, 2137,
    2287, 2292, 2313, 2319, 2371, 2411, 2413,
    2420, 3107, 4301, 4607, 4669, 4766,
    4804, 4819
Utopie 100, 713, 740, 3617, 3618
Utopisme 100, 740, 2926, 3544, 4163, 4297
Vacances 2482, 2778, 4350
Vaches sacrées 3292
Vailland, Roger 2453
Valeur 327, 2328, 2329, 2349, 2375, 2381,
    2593, 2605, 2956, 2963, 3196
Valeur travail 2342
Valeurs 2097, 2160, 2388, 2478, 2668, 3020,
    3083, 3137, 3348, 3551, 3661, 4418,
    4510, 4536, 4548, 4556, 4660
Valeurs culturelles 1475, 2166, 2691, 2694,
    2762, 3036, 3059, 3660, 3693, 4570, 4625
Valeurs sociales 1766, 2156
Validité 306, 2750, 3019, 3182, 4676

Valikhanov, Chokan 150, 382
Vallées 303, 721, 1241, 2437, 2438, 4263
Variance 70, 1457, 1462, 1488, 1528, 1567, 1709, 1721, 1764, 3970
Variole 1489
Veblen, Thorstein Bunde 2946, 4116
Védas 3301, 3316, 3319
Védisme 22, 457, 2623, 2973, 3173, 3213, 3277, 3280, 3282, 3295, 3297, 3298, 3301, 3303, 3306-3308, 3310, 3313, 3316, 3318, 3319, 3466, 3683, 3857
Végétarisme 3288
Vendeurs 2210
Vengeance 510, 790, 2536, 2653, 2977
Verbes 1724, 1751, 1769, 1812, 1854, 1860, 1872, 1879, 1889, 1910, 1939, 1940, 1947-1949, 1962, 1986, 1989, 2002, 2006, 2014, 2024, 2025, 2031, 2040, 2042, 2046, 2053, 3147, 3290
Vérification 1764
Vérification comptable 4709
Verité 95, 159, 217, 234, 291, 428, 1538, 3170, 3383, 3388, 3499, 3877, 4006, 4063, 4508
Verrerie 1447
Vêtements 174, 760, 1360, 1423, 2928, 2936, 2942, 2943, 2951, 2957, 2960, 4003, 4121, 4164
Veuvage 2793
Veuve 2753, 2793, 2906, 4231
Vezo 4507
Viande 2352, 4380, 4389, 4391
    voir aussi: Boucherie
Viaud, Gustave 4263
Viaud, Julien 4263
Victimes 2137, 4508, 4538
Vidal, Peire 4035
Vidéo 357, 440, 4119
Vie 103, 297, 357, 1481, 1546, 1718, 2938, 3870, 4574, 4575, 4577
Vie économique 276, 2364
Vie familiale 2394, 2655, 2770, 2878, 3157, 3788, 4877
Vie politique 110, 2551, 2554, 3799
Vie privée 2459
Vie quotidienne 32, 103, 161, 291, 323, 487, 656, 707, 911, 1430, 2200, 2210, 2213, 2217, 2259, 2294, 2459, 2462, 2946, 3034, 3523, 3538, 3580, 3581, 3601, 3870, 3974, 4038, 4105, 4116, 4356, 4378, 4495, 4523, 4570, 4572, 4754
Vie religieuse 210, 766, 2617, 2811, 2979, 3204, 3349, 3512, 3517, 3526, 3531, 3561, 3562, 3574, 3579

Vie rurale 667, 917, 1759, 2197, 2200, 2203, 2205, 2206, 2256, 2388, 2423, 2463, 2655, 2702, 2770, 2949, 3005, 3669, 3775, 4135, 4369, 4448, 4764, 4799, 4884, 4909, 4922
Vie sociale 137, 267, 271, 277, 299, 373, 393, 422, 531, 651, 756, 760, 1502, 2217, 2291, 2374, 2386, 2472, 2474, 2583, 2611, 2613, 2647, 2649, 2684, 2738, 2785, 2790, 2919, 2942, 3034, 3052, 3065, 3109, 3575, 3807, 4358, 4376, 4403, 4540, 4579
Vie urbaine 917, 1272, 2206, 3900, 3907, 4075
Vieillesse 813, 2655, 2770, 2773, 2774, 2898
Vieillissement 565, 813, 1545, 1564, 1633, 2174, 2655, 2761-2763, 2765-2767, 2769-2772, 2774, 2776, 2804, 2845, 2925, 3540
VIH 44, 52, 264, 419, 1580, 2156, 2695, 2865, 2866, 2869, 2874, 2884, 2885, 2889, 2892, 2896, 2902, 2903, 2908, 2913, 2916, 3761, 3762, 3770, 3771, 3773, 3780, 3782, 3796, 3810, 3820, 3831, 3834, 4863, 4869, 4873, 4889, 4893, 4897, 4898
Vikings 2360
Vila, Vargas 4277
Villages 37, 41, 114, 190, 402, 942, 951, 1037, 1061, 1117, 1176, 1265, 1454, 1477, 1577, 1993, 2085, 2127, 2187, 2188, 2192, 2194, 2195, 2200, 2404, 2417, 2557, 2663, 2669, 2676, 2943, 3018, 3094, 3176, 3530, 3811, 3889, 3930, 3988, 4008, 4310, 4320, 4345, 4369, 4448, 4598, 4684, 4689, 4718, 4777, 4799, 4822, 4849, 4852
Villages de pêcheurs 2194
Villegaignon, Nicolas Durand de 756
Villes 529, 895, 1265, 1386, 1447, 2159, 2180, 3660, 4317
    voir aussi: Bidonville
Villes capitales 450, 466, 521, 2154
Vin 1106, 1236, 4382, 4397
Viol 2533, 3073
Violence 192, 291, 292, 299, 395, 618, 717, 780, 790, 977, 2076, 2222, 2439, 2456, 2502, 2533, 2558, 2583, 2609, 2635, 2714, 2961, 3013, 3021, 3022, 3024-3027, 3029, 3031-3035, 3048, 3050, 3052, 3073, 3107, 3199, 3572, 3603, 3608, 3730, 3900, 4100, 4450, 4471, 4477, 4520, 4538, 4543, 4741, 4828, 4872
Violence dans la famille 2987, 3028, 3030, 4872

Violence politique 395, 2515, 2558, 2714,
   3029, 3050
Violon 3967
Viticulture 1106, 1236, 4382, 4397
Vivekananda 3312
Vocabulaire 68, 745, 1723, 1728, 1730, 1737,
   1768, 1791, 1806, 1873, 1889, 1926,
   1932, 1992, 1993, 2039, 2048, 2055, 2056
Voies navigable 2070
Voile 3240, 3384
Vol 342, 2382, 2384
Volcans 2432
Voleurs 4015
Voulet, Paul 3608
Voyages 88, 99, 584, 596, 690, 742, 779,
   1419, 1611, 2092, 3111, 4171, 4208, 4226,
   4302, 4316, 4318, 4324, 4332, 4340,
   4341, 4347, 4565
   voir aussi: Histoire des voyages
Voyages internationaux 594, 674, 756, 1820,
   3600, 3749, 3797, 3821, 3952, 4263,
   4320, 4328, 4334, 4565, 4598, 4618, 4794
Voyages par mer 455, 820, 2225
Voyelle 1722, 1801, 1858, 1870, 1912, 1957,
   1997, 2051
Vue 1688, 3728
Vulgarisation agricole 4701
Wa 3715
Walcott, Derek 4200
Wallach, Yona 4040
Walsperger, Andreas 768
Wancho 2048
Wang, Fuzhi 588
Wapishana 3069
Ward, Henry George 1428
Warhol, Andy 4093
Washburn, Sherwood Larned 144
Wayana 3570, 3783
Welby, Victoria 3728
Wells, H.G. 3746
Wesley, John 3239
Westermarck, Edvard 142, 3599
Whitehead, Alfred North 3170
Wiéner, Jean 3929
Wierzbicka, Anna 1723
Wijeyewardene, Gehan 35, 104
Wilber, Ken 186, 3149
Williams, Tennessee 2857, 3076
Willumsen, J.F. 371
Wiru 809
Wittgenstein, Ludwig 3728
Wo'daa'be 2064
Wojciech [Saint] 3554
Wolf, Eric R. 98, 2503
Wright, Melissa W. 2955

Wu-chu, Hsia 481
Xénophobie 2802, 3060, 3607, 4395
Xhosa 813, 2774, 3829, 4082
Xie, Wanying 4042
Xingu 3605
Yagnik, Indulal 4571
Yahi 887
Yang, Shang 2985
Yanomami 24, 135, 148, 416, 1577, 3750,
   4822
Yao (Thaïlande) 4689
Yap 2384
Yāska, Acharya 1738
Yazīd Makhlad, Abū 470, 2567
Yeats, William Butler 3698, 4563
Yehudah, Yeshu'ah ben 3393
Yerukula 1490
Yoga 3299, 3304, 3372, 3496, 4207
Yolngu 2670, 2747, 3955
Yombe 3557
Yoruba 2252, 2320, 2584, 2682, 3533, 3732,
   3835, 4090, 4289, 4862
Yuan 4089
Yucatèque 1970, 3753
Yukagir 1825
Yupik 3514
Yuson, Alfred A. 4199
Zapotèque 733, 993, 1812, 1967
Zarma 1749
Zedong, Mao 2936
Zen 3168
Zhang, Tianyi 4194
Zheng, Liu 2933
Zigmund-Cerbu, Anton 6, 94
Zigmund-Cerbu, Liza 6, 94
Zionisme 3438, 4427
Zola, Émile 3005
Zone tempérée 2275
Zone tropicale 900, 1717, 2091, 2443, 3746,
   3809
Zones arides 957
Zones résidentielles 1083, 3660
Zones rurales 2133, 2137, 2138, 2180, 2185,
   2202, 2286, 2336, 2396, 2413, 2441,
   2599, 2620, 2718, 2793, 2818, 3629,
   3678, 3800, 3814, 3819, 3858, 4291,
   4353, 4669, 4699, 4757, 4766, 4796,
   4858, 4866, 4902, 4905, 4906, 4908,
   4909, 4918-4920, 4922, 4925
Zones suburbaines 417, 2215
   voir aussi: Périurbanisation
Zones urbaines 1576, 2133, 2180, 2181, 2209,
   2218, 2220, 2222, 2502, 3068, 3505,
   3572, 3660, 4533, 4765, 4927

Zoologie 371, 974, 1673, 1819, 3785
    voir aussi: Archéozoologie, Paléozoologie

Zulou 817, 2006, 2739, 3012, 4363
Zuni 4103